# multinational
# **management**

*A Strategic Approach* 6e

# multinational
# management
*A Strategic Approach* 6e

## John B. **Cullen**
*Washington State University*

## K. Praveen **Parboteeah**
*University of Wisconsin, Whitewater*

SOUTH-WESTERN
CENGAGE Learning

Australia • Brazil • Japan • Korea • Mexico • Singapore • Spain • United Kingdom • United States

**SOUTH-WESTERN**
CENGAGE Learning·

**Multinational Management: A Strategic Approach, 6e, International Edition**
John B. Cullen and K. Praveen Parboteeah

Senior Vice President, LRS/Acquisitions & Solutions Planning: Jack W. Calhoun

Editorial Director, Business & Economics: Erin Joyner

Editor-in-Chief: Joe Sabatino

Senior Acquisition Editor: Michele Rhoades

Developmental Editor: Ted Knight

Editorial Assistant: Tamara Grega

Market Development Manager: Jonathan Monahan

Marketing Brand Manager: Robin LeFevre

Art and Cover Direction, Production Management, and Composition: PreMediaGlobal

Media Editor: Rob Ellington

Senior Manufacturing Planner: Ron Montgomery

Rights Acquisition Specialist, Text and Image: Amber Hosea

Cover Image: © iStockphoto/szefei

International Edition:

ISBN-13: 978-1-285-09622-3

ISBN-10: 1-285-09622-3

Cengage Learning International Offices

**Asia**
www.cengageasia.com
tel: (65) 6410 1200

**Australia/New Zealand**
www.cengage.com.au
tel: (61) 3 9685 4111

**Brazil**
www.cengage.com.br
tel: (55) 11 3665 9900

**India**
www.cengage.co.in
tel: (91) 11 4364 1111

**Latin America**
www.cengage.com.mx
tel: (52) 55 1500 6000

**UK/Europe/Middle East/Africa**
www.cengage.co.uk
tel: (44) 0 1264 332 424

**Represented in Canada by Nelson Education, Ltd.**
www.nelson.com
tel: (416) 752 9100/(800) 668 0671

Cengage Learning is a leading provider of customized learning solutions with office locations around the globe, including Singapore, the United Kingdom, Australia, Mexico, Brazil, and Japan. Locate your local office at: **www.cengage.com/global**

For product information and free companion resources:
**www.cengage.com/international**

Visit your local office: **www.cengage.com/global**

Visit our corporate website: **www.cengage.com**

Printed in the United States of America
1 2 3 4 5 6 7 17 16 15 14 13

To les deux

J & J

and

to Kyong, Alisha, and Davin

# BRIEF CONTENTS

# CONTENTS

*part three*

# Management Processes in Strategy Implementation: Design Choices for Multinational Companies   303

*part four*

## Strategy Implementation for Multinational Companies: Human Resource Management   443

*part five*

# Strategy Implementation for Multinational Companies: Interaction Processes   557

Defining the nature of today's business are the globalization of markets, financial institutions, and companies; the growing importance of the emerging markets of Brazil, China, India, and Russia (the BRIC markets) and other markets in the continent of Africa; and the global impact of financial crises, wars, terrorism, and even disease. Developing and making strategic choices are the mainstays of successful decision making in this increasingly complex global environment. To help students develop the essential skills needed to formulate and implement successful strategic moves in the new competitive and interlaced global environment, this sixth edition of *Multinational Management: A Strategic Approach* continues its tradition of providing a thorough review and analysis of the latest research on international management. In addition, by using a strategic perspective as a unifying theme to explore the global economy and the impact of managerial decisions, we bring a distinctive method to the teaching and learning of international management. This text was the first international management text to use this critical emphasis on strategic decision making as the cornerstone of its approach, and each subsequent edition has built on this tradition.

After reading this text, students will understand that successful multinational managers view the world as an integrated market where competition and collaboration evolve from almost anywhere and anyone. At the same time, these future managers must appreciate the wide array of differences that exist in cultures and social institutions. This text considers how cultural differences affect strategies and operations and gives the student an appreciation of how social institutions such as the economic system, the polity, the educational system, and religion play an important role in any multinational operation. As such, the reader is not limited to understanding multinational management from the perspective of any one nation or group.

# New to This Edition

The entire text has been updated to reflect current research and examples from the field of international management. All chapters have new boxed features to reflect the latest trends. Additionally, most of the statistics reported in the chapters reflect the latest numbers. Many of the updates pertain to the opportunities presented by the emerging markets such as Brazil, China, India, and Russia, and the text recognizes the emergence of the class of emerging market competitors. Furthermore, the text recognizes the impressive progress made by nations in the African continent. It also acknowledges the growth of state-owned enterprises. Finally, chapters were written keeping in mind the current economic crisis, while acknowledging that, as most experts predict, emerging markets will recover much more quickly than developed nations.

Among many changes, some specific revisions to the text material include the following:

### New Cases

All chapters and each major section of the text have their own cases with specific case-based discussion questions. Around 30 percent of the cases are new to this edition. Case topics reflect the current global environment and cover most of the world's continents.

- Some cases pertain to companies operating in the world's biggest as well as emerging markets, such as India, China, and Malaysia. One case deals with Tata Motors in India, providing valuable insights into the Indian markets and the emergence of this potential world competitor.

- Cases include companies in the Czech Republic and Poland to reflect the challenges faced as these countries transition to market-based economies.

- Cases on Asian economies, such as South Korea and Japan, illustrate some of the difficulties encountered as these countries deal with an environment that is counter to collectivist values.

- The case on Kimberly-Clark in Latin American illustrates some of the unique challenges multinationals experience in this region of the world.

- Other cases, such as Google in China and Alibaba versus Yahoo, reflect some of the challenges and the opportunities of e-commerce strategies.

- Many new cases on international ethics and corporate social responsibility (e.g., Yahoo and Customer Privacy, Procter and Gamble and Safe Drinking Water, Micro-credit in Armenia) have been added to reflect the increasingly crucial importance of this area.

- The text now features a new case on the Middle East to reflect the growing importance of the region to global trade. Case material pertaining to Nigeria has also been included.

- Case material on Europe and Canada show that these places also represent particular difficulties for multinationals.

## New Topical Areas

All chapters include the latest developments in the international management field.

## part one

- *Chapter 1—Multinational Management in a Changing World* has been thoroughly updated to reflect the latest trends in the field. A significant emphasis in the chapter pertains to the emergence of powerful new competitors from emerging markets. The chapter details the reasons why these new competitors are emerging and how they are drastically influencing strategies of the well-established multinationals. The chapter also recognizes the growing emergence of state-owned companies and their influence on the global business environment.

- *Chapter 2—Culture and Multinational Management* has been updated and remains one of the most balanced presentations of culture, including the popular Hofstede framework and the most recent GLOBE framework. The implications of each cultural dimension for management functions such as leadership styles, HRM, etc., are clearly summarized through figures. Readers are also alerted to the dangers of relying too much on culture.

- *Chapter 3—The Institutional Context of Multinational Management* has been updated and now emphasizes important information on social inequality and its impact on multinational management. The chapter also presents a balanced overview of the world's main religions, underscoring the importance of religion to the global business environment.

- *Chapter 6—Multinational and Entry-mode Strategies: Content and Formulation* now emphasizes the section on political risk and what companies can do to mitigate it. The chapter includes more discussion of the new emerging market competitors.

- *Chapter 7—Small Businesses and International Entrepreneurship* has also been updated to reflect the sustained importance of the topic to international management. Students will read about potential barriers faced by small businesses as they go global. However, the chapter also discusses the many benefits small businesses may gain by going international. This text remains one of the few on the market to acknowledge the growing importance of international entrepreneurship.

- *Chapter 8—Organizational Designs for Multinational Companies* continues the extensive discussion of knowledge management, adding a timely and interesting topic to the traditional discussion of multinational organizational structures. This reflects the growing importance to multinationals of knowledge management systems.

- *Chapter 10—Multinational E-Commerce: Strategies and Structures* is included in this sixth edition making it one of the only texts with a chapter on this important topic. More detail is now provided on the growing importance of multinational e-commerce security and the many aspects of IT security. The latest figures and statistics on e-commerce are discussed providing evidence of the sustained growth of the sector.

- *Chapters 11 and 12—International Human Resource Management* continues the strong tradition of considering human resource management issues for both expatriates and other employees. Special emphasis is placed on emerging markets and the more sustained difficulty of finding and retaining qualified workers.

- *Chapter 15—Leadership and Management Behavior in Multinational Companies* continues the examination of leadership in a global context and integrates the latest GLOBE research on leadership in over 60 nations.

## Current Data

All chapters have been updated to include the latest research, examples, and statistics in multinational management, creating the most accurate and current presentation possible:

- Current multinational management examples in the Case in Point and other chapter features, including Multinational Management Briefs, Multinational Management Challenges, and Multinational Management Skill Builders.

- Updated tables and figures using recent findings on multinational leadership from *GLOBE: The Global Leadership and Organizational Behavior Effectiveness Research Program*.

- Updated tables and figures using recent findings on organizational behavior issues from the *World Values Survey* and the *International Social Survey Program*.

- Updated tables and figures using recent publications from the latest World Bank's *World Trade Report*, other critical information from the United Nations Conference on Trade and Development (UNCTAD), and the United Nation's *World Investment Report*.

- Prepublication information from the authors' own research on the effects of social institutions on work values and international recruiting.

- A large selection of new cases.

# Pedagogical Approach

In addition to providing a thorough review and analysis of multinational management, *Multinational Management: A Strategic Approach*, sixth edition, includes several unique pedagogical learning tools:

- *Strategic viewpoint:* This viewpoint provides a unifying theme that guides the reader through the material. It highlights for students the process that multinational companies engage in when deciding to compete in the global economy and the management consequences of these strategic choices.

- *Comparative management issues:* Multinational managers must understand the strengths, weaknesses, and strategies of competitors from anywhere in the world. In addition, they must know when and how to adapt their organizational practices to accommodate local situations. Where relevant, the comparative sections of the text assist students in understanding the complexities of the cultures and business practices of other nations.

- *Review of management principles:* The text contains several chapters that assume some background knowledge in management, specifically strategic management, organizational design, human resource management, and organizational behavior. For students with limited previous coursework in management, or for those who need a review, each chapter provides background primers with brief explanations of key concepts and ideas.

- *Small business and entrepreneurship applications:* Unlike most international management texts, this book explains the multinational activities of small businesses. An entire chapter focuses specifically on the problems and prospects for entrepreneurs and small businesses looking to become multinational competitors.

- *Application based:* Each chapter gives the learner three different opportunities to apply the knowledge gained from reading the chapter: Multinational Management Skill Builders, chapter Internet Activities (located on the book's website, www.cengage.com/management/cullen), and end-of-chapter cases. These exercises simulate the challenges that practicing multinational managers encounter on the job.

# Key Features

- *Chapter Cases and Multinational Management Skill Builders:* End-of-chapter projects include cases and activities, which give the learner the opportunity to apply the text material to real-life managerial problems.

- *Multinational Management Internet Exercise:* For this sixth edition, we have added a new feature to take advantage of the wealth of resources available on the Internet. For each chapter, students will now have the option of researching a website relevant to the chapter and reporting the latest findings to the class. This will encourage students to explore the wealth of resources on the Web while at the same time learning about the most recent data.

- *Integrating Cases:* Each major section offers at least one full-length case that requires the integration of material from all preceding chapters. These cases were chosen to challenge the reader with the complexities of the global environment.

- *Extensive examples:* Throughout the text, many examples enhance the text material by showing actual multinational management situations. These examples are illustrated in six different formats:

  - *Preview Case in Point:* These brief cases open each chapter and focus the reader's interest on the chapter content.

  - *Focus on Emerging Markets:* This edition strengthens a feature that was introduced in the fourth edition focusing on the growing importance of the BRIC emerging markets in Asia, Latin America, and Europe. Each chapter discusses the many opportunities and threats presented by emerging markets in the context of the chapter. Furthermore, many of these examples emphasize the two dominant emerging markets, India and China.

  - *Case in Point:* These real-life examples of multinational companies discuss relevant topics in each chapter.

  - *Multinational Management Challenge:* These cases explore challenging situations faced by multinational managers in actual companies and situations.

  - *Multinational Management Brief:* Brief examples elaborate on an issue discussed in the text.

  - *Comparative Management Brief:* These examples show how a unique cultural or social institutional setting can influence management decisions.

- *Models as examples:* The authors created numerous models to act as visual aids for students as they study key principles.

- *Learning aids:* The Multinational Management Electronic Study Tools for students, product support website, and supporting video make learning easy and fun while exposing the learner to the complex issues of multinational management. In addition, included on the product support website are Internet Activities that challenge students to use Internet resources in locating international business information. The Web site also contains an extensive selection of Internet links to resources and information that are updated regularly.

# Contents

The text is structured into five major parts. Part One is divided into four chapters: three introductory chapters that provide essential background on the nature of multinational management and a fourth on international ethics. These chapters address the challenges facing managers in the new global economy, how national cultures affect management, the institutional context of multinational companies, and the ethical challenges these firms encounter.

Part Two includes three chapters that review how multinational companies formulate successful strategies to compete internationally. Chapter 5 provides a broad overview of strategic management with global implications. Chapter 6 focuses on the strategies required to "go international." Chapter 7 applies the concepts from the previous two chapters to the unique problems faced by small, entrepreneurial organizations.

Part Three addresses the management systems used to implement multinational strategies. Specifically, Chapter 8 considers how multinational companies design and structure their organizations to implement their strategies. Chapter 9 examines the management and design issues involved in building global strategic alliances. Chapter 10 considers how companies can use e-commerce in multinational operations.

Part Four contains two chapters dealing with the human resource management issues related to implementing strategy. Topics considered include international human resource practices and the adaptation of these practices across cultures.

Finally, Part Five continues to examine strategy implementation at the level of the individual in the organization. Chapters consider international negotiation and cross-cultural communication, motivating people in different nations, and leadership challenges in multinational companies.

# Ancillary Materials

*Multinational Management: A Strategic Approach,* sixth edition, offers a highly intensive learning and teaching package of ancillary tools for both students and instructors. These supplements give students and instructors many options for learning and teaching.

- *Website:* Visitors to the website (www.cengagebrain.com) will find these teaching ancillaries available for download in the password-protected Instructor Resources section. The student companion website provides key instructional materials, and a Premium Website for students features additional Internet-based learning activities related to international business for each chapter.

---

**Accessing CengageBrain**

1. Use your browser to go to www.CengageBrain.com.
2. The first time you go to the site, you will need to register. It's free. Click on "Sign Up" in the top right corner of the page and fill out the registration information. (After you have signed in once, whenever you return to CengageBrain, you will enter the user name and password you have chosen and you will be taken directly to the companion site for your book.)
3. Once you have registered and logged in for the first time, go to the "Search for Books or Materials" bar and enter the author or ISBN for your textbook. When the title of your text appears, click on it and you will be taken to the companion site. There you can chose among the various folders provided on the Student side of the site. NOTE: If you are currently using more than one Cengage textbook, the same user name and password will give you access to all the companion sites for your Cengage titles. After you have entered the information for each title, all the titles you are using will appear listed in the pull-down menu in the "Search for Books or Materials" bar. Whenever you return to CengageBrain, you can click on the title of the site you wish to visit and go directly there.

---

## For Instructors

- *Instructor's Manual:* The Instructor's Manual offers instructional materials, case solutions, and questions. For this sixth edition, we continue to provide case solutions for each chapter in a consistent format. Instructors are provided with a list of suggested questions and solutions, along with a synopsis and case objectives that show the academic value of each case.
- *PowerPoint® Slide Presentations:* The authors have created more than 450 slides illustrating the concepts of each chapter.

- **ExamView:** ExamView Computerized Testing Software, located on the Instructor's Resource CD-ROM, contains all of the questions in the test bank, which are available on the instructor's companion website. This program is easy-to-use test creation software, compatible with Microsoft Windows. Instructors can add or edit questions, instructions, and answers, and select questions by previewing them on the screen, selecting them randomly, or selecting them by number.

- **Instructor's Resource CD-ROM:** This CD-ROM includes the key instructor support materials—Instructor's Manual, ExamView Test Bank, and PowerPoint® Slides—and provides instructors with a comprehensive capability for customizing lectures and presentations.

- **DVD:** The DVD to accompany *Multinational Management: A Strategic Approach,* sixth edition, offers video clips featuring real-world companies and illustrating the international business concepts outlined in the text. Focusing on both small and large businesses, the video clips help students apply the theories presented in the book to actual situations and issues that global corporations face. A set of video case-based discussion questions and answers are included in the Instructor's Manual.

# Acknowledgments

Most of all, we must thank our families for giving us the time and quiet to accomplish this task. Numerous individuals helped make this book possible. Jean Johnson, professor of marketing at Washington State University, an experienced internationalist and John's wife read and commented on all chapters. Her insights were invaluable, as was her suggestion to organize the book around the strategic management perspective. Kyong Pyun, Praveen's wife, remained patient during the revision process. She was very supportive as Praveen started this revision as soon as another book project was finished. Praveen's eleven-year-old daughter, Alisha, is no longer as fascinated with revisions. Davin, Praveen's six-year-old son, no longer bothers dad during the revision process. Praveen misses being bothered!

This text would not be possible without the support of a team of professionals at Cengage Learning. Our initial thanks go to John Szilagyi, former executive editor of South-Western's management list, who encouraged us to write earlier editions of this book, as well as Senior Acquisitions Editor Michele Rhoades. We also appreciate the hard work of individuals involved on the production side, particularly End-to-End Production Site Lead/Content Project Manager Jean Buttrom.

Several colleagues who read and offered insightful comments on this and previous editions include the following:

Len J. Trevino, *Washington State University*
William Y. Jiang, *San Jose State University*
Manjula Salimath, PhD, *University of North Texas*
Carol Sanchez, *Grand Valley State University*
Raffaele DeVito, *Emporia State University*
David F. Martin, *Murray State University*
Anthony J. Avallone Jr., *Point Loma Nazarene University*
Gerry N. Muuka, *Murray State University*
Maru Etta-Nkwelle, *Howard University*
Gary Baker, *Buena Vista University*
Douglas M. Kline, *Sam Houston State University*

Michael J. Pisani, *Texas A&M International University*
Tracy A. Thompson, *University of Washington, Tacoma*
Bonita Barger, *Tennessee Technological University*
Dave Flynn, *Hofstra University*
Songpol Kulviwat, *Hofstra University*
Joan C. Hubbard, *University of North Texas*
Manisha Singal, *Virginia Tech*
Mike Giambattista, *University of Washington*
Kamala Gollakota, *University of South Dakota*
Stephen Jenner, *California State University, Dominguez Hills*
John A. Kilpatrick, *Idaho State University*
Richard Lovacek, *North Central College*
Scott L. Boyar, *University of South Alabama*
Carl R. Broadhurst, *Campbell University*
Linda L. Blodgett, *Indiana University South Bend*
Joseph Peyrefitte, *University of Southern Mississippi*
Lawrence A. Beer, *Arizona State University*
Janet S. Adams, *Kennesaw State University*

The following authors deserve special recognition for contributing their cases to this book: Thomas A. Fruscello and Jenny Mead: Yahoo! and Customer Privacy; Krystyna Joanna Zaleska: Organizational and National Cultures in a Polish/U.S. Joint Venture; Prahar Shah: Google in China; Klaus Meyer: Ethics of Offshoring: Novo Nordisk and Clinical Trials in Emerging Economies; Isaiah A. Litvak: Royal Dutch Shell in Nigeria: Operating in a Fragile State; Laura P. Hartman, Justin Sheehan, and Jenny Mead: Procter & Gamble: Children's Safe Drinking Water; James W. Bronson and Graham Beaver: Harley-Davidson and the International Market for Luxury Goods; Rua-Huan Tsaih and Darren Meister: Polaris 2008; Marlene Reed: Aregak Micro-Credit Organization in Armenia; Prashant Salwan: Tata Motors; Marlene Reed and Rochelle R. Brunson: The Fleet Sheet; Mikolaj Jan Piskorski and Alessandro L. Spadini: Procter & Gamble: Organization 2005; Jordan Mitchell and Brian Hohl: Fiat's Strategic Alliance with Tata; Katherine Xin, Winter Nie, and Vladimir Pucik: Alibaba versus eBay: Competing in the Chinese C2C Market; Sonia Ferencikova: Transition at Whirlpool Tatramat: From Joint Venture to Acquisition; Sandeep Krisnamurthy: The Failure of Boo.com; Gareth Evans: The Road to Hell; Preeti Goyal: People Management, The Mantra for Success: The Case of Singhania and Partners; Debi S. Saini: People Management Fiasco in Honda Motorcycles and Scooters India Ltd.; Markus Pudelko, Brian Stewart, Sally Stewart, and Xunyi Xu: Cross-Cultural Negotiation: Americans Negotiating a Contract in China; Brian J. Hall and Nicole S. Bennett: Insulting Andrew; Asianweek.com and Sang-Hun Choe: Old Corporate Ways Fade as New Korean Generation Asserts Itself; Stephen Ko: Cheung Yan: China's Paper Queen; Megan Anderson: Kimberly-Clark Andean Region: Creating a Winning Culture

John B. Cullen
K. Praveen Parboteeah

## John B. Cullen

John Cullen is Professor of Management, Ph.D. Program Director, and the Huber Chair of Entrepreneurial Studies at Washington State University, where he teaches courses on international management, organizational theory, strategic management, and business ethics. He has also taught on the faculties of the University of Amsterdam, the University of Nebraska, the University of Rhode Island, Waseda and Keio Universities in Japan (as a Fulbright lecturer), and the Catholic University of Lille in France. He received his PhD from Columbia University. He consults regularly with U.S. and Japanese organizations regarding international strategic alliances and the management of ethical behavior.

Professor Cullen is the author or coauthor of four books and over 70 journal articles, which have appeared in journals such as *Administrative Science Quarterly, Journal of International Business Studies, Academy of Management Journal, Organization Science, Entrepreneurship Theory and Practice, Journal of Management, Organizational Studies, Management International Review, Journal of Vocational Behavior, American Journal of Sociology, Organizational Dynamics, Journal of Business Ethics,* and the *Journal of World Business.* He also has given over 100 presentations at national and regional meetings. His major research interests include the effects of national culture and social institutions on entrepreneurial activities, the management of trust and commitment in international strategic alliances, ethical climates in multinational organizations, and the dynamics of organizational structure. Professor Cullen is a Senior Editor for the *Journal of World Business* and serves or has served on various editorial boards including the *Academy of Management Journal* and *Advances in International Management* and reviews for major journals in management and international business.

## K. Praveen Parboteeah

K. Praveen Parboteeah is Professor of International Management in the Department of Management, University of Wisconsin–Whitewater. He received his Ph.D. from Washington State University and holds an M.B.A. from California State University–Chico and a B.Sc. (Honors) in management studies from the University of Mauritius.

Parboteeah's research interests include international management, ethics, and technology and innovation management. He has been actively involved in developing alternative models to national culture to explain cross-national differences in individual behaviors. He has published over 35 articles in journals such as the *Academy of Management Journal, Organization Science, Journal of International Business Studies, Decision Sciences, Human Relations, Journal of Business Ethics, Management International Review, Journal of World Business, Journal of Engineering and Technology Management, Entrepreneurship Theory and Practice, Journal of Business Research,* and *Journal of Product Innovation Management.*

Parboteeah has received numerous awards for his research. He was the 2005 Western Academy of Management Ascendant Scholar and has won the University of Wisconsin–Whitewater Award for Outstanding Research.

Parboteeah has been involved in many aspects of international education at the University of Wisconsin–Whitewater. He chaired the International Business Committee, helping create criteria to evaluate strategic alliances with other universities for exchanges. He is the coordinator for exchanges with two French universities,

ESC Rouen and the Burgundy School of Business in Dijon. In 2012, he also developed and implemented an undergraduate International Business degree.

He has also lectured in many countries, including Mexico, South Korea, Taiwan, Trinidad and Tobago, and the United Kingdom. He now regularly lectures at Germany's leading business school, the Otto Beisheim School of Management, and Sun Yat-Sen University in Taiwan.

Of Indian ancestry, Parboteeah grew up on the African island of Mauritius and speaks English, French, and Creole. He currently lives in Whitewater, Wisconsin, with his South Korean wife Kyong, his daughter Alisha, and his son Davin.

# multinational
# management
*A Strategic Approach* 6e

# Foundations of Multinational Management

# 1 Multinational Management in a Changing World

## Learning Objectives

*After reading this chapter you should be able to:*

- Define multinational management.

- Understand the characteristics of a multinational company.

- Understand the nature of the global economy and the key forces that drive globalization.

- Know the basic classification of the world's economies.

- Identify the characteristics of the next generation of multinational managers.

## *Preview* CASE IN POINT

### Emerging Market Multinationals

The latest trend in global business is the rise of new multinationals hailing from emerging markets such as India, China, Brazil, and Russia. Furthermore, successful companies are also emerging from African nations. These new multinationals are using innovative strategies to compete effectively with their established counterparts from developed countries. Often, these emerging market multinationals use their local markets for testing before deploying their products to Western markets.

Take the cases of companies based in India and South America. For example, in 2008, Tata Motors, one of India's biggest industrial conglomerates, acquired the British automakers Jaguar and Land Rover and began developing cars for these prestigious companies. Moreover, the world's leading maker of regional jets is based in Brazil. Embraer, a Brazilian company, has taken advantage of its local engineering experience to innovate at a global level. It now manufactures small, sleek, fast jets for the international market.

Multinationals from developed nations are also paying attention to emerging companies from China and Mexico. For example, Chery International, China's leading car exporter, has plans to build plants in the Middle East, Africa, and Eastern Europe. Furthermore, collectively, the leading exporters of cars in China exported almost 900,000 cars in 2011. Cemex, one of the world's largest suppliers of cement, is based in Mexico, and has improved on its local business model to go international.

Recent trends also suggest that new multinationals are emerging in Africa. Safaricom, Kenya's most popular mobile phone company, listed its shares on the Nairobi Stock Exchange and was able to raise over $800 million in one of the biggest initial public offerings in sub-Saharan Africa. In fact, Kenya is fast becoming the African tech hub; hundreds of start-ups have sprung up there over the past few years. Furthermore, companies such as Celtel are banking on Africa's thirst for mobile phones.

The overwhelming agreement among experts is that emerging market countries and their multinationals have already become, or are expected to become, major players in world trade. Such trends are dramatically changing the environmental landscape for established Western multinationals.

*Sources: Based on* Economist. *2012. "Still in second gear." May 5, 62–63;* Economist. *2012. "Upwardly mobile." August 25, 53–54;* Economist. *2008. "The new champions." September 20, 53;* Economist. *2008. "The challengers—Emerging market multinationals." January 12, 61; Mo, I. 2012. "Celtel's founder on building a business on the world's poorest continent."* Harvard Business Review, *October, 41–44.*

A s the examples in the Preview Case in Point show, businesses and individuals, whether from the old or the new economy, increasingly see the entire world as a source of business opportunities. The world is becoming one interconnected economy in which companies conduct business and compete anywhere and with anyone, regardless of national boundaries. New multinationals with the clout to compete effectively against established multinationals are emerging worldwide. In a global economy, any company or individual from any country can become a competitor. The Internet crosses national boundaries with the click of a mouse, allowing even the smallest businesses to go global immediately. Consequently, companies can no longer afford the luxury of assuming that success in their home markets equates to long-term profitability—or even survival. Furthermore, although the integrated global economy presents challenges and threats such as terrorism, war, and recession, it also presents significant opportunities for most companies. Consider the next Focus on Emerging Markets.

What does this trend mean to the student of international business? With companies increasingly looking at global rather than domestic markets, managers will

## Focus on Emerging Markets

### Growing Opportunities

As mentioned in the Preview Case in Point, emerging markets are providing the base for the development of a new breed of powerful competitors. However, emerging markets also provide established companies with significant opportunities. As of 2012, while much of the developed world reeled from the economic recession, emerging markets were proving able to weather the storm better. The ability to grow despite the recession has largely been due to healthy demand in local markets. For example, although car sales in the developed markets fell during the recession, they increased significantly in China. China is now the world's largest market for cars, with sales of 18.5 million cars, compared to only 13.1 million in the United States.

Such upward trends are likely to continue. In fact, while recent data show a slowdown in the growth of emerging markets, they are still experiencing much more robust growth than Western countries. Goldman Sachs estimates that the global middle class is growing by over 70 million a year, and it is expected to continue growing. By 2030, experts predict that over two billion people will have joined the middle class worldwide. Such trends suggest tremendous opportunities for multinationals.

*Sources:* Economist. *2008. "The new champions." September 20, 53;* Economist. *2009. "Not so Nano; Emerging market multinationals." March 28, 20–21.* Economist. *2012. "Still in second gear." May 5, 62–63;* Economist. *2012. "Dream on?" July 21, 59–60.*

have little choice in the future but to be multinational in their outlook and strategies. Consequently, all students of business should have at least a basic background in multinational management. **Multinational management** is the formulation of strategies and the design of management systems that successfully take advantage of international opportunities and respond to international threats. Successful multinational managers are executives with the ability and motivation to meet and beat the challenges of multinational management.

To provide you with a basic background in multinational management, this book introduces you to the latest information on how managers throughout the world respond to the challenges of globalization. You will see how businesses, both large and small, deal with the complexities of national differences in cultures, economies, and political systems. You will learn how multinational managers use their understanding of these national differences to formulate strategies to maximize their companies' success in globalizing industries. But, because having good strategies is not enough to succeed in today's economy, you will learn how multinational managers carry out their global strategies.

To give you insights into the real world of multinational management, you will find several features in this and the following chapters.

- The *Preview Case in Point* shows you examples of how multinational companies deal with a key issue discussed in the chapter.
- *Cases in Point* give information on how multinational companies handle other issues raised in the course of the chapter.
- *Multinational Management Briefs* provide further details and examples that extend the discussion.
- *Multinational Management Challenges* describe problems and dilemmas that real multinational managers face, and for which there are no easy answers.
- *Comparative Management Briefs* provide examples of management issues that are influenced by a unique cultural or social institutional setting.
- Finally, the *Focus on Emerging Markets* feature reflects the sustained importance of emerging markets in world trade.

Multinational management takes place within the multinational company. But what exactly is a multinational company? The next section gives a definition and brief introduction to the major players in multinational competition.

# The Nature of the Multinational Company

The **multinational company (MNC)** is broadly defined as any company that engages in business functions beyond its domestic borders. This definition includes all types of companies, large and small, that engage in international business. Most MNCs, however, are multinational corporations; that is, the companies are publicly owned through stocks. Usually, when you see references to MNCs in the popular business press, the reference is to multinational corporations. The largest multinationals are all public corporations.

Exhibit 1.1 lists the top 20 multinational corporations ranked by sales revenue. As the exhibit shows, many of the largest corporations are in the petroleum industry—not surprisingly, given the continuous increase in oil prices. However, out of the top 10 companies, some are automotive companies and big *consumers* of the oil industry. Wal-Mart is the only retailer, and a few of the remaining

**Multinational management**
The formulation of strategies and the design of management systems that successfully take advantage of international opportunities and that respond to international threats.

**Multinational company (MNC)**
Any company that engages in business functions beyond its domestic borders.

**EXHIBIT 1.1**    Largest Companies in the World

| Rank | Company | Industry | Headquarters Country | Revenues (US$ million) |
|---|---|---|---|---|
| 1 | Royal Dutch Shell | Petroleum | Netherlands | 484,489 |
| 2 | Exxon Mobil | Petroleum | USA | 452,926 |
| 3 | Wal-Mart Stores | Retailing | USA | 446,960 |
| 4 | BP | Petroleum | UK | 386,463 |
| 5 | Sinopec Group | Petroleum | China | 375,214 |
| 6 | China National Petroleum | Petroleum | China | 352,338 |
| 7 | State Grid | Power Supply | China | 259,142 |
| 8 | Chevron | Petroleum | USA | 245,621 |
| 9 | ConocoPhillips | Petroleum | USA | 237,272 |
| 10 | Toyota Motor | Automotive | Japan | 253,364 |
| 11 | Total | Petroleum | USA | 231,580 |
| 12 | Volkswagen | Automotive | Germany | 221,551 |
| 13 | Japan Post Holdings | Finance | Japan | 211,019 |
| 14 | Glencore International | Manufacturing | Switzerland | 186,152 |
| 15 | Gazprom | Petroleum | Russia | 157,831 |
| 16 | E.On | Energy | U.K. | 157,057 |
| 17 | ENI | Petroleum | Italy | 153,676 |
| 18 | ING Group | Insurance | USA | 150,571 |
| 19 | General Motors | Automotive | USA | 150,276 |
| 20 | Samsung Electronics | Electronics | South Korea | 148,944 |

Source: Adapted from Fortune 2012. "Fortune Global 500." http://www.fortune.com/fortune/global500.

companies are from the financial and insurance industries. However, it is also important to note that not all top-20 companies are from Western countries. For example, the companies ranked fifth (Sinopec) and sixth (China National Petroleum) are both Chinese multinationals. Furthermore, the list also includes previously unknown multinationals such as E.On and ENI.

Where are most of the global multinationals located? Exhibit 1.2 lists selected countries with higher numbers of Fortune Global 500 companies. As you can see, global multinationals are concentrated not just in major Western cities. Prominent new competitors can be found in countries such as China, South Korea, Brazil, and Mexico. As of 2012, the United States had about 132 global multinationals, with China having the next highest number at 73. This is in sharp contrast to the situation in 2008, when the United States had 153 global multinationals and Japan had 64, the second-highest number. Such trends show the impressive growth of companies from emerging markets such as Brazil (8 global multinationals), Russia (7 global multinationals) India (8 global multinationals), and China (73 global multinationals). This exhibit also shows that global companies can be located anywhere in the world and are not confined to European or U.S. cities.

What kinds of business activities might make a company multinational? The most apparent activity, of course, is international sales. When a company produces in its own country and sells in another country, it engages in the simplest form of multinational activity. However, as you will see in much more detail, crossing national borders opens up more options than simply selling internationally.

To introduce some of these options, consider the following hypothetical U.S. company that produces and sells men's shirts. As a domestic-only company,

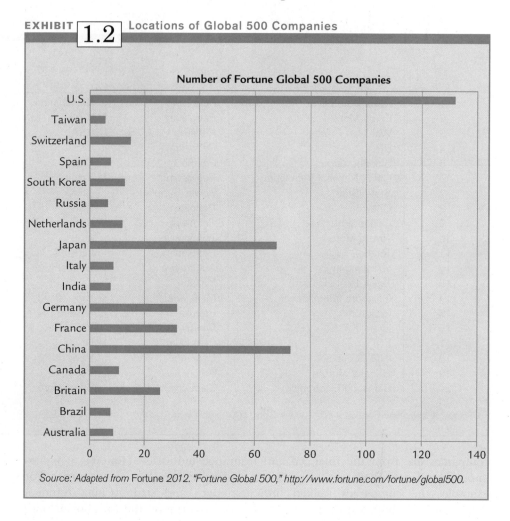

**EXHIBIT 1.2**     Locations of Global 500 Companies

*Source: Adapted from* Fortune *2012. "Fortune Global 500,"* http://www.fortune.com/fortune/global500.

it could buy the dye, make the fabric, cut and sew the garment, and sell the shirt, all in the United States. However, the firm might not be able to compete successfully using this approach. The U.S. market might be stagnant, with competitive pricing and decreased profit margins. Competitors might find higher-quality fabric or dye from overseas suppliers. Competitors might also find lower production costs in low-wage countries, allowing them to offer lower prices. What can this company do?

As a multinational company, the firm might sell its shirts to overseas buyers with less competition and at higher prices. Several other multinational activities might also increase its competitive strength. For example, the shirt maker might locate any of the steps in obtaining raw materials or completing production in another country. It might buy the highest-quality dye from Italy; use low-cost, high-quality fabric producers in Hong Kong; and have the cutting and sewing done in Vietnam, with its very low labor costs. For any of these steps, the company might contract with local companies in another country, or it may own its own factories in the other country. As you will see in later chapters, MNCs must develop strategies and systems to accomplish all or some of the multinational business tasks of this hypothetical U.S. firm.

Next, we will consider the forces that drive the new economic reality that faces the next generation of multinational managers and MNCs.

# The Globalizing Economy: A Changing (but Not Always Stable) Environment for Business

Trade barriers are falling, and in the first decade of this century, world trade among countries in goods and services grew faster than domestic production. Money is flowing more freely across national borders, allowing companies to seek the best rates for financing—and allowing investors to look for the best returns—anywhere in the world. All of these processes, known as globalization, represent the trend whereby the world's economies are becoming borderless and interlinked. Companies are no longer limited by their domestic boundaries and may conduct any kind of business activity anywhere in the world. Globalization means that companies are more likely to compete anywhere, source their raw material or research and development (R&D) anywhere, and produce their products anywhere.

Globalization, however, is not a uniform evolutionary process, and not all economies of the world are benefiting or participating equally in it. Terrorism, wars, and at times a worldwide economic stagnation have limited or in some cases even reversed some aspects of globalization. Additionally, globalization is producing such worrisome effects as natural resource scarcity, environmental pollution, negative social impacts, and increased interdependence of the world's economies.[1] Furthermore, some even argue that globalization is widening the gap between rich and poor countries.

However, others see globalization as beneficial to the world's economies. For instance, globalization is resulting in lower prices in many countries as multinationals become more efficient. Lower prices give consumers more for their money while encouraging local productivity through competition.[2] Furthermore, globalization is clearly benefiting many emerging markets such as India and China because these countries enjoy greater availability of jobs and better access to technology. Globalization has been the major reason why many new companies from countries such as Mexico, Brazil, China, India, and South Korea are among the new dominant global competitors.

Several key trends drive the globalization of the world economy, and in turn—even with shakeups to the world economy—force businesses to become more multinational to survive and prosper. Some of the most important trends include falling borders, growing cross-border trade and investment, the rise of global products and global customers, the growing use of the Internet and sophisticated information technology (IT), privatizations of formerly government-owned companies, the emergence of new competitors in the world market, and the rise of global standards for quality and production.

Before discussing the key globalization trends that affect multinational managers and their companies, it is useful to look at some commonly used classifications of the world's countries. The classifications roughly indicate a country's GDP and its growth in GDP. The classifications are not exact, but they simplify discussions of world trade and investments.

## Countries of the World: The Arrived, the Coming, and the Struggling

Exhibit 1.3 shows some divisions of the world's economies based roughly on classifications used by the United Nations and the *Economist*. **Developed countries** have mature economies with substantial per-capita GDPs and international trade and investments. **Developing countries**, such as Hong Kong, Singapore, and Taiwan, have economies that have grown extensively over the past two decades, yet have sometimes struggled, especially during the setbacks of the Asian crisis in the late

**Globalization**
The worldwide trend of cross-border economic integration that allows businesses to expand beyond their domestic boundaries.

**Developed countries**
Countries with mature economies, high GDPs, and high levels of trade and investment.

**Developing countries**
Countries with economies that have grown extensively in the past two decades.

**EXHIBIT 1.3**    Selected Economies of the World

| Developed Economies | Developing Economies | Transition Economies | Emerging Markets |
|---|---|---|---|
| Australia | Hong Kong | Czech Republic | Argentina |
| Austria | Singapore | Hungary | Brazil |
| Belgium | Taiwan | Poland | China |
| Britain | Malaysia | Russia | Chile |
| Canada | Indonesia | | Colombia |
| Denmark | Thailand | | India |
| France | | | Malaysia |
| Germany | | | Mexico |
| Italy | | | Philippines |
| Ireland | | | South Africa |
| Japan | | | South Korea |
| Netherlands | | | Turkey |
| Spain | | | Venezuela |
| Sweden | | | |
| Switzerland | | | |
| United States | | | |

*Sources: Adapted from Economist. 2003. "Markets and data, weekly indicators." http://www.economist.com, June 7; Economist. 2006. "Emerging markets and interest rates." August 5, 65; Economist. 2012. "Dream on?" July 21, 59–60.*

**Transition economies**
Countries in the process of changing from government-controlled economic systems to free market or capitalistic systems.

**Emerging markets**
Countries that are currently between developed and developing countries and are rapidly growing.

1990s. Other economies to watch are what the UN calls the **transition economies** of Central and Eastern Europe, such as the Czech Republic, Hungary, Poland, and Russia. Transition economies are countries that have changed from government-controlled, mostly Communist, economic systems to free market or capitalistic systems. The former systems relied on state-controlled organizations and centralized government control to run the economy. In the transition to free market and capitalistic systems, many government-owned companies were converted to private ownership. From that point, the market, not the government, determined the success of companies. Several of these transition economies, such as Hungary, Poland, Slovakia, and the Czech Republic, have developed market economies and are now members of the European Union (EU).

Finally, **emerging markets** are currently economies that are growing rapidly. Although it is difficult to determine the exact list of emerging markets, prominent countries such as India, China, Brazil, and Russia are considered to be emerging. In fact, the term BRIC, standing for Brazil, Russia, India, and China, has also been suggested to represent the strongest among the emerging economies.

The term *emerging markets,* coined by the World Bank around 25 years ago, represents markets that present tremendous opportunities for all multinationals.[3] In fact, emerging markets have about five-sixths of the world's population with only half of the output. Furthermore, the purchasing power in many emerging markets has been increasing steadily. It is therefore not surprising to see that emerging markets now account for 30 percent of exports, compared to only 20 percent in 1970. Recent trends also show that developed countries' trade with emerging markets has been growing twice as much compared to trade with each other.[4] Furthermore, while emerging markets are now experiencing a significant slowdown in growth, they are still expected to grow at a much faster pace than developed economies.

However, despite these classifications, we acknowledge that many of the economies classified as developing or transition economies can also be classified as emerging economies. In fact, countries such as Russia, Poland, and Singapore are rightly being classified as emerging markets in some reports. Such trends suggest that we will not see such a broad classification in the future, as countries will be seen as either developed or emerging.

Finally, although these nations have not necessarily received any specific designation, African nations are getting attention for their strong economic development.[5] Many countries in Africa are growing at a faster pace than the rest of the world. Consider the following Case in Point.

With this overview of the major economies of the world, we can now look more closely at the driving forces of the new world economy. Exhibit 1.4 illustrates these important forces. Each will be discussed more fully in the following pages.

## Disintegrating Borders: The World Trade Organization and Free Trade Areas

In 1947, several nations began negotiating to limit worldwide tariffs and encourage free trade. At that time, worldwide tariffs averaged 45 percent. Seven rounds of tariff negotiations reduced the average worldwide tariffs on manufactured goods from 45 percent to less than 7 percent. These negotiations were known as the **General Agreement on Tariffs and Trade (GATT)**.

**General Agreement on Tariffs and Trade (GATT)**
Tariff negotiations among several nations that reduced the average worldwide tariff on manufactured goods.

---

### CASE IN POINT

### Africa Rising?

Mo Ibrahim is one of Africa's noted entrepreneurs and is also the founder of the Mo Ibrahim Foundation, dedicated to supporting good governance in sub-Saharan Africa. When he was running MSI, a software and consulting company based in the United Kingdom, he started asking his telecommunications clients why they were not going to Africa. He saw tremendous opportunities in Africa, but most of his Western-based clients seemed ignorant of such opportunities. He therefore decided to form Celtel out of another telecommunications project that started in 1998. Through smart entry into lucrative markets and by buying only those licenses that were acquired through open bidding or cheap license costs, Celtel grew quickly, experiencing a growth of 216 percent in revenue between 2001 and 2010. Today, Celtel is owned by one of India's major telecommunications companies, Bharti Airtel, and is one of Africa's leading multinationals.

The above is just one example of the vast opportunities that African nations present to the world today. Many African nations are growing faster than the rest of the world. A number of other factors are fueling this growth, and will sustain it in the future. For instance, by 2015, around 100 million households in Africa will have reached middle-class status, thereby supporting local demand. Furthermore, the African population will be significantly younger than the rest of the world. (The median age in Africa is now 20, as compared to 30 in Asia and 40 in Europe). Such demographic dividends are likely to support growth. Additionally, many African nations have seen significant regulatory changes that have improved the business climate. Many countries have reduced or eliminated trade barriers. Improvement in transportation also means that Africans are increasingly engaging in cross-border trade with each other. Finally, African nations are no longer solely relying on oil or other commodities for survival. Foreign investors are finding that other industries, such as technology and other services, are also worthy of investment.

*Sources: Based on* Economist. *2011. "The sun shines bright." December 3, 82–84; Mo, I. 2012. "Celtel's founder on building a business on the world's poorest continent." Harvard Business Review, October, 41–43.*

**EXHIBIT** 1.4     The Globalizing Economy

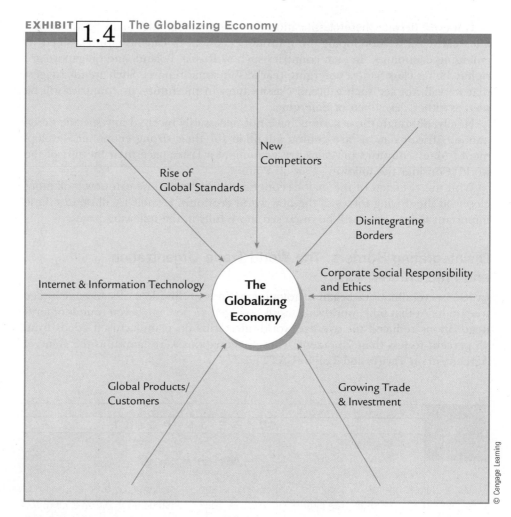

Negotiations in Uruguay began in 1986, and ended in 1993 with agreements to reduce tariffs even further; to liberalize trade in agriculture and services; and to eliminate some nontariff barriers to international trade, such as excessive use of health regulations to keep out imports.[6] The Uruguay talks also established the **World Trade Organization (WTO)** to succeed GATT. The WTO provides a formal structure for continued negotiations and for settling trade disputes among nations. There are now more than 150 nations in the WTO, up from 92 when the 1986 GATT talks began, including 29 of the UN-classified least-developed countries. Thirty other countries, including Russia, seek WTO membership. Since 1995, tariffs on industrial products have fallen from an average of 6.3 percent to 3.8 percent.[7]

In March 1997, trade ministers from countries representing 92 percent of world trade in IT products agreed to end tariffs on trade in software, computer chips, telecommunications equipment, and computers by the year 2005. The immediate result was that, with tariffs eliminated, high-tech exports to Europe from Asia and the United States doubled. Developing countries, even those not party to the agreement, also benefited, as prices began to go down on products such as phones, faxes, and computers produced in tariff-free locations.[8]

Is free trade working? The WTO thinks so, and the data seem to support its conclusion. Since the early GATT agreements, world trade has grown at more than

**World Trade Organization (WTO)**
A formal structure for continued negotiations to reduce trade barriers and a mechanism for settling trade disputes.

four times the output of the world's gross domestic product. This suggests that the world's economies are increasingly more intertwined and mutually stimulated.

There are critics, however. Some argue that the WTO favors the developed nations because it is more difficult for poorer nations to compete in an unregulated world. Environmentalists note that free trade encourages large multinational companies to move environmentally damaging production to poorer and often environmentally sensitive countries; that is, commercial interests have priority over the environment, health, and safety. Labor unions see free trade leading to the migration of jobs from higher-wage countries to lower-wage countries.

The WTO is not the only group encouraging the elimination of trade barriers. Regional trade agreements, or free trade areas, are agreements among groups of nations to reduce tariffs and to develop similar technical and economic standards. With the breakdown of the Doha Development Round talks in 2008, regional trade agreements are very likely to continue growing in importance.[9] Such agreements have usually led to more trade among the member nations. Some argue that these agreements are the first step toward complete globalization. Others criticize the agreements as benefiting only trade group members and being harmful for the poorer nations left out of the agreements, such as the Caribbean countries that are not North American Free Trade Agreement (NAFTA) members.[10] From a practical point of view, regional agreements benefit world trade more than they hurt it. Although they do benefit member countries the most, such agreements are more politically manageable than worldwide trade agreements.[11]

The three largest agreements account for nearly half of the world's trade. These groups are the EU, NAFTA, and APEC.

The EU (European Union) includes 27 members, namely, Austria, Belgium, Britain, Bulgaria, Cyprus, Czech Republic, Denmark, Estonia, Finland, France, Germany, Greece, Hungary, Ireland, Italy, Latvia, Lithuania, Luxembourg, Malta, the Netherlands, Poland, Portugal, Romania, Slovakia, Slovenia, Spain, and Sweden. Croatia becomes the 28th member in July of 2013. Although the idea of the European Union originated during World War II, the EU took off in 1992, when countries allowed goods and services to move across borders without customs duties and quotas. More recently, EU member countries adopted a unified currency called euro. EU member countries currently represent 450 million individuals and an area of significant economic importance. The EU is also currently considering applications for membership from countries such as Croatia, Macedonia, and Turkey. You can check the current status of the EU at http://europa.eu.

The North American Free Trade Agreement (NAFTA) links the United States, Canada, and Mexico in an economic bloc that allows the relatively free exchange of goods and services. After the agreement went into effect in the early 1990s, all three countries experienced immediate increases in trade. However, the Mexican economy soon went into a tailspin, with inflation running as high as 45 percent.[12] Emergency loans from the United States helped stabilize the situation, and by 1996, Mexico had paid back the loans—before the due date. The next step for NAFTA may be FTAA, or the Free Trade Area of Americas. This group will include not only the United States, Canada, and Mexico, but also most of the other Caribbean, Central American, and South American nations.

Compared with the EU or NAFTA, the Asia-Pacific Economic Cooperation (APEC) is a loose confederation of 21 nations with less-specific agreements on trade facilitation. However, its ultimate goals call for total free trade in the Pacific region by 2020.[13] Some of the major players in APEC include China, the United States, Japan, Taiwan, South Korea, Hong Kong, Australia, Singapore, Thailand, and Malaysia.

Exhibit 1.5 shows all the major regional trade agreements and their member countries.

**Regional trade agreements**
Agreements among nations in a particular region to reduce tariffs and develop similar technical and economic standards.

**European Union (EU)**
Austria, Belgium, Bulgaria, Britain, Denmark, Finland, France, Germany, Greece, Ireland, Italy, Luxembourg, the Netherlands, Portugal, Romania, Spain, and Sweden, plus Norway and Switzerland in the related European Free Trade Area.

**North American Free Trade Agreement (NAFTA)**
A multilateral treaty that links the United States, Canada, and Mexico in an economic bloc that allows freer exchange of goods and services.

**Asia-Pacific Economic Cooperation (APEC)**
A confederation of 19 nations with less-specific agreements on trade facilitation in the Pacific region.

**EXHIBIT 1.5**   Regional Trade Agreements around the World

| Andean Common Market | ASEAN (Association of Southeast Asian Nations) | Baltic Countries | CEPGL (Economic Community of the Great Lakes Countries) | APEC (Asia-Pacific Economic Cooperation) | UEMOA (West African Economic and Monetary Union) |
|---|---|---|---|---|---|
| Bolivia | Brunei Darussalam | Estonia | Burundi | Australia | Benin |
| Colombia | Cambodia | Latvia | Democratic Republic of the Congo | Brunei Darussalam | Burkina Faso |
| Ecuador | Indonesia | Lithuania | Rwanda | Canada | Cote d'Ivoire |
| Peru | Lao People's Democratic Republic | | | Chile | Guinea-Bissau |
| Venezuela | Malaysia | | | China | Mali |
| | Myanmar | | | Hong Kong, China | Niger |
| | Philippines | | | Indonesia | Senegal |
| | Singapore | | | Japan | Togo |
| | Thailand | | | Malaysia | |
| | Vietnam | | | Mexico | |
| | | | | New Zealand | |
| | | | | Papua New Guinea | |
| | | | | Peru | |
| | | | | Philippines | |
| | | | | Republic of Korea | |
| | | | | Russian Federation | |
| | | | | Singapore | |
| | | | | Taiwan | |
| | | | | Thailand | |
| | | | | United States of America | |

| CARICOM (Caribbean Community) | ECO (Economic Cooperation Organization) | EU (European Union) | UMA (Arab Maghreb Union) | CIS (Commonwealth of Independent States) | OECS (Organization of Eastern Caribbean States) |
|---|---|---|---|---|---|
| Antigua and Barbuda | Afghanistan | Austria | Algeria | Armenia | Anguilla |
| Bahamas | Azerbaijan | Belgium | Libya | Azerbaijan | Antigua and Barbuda |
| Barbados | Islamic Republic of Iran | Denmark | Mauritania | Belarus | British Virgin Islands |
| Belize | Kazakhstan | Finland | Morocco | Georgia | Dominica |
| Dominica | Kyrgyzstan | France | Tunisia | Kazakhstan | Grenada |
| Grenada | Pakistan | Germany | | Kyrgyzstan | Montserrat |
| Guyana | Tajikistan | Greece | | Moldova | Saint Kitts and Nevis |
| Jamaica | Turkey | Ireland | | Russian Federation | Saint Lucia |
| Montserrat | Turkmenistan | Italy | | Tajikistan | Saint Vincent and the Grenadines |
| Saint Kitts and Nevis | Uzbekistan | Luxembourg | | Turkmenistan | |
| Saint Lucia | | Netherlands | | Ukraine | |
| Saint Vincent and the Grenadines | | Portugal | | Uzbekistan | |
| Suriname | | Spain | | | |
| Trinidad and Tobago | | Sweden | | | |
| | | United Kingdom | | | |

### FTAA (Free Trade Area of the Americas)

Antigua and Barbuda
Argentina
Bahamas
Barbados
Belize
Bolivia
Brazil
Canada
Chile
Colombia
Costa Rica
Dominica
Dominican Republic
Ecuador
El Salvador
Grenada
Guatemala
Guyana
Haiti
Honduras
Jamaica
Mexico
Nicaragua
Panama
Paraguay
Peru
Saint Kitts and Nevis
Saint Lucia
Saint Vincent and the Grenadines
Suriname
Trinidad and Tobago
United States of America
Uruguay
Venezuela

### GCC (Gulf Cooperation Council)

Bahrain
Kuwait
Oman
Qatar
Saudi Arabia
United Arab Emirates

### EU (European Union and Accession Countries)

Member States:
Austria
Belgium
Denmark
Finland
France
Germany
Greece
Ireland
Italy
Luxembourg
Netherlands
Portugal
Spain
Sweden
United Kingdom

New Member States:
Cyprus
Czech Republic
Estonia
Hungary
Latvia
Lithuania
Malta
Poland
Slovakia
Slovenia

Ascension States:
Romania
Slovakia
Turkey

### ECOWAS (Economic Community of West African States)

Benin
Burkina Faso
Cape Verde
Cote d'Ivoire
Gambia
Ghana
Guinea
Guinea-Bissau
Liberia
Mali
Niger
Nigeria
Senegal
Sierra Leone
Togo

### MERCOSUR (Southern Cone Common Market)

Argentina
Brazil
Paraguay
Uruguay

### SAARC (South Asian Association for Regional Cooperation)

Bangladesh
Bhutan
India
Maldives
Nepal
Pakistan
Sri Lanka

### ECCAS (Economic Community of Central African States)

Angola
Burundi
Cameroon
Central African Republic
Chad
Congo
Democratic Republic of the Congo
Equatorial Guinea
Gabon
Rwanda
Sao Tome and Principe

*Source: Adapted from UNCTAD (UN Conference on Trade and Development). 2003. "Prospects for global and regional FDI inflows, UNCTAD's worldwide survey of investment promotion agencies." Research Note, May 14.*

## Sell Anywhere, Locate Anywhere: Trade and Foreign Investment Are Growing but Setbacks Are Part of the Challenge

World trade among countries (imports and exports) grew at an average rate of 6.5 percent per year between 1990 and 2000,[14] slowed to 4 percent by 2004, and grew again to 6 percent in 2005.[15] World trade grew by 8.5 percent in 2006. However, the latest available figures suggest that trade then slowed down because of the economic recession. World trade was predicted to grow at only 2.5 percent in 2012, and the forecast for 2013 was 4.5 percent (see the WTO website for current information).

Exhibit 1.6 shows the annual change of exports and imports for developed economies and developing economies based on the most recent WTO data. As this exhibit shows, developing nations and mostly emerging nations have experienced much stronger growth in both exports and imports in recent years. This exhibit also provides further evidence of robustness of growth and trade in emerging markets relative to developed economies. Exhibit 1.6 provides strong support for the importance of such economies to world trade.

The latest report on world trade from the WTO (see http://www.wto.org) suggests a few trends. First, the global economy is suffering a very severe slowdown caused by weak economic performance in most of the world's biggest economies.

**EXHIBIT 1.6**     Change in Exports and Imports (Developed and Developing Economies)

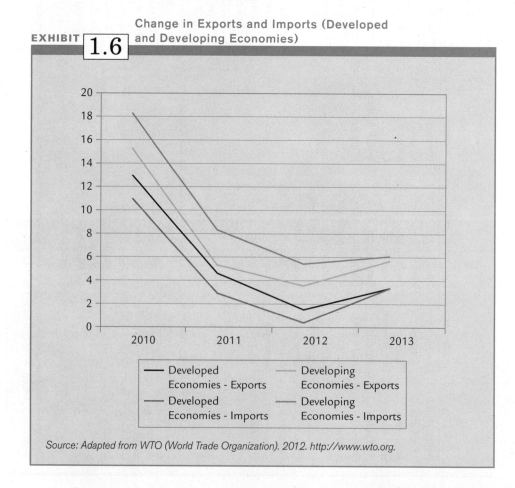

Source: Adapted from WTO (World Trade Organization). 2012. http://www.wto.org.

European countries are suffering the worst sovereign debt crisis they have ever faced. Furthermore, employment and output data continue to be disappointing in the United States. Finally, China is also experiencing a slowdown because of weakened domestic demand and soft demand from foreign countries. A second important trend is that for both imports and exports, the annual percentage changes in developing and emerging economies were higher than those from developed economies. Such trends also suggest that emerging economies are still performing at a higher level.

Multinational companies not only trade across borders with exports and imports but also build global networks that link R&D, supply, production, and sales units around the globe. The result is that cross-border ownership, called foreign direct investment, is on the rise, more than doubling between 1998 and 2001.[16] **Foreign direct investment (FDI)** occurs when a multinational company from one country has an ownership position in an organizational unit located in another country. Fueled by cross-border mergers and acquisitions, such as the merger of Chrysler and Daimler-Benz, cross-border ownership was especially high in the late 1990s, up to the year 2000.

Foreign direct investment soared by more than 36 percent between 1996 and 2000 and reached a record of more than $1.5 trillion in 2000.[17] Following a pattern similar to international trade, however, FDI declined to $735 billion in 2001, less than half of the previous year, and declined another 25 percent in 2002. The global environment for FDI seems to be declining significantly. According to the 2008 statistics provided by the Organization for Economic Co-operation and Development (OECD) website, countries in the OECD group saw declines in foreign direct investment for both incoming investment (35 percent) and outgoing investment (19 percent). Data for 2012 indicate that the decline of FDI seems sustained. The OECD group investment inflows for the first quarter of 2012 declined by 18 percent.

Despite these declines, the importance of emerging markets is reflected in the growth of FDI in these economies (see http://www.oecd.org for this report). The emerging economies of China, Brazil, and Russia were significant FDI destinations, receiving US$182 billion, US$15 billion, and US$13 billion, respectively. However, emerging nations were also significant investors abroad. The most recent OECD report shows that investment by Argentina, China, and India increased by more than 50 percent in the first quarter of 2012. Furthermore, Indonesia experienced its highest FDI outflow, investing US$3 billion in the first quarter of 2012.

What does this mean for individual companies? Trends suggest that, despite the slowdown, FDI will probably resume its steady growth and stay steady, with mergers and acquisitions playing an important role in these markets. Perhaps the most important implication is that multinational companies now manufacture and sell anywhere.

Although OECD countries dominate the bulk of world FDI and will continue to do so in the immediate future, astute multinational managers are looking to other areas of the world for future investments. Specifically, emerging markets will continue to attract significant inflows of FDI. As we see here, many countries, such as India, China, Brazil, Russia, and others, will continue to present tremendous opportunities. However, succeeding in these markets will not be easy. Consider the next Case in Point.

Despite these challenges, multinationals will likely continue to invest in these markets, but Western-based multinationals will have to be very creative to succeed and beat local companies. As the Case in Point suggests, a good knowledge of the local market is necessary for any company to succeed. In addition, multinationals will have to develop strategies that local companies cannot easily copy.

**Foreign direct investment (FDI)**
Multinational firm's ownership, in part or in whole, of an operation in another country.

## CASE IN POINT

### Succeeding in Emerging Markets

It is not easy to succeed in emerging markets, which often present significant challenges that may discourage the most well-intentioned companies. For instance, the roads in some emerging markets may still be impassable, or local products may be sold at prices well below the cost of production. Other markets have local products with intensely loyal customers. How can multinationals succeed in such markets? A recent study of successful multinationals suggests some common best practices. Successful multinationals:

- *Enter the mass market to achieve economies of scale.* Although multinationals in the past would target only premium segments, it is becoming increasingly evident that the mass market presents significant opportunities.

- *Localize as much as possible.* If companies take the time to understand local market needs, they increase their chance of succeeding. Consider the case of Procter & Gamble and its toothpaste Crest, reformulated in fruit and tea flavors with herbal elements. Such localization gives the product a very local flavor.

- *Develop a good-enough mentality.* Rather than focusing on the upscale or low-end target,

successful multinationals develop products that are of better quality than those of the low end but not in the premium category. Such products then become more affordable to the local population. Consider the efforts by African telecommunication companies to develop affordable mobile phones for poor consumers.

- *Hire local managers rather than expatriates.* Local managers have better knowledge of the local market.

- *Understand the role of states in the business world.* Most Western countries are not used to national states owning and running companies. However, many of the emerging markets of China, India, and Brazil have significant state companies that are major business players. It therefore becomes critical for companies to understand how to do business with these state entities.

*Sources: Based on* Economist. 2012. *"The visible hand," January 21, 3–5; Mo, I. 2012. "Celtel's founder on building a business on the world's poorest continent."* Harvard Business Review, *October, 41–43; Shankar, S., C. Ormiston, N. Bloch, R. Schaus, and V. Viswhwanath. 2008. "How to win in emerging markets."* MIT Sloan Management Review, *49(3): 19–23.*

Additionally, although developing countries may provide great opportunities for multinational companies, they are also among the most risky locations in the world. We usually think of two types of risks in multinational business: economic and political. As you will see in more detail in Chapter 5, political risk is anything a government might do (or not do) that might adversely affect a company. In extreme circumstances—and now very rarely—governments have expropriated or taken over foreign firms with little or no compensation. More often, though, a government's instability and the uncertainty of its reactions to foreign investment are the most important considerations. Economic risk considers all factors of a nation's economic climate that may affect a foreign investor. Government policies affect some of these factors, such as mandating artificially high or low interest rates. Other factors, such as a volatile exchange rate, may respond to economic forces from outside the country.

## The Internet and Information Technology Are Making It All Easier

The explosive growth of the Internet, as well as major growth in the capabilities of information technology, has increased multinational companies' ability to deal with a global economy. The Internet makes it easy for companies to go global because anyone in the world can access any website. Thus, companies and individuals can shop and sell anywhere. Because of the growing importance of e-commerce, Chapter 10 discusses the impact of the Internet on multinational management in detail.

Electronic communication vehicles, such as e-mail and the World Wide Web, allow multinational companies to communicate with company locations around the world, and information technology expands the global reach of an organization. Multinational companies can now monitor worldwide operations to an extent never before possible. Text and graphic information can flow to any part of the world nearly instantaneously. Headquarters, R&D, manufacturing, and sales can be located anywhere there is a computer. Because employees, suppliers, and customers are geographically dispersed, organizations are becoming virtual—linked by networks of computers. Information technology makes it all happen.

Information technology is also spurring a borderless financial market. Investors are going global, and companies of the future will get their financing not in local stock or bond markets but in global markets that seek the best companies worldwide. Consider this *Business Week* comment, which captures the feel of financial markets in the twenty-first century:

> It's January 20, 2015, a fine summer day in Sydney. You stroll up to a Citibank automated-teller machine and, after the eye retina scan log on, a computer in Bombay greets you, and you get down to business. First, you shift 10,000 Euros into today's special—a NAFTA-dollar certificate of deposit issued by GEC Capital in Rome. Equities are looking good, so you punch in an order for 500 shares of Telefonos de Mexico on the New York Stock Exchange. Then, at the press of a button, an account officer in Singapore comes onto the screen to answer your questions about a loan for your factory in Argentina.[18]

As we will see in Chapter 7, information technologies are allowing small companies to get very easy access to resources worldwide (capital, human resources, and machinery).

Information technologies make available many new tools that facilitate business operations. For instance, Voice-Over-Internet Protocol (VOIP) companies such as Skype now allow employees to communicate worldwide at very low costs. WIKI companies allow companies to set up collaborative networks at very low cost. Instant messaging through such services as MSN Messenger and AOL also allow employees to stay in constant communication. Finally, increasingly sophisticated search engines like Google allow anyone to find crucial information. Many small companies typically use such searches to find suppliers or manufacturers in emerging markets such as India or China.

Information technology is thus presenting multinationals with many new opportunities. Consider the next Multinational Management Brief.

The use of information technology and the Internet is also speeding up another globalization driver. Because many companies now use the Web to search for suppliers, being a global customer is much easier than it used to be.

## The Rise of Global Products and Global Customers

Although large differences still exist among countries in terms of national cultures and political and economic systems, the needs of customers around the world for many products and services are growing more similar. For example, the products

## Multinational Management **Brief**

### Information Technology Opportunities for Multinationals

The spread of computing power and technology and the Internet has become so pervasive that the *Economist* has dubbed the dramatic changes affecting the business environment as the third industrial revolution. Developments in computing technology mean that the manufacturing sector will no longer see hammers, lathes, drills, and stamping presses. Instead, at the latest manufacturing trade fair, Euromold, held in Frankfurt, displays consisted of hall after hall of clean and highly automated machine tools. Most of the operators sat in front of computer screens.

One of the most significant recent technologies is the 3D printer. These printers work very similarly to regular printers. However, instead of ink, the 3D printer uses materials such as plastic. As an object is being printed, the printer successfully adds thin layers of the material until a solid object emerges.

The potential for the 3D printer to revolutionize multinational operations is tremendous. Prototypes can now be easily and cheaply printed to get approval from engineers, stylists, and even customers. Three-dimensional printing can also allow engineers located around the world to collaborate with minimal costs. Furthermore, this type of printing is also allowing the development of complex prototypes at relatively low costs and even weight savings.

Companies such as Shapeways in the Netherlands are already taking advantage of 3D printing. They have already shipped over 750,000 products using 3D printers in 2011 and the numbers are growing. Users can upload their designs and get quotes using different materials. Such possibilities mean that products can now go to market much faster. Furthermore, entrepreneurs may no longer have to wait for product failures in the market before they release such products. Three-dimensional printing allows prototypes to be extensively tested in efficient ways.

*Sources: Based on* Economist. 2012. *"A third industrial revolution." April 21, 3–4;* Economist. 2012. *"Solid print." April 21, 14–18;* Economist. 2012. *"All together now." April 21, 18–19.*

offered by fast-food chains like McDonald's, aircraft manufacturers like Boeing, and automakers like Toyota are quite similar and successful no matter where they are sold in the world. In industries where customers' needs are similar across national boundaries, global competition is more likely.[19]

Along with the rise of worldwide customer needs, a new type of customer is increasingly common: the global customer. Global customers search the world for their supplies without regard for national boundaries. Price and quality affect purchase decisions more than nationality does. At present, most global customers are companies making industrial purchases. This explains why 70 percent of global e-commerce comes from business-to-business transactions. However, with the globalization of mail order businesses and the increased use of Web stores for purchasing consumer goods, including everything from athletic equipment to PCs, soon anyone can be a global customer.

Similar customer needs and globally minded customers link economies because companies can produce one product for everybody, and anyone can buy anything from anywhere. These trends will continue as developing nations become more than sources of cheap production and turn into the areas of the greatest consumer growth.

## New Competitors Are Emerging

The free market reforms in emerging countries are creating a potential group of new competitors around the world. As you have seen in this chapter, experts now recognize the existence of powerful emerging market competitors that are using many new techniques and strategies to compete successfully in their local markets. In many cases, these new competitors had to survive brutal competition in their domestic markets to become successful. By competing every day with both domestic rivals and Western multinationals, they were able to develop strategies to generate profits at very low prices.

Global trade has two important effects in developing new competitors. First, when large multinationals use developing countries as low-wage platforms for high-tech assembly, they facilitate the transfer of technology. Workers and companies in developing countries often learn new skills when large multinationals use them for low-cost production and assembly. In countries where workers are well educated and motivated, the former assemblers often become the creators rather than the builders of advanced technologies. Second, aggressive multinational companies from emerging market countries are also expanding beyond their own borders. Consider the following Case in Point about the rise of state firms.

As the above Case in Point shows, companies worldwide will increasingly have to contend with formidable state competitors. These companies are often well run

### CASE IN POINT

### Rise of State Firms

Western multinationals are increasingly competing with state multinationals based in emerging nations worldwide. These enterprises have often been very successful while relying on state support. Consider the China National Offshore Oil Corporation, which has built an impressive headquarters that resembles an oil tanker emerging from the sea. Petronas, Malaysia's state-owned oil company, has built an 88-story tower in Kuala Lumpur. Furthermore, the Moskva City Business Complex in Moscow houses two new sleek skyscrapers where Russia's first- and second-largest banks are headquartered. Such impressive buildings display the might of these new state multinationals.

An understanding of the characteristics of such state-owned firms is critical to understand the implications for international management. First, these companies are succeeding because of prudent governmental strategies. Most state-owned companies have been pruned and restructured to become lean. They therefore have cash that they can use for expanding. State companies are no longer poorly run enterprises.

Second, they have been extremely successful in emerging markets defying expert prediction about the downfall of government-owned enterprises. Because of the potential offered by such markets and their local knowledge of such markets, they have been more readily able to take advantage of such opportunities. Third, they are no longer content to operate domestically. Many of the national energy companies have invested aggressively in other countries. Chinese oil companies have been striking many deals in Africa. Fourth, they are not necessarily limited to oil and energy industries. State-owned enterprises are also successful in the finance industries running sovereign wealth funds. Finally, some state-owned companies also have strong support from their respective governments. Consider the case of Lenovo, the computer manufacturer, which has been provided repeatedly with seed money from the Chinese Academy of Sciences in order to smooth out growth.

*Source: Based on* Economist. *2012. "Special report: State capitalism." January 21, 3–12.*

but can also rely on the state for financial support. Furthermore, they also have better knowledge of local markets and can therefore better tailor products to satisfy these markets. Worldwide multinationals will therefore have to adapt their strategies to these new competitors.

## The Rise of Global Standards

Increasingly, especially in technical industries, global product standards are common. For example, you can buy an AA battery anywhere in the world, and it will fit into your flashlight. A driving factor is that, when a product standard is accepted globally or regionally, companies can make one or only a few versions of a product for the world market. This is much cheaper than making 100 different versions for 100 different countries. Component makers also benefit because they can take advantage of the same efficiencies with fewer product designs.

Certainly, there are still many diverse technical standards throughout the world. For example, Europe and North America have different formats for TVs and DVDs. Differences in electrical currents and plugs are common examples of difficulties that international travelers face. However, many electronic devices are now smart enough to overcome these differences. Power sources for computers, for example, often can adjust automatically for differences in voltage.

As new products are introduced into the world market, there is increasing competitive pressure to save money by developing one product for everyone. Therefore, the company that can establish its standard as dominant, either regionally or worldwide, has a tremendous strategic advantage. For example, the U.S. company Motorola is locked in a fierce competitive battle with Finland's Nokia and Sweden's Ericsson over setting the standard for the next generation of digital cellphone technology.

Consistency in quality also has become a requirement for doing business in many countries. The International Organization for Standardization (ISO) in Geneva, Switzerland, has developed a set of technical standards known originally as ISO 9000 and now called the **ISO 9001:2000** series (International Standards Organization 2006). There are also environmental protection standards known as **ISO 14000**.

In 1992, ISO compliance became part of product safety laws in many European countries. Many large European multinationals, such as Germany's Siemens, now require suppliers to be ISO certified. As a result, in order to do business in the EU, the pressure is increasing for the United States and other countries to adopt ISO quality requirements and standardization.[20]

## Corporate Social Responsibility and Business Ethics

Multinationals are facing increased pressure to be socially responsible. Although many multinationals have significant clout and power to influence local governments because of their size, these firms are now under increased scrutiny from both the media and the public. As a result, many multinationals are now very cognizant of the impact of their actions on the societies and countries in which they operate. Such companies need to pay attention to climate change, environmental degradation and pollution, sweatshop conditions, and bribery, to name only a few issues, because ignoring business ethics and corporate social responsibility issues can be perilous. Such multinationals can face significant backlash at home and in international markets, suffering significant losses in terms of both reputation and finance.

Proactive multinationals are therefore paying close attention to such issues. Consider the examples in the next Case in Point. As we will see, multinationals

**ISO 9001:2000**
The current name for the technical and quality standards of the International Organization for Standardization.

**ISO 14000**
The current name for the environmental protection standards of the International Organization for Standardization.

are finding ways to become more ethical. This issue is so important that we devote an entire chapter (Chapter 4) to understanding business ethics in the global environment.

Other evidence of the importance of business ethics to multinationals is the appearance of rankings on ethics. In that context, Ethispsphere is a renowned think-tank dedicated to furthering business ethics and corporate social responsibility. On a yearly basis, the organization conducts a global survey to identify companies that are seen as most ethical. Such companies not only exceed the legal minimum requirements for compliance in their industries, but they also are the leaders in terms of adoption of best ethical practices in their industries. Exhibit 1.7 shows selected companies from the 2012 list of the World's Most Ethical Companies, as identified by the most recent Ethisphere survey.

The next section describes some of the characteristics of the next generation of multinational managers.

---

## CASE IN POINT

### Corporate Social Responsibility and Multinationals

Multinationals worldwide are working hard to implement corporate social responsibility programs to show their approach to managing social responsibility and business ethics issues. Consider the following initiatives:

- A British nonprofit organization, Carbon Disclosure Project, is coordinating an important project to help major multinationals curb greenhouse gas emissions. Companies such as Cadbury Schweppes, Dell, Nestle, Pepsi, Procter & Gamble, and Tesco are working closely with their suppliers to identify sources of carbon emissions in their supply chain. These companies then intend to work together to identify ways to gradually reduce carbon emissions.

- Some multinationals are creating separate local social enterprises to tackle local problems. Consider the case of Indian chulas, which are wood-burning ovens made from mud. Although the chulas are very cheap to operate, they can often cause burns because of uncontrolled flames. Furthermore, the smoke can frequently fill the users' rooms, creating a sooty film in the kitchen and making breathing difficult. The electronics giant Royal Philips Electronics decided to partner with local chula users to find a better design. Only a year later, households were using the model designed by Philips. Rather than using a single length of pipe as a chimney, Philips

devised a three-part chimney that can be easily disassembled for cleaning. Chula users now breathe much more easily. Philips is also obtaining tremendous in-depth knowledge of product preferences.

- Companies such as IBM, Goldman Sachs, Google, and Community Business have partnered to create a resource guide to make the workplace more inclusive for Lesbian, Gay, Bisexual, and Transgender (LGBT) employees in India. The publication discusses the best practices regarding such inclusiveness. Leading companies are slowly recognizing the benefits of having diversity in the workplace.

- In Thailand, a joint venture between the South Korean electronics giant Samsung and the British retailer Tesco recognizes the importance of corporate social responsibility. The joint venture, Homeplus, has spent significant money towards CSR projects in four main areas: the environment, sharing, families, and neighbors. The company feels that if it spends on CSR, it will build better perception of the brand in the long run and lead to a better reputation.

*Sources: Based on Asia News Monitor. 2012. "Thailand: Tesco-Samsung JV sings praise of CSR." October 1, online edition; Capell, K., and N. Lakshman. 2008. "Philanthropy by design." BusinessWeek, September 22, 66; New York Times. 2008. "Multinationals fight climate change." January 21, C5; Saswati, M. 2012. "Inclusive workplace for LGBT employees in India." Times of India, October 13, online edition.*

**EXHIBIT 1.7**     Ethisphere's Most Ethical Companies (By Industry and Nationality)

| Industry | Company | Nationality |
|---|---|---|
| Apparel | Comme Il Faut | Israel |
| Apparel | Gap, Inc. | USA |
| Automotive | Cummins, Inc. | USA |
| Automotive | Ford Motor Company | USA |
| Banking | National Australia Bank | Australia |
| Banking | Rabobank | Netherlands |
| Banking | Standard Chartered Bank | UK |
| Business Services | Accenture | Ireland |
| Business Services | Dun & Bradstreet | USA |
| Computer Software | Symantec Corporation | USA |
| Computer Software | Wipro, Ltd. | India |
| Consumer Electronics | Ricoh | Japan |
| Energy: Electric | ENMAX Corporation | Canada |
| Energy: Natural Gas | Encana Corporation | Canada |
| Energy: Wind | Vestas | Denmark |
| Food and Beverages | Kellogg | USA |
| Food and Beverages | Pepsico | USA |
| Health and Beauty | L'Oreal | France |
| Health and Beauty | Shiseido | Japan |
| Medical Devices | Coloplast | Denmark |
| Medical Devices | Royal Philips | Netherlands |
| Retail | Kesko | Finland |
| Retail | Safeway | USA |
| Retail | Marks and Spencer | UK |
| Retail | Costco | USA |
| Transportation | Nippon Yusen Kabishiki Kaisha | Japan |
| Transportation | Panama Canal Authority | Panama |

*Source: Adapted from Ethisphere Institute. 2012. World's Most Ethical Companies. http://www.ethisphere.com.*

# The Next Generation of Multinational Managers

Consider what the experts say about the need for multinational managers and leaders:

> *It takes more than a lot of frequent flyer miles to become a global leader. Today's cosmopolitan executive must know what to do when competitive advantage is fleeting, when change becomes chaos, and when home base is the globe.[21]*
>
> *We need global leaders at a time when markets and companies are changing faster than the ability of leaders to reinvent themselves. We have a shortage of global leaders at a time when international exposure and experience are vital to business success. And we need internationally minded, globally literate leaders at a time when leadership styles are in transition around the world.[22]*

To become global leaders and to keep pace with the dizzying rate of globalization, most managers will need additional strengths to meet the related challenges.

According to some experts, the next generation of successful multinational managers must have the following characteristics:[23]

- *A global mindset:* A person with a **global mindset** understands that the world of business is changing rapidly and that the world is more interdependent in business transactions. A global mindset requires managers to think globally but act locally. Managers must see similarities in the global market while being able to adapt to local conditions in any country. A global mindset is necessary for all employees, from the CEO to the rank and file, if a company is to support and implement a global strategic vision. What does it mean to have a global mindset? Consider the following Multinational Management Brief.

- *Emotional intelligence:* There is growing evidence that being able to manage one's emotions, or emotional intelligence, is a crucial requirement for the multinational manager. Previous research has shown that emotional intelligence prepares the manager to better adjust to and deal with new cultures and people.

- *A long-range perspective:* A short-term view seldom succeeds in the new global economy. Credited with responsibility for turning Motorola into a global player, former CEO Robert W. Galvin put a representative in Beijing more than

**Global mindset**
Mindset that requires managers to think globally but act locally.

## Multinational Management **Brief**

### Global Managers

It is undeniable that acquiring skills to be able to navigate foreign cultures and succeed in other countries are critical skills for the twenty-first-century manager. But how can managers develop such skills? A recent study of around 200 senior managers and over 5000 managers provided insights. The study reports that success is dependent on three main components: intellectual capital, psychological capital, and social capital.

Intellectual capital refers to one's knowledge of international business and the ability and capacity to learn. It includes being global-business savvy and comfortable with complexity and having a cosmopolitan outlook. Intellectual capital tends to be the easiest of the three forms of capital to develop. A manager can learn about new cultures through magazines, texts, and shows. And as you will see later, managers can also experience short stays in the host country ahead of the actual assignment.

Psychological capital tends to be the hardest to build, as it is often reflected in personalities. Psychological capital refers to one's openness to differences and change. A person with high psychological capital is passionate about diversity and is open to adventures and change. To develop psychological capital, managers need to become more self-aware by gauging their feelings for foreign countries and people and their openness to change. This means broadening one's outlook by expanding one's social circle and being willing to try new experiences consistently.

Finally, social capital is the ability of a manager to build trusting relationships with individuals from other cultures. This aspect includes skills such as intercultural sympathy and diplomacy. These skills tend to be mostly relationship based and acquired through experience. Managers can develop such skills by expanding their social skills and including individuals with diverse interests. Participating in international missions and other foreign assignments is also likely to help develop such skills.

*Sources: Based on Javidan, M., M. Teagarden, and D. Bowen. 2010. "Making it overseas." Harvard Business Review, April, 109–113; Molinksy, A. L. 2012. "Code switching between cultures." Harvard Business Review, January–February, 139–140.*

10 years ago. Now Motorola is the largest U.S. investor in China. Successful companies must be persistent if they are to overcome the complexities of dealing with the international environment.

- *The talent to motivate all employees to achieve excellence:* The ability to motivate has always been a hallmark of leadership. In the next generation of organizations, the leader will face additional challenges of motivation. Employees may come from any country and may live in any country. Leaders will face the motivational challenge of having employees identify with the organization rather than with their country. Leaders also will need to develop motivational strategies that transcend cultures.

- *Accomplished negotiating skills:* All business transactions require negotiation. However, leaders in the global economy will spend considerably more time negotiating cross-culturally. Such skills will be more challenging to acquire and more necessary to apply.

- *The willingness to seek overseas assignments:* The next generation of leaders will have significant international experience. They will demonstrate management skills and success in more than one cultural environment.

- *An understanding of national cultures:* In spite of the pressures of globalization to treat the world as one market, large differences still exist among national cultures. No multinational leader or business can succeed without a deep understanding of the national cultures in which they do business. Multinational managers often will be required to learn two or more additional languages as well as the nuances of local cultural differences.

Can you develop the skills necessary to be a successful multinational manager? One of the first tasks is to learn all you can about multinational management and international business. In the next section, we will discuss how this text can contribute to this goal.

# Multinational Management: A Strategic Approach

**Strategy**
The maneuvers or activities that managers use to sustain and increase organizational performance.

**Strategy formulation**
Process by which managers select the strategies to be used by their company.

**Strategy implementation**
All the activities that managers and an organization must perform to achieve strategic objectives.

Why should you study multinational management? In today's Internet-connected world, you may have little choice but to be a multinational manager. Foreign competition and doing business in foreign markets are daily facts of life for today's managers. The study of multinational management helps you prepare for dealing with this evolving global economy and for developing the skills necessary to succeed as a multinational manager. This text will introduce some of the basic requisite skills.

Competing successfully in the global economy requires a strategic approach to multinational management, and multinational managers formulate and implement such strategies. **Strategy** is defined here as the maneuvers or activities that managers use to sustain and increase organizational performance. **Strategy formulation** is the process of choosing or crafting a strategy. **Strategy implementation** encompasses all the activities that managers and an organization must perform to achieve strategic objectives.

From the perspective of the multinational company and managers, strategies must include maneuvers that deal with operating in more than one country and culture. Therefore, multinational strategy formulation takes on the added challenges of dealing with opportunities and competition located anywhere in the world. Multinational strategy implementation carries added challenges, including the need to develop complex management systems to carry out strategies that reach beyond domestic boundaries.

The rules of competition are constantly evolving. Today's multinationals face an environment that is drastically different from the environment that multinationals faced in the past. A company can be a dominant player and then lose its competitive edge rapidly. As we examine international management from a strategic perspective, it is important to understand trends that will shape the future business environment. These include:[24]

- *Blurring of industry boundaries:* Information and other communication technologies have made industry boundaries less clear. For instance, the South Korean company Samsung now produces products ranging from televisions to cell phones to microprocessors. This blurring of boundaries makes it much harder to identify and understand competitors.

- *Flexibility matters more than size:* Recent failures of large companies suggest that being big may no longer be useful. Consider that many giants such as GM, Microsoft, Dell, and IBM have all hit market caps. As outsourcing, alliances, and partnering gather steam, companies are finding that they can convert many fixed costs into variable costs. Such changes make scale less useful.

- *Finding your niche:* Multinationals have traditionally strived to be the leaders in their respective industries. However, such thinking is now changing. Kim and Mauborgne's Blue Ocean Strategy suggests that finding those uncontested niches also leads to success. In fact, many companies are finding that they can do well by finding niches and satisfying the needs in that niche.[25]

- *Hypercompetition:* The new environment is characterized by intense competition coming from companies located in all parts of the world. Businesses cannot expect to be stable and be around for a long time. For instance, consider that Haier, a Chinese company that entered the U.S. market in 1999, is now the topselling brand of dorm fridges. It also is the market leader in home wine coolers and ranks third in freezers.

- *Emphasis on innovation and the learning organization:* Successful companies are going to be those that can draw on local knowledge to innovate and compete globally. For instance, many of the successful South Korean and Japanese companies were able to use their domestic markets as tests to improve and launch their products globally. To achieve such success, any multinational will need to develop the appropriate mechanisms and systems to integrate local knowledge to produce value for the company.

Given these requirements, a fundamental assumption of this book is that successful multinational management requires managers to understand their potential competitors and collaborators.[26]

> *When you understand your competitors and yourself, you will always win.*
>
> —Sun Tzu, The Art of War

Multinational companies and managers must be prepared to compete with other firms from any country. In addition, they must be prepared to collaborate with companies and people from anywhere in the world as suppliers, alliance partners, and customers. Accomplishing these tasks means that multinational managers must understand more than the basics of national culture. They must understand how people from different nations view organizational strategies and organizations. To provide such a background, this text devotes several chapters to comparative management—the comparison of management practices used by people from different nations.

## Summary and Conclusions

This chapter provided you with key background information that supports the study of multinational management, defining multinational management and the multinational company. You saw examples of the world's largest multinationals. However, as the Preview Case in Point showed, companies of all sizes can be multinational.

Because we exist in a globalizing world, considerable attention has been devoted to the forces that drive globalization. These are key environmental issues that affect every multinational company and its managers. World trade and investments are growing rapidly, but not always consistently, making all economies more linked and creating both opportunities and threats for both domestic and multinational companies. New competitors, strong and motivated, are coming from developing nations in Asia, the Americas, and the transitioning economies of Eastern Europe. Customers, products, and standards are becoming more global. The increasing sophistication and lower cost of information technology fuel the development of global companies that can more easily manage worldwide operation.

Multinational managers of the next generation will need skills not always considered necessary for domestic-only managers. This chapter described key characteristics of successful multinational managers, as identified by several experts. Perhaps the most encompassing characteristic is the global mindset. Managers with such a mindset understand the rapidly changing business and economic environment. They can see the world as an integrated market, yet appreciate and understand the wide array of differences among world cultures and social institutions.

The next two chapters in this section will begin building the foundation of your global mindset. You will see how cultural differences affect business practices. You will see not only how understanding national culture is crucial to your success as a multinational manager, but also how social institutions, such as religion and law, influence multinational management. This combination of national culture and social institutions is called national context.

After reading this text, you should have the foundation necessary for understanding the latest challenges and practices of multinational management. However, the field is dynamic, and your learning will never be complete. Successful multinational managers will view the process of understanding their field as a lifelong endeavor.

## Discussion Questions

1. Discuss how any company can become a multinational company. What are some of the options available to companies that allow them to use international markets and locations competitively?

2. Discuss some reasons why reductions in world trade barriers are driving the world toward a global economy.

3. Consider how phenomena such as wars, terrorist activities, and bird flu might alter the progression of globalization. What should a multinational manager do to deal with such situations?

4. Discuss the differences between foreign trade and foreign direct investment.

5. Discuss some of the advantages and disadvantages of setting up production in developing nations.

6. Look at the information on developing economies and competition discussed in the text. Where do you think the next generation of world-class competitors will come from? Why?

7. Discuss the characteristics of a next-generation multinational manager. How can you develop those characteristics through education and experience?

8. What are some of the new rules of competition? How are these new rules going to affect global trade?

## Multinational Management **Internet Exercise**

1. Go to the WTO website, http://www.wto.org.

2. Locate the most recent trade report under "Documents and Resources."

3. Discuss the most recent findings. How are developed countries doing? Are emerging nations still dominating trade growth?

4. What are the findings for Africa? Are African nations continuing their steady growth?

5. What are some of the long-term forecasts of the report?

## Multinational Management **Skill Builder**

### Interview a Multinational Manager

**Step 1.** As a member of a team or as an individual, contact a current or former multinational manager. Where can you find such a manager? Perhaps some are close by. In a business college, many graduate students and professors have work experience as multinational managers. Also, the parents of many students are similarly experienced. Most likely, however, you will need to contact a company and ask to speak with the individual in charge of international operations. Do not overlook small companies. Although it may not be a full-time responsibility, international sales may be the responsibility of someone in many companies.

**Step 2.** Set up an appointment for an interview.

**Step 3.** Arrive on time, professionally dressed, with a list of prepared questions. Some possible questions are:

- What circumstances led you to assume a position with international responsibilities?
- What are the major challenges in the international part of your job?
- How would you describe the international strategy of your company?
- How important is international work to advancement in your company?
- How do you deal with and prepare for cultural differences?
- Do you ever have to manage employees from other countries directly? If so, what are the challenges in doing that?
- How are people selected for international assignments?
- Do you face any unique ethical situations in your job?

## *Endnotes*

[1] Lamy, Pascale. 2006. "Humanizing globalization." *International Trade Forum,* 1, 5–6.

[2] *Economist.* 2006. "The future of globalization," July 29, 11.

[3] *Economist.* 2006. "Climbing back," January 21, 69.

[4] Ibid.

[5] *Economist.* 2011. "The sun shines bright." December 3, 82–84; Mo, I. 2012. "Celtel's founder on building a business on the world's poorest continent." *Harvard Business Review,* October, 41–43.

[6] *Economist.* 1996. "All free traders now?" December 7, 23–25.

[7] *Economist.* 2003. "Heading east." http://www.economist.com, March 27.

[8] WTO (World Trade Organization). 2009. *http://www.wto.org.*

[9] *Economist.* 2006. "In the twilight of Doha," July 29, 69–70.

[10] *Economist.* 1996. "Spoiling world trade." December 7, 15–16.

[11] Lubbers, R. F. M. 1996. "Globalization: An exploration." *Nijenrode Management Review,* 1.

[12] Boscheck, Ralph. 1996. "Managed trade and regional preference." In IMD, *World Competitiveness Yearbook 1996,* 333–334. Lausanne, Switzerland: Institute for Management Development.

[13] *Economist.* "Spoiling world trade."

[14] WTO (World Trade Organization). *World Trade Organization: Trading into the Future* (2002). Geneva: World Trade Organization.

[15] WTO (World Trade Organization), *World Trade Report.* 2009.

[16] Organisation for Economic Co-operation and Development. 2009. http://www.oecd.org.

[17] UNCTAD (UN Conference on Trade and Development). 2000. *World Investment Report.* New York and Geneva: United Nations; UNCTAD (UN Conference on Trade and Development). 2000.

"World FDI flows exceed US$1.1 trillion in 2000." UNCTAD Press Release, December 7.

[18] Javetski, Bill, and William Glasgall. 1994. "Borderless finance: Fuel for growth." *BusinessWeek,* November 18, 40–50.

[19] Yip, George S. 2002. *Total Global Strategy II.* Englewood Cliffs: Prentice Hall.

[20] Levine, Jonathan B. 1992. "Want EC business? You have two choices." *Business Week,* October 19, 58–59.

[21] Rhinesmith, Steven H., John N. Williamson, David M. Ehlen, and Denise S. Maxwell. 1989. "Developing leaders for the global enterprise." *Training and Development Journal,* April, 25–34.

[22] Rosen, Robert H., Patricia Digh, Marshall Singer, and Carl Phillips. 1999. *Global Literacies: Lessons on Business Leaders and National Cultures.* Riverside, NJ: Simon & Schuster.

[23] Beamish, Allen, J. Morrison, Andrew Inkpen, and Philip Rosenzweig. 2003. *International Management.* New York: McGraw Hill-Irwin; Gabel, Racheli Shmueli, Shimon L. Dolan, and Jean Luc Cerdin. 2005. "Emotional intelligence as predictor of cultural adjustment for success in global assignments." *Career Development International,* 10(5): 375–395; Moran, Robert T., and John R. Riesenberger. 1994. *The Global Challenge.* London: McGraw-Hill.

[24] Hitt, Michael A., Barbara W. Keats, and Samuel M. DeMarie. 1998. "Navigating in the new competitive landscape: Building strategic flexibility and competitive advantage in the 21st century." *Academy of Management Executive,* 12(4): 22–42; Kim, Chan W., and Renee Mauborgne. 2005. "Value innovation: A leap into the blue ocean." *The Journal of Business Strategy,* 26(4): 22–28; Morris, Betsy. 2006. "The new rules." *Fortune,* July 24, 70–87.

[25] Kim and Mauborgne, "Value innovation: A leap into the blue ocean."

[26] Hamel, Cary, and C. K. Prahalad. 1989. "Strategic intent." *Harvard Business Review,* May–June, 63–76.

# Foreign Direct Investment in the Middle East: Riyadh and Dubai

F. JOHN MATHIS, TIM ROGMANS, RAJA ALMARZOQI ALBQAMI

SCHOOL OF GLOBAL MANAGEMENT

## Introduction

"Follow the money" and it will lead you to business opportunities. Several times during the past decade, oil prices have reached record highs, pouring petro-dollars into the Middle East, and now—May 2011—is one of those times. Thus, we visited the Middle East, particularly Riyadh, Saudi Arabia, and Dubai, United Arab Emirates, to research a sample of the foreign companies that have invested there, examine why they have done so, and determine what their business model is. Our specific focus was primarily on the financial service sector, and secondarily on other selected foreign investments in the service sector. The resulting survey data are aggregated to protect the companies interviewed, which included (alpha-betically) for financial services: Barclays (UK), Credit Suisse (Swiss), Robeco (Dutch), and for other ser-vices: FedEx (U.S.), Hay Group (U.S.), Yum Brands (U.S.), and Maersk (Denmark). The research identified what changes these companies considered impor-tant to improve their operations and performance now that they have been functioning in the region for some time.

We examined the key drivers of foreign direct investment in the region. Our research had three objectives:

* To show how laws, requirements, and regulations have changed and become more receptive to for-eign investment in recent years by comparing sev-eral business environmental characteristic indices and their change over time.

* To examine the exchange arrangements and frame-work for financial and capital transactions in the countries.

* To determine the experiences of several companies in the financial services and other sectors that invested in the region by looking at the key drivers of foreign direct investment from the company's perspective.

## Financial and Political Context

Political and economic conditions tend to be quite volatile in the Middle East, as evidenced by the 2007-2009 global financial crisis and a severe worldwide recession accompanied by falling oil prices, followed by rising but volatile oil prices in 2010-2011. More recently (at the time of writing this case, mid-2011), political unrest occurred in North Africa and throughout much of the Middle East, including Iraq, Iran, Bahrain, Yemen, and Syria. The global financial crisis of 2007-2009 caused several changes to be made in macro-economic policy management in Saudi Arabia and the UAE in order to reduce the impact of the global crisis on the local economy.

The United Arab Emirates and Saudi Arabia stimu-lated their economies with monetary and fiscal policy, but because Saudi Arabia is less integrated with global financial markets than the UAE, their approaches dif-fered. Saudi Arabia made concerted attempts to attract FDI for natural gas investment and the petrochemical industry. This effort in Saudi Arabia reflected an attempt to reduce dependency on export of oil to increased domestic demand-led growth, stimulated by expansive economic policy and an attempt to attract investment inflows. In contrast, in the UAE, when Dubai's real estate bubble burst in 2009, initially causing capital flight, the government quickly made successful fiscal moves to ensure financial stability.

Additionally, a major structural change impacting the Middle East has been the globalization of financial flows. As financial markets worldwide liberalized, developments in information technology and telecommunications accelerated the size and volatility of global money flows. As a result, there has been an increase in the competition for funds (both portfolio investment and FDI) between countries. Open financial markets attract foreign capital inflows, and Asia and Latin America have been recent benefactors. These inflows can bring benefits in the form of technology and knowledge transfer. But there can sometimes also be an economic cost—inflation and the potential for financial crisis. Thus, the significant change in the global financial environment has affected the Middle East region.

## Changing Significance and Structure of Global Capital Flows

A recent study of the impact of global capital flows in causing a financial crisis provided the following three-step analytical framework:[1]

- Identify the determinants of the size of the shock,

- Identify the nature and quality of the cushion or, alternatively, the factors affecting the absorption of the impact, and

- Evaluate the response to the impact.

Regarding the possible channels for the impact, the degree of economic globalization needs to be considered. This is based on financial and investment-related links and the level of cross-border capital flows, both foreign direct investment and portfolio flows, into financial instruments. It is also a function of trade-related links. Finally, consumer confidence-related links such as the strength or weakness of the currency are also important. Regarding the nature and quality of the shock safety net, countries with sound monetary and fiscal policies and more diversified economies tend to be insulated from impact. The degree of a state's control on its economy is also important in absorbing the impact of financial inflows. In responding to the global financial crisis, policies that work best include a shift from export-led to a domestic demand-led growth and a diversion of economic links.

The degree of the macro-financial linkages and the impact of the global financial crisis on Saudi Arabia might have at first been thought to be small because of its lower degree of economic integration. Economic activity in Saudi Arabia is more tightly controlled by the government than is Dubai, for example (see below), although the private sector is now developing rapidly. However, Saudi Arabia is very dependent on the oil sector, which accounts for roughly 86% of budget revenues, 46% of GDP, and 90+% of export earnings as of 2010. Therefore, in some respects, Saudi Arabia could be considered to be more globally vulnerable than the economy of the United Arab Emirates.

Although the United Arab Emirates is more open to various activities, it may be only indirectly impacted by external financial events and more dependent on local financial events. Thus, in Dubai in 2009, there was a local real estate and foreign investment crisis that resulted in a significant outflow of funds and a subsequent $10 billion rescue loan from Abu Dhabi. Overall, real GDP growth was slightly higher in the UAE compared to Saudi Arabia during the period 2007 to 2010.

In an article by Dell'Ariccia et al. (2008),[2] the mechanisms for transmission of financial globalization are identified as:

- Well-developed domestic financial markets which can moderate boom/bust cycles triggered by sudden stops in financial flows by efficiently allocating foreign financial flows to competing investment projects,

- Stronger financial institutions shift the composition of financial flows toward FDI and portfolio equity, thereby enhancing growth and macroeconomic stability, and the stronger the institutions, the greater the economic growth benefits from financial integration,

- Lack of sound macroeconomic policies in international financial integration may lead to excessive borrowing, debt accumulation, and possibly crisis, and

- Trade openness and integration facilitate recoveries from financial crisis and mitigate adverse growth effects.

These factors would tend to support greater FDI flows to Dubai, which has more advanced and more sophisticated financial services sector than Saudi Arabia. "Recent empirical research supports the view that financial sector development amplifies the growth benefits associated with FDI flows, with some authors finding that a threshold level of financial sector development is necessary for a country to realize any growth benefits from FDI."[3] See also Hermes and Lensink (2003), Alfaro et al. (2004), and Durham (2004). Furthermore, financial development (deepening of robust financial markets) has a positive impact on macroeconomic stability, which tends to be attractive to further capital inflows.[4] Better-developed financial institutions help reduce volatility from external capital inflows. The share of FDI in a country's capital inflows is negatively associated with the probability of a currency crisis. But more rigid or fixed exchange rate regimes can be more vulnerable to crisis. So countries like Saudi Arabia and UAE, which both have fixed exchange rates, will—if they have more open financial flows—feel greater pressure on other policies and structural features of the economy and are prone to experience currency crises.[5]

## Environmental Scan: Recent Improvements

When we examined various ratings of countries based on a range of risk factors, the ranking of Saudi Arabia and the UAE were stable or improving in recent years. The country risk rating reported by A.M. Best Company focusing on comparative political and economic conditions for insurance purposes showed Saudi Arabia and the UAE both at a CRT-3—about average country risk. A multifactor model created by Barra, Inc., measured the overall risk associated with a

security or credit risk relative to the market. Barra Risk Factor Analysis incorporated more than 40 data metrics, including earnings growth, share turnover, and senior debt rating. The model then measured risk factors associated with three main components: industry risk, risk from exposure to different investment themes, and company-specific risk. The Barra risk rating for Saudi Arabia was BBB to single B for political risk and BB for banking sector risk. The UAE's rating was slightly better at BB overall, and several measures were a single B due to economic factors and more diverse economic and banking sector factors. In general, as reflected in Table 1, most country risk rating agencies, and even the AT Kearney FDI Confidence survey of executives, show the UAE to be rated more positively than Saudi Arabia. In part, this difference is due to tighter regulations in Saudi Arabia than in the UEA, as discussed in the next section.

## Summary of Regulations and Capital Controls

This section of the case offers a detailed description of the exchange arrangements and exchange controls that existed in Saudi Arabia and the United Arab Emirates in 2010. It includes regulations on any financial flows into or out of the country, trade restrictions, and regulations that impact operation of a financial service company in either country. Table 2 summarizes the differences between the two areas.

**TABLE 1** Sample Country Risk Ratings for UAE and Saudi Arabia

| March 2011 | Country Risk | Political Risk | Corruption | Economic Risk | Credit Risk | Banking Risk |
|---|---|---|---|---|---|---|
| A.M. Best | UAE—3 KSA—3 | | | | UAE—3 KSA—3 | |
| Barra | UAE—BB KSA—BBB | UAE—BB KSA—B | | UAE—B KSA—BBB | | UAE—B KSA—BB |
| Transparency Intl. | | | UAE—28 KSA—50 | | | |
| Euromoney | UAE—33 KSA—38 | UAE—59 KSA—52 | | UAE—67 KSA—72 | UAE—8/10 KSA—8/10 | |
| S&P | | | | | | |
| OECD | UAE—3/10 KSA—2/10 | | | | | |
| A.T. Kearney FDI Rankings | UAE—1.29/3 KSA—1.26/3 | | | | | |

## Saudi Arabia[6]

***Exchange Rate***—The exchange rate of the Saudi riyal is a conventional peg to the U.S. dollar at the official rate of SRI 3.75 per $1, and is set by the Saudi Arabian Monetary Agency (SAMA). The rate has been stable since June 1986. Banks may charge up to 0.125% above the official rate. Commercial banks have an active forward market to cover exchange risk for up to 12 months. Transactions with and use of Israeli currency are prohibited. Controls on payments and receipts are administered by SAMA. No payment arrears are permitted. There are no controls on export and import of bank notes. Foreign exchange accounts are permitted domestically and abroad, and domestic currency accounts are convertible into foreign currency, but no domestic currency accounts are permitted abroad. All of these accounts must be approved.

***Imports and Import Payments***—Import restrictions on a few commodities are maintained for religious, health, and security reasons. Trade with Israel is prohibited. A maximum of 5% tax is applied on most dutiable goods. For a few goods, the rate is 12% and 20%, and for tobacco products, the tax is 100%. Imports from GCC members are exempt. There is no state import monopoly.

***Exports and Export Proceeds***—There are no repatriation, financing, or documentation requirements. The re-export of certain imported items benefiting from government subsidies is prohibited. There are no export taxes. There are no controls on payments for invisible transactions and current transfers. There are no repatriation requirements or restriction on the use of funds for proceeds from invisible transactions and current transfers.

***Capital Transactions***—There are controls on capital transactions, but there are no requirements on repatriation. Under the regulations for the licensing of both bank-affiliated and nonbank brokerage and investment companies (released by the Capital Market Authority), four categories of companies are allowed to engage in brokerage and investment fund management: (1) local bank subsidiaries, (2) Saudi Arabian joint stock companies, (3) subsidiaries of Saudi Arabian joint-stock companies that are engaged in the financial services business, and (4) subsidiaries of foreign financial institutions that are licensed under the Banking Control Law issued by Royal Decree No. M/5 dated 22/2/1386H (June 11, 1966).

***Shares***—Resident foreign nationals may invest in shares of listed KSA joint-stock companies. Nonresident foreign nationals are limited to indirect investment through authorized mutual funds. Nonresidents must seek permission of the minister of commerce and industry and the Capital Market Authority to sell or issue securities in KSA. There are no controls on the repatriation of proceeds from the sale of securities issued by nonresidents. Residents may purchase or sell nonresident securities via brokerage services offered by licensed brokerage firms. In the case of a KSA joint-stock company, the rules on the purchase locally by nonresidents apply.

***Bonds***—Purchase locally by nonresidents: there are no controls on portfolio investment in government securities by foreign nationals. Sale or issue locally by nonresidents: the regulations governing shares or other securities of a participating nature apply. For money market instruments, the sale or issue locally by nonresidents: the regulations governing shares or other securities of a participating nature apply. For sale or issue abroad by residents: in the case of collective investment securities when the underlying assets are shares of KSA joint-stock companies, the regulations governing shares or other securities of a participating nature apply. For controls on derivatives and other instruments: the regulations governing shares or other securities of a participating nature apply.

***Controls on Credit Operations***—For commercial credit to nonresidents: KSA banks must seek permission from the SAMA. To residents from nonresidents: the SAMA's permission is required for riyal-denominated loans made through KSA banks. For financial credits: the SAMA's permission is required for all financial credit operations. For guarantees, sureties, and financial backup facilities by residents or nonresidents: SAMA's permission is required. But for these facilities to residents from nonresidents: financial institutions that give guarantees to government projects must appear on the SAMA-approved list.

***Controls on Direct Investment***—Approved foreign investments in KSA enjoy the same privileges as domestic capital. The foreign investment law allows foreign investors to make direct investment in most of the country's economic sectors—with or without local participation—and imposes a tax rate of 20% on most foreign company profits, with two exceptions: (1) an 85% tax rate is charged on profits of investment in the oil and hydrocarbon sector, and (2) a basic rate of 30% is imposed on profits of investment in the natural gas sector as long as the internal rate of return (IRR) of the project does not exceed 8%. For investments with an IRR exceeding 8%, a sliding scale of higher tax rates apply with a maximum rate of 85% for an IRR exceeding 20%. The Supreme Economic Council has issued a list of economic sectors that remain off limits to foreign investors. The list is reviewed regularly and includes projects related to exploration, drilling, and production of oil; production of military equipment and uniforms; production of explosives for civil purposes; certain printing and publishing activities; certain telecommunications services; land and air transportation; real estate investment in Mecca and Medina; services involving fishing; distribution services, including wholesale and retail trade and commercial agencies; and a few other sectors. In accordance with the Cooperative Insurance Companies Control Law, the SAMA accepts licensing applications from insurance companies transacting insurance and reinsurance business in KSA. Under the regulations, foreign insurance companies are allowed to own up to 49% of these local companies. There are no controls on the liquidation of direct investment.

*Controls on Real Estate Transactions*—For real estate purchased locally by nonresidents: in principle, the purchase of real estate is restricted to KSA nationals, Saudi corporations, Saudi institutions, and nationals of GCC member countries. However, under the foreign investment law, foreign investors are allowed to purchase real estate as needed for their business, including housing for their staff. In addition, nonresidents are allowed to purchase real estate for conducting real estate business in all cities except Mecca and Medina, provided the investment in the real estate business is not less than SRl 30 million.

*Controls on Personal Capital Transactions*—Price earnings are transferable; gambling is prohibited.

*Provisions Specific to the Financial Sector*—Lending to nonresidents: KSA banks require SAMA's permission to lend to nonresidents, except for interbank transactions and commercial credits. In the case of deposits originating from foreign banks, only domestic currency deposits are subject to SAMA's reserve requirement. SAMA's approval is required for KSA banks only; domestic currency deposits are subject to SAMA's reserve requirement. SAMA's approval is required for Saudi banks to acquire shares in foreign companies. There is a limit of 40% of capital and permission of the authorities for nonresidents to invest in KSA banks. Open foreign exchange positions are monitored by means of prudential reports.

*Provisions Specific to Institutional Investors*—Foreign insurance companies may open branches in

KSA subject to the Law on Supervision of Cooperative Insurance Companies and to the Insurance Implementing Regulations issued by SAMA. These regulations impose certain restrictions on investments by insurance companies. Existing insurance companies had until March 2008 to bring their operations into conformity with these regulations. SAMA guidelines for KSA branches of foreign insurance companies are, in effect, requiring minimum levels of investment locally in riyals; maximum limits on investment in foreign equities and foreign bonds, both government and corporate; and adherence to Articles 59 and 61 of the Insurance Implementing Regulations. There is a limit on securities issued by nonresidents of 20% unless approved by SAMA. In addition, a limit of 10% applies to foreign currency-denominated investments and 5% to foreign government bonds and bonds issued by foreign companies. Regulations regarding limits on investment portfolios held abroad are related to nonresidents only. The limits on investment portfolios held locally are 50% of the total assets in riyals. Moreover, unless otherwise approved by SAMA, insurance companies and branches are required to keep 20% of their investments in authorized banks and 20% in KSA government bonds for companies and branches engaged in property and life insurance.[7]

### United Arab Emirates[8]

*Exchange Measures and Arrangement*—There are no restrictions. In accordance with UN Security Council Resolution No. 1373 (2001), accounts belonging to individuals and/or organizations associated with terrorism have been frozen. Banks are required to verify identity for transfers exceeding Dhs 3,500 or its equivalent. Money changers are required to do the same for transfers exceeding Dhs 2,000. Free zones in the United Arab Emirates are required to verify the identity of persons wishing to establish businesses. The currency of the UAE is the dirham. The dirham is pegged to the dollar, the intervention currency, at Dhs 3.6725 per $1. There is no exchange tax or subsidy. The spot exchange market is operated by the Central Bank. The forward exchange market— the UAE Central Bank (UAECB)—maintains a swap facility which commercial banks may use to purchase dirhams spot and sell dirhams forward for periods of one week, one month, and three months. For each bank, maximum limits of $20 million outstanding for one-month and three-month swaps and $10 million outstanding for one-week swaps are in effect. There is also a daily limit of $3 million on purchases by each bank for one-month and three-month swaps. This facility is designed to provide temporary dirham liquidity to commercial banks. Swap facilities are not available to banks having a short position in dirhams except for covering forward transactions for commercial purposes. Official cover for forward positions is required.

*Arrangements for Payments and Receipts*—There are no currency requirements, but settlements with Israel are prohibited. The UAE is a member of the GCC Customs Union. There are no payment arrears, controls on trade in gold, controls on export, and imports of banknotes.

*Resident Accounts*—The following are permitted: foreign exchange accounts, held domestically, held abroad; accounts in domestic currency convertible into foreign currency. Accounts in domestic currency held abroad may be maintained in offshore affiliates of domestic banks.

*Nonresident Accounts*—These accounts may be opened by banks and trade, financial, and industrial companies incorporated outside of the UAE that have no local branches; by branches of local institutions in foreign countries; and by embassies and diplomatic agencies. These accounts may also be opened by UAE citizens working abroad and by nonresident foreigners working in the UAE. Domestic currency accounts are allowed and may be convertible into foreign currency. There are no blocked accounts.

*Imports and Import Payments*—No foreign exchange budget is required, nor is there a financing requirement for imports, or documentation requirements for the release of foreign exchange. Only licensed parties may engage in import trade. Importers may import only the goods specified in their licenses. Imports of a few products are prohibited for health, security, or moral reasons. Imports from Israel are prohibited, as are imports of products manufactured by foreign companies blacklisted by the Arab League. In accordance with the GCC Customs Union, a unified tariff of 5% applies on most dutiable goods. There is no state monopoly.

*Exports and Export Proceeds*—There are no repatriation requirements, financing requirements, documentation requirements, export licenses, export taxes.

*Payments for Invisible Transactions and Current Transfers*—There are no controls.

*Proceeds from Invisible Transactions and Current Transfers*—There are no repatriation requirements, or restrictions on use of funds.

*Capital Transactions*—There are controls on capital transactions. At least 51% of the shares of UAE corporations must be held by UAE nationals or organizations. Companies domiciled in free zones are exempt from this requirement and may be up to 100% foreign owned. Nonresidents may sell or issue stocks and bonds, and purchases by GCC residents are exempt from controls. Nonresidents may issue some mutual funds. There are no controls on derivatives or credit operations.

*Controls on Direct Investment*—At least 51% of the equity of companies other than branches of foreign companies must be held by nationals of the UAE. GCC nationals are permitted to hold (1) up to 75% of the equity of companies in the industrial, agricultural, fisheries, and construction sectors; and (2) up to 100% of the equity of companies in the hotel industry. GCC nationals are also permitted to engage in wholesale and retail trade activities, except in the form of companies, in which case they are subject to the company law. In free zones, foreign ownership is permitted up to 100%. There are no controls on the liquidation of direct investment. A new system of freehold properties allows nonresidents subject to each Emirate's specific conditions to own real estate. The new system was first introduced in Dubai and is now generalized to other main Emirates, particularly Abu Dhabi, Sharjah, Ajman, and Ras Al-Khaimah. There are no controls on personal capital transactions.

*Provision Specific to the Financial Sector*—Commercial banks operating in the UAE are prohibited from engaging in nonbanking operations. Banks operating in the UAE are required to maintain special deposits with the UAECB equal to 30% of their dirham placements with or loans to nonresident banks when these transactions have a remaining maturity of one year or less. The profits of foreign banks are subject to a profit tax levied by the local authorities at an annual rate of 20%. Banks are not allowed to lend more than 7% of their capital base to one foreign institution. Also, they are not allowed to invest more than 25% of their own funds in shares or bonds issued by commercial companies. Loans to foreign governments with a first-class credit rating and placement in such countries' financial institutions are exempt from such limits. Nonresidents may not acquire more than 20% of the share capital of any national bank. For the acquisition by nonresidents of shares of national banks, the UAE company law applies, i.e., nonresidents are allowed to acquire up to 49% of the total shares. Table 2 shows a comparative summary of exchange and financial restrictions in the two countries, the UAE and Saudi Arabia, in 2010.

**Summary Features of Exchange Arrangements and Regulatory Frameworks for Current and Capital Transactions in U.S., Saudi Arabia, and UAE***

**TABLE 2** (As of date shown on first county page)

| | United States | Saudi Arabia | United Arab Emirates |
|---|:---:|:---:|:---:|
| **Status under IMF Articles of Agreement** | | | |
| Article VIII | | | |
| Article XIV | | | |
| **Exchange rate arrangements** | | | |
| No separate legal tender | | | |
| Currency board | | ◆ | ◆ |
| Conventional peg | | | |
| Stabilized arrangement | | | |
| Crawling peg | | | |
| Crawl-like arrangement | | | |
| Pegged exchange rate within horizontal bands | | | |
| Other managed arrangement | | | |
| Floating | | | |
| Free floating | • | | |
| **Exchange rate structure** | | | |
| Dual exchange rate | | | |
| Multiple exchange rates | | | |
| **Arrangements for payments and receipts** | | | |
| Bilateral payments arrangements | • | | |
| Payments arrears | | | |
| **Controls on payments for invisible transactions and current transfers** | | | |
| **Proceeds from exports and/or invisible transactions**\*\* | | | |
| Repatriation requirements | | | |
| Surrender requirements | | | |
| **Capital transactions** | | | |
| Controls on: | | | |
|   Capital market securities | • | • | • |
|   Money market instruments | • | • | |
|   Collective investment securities | • | • | • |
|   Derivatives and other, instruments | • | • | |
|   Commercial credits | | • | |
|   Financial credits | | • | |
|   Guarantees, sureties, and financial backup facilities | • | • | |
|   Direct investment | • | • | • |
|   Liquidation of direct investment | | | |
|   Real estate transactions | • | • | • |
|   Personal capital movements | | | |
| Provisions specific to: | | | |
|   Commercial banks and other credit institutions | | • | • |
|   Institutional investors | • | • | — |

• The specified practice is a feature of the exchange system.

— Data were not available at the time of publication.

◆ Flexibility is limited vis-a-vis the U.S. dollar.

\* Data are also included for Aruba (Netherlands), Hong Kong SAR (People's Republic of China), and the Netherlands Antilles.

\*\* These items now refer to corresponding requirements for both exports proceeds, and proceeds from invisible transactions and current transfers (e.g., it would be sufficient for surrender requirement to be indicated as a feature of the exchange system if at least one of them is subject to a surrender requirement).

*Source: IMF "Annual Report on Exchange Arrangements and Exchange Restrictions, 2010."*

***Capital Controls and Their Effectiveness***—"The magnitude of cross-border financial assets has grown in recent years at a rising speed, from under 50% of world GDP in 1970 to over 300% in 2006, and doubling over the last 10 years."[9] From a country's perspective, there is concern about the risks outweighing the benefits of financial inflows and, if so, should capital inflow be regulated and controlled? Many countries in Asia are facing this question today as financial inflows have accelerated to record levels. Even so, in some cases de jure controls as presented in the IMF "Annual Report on Exchange Arrangements and Exchange Restrictions, 2010," may not represent actual de facto outcomes. Thus, Schindler (2009) found that even in countries with de jure restrictions and capital controls, there may still be sizeable de facto financial inflows. While de jure restrictions on foreign direct investment may be somewhat more effective, Lane and Milesi-Ferretti (2007) found that there have been de facto significant increases in financial flows, and that there is a growing reliance on equity financing in emerging markets in contrast to the use of debt financing in industrial countries.[10]

## Saudi Arabia

The Kingdom of Saudi Arabia (KSA) has a population of 25 million people. Of these, 35% are under the age of 15 and only 4% are over the age of 60, with a life expectancy of 71 years for men and 75 years for women. Seventy-two percent of employment is in the service sector, 21% is in industry (energy and related activities), while the remaining 7% is in agriculture. Unemployment during the past decade has run just under 5%. Similar to the United States, 97% of households have color television sets and 78% have cell phones, but only 14 people out of 100 have computers, compared to 76 in the United States and 47 in the European Union.[11]

***Global Competitiveness***   In an annual survey of global competitiveness done by the International Institute for Management Development (IMD), Saudi Arabia ranked 35th out of 131 participating countries.[12] One of the most important factors contributing to this high ranking was macroeconomic stability, where it ranked third out of 131 countries. However, the sophistication of company operations and strategy and the quality of the national business environment ranked about 50th out of 127 countries (four countries did not report). The five major problems identified and ranked as issues for doing business in the Kingdom were:

- Inefficient government bureaucracy,
- Inadequately educated workforce,
- Restrictive labor regulations,
- Inadequate supply of infrastructure, and
- Lack of access to financing.

Consequently, a dependency on imported foreign workers has developed, resulting in anxiety among some of the local unemployed Saudi workers. As a result, the government put into place a program that required companies to hire Saudi nationals.

Saudi Arabia has launched a program to attract foreign investment into the country in support of its new "Economic Cities," which it is promoting strongly. Several changes were under way by the government to address some of the weaker aspects of its global competitiveness ranking. One of the most important of these improvement efforts was the centralization in one government ministry—the Saudi Arabian General Investment Authority (SAGIA)—of all of the various applications, rules, and regulations that had to be completed by a foreign company in order to start a business in Saudi Arabia. The government was making a concerted effort to significantly increase foreign investment coming into the country. In this respect, tax rates and tax regulations were ranked as one of the least problematic factors for doing business, along with a low-level burden of government regulation. Foreign investment is seen as a way to diversify the economy away from its concentration on energy, transfer new knowledge and technology into the country, and provide an alternative source of revenue for the Kingdom.

***Foreign Investment Environment***   SAGIA combined three departments and nine ministries into one office at one location to assist foreign investors. In a statement by the governor of SAGIA, Amr bin Abdullah Al-Dabbagh,[13] he described SAGIA's role as, "… to attract sufficient investment to achieve sustainable rapid economic growth while capitalizing on the Kingdom's competitive strengths as the global capital of energy, and as a major hub between East and West."[14] SAGIA intended to position Saudi Arabia among the top ten most competitive nations by 2010 through the creation of a pro-business environment and a knowledge-based society while putting forth its best effort to make Saudi Arabia a favorable investment destination in the region and throughout world.

SAGIA's role was to provide comprehensive licensing and support services to foreign investors. In addition, SAGIA is working to become the investors' information clearinghouse, serving as a central repository of information regarding business in the country, including key economic news and indicator reports, competitiveness studies, general statistics and economic research, and the country's laws and regulations. While they intended to provide services to investors in all sectors of the Saudi economy, SAGIA emphasizes three sectors: energy, transportation, and information and communications technology (ICT).

SAGIA cooperated with other government agencies and private sector organizations to improve the country's business laws and policies according to international best practices so that a healthy investment environment develops and continues in future years. An increasingly globalized economy required Saudi Arabia's business climate to be attractive and competitive. As a start, in August 2004, SAGIA (1) updated its list of policies and procedures that required revision, (2) compared the country's practices to its benchmarked countries, and (3) began cooperating

with relevant government authorities on procedural improvements.

To maximize users' ease and efficiency, SAGIA's One-Step Shops (OSS) has centralized a wide range of critical services—all focused on making it as easy as possible to invest in or set up and operate a business in the Kingdom. A large number of government departments were represented in each OSS, providing investors with fast, hassle-free access to 128 business-related services, ranging from government licensing to telecommunications and banking services. As the government agency responsible for both promoting and licensing investments within the Kingdom, SAGIA is the sole contact point between investors and the Saudi Government, and would provide all government services through its OSS operations.[15] The SAGIA OSS service operations are listed below.

**Government Procedures Licensing Conditions.** The conditions for granting a Foreign Investment license by The Authority shall include the following:

1. The investment activity to be licensed should not be in the list of *Excluded Activities from Foreign Investment.*

2. The intended Product should comply with the *Kingdom's rules and regulations*, or the laws of the European Union or the United States of America in the absence of those laws, in terms of standards and specifications, raw materials and production processes.

3. The license applicant should be a natural or nominal person who has come to the Kingdom for investment.

4. The Foreign Investor should not have been convicted in the past for substantial violations of the provisions of The Act.

5. The Foreign Investor should not have been convicted in the past of financial or commercial violations whether in the Kingdom or in other countries.

6. The grant of a license shall not result in the breach of any international or regional agreement to which the Kingdom is a party.

**Starting a Business Investment License.** A foreign investor may obtain more than one license to practice the same activity or different activities. License application must be completed in full; all documentary requirements must be submitted in full; all of which must be signed by the applicant or his duly authorized representative.

**Guides for Licensing a New Project.** The required documents for governmental procedures are referenced here: Required Documents.

**Business Visit Visas.** Business Visit Visas are issued from the Saudi Arabian Embassies worldwide to facilitate the business community.

**Commercial Registration.** Companies operating in Saudi Arabia must register their businesses with the Ministry of Commerce and Industry and obtain a Commercial Registration (CR) number.

SAGIA provides examples of success stories in the area of telecommunications, summarized below.

***Mobile Telephone***—In 2004, United Arab Emirates operator Etisalat paid US$3.3 billion for the Kingdom's second GSM license. Etihad Etisalat has since gained 30% of the Saudi mobile market and offers a range of 3G services. The Kingdom's third mobile license was awarded to a Kuwaiti-led consortium, which made a US$6 billion bid against six other companies. Competition is propelling Saudi Arabia towards its goal of acquiring one of the region's most advanced and diversified telecommunications markets. Rapid growth is expected to continue due to still-low penetration rates across many fixed-line and mobile services. Newly appointed Saudi providers, the Bahrain Telecommunications Company (Batelco), Hong Kong-based PCCW, and U.S.-based Verizon Communications have formed consortia with local interests.

***SAP***—Many of the largest clients in SAP's portfolio are based in Saudi Arabia, including world-class players such as Saudi Aramco, Saudi Electricity Company, Saudi Arabian Airlines, Saudi Basic Industries Corporation, and the Saudi Arabian General Investment Authority. To accommodate its aggressive growth targets in the region, SAP announced in 2008 that it plans to locate 30% of its Middle East headcount in the Kingdom. In March 2008, Sergio Maccotta, managing director of SAP's MENA division, indicated that the majority of new Saudi-based staff would be local hires. "Saudi Arabia has always been one of our strongest countries in the Middle East, and we are continuing to reinforce our own presence there. Customers demand more local presence; we can't have only people from outside," he said. Following the acquisition of SAP Arabia, SAP now operates in Saudi Arabia as SAP KSA, with offices in Riyadh and Khobar.

***Cisco***—Cisco has signed agreements to design the information and communications (ICT) infrastructure for three of Saudi Arabia's planned Economic Cities. The scale of this Greenfield project provides a "blank slate" opportunity for Cisco to pioneer the most advanced innovations in communications infrastructure. Cisco plans to design the infrastructure for fully networked buildings and residences, linked together by a high-capacity fiber-optic backbone, along with ubiquitous wireless connectivity. These investments are integral to providing the Economic Cities with the most advanced basis for 21st century commerce, and will enable applications such as smart elevators, "invisible" security, RFID inventory tracking, and automated transportations systems. In addition, Cisco has announced plans to invest US$265 million in Saudi Arabia as part of the country's initiative to become a "connected Kingdom." Over the next five years, Cisco plans to: increase its workforce in the Kingdom from 70 to 600; provide leasing and other financial options to Cisco customers; create a Cisco technology and entrepreneurship innovation center; sponsor a Saudi technology and entrepreneurship institute; establish 100 networking training centers to provide joint technical programs with local universities; support provision of Internet connections to 2,000 underserved homes.

Cisco's NETVERSITY (Networking Academy program) has partnered with public education organizations to provide advanced business and technical training to Saudi students, and Cisco has hired 100% of the program's graduates. Cisco has operated in the Kingdom since 1998, with offices in Riyadh, Jeddah, and Khobar. In 2006, Cisco called Saudi Arabia the world's fastest growing region in terms of networking technology adoption. Cisco has worked on other "smart city" projects such as Dubai Internet City, Hong Kong's Cyberport, and Belgium's I-City. Its recent and planned investments in the Kingdom are examples of the large-scale opportunities provided by the Kingdom's expansive investment initiatives.

## Sample Company Surveys and Interviews

Several companies were interviewed to discover what they considered to be the most important factors guiding their location in the Middle East. While the primary target industry was financial services, several other service industry companies were also interviewed to validate or reveal differences in the criteria considered. The results are organized along the following themes: strategic considerations (why invest?), location decision factors, ownership mode decisions (licensing vs. joint venture vs. wholly owned subsidiary), and the decision-making process.

### Strategic Considerations

All companies interviewed invested in the region with a market-seeking purpose. In the case of financial services, the focus was primarily on sourcing of funds via the provision of private banking or wealth management services to the affluent. MENA markets are considered attractive with high-growth prospects. The financial services companies all found that it was increasingly inappropriate to service MENA clients from their

European base in the United Kingdom. Given an increasing aversion to suitcase bankers among clients and prospects, financial services companies decided to establish local bases to grow their business. Other companies interviewed had a global strategy and needed to be in all parts of the world as part of this strategy. This was particularly true for companies who needed to follow their clients across the globe (for example, logistics companies), who managed global relationships with the world's largest and most international companies. In such cases, investment in a particular national market might not be profitable on a standalone basis, but was necessary in order to support strategic, global client relationships.

Several companies also expressed elements of strategic asset-seeking considerations. This was the case, for example, for a logistics provider who invested in the UAE and Bahrain in order to perform hub functions for its global logistics network. Other companies investing in Dubai also did so in order to have a regional hub, which in several cases stretched farther in geographic scope than just the MENA region to encompass the whole of Africa or South Asia.

Natural resource-seeking or factor-seeking considerations were hardly mentioned as reasons to invest. This was to be expected, given the fact that all companies interviewed were service companies operating outside the energy sector. The availability of qualified staff and the possibility to attract staff into a particular location were mentioned as factors to decide for a particular location within the MENA region, but such considerations were not mentioned as reasons to support the investment decision in the MENA region overall.

Therefore, among the interviewees, market-seeking considerations were by far the most important motivation for the companies in the sample to be in the MENA region.

## Location Choice Criteria

The main reasons for considering or choosing specific locations can be classified into the following categories:

1. **Market Potential**

    Since all companies in the sample were investing primarily for market-seeking purposes, market potential was clearly a major location decision criterion. Although Saudi Arabia is the largest market for many investors, most companies decided to set up operations first in countries other than Saudi Arabia. Especially Bahrain and the UAE, which are within close proximity of Saudi Arabia, were preferred based on the other location decision factors that are discussed below. Several

companies subsequently started their own operations in Saudi Arabia as the market opportunity grew, Saudi Arabia's regulatory framework improved, and as investors gained familiarity with the region. Other MENA countries were entered in the same way, with a regional headquarters planning and coordinating entry into adjacent markets. In this sense, the findings are consistent with the Uppsala model of the company internationalization process (Johanson and Vahlne, 1977, 1990), whereby companies commit increasing amounts of resources to a market as their knowledge of foreign markets increases with experience.

2. **Regulatory Environment**

    The regulatory environment is a driver of both investment location decisions and operation mode decisions for all investors. The regulatory environment has changed significantly in many MENA countries in the last decade. As a result, several companies said they would have taken a different location and ownership mode decision in today's environment compared to the time that they made their original decision.

    Specifically, Bahrain attracted investment in the financial services industry because it was the first GCC country with a clear regulatory framework and the opportunity for foreigners to obtain 100% ownership. With the subsequent establishment of the Dubai International Financial Center (DIFC) in 2004, financial services companies had a choice of locations in which they could retain full ownership. More recently, Saudi Arabia also allowed foreign investors to obtain full ownership in certain sectors (including financial services) and Qatar established the Qatar Financial Center.

    Several financial services companies said that the fact that the DIFC regulations were modeled on UK regulations provided a major reason for establishing at the DIFC. In Dubai, the Dubai Financial Services Authority (DFSA) is the regulator for the DIFC. Its rules and ways of enforcing the rules are familiar to international bankers, particularly to those with experience in the UK and the United Sates. This consistency in regulation between the DIFC and other international financial centers made it easier for legal departments at headquarters to accept the DIFC as a location compared to other locations where the regulatory framework might be less familiar.

    Other regulatory factors mentioned included those from among the World Bank's Doing Business indicators and other rankings, such as ease of setting up a business, the efficiency of the bureaucracy, and the level of corruption.

3. **Quality of Life**

Quality of life for employees and their families is a major determinant for location decisions since new investments require new staff which may not be working in the region yet. Aspects of quality of life that were mentioned include:

- The availability of good international schools
- Community life and entertainment possibilities
- Safety
- The accessibility of the location by air

Several respondents stressed the importance of this point in the context of the large proportion of time that staff spends traveling. Company management wants to make sure that their families are in an optimal environment when staff are away from home. These factors were mentioned as particularly important by companies that chose the UAE (specifically Dubai) as their hub.

4. **Physical Infrastructure**

Infrastructure was mentioned as an important location decision factor by all respondents, particularly for those companies choosing their location for a regional hub. In these cases, the available international flight network was mentioned several times as a factor in favor of the UAE.

5. **Cost Considerations**

Cost by itself was not mentioned frequently as a major driving factor for a location decision, indicating again the market-seeking motive rather than a resource-seeking motive for the companies in the sample. Every investment decision was typically supported by a business case which outlined the revenues, costs, investments, and risks associated with the investment proposal. Cost was therefore clearly one of the main factors driving the attractiveness of a project, but was not by itself a deciding factor for investors choosing one location over another or for companies investing in particular countries.

A comment made by several companies was that Dubai's attractiveness as a location increased significantly since 2008 due to the large drop in rents for office and housing costs (housing for expatriate staff is usually paid for by the employer).

*Quotes from Interviewees:*
*"We considered Bahrain and Dubai as locations for our first Middle East office. At the time, flight connections in and out of Bahrain were actually reducing due to the Gulf Air restructuring, while Emirates was rapidly expanding its network. This was an important factor in choosing for Dubai."*

**The Role of Environmental Risk**

Environmental or political risk was considered in the investment decision-making process of all interviewees. The role that this risk factor played depended on the circumstances of the company and the investment decision. If the investment decision was a stand-alone project, then political risk influenced the decision-making process by increasing the discount rate that was used to evaluate a project's attractiveness. In this case, the hurdle rate for a project in a country with high political risk was increased and projects with relatively low profitability might be rejected in high-risk countries but accepted in low-risk countries.

If the project being considered had alternative locations (such as for a regional hub), then, ceteris paribus, the location with lower political risk was preferred. For example, Beirut was mentioned several times as a potential regional headquarters location for financial services firms, but political instability prevented companies from establishing their hub there.

The idea of threshold levels of risk was supported to some extent by the interviewees. If political risk was below a certain level, it had no impact on the discount rate used to evaluate the project. At higher levels of risk, the discount rate increased. Above a certain level of political risk, most companies concluded that it was not feasible to provide a service in the country. However, this threshold level of risk was high and seemed to be related specifically to security concerns rather than overall political considerations. No country in the MENA region seemed to be barred from consideration, and several respondents said they were actively considering investment in Iraq. For companies who needed to maintain control over key processes in their service delivery, the criterion to invest in a country was whether certain activities could be carried out by the company's own staff. If a company's own staff was not able to perform core functions because of security concerns, then the market was not entered. Only in one case was political risk found to affect the operation mode; if risk was high, the company was more likely to operate through a licensee rather than through a wholly owned subsidiary.

Political risk was typically a section in the company's business case document, enabling a structured discussion of political risk factors. There appeared to be little knowledge or use of publicly available political risk ratings among interviewees. Several companies had their own risk rating methodology used by head-quarters staff to evaluate and measure political risk. On the whole, it seemed that systematic political risk analysis was left to headquarters staff to ensure consistency of analysis methods across the company globally.

> ### Quotes from Interviewees:
> *"Political risk is a structural feature of the region and needs to be accepted as an element of doing business."*
>
> *"We did not carry out a specific political risk assessment, except for an analysis of the regulations specific to our business."*
>
> *"Although political risk is an important consideration, it will not by itself cause us to abandon a project."*
>
> *"We don't see joint ventures as a way to manage political risk."*

## Entry Modes and Operation Modes

The companies interviewed operated with a large variety of operation modes, including 100% ownership (either onshore or in free zones), joint ventures, and licensing agreements. In nearly all cases, the operation mode was the same as the entry mode, meaning that there were only few and minor changes to a company's ownership and control arrangements after the initial entry was made.

Nearly all companies demonstrated a strong preference for maximum ownership and control in all their markets in the MENA region. The reason that not all companies operated exclusively in their preferred ownership mode in practice was either due to regulatory factors, historical reasons, or a combination of both.

Regulatory factors inhibited companies from having full ownership in many MENA countries, although variations tended to exist by industry sector within a country. In all GCC countries except for Bahrain, an onshore presence could only be obtained in partnership with a local sponsor, whereby the sponsor must own a minimum of 51% in the venture. Several interviewees that operated under such an arrangement commented that they saw this not as a true joint venture but mostly an effective way to operate in a market under the regulations existing at the time of entry. Among companies interviewed, such joint venture arrangements often had a service contract in addition to the joint venture agreement, whereby the partner/sponsor provided visa processing and administrative services to the foreign investor for a fee. The actual profits from the business flowed entirely to the foreign investor. The local joint venture partner therefore did not take a risk by participating in the venture, got no share of the profits, and only received a fee for services rendered. In one case, the foreign investor did mention that the sponsor provided assistance in obtaining payment from a government entity.

In some cases, joint ventures existed because the government required part ownership of a business as part of a privatization effort, or because the government was a strategic participant in the company's parent.

In one case, a joint venture existed for historical reasons as it had been put in place by previous management who considered a joint venture as an effective way to obtain local market knowledge and access to decision makers. In this case, current management is continuing the existing arrangement, even though its preference would be for full control and ownership.

The forces of regulations and historical considerations come together in the sense that those companies that opened in the region before full ownership became possible were still operating as joint ventures through local sponsors, whereas several companies indicated they would prefer to set up in one of the free zones in order to benefit from full ownership and control. However, switching costs (including administrative costs, office moves, and increases in office rent), as well as a concern that the existing sponsor might respond negatively to the termination of the sponsorship agreement, were factors that inhibited a change in operation mode.

The reasons given by companies to prefer full ownership and to shy away from agency agreements or joint ventures showed a large degree of consistency among respondents, with the main theme being fears of opportunism among joint venture partners. In several cases, it was argued that the interests of joint venture partners might not be aligned. First, a local joint venture partner might be interested in local profitability, whereas the multinational company was managing for global profitability. This concern arose particularly in the treatment of strategic global customers. A second concern mentioned was that the joint venture partner might not be sufficiently interested in the profitability of the venture, as it might be just one of many business activities the partner engaged in. The partnership could be seen as a vehicle for prestige rather than profit. Third, foreign investors in knowledge-intensive industries were keen to protect their intellectual property, particularly in markets where intellectual property rights are not rigorously enforced. Fourth, companies with important operations in the U.S. all mentioned the importance attached to full compliance with the Foreign Corrupt Practices Act (FCPA). This legislation, as well as equivalent legislation in the UK and other countries, places restrictions on the partners of multinational companies and their activities. Foreign investors wanted to ensure that communication with host governments was done by them directly in a way that complied with the FCPA rather than by a partner whose compliance with the FCPA was difficult to monitor in practice. Several companies said, "Only we can represent ourselves to foreign governments." Finally, several companies mentioned financial and reporting factors as reasons to prefer full or majority ownership. Majority ownership was required to be able to consolidate investments in the company's financial statements. Similarly, majority or full ownership was also mentioned as superior from a shareholder value-creation perspective, particularly if a company was quoted on the stock market.

Generally, the issue of dealing with host governments was seen as a reason to maintain full control over an investment rather than sharing ownership. In addition to the FCPA considerations mentioned, companies with operations in many countries (including emerging markets) considered dealing with host governments as one of their main competencies with which they required little outside help. Several of the companies indicated that when required, support was provided by the relevant Embassy or Consulate in the host country. If additional outside help was needed in this area, a company might use a consult for a fee, without any need to share ownership over the investment.

More generally, interviewees saw no major differences between the way the company operated in the MENA region compared to the home market in terms of how decisions were made on what should be done by the company itself and what could best be done by outsiders. If there were certain activities that were considered as not being core to the company, then these could be subcontracted or outsourced. The fact that the MENA operation was in a country other than the company's home base did not provide a reason by itself to enter into equity-sharing arrangements. Subcontracting and outsourcing were considered to provide greater flexibility to change partners when required.

The internationalization of the management base at multinational companies was an additional reason that local partnerships were not always viewed as necessary. The MENA operations of most of the companies interviewed were managed by staff from the region or had extensive experience in the region, combined with higher education and work experience in Europe or the United States. This internationalization of the multinationals' HR strategy helped reduce the liability of foreignness for these investors, and also reduced the need for local partners.

Therefore, most companies had a strong preference for maximum control and ownership of their operations.

***Quotes from Interviewees:***
*"Local partners don't bring much to the table. They are not needed for financial strength and not for operational skills."*

*"The sponsor is not really needed to open doors in a country. This can be done just as well by local employees."*

*"If our name is on the venture, then we must have majority ownership."*

*"A joint venture is seen as risky, since it ties the company to one partner, who may later turn out to be the wrong partner."*

*"Our strategy is to have as much ownership share as the local regulations will allow."*

*"According to the FCPA regulations, we must avoid partnerships which can be seen as political partnerships."*

**The Decision-Making Process**
Except for one acquisition, all market entries were made through greenfield investments. Nearly all companies considered several locations when they entered the MENA region for the first time, although several companies were able to narrow down the list of location options quickly.

In each case, a formal business case document was prepared and presented to the company's highest decision-making body, typically the Managing Board. The business case development process, the decision-making process, and its implementation were standardized to a high degree for the larger companies in the sample. Typically, the business case document itself was not completely standardized, even for the larger companies, but there was a clear expectation of the topics that should be covered in the document.

At the same time, the informal involvement of the company's senior management was seen as critical in obtaining subsequent approval of a business case. Such involvement typically consisted of visits of senior management from company headquarters to proposed investment destinations in the MENA region.

The duration of the decision-making project varied between six months and several years.

### Quotes from Interviewees

*"Deciding on an office location is an iterative process. First, we serve customers from the country, we build up tacit knowledge, and then prepare a business case."*

*"Getting people from head office to visit the region helped a great deal in getting decisions made."*

## CASE DISCUSSION QUESTIONS

1. Discuss how laws and regulations regarding foreign direct investment (FDI) have changed over the years.
2. What are some of the major factors companies consider when investing in the countries discussed in the case? Do these companies consider one set of factors more important than others? Why?
3. What are some of the major challenges facing multinationals as they invest in countries such as Dubai or Saudi Arabia?
4. Why are most foreign multinationals unwilling to form joint ventures as they enter markets in Saudi Arabia and Dubai? Do you believe that these fears are justified?

## CASE NOTES

[1] Nir Kshetri, "Emerging Economies and the Global Financial Crisis: Evidence from China and India," *Thunderbird International Business Review*, Vol. 53, No. 2, March/April 2011.

[2] Giovanni Dell'Aricca, Julian Giovanni, Andre Faria, M. Aythan Kose, Paolo Mauro, Jonathan D. Ostray, Martin Schindler, and Marco Terrones, "Reaping the Benefits of Financial Globalization," *IMF Occasional Paper No. 264*, 2008.

[3] M. Ayhan Kose, Eswar Prasad, Kenneth Rogoff, and Shang-Jin Wei, "Financial Globalization: A Reappraisal," *IMF Staff Papers*, Vol. 56, No. 1, 2009.

[4] Ibid.

[5] Ibid.

[6] This section is summarized from the IMF "Annual Report on Exchange Arrangements and Exchange Restrictions, 2010," Saudi Arabia, pp. 1208–1213.

[7] www.sama.gov.sa/en/insurance;www.cma.org.sa/cma_en/default.aspx.

[8] Information for this section is taken from the IMF "Annual Report on Exchange Arrangements and Exchange Restrictions, 2010," United Arab Emirates, pp. 1509–1513.

[9] Martin Schindler, "Measuring Financial Integration: A New Data Set," *IMF Staff Papers*, Vol. 56, No. 1, 2009.

[10] Philip R. Lane, and Gian Maria Milesi_Ferretti, "The External Wealth of Nations Mark II: Revised and Extended Estimates of Foreign Assets and Liabilities, 1970-2004," *Journal of International Economics*, Vol. 73, No. 2, 2007.

[11] IMD "World Competitiveness Yearbook, 2009."

[12] Ibid.

[13] His Excellency Mr. Amr Al-Dabbagh is the Governor and Chairman of the Board of the Saudi Arabian General Investment Authority (SAGIA), with the rank of Minister. In the years since assuming the position in March 2004, SAGIA has seen the value of investment licenses grow to 19 times the total since it was created in 2000 (from US$4.5 billion to US$80 billion). Al-Dabbagh has been lauded by government and private sector leaders for his visionary and highly ambitious leadership, which recently garnered several awards for him, including Man of Year from *Arabian Business Magazine*, Global Leader of Tomorrow from the Executive Board of the World Economic Forum and the Editorial Board of *Worldlink* magazine, and the Leadership Award of the 12th Arab Economic Forum. Since 2005, SAGIA has been the architect behind the launch of an entirely new global product called "Economic Cities." These super-high-tech, 100% privately held total living and investing environments will, by 2020, have added more than US$150 billion to the Saudi GDP, 1.5 million jobs, raised the per capital GDP from 13,000 to 33,500 riyals, and provided ultimate living destinations to more than 4.5 million people. Five of six cities have already been launched, with a total value of more than US$80 billion. These include King Abdullah Economic City in Rabigh, Prince Abdul Aziz Bin Mousaed Economic City in Hail, Knowledge Economic City in Madina, and Jizan Economic City in Jizan. [http://www.sagia.gov.sa/english/uploads/HEBio_2008October.pdf, downloaded 8/19/09]

[14] Information about SAGIA is taken from www.SAGIA.gov.sa.

[15] Web links to Saudi Arabia government procedures and licensing requirements: http://www.sagia.gov.sa/english/uploads/Government%20Procedures_%D9%90En_2.2.1.2.pdf; http://www.sagia.gov.sa/english/index.php?page=documents-downloads.

# Culture and Multinational Management

2

## Different and the Same: Explorations in Culture

The poem "We and They" by Rudyard Kipling captures some of the feelings associated with intercultural experiences,

Father, Mother, and Me
Sister and Auntie say
All the people like us are We,
And everyone else is They,
And They live over the sea
While We live over the way,
But—would you believe it?—They look upon We
As only a sort of They!

We eat pork and beef
With cow-horn-handled knives,
They who gobble Their rice off a leaf
Are horrified out of Their lives:
While They who live up a tree,
Feast on grubs and clay,
(Isn't it scandalous?) look upon We
As a simply disgusting They!

We eat kitcheny food,
We have doors that latch,
They drink milk and blood
Under an open thatch. We have doctors to fee,
They have wizards to pay,
And (impudent heathen!) They look upon We
As a quite impossible They!

All good people agree,
And all good people say,
All nice people, like us, are We

## Learning Objectives

*After reading this chapter you should be able to:*

- Define culture and understand the basic components of culture.

- Identify instances of cultural stereotyping and ethnocentrism.

- Understand how various levels of culture influence multinational operations.

- Apply the Hofstede, GLOBE, and 7d models to diagnose and understand the impact of cultural differences on management processes.

- Appreciate the complex differences among cultures and use these differences to build better organizations.

- Recognize the complexity of understanding new cultures and the dangers of stereotyping and cultural paradoxes.

And everyone else is They
But if you cross over the sea,
Instead of over the way,
You may end by (think of it!) looking on We
As only a sort of They!

*Source: Kipling, Rudyard. "We and They." 1923. In Storti, Craig. 1990.* The Art of Crossing Cultures. *Yarmouth, ME: Intercultural Press, 92–91.*

---

The Preview Case in Point shows the feelings that many individuals have when they meet people from other cultures. They see behavior that they have trouble understanding. They see, hear, smell, and taste things that are strange and unpredictable. However, in today's business world, these seemingly strange people are often your customers, employees, suppliers, and business partners.

To remain competitive and to flourish in the complex and fast-changing world of multinational business, multinational managers look worldwide not only for potential markets but also for sources of high quality and less expensive raw materials and labor. Even managers who never leave their home country must deal with markets and workforces whose cultural backgrounds are increasingly diverse. Managers with the skills to understand and adapt to different cultures are better positioned to succeed in these endeavors and to compete successfully in the world market.

Throughout this text you will encounter numerous cultural differences in management practices from countries around the world. To help you better understand these cultural underpinnings of management, this chapter considers two basic questions: (1) What is culture?, and (2) How does culture affect management and organizations? The concept of culture will be revisited in other chapters to show how an understanding of cultural differences in management practices can contribute to more effective management of multinational organizations.

## What Is Culture?

Culture is a concept borrowed from cultural anthropology. Anthropologists believe that cultures provide solutions to problems of adaptation to the environment. Culture helps people become attached to their society. It tells us who we are and to what groups we belong. Culture provides mechanisms that enable the continuation of the group. For example, culture determines how children are educated and tells us when and whom to marry. Culture pervades most areas of our life, determining, for example, how we should dress and what we should eat.

Anthropologists have numerous and subtly different definitions of culture.[1] However, for the purposes of this book, with its focus on multinational management, **culture** is defined as the pervasive and shared beliefs, norms, and values that guide the everyday life of a group. These beliefs, norms, and values are expressed to current group members and passed on to future group members through rituals, stories, and symbols.

**Cultural norms** both prescribe and proscribe behaviors; that is, they tell us what we can and cannot do. For example, norms prescribe when and whom we can

**Culture**
The pervasive and shared beliefs, norms, and values that guide the everyday life of a group.

**Cultural norms**
Prescribed and proscribed behaviors, telling us what we can do and what we cannot do.

marry and what clothes we can or cannot wear to a funeral or to the office. Cultural values tell us such things as what is good, what is beautiful, what is holy, and what are legitimate goals in life. Cultural beliefs represent our understandings about what is true. For example, most people in the United States accept the scientific method as a valid way of discovering facts. In contrast, other cultures may have the belief that facts can be revealed only by God.

Cultural symbols, stories, and rituals communicate the norms, values, and beliefs of a society or a group to its members. Each generation passes its culture to the next generation through certain symbols, stories, and rituals. A culture is continuously reinforced when people see particular symbols, hear particular stories, and engage in specific rituals.

Rituals include ceremonies such as baptism and graduation, as well as the tricks played on a new worker or the pledge to a sorority or fraternity. Stories include such things as nursery rhymes, proverbs, and traditional legends (such as the U.S. legend that George Washington could not tell a lie). Symbols may be physical, such as national flags or holy artifacts. In the workplace, office size and location can serve as cultural symbols. North American managers, for example, use large offices with physical barriers such as outer offices as symbols to communicate their power. In contrast, Japanese managers avoid physical barriers. They prefer instead to locate their desks at the center of communication networks, where their desks are surrounded by coworkers.

Culture is pervasive in societies. It affects almost everything we do, see, feel, and believe. Pick any aspect of your life, and it is likely influenced by your culture. What you sleep on, what you eat, what clothes you wear, how you address your family members and boss, whether you believe that old age is good or bad, what your toilet looks like, all relate to cultural differences. In each of these areas, societies develop pervasive cultural norms, values, and beliefs to assist their members in adapting to their environments.

Because culture affects so many aspects of our lives, many of the core values, norms, and beliefs about what should happen in everyday life are taken for granted. People do not consciously think about how culture affects their behaviors and attitudes. They just do what they believe is "right and natural" (see the Preview Case in Point). They may not fully understand why they behave as they do.

Another key component of the definition of culture is that cultural values, norms, and beliefs must be shared by a group of people. The group must accept, for the most part, that the norms, values, and beliefs of their group are correct and compelling.[2] The phrase "correct and compelling" means that, although all people in any culture do not behave the same way all the time, behaviors are predictable most of the time. Imagine, for example, the chaos that would exist if we did not have norms to guide our driving. For example, when driving on two-lane roads in Ireland, drivers routinely pass slower vehicles even when faced with oncoming traffic. Unlike in the United States, oncoming drivers expect this tactic and routinely move to the breakdown lane. Although this norm makes driving different than it is in the United States, the majority of people in Ireland manage to drive without running into each other. For the multinational manager, dealing with cultural differences is unavoidable. To succeed cross-culturally, multinational managers must learn as much as they can about the important cultural norms, values, and beliefs of the societies in which they work. They also must learn to recognize the important symbols, values, and rituals of a culture. Such knowledge helps the multinational manager understand the "why" behind the behavior of their customers, workers, and colleagues.

**Cultural values**
Values that tell us such things as what is good, what is beautiful, what is holy, and what are legitimate goals in life.

**Cultural beliefs**
Our understandings about what is true.

**Cultural symbols**
These may be physical, such as national flags or holy artifacts. In the workplace, office size and location can serve as cultural symbols.

**Cultural stories**
These include such things as nursery rhymes and traditional legends.

**Cultural rituals**
Ceremonies such as baptism, graduation, the tricks played on a new worker, or the pledge to a sorority or fraternity.

**Pervasive**
The idea that culture affects almost everything we do, everything we see, and everything we feel and believe.

**Shared cultural values, norms, and beliefs**
The idea that people in different cultural groups have similar views of the world.

**CASE IN POINT**

## Cultural Misunderstandings

- You negotiate extensively with a Chinese company to enter into an alliance to penetrate the Chinese market. After agreeing on the alliance, you visit the Chinese company and present management with an extremely thorough document discussing the details of the agreement. You then find that the Chinese are reluctant to establish the alliance. Why? The Chinese are more interested in developing a relationship than in signing a contract.

- You spend considerable time preparing for your meeting in Tokyo. Your meeting goes well, and you are able to answer everyone's questions about the proposed joint venture without hesitation. However, you do not hear from your contacts when you get back to the United States. Why? During your proposal, you crossed your ankle over your knee, a posture that is considered rude in Japan.

- Your meeting with your Chinese counterparts goes very well. After the negotiations end, you exchange gifts with your Chinese hosts. However, your gift is met with looks of disapproval. Why? Although your gift was an expensive clock with the corporate logo, clocks tend to be reminders of funerals in China.

- BenQ, a Taiwan-based company, was in the headlines in 2005 when it acquired the money-losing mobile phone subsidiary of Siemens. The chairman of BenQ was convinced that the company could achieve synergy with the new acquisition and return to profitability. Unfortunately, the acquisition failed and BenQ was forced to file for bankruptcy protection in Germany. One of the major reasons for the failure was the communication gaps between Taiwanese and Germans. Germans prefer to express themselves openly and directly, while the Taiwanese prefer a more subtle mode of expression, avoiding overt agreement or disagreement. This difference led to the two companies' workers becoming suspicious of each other, and led to the financial disaster.

*Sources: Based on Cheng, S. S. & M. W. Seeger. 2012. "Cultural differences and communication issues in international mergers and acquisitions: A case study of BenQ debacle." International Journal of Business and Social Science, 3(3): 116–127; Llorente, Elizabeth. 2006. "A little cultural savvy can go a long way toward sealing a deal: Avoid faux pas that can cost business." The Record, February 7, X28; Orkin, Neil. 2008. "Focus on China." Training, 45(6): 18.*

The above Case in Point shows the challenges caused by a lack of sensitivity to local cultural values. As you can see, appropriately understanding a country's culture can lessen the likelihood of the misunderstandings discussed in the Case in Point. A lack of sensitivity can be disastrous for the company involved and result in failure. Understanding culture is therefore a critical component of doing business in today's global environment.

The next section expands our discussion of culture by looking at how the various levels of culture affect the multinational manager in the business world.

**Levels of culture**
The levels of cultural influence, including national, business, and occupational and organizational culture.

# Levels of Culture

The international businessperson needs to be aware of three **levels of culture** that may influence multinational operations: national culture, business culture, and occupational and organizational cultures. Exhibit 2.1 shows the levels of culture that affect multinational management.

**National culture**
The dominant culture within the political boundaries of the nation-state.

## National Culture

**National culture** is the dominant culture within the political boundaries of the nation-state. The dominant national culture is usually the culture of those in the majority, or

**EXHIBIT 2.1**   Levels of Culture in Multinational Management

© Cengage Learning

those with the greatest political or economic power. Formal education is generally taught, and business is usually conducted, in the language of the dominant culture.

Political boundaries, however, do not necessarily reflect cultural boundaries. Many countries, such as Canada and Singapore, have more than one major cultural group within their political boundaries. Even states with relatively homogeneous cultures have subcultures that represent regional and rural/urban cultural differences and influence business transactions.

Most business takes place within the political boundaries of the nation-state. As a result, the dominant culture of the nation-state has the greatest effect on international business. In particular, the dominant national culture usually influences not only the language of business transactions but also the nature and types of laws that govern businesses.

## Business Culture

To a large degree, when multinational managers express concern about the impact of culture on international operations, they focus on how national cultures influence business operations. They ask, "How do the [Germans, Indians, Japanese, Koreans, South Americans, Africans, Israelis, etc.] do business?" What concerns these managers is **business culture**. More than cultural differences in business etiquette, business culture represents norms, values, and beliefs that pertain to all aspects of doing business in a culture.[3] Business cultures tell people the correct, acceptable ways to conduct business in a society.

Each national culture produces its own business culture. As such, business cultures are not separate from the broader national culture. Rather, the more pervasive national culture constrains and guides the development of business culture in a society. In any society, business is closely interwoven with the values, norms, and beliefs of a culture as a whole. Examples are the priorities given to age and seniority, the role expectations for women with their families, and expectations concerning how superiors should behave toward subordinates.

At a very broad level, business culture, as a reflection of national culture, influences all aspects of work and organizational life. This includes how managers select and promote employees, lead and motivate their subordinates, structure their organizations, select and formulate their strategies, and negotiate with other businesspeople. Much

**Business culture**
The norms, values, and beliefs that pertain to all aspects of doing business in a culture.

## Focus on Emerging Markets

### Business Culture in China

As one of the world's fastest growing economies, China remains an important market that most Western-based multinationals want to break into. Understanding China's business culture is critical to such endeavors. However, China's business culture is undergoing dramatic and constant change. China's Cultural Revolution sent many young professionals to work in rural areas while denying education to others. Also, because most Chinese enterprises were state owned, most Chinese did not have the opportunity to study business-related subjects to help craft the Chinese business culture. However, over the past two decades, more Chinese have had the chance to pursue business education and careers, and they are helping to define Chinese business culture.

Although Chinese business culture is rapidly evolving, a number of key issues need to be addressed when doing business in China:

- *Understand that business moves slowly:* Business happens at a much slower pace in China than in the United States. Companies wanting to do business may need to visit China numerous times before purchasing or negotiating anything.

- *Know the organizational hierarchy:* Chinese companies remain very hierarchical, and it helps to know the most-senior individuals at the negotiating table because they are most likely the decision makers.

- *Get it in writing:* Chinese companies are reluctant to say no, and what may seem to have been agreed upon may not necessarily be what has been agreed upon. It is therefore important to get as much of an agreement in writing as possible for future consideration.

- *Respect Chinese business etiquette:* Individuals hoping to do business with Chinese companies should respect the many facets of Chinese business etiquette. For instance, dressing conservatively and arriving promptly for appointments is strongly advised. The negotiator is also expected to present business cards with both hands. It is advantageous to carry business cards in English on one side and in Chinese on the other. Because of the emphasis on formality, it is also advisable to use last names unless asked to do otherwise. Chinese companies also treat their visitors with lavish banquets, and negotiators should expect to participate in some form of drinking.

- *Value harmony and order:* The Chinese value harmony and order. Therefore, you do not want to highlight individual performances or to praise members of a group. It is typically better to focus on the group performance.

*Sources: Based on Hannon, David. 2006. "Dos and DON'Ts of doing business in China." Purchasing, May 18, 135(8): 52–54; Jung-a, S. & R. Kwong. 2012. "Kim's trip helps make inroads into Chinese market." Financial Times, May 21, 17; Orkin, Neil. 2008. "Focus on China." Training, July–August, 45(6):18; Penzner, Betty. 2006. "The art of Chinese business etiquette: Ancient traditions form the basis of strategy." AFP Exchange, May, 26(4): 61–63.*

of what you read in this text will help you understand how national and business cultures affect organizations and management. Consider the Focus on Emerging Markets above which explores the evolving business culture in China.

Business culture also guides everyday business interactions, and the business cultures of different nations vary widely in terms of the codes of conduct that represent proper business etiquette. As we saw in the last Focus on Emerging Markets, what to wear to a meeting, when and how to use business cards, and how to treat members of a group are examples of business etiquette that vary according to national cultures.

Understanding the basic etiquette of a business culture is a minimal requirement for the multinational manager. In Germany, for example, "[s]how up half an hour late [for a business meeting] and it makes no matter how bad the traffic and how tight your schedule. You've likely lost the appointment and may have a tough time getting another."[4]

## Occupational Culture and Organizational Culture

Although differences in national and business cultures usually present challenges to the multinational manager, other distinct cultures develop around work roles and organizations. These cultures are called occupational and organizational cultures.

Different occupational groups, such as physicians, lawyers, accountants, and craftspeople, have distinct cultures called occupational cultures. Occupational cultures are the norms, values, beliefs, and expected ways of behaving for people in the same occupational group, regardless of their organizational employer.

In spite of the importance of national and business cultures, the multinational manager cannot ignore differences in occupational cultures. To demonstrate this point, a study by Hofstede including more than 40 different national cultures found that people with similar jobs often had very similar cultural values. Moreover, the people from different occupational groups were often more similar to one another than to people from their own national cultures.

Occupational cultures are more commonly found among professional and technical occupations, such as physicians. This distinction occurs because professionals have similar educational backgrounds and have access to the free flow of technical information across national boundaries.

During the last decade, managers and academics realized that the concept of culture also applies to individual organizations. Differences in organizational cultures seemed to explain why two organizations with similar structures and strategies would have different performance levels and why a merger of two otherwise successful companies would fail. In particular, the idea of an organizational culture helps us understand how organizations are affected by more than their formally designed systems, such as their organizational structure.

Vijay Sathe defined organizational culture as "the set of important understandings (often unstated) that members of a community share in common." Edgar Schein of MIT added that these assumptions, values, and beliefs concerning the organization are discovered and created when members learn to cope with external and internal problems, such as developing a strategy or the criteria for allocating organizational rewards. When coping strategies—such as Hewlett-Packard's "management by wandering around"—work successfully, they are taught to new members as "the correct way to perceive, think, and feel in relation to those problems."

Organizations seldom have only one organizational culture, nor perhaps should they. Because organizational subunits (i.e., divisions, departments) all face different situations, most subunits develop distinct subcultures. Subunits may retain many of the overall characteristics of the parent company, but, for example, few would expect an R&D department to have the same culture as a manufacturing plant.

Although various parts of an organization may have different organizational cultures, it is important to note that organizational cultures may also have as important an influence on employees as the national culture does. For instance, consider

**Occupational cultures**
Distinct cultures of occupational groups such as physicians, lawyers, accountants, and craftspeople.

**Organizational culture**
The norms, values, and beliefs concerning an organization that are shared by members of the organization.

## CASE IN POINT

### Influence of Power Distance on Communication among Mexican Workers

A study of 168 Mexican employees in Mexican organizations examined the interplay between national culture and organizational culture. The author of the study argued that compatibility between an organizational culture and the national culture would be more satisfying for workers. Power distance (the degree to which individuals accept that there are inequalities among people at different positions of formal power, a concept that will be covered in more detail in the next section) was assessed at both the company level and the national level. Given that Mexico is a high-power-distance country, it would seem likely that workers would expect to be told what to do. However, because of status differences and the fact that most communication is top down, it may also be expected that workers will experience high communication apprehension (subordinates' aversion to communicating with superiors because they are consistently being told what to do) and high approach avoidance (the act of being abrupt, such as cutting someone off or acting in an offensive or condescending manner).

In the study, the author does indeed find that Mexican workers experience high communication apprehension and high approach avoidance. However, the most surprising aspect of the study's results was the fact that the more an organization had high power distance (and hence the more closely it hewed to the high power distance in the nation as a whole), the more the Mexican workers were satisfied with the various aspects of organizational communication. Furthermore, the more satisfied with communication they were, the more likely the workers were to be satisfied with their jobs and committed to their organizations.

*Source: Based on Madlock, P. E. 2012. "The influence of power distance and communication on Mexican workers." Journal of Business Communication, 49(2): 169–184.*

that many U.S. companies promote the use of first names as a way to encourage employees to bond and feel comfortable with each other. Such practices may not work well in more hierarchical societies such as Germany and France, where it is important to respect titles and hierarchy. However, organizational cultures in smaller firms may actually make the use of first names more acceptable because their small size encourages employees to be more familiar with each other. Consequently, it is critical for the multinational manager to understand the influences of the various levels of culture on employees. In fact, research shows that when an organizational culture is compatible with the national culture, employees are more likely to feel at ease at work. Conisder the above Case in Point

The above Case in Point clearly shows the interplay between organizational culture and national culture. U.S. society generally views communication aversion and approach avoidance as negative. Subordinates in the United States will generally pay attention to supervisors and will not appear disengaged. Furthermore, approach avoidance is also frowned upon, as in general, U.S. workers will not tolerate being talked to in a condescending manner. However, Mexican workers are used to these behaviors because they live in a society in which workers accept high power distance. These workers tend to be more satisfied if they work in companies with high power distance. Companies that have higher power distance have organizational cultures that are more compatible with the higher power distance of Mexican culture as a whole. In sum, the compatibility between organizational cultures and national cultures is an important issue to take into consideration as multinationals enter new cultures.

In the next section, we discuss some of the more popular frameworks for understanding national culture.

## Cultural Differences and Basic Values: Three Diagnostic Models to Aid the Multinational Manager

Multinational managers face a complex and challenging array of cultural differences. To be successful, multinational managers must understand the important ways in which national and business cultures differ. The following sections therefore describe three popular models of culture.

The Dutch scientist Geert Hofstede introduced the first model in the early 1980s and continued his research on national culture for over two decades.[5] Management scholars now use Hofstede's work extensively as a way of grasping cultural differences. We call his model the Hofstede model of national culture. Hofstede based his model primarily on differences in values and beliefs regarding work goals. This model has easily identifiable implications for business because it provides a clear link between national and business cultures. It also serves as a basis for extensive research on cross-cultural management.[6] Later in the text, you will see numerous examples of Hofstede's ideas providing the background for attempts to understand differences in management practices.

The second model, the most recent development of a framework for understanding national culture, is represented by the Global Leadership and Organizational Behavior Effectiveness (GLOBE) project.[7] This model, based heavily on Hofstede's national culture model, involves nine cultural dimensions. Seven of these nine dimensions are directly related to the five Hofstede dimensions, while two of those nine dimensions were developed independently of the Hofstede model. We will therefore focus our discussion of the GLOBE national culture model on these two dimensions.

Finally, the third model, created by Fons Trompenaars, is called the 7d culture model because it represents seven dimensions of culture. This model has emerged from extensive and continuing cross-national research by Trompenaars and his colleagues.[8]

All three models equip managers with the basic tools necessary to analyze the cultures in which they do business. Furthermore, these approaches also provide useful terms to help you understand the complexities of different cultural values. By using these models, you will develop an initial understanding of important cultural differences and key cultural traits.

The next section provides more detail on the Hofstede model, followed by a briefer section describing the GLOBE model. The section concludes with Trompenaars's 7d model.

## Hofstede's Model of National Culture

To describe national cultures, Hofstede[9] uses five dimensions that speak to basic cultural values:

1. *Power distance:* Expectations regarding equality among people.
2. *Uncertainty avoidance:* Typical reactions to situations considered different and dangerous.
3. *Individualism:* Relationship between the individual and the group in society.
4. *Masculinity:* Expectations regarding gender roles.
5. *Long-term orientation:* Basic orientation toward time.

Hofstede's framework was based on 116,000 surveys from 88,000 employees of IBM subsidiaries around the world. Although the original sample included 72 countries,

**Hofstede model of national culture**
A model mainly based on differences in values and beliefs regarding work goals.

**Global Leadership and Organizational Behavior Effectiveness (GLOBE) project**
A recent large-scale project based on Hofstede's model and aimed at determining 9 cultural dimensions of 62 countries.

**7d culture model**
A seven-dimension model based on beliefs regarding how people relate to each other, how people manage time, and how people deal with nature.

Hofstede used only the countries that provided more than 50 responses.[10] Hofstede thus identified four of these cultural value dimensions in the reduced sample of 40 countries.[11] However, the database was later expanded to include 10 additional countries from three regions, specifically Arab countries and East and West Africa. Later research by Hofstede and others added to the number of countries studied and introduced the fifth dimension, long-term orientation.[12]

Research on the long-term orientation dimension was unique. Rather than using survey questions developed by Western researchers, Michael Bond and several Chinese colleagues designed a new survey based on questions developed by Asian researchers that reflected Confucian values. Hofstede and Bond have related long-term orientation to the recent economic growth in the mini-dragons (e.g., Singapore, South Korea) of the rising Asian economies.[13]

## Hofstede's Cultural Model Applied to Organizations and Management

The following section defines Hofstede's dimensions of national culture.[14] It also adapts and extends this work to show how cultural values affect numerous management practices in different cultures. The management practices considered in the discussion of Hofstede's model are:

1. *Human resources management:*
   a. Management selection: how people are chosen for jobs.
   b. Training: what the focus of job training is.
   c. Evaluation and promotion: what counts to get ahead.
   d. Remuneration: what accounts for differences in pay.
2. *Leadership styles:* How leaders behave.
3. *Motivational assumptions:* Beliefs regarding how people respond to work.
4. *Decision making and organizational design:* How managers structure their organizations and make decisions.
5. *Strategy:* Effects of culture on selecting and implementing strategies.

## Power Distance

**Power distance**
Expectations regarding equality among people.

**Power distance** is concerned with how cultures deal with inequality. It focuses on (1) the norms that tell superiors (bosses, leaders) to what extent they can determine the behavior of their subordinates, and (2) the belief that superiors and subordinates are fundamentally different kinds of people.

High-power-distance countries have norms, values, and beliefs such as the following:[15]

- Inequality is fundamentally good.
- Everyone has a place; some are high, some are low.
- Most people should be dependent on a leader.
- The powerful are entitled to privileges.
- The powerful should not hide their power.

Organizations in countries with a high level of power distance use management systems and processes that reflect a strong concern with hierarchy. As shown later in the chapter in Exhibit 2.7, Latin American, Latin European, and Far Eastern countries demonstrate the highest levels of power distance.

The concern for hierarchy and inequality in organizations is rooted in early socialization in the family and school. In high-power-distance cultures, children are expected to be obedient to parents and elders. This deference continues as long as parents are alive. When children enter school, teachers assume the dominant role. Children must show extreme respect and they seldom challenge a teacher's authority. Later in life, organizations assume many of the roles of parents and teachers.

In high-power-distance countries, the ideal people for a managerial job have either come from a high social class or graduated from an elite university. These characteristics define the person as having the intrinsic or built-in qualities of a leader. Who you are in terms of elite associations is more important than past performance. Leaders and subordinates expect large wage differences between management and workers.

The basic motivational assumption in high-power-distance countries is that people dislike work and try to avoid it. Consequently, managers believe that they must adopt a Theory X leadership style; that is, they must be authoritarian, must force workers to perform, and must closely supervise their subordinates. Similarly, employee training emphasizes compliance (following orders) and trustworthiness.

Organizational structures and systems match the assumptions regarding leadership and motivation. Decision making is centralized. Those at the top make most of the decisions. The close supervision of workers requires many supervisors and a tall organizational pyramid (an organization with many levels). Strategic decisions in high-power-distance countries are influenced by the need to maintain and support those in power.

The following Comparative Management Brief describes how differences in power distance affect specific U.S. and Mexican business practices.

Exhibit 2.2 gives a summary of the managerial implications for power distance. The next section considers uncertainty avoidance.

## Uncertainty Avoidance

**Uncertainty avoidance** relates to norms, values, and beliefs regarding a tolerance for ambiguity. A higher-uncertainty-avoidance culture seeks to structure social systems (such as politics, education, and business) in such a way that order and predictability are paramount and rules and regulations dominate. In such a culture, risky situations create stress and upset people. Consequently, people avoid behaviors such as changing jobs.

High-uncertainty-avoidance countries have norms, values, and beliefs such as the following:[16]

- Conflict should be avoided.
- Deviant people and ideas should not be tolerated.
- Laws are very important and should be followed.
- Experts and authorities are usually correct.
- Consensus is important.

The business cultures in countries high on uncertainty avoidance have management systems and processes that make organizations and employees dependable and predictable. People in such cultures react with stress and anxiety when the rules of

**Uncertainty avoidance**
How people react to what they perceive as different and dangerous.

## Comparative Management **Brief**

### Respect and Power in Mexico versus Respect and Fair Play in the United States

In describing Mexican business culture, a high-power-distance culture, Marc J. Erlich, a psychologist who works with U.S. businesses in Mexico, noted:

> Within Mexican society, there is a tendency to respect those in power. The boss's respectability is manifested by maintaining a definite social distance, through an unwillingness to delegate.
>
> Fair play, shared responsibility, and playing by the rules are characteristics of respect for the [North] American. Respect is earned, not given. North of the border, the ability to be one of the team reflects responsibility.
>
> The U.S. executive frequently perceives Mexican submission to authority as a lack of resolve and an unfortunate passivity. The Mexican will typically view the U.S. executive's insistence on fair play and desire to delegate as an inability to accept the power associated with position.
>
> The power distance is also reflected in Mexican organizations, which are hierarchical. Top management uses and is expected to use power. This organizational structure results in many layers of management and slow decision making. Building trust is thus a key component of Mexican business culture and can speed up decision making for foreign firms. However, impatience is perceived as a weakness in Mexican culture; so foreign multinational managers should avoid moving too quickly.

The high power of distance of Mexican society means that Mexican workers are likely to accept that those who hold higher positions have more power. Because of this power differential, communication tends to be more one way and top down. Subordinates typically expect to be told what to do and how to do their work. Mexican workers will also typically engage in communication patterns with their supervisors based on a power differential and an acceptance of authority.

*Source: Erlich, Mark J. 1993. "Making sense of the bicultural workplace." Business Mexico, August, 18; Madlock, P. E. 2012. "The influence of power distance and communication on Mexican workers." Journal of Business Communication, 49(2): 169–184.*

behavior are not clear in organizational settings. Generally, Nordic and Anglo countries are low on uncertainty avoidance, whereas Latin European and Latin American countries are high. As the next Case in Point shows, Belgian students have little uncertainty when deciding whether to enter their professors' offices.

In high-uncertainty-avoidance cultures, entry-level people are chosen for their potential fit with and loyalty to the organization. Managers follow the logic, "If people are like me, come from my town or my family, then I understand them and trust them more." This minimizes interpersonal conflict, reduces potential employee turnover, and makes people more predictable.

In some cultures, uncertainty regarding employees is further reduced through the selection and promotion of people with specialized expertise. Employers seek out people who will be loyal and committed to them and to the organization. Later, seniority, long-term commitment to the organization, and expertise in the area of management become the prime bases for promotion and payment. Both

**EXHIBIT 2.2**   Management Implications of Power Distance

| Management Processes | Low Power Distance | High Power Distance |
|---|---|---|
| Human resources management | | |
|   Management selection | Educational achievement | Social class; elite education |
|   Training | For autonomy | For conformity/obedience |
|   Evaluations/promotion | Performance | Compliance; trustworthiness |
|   Remuneration | Small wage difference between management and worker | Large wage difference between management and worker |
| Leadership styles | Participative; less direct supervision | Theory X; authoritarian, with close supervision |
| Motivational assumptions | People like work; extrinsic and intrinsic rewards | Assume people dislike work; coercion |
| Decision making/organizational design | Decentralized; flat pyramids; small proportion of supervisors | Tall pyramids; large proportion of supervisors |
| Strategy issues | Varied | Crafted to support the power elite or government |

*Sources: Adapted from Hofstede, Geert. 1980.* Culture's Consequences: International Differences in Work-Related Values. *London: Sage; Hofstede, Geert. 1991.* Cultures and Organizations: Software of the Mind. *London: McGraw-Hill; and Hofstede, Geert. 1993. "Cultural dimensions in people management." In Vladimir Pucik, Noel M. Tichy, and Carole K. Barnette,* Globalizing Management. *Hoboken, NJ: Wiley, 139–158.*

## CASE IN POINT

## Uncertainty Avoidance in a Belgian University

Despite the global financial crisis, Belgium has enjoyed a robust recovery and represents a strong economy in the European Union. However, as multinationals ponder Belgium, they will need to take into consideration Belgium's uncertainty avoidance. Belgium ranks in the top 10 percent (91st percentile) on Hofstede's uncertainty avoidance dimension. As a result, one expects Belgian organizations to have many of the characteristics for high uncertainty avoidance, as shown in Exhibit 2.3. This seems true even for Belgium's universities.

At the University of Leuven, an old Belgian university, three lights stand over a professor's door: green, yellow, and red. Students wishing to see their professor must ring a bell and wait for an appropriate response. Green means come in, yellow means wait a few minutes, and red means go away. There is no ambiguity in these situations. Students do not have to interpret the situation to see whether the professor is busy. In contrast, most students from the United States, a low-uncertainty-avoidance country (21st percentile), would probably find this degree of formality impersonal at best and perhaps even insulting.

*Sources: Based on Business Monitor International. 2012. Belgium—Business Forecast Report. http://www.business monitor.com; Gannon, Martin J., and Associates. 1994. Understanding Global Cultures. Thousand Oaks, CA: Sage Publications; McGinnis, A. Seleim, and N. Bontis. 2009. "The relationship between culture and corruption: A cross-national study." Journal of Intellectual Capital, 10(1): 165–184.*

managers and employees believe that loyalty to the organization is a virtue and that conflict and competition should be avoided.

Task-directed leaders give clear and explicit directions to subordinates. This reduces ambiguity regarding job expectations. The boss tells workers exactly what to do. Task-directed leaders are the preferred leaders in high-uncertainty-avoidance cultures. Such leaders make subordinates less anxious because subordinates know

**EXHIBIT 2.3**     Management Implications of Uncertainty Avoidance

| Management Processes | High Uncertainty Avoidance | Low Uncertainty Avoidance |
|---|---|---|
| Human resources management | | |
|    Management selection | Seniority; expected loyalty | Past job performance; education |
|    Training | Specialized | Training to adapt |
|    Evaluation/promotion | Seniority; expertise; loyalty | Objective individual performance data; job switching for promotions |
| Remuneration | Based on seniority or expertise | Based on performance |
| Leadership styles | Task-oriented | Nondirective; person-oriented; flexible |
| Motivational assumptions | People seek security, avoid competition | People are self-motivated, competitive |
| Decision making/organizational design | Larger organization; tall hierarchy; formalized; many standardized procedures | Smaller organizations; flat hierarchy, less formalized, with fewer written rules and standardized procedures |
| Strategy issues | Averse to risk | Risk taking |

*Sources: Adapted from Hofstede, Geert. 1980.* Culture's Consequences: International Differences in Work-Related Values. *London: Sage; Hofstede, Geert. 1991.* Cultures and Organizations: Software of the Mind. *London: McGraw-Hill; and Hofstede, Geert. 1993. "Cultural dimensions in people management." In Vladimir Pucik, Noel M. Tichy, and Carole K. Barnette,* Globalizing Management. *Hoboken, NJ: Wiley, 139–158.*

exactly what is expected of them. Similarly, organizations in these cultures have many written rules and procedures that tell employees exactly what the organization expects of them. Consequently, employees tend to believe that these rules should not be broken.

In contrast, leaders in low-uncertainty-avoidance cultures favor more flexibility and allow subordinates more choices on the job. The design of their organizations also builds in more freedom, imposing fewer rules and regulations. There are also more subordinates per manager, which results in less supervision and greater autonomy for workers.

People in high-uncertainty-avoidance cultures do not like risk, and they often fear failure. As decision makers, they are conservative. It is unlikely that individual managers will choose risky strategies for their organizations. Hofstede[17] notes, however, that neither low nor high uncertainty avoidance necessarily relates to success. Innovations may be more likely in low-uncertainty-avoidance countries like the United States, but the implementation of innovations may be more likely in high-uncertainty-avoidance countries such as Japan.

Exhibit 2.3 summarizes the managerial implications of uncertainty avoidance.

## Individualism/Collectivism

The values, norms, and beliefs associated with individualism focus on the relationship between the individual and the group. Individualistic cultures view people as unique. People are valued in terms of their own achievements, status, and other unique characteristics.

The cultural values associated with individualism are often discussed with the opposing set of values, called collectivism. Collectivist cultures view people largely

**Individualism**
A relationship between the individual and the group in society that privileges individual traits and achievements.

**Collectivism**
A set of cultural values that views people largely on the basis of the groups to which they belong.

in terms of the groups to which they belong. Social groups such as family, social class, organization, and team all take precedence over the individual.

Countries high on individualism have norms, values, and beliefs such as the following:[18]

- People are responsible for themselves.
- Individual achievement is ideal.
- People need not be emotionally dependent on organizations or groups.

In contrast, collectivist countries have norms, values, and beliefs such as the following:[19]

- One's identity is based on group membership.
- Group decision making is best.
- Groups protect individuals in exchange for their loyalty.

Countries with low individualism have collectivist norms, values, and beliefs that influence a variety of managerial practices. Organizations in collectivist cultures tend to select managers who belong to favored groups. Usually, the favored group is the extended family and friends of the extended family. Being a relative or someone known by the family becomes more important than an individual's personal qualifications. In contrast, people in highly individualistic societies, such as the United States (the most individualistic society by Hofstede's measurement), often view favoritism toward family and friends as unfair and perhaps illegal. In such societies, most people believe that job selection should be based on universalistic qualification, which means that the same qualifications apply universally to all candidates. The cultural belief is that open competition allows the most qualified individual to get the job.

Organizations in collectivist cultures base promotions mostly on seniority and age. People tend to move up the organizational hierarchy by being promoted with their age cohort (people of the same age). People feel that a major reward for working is being taken care of by their organizations, a type of organizational paternalism. The senior managers in the organization act as father figures. Unlike individualistic societies, where people expect extrinsic rewards such as money and promotions, managers in collectivist societies use "a call to duty" as an emotional appeal to work for the good of the group.

The effects of collectivism on aspects of various Asian countries are described in the following Multinational Management Brief.

Exhibit 2.4 summarizes the managerial implications of high-individualism versus collectivist (low-individualism) norms, values, and beliefs.

## Masculinity

Different cultural expectations for men and women occur in all societies. In all cultures, men and women are socialized differently and usually perform different roles. A variety of studies shows that in most—but certainly not all—cultures, male socialization places a greater emphasis on achievement, motivation, and self-reliance. In contrast, the socialization of women emphasizes nurturance and responsibility.[20]

As a cultural dimension, masculinity represents the overall tendency of a culture to support the traditional masculine orientation; that is, higher masculinity means that the business culture of a society takes on traditional masculine values, such as

**Masculinity**
Tendency of a society to emphasize traditional gender roles.

## Multinational Management **Brief**

### Asian Countries and Collectivism

China continues to be an extremely important economy and its growth is not expected to slow down soon. Understanding Chinese businesspeople is therefore critical. Furthermore, Chinese businesspeople outside the People's Republic of China, whom Hofstede calls "the overseas Chinese," have developed highly performing businesses in Taiwan, Hong Kong, and Singapore, as well as throughout the world. Many of their organizations, however, lack the trappings of modern management. They tend to be feudal (i.e., dominated by the entrepreneurial father), family owned, and small, and they have few if any professional managers. Most focus on only one product, and cooperation with networks of other small organizations is based on personal family friendships.

There are seldom any formal systems within or between organizations—only networks of people guided roughly by Confucian ethics. For example, in the father-dominated family firm, Confucian ethics dictate that the son must show respect and obedience to the father and that the father must protect and show consideration for the son. In a practical sense, this means that the father will dominate organizational decision making. As the son gets older, he may be given considerations such as managing a new firm venture. However, on inheriting the family firm, brothers may engage in more horizontal decision making because their family obligations are less vertical.

This family aspect to business is not unique to China. Japan and South Korea are also collectivistic societies, and how businesses operate is determined by collectivism. For instance, many Western-based companies are willing to sever relationships with suppliers in an effort to cut cost. However, this practice is not acceptable in Japan, where collectivism encourages Japanese companies to hold long-term and often personal relationships with suppliers.

However, as you will see later, although many Asian countries are collectivistic, they are not necessarily similar. For instance, Japanese companies are well known for providing lifetime employment. In contrast, Chinese companies do not necessarily offer such benefits. Furthermore, although Japanese employees may not address salary inequities with their supervisors, Chinese employees are likely to discuss salary with each other and with their supervisors.

*Sources: Based on Dvorak, Phred. 2006. "Managing: Making U.S. ideas work elsewhere: Firms work to adapt management theory to local practices." Wall Street Journal, May 22, 31; Economist. 2012. "Pedalling prosperity." May 26, 3–5; Hofstede, Geert. 1993. "Cultural constraints in management theories." Academy of Management Executive, 7, 1; Li, Xinjian, and Martin Puettrill. 2007. "Strategy implications of business culture differences between Japan and China." Business Strategy Series, 8(2): 148–154. and Syu, Agnes. 1994. "A linkage between Confucianism and the Chinese family firm in the Republic of China." In Dorothy Marcic and Sheila M. Puffer, eds. Management International. Minneapolis, MN: West.*

an emphasis on advancement and earnings. However, within each culture, there remain gender differences in values and attitudes.

High-masculinity countries have norms, values, and beliefs such as the following:[21]

- Gender roles should be clearly distinguished.
- Men are assertive and dominant.
- Machismo or exaggerated maleness in men is good.

**EXHIBIT** 2.4   Management Implications of Individualism

| Management Processes | Low Individualism | High Individualism |
|---|---|---|
| Human resources management | | |
| Management selection | Group membership; school or university | Universalistic based on individual traits |
| Training | Focus on company-based skills | General skills for individual achievement |
| Evaluation/promotion | Slow, with group; seniority | Based on individual performance |
| Remuneration | Based on group membership/organizational paternalism | Extrinsic rewards (money, promotion) based on market value |
| Leadership styles | Appeals to duty and commitment | Individual rewards and punishments based on performance |
| Motivational assumptions | Moral involvement | Calculative; individual cost/benefit |
| Decision making/organizational design | Group; slow; preference for larger organization | Individual responsibility; preference for smaller organizations |
| Strategy issues | Incremental changes with periodic revolutions | Aggressive |

*Sources: Adapted from Hofstede, Geert. 1980.* Culture's Consequences: International Differences in Work-Related Values. *London: Sage; Hofstede, Geert. 1991.* Cultures and Organizations: Software of the Mind. *London: McGraw-Hill; and Hofstede, Geert. 1993. "Cultural dimensions in people management." In Vladimir Pucik, Noel M. Tichy, and Carole K. Barnette*, Globalizing Management. *Hoboken, NJ: Wiley, 139–158.*

- People—especially men—should be decisive.
- Work takes priority over other duties, such as family.
- Advancement, success, and money are important.

In highly masculine societies, jobs are clearly defined by gender. There are men's jobs and women's jobs. Men usually choose jobs that are associated with long-term careers. Women usually choose jobs that are associated with short-term employment, before marriage and children. However, smaller families, delayed childbirth, pressure for dual-career earnings, and changing national cultural values may be eroding the traditional views of masculinity. Consider the cases of working women in Japan and Sweden, as described in the next Comparative Management Brief.

In addition to clear work-related roles based on gender, work in masculine cultures tends to be very central and important to people, especially men. In cultures like Japan, men often take assignments for over a year in other cities or other countries while their family members remain at home.

In a high-masculinity culture, recognition on the job is considered a prime motivator. People work long hours, often work more than five days a week, and take short vacations. In most low-masculinity countries, work is typically less central. People take more time off, take longer vacations, and emphasize quality of life. There are, however, some exceptions. In the highly masculine Mexican culture, for example, gender differences are strong but work is less central. The cultural value is that people "work to live."

In masculine cultures, managers act decisively. They avoid the appearance of intuitive decision making, which is often regarded as feminine. They prefer to work in large organizations, and they emphasize performance and growth in strategic decision making.

## Comparative Management **Brief**

### Working Women in Japan and Sweden: Contrasts in Cultural Masculinity

Japan is currently the highest-ranking masculine culture. Nevertheless, it now faces a challenge to its traditional cultural values regarding masculinity and the role of women. Traditionally, Japanese companies expected most women, even college graduates, to quit their jobs by the age of 25. Women occupy most of the part-time jobs and have less access to the fabled lifetime employment than do men. However, with the slowdown in the Japanese economy, many women are not leaving as expected. The Japanese popular press now prints many stories about companies that "have problems with their women." Such phraseology reflects the conflict of changing values regarding masculinity in Japan. Although there are traditional cultural expectations about what women "should" do regarding work and family, there is no legal or accepted way to force Japanese women to leave their jobs when they choose to remain employed.

Perhaps because of strong norms of equality, the Nordic countries rank lowest in masculinity. In contrast to masculine Japan, where support for working women, such as day care, is rare, the Swedish government provides day care to all who need it. Since more than 85 percent of Swedish women work outside the home, day care is essential. In addition, with the birth of a child, one year of parental leave is available for both parents. Approximately 20 percent of Swedish men take this option.

Another indicator of the impact of masculinity and femininity is the percentage of women on boards of directors within a country. Most developed nations are working to encourage companies to increase the proportion of women on their boards. Such thinking stems from the fact that research has shown that companies that have more women in executive and board positions tend to outperform those with fewer women. Therefore, it is undeniable that the cultural dimension of masculinity/femininity has an impact on the proportion of women on board of directors. For example, in Norway, a society with a high level of femininity, around 40 percent of company boards of directors are now made up of women. Other feminine societies such as those of Finland and Sweden have percentages above 20%. In contrast, masculine societies such as Austria, the United States, the United Kingdom, and Japan have a low percentage of women on their boards, at 6.7, 11.4, 7.8, and 0.9 percent respectively.

*Sources: Based in part on* Economist. *2012. "Waving a big stick." March 10th, 77; Gannon, Martin J., and Associates. 1994.* Understanding Global Cultures. *Thousand Oaks, CA: Sage; Governance Metrics International. 2012. "Women on boards." http://www.gmiratings.com.*

Exhibit 2.5 shows the major effects of high masculinity on work and organizations.

The next section deals with the impact of long-term orientation on work and organizations.

## Long-Term Orientation

**Long-term (Confucian) orientation**
An orientation toward time that values patience.

Because we have data on the long-term (Confucian) orientation for only a few countries, Hofstede and others have produced less research on how this orientation relates to work and organizations. Consequently, the discussion is more speculative on this issue than on others.

EXHIBIT **2.5**    Management Implications of Masculinity

| Management Processes | Low Masculinity | High Masculinity |
|---|---|---|
| Human resources management | | |
|   Management selection | Independent of gender, school ties less important; androgyny | Jobs gender identified; school performance and ties important |
|   Training | Job-oriented | Career-oriented |
|   Evaluation/promotion | Job performance, with less gender-based assignments | Continues gender-tracking |
|   Remuneration | Less salary difference between levels; more time off | More salary preferred to fewer hours |
| Leadership styles | More participative | More Theory X; authoritarian |
| Motivational assumptions | Emphasis on quality of life, time off, vacations; work not central | Emphasis on performance and growth; excelling to be best; work central to life; job recognition important |
| Decision making/organizational design | Intuitive/group; smaller organizations | Decisive/individual; larger organization preferred |
| Strategy issues | Preference for consistent growth | Aggressive |

*Sources: Adapted from Hofstede, Geert. 1980.* Culture's Consequences: International Differences in Work-Related Values. *London: Sage; Hofstede, Geert. 1991.* Cultures and Organizations: Software of the Mind. *London: McGraw-Hill; and Hofstede, Geert. 1993. "Cultural dimensions in people management." In Vladimir Pucik, Noel M. Tichy, and Carole K. Barnette,* Globalizing Management. *Hoboken, NJ: Wiley, 139–158.*

Because of the need to be sensitive to social relationships, managers in cultures high on long-term orientation are selected based on the fit of their personal and educational characteristics to the company. A prospective employee's particular skills have less importance in the hiring decision than they do in cultures with short-term orientation. Training and socialization for a long-term commitment to the organization compensate for any initial weaknesses in work-related skills. Organizations in cultures with short-term orientation, in contrast, must focus on immediately usable skills. Managers do not assume that employees will remain with the company for an extended period of time. They cannot be assured of a return on any investment in employee training and socialization.

In short-term-oriented cultures, leaders use quick rewards that focus on pay and rapid promotion. Employees in long-term-oriented cultures value security, and leaders work on developing social obligations.

Hofstede notes that Western cultures,[22] which tend to have short-term orientations, value logical analysis in their approach to organizational decisions. Managers believe in logically analyzing the situation for their company and following up with a solid game plan. In contrast, Eastern cultures, which rank the highest in long-term orientation, value synthesis in organizational decisions. Synthesis is not a search for the correct answer or strategy; rather, it takes apparently conflicting points of view and logic and seeks practical solutions. Not surprisingly, organizations in short-term-oriented cultures are designed and managed purposefully to respond to immediate pressures from the environment. Managers often use quick layoffs of "excess" employees to adjust to shrinking demand for products. Organizations in long-term-oriented cultures are designed first to manage internal social relationships. The assumption is that good social relationships eventually lead to successful organizations. The difference between long- and short-term-oriented

EXHIBIT **2.6**   Management Implications of Long-Term Orientation

| Management Processes | Short-Term Orientation | Long-Term Orientation |
|---|---|---|
| Human resources management | | |
|   Management selection | Objective skill assessment for immediate use to company | Fit of personal and background characteristics |
|   Training | Limited to immediate company needs | Investment in long-term employment skills |
|   Evaluation/promotion | Fast; based on skill contributions | Slow; develop skills and loyalty |
|   Remuneration | Pay, promotions | Security |
| Leadership styles | Use of incentives for economic advancement | Building social obligations |
| Motivational assumptions | Immediate rewards necessary | Immediate gratification subordinate to long-term individual and company goals |
| Decision making/organizational design | Logical analyses of problems; design for logic of company situation | Synthesis to reach consensus; design for social relationships |
| Strategy issues | Fast; measurable payback | Long-term profits and growth; incrementalism |

*Sources: Adapted from Hofstede, Geert. 1980. Culture's Consequences: International Differences in Work-Related Values. London: Sage; Hofstede, Geert. 1991. Cultures and Organizations: Software of the Mind. London: McGraw-Hill; and Hofstede, Geert. 1993. "Cultural dimensions in people management." In Vladimir Pucik, Noel M. Tichy, and Carole K. Barnette, Globalizing Management. Hoboken, NJ: Wiley, 139–158.*

cultures is apparent in the goals that companies set in strategic decision making. Managers in countries such as the United States want immediate financial returns. They are most comfortable with fast, measurable success. Countries with more long-term orientations do not ignore financial objectives, but they prioritize growth and long-term paybacks. Long time horizons allow managers to experiment and seek success by developing their "game plans" as they go along.

Exhibit 2.6 summarizes the managerial implications of long-term (Confucian) orientation.

To apply Hofstede's model to specific countries, look at Exhibit 2.7, which displays the percentile ranks of selected countries for five of Hofstede's dimensions of national culture. To interpret this exhibit, you need to understand that the percentile for each country tells you the percentage of other countries that rank below it. For example, the United States has the highest scores on individualism, so its percentile rank tells you that 100 percent of the countries are equal to or below the United States on individualism. A percentile rank of 75 percent tells you that 75 percent of the other countries have equal or lower ranks on a cultural dimension.

To simplify generalizations from Hofstede's data, the table groups countries by country clusters.[23] **Country clusters** are groups of countries—such as Anglo, Latin American, and Latin European—with roughly similar cultural patterns. Although cultures differ within these broad classifications, such summaries are useful for condensing cultural information. They are also useful in predicting likely cultural traits when specific information is not available.

Next, we consider the GLOBE model of culture.[24] This model is heavily based on Hofstede's dimensions, and we focus mainly on the two dimensions unique to the model.

**Country clusters**
Groups of countries with similar cultural patterns.

EXHIBIT  2.7  Percentile Ranks for Hofstede's Cultural Dimensions for Selected Countries by Cultural Cluster (100 = highest, 50 = middle)

| Cultural Group/ Country | Power Distance | Uncertainty Avoidance | Individualism | Masculinity | Long-Term Orientation |
|---|---|---|---|---|---|
| Anglo: | | | | | |
| Australia | 25 | 32 | 98 | 72 | 48 |
| Canada | 28 | 24 | 93 | 57 | 19 |
| Great Britain | 21 | 12 | 96 | 84 | 27 |
| United States | 30 | 21 | 100 | 74 | 35 |
| Arab: | | | | | |
| Arab countries | 89 | 51 | 52 | 58 | n/a |
| Far Eastern: | | | | | |
| China | 89 | 44 | 39 | 54 | 100 |
| Hong Kong | 73 | 8 | 32 | 67 | 96 |
| Singapore | 77 | 2 | 26 | 49 | 69 |
| Taiwan | 46 | 53 | 19 | 41 | 92 |
| Germanic: | | | | | |
| Austria | 2 | 56 | 68 | 98 | n/a |
| Germany | 21 | 47 | 74 | 84 | 48 |
| Netherlands | 26 | 36 | 93 | 6 | 65 |
| Switzerland | 17 | 40 | 75 | 93 | n/a |
| Latin America: | | | | | |
| Argentina | 35 | 78 | 59 | 63 | n/a |
| Colombia | 70 | 64 | 9 | 80 | n/a |
| Mexico | 92 | 68 | 42 | 91 | n/a |
| Venezuela | 92 | 61 | 8 | 96 | n/a |
| Latin European: | | | | | |
| Belgium | 64 | 92 | 87 | 60 | n/a |
| France | 73 | 78 | 82 | 35 | n/a |
| Italy | 38 | 58 | 89 | 93 | n/a |
| Spain | 43 | 78 | 64 | 31 | n/a |
| Near Eastern: | | | | | |
| Greece | 50 | 100 | 45 | 67 | n/a |
| Iran | 46 | 42 | 57 | 35 | n/a |
| Turkey | 67 | 71 | 49 | 41 | n/a |
| Nordic: | | | | | |
| Denmark | 6 | 6 | 85 | 8 | n/a |
| Finland | 15 | 42 | 70 | 13 | n/a |
| Norway | 12 | 30 | 77 | 4 | n/a |
| Sweden | 12 | 8 | 82 | 2 | 58 |
| Independent: | | | | | |
| Brazil | 75 | 61 | 52 | 51 | 81 |
| India | 82 | 17 | 62 | 63 | 71 |
| Israel | 4 | 66 | 66 | 47 | n/a |
| Japan | 32 | 89 | 55 | 100 | n/a |

*Sources: Adapted from Hofstede, Geert. 1980.* Culture's Consequences: International Differences in Work-Related Values. *London: Sage; Hofstede, Geert. 1991.* Cultures and Organizations: Software of the Mind. *London: McGraw-Hill; Hofstede, Geert. 1993. "Cultural dimensions in people management." In Vladimir Pucik, Noel M. Tichy, and Carole K. Barnette,* Globalizing Management. *Hoboken, NJ: Wiley, 139–158; Ronen, S., and O. Shenkar. 1985. "Clustering countries on attitudinal dimensions: A review and synthesis."* Academy of Management Review, *September.*

# GLOBE National Culture Framework

The GLOBE project involves 170 researchers who collected data on 17,000 managers from 62 countries around the world.[25] Using the Hofstede model as their foundation, the GLOBE researchers conceptualized and developed nine cultural dimensions. Of the nine dimensions, only two are independent of the Hofstede model. The seven GLOBE dimensions that are similar to Hofstede's model are:

- Assertiveness orientation and gender egalitarianism (similar to masculinity-femininity).
- Institutional and family collectivism (similar to individualism-collectivism).
- Future orientation (similar to long-term orientation).
- Power distance.
- Uncertainty avoidance.[26]

Many of the implications discussed earlier for Hofstede's cultural dimensions apply to the corresponding GLOBE dimensions. The two dimensions unique to the GLOBE project are performance orientation and humane orientation.

**Performance orientation** refers to the degree to which a society encourages its members to innovate, improve their performance, and strive for excellence. This dimension is similar to Weber's Protestant work ethic and reflects the desire for achievement in society.[27] Countries such as the United States and Singapore have high scores on performance orientation, whereas countries such as Russia and Greece have low scores on that dimension. Javidan, Dorfman, de Luque, and House argue that countries with high performance orientation scores tend to favor training and development, whereas in countries low on performance orientation, family and background are more important.[28] In societies with high performance orientation, people are rewarded for taking initiative and performing with the belief that one can succeed by trying hard. In contrast, low-performance-oriented societies reward harmony with the environment; they emphasize loyalty and integrity while regarding assertiveness as unacceptable. Consider the following Case in Point.

Exhibit 2.8 summarizes some of the implications of performance orientation for management.

**Humane orientation** is an indicator of the extent to which individuals are expected to be fair, altruistic, caring, and generous. In high-humane-oriented societies, the need for belonging and affiliation is emphasized more than needs such as material possessions, self-fulfillment, and pleasure. Societies that are less humane oriented are more likely to value self-interest and self-gratification.[29]

Countries such as Malaysia and Egypt score highly in terms of humane orientation, whereas France and Germany have low scores. As such, companies in high-humane-oriented countries such as Egypt are generally expected to be caring and offer benefits that seem unusual for U.S. companies. For instance, companies may offer tuition assistance to employees' children, paid family vacations, or even home appliances.[30] Exhibit 2.9 lists some of the management implications of humane orientation.

The GLOBE data show that countries can be categorized by ten clusters and that these clusters differ with respect to the nine cultural dimensions. Clusters in the GLOBE project include Anglo, Confucian Asia, Eastern Europe, Germanic Europe, Latin America, Latin Europe, Middle East, Nordic Europe, Southern Asia, and Sub-Saharan. Exhibit 2.10 shows the various clusters and their

---

**Performance orientation**

The degree to which the society encourages its members to innovate, improve their performance, and strive for excellence.

**Humane orientation**

An indication of the extent to which individuals are expected to be fair, altruistic, caring, and generous.

## Performance Orientation and Propensity to Support Sustainability Initiatives

Multinational corporations are facing strong calls to implement more sustainable practices as they conduct operations around the world. Multinationals have been criticized for not doing enough to minimize the impact of their operations on the environment. However, as they embark on new programs to become more sustainable, multinationals are finding that success at such programs is dependent on engaged employees. The more favorable the attitudes that employees hold about the environment and contributing to the environment, the more likely environmental programs are to work. It therefore becomes critical to understand how employees from different societies view sustainability.

In a study of 42,346 individuals from 33 countries, the effects of national culture on propensity to support sustainability initiatives were investigated. Propensity to support sustainability initiatives simply refers to the willingness of individuals to support environmental programs. This was measured by asking respondents whether they were likely give part of their income for programs aimed at reducing environmental pollution or whether they would be willing to pay more taxes if they knew that the money would go towards reducing environmental pollution.

One of the important cultural dimensions measured was performance orientation. As mentioned in the chapter, performance orientation refers to the degree to which societies value achievement and excellence in society. High-performance-oriented societies have individuals who believe they can dominate the outside world in their ambition to achieve their goals and objectives. Such societies are also less likely to have individuals with a propensity to support sustainability initiatives. Because their focus is on achievement and materialism, individuals in high-performance-orientation societies are less likely to be concerned about personal sacrifices to reduce environmental pollution.

The study indeed showed that in the sample of countries ranging from Albania and Argentina to Poland and Zimbabwe, individuals had a higher propensity to support sustainability initiatives if they resided in lower-performance-orientation societies. Such results suggest that if multinational corporations want to succeed with environmental programs in high-performance-orientation societies, they will need to work harder and more aggressively to convince these employees of the importance of reducing environmental pollution.

*Source: Based on Parboteeah, K. P., H. M. Addae, & J. B. Cullen. 2012. "Propensity to support sustainability initiatives: A cross-national model." Journal of Business Ethics, 105: 403–413.*

corresponding cultural scores. Refer to Exhibit 15.7 in Chapter 15 to see which countries are included in each cluster. Many of the management implications of Hofstede's cultural dimensions can be used for the seven GLOBE dimensions that are similar to Hofstede's.

Next we consider the model developed by Trompenaars and his colleagues. You will see that this model is also similar in some respects to Hofstede's, but it contains more dimensions and deals with a broader array of countries.

## 7d Cultural Dimensions Model

The 7d cultural model builds on traditional anthropological approaches to understanding culture. Anthropologists argue that culture comes into existence because all humans must solve basic problems of survival.[31] These challenges include how people relate to others, such as family members, supervisors, friends, and fellow workers; how people deal with the passage of time; and how people relate to their environment. All cultures develop ways to confront these basic issues, but their strategies are not the same, which is why cultures differ significantly.

**EXHIBIT** 2.8    Management Implications of Performance Orientation

| Management Processes | High Performance Orientation | Low Performance Orientation |
| --- | --- | --- |
| **Human resources management** | | |
| Management selection | Based on individual achievement and merit | Emphasis on seniority and experience |
| Training | Value training and development | Value societal and family relationships |
| Evaluation/promotion | Based on merit and achievement | Based on age |
| Remuneration | Pay, promotions | Tradition |
| Performance appraisal | Systems emphasize results | Systems emphasize integrity and loyalty |
| Leadership styles | Have can-do attitude | Emphasize loyalty and belongingness |
| Motivational assumptions | Value bonuses and rewards | Value harmony with environment and quality of life |
| Communication | Value direct and to-the-point communication | Value subtlety and ambiguity in communication |

*Source: Adapted from House, R., P. Hanges, M. Javidan, P. Dorfman, and V. Gupta. 2004.* Culture, Leadership and Organizations: The GLOBE Study of 62 Societies. *Thousand Oaks, CA: Sage Publications.*

**EXHIBIT** 2.9    Management Implications of Humane Orientation

| Management Processes | High Humane Orientation | Low Humane Orientation |
| --- | --- | --- |
| Relationships | Importance of others (i.e., family, friends, and community) | Emphasis on self-interest |
| **Leadership styles** | | |
| Style | More consideration-oriented leadership | Less consideration-oriented leadership |
| Concern for subordinates | Individualized/holistic consideration | Standardized/limited consideration |
| Approach | More benevolent | Less benevolent |
| Relationship with subordinates | More personal and less informal | More informal and less personal |
| Motivational assumptions | Need for belongingness | Motivation by power and material possessions |
| Company role | Support for employees | Expectation of people to solve problems on their own |

*Source: Adapted from House, R., P. Hanges, M. Javidan, P. Dorfman, and V. Gupta. 2004.* Culture, Leadership and Organizations: The GLOBE Study of 62 Societies. *Thousand Oaks, CA: Sage Publications.*

Five of the seven dimensions of the 7d cultural model deal with the challenges of how people relate to each other. Each dimension is a continuum or range of cultural differences. The five dimensions that deal with relationships among people are:

1. *Universalism versus particularism:* The choice of dealing with other people based on rules or based on personal relationships.

2. *Collectivism versus individualism:* The focus on group membership versus individual characteristics.

EXHIBIT 2.10   The GLOBE Model of Culture

| Cluster | Performance Orientation | Assertiveness | Future Orientation | Humane Orientation | Institutional Collectivism | In-Group Collectivism | Gender Egalitarianism | Power Distance | Uncertainty Avoidance |
|---|---|---|---|---|---|---|---|---|---|
| Anglo | High | Medium | Medium | Medium | Medium | Low | Medium | Medium | Medium |
| Confucian Asia | High | Medium | Medium | Medium | High | High | Medium | Medium | Medium |
| Eastern Europe | Low | High | Low | Medium | Medium | High | High | Medium | Low |
| Germanic Europe | High | High | High | Low | Low | Low | Medium | Medium | High |
| Latin America | Low | Medium | Low | Medium | Low | High | Medium | Medium | Low |
| Latin Europe | Medium | Medium | Medium | Medium | Low | Medium | Medium | Medium | Medium |
| Middle East | Medium | Medium | Low | Medium | Medium | High | Low | Medium | Low |
| Nordic Europe | Medium | Low | High | Medium | High | Low | High | Low | High |
| Southern Asia | Medium | Medium | Medium | High | Medium | High | Medium | Medium | Medium |
| Sub-Saharan Africa | Medium | Medium | Medium | High | Medium | Medium | Medium | Medium | Medium |

*Source: Based on Javidan, Mansour, Peter W. Dorfman, Mary Sully de Luque, and Robert House. 2006. "In the eye of the beholder: Cross cultural lessons in leadership for project GLOBE." The Academy of Management Perspectives, February, 20(1): 67–90.*

3. *Neutral versus affective:* The range of feelings outwardly expressed in the society.

4. *Diffuse versus specific:* The types of involvement people have with each other, ranging from all aspects of life to specific components.

5. *Achievement versus ascription:* The assignment of status in a society based on performance (e.g., college graduation) versus assignment based on heritage.

The two final dimensions deal with how a culture manages time and how it deals with nature:

6. *Past, present, future, or a mixture:* The orientation of the society to the past, present, or future or some combination of the three.

7. *"Control of" versus "accommodation with" nature:* Nature viewed as something to be controlled versus something to be accepted.

Exhibit 2.11 gives a summary of the 7d model and the issues addressed by each dimension. The following sections define the dimensions and show their managerial applications.

## Universalism versus Particularism

**Universalism**
Dealing with other people based on rules.

**Particularism**
Dealing with other people based on personal relationships.

**Universalism** and **particularism** pertain to how people from a culture treat each other based on equally applied rules rather than personal relationships. In a universalistic culture, how people are treated is based on abstract principles such as the rules of law, religion, or cultural principles (e.g., "Do unto others as you would have them do unto you"). Thus, universalism suggests that there are rules

**EXHIBIT 2.11**    The 7d Model of Culture

| Cultural Dimension | Critical Question |
|---|---|
| **Relationships with people:** | |
| Universalism versus particularism | Do we consider rules or relationships more important? |
| Individualism versus collectivism | Do we act mostly as individuals or as groups? |
| Specific versus diffuse | How extensively are we involved with the lives of other people? |
| Neutral versus affective | Are we free to express our emotions, or are we restrained? |
| Achievement versus ascription | Do we achieve status through accomplishment, or is it part of our situation in life e.g., gender, age, social class)? |
| **Perspective on time:** | |
| Sequential versus synchronic | Do we do tasks in sequence or several tasks at once? |
| **Relationship with the environment:** | |
| Internal versus external control | Do we control the environment, or does it control us? |

*Source: Adapted from Trompenaars, Fons, and Charles Hampden-Turner. 1998.* Riding the Waves of Culture: Understanding Cultural Diversity in Global Business. *New York: McGraw-Hill.*

or appropriate and acceptable ways of doing things, and we look to those precise guides in all situations.

In contrast, in particularistic cultures, rules represent only a rough guide to life. Each judgment represents a unique situation and the "right" way of behaving must take into account who the person is and his or her relationship to the one doing the judging. In particularistic cultures, rules may be in place and fully recognized, but people expect exceptions to be made for friends, family relations, and others. The focus is on situation-to-situation judgments and on the exceptional nature of changing circumstances.[32]

In developing his 7d model, Trompenaars uses dilemmas that show contrasts in cultural values. Consider the following dilemma and the different cultural assumptions that people use to make the "right" choice.

One of the dilemmas used to show differences between universalistic and particularistic cultures concerns the story of a motorist hitting a pedestrian while going 35 miles per hour in a 20-mile-per-hour zone. The driver's lawyer notes that if a witness says the driver was going only 20 miles per hour, the judge will be lenient. The question is this: Should a friend who is a witness be expected to—or feel obligated to—testify to the lower speed? In universalistic cultures such as the United States and Switzerland, more than 93 percent say no. The principle of telling the truth supersedes friendship. In particularistic cultures such as South Korea, Nepal, and Venezuela, close to 40 percent say yes. Friendship supersedes the law.[33]

No culture is purely universalistic or particularistic. However, the tendency to lean in one direction or the other influences business practices and relationships between business partners from different cultures. In particular, more universalistic cultures tend to use contracts and law as a basis for business. Managers from such cultures are often uncomfortable when written documents are ignored and the personal relationships between partners become paramount. Consequently, managers from universalistic cultures doing business in particularistic cultures must be sensitive to building relationships. However, managers from particularistic cultures must make efforts to realize that the emphasis on law and contract does not mean a distrust of the business partner in a universalistic culture.

Exhibit 2.12 gives a brief description of universalism and particularism as cultural dimensions and shows the managerial implications for doing business in each.

## Individualism versus Collectivism

In the preceding sections, we examined Hofstede's view of individualism and collectivism. The 7d model considers the same distinctions. Although the 7d view of individualism is similar to Hofstede's in concept, the rankings of countries do not match exactly. One explanation for this difference may be that Trompenaars's ranking comes from more recent data. Another reason is that the 7d model uses a different methodology from Hofstede's model and captures more subtle aspects of the individualism-collectivism continuum.

One of the questions that Trompenaars used to examine cultural differences in individualism asked about typical organizations in each country. One choice represented organizations where individual work and individual credit were common. The other choice represented group work and group credit. In the more collectivist societies, such as India and Mexico, fewer than 45 percent of the workers said that their jobs involved individual work with individual credit. Somewhat surprising was the finding that the former Eastern Bloc countries of the Czech Republic,

**EXHIBIT** | **2.12** | Universalism versus Particularism: Differences and Managerial Implications

| Universalism | | | | | Particularism |
|---|---|---|---|---|---|
| United States | United Kingdom | Czech Rep. | Nigeria | Mexico | South Korea |

### Differences

| | |
|---|---|
| Focus on rules | Focus on relationships |
| Contracts difficult to break | Contracts easy to modify |
| Trustworthy people honor their word | Trustworthy people adapt to each other's needs based on trust |
| Belief is in only one reality | Reality is relative to each person's situation |
| "Deals" are obligations | "Deals" are flexible based on the situation and the person |

### Managerial Implications

| | |
|---|---|
| Use procedures applied to all | Use informal networks to create understanding |
| Formalize business practices | Make changes subtly and privately |
| Treat all cases similarly | Treat each case based on its unique circumstances |
| Announce changes publicly | Keep only insiders informed |

*Sources: Adapted from Economides, A. A. 2008. "Culture-aware collaborative learning."* Multicultural and Technology Journal, *2(4): 243–267; Trompenaars, Fons, and Charles, Hampden-Turner. 1998.* Riding the Waves of Culture: Understanding Cultural Diversity in Global Business. *New York: McGraw-Hill.*

Russia, Hungary, and Bulgaria were the most individualistic in their organizations, ranking ahead of the United States.

Exhibit 2.13 gives a brief description of individualistic and collectivistic cultural dimensions and the managerial implications of doing business in each.

## Neutral versus Affective

**Neutral versus affective**
The acceptability of expressing emotions.

The **neutral versus affective** dimension of the 7d model concerns the acceptability of expressing emotions. In cultures with a more neutral orientation, people expect interactions to be objective and detached. The focus is more on the task and less on the emotional nature of the interaction. People emphasize the achievement of objectives without the messy interference of emotions. In contrast, in cultures with a more affective orientation, all forms of emotion are appropriate in almost every situation. Expressions of anger, laughter, gesturing, and a range of emotional outbursts are considered normal and acceptable. It is natural and preferred to find an immediate outlet for emotions.[34]

You can test yourself on this dimension by responding to one of Trompenaars's dilemmas: How would you respond in a negotiation if your partner called your proposal insane? People from neutral cultures attempt to hide their emotional reactions to this insult. Revelation of the hurt would show weakness and vulnerability. People from affective cultures would react immediately. They realize that such a reaction shows that they are insulted and they believe that their partner should know this. This is expected behavior and is not viewed negatively by people in an affective culture.[35]

**EXHIBIT** **2.13** Individualism versus Collectivism: Differences and Managerial Implications

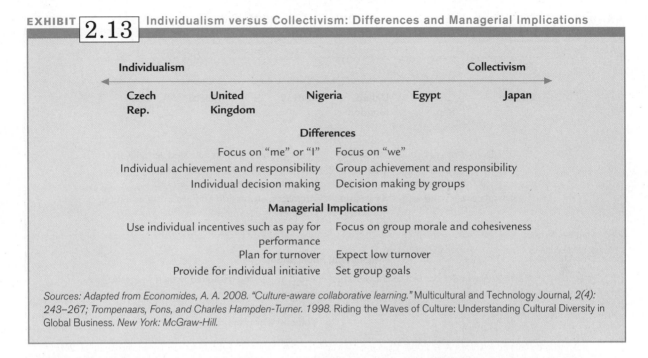

Sources: Adapted from Economides, A. A. 2008. "Culture-aware collaborative learning." Multicultural and Technology Journal, 2(4): 243–267; Trompenaars, Fons, and Charles Hampden-Turner. 1998. Riding the Waves of Culture: Understanding Cultural Diversity in Global Business. New York: McGraw-Hill.

Exhibit 2.14 gives a brief description of the neutral versus affective cultural dimensions and the managerial implications of doing business in these different contexts.

## Specific versus Diffuse

The **specific versus diffuse** cultural dimension addresses the extent to which an individual's life is involved in his or her work relationships. In a specific-oriented culture, business is segregated from other parts of life. People in business-exchange and work relationships know each other, but the knowledge is very limited and shared for only very specific purposes. In such societies, written contracts frequently prescribe and delineate such relationships. Conversely, in diffuse-oriented cultures, business relationships are more encompassing and inclusive. The preference is to involve multiple areas and levels of life simultaneously; truly private and segregated spaces in life are quite small. In doing business, the parties come to know each other personally and more thoroughly, and they become acquainted with each other across a variety of life's dimensions and levels.[36]

> **Specific versus diffuse**
> The extent to which all aspects of an individual's life are involved in his or her work relationships.

The example Trompenaars uses to test the differences between specific and diffuse cultures concerns a boss who asks a subordinate to help him paint his house. In specific cultures, most people believe that the worker has no obligation to help because the boss has no authority outside work. In diffuse cultures, people feel an obligation to help the boss in any way possible, even beyond the job's requirements.[37]

Exhibit 2.15 gives a brief description of specific versus diffuse cultural dimensions and the managerial implications of doing business in these different contexts.

## Achievement versus Ascription

The dimension identified as **achievement versus ascription** addresses how a particular society accords or gives status. In achievement-oriented cultures, people earn status through their performance and accomplishments. In contrast, when a culture

> **Achievement versus ascription**
> How a society accords or gives status.

**EXHIBIT 2.14**     Neutral versus Affective: Differences and Managerial Implications

Neutral ←——————————————————————————————————→ Affective

| Sweden | Czech Rep. | United Kingdom | Norway | Mexico | China |

**Differences**

| | |
|---|---|
| Do not reveal thoughts or feelings | Feelings and thoughts revealed verbally and nonverbally |
| Control over emotions admired | Emotional expression uninhibited |
| Physical contact and expressive gestures avoided | Animated expression and gesturing admired; touching is common |

**Managerial Implications**

| | |
|---|---|
| Act under control to show status | Avoid appearing detached, which suggests distance |
| Keep dialogue to the point | Expect strong commitment to positions |
| | Tolerate emotional outbursts |

*Sources: Adapted from Economides, A. A. 2008. "Culture-aware collaborative learning." Multicultural and Technology Journal, 2(4): 243–267; Trompenaars, Fons, and Charles Hampden-Turner. 1998. Riding the Waves of Culture: Understanding Cultural Diversity in Global Business. New York: McGraw-Hill.*

**EXHIBIT 2.15**     Specific versus Diffuse: Differences and Managerial Implications

Specific ←——————————————————————————————————→ Diffuse

| Sweden | Czech Rep. | United Kingdom | Norway | Mexico | China |

**Differences**

| | |
|---|---|
| Direct in relationships | Indirect and subtle in relationships |
| Blunt and precise in communication | Ambiguous or evasive in communication |
| Principled moral reasoning | Situation-based moral decision making |

**Managerial Implications**

| | |
|---|---|
| Use of objectives and standards | Attempt continuous improvement |
| Separate private and business lives | Mix private and business lives |
| Give clear and precise directions | Use ambiguous directions to give employees latitude |

*Sources: Adapted from Economides, A. A. 2008. "Culture-aware collaborative learning." Multicultural and Technology Journal, 2(4): 243–267; Trompenaars, Fons, and Charles Hampden-Turner. 1998. Riding the Waves of Culture: Understanding Cultural Diversity in Global Business. New York: McGraw-Hill.*

**EXHIBIT** **2.16**    Achievement versus Ascription: Differences and Managerial Implications

Achievement ← → Ascription

| Norway | Ireland | Austria | Japan | Hong Kong | Argentina |

**Differences**

| Use title only when relevant | Use of titles common and expected |
| Superiors earn respect through job performance | Respect for superior shows commitment to organization |
| Mixture of age and gender in management | Background and age main qualification for management |

**Managerial Implications**

| Emphasize rewards and respect based on skills and accomplishments | Emphasize seniority |
| Senior-level managers defer to technical and functional specialists | Use personal power of superior for rewards |
| | Emphasize the chain of command |

*Sources: Adapted from Economides, A. A. 2008. "Culture-aware collaborative learning."* Multicultural and Technology Journal, *2(4): 243–267; Trompenaars, Fons, and Charles Hampden-Turner. 1998.* Riding the Waves of Culture: Understanding Cultural Diversity in Global Business. *New York: McGraw-Hill.*

bases status on ascription, one's inherent characteristics or associations define status. For example, ascription-oriented societies often assign status based on schools or universities attended, or on age. Ascribed status does not require any justification. It simply exists. In such cultures, titles and their frequent usage play a large part in interactions.[38]

Exhibit 2.16 gives a brief description of the achievement versus ascription cultural dimensions and the managerial implications of doing business in each.

To better understand this cultural dimension, consider the next Multinational Management Challenge. It describes the culture clash experienced by a young female manager from an achievement-oriented society who is working in an ascription-oriented society.

## Time Orientation

To coordinate any business, managers must have a shared understanding of time. Experts on culture find vast differences in how people deal with time, and these differences become apparent when people from different cultures engage in business exchanges. One dimension of time that is important to managers is the time horizon. The **time horizon** concerns how cultures deal with the past, present, and future, as well as the boundaries among these time zones. Mexicans and Chinese, for example, have long time horizons and distinct boundaries among the time zones.[39]

Exhibit 2.17 summarizes the cultural characteristics of different time horizons. It also gives some managerial implications of differing time orientations.

In future-oriented societies, such as the United States, organizational change is considered necessary and beneficial. A static organization is a dying organization. However, in past-oriented societies, people often assume that life follows a preordained

**Time horizon**
The way cultures deal with the past, present, and future.

## Multinational Management **Challenge**

### Achievement-Based Management in an Ascription-Based Culture

What happens when young and previously successful managers from achievement-oriented Western societies find themselves in an ascription-based culture? Ms. Moore, a successful 34-year-old female manager from a U.S. company, takes a promotion as director of marketing in Ankara, Turkey. She has international experience in Britain and is confident that she can replicate her success at winning the support and trust of her subordinates and colleagues in Turkey.

Within a few months, however, Ms. Moore finds her authority eroding. Hasan, a 63-year-old Turk, is gradually and consciously taking over her authority as the boss and is becoming the driving force behind marketing projects. Although everyone recognizes that Ms. Moore's marketing knowledge is much greater than Hasan's, her attempts to fulfill her function meet with increased resistance. The company follows Hasan's direction even though the results are not satisfactory. Later, Ms. Moore learns that her predecessor, a U.S. man her age, was fired for "failure to command local managers."

If you were sending a young, female manager to this assignment, what strategies would you recommend?

*Source: Based on Trompenaars, Fons, and Charles Hampden-Turner. 1998.* Riding the Waves of Culture: Understanding Cultural Diversity in Global Business. *New York: McGraw-Hill.*

---

**EXHIBIT 2.17**   **Time Horizon: Differences and Managerial Implications**

Past/Present ←————————————————————————————→ Future

| Hong Kong | Israel | Russia | Korea | Hong Kong |
|-----------|--------|--------|-------|-----------|

#### Differences

| Past | Present | Future |
|------|---------|--------|
| Communication references history and origins of country, business, and family | Enjoy the moment | Communication refers to potential achievements |
| Respect for past glory and elder | Planning seldom results in execution | Planning important |
| History provides a context for present actions | Immediate impact most important | Potential for future advantage emphasized |

#### Managerial Implications

| Past and Present | Future |
|------------------|--------|
| Emphasize and be sensitive to history and tradition | Motivate by emphasis on opportunities |
| Avoid strict deadlines for completion of tasks | Set specific deadlines |

*Sources: Adapted from Economides, A. A. 2008. "Culture-aware collaborative learning." Multicultural and Technology Journal, 2(4): 243–267; Trompenaars, Fons, and Charles Hampden-Turner. 1998. Riding the Waves of Culture: Understanding Cultural Diversity in Global Business. New York: McGraw-Hill.*

course based on traditions or the will of God. As a result, strategic planning has little importance for the organization. A changing organization is suspicious to both employees and society. Stability is revered. Within these organizations, senior people are thought to make the best decisions because they have the authority and wisdom to know the right way to do things. Symbols and rituals dominate the organizational culture.

To consider your own time horizon, ask yourself how long ago your past started and ended, how long ago your present started and ended, and when your future will start and end. Trompenaars uses similar questions to measure the time horizons of different cultural groups.[40]

## Internal versus External Control

The cultural dimension of **internal versus external control** concerns beliefs regarding control over one's fate. This cultural dimension is perhaps best reflected in how people interact with their natural environment. Does nature dominate us, or do we dominate nature?

To measure this dimension, Trompenaars and his colleagues presented managers with the following options: "It is worthwhile trying to control important natural forces like the weather," and "Nature should take its course, and we just have to accept it the way it comes and do the best we can."[41] Managers in Arabic countries, such as Bahrain, Egypt, and Kuwait, were the most fatalistic, with fewer than 20 percent of them choosing the option of control over nature. This contrasts with more than 50 percent of the managers from Spain and Cuba, who chose the option of control over nature.

Exhibit 2.18 summarizes internal versus external cultural dimensions and their managerial implications.

Cultural values regarding relationships with nature can affect how organizations and managers approach strategic and operational problems. In cultures where

> **Internal versus external control**
> Beliefs regarding whether one controls one's own fate.

**EXHIBIT 2.18**    Internal versus External Control: Differences and Managerial Implications

| Internal Control | | | External Control | |
|---|---|---|---|---|
| Poland | Brazil | Greece | Ethiopia | China |

**Differences**

| | |
|---|---|
| Dominate the environment | Emphasis on compromise |
| Show convictions | Harmony and adjustment is good |
| Focus on self or own group | Adaptation to cycles |

**Managerial Implications**

| | |
|---|---|
| Emphasize authority | Emphasize patience |
| Dominate subordinates | Build and maintain relationships with subordinates, equals, and superiors |
| | Emphasize win-win relationships |

*Sources: Adapted from Economides, A. A. 2008. "Culture-aware collaborative learning." Multicultural and Technology Journal, 2(4): 243–267; Trompenaars, Fons, and Charles Hampden-Turner. 1998. Riding the Waves of Culture: Understanding Cultural Diversity in Global Business. New York: McGraw-Hill.*

nature is believed to dominate people, managers are likely to be fatalistic. They believe that situations must be accepted and reacted to rather than changed. In such cultures, people do not emphasize planning and scheduling. Work schedules must adjust to other priorities, such as family.

In contrast, where cultural values support the notion that people dominate nature, managers tend to be proactive. They believe that situations can be changed. Strategic plans and operations reflect the assumption that obstacles can be conquered. What works is what is important. Organizations focus on using concrete data that suggest the best way to solve problems.

This section concludes our examination of the 7d view of culture. As Exhibit 2.7 did for the Hofstede model, Exhibit 2.19 gives percentile rankings for these dimensions in selected countries.

From the sections on cultural models, you should have acquired two skills. First, you should now be able to apply the models to diagnose and understand the basic cultural values of a society. Second, you should be able to apply this information to assess how the characteristics of a particular culture affect business operations. Later chapters will build on your knowledge of culture and of the concepts introduced here. However, developing an in-depth understanding of any culture goes beyond the simple application of cultural models. The successful multinational manager will seek information continually from all sources. Consider, for example, how Exhibit 2.20 shows that proverbs provide informal insights into national cultures.

The chapter concludes with some cautions for all who venture into international operations.

# Caveats and Cautions

Although understanding the cultures of people and organizations is crucial for international business success, multinational managers in particular must realize that cultures provide only broad guidelines for behavior. For instance, although the United States scores very highly on individualism, it has the highest percentage of charity giving in the world (clearly a collectivistic behavior). Similarly, whereas many Latin American cultures prefer warm interpersonal relationships, researchers were surprised to find that Costa Ricans preferred automatic tellers over human tellers.[42] These are examples of **cultural paradoxes**, where individual situations seem to contradict cultural prescriptions. However, if one assumes that all people within a culture behave, believe, feel, and act the same, it is known as **stereotyping**.

Using the cultural stereotype—the typical way people act—to understand a culture is not necessarily wrong if done carefully. Broad generalizations about a culture can serve as a starting point for understanding the complexities of cultural differences. Most books that explain how to do business with the _____ [name a culture] use stereotypical cultural generalizations. Such books are helpful in understanding a culture as a whole, not in perceiving the variations within it. However, managers must also understand that there are differences even among people from the same cultures. Consider the following Case in Point.

After considering such information about significant local differences, however, the multinational manager must realize that organizational and occupational cultures differ within a national context and that individuals vary widely within each level of culture. Consequently, management functions such as planning, organizational

**Cultural paradoxes**
When individual situations seem to contradict cultural prescriptions.

**Stereotyping**
When one assumes that all people within a culture behave, believe, feel, and act the same.

CASE IN POINT

## Ethnic Cultures in China, Hong Kong, and Taiwan

Cross-cultural management research assumes that countries differ based on culture. However, although there are wide cultural differences between countries, significant differences can also exist between countries that share the same cultural values. Consider the case of three ethnic Chinese societies: Hong Kong, Taiwan and China. All three countries share similar national cultural profiles. However, in a recent study of 151 Hong Kong respondents, 95 Taiwanese respondents, and 127 Chinese respondents, significant differences were found in several dimensions. For instance, the Chinese respondents scored higher on materialism (priority on immediate material gain) than the respondents from the other two nations. The authors explain such findings with the fact that the Chinese are only now enjoying a capitalist economy after years of communism. In contrast, both Hong Kong and Taiwan have already had decades of affluence and materialism is not as important. Another

important difference noted was the time (pace of life) difference. With respect to the time dimension, Taiwan scored significantly higher than Hong Kong and China. This difference can likely be attributed to the fact that Taiwan has a much higher degree of economic development and the pace of life tends to be higher in countries with higher economic development. Another difference explored was efficiency, reflecting the degree to which a society emphasizes goal attainment with minimal time and effort. Both Hong Kong and Taiwan scored higher on efficiency than China. Such results make sense given that Hong Kong and Taiwan are more economically developed than China, and more economically developed societies tend to place more importance on efficiency.

*Source: Based on Price, W. D. 2012. "The effect of ethnic culture on managerial attitudes and practices: A survey in Hong Kong, Taiwan and China." International Journal of Management, 29(2): 267–278.*

design, and personnel management must account not only for differences in national culture, but also for differences in occupational and organizational cultures. Similarly, successful leadership, motivation, and the development of individual employees must take into account the unique characteristics of each employee.

Perhaps the greatest cultural danger facing the multinational manager is **ethnocentrism**, which occurs when people from one culture believe that theirs are the only correct norms, values, and beliefs. The ethnocentric person may look down on people from other cultures and may even consider them backward, dirty, weird, or stupid. The work of many anthropologists leads to the conclusion that the multinational manager can offset ethnocentric tendencies and truly understand other cultures only by adopting a mindset of **cultural relativism**. This is the philosophical stance that all cultures, no matter how different, are correct and moral for the people of those cultures.

Few multinational managers are so ethnocentric that they fail to realize that people from other cultures just do things differently. Rather, the danger is a subtle form of ethnocentrism; that is, managers may find it difficult to remain entirely neutral in response to other cultures. For example, issues such as the variations in the pace of work in other countries, the unwillingness of subordinates to take responsibility, or practices such as bribery often frustrate North American managers. Especially when first assigned overseas, managers must be wary of judging subordinates in terms of their own cultural values. A common ethnocentric reaction is, "Why don't they do it right, as we do?"

Given the complexities and subtleties associated with national cultures, multinational managers have to work diligently to adequately understand any culture.

**Ethnocentrism**
When people from one culture believe that theirs are the only correct norms, values, and beliefs.

**Cultural relativism**
A philosophical position arguing that all cultures, no matter how different, are correct and moral for the people of those cultures.

**EXHIBIT 2.19    Percentile Ranks for the 7d Model Cultural Dimensions in Selected Countries**

| | Universalism | Individualism | Neutral | Specific | Achievement | Past Orientation | Future Orientation | Internal Control |
|---|---|---|---|---|---|---|---|---|
| Argentina | n/a | n/a | 21 | n/a | 8 | n/a | n/a | 59 |
| Australia | n/a | 71 | 69 | 73 | 84 | 32 | n/a | 78 |
| Austria | n/a | n/a | 90 | 60 | 3 | n/a | n/a | 63 |
| Belgium | n/a | 52 | 46 | n/a | n/a | n/a | n/a | 43 |
| Brazil | n/a | 19 | 46 | n/a | 34 | 18 | n/a | 73 |
| Bulgaria | n/a | 84 | 81 | n/a | 29 | n/a | n/a | 20 |
| Canada | 95 | 74 | 77 | 80 | 92 | n/a | 47 | 88 |
| China | 26 | 26 | 85 | 3 | 58 | 82 | 89 | 2 |
| Cuba | n/a | n/a | 4 | n/a | 11 | n/a | n/a | 98 |
| Czech Rep. | 16 | 100 | 56 | 37 | 45 | n/a | 84 | n/a |
| Denmark | n/a | 61 | 33 | 70 | 82 | n/a | n/a | 80 |
| Egypt | n/a | 10 | 2 | n/a | n/a | n/a | n/a | n/a |
| Ethiopia | n/a | n/a | 100 | 97 | 37 | n/a | n/a | 24 |
| Finland | n/a | 58 | 50 | 63 | 76 | n/a | n/a | 39 |
| France | 63 | n/a | 25 | 53 | 71 | 77 | 74 | 90 |
| Germany | n/a | 35 | 35 | n/a | 61 | 64 | 53 | 34 |
| Greece | 42 | 32 | 38 | 40 | 55 | n/a | n/a | 51 |
| Hong Kong | n/a | n/a | 92 | 87 | 13 | 100 | 100 | 29 |
| Hungary | 79 | 94 | 58 | 23 | 47 | n/a | n/a | n/a |
| India | 21 | 16 | 83 | 27 | 18 | 9 | 39 | 27 |
| Indonesia | 47 | n/a | 85 | 17 | n/a | 36 | 39 | 32 |
| Ireland | 84 | 48 | 23 | n/a | 95 | n/a | n/a | 71 |

| | | | | | | | |
|---|---|---|---|---|---|---|---|
| Italy | n/a | 31 | n/a | 66 | n/a | 16 | 43 |
| Japan | 6 | 98 | 57 | 53 | 59 | 63 | n/a |
| Kenya | n/a | n/a | n/a | 26 | n/a | n/a | 17 |
| Malaysia | 29 | 25 | 43 | n/a | n/a | n/a | n/a |
| Mexico | 13 | 50 | n/a | 63 | n/a | n/a | n/a |
| Netherlands | 55 | 63 | 93 | n/a | 41 | 32 | 54 |
| Nigeria | 81 | 69 | 13 | n/a | n/a | n/a | 76 |
| Norway | n/a | 44 | 50 | 100 | 23 | n/a | 95 |
| Pakistan | 42 | n/a | n/a | n/a | n/a | n/a | n/a |
| Philippines | n/a | 15 | 33 | 21 | n/a | n/a | n/a |
| Poland | 87 | 96 | 90 | 39 | 27 | n/a | 100 |
| Portugal | 39 | 67 | n/a | 74 | n/a | n/a | 46 |
| Romania | 90 | n/a | n/a | n/a | n/a | n/a | n/a |
| Russia | 97 | 17 | 10 | 42 | 50 | 11 | 12 |
| Korea | 11 | n/a | n/a | 24 | 91 | 79 | 61 |
| Singapore | 23 | 69 | 47 | 68 | 73 | 5 | 10 |
| Spain | 68 | 4 | n/a | 32 | 55 | n/a | 93 |
| Sweden | 45 | 63 | 100 | 79 | 86 | 68 | 22 |
| Switzerland | 100 | 29 | 67 | 50 | 68 | 58 | 49 |
| Thailand | n/a | 58 | n/a | 16 | n/a | n/a | 56 |
| United Kingdom | 65 | n/a | 83 | 87 | 45 | 26 | 68 |
| United States | 77 | 54 | 77 | 97 | 14 | 21 | 66 |
| Russia | 5 | 17 | 10 | 42 | 50 | 11 | 12 |

*Source: Computed from data reported in Trompenaars, Fons, and Charles Hampden-Turner. 1998. Riding the Waves of Culture: Understanding Cultural Diversity in Global Business. New York: McGraw-Hill.*

**EXHIBIT**  **2.20**    Proverbs: Windows into National Cultures

| Cultural Belief/ Value | Country or Culture | Proverb |
| --- | --- | --- |
| Time | United States | Time is money. |
| | China | Drips of water wear through stone. |
| Directness | Mexico | Only little children and drunks always tell the truth. |
| | Arab | If I have regretted my silence once, I have regretted my chatter many times. |
| Modesty | Japan | The nail that sticks up gets pounded down. |
| | Korea | A barking dog is never a good hunter. |
| Collectivism | Arab | My brother and I against my cousin. My cousin and I against the stranger. |
| | Indonesia | Both a light burden and a heavy burden should be carried together. |
| Value of age | Turkey | Beauty passes, wisdom remains. |
| | Nigeria | The elders of a community are the voice of God. |
| Power distance | Romania | There is no good accord where every man would be a lord. |
| | China | When you are an anvil, hold still. When you are a hammer, strike at will. |
| Fate | Arab | Man does not attain everything he desires; winds don't always blow as the vessels wish. |
| | China | A wise person adapts to circumstances as water conforms to the jar that contains it. |
| Risk | Korea | Even if it is a stone bridge, make sure it is safe. |
| | Arab | Only a fool tests the depth of water with both feet. |

*Source: Wederspahn, Cary M. 2003. "Proverbs: Windows into other cultures." Executive Planet, October 4, 2002. http://www. executiveplanet.com/business-culture.*

Often this process can take years of living and working in the new country. Chapter 11 discusses how multinational firms can provide cultural training to their managers who are about to take foreign assignments in new cultures. Some training can be very rigorous and include stays in the local culture. However, in other cases, such as work being outsourced, the local employees may, of necessity, receive less rigorous cross-cultural training. Consider the following Multinational Management Brief.

**Cultural intellingence**
Ability to interact effectively in multiple cultures.

The goal of the multinational manager is ultimately to become culturally intelligent. Researchers such as Crowe define **cultural intelligence** as the ability to interact effectively in multiple cultures.[43] A culturally intelligent manager is able to understand diverse cultural situations and act appropriately. For instance, the culturally savvy and intelligent manager can be proactive and avoid many of the cultural misunderstandings discussed in the first Case in Point in this chapter (page 46).

How can managers become culturally intelligent? Crowe's research suggests that exposure to new cultural experiences in other countries heightens cultural intelligence. A multinational company may therefore send its employees on foreign trips for this kind of exposure. Crowe's research also points to the importance during one's education of studying abroad and seeking foreign internships as a means to start developing cultural intelligence. Crowe's research also suggests that the depth of exposure increases cultural intelligence. Multinationals may therefore benefit from sending their employees on frequent and different foreign assignments.

## Multinational Management **Brief**

### Outsourcing and Cross-Cultural Training

Many multinationals are outsourcing customer services to achieve cost savings. However, U.S. consumers do not always react positively to such outsourced services. U.S. consumers often find it more difficult to interact with customer service providers located in foreign countries. Issues such as communication and cultural barriers as well as accents often prevent consumers from having a successful exchange; consumers may also become reluctant to provide private information as they become concerned about security of information in foreign countries. In fact, research has shown that Indian operators in call centers in India will experience one disgruntled customer per hour. In some cases, individuals will call customer service centers in India simply to berate the customer service representatives. Multinationals therefore have to deal with many problematic issues while also pursuing cost advantages.

One of the most important ways that multinationals can counteract the difficulties associated with using foreign customer service representatives is through cross-cultural training. Cross-cultural training can be as simple as neutralizing the presence of accents. Such efforts can often result in better interactions. In other cases, cross-cultural training can take the form of familiarization with aspects of local culture such as holidays, popular TV shows, sports, and typical activities of U.S. families. For instance, understanding expressions such as "hitting a sixer" or "scoring a touchdown" may mean the difference between success and failure in an exchange. In yet other cases, the local call centers are physically designed to mirror local cultures. For example, in Indian call centers, maps and other physical representations of the United States are prominently displayed. Times of different cities are also shown on several clocks. Furthermore, call center employees are only allowed to converse in English.

*Source: Based on Honeycutt, E. D., Magnini, V. P. and Thelen, S. T. 2012. "Solutions for customer complaints about offshoring and outsourcing services." Business Horizon, 55, 33–42.*

## Summary and Conclusions

After completing this chapter you should know that a variety of cultural levels affect multinational managers and organizations. However, the descriptions and examples of cultural effects on management are broad illustrations. No one book or chapter can do justice to the immense variety of cultures that exist in the world. This chapter hopes only to sensitize readers to the extremely complex and subtle influences that culture has on management and organizations.

The models of cultural values proposed by the GLOBE researchers, by Hofstede, and by Trompenaars and his colleagues provide basic concepts for analyzing cultural differences. They are tools to help you understand a culture and adjust your business practices to various cultural environments.

The most successful multinational managers realize that understanding a different culture is a neverending learning process. They will prepare for their international assignments by studying as much as they can about the country in which they will work, including but not limited to business etiquette. Understanding the national culture as well as important historical, social, aesthetic, political, and economic trends builds a foundation. They will study the language, for few can really get behind the front stage of culture without speaking the local language. Finally, they will be sensitive and observant, continually adjusting their behavior to conform to what works locally.

This chapter presents only a brief introduction. As you read later chapters, especially those with a comparative focus, you will broaden your understanding of cultural differences. You also will learn to seek advantage in differences and to avoid looking at culture as a potential obstacle.

## Discussion Questions

1. Identify five cultural rituals, stories, or symbols from your native culture. Examples might include national holidays, the country's flag, nursery rhymes, childhood traditional stories, and sayings such as "A stitch in time saves nine." Discuss how each of these communicates cultural values, norms, and beliefs.

2. Define and contrast backstage and front stage culture. Discuss how someone not familiar with your culture could misunderstand a front stage behavior.

3. Discuss several ways that stereotyping and ethnocentrism limit successful multinational management.

4. Define levels of culture, and discuss the interrelationships among the levels.

5. Compare and contrast Hofstede's model of culture with the 7d model. Which model do you think is more valuable for managers? Why?

6. Compare and contrast the GLOBE model with the 7d model.

7. Pick three countries from Exhibits 2.7 and 2.19. Summarize and discuss the managerial implications of cultural differences by applying the Hofstede and 7d models.

8. What are cultural paradoxes? How can a manager prepare for such paradoxes?

## Multinational Management **Internet Exercise**

1. Go to the Executive Planet website at http://www.executiveplanet.com.

2. Choose at least four countries based on your personal interest. (The BRIC [Brazil, Russia, India, and China] group may be a good choice.)

3. Present the business etiquette of these countries to your class. Discuss issues such as "Let's make a deal" or "Prosperous Entertaining" or "Conversation."

4. Are your findings consistent with what is discussed in the book? In other words, based on your understanding of the cultural scores in the book for the countries you selected, are the business etiquette recommendations consistent with such scores?

## Multinational Management **Skill Builder**

**A Briefing Paper**

**Step 1.**  Read the following scenario.

You are a recent college graduate and a junior-level executive in a midsize multinational firm. Your CEO will depart next week on a one-month business trip to meet potential joint venture partners in Saudi Arabia, Poland, Hong Kong, Germany, Greece, and Brazil. Because of your expertise in international business, the CEO has asked you to prepare a cultural brief dealing with the national and business cultures she will be visiting. She does not want to make any cultural faux pas. She expects a high-quality oral and written presentation. Because this is your first major assignment, it is important that you perform well. First impressions are lasting, and your job may depend on it.

**Step 2.**  Your instructor will divide the class into six groups and assign each group at least one country.

**Step 3.**  Using sources on the World Wide Web and in the library, research general cultural issues such as (but not limited to) basic cultural norms, values, and beliefs that may affect work (e.g., attitudes toward work in general, the role of the family in work, food and diet, the role of religion, language). Research specific business cultural issues such as expectations regarding dress, appointments, business entertaining, business cards, titles and forms of address, greetings, gestures, gift giving, the language of business, interaction styles, the timing for closing deals, and the potential reactions to a woman executive.

**Step 4.**  Present your findings to the class.

## *Endnotes*

[1] Kroeber, A. L., and C. Kluckhohn. 1952. "Culture: A critical review of concepts and definitions." *Papers of the Peabody Museum of American Archaeology and Ethnology*, 47, 1.

[2] Terpstra, Vern, and Kenneth David. 1991. *The Cultural Environment of International Business*. Cincinnati: South-Western.

[3] Ibid.

[4] *Craighead's International Business, Travel, and Relocation Guide 2000*. Detroit: Gale Research.

[5] Hofstede, Geert. 2001. *Culture's Consequences: International Differences in Work-Related Values*, 2nd ed. Thousand Oaks, CA: Sage Publications.

[6] Ibid.

[7] House, R., P. Hanges, M. Javidan, P. Dorfman, and V. Gupta. 2004. *Culture, Leadership and Organizations: The GLOBE Study of 62 Societies*. Thousand Oaks, CA: Sage Publications.

[8] Trompenaars, Fons, and Charles, Hampden-Turner. 1998. *Riding the Waves of Culture: Understanding Cultural Diversity in Global Business*. New York: McGraw-Hill. 2000. http://www.7d-culture.nl/.

[9] Hofstede, *Culture's Consequences*.

[10] Kirkman, Bradley L., Kevin B. Lowe, and Cristina B. Gibson. 2006. "A quarter century of *Culture's Consequences*: A review of empirical research incorporating Hofstede's cultural values framework." *Journal of International Business Studies*, 10(4): 1–36.

[11] Hofstede, *Culture's Consequences*.

[12] Hofstede, Geert. 1991. *Cultures and Organizations: Software of the Mind*. London: McGraw-Hill; Hofstede, Geert and Michael Harris Bond. 1988. "The Confucian connection: From cultural roots to economic growth." *Organizational Dynamics*, 16: 4, 4–21.

[13] Hofstede and Bond.

[14] Ibid.

[15] Hofstede, *Culture's Consequences*.

[16] Ibid.

[17] Ibid.

[18] Ibid.

[19] Ibid.

[20] Ibid.

[21] Ibid.

[22] Hofstede, *Cultures and Organizations*.

[23] Ronen, S., and O. Shenkar. 1985. "Clustering countries on attitudinal dimensions: A review and synthesis." *Academy of Management Review*, September, 435–454.

[24] House et al.

[25] Ibid.

[26] Leung, Kwok, Rabi S. Bhagat, Nancy R. Buchan, and Cristina B. Gibson. 2005. "Culture and international business: Recent advances and their implications for future research." *Journal of International Business Studies*, 36, 357–378.

[27] House et al.

[28] Javidan, Mansour, Peter W. Dorfman, Mary Sully de Luque, and Robert J. House. 2006. "In the eye of the beholder: Cross cultural lessons in leadership for project GLOBE." *The Academy of Management Perspectives*, February, 20(1): 67–90.

[29] House et al.

[30] Javidan et al.

[31] Kluckhohn, Florence, and F. L. Strodtbeck. 1961. *Variations in Value Orientations*. New York: Harper & Row.

[32] Trompenaars et al.

[33] Ibid.

[34] Ibid.

[35] Ibid.

[36] Ibid.

[37] Ibid.

[38] Ibid.

[39] Ibid.

[40] Ibid.

[41] Ibid.

[42] Osland, Joyce S., Allan Bird, June Delano, and Mathew Jacob. 2000. "Beyond sophisticated stereotyping: Cultural sensemaking in context." *The Academy of Management Executive*, February, 14(1): 65–79.

[43] Crowe, K. A. 2008. "What leads to cultural intelligence." *Business Horizons*, 51, 391–399.

# Jextra Neighbourhood Stores in Malaysia

ANDREW INKPEN

**THUNDERBIRD**
SCHOOL OF GLOBAL MANAGEMENT

In October 2010, Tom Chong was on his way to his office and thinking about several issues he would have to deal with in the coming weeks. Chong was Jextra Stores (Jextra) country manager for the Neighbourhood Markets Division in Malaysia. One issue involved a conversation with the mayor of Klang, a town near Malaysia's capital city of Kuala Lumpur. Chong had been seeking to expand to Klang for some time. The mayor surprised Chong with an offer to help with land zoning if Jextra would help finance a new primary school (or at least Chong thought that was what he had been asked for).

The second issue involved the job performance of Arif Alam, Jextra's top-performing buyer. Alam, a buyer of fresh fruit and vegetables, consistently negotiated better contracts than Jextra's fifteen other buyers and, Chong believed, better than Jextra's competitors. The contracts negotiated by Alam certainly contributed to the excellent financial performance of Jextra Malaysia. Nevertheless, Chong could not help wondering if there was more to the picture than he was aware of. The retail industry in Malaysia was notorious for buyers accepting money and gifts from suppliers. A few days ago, Chong had accidentally overheard two of his accounting employees speculating that Alam must be accepting gifts, or even taking bribes—how else could he get such good contracts?

Chong was not sure what to do. Should he confront Alam? Or, to use one of his English colleague's favorite expressions, should he let sleeping dogs lie? Chong knew that his boss expected him to aggressively grow the business, so perhaps it would be best to accept the mayor's offer and deal with Alam later.

## Jextra Malaysia

Jextra Stores, a large Asian retailer, was based in Hong Kong and was owned by Sim Lim Holdings, a large publicly traded industrial group. Sim Lim Holdings was traded on the Hong Kong and London stock exchanges. Jextra operated retail stores in Hong Kong, China, Philippines, Viet Nam, Malaysia, Thailand, and Singapore. The company operated supermarkets, hypermarkets, and convenience stores.

Jextra entered Malaysia, a stable and prosperous nation of 28 million multi-ethnic people, in 2005 and was very successful. The company operated supermarkets in Malaysia using the name Neighbourhood Markets. There were now ten Neighbourhood Markets, and breakeven had been reached quickly. Jextra was planning to enter the Malaysian convenience store sector in a few years. Although other Asian and European retailers were entering Malaysia, Tom Chong saw plenty of growth opportunities for supermarkets, and his boss in Hong Kong had approved an aggressive five-year investment strategy.

## Tom Chong

Tom Chong, a Hong Kong native, had been in his position for eight months, and expected to remain there for another two to three years. Malaysia was Chong's first assignment as country manager. Prior to moving to Malaysia, Chong held various positions in corporate headquarters in Hong Kong, and then moved to Malaysia as finance director. After two years in finance, he moved into his current role as country manager for Neighbourhood Markets. His new assignment in Malaysia was his first experience with real operational issues and profit and loss responsibilities.

Chong reported to a Regional Operating Officer responsible for Singapore, Malaysia, and Thailand, and was in constant contact with the CEO and the CFO of the Supermarket and Hypermarket Divisions of Jextra in Hong Kong. Chong was evaluated based on various financial measures, including Economic Value Added. As a country manager in a young market, the number of new stores opened was an important element in his overall evaluation, and a factor in determining his career prospects. In a fast-growing market like Malaysia, a failure to open new stores would be viewed negatively at corporate headquarters. The number of new stores opened would also be a factor in determining his discretionary bonus. In recent years, Chong's performance had been among the best for Jextra managers of his age and experience.

## A New Store in Klang

Jextra was doing well in Malaysia and actively seeking to expand. Chong and his team had identified a potential site in Klang for a new Neighbourhood Market. Klang, a town located about 30 km west of Malaysia's capital, Kuala Lumpur, was growing and was viewed as an attractive location for a new store. Although the potential site was not zoned for retail and commercial purposes, it had good road access and plenty of space for parking. Chong knew that several other retailers were also interested in expansion in Klang, especially with the opening of a new highway connecting Klang to the southeastern edge of Kuala Lumpur.

At a recent meeting between Chong and the mayor of Klang:

*Chong:* As you know, we have identified Klang as one of the most attractive cities in Malaysia for Jextra investment. We are interested in opening a Jextra Neighbourhood Market there.

*Mayor:* We are pleased that you are considering our city for your next investment. Klang is a growing community, and the new highway makes our city much more attractive as a place for families to live and commute to the capital. Where does your investment analysis stand?

*Chong:* We have done some preliminary work. We have identified some potential sites. There is one site of interest near the new sports arena, and we have had some conversations with your offcials since the land is currently not zoned for commercial use. Unfortunately, our previous investments in Malaysia have all encountered diffculty with land development. Our newest store was delayed by more than eight months because of zoning issues. We hope that will not be a problem in Klang.

*Mayor:* We have a unique community in Klang, and want to protect our cultural heritage. We scrutinize all proposed real estate developments very carefully. With your store, perhaps we can help each other.

*Chong:* Can you be more specific?

*Mayor:* Our community is growing quite rapidly, and we have a lot of young families moving in. We desperately need a new primary school. Without it, families may choose to live elsewhere. People do not want to live in a city with inadequate school facilities. Unfortunately, our school budget is quite tight, and we may not be able to build the school for at least two years. If Jextra were willing to consider supporting a primary school development fund, I am sure I could speed up the land zoning process.

*Chong:* Interesting….Can you tell me a bit more about the primary school project? Do you have any preliminary estimates of the cost?

*Mayor:* My Director of Schools has told me that we need about 350,000 ringgit to make up a budget shortfall for a new primary school. Jextra's support would greatly help the community. Also, if you were to build your store on the proposed site, road and electricity developments would be necessary. A flyover at the intersection of Jalan Mantin and Jalan Subang on the east side of the site would be necessary to ensure smooth traffic flow. We would, of course, expect Jextra to help pay for the flyover. I understand one of your competitors in Shah Alam [a community close to Klang] helped pay for a new fire truck when they entered the market. This is quite normal for new investment in Malaysia.

*Chong:* Well, Mr. Mayor, thank you for your time. We will continue with our analysis, and certainly hope that we can do something that is good for Klang and good for Jextra.

With that, Chong left the meeting. The conversation with the mayor had caught him by surprise. The mayor's zoning proposal was unexpected, but could certainly speed up development. However, Chong was not sure what he asked for. Was he being asked to pay the entire 5 million ringgit or just a part of the cost? Would he pay for it before the primary school was built, or after? Would he pay the city or a contractor? If he said no, would that mean a denial of the zoning change?

Chong made a few calls, and learned that the mayor's sister was on the school board and was one of the major supporters of a new primary school. Chong also learned that planning for the flyover had started several months before Jextra had ever expressed an interest in the nearby site. In addition, Jextra had already determined that traffic to and from the store parking lot would be routed through the west side of the lot, using a lightly used commercial street and not on either of the roads close to the planned flyover. Chong wondered about the mayor's motives in asking Jextra to pay for the flyover.

## Jextra Business Conduct Code

Jextra's Business Conduct Code was very clear: employees could not offer benefits to third parties in connection with business matters (see the Appendix for excerpts from the Code). If Jextra were to contribute to a primary school, the benefit would be a contribution to a school development fund, and the benefit would go to the school and the community, not individuals. Chong had discussed a hypothetical situation with a Malaysian friend who was also a lawyer (he did not reveal the specifics of the mayor's request). He was told that Malaysian law was unclear in the area of business payments for social purposes made specifically for regulatory approval. He was also told that although not widespread in Malaysia, the practice of businesses contributing to city projects was common in Klang and other areas around Kuala Lumpur, and the local mayor prided himself on being able to obtain these payments for schools and roads in particular.

Jextra's corporate office in Hong Kong had a small group of employees that managed the Jextra Social Fund. The Jextra Social Fund provided funding for various social and educational programs, mainly in Hong Kong. One of the fund's specific initiatives was providing university scholarships in Hong Kong for children of lower-income families. As Jextra expanded in Asia, the fund was slowly looking at ways to contribute to more local programs.

However, Chong knew that recently there had been some concerns in the Philippines involving the Jextra Social Fund and some funds for a community center in a city in which Jextra planned to build a store. Chong did not know the details, but the rumors were that much of the money went to local politicians instead of the community center. Not long after the incident, Jextra's country manager in the Philippines was transferred back to Hong Kong to a position that looked like a demotion.

## Legal in Malaysia?

Chong thought that the primary school contribution could be illegal in Hong Kong if it circumvented the Jextra Social Fund. But, perhaps this was normal practice in Malaysia. Chong's friend said that some local lawyers would probably advise him to make the payments, but to keep the school and flyover payments independent, which would blur the line as to whether the behavior was indeed illegal. Complicating the issue was the question of the expected outcome from the primary school payment. If the school payment speeded up the development process, it could be legal; if it was necessary to make the payment solely as a prerequisite to obtaining the permit, it could be considered a bribe. If the payment was made after the store was built and went directly to a school board budget for future operating expenses, would that be illegal? Chong did not know the answer to these questions.

Various scandals involving alleged bribes and corporate contributions had contributed to the recent "retirement" of various elected officials in Malaysia. Both state and federal politicians were using "clean government" as part of their political platforms. The State Investment, Trade and Industry Committee Chairman said that his government would separate itself from the historically tight ties between business, government, and political campaign contributions. At the federal level, the government had promised that foreign direct investment in Malaysia would become transparent, and that giveaways to foreign investors would stop (exactly what giveaways he meant were never specifically identified).

Chong knew that, in the last year, there had been several foreign investors who were rumored to have helped fund different government programs in exchange for favorable treatment. So far, there was no evidence that any of these efforts were illegal or even of much interest to voters and legislators. When a European electronics company opened a new plant in Malaysia, there were many rumors that the company paid a substantial amount of money to a government "education fund." Chong's teammate from his football club told him confidentially that the company had paid 2.5 million ringgit to the fund, and that the fund was controlled personally by the Industry and Development Minister, a well-known businessman turned politician, whose wife was dean of the Communications School at the Malaysian Institute of Technology.

## Jextra's Competitors and the Mayor's Offer

Chong was aware that Super-Value, one of Jextra's competitors, was also actively looking at Klang for a new store. Would the mayor make the same offer to Super-Value as he had made to Jextra? If so, when would the offer be made, and would Super-Value be willing to accept it? Perhaps Super-Value was interested in the same site as Jextra. Before Chong could even consider agreeing to the mayor's primary school request, he needed to think through the details. How would he get the money for the school? Would he identify it in the investment proposal, or try to hide it with other items? Should he get legal advice on his possible criminal liability in Hong Kong? What if he went ahead with the payment, and the money ended up not going to the school? If the press found out, Jextra and Chong could be in big trouble.

Perhaps the best approach would be to decline the mayor's offer and work through regular channels to get the zoning approval. If that was successful, he would worry about the fyover request later. On the other hand, he did not want to lose access to a prime retail site, and his boss, who was aware of the Klang site, wanted an update on the project next week.

## Category Management

A very simplified view of Jextra's category management and buying process is as follows. Category managers (CMs) were responsible for driving category direction and leading an operationally efficient category team to deliver the budget within the framework of the corporate goals. A key area of responsibility for category managers was working with suppliers to determine the products to order, together with their negotiating prices. For a new supplier, establishing a relationship with a category manager was crucial in getting its products listed by Neighbourhood Markets. Category managers negotiated contracts, rebates, equipment, placement, incentives, and other financial and logistical arrangement for their category. Neighbourhood Markets in Malaysia had category managers for product lines such as fruits and vegetables, meat, frozen foods, and beverages. Product buyers managed the bundling of orders and actual buying from suppliers at the negotiated prices. Over and above this organizational setup, there were few defined processes, leaving a fair amount of leeway to the category managers because they decided what to order and what not to order.

## Arif Alam

Arif Alam was 32 years old, and had been with Jextra in Malaysia since the company entered the market. He had worked his way up from a sales apprentice position to category manager for fruits and vegetables. His responsibilities included building and managing contacts with suppliers, listing suppliers and products, negotiating prices, and working closely with buyers to ensure that the supplier relationship was smoothly managed.

As Alam's boss, Chong had a reasonable understanding of how the Malaysian buying process worked, but he did not know all the details, and certainly was not involved in day-to-day activities. What Chong had learned over the past few months was that there were ample opportunities for CMs to exploit the system for personal gain. One typical scheme involved company samples and rewards. Most suppliers provided CMs with a large supply of product samples that could be sold on the grey market. CMs and their spouses often traveled extensively to product presentations of certain suppliers. These events usually took place at luxury hotels, and often in resort settings. Since Alam was a CM for fruits and vegetables, he might be provided with other products, such as small appliances like toasters or coffeemakers. Another typical scheme was for suppliers to provide rewards tied to performance and sales. These could range from household appliances to expensive jewelry and watches. These rewards could be kept or sold. There were even cases where companies owned by relatives of CMs had to be paid by suppliers in order for the suppliers to get their products sold by Jextra.

Besides his suspicions that Alam was accepting gifts, or even taking bribes, Chong had heard rumors about a scheme between Alam and his father-in-law. Alam referred suppliers willing to be listed for a new product to his father-in-law who, as a side job, ran a trading agency that "established contact to Jextra Stores." The agency received a commission of 0.5 percent for all goods covered by the agency agreement. It was rumored that Alam rarely listed suppliers and products not covered by the agency.

## Bribery

The bribery issue was particularly troubling. Bribery of retail buyers was as old as the retail industry itself. The bribery process works as shown in the following example. A buyer who paid 50 ringgit for a pair of blue jeans the previous year negotiates a 45 ringgit price based on a larger order. Another clothesmaker offers the same pants for 42 ringgit each. In order to retain the big order, the first vendor matches the 42 ringgit price and gives the buyer 2 ringgit for each pair of blue jeans. The bribe is undetectable, because the buyer sets up a phony company that serves as a middleman in the transaction. The vendor bills the retailer for 42 ringgit a pair and funnels the 2 ringgit to the buyer through the dummy corporation, calling it "an agency commission." After the deal is done, the vendor keeps the order and the retailer pays less for the pants than a year ago. The buyer looks good because the price paid was lower than a year ago. The buyer believes, "I deserve the money because I am helping the company." For a few years, the retailer may benefit by having lower costs. Longer term, the retailer's costs may increase because the buyer has an obligation to the vendor and may end up paying less-competitive prices. The retailer may also end up with merchandise that is inferior in quality and difficult to sell because it was purchased by a corrupt buyer.

## Chong's Decision

Chong had a dilemma. Although he suspected that Alam was involved in "dirty" buying, how could he find out? His colleagues might know, but they could be involved in the same activities. Jextra was doing well and, as far as Chong knew, except for bribery, most of the behaviors were not criminal in Malaysia. What if he set up an investigation? If he found nothing, he could alienate his people and lose personal credibility. He might find that large parts of his product category management were engaged in similar actions. What should he do then? The whole business might be at risk if he were to shut it down. He could lose his top CMs and disrupt supplier relationships. Plus, how would he actually investigate the CMs—hire an outside investigator? Talk with suppliers? Find a disgruntled employee? Spy on his employees? This was all new to him.

Proving any of his suspicions would be difficult. Alam was a respected member of the team. Aside from rumors and hearsay, Chong had no real evidence of bribery or kickbacks. Alam's lifestyle did not seem out of the ordinary. Chong would need clear evidence, and an outside investigator would mean added cost. The investigation could take months, or even years, and Chong might be gone from Malaysia by the time the process was completed. In addition, this would take a lot of his time, and he was already working almost 60 hours a week.

Chong needed to keep growing the business and meet his financial targets. It was critical for him to deal with the mayor's proposal appropriately and ensure that Jextra's chosen site did not end up with one of his competitors. Maybe he should wait before doing anything about Alam.

## Appendix: Excerpts from Jextra's Business Conduct Code

### Summary

Jextra is an international company with a strong reputation for providing quality products. We continually seek to deliver the best results for the Company the highest return to our shareholders, and the most beneficial service to our customers.

Ethical conduct is defined as conduct that is morally correct and honourable. To maintain our valuable reputation and to build on our success, we must conduct our business in a manner that is ethical as well as legal. This Business Conduct Code establishes Jextra's commitment to following ethical business practices. It details the fundamental principles of ethical business behaviour, and defines the responsibilities of all directors, officers, associates, and Company representatives.

Jextra is committed to conducting business lawfully and ethically. Every associate is obligated to act at all times with honesty and integrity. We expect you to bring good judgment and a sense of integrity to all your business decisions. While it is not possible to list all policies and laws to be observed, or all conflicts of interest or prohibited business practices to be avoided, this Business Conduct Code details the company's expectations for associate conduct, and helps associates make the right decisions. Associates are expected to know the company's policies and comply with them.

### Applicability

Associates who supervise others have an important responsibility to lead by example and maintain the highest standards of behaviour. If you supervise others, you should create an environment where employees understand their responsibilities and feel comfortable raising issues and concerns without fear of retaliation. If an issue is raised, you must take prompt action to address the concerns and correct problems that arise.

You must also make sure that each associate under your supervision understands our Code and the policies, laws, and regulations that affect our workplace. Most importantly, you must ensure that employees understand that business performance is never more important than ethical business conduct.

As a Jextra employee, you are expected to comply with both the letter and the spirit of our Code. This means you must understand and comply with all of the company policies, laws, and regulations that apply to your job, even if you feel pressured to do otherwise. Our Code also requires you to seek guidance if you have questions or concerns, and to cooperate fully in any investigation of suspected violations of the Code that may arise in the course of your employment.

### Bribery

It is illegal to pay or receive a bribe intended to influence business conduct or behaviour. Our guideline goes beyond the standard set by the law, and prohibits any activity that creates the appearance of anything improper, anything that may embarrass the company or anything that may harm our corporate reputation. No assets of the company or other funds may be used to bribe or influence any decision by an officer, director, employee, or agent of another company, or any governmental employee or official.

It may be acceptable to entertain or provide minor gifts to guests or suppliers, as long as the expenses are reasonable, consistent with good business practices, and do not appear improper. Any gift, entertainment, or benefit provided must be modest in scope and value. You should consult with your supervisor if you have any questions about whether any gift-giving activity is appropriate. Never provide a gift, entertainment, or benefit that contravenes any applicable law or contract term or that is large enough to influence, or appear to influence, the recipient's business decisions.

Associates should not accept money, gifts, or excessive entertainment from any guest, contractor, or supplier at any time. For more information on gifts, entertainment, and related issues, see the Conflicts of Interest guidelines.

International laws strictly prohibit giving, promising, or offering money, or anything else of value, directly or indirectly, to officials of foreign governments or foreign political candidates in order to obtain or retain business or any improper business advantage. Never give, promise, offer or authorize, directly or indirectly, any payments to government officials of any country.

### Conflicts of Interest

Associates must avoid any situation in which their personal interests conflict with the interests of Jextra. If a circumstance arises in which your interests could potentially conflict with the interests of Jextra, it must be disclosed immediately to both your supervisor and Human Resources for review. Associates should be vigilant about recognizing potential conflicts. You must always consider whether your activities and associations with other individuals could negatively affect your ability to make business decisions in the best interest of the company or result in disclosing

nonpublic company information. If so, you may have a real or perceived conflict of interest. Below is a list of potential conflicts of interest.

- Owning a substantial amount of stock in any competing business or in any organization that does business with us.
- Serving as a director, manager, consultant, employee, or independent contractor for any organisation that does business with us, or is a competitor—except with our company's specific prior knowledge and consent.
- Accepting or receiving gifts of any value or favours, compensation, loans, excessive entertainment, or similar activities from any individual or organization that does business or wants to do business with us, or is a competitor.
- Taking personal advantage of a business opportunity that is within the scope of Jextra's business—such as by purchasing property that Jextra is interested in acquiring.

### Related Party Transactions

Employees and immediate family or household members may not serve as a supplier or customer of the Company, or otherwise engage in business dealings with the Company, without the written consent of a member of the Executive Management Team. You or a member of your immediate family or household may not accept business opportunities, commissions, or advantageous financial arrangements from a customer, supplier, or business partner of the Company. You may not purchase for personal use the goods or services of the Company's suppliers on terms other than those available to the general public or established by Company policy. You may not take advantage of any business opportunity that you learn about in the course of your employment.

### CASE DISCUSSION QUESTIONS

1. Consider the GLOBE study discussed earlier in the chapter. Where does Malaysia rank on the various cultural dimensions? Does Malaysia's ranking help explain some of Jextra's experiences as they try to open a new store?
2. What cultural dimensions may help explain the need for Malaysian investors to contribute to corporate social responsibility funds? Is humane orientation relevant here?
3. Based on your understanding of Malaysia's culture, what should Mr. Chong do? Why?

# 3 The Institutional Context of Multinational Management

## Learning Objectives

*After reading this chapter you should be able to:*

- Understand the national context and how it affects the business environment.

- Understand the influence of the institutional context of countries on individuals and organizations.

- Define social institutions and understand their basic forms.

- Explain how social institutions influence both people and organizations.

- Describe the basic economic systems and their influence on multinational operations.

- Understand the basic stages of industrialization and their implications for multinationals.

- Discuss the world's basic religions and how they shape the local business environment.

- Develop an understanding of education and its effects on multinational operations.

- Define social inequality and its implications for multinationals.

- Understand the importance of the national context and its connection with other international management areas.

## *Preview* CASE IN POINT

### Shell and Oil Drilling in Alaska

Alaska's outer continental shelf includes many of the arctic wildlife wonders. The ocean surrounding the region includes vital migration routes for many species such as whales, walruses and other critical marine life. The ocean ecosystem is also viewed as one of the most unspoiled. However, in addition to its environmental wonders, Alaska holds around 27 billion barrels of recoverable oil under its continental shelf. Furthermore, Alaska is believed to contain around 130 trillion cubic inches of natural gas. The commercial potential of these resources is enormous, given the insatiable demand for fossil fuels such as oil and natural gas. Companies that are able to exploit such resources have the ability to earn significant returns on their investments if the price of oil stays high.

One of the oil companies preparing to start exploration of Alaska's outer continental shelf is the Dutch-based multinational Shell. After years of seeking all of the major permits, Shell can now start exploratory drilling. Shell has not found obtaining the required permits to be easy. After taking two years to get the proper drilling permits, the BP Deepwater Horizon disaster struck and the U.S. Environmental Protection Agency decided to halt Shell's planned 2010 drilling. The governmental arm requested that Shell install some $60 million exhaust filtration equipment on its ships. Shell halted exploration in order to seek the appropriate permits.

Obtaining the proper permits has taken significant time and resources for Shell. Shell officials argue that the regulatory process has been far too open-ended in their case. They have claimed that they found conflicting demands from different U.S. agencies and no clear final outcome. Many environmental groups have filed legal challenges to prevent Shell from starting drilling. In an attempt to prevent any last-minute surprises, Shell decided to file preemptive lawsuits against environmental groups. If it is successful in starting the drilling in 2012, Shell is expected to make one of the largest recent U.S. oil discoveries.

*Source: Based Birger, J. "Why Shell is betting billions to drill oil ... here." Fortune, June 11, 121–130.*

I n Chapter 2, we discussed some of the ways societies can be compared in terms of their national cultures. However, as the Preview Case in Point shows, other elements of a society besides national culture, such as education, the government and the legal system, can affect important business-related differences among societies. In the Shell case, you see how the role of the government and the law can shape how business is done. These factors are critical in how businesses are conducted in societies, and some of them may even encourage individuals to adopt values that are not consistent with their national cultures. It is therefore important to understand the dominant institutional context of any society and to appreciate its influence on both individuals and organizations.

Specifically, understanding the institutional context is extremely critical to effective multinational management. At a basic level, a manager cannot completely understand any society without examining its national culture and its institutional context.[1] Both are key elements of societies, and both have important influences on issues related to strategic multinational management. Exhibit 3.1 shows a model of how the national context (i.e., institutional context, national culture, and business culture) leads to national differences that have implications for the business environment of a country.

**EXHIBIT 3.1**   The National Context and Multinational Companies

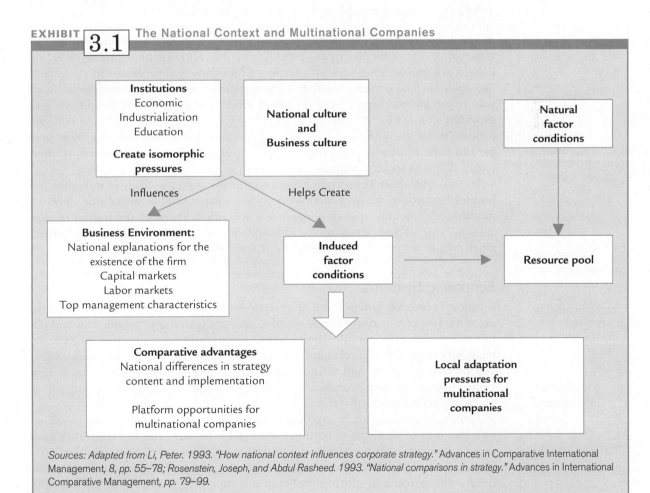

Sources: Adapted from Li, Peter. 1993. "How national context influences corporate strategy." Advances in Comparative International Management, 8, pp. 55–78; Rosenstein, Joseph, and Abdul Rasheed. 1993. "National comparisons in strategy." Advances in International Comparative Management, pp. 79–99.

The **national context** is made up of the respective national cultures and social institutions of a society. As we saw in Chapter 2, the national culture of a society shapes its important norms, values, and beliefs. These cultural components exert important influences on the nation's business culture, that is, on acceptable and correct ways of doing business. However, closely intertwined with national cultural forces are social institutions such as the economic system, religion, and education. As we will see later in this chapter and in other chapters, these social institutions also exert a significant influence on people's norms, values, and beliefs, and have implications for a nation's business culture.

This chapter thus provides a basic understanding of the institutional context of societies. In the next section, we discuss briefly the main elements of a country's institutional environments; that is, social institutions and how they influence society. In subsequent sections, we discuss each of these social institutions in depth as well as their implications for multinational strategic management. We conclude this chapter by looking at some of the ways in which social institutions are relevant to the material covered in later chapters.

# Social Institutions and Their Influence on Society

A **social institution** can be defined as "a complex of positions, roles, norms, and values lodged in particular types of social structures and organizing relatively stable patterns of human resources with respect to fundamental problems in … sustaining viable societal structures within a given environment."[2] In addition to national culture, social institutions have profound effects on people's life conditions and provide a context for psychological differences among people. Similar to national culture, social institutions provide boundaries and norms that prescribe how people will behave; that is, they provide people with behavioral guides to follow when facing different social situations.

We consider three key social institutions that are the most likely to influence the business environment: economic system (e.g., capitalism or socialism), level of industrialization, and types of religion. We also briefly consider the impact of educational systems and levels of social inequality because both have been linked, albeit to a lesser extent, with the business environment.

## Economic Systems

A nation's **economic system** is the "interrelated network or system of beliefs (concerning work, property, constructs, and wealth), activities (extraction, production, and distribution), organizations (business firms, labor unions, consumer associations, regulatory agencies), and relationships (ownership, management, employment, sales) that provide the goods and services consumed by the members of a society."[3] Economic systems are usually reflected in their governments' influence, specifically in terms of whether productive activities are state owned or privately owned.

Economic systems can be typified by the extremes of capitalism and socialism, with mixtures of elements of both in the mixed economy. The **capitalist or market economy** refers to an economic system where production activities are "decentralized to private-property-rights holders (or their agents) who carry out these activities for the purpose of making profits in a competitive market."[4] In contrast, the **socialist or command economy** is one in which production resources are owned by the state and production decisions are centrally coordinated.[5] The ideal socialist economies pursue collective goals such as social equality and solidarity. Consider the following Case in Point.

Finally, the **mixed economy** combines aspects of capitalist and socialist economic systems. In such economies, certain sectors of the economy are left to private ownership while the state runs others, such as health care and education. The state determines that private interests cannot run some sectors of the economy and thus takes control of such sectors, making resource allocation and production decisions. Countries such as Sweden, France, Denmark, Italy, and India are examples of mixed economies.

**Mixed economy**
Combines aspects of capitalist and socialist economies.

Although it is impossible to cover all their possible business implications, economic systems have two major implications for strategic multinational management:

1. Dominant market type.
2. Market transitions.

---

## CASE IN POINT

### Cuba and Capitalism

Cuba has long been run as a communist nation under Fidel Castro. Castro centralized power while also imposing a utopian view of egalitarianism. He expropriated private property and mostly eliminated private businesses. The state took over farming operations, and state farms now occupy over 75 percent of agricultural land. The state also took responsibility for economic activities such as selling products and services, providing credit, providing housing, etc.

While nationalizing all economic sectors, Castro also budgeted significant resources to fund social programs ranging from free education to free healthcare and pensions. As a result, Cuba boasted superior socioeconomic indicators such as life expectancy close to U.S. levels, and the elimination of illiteracy and child malnutrition.

Much of Cuba's success before the 1990s was due to subsidies from the Soviet Union. However, after the Soviet Union collapsed in 1991, most of the subsidies dried up and many thought communism in Cuba was set to die. However, Castro found another way to counteract the decline of Soviet subsidies. In exchange for 20,000 Cuban doctors and other services, Venezuela started providing Cuba with cheap oil. The Chinese government also started providing support and Castro's model was suddenly revived.

This communist model is now under severe attack. Most of Castro's policies resulted in a paternalistic state that removed any incentive to work. Most Cubans came to rely on the Cuban state to provide services. Furthermore, nationalization of most sectors has resulted in very low efficiency and productivity. The high costs associated with social services have meant that the quality of such services has declined considerably.

In 2006, Fidel Castro had to undergo emergency surgery and his brother, Raul Castro, took over. Raul Castro is slowly transferring the economy from state hands to private companies. In 2011, the Communist party approved 313 different types of economic reforms aimed at moving Cuba towards capitalism. Individuals can now more easily obtain permits to sell products and services. Other reforms have included providing idle state lands to private farmers, laying off surplus public workers, removing barriers to the creation of small businesses, and approval of credit. For the first time in decades, Cubans are now allowed to buy and sell houses and cars while also owning items such as cell phones and computers.

*Source: Based on Economist. 2012. "Revolution in retreat." March 24, 3–4; Economist. 2012. "The deal's off." March 24, 5–7; Economist. 2012. "Edging towards capitalism." March 24, 7–9.*

## Dominant Market Type

At a basic level, decisions to operate in a country can be made based on the dominant economic type. For instance, to operate relatively free from governmental interference, a multinational may want to set up operations in a capitalist society like the United States or Britain. However, if multinationals expect to do business in mixed economies like France and Italy, they should expect to subordinate their economic goals and respect social objectives. Emerging markets also present peculiar challenges for investors. Consider the next Focus on Emerging Markets.

The Focus on Emerging Markets clearly shows the impact of governmental interference on a multinational's operations. As a rough guide, multinational managers may want to consider a country's **index of economic freedom** to determine the extent of

**Index of economic freedom**
Determines the extent of governmental intervention in a country.

---

### **Focus** on Emerging Markets

#### Governmental Interference in China

It is undeniable that the potential presented by the Chinese economy will continue to attract investment interests by Western-based multinationals. However, such multinationals have to contend with significant government interference. For example, research by Luo shows how companies deal with difficulties when forming joint ventures in China. The international joint venture contract, which governs how many joint ventures are operated, incorporates three important components: (1) term specificity (the degree to which contractual terms are clearly specified), (2) contingency adaptability (the degree to which companies can adapt to changing situations), and (3) contractual "obligatoriness" (the degree to which companies are bound by the contract). Using surveys from 110 executives involved in international joint ventures, Luo showed that the more the respondents experienced governmental interference, the more highly they rated the need for contingency adaptability in the contract. In other words, the more governmental interference, the more the contract needs to leave room for adaptation to new situations. Luo also found that governmental interference had a negative impact on contract specificity because the more the government intervened, the less possible it was to specify the contract clearly. Such research provides some important guidelines regarding how companies need to structure their contracts to counteract Chinese local and central governmental interventions.

Other events point to the role played by the Chinese government in other cases. For instance, Coca-Cola attempted to buy China Huiyan, China's largest juice company, offering $2.4 billion, an amount that represented about three times the value of the company. For the privately run company, the offer was very appealing, but the Chinese government rejected the offer. Many experts see the move as an effort to prevent foreign companies from dominating the Chinese market. Although Coca-Cola controls half of the market for soft drinks, the juice market is highly fragmented. The successful acquisition of China Huiyan would have given Coca-Cola control of 20 percent of the market. Other industries, such as aviation, banking, and automaking, are seeing significant governmental control through nationalization.

*Sources: Based on* Economist. *2012. "Pedalling prosperity. Special Report. China's Economy." May 26, 1–18;* Economist. *2009. "Business in China. So much for capitalism." March 7, 72;* Economist. *2009. "Coca-Cola and China. Hard to swallow." March 21, 68–69; Luo, Yadong. 2005. "Transactional characteristics, institutional environment and joint venture contracts."* Journal of International Business Studies, *36, 209–230.*

its governmental intervention. Since 1995, the Heritage Foundation, a U.S.-based research foundation, has been constructing the index. It defines economic freedom as "the absence of government coercion or constraint on the production, distribution, or consumption of goods and services beyond the extent necessary for citizens to protect and maintain liberty itself." The index includes 10 indicators, ranging from trade freedom (i.e., the degree to which the government hinders free trade through tariffs); taxation policies; and the level of governmental intervention in the economy, to property rights (freedom to accumulate private property) and business freedom (i.e., ease of obtaining a business license). The foundation assigns scores of 0 through 100, with 100 being the highest degree of economic freedom. Exhibit 3.2 shows selected top and bottom 10 countries on the 2012 assessment.

The indices shown in Exhibit 3.2 are not surprising. Capitalist societies such as Canada, Australia, the United States, Singapore, and Hong Kong figure prominently in the list of top 10 countries. Communist societies such as Cuba and North Korea are in the bottom 10. Additionally, countries with repressive governments such as Zimbabwe, Libya, and Iran are also in the bottom 10.

**Market transitions**
Changes that societies go through as they move from socialism toward a market-based economy.

## Market Transitions

The second economic system implication involves **market transitions,** which are the changes often experienced by societies that are moving from socialism toward

**EXHIBIT 3.2**

Index of Economic Freedom (5=lowest economic freedom, 1 = highest economic freedom)

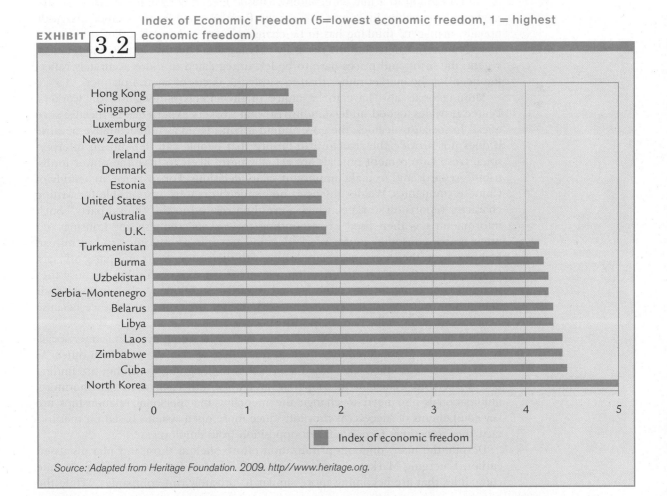

Source: Adapted from Heritage Foundation. 2009. http//www.heritage.org.

a market-based system. The decades following the 1980s have seen a large number of countries in Russia, Eastern Europe, and Asia (i.e., China and Vietnam) undergo marked attempts by the governments to infuse heavy doses of capitalism. For most multinationals, such open-market policies have presented incredible opportunities because they represent new markets and access to skilled but relatively cheap labor. An important aspect of this transition for many multinationals has been an increase in international strategic alliances with local companies, as described in Chapter 9.

For most multinationals, an important component of market transitions has been to understand socialism and its effects on both people and organizations in order to better understand the workers' reactions to market mechanisms. Under socialism, most enterprises were only factories, with no need for cost control.[6] Often these enterprises did not have any strategic planning, accounting, or marketing departments. Furthermore, central planners guaranteed the survival of these firms—despite their inefficiencies—by setting up prices that were not accurate reflections of costs. Instead, prices were sometimes kept low to encourage the heavy consumption of goods manufactured on the orders of the central planners. Banks also were managed according to the needs of central planners. Loans were often made on the basis of connections and personal relationships rather than creditworthiness.

It is not difficult to understand, then, what multinationals experience in facilitating the transition to a market economy. Drastic measures have to be taken to turn inefficient companies into firms that can perform essential business functions. Additionally, managers' thinking has to be changed completely so that they understand management functions and the necessity of being cost-effective. Finally, the financial system, the firms, and prices have to be left unregulated to more accurately reflect the needs of the market rather than to satisfy the needs of central planners.

Multinationals also have to be aware of the effects of socialism on workers. Pearce provides a good understanding of what workers experience in socialist societies.[7] In socialist societies, the government is considered as nonfacilitative because it does not provide the structure to ensure that people can depend on interpersonal trust. Government officials are actually more likely to have the power to distribute rewards and to make important salary decisions. For instance, in a study of Chinese companies, Walder discusses how supervisors were responsible for writing character reports on workers, which were then relayed to the central party.[8] Such information was then used in responding to workers' requests for housing and other scarce consumer items. Workers could not rely on meritocracy but instead had to rely on their personal relationships with their supervisors and party officials. Consequently, they tended to develop a severe distrust of each other because they were all competing for the same limited rewards. Additionally, they focused their energies on refining their personal networks rather than on performance because networks were more likely to help with success.

Multinationals have incredible challenges as they hire employees in former socialist societies. At a basic level, they need to train these workers to trust each other. As multinationals introduce team-based approaches to designing work, they are finding that workers are reluctant to cooperate and work with each other. Furthermore, multinationals also need to change the mentality that personal relationships are key components of success. As they introduce more open systems based on meritocracy, they sometimes face significant opposition from employees.

Despite the many ongoing privatization efforts such as those in Cuba discussed earlier, Emerging Market Countries such as China and Brazil are relying on state companies that are becoming more similar to privately run companies. While the stereotype has been that state-run enterprises are inefficient, unproductive, and unnecessarily bloated, these new state-run companies have shown that state-run companies can also do well. Consider the following Case in Point.

Clearly, economic systems have important implications for the strategic management of multinationals, impacting relationships among companies as well as how these companies are structured. Specifically, the transition of many former socialist countries to a market-based approach presents significant challenges for multinationals. However, economic systems also affect individuals, and specifically how workers view work and even how they justify ethical behaviors, as we will see in subsequent chapters.

In the next section, we consider another critical social institution: the levels of economic development through different degrees of industrialization.

## Industrialization

The application of the steam engine to the gathering and production processes helped spark the Industrial Revolution in Europe.[9] The machine eliminated

---

### C A S E   I N   P O I N T

## Rise of State-Run Companies

While most of the Western world has praised the merits of capitalism to promote economic growth, emerging market economies have been increasingly relying on state-run companies to encourage growth. Consider the case of China, which has seen its gross domestic product triple over the last decade. China is now the world's second biggest economy. However, an interesting aspect of the Chinese economy is that the Chinese state is actually the biggest shareholder in the country's 150 biggest companies. While most Western-based economies have shunned the state-run model, preferring private companies, the Chinese example shows that state capitalism can work. Experts had previously warned that state-run companies could never capitalize on their successes and that they were slow to innovate. However, examples of companies in both Brazil and China have shown that such assertions may not always be true. How have these state-owned companies defied these stereotypes?

Examination of the state-owned companies worldwide shows several trends. First, states are becoming more sophisticated at managing companies. They routinely move company bosses for improper management while also exercising strict control over boards of directors, etc. Second, states are also becoming more efficient at using the assets at their disposal. Chinese state-owned companies have

undergone significant pruning and restructuring resulting in leaner organizations. Third, states also have access to unlimited funds that they can pump into these companies. Consider that the Chinese state still plays a big role in Lenovo through provision of funds, although Lenovo considers itself a private company. Finally, states have also taken advantage of globalization and have struck joint ventures worldwide. This is especially true of Chinese oil companies that have forged ventures in Africa.

Will this model hold? Experts think that state-owned companies may not fare as well as privately run companies in the face of unfavorable environments. First, government companies are still less adept at innovation. There are countless examples of state-owned companies that have been unable to perform as expected (e.g., Malaysia's $150 million bio-valley). Second, state-owned companies are also less productive and efficient than believed because they rely on government subsidies, and accurately measuring their performance is difficult. Finally, an inherent level of corruption exists, as state-owned companies' management is often linked to the ruling elite.

*Sources: Based on* Economist. *2012. "The visible hand." January 21, 3–5;* Economist. *2012. "New master of the universe." Jan 21, 6–8;* Economist. *2012. "Theme and variations." January 21, 9–12;* Economist. *2012. "Mixed bag." January 21, 13–15.*

**EXHIBIT 3.3**    Distribution of Production Activities by Sectzor

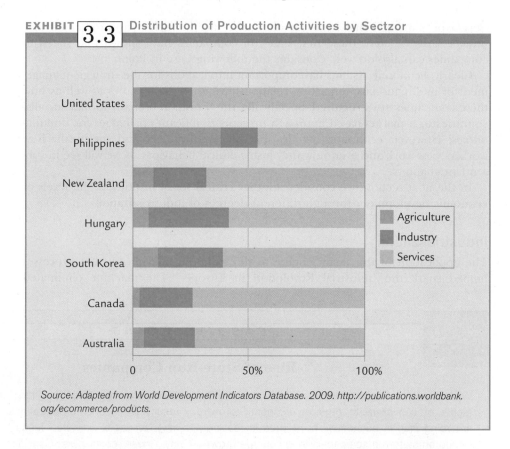

*Source: Adapted from World Development Indicators Database. 2009. http://publications.worldbank. org/ecommerce/products.*

**Industrialization**
Cultural and economic changes that occur because of how production is organized and distributed in society.

**Preindustrial society**
Characterized by agricultural dominance and shaping of the economic environment.

**Industrial society**
Characterized by the dominance of the secondary or manufacturing sectors.

**Postindustrial society**
Characterized by emphasis on the service sectors.

reliance on animal power and allowed the building and use of efficient new machines and equipment. This new ability to gather and transform resources led to the rapid development in many Western societies of large factories with large numbers of workers assembled around networks of machines. Such changes dramatically influenced all aspects of society.

**Industrialization** refers to the cultural and economic changes that are brought about by fundamental changes in how production is organized and distributed in society. Industrialization can be categorized in several ways. In a **preindustrial society,** agriculture dominates and shapes the economic environment. Religious norms and tradition are emphasized, and social mobility is discouraged.[10] Occupational placement tends to be based on ascription (family background), and social status is largely determined through inheritance. An **industrial society** tends to be characterized by the dominance of the manufacturing or secondary sector. Such societies reflect the prevalence of technological development that makes rapid economic growth possible. Industrial societies tend to require wider ranges of skills in their workforce relative to preindustrial societies. Occupational placement is based on universalistic criteria, such as achievement. Finally, the **postindustrial society** emphasizes the service sector. The dominance of employment by the service sector leads to a drastic expansion of the role of formal education due to the need for highly trained workers with specialized skills. Exhibit 3.3 shows selected countries and the distribution of employment by primary, secondary, and tertiary sectors.

The level of industrialization has important implications for strategic multinational management. Consider the next Case in Point.

## CASE IN POINT

### Industrialization and India

India is currently experiencing tremendous changes because of industrialization. Even though a significant percentage of the population remains in poverty, India has nevertheless seen a growing middle class with the rise of service companies such as Infosys. Such experiences are bringing major changes that will likely affect the future work environment in that country. Furthermore, even the poorest Indians are doing better. A recent report suggests that around 52 million Indians have escaped poverty.

One of the many changes has been a new celebration of entrepreneurial success. Many Indians are now willing to leave or turn their backs on jobs at well-known companies to start their own businesses. Such efforts are also spurred by new entrepreneurship competitions, such as the National Entrepreneurship Network's competition to find India's hottest start-ups. One company shortlisted for the competition is Sammaan ("dignity"). Irfan Alam came up with the idea when he was sitting in a rickshaw on a hot summer day. He asked the rickshaw puller for a drink of water and realized that rickshaws cover over six miles a day. He realized that the rickshaw pullers could supplement their meager income by selling water and even advertising on their rickshaws. He thus sells ads through the rickshaws.

*Source: Economist. 2012. "Unfinished journey." March 24, 27–30; Economist. 2008. "Start-ups in India. A suitable business." December 20, 111–112.*

What does the Case in Point mean in terms of international management? There is a direct correspondence between the level of economic development and industrialization, so preindustrial societies tend to be the least economically developed. Multinational companies can use such indicators to determine the feasibility of doing business in preindustrial societies. Given that the long-term prospect of a business in any country depends on market size and income, preindustrial societies tend to provide fewer opportunities. However, preindustrial societies also provide relatively cheap labor compared to industrialized societies, so, not surprisingly, many companies tend to locate their plants in preindustrial countries. Also, preindustrial societies tend to have poor infrastructure and business support. Operating in such countries may be more costly because a multinational company may have to provide its own infrastructure and support services. Many African countries unfortunately fall into this preindustrial category, and multinationals have generally shunned most of them because of political instability. However, as the Case in Point below, "What Does the Future Hold for Africa?" shows, the future for some African countries is bright, and multinationals have to be aware of the role they can play in such developments.

As technological developments make it possible to shift production to the manufacturing sector, important changes in a society's economic environment affect strategic management. Instead of emphasizing tradition and communal obligations that are heavily influenced by the religious norms typical of preindustrial societies, industrial societies tend to favor innovation and individualism. Economic achievement becomes the top priority for industrial societies, and discipline and achievement-oriented norms predominate.[11] Industrial societies tend to present significant opportunities for multinational companies. Multinational companies have access to an environment that is very favorable to businesses and a labor force that is often educated and motivated. Additionally, industrialized societies tend to have governments that are favorable to businesses. Multinational companies can generally expect that their business endeavors will be facilitated. Furthermore, industrial nations tend to present lower nonmarket risks, such as government appropriation.

## What Does the Future Hold for Africa?

For decades, few African economies had been able to sustain growth in real per-capita gross domestic product, one indicator of industrialization. The reality was that African nations had been growing much more slowly than other developing nations. Why had most African countries been left behind in terms of industrialization? It was often argued that after many African nations experienced independence from the three major colonizers (France, Belgium, and Great Britain), their respective elites established one-party rule, "promising stability and economic development in return for a monopoly on political power." However, these countries did not have previous experience in governing and in capital accumulation. Furthermore, any outward-oriented growth potential was viewed with suspicion because it was seen as foreign interference from the previous colonizers. Consequently, most governments, because of internal pressures, engaged in more state-led and inward-looking industrialization efforts. Coupled with internal strife and

governments' response to interest groups, African nations had not achieved much economic progress.

However, recent economic indicators suggest that many African nations are experiencing tremendous growth. Consider that at least six African nations have been experiencing growth of 6 percent or more over the past six years. Many African nations have been experiencing sustained industrialization, and countries such as Ghana and Mozambique have been experiencing growth higher than most other parts of the world. This has led to the emergence of a middle class (predicted to be around 100 million by 2015) with significant purchasing power. Furthermore, not all growth is coming from commodities such as minerals and copper, gold, and other metals. Despite having little oil and other commodities, East African nations such as Burkina Faso and Ghana have experienced more growth than most other African nations. Such growth has been very encouraging for countries in what was once called the "hopeless" continent. The

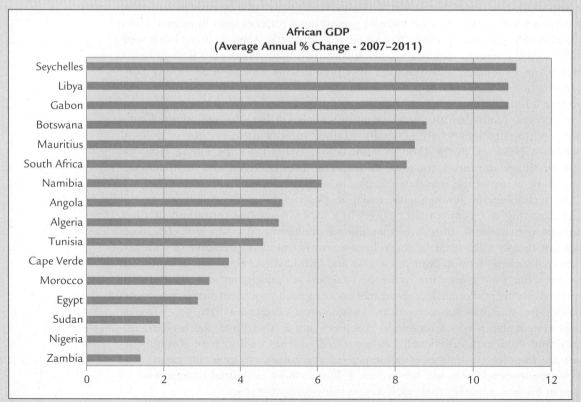

African GDP
(Average Annual % Change - 2007–2011)

*continued*

Exhibit above shows selected high-performing African countries and their growth rates.

Multinational companies thus have significant roles to play in Africa's future development and growth. Africa has sizable physical and human resources, and it represents significant market opportunities. Many countries are gradually moving toward multiparty regimes with an emphasis on political stability. As more and more of African nations gain political freedom, the economic environment will become more conducive to capital accumulation and growth. Furthermore, despite protests and potential for political instability in countries such as Angola and Equatorial Guinea, Africa's significant and growing middle class suggests that the continent will present tremendous potential.

*Sources: Adapted from Bollen, Kenneth. 1993. "Liberal democracy: Validity and method factors in cross-national measures."* American Journal of Political Science, *37, 1207–1230;* Economist. *2012. "A sub-Saharan spring? The World in 2012," 76;* Economist. *2011. "The sun shines bright." December 3, 82–84.*

Exhibit 3.4 shows the materialist scores of selected countries. These scores indicate how much societies value such goals as economic growth and maintaining discipline, both indicators of the degree of industrialization. As the exhibit shows, many countries that are currently undergoing industrialization (e.g., China, Hungary, India, and Brazil) have high rankings on the materialist index, suggesting that individuals in such societies are achievement oriented and favor material gains. The emphasis on economic achievement implies that multinational companies are well advised to motivate employees with monetary rewards.

In addition to shaping norms for individuals, industrialization also has implications for how industries are shaped. Industrialization can therefore take many forms and have various effects based on social conditions. In some cases, industrialization efforts

**EXHIBIT 3.4**    **Materialist Values for Selected Countries**

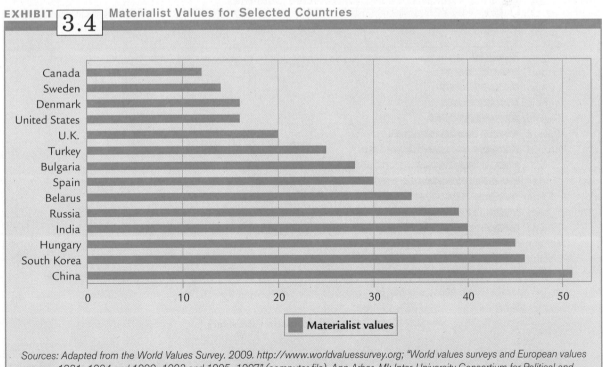

*Sources: Adapted from the* World Values Survey. *2009. http://www.worldvaluessurvey.org; "World values surveys and European values surveys. 1981–1984 and 1990–1993 and 1995–1997" (computer file). Ann Arbor, MI: Inter-University Consortium for Political and Social Research.*

can be inwardly oriented, where local industries are promoted to satisfy the domestic market and preserve foreign exchange.[12] In contrast, some countries also have more outwardly oriented industrialization strategies, where foreign investment is encouraged and export is heavily promoted.

A postindustrial society is characterized by the dominance of the service sectors in production activities.[13] In such a society, productivity and growth tend to come from the generation of knowledge, which is applied to all economic sectors through information processing. Countries transitioning from an industrial to a postindustrial society experience an almost complete demise of the agricultural sector, along with a significant decline in the manufacturing sector. Because services delivery becomes prevalent, there is a significant rise in information-rich occupations, such as managerial, professional, and technical jobs. As societies become more postindustrial, more jobs require increased skills and advanced educational achievements.

Postindustrialization is leading to a postmodern shift in many societies. Inglehart et al. argue that the disciplined and achievement-oriented norms and values typical of industrialized societies have reached a peak.[14] In post-industrial societies, the "emphasis on economic achievement as the top priority is now giving way to an increasing emphasis on the quality of life."[15] As a result, people are more likely to espouse values related to individual expression and a movement toward a more humane society.

Exhibit 3.5 shows selected countries and their scores on the postmaterialist scale. As the exhibit shows, many of the most developed societies have high postmaterialist scores. Multinational companies operating in such countries have to be

**EXHIBIT 3.5    Postmaterialist Values for Selected Countries**

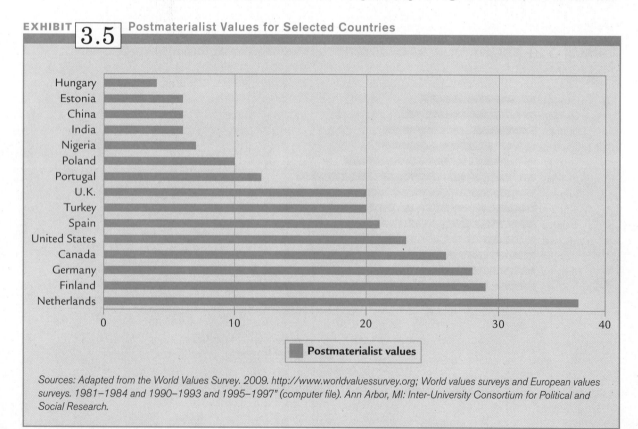

Sources: Adapted from the World Values Survey. 2009. http://www.worldvaluessurvey.org; World values surveys and European values surveys. 1981–1984 and 1990–1993 and 1995–1997" (computer file). Ann Arbor, MI: Inter-University Consortium for Political and Social Research.

aware of the changing needs of workers in these countries. Specifically, people are likely to value those jobs over which they have most control. Such workers also are more likely to prefer noneconomic incentives rather than monetary rewards. Companies should strive to find ways to satisfy such needs.

In this section, we described some of the possible effects of industrialization on societies. Specifically, we looked at industrialization levels and how they affect individuals as well as organizations. In the next section, we consider another critical social institution: religion.

## Religion

A **religion** can be defined as a shared set of beliefs, activities, and institutions based on faith in supernatural forces. Religions continue to be an important aspect of most societies. The reemergence of Christianity in the United States, the rise of Islamic fundamentalism in the Middle East, the rapid growth of Protestantism in Latin America, and the religious devotion in the former Soviet Union and Eastern Europe all signal that religions continue to be pervasive and influential in people's lives.[16]

Religion and work and their interrelationships form the very foundations of human society.[17] In fact, the link between religion and the ways in which societal systems are structured for economic purposes forms the basis of Max Weber's famous formulation of the Protestant work ethic.[18] Weber, a well-known German sociologist, proposed that the dominance of Protestant religions led to the emergence of modern capitalism in Western Europe. He argued that Protestant beliefs emphasize hard work, the creation of wealth, and frugality. This combination of values led individuals to work hard to accumulate wealth. However, because Protestant beliefs encouraged believers to reinvest their wealth rather than spend it, they formed the basis of Western European capitalist expansion.

Religions exert an important influence on society, providing their members with a way of dealing with issues that reflect individual wishes and activities.[19] However, religions also affect business and other organizational procedures. Consider that Islam has productivity implications during the Ramadan months and that Christianity has obvious consumer behavior implications during Christmastime.[20] As we will see, for instance, in Chapter 4, religions shape how people do business in different parts of the world. Consider the following Case in Point.

As the Case in Point shows, religion has profound influences on work and other aspects related to multinational management. As multinationals conduct operations in foreign locales, they need to be sensitive to religion. We therefore consider various aspects of religion in this section.

Despite the great variety of religions around the world, only four are practiced by a large percentage of the world's population. In the next few sections, we look at Christianity, Islam, Hinduism, and Buddhism, along with their implications for multinational strategic management. Exhibit 3.6 shows the distribution of religions around the world, both in percentage of world population and in number of followers. As the exhibit shows, taken together, Christianity, Hinduism, Islam, and Buddhism are followed by almost 71 percent of the world's population; of the remaining 29 percent, approximately 20 percent are considered nonreligious.

"**Christianity** is a faith based on the life, teachings, death, and resurrection of Jesus,"[21] and is the most practiced religion around the world. Christianity started with the birth of Jesus Christ approximately 2,000 years ago and has evolved considerably into different forms as a result of many internal feuds and divisions. A major separation occurred in 1054 when the Roman Catholic Church split from

**Religion**
Shared set of beliefs, activities, and institutions based on faith in supernatural forces.

**Christianity**
Religion based on the life and teachings of Jesus.

## Religion and Work

The issue of how religion affects work has attracted significant attention, but only recently have the important effects of religion on work been demonstrated. A study by Parboteeah, Hoegl, and Cullen examined the effects of religion on work obligations—that is, the degree to which individuals believe they have a societal duty to work. The researchers argued that all religions view work as an important obligation and, more importantly, as having religious dimensions. Analysis of a large-scale set of data from 45 countries showed that the belief in God and the behavioral aspects of religion, such as church attendance, have positive effects on work obligations. Multinationals may therefore want to weigh religion in determining how their employees view work.

In another study, Parboteeah and colleagues looked at how four specific religions (Buddhism, Christianity, Hinduism, and Islam) influence work values. Employees typically have preferences for what they want from their work. Some prefer extrinsic work values, such as income and job security, while others prefer intrinsic work values, such as autonomy and the use of initiative at work. Analysis of another large-scale data set from 40 countries showed that all

four religions have positive influences on intrinsic work values. Furthermore, the results show that three of the four religions (Christianity excluded) have positive effects on extrinsic work values.

However, religion has an impact on many other issues related to how multinationals conduct their operations in different societies. Consider the study by McGuire, Omer, and Sharp (2012). These researchers argued that companies in countries that have high religious norms should also have lower incidences of financial reporting irregularities because religiosity is often linked with reduced acceptance of unethical business practices. Their study does indeed show that companies located in more religious environments tend to report fewer financial irregularities.

*Sources: Based on McGuire, S. T., T. C. Omer, and N. Y. Sharp. 2012. "The impact of religion on financial reporting irregularities."* The Accounting Review, *87(2), 645–673; Parboteeah, K. P., Y. Paik, and J. B. Cullen. 2009. "Religious groups and work values."* International Journal of Cross Cultural Management, *9(1): 51–67; Parboteeah, K. P., M. Hoegl, and J. B. Cullen. 2009. "Religious dimensions and work obligations: A country institutional profile approach."* Human Relations, *62(1): 119–148.*

**EXHIBIT 3.6**    Religion by Percentage of World Population and Number of Followers

| Religion | Percentage of World Population Following Religion (%) | Number of Followers (000) |
|---|---|---|
| Christians | 33.60 | 1,900,174 |
| Nonreligious | 20.50 | 1,163,189 |
| Muslims | 18.25 | 1,033,453 |
| Hindus | 13.50 | 764,000 |
| Others | 7.33 | 414,725 |
| Buddhists | 5.99 | 338,621 |
| Sikhs | 0.36 | 20,204 |
| Jews | 0.24 | 13,451 |
| Confucians | 0.10 | 6,334 |
| Jains | 0.07 | 3,951 |
| Shintoists | 0.06 | 3,387 |

*Sources: Adapted from Fisher, Mary P. 2010.* Living Religions, *8th ed. Upper Saddle River, NJ: Prentice-Hall.*

the Eastern Orthodox Church. The majority of Orthodox Christians today live in Russia, Serbia, Bulgaria, Romania, Albania, Poland, and the Czech Republic, and most Roman Catholics live in Western Europe and the Americas. In 1517, another major division occurred in Christian history. Disillusioned with the Roman Catholic Church's authority and practices, Martin Luther, a German monk and priest, initiated different interpretations of the Bible that led to the formation of the Protestant branch of Christianity.

Despite the many divisions within Christianity, all Christians share the belief that Jesus is the incarnation of God who was sent to cleanse the sinfulness of humanity. Jesus is often associated with love, and allows humans to connect with God through penance, confession of sins, self-discipline, and purification.

The impact of Protestantism on the development of capitalism is seen as major evidence of the link between religion and economic structuring of societies. Because Protestantism emphasized wealth and hard work for the glory of God, it allowed the focus on goals related to economic development and wealth accumulation. In contrast, Catholics were more likely to question the pursuit and accumulation of wealth. This difference explains the sustained development of capitalism in Western Protestant societies.

In general, Christians agree "on the value and dignity of human life, labor, and happiness."[22] There is a general support for the freedom to accumulate wealth and possessions. However, human greed and selfishness are viewed with contempt, and attempts are made to ensure equality of opportunity and fairness for the less fortunate. Additionally, Christianity, through the Ten Commandments, provides the basis for what are considered ethical behaviors. Although not all individuals follow these commandments, they are nevertheless seen as norms guiding behaviors with respect to such things as theft ("You shall not steal"), murder ("You shall not kill"), and protection of private property ("You shall not covet your neighbor's house or anything that is his"). Multinational companies therefore have access to environments that are conducive to conducting business.

The essence of Islam, as described in the *Qur'an*, is submission to the will of Allah (God). Islam can be traced back to Muhammad, a prophet born in 570 BC. However, unlike the Christian view that the founder Jesus was divine, Muslims do not ascribe divinity to Muhammad. Rather, he is seen as the messenger of Allah's revelations and the last in a line of prophets starting with Adam and continuing through Abraham, Moses and Jesus.[23] Islam is currently the second largest of the world's religions and has adherents in Africa, the Middle East, China, Malaysia, and the Far East. It continues to grow rapidly in many countries, especially in Europe.

**Islam**
Religion based on the submission of the will to Allah (God).

Muslim society is heavily influenced by Islamic standards and norms. Islam provides encompassing guidance in all spheres of life, both social and economic. Muslims believe that those who serve Allah and have faith in the reality and oneness of Allah will go to paradise in the afterlife.[24] Muslims also believe that Allah wants them to live according to the *Shari'ah* (Law). The *Shari'ah* requires Muslims to follow five pillars: confession, prayer, alms giving, fasting, and pilgrimage to Mecca.[25]

These pillars have important implications for multinational strategic management. First, a multinational company operating in a Muslim country has to accommodate the Muslim's need to pray five times a day. Muslims need to pray in the early morning, noon, midafternoon, sunset, and evening.[26] Furthermore, during Ramadan, a month of fasting, multinational companies face some decline in productivity. During that month, Muslims are not allowed to eat, drink, smoke, or even take medicines from dawn until dusk. Therefore, multinational managers are advised to take steps to ensure that business activities are not disrupted. The month is also considered very spiritual, and multinational companies should expect their workers to be more concerned with sacred matters and a heightened spiritual atmosphere.

The alms-giving pillar also has critical implications for multinational strategic management and how Islam views business. In general, the *Qur'an* is supportive of entrepreneurship and the earning of profits through legitimate business activities. The *Qur'an* also allows the accumulation and protection of private property. However, Muslims are naturally concerned with issues of social justice and fairness, and they are likely to condemn the pursuit of profits through the exploitation of others. Multinational companies therefore have to ensure that their business activities are conducted in a socially just manner and that some form of alms giving is practiced. Individual Muslims, as well as organizations, are required to share their accumulated wealth by charitable giving to the poor. This practice is seen as necessary to decrease social inequalities and personal greed. Multinational companies may be well served by participating in such donations.

An important consequence of Islam's condemnation of the exploitation of others is that Muslims may not pay or receive interest. Islam regards the payment or acceptance of interest as a serious sin. Such beliefs are not just ideals but are actually put into practice in many countries, including Pakistan. In such countries, governments have instituted financial laws declaring interest illegal. For a multinational company operating in a Muslim country, the prohibition of interest presents a serious challenge. However, many Muslim societies have been working in profit-sharing plans to avoid the payment or receipt of interest. For instance, if a multinational company borrows money from a bank in a Muslim country, it should expect to be asked to share the profits from the investment as an alternative to paying interest. Multinational companies should thus be prepared to formulate creative but acceptable ways to manage their finances.

Multinational firms are likely to be presented with significant opportunities in Muslim countries in years to come. For instance, it has been estimated that the Middle East alone has approximately 300 infrastructure projects representing $45–$60 billion of possible private investment,[27] and it is likely that multinational companies will have to provide significant financing for these projects. The challenges of financial exchanges, therefore, will become more urgent and will have to be dealt with. Consider the next Comparative Management Brief on the challenges of Islamic laws.

A final multinational strategic management implication of Islam pertains to the role of women in Muslim countries. Although the *Qur'an* puts men and women on an equal footing as individuals, the guidelines for the roles of men and women differ.[28] While the man's role is to work and support the family, the woman's role is to provide care and stability to the family in the home. Not surprisingly, many Muslim societies are strictly divided by gender. Multinational companies must be aware of the effects of their business actions related to gender roles. For instance, given the dominance of the male sector, it is not advisable for multinational companies to post women in executive positions in Muslim countries. Additionally, human resource management practices need to take into consideration the limited role of women in such societies. Although there has been much progress in many Muslim societies regarding gender equality, respecting local gender norms is clearly important for any multinational firm operating in a Muslim country.

**Hinduism** is a broad and inclusive religion encompassing individuals who respect and accept the ancient traditions of India, "especially the Vedic scriptures and the social class structure with its special respect for *Brahmans* (the priestly class)."[29] Unlike Christianity and Islam, Hinduism has no specific founder, and

**Hinduism**
Acceptance of the ancient traditions of India that are based on the Vedic scriptures.

## Comparative Management **Brief**

### Islamic and Financial Operations

In an effort to revitalize its economy after the Gulf War, the Kuwaiti government embarked on a strategy of attracting foreign investment to make up for the deficits incurred in reconstruction. Kuwait is an Islamic society and observes the *Shari'ah,* or religious law, which prohibits receiving or paying interest. However, although interest cannot be paid, this does not necessarily mean that Islam prevents the lender to earn a return on his or her investment. Rather than specify an interest rate, the *Shari'ah* basically suggests that the lender needs to share both the profits and the loss that the borrower incurs. Thus, the financier is still allowed to earn profits.

In addition to this well-known financial requirement of Islam, the *Shari'ah* also prohibits uncertainty and gambling, and it stresses honesty in business and monetary transactions. As a consequence, the contents of all contracts must be spelled out in great detail. Additionally, because futures and options are speculative in natures, they are regarded as gambling and are therefore illegal. Such prohibitions represent significant challenges for international capital providers.

The EQUATE (Ethylene Products from Kuwait) project was a joint venture between Petrochemical Industries Company, a subsidiary of the Kuwaiti national oil company, and Union Carbide Corporation. The joint venture, formed to finance the construction and operation of a $2 billion petrochemical plant, faced a number of significant financing challenges. For instance, the venture participants wanted part of the financing to come from Islamic banks in an effort to involve Kuwaiti citizens and investors. However, the Islamic banks could not loan the money directly; they had to be involved indirectly in the venture so that they could share in the profits instead of earning interest. Eventually, the Islamic banks purchased assets and leased them to the joint venture.

Compared to a regular loan, these financial arrangements present significant challenges. With the ownership of assets in a company comes ownership risk. For instance, how much should the Islamic banks be liable for if the plant causes serious environmental damage? This problem was addressed by placing the assets in a special-purpose vehicle with limited liability. Another challenge pertained to the leasing aspect of the financial arrangement: the Islamic banks owned the assets while the venture was the actual user. As with any lease agreement, the Islamic banks are responsible for maintaining the assets of the plant and for insuring against losses that may occur should the assets break down. A major expectation for the venture was therefore to ensure that the Islamic banks took such insurance and maintenance precautions. Another challenge dealt with the application of the law in the event of default: Should Islamic or other law apply to the contract? Additionally, the Islamic investors were at a great disadvantage if payments were late because of their inability to collect penalty interest, which would have to be donated to charities. Finally, in the event of a bankruptcy, the Islamic bank still owned the assets and would be able to claim them from the venture. However, such actions would destroy the ongoing value of the project and reduce any chance of recovery.

*Sources: Based on Al-Kashif, A. M. 2009. "Shari'ah's normative framework as to financial crime and abuse." Journal of Financial Crime, 16(1): 86–98; Esty, Benjamin C. 2000. "The EQUATE project: An introduction to Islamic project finance." Journal of Project Finance, 5, 7–20; Shaj, S. F., M. W. Raza, and M. R. Khurshid. 2012. "Islamic bank controversies and challenges." Interdisciplinary Journal of Contemporary Research in Business, 3(10), 1018–1026.*

Hindus place no special significance on historical events or on a specific sequence of events. Rather, Hinduism, through the Vedic scriptures, is seen as timeless and eternal. Currently about 760 million Hindus reside in India, Malaysia, Nepal, Suriname, and Sri Lanka. Many Hindus outside of India typically have ancestors from India.

The quest for *Brahman* is the ultimate goal for most Hindus. *Brahman* refers to the ultimate reality and truth, the "sacred power that pervades and maintains all things."[30] To discover *Brahman,* one needs to look into one's *atma,* or soul. Hinduism generally believes in the reincarnation of the *atma* based on one's *karma,* or the effects of one's past actions. Hindus believe that whoever tries hard to live life according to the principles of *dharma,* or principles of righteousness and moral order, will be reincarnated in successively more favorable *atmas* until one reaches *Brahman.*

One aspect of Hinduism that is most likely to have implications for multinational companies in India is the caste system, which is the ordering of Indian society into four occupational groups. The highest caste includes the priests, followed by the kings and warriors, and then merchants and farmers. The fourth caste includes the manual laborers and artisans. Although the caste system is illegal in India, its original purpose was to create a higher law that would subordinate individual interests to the collective good. The system remains a dominant feature of life in India today, and multinational companies operating in India have to be aware of it. For instance, having a member of a lower caste supervise higher-caste individuals can be problematic. Additionally, members of lower castes may face promotion ceilings in organizations because of their caste membership. Finally, at meetings, it is important to consider how the various castes interact.

Consider the experience of FoodWorld supermarket chains in India.[31] While opening new retail supermarkets in India, the firm had to hire and train managers. However, a retail manager is not seen as having a high social status in India, and only members of the lower caste were willing to take the jobs. Given the pervasiveness of the caste system in India, these workers felt that they had significantly lower status. Training programs therefore had to be designed to emphasize confidence in the workers in order to get them to perform their duties adequately. Another major challenge was to find ways to alleviate the concerns of traditional Indian customers who may not want to make contact with someone from a lower caste.

Some, however, argue that the caste system is slowly dying. The next Case in Point provides evidence of fundamental changes in Indian society and how Indians view the caste system.

Hinduism's teachings and philosophies have other implications for multinational strategic management. The religion provides clear guidelines on ethical behaviors, among which performing one's duty and respect for one's parents are prominent. In connection with the caste system, most people have clearly defined paths that they should follow. Multinational companies would be well advised to take such guidelines into consideration. The Hindu's respect for parents also has business implications. Multinationals will often find that families run Indian businesses and that the elder males in the business typically make the major decisions. Therefore, multinational companies should be ready to accept parental influence even when dealing with younger family members. Finally, Hindus believe that they should aim for four goals in life: spiritual achievement, material prosperity, pleasure, and liberation, although the aims vary depending on the stage of life.[32] Nevertheless, multinational firms should be aware that Hinduism does not condemn

### CASE IN POINT

## Is the Caste System Dying?

The caste system was devised around 2000 years ago to clearly define division of labor into four castes: priests (brahmins), warriors (kshatryias), businesspeople (vaishyas), and workers (sudras). This mandated division has endured over the centuries and has resulted in significant discriminatory practices. However, the silver lining for multinationals is that most Indian enterprises belong to the vaishyas. Centuries of mandated divisions of labor have meant that the vaishyas have been able to hone their business skills and multinationals therefore deal with well-established companies tightly linked in networks.

Despite the endurance of the caste system, more recent evidence suggests that the demise of this discriminatory system may be on the horizon. Consider the following example. The villagers of Seetanagaram were tired of their water pumps breaking down. Despite their complaints to local officials, the pumps were seldom repaired. The women of the village would then have to walk for two hours to get water from the Sarada River, and the water would often make them sick. Things changed when Mr. Rao, a 23-year-old resident of Seetanagaram, was sent to attend the pump repair training program offered by a British charity, Water Aid. After he attended the training, his services were much in demand. However, Mr. Rao is a member of the *Dalit*, or untouchable caste, a fifth class below the other four castes. Furthermore,

Seetanagaram is a very segregated village, where the upper castes live in a separate colony and exclude the *Dalits* even from participation in marriages and festivals. At first, upper-caste members were reluctant to interact with the *Dalits*. However, faced with the possibility of nonfunctioning pumps, the upper castes gradually accepted the idea of a *Dalit* helping them fix the pumps. Such programs, like Water Aid's efforts to train 490 lower-caste villagers, are slowly eroding caste-based prejudice.

The political environment also shows some evidence that the caste system is slowly dying. India has extended quotas in various occupations to ensure that the lower castes get fair representation. Indian companies are also implementing voluntary plans to increase the numbers of lower castes in the workforce. Some companies are thinking about offering better educational and training opportunities, while others are investigating coaching classes to encourage lower castes to achieve higher education. The Indian government is also offering tax breaks for companies offering employment to lower-caste people in poor areas.

*Sources: Based on* Economist. *2006. "Asia: Caste and cash," April 29, 67; Harding, Luke. 2002. "Indian villagers given a taste of equality: Lower-caste Dalits trained to fix pumps gain clean water and modicum of respect." Guardian, December 7, 20; Rao, A. 2012. Managing diversity: Impact of religion in the Indian workplace.* Journal of World Business, *47, 232–239.*

the pursuit of material possessions; they can generally expect an environment that is conducive to business and wealth accumulation.

**Buddhism** is the broad and multifaceted religious tradition that focuses primarily on the reality of worldly suffering and on the ways in which all beings can be freed from it. Gautama Buddha, the founder of Buddhism, was born as a prince in the sixth century BCE in India. Buddhist accounts of his life suggest that his father tried to protect him from seeing suffering to prepare him to be a king. Buddha was, however, dissatisfied with the impermanence of life, and, when he turned 29, he abandoned all riches to become "a wandering ascetic, searching for truth."[33] Today, Buddhism is popular in Europe and the United States, although most of its followers are found in countries such as Cambodia, China, Japan, Korea, Laos, Sri Lanka, and Thailand.

The essence of Buddhism is that craving and desires inevitably produce suffering. It is, however, possible to reach a state where there is no longer any suffering. Buddha proposed that, to remove suffering, one had to follow the Eightfold Path

**Buddhism**
Religious tradition that focuses primarily on the reality of world suffering and the ways in which all beings can be freed from suffering.

of right understanding, right intention, right speech, right action, right livelihood, right effort, right mindfulness, and right concentration. Buddhists also believe that the way to end suffering is to meditate in order to train and soothe the mind and ultimately reach enlightenment, or *Nirvana.*

Nanayakkara's interpretations of Buddha's teachings suggest that Buddha saw poverty as the major reason for the decline of ethical behavior in society.[34] Buddhism therefore prescribed a work ethic that encouraged workers to engage in their best efforts, and that promoted qualities such as taking initiative, persistence, and hard work. Laziness is seen as a very negative quality and is heavily discouraged. Buddhist workers may be expected to have a generally positive view of work, but multinational managers must be aware that Buddhism proposes a work ethic that emphasizes teamwork and ethical means to achieve success. Multinational companies would be well advised to provide environments that take advantage of such values.

Given Buddhism's strong emphasis on compassion and love, some have suggested that Western profit-oriented companies should adopt Buddhist principles. In that context, Gould proposes that employees (and multinational managers) engage in a number of exercises to enhance their ethical orientation to business.[35] For instance, if everyone is considered as a mother, father, brother, or sister, one is more careful about the consequences of one's actions on others. Furthermore, the compassion and love inherent in considering others as close relatives may be helpful in dealing with the employee diversity of multinational companies. Another Buddhist principle is the acknowledgment that the positive action of others makes life possible. Hence, if multinational managers recognize the efforts of their workers through ethical treatment, they are likely to enjoy long-term benefits. Finally, although work is a key component of life, other areas need to be balanced. Multinational companies can respect a balanced work design for their employees.

These descriptions of the four major world religions show that they all have implications for the economic environment.

In this section, we looked at four of the world's main religions and examined the implications for multinational strategic management. In the next section, we look at two final social institutions: education and social inequality. Both are central to most societies, even though their effects on multinational strategic management may not be as great as that of the other three social institutions.

## Education

**Education**
Organized networks of socialization experiences that prepare individuals to act in society.

**Education** consists of the "organized networks of socializing experiences which prepare individuals to act in society," and it "is also a central element in the table of organization of society, constructing competencies and helping create professions and professionals."[36] Education is seen as a critical path to economic development and progress. Most countries want to achieve universal educational enrollment[37] because education enables society to instill the skills, attitudes, behaviors, and knowledge that allow people to demand more and give more to society. Such exchanges enhance the societal expansion and modernization. Consider the following Case in Point.

Education has obvious implications for multinational strategic management. For one thing, educational levels indicate the skill and productivity of workers.[38] The more educated workers are, the more skills they possess, and the more likely they are to contribute to a country's productivity, both in products and services. As you will see in Chapters 11 and 12, educational systems have implications for how labor

## CASE IN POINT

### Education and Entrepreneurship in Nigeria

Countries aim to fulfill various goals through the provision of education. Most of them expect that the educational system will provide members of society with the necessary capabilities and skills to be fully functioning citizens. However, Nigeria is hoping to take a different path through its educational system. The recent economic downturn has had significant impact on the Nigerian economy, whereby employment opportunities have decreased while wages are declining. This issue is exacerbated by the fact that youths in Nigeria are usually the ones who are hit the worst by lack of opportunity. For this group, escaping poverty is very difficult.

One of the ways that people can escape poverty is through starting their own businesses. Experts believe that the introduction of entrepreneurship in the Nigerian

educational curriculum would greatly enhance the ability of Nigerian youths to escape poverty. A recent report discusses introduction of entrepreneurship education starting at the primary levels (basic exposure of students to the importance of entrepreneurship with some emphasis on entrepreneurship skills) and continuing to the tertiary levels (more advanced curriculum focuses on the entrepreneur, the marketing and business plans, legal requirements). The primary aim of such education would be to promote the notion of entrepreneurship as a viable employment option while also cultivating Nigerians' confidence in their ability to start their own new ventures.

*Source: Based on Ejiogu, A. O. and C. A. Nwajiuba. 2012. The need for inclusion of entrepreneurship in Nigerian school curricula.* Thunderbird International Business Review, 54(1), 7–13.

force issues are approached and how policies are implemented. Educational systems determine the nature of the workforce, and having an abundant supply of well-educated individuals allows countries to facilitate the absorption of technology from developed countries. Multinational companies can thus gauge the educational levels of various countries to determine what to expect from workers. Specifically, multinational companies can look at the mean years of education or educational attainment scores to get an idea of the human-capital potential in a society. To estimate the availability of service-oriented multinationals, multinational companies can look at the percentage of a population enrolled in tertiary education. Exhibit 3.7 shows, for a selected number of countries, the percentages of individuals within the relevant age groups enrolled in tertiary education. The scores reported in Exhibit 3.7 give a very rough estimate of educational potential.

Nevertheless, the focus of education varies widely. As you will see in Chapter 11, some societal educational systems value only academic education, while others, like that of Germany, strike a balance between the academic and vocational components of the workforce. Multinational companies may therefore be interested in the skills and experience to be gained from a country's educational system by considering the test scores of students on internationally comparable tests. For instance, the test scores on mathematics and science, as conducted by the International Evaluation of Educational Achievement and International Assessment of Educational Progress, provide a good idea of the quality of a workforce and the educational system's preference for specific areas. Furthermore, if a multinational company is engaged in high-level R&D, it may find that locating in countries with high research and development may be necessary. Exhibit 3.8 shows the percentage of GDP that goes to research and development in selected countries.

As Exhibit 3.8 shows, an important issue is the extent to which educational systems actually encourage students to be innovative and creative. Many Asian societies have

**EXHIBIT 3.7**   Tertiary Enrollment as Percentage of Relevant Age Group (%)

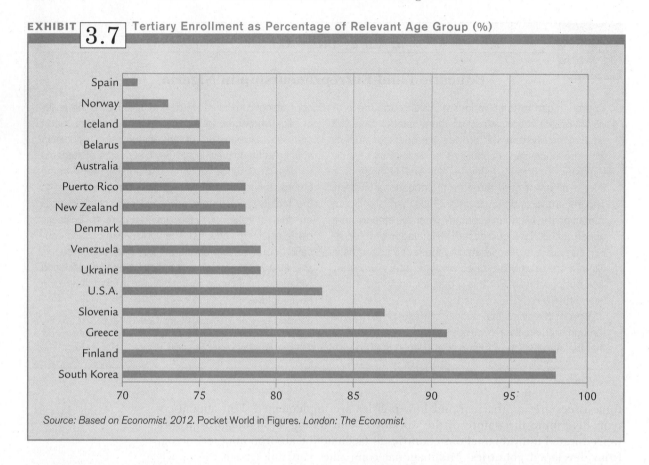

Source: Based on Economist. 2012. Pocket World in Figures. *London: The Economist.*

**EXHIBIT 3.8**   Total Expenditures on R&D as Percentage of GDP (%)

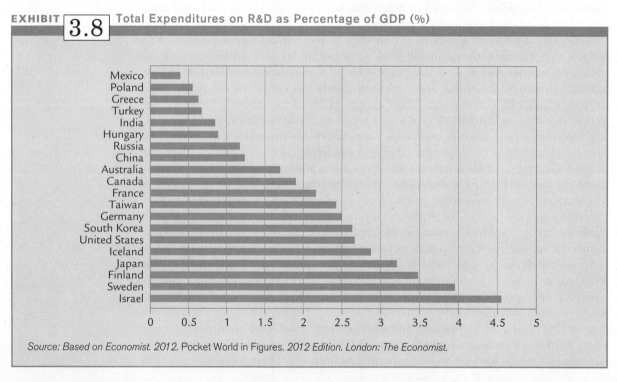

Source: Based on Economist. 2012. Pocket World in Figures. *2012 Edition. London: The Economist.*

### Research and Development in Asia

China is currently struggling with efforts to redesign its educational system. For decades, its system was based on rote learning; both parents and teachers would encourage students to memorize very large amounts of information and cram for extremely competitive examinations. However, current critics argue that the system stifles creativity and is producing a very unhappy student force. A survey conducted in 2002 found that about 50 percent of senior secondary students and first-year university students had actually considered committing suicide as a way to cope with the difficulties associated with being a student.

The nature of the changes has been to reformulate textbooks to make them more interesting, integrating practical situations with theoretical explanations. Instead of merely memorizing facts, students are encouraged to see how facts relate to solutions to practical problems. Students are also encouraged to be imaginative and to view texts as the foundation for learning rather than as sacred books.

These reforms, however, cost money, and many schools are having difficulty implementing them.

Some also argue that, as long as students have to take nearly impossible entrance examinations to secondary and tertiary schools based on memorization, parents will continue to pressure their children in the old way.

Despite these difficulties, the future looks bright for Asian nations. Observations show that research and development in countries like China and South Korea has increased substantially. For example, Samsung spent more on R&D in 2007 than IBM. Corporate spending on R&D in China grew 23 percent between 2001 and 2006, while it grew only 1–2 percent in Europe and the United States. Other statistics show that Taiwan has more high-tech researchers than the United Kingdom. Furthermore, recent data show that the top five countries granted patents per resident included four Asian nations (Japan, South Korea, China, and Taiwan) in addition to the United States.

*Sources: Based on* Economist. *2012. Pocket World in Figures. 2012 Edition. London: The Economist.* Economist. *2009. "Rising in the East," January 3, 47;* Economist. *2003. "Roll over, Confucius," January 25, 40–41.*

been grappling with the redesign of educational systems that are extremely competitive at the secondary level but that rely heavily on rote learning. Nevertheless, some of these societies have been extremely successful in research and development. Consider the Case in Point, which shows that, in many Asian societies, students may go through extreme hardship to succeed. Multinational companies have to be aware that their workers have gone through schooling experiences based sometimes on rote memorization. However, the evidence also suggests that Asia will play a key role in the future with regard to innovation.

This section has explained that education has important effects on how societies are structured economically. In the next and final section, we look at social inequality.

## Social Inequality

**Social inequality** is the degree to which people have privileged access to resources and positions within societies.[39] In high-social-inequality societies, a few individuals have the ability to control and use important resources. This access to resources also enables the select few to use this power to gain access to even more power and in turn to use it to perpetuate inequality. Additionally, the level of inequality is typically taken for granted by people, as various socialization agents, such as schools and parents, tend to teach their children to justify such social stratification.

**Social inequality**
Degree to which people have privileged access to resources and positions within societies.

Social inequality has important implications for multinational management. As you will see in the next chapter on international ethics, multinational companies are subject to significant criticism for their operations in countries with high social inequalities. Many firms endure negative publicity for paying low wages or using child labor, and the high levels of social inequality only magnify the publicity. As a result, many multinational companies are realizing that it is sometimes in their interests to be socially active to mitigate social inequalities. Consider the following Case in Point, which considers social inequality from a gender perspective.

As the Case in Point implies, social inequality can have important implications for location decisions. Many multinational companies now actively avoid countries with high inequalities to prevent potential negative publicity. As we will see in Chapter 4, many key ethical issues arise in countries with high levels of social inequality. For that reason, multinational companies can consider the GINI index as an indicator of the degree of social inequality. The GINI index measures the degree to which people's income deviates from a perfectly equal income distribution. Exhibit 3.9 shows GINI indices for selected countries.

## CASE IN POINT

### Gender Inequality and Chiquita Bananas

Multinational companies involved in trading bananas have been under intense pressure to improve the labor conditions of both their workers and their suppliers' workers. Chiquita, for example, has developed a comprehensive corporate social responsibility policy. A major component of this policy is a voluntary code of conduct, which both Chiquita and its independent producers must implement. However, a survey of Nicaraguan women banana workers revealed that the code of conduct has not made much difference in their lives.

Why has the code been less effective for Nicaraguan women and women in other countries? Prieto-Carron argues that, among other factors, structural gender inequalities have mitigated the effectiveness of such codes. The banana industry employs approximately 482,000 women in countries such as Guatemala, Honduras, Nicaragua, Colombia, and Ecuador. However, most of these women are involved in very low-paying, high-hour packing jobs. They face significant inequalities compared to their male counterparts. Additionally, they are employed in a very seasonal industry, and many more women workers are usually available to perform these jobs. Coupled with a social context where domestic violence and the negative perception of women are common, these inequalities have resulted in women workers facing much harder working conditions than men.

What can Chiquita do to reduce gender inequalities? Most experts agree that improving the conditions of women is a challenging task. However, local governments and companies can work to provide equal pay for equal work. Furthermore, gender awareness training may be useful to encourage male workers to change their perception of female counterparts. Additionally, more female supervisors can be hired to reduce cases of sexual harassment, and systems can be implemented so that women can safely report incidents and violators can be sanctioned. Finally, companies can be proactive and work to provide a better environment for maternity rights.

However, it is important to note that even governmental institutions are taking measures to reduce the effects of social inequalities on individuals. Consider that many of the research initiatives of the European Union are in the areas of poverty alleviation. Programs such as SAMPLE and GUSTO are both initiatives targeted at better understanding of social inequality in Europe and finding ways to reduce such inequality.

*Sources: Based on Harkiolakis, N., D. Prinia, and L. Mourad. 2012. Research initiatives of the European Union in the areas of sustainability, entrepreneurship, and poverty alleviation. Thunderbird International Business Review, 54(1), 73–78; Prieto-Carron, Marina. 2006. "Corporate social responsibility in Latin America." Journal of Corporate Citizenship, 21, 85–94.*

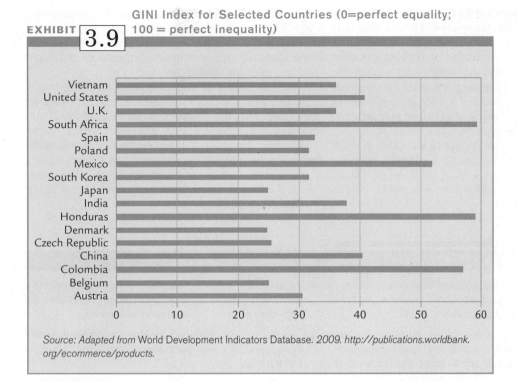

EXHIBIT   3.9

GINI Index for Selected Countries (0=perfect equality; 100 = perfect inequality)

Source: Adapted from World Development Indicators Database. 2009. http://publications.worldbank. org/ecommerce/products.

Few cross-cultural studies have examined the effect of social inequality on work-related variables. However, in an innovative study of 30,270 individuals from 26 nations, Parboteeah and Cullen showed that social inequality negatively impacts the degree to which people are attached to work.[40] Social inequality provides job opportunities only to some highly placed individuals. Furthermore, high levels of social inequality may result in more demoralized workers who are suspicious of their "exploiters." It is therefore less likely that people in high-social-inequality societies will see work as more important in their lives. In fact, high levels of social inequality likely result in a less-favorable work environment.

This study clearly shows the importance of social inequality and its potential impact on multinational companies.

## Summary and Conclusions

To get a full understanding of any society, it is essential to understand both national culture and institutional context. We first looked at a model to examine how national culture and social institution combine to form the national context that influences the business culture of a society. The chapter then complemented Chapter 2 by providing more specific background information on four important social institutions and their implications both for companies and the people they employ.

First, the chapter defined social institutions and provided an explanation of how social institutions affect individuals and organizations. It then described economic systems, especially their extreme types. It was shown that in societies arranged along socialist systems, the government owns the systems of production, whereas in capitalist systems private individuals make production decisions. Between these two extremes is the mixed economy. Two major implications of economic systems for multinational strategic management were then discussed: the extent of governmental intervention in the business arena and the transition from a socialist economy to a free-market economy.

The institutional context includes industrialization. In that context, the chapter discussed preindustrial, industrial, and postindustrial societies and their implications for multinational strategic management. Preindustrial societies are typically less developed and thus present significant challenges for multinational companies. In contrast, industrial societies tend to be more economically advanced, with the manufacturing sector dominating the economic environment. Finally, in the postindustrial society, services become the dominant sector, and people start shifting from achievement values to more quality-of-life values.

Religion is also an important social institution in most societies. We discussed four of the major religions around the world: Christianity, Islam, Hinduism, and Buddhism. The chapter also outlined the important business implications for each.

Educational systems have important implications regarding the available skills and experiences of the workforce in a society. However, other aspects of educational systems, such as emphasis on sciences and mathematics, were also discussed.

Finally, we saw that social inequality can have important implications for multinational companies. The chapter concluded with the theme that social institutional differences are important now and will continue to be important in the future. We argued that successful multinational managers are the ones who can properly assess the institutional context of the society in which they operate and who can design work environments that fit the institutional context.

## Discussion Questions

1. What are the three major types of economic systems? What are the effects of economic systems on how organizations are structured in societies?

2. What are some implications of the market transition that many formerly communist societies are experiencing? What are some major challenges that companies are facing in such societies as they try to motivate workers?

3. Why has Africa lagged behind other countries in economic development? What can multinational companies do to encourage economic progress on that continent?

4. What are the major philosophies of each of the world's four major religions? Pick two religions and discuss how they affect the business environment.

5. Discuss specific Buddhist principles and how they can be applied to help multinational managers become more ethical.

6. How does a country's educational system influence its business environment?

7. What is social inequality? What important areas of business can social inequality impact?

## Multinational Management **Internet Exercise**

### Index of Economic Freedom

1. Go to the Heritage Foundation website (http://www.heritage.org) and search for the latest Index of Economic Freedom report.

2. What is economic freedom? Why is economic freedom so critical to multinationals?

3. Discuss how the Index of Economic Freedom was computed. What are the 10 factors the foundation uses to create the index?

4. Which countries figure on the top 10 list of the Index of Economic Freedom? Which countries are in the bottom 10 list?

## Multinational Management **Skill Builder**

### A Briefing Paper

You have just been informed that your company has agreed to a joint venture with a company in the Czech Republic. You not only will provide new technology to manufacture light bulbs but also will have to provide your managerial expertise to manage and motivate workers. Your understanding is that you will take over the

managerial aspects of the joint venture at the beginning, and gradually train Czechs in management positions.

Using the World Wide Web and the library, research general issues such as Czech culture, Czech workers' attitudes toward work, the appropriateness for Czech partners of the Western-based motivational practices typically used in your company, and the managerial potential of

Czech workers. Identify key challenges you will face as you make the merger work. Discuss some potential solutions to these challenges. What are some challenges you may face when you try to train Czechs to become managers? Discuss some of the training methods you may want to use. Present your findings to the class.

## *Endnotes*

[1] Schooler, C. 1996. "Cultural and socio-cultural explanations of cross-national psychological differences." *Annual Review of Sociology,* 22, 323–319.

[2] Turner, J. H. 1997. *The Institutional Order.* New York: Addison-Wesley, 6.

[3] Olsen, M. E. 1991. *Societal Dynamics: Exploring Macrosociology.* Englewood Cliffs, NJ: Prentice-Hall, 35.

[4] Tsoukas, Haradimos. 1994. "Socio-economic systems and organizational management: An institutional perspective on the socialist firm." *Organization Studies,* 15, 21–45.

[5] Ibid.

[6] Healey, Nigel M. 1996. "Economic transformation in Central and Eastern Europe and the commonwealth of independent states: An interim report." *Contemporary Review,* 268, 229–236.

[7] Pearce, Jones L. 2001. *Organization and Management in the Embrace of Government.* Mahwah, NJ: Lawrence Erlbaum Associates.

[8] Walder, A. G. 1986. *Communist Neo-Traditionalism.* Berkeley: University of California Press.

[9] Turner, *The Institutional Order.*

[10] Blau, Peter, and Otis Duncan. 1967. *The American Occupational Structure.* Hoboken, NJ: Wiley.

[11] Inglehart, Ronald, Miguel Basanez, and Alejandro Moreno. 1998. *Human Values and Beliefs: A Cross-Cultural Sourcebook.* Ann Arbor: University of Michigan Press.

[12] Gereffi, Garry, and Donald L. Wyman. 1990. *Manufacturing Miracles: Paths of Industrialization in Latin America and East Asia.* Princeton: Princeton University Press.

[13] Kuruvilla, Sarosh. 1996. "Linkages between industrialization strategies and industrial relations/human resource policies: Singapore, Malaysia, the Philippines, and India." *Industrial and Labor Relations Review,* 49, 635–657.

[14] Ibid., 652.

[15] Bell, Daniel. 1973. *The Coming of Postindustrial Society.* New York: Basic Books.

[16] Stark, Rodney, and William S. Bainbridge. 1985. *The Future of Religion.* Berkeley: University of California Press.

[17] Iannaconne, Laurence R. 1998. "Introduction to the economics of religion." *Journal of Economic Literature,* 36, 1465–1496.

[18] Harpaz, Itzhak. 1998. "Cross-national comparison of religious conviction and the meaning of work." *Cross-Cultural Research,* 32, 143–170.

[19] Weber, Max. 1958. *The Protestant Ethic and the Spirit of Capitalism.* Translated by T. Parsons. New York: Scribner's.

[20] Terpstra, V., and K. David. 1991. *The Cultural Environment of International Business.* Cincinnati: South-Western.

[21] Harpaz.

[22] Fisher, Mary P. 1999. *Living Religions,* 7th ed. Upper Saddle River, NJ: Prentice Hall 273.

[23] Ludwig, Theodore M. 2001. *The Sacred Paths,* 3rd ed. Upper Saddle River, NJ: Prentice Hall, 425.

[24] Fisher.

[25] Ibid.

[26] Ludwig.

[27] Esty, Benjamin C. 2000. "The EQUATE project: An introduction to Islamic project finance." *Journal of Project Finance,* 5, 7–20.

[28] Ludwig.

[29] Ibid., 64.

[30] Ibid., 84.

[31] Wylie, David. 1996. "FoodWorld supermarkets in India." In A. A. Thompson and A. J. Strickland, *Strategic Management,* 11th ed. Boston: Irwin/McGraw-Hill.

[32] Ludwig.

[33] Ibid., 117.

[34] Nanayakkara, S. 1992. *Ethics of Material Progress: The Buddhist Attitude.* Colombo, Sri Lanka: The World Fellowship of Buddhist Activities Committee.

[35] Gould, Stephen J. 1995. "The Buddhist perspective on business ethics: Experiential exercises for exploration and practice." *Journal of Business Ethics,* 14, 63–70.

[36] Meyer, John W. 1977. "The effects of education as an institution." *American Journal of Sociology,* 83, 55–77.

[37] Meyer, John W., Francisco O. Ramirez, and Yasemin N. Soysal. 1992. "World expansion of mass education, 1870–1980." *Sociology of Education,* 65, 128–149.

[38] Barro, Robert J., and Jong-Wha Lee. 2000. "International data on educational attainment: Updates and implications." Working Papers, Center for International Development at Harvard University.

[39] Olsen.

[40] Parboteeah, K. Praveen, and John B. Cullen. 2003. "Social institutions and work centrality: Explorations beyond national culture." *Organization Science,* 14(2): 137–148.

CHAPTER CASE

# Google in China[1]

Richard Ivey School of Business
The University of Western Ontario     **IVEY**     Institute for
Entrepreneurship

*Prahar Shah wrote this case under the supervision of Professor Deborah Compeau solely to provide material for class discussion. The authors do not intend to illustrate either effective or ineffective handling of a managerial situation. The authors may have disguised certain names and other identifying information to protect confidentiality.*

*Ivey Management Services prohibits any form of reproduction, storage or transmittal without its written permission. Reproduction of this material is not covered under authorization by any reproduction rights organization. To order copies or request permission to reproduce materials, contact Ivey Publishing, Ivey Management Services, c/o Richard Ivey School of Business, The University of Western Ontario, London, Ontario, Canada, N6A 3K7; phone (519) 661-3208; fax (519) 661-3882; e-mail cases@ivey.uwo.ca.*

In less than 10 years of existence, Google had truly become a global success story. The internet giant had experienced unprecedented growth, wooed highly acclaimed talent from rival Microsoft and other competitors to join the company—including the "father of the internet," Vinton Cerf—and entered new markets across the world at a rapid pace. The company prided itself on its philosophy of "Do No Evil"—something that had served them well while operating in North America. However, in early 2006, they faced an ethical dilemma that put this philosophy to the test. According to some, Google's decision to censor search results in China left their motto "in smithereens."[2] The company faced intense international criticism and a backlash that made them question if their decision had been the right one.

## The Birth of the Search Engine

Throughout the 1990s and into the new millennium, the world had seen the creation of a new "communications superhighway" which changed the way people accessed resources and shared knowledge. Perhaps the fastest-growing and farthest-reaching creation since the telephone, the Internet and the World Wide Web had forever changed the way people communicated and delivered information, products and services without any international boundaries. By 2005, almost 14.6 per cent of the world's population—close to one billion people—accessed it.[3]

During this time, as the web blossomed so did the need for a tool that enabled users to quickly and efficiently search the hundreds and thousands of isolated web-pages available online. Computer engineers and developers all over the world attempted to create a search engine that indexed these websites, and in 1990 the first tool to search the Internet, nicknamed "Archie," was introduced by McGill University student Alan Emtage. The program downloaded directory listings of all the files located on a File Transfer Protocol (FTP) site into a searchable database. Shortly thereafter, Mark McCahill and a team from the University of Minnesota launched "Gopher"—the first search engine that organized and enabled access to plain text files from across the web.[4]

As it became clear that this tool could quickly become a backbone of the Internet, investors and developers began simplifying, streamlining and marketing online search engines. Competition within the industry was intense, and with minimal barriers to entry and minimal capital required to launch a successful search engine, competitive advantage was not easily sustained. Between 1990 and 1997, dozens of Internet search engines were created, including Excite, Galaxy, Yahoo, WebCrawler, Lycos, Infoseek, AltaVista, Inktomi, Overture, AskJeeves and MSN Search. They each had their own algorithm of organizing, ranking and displaying search results and serviced a multitude of users. In 1998, two students at Stanford University—as part of a research project—launched Google, using a new and unique method of inbound links to rank sites.[5]

## Google.Com

Co-founders Larry Page, president of products, and Sergey Brin, president of technology, brought Google to life in September 1998. By 2006, the company had grown to more than 5,000 employees worldwide, with a management team representing some of the most experienced technology professionals in the industry. Dr. Eric Schmidt joined Google as chairman and chief executive officer in 2001 while Vinton Cerf joined in 2005 as Google's vice-president and chief Internet evangelist.[6] While Page, Brin and Schmidt were largely responsible for the company's day-to-day operations and developing sustainable longer-term strategies, Cerf focused primarily on developing new ideas to launch products and find new sources of revenue apart from its search engine business. See Exhibits 1 and 2 for Google Inc.'s 2004 and 2005 financial statements.

## Google's Business Model

Google's search engine used a pay-per-click (PPC) method to earn advertising revenue and provide

**EXHIBIT 1**  Consolidated Statements of Income (in thousands, except per share amounts)

| | Year Ended December 31, | | |
| --- | --- | --- | --- |
| | 2003 | 2004 | 2005 |
| Revenues | $1,465,934 | $3,189,223 | $6,138,560 |
| Costs and expenses: | | | |
| Cost of revenues | 625,854 | 1,457,653 | 2,571,509 |
| Research and development | 91,228 | 225,632 | 483,978 |
| Sales and marketing | 120,328 | 246.300 | 439,741 |
| General and administrative | 56,699 | 139.700 | 335,345 |
| Stock-based compensation[1] | 229,361 | 278,746 | 200,709 |
| Contribution to Google Foundation | — | — | 90,000 |
| Non-recurring portion of settlement of disputes with Yahoo | — | 201,000 | — |
| Total costs and expenses | 1,123,470 | 2,549,031 | 4,121,282 |
| Income from operations | 342,464 | 640,192 | 2,017,278 |
| Interest income and other, net | 4,190 | 10,042 | 124,399 |
| Income before income taxes | 346,654 | 650,234 | 2,141,677 |
| Provision for income taxes | 241,006 | 251,115 | 676,280 |
| Net income | $105,648 | $399,119 | $1,465,397 |
| Net income per share: | | | |
| Basic | $    0.77 | $    2.07 | $    5.31 |
| Diluted | $    0.41 | $    1.46 | $    5.02 |
| Number of shares used in per share calculations: | | | |
| Basic | 137,697 | 193,176 | 275,844 |
| Diluted | 256,638 | 272,781 | 291,874 |

| | Year Ended December 31, | | |
| --- | --- | --- | --- |
| | 2003 | 2004 | 2005 |
| Cost of revenues | $   8,557 | $  11,314 | $   5,579 |
| Research and development | 138,377 | 169,532 | 115,532 |
| Sales and marketing | 44,607 | 49,449 | 28,411 |
| General and administrative | 37,820 | 48,451 | 51,187 |
| | $229,361 | $278,746 | $200,709 |

[1]Stock-based compensation is allocated as follows.
Source: Google Inc. Annual Report 2005.

**EXHIBIT 2**  Consolidated Balance Sheets (in thousands, except par value)

| | December 31, 2004 | December 31, 2005 |
|---|---|---|
| **Assets** | | |
| **Current assets:** | | |
| Cash and cash equivalents | $ 426,873 | $3,877,174 |
| Marketable securities | 1,705,424 | 4,157,073 |
| Accounts receivable, net of allowances of $3,962 and $14,852 | 311,836 | 687,976 |
| Income taxes receivable | 70,509 | – |
| Deferred income taxes, net | 19,463 | 49,341 |
| Prepaid revenue share, expenses and other assets | 159,360 | 229,507 |
| Total current assets | 2,693,465 | 9,001,071 |
| Property and equipment, net | 378,916 | 961,749 |
| Goodwill | 122,818 | 194,900 |
| Intangible assets, net | 71,069 | 82,783 |
| Deferred income taxes, net, non-current | 11,590 | – |
| Prepaid revenue share, expenses and other assets, non-current | 35,493 | 31,310 |
| Total assets | $3,313,351 | $10,271,813 |
| **Liabilities and Stockholders' Equity** | | |
| **Current liabilities:** | | |
| Accounts payable | $32,672 | $115,575 |
| Accrued compensation and benefits | 82,631 | 198,788 |
| Accrued expenses and other current liabilities | 64,111 | 114,377 |
| Accrued revenue share | 122,544 | 215,771 |
| Deferred revenue | 36,508 | 73,099 |
| Income taxes payable | — | 27,774 |
| Current portion of equipment leases | 1,902 | — |
| Total current liabilities | 340,368 | 745,384 |
| Deferred revenue, long-term | 7,443 | 10,468 |
| Liability for stock options exercised early long-term | 5,982 | 2,083 |
| Deferred income taxes, net | — | 35,419 |
| Other long-term liabilities | 30,502 | 59,502 |
| Commitments and contingencies | | |
| **Stockholders' equity:** | | |
| Class A and Class B common stock, $0.001 per value: 9,000,000 shares authorized at December 31, 2004 and December 31, 2005, 266,917, and 293,027 shares issued and outstanding, excluding 7,605 and 3,303 shares subject to repurchase | 267 | 293 |
| Additional paid-in capital | 2,582,352 | 7,477,792 |
| Preferred stock-based compensation | (249,470) | (119,015) |
| Accumulated other comprehensive income | 5,436 | 4,019 |
| Retained earnings | 590,471 | 2,055,868 |
| Total stockholders' equity | 2,929,056 | 9,418,957 |
| Total liabilities and stockholders' equity | $ 3,313,351 | $10,271,813 |

*Source: Google, Inc. Annual Report 2005.*

companies with a vehicle to promote their products and services. According to wikipedia:

> Pay-per-click is often used to kick-start website visibility when a new website or page is promoted, and is basically a bidding system for advertisers who pay a fee to the promotion vehicle (search engine or directory) whenever a surfer clicks on their advertisement. The more the customer pays, the higher the bid, and the more highly placed—prominent—the advertisement appears. Advertisers specify the words that should trigger their ads and the maximum amount they are willing to pay per click. When a user searches Google's search engine on www.google.com, ads for relevant words are shown as "sponsored link" on the right side of the screen, and sometimes above the main search results.[7]

The technology Google used to accomplish this was called AdWords. AdWords used a combination of pricing and relevance to place ads. If an ad was clicked through frequently, it would be displayed more prominently. An ad which fell below a threshold clickthrough rate would be deemed not relevant, and thus would be removed from that particular search. The key benefit of Google's approach was its targeting of ads. Ads were served in the places where they would be of most relevance to users, which had the dual effect of minimizing user frustration with advertising and optimizing clickthrough rates for advertisers.

Google's AdSense technology was created based on the success of AdWords. Google recognized a much more vast marketing opportunity and released a system for webmasters and site owners to publish Google advertisements on their websites. Essentially, a website owner could choose to have Google ads served up on its pages using the same process as Google used for its own sites. When users clicked through these ads, Google and the referring site shared the revenue.

## Other Google Products

The AdWords promotional engine had catapulted the company's commercial worth into the multi-billion dollar league and funded development of spin-off search technology such as their desktop search. It had also led to further marketing opportunities for businesses as the search engine giant expanded into such areas as email and map marketing. In 2004, Google launched its first beta version of Google Desktop, a free downloadable application for locating one's personal computer files (including email, work files, web history and instant message chats) using Google-quality search. It also introduced Gmail in 2004, an email application service that received world-wide publicity during its launch. Gmail offered a powerful built-in search function, messages grouped by subject line into conversations and enough free storage to hold years' worth of messages.[8] Using AdSense technology, Gmail was designed to deliver relevant ads adjacent to mail messages, giving recipients a way to act on this information. By early 2006, Google offered a range of products (see Exhibit 3).

## Google in China

On July 19, 2005, Google announced the opening of a product research and development center in China, to be led by renowned computer scientist and industry pioneer Dr. Kai-Fu Lee. Dr. Lee served as the company's first president and hoped to exploit China's thriving economy, excellent universities and multitude of talent to help Google develop new products and expand its international business operations. "The opening of a research and development (R&D) center in China will strengthen Google's efforts in delivering the best search experience to our users and partners worldwide," said Alan Eustace, vice-president of engineering at Google. "Under the leadership of Dr. Lee, with his proven track record of innovation and his passion for technology and research, the Google China R&D center will enable us to develop more innovative products and technologies for millions of users in China and around the world."[9]

One of the company's goals was to revitalize the Google website and offer a search engine catered specifically to the Chinese population. As Andrew McLaughlin, senior policy counsel for Google, explained in January of 2006:

> Google users in China today struggle with a service that, to be blunt, isn't very good. Google.com appears to be down around 10 per cent of the time. Even when users can reach it, the website is slow, and sometimes produces results that when clicked on, stall out the user's browser. Our Google News service is never available; Google Images is accessible only half the time. At Google we work hard to create a great experience for our users, and the level of service we've been able to provide in China is not something we're proud of. This problem could only be resolved by creating a local presence, and this week we did so, by launching our website for the People's Republic of China.[10]

**EXHIBIT** **3**    Selected Google Products

Alerts

— a service which provides emails of news and search results for a particular topic area

Answers

— a service where users can post queries for which they are willing to pay others to do research; the user sets the price they are willing to pay

Blogs

— Google's own blog site is "blogger"
— They also provide a blog search utility

Book & catalog search

— allows users to search the full text of books and to search and browse online catalogs for mail order businesses

Images and Video

— Google's sites for searching pictures on the web and videos

Google Earth & Google Maps

— global maps and driving directions
— also includes the capability to search for various businesses etc. within a map and display the results graphically

Google Scholar

— allows users to search academic papers

Google Groups

— a site to allow users to create mailing lists and discussion groups

Google Desktop Search

— uses Google's search technology to track information on the user's PC

GMail

— Google's mail application

For a complete listing of Google products and services, see http://www.google.ca/intl/en/options/index.html

## Google.cn

The launch of the new website and search engine, Google.cn, enabled the company to create a greater presence in the growing Chinese market and offered a customized region-specific tool with features (such as Chinese-language character inputs) that made the Chinese user experience much simpler. It also sparked the greatest controversy in the company's history. In order to gain the Chinese government's approval and acceptance, it agreed to self-censor and purge any search results of which the government disapproved.

Otherwise, the new website risked being blocked in the same way the previous Google.com was blocked by the Chinese authorities. Google conceded. Type in "Falun Gong" or "Tiananmen Square" on Google.com and thousands of search results will appear; however, when typed into Google.cn all the links will have disappeared. Google will have censored them completely. Google's decision did not go over well in the United States. In February 2006, company executives were called into Congressional hearings and compared to Nazi collaborators. The company's stock fell, and protesters waved placards outside the company's headquarters in Mountain View, California.

## Google's Defense

Google defended its position, insisting that while the decision was a difficult one, it served the greater advantage to the greatest number of people.

*We know that many people are upset about this decision, and frankly, we understand their point of view. This wasn't an easy choice, but in the end, we believe the course of action we've chosen will prove to be the right one.*

*Launching a Google domain that restricts information in any way isn't a step we took lightly. For several years, we've debated whether entering the Chinese market at this point in history could be consistent with our mission and values. Our executives have spent a lot of time in recent months talking with many people, ranging from those who applaud the Chinese government for its embrace of a market economy and its lifting of 400 million people out of poverty to those who disagree with many of the Chinese government's policies, but who wish the best for China and its people. We ultimately reached our decision by asking ourselves which course would most effectively further Google's mission to organize the world's information and make it universally useful and accessible. Or, put simply: how can we provide the greatest access to information to the greatest number of people?*

*Filtering our search results clearly compromises our mission. Failing to offer Google search at all to a fifth of the world's population, however, does so far more severely. Whether our critics agree with our decision or not, due to the severe quality problems faced by users trying to access Google.com from within China, this is precisely the choice we believe we faced. By launching Google.cn and making a major ongoing investment in people and infrastructure within China, we intend to change that.*

*No, we're not going to offer some Google products, such as Gmail or Blogger, on Google.cn until we're comfortable that we can do so in a manner that respects our users' interests in the privacy of their personal communications. And yes, Chinese regulations will require us to remove some sensitive information from our search results. When we do so, we'll disclose this to users, just as we already do in those rare instances where we*

*alter results in order to comply with local laws in France, Germany and the U.S.*

*Obviously, the situation in China is far different than it is in those other countries; while China has made great strides in the past decades, it remains in many ways closed. We aren't happy about what we had to do this week, and we hope that over time everyone in the world will come to enjoy full access to information. But how is that full access most likely to be achieved? We are convinced that the Internet, and its continued development through the efforts of companies like Google, will effectively contribute to openness and prosperity in the world. Our continued engagement with China is the best (perhaps only) way for Google to help bring the tremendous benefits of universal information access to all our users there.*

*We're in this for the long haul. In the years to come, we'll be making significant and growing investments in China. Our launch of Google.cn, though filtered, is a necessary first step toward achieving a productive presence in a rapidly changing country that will be one of the world's most important and dynamic for decades to come. To some people, a hard compromise may not feel as satisfying as a withdrawal on principle, but we believe it's the best way to work toward the results we all desire.[11]*

Dr. Lee, a Chinese citizen, also defended Google's decision to censor the search results for Google.cn, stating that the Chinese students he meets and employs "do not hunger for democracy." He claims that,

*People are actually quite free to talk about the subject (of democracy and human rights in China). I don't think they care that much. I think people would say: "Hey, U.S. democracy, that's a good form of government. Chinese government, good and stable, that's a good form of government. Whatever, as long as I get to go to my favorite web site, see my friends, live happily." Certainly, the idea of personal expression, of speaking out publicly, had become vastly more popular among young Chinese as the Internet had grown and as blogging and online chat had become widespread. But I don't think of this as a political statement at all. I think it's more people finding that they can express themselves and be heard, and they love to keep doing that.[12]*

Google's management team, although publicly supporting their decision, were disturbed nonetheless by the growing anti-censorship campaign targeting Google. Led by groups such as the "Students for a Free Tibet" and Amnesty International, mass public rallies and demonstrations were staged outside Google offices, more than 50,000 letters were sent to Google CEO Eric Schmidt demanding the removal of search filters, and the company received intense negative publicity in the media.[13]

> *The web is a great tool for sharing ideas and freedom of expression. However, efforts to try and control the Internet are growing. People are persecuted and imprisoned simply for criticizing their government, calling for democracy and greater press freedom, or exposing human rights abuses, online.*
>
> *But Internet repression is not just about governments. IT companies have helped build the systems that enable surveillance and censorship to take place. Yahoo! has supplied email users' private data to the Chinese authorities, helping to facilitate cases of wrongful imprisonment. Microsoft and Google have both complied with government demands to actively censor Chinese users of their services.*
>
> *Freedom of expression is a fundamental human right. It is one of the most precious of all rights. We should fight to protect it.[14]*

As the debate continued, Google executives realized that statements such as "We actually did an evil scale and decided that not to serve at all was worse evil"[15] made by Schmidt were not resonating with the public. It wondered what the immediate and longer-term implications of their action would be, and whether they really were staying true to their motto "Don't Be Evil."

## CASE DISCUSSION QUESTIONS

1. What immediate and longer-term issues does Google's censorship decision create?
2. Prior to the launch of Google.cn, what factors should Google have considered in reaching their decision to comply with Chinese government censorship laws?
3. Assess Dr. Schmidt's statement, "We actually did an evil scale and decided that not to serve at all was worse evil." Was Google being evil?

4. Using Thomas Donaldson's *Ethical Algorithm*, assess the censorship issue and determine whether Google could be said to have acted ethically based on this model. Is the Ethical Algorithm model adequate when making ethical decisions outside of a company's home country?
5. It has been said that "[in the U.S. Constitution] the First Amendment does not reflect universal values. There is very little to say in favor of a single global standard of speech." Do you agree/disagree with this statement, and how would you relate it to this case?
6. What should Google do?

## CASE NOTES

[1] This case has been written on the basis of published sources only. Consequently, the interpretation and perspectives presented in this case are not necessarily those of Google Inc. or any of its employees.

[2] "Google move 'black day' for China," http://news.bbc.co.uk/2/hi/technology/4647398.stm, accessed August 2006.

[3] Sergey Brin and Lawrence Page, "The Anatomy of a Large-Scale Hypertextual Web Search Engine," Stanford University. 1998, accessed August 2006.

[4] Ibid.

[5] http://en.wikipedia.org/wiki/Search_engine, accessed August 2006.

[6] "Vint Cerf: Google's New Idea Man," http://www.wired.com/news/business/0,1367,68808,00.html, accessed August 2006.

[7] Ad Words, http://en.wikipedia.org/wiki/AdWords, accessed August 2006.

[8] http://www.google.com/corporate/history.html, accessed August 2006.

[9] http://news.bbc.co.uk/2/hi/technology/4647398.stm, accessed August 2006.

[10] http://googleblog.blogspot.com/2006/01/google-in-china.html, accessed August 2006.

[11] http://googleblog.blogspot.com/2006/01/google-in-china.html, accessed August 2006.

[12] Google—New York Times, http://www.nytimes.com/2006/04/23/magazine/23google.html?ei=5090&en=972002761056363f&ex=1303444800.&adxnnl=1&adxnnlx=1156925160-KvHRNCAA/InAFCXMUlz/+g, accessed August 2006.

[13] http://politics.slashdot.org/politics/06/02/20/0238233.shtml, accessed August 2006.

[14] http://irrepressible.info/about, accessed August 2006.

[15] http://www.rfa.org/english/news/technology/2006/02/01/china_google, accessed August 2006.

# Managing Ethical and Social Responsibility Challenges in Multinational Companies

# 4

## Preview CASE IN POINT

### Unethical Behavior Worldwide

While most societies now expect stronger ethics from their companies, recent evidence suggest that unethical behavior remains common worldwide. Consider the following examples:

- Alibaba.com is China's leading e-commerce platform. Similar to Amazon.com, it brings together buyers and sellers and acts as the online intermediary through which business transactions occur. It is experiencing strong growth and has around 56 million people using its business to business website and about 370 million using its online mall. The company frequently touts its strong commitment to integrity and its passion regarding ethics. However, it was discovered that around 100 of its employees were engaging in fraud. Unlike other online platforms, Alibaba.com does not make money by charging commissions on sales. Rather, it derives its revenues from extras such as fees for gold status. Sellers on the website need to go through an extensive verification process to get the gold status. As early as 2009, it was discovered that around 2300 sellers had used fraudulent credentials, sometimes with the help of Alibaba.com, to gain gold status. This resulted in a large number of buyers dealing with fraudulent companies. In many cases, buyers paid for goods they never received. Alibaba.com now has to work hard to regain credibility among buyers in the Chinese booming e-commerce market.

- Christian Sapsizian, a French citizen and former executive at Alcatel, a well-known French telecommunications firm, was sentenced to 30 months in prison and had to forfeit around $261,500. He pled guilty to bribing senior Costa Rican government officials in exchange for a mobile telephone contract with the Costa Rican state-owned telecommunications company. He paid more than $2.5 million in bribes to various Costa Rican officials. Although Alcatel is not a U.S. company and Sapsizian is not a U.S. citizen, Sapsizian was convicted in a U.S. court because Alcatel is listed on the New York Stock Exchange and his actions violated the Foreign Corrupt Practices Act.

## Learning Objectives
*After reading this chapter you should be able to:*

- Know the definitions of international business ethics and social responsibility.

- Understand some basic principles of ethical philosophy relevant to business ethics.

- Understand how social institutions and national culture affect ethical decision making and management.

- Understand the implications of using ethical relativism and ethical universalism in ethics management.

- Identify the basic principles and consequences of the U.S. Foreign Corrupt Practices Act.

- Understand how international agreements affect international business ethics.

- Understand the differences among economic, legal, and ethical analyses of business problems.

- Develop skills in international decision making with ethical consequences.

- On February 3, 2012, Hanwha Group of South Korea announced that its chairman, Kim Sueng-yeon, was being investigated for embezzlement. Chey Tae-won, chairman of the SK group, was also being investigated for the disappearance of 99 billion won from the company. It is alleged that Chey worked with his brother and used the money to cover a futures trading loss. Both cases involve large companies part of the family-run *chaebol* companies in South Korea. These companies have played an important role in elevating South Korea to one of the most developed countries in the world. Unfortunately, because of poor corporate governance, many of these companies are managed in ways detrimental to small investors. *Chaebols* are known to practice in tunneling, whereby contracts are awarded to other firms owned by family members. These companies also engage in propping, whereby failing units get financial support from sister companies. Such transactions inevitably benefit family insiders at the expense of small investors.

- Satyam, one of India's biggest software and services companies, is now considered India's Enron. For several years, Satyam's founder and chairman, Mr. Raju, was involved in many actions that resulted in fraud amounting to more than $1.47 million. For instance, he inflated profits while reporting cash and reported earning interest that never existed. Furthermore, the company overstated the amount of money it was owed. The pattern of deception finally came to an end when the company tried to buy two other firms owned by members of the family. Shareholders revolted and the deal was aborted. However, the scheme was discovered, leading to major questions for India's corporations to answer.

- Similarly, Siemens, Germany's powerhouse and one of Europe's largest engineering firms, had to face a major bribery scandal. For decades, Siemens had three "cash desks," where employees could bring suitcases to be filled with cash, which was then used to bribe individuals to win contracts. Reportedly, over $850 million was paid to foreign officials to help Siemens win contracts around the world.

*Sources: Based on Chao, L. 2011. "Alibaba starts to repair reputation." Wall Street Journal, February 23, B5; Chao, L. and Lee, Y. 2011. "Alibaba frauds lead to shake-up." Wall Street Journal, February 22, B1; Economist. 2012. "Minority report." February 11, 74; Economist. 2011. "Alibaba and the 2,236 thieves: An online retailing scandal in India." February 26, 73–74; Based on Economist. 2008. "Bavarian baksheesh," December 20, 112–113; Economist. 2009. "India's Enron," January 10, 56–57. Sanyal, R. 2012. "Patterns in international bribery: Violations of the Foreign Corrupt Practices Act." Thunderbird International Business Review, 54(3), 299–309.*

While the business community has been exposed to well-known cases such as Enron, WorldCom, and others, the Preview Case in Point shows that unethical behavior continues to occur regularly worldwide. In fact, the cases only represent a few examples of worldwide multinationals engaging in unethical behaviors. Such unethical activities are usually detrimental to these companies and to the societies they operate in. Multinationals engaging in questionable behaviors receive bad publicity and can lose significant reputation and goodwill. In other cases, multinationals can get sued and suffer losses as they pay fines. Finally, offending companies can also lose customers as they lose trust. As a result, global ethics are likely to remain an extremely critical issue for most multinationals.

This chapter will present an overview of business ethics and build on this information to discuss ethical and social responsibilities unique to multinational management. Managers at all levels face ethical issues every day. For example, "If I fire a poorly performing employee, what will happen to his children?"; "If we can get cheap child labor overseas, and it is legal there, should we use it because our competitors do?"; "Should we refuse to give a bribe to an underpaid government official and lose the contract in favor of our competitor?"; "Should we dump our waste in the river, knowing well that it will pose pollution risks although the dumping is not illegal in this country?"

Why is so much attention being paid to ethical issues in multinational companies? Woods argues that approximately 60,000 multinationals are operating across national borders today but that an overwhelming majority of them and their 500,000 subsidiaries are based in developing countries.[1] Multinational firms have access to vast financial, capital, and human resources, and such access provides power that limits the ability of the developing countries' governments to regulate these companies. In some cases, the governments of developing countries are not willing to regulate because they are competing for foreign investment. Multinationals are therefore being scrutinized for their ability to make the ethical decisions when faced with such power.

In addition to the potential of being exposed for unethical behavior and suffering consequent loss of goodwill and reputation, current research suggests that operating in an ethical manner has many benefits for companies. A recent review of hundreds of studies by van Beurden & Gossling (2008) shows that more-ethical companies enjoy positive effects in many aspects of performance, such as 1) firm financial performance, 2) firm market value, 3) stock market value, 4) stock market returns, and 5) perceived future financial performance. Ethical companies thus enjoy better financial performance. How important is business ethics? Consider the following Case in Point.

## CASE IN POINT

### The Ethisphere Institute

The Ethisphere Institute describes itself as a "leading international think-tank dedicated to the creation, advancement and sharing of best practices in business ethics, corporate social responsibility, anti-corruption and sustainability." On an annual basis, it recognizes an elite list of companies as part of the "World's Most Ethical Companies" award. The company receives nominations from companies worldwide and assesses the Ethics Quotient of these nominees. The Ethics Quotient is derived based on five categories, including the ethics and compliance structure, reputation in the marketplace, strong governance, corporate social responsibility, and the existence of an ethics culture. Once the Ethics Quotient of the nominees is assessed, the Ethisphere Institute then devises a list of the World's Most Ethical Companies.

Why is being listed as among the World's Most Ethical Companies desirable? Testimonials from award winners attest to the importance of being recognized for ethical effort. For instance, Johnson

Controls, a global diversified company that has won the award for six years in a row, sees the honor as a testament to the hard work of the more than 162,000 employees who are committed to ethics on a daily basis. Furthermore, Johnson Controls also understands the importance of a strong ethics to competitive advantage, as its approach to corporate social responsibility has resulted in significant advantages over competitors.

The World's Most Ethical Companies list includes companies located worldwide. Exhibit 4.1 shows the selected companies by industry and their location.

Given the importance of business ethics, this chapter will provide some of the background and skills required to deal with the ethical situations faced by multinational managers.

*Source: Based on http://www.ethisphere.com;* Transportation Business Journal. *2012. "Johnson Controls named one of 'World's Most Ethical Companies' for Sixth consecutive year." April 8, 59.*

| Industry | Company | Country of Origin |
|---|---|---|
| **Agriculture** | Ethical Fruit Company Limited | United Kingdom |
| **Apparel** | Comme Il Faut | Israel |
| **Apparel** | Gap, Inc. | United States |
| **Apparel** | Patagonia | United States |
| **Automotive** | Johnson Controls | United States |
| **Banking** | National Australia Bank | Australia |
| **Banking** | Rabobank | Netherlands |
| **Business Services** | Accenture | Ireland |
| **Computer Software** | Adobe Systems | United States |
| **Computer Software** | Wipro | India |
| **Consumer Electronics** | Electrolux | Sweden |
| **Consumer Electronics** | Texas Instruments | United States |
| **Energy: Oil** | Alyeska Pipeline Service Co. | United States |
| **Energy: Oil** | Statoil | Norway |
| **Health and Beauty** | L'Oreal | France |
| **Health and Beauty** | Shisheido Co. | Japan |
| **Restaurants and Cafes** | Starbucks Coffee Co. | United States |
| **Retail: Food Stores** | Kesko | Finland |
| **Retail: Food Stores** | SONAE | Portugal |
| **Retail: General** | Costco | United States |
| **Transportation and Logistics** | Nippon Yusen Kabuship Kaisha | Japan |
| **Transportation and Logistics** | Panama Canal Authority | Panama |
| **Transportation and Logistics** | UPS | United States |

# What Are International Business Ethics and Social Responsibility?

Before you can understand the ethical dilemmas faced by multinational managers, you need a working definition of business ethics. Most experts consider business ethics as an application of the broader concern for all ethical behavior and reasoning, which pertains to behaviors or actions that affect people and their welfare. A decision by managers to knowingly sell a useful but dangerous product is an ethical decision. Ethics deal with the "shoulds" of life—that is, the rules and values that determine the goals and actions people should follow when dealing with other human beings.[2]

Although economic logic (i.e., making money) dominates business decision making, most business decisions have consequences for people (workers, suppliers, customers, and society). Thus, ethical decision making permeates organizational life. For example, decisions such as those regarding product safety, layoffs, closing or relocating a plant, or the truthfulness of an advertisement have consequences for people. When managers make such decisions, they make decisions with ethical consequences—whether consciously or not.

However, ethical questions seldom have clear or unambiguous answers that all people accept. For example, producing automobiles that are safer than those currently on the market is possible. However, if such vehicles were required by law, they would be extremely expensive (only the rich could drive), they would probably result in smaller automobile production plants (putting people out of work), they would likely require larger engines (increasing oil consumption and pollution), and they would likely reduce profits (violating the ethical responsibilities of the managers to stockholders). So automobile manufacturers always deal with the ethical dilemma of whether a vehicle is sufficiently safe versus sufficiently affordable.

**International business ethics** pertain to the unique ethical problems faced by managers conducting business operations across national boundaries. International business ethics differ from domestic business ethics on two accounts. First, and perhaps most important, international business is more complex because business is conducted cross-nationally. Different cultural values and institutional systems necessarily mean that people may not always agree on how one should behave in a given situation. Expatriate managers may face situations where local business practices violate their culturally based sensibilities or home country laws. Second, very large multinational companies often have powers and assets that equal those of some foreign governments. Managers in these large and powerful multinationals may encounter challenging ethical dilemmas regarding how to use this power.

Closely related to business ethics is the concept of **corporate social responsibility**, which is the idea that businesses have a responsibility to society beyond making profits. Corporate social responsibility means that a company must take into account the welfare of other constituents (e.g., customers, suppliers) in addition to stockholders. While business ethics usually concern the ethical dilemmas faced by managers as individuals, corporate social responsibility is usually associated with the ethical consequences of a company's policies and procedures. Monitoring the working conditions of your suppliers, paying for the education of the children of workers, and donating money to the local community are examples of corporate social responsibility in action. Consider the Emerging Markets Insight below.

**International business ethics**
Unique ethical problems faced by managers conducting business operations across national boundaries.

**Corporate social responsibility**
The idea that businesses have a responsibility to society beyond making profits.

## **Focus** on Emerging Markets

### Infosys and Corporate Social Responsibility

Infosys is one of India's leading software companies. However, although it is headquartered in a country rife with corruption, Infosys decided to follow an ethical path from the day it was created. In a recent interview, the founder of Infosys, N. R. N. Murthy, recounts how he quit his job in a professionally managed software company to form his own company. He invited six colleagues to meet in his apartment in Mumbai. During the meeting, they discussed what they wanted Infosys to be. Some suggested, "India's largest company." However, when it was Murthy's turn, he proposed, "Why don't we aim to be India's most respected company?" Thus, Infosys's dedication and commitment to ethics was born.

The company's approach to its operations is simple. It operates on the C-LIFE value system, which stands for Client focus, Leadership by example, Integrity and transparency, Fairness, and Excellence. These values have guided Infosys from its creation, and it approaches how it deals with each and every stakeholder though the application of these values.

Infosys has also embraced corporate social responsibility. It has created the Infosys Foundation, which contributes a percentage of profits annually to charity. In India, the foundation has helped the poorest, building hospitals and homes and providing educational scholarships to poor children. Infosys has also built libraries in over 15,000 villages while also donating PCs to thousands of schools. Furthermore, Infosys is supporting science and mathematics initiatives in U.S. inner-city schools.

*Source: Based on Raman, A. 2011. "Why don't we try to be India's most respected company?"* Harvard Business Review, *November, 2–7.*

In practice, ethics and social responsibility are not easily distinguished. Usually, procedures and policies in a company regarding social responsibility reflect the ethical values and decisions of the top management team.[3] Furthermore, the ethical and social responsibility issues faced by multinational companies are complex and varied. Exhibit 4.2 identifies some of the stakeholders in a multinational company and shows typical problems that multinational companies face and that affect their stakeholders. As the exhibit shows, multinational companies have both primary and secondary stakeholders. **Primary stakeholders** are directly linked to a company's survival and include customers, suppliers, employees, and shareholders. In contrast, **secondary stakeholders** are less directly linked to the company's survival and include the media, trade associations, and special interest groups.[4] Although secondary stakeholders may seem to have less potential impact on multinational companies, recent examples show that they are as important as primary shareholders in terms of their effect. Consider, for example, that Shell Oil has been forced to acknowledge its relationship with a corrupt government in Nigeria. Similarly, the agricultural giant Monsanto has been forced to deal with secondary stakeholders such as Greenpeace and Friends of the Earth as it tries to develop agricultural biotechnology products.[5] Such examples show that addressing the needs of both groups of shareholders is critical.

How can international managers deal with the constant ethical challenges such as those in Exhibit 4.2? To succeed and be profitable in a socially responsible fashion, multinational company managers must weigh and balance the economic, legal, and ethical consequences of their decisions. The next sections discuss how managers must analyze situations with ethical consequences. The first section presents an overview of basic ethical philosophies used by managers as guides for ethical decision making. The second section deals with national differences in business ethics and social responsibility. The third considers the development of transnational business ethics—an ethical system for the multinational company that does not rely on the ethical principles and philosophies of any one country. In the final section, we look at the practical considerations involved in balancing the needs of the company and managerial actions with ethical consequences.

# Ethical Philosophy

In this section, we examine two approaches to ethical decision making. The first comes from traditional ethical philosophy. The second is a contemporary philosophical view of how we can think about ethics.

## Traditional Views

Two basic systems of ethical reasoning dominate ethical philosophy: the teleological and the deontological systems.

In **teleological ethical theories**, the morality of an act or practice proceeds from its consequences. The most popular teleological theory is **utilitarianism**. Utilitarianism argues that what is good and moral comes from acts that produce the greatest good for the greatest number of people. For example, from a utilitarian perspective, one might argue that stealing a loaf of bread to feed a hungry family is moral because eating the bread is crucial to the family's survival. Many multinational economic decisions are based on utilitarianism. For instance, a multinational company can choose a plant location among a number of candidate countries by doing a cost-and-benefit analysis, which

**Primary stakeholders**
Groups or entities directly linked to a company's survival, including customers, suppliers, employees, and shareholders.

**Secondary stakeholders**
Groups or entities less directly linked to a company's survival, including the media, trade associations, and special interest groups.

**Teleological ethical theory**
A theory that suggests that the morality of an act or practice comes from its consequences.

**Utilitarianism**
The argument that what is good and moral proceeds from acts that produce the greatest good for the greatest number of people.

**4.2**

**Areas of Ethical and Social Responsibility Concerns for the Multinational Company (MNC)**

| Stakeholder Affected | Ethical/Social Responsibility Issue | Example Problems for the MNC |
|---|---|---|
| Customers | Product safety | Should an MNC delete safety features to make a product more affordable for people in a poorer nation? |
| | Fair price | Should a sole supplier in a country take advantage of its monopoly? |
| | Proper disclosures and information | Should an MNC assume the cost of translating all its product information into other languages? |
| Stockholders | Fair return on investment | If a product is banned because it is unsafe in one country, should it be sold in countries where it is not banned to maintain profit margins? |
| | | What should a company do if it is found that the corporate executives have been involved in accounting scandals? What protection measures should be taken to protect shareholders' interests? |
| | | How much should CEOs be paid? Should shareholders ignore extremely generous severance packages? |
| | Fair wages | Should a company pay more than market wages when such wages result in other people living in poverty? |
| | Safety of working conditions | Should a company be responsible for the working conditions of its suppliers' employees? |
| Employees | Child labor | Should an MNC use child labor if it is legal in the host country? |
| | Discrimination by sex, race, color, or creed | Should a company assign a woman to a country where women are expected to remain separate from men in public? |
| | Impact on local economies | Should an MNC use transfer pricing and other internal accounting measures to reduce its actual tax base in a foreign country? |
| Host country | Following local laws | Should an MNC follow local laws that violate home country laws against discrimination? |
| | Impact on local social institutions | Should an MNC require its workers to work on religious holidays? |
| | Environmental protection | Is an MNC obligated to control its hazardous waste to a degree higher than local laws require? |
| Society in general | Raw material depletion | Should MNCs deplete natural resources in countries that are willing to let them do so? |

represents one of the most popular applications of utilitarianism. What happens when utilitarian is pushed to the extreme? Consider the following Case in Point.

The Case in Point below clearly shows application of utilitarian thinking. From its inception, *News of the World* decided that it would do whatever it took to get information to be able to publish sensational stories. *News of the World* reporters justified bribing the police to get access to tips and confidential information that would help sell newspapers. The benefits of such unethical activities as phone hacking, email hacking, and police bribery seemed to far outweigh the costs associated with such activities. Unfortunately, recent events suggest that both Newscorp and *News of the World* underestimated the costs associated with such unethical behaviors.

However, not all companies espouse utilitarian thinking. In contrast to teleological ethical theories, **deontological ethical theories** do not focus on consequences. Rather, in this way of thinking, actions by themselves have a good or bad morality regardless of their outcomes. For example, a person who chooses not to steal a loaf of bread because stealing is immoral, even if people starve because of this action, behaves ethically according to the deontological argument. In this case, the moral principle forbidding stealing, common in many religious doctrines, takes

**Deontological ethical theory**
A focus on actions that, by themselves, have a good or bad morality regardless of their outcomes.

## CASE IN POINT

## Robert Murdoch and Newscorp

News Corporation (Newscorp) is a diversified global company organized around business segments linked to the entertainment industry. Business segments include areas such as television, cable network programming, satellite services, and newspaper and book publishing services. In the United States, most people know Newscorp through its ownership of the Fox television channels.

In 2011, Newscorp became embroiled in a major scandal that has the potential to destroy the company. One of the newspapers that Newscorp owns is *News of the World*, published in the United Kingdom. Investigations during late 2011 revealed that employees of the newspaper were engaging in phone hacking to gain access to private information regarding celebrities, politicians, and sports figures. It was also revealed that Newscorp employees hacked into the cell phone of an abducted young girl and the employee deleted several voice mails. This not only gave the girl's parents hope that she was alive, it also hampered the police investigations. Other emails also showed that Newscorp was bribing the police to get access to sensitive information.

Throughout the investigations, most Newscorp executives argued that they were not aware of these various tactics to access confidential information. However, new evidence suggests that many of

the executives were not only aware of these illegal and unethical activities but were also approving such activities. In fact, London's Metropolitan police department (Met) is also under fire, as the investigations revealed that some of the highest-ranking members of the Met were complicit in providing confidential information and tips to Newscorp reporters while also not adequately investigating alleged illegal activities.

The scandal has been devastating for Newscorp. *News of the World* is no longer being published. Furthermore, James Murdoch, son of Robert Murdoch, founder of Newscorp, has also resigned from the newspaper business and many doubt his future at Newscorp. Robert Murdoch continues to reel from the various scandals and shareholders are asking for his resignation. The U.S. Federal Bureau of Investigation (FBI) is also conducting an inquiry into whether Newscorp employees hacked into phones of 9/11 victims. Furthermore, Newscorp is being investigated for allegations of bribery in Russia.

*Source: Based on* Economist. *2011. "Officers down." July 21, online edition;* Economist. *2012a. "Rising sun, setting son." March 3, online edition;* Economist. *2012b. "An old new scandal." March 31, online edition. Katz, G. 2011. "News of the World hacked into murdered girl Milly Dowler's phone." July 5,* Huffington Post; *http://www.huffingtonpost.com.*

precedence over a bad outcome. Similarly, deontologists have argued that closing a plant is unethical because workers are not being treated with dignity.

Some deontological ethical philosophers argue that morality is intuitive and self-evident; that is, moral people just know what is right because it is obvious how an ethical person should behave. Other deontologists argue that we cannot rely on intuition. Instead, we should follow an essential moral principle or value, such as the Golden Rule or a concern for justice. Still others argue for a more comprehensive set of moral principles or rules that can guide our behavior, such as the Ten Commandments or the precepts contained in the *Qur'an*.[6]

## Moral Languages

A more contemporary way of looking at ethics, favored by Thomas Donaldson, an expert on international business ethics, broadens the rough distinction between the teleological and deontological ethical theories. Donaldson argues that international business ethics are best understood by focusing on the "language of international corporate ethics."[7] According to Donaldson, **moral languages** describe the basic ways that people think about ethical decisions and to explain their ethical choices. The six basic ethical languages identified by Donaldson are:[8]

1. *Virtue and vice:* This language identifies a person's good or virtuous properties and contrasts them with vices. For example, temperance might be contrasted with lust. People or groups who exhibit or who have virtuous characteristics are seen as ethical. It is not important what results from an action, but rather the virtuous intent of the action.

2. *Self-control:* This language emphasizes achieving perfection at controlling thoughts and actions, such as passion. It is apparent in the Buddhist and Hindu views of the world but also appears in many Western traditions, such as in the philosophy of Plato and in the control of "appetites."

3. *Maximizing human welfare:* This is the basic language of the utilitarian view, emphasizing the greatest good for the greatest number of people. For example, using this language of ethical thought, one might argue that exposing a few people to dangerous chemicals is acceptable if most people in the society benefit.

4. *Avoiding harm:* Like the emphasis on the greatest good for the greatest number, this language of ethics sees good or bad in terms of consequences. However, rather than maximizing benefits, it focuses on avoiding unpleasant outcomes or consequences. For example, one might argue, "If it doesn't hurt anyone, it's okay."

5. *Rights and duties:* This language focuses on principles that guide ethical behaviors. The principles specify required duties, such as the duties of a parent to care for a child. The principles also specify the rights of people, such as the right to free speech. According to Donaldson, the language of rights and duties fits well in a legal context.

6. *Social contract:* The social contract language structures ethics as a form of agreement among people. These agreements need not be written but may be taken for granted by all parties. In this sense, what is ethical is what the people in our culture or in our organization have come to agree is ethical.

Ethical philosophies provide a language or structure for thinking about ethical decisions and dilemmas. They help managers understand the philosophical bases

**Moral languages**
Descriptions of the basic ways that people use to think about ethical decisions and to explain their ethical choices.

of their decision making and of the company's ethical or social responsibility policies. International managers face the additional challenge of understanding the unfamiliar cultural and institutional contexts surrounding their ethical decision making. The next section shows how culture and social institutions come into play in the complexities of ethical decision making.

# National Differences in Business Ethics and Social Responsibility

As with most multinational business practices, national culture and social institutions play a role; in this case, they affect how businesses manage ethical behavior and social responsibility. Exhibit 4.3 presents a simple model of the

**EXHIBIT 4.3**  A Model of Institutional and Cultural Effects on Business Ethics Issues and Management

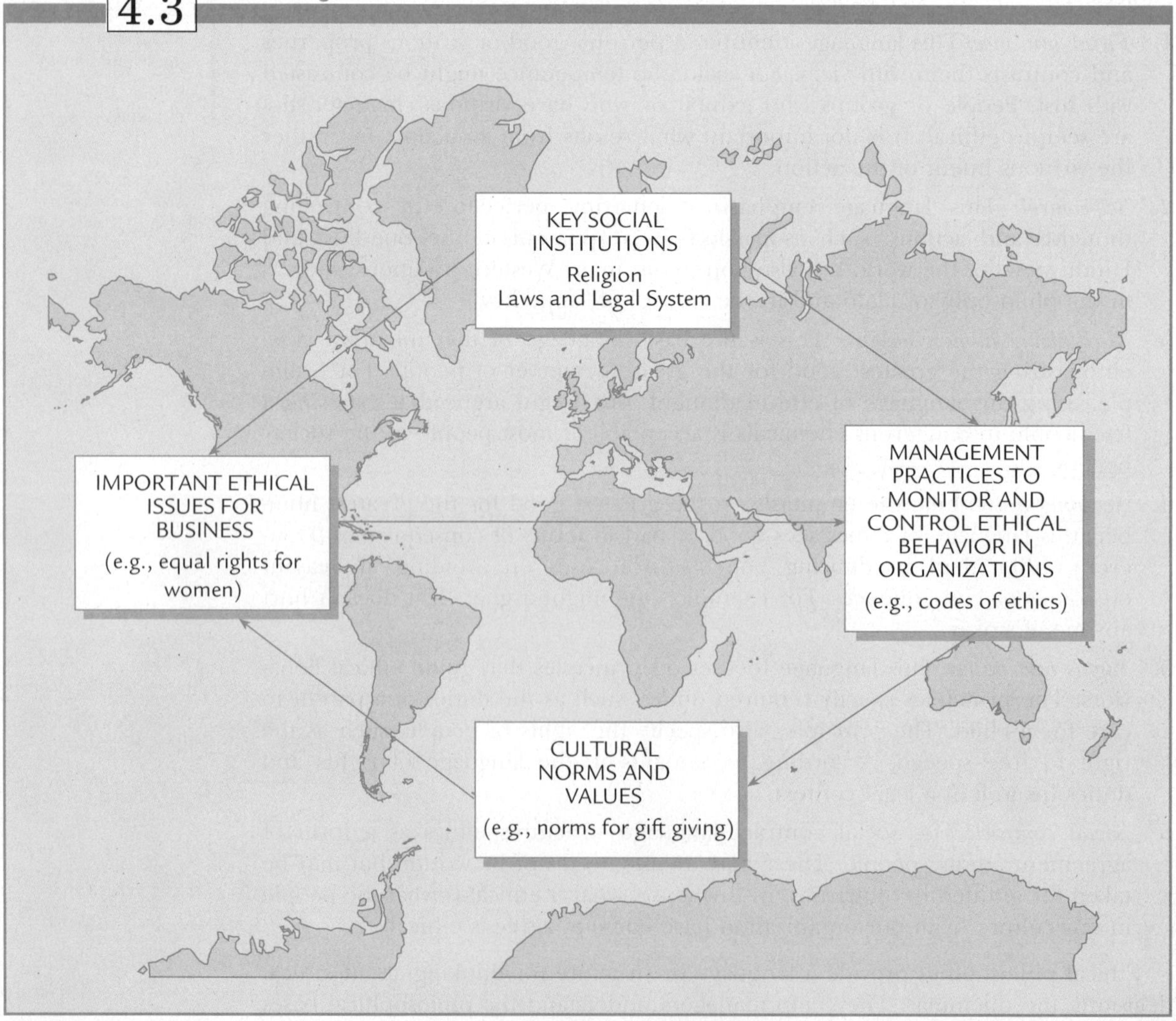

KEY SOCIAL INSTITUTIONS
Religion
Laws and Legal System

IMPORTANT ETHICAL ISSUES FOR BUSINESS
(e.g., equal rights for women)

MANAGEMENT PRACTICES TO MONITOR AND CONTROL ETHICAL BEHAVIOR IN ORGANIZATIONS
(e.g., codes of ethics)

CULTURAL NORMS AND VALUES
(e.g., norms for gift giving)

© Cengage Learning

relationships among national culture, social institutions, and business ethics. As explained in Chapter 2, national culture, by means of cultural norms and values, influences important business practices such as how women and minorities are treated on the job, attitudes toward gift giving and bribery, and expectations regarding conformity to written laws. Similarly, the social institutions described in Chapter 3, such as religion and the legal system, are probably the key institutions that affect what ethical issues are important in a society and how they are typically managed.

Although there are significant differences in how people view ethics, Forsyth, O'Boyle, Jr., and McDaniel argue that some actions are universally condemned from an ethical standpoint.[9] For instance, lying to others, harming or killing children, failing to keep one's promises, and taking valuables from others are all often morally condemned. However, despite these universals, other actions are viewed with significantly more variation. Consider Exhibit 4.4, which clearly shows that there are significant differences in how actions with moral consequences are viewed.

How can such differences be explained? Although no comprehensive body of knowledge identifies exactly how national culture and social institutions affect business ethics and under what conditions, work by Cullen, Parboteeah, and Hoegl suggests possible applications to multinational ethics.[10] Basing their study on Messner and Rosenfeld's institutional anomie theory,[11] they argue

---

**EXHIBIT 4.4**    Some Examples of Cultural Variations Regarding Acceptance of Ethically Suspect Behaviors

**Results of Cross-Cultural Studies**

- U.S. students consider it morally wrong for employees of an auto repair shop to lie to customers about repairs done. However, the practice is seen as more morally acceptable to Russian students.
- Most Westerners violate copyright laws, even though they recognize that violation of such laws is wrong.
- Requesting money to smooth out business transactions is standard practice in many countries such as Mexico, Russia, Thailand, and Haiti. In the United States, such practices are frowned upon.
- Austrians do not find it immoral for a male boss to promote only women who see him socially. U.S. managers find such actions unethical.
- Muslim and Caucasian managers working in Malaysia had the highest regard for profits, while Australian managers tended to be more socially considerate toward employees, customers, and the environment.
- It is acceptable to evaluate one's bosses in the United States, but it is considered immoral in many other societies.
- In a study comparing whistle-blowing forms, students from the United Kingdom had a much higher preference for internal forms of whistle-blowing relative to students from Turkey and South Korea.

*Sources: Based on Forsyth, D. R., E. H. Boyle, Jr., and M. A. McDaniel. 2008. "East meets West: A meta-analytic investigation of cultural variations in idealism and relativism." Journal of Business Ethics, 83(4): 813–833; Park, H., J. Blenkinsopp, M. K. Oktem, and U. Omurgonulsen. 2008. "Cultural orientation and attitudes toward different forms of whistle blowing: A comparison of South Korea, Turkey and the U.K." Journal of Business Ethics, 82, 929–929; Yong, A. 2008. "Cross-cultural comparisons of managerial perceptions on profit." Journal of Business Ethics, 82, 775–791.*

that specific national culture and social institutions are likely to encourage people to break norms and thereby justify ethically suspect behaviors. Cullen and colleagues argued that societies with national cultural values of high achievement (i.e., people value achievement), high individualism (i.e., people value their own personal freedom), high universalism (i.e., people are more ambitious because they expect to be treated fairly), and high pecuniary materialism (i.e., people have high materialist tendencies) are likely to have a greater number of people engaging in deviant acts such as crime. In addition to these national cultural values, they also specified that social institutions, such as industrialization, the type of economic system, family, and education, should be related to the breaking of norms. They suggest that societies with relatively high levels of industrialization, capitalist systems, low degrees of family breakdown, and easily accessible education should encourage more deviance. Testing their theory on 3,450 managers from 28 countries, the researchers found support for most of their hypotheses. Multinational managers can use this theory to understand how people approach ethics. However, managers often have access only to their own knowledge of a country's social institutions and culture to make inferences about which ethical issues are important and how they are best managed.

Other research has been done on how the national institutional context affects business ethics. For example, Seleim and Bontis examined how the cultural dimensions of the GLOBE studies (Chapter 2) influence corruption.[12] They found that countries that rate high on future orientation have relatively low levels of corruption. Possibly the focus on future-oriented behaviors, such as strategic planning and creating vision statements, discourages corruption. The researchers also found that societies high on institutional collectivism practices also tend to have low levels of corruption. The high levels of integration and bonding of people in such societies very likely reinforce ethical standards. Among other results, the study found that societies high on in-group collectivism have relatively high levels of corruption. Such results suggest that people in these societies engage in actions that will benefit their own groups and friends rather than the wider good, thereby encouraging corruption.

With its extensive legal control over the management of ethical behaviors, the United States is unique in the world. The next section discusses a major law governing ethical behavior in international business that has possibly the greatest impact of all legislation on U.S. multinational companies.

## Questionable Payments and Bribery

In addition to the many possible ethical issues presented in Exhibit 4.2, a particular ethical difficulty for many multinational companies relates to bribery, or what some call questionable payments. In many societies, people routinely offer bribes or gifts to expedite government actions or to gain advantage in business deals. Even the major German multinational Siemens was involved in a major bribery scandal. "Grease money" can speed up the import or export of goods or get customs agents to look the other way. A gift or a kickback may be expected by a purchasing agent to select your company's product over another. Words for these types of actions exist in all countries. For example, in Mexico the bribe is known as *mordida,* or bite; in France, the *pot –de vin,* or jug of wine; in Germany, *die "N.A.,"* an abbreviation of *nutzliche Abagabe,* the useful contribution; and in Japan, the *jeitinho,* or fix.[13] Consider the following Multinational Management Challenge.

## Multinational Management **Challenge**

### Wal-Mart in Mexico

Wal-Mart, the well-known U.S. retailer, is currently under investigation for bribery in Mexico. Following a series of investigations, *Time* published a scathing report alleging that Wal-Mart had bribed Mexican officials with over $24 million. Wal-Mart's success in Mexico has been tremendous. It has expanded rapidly, creating thousands of jobs in the formal sector. Furthermore, it is selling products at prices that are highly attractive to Mexican consumers. However, some are starting to question whether such success came at a price.

Mexico is widely seen as a country rampant with corruption. To succeed in this environment, Wal-Mart decided to resort to bribery. As such, it is alleged that Wal-Mart paid Mexican officials to win permits in days or weeks rather than the usual months or years. Documents from the *Time* investigations show that the company made these payments before 2006 to speed up permits for new stores. One of the individuals interviewed, a former Wal-Mart executive, who discussed how he personally sent two trusted lawyers with envelopes full of cash to be given to mayors and city council members as well as low-level bureaucrats. However, most troubling is the allegation that Wal-Mart executives were aware of such bribery activities. In fact, it is argued that the arrival of an ambitious new Wal-Mart CEO of Mexico hastened the bribery. The new CEO, Mr. Castro-Wright, argued that such bribery was necessary to strategically build as many stores as possible and prevent competitors from reacting. His efforts were quite successful and he was promoted to a more senior position in the United States.

*Sources: Based on Barstow, D. 2012. "Wal-Mart hushed up a vast Mexican bribery case."* New York Times, *April 21, online edition; Jenkins, H. W. 2012. "Wal-Mart innocents abroad."* Wall Street Journal, *April 25, A13.*

The above Multinational Management Challenge alleges that Wal-Mart engaged in a pattern of bribery over a period of years to speed up permits in Mexico. If these allegations are found to be true, Wal-Mart will likely have to pay a significant fine under the Foreign Corrupt Practices Act, a law we will discuss later. Bribery can thus be very damaging for companies engaged in the practice. However, corruption and bribery can also have devastating effects on societies. Compte, Lambert-Mogiliansky, and Verdier argue that companies typically make up for bribery by increasing the contract price by the amount of the bribe.[14] As such, many developing countries suffer because they are charged higher prices. However, companies also routinely use poorer-quality products or materials to make up for the bribe, thus putting out inferior products. Furthermore, corruption can also result in collusion among firms, resulting in even higher prices. As a result, corruption and bribery usually result in higher public spending, lower-quality projects, undermined competition, and the inefficient allocation of resources. Additionally, some argue that corruption discourages entrepreneurship because bribery becomes a form of taxation.[15] Such impediments to entrepreneurship affect investment growth and development, leading to lessened economic performance.[16]

To understand the level of corruption in countries, multinational companies can rely on the corruption perception index (CPI). The CPI, developed by Transparency International, is a rating of the perceived levels of corruption in a country. Exhibit 4.5 shows the CPI for selected countries; high CPIs indicate the least corruption.[17]

**EXHIBIT** 4.5    CPIs for Selected Countries (2008; 0 = most corruption, 10 = least corruption)

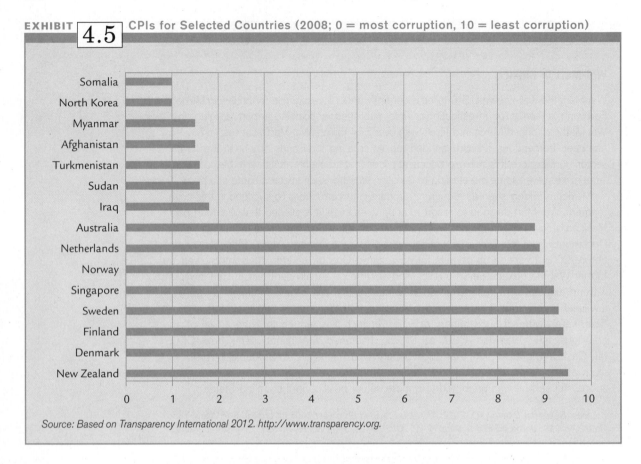

Source: Based on Transparency International 2012. http://www.transparency.org.

As in the United States, most countries have formal laws forbidding corrupt practices. However, because of wide differences among countries in legal traditions, enforcement differs greatly. The accepted amounts of gift giving and entertainment associated with business transactions vary enormously. For example, even for academic research grants, Japanese professors will budget as a legitimate expense about 20 percent of the grant for entertainment costs—something unheard of in U.S. academic research.

In 1977, in response to several investigations by U.S. government agencies, President Jimmy Carter signed the Foreign Corrupt Practices Act (FCPA).[18] Exhibit 4.6 shows excerpts taken directly from the FCPA.

The FCPA forbids U.S. companies from making or offering payments or gifts to foreign government officials for the sake of obtaining or retaining business. However, the act does not prohibit some forms of payments that may occur in international business. Payments made under duress to avoid injury or violence are acceptable. For example, in an unstable political environment, a company may pay local officials "bribes" to avoid harassment of its employees. Small payments that merely encourage officials to do their legitimate and routine jobs are legal. Payments made that are lawful in a country are also acceptable. These "grease" payments must not seek illegal ends but just speed up or make possible normal business functions, such as necessary paperwork.

A tricky component of the FCPA for U.S. companies is the law's reason-to-know provision. This provision means that a firm is liable for bribes or questionable

**Foreign Corrupt Practices Act (FCPA)**
Forbids U.S. companies to make or offer illegal payments or gifts to officials of foreign governments for the sake of obtaining or retaining business.

**EXHIBIT 4.6**    Excerpts from the Foreign Corrupt Practices Act

### Prohibited Foreign Trade Practices

It shall be unlawful for *any domestic concern* or for any officer, director, employee, or agent of such domestic concern or any stockholder thereof acting on behalf of such domestic concern, to make use of the mails or any means or instrumentality of interstate commerce corruptly in furtherance of an offer, payment, promise to pay, or authorization of the payment of any money, or offer, gift, promise to give, or authorization of the giving of anything of value to any foreign official for purposes of:

A.  influencing any act or decision of such foreign official, political party, party official, or candidate in his or its official capacity, or
B.  inducing such foreign official, political party, party official, or candidate to do or omit to do any act in violation of the lawful duty of such foreign official, political party, party official, or candidate, or
C.  inducing such foreign official, political party, party official, or candidate to use his or its influence with a foreign government or instrumentality thereof to affect or influence any act or decision of such government or instrumentality, in order to assist such issuer in obtaining or retaining business for or with, or directing business to, any person.

Also prohibited is any offer, payment, promise to pay, or authorization of the payment of any money, or offer, gift, promise to give, or authorization of the giving of anything of value *when given to any person, while knowing* that all or a portion of such money or thing of value will be offered, given, or promised, directly or indirectly, to any foreign official, to any foreign political party or official thereof, or to any candidate for foreign political office, for purposes of A through C above.

### Definitions

1.  The term "*domestic concern*" means any individual who is a citizen, national, or resident of the United States; and any corporation, partnership, association, joint-stock company, business trust, unincorporated organization, or sole proprietorship which has its principal place of business in the United States, or which is organized under the laws of a State of the United States or a territory, possession, or commonwealth of the United States.
2.  The term "*foreign official*" means any officer or employee of a foreign government or any department, agency, or instrumentality thereof, or any person acting in an official capacity for or on behalf of any such government or department, agency, or instrumentality.
3.  A person's state of mind is "*knowing*" with respect to conduct, a circumstance, or a result if:
    (i)  such person is aware that such person is engaging in such conduct, that such circumstance exists, or that such result is substantially certain to occur; or
    (ii)  such person has a firm belief that such circumstance exists or that such result is substantially certain to occur. Knowledge is established if a person is aware of a high probability of the existence of such circumstance, unless the person actually believes that such circumstance does not exist.

4.  The term "*routine government action*" means only an action which is ordinarily and commonly performed by a foreign official in such cases as obtaining permits, licenses, or other official documents to qualify a person to do business in a foreign country. The term "routine governmental action" does not include any decision by a foreign official whether, or on what terms, to award new business to or to continue business with a particular party, or any action taken by a foreign official involved in the decision-making process to encourage a decision to award new business to or continue business with a particular party.
5.  The term "*interstate commerce*" means trade, commerce, transportation, or communication among the several States, or between any foreign country and any State or between any State and any place or ship outside thereof.

### Exceptions

A.  Facilitating or expediting payment to a foreign official, political party, or party official the purpose of which is to expedite or *to secure the performance of a routine governmental action* by a foreign official, political party, or party official.
B.  The payment, gift, offer, or promise of anything of value that was made, *was lawful under the written laws and regulations of the foreign official's, political party's, party official's, or candidate's country*; or
C.  The payment, gift, offer, or promise of anything of value that was made, was a *reasonable and bona fide expenditure,* such as travel and lodging expenses, incurred by or on behalf of a foreign official, party, party official, or candidate and was directly related to the promotion, demonstration, or explanation of products or services; or the execution or performance of a contract with a foreign government or agency thereof.

*continued*

**EXHIBIT** 4.6 Continued

**Penalties**

1. Any domestic concern that violates this section shall be fined not more than $2,000,000 and shall be subject to a civil penalty of not more than $10,000 imposed in an action brought by the Attorney General.
2. Any officer or director of a domestic concern, or stockholder acting on behalf of such domestic concern, who willfully violates this section shall be fined not more than $100,000, or imprisoned not more than 5 years, or both.
3. Any employee or agent of a domestic concern who is a United States citizen, national, or resident or is otherwise subject to the jurisdiction of the United States (other than an officer, director, or stockholder acting on behalf of such domestic concern), and who willfully violates this section, shall be fined not more than $100,000, or imprisoned not more than 5 years, or both.
4. Any officer, director, employee, or agent of a domestic concern, or stockholder acting on behalf of such domestic concern, who violates this section shall be subject to a civil penalty of not more than $10,000 imposed in an action brought by the Attorney General.
5. Whenever a fine is imposed upon any officer, director, employee, agent, or stockholder of a domestic concern, such fine may not be paid, directly or indirectly, by such domestic concern.

*Source: U.S. Code, Title 15—Commerce and Trade, Chapter2B-Securities Exchanges, Section 78dd—1.*

payments made by agents hired by the firm, even if members of the firm did not actually make the payments or see them being made. To take advantage of a local person's knowledge of "how to get things done" in a country, U.S. multinational managers often use local people as agents to conduct business. If it is common knowledge that these agents use part of their fees to bribe local officials to commit illegal acts, then the U.S. firm is breaking the law. If, however, the U.S. firm has no knowledge of the behavior of the agent and no reason to expect illegal behavior by the agent, then the firm has no liability under the FCPA. The term "knowing" means that the person actually knows an illegal bribe will be given, knows that the circumstances surrounding the situation make it likely that an illegal bribe will be given, or is aware of the high probability that an illegal act will occur. Exhibit 4.6 states the types of penalties included in the FCPA. Note that the penalties apply to individuals as well as to companies and that individual fines cannot be paid by the company.

Although the FCPA was passed in 1977, it went generally unenforced for several decades. However, starting in 2007, several firms have been punished under the FCPA. Furthermore, recent evidence suggests that the U.S. Department of Justice is also actively suing individuals for violating the act. A recent report mentions the conviction of several individuals, including Joel Esquenazi (sued as CEO of a company that facilitated a bribe of $890,000 to officials at Haiti Telecom and given a prison term of 15 years) (Berger, Yannett, Hecker, Fuhr, and Gorhmann, 2012).

Exhibits 4.7 and 4.8 show the number of convictions and the amount of fines levied under the FCPA from 2002 to 2011. As Exhibits 4.7 and 4.8 show, it is clear that multinationals will have to ensure that their operations do not violate FCPA provisions.

## Toward Transnational Ethics

Globalization dramatically increases contact among people from different ethical and cultural systems. This contact is creating pressure for ethical convergence and for the development of transnational agreements among nations to govern business practices. The next Case in Point shows that the battle is on against corrupt relationships between business and government.

Next, we review some of the trends toward ethical convergence and transnational ethical agreements.

**EXHIBIT 4.7** Number of Convictions under FCPA

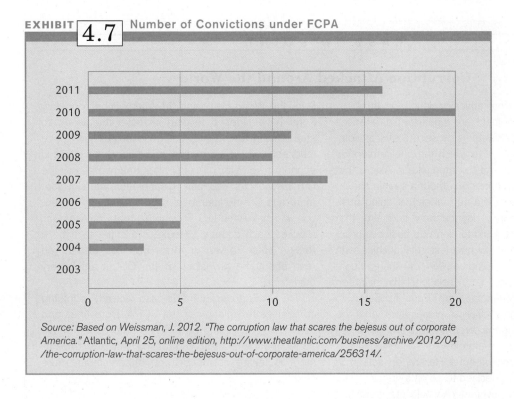

*Source: Based on Weissman, J. 2012. "The corruption law that scares the bejesus out of corporate America." Atlantic, April 25, online edition, http://www.theatlantic.com/business/archive/2012/04/the-corruption-law-that-scares-the-bejesus-out-of-corporate-america/256314/.*

**EXHIBIT 4.8** FCPA Civil and Criminal Fines (Millions of US $)

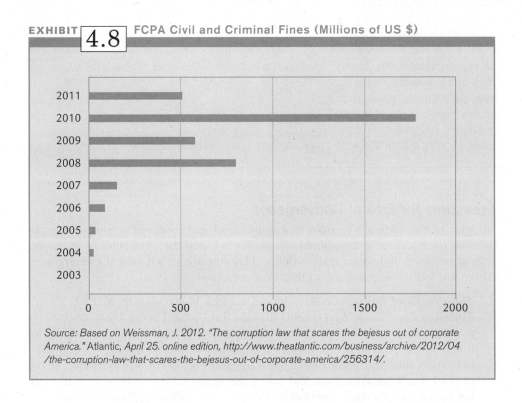

*Source: Based on Weissman, J. 2012. "The corruption law that scares the bejesus out of corporate America." Atlantic, April 25. online edition, http://www.theatlantic.com/business/archive/2012/04/the-corruption-law-that-scares-the-bejesus-out-of-corporate-america/256314/.*

## Corruption Attacked Around the World

No nation is free from ethical violations in business practices. However, there are significant differences in how national legal systems prosecute ethical violations and in the degree to which the public tolerates violations. For instance, a common joke in Asia is that it is futile to pursue contracts without a sizable checkbook because bribery is a normal part of doing business. However, some evidence now suggests that there is a worldwide trend to clean up business practices, especially unethical business relationships with government. The growing power of shareholders challenges the once cozy relationships between business and government, from Paris to Seoul to Mexico City. Ordinary citizens, prosecutors, and the press are challenging the corporate elite and clamoring for ethical corporate governance.

Consider the case of Anna Hazare, an activist in India. In 2011, Hazare decided to go on a hunger strike because the Indian government would not create an anti-corruption body as he had stipulated in a bill proposal. Rather than respond to his demands, the Indian government arrested Hazare to keep him in "preventive" custody. However, because of major cases of corruption in 2010, the Indian population started demonstrating to support Hazare. The Indian government had no choice but to release Hazare to continue his hunger strike. Furthermore, Hazare has said that he would start a new hunger strike in August of 2012 if the Indian government does not investigate 14 Cabinet ministers for corruption. At the international

level, the World Bank and the International Monetary Fund have stopped lending or have threatened to stop lending to countries such as Kenya, Nigeria, and Indonesia, where corruption and bribery have stifled economic growth. Twenty-nine members of the Organisation for Economic Cooperation and Development and five nonmembers signed a bribery convention, which, like the U.S. Foreign Corrupt Practices Act, requires each country to make it a crime to bribe a foreign office to win or retain business. Earlier, you read about the provisions of the OECD anti-bribery guidelines.

The U.S. government is also actively pursuing companies in violation of the FCPA. Both fines and convictions stemming from FCPA enforcement have gone up dramatically, suggesting that the government is taking corruption and bribery much more seriously.

*Sources: BBC Monitoring South Asia. 2012. "Indian activist warns government if anti-corruption law not passed." March 26, online edition; Economist. 2011. "No modern-day Mahatma. There are better ways to curb corruption than those proposed by Anna Hazare." August 27, online edition. "A global war against bribery." Economist.com, January 16, Story_1 D-18208; Financial Times. 2009. "Battling bribery," February 16, p. 8; Rossant, John. 1995. "Dirty money." BusinessWeek Online, international edition, December 18; Weissman, J. 2012. "The corruption law that scares the bejusus out of corporate America." Atlantic, April 25, online edition, http://www.theatlantic.com /business/archive/2012/04/the-corruption-law-that-scares-the -bejesus-out-of-corporate-america/256314/.*

## Pressures for Ethical Convergence

In spite of the wide differences in cultures and in social institutions, there are growing pressures for multinational companies to follow the same rules in managing ethical behavior and social responsibility. This trend is called **ethical convergence**. There are four basic reasons for ethical convergence:

**Ethical convergence**
The growing pressures for multinational companies to follow the same rules in managing ethical behavior and social responsibility.

1. The growth of international trade and trading blocs, such as NAFTA (North American Free Trade Agreement) and the European Union, creates pressures to have common ethical practices that transcend national cultures and institutional differences. Predictable interactions and behaviors among trading partners from different countries make trade more efficient. Furthermore, many of these trade organizations and other international associations are developing measures to reduce corruption. Consider the following Case in Point.

CASE IN POINT

## Anti-Bribery Eradication Worldwide

While the earlier section discussed the U.S. approach to fighting corruption with the FCPA, the pressures for ethical convergence have also encouraged other organizations worldwide to develop anti-bribery measures. The OECD is an association of 30 of the world's largest economies in terms of gross domestic product, including countries such as Belgium, Canada, Ireland, South Korea, New Zealand, Spain, the United Kingdom, and the United States. The OECD members have also ratified guidelines to combat bribery (http://www.oecd.org). Specifically, the members have agreed to take measures to make bribery a criminal offence. Furthermore, members are expected to provide legal assistance to each other to prosecute nationals who are engaged in bribery. Additionally, members are also expected to take the necessary measures to prevent or tackle money laundering related to bribery. Furthermore, in addition to providing clear guidelines regarding the eradication of bribery, the OECD has also enacted regulations to address bribery in companies. Multinationals operating in OECD and other countries are expected to have adequate accounting practices and internal controls and audits to ensure that they are complying with anti-bribery laws.

*Source: Based on http://www.oecd.org.*

2. Interaction between trading partners promotes imitating the business practices of other countries. As people from different cultural backgrounds increase their interactions, exposure to varying ethical traditions encourages people to adjust to, imitate, and adopt new behaviors and attitudes.

3. Companies that do business throughout the world have employees from varied cultural backgrounds who need common standards and rules regarding how to behave. Multinational companies often rely on their corporate culture to provide consistent norms and values that govern ethical issues.

4. An increasing number of business watchdogs, such as ethical investment companies and nongovernmental organizations, also are encouraging multinational companies to be ethical.

In addition to moral pressure to eliminate corrupt activity, there is increasing financial pressure to do so. Extensive corruption costs money, makes businesses less competitive internationally, and risks embarrassing and costly scandals.

## Prescriptive Ethics for the Multinational

Donaldson argues that the three moral languages of avoiding harm, rights and duties, and the social contract should guide multinational companies. He advocates **prescriptive ethics for multinationals**; that is, he argues that multinational companies should engage in business practices that avoid negative consequences to their stakeholders (e.g., employees, the local environment). Although multinationals retain basic rights, such as seeking a fair profit, these rights imply duties, such as providing a fair wage to local employees. The multinational company also has a social contract with its stakeholders, which, even if taken for granted, defines the nature of the relationships. For example, when a multinational company enters a country, it accepts the social contract to follow local laws.

These three moral languages are the easiest of ethical systems to specify in written codes, such as contracts and international laws. Donaldson believes that these moral languages are the most appropriate for managing ethical behaviors among culturally

**Prescriptive ethics for multinationals**
Suggested guidelines for the ethical behavior of multinational companies.

heterogeneous multinationals; that is, regardless of their national culture, companies can agree with their stakeholders on the basic rules of moral behavior.[19]

For Donaldson's ideas to work, there must be a code of conduct to guide multinational companies that is independent of national boundaries. The code must include prescriptive and proscriptive rules to guide multinational behavior. Prescriptive rules tell multinational managers and companies what they should do, whereas proscriptive rules tell them what they may not do.

Some scholars argue that such ethical guides currently exist in various international agreements and in the codes of international governing bodies, such as the United Nations and the International Labor Office.[20]

Exhibit 4.9 summarizes ethical stipulations for the multinational company derived from the following international sources:

- The United Nations Universal Declaration of Human Rights
- The United Nations Code of Conduct on Transnational Corporations
- The European Convention on Human Rights
- The International Chamber of Commerce Guidelines for International Investment
- The Organization for Economic Cooperation and Development Guidelines for Multinational Enterprises
- The Helsinki Final Act
- The International Labor Office Tripartite Declarations of Principles Concerning Multinational Enterprises and Social Policy

The principles in the code of conduct for the multinational company shown in Exhibit 4.9 have two supporting rationales. The first rationale comes from the basic deontological principles dealing with human rights, such as the right to work and the right to be safe. To a large degree, the international agreements specify the rights and duties of multinational companies that are presumed to be transcultural; that is, the basic ethical principles apply to all, regardless of a company's country of origin or its current business location. The second rationale comes from the history of experiences in international business interactions.[21] For example, because multinational companies often ignore the environmental impact of their operations in other countries, several international agreements specify their duties regarding the environment.

Although such agreements are diverse and not always enforceable, they are useful in that they provide a safe guide to ethical management for multinational managers. It is likely that, if managers follow the code of conduct shown in Exhibit 4.9, both in individual behavior and in guiding a company, they will generally be on safe ethical and legal ground in nearly all situations.

The next Multinational Management Brief discusses Cisco's efforts to change its corporate culture to become more ethical.

The next section concludes this chapter with a focus on ethical decision making for the individual multinational manager.

## The Ethical Dilemma in Multinational Management: How Will You Decide?

The potentially significant differences in ethical systems and in how ethics are managed create dilemmas for multinational managers. This section looks first at the issue of which ethical system you should use—your own country's or that of the host country. It concludes with a description of an ethical decision model for the multinational manager.

**EXHIBIT 4.9**    A Code of Conduct for the Multinational Company

**Respect Basic Human Rights and Freedoms**

- Respect fundamental human rights of life, liberty, security, and privacy.
- Do not discriminate on the basis of race, color, gender, religion, language, ethnic origin, or political affiliation.
- Respect personal freedoms (e.g., religion, opinion).

**Maintain High Standards of Local Political Involvement**

- Avoid illegal involvement in local politics.
- Don't pay bribes or other improper payments.
- Do not interfere in local government internal relations.

**Transfer Technology**

- Enhance the transfer of technology to developing nations.
- Adapt technologies to local needs.
- Conduct local R&D when possible.
- Grant fair licenses to use technology.

**Protect the Environment**

- Follow local environmental-protection laws.
- Actively protect the environment.
- Repair damage to the environment done by company operations.

- Help develop local standards.
- Provide accurate assessments of environmental impact of the company.
- Provide complete disclosure of the environmental effects of operations.
- Develop standards to monitor environmental effects.

**Consumer Protection**

- Follow local consumer-protection laws.
- Ensure accurate and proper safety disclosures.

**Employment Practices**

- Follow relevant policies and employment laws of host nation.
- Help create jobs in needed areas.
- Increase local employment opportunities and standards.
- Provide local workers stable employment and job security.
- Promote equal employment opportunities.
- Give priority to local national residents when possible.
- Provide training opportunities at all levels for local employees.
- Promote local nationals to management positions.
- Respect local collective-bargaining rights.
- Cooperate with local collective-bargaining units.
- Give notice of plant closings.
- Do not use threat of leaving country in collective-bargaining dealings.
- Provide income protection to terminated workers.
- Match or improve local standards of employment.
- Protect employees with adequate health and safety standards.
- Provide employees information on job-related health hazards.

*Sources: Adapted from Getz, Kathleen A. 1990. "International codes of conduct: An analysis of ethical reasoning." Journal of Business Ethics, 9, 567–578; HR Focus. 2008. "Why global ethics count and how HR can help." October, 85(10): 13–15; Frederick, William C. 1991. "The moral authority of transnational corporate codes." Journal of Business Ethics, 10, 165–177.*

## Ethical Relativism versus Ethical Universalism

The extensive effects of cultural value differences on all areas of management are never more apparent than when multinational companies have to determine how to deal with ethical differences among the countries in which they do business. Do you impose your own country's ethical system everywhere, or do you follow the maxim, "When in Rome, do as the Romans do"?

---

## Multinational Management **Brief**

### Building an Ethical Culture at Cisco

Cisco has over 63,000 employees worldwide. Despite the large number of employees located in numerous foreign offices, they have been able to sustain an ethical culture. In fact, Cisco has been on the Corporate Responsibility Officer's 100 best corporate citizen list more than once. Furthermore, it has now been listed on Ethisphere Institute's World's Most Ethical Companies for five consecutive years. How does the firm achieve such a culture?

Top management at Cisco encourages and supports the ethics effort. The top-level managers strive to be role models for the organization. Cisco also regularly updates its code of ethics. For instance, it recently revised the code of ethics and used active-voice language throughout the document. About 95 percent of Cisco's employees surveyed mentioned that the Code of Ethics is very easy to understand. In addition to having a regularly updated code of ethics, Cisco also makes the training process fun. For instance, they recently started an Ethics Idol program similar to the popular Idols music series. To get the ethics message out to a highly technical workforce, Cisco devised four fun modules, in which animated contestants sing their ethical dilemmas and judges provide their opinions. Employees then have to rate the judges' opinions based on how they feel they addressed the ethical dilemmas. This program has created company-wide buzz regarding ethics at Cisco. Finally, ethics is considered a way of doing business at Cisco. Rather than having an ethics program, Cisco sends frequent communications about ethics issues. Ethical behavior is kept at the forefront through regular ethics meeting, and communication is made regularly in employees' native languages. Such actions ensure that ethics is always prominent at Cisco.

*Source: Based on Ethisphere Institute. 2012. "Ethisphere Institute unveils the 2012 World's Most Ethical Companies." http://ethisphere.com/ethisphere-institute-unveils-2012-worlds-most-ethical -companies/; Ramos, Luis. 2009. "Outside-the-box ethics."* Leadership Excellence, *26(4): 19.*

---

Recall the concept of cultural relativism (Chapter 2), the philosophical position in anthropology that all cultures are legitimate and viable as a means for people to guide their lives. In other words, what people consider right or wrong, pretty or ugly, good or bad all depends on their cultural norms and values.

**Ethical relativism**
The theory that each society's view of ethics must be considered legitimate.

A similar concept in business ethics is called **ethical relativism**, which means that a multinational manager considers each society's view of ethics as legitimate. For example, if the people in one country believe something like assisted suicide is morally wrong, then for them it is wrong. If, on the other hand, people in another country believe that assisted suicide is morally correct, then for them it is correct. For multinational companies, ethical relativism means that managers need only follow local ethical conventions. Thus, for example, if bribery is an accepted way of doing business in a country, then it is okay for a multinational manager to follow local examples, even if the practice would be illegal at home. Consider the next Comparative Management Brief.

**Ethical universalism**
The theory that basic moral principles transcend cultural and national boundaries.

The opposite of ethical relativism is **ethical universalism**, which holds that basic moral principles transcend cultural and national boundaries. All cultures, for example, have rules that prohibit murder, at least of their own people.

The difficulty in using ethical universalism as a guide for multinational business practices is that there is little agreement on which moral principles exist in all cultures. Moreover, even when the same principles are used, there is no guarantee that all societies use the principles in the same way. For example, two societies may prohibit murder. However, for the group to have a better chance of surviving at a time when food resources are marginal, the aged might be obliged to commit suicide or newborn girls might be killed. The members of the society do not consider such practices to be murder, but rather an ethical way to ensure the survival of the group. Most societies tolerate some form of killing, such as in executions of criminals or in wars. Even though people die as a result of human actions, these acts are not defined as murder but as legitimate acts of society.

For the multinational company, however, practical problems come with following either ethical relativism or ethical universalism. Some ethicists argue that cultural relativism, while a necessary condition for conducting unbiased

## Comparative Management **Brief**

### Chinese Guanxis: Are They Ethical?

Most experts agree that the Chinese economy will continue to experience tremendous growth and that the opportunities for business in China will likely stay strong. However, doing business will also become more complex and challenging. Experts agree that having personal connections is often better than having business acumen to do business in China.

Consider the case of *guanxis*, which are special relationships among Chinese companies that rely on trust, favor, and interdependence. Companies that are within the same network, or *guanxi*, are bound by expectations of reciprocal obligations and are expected to give preferential treatments to other members within the network. Western companies have often argued that such arrangements lead to unethical behaviors, bribery, and corruption. In the absence of a good legal infrastructure, *guanxis* lead to unethical behaviors because members within the same network engage in under-the-table dealings and give preferential treatment to each other.

However, for the Chinese, a *guanxi* network is indispensable for efficiently doing business and is therefore ethical. *Guanxis* substitute for the poorly developed legal and distribution systems in China. For instance, Chinese export companies are faced with dealing with complicated administrative procedures regarding distribution involving complex customs clearance rules and difficulties with securing raw materials and finished goods. These companies are more likely to develop special relationships with local customs officials and other trading firms to ensure a smooth and speedy delivery. Similarly, the Chinese are more likely to engage in conflict resolution based on trust within their network rather than relying on the poorly developed commercial laws.

For the ethical relativist, *guanxis* are acceptable because they represent the legitimate views of Chinese business society. Furthermore, most foreign companies find that they need to rely on these personal connections to do business. However, ethical universalists most likely view *guanxis* as unethical because they violate transparency norms.

*Sources: Based on Chan, Ricky, Y. K. Louis, T. W. Cheng, and Ricky W. F. Szeto. 2002. "The dynamics of guanxi and ethics for Chinese executives." Journal of Business Ethics, 41, 327–336; Kissel, M. 2009. "A web of connections." Wall Street Journal, March 10, C4; St. Clair, N. S. and J. T. Norris. 2012. "Business ethics and social responsibility in contemporary China." Journal of Academic and Business Ethics, 5, 1–9; Su, Chenting M., Joseph Sirgy, and James L. Littlefield. 2003. "Is guanxi orientation bad, ethically speaking? A study of Chinese enterprises." Journal of Business Ethics, 44, 303–312.*

anthropological research, cannot be applied to ethics. Thomas Donaldson, for example, argues that multinational companies have a higher moral responsibility than ethical relativism.[22] He notes that, at the extreme, ethical relativism can become **convenient relativism**. Convenient relativism occurs when companies use the logic of ethical relativism to behave any way they please, using differences in cultures as an excuse. Donaldson gives the example of child labor in developing countries. In some cases, children as young as seven years of age work for a pittance, producing products that eventually are used by large multinational companies.

> **Convenient relativism**
>
> What occurs when companies use the logic of ethical relativism to behave any way they please, using the excuse of differences in cultures.

Extreme moral universalism also has its pitfalls. The assumption that one can identify universal ethics that all people should follow can lead to a type of ethnocentrism that Donaldson calls cultural imperialism. Managers who assume that they know the correct and ethical ways of behaving can easily view the moral systems of foreign cultures as inferior or immoral. This is particularly dangerous when the multinational is a big and financially powerful company with subsidiaries located in the developing world.

Given the above factors, how can a manager decide which of the two approaches is the best option? Consider the following Case in Point.

---

## CASE IN POINT

### Follow Local or Global Norms?

Hamilton, Knouse, and Hill (2009) provide a good guide for deciding which option works best. They suggest that managers use a number of heuristic questions to decide whether to follow local or global norms. The first step in the process involves the identification of the questionable practice of any decision. In such cases, there is often a conflict between what the company wants to do and what values local norms and practices represent. A manager needs to clearly understand the nature of the questionable practice. The second step is to understand whether the questionable practice violates any laws. If the practice violates laws, it seems logical that the manager would suggest not engaging in the decision. However, if the questionable practice does not involve breaking laws, a manager can move on to the third step. In the third step, a manager needs to decide whether the questionable practice is simply a cultural difference or whether it could be an ethics problem. According to Hamilton, Knouse, and Hill (2009), a decision is an ethics problem if it harms someone or violates generally accepted principles. Once the step has been assessed, a manager will then move on to the fourth step, which involves assessing whether the ethics problem or cultural difference violates any industry or

other international code. Whether a questionable practice is an ethics problem or simply a cultural difference, managers are well advised to follow local norms if the questionable practice does not violate any industry-wide code or the company's own code of conduct. However, if the questionable practice violates any form of codes, the manager can move to the fifth and final step. In the fifth step, a manager needs to assess whether a company has leverage (something of value to give) in the host country so that it can follow its own practices. If the firm has leverage, managers are well advised to do business the firm's way. However, if it has no leverage, a manager is well advised to leave the country altogether.

As such, by assessing the various steps, a company can determine whether it can follow local norms or do business its own way. One of the strengths of the method is the fact that it acknowledges that a company may sometimes need to leave a country altogether and not do business either the local way or its own way.

*Source: Based on Hamilton, J. B., S. B. Knouse, and V. Hill. 2009. "Google in China: A manager-friendly heuristic model for resolving cross-cultural ethical conflicts." Journal of Business Ethics, 86, 143–157.*

## Individual Ethical Decision Making for the Multinational Manager

Although companies develop policies, procedures, organizational cultures, and business practices that have ethical consequences, individual managers are ultimately the ones who must make decisions.

The first duty of a manager is to consider whether a decision makes business sense. This is called economic analysis. In economic analysis, the prime interest is in making the best decision in terms of a company's profits. However, if profits alone guide ethical decision making, managers could worry little about how their decisions affect anyone except the owners of the company. Some argue that this type of decision making is not ethics at all because businesses could engage in deceptive and dangerous practices with only the marketplace to control their actions.

After considering the business impact of a decision, multinational managers must consider the legal and ethical consequences of their actions.[23] Exhibit 4.10 shows a decision flowchart illustrating the issues that multinational managers must consider beyond profits when confronted with ethical decisions.

In the legal analysis of an ethical problem, managers focus first on complying with the laws of the country in which their company is operating and, if required, the laws of their home country. Should the law not forbid something, it is ethical. In a combination of pure economic and legal analyses, managers should seek to maximize profits within the confines of the letter of the law. The law in this sense provides the rules of the game by which companies and people compete. Because legal systems vary from country to country, multinational managers who use only a legal analysis of an ethical problem are free to act in accordance with the law in each country, provided their own country does not have other requirements. Some scholars, such as the Nobel Laureate Milton Friedman, believe that profit maximization—within the rules of the game of open and free competition—is the main ethical responsibility of business.[24] Many multinational managers also believe that the legal analysis includes not only a test of whether behaviors or their consequences meet legal standards in the home and host countries, but also a comparison against international standards. These standards come from the international agreements among nations and the resulting code, summarized in Exhibit 4.9.

An important piece of legislation that pertains to business behavior with ethical implications is the 2002 Sarbanes-Oxley Act. The act requires multinational companies to hold their executives and senior management accountable for ethical conduct. Additionally, the legislation addresses the auditor–client relationship. This act was proposed by the Securities and Exchange Commission in reaction to the accounting scandals at companies like Enron and WorldCom. However, as we saw at the beginning of the chapter, U.S. companies are not alone in being affected by accounting scandals. European and Asian companies have also engaged in numbers manipulation, usually to inflate profits. As multinational companies get more involved in businesses in other countries, executives around the world are facing increasing pressure to operate legally, especially regarding accounting issues. In Canada and the United Kingdom, legislation similar to the Sarbanes-Oxley Act is being implemented. The future will most likely see similar groundbreaking legislation adopted around the world.

Although managers in for-profit businesses must consider the economic and legal implications of their decisions, few managers fail to consider the ethical

**Economic analysis**
In relation to an ethical problem, this analysis focuses on what is the best decision in terms of a company's profits.

**Legal analysis**
In relation to an ethical problem, this type of analysis focuses only on meeting legal requirements of host and parent countries.

**EXHIBIT** 4.10     Decision Points for Ethical Decision Making in Multinational Management

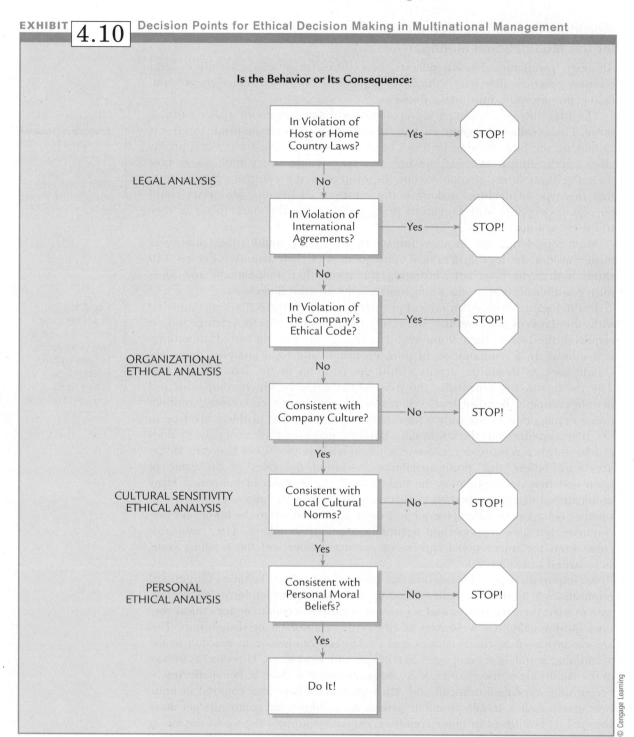

**Is the Behavior or Its Consequence:**

LEGAL ANALYSIS

In Violation of Host or Home Country Laws? — Yes → STOP!

No

In Violation of International Agreements? — Yes → STOP!

No

In Violation of the Company's Ethical Code? — Yes → STOP!

ORGANIZATIONAL ETHICAL ANALYSIS

No

Consistent with Company Culture? — No → STOP!

Yes

CULTURAL SENSITIVITY ETHICAL ANALYSIS

Consistent with Local Cultural Norms? — No → STOP!

Yes

PERSONAL ETHICAL ANALYSIS

Consistent with Personal Moral Beliefs? — No → STOP!

Yes

Do It!

© Cengage Learning

implications of their actions or practices as well. These issues involve the decision makers' individual moral beliefs on how to act; the company's policies regarding the proper way to treat all constituents (e.g., customers, employees, society); and the cultural context of the ethical issue.[25] Thus, besides the economic and legal

## CASE IN POINT

## Creating a Code of Conduct for a Multinational

As this chapter explains, there are cultural variations regarding how ethics are viewed in different countries. For instance, the French privacy watchdog did not allow McDonald's to enact its whistle-blower initiatives because the group said it was against French privacy law. How, then, can a multinational develop an enforceable code of conduct for its many subsidiaries? Experts suggest the following:

- *Involve the human resources management department:* Rather than turning to the legal department, experts suggest making use of the human resources management department. This department can help with developing a values-based approach to ethics rather than just a compliance- or legal-based approach.

- *Create an international advisory board:* Involve employees who are knowledgeable about the cultural demands of the regions they work in. Avoid using expatriates, who may not have as much in-depth cultural knowledge.

- *Draft a contents list and ensure that the code is culturally neutral:* The advisory board can get input from its different subsidiaries to determine the areas the code should address. Drafting of the contents should be done in as culturally neutral a way as possible.

- *Finalize contents:* Hold focus groups in the different areas to finalize the contents. Address any cultural discrepancies.

- *Translate the code of conduct:* Translate the code of conduct to the native languages of all employees. This will ensure maximal comprehension of the document.

*Source: Based on HR Focus. 2008. "Why global ethics count and how HR can help," October, 85(10): 13–15.*

analyses, multinational managers must subject problems to an **ethical analysis**; that is, they must go beyond simply responding to profit goals and legal regulations. To determine what is *really* the right thing to do, managers must take into account additional issues in their business decisions.

Ethical analysis has three components: one's organization, the national culture in which the business operates, and personal ethical beliefs.

In organizational ethical analysis, managers must look to their written codes of ethics and the unwritten norms of the company culture. Many organizations have ethical codes that specify the principles to guide managers' decision making and behaviors. When referring to the ethical code as a guide, managers use deontological ethical reasoning; they know and follow the written rules. In addition, all organizations have company cultures with unwritten rules that prescribe or proscribe behaviors. In some companies, for example, all managers would know the informal rules, such as, "Profit is more important than the environment as long as you follow the letter of the law," or, "Give the bribe if it gets the job done and no one gets hurt or caught." A manager might better understand the ethical bases of the company's culture by understanding the moral language used. For example, is it maximizing the greatest welfare or is it avoiding harm?

In setting a code of conduct, one important challenge that most multinationals face is enforcing such codes worldwide. How can a multinational work to ensure that such codes work globally? The following Multinational Management Brief provides some insights.

Multinational managers are guests in other nations. As such, their ethical decision making must go beyond legal constraints and following company

**Ethical analysis**
An analysis that goes beyond focusing on profit goals and legal regulations.

## Multinational Management **Brief**

### General Electric and Code of Conduct

General Electric (GE) is ranked sixth among the Fortune 500 companies and eleventh among the Fortune Global 500 companies. It is involved in varied industries, such as transportation equipment manufacturing, electrical products manufacturing, media, and healthcare products manufacturing. It produces such things as turbines, trains, TVs, and ultrasound machines, and also provides financial services. It also operates in a large number of countries that have widely different norms and standards. However, despite this variety of industries and countries, it is seen as a company with high ethics and integrity. How can it maintain such consistency? GE follows a number of important principles:

- *Committed leadership and leading by example:* One of the key reasons why GE can maintain consistency worldwide is that top executives are committed to performance with integrity. All executives are committed to ethics and show such commitment in all activities. Furthermore, top executives are also held to the same strict standards as everyone in the company. In two cases, GE did not hesitate to terminate top executives who violated GE ethics, although these executives had valuable in-depth country knowledge. Such actions send an important message that no one can violate the ethics standards under any circumstances.

- *Going beyond financial, legal and country rules:* In order to maintain the same standards worldwide, GE will often adopt the most rigorous standards that are applied consistently worldwide. The company consults with stakeholders to determine those critical areas that need to be addressed. GE has instituted a corporate risk committee made up of top officers. The committee meets regularly to discuss which areas need standards and to determine the most rigorous to be applied.

- *Staying ahead of regulators:* GE also makes sure that it is constantly being proactive to stay ahead of regulators. It has a team of employees that constantly reviews trends worldwide to determine what new regulations might be passed. It then reviews its own regulations to ensure that it stays ahead of new rules.

- *Assigning responsibility to all employees:* GE ensures that everyone is responsible for leadership in their own areas. Instead of the typical procedure of assigning ethics responsibility to employees in the legal or finance department, GE acknowledges that employees are more aware of ethical dilemmas in their work than others. As such, employees are given the authority and responsibility of maintaining and improving ethical standards in their respective areas. For example, plant managers are formally responsible for environmental, health, and safety issues in their plants.

- *Letting employees have a say in ethics:* GE discovered that educating and training employees, especially in newly acquired companies or emerging markets, is extremely critical. However, such training cannot function effectively unless employees can also voice their concern about current standards or new ethical issues. GE therefore gives employees several channels to voice their concerns. For example, GE has an ombuds system that lets employees voice their views without fear of retaliation.

*continued*

- *Holding leaders accountable with ethics metrics:* GE ensures that employees receive the necessary feedback regarding integrity and ethics. Each and every business leader is evaluated in terms of how they have fulfilled their ethics responsibilities. Have the proper systems been implemented? Have the leaders set appropriate goals? Have they integrated high ethics in all areas? Based on such evaluations, GE then rewards employees as appropriate.

*Sources: Based on* Ethisphere Institute. *2012. "Ethisphere Institute unveils the 2012 World's Most Ethical Companies."   http://ethisphere.com/ethisphere-institute-unveils-2012-worlds-most-ethical-companies/; Heineman, B., Jr. 2007. "Avoiding integrity land mines."* Harvard Business Review, *April, 100–108.*

rules and cultural norms. The managers must ask themselves whether what they are doing is consistent with and respectful of local cultural norms. For example, should they require employees to work on a religious holiday in one country because other units throughout the world are having regular business days?

Managers may begin these analyses at different points. For some issues, they may consider personal moral beliefs first. For other issues, it may make more sense to start with the law. At some point, however, after considering all the components in managerial decision making, you, as the manager, must make a personal moral judgment. Is it right for you? You are ultimately responsible. Most courts of law throughout the world will not accept the defense, "The organization made me do it."

Thus, for the multinational manager, the purely ethical issues in a decision must be weighed against the economic and legal analyses. A business must make a profit to survive, people do not want to go to jail or be fined, and most people want to behave ethically. Often there is no easy answer. For example, should a manager move a factory to a country with a cheap labor force, even if the move hurts the people who will lose their jobs? Should a multinational company sell potentially dangerous but useful products to a Third World country because the people in that country cannot afford the higher-priced, safer products? Should a multinational company ignore the use of child labor by some of its suppliers because the children's families desperately need the money and their competitors will use these suppliers anyway?

When faced with such complex conflicts among economics, law, and ethics, how do managers know whether they are behaving ethically? Although not every ethical dilemma faced by every individual in every culture has a resolution, one aid to ethical decision making is to approach decisions using philosophical ethical theories. Unfortunately, there is no single accepted ethical theory or system that managers can use as a guide when they face difficult ethical problems. Philosophers have debated the merits of various systems for millennia. Nevertheless, managers can make use of generally accepted ethical theories to understand ethical problems and the nature of their ethical decisions.

Although an ethical analysis like the one suggested in Exhibit 4.8 does not provide the "right" answer to an ethical problem, it does help to clarify the reasons behind ethical choices. It also raises the businessperson's awareness of the ethical nature of business decisions.

## Summary and Conclusions

The multinational manager faces ethical challenges similar to the domestic manager, but the challenges are magnified by the complexity of working in different countries and cultures. Part of this chapter provided essential background information on business ethics that is useful for ethics management in all settings. The chapter proposes a starting point for understanding international business ethics: understanding the relationship between ethics and social responsibility; understanding how ethical philosophies underlay much of our ethical reasoning; and understanding the differences among financial, legal, and ethical analyses.

Unlike the domestic-only manager, multinational managers must be able to assess how a country's social institutions and culture will affect their ability to manage ethical behavior. The examples showed that differences in legal and religious institutions and in basic cultural values often lead to different perceptions of what is ethical in business. Although there is some evidence of a convergence in business ethics due to the increase in international trade and investment, a multinational manager can never be too sensitive to issues as important as moral behavior in another culture.

Besides understanding the cultural setting in which they operate, multinational managers can never ignore their home country's laws. In this regard, the U.S. manager probably faces the strictest constraints. The FCPA constrains U.S. managers from behaving in ways that, while accepted in other societies, are off limits to U.S. managers. All multinational managers, regardless of national origin, should be aware of the international agreements to which their country is party. Following the summary of these agreements, as shown in Exhibit 4.9, will likely help managers avoid legal and ethical difficulties in their international operations.

The chapter concluded with a decision model for making ethical decisions in a multinational setting. Although the model does not tell you what to do, it does provide a variety of issues that a manager should consider. Managing ethically in the international environment is not always easy, and certainly the challenges will continue to grow with increasing interactions among nations.

## Discussion Questions

1. Discuss some of the issues that make international business ethics more complex than domestic business ethics.

2. What is ethical relativism? What are some of the dangers of using ethical relativism to justify all ethical decisions?

3. How do legal and ethical analyses differ? Give examples. Can a manager behave ethically just by following the host country's laws? Explain.

4. Discuss the difference between teleological and deontological theories of ethics. Give examples of how an international manager might appeal to either type of theory when faced with the opportunity to offer a bribe.

5. How do social institutions and culture affect the practice of business ethics in different countries? How do these differences affect managers who take the moral positions of ethical relativism and ethical universalism?

6. Discuss the arguments regarding whether businesses from other nations should follow the U.S. FCPA.

7. Discuss reasons for the trend toward a universal code of business ethics.

## Multinational Management **Internet Exercise**

1. Go to the Transparency International Website (http://www.transparency.org/).

2. Find information on Corruption Perception Index (CPI). How is the CPI measured? What is the logic for including the various indicators in measuring CPI?

3. Find information on the Bribe Payer's Index (BPI). How is the Bribe Payer's Index measured?

4. Compare and contrast the CPI and BPI. Do countries rank similarly on both lists? Why or why not?

5. What are some essential characteristics of countries that score highly on the CPI? How are they different from countries that have low CPI scores?

## Multinational Management **Skill Builder**

### Rex Lewis's Ethical Dilemma

**Step 1.** Reread the section on Thomas Donaldson's views on moral languages.

**Step 2.** Read the following scenario. Rex Lewis is a 25-year-old manager for ICS Corp., a small U.S. manufacturer of dietary supplements. After graduation, Mr. Lewis worked at company headquarters in Lexington, Nebraska, in a variety of positions. As an international business major, Mr. Lewis jumped at the chance to take a position as country manager in Matinea. Mr. Lewis studied the Matinean language for four years and visited the country for a summer while an undergraduate. He feels confident that he can handle this position because he has both the managerial and cultural experience.

ICS's major product is SUPALL, a dietary supplement that is inexpensive to produce and that can provide children with all of their basic nutritional needs. This product is very attractive to poor countries such as Matinea, where agricultural production is not sufficient to feed the population and recent droughts have made the situation even worse. Although cheaper than a well-rounded basic diet, one child's monthly supply of SUPALL costs about one-quarter of an average worker's salary at current prices, and most families are quite large.

In his first week in Matinea, Mr. Lewis makes a variety of startling discoveries. In spite of the relatively high price of SUPALL, demand in the Matinean market is strong. Moreover, ICS is making a 50 percent return on the product! Now Mr. Lewis realizes why the revenues from SUPALL have been able to support his company's crucial R&D research on other products. When he worked back in the United States, the CEO told him personally that if ICS doesn't come up with new products soon, the big companies will soon have a SUPALL-type product, and the price will fall drastically.

Mr. Lewis, who considers himself a good Christian, begins to wonder whether the price is fair for the Matineans. The price of SUPALL is cheaper than food, but it takes virtually all of a family's income to buy it. Yet ICS needs the profits to survive. Mr. Lewis has the authority to set prices in the country, but he must justify his decision to headquarters back in the United States.

**Step 3.** Divide the class into six teams, one for each moral language. Each team represents a version of the ICS Corp., but with a corporate culture dominated by one of the moral languages.

**Step 4.** As a team, review Exhibit 4.7 and conduct the relevant analyses. Come to a consensus and give a recommendation to Rex Lewis.

**Step 5.** Present and discuss your findings with the entire class.

---

## *Endnotes*

[1] Woods, Walter. 2006. "Hyundai scandal delays 2nd plant." *The Atlanta Journal-Constitution*, April 25, C4; Beurden, Pieter van and Tobias Gossling. 2008. "The worth of values—A literature review on the relation between corporate social and financial performance." *Journal of Business Ethics*, 82, 407–424.

[2] Buchholz, Rogene A. 1989. *Fundamental Concepts and Problems in Business Ethics*. Englewood Cliffs, NJ: Prentice Hall.

[3] Cullen, John B., Bart Victor, and Carroll Stephens. 1989. "An ethical weather report: Assessing the organization's ethical climate." *Organizational Dynamics*, 18, 50–62.

[4] Ferrell, O. C., John Fraedrich, and Linda Ferrell. 2005. *Business Ethics*. New York: Houghton Mifflin.

[5] Hall, Jeremy, and Harrie Vredenburg. 2005. "Managing stakeholder ambiguity." *MIT Sloan Management Review*, 47(1), 11–13.

[6] Buchholz.

[7] Donaldson, Thomas. 1992. "The language of international corporate ethics." *Business Ethics Quarterly*, 2, 271–281.

[8] Ibid.

[9] Foryth, Donelson R., Ernest H. O'Boyle, and Michael A. McDaniel. 2008. "East meets West: A meta-analytic investigation of cultural variations in idealism and relativism." *Journal of Business Ethics*, 83(4): 813–833.

[10] Cullen, J. B., K. Praveen Parboteeah, and Martin Hoegl. 2004. "Cross-national differences in managers' willingness to justify ethically suspect behaviors: A test of institutional anomie theory." *Academy of Management Journal*, 47(3): 410–421.

[11] Messner, S. F., and R. Rosenfeld. 2001. *Crime and the American Dream*. Belmont, CA: Wadsworth.

[12] Seleim, A., and N. Bontis. 2009. "The relationship between culture and corruption: A cross-national study." *Journal of Intellectual Capital*, 10(1): 165–184.

[13] Mendenhall, Mark E., Betty Jane Punnet, and David Ricks. 1994. *Global Management*. Cambridge, MA: Blackwell.

[14] Comte, O., A. Lambert-Mogiliansky, and T. Verdier. 2005. "Corruption and competition in procurement actions." *The Rand Journal of Economics*, 36(1): 1–15.

[15] Bayar, Guzin. 2005. "The role of intermediaries in corruption." *Public Choice*, 122, 277–298.

[16] Soon, Lim Ghee. 2006. "Macro-economic outcomes of corruption: A longitudinal empirical study." *Singapore Management Review*, 28(1): 63–72.

[17] Transparency International 2012. http://www.transparency.org.

[18] Gleich, Oren, and Ryan Woodward. 2005. "Foreign corrupt practices act." *The American Criminal Law Review*, 42(2): 545–571; Berger, R. P., B. E. Yannett, S. Hecker, D. M. Fuhr, and N. D. Grohmann. 2012. "The FCPA in 2011: The year of the trial shapes PCPA enforcement." Debevoise and Plimption LLP. Online edition, http://www.debevoise .com/files/Publication/f1606dac-62eb-4299-9bfa-5de993090940 /Presentation/PublicationAttachment/db0149b4-0ec7-4633-87b6 -69b728577aa1/FCPA_Update_Feb_2012.pdf.

[19] Donaldson, Thomas. 1989. *The Ethics of International Business*. New York: Oxford University Press.

[20] Frederick, William C. 1991. "The moral authority of transnational corporate codes." *Journal of Business Ethics*, 10, 165–1 77; Getz, Kathleen A. 1990. "International codes of conduct: An analysis of ethical reasoning." *Journal of Business Ethics*, 9, 567–578.

[21] Frederick.

[22] Donaldson, Thomas. 1992. "Can multinationals stage a universal morality play?" *Business and Society Review*, 81, 51–55.

[23] Hosmer, Larue Tone. 1987. *The Ethics of Management*. Homewood, IL: Irwin.

[24] Friedman, Milton. 1970. "The social responsibility of business is to increase its profits." *New York Times Magazine*, September 13, 122–126.

[25] Victor, Bart, and John B. Cullen. 1988. "The organizational bases of ethical work climates." *Administrative Science Quarterly*, 33, 101–125.

# Ethics of Offshoring: Novo Nordisk and Clinical Trials in Emerging Economies

Richard Ivey School of Business
The University of Western Ontario   IVEY   | Institute for
Entrepreneurship

On a warm day in early spring 2008, the telephone is ringing in the office of Anders Dejgaard, chief medical officer of Novo Nordisk, a leading developer and manufacturer of insulin and related products. A business journalist of the Danish national newspaper *Berlingske Tidende* is on the line and asking for an interview. Dejgaard knows her from several conversations relating to business practices in the pharmaceutical industry.

The journalist is investigating the offshoring of clinical trials by Danish companies. A report recently published in the Netherlands alleges that multinational pharmaceutical companies routinely conduct trials in

developing countries under allegedly unethical conditions. Also, the Danish National Committee on Biomedical Research Ethics has expressed concerns because Danish pharmaceutical companies are not obtaining ethical reviews in Denmark for such trials despite the offer from this committee. Thus, she wants to discuss Novo Nordisk's position on these issues.

Dejgaard reflects on how to react. Several articles on ethical aspects related to medical research in the Third World had appeared in the Danish press in recent months, creating an atmosphere of suspicion toward the industry.[1] Should he meet with the journalist and if so, what should he tell her? Or should he rather focus on his forthcoming business trip to new production facilities and send Novo Nordisk's press officer to meet the journalist? In his mind flashes the possibility of derogatory headlines in the tabloid press. As a company emphasizing corporate responsibility, the interaction with the media presents both opportunities and risks to Novo Nordisk.

## Novo Nordisk[2]

Novo Nordisk A/S had been created in 1989 through a merger between two Danish companies, Novo Industri A/S and Nordisk Gentofte A/S. Both had been established in the 1920s as manufacturers of insulin, a crucial medication for diabetes. Over decades of fierce competition, they had become leading providers of insulin and related pharmaceutical products. Novo Industri had been pursuing an internationally oriented strategy from the outset, and by 1936 was supplying insulin to 40 countries. A significant step in the internationalization of the company was a major push into the U.S. market in 1979. At the time, Food and Drug Administration (FDA) regulations required Novo Industri to replicate its clinical studies in the United States to obtain the approval of the marketing of their new products. In 1989, the two companies merged and in 2000 the merged company spun off the enzyme business "Novozymes."

In 2008, Novo Nordisk presents itself as a focused company within the healthcare industry and a world leader in diabetes care. It claims the broadest and most innovative diabetes product portfolio in the industry, including the most advanced insulin delivery systems. In addition, Novo Nordisk holds leading positions in areas such as haemostasis management, growth hormone therapy, and hormone replacement therapy. Sales reached DKr 41.8 billion (about US$8 billion) in 2007, of which DKr 30.5 billion were in diabetes care and DKr 11.4 billion were in biopharmaceuticals.

Innovation is considered pivotal to the success of Novo Nordisk, as it was to its predecessor companies. Continuous innovations allow the development of more refined, and thus more effective, insulin preparations, and new delivery systems, such as Novopen, that facilitate the administration of the treatment, including self-administration by patients. In 2008, about 18 percent of employees are working within research and development.

In 2008, Novo Nordisk holds market shares for insulin of about 56 percent in Europe, 41 percent in North America and 73 percent in Japan and employs about 26,000 people, of whom 12,689 are located in Denmark, 3,411 in the rest of Europe, 3,940 in North America, and the remainder in Asia Pacific and the rest of the world. Production facilities are located in six countries and products are marketed in 179 countries.

The shares of Novo Industri were first listed on the Copenhagen Stock Exchange in 1974 and on the London Stock Exchange in 1981 as the first Scandinavian company to be listed in London. In 2008, Novo Nordisk's B shares are listed on the stock exchanges in both Copenhagen and London, while its American depositary receipts (ADRs) are listed on the New York Stock Exchange.

Novo Nordisk emphasizes corporate social responsibility as part of its image, pursuing a triple bottom line approach: environmental and social responsibility along with economic viability. This commitment is demonstrated through its values and its environmental and social responsibility policies that are reported on its website (see Appendix 1).

---

### Appendix 1    Corporate Sustainability at Novo Nordisk (Extracts)

At Novo Nordisk, we refer to corporate sustainability as companies' ability to sustain and develop their business in the long-term perspective, in harmony with society. This implies a more inclusive view of business and its role: one in which engagements with stakeholders are not just used to legitimize corporate decisions, but rather the foundation for how a company conducts and grows its business. It is about innovation, opportunity and planning for the long term.

The Triple Bottom is the principle behind our way of doing business. The company's Articles of Association state that it "strives to conduct its activities in a financially, environmentally and socially responsible way." This is a commitment to sustainable development and balanced growth, and it has been built into corporate governance structures, management tools and methods of assessing and rewarding individuals' performance....

**The stakeholder dimension:** Novo Nordisk needs to stay attuned to emerging trends and 'hot issues' on the global agenda in order to respond and to contribute to the debate. Stakeholder engagement is an integrated part of our business philosophy. We have long-standing engagements with stakeholders that are vital for building trust and understanding of a variety of issues. By involving stakeholders in the decision-making processes, decisions are better founded and solutions more likely to succeed. Stakeholders are defined as any individual or group that may affect or be affected by a company's activities.

**Translating commitment to action:** Corporate sustainability has made a meaningful difference to our business, and we believe it is a driver of our business success. This is best illustrated in three examples:

**Business ethics:** Surveys indicate that ethical behavior in business is today the number one driver of reputation for pharmaceutical companies. Any company that is not perceived by the public as behaving in an ethical manner is likely to lose business, and it takes a long time to regain trust. While the Novo Nordisk Way of Management is a strong guide to our behavior, we decided we needed more detailed guidance in the area of business ethics. In 2005 we therefore framed a new business ethics policy, in line with universally accepted high standards, backed by a set of procedures. Since then we have trained managers and employees, held workshops, and offered e-learning on the new policy.

*continued*

Appendix 1 Continued

**Climate change:** We need to act to put a brake to human-induced climate change. While the implications of climate change pose major business risks, there are also opportunities. We have partnered with the WWF [World Wildlife Fund] in the Climate Savers program and set an ambitious target to achieve a 10% reduction in our company's $CO_2$ emissions by 2014, compared with 2004 emission levels. This will occur through optimized production, energy savings, and greater use of renewable energy supplies.

**The diabetes pandemic:** Today, diabetes is recognized as a pandemic. Novo Nordisk responds to this major societal challenge by working in partnerships with many others to rally the attention of policy-makers and influencers to change diabetes. We have made a promise of **Changing Diabetes®** and have framed **a strategy for inclusive access to diabetes care.** We established the **World Diabetes Foundation,** and have made several initiatives to advocate for change and build evidence of diabetes developments. **The National Changing Diabetes®** program and **DAWN** are examples of education and awareness programs implemented by Novo Nordisk affiliates in their respective countries. Our **Changing Diabetes®** Bus that promotes Novo Nor-disk's global **Changing Diabetes®** activities had reached 86,000 people by the end of 2007 during its world tour. Its primary goal is to support the **UN Resolution on diabetes,** which was passed in December 2006.

*Source: www.novonordisk.com, accessed November 2008.*

Critical milestones in Novo Nordisk's ambition to be recognized as a leader of corporate sustainability include the publication in 1994 of its Environmental Report. It was the first company in Denmark and one of the first in the world to do so. This was followed in 1999 by the first annual Social Report. In 2001, Novo Nordisk established the World Diabetes Foundation, a charity aiming to improve diabetes care in developing countries, where diabetes is becoming an epidemic as it had in Europe and North America a few decades earlier.

In recognition of its sustainability engagement, Novo Nordisk had been included in the Dow Jones Global Sustainability Indices, where it was ranked as "best in class" in the healthcare category in 2007. At home, Novo Nordisk is frequently ranked as having the most highly regarded corporate image by Danish magazines *Berlingske Nyhedmagasin, Børsen,* and *Ingeniøren.*

## New Medications: Development and Approval

Novo Nordisk, like other pharmaceutical and medical companies, heavily invests in the development of new medications offering more effective, safe, and user-friendly treatments. New product development involves the creation of new drugs or modifications in their use, for instance their dosage and the form of administration. To bring new drugs or medical devices to market, they must be approved by the relevant authorities—the FDA in the United States and European Medicines Agency (EMEA) in the European Union. The approval of drugs and medical devices requires proof of their efficacy and

their safety. Efficacy refers to scientific evidence that the drug improves patients' conditions as claimed by the manufacturer. Safety refers to the absence of substantive negative side-effects. Thus, to obtain approval, pharmaceutical companies have to provide scientific evidence that the drug improves the conditions of patients and is free of disproportional side-effects.

This evidence has to be based on, among other data, clinical trials in which the drug has been tested on actual patients. The clinical trials are normally conducted in four stages. Phase 1 involves a small number of healthy volunteers and serves to assess the kinetic properties and tolerability of the drug. Phase 2 is performed on larger groups of patients to assess how well the drug works and to establish the doses that give the desired effect and to continue its safety assessment. Phase 3 trials often involve thousands of patients and aims to provide a definitive assessment of how effective and safe the drug is. All data generated in the three phases form an essential part of submissions to the regulatory authorities (FDA, EMEA, and their counterparts in other countries) for drug approval. With this approval, the drug can then be marketed for the approved indications. Further trials, in phase 4, may be required to obtain permission to extend the labeling of a drug to new indications (e.g. a different disease) or specific groups, such as children or pregnant women.

Phase 3 and 4 trials require a large number of patients with the specific disease that the drug is to improve. A typical approval process conducted by Novo Nordisk might require six to eight different phase 3 trials with different patient groups or combinations of the drug component, each involving about 400 to 800 patients. Such trials are often conducted as multinational studies involving up to 15 countries. With increasing requirements for patient exposure for approval and increasing numbers of drugs being tested, the recruitment of patients is often a major challenge. Typically, trials are conducted at multiple hospitals that all must follow the same trial protocol to ensure the consistency of data and compliance with existing "good clinical practice" (GCP) guidelines. Multi-site trials also facilitate the recruitment of patients with diverse backgrounds, for instance different ethnicities and diets, while helping to demonstrate their universal properties. Doctors and nurses but not patients are normally paid for this work and hospitals often find it attractive to participate in trials that allow access to new medications and front line research. Clinical trials, especially phase 3, are a major cost factor in the development of new medications and they often take many years to conduct (on average eight years).

In the early 2000s, major pharmaceutical industries increasingly moved parts of their trials, especially phases 3 and 4, to countries outside their traditional areas of operations, especially to Eastern Europe, South America, India, and China. Hospitals in these areas provide access to qualified medical staff and larger numbers of patients with the specific conditions, while potentially being able to administer a trial at lower costs. Moreover, the efficacy of drugs may also vary across contexts, for instance due to genetic, dietary, climatic, or other environmental conditions. In such cases, multi-site trials help to establish the efficacy of medications across contexts. Some countries, such as Japan, India, and China, in fact require that trials are at least in part conducted locally to approve a new medication in the respective countries. However, the conduct of clinical trials in these areas also raises a range of ethical issues.

## Ethical Issues in Medical Research[3]

Ethical issues in the pharmaceutical industry have received considerable media attention over several decades, as the industry has failed to live up to the expectations of some interest groups. In particular, clinical trials raise a number of widely recognized issues. Medical professionals, and with them many NGOs and media, focus on the medical ethics grounded in the Hippocratic oath that commits doctors to treat each patient to the best of their abilities, never to cause intentional harm, and to maintain patient confidentiality. Scientists and approval authorities have been concerned about the scientific rigor of the tests to provide solid evidence of the effects of a new drug, and thus to protect potential future users of the drug. At the same time, pharmaceutical companies have to operate with limited financial resources and to satisfy shareholders and thus cannot spend more resources than expected future revenues would justify. Accordingly, the industry has been accused of performing trials in developing countries with lower attention to ethical principles—"ethical bribing," with patients acting as guinea pigs that do not understand and/or care about the risk involved but just want to get free medication and with investigators not meeting the competence requirements, etc. Allegedly, all this just serves to generate documentation for compounds that are to be sold only in developed countries.

**Medical (Hippocratic) ethics** concern primarily the individual patients that are participating in any experiment. The relationship between the doctor and the subject participating in a trial is thus governed by the doctor's responsibility to care for his or her patient. Past incidences where this principle had been violated continue to affect popular perceptions of medical research. Most infamously, the Tuskegee syphilis study left 400 impoverished and unwitting African-American men in Macon County, Alabama, untreated to study how they developed the disease—an experiment initiated in 1932 and terminated only in the 1970s.

To prevent such scandals, professional medical organizations have developed guidelines and principles of ethics to guide their research, notably the Helsinki Declaration of the World Medical Association (see Appendix 2). These widely accepted ethical principles aim to protect subjects, e.g., patients, participating in such research. These include:

- *Voluntary informed consent:* Each patient has to agree voluntarily to participate in the research based on being fully informed about the purposes of the study and potential risks for the individual. Sponsors and local site investigators thus normally write an "informed consent" document that informs potential subjects of the true risks and potential benefits, which is signed by each patient or their legal guardian before any trial procedure.

- *Respect of patients:* The privacy of the subject should be protected and they should be free to withdraw from the experiment at any time without reasoning. The doctor's professional responsibility to the patient should take precedence over any other considerations.

- *Independent review:* Any medical and pharmacological research has to be assessed on its scientific merits and ethicality by an independent review board (IRB) that is independent from those involved in or sponsoring the research.

**Appendix 2   Helsinki Declaration of the World Medical Association (Excerpts)**

10. It is the duty of the physician in medical research to protect the life, health, privacy, and dignity of the human subject.

13. The design and performance of each experimental procedure involving human subjects should be clearly formulated in an experimental protocol. This protocol should be submitted for consideration, comment, guidance, and where appropriate, approval to a specially appointed ethical review committee, which must be independent of the investigator, the sponsor or any other kind of undue influence. This independent committee should be in conformity with the laws and regulations of the country in which the research experiment is performed. The committee has the right to monitor ongoing trials. The researcher has the obligation to provide monitoring information to the committee, especially any serious adverse events. The researcher should also submit to the committee, for review, information regarding funding, sponsors, institutional affiliations, other potential conflicts of interest and incentives for subjects.

14. The research protocol should always contain a statement of the ethical considerations involved and should indicate that there is compliance with the principles enunciated in this Declaration.

15. Medical research involving human subjects should be conducted only by scientifically qualified persons and under the supervision of a clinically competent medical person. The responsibility for the human subject must always rest with a medically qualified person and never rest on the subject of the research, even though the subject has given consent.

16. Every medical research project involving human subjects should be preceded by careful assessment of predictable risks and burdens in comparison with foreseeable benefits to the subject or to others. This does not preclude the participation of healthy volunteers in medical research. The design of all studies should be publicly available.

17. Physicians should abstain from engaging in research projects involving human subjects unless they are confident that the risks involved have been adequately assessed and can be satisfactorily managed. Physicians should cease any investigation if the risks are found to outweigh the potential benefits or if there is conclusive proof of positive and beneficial results.

18. Medical research involving human subjects should only be conducted if the importance of the objective outweighs the inherent risks and burdens to the subject. This is especially important when the human subjects are healthy volunteers.

19. Medical research is only justified if there is a reasonable likelihood that the populations in which the research is carried out stand to benefit from the results of the research.

20. The subjects must be volunteers and informed participants in the research project.

21. The right of research subjects to safeguard their integrity must always be respected. Every precaution should be taken to respect the privacy of the subject, the confidentiality of the patient's information and to minimize the impact of the study on the subject's physical and mental integrity and on the personality of the subject.

22. In any research on human beings, each potential subject must be adequately informed of the aims, methods, sources of funding, any possible conflicts of interest, institutional affiliations of the researcher, the anticipated benefits and potential risks of the study and the discomfort it may entail. The subject should be informed of the right to abstain from participation in the study or to withdraw consent to participate at any time without reprisal. After ensuring that the subject has understood the information, the physician should then obtain the subject's freely given informed consent, preferably in writing. If the consent cannot be obtained in writing, the non-written consent must be formally documented and witnessed.

23. When obtaining informed consent for the research project the physician should be particularly cautious if the subject is in a dependent relationship with the physician or may consent under duress. In that case the informed consent should be obtained by a well-informed physician who is not engaged in the investigation and who is completely independent of this relationship.

*continued*

---

29. The benefits, risks, burdens, and effectiveness of a new method should be tested against those of the best current prophylactic, diagnostic, and therapeutic methods. This does not exclude the use of placebo, or no treatment, in studies where no proven prophylactic, diagnostic or therapeutic method exists.

    Note of clarification on paragraph 29 of the WMA Declaration of Helsinki

    The WMA hereby reaffirms its position that extreme care must be taken in making use of a placebo-controlled trial and that in general this methodology should only be used in the absence of existing proven therapy. However, a placebo-controlled trial may be ethically acceptable, even if proven therapy is available, under the following circumstances:

    • Where for compelling and scientifically sound methodological reasons its use is necessary to determine the efficacy or safety of a prophylactic, diagnostic, or therapeutic method; or

    • Where a prophylactic, diagnostic, or therapeutic method is being investigated for a minor condition and the patients who receive placebo will not be subject to any additional risk of serious or irreversible harm.

    All other provisions of the Declaration of Helsinki must be adhered to, especially the need for appropriate ethical and scientific review.

30. At the conclusion of the study, every patient entered into the study should be assured of access to the best-proven prophylactic, diagnostic, and therapeutic methods identified by the study.

    Note of clarification on paragraph 30 of the WMA Declaration of Helsinki

    The WMA hereby reaffirms its position that it is necessary during the study planning process to identify post-trial access by study participants to prophylactic, diagnostic, and therapeutic procedures identified as beneficial in the study or access to other appropriate care. Post-trial access arrangements or other care must be described in the study protocol so the ethical review committee may consider such arrangements during its review.

*Source: www.wma.net/e/policy/b3.htm, accessed October 2008.*

---

**Scientific ethics** are concerned about the validity of the results of the scientific inquiry and thus the methodological rigor of the study. Thus, a study has to use valid measurements and statistical techniques and samples that are unbiased and sufficiently large that they can generate trustworthy and valid results.

Such scientific rigor is important to anyone who may in the future use an approved drug or medical device. Awareness of the need for rigorous tests prior to launching new medications had been triggered by various scandals of the 1960s, notably the Thalidomide scandal involving a pain killer used by women to ease sleep problems and pregnancy sickness. Due to side-effects of this medication, thousands of children worldwide were born with incomplete arms or legs, before the drug was withdrawn. In consequence to this and other scandals, the licensing and approval procedures for drugs have been tightened to ensure that only drugs with scientifically proven efficacy and safety are marketed.

**Ethical businesses** have to balance activities done in the interest of the wider society with their pursuit of profits. The late Nobel prize-winning economist Milton Friedman famously declared that the primary social responsibility of business is to make profits.[4] Under efficient markets, which he firmly believed in, this would generate the most mutually beneficial outcome. Thus, he argued, firms ought to give precedence to shareholders over any other interest groups.

Others argue that firms should engage in corporate social responsibility because it can be expected to benefit their bottom line in the long run, for instance through reputation effects. Yet others argue that firms have an intrinsic, normative responsibility to use their influence to do good for society and to aspire to the highest moral standards, independent of the profit motive. However, even so, their financial resources will be limited. Like organizations in the governmental or non-profit sector, businesses have to make critical decisions about how best to use their scarce resources.

## Ethics of Placebo Experiments[5]

Particular concerns have arisen for placebo trials, that is, trials where a control group of patients receives a treatment without any active ingredient for the disease. The purpose of placebo trials is, normally, to provide evidence of product efficacy by showing statistically significant improvements of the conditions of patients receiving the active treatment, compared to those receiving a placebo treatment.

Placebo trials are especially important for diseases that are affected by the so-called placebo effect, that is, patients' conditions improving because of the positive effect of receiving a form of treatment rather than the specific medication. This has been shown to be quite substantive, for instance, for schizophrenia and other psychiatric conditions. Both American and European authorities thus often require placebo trials as prerequisite for the approval of new medications.

Alternatives to placebo trials include the use of active controls, in which the control groups receive a previously marketed medication with known properties. Yet these types of trials are often not sufficient to provide the required rigorous evidence regarding the efficacy of the medication.[6] Placebo trials may create risks for patients in the placebo group, in particular when patients are denied a treatment that is known to improve their condition. The Helsinki Declaration therefore requires avoiding placebo experiments unless very special reasons require them or no alternative treatment of the illness is available (see Appendix 2, item 29). Ethics review boards have become very restrictive in permitting placebo trials. There have been arguments from some groups that one reason for the pharmaceutical industry to place studies in developing countries is the possibility of performing placebo trials that otherwise can be difficult to get approval for in developed countries.

Novo Nordisk generally avoids placebo trials. Usually, they are used only in phase 1 trials in healthy volunteers when new drug candidates are being developed. These trials are normally located near its main research centers in Europe and rarely in non-Western countries.

## Media Spotlights

In February 2008, a report from the Dutch NGO SOMO raised public awareness of placebo trials conducted by major pharmaceutical companies in developing countries.[7] The report was critical of trials that had been submitted to the FDA and the EMEA for drug approval. Its primary concern was that key information about ethical aspects of these clinical trials was not available to it as an external observer and it found incidences where patients suffered serious harm after receiving a placebo in a trial.

The report focused on three case studies of clinical trials for recently approved drugs conducted in Eastern Europe and Asia, based on publicly available information. It concluded that

> trial subjects in these countries are more vulnerable and their rights are less secured than in high income countries. Conditions such as poverty, illiteracy, poor health systems and inadequate research ethics committees result in international ethical standards not being met. Current EU legislation requires that results from unethical clinical trials … not be accepted for marketing authorization. With three case studies on recently approved drugs in the EU (Abilify, Olmetec, and Seroquel), SOMO demonstrates that this principle is being violated. European authorities devote little to no attention to the ethical aspects of the clinical trials submitted, and they accept unethical trials as well as trials of poor quality.[8]

In its conclusions, the report alleges that local regulation and the enforcement of ethical principles are less strict, partly because local independent review boards are less qualified and partly because they are less keen on restricting what is potentially a revenue earner. The authors thus advocate global harmonization of ethical criteria along the principles currently used by ethics committees in Europe: "… there must be no discrepancy between the ethical criteria used to approve research protocols in Western Europe and in low and middle income economies to avoid the creation of 'easy countries.'"[9]

The media picked up, in particular, the case of a schizophrenic patient committing suicide while participating in a trial of the anti-schizophrenia medicine Seroquel by Astra-Zeneca. Moreover, media reported that 10 percent of recipients in the placebo group had to be hospitalized because of worsening conditions. Careful reading of the original report suggests that 8.3 percent (p. 64) of a group of 87 patients (p. 62) were affected, which adds up to seven persons. No assessment of the likelihood of such incidents under alternative medication available at the time had been included in the report.

Concerns have also been raised by the Danish National Committee on Biomedical Research Ethics.[10] In particular, the committee criticizes the industry for not accepting the committee's offer to provide independent ethical reviews before submitting to local ethics committees as a service to the industry. The chairperson for the committee, Johannes Gaub, chief medical officer at Odense Hospital, told the media:

> Like production companies locate their factories in low wage areas, the medical industry is

*outsourcing its scientific experiments in the same way. The costs of conducting medical trials in developing countries are only a fraction of what they are in the West because of the low wages.... In the USA it costs about DKr 150,000 to move one patient through a trial. In Denmark, it costs DKr 80,000. I don't really know the price in developing countries, but it is a fraction of that.*

Gaub also rejects the concern of the industry that hospitals in Denmark would not be able to conduct trials of the necessary scale, given the growing requirements worldwide to provide clinical trial data for approvals around the world:

*We have considerable spare capacity in Denmark. Despite the high costs we have a well-functioning health system. We have data about patients because of our national identity number system, and there are many clinical researchers in the hospitals who would be happy to participate in the trials of new medications.... It is actually worrying that we do not receive more applications in Denmark. We need clinical research to maintain the high level of health science that we so far have had in the country.*[11]

Danish politicians also joined the debate. In a statement to the health committee of the national parliament, the minister for health emphasized that E.U. regulation for the approval of new medicines requires that trials conducted outside the European Union have been implemented in accordance with the European Union's own rules as well as with ethical principles such as the Helsinki Declaration. The minister thus concluded:

*I find no reason to take initiatives to constrain research projects by the Danish medical industry outside the EU. In this context, I consider it important to emphasize that all clinical trials that shall be used as a basis for applications for approval of marketing of a medication in the EU must comply with the EU's laws on good clinical practice and the ethical principles regarding medical research with human subjects.*[12]

Also, other politicians joined the debate. For example, Member of Parliament Birgitte Josefsen (V)[13] urged Danish pharmaceutical companies to hold the ethical flag high: "The medical industry ought to be very careful about whom they use as test persons. That should be people who have resources to say 'no'. A poor Indian mother with three children is not the right one to become a test person."[14]

## Novo Nordisk's Position on Clinical Trials

Anders Dejgaard is pondering the complexity of the ethical issues. As corporate sustainability features highly on Novo Nordisk's agenda, the ethically appropriate handling of clinical trials is important to the company. It conducts clinical trials globally to test the safety and efficacy of new drug candidates in order to obtain global marketing authorization. These trials always follow a common protocol and thus the same standards at all trials sites. Trials sites are selected based on a variety of criteria, including the quality of regulatory authorities, ethical review processes, and medical practices. Moreover, drugs have to be tested on the types of patients who will later become users of the drug and trial subjects should have access to the drugs after the process has been completed. In addition, Novo Nordisk will only conduct trials in countries where it has affiliates with the necessary competence to arrange and monitor the trials. In 2008, these criteria were met in about 65 countries worldwide.

Novo Nordisk has adapted the global guidelines and recommendations by all the professional bodies and publishes its policies on clinical trials on its website (see Appendix 3). This includes enhanced global exposure of investigated products through its own website as well as websites sponsored by the FDA (see Appendix 3). Novo Nordisk conducts research in therapies that require global trials and the inclusion of different ethnic populations. The company also anticipates a need to increase the number of clinical trials due to an expanding pipeline and more extensive global and local regulatory requirements. Its ethical principles and standard operating procedures, which apply globally, are designed to ensure due respect for the safety, rights, integrity, dignity, confidentiality, and well-being of all human beings participating in Novo Nordisk-sponsored trials. Novo Nordisk is auditing 10 percent of all trials, while at the same time the American and European authorities, FDA and EMEA, are making random checks of about 1 percent of Novo Nordisk's clinical trials. These random checks have never identified ethical problems in clinical trials in developing countries. Since trials are normally conducted in multiple countries, the same standards are applied everywhere, for both ethical and scientific reasons (consistency of results).

At the same time, Dejgaard is irritated about the request for an additional ethics approval by the Danish National Committee on Biomedical Research Ethics. He estimates that it would add three months to the preparation of each new trial. In his own experience, the ethical

**Appendix 3   Clinical Trials: Novo Nordisk's Position**

- Clinical trials sponsored by Novo Nordisk will always be conducted according to the Helsinki Declaration, which describes human rights for patients participating in clinical trials, and similar international ethical guidelines such as the Nuremberg code, the Belmont report and CIOMMS, and the International Conference of Harmonisation (ICH) guidelines for current good clinical practice (cGCP).

- The above guidelines and regulations are the foundation for our clinical Standard Operating Procedures (SOPs) including the SOP on the 'principles of clinical trials'. These standards are laid out to ensure the safety, rights, integrity, confidentiality, and well-being of persons involved in Novo Nordisk trials globally.

- Novo Nordisk will apply the same procedures wherever we sponsor clinical trials. This means that all subjects enrolled in Novo Nordisk trials are protected by the same rights, high ethical standards, and regulations irrespective of location of the study.

- The interest and well-being of the trial subject should always prevail over the interest of science, society, and commerce.

- Novo Nordisk will not conduct clinical trials for drug development in countries where we do not intend to market the investigational drug. In any country where we do undertake clinical trials we will ensure that a proper internal organization and a proper regulated external environment exist.

- Clinical trials should only be done if they can be scientifically and medically justified, and all Novo Nordisk-sponsored trials should be based on sound scientific methodology described in a clear and detailed protocol. Placebo will only be used as comparator when scientifically and ethically justified.

- No trial activity in Novo Nordisk-sponsored trials will start before approval is obtained from external local ethics committees and health authorities.

- We will always ensure that investigators involved in Novo Nordisk clinical trials are skilled in the therapeutic area and are trained in GCP. No procedure involving a person undergoing clinical trial activities will take place before the appropriate freely given informed consent is obtained based on proper information on potential risk of participation in the trial. A patient can at any time withdraw from a clinical trial without giving any reason. In cases where trial subjects are incompetent, physically or mentally incapable of giving consent, or if the person is a minor, Novo Nordisk will follow local regulations for obtaining consent.

- Products used in Novo Nordisk-sponsored clinical trials will be manufactured and controlled according to international and local regulations and laws. Novo Nordisk will conduct frequent site monitoring to ensure that the study is executed according to the study protocol, and that data used in statistical analysis and reporting reflect the data obtained from the involved patients during the trial. Safety information from any Novo Nordisk trial will be monitored on a continuous basis and appropriate actions will be taken if risks of the investigational product outweigh the potential benefits.

- Patients participating in Novo Nordisk-sponsored clinical trials will always be offered best available and proven treatment after study termination. The treatment will be offered at the discretion of the responsible physician. If study medication is not marketed the responsible physician can apply for medication on a named patient basis. Post-study medication will be described in the protocol and informed consent.

- Novo Nordisk will ensure proper indemnification of trial subjects in case a trial product or procedures in a Novo Nordisk-sponsored trial cause bodily harm to a trial subject.

- Novo Nordisk strives to have all clinical trial results published according to accepted international guidelines, and we will always ensure transparency of our studies by publishing protocol synopses on the external website: www.clinicaltrials.gov. Study results from trials involving marketed drugs can be accessed via www.clinicalstudyresults.org. Furthermore, Novo Nordisk has its own online repository for clinical trials activities: novonordisk-trials.com. Novo Nordisk is collating all information about bioethics in the R&D area on www.novonordisk.com/R&D/bioethics.

*Source: www.novonordisk.com, accessed November 2008.*

reviews in those locations he worked in are as rigorous as in Western countries and he does not recognize an added benefit, as the Danish committee would be no better in assessing a trial than a local ethics committee. On the contrary, he finds the suggestion more appropriate for a colonial empire. Moreover, specific local issues, such as ethnic or religious minorities, would be better understood by local committees.

Yet various issues come to mind. Is Novo Nordisk doing its research and development in an appropriate manner or are there issues that could be done better in view of Novo Nordisk's triple bottom line commitments? Are Novo Nordisk's standard operating procedures being properly implemented in all developing countries that participate in the programs and how is such compliance to be monitored? How should Novo Nordisk manage its simultaneous relationships with various regulatory authorities, independent review boards at various sites, and with the Danish National Committee on Biomedical Research Ethics?

Most pressing is the decision on how to handle the journalist. Should he meet her in person, send a public relations person, or not meet at all and reply in writing, citing the corporate website? If he is to meet her, what should be the key messages that he should get across and how should he prepare himself for any questions she might raise during the meeting?

## CASE DISCUSSION QUESTIONS

The case is written from the perspective of Anders Dejgaard, chief medical officer. Assignment questions thus may take his perspective.

1. Considering both economic and ethical aspects, is it appropriate for companies like Novo Nordisk to conduct clinical trials in, for example, India? What exactly are the principles that should guide such a decision?
2. If trials are conducted in an emerging economy, how should they be managed, and which standards should apply?
3. What interest groups are joining the public debate and why? How should businesses handle them? What is the role, respectively, of Danish, European, American, and host country authorities and ethics committees in this process?
4. How should Anders Dejgaard react when the journalist calls to discuss Novo Nordisk's practices? What is the most effective way to communicate with the public?

## CASE NOTES

[1] See in particular Alfter, B. 2008. "De fattige er verdens nye forsogskaniner. Krav om kontrol med medicinalindustrien," *Information*, Feb. 26, pp. 4–5, and Lambeck, B. and S. G. Jensen. 2007. "Halvdelen at al medicin afproves i den tredje verden," *Politiken*, October 6.

[2] This section draws on the company Web site, www.novonordisk .com, and an undated (circa 2002) document, "Novo Nordisk History," available via this website.

[3] This section draws in particular on Emanuel, E. J., D. Wendler, and C. Grady. 2000. "What makes clinical research ethical?" *Journal of the American Medical Association*, 284:20, pp. 2701–2711, and Michael A. Santoro and Thomas M. Gorrie, *Ethics and the Pharmaceutical Industry*, Cambridge University Press, 2005.

[4] Friedman M. 1970. "The social responsibility of business is to increase profits," *The New York Times Magazine*, September 13; reprinted in Meyer, K. E. 2009. *Multinational Enterprises and Host Economies*, Elgar, Cheltenham.

[5] This section draws on contemporary discussions in the medical literature, in particular Emanuel, E. J. and F. G. Miller. 2001. "The ethics of placebo-controlled trials: A middle ground." *New England Journal of Medicine*, 345:12, pp. 915–919, and Temple, R. and S. S. Ellenberg. 2000. "Placebo-controlled trials and active-controlled trials in the evaluation of new treatments," *Annals of Internal Medicine*, 133:6, pp. 455–463.

[6] An active-control trial infers efficacy from non-significant differences of performance compared to the active-control drug. Such non-significance, however, can be caused by a number of other influences. Moreover, this test is problematic if the active-control drug is subject to large placebo effects varying with study designs. On the merits and concerns of active-control trials, see e.g., Temple, R. and S. S. Ellenberg. 2000. "Placebo-controlled trials and active-controlled trials in the evaluation of new treatments," and Walsh, B. T., S. N. Seidman, R. Sysko and M. Gould. 2002. "Placebo response in studies of major depression: Variable, substantial and growing," *Journal of the American Medical Association*, 287:14, pp. 1840–1847.

[7] Schipper, I. and F. Weyzing. 2008. "Ethics for drug testing in low and middle income countries: Considerations for European market authorisation," *Stichting Onderzoek Multinationale Ondernemingen* (SOMO), http://somo.nl/publications-en/Publication_2472, accessed October 2008.

[8] Ibid., abstract on the cover page.

[9] Ibid, p. 68.

[10] For further information on the Danish National Committee on Biomedical Research Ethics, see www.cvk.im.dk/cvk/site.aspx?p=119.

[11] Both citations are from Erhardtsen, B. 2008. "Medicinalindustrien dropper frivillig etisk blastempling," *Berlingske Tidende*, April 5, Inland section, pp. 6–7 (case author's translation).

[12] Nielsen, J.K. 2008. Besvarlse af sporgsmal nr. 20 (aim. del) som Folketingets Sundhedsudvalg har stillet til indenrigs - og sundhedsministeren (Written reply to a question in the health committee of the Danish parliament), January 9. (Archives of the Danish government: Indenrigs or Sundhedministeriet, Laegemiddelkontoret, J.nr. 2007-13009-599, Sagsbeh: nhj) (case author's translation).

[13] (V) refers to Venstre, one of the parties of the minority government at the time.

[14] Berlingske Tidende Web site. 2008. www.berlingske.dk/article /20080403/danmark/704030057, April 3, accessed October 2008 (case author's translation).

# Shell Oil in Nigeria

## Introduction

Nigeria is a country that is slightly more than twice the size of California. In July of 2011, its population was estimated at just over 155 million people making it the 8th most populated country in the world. It is Africa's most populous country and is composed of more than 250 ethnic groups. The country has the second highest rate of HIV/AIDS deaths and is ranked number three with respect to total number of people living with HIV/AIDS in the country.

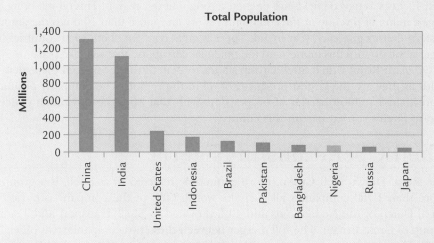

The country itself is full of rich natural resources such as natural gas, petroleum, tin, iron, coal, and limestone. Despite these rich resources, the country has been crippled by civil wars, military rule, religious tensions, and corruption. Even more devastating was the poor macroeconomic management that has left the country completely dependent upon its number one resource which is petroleum. Petroleum provides 95% of the foreign exchange earnings and close to 80% of its budgetary revenues. In 2010, Nigeria surpassed Iran to become the second largest oil producer behind Saudi Arabia. It shipped 2.464 million barrels of oil per day compared to Iran who shipped 2.248 million barrels per day.

The United States imports 17% of its petroleum from West Africa with Nigeria being the key supplier. That number is estimated to rise to over 25% in the year 2015. Despite the potential for oil to change the lives of this resource rich country, the majority of the Nigerians live on less than $1USD per day. The poor living conditions, low wages, and lack of quality of life improvement is attributed to the large amount of corruption by the citizens, politicians, and companies who exist within the country.

# A History of Corruption

While petroleum drives the majority of the economy, it also drives the majority of the corruption. Nigeria has long been considered the most corrupt country in the world. Its citizens, government and corporations have been party to and involved in political corruption, bureaucratic corruption, electoral corruption, embezzlement, and bribery. In fact, it has been said the corruption is actually a viable enterprise in the society with no way to trace these activities or prosecute those involved.

The companies operating in this region have long been blamed for allowing, participating, and even creating the corruption that has taken place. Not only have they failed to engage reformers but they have been accused of doing things like bribing officials, obscuring oil revenue figures, and failing to invest in the infrastructure and improvement of the people in the country. While the oil companies point to millions of dollars of investment into the region, one look at the impoverished conditions common to the people of Nigeria and its difficult to say it was enough.

An estimated $200 billion in revenues is planned to go to African treasuries in the next 10 years as new oil fields are opened throughout this region. This oil will bring the largest influx of revenue in the continents history and more than 10 times the amount western donors give each year in aid. There is great concern about what countries like Nigeria will do with this money and the potential corruption that will take place.

Oil giant Royal Dutch Shell Group stands to benefit the most from these new oil fields as they are the largest producer of oil in the region. The company produces more than 1 million barrels of oil per day. With that said, there is much concern due to Shell's storied past in this country.

# Shell Operations in Nigeria

The Royal Dutch Shell Group, more commonly referred to as Shell, is a group of more than 1,700 companies all over the world. 60% of the company is owned by Royal Dutch of the Netherlands and 40% is owned by Shell Transport and Trading Group of Great Britain. The full merger between these two companies was official in 1907. This conglomerate of companies includes companies such as Shell Petroleum of the USA, Shell Nigeria, and Shell Argentina. The company's mission was to bulk ship and export oil revolutionizing the transport of this precious resource. Soon after the merger was complete, the company rapidly expanded across the world with both marketing offices and exploration and production facilities. Within twelve months, both of the struggling entities were transformed into successful ones.

In 1937, Shell entered the Nigeria making it the first energy company to enter the market in this country. By 1938 they were granted an exploration license that allowed them to prospect for oil in the region. It was not until January of 1956 that the company drilled its first well. Later that year, the company changed its name to Shell-BP Petroleum Development Company of Nigeria Limited (SPDC). Over the course of the next twenty years Shell entered into a number of agreements with the Nigerian government that gradually increased the government's ownership of the company from 35% all the way up to 80% in 1979.

As it stands today, Shell operates two businesses related to the exploration, production, and transportation of oil and gas within Nigeria. The SPDC still exists and is the largest private sector oil and gas company in Nigeria. It is a joint venture between the government owned Nigerian National Petroleum Corporation (NNPC) which owns 55%, Shell which owns 30%, Elf Petroleum Nigeria Limited which owns 10%, and Agip which owns 5%. The other business operated by Shell in Nigeria is called Shell Nigeria Exploration and Production Company (SNEPCO) which was formed in 1993 to develop deep water drilling resources. It operates two deep water licenses and a production sharing contract with the NNPC.

The SPDC's operations are spread over a 30,000 square kilometer area in the Niger Delta. Its network consists of 6,000 kilometers of flowlines and pipelines, 90 oil fields, 1,000 producing wells, 72 flowstations, 10 gas plants, and two major oil export terminals. This business unit is capable of producing up to one million barrels of oil per day on average. The SNEPCO is committed to the discovery of new resources and sources of oil and is charging towards the goal set by the Nigerian government of being able to have a capacity of four million barrels per day.

While Nigeria was once the shining star of Shell's portfolio, it is now a large black cloud that hangs over the entire organization. Shell Nigeria has been accused of pollution, collusion, corruption, bribery, and false accounting. Every time the company settles a claim or accusation, another one pops right up. The following provides an account of the accusations and corruption that have scared this organization throughout its history.

## Ken Saro-Wiwa

Shell's first problems began in the early 1990's when criticism of human rights policies and the destruction of the environment in Nigeria became a hot topic. Ken Saro-Wiwa was a leading environmentalist and author who happened to be a Nigerian native and part of the Ogoni tribe. He was one of the more determined and articulate critics of the government and of Shell Oil's destruction of his homeland. He argued that neither party had appropriate regulations for protecting the Ogoni people's land and did not return any of the immense wealth that was taken from their region.

Saro-Wiwa organized a group called the Movement for Survival of the Ogoni People and quickly grew to be the largest political organization in the region. This group began to protest and demonstrate for an end to destructive behaviors such as oil spills, gas flaring, and the destruction of property to make way for pipelines that Shell was building. They also began demanding they be given a share of the revenues from the land Shell was using. Shell denied these claims and stated the group was greatly exaggerating their claims.

Nigeria's military began to respond to the groups claim through a strategy that has been referred to as a "scorched earth campaign against the Ogoni" which included burning villages and committing rapes and murders. Shell refused to get involved stating that the company does not get involved in politics. This led to Saro-Wiwa and eight other Ogoni members were arrested on charges that western governments and human rights groups called trumped up. The Nigerian government ultimately executed all nine with Saro-Wiwa's body being burned with acid and buried in an unmarked grave.

This event ignited world-wide protests and criticism against Nigeria, the African oil industry, and Shell. Shell was sued in a New York court by Saro-Wiwa's family and was accused of bribing soldiers who carried out human rights abuses in addition to playing a role in the capture and execution of the nine. Shell eventually settled this case out of court for $15.5M.

## Oil Spills

Oil spills are quite prevalent in the Niger Delta and it is estimated that the equivalent of the Exxon Valdez spill has occurred every year for the past 50 years. There is no other place in the world that has been as battered by oil as this region. The

Nigerian Government and international environmental groups sponsored a report in 2006 that concluded as many as 546 million gallons of oil have spilled into the region of the past five decades. This has led to the destruction of swamps, aquatic life, and the main food source for many of the tribes.

Shell is the major player with thousands of miles of pipes that have been laid through the swamps and fertile land. The majority of the spillage is attributed to poorly maintained and aging pipes however Shell maintains the position that the majority of the spills are due to oil thieves and sabotage. A spokesperson for Shell stated that the company does not discuss individual oil spills but only two percent of the total spills are due to equipment failure. Richard Steiner, a consultant on oil spills, concluded in a 2008 report that historically "the pipeline failure rate in Nigeria is many times that found elsewhere in the world". He also noted that Shell has acknowledged almost every year a spill due to corroded pipes.

Shell has repeatedly received pressure from the Niger Delta people and internationally to clean up its processes and spills. In 2008, there were two major oil spills that occurred. One of the spills was due to a leak in a major pipeline that went undetected for close to four months before something was done about it. This completely devastated the twenty square kilometer network of creeks and inlets in which the Bodo people inhabit. The company initially offered the people £3,500 along with 50 bags of rice, 50 bags of beans, and a few cartons of sugar, tomatoes, and groundnut oil. The offers were rejected and the Bodo filed a class action lawsuit.

Shell finally admitted that the spills were due to operational issues and stated that it will take full responsibility for these two spills in accordance with Nigerian Law. Many estimate that Shell's exposure could be close to a hundred million dollars for the cleanup and potentially take up to 20 years to fully revive this area. They are also responsible for paying compensation to those that are entitled to receive such under the Nigerian Law.

# Bribery

As discussed previously, bribery is common in Nigeria especially in doing business with the government. Shell has long been suspected of using bribery as a way of securing new territories, new licenses, and circumventing customs laws. However, up until recently no one was able to provide any proof that these things were happening.

In 2007, the SEC learned that Shell was doing business with a company named Panalpina. Panalpina was doing business with lots of different organizations that operated in high-risk countries as a freight forwarder. It was learned that Panalpina was bribing the Nigerian government on behalf of several companies including Shell. The bribes went to the government to secure preferential treatment when moving rigs, ships, workboats, and other equipment throughout the country. It was learned that the money was used to go around the customs process allowing Shell to benefit from faster movement of goods, using military aircraft to transport special goods, overlooking visa inspections, and avoiding employees being deported for overstaying visas. Panalpina provided information that Shell specifically requested for fake invoices to be drawn up with line items to mask the nature of the bribes and avoid any suspicion in case of an audit.

In addition to Panalpina confirming the bribes on behalf of Shell, Shell also admitted to separate incidents of paying $2 million dollars in bribes to Nigerian Subcontractors on its deepwater Bonga Project. It is estimated that Shell profited about $14 million because of these payments. Because of these two incidents, Shell has been ordered to pay fines of $48.1 million.

# Shell Today

Even with all of these accusations, bad press, fines, and unethical issues surrounding the company, Shell continues to do business in Nigeria. The company maintains that it continues to support and improve the communities of the Niger Delta region through the taxes and royalties they pay to the Nigerian Federal Government. Shell claims to have contributed approximately $31 billion to the government over the past five years and that the government receives 95% of the revenue after costs from the SPDC joint venture.

In addition to generating revenue, the company actively promotes projects in the region. These projects support small businesses, agriculture, training, education, and health care throughout the region with many of the details of each being available from the company's Nigeria website. Education is a strong part of their contributions as they pay a portion of their profit into an educational fund for the restoration and consolidation of education in Nigeria.

# Bibliography

BBC News. *Ogoniland Oil Spills: Shell Admits Nigeria Liability*. 3 August 2011. 5 August 2011 <http://www.bbc.co.uk/news/world-africa-14391015>.

Blackden, Rowena Mason and Richard. *Shell to Pay $48M Nigerian Bribe Fine*. 4 November 2010. 5 August 2011 <http://www.telegraph.co.uk/finance /newsbysector/energy/oilandgas/8111277/Shell-to-pay-48m-Nigerian -bribe-fine.html>.

Bloomberg. *Nigeria Exported More Than Second Largest OPEC Nation Iran*. 18 July 2011. 21 July 2011 <http://www.bloomberg.com/news/2011-07-18 /nigeria-exported-more-than-second-largest-opec-nation-iran-1-.html>.

Calkins, David Voreacos and Laurel Brubaker. *Shell Bribes Among "Culture of Corruption" Panalpina Admits*. 5 November 2010. 5 August 2011 <http://www .businessweek.com/news/2010-11-05/shell-bribes-among-culture-of-corruption -panalpina-admits.html>.

CIA. *The World Fact Book*. 5 July 2011. 21 July 2011 <https://www.cia.gov/library /publications/the-world-factbook/geos/ni.html>.

Donovan, John. *$15.5M Settlement: Shell Has Another Day In Court*. 13 June 2009. 4 August 2011 <http://royaldutchshellplc.com/2009/06/13/155m-settlement -shell-has-another-day-in-court/>.

Investigative Africa. *Shell to Pay $30M in Nigeria Corruption Settlement*. 17 October 2010. 3 August 2011 <http://investigativezim.com/2010/10/17/shell-to-pay -30-million-in-nigeria-corruption-settlement/>.

Shell Global. *The Beginnings*. 2 August 2011 <http://www.shell.com/home /content/aboutshell/who_we_are/our_history/the_beginnings/>.

Shell Nigeria. *Shell At a Glance*. 30 July 2011 <http://www.shell.com.ng/home /content/nga/aboutshell/at_a_glance/>.

Shell Oil. *SNEPCO*. 30 July 2011 <http://www.shell.com.ng/home/content/nga /aboutshell/shell_businesses/e_and_p/snepco/>.

The New York Times. *Far From Gulf, a Spill Scourge 5 Decades Old*. 16 June 2010. 2 August 2011 <http://www.nytimes.com/2010/06/17/world/africa/17nigeria. html>.

———. *Ken Saro-Wiwa*. 22 May 2009. 3 August 2011 <http://topics.nytimes.com /topics/reference/timestopics/people/s/ken_sarowiwa/index.html>.

The Telegraph. *Shell Execs Accused of "Collaboration" Over Hanging of Nigerian Activist Ken Saro-Wiwa.* 31 May 2009. 2 August 2011 <http://www.telegraph.co.uk /news/worldnews/africaandindianocean/niger/5413171/Shell-execs-accused -of-collaboration-over-hanging-of-Nigerian-activist-Ken-Saro-Wiwa.html>.

UPI.com. *Shell Admits to Oil Spills in Nigeria.* 4 August 2011. 5 August 2011 <http:// www.upi.com/Business_News/Energy-Resources/2011/08/04/Shell-admits-to -oil-spills-in-Nigeria/UPI-69831312459493/>.

Vidal, John. *Shell Accepts Liability for Two Oil Spills in Nigeria.* 3 August 2011. 5 August 2011 <http://www.guardian.co.uk/environment/2011/aug/03/shell-liability-oil -spills-nigeria>.

### CASE DISCUSSION QUESTIONS

1. What are some of the factors explaining why corruption and bribery are so high in Nigeria?
2. Was Shell involved in the execution of the poet Ken Saro-Wiwa? What impact did the poet's death have on Shell?
3. Was Shell taking advantage of weak local regulation?
4. What can a company do to ensure that it operates ethically in societies with weak institutions?

### CASE CREDIT

Reprinted with permissions from Andrew Flint.

# Organizational and National Cultures in a Polish–U.S. Joint Venture

T his case looks at differences in the cultural values and beliefs of Polish and U.S. managers employed in a joint venture in Poland. The case comes from data collected from interviews with Polish and expatriate U.S. managers.

## Background

### The U.S./Polish Company

The company was a joint venture with a Polish partner and a wholly owned subsidiary of a U.S. multinational corporation located in Poland. The U.S. company started operations in Poland in 1990. The joint venture started two years later.

The joint venture was a small, nonbureaucratic organization with 140 employees. Everybody knew each other and a family type of relationship existed among the managers. Both local Polish managers and U.S. expatriates reported a friendly work climate even though all top managerial positions were held by the U.S. expatriates.

## Polish Attitudes Regarding U.S. Management

When asked why they chose to work for this company, Polish managers often described U.S. business as "real," "healthy," "tough," "honest," and "fair," even though they had never had the opportunity to work with U.S. Americans. In addition, they felt that the features of Polish national culture such as "ability to work in difficult situations" and "experience of struggle with hardship of communism" combined well with American management expertise. In addition, Polish managers reported that working for a U.S. company was a major bonus for their future success and careers. Multinational corporations give employment security because they have a low risk of bankruptcy. In comparison with state-owned companies, the organization was perceived as having a very efficient organizational design dedicated to efficiency and profit making. Reflecting on his experience in state-owned operations, a Polish manager from the customer service operation unit noted:

> The basic difference between state companies and this company is that the organization of U.S. firms contains many necessary and indispensable elements. Whereas, in Polish companies, many elements were not needed and, even in some cases, disturbed the effective functioning of the company as a whole. Profit was not a major goal, only apparent activities. Many jobs and even whole companies were created when they were not needed. They were unproductive. Here we have only jobs and departments which help the company to function effectively.

The Polish managers expressed a great deal of enthusiasm and excitement for learning U.S. business know-how. Polish managers felt that they learned something new each day, not only from formal training but also from on-the-job training. Often Polish managers compared the company to a university. For the first time since entering a market economy, they felt they had the opportunity to learn business functions such as marketing, distribution, and logistics. These pro-American attitudes created an eagerness among the Polish managers to accept expatriate ideas concerning new work priorities. The attitudes also worked to legitimize the power and leadership of the U.S. Americans in the company.

The Polish managers believed that, unlike under the previous communist system, the new organization encouraged the development of the individual. They believed that the U.S. system of management inspired self-expression and achievement, respecting individuals and their unique personalities. There was a strong belief that hard work would bring success. Talented people who were willing to work could advance and succeed.

These organizational values were quite new for the Polish managers. In their previously state-controlled organizations, competence and good performance were not the main bases for a promotion and compensation. Party membership was the key to a successful managerial career. Rewards and promotions depended on fulfilling a political role rather than on achieving economic goals.

# The Cultural Conflicts

In spite of the very positive attitudes of the Polish managers toward a U.S. management style, there were still many conflicts between expectations based on Polish cultural traditions and an organizational culture based on the national culture of the United States.

## Managerial Selection

Many Polish employees wanted to be hired immediately as managers, without any experience in basic business functions. They associated the magic word *manager* with a higher status and success. U.S. managers, however, felt that "you had to earn your spurs first." The U.S. expatriate district manager recalled:

> *People applying for positions in the sales department do not want to do basic business first, to be a sales representative, they want to be immediately managers. People that I interview want to be only managers. How you can manage sales representatives if you don't know what they do? They lack a concrete answer for my question.*

## Merit, Age, and Seniority

The corporate culture encouraged rewards primarily based on competence in key skills and performance against objective criteria. Both local and expatriate managers believed that individuals were appointed and promoted based on their knowledge and professional expertise. This situation often resulted in much younger managers having older subordinates. As one U.S. manager from the finance department stated:

> *The company gives a lot of authority to young people very quickly. You never know, the guy who is looking younger than you could be a vice president already.*

Although Polish managers appreciated promotions based on competence, the issue of age presented some adjustment problems. Traditional expectations hold that, when one is young, it is impossible to be knowledgeable and to have the necessary experience and competence to manage successfully. As a Polish assistant manager from the marketing department admitted:

> *I prefer to have an older boss because it would be very stupid if I have a boss younger than me. He has less life experience and a shorter marriage. He is younger and he is not authority to me. I would prefer someone who has more life experience. I realize that it is a very Polish thing that I find this to be a problem.*

## The Salary System

Polish managers expressed difficulty in adjusting to the confidentiality of the new salary system. The Polish and U.S. managers differed in their beliefs regarding what kind of information was personal and what kind should be public. Polish managers wanted to know as much about each other's salaries as possible. They had no problems asking another employee about exactly how much they were paid. To the Polish managers, this served as a means of establishing their relative status. As a Polish assistant brand manager indicated:

> *I like this system but I would like to know how I am in comparison with the others. If I knew that the person who works together with me had a higher salary than me, I would be very unhappy.*

For the expatriate U.S. Americans, however, it was not part of the company culture to reveal explicit salary information. Salary information was considered personal and confidential. Most felt that revealing salary information disrupted the family climate of the organization. Instead, the Americans expressed faith in the system of assessment and reward allocation. As the expatriate head of the finance department noted:

> *Poles make mistakes when they say: "Americans don't share salaries in this system." I would say it is not that straightforward at all. In the American system, in our company's system, we don't share specifics on what any one person makes. We try very hard to share the system by which you make more salary. We make it very clear that your salary is based on your performance. If you perform well you will make a lot of money.*

## Team Goals

Working not only for your own interests but also for the success of the team or the whole company was a challenge for many Polish managers, especially for those who had their initial managerial experiences in a state-controlled economy. One Polish manager noted:

> *Americans want to hire the best, because the organization will gain from them and you as a boss should be not afraid if you hire a person who is more clever than you. You will benefit from it because the company will benefit. In state companies you had to protect yourself by not cooperating—a new, better employee was your potential enemy.*

Another Polish assistant marketing manager mentioned:

> *In a state company, if somebody has a problem, he or she solves it with their own interests in mind. Here we are thinking in terms of the benefit of the whole company. I made a mistake and I regarded it as my mistake because I was responsible for it. But the problem was judged [by the Americans] as a problem and loss for all of us. This is a different way of thinking, and this is the attitude of this company. Success belongs to everybody and so does failure. This is better than making one person responsible for it.*

## The Psychological Contract

In the eyes of the Polish managers, the organization required them to accept a new psychological contract between the organization and the individual. On the one hand, they felt positive about the degree of personal involvement and responsibility in the daily activities of company affairs. On the other hand, they were confused where to draw the line between professional and private lives. Many of the Polish managers felt that, for them to succeed as employees, the organization demanded too much of their private lives. As the Polish marketing manager said:

> *Americans look differently at the firm. They associate themselves very closely with it. They are part of the firm. In the past I never felt such a relationship with the firm.*

Another Polish district manager mentioned:

> *This new way of thinking, that you have to have a strong psychological connection with the firm, surprised me. You have to show you are interested. In the past you escaped from your job as quickly as possible.*

## Trust

A U.S. cultural trait that surprised Polish employees was the perception of an underlying good faith in people. Both the company culture and the expatriate managers had positive valuations regarding the intentions of people within the organization. As a Polish accountant stated:

> *What was new for me was that Americans have the assumption that you are acting for the good of the firm and that you are honest and that people are good. If you go to a restaurant for a business meal, nobody will tell you that you are nasty and that you used the company money and did it for a bad purpose.*

A Polish assistant brand manager added:

> *A positive attitude toward people, trust in people—this is a basis for everything. Americans don't wait to catch you in a mistake. We are more suspicious of people. Our immediate assumption is that a person wants to do something bad.*

Polish managers expressed much more negative attitudes regarding the nature of people. These were evidenced in many aspects of the daily business life of the organization: subordinate–superiors ("My boss wants to harm me"), employee–peers ("My colleagues would only criticize me"), customer–product ("Americans are trying to sell us bad products"), employee–product ("I don't believe in the value of this product"). A U.S. expatriate brand manager, describing the Polish managers, indicated:

> *I have never met a group of people that was more skeptical of the future and more distrusting. Everyone we do business with is convinced that we are dumping a less quality product on the market. The Polish customer is very skeptical. They don't believe that they can get products as good as anybody else in the world.*

Distrust, fear, and a disbelief that the boss wishes well for the employees were common attitudes observed by the U.S. expatriates. One U.S. expatriate from customer service operations remarked:

> *Sometimes they [the Polish managers] don't understand that the company is trying to do the right things for individuals. Sometimes there will be questions which assume that the employer is going to take advantage of them and is going to treat locals badly. It is not a good assumption that the company and manager are not trying to help them if they have a problem.*

## Informality

U.S. managers valued blunt and direct speaking. Saying exactly what you mean was considered a virtue, and the U.S. managers had a low tolerance for ambiguity. Therefore, expatriate managers took most explanations at face value. Reacting to this, Polish managers often described Americans as very "open," "direct," "spontaneous," and "natural" during communication. However, this style of communication clashed with the indirect communication habits of Polish employees. As the American head of the marketing department stated:

*Communication with Polish employees is difficult, especially when an employee has a problem. There is a general unwillingness to talk directly about oneself and one's problems. Poles will gladly talk about somebody else. They will not talk about their own needs. They don't like direct questions about things which are important to them. Perhaps it is considered impolite, too bold, or inappropriate for them.*

Polish managers adapted to the U.S. directness by developing an informal network of communication among themselves, which served as a buffer between the U.S. and Polish managers. To deal with their U.S. superiors, Polish managers first talked among themselves. Then one person would become responsible for going to a U.S. manager and telling him or her about someone else's problems. Expatriate managers found it unusual when subordinates who needed to communicate problems resorted to this informal channel. However, this buffer in communication provided a comfort zone for the Polish managers. As the Polish assistant marketing manager noted:

*Poles more easily criticize things among themselves, but it is difficult for them to criticize things in the presence of Americans. It is as if they don't believe in their strengths, and are afraid that their opinions are either untrue or irrational. They are afraid of being funny.*

Americans also introduced an informal style of communication by addressing everyone in the office on a first-name basis. Expatriates expressed the belief that their organizational culture provides an opportunity to "lead by competence, not by formality in relationships between superiors and subordinates." They were proud of their openness and equality in forming business relations. To the expatriates, the Polish managers who resisted the informality appeared to be cold and distrusting. Expatriates interpreted it as the "director syndrome" or as an example of an attitude from the communist-controlled past. The expatriate head of the sales department described it as follows:

*I respect their history. I respect the cultural aspects. Every time they call me "Mister Director" I remind them to call me by my first name. I am constantly telling them that I have a culture, too. This company has a culture, one that I want to build here. I don't like the environment that formality fosters and the environment that it creates. It is a barrier for effective communication. You almost have too much respect, and then you stop talking to me, soon you stop coming and saying, "I have a problem."*

The majority of Polish managers adjusted to the norm of a first-name basis very quickly in dealing with the Americans. However, this did not mean that they wished to be on a first-name basis when speaking among Polish managers, especially with their Polish subordinates. Using first names for older people or for superiors is not a Polish norm. Some Polish managers were afraid that they would lose the ability to lead by being so informal. They believed that distance between superiors and subordinates helped them in the direct management of lower staff. The Polish head of the human resource department said:

> *There are some people in the firm with whom I will never be on a first-name basis. I am on a first-name basis with some people and on a Ms./Mr. basis with others. I don't know why, but I will not change that.*

Informality also contrasted with Polish views that managers should symbolically show their status and success. Polish managers gave much value to formality, titles, and signs of status, such as having a good make of car. Superiors were expected to have these trappings as a demonstration of their authority over subordinates. In contrast, the U.S. expatriates regarded many of these status symbols as counterproductive and meaningless. A U.S. brand manager mentioned:

> *Poles are passionate about getting ahead in status. People are looking for examples of badges to wear for the rest of the populace to know that you have made it. My boss must be in a big car. "What car are you going to drive?" I was asked by a Pole in the first meeting in Poland.*

### Positive Feedback on the Job

There were significant differences between Polish managers and expatriate Americans in the type of feedback given on the job. Consistent with their views of management practices, the U.S. managers were quick to recognize achievements publicly and privately. Polish managers were generally positive about this approach and perceived it as motivating. However, in spite of this reaction, positive feedback was not a popular management technique among the Polish managers. They preferred to give criticism and generally negative feedback in front of subordinates and peers. Reacting to the U.S. approach, a Polish district manager described the situation:

> *If you are good, Americans can send you a congratulatory letter. Once I had got such a letter from an American colleague of mine even though he had no particular responsibility for my job. He was not my boss. I would never think of doing so. It was so spontaneous.*

## Conclusions

Coming from a culture that lacked experience and contact with U.S. businesses before 1989, Polish managers generally had positive but stereotypical views of U. S. business practices. In the short term, such attitudes played a highly motivating role in attracting managers to the joint venture. In the long term, however, despite the initial enthusiasm, basic cultural differences may lead to disillusionment among Polish managers.

**CASE DISCUSSION QUESTIONS**

1. What are some important cultural differences between the Poles and the U.S. expatriates?
2. Using Hofstede's and the 7d cultural dimension models, explain some of the cultural differences noted in the case.
3. What are some institutional explanations for how the Polish workers are reacting to U.S. management style?
4. How can the joint venture take advantage of the initial enthusiasm of the Polish managers to build a stronger organization?
5. What cultural adaptations would you suggest to the U. S. expatriate managers regarding their management styles?

**CASE CREDIT**

This case was prepared by Krystyna Joanna Zaleska of the Canterbury Business School, University of Kent, Canterbury, England, while a postgraduate student at the Central European University, Prague. Reprinted with permission of the author.

# Strategy Content and Formulation for Multinational Companies

Cuiphoto/Shutterstock.com

# 5

# Strategic Management in the Multinational Company: Content and Formulation

## Learning Objectives

*After reading this chapter you should be able to:*

- Define the generic strategies of differentiation and low cost.

- Understand how low-cost and differentiation strategists make money.

- Recall multinational examples of the use of generic strategies.

- Understand competitive advantage and the value chain and how they apply to multinational operations.

- Understand how multinational firms use offensive and defensive strategies.

- Understand the basics of multinational diversification.

- Understand how to apply the traditional strategy formulation techniques, industry and competitive analysis, and company situation analysis to the multinational company.

- Realize that national context affects both convergence and divergence in the strategies used by multinational companies.

## *Preview* CASE IN POINT

### IKEA Battles the Recession

IKEA, the world's largest furniture retailer, specializes in inexpensive Scandinavian-style furniture. IKEA operates 338 stores in 40 countries. It has been a success story since its founding in the early 1940s.

The thrust of IKEA's strategy is to provide attractive furniture at low prices. Since 2000, the company has dropped prices an average of 2 to 3 percent. To succeed at this strategy, IKEA must keep costs down. The company uses low-cost manufacturing processes, purchases raw material in large quantities, minimizes transportation and storage with flat packaging, and has customers assemble their own furniture. As IKEA's website notes, "IKEA designers do their part to keep prices low by using production capabilities from other areas in unique and previously unimagined ways—like having shirt factories produce furniture upholstery. Or using leftover materials from the production of one product to create an entirely new one."

Even very successful multinational companies such as IKEA face challenges when the economic environment sours. In 2008, with most of the world in a recession, IKEA faced rising prices for its supplies, while demand from its core market of new homeowners and the middle class was decreasing.

In spite of daunting economic conditions, IKEA has kept to its strategy of offering affordable furniture. Ian Worling, a top executive at IKEA, notes that the company was doing so well in the early 2000s that it got "a bit fat" on the cost side. To attack rising costs, and rather than reduce its number of stores, IKEA targeted four areas, most of which customers do not see. First, the company sought to lower operational costs. According to Worling, small things like everyone flying economy class and staying in inexpensive hotels make a real difference. Second, it increased volume by offering more and lower-priced products, gaining efficiency not by increasing the number of stores but by increasing the sales revenue for existing stores. Third, it looked at every step in the supply chain to find cost savings. Fourth, it empowered workers to make decisions in stores or factories close to suppliers or customers to help keep headquarters lean.

Based on rising sales in emerging markets, cost reductions, and lower interest payments, IKEA announced a profit increase of 10.3 percent, to three billion euro, in early 2012—at the same time decreasing prices an average of 2.6 percent in the previous year.

*Sources: Based on Caglar, D., M. Kesteloo, and A. Kleiner. 2012. "How Ikea reassembled its growth strategy." strategy+business, online, May 7; Cripps, P. 2012. "Ikea profits up 10%." The Independent, January 20 http://www.independent.co.uk/news/business/news/ikea-profits-up-10-6292433.html; www.ideafans.com/idea /idea-whyidea; http://franchisor.ikea.com/range.html.*

The Preview Case in Point indicates how firms can adjust their strategies in the new competitive landscape. Although IKEA faced challenging economic conditions, the company prevailed by honing its low-cost strategy. Successful companies like IKEA are able to accurately predict and be prepared for quick changes in the business landscape. Furthermore, the environment facing companies has never been more complex. Companies now face global competition, extremely unpredictable environments, rapid technological change, hypercompetitive markets, and an increasing emphasis on price and quality by demanding customers.[1] In such a highly competitive environment, multinational managers must craft the competitive strategies to guide their companies toward profitability and long-term success. This chapter introduces the basic strategies that all multinational managers must be prepared to face and to master.

To develop an understanding of these strategies, this chapter presents the major components of the strategic management process in three main sections. The first section provides background on basic strategic content as applied to the multinational firm, including the available strategic options. The second section reviews the principles of strategy formulation with applications for the multinational company, including the processes by which managers analyze their industries and companies to select a strategy.

After reading this chapter, you should understand how the basic elements of the strategic management process apply to multinational operations. You also should understand that the multinational manager is faced with more complex challenges than those a domestic-only manager encounters.

# Basic Strategic Content Applied to the Multinational Company

What is a strategy? Strategy experts Hambrick and Fredrickson argue that statements such as "Our strategy is to be the low-cost provider" or "Our strategy is to provide excellent customer service" are not really strategies.[2] These statements represent only elements of strategies. Instead, a **strategy** is the central, comprehensive, integrated, and externally oriented set of choices structuring how a company exploits its core competencies to achieve its objectives.[3] Ideally, a strategy needs to address important areas such as which businesses a company wants to be in, what the company will use to create presence in a market, and how the company will win customers. For a multinational company's strategy, a major question is which country to enter at what time or what products to produce. Consider the next Case in Point, in which both Airbus and Boeing are poised for success by targeting different customer groups with different products.

Multinational companies use many of the same strategies practiced by domestic companies, of which we present an overview next. For students with coursework in

**Strategy**
The central, comprehensive, integrated, and externally oriented set of choices determining how a company will achieve its objectives.

## Airbus and Boeing: Targeting Different Customer Groups

Investing millions, Airbus and Boeing developed dramatically different commercial airplanes, each hoping its assumptions about the market were correct. Airbus offers the A380, believing that airlines want an airplane that can carry 550 or more passengers between hubs, from which travelers would then transfer to smaller planes going to their final destinations. The A380 replaced Boeing's 747 as the world's largest commercial jet. In contrast, Boeing assumed that airlines need a plane that flies long distance very efficiently. Its product, the Dreamliner (Boeing 787), was the company's first new plane in ten years. The Dreamliner set the world distance record of 10,710 nautical miles for its weight class in December of 2011 and circled the world in a record of less than 43 hours. The Dreamliner has a lightweight structure made of composite material and new engines, making it 20 percent more efficient than similar planes carrying more than 200 passengers.

As is common with new aircraft, both companies had their share of delays with their planes. Although Airbus received many early orders for the A380, manufacturing difficulties have caused missed delivery dates. Boeing also faced similar difficulties with its Dreamliner. Some airlines demanded refunds of deposits.

With many of the early difficulties solved, which company is winning? Perhaps both, as different airlines have different customer niches and needs. Airbus was first in business in 2007 and now has 257 orders, with 81 delivered as of August 2012, each with a price tag of $389.9 million. Although Boeing did not deliver its first plane until September 2011, it has 835 orders, with 25 delivered for a price of $206.8 to $243.6 million, depending on the variant ordered.

*Sources: Based on Betts, P. 2009. "Boeing and Airbus fly in face of industry's tailspin." FT.com, April 20; Daily Mail. 2006. "Setback for Boeing's Dreamliner," June 20, 68; Michaels, Daniel. 2006. "Leading the news: Airbus scrambles to fix wiring problems; Effort aims to put production, delivery of 380 back on track." Wall Street Journal Asia, June 26, 3; www.boeing.com /commercial/prices/;http://active.boeing.com/commercial /orders/index.cfm; www.airbus.com/company/market/orders -deliveries/; www.airbus.com/newsevents/news-events-single /detail/new-airbus-aircraft-list-prices-for-2012/.*

---

**Generic strategies**
Basic ways that both domestic and multinational companies keep and achieve competitive advantage.

**Competitive advantage**
When a company can outmatch its rivals in attracting and maintaining its targeted customers.

**Differentiation strategy**
Strategy based on finding ways to provide superior value to customers.

**Low-cost strategy**
Producing products or services equal to those of competitors at a lower cost.

strategic management, this will serve as a partial review. However, the discussion illustrates specifically how multinational companies use basic strategies. In particular, the Cases in Point in this chapter show how real multinational firms use basic strategic options in international business. After this introductory chapter, the text focuses on the strategic options that are unique to the multinational company.

## Competitive Advantage and Multinational Applications of Generic Strategies

**Generic strategies** represent very basic ways in which both domestic and multinational companies achieve and sustain competitive advantage. **Competitive advantage** occurs when a company's strategy creates superior value for targeted customers and is difficult or too costly for competitors to copy.[4] Porter identifies the two primary generic strategies that companies use to gain competitive advantage as differentiation and low cost.[5]

Companies that adopt a **differentiation strategy** find ways to provide superior value to customers from sources such as exceptional product quality, unique product features, rapid innovation, or high-quality service. For example, BMW competes in the world market by providing customers with very high-quality and high-performance sport touring cars. Caterpillar competes worldwide in its heavy construction equipment business by offering not only high-quality machinery but also, and more importantly, with after-sales service committed to delivering spare parts anywhere in the world.

In contrast, companies that adopt a **low-cost strategy** produce or deliver products or services equal to those of their competitors, but they find a way to produce their products or to deliver their services more efficiently than the competition. In other words, they lower costs without sacrificing the level of quality that is acceptable to customers. The cost savings may occur anywhere from the creation of the product to its final sale: finding sources of cheaper raw materials, employing cheaper labor, using more efficient production methods, or using more efficient delivery methods. Porter notes, for example, that Korean steel and semiconductor firms often perform well against U.S. and Japanese firms by using low-cost strategies.[6] The Korean firms save money with low-cost and productive labor, combined with advanced and efficient production methods. As discussed in the Preview Case in Point, IKEA is the master of the low-cost strategy, searching for cost cutting everywhere in its operations while still delivering a quality product to loyal customers.

## How Do Low-Cost and Differentiation Firms Make Money?

Differentiation leads to higher profits because people often pay a higher price for the extra value of a superior product or service. Levi's jeans have relatively high prices in the world market because of the special appeal of the Levi's brand. The Swiss firm Tobler/Jacobs can charge more for its specially produced chocolate than Hershey can for its mass-produced product. Tobler/Jacobs uses higher-quality ingredients, a longer processing time, and specialized distribution channels. These factors produce a high-quality product that commands a high price.[7]

High quality, service, and other unique characteristics of a differentiated product usually increase costs; that is, it takes more expensive labor or higher-quality materials to make a differentiated product or to provide a differentiated service. In addition, to make customers aware of the special value of their products or services, firms must spend more on marketing. Consequently, to maintain an acceptable profit margin, the differentiating company must increase prices to offset its additional costs.

Low-cost firms produce products or services similar to their competitors in price and value. Their competitive advantage and their additional profits come from cost savings. Every dollar, euro, or yen they save contributes to the bottom line by increasing their profit margins. Exhibit 5.1 shows how the relationships among costs, prices, and profits work for the differentiator and the low-cost strategists,

**EXHIBIT 5.1** Costs, Prices, and Profits for Differentiation and Low-Cost Strategies

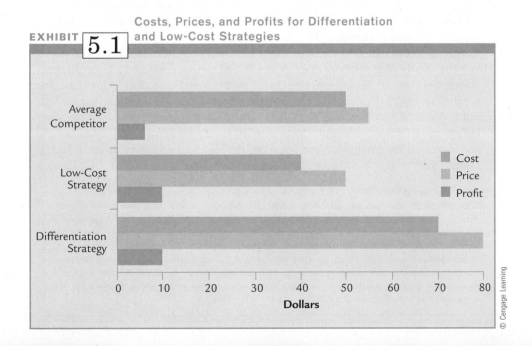

© Cengage Learning

compared to the average competitor. As the exhibit shows, both the differentiator and the low-cost strategist have higher profits than those of the average competitor. The next Multinational Management Brief on Ryanair shows how a low-cost competitor is dominating other airlines in Europe.

---

## Multinational Management **Brief**

### Ryanair: Taking Cost Leadership to the Next Level

Ryanair has become one of Europe's most popular and profitable airlines. While other European airlines struggled, Ryanair's obsessive commitment to keeping costs low resulted in an impressive 23 percent increase in profits in the company's most recent annual report. Ryanair's similarity to Southwest Airlines is not coincidental. Michael O'Leary, the company CEO, went to Dallas to meet Southwest Airlines executives to learn some lessons that could be used in Ireland. Similar to Southwest Airlines, Ryanair uses a single type of aircraft and flies to smaller and cheaper airports. Passengers are offered open seating, meaning that Ryanair does not need to maintain complicated seating systems. However, Ryanair has also found other innovative ways to cut costs. For instance, it decided to remove all seat-back pockets in its airplanes. This move reduces not only weight, resulting in better fuel efficiency, but also cleaning expenses.

However, Ryanair focuses on cost-leadership, like the airline industry as a whole, and continues to seek new ways to get more revenue from each traveler. For instance, some of Ryanair's fees include a Boarding Pass Reprint Fee (60€ per person), Name Change Fee (160€ per person if paying at the airport), Excess Luggage Fee (20€ per kilo), Credit/Debit Card Fee (5€ per person per flight), Priority Boarding Fee (5€ per person), and expensive in-flight food and drink (the most expensive of all British and Irish airlines).

Ninety-eight percent of Ryanair's customers buy their tickets online, making its website the largest travel site in Europe. This has enabled Ryanair to use its site for marketing purposes while getting commissions on other items such as car rentals or hotel room bookings. Ryanair also sells advertising opportunities when repainting the exterior of its planes. The company is considering removing all but one toilet on its aircraft to add about 50 more seats. While passengers have reacted to the news with incredulity, this intense focus on finding new sources of revenue and on reducing costs is indicative of Ryanair's financial success.

Ryanair's cost-leadership strategy is not without its risks. Cost leaders must maintain the quality and safety of their products and services. Recently, three Ryanair planes were forced to request emergency landings in Spain due to low fuel. To avoid extra weight, Ryanair instructs its pilots to carry only the fuel required for the flight. The legal minimum is 30 minutes' worth of fuel beyond the amount required to fly to the intended destination. When diverted to another airport, the Ryanair planes had to request the emergency landings when the fuel reached minimum levels. These events have resulted in some critical press and investigations in Europe.

*Sources: Adapted from CAPA. 2012. "Ryanair defeats European recession and posts all-time annual high net profit, but outlook less rosy." May 25 http://centreforaviation.com/analysis/financials /ryanair-defeats-european-recession-and-posts-all-time-annual-high-net-profit-but-outlook-is-less-ro-74750; M2 Presswire. 2009. "Ryanair's 5.3 April passengers double those of British Airways," May 6; Maier, Matthew. 2006. "A radical fix for airlines: Make flying free." Business 2.0, April, 32–34; Reilly, J. 2012. "Three Ryanair mayday calls go out on same day." August 12, http://www.independent.ie/national-news /three-ryanair-mayday-calls-go-out-on-same-day-3197081.html; Smyth, C. 2009. "Ryanair may charge passengers 1 pound to use lavatories on flights." Wall Street Journal, online edition, February 28; http:// www.ryanair.com/doc/investor/2011/Annual_Report_2011_Final.pdf.*

**EXHIBIT 5.2** Porter's Generic Strategies

| Scope of Competitive Target | Source of Competitive Advantage | |
| --- | --- | --- |
| | Lower Cost | Differentiation |
| Broad market | General cost leader | General differentiator |
| Niche market | Focused cost leader | Focused differentiator |

*Source: Adapted from Porter, Michael E. 1990.* Competitive Advantage of Nations. *New York: Free Press.*

Porter identifies another competitive issue regarding the two basic generic strategies, called the **focus strategy,** which is the application of a differentiation or low-cost strategy to a narrow market niche.[8] Focus strategy is based on **competitive scope,** which represents how broadly a firm targets its products or services. For example, companies with a narrow competitive scope may focus only on limited products, certain types of buyers, or specific geographical areas. Companies with a broad competitive scope may have many products targeted at a wide range of buyers. Auto manufacturers such as BMW target a high-income market with a few models, whereas most U.S. and Japanese auto manufacturers target a broad-income market with many models. Exhibit 5.2 shows the four subdivisions of Porter's generic strategies, including the basic differentiation and cost-leadership strategies with their broad-market or narrow-market options.

## Competitive Advantage and the Value Chain

A firm can gain a competitive advantage over other firms by finding sources of lower cost or differentiation in any of its activities—from getting the necessary raw materials through production to sales, and eventually to follow-up with after-sales service. For example, a company may lower costs by obtaining cheap raw materials or cheap labor in other countries. A multinational company may base its differentiation on the excellent R&D of its subsidiary in a country where high-quality engineering talent is cheap. Many multinational software design companies, for example, take advantage of the very high number of quality engineers in India and Singapore.

A convenient way of thinking about a firm's activities is in terms of the **value chain.** According to Michael Porter, the term "value chain" represents all the activities that a firm uses "to design, produce, market, deliver, and support its product."[9] The value chain consists of areas where a firm can create value for customers. Better designs, more efficient production, and better service all represent value added in the chain. Ultimately, the value a company produces represents what customers will pay for a product or service. Exhibit 5.3 shows a picture of the value chain. Later, you will see that the value chain provides a useful way of thinking about how multinational companies operate.

Porter divides the value chain into primary and support activities. These activities represent (1) the processes of creating goods or services and (2) the organizational mechanisms necessary to support the creative activities. *Primary activities* involve the physical actions of creating (or serving), selling, and providing after-sale service for, products. Early activities in the value chain, such as R&D and dealing with suppliers, are called *upstream.* Later value chain activities, such as sales and dealing with distribution channels, represent *downstream* activities. *Support activities* include systems for human resources management (e.g., recruitment and selection

**Focus strategy**
Applying a differentiation or low-cost strategy to a narrow market.

**Competitive scope**
How broadly a firm targets its products or services.

**Value chain**
All the activities that a firm uses to design, produce, market, deliver, and support its product.

**EXHIBIT** 5.3     The Value Chain

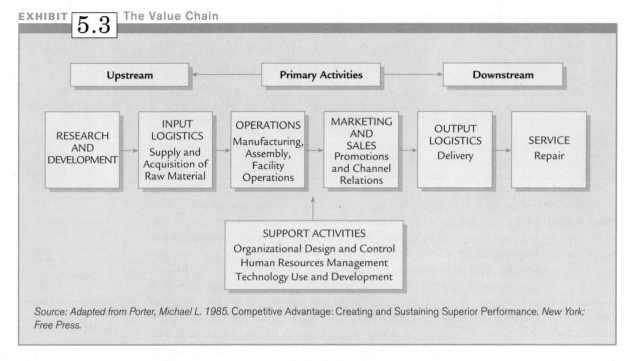

Source: Adapted from Porter, Michael L. 1985. Competitive Advantage: Creating and Sustaining Superior Performance. New York: Free Press.

procedures), organizational design and control (e.g., structural form and accounting procedures), and a firm's basic technology.

One common use of the value chain is to enable companies to determine their internal cost structures by assessing the cost levels associated with the different activities.[10] Comparing internal cost structure against the industry or other competitors provides the multinational company with information about the relative efficiency of its internal activities. This benchmarking exercise also provides important guidance on which activities are sources of internal cost advantage or disadvantage. To become more competitive, most multinational firms need to find ways to correct cost disadvantages.

Of all the ways to correct internal cost disadvantages, one of the most popular and controversial is **outsourcing**, which is the deliberate decision to have outsiders or strategic allies perform certain activities in the value chain.[11] Although outsourcing can occur within countries, there is an increasing tendency for multinational companies to outsource across borders to take advantage of lower costs in other countries. In 2011, over 2.2 million jobs in the United States were outsourced to foreign countries. These jobs were from the total value chain, including manufacturing (53 percent), IT services (43 percent), R&D (38 percent), distribution (18 percent), and call/help centers (12 percent). Although cost control or reduction is the most common reason cited for outsourcing, the majority of outsourcing is driven by other factors, such as better quality than is available locally.[12]

When should a multinational company outsource? In general, outsourcing makes sense if an outsider can perform a value chain task better or more cheaply.[13] However, outsourced tasks should be ones that are not crucial to the company's ability to achieve competitive advantage. Otherwise, the company runs the risk of creating new competitors. As a result, functions of low strategic value (e.g., billing services, maintenance services, benefits management) are outsourced more frequently.

Nevertheless, many multinational companies are shifting manufacturing and IT services to emerging markets such as the BRIC countries—Brazil, Russia, India,

**Outsourcing**
The deliberate decision to have outsiders or strategic allies perform certain activities in the value chain.

and China—because of the cost savings. Consider the next Focus on Emerging Markets regarding outsourcing locations.

The value chain thus identifies the areas in the input, throughput, and output processes where multinational companies can find sources of differentiation or lower costs. In the search for those sources, the company must take advantage of the distinctive competencies in its value chain. What distinctive competencies are and where they come from are the topics of the next section.

## Distinctive Competencies

**Distinctive competencies** are the strengths anywhere in the value chain that allow a company to outperform rivals in areas such as efficiency, quality, innovation, or customer service.[14] Distinctive competencies come from two related sources: resources and capabilities. **Resources** are the inputs into a company's production or services processes. Resources can be *tangible assets,* such as borrowing capacity, buildings, land, equipment, and highly trained employees, or *intangible assets,* such as reputation with customers, patents, trademarks, organizational knowledge, and innovative research abilities. **Capabilities** represent the ability of companies to assemble and coordinate their available resources in ways that lead to lower costs or differentiated output.

Thus, resources provide a company with potential capabilities. They are the raw materials—much like a person's athletic or intellectual potential—that become actual capabilities only when used effectively. In turn, capabilities are the building blocks of a distinctive competence. However, although capabilities are the prerequisites for building distinctive competencies, they are not enough. To result in long-term profitability and success, capabilities must lead to a sustainable competitive advantage. Next, we consider how companies achieve this state.

## Sustaining Competitive Advantage

For a company to have long-term profitability, a successful low-cost or differentiation strategy must be sustainable. **Sustainable** means that strategies are not easily neutralized or attacked by competitors.[15] Sustainability is traced to the nature of a company's capabilities. Capabilities that lead to competitive advantage must have four characteristics:[16] they must be valuable, rare, difficult to imitate, and nonsubstitutable.

*Valuable capabilities* create demand for a company's services or products or give companies cost advantages.

*Rare capabilities* are those that a company has but that are possessed by no competitor or by only a few competitors. For example, Boeing and Airbus are two companies with the rare technological capability to design and manufacture large commercial aircraft.

As we have seen, either providing customers with superior value or delivering products or services at lower cost results in increased profit margins. Competitors seek high profits by imitating or substituting for these capabilities. Thus, for a competitive advantage to be sustainable or long term, a company's capabilities must be not only valuable and rare, but also difficult to imitate or nonsubstitutable.

*Difficult-to-imitate capabilities* are those not easily copied by competitors. One of the most imitated sources of lower costs in the international marketplace is cheap labor. Competitors with access to the same international labor pools quickly duplicate the cost advantage of locating manufacturing facilities in countries with cheap labor. In addition, wage rates in countries with cheap labor often rise faster than productivity, gradually undermining those cost advantages.

*Nonsubstitutable capabilities* leave no strategic equivalent available to competitors. For example, many early e-commerce companies, such as Amazon.com, developed

**Distinctive competencies**
Strengths that allow companies to outperform rivals.

**Resources**
Inputs into the production or service processes.

**Capabilities**
The ability to assemble and coordinate resources effectively.

**Sustainable**
Characteristic of strategies that are not easily defeated by competitors.

## Focus on Emerging Markets

### Where to Outsource?

Emerging market countries provide many opportunities for multinational companies to outsource value chain activities. The leading destinations are China and India. China provides many multinational companies with a platform for low-cost manufacturing. India has proven to be the country of choice for IT outsourcing. The top 10 Indian IT companies, including Infosys and Satyam, make up nearly 45 percent of the global IT market. However, there are many factors to consider when a multinational company looks for an outsourcing location.

SourcingLine, a consulting and research firm specializing in outsourcing, ranks countries for outsourcing potential using dozens of key statistics representing three broad areas: Cost Competitiveness, Resources & Skills, and Business & Economic Environment. Although India ranked first in its recent survey by having the best mix of factors, it did not lead in all dimensions. English language skills and a large skill base are attractive, but wages in India are rising. Consider the table below, showing selected countries and their respective resources.

| Top Rated Outsourcing Countries for Services by *Sourcing Line* | | | | | |
|---|---|---|---|---|---|
| Country | Overall Rating | Business Environment | Cost Index | Resources/ Skills | Effective Workforce |
| India | 7.1 | 4.2 | 8.3 | 6 | 1,430,000,000 |
| Indonesia | 6.9 | 4.4 | 8.6 | 4.3 | 1,033,000,000 |
| China | 6.4 | 5.6 | 7 | 5.6 | 780,000,000 |
| Bulgaria | 6.4 | 5.2 | 8.8 | 2.9 | 3,000,000 |
| Philippines | 6.3 | 3.9 | 9 | 2.8 | 39,000,000 |

*Sources: Based on Kathawala, Y. and C. Heeren. 2009. "China presents a major threat to India in the global IT outsourcing industry." Graziadio Business Review, 12, gbr.pepperdine.edu; Overby, S. 2010. "Offshore outsourcing: 24 ways to compare India vs. China." November 29, www.cio.com; www.statisticbrain.com/outsourcing-statistics-by-country/; www.sourcingline.com/top-outsourcing-countries.*

capabilities to conduct business over the Internet. Not only have these models been easy to copy, but competitors have also substituted for these capabilities by outsourcing such procedures as website building and translation. In contrast, consider the example of Toyota in the next Case in Point, which shows how Toyota uses strategic capabilities that competitors have found difficult to copy or for which competitors have been unable to create substitutes.

Exhibit 5.4 summarizes the relationships among resources, capabilities, distinctive competencies, and eventual profitability.

Companies also develop strategies that directly target rival firms, some of which the following section reviews from the vantage point of the multinational company.

**Competitive strategies**
Moves multinational firms use to defeat competitors.

## Offensive and Defensive Competitive Strategies in International Markets

Besides using basic generic strategies in their operations, multinational companies use several strategic moves called **competitive strategies.** Competitive strategies can

## Toyota's Distinctive Competencies along the Value Chain: Strategic Capabilities in Cost Reductions, Quality, and Service

Toyota is the world's number one car manufacturer in terms of volume of sales. Its competitive advantages over other automakers from Japan, Europe, and the United States are the firm's distinctive competencies in cost reduction and high-quality materials and service. Using techniques such as just-in-time production and lean manufacturing, Toyota has transformed itself from a small car manufacturer to a global giant.

How did it achieve such a feat? Upstream in the value chain, to bring new models to market more quickly and cheaply, Toyota combines manufacturing and production engineering, thereby eliminating mistakes in production design and reducing cost. Toyota designs cars with the objectives of using fewer parts, tying up fewer production machines, and reducing production times. For example, the company's redesigned Corolla model had 25 percent fewer parts, was 10 percent lighter, and was more fuel efficient than previous models. Of the $1 billion necessary to design a new model and build the plants to produce it, tools and machinery can account for three-quarters of the cost.

The mastery of *kanban,* the just-in-time production system, provides a basis of cost reduction and customer service. Not only do suppliers deliver materials just in time, as now happens for many U.S. manufacturers, but the whole value chain also works just in time.

Downstream, in the marketing and sales component of the value chain, Toyota dealers use online computers to order models directly from the factory. A built-to-order car can be delivered in as few as five days using its virtual production system. The system precisely calculates the types and timing of parts to arrive on the assembly line exactly when needed for a particular production mix. Even with this design flexibility, Toyota uses only 14 person-hours to assemble a car, compared with 22 for Honda and Ford.

Toyota also continues to develop innovations in plant efficiency, which the company says is extremely important, as 60 percent of the cost of the car is investment into the plant. In its newest plant in Ohira, two hours from Tokyo, the U-shaped assembly line produces cars in 1/3 of the time of other Toyota plants. Rather than hanging from the ceiling, cars roll on a simple raised platform that requires a smaller and cheaper building. A conveyor system is simply bolted to the floor, making it cheaper to build, shorten, or lengthen, or even move to another site. Cars do not move in a line as in traditional factories, but move side by side like in a parking lot, creating a 35 percent shorter and cheaper line.

Such manufacturing efficiency also translates into bigger profits, with Toyota's average profit margin per vehicle at 9.4 percent compared to GM's 3 percent. Therefore Toyota has the advantage not only of being the cost leader but also of being perceived by consumers as being among the highest-quality manufacturers. In spite of a strong yen, recalls on some models, and the natural disasters of 2011, in 2012 Toyota became the first car maker to top 10 million vehicles in one year.

*Sources: Based on Bunkley, Nick. 2006. "Gas prices stall U.S. sales of big vehicles: Detroit's Asian rivals benefit, helped by fuel-efficiency reputation." International Herald Tribune, June 5, 11; Jiji Press English News Service. 1999. "Toyota shrinks car production time to 5 days." August 6; Norton, L. P. 2009. "Toyota hits a roadblock." Barron's, April 27, 89(17), M9; Peterson, Thane. 2000. "Toyota's Fujio Cho: Price competition will be brutal." April, http:www.businessweek.com; Pande, S. 2009. "Lean manufacturing, just-in-time are hallmark manufacturing philosophies that have dominated production practices since the 1950s." Business Today, April 19; Williams, Chambers G., III. 2003. "Toyota strategy includes San Antonio expansion." Knight Ridder Tribune Business News, February 7; Schmitt, B. 2011. "Toyota's secret weapon: Low cost car factories." February 16, www.the-truthaboutcars.com; Tabuchi, H., 2012. "After recalls and woes, Toyota posts huge profit." August, 3, www.nytimes.com.*

be offensive or defensive. In *offensive* strategies, companies directly target rivals from whom they wish to capture market share. For example, an attacking company may suddenly drop its prices or add new features to its products that compete with its rival's products. In *defensive* strategies, companies seek to beat back or discourage their rivals' offensive strategies. For example, a firm might match a rival's

**EXHIBIT** 5.4     How Distinctive Competencies Lead to Successful Strategies

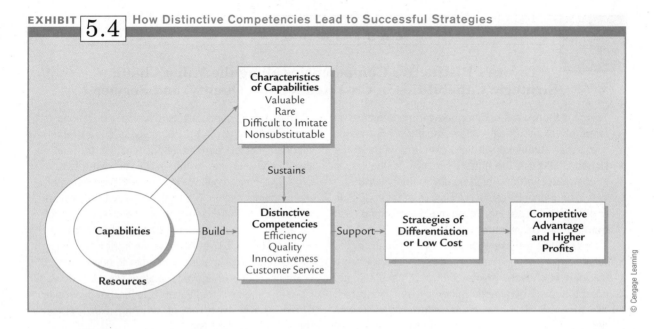

© Cengage Learning

lower prices or give distributors volume discounts to discourage customers from shifting to a rival's products.

**Offensive competitive strategies**
Direct attacks, end-run offensives, preemptive strategies, and acquisitions.

Examples of **offensive competitive strategies** include direct attacks, end-run offensives, preemptive strategies, and acquisitions.[17]

- *Direct attacks:* Direct attacks include price cutting, adding new features, comparison advertisements that show lesser quality in a competitor's products, or going after neglected or poorly served market segments.

- *End-run offensives:* Companies try to avoid direct competition and seek unoccupied markets. In international competition, unoccupied markets are usually countries ignored or underserved by competitors.

- *Preemptive competitive strategies:* These strategies involve being the first to gain a particular advantageous position. Advantages might include getting the best suppliers of raw material, buying the best locations, or getting the best customers. In international markets, being the first company with a global strategy can bring great advantages. For example, a multinational company can seek the best raw material anywhere in the world, or it can work to become the first company to have its brand recognized worldwide.

- *Acquisitions:* In this type of acquisition, a firm buys its competitor. This can be the most effective competitive strategy against rivals because the acquired competitor no longer exists. However, if the purchased company does not contribute to the overall company's performance, the strategy may not contribute to bottom-line effectiveness. For the multinational firm, acquiring a firm from another country might include other strategic benefits besides profit, such as improving geographical coverage or strengthening the firm's position in important countries.

Usually, multinational managers analyze the strengths and weaknesses of their competitors country by country. Different countries represent different markets and often require different attack strategies. Consequently, managers develop country-specific plans for dealing with their competitors and deciding whether to attack, take an end-run approach (avoid direct competition), or acquire the rivals.

In a competitive industry, all managers should expect attacks from rival firms. To counteract these attacks, companies use **defensive competitive strategies.** Defensive strategies attempt to reduce the risk of being attacked, to convince attacking firms to seek other targets, or to blunt the impact of an attack. Companies may defend themselves at several points on the value chain. For example, a firm may sign exclusive contracts with the best suppliers, thus blocking competitors' access to raw materials. A company can introduce new models and match its competitors' lower prices. A firm may get exclusive contracts with distributors or provide better warranties or after-sales service. To scare off potential challengers, firms may make public announcements about their willingness to fight. Rivals then realize that an attack will be costly, and they often decide it is not worth the risk. Attacked firms can also **counter-parry,** a popular strategy for multinationals.

In international markets, companies use the counter-parry to fend off a competitor's attack in one country by attacking it in another country, usually the competitor's home country. This strategy draws resources from the competitor and weakens its attack. The tactic is most successful when the rival firm is forced to protect its established home markets. Goodyear used this strategy against the French tire manufacturer Michelin.

Michelin entered the U.S. market with a low-price strategy, expecting that Goodyear would be forced to match the lower prices. Faced with a likely drastic drop in revenue, Goodyear did not match the lower prices. Instead, unexpected by Michelin, Goodyear responded by lowering its prices in Michelin's core European markets. Goodyear's counter-parry of price reductions in Europe caused significant losses for Michelin. Eventually, Michelin returned its U.S. prices to their previous levels.[18]

Next, we discuss how multinational companies use diversification in the international marketplace.

## Multinational Diversification Strategy

Most of the strategic options discussed so far pertain to the operation of a single business, and they are called **business-level strategies.** However, many corporations have more than one type of business. Strategies for multi-business companies are called **corporate-level strategies,** and these concern how companies choose their mix of different businesses. When a company moves from a single type of business into two or more businesses, this type of move is called diversification. There are two types of diversification: related and unrelated.

In **related diversification,** companies start or acquire businesses that are similar in some way to their original or core business. These similarities can exist all along the value chain. Firms choose related diversification for three basic reasons: sharing activities, transferring core competencies, and developing market power.[19] *Sharing activities* along the value chain can include the common purchasing of similar raw material, the common production of similar components, and the sharing of sales forces, advertising, and distribution activities. Companies such as Honda *transfer core competencies* across units by using similar technologies in their internal combustion engines for motorcycles and lawn mowers. Nike transferred its core competency in brand recognition when it added a clothing line to its athletic

**Defensive competitive strategies** Attempts to reduce the risks of being attacked, to convince an attacking firm to seek other targets, or to blunt the impact of any attack.

**Counter-parry** Fending off a competitor's attack in one country by attacking in another country, usually the competitor's home country.

**Business-level strategies** Strategies for a single-business operation.

**Corporate-level strategies** How companies choose their mixture of different businesses.

**Related diversification** A mix of businesses with similar products and markets.

shoe operations. Firms use related diversification to build *market power* by attacking rivals with multipoint competition or with competition in more than one area and by vertical integration. Vertical integration allows firms to internalize supply (e.g., coffee growing for a company like Starbucks) or other downstream components of their value chain (e.g., direct sales). Integration can result in greater profits if it leads to lower costs or to improved bases of diversification.

**Unrelated diversification**
A mix of businesses in any industry.

In **unrelated diversification,** firms acquire businesses in any industry, and their main concern is only whether an acquisition is a good financial investment.[20] Businesses can be acquired as long-term investments. If so, the acquired firm has potential for growth, but it does not have the financial or other resources necessary to grow without help. To reach its potential, the acquired company needs the parent company's financial or managerial resources. Businesses can also be acquired as short-term investments. In this case, the parent company hopes to sell off the acquired firm's assets for more than the cost of acquisition. In addition, some firms look for businesses in industries with different economic cycles. In this way, the parent firm can remain profitable even if one industry is in an unprofitable economic cycle.

Like domestic companies, multinational firms also pursue diversification strategies. Acquiring a business in another country is a quick way to gain a presence and often a recognized brand name. The multinational company with related diversification can also coordinate and use resources, such as R&D from different businesses located anywhere in the world, to gain competitive advantages. It can more easily establish global brand names for different but related products. Diversified multinational companies can cross-subsidize, both across countries and across companies, to attack rivals in different countries. Cross-subsidization means that money generated in one country or from one company within a corporation provides resources to sister organizations in other countries or other companies to undercut their local competition.

However, diversification is not without its costs, and multinationals need to balance its benefits with the added costs. For instance, companies diversifying into new countries face the liability and related costs of newness and foreignness (i.e., being new and foreign in a country) and the coordination and administration costs of managing a more complex organization. Differences in culture and social institutions as well as geographic distance make multinational diversification more challenging. However, recent research by Qian, Li, Li, and Qian suggests that multinationals can benefit tremendously by diversifying on a regional basis up to some point.[21] Diversification into regions allows the multinational to enter markets that are fairly similar, reducing costs associated with the diversification efforts. However, beyond a certain point, higher levels of diversification actually hurt a multinationals' profits. Multinationals that operate in a moderate number of regions optimize their performance. Exhibit 5.5 shows a selection of Global Fortune 500 diversified multinational companies with their major lines of businesses.

## Strategy Content: Brief Conclusions

The first section of this chapter provided an overview of the content or makeup of basic strategies: generic, competitive, and diversified. Like solely domestic firms, multinational companies use these strategies to achieve and maintain competitive advantage over rivals. The next section reviews traditional strategy formulation techniques as applied to the multinational company.

**EXHIBIT 5.5**    Examples of Diversified Multinationals

| Company (Headquarters Location) | Major Lines of Business | Countries | Number of Employees | Revenues ($ million) | Profits ($ million) |
|---|---|---|---|---|---|
| GE (United States) | Aircraft engines, aerospace, appliances, communications and services, electrical distribution and control, financial services, industrial and power systems, lighting, medical systems, motors, NBC, plastics, transportation | 150+ | 301,000 | 147,606 | 13,900.00 |
| Siemens (Germany) | Automation and drives, automotive systems, computers, industrial projects and technical services, mobile information and communication, information and communication networks, medical engineering, power distribution and transmission, power generation, production and logistics system, building technologies, business services, design and exhibition, financial services, real estate management, transportation systems | 190 | 360,000 | 113,349 | 8,562 |
| Samsung (Korea) | Electronics, precision materials, mobile display, digital imaging, heavy industries (shipbuilding), construction, petrochemicals, fine chemicals, life insurance, fire and marine insurance, securities, investment trust management, venture investment, advertising, Shilla Hotels & Resorts | 97 | 221,726 | 148,944 | 12,059 |
| Procter & Gamble (United States) | Health, beauty care, industrial chemicals, beverages and food, laundry and cleaning detergents, food services and lodging, paper | 140 | 129,000 | 11,797 | 3,763.00 |
| Mitsui (Japan) | Iron and steel, non-ferrous metals, property, service, construction, machinery, chemicals, energy, foods, textiles, general merchandise | 88 | 44,937 | 5,503 | 116.5 |
| Philips (Netherlands) | Lighting, components, consumer electronics, household appliances and personal care, medical systems, industrial and electric acoustic systems, information systems, communication systems, semiconductors, office equipment | 100+ | 184,000 | 32,339.00 | (1,371.0) |

Sources: Based on http://money.cnn.com/magazines/fortune/global500/2012/full_list/index.html and company websites.

# Strategy Formulation: Traditional Approaches

**Strategy formulation**

Process by which managers select the strategies to be used by their company.

Managers use several common techniques as aids in formulating their strategies. In general, **strategy formulation** is the process by which managers select the strategies to be used by their company.

In this section, we review some of the popular types of analyses that provide managers with the information to formulate successful strategies. These analyses help managers understand: (1) the competitive dynamics of their industry, (2) their company's competitive position in the industry, (3) the opportunities and threats faced by their company, and (4) their organization's strengths and weaknesses. This information allows managers to choose strategies that best fit their firm's unique situation.

## Industry and Competitive Analyses

Companies compete within industries, meaning that industries are the main competitive arenas of a company's business activities. To formulate effective strategies, managers must understand their industries well. They must know the forces affecting the industry, its economic characteristics, and the driving forces of change and competition within it.

**Porter's five forces model**

A popular technique that can help a multinational firm understand the major forces at work in the industry and the industry's degree of attractiveness.

**Porter's five forces model** is a popular technique that can help a multinational manager understand the major forces at work in the industry and the industry's degree of attractiveness.[22] The first important force to consider is the degree of competition in the industry. For instance, there is a high degree of global competition among auto manufacturers, and such competition has a significant influence on the profitability of the industry and on the strategic moves of the players.

The second force to evaluate is the threat of new entrants. Companies need to consider the degree to which they may face new competitors in their industries. The threat of new entrants is generally dependent on barriers to entry, as shown in the next Case in Point.

The third force in Porter's model is the bargaining power of buyers, which is the degree to which buyers of the industry's products can influence competitors within the industry. Most experts argue that buyers are becoming increasingly sophisticated globally and will have an ever-growing influence on most industries. To remain competitive, therefore, most companies will have to create innovative products and services at low prices.[23]

To understand any industry, multinational companies must also look at the bargaining power of suppliers, the fourth force. Suppliers tend to have high power if they can exert significant influence on competitors within the industry. DeBeers, for example, controls a significant proportion of the supply of diamonds and has significant influence on the global diamond market.

The final force is the threat of substitutes: the extent to which competitors are confronted with alternatives to their products. For instance, Netflix, the company that pioneered web-based DVD rental, along with other competitors like Amazon.com, is threatened by substitutes in the form of web-based movies on demand.[24] In such industries, the threat of substitutes is high.

Although Porter's five forces model is a powerful technique for understanding domestic competition, multinational firms can also use it to examine their industries in other countries. The model allows multinational firms to determine the attractiveness of their industries and to ascertain which forces require attention. Such analyses can be very helpful as strategies are crafted.

### Barriers to Entry: Where Are the Chinese Cars in the United States?

China leads the world in the production of automobiles. Chinese manufacturers are exporting over one million cars a year. This begs the question of why we have not seen Chinese cars in the United States following the strategies pioneered by the Japanese and later the Korean automobile manufacturers.

Since 2005, Chinese auto manufacturers, including Brilliance, Geely, Great Wall, and BYD Auto have shown their cars at U.S. auto shows, announcing plans to sell their cars in the United States. As domestic growth has slowed, Chinese manufacturers have been increasing exports but primarily to developing countries in Africa, Asia, and Latin America. However, these cars do not meet the safety standards and consumer expectations for most of the developed world, including the United States. To keep prices low, near $6000 for some models, manufacturers cut features like air conditioning and power windows, but also short-cut safety testing typical of established makers. The Chinese government imposes no safety standards on automobiles. To enter the U.S. market, the Chinese would need to develop different products.

Chinese manufacturers not only need different products but also, as Bill Visnic, a senior analyst at Edmunds.com, notes, "You need some dealerships, and those things are tremendous investments of time and resources." Additionally, Chinese companies entering the U.S. market would have to invest heavily in marketing to overcome an image of poorer quality and safety. The lower-cost end of the automobile market is highly competitive and getting consumers to switch brands would be difficult.

Some Chinese companies might overcome these barriers to entry by acquiring known brands to export to the United States using existing dealers. Geely, which recently acquired Volvo, is a candidate for such a strategy. Some suggest that the Chinese will focus primarily on the niche market of electric vehicles.

*Sources: Based on Belson, K. 2011. "Where are the Chinese cars?" New York Times, February 18, www.ny times.com; ChinaAuto Web. 2010. "Why haven't Chinese car come to the US?" September 13, www.chinaautobeb.com; Dawson, C., and S. Terlep. 2012. "China ramps up auto exports." Wall Street Journal, April 24, online.wsj.co; Forbes. 2012. "How China will conquer the U.S. auto industry." January 31, www.forbes.com; Shirouzu, N. 2012. "Special report: China's car makers cut corners to success." September 18, www .reuters.com.*

The next important step in understanding an industry is to assess its dominant economic characteristics, which affect how strategies work. Issues that influence strategy selection include market size, ease of entry and exit, and whether there are economies of scale in production.[25] For example, markets with high growth rates often attract new competitors, and companies in such industries must be prepared to execute defensive strategies against the new rivals. Michael Porter argues that strategists must also monitor several driving forces of change in an industry.[26] These forces include the speed of new product innovations, technological changes, and changing societal attitudes and lifestyles. For example, rapidly changing technology creates the risk of being quickly overtaken by competitors; firms must respond by emphasizing innovation. Industries are also affected by the extent of competition. Competition is increased by such forces as the power of key suppliers and buyers or the threat of potential new entries into the industry.[27] Knowing your industry can be the key to strategic survival.

An analysis of an industry helps the manager identify the characteristics of companies and of their products or services that lead to competitive success. For example, in some industries, speed to market with a new product might be the key. Intel maintains dominance in the microprocessor industry by continually beating its rivals to the market with the next generation of computer chips. In other industries, high-quality designs may be critical for competitive success.

**Key success factors (KSFs)**
Important characteristics of a company or its product that lead to success in an industry.

The factors that lead to success in an industry are called **key success factors (KSFs).** Each factor can have a different degree of importance in various industries or within the same industry at different points in time. Possible KSFs are:[28]

- Innovative technology or products
- A broad product line
- Effective distribution channels
- Price advantages
- Effective promotion
- Superior physical facilities or skilled labor
- Experience of the firm in business
- The cost position for raw materials
- The cost position for production
- R&D quality
- Financial assets
- Product quality
- The quality of human resources

The knowledge of industry dynamics and KSFs helps both multinational and domestic managers formulate strategies to achieve their key goals. With an understanding of what drives competition in the industry and what the successful firms do to achieve and maintain their profitability, managers can formulate strategies that have the best chance of success for their firms. The next Case in Point shows how South African Breweries uses knowledge of KSFs to defend its monopoly in the South African beer market.

Understanding an industry and identifying KSFs represent only some of the analysis necessary to formulate successful strategies. Managers must also understand and anticipate their competitors' strategies. One technique used to assess rivals is a **competitor analysis,** which is a profile of a competitor's strategies and objectives. It can help you select an offensive or defensive competitive strategy based on the current or anticipated actions of your rivals.

**Competitor analysis**
Profile of a competitor's strategies and objectives.

The competitor analysis has four steps:

1. *Identifying the basic strategic intent of competitors:* Strategic intent consists of the broad strategic objectives of the firm, such as to be the market share leader or to be a company known for its technological innovation.

2. *Identifying the generic strategies used and anticipated to be used by competitors (e. g., producing at the lowest cost):* This information helps managers determine which KSFs are currently the most important to competitors and the most likely to be important in the future. For example, cheap labor cost might be an important KSF for a competitor's low-cost strategy.

3. *Identifying the offensive and defensive competitive strategies currently used or anticipated to be used by rivals.*

4. *Assessing the current positions of competitors:* An example is identifying the market leader or the competitors losing market share.

Understanding current and anticipated competitive moves by rival firms allows managers to plan offensive or defensive strategies for their own firms. For example, if a competitor uses a differentiation strategy based on high-quality products, a company may attack by matching or exceeding that quality at a lower price.

To formulate their competitive strategies, multinational companies use a country-by-country competitive analysis. In this way, a company can make competitive moves based on a specific competitive strategy for each competitor in each country. Exhibit 5.6 shows hypothetical competitive profiles of four companies in

**EXHIBIT 5.6**   Hypothetical Country-by-Country Competitive Analysis of Rivals

| Rivals | Strategic Issues | Countries | | | |
|---|---|---|---|---|---|
| | | Canada | Mexico | France | Taiwan |
| Bronson, Inc. (United States) | • Strategic Intent | Dominant leader | Maintain position | Dominant leader | Move into the top five |
| | • Generic Strategies | Low cost | Low cost | Low cost | Differentiation based on foreign image |
| | • Competitive Strategies | Defensive based on threat of retaliation | None | Offensive price cutting | Offensive price cutting |
| | • Current Position | Market leader | Middle of the pack | Increasing share: No. 2 | New entry |
| Leroux (Belgium) | • Strategic Intent | Overtake the leader | Move up a notch | Dominant leader | Survive |
| | • Generic Strategies | Differentiation based on brand name | Differentiation based on brand name | Differentiation based on brand name | Differentiation based on brand name |
| | • Competitive Strategies | Price cutting based on counter-parry | Price cutting based on counter-parry | Provide resources for counter-parries | Price cutting based on counter-parry |
| | • Current Position | Holding at No. 3 | Market leader | New entry; too early to tell | Holding at No. 2 |
| Shin, Ltd. (Singapore) | • Strategic Intent | Gain and hold market share | Gain and hold market share | Gain and hold market share | Gain and hold market share |
| | • Generic Strategies | Differentiation based on high quality | Differentiation based on high quality | Differentiation based on high quality | Differentiation based on high quality |
| | • Competitive Strategies | Offensive by comparative advertisements | Offensive by comparative advertisements | Defensive, lock in long-term contracts | Defensive, lock in long-term contracts |
| | • Current Position | Middle of the pack | Middle of the pack, but rising | Market leader | Market leader |
| Keio, Ltd. (Japan) | • Strategic Intent | New entry, rising fast | New entry, rising fast | Expected to enter this year | New entry, rising fast |
| | • Generic Strategies | To catch and pass the leaders | To catch and pass the leaders | To catch and pass the leaders | To catch and pass the leaders |
| | • Competitive Strategies | Low cost based on cheap labor | Low cost based on cheap labor | Low cost based on cheap labor | Low cost based on cheap labor |
| | • Current Position | Heavy discounts based on volume purchases | Heavy discounts based on volume purchases | Heavy discounts based on volume purchases | Heavy discounts based on volume purchases |

## Mastery of Local KSFs: The Case of SABMiller (South African Breweries Miller)

SABMiller is touted as one of South Africa's major multinationals, growing from a small local brewery to the world's second largest. Having merged with Coors and Miller, it now has operations in 75 countries on six continents. How has it become so strong?

One of SABMiller's key success factors is its mastery of local markets. It is one of the dominant players in the South African alcoholic beverages market, with a 97 percent market share in beer and more than 60 percent of the liquor market. However, SABMiller dominates the South African market not because its beers have a unique taste or quality but rather because the company has the distinctive competency to meet the complex demands of the local market.

The key success factor for selling beer in South Africa is mastery of the distribution channel. In South Africa, most beer is sold through *shebeens*. Left over from the time of apartheid, these pubs were unlicensed because the sale of alcohol to blacks was illegal. Currently, although there is a push by the government to bring the *shebeens* into the government's liquor control system, the majority remain unlicensed, and are small local operations. SAB estimates that

there are over 265,000 points of sale in the country, over half of which are unlicensed.

SABMiller does not sell directly to the illegal pubs but works through local distributors and independent truck drivers. Loyal to SAB, many of the truck drivers are former employees who started their delivery businesses with help from SAB. Although technically drivers and distributors should only sell to licensed outlets, selling to the *shebeens*, as entities outside of government control, is institutionalized in the black townships. Although SAB successfully navigates the existing system, the company is also working to move the *shebeens* into the licensed domain where they could serve their customers directly.

*Sources: Based on* Business Report. *2011. "License shebeens to tackle abuse—SAB," November 18, www.iol.co.za; Fin24. 2012. "Gauteng shebeens granted permit extension," July 4, www.fin24.com; Gilmour, C. 2005. "Distribution holds the key to brewer's success,"* Financial Mail, *August 12, free.financialmail.co.za; Mawson, N. 2009. "SABMiller grows from 'dusty operation' into a global giant."* BusinessDay, *March 27; Reed, John. 2005. "How SAB Miller stayed dominant at home while aiming to go global."* Financial Times, *October 12.*

different countries. Using this hypothetical illustration, a multinational manager might decide to avoid attacking Bronson, Inc., the dominant leader, in its home market. Bronson has threatened retaliation.

## Company-Situation Analysis

Each company faces a unique situation in the competitive business world. Managers must understand what *their* particular company can and cannot do best, realistically assessing their company's resources and strategic capabilities. In addition, they must identify any opportunities for or threats to their company's unique position in the industry.

The most common tool for a company-situation analysis is called the **SWOT**, an acronym for strengths, weaknesses, opportunities, and threats. The SWOT has an internal component, which focuses on an organization's *strengths* and *weaknesses*, and an external component, which focuses on *opportunities* or *threats* from the environment.

A *strength* is a distinctive capability, resource, skill, or other advantage of an organization relative to its competitors. Strengths may come from technological superiority, innovative products, high efficiencies and low costs, human resource capabilities, marketing and promotional strengths, or other factors.

**SWOT**
The analysis of an organization's internal strengths and weaknesses and the opportunities or threats from the environment.

A *weakness* is any competitive disadvantage of a company relative to its competitors. To identify relevant strengths or weaknesses, managers must assess their organizations' distinctive competencies that can lead to sustainable competitive advantage when matched with an appropriate strategy. Relevant strengths and weaknesses are often industry specific and depend on the KSFs in a company's industry. Companies attempt to build their strategies on their strengths. For example, if you can produce at lower costs, you can underprice your rivals. If you can innovate quickly, you can be first to market with a new product.

*Opportunities* are favorable conditions in a firm's environment. *Threats* are unfavorable conditions in the environment. Threats come from any changes that challenge a company's position in its industry, for example, new competitors, such as Korean electronics makers in the United States; technological change; political change; or changes in import regulations. Opportunities often come from the same sources as threats. Hence, what may appear as a threat for one company may seem like an opportunity for another. For example, growth in the tablet market and smart phone market offers opportunities for companies like Apple and Samsung to sell new products that replace some of the functions of a PC. Yet this same trend may be a threat to Microsoft, with an operating system tied so closely to PCs. New markets often constitute important opportunities. Consider the next Multinational Management Brief on challenges and opportunities for retail sales in China.

## Multinational Management **Brief**

### Emerging Market Opportunities: The Challenge of China for Wal-Mart and Home Depot

When Wal-Mart drew 80,000 shoppers on opening day for its first supercenter in China, the top global retailers saw a golden opportunity. More than a decade later, things are not so rosy and China has proven to be a tough market for the global companies.

Wal-Mart does have 364 stores in China but its stores no longer draw the monster crowds. Competition is heated with the two other largest retailers, Carrefour SA and Tesco, and the market leader, Sun Art, a joint venture between France's Auchan and Taiwan's Ruentex Group. Sun Art has 12.8 percent of the hypermarket segment to Wal-Mart's 11.2 percent. However, Wal-Mart, with a shift in strategy, is moving forward aggressively by acquiring Yihaodian, a recognized Chinese online retailer. Yihaodian provides Wal-Mart an established brand that sells groceries and other everyday items.

For Home Depot, the China experience is pretty much a failure. In September of 2012, Home Depot announced that it was closing its remaining seven big-box stores. The company will continue to own two specialty stores and an online business. Although the Chinese middle class is growing and many are purchasing newly built apartments, often just shells that lack flooring, appliances, and even doors, the Chinese consumer seems adverse to the "do it yourself" mentality. Home Depot joined a growing list of retailers who misjudged the local culture and the difficulties of importing a foreign business model. As a Home Depot spokesperson noted, "The market trend says this is more of a do-it-for-me culture."

*Sources: Based on Burkitt, L. 2012. "Wal-Mart to work harder on growth in China." The Wall Street Journal, April 15, www.online.wsj.com; Burkitt, L. 2012. "Home Depot learns Chinese prefer 'do-it-for me,'" September 14, www.online.wjs.com; DuBois, S. 2012. "Home Depot knows when to call it quits," October 26, www.fortune.com; Einhorn, B. 2012. "Wal-Mart moves into China's hot e-commerce sector," August 15, www.businessweek.com.*

The SWOT analysis for the multinational company is more complex than for the domestic company, especially for assessing opportunities and threats. Multinational companies face more complex general and operating environments because they compete in two or more countries. Each country provides its own national context, which may present its particular opportunities or threats. Import or export barriers may make shipping products or bringing in supplies prohibitively expensive. Volatile exchange rates may make an otherwise attractive business environment threatening. Local inflation may play havoc with prices for the international market. Changes in government policies may affect the ability to repatriate earnings (i.e., get the company's money out of the country). In conducting a SWOT, therefore, multinational managers must conduct an extremely thorough analysis of the business environment in each country, and a country-by-country SWOT is probably the most prudent approach.

## Corporate Strategy Selection

A diversified corporation has a portfolio (a selection) of businesses, with the primary goal of investing in profitable businesses. The major strategic question is which businesses in the portfolio are targets for growth and investment and which are targets for divestment or harvesting. Targets for growth and investment receive additional corporate resources because managers anticipate high returns. Targets for divestment are businesses that managers decide to sell or liquidate. Targets for harvesting are usually mature and profitable businesses that managers see as sources of cash for other investments.

One way of assessing a corporate business portfolio is through a matrix analysis. While several consultants and companies have developed their own business matrix systems to assess business portfolios, a popular one is the growth-share matrix of the Boston Consulting Group (BCG). This matrix is used to decide how much of its resources a corporation should devote to any unit. The BCG growth-share matrix divides businesses into four categories based on the industry growth rate and the relative market share of the business in question. The most attractive businesses are those in fast-growing industries in which the business has a relatively large market share compared to the most successful firm in the industry. Businesses in this category are called *stars*. In contrast, *dogs* are businesses with relatively low market shares in low-growth industries. *Cash cows* are businesses in slow-growth industries where the company has a strong market share. *Problem children* are businesses in high-growth industries where the company has a poor market share. For each type of business, the growth-share matrix has a suggested strategy, as shown in Exhibit 5.7.

Another popular portfolio matrix is the GE portfolio matrix. This matrix contains nine cells based on high, medium, and low levels of industry attractiveness and on strong, average, and weak levels of a business's competitive position in the industry. Some indicators of industry strength are market size and growth rate. Competitive position is based on the strategic capabilities of a business, such as lower costs for production. The matrix is used to determine the competitive position of a business in its industry.

For the diversified multinational company, the portfolio assessment becomes more complex because market share and industry growth are seldom the same in all the countries in which a multinational competes. Thus, as illustrated in Exhibit 5.7 showing a cross-country BCG analysis, portfolio analyses must be conducted for each business in each country or region of operation.

This is only a brief review of some of the analytical techniques used to formulate strategy for the multinational company. The challenge for the multinational

**EXHIBIT** **5.7**   BCG Growth-Share Matrix for a Diversified Multinational Company

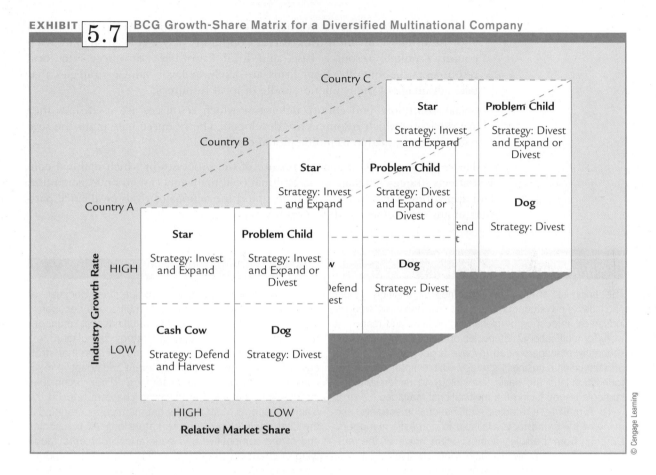

manager is to use these and other techniques in the highly complex and evolving world of international competition.

The next section shows how broad institutional forces can affect the choice of strategies for the multinational company and its competitors. Specifically, the final section presents an overview of how the national context leads to country-by-country differences in strategic management practices.

# The National Context and Organizational Strategy: Overview and Observations

The national context—the immediate environment where firms compete—directly affects organizational strategy and design. These environments provide firms with nation-specific opportunities and threats; that is, the specific combinations of opportunities and threats in any given nation that are different from those in other nations. As a result, the varieties of national contexts enable different industries to flourish and different strategies to be effective.

National context affects organizational design and strategy formulation and content through the following processes:

• The social institutions and national and business cultures encourage or discourage certain forms of businesses and strategies in each nation. There are generally acceptable and unacceptable ways of conducting business.

- Each nation must rely on its available factor conditions for developing industries and the firms within industries. Factor conditions play a role in shaping each country's unique resource base, and local firms have easy access to local resources. Consequently, local firms are likely to favor similar strategies that take advantage of their unique bundle of local resources.

- Social institutions and culture determine which resources are used, how they are used, and which resources are developed. The resource base limits the strategic options available to multinational companies.

These points provide a general picture of the processes by which national context affects strategic management. Multinational managers can go on to generalize and apply these ideas in order to understand the actions of rivals or alliance partners in any country where their firms do business.

## Summary and Conclusions

The business environment becomes increasingly global each day. Few students who read this book will work in industries untouched by global competition, and many will work for multinational companies or their subsidiaries. Consequently, managers need to have a good understanding of multinational business strategy. This chapter provides a foundation and the basic terminology to understand the strategic issues facing the multinational manager.

To formulate strategies, multinational managers use many of the same tools available to domestic managers. Differing from the solely domestic firm, however, the multinational company always faces more complex situations. Basic strategies that work in one country may not work in another. Competitive strategies must be considered on a country-by-country basis. The multinational company and its rivals are seldom in the same competitive positions in all the countries in which they compete. Although there are global trends of convergence in strategies, the institutional and cultural conditions favor different strategies by competitors from different nations. Multinational managers must be aware of these differences because they

affect both collaborators and competitors. Because of these complexities and those of a multicountry economic and political environment, the multinational manager faces continuous challenges in strategy formulation.

The multinational manager also must realize that strategy is a combination of planned intent and adaptive reactions to changing circumstances. The techniques discussed in this and the following chapters refer to the planned aspects of strategy: what managers determine is the best game plan given the nature of their companies and of the competitive and general environments. Modifying or changing strategies in response to new opportunities and new threats is a necessity in today's world of rapid cross-border competition.

Beyond the traditional strategic questions facing all managers, the multinational manager must confront other issues related to strategy. Chapter 6 will deal directly with these issues and introduce the global-local dilemma facing multinational companies. Chapter 6 will also present an array of strategies that multinational companies use to participate in different markets.

## Discussion Questions

1. Discuss how a multinational firm might use a low-cost strategy in one country while using a differentiation strategy in another country.

2. Identify examples of how multinational companies have used the offensive competitive strategies discussed in the chapter.

3. How can a multinational competitor such as Wal-Mart attack multinational rivals using the counter-parry?

4. Discuss the advantages that multinational companies might have over domestic rivals in sustaining competitive advantage.

5. Identify and discuss the KSFs that are most likely to vary by national context. Explain your answer.

## Multinational Management **Internet Exercise**

### Opportunities and Threats in India

**Step 1.** Find online copies of the business press in India.

**Step 2.** Identify recent changes in Indian law and popular reactions to foreign companies.

**Step 3.** Based on your findings, discuss opportunities and threats for different types of businesses considering entering India.

**Step 4.** Prepare a report for a company in a relevant industry.

## Multinational Management **Skill Builder**

### Identifying Distinctive Competencies and Generic Strategies

**Step 1.** Choose a global industry, such as the automobile industry or the cell phone industry, and identify two to four major competitors in the industry.

**Step 2.** Research the selected companies in the popular business press and make a list of the unique capabilities of each company. Identify where on the value chain these capabilities exist.

**Step 3.** For each company, write a one-page analysis showing how these capabilities lead to distinctive competencies.

**Step 4.** For each company, write a one-page analysis showing how the company attempts to use its distinctive competencies to successfully implement a generic strategy. Note whether companies have different generic strategies for different products or for different market segments.

## *Endnotes*

1 Hitt, Michael A., B. W. Keats, and S. M. DeMarie. 1998. "Navigating in the new competitive landscape: Building competitive advantage and strategic flexibility in the 21st century." *Academy of Management Executive,* 12, 22–42.

2 Hambrick, Donald C., and James W. Fredrickson. 2005. "Are you sure you have a strategy?" *Academy of Management Executive,* 19(4), 51–62.

3 Hitt, Michael A., Ireland, R. Duane, and Hoskisson, Robert E. 2013. *Strategic Management.* Mason, OH: South-Western.

4 Hitt, p. 4.

5 Porter, Michael E. 1990. *Competitive Advantage of Nations.* New York: Free Press.

6 Ibid.

7 Ibid.

8 Ibid.

9 Porter, Michael E. 1985. *Competitive Advantage: Creating and Sustaining Superior Performance.* New York: Free Press.

10 Thompson, Arthur A., Jr., Margaret A. Peteraf, A. J. Strickland III, and John E. Gamble. 2012. *Crafting and Executing Strategy.* Homewood, IL: McGraw-Hill Irwin.

11 Ibid.

12 http://www.statisticbrain.com/outsourcing-statistics-by-country/; http://www.sourcingline.com/top-outsourcing-countries.

13 Kakumanu, Prasad, and Anthony Portanova. 2006. "Outsourcing: Its benefits, drawbacks and other related issues. *Journal of American Academy of Business,* September, 9(2), 1–7.

14 Hill, Charles and G. R. Jones. 2013. *Strategic Management Theory.* Cengage Learning: Mason, OH.

15 Barney, J. B. 1991. "Firm resources and sustained competitive advantage." *Journal of Management,* 17, 99–120.

16 Ibid.

17 Thompson, Peteraf, Strickland, and Gamble; Yip, G. S., and G. T. Hult. 2012. *Total Global Strategy.* Englewood Cliffs, NJ: Prentice Hall.

18 Yannopoulos, P. 2011. "Defensive and offensive strategies for market success." *International Journal of Business and Social Science,* 2, 1–12.

19 Thompson, Peteraf, Strickland, and Gamble.

20 Thompson, Peteraf, Strickland, and Gamble.

21 Qian, G., L. Li, J. Li, and Z. Qian. 2008. "Regional diversification and firm performance. *Journal of International Business Studies,* 39, 197–214.

22 Porter, Michael E. 1979. "How competitive forces shape strategy." *Harvard Business Review,* 57, March–April, pp. 137–145.

23 Porter, Michael E. 1979. "How competitive forces shape strategy." *Harvard Business Review,* 57, March–April, pp. 137–145.

24 Heilemann, John. 2005. "Showtime for Netflix." *Business 2.0,* March, 36–38.

25 Thompson, Strickland, and Gamble.

26 Porter, Michael E. 1979. "How competitive forces shape strategy." *Harvard Business Review,* 57, March–April, pp. 137–145.

27 Porter, Michael E. 1979. "How competitive forces shape strategy." *Harvard Business Review,* 57, March–April, pp. 137–145.

28 Thompson, Strickland, and Gamble.

# Harley-Davidson, Inc.: Troubled Times Increase H-D's Reliance on International Sales

JAMES W. BRONSON, UNIVERSITY OF WISCONSIN–WHITEWATER

MARGARET L. KUCHAN, UNIVERSITY OF WISCONSIN–WHITEWATER

***2009 Mission Statement, as stated on the company Web site:*** *We inspire and fulfill dreams around the world through Harley-Davidson motorcycling experiences.*

***2007 Mission Statement:*** *We fulfill dreams through the experience of motorcycling, by providing to motorcyclists, and to the general public, an expanding line of motorcycles, branded products, and services in selected market segments.*

Harley-Davidson, the over-100-year-old manufacturer of motorcycles, turned a corner in 2008–2009, but it was largely the wrong corner. Total sales for 2008 were down 4 percent from the company's 2006 high. Sales in North America, the company's dominant market, were off 17 percent, and the company estimated its total sales would be down an additional 10–13 percent in 2009. Part of the problem could be attributed to selling a luxury good during a recession, but Harley-Davidson (H-D) had also made some notable tactical errors.

Harley-Davidson's Financial Services (HDFS) had financed the sale of motorcycles to buyers of questionable financial means. These motorcycle loans were resulting in a high default rate. H-D's questionable loans and high default rate closely paralleled the 2008–2009 bank crisis brought on by subprime mortgages. H-D wrote off $80 million in loans in 2008, and 2009 is expected to be worse. Where H-D had been a Wall Street darling since the early 1990s, as of mid-2009 it is on many sell lists.

The most damaging aspect of loan default was not the loss on the loans, but the thousands of used H-D motorcycles that entered the marketplace at bargain prices. Traditionally, used H-D motorcycles had retained their value, and value retention was a major selling point. However, the glut of used H-D motorcycles not only eroded the sales of new H-D motorcycles but significantly reduced the value of H-D owners' investments.

H-D had been touted as a model for favorable labor relations management for many years. This era may have come to an end in 2008 when H-D announced the layoff of up to 1,500 employees, or about 15 percent of the company's workforce. While the labor force was being reduced as the result of declining domestic sales and diminished profits, outgoing CEO James Ziemer's pay jumped from $4,447,713 in 2007 to $5,625,595 in 2008, a 26.5 percent increase.

The bright spot for H-D was international sales. Between 2006 and 2008 H-D's international revenue increased by 49 percent. During the same period the number of motorcycles sold in international markets grew 28 percent, while the domestic market decreased 25 percent.

H-D produces and sells only heavyweight motorcycles under the H-D brand. These motorcycles, showcasing chrome and flawless paint, are intended to make a statement for their owners. It can be an expensive statement; 2009 base prices ranged from $6,999 for the smallest model, the venerable Sportster, to over $29,999 for the massive Tri Glide Ultra Classic. Accessories, shipping, import tariffs, and other duties and licenses can more than double the factory price in offshore markets. The company also manufactures about 13,000 motorcycles a year under the Buell brand.

The company has defined the heavyweight segment as motorcycles with engines displacing a minimum of 651 cc. Following a decade of short supply, the production of H-D heavyweight motorcycles rose markedly

demand for the company's motorcycles far outstripping supply. During this period it was not unusual for a buyer to have to wait as long as two years to take delivery on the company's most popular models. Profits soared and H-D became the darling of Wall Street. By 2005 management had narrowed the gap between demand and supply. By carefully managing growth, the company ensures that its bikes are not too easy to come by. Starting in 2007, the company was forced to cut back on manufacturing to avoid over-supplying the market. Managing the supply of H-D motorcycles maintains high prices and permits H-D to avoid having to offer promotions and discounts to sell its product. Promotions and discounts are practices that are inconsistent with a luxury good.

H-D's premium pricing limits the number of young buyers. Two-thirds of its customers are between the ages of 35 and 54 years. H-D has redesigned some of its bikes to better accommodate female riders. The percentage of female buyers has reached 12 percent and continues to move slowly upward. H-D also offers motorcycle driver education courses, where 40 percent of the participants are women.

For the most part, the company has failed in its attempts to diversify into related industries. The economic downturn of 2007–2008 negatively impacted Harley-Davidson Financial Services (HDFS). HDFS's primary business is to provide financing and insurance to H-D dealers and buyers. In 1998 H-D moved to expand its presence within the motorcycle industry when it acquired the outstanding shares of the Buell Motorcycle Company. While sharing components and technology with H-D, the performance-oriented Buell is intended to attract younger and nontraditional riders to the H-D family. In 2008 H-D acquired the European motorcycle manufacturer, MV Agusta, which includes the MV Agusta and Cagiva brand names. MV Agusta products emphasize design and performance and feature a liquid-cooled, four-cylinder engine design. Caviga products are lightweight sport bikes featuring 125-cc air-cooled engines.

*H-D Strategy* In 2008 H-D's strategy incorporated three objectives, at least two of which are a direct result of the economy: (1) investing in the H-D brand, (2) restructuring operations and reducing the cost structure, and (3) obtaining funding for HDFS.

The first objective, investing in the brand, is to be achieved through a two-pronged approach. First, the company intends to increase its market base by reaching out to nontraditional rider groups, including women and minorities. The second prong is directed at its traditional rider group, and product innovation is the vehicle of choice for reaching this group.

The second objective, restructuring operations, is to be accomplished by plant closing and outsourcing. The company will close two engine and transmission plants in Milwaukee and move their operations to a third plant in Menomonee Falls, Wisconsin. Paint and frame operations in York, Pennsylvania, will be combined with other operations at that site. A distribution facility in Franklin, Wisconsin, that handles parts and accessories will be closed and its operations outsourced. Finally, the company's trucking operation will be terminated and its activities outsourced. It is expected that restructuring and reduced product demand will result in the loss of 1,500 hourly and salaried positions.

The third objective, obtaining funding for HDFS will be the most problematic and includes:

- Accessing the unsecured debt capital markets.
- Increasing asset-backed credit.
- Renewing existing lines of credit.
- Accessing the asset-backed securitization market through the U.S. Federal Reserve programs.

H-D has found it difficult to sell motorcycles without providing a source for financing. Consequently, the company's well-being hinges on the liquidity of HDFS.

*H-D Human Resources Management* H-D prides itself on open communication with its union and non-union employees and on its team-based culture. Employees are involved in goal setting, and this practice facilitates a shared vision of the company's direction. Self-directed work groups are the norm. Departmental differences are minimized through a focus on cross-functional communications. These types of personnel practices are known as partnering at H-D; partnering results include increased employee motivation and a reduced need for supervision.

The company developed its Performance Effectiveness Process to foster both employee performance and career development. Employees are rated on a form that includes over 90 descriptors, which include: (1) values diversity in the workforce, (2) does what he/she says he/she will do, and (3) responds in a positive manner to criticism. The performance evaluation was tested and refined on managers before it was used on the workforce. H-D takes career development seriously and has formalized all the company's learning, training, and development initiatives under its Leadership Institute. Each year over a third of the company's employees attend the institute's courses. Management believes these courses improve the company's competitiveness, while giving employees the knowledge and skills needed for advancement and personal growth. H-D prefers to promote from within the company to give employees opportunities for advancement and to demonstrate the company's commitment to retaining talent. This is why they also have an extensive tuition reimbursement program, including undergraduate and graduate programs offered through Marquette University and Milwaukee Area Technical College. H-D even developed a program to assist its distributors. Classes offered at H-D University (HDU) help distributors improve customer satisfaction, store layout, and merchandising.

An emphasis for HDU is teaching dealers how to market and sell motorcycles. Until 2005—2006, the H-D's dealers functioned as order takers. Demand for H-D motorcycles exceeded manufacturing capacity, and most buyers had to wait a few months before receiving their bikes. During the transition from the 2005 to the 2006 model years, supply briefly exceeded demand. For the first time in the memory of most dealers, unsold motorcycles were sitting on the showroom floor. The fact that dealers simply didn't know how to handle this situation became painfully evident when sales trended downward in 2007. HDU stepped in to help H-D dealers learn what every successful car dealership already knows: how to sell your product.

In 2008 the company employed approximately 9,000 employees in the manufacture of motorcycles. As a function of their geographical location, unionized employees are represented by one of two unions. H-D had incurred only one previous strike since the AMF buyout in 1981 when in 2007 the employees at the York, Pennsylvania, plant went on strike for three weeks. The bones of contention were pay, a tiered wage system, and copay for medical benefits. In the end workers received a 12 percent wage increase over three years, and the company received a lower starting wage for new employees. The tiered wage system flew in the face of Harley's compensation structure, which had traditionally been driven by two guidelines: (1) make a larger portion of the employee's pay at risk or variable and (2) compensate all employees in the same manner. An example of a bonus compensation system used for employees is giving equal percentage bonuses, based on 15 percent of sales. It is believed that this practice minimizes differences in employee pay and promotes teamwork and lessens jealousy among employees. H-D generally evokes a deep commitment from employees. Building consensus with union employees is H-D's standard practice. Resolving the occasional union grievance is left to the employee's filing the grievance, the union steward, the work group, and the work group's advisor (manager). The grievance resolution is considered binding by the union and the company.

Harley has a time-tested device for keeping up with customer demands and ensuring product quality. Half of the company's 9,000 employees ride a H-D, yet every employee, including the CEO, must go through a dealer to get a bike. This is just a testament to H-D being a company driven by the human resources function. Fairness and equality are driving this company into the future with a workforce that believes they are part of something special.

***H-D Operations*** H-D has an ongoing production strategy of increasing the supply of its motorcycles, but at a rate less than that demanded by the market. To this end, the company expanded its manufacturing capacity through 2006. The company tries to position its product development staff in proximity to its manufacturing operations in order to ensure that new product and model changes are coordinated prior to and during ramp-up.

## Harley-Davidson Manufacturing Facilities

| Facility | Size (sq. ft.) | Part(s) Supplied |
|---|---|---|
| Wauwatosa, Wisconsin | 430,000 | Powertrain |
| Menomonee Falls, Wisconsin | 881,000 | Powertrain |
| Tomahawk, Wisconsin | 211,000 | Fiberglass parts and painting |
| York, Pennsylvania | 1,331,000 | Parts fabrication, painting, and assembly |
| Kansas City, Missouri | 450,000 | Sportster assembly, V-Rod powertrain |
| East Troy, Wisconsin (Buell) | 40,000 | Buell assembly |
| Manaus, Brazil | 82,000 | Office and subassembly for local markets |
| Varese, Italy | 1,378,000 | MV Agusta facilities |
| Adelaide, Australia | 485,000 | Motorcycle wheels |

A company operation in South America imports parts and subassemblies from the United States for final assembly in Brazil. Assembling the bikes in Brazil reduces duties and taxes, thus reducing the selling price and increasing the company's market. However, the volume of this facility remains under 1,000 units per year. Bikes for all other international markets are exported from the United States.

H-D actively practices lean manufacturing and quality management. The company continuously strives to improve the quality of its operations while controlling costs. Quality management practices include statistical process control, employee involvement in operations-related decisions, supplier participation, just-in-time inventory control, and partnerships with the company's unions. H-D trains its employees in the use of statistical methods and problem solving through its Leadership Institute courses. The company is proud of its relationship with employees and encourages employee involvement, emphasizing a highly flexible and participative workforce. The company employs this flexibility in cross-functional teams that review every aspect of the production process.

H-D strives to establish long-term mutually beneficial relationships with its suppliers. The company involves suppliers in the design and manufacturing of its products and quality improvement programs. Harley requires that its suppliers be committed to annual cost reductions even when labor and material costs are rising. The company believes that vendor involvement results in improved products, the adoption of new technologies, and the smoother introduction of new products and product changes. Supplier involvement is not without its costs and has led to an increase in the number of purchasing engineers from 4 to 30 in the 1990s. The involvement of suppliers has resulted in improvements in productivity and product quality, and a four- to five-day component inventory, all of which translates into an estimated savings of over $10 million per year.

In conjunction with its just-in-time inventory and assembly controls, H-D has introduced an automated electrified monorail (AEM) system in its two Wisconsin engine assembly plants. The AEM systems have increased productivity, improved ergonomics and increased the speed of changeover between different assemblies, while freeing up space on the factory floor. Similarly, the company's parts and accessories distribution centers have been highly automated leading to increased speed of delivery and a 99.7 percent level of accuracy.

***H-D Marketing*** August 2003 saw the culmination of H-D's hundredth anniversary celebration when an estimated 200,000 people participated in events in and around Harley's hometown of Milwaukee, Wisconsin. Riders came from every state and from every inhabited continent. H-D's anniversary was one of the biggest—some said the biggest—events in Milwaukee's history. H-D's public exposure from the carefully orchestrated event was beyond price, but events and promotions are the norm for H-D. Countless features in the media focus on the company, its bikes, and the image of Harley riders. The company has a long history of successful promotion, and its bikes have costarred in numerous major film productions.

The 130,000-square-foot H-D Museum opened in Milwaukee in 2008. The museum, showcasing both historic and current motorcycles, is intended to strengthen the company's bonds with riders and the general public. The museum includes a restaurant, café, retail, and meeting spaces. The company will use the space to host special events for the Harley Owners Group (HOG®).

The company's traditional advertising and promotional venues include dealer promotions and cooperative programs, magazine and direct mail advertising, and its famous HOG customer events. The annual gathering in Sturgis, South Dakota, has been the subject of public television documentaries. H-D's Web site offers an interactive and exhaustive online catalog. Customers can order accessories and customize bikes with hundreds of options. It wasn't until 2002 that Harley-Davison felt the need to advertise its products on television. The result of the company's marketing actions is that Harley-Davison ranks near the top among iconic brands, along with Disney and Apple Computer.

Formed in 1983, the company-sponsored HOG had over 1.1 million members worldwide in 2008. The group sponsors events, including national rides and rallies, and the company sponsors racing activities. Harley's buyers are not locked into any social class. You are just as likely to find a CEO on a Harley as a worker off the assembly line. Harley owners are loyal, with 90 percent of buyers reporting the intention of purchasing another Harley bike. Clearly image sells to this demographic, Harley ranks near the 100th percentile on the Brand Asset Valuator scale for such qualities as authentic, rugged, daring, dynamic, distinctive, and high performance. As one Harley owner put it, "What Harley-Davidson appeals to me is that we all think we're cooler than we really are." (*Milwaukee Journal Sentinel*, August 24, 2003)

A creative tool in H-D's marketing program is its Authorized Rental and Tour program. Operated in the

United States and overseas, this program puts riders on factory-maintained Harleys for guided tours. Included in the tour are some meals, lodging, and a support vehicle to carry the heavy luggage and take care of any mechanical malfunctions. A lot of development ideas come from bike-riding employees and from employee attendance at the Harley rallies that are held around the country. Harley riders traditionally customize their bikes, and this practice led H-D to offer custom bikes in 1998. This ongoing product group allows buyers to alter their factory bikes with a wide range of accessories and paint. With an average of $9,000 in extras, these bikes go for more than $27,000 and carry a 40 percent profit margin. Delivery time for the factory-custom bikes can run up to year. The company's marketing efforts were recognized when H-D was inducted into the 2001 Marketing Hall of Fame. Their selection was based on "an outstanding job of building and sustaining their brand through smart marketing" (http://proquest.umi.com). The honor recognized what Harley followers have known for years: Brand equity plus superior manufacturing has positioned H-D as the elite manufacturer in the North American motorcycle market.

**H-D Distribution** H-D products are sold through a network of 686 independently owned full-service dealerships in the United States. The company maintains a European headquarters in England. Dealerships can be found in 36 European, Middle Eastern, and African countries, in 8 Asian countries, and in 15 Latin America countries. Most dealerships sell only H-D and Buell products.

Uke's H-D/Buell dealership in Kenosha, Wisconsin, is fairly typical of Harley dealers. Uke's recently completed a new 54,000-square-foot facility alongside I-94. What may be unique to Uke's is a six-story glass tower that displays custom bikes like jewels in a showcase. The new building features a 15,000-square-foot showroom and a 10,000-square-foot service area. The basement is given over to the winter storage of customer's bikes, while the second-floor mezzanine houses a museum and art gallery. The architectural firm of Kubala Washatko of Cedarburg, Wisconsin, designed the new facility. Kubala Washatko has designed dozens of Harley dealerships around the United States.

**H-D Research and Development** H-D believes research and development is a key component of its ability to lead the touring bike market. The company maintains a 409,000-square-foot product development center and a separate 79,000-square-foot development center for the Buell product line. The product development centers are staffed with

| Harley-Davidson Dealership Locations in 2007 | |
|---|---|
| Country/Region | H-D/Buell Dealerships |
| United States | 684 |
| Canada | 74 |
| Europe | 370 |
| All other | 240 |
| Total | 1,368 |

employees from styling, purchasing, and manufacturing, as well as supplier representatives. The practice is consistent with H-D's commitment to quality management and results in seamless product development. Due to the increasing prevalence of environmental and safety regulations, the product development centers are staffed with professionals specializing in the regulatory process. The company has sought to be proactive in meeting environmental and safety regulations in both its products and facilities. The company spent $163.5 million in 2008, $185.5 million in 2007, and $177.7 million in 2006 on product development.

The company's products are in compliance with all current federal and state emission and noise standards. H-D has made the investment necessary to comply with the Environmental Protection Agency's tailpipe emission standards that became effective in 2010. A more pressing problem for H-D may come from more stringent noise standards in the European Union and Japan. Such standards may interfere with one of Harley's most sacred traditions: the bike's distinctive, and loud, exhaust.

**H-D Motorcycle Unit** According to H-D:

*The total on-highway motorcycle market, including the heavyweight portion of the market, is comprised of the following four segments:*

- *standard (emphasizes simplicity and cost)*
- *performance (emphasizes handling and acceleration)*
- *custom (emphasizes styling and individual owner customization)*
- *touring (emphasizes comfort and amenities for long-distance travel) (2008 Form 10-K)*

The company currently addresses all categories with its offerings from the MV Agusta line in the performance segment, with the Buell lineup in the standard and performance segments, and with H-D offerings in the standard, performance, touring, and custom segments. The larger displacement custom and touring models are the most profitable for the company.

The company's motorcycle unit consists of H-D Motor Company, the Buell Motorcycle Company, and MV Agusta. The motorcycle unit designs, manufactures, and markets primarily heavyweight bikes, as well as motorcycle parts, accessories, and merchandise. The company is the only major U.S. manufacturer of motorcycles and has led the heavyweight market since going public in 1986. The Motorcycle Industry Council figures give H-D a 45.5 percent share of the domestic heavyweight market for 2008. For some years the motorcycle unit generated about 80.0 percent of the total net sales of Harley-Davidson, Inc.

Harley's heavyweight bikes are, by the company's own definition, more than 650 cc of engine displacement. The company currently markets 33 models of performance, touring, and custom bikes with suggested retail prices up to $29,999 for a limited-edition factory-customized model. These bikes are built on five basic chassis designs (Softail, Sportster, Dyna Glide, Touring, and the VRSC, or V-Rod) and are powered by one of four 45-degree V-twin air-cooled engines ranging from 883 cc to a huge 1803-cc brute (the V-Rod utilizes a liquid-cooled engine). The company pioneered the touring heavyweight motorcycle, and this segment includes well-equipped bikes with fairings, windshields, and luggage carriers. The custom segment includes the retro-look bikes that are typically highly customized through the use of chrome, paint, and accessories. These bikes sell for prices that are about 50 percent higher than competitors' comparable models.

The V-Rod or VRSC model is the first in a new series of bikes aimed at the performance café racer market. The VRSC shares nothing with existing bikes and is equipped with the Porsche-designed, liquid-cooled, 60-degree V-twin, 1130-cc, 110+-hp, Revolution engine. It is the most expensive development project in the company's history, but H-D has not revealed the numbers. The VRSC model has met grudging acceptance at best with H-D's traditional buyers, but has done well with nontraditional buyers and the international market. Harley's previous foray into the performance segment with its Buell line of motorcycles has met with only limited success.

H-D manufactured and shipped 303,479 motorcycles in 2008 down from 330,619 in 2007. About half of all bikes on the road are Harley's big street cruisers, like the Softail, that sell for about $18,000. Around 30 percent are the true heavyweight touring

machines; equipped with fiberglass saddlebags, CD players, radios, and cruise control, these bikes sell for $20,000 or more. The remaining bikes are mostly the $7,000-or-more Sportsters; with ongoing cosmetic upgrades, the Sportster remains Harley's oldest and most affordable model.

*H-D Parts and Accessories* Parts and accessories include genuine H-D replacement parts and cosmetic bike accessories. Parts and accessories comprised 15.4 percent of sales in the motorcycle segment in 2008. This segment includes general merchandise, an area encompassing such items as clothes and collectibles. Around the country are 80 dealerships with shops that feature H-D clothes and collectibles, as well as an additional 52 Harley stores in malls, airports, and vacation destinations and another 20 seasonal shops. General merchandise constitutes 5.6 percent of sales in the motorcycle segment. While general merchandise is a small entry on H-D's income statement, it is an important form of advertising and a major player in the company's quest to turn the brand into a lifestyle. H-D licenses its name and logo for such items as T-shirts, jewelry, and toys. The company believes that licensing is a useful tool for promotion and routinely polices the unauthorized use of its name and logo. Royalty revenues totaled $45.4 million in 2008. While royalties are not great, the margins are high.

*H-D Financial Services Unit* The 700 employees of HDFS engage in the financing of dealer inventories and retail consumer installment sales contracts. The growth area in this market appears to be in the financing of new motorcycles. During 2008, 53.5 percent of all new H-D motorcycles retailed in the United States were financed by HDFS, up from 40 percent in 2004. H-D also reports that it provided financing to 95 percent of its dealers in 2008. Operating income from financial services was $82,765,000 in 2008, down 61 percent from 2007. While most of its business is directed at H-D dealers and the dealer's customers, Financial Services also provides financing for noncommercial aircraft, as well as broker's insurance and service contracts for motorcycle owners.

## H-D Financial Statements

In the face of the 2008–2009 recession, H-D's net profit remained strong but significantly off the 2006 high of $1,043,153. Profits in 2008 were $654,718, down 37 percent from 2006. The company has relatively little debt. Needless to say, H-D is no longer the darling of investors and the financial press. The board of directors has authorized the company to repurchase shares of the company's common stock. Under these plans, large blocks of stock have been repurchased by the company in recent years and have helped to keep H-D's stock price up in an often down market. Nonetheless, the company's stock value has declined markedly. The high value in the first quarter of 2007 was $74.03 per share, which may be contrasted against a low value of $11.54 per share in the fourth quarter of 2008.

H-D has taken steps to reduce its exposure to fluctuations in the international financial markets. The company made $95 million on foreign exchange adjustments in 2008, largely due to the decline in the dollar. The company expects to lose on foreign exchange adjustments in 2009. To reduce foreign exchange risks, the company selectively uses financial instruments. Forward foreign exchange contracts are used to hedge the effect of earnings fluctuation on the dollar. H-D is also exposed to loan defaults and interest rate fluctuations through its financial services division. To minimize its risk, HDFS packages and resells most of its loans. Harley's pension and SERPA benefit obligation has increased from $963,824 in 2005 to $1,178,283 in 2008. The postretirement health care liability went from $298,340 to $372,631 in 2005 and 2006, respectively. These liabilities will need to be closely monitored in the years to come.

## CASE DISCUSSION QUESTIONS

1. Which of Porter's generic strategies is H-D using? Will this strategy work for all of the countries described in the case? Why or why not?
2. What does a Porter's five forces analysis reveal about the strategies H-D has employed in recent years?
3. How does H-D compare to its competitors?

## CASE CREDIT

Harley-Davidson, Inc., 3700 West Juneau Avenue, Milwaukee, Wisconsin 53208. http://www.harley-davidson.com. SIC: 3751—Motorcycles, bicycles & parts.

## CASE NOTES

[1] Barrett, R. 2009. "New Harley CEO brings the chops." *Milwaukee Journal Sentinel*, April 12.

[2] Barrett, R. 2009. "Job cuts, outsourcing questioned at Harley shareholders meeting." *Milwaukee Journal Sentinel*, April 26.

[3] Barrett, R. 2009. "Job auction services, tent sales market repossessed bikes." *Milwaukee Journal Sentinel*, April 26.

[4] Carpenter, S. 2008. "Bumpy road ahead for industry." *Los Angeles Times*, January 23.

[5] Content, T. 2003. "Harley looks to a new breed of bike for growth." *Milwaukee Journal Sentinel*, August 24.

[6] Half-yearly report of Ducati Motor Holding S.p.A. as of June 30, 2008.

[7] Hamner, Susanna. 2009. "Harley, you're not getting any younger." *New York Times*, March 22.

[8] Harley Davidson, Inc., Form 10-K, December 31, 2004.

[9] Ibid., 2005.

[10] Ibid., 2006.

[11] Ibid., 2007.

[12] Ibid., 2008.

[13] *PR Newswire*, "Harley-Davidson and Staples elected to the 2001 Marketing Hall of Fame." April, p. 1.

[14] *Journal of Business and Design*. 2002. "Harley-Davidson: Marketing an American icon." January 05. http://www.cdf.org/cdf/atissue/vol2_1/harley/harley.html.

[15] *Economist*. 2004. "Luxury's new empire," June 17. http://www.economist.com/business/displaystory.cfm?story_id=2771531.

[16] Narayan, S. 2006. "India's lust for Luxe." *Time: Asia*, April. http://www.time.com/time/asia/magazine/printout/0,13675,501. 060410-1179415,00.html.

[17] O'Connell, V. 2009. "Sales of luxury goods seen falling by 10 percent." WSJ.com, April 11.

[18] Spivak, C. 2009. "Earning their keep?" *Milwaukee Journal Sentinel*, May 24.

[19] Steverman, B. 2009. "Harley-Davidson: Cruising on recovery road." *Business Week Online*, April 20.

[20] Teerlink, R., and L. Ozley. 2000. *More than a motorcycle: The leadership journey at Harley-Davidson*. Harvard Business School Press Boston, MA: Harvard Business School Press.

[21] Teerlink, R. 2000. "Harley's leadership U-turn." *Harvard Business Review*, July–August, pp. 43–48.

[22] Tortoiella, R., S. Kessler, E. Kolb, C. Montevirgen, and M. Basham. 2009. "S&P picks and pans: GE, Google, Harley-Davidson, AMD, Microsemi, Chipotle." *Business Week Online*, January 26.

[23] Weisman, K. 2005. "America's take on new luxury." *International Herald Tribune*, December 5.

[24] Windle, C. 2005. "China luxury industry prepares for boom." BBC News, September 27. http://news.bbc.co.uk/2/hi/business/4271970.stm.

[25] http://www.harley-davidson.com.

[26] http://www.hoovers.com.

[27] Zielinski, G. 2003. "Milwaukee gears up for motorcycle mania." *Milwaukee Journal Sentinel*, August 24.

# Multinational and Entry-Mode Strategies: Content and Formulation

# 6

## Preview CASE IN POINT

### BMW: Success in Selling Premium Cars

By automotive industry standards, BMW is a small auto manufacturer; while automotive giants such as Toyota or GM are selling cars by the tens of millions, BMW sells less than 2 million a year. However, even though BMW is often seen as too small, too exclusive, and too Euro-centric to achieve worldwide success, the carmaker has been extremely profitable in the premium car market. How has BMW become such a successful seller of premium cars?

A look at its strategic approaches provides some answers. Because BMW is a small company, many expect marketing to dominate its orientation. However, four of the last five BMW CEOs have been manufacturing experts, and BMW has always been guided by manufacturing excellence and technological innovation. Furthermore, this zeal for manufacturing performance has encouraged the company to strive constantly for efficiency, For instance, both the 1 and 3 series share about 60 percent of their parts.

However, BMW is clearly considered a premium car manufacturer and cannot rely solely on efficiency to remain successful. A big component of BMW's success depends on technological innovations. To stay at or near the top of the luxury car market, BMW uses a worldwide network of innovation centers, both to understand and adapt to local markets and to share innovations throughout the system. BMW has research and innovation centers in Munich, Germany; Steyr, Austria; Tokyo, Japan; and Beijing, China, as well in three locations in the United States (Newbury Park, Oxnard, and Palo Alto, California). In addition, BMW has 17 production facilities in 6 countries with additional assembly plants in 12 countries. BMW has marketing subsidiaries in 34 countries. Regarding their worldwide collaboration among subsidiaries, BMW notes, "Worldwide teamwork is the underlying principle in daily work at BMW. The BMW Group's agile network, which includes its innovation and production networks, is distinguished by unconventional, flexible thought and action."

*Source: Based on Taylor III, Alex. 2009. "Bavaria's next top model." Fortune, March 30, 100–105; BMW Group. 2012. http://www.bmwgroup.com/bmwgroup_prod/e/nav/index.html?http://www.bmwgroup.com/bmwgroup_prod/e/0_0_www_bmwgroup_com/unternehmen/unternehmensprofil/strategie/strategie.html.*

## Learning Objectives
*After reading this chapter you should be able to:*

- Appreciate the complexities of the global-local dilemma facing the multinational company.

- Understand the content of the multinational strategies: transnational, international, multidomestic, and regional.

- Formulate a multinational strategy by applying the diagnostic questions that aid multinational companies in solving the global-local dilemma.

- Understand the content of the entry-mode strategies: exporting, alliances/international joint ventures (IJVs), licensing, and foreign direct investment.

- Formulate an entry-mode strategy based on the strengths and weaknesses of each approach and the needs of the multinational company.

- Understand political risk and how multinational companies can manage such risks.

The Preview Case in Point describes BMW and the many facets of its innovation-based global strategy. Whether BMW is deciding on which market to enter or where to build its next factory or which car to build next, it relies on many aspects of its multinational strategy to make the best decisions. BMW shows how a company can benefit from geographical dispersion by being close to customers throughout the world and seeking innovations from these locations to share across the company.

In this chapter you will find a review of the essential strategies that multinationals use to bring their companies to international markets and to compete successfully in them. This chapter contains three major sections. The first section introduces general strategies for multinational operations. The second section explains the specific techniques that multinationals use to enter markets. The final section provides an understanding of political risk, an important risk that many multinational companies face.

# Multinational Strategies: Dealing with the Global-Local Dilemma

Multinational companies face a fundamental strategic dilemma when competing internationally: the global-local dilemma. On one hand, there are pressures to respond to the unique needs of the markets in each country or region in which a company does business. When a company chooses this option, it adopts the **local-responsiveness solution**. On the other hand, there are efficiency pressures that encourage companies to deemphasize local differences and to conduct business similarly throughout the world. Companies that lean in this direction choose the **global integration solution**.

The solution for the so-called **global-local dilemma**—the choice between local responsiveness or global integration—forms the basic strategic orientation of a multinational company.[1] This strategic orientation affects the design of organization and management systems as well as of supporting functional strategies in areas such as production, marketing, and finance. Here we consider only the strategic implications. In later chapters, you will see how this fundamental problem influences other areas of multinational management, such as human resources management and the choice of an organizational design.

Companies that lean toward the local-responsiveness solution stress customizing their organizations and products to accommodate country or regional differences, with the focus on tailoring products or services to satisfy local customer needs. Forces that favor a local-responsiveness solution come primarily from national or cultural differences in consumer tastes and variations in customer needs, as well as from how industries work and institutional pressures. For an example of an institutional pressure, government regulations can require a company to share ownership with a local firm, and some governments require companies to produce their products in the countries in which they sell.[2]

Multinational companies that lean toward a global integration solution attempt to reduce costs to the largest degree possible by using standardized products, promotional strategies, and distribution channels in every market they enter. Some globally oriented multinational firms exploit the differences among the countries in which they operate. To do this, they locate value chain activities in different countries seeking sources of lower costs or higher quality anywhere in the world. For example, in such companies, headquarters, R&D, production, or distribution

**Local-responsiveness solution**

Responding to differences in the markets in all the countries in which a company operates.

**Global integration solution**

Conducting business similarly throughout the world and locating company units wherever there is high quality and low cost.

**Global-local dilemma**

Choice between a local-responsiveness or global approach to a multinational's strategies.

centers may be located anywhere they can obtain the best value while maintaining quality or lowering cost.[3]

For each product or business, multinational firms must choose carefully how globally or locally to orient their strategies. Later in the chapter, you will see some of the questions that managers must answer before selecting an appropriate multinational strategy. Before that, however, we will review the broad strategic choices for the multinational manager dealing with the global-local dilemma.

Four broad multinational strategies offer solutions to this dilemma: multidomestic, transnational, international, and regional. The multidomestic and transnational strategies represent the bipolar reactions to the global-local dilemma. The international and regional strategies reflect compromises that attempt to balance these conflicting drives. Few multinational companies adopt pure versions of these strategies. Rather, companies tend to emphasize one or a combination of orientations that managers feel best fits their industry, products, and internal capabilities.

## Multidomestic Strategy

The **multidomestic strategy** gives top priority to local responsiveness. The multidomestic strategy is in many respects a form of differentiation strategy. The company attempts to offer products or services that attract customers by closely satisfying cultural needs and expectations unique to particular countries. For example, advertisements, packaging, sales outlets, and pricing are adapted to local standards.

As with most types of differentiation, it usually costs more for multinational companies to produce and sell unique or special products or services for different countries than to standardize for all countries. There are extra costs to adapt each product to local requirements, such as different package sizes and colors. Thus, to succeed, a multidomestic strategy usually requires the company to charge higher prices to recoup the costs of tailoring products. Customers will pay the higher prices if they perceive an extra value in having a company's products adapted to their tastes, distribution systems, and industry structures.[4]

Although there is consensus that the world is becoming "flatter" or more similar with globalization, multinational companies cannot ignore that differences may still matter.[5] Consider the Case in Point below contrasting Wal-Mart's and Tesco's experiences in South Korea. Similarly, the Focus on Emerging Markets below suggests that a multidomestic strategy may work best in these less-developed economies.

A multidomestic strategy is not limited to large multinational companies that can afford to set up overseas subsidiaries. Even a small firm that exports only its products may use a multidomestic strategy by extensively adapting its product line to different countries and cultures. However, for larger organizations, with production and sales units in many countries, using a multidomestic strategy often means treating foreign subsidiaries as independent businesses. Headquarters focuses on the bottom line, viewing each country as a profit center. Each country's subsidiary is free to manage its own operations as necessary, but it must generate a profit to receive resources. Besides having its own local production facilities, marketing strategy, sales staff, and distribution system, the subsidiary of the multidomestic company often uses local sources for raw materials and employs mostly local people.

## Transnational Strategy

The **transnational strategy** gives two goals top priority: seeking location advantages and gaining economic efficiencies from operating worldwide.[6] Using **location advantages** means that the transnational company disperses or locates its value

**Multidomestic strategy**
A strategy that emphasizes local-responsiveness issues.

**Transnational strategy**
An approach that seeks location advantages and economic efficiency through operating worldwide.

**Location advantages**
Dispersing value chain activities anywhere in the world where the company can do them best or cheapest.

**CASE IN POINT**

## Local Adaptation: Some of the Biggest Companies in the World Make Mistakes

After a nearly 10-year tryout, Wal-Mart sold its stores to a local Korean competitor and left the country. Why? According to Na Hon Seok, an analyst at Goodmorning Shinhan Securities in Seoul, "Wal-Mart is a typical example of a global giant who has failed to localize its operations in South Korea. It failed to read what South Korean housewives want when they go shopping. Some necessary local adaptations Wal-Mart missed:

• Koreans prefer quality to less-expensive products.

• Koreans expect high levels of customer service by retailers.

• Koreans did not respond well to the warehouse model that gave the image of low quality.

• Koreans value the freshness of food products and make frequent trips to markets and buy small volumes of fresh food.

In contrast to Wal-Mart, Tesco, a major international rival from the United Kingdom, has exceeded expectations in Korea by adopting a local responsiveness strategy. By 2011, South Korea was Tesco's most profitable international operation. Tesco entered the Korean market with Samsung as a local joint venture partner and used Samsung's knowledge and expertise of the local market to adapt to Korean preferences. Tesco did not attempt to impose a home-country retail format in Korea, instead balancing the efficiency of the Western retail format with the Korean retail format of extra services, smaller packaging, and higher quality. Most recently, Tesco has tapped into another local phenomenon based on Korea being one of the most wired countries of the world. Tesco's virtual supermarkets allow Koreans to shop by smart phones using QR codes from virtual supermarkets located in public places. The target market is younger Koreans who no longer have time to shop (Koreans have among the longest working hours in the world) and do many tasks with their smart phones.

*Sources: Based on Choe, Sang-Hun. 2006. "Wal-Mart quitting South Korea."* The New York Times, *March 26; Kim, Renee B. 2008. "Wal-Mart Korea: Challenges of entering a foreign market."* Journal of Asia-Pacific Business, *9, 344–357; Strother, Jason. 2011. "Shopping by phone at South Korea's virtual grocery."* BBC News, *October 20.*

chain activities (e.g., manufacturing, R&D, and sales—see the previous chapter for more detail) anywhere in the world where the company can "do it best or cheapest" as the situation requires. For example, many U.S. and Japanese multinational companies have production facilities in Southeast Asian countries where labor is currently cheap. Michael Porter argues that, for global competition, firms must look at countries not only as potential markets but also as what he calls global platforms.[7] A **global platform** is a country location where a firm can best perform some, but not necessarily all, of its value chain activities.

Often costs or quality advantages associated with a particular nation are called national **comparative advantage**. This is different from *competitive* advantage, which refers to the advantages of individual firms over other firms. *Comparative* advantage refers to advantages of *nations over other nations*. For example, a country with cheaper and better-educated labor has a comparative advantage over other nations. Comparative advantage is important to domestic organizations because they can use their nation's comparative advantages to gain competitive advantages over rivals from other nations.

Historically, international firms took advantage of their nations' comparative advantages—such as, for example, the United States' abundant natural resources—to compete on the world market. However, the comparative advantage of a nation

**Global platform**
Country location where a firm can best perform some, but not necessarily all, of its value chain activities.

**Comparative advantage**
The advantage arising from cost, quality, or resource advantages associated with a particular nation.

## Focus on Emerging Markets

### LG Electronics Succeeds in Emerging Markets with a Multidomestic Strategy

LG Electronics is currently the world's top producer of air conditioners and is among the top three producers in other appliances, such as washing machines, microwave ovens, and refrigerators. It is the dominant player in emerging markets in nearly every appliance and electronics category, particularly in the BRIC countries of India and Brazil. It has a 40 percent market share of plasma TVs in the Middle East and Africa. Furthermore, although it is a relative newcomer in the Chinese market, LG has been successful and has achieved sales of $8 billion in China.

LG uses an in-depth localized strategy. It tries to understand the realities and subtleties of the local market by establishing local research, manufacturing, and marketing facilities. LG's localization strategy in India provides a good example of its approach. To meet local Indian needs, LG offers refrigerators with large compartments for vegetables and water storage and with surge-resistant power supplies to deal with frequent power outages. LG even customizes its products to suit local customers' color preferences, selling red refrigerators in the south and green ones in Kashmir. It offers microwave ovens with dark interiors to mask staining from curries. Its TVs include on-screen-displays and directors that include all 16 of India's official languages. Unlike its competitor, Samsung, which used TV ads aimed only at the wealthiest Indians, LG used "van marketing," loading trucks with their products and visiting remote areas where consumers had no access to TVs. Additionally, to take advantage of the Indian passion for cricket, LG offers televisions that come with cricket video games.

LG's localization strategy in the Middle East is also noteworthy. It developed the *Qur'an* TV with the entire text of the *Qur'an* installed on screen. Viewers can also have this holy book read to them. LG already incorporated Bluetooth connectivity to its plasma TVs because more consumers want that connectivity. For instance, consumers can use their TVs to view pictures taken on their mobile phones.

LG's localization approach in emerging markets has been successful because it took into account that customers in emerging markets generally do not yet have strong brand loyalties. By offering products adapted to the local needs, LG can start to build its own brand. For example, LG's research in other markets has resulted in products such as microwaves with preset shish kebab heat settings in Iran and refrigerators with special compartments to store dates in the Middle East. Research in Russia revealed that people are more likely to entertain indoors during the harsh winters. LG then developed a popular karaoke phone that can hold more than 100 Russian songs.

*Sources: Based on Choe, Son-kyoo. 2012. "Unique case: How LG surpassed Samsung in India." The Korean Times, April 6. Kim, Yoo-chul. 2007. "LG seeks localization in emerging markets." The Korean Times, August 30; Middle East Company News. 2009. "LG—A plasma powerhouse in Korea, Middle East and Africa," April 27.*

no longer gives competitive advantages only to domestic firms; that is, the induced (created) or natural resources available in different nations provide the transnational firm with potential global platforms for location-based competitive advantages in costs and quality. For the most part, these resources support upstream activities in the value chain, such as R&D and production. Thus, a transnational strategy enables a company to base activities upstream in its value chain not only on lower costs but also on the potential for creating additional value for its products or services.

However, location advantages can also exist for other value chain activities, such as being close to suppliers, key customers, and the most demanding customers. Location in the Japanese market, for example, usually requires a firm to maintain a product quality level that is acceptable to the whole world. Thus, the transnational firm views *any country* as a global platform where it can perform *any value chain activity*. Thus, the comparative advantage of a nation is no longer just for locals. With increasingly free and open borders, any firm, regardless of its nation of ownership, can turn any national advantage into a competitive advantage—if the firm has the flexibility and willingness to locate anywhere. However, not all location advantages are sustainable and competitors easily copy some. The next Case in Point addresses the issues regarding seeking low cost manufacturing sites. Recent data now suggest that some of the location advantages of producing in low-cost countries may be eroding.

Location advantages provide the transnational company with cost or quality gains for different value chain activities. To reduce costs even further, transnational firms strive, where possible, for uniform marketing and promotional activities throughout the world; these companies use the same brand names, advertisements, and promotional brochures wherever they sell their products or services. The soft drink companies, such as Coca-Cola, have been among the most successful in taking their brands worldwide. When a company can do things similarly throughout the world, it can take advantage of economies of scale. For

---

### CASE IN POINT

## Comparative Advantage and the "Boomerang Effect" for Low-Cost Manufacturing

Manufacturing in low-cost countries, primarily developing nations, started gaining popularity as early as the 1960s. When China started its Special Economic Zones, production factories blossomed, and the first location, Shenzhen, is now one of the richest cities in China. Departing countries like Taiwan, South Korea, and Mexico, multinational manufacturing companies from around the world sought China's comparative advantage in low wages to build their own competitive advantage as low cost producers. However, like other former low-cost countries, Chinese wages are rising at an estimated 20 percent a year. Countries like Bangladesh, Cambodia, Indonesia, and Vietnam are becoming new destinations. Vietnam is now the primary production site for Nike. There is already near wage parity between China and Mexico and shipping costs are more advantageous for U.S. companies using Mexico.

As wages converge around the world, many multinational companies are rethinking their decisions to move production to low-cost countries. Labor costs are only one consideration for a multinational company and

multinational managers must factor issues such as distance, taxes, ease of management, quality of labor, and protection of intellectual property rights into such a move. Consider that the Apple iPad, which retails for around $500 has only $33 of labor costs. Indeed, some U.S. companies have already reached the tipping point and see advantages of returning production to the United States. The Boston Consulting Group expects manufacturing costs for the United States and China to converge in 2015. For example, Caterpillar chose Texas over foreign locations for its new manufacturing facility. NCR Corp. returned its production facilities to Columbus, Georgia, to decrease time to market. Wham-O, Inc., returned 50 percent of its Frisbee and Hula Hoop production to the United States from Mexico and China.

*Sources: Based on Boston Consulting Group. 2011. "Made in the USA again: Manufacturing is expected to return to America as China's rising labor costs erase most savings from offshoring." May 5; Economist. 2012. "Comparative advantage: The boomerang effect." April 21; Offshore Group. 2012. "Mexico closes manufacturing competitiveness gap with China," May 16.*

example, it is most efficient to have one package of the same color and size produced worldwide in centralized production facilities.

## International Strategy

Companies pursuing largely international strategies, such as Toys "R" Us and Boeing, take a compromise approach to the global-local dilemma. Like transnational strategists, firms pursuing international strategies attempt to sell global products and use similar marketing techniques worldwide. Adaptation to local customs and culture, if it exists at all, is limited to minor adjustments in product offerings and marketing strategies. However, international strategist firms differ from transnational companies in that they choose to avoid locating their value chain activities anywhere in the world. In particular, upstream and support activities remain concentrated at home country headquarters. The international strategist hopes that the concentration of its R&D and manufacturing strengths at home will bring greater economies of scale and quality and lower coordination costs than the dispersed activities of the transnational. For example, Boeing, based in the United States, traditionally kept most of its production and development at home while selling planes such as the 757 worldwide using the same sales force. Its marketing approach focuses on price and technology, and even quotes the prices and payments in U.S. currency.

In a partial nod to the benefits of a transnational strategy, Boeing outsourced much of the work on its newest plane, the 787 Dreamliner, to companies around the globe, including, for example, Mitsubishi, Kawasaki, Fuji, Saab, and Italy's Alenia Aeronautica. Difficulties with coordinating and managing the work of this diverse supply chain led to considerable delays in the Dreamliner. In consequence, according to Boeing's commercial division CEO, "we are pulling more of the engineering back inside to try and alleviate some of the issue we had."[8]

When necessary for economic or political reasons, companies with international strategies frequently set up sales and production units in major countries of operation. However, the home country headquarters retains control of local strategies, marketing, R&D, finances, and production. Local facilities become only scaled-down replicas of production and sales facilities at home.[9]

## Regional Strategy

The regional strategy is another compromise strategy. It attempts to balance the economic efficiency and location advantages of the transnational and international strategies with some of the local-adaptation advantages of the multidomestic strategy. Rather than having worldwide products and a worldwide value chain, the regional strategist manages raw material sourcing, production, marketing, and some support activities within a particular region. For example, a regional strategist might have one set of products for North America and another for Mexico and South America. This strategy not only allows some cost savings similar to those of the transnational and international strategists, but also gives the firm flexibility for regional responsiveness. Managers have the opportunity to deal regionally with regional problems, such as competitive position, product mix, promotional strategy, and sources of capital.[10]

Regional trading blocs, such as the European Union (EU) and the North American Free Trade Agreement (NAFTA), have led to relative uniformity of customer needs and expectations within member nations. Trading blocs also reduce differences in government- and industry-required specifications for products. As a result, companies within the trading bloc can use regional products and regional location advantages for all value chain activities. The rise of trading blocs also forced some

**International strategies**
Selling global products and using similar marketing techniques worldwide.

**Regional strategy**
An approach that manages raw material sourcing, production, marketing, and support activities within a particular region.

former multidomestic strategists, especially in Europe and the United States, to adopt regional strategies. For example, Procter & Gamble and DuPont combined their respective subunits in Mexico, the United States, and Canada into one regional organization. With this strategy, these companies gain some of the advantages of both local adaptation and a transnational strategy.

## A Brief Summary and Caveat

Students of multinational management should realize that all these strategies are general descriptions of multinational strategic options and companies seldom adopt any pure form. Companies with more than one business may use a different multinational strategy for each unit. Even single-business companies may alter strategies to adjust for product differences. In addition, governmental regulations regarding trade, historical evolution of the company, and the cost of switching strategies may prevent a firm from a full implementation of any given strategy.

Exhibit 6.1 summarizes the content of the four basic multinational strategies. As the exhibit shows, the array of multinational strategic options means that managers must carefully analyze the situation for their companies when formulating or choosing a strategy. Which strategy works best? Different companies use different approaches to suit their needs. Consider LG Electronics' successful localized approach in its various markets in the previous Focus on Emerging Markets.

**EXHIBIT 6.1** Multinational Strategy Content

| Strategy Content | Transnational Strategy | International Strategy | Multidomestic Strategy | Regional Strategy |
|---|---|---|---|---|
| Worldwide markets | Yes, as much as possible, with flexibility to adapt to local conditions | Yes, with little flexibility for local adaptation | No, each country treated as a separate market | No, but major regions treated as similar market (e.g., Europe) |
| Worldwide location of separate value chain activities | Yes, anywhere, based on best value to company—lowest cost for highest quality | No, or limited to sales or local production replicating headquarters | No, all or most value chain activities located in country of production and sales | No, but region can provide some different country location of activities |
| Global products | Yes, to the highest degree possible, with some local products if necessary; reliance on worldwide brand recognition | Yes, to the highest degree possible, with little local adaptation; companies rely on worldwide brand recognition | No, products made in and tailored to the country of location to best serve needs of local customers | No, but similar products offered throughout a major economic region |
| Global marketing | Yes, similar strategy to global product development | Yes, to the highest degree possible | No, marketing focuses on local country customers | No, but region is often treated similarly |
| Global competitive moves | Resources from any country used to attack or defend | Attacks and defenses in all countries, but resources must come from headquarters | No, competitive moves planned and financed by country units | No, but resources from region can be used to attack or defend |

The following section presents diagnostic questions that multinational managers can use to select a strategy appropriate for their company. These diagnostic questions guide multinational companies in resolving the global-local dilemma.

## Resolving the Global-Local Dilemma: Formulating a Multinational Strategy

As Exhibit 6.2 shows, and as you have seen in the examples above, multinational companies face conflicting pressures regarding the strategic options for going international. The selection of a transnational, multidomestic, international, or

**EXHIBIT 6.2**    The Balancing Act of Multinational Strategy Formulation

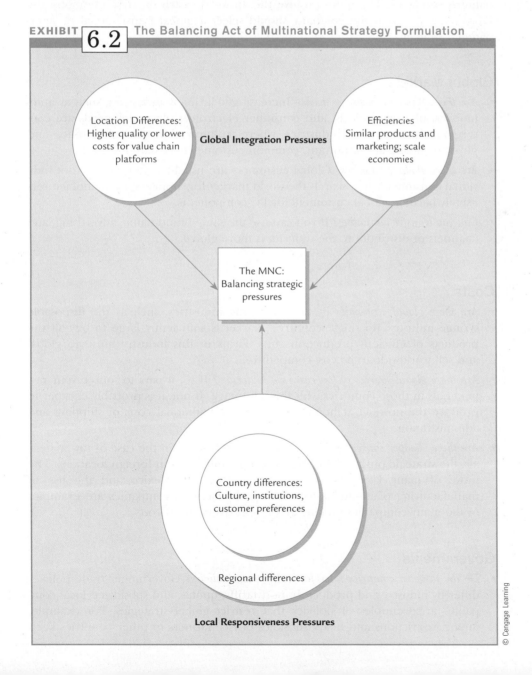

© Cengage Learning

regional strategy, or some combination of these orientations, depends to a large degree on the globalization of the industry in which a company competes. Multi-business companies need to consider the degree of globalization within all the industries in which they compete.

What makes an industry global? George Yip calls the trends that globalize an industry the "globalization drivers." **Globalization drivers** are conditions in an industry that favor the more globally oriented transnational or international strategies over the locally oriented multidomestic or regional strategies.[11]

The globalization drivers fall into four categories: markets, costs, governments, and competition. Associated with each of these areas are key diagnostic questions that strategists must answer in selecting the degree of globalization of their multinational strategies. The more positive the answer to each of these questions, the more likely it is that the company should select a global transnational or international strategy.

**Globalization drivers**

Conditions in an industry that favor transnational or international strategies over multidomestic or regional strategies.

## Global Markets

- *Are there common customer needs?* Increasingly, in many industries, such as automobiles, pharmaceuticals, and consumer electronics, customer needs are converging. However, in industries where cultural differences, income, and physical climate are important, common customer needs are less likely.

- *Are there global customers?* Global customers are usually organizations (not individual consumers) that search the world market for suppliers. PC manufacturers usually become global customers for PC components.

- *Can you transfer marketing?* If you can use the same brand name, advertising, and channels of distribution, the industry is more global.

## Costs

- *Are there global economies of scale?* In some industries, such as the disposable syringe industry, no single country's market is sufficiently large to buy all the products of efficient production runs. Firms in this industry must go global and sell worldwide to be cost-competitive.

- *Are there global sources of low-cost raw materials?* If so, it pays to source your raw materials in those countries with this advantage. If not, it is probably cheaper to produce the product at home and avoid the additional costs of shipping and administration.

- *Are there cheaper sources of highly skilled labor?* If so, as in the case of raw materials, the strategic push is for companies to manufacture in foreign locations. The move of many U.S. manufacturing operations to Mexico and the use of manufacturing plants in Eastern Europe by German companies are examples of the many companies seeking global sources of lower costs.

## Governments

- *Do the targeted countries have favorable trade policies?* Government trade policies differ by industry and product. Import tariffs, quotas, and subsidized local companies are examples of policies that restrict global strategies. For example, import restrictions and heavy subsidies of rice farmers in other countries keep foreign competition out of Japan and maintain domestic prices that often approach four times the world market price. Trade agreements such as the World Trade Organization and trading blocs such as NAFTA and the EU encourage global strategies by lowering governmental trade restrictions, at least among member nations.

- *Do the target countries have regulations that restrict operations?* Restrictions on foreign ownership, on advertising and promotional content, and on the extent of expatriate management present barriers to full implementation of a transnational or international strategy.

## Competition

- *What strategies do your competitors use?* If transnational or international companies successfully attack the markets of multidomestic companies, then the multidomestic company may have to become more global.
- *What is the volume of imports and exports in the industry?* A high volume of trade suggests that companies see advantages in strategies that are more global.

## Caution

The increasingly popular strategy of going global by making uniform products for the world market can sometimes backfire. Cultural and national differences still exist, and even transnational and international strategists must adjust to key differences in national or regional needs.

Next, we discuss how the globalization drivers push some firms toward the transnational strategy and others toward the international strategy.

Some firms may have competitive strengths in downstream activities, such as customer service, but compete in industries with strong globalization drivers. Other companies may produce high-quality products efficiently but compete in industries with strong pressures for local adaptation. In such circumstances, multinational companies often compromise and select a regional strategy. For the firm with upstream competitive strengths, such as high-quality R&D, the regional strategy allows some downstream adaptation of products to regional differences. For the firm with downstream competitive strengths, such as after-market service, the regional strategy allows some of the economies of scale produced by activities such as centralized purchasing and uniform products.

Exhibit 6.3 shows how these factors and the pressures for globalization and local responsiveness combine to suggest different multinational strategies.

## Transnational or International: Which Way for the Global Company?

In globalized industries, companies with more global strategies (strategies closer to international or transnational) tend to perform better than multidomestic or regional strategies because they can usually offer cheaper or higher-quality products or services. How do companies choose between these two approaches to globalization—the transnational and the international?

To select a transnational over an international strategy, the multinational manager must believe that the benefits of dispersing activities worldwide offset the costs of coordinating a more complex organization. For example, a company may do R&D in one country, parts manufacturing in another, final assembly in another,

## Multinational Management **Challenge**

### Knowing When to Change Your Multinational Strategy: Lessons from IBM

IBM has been at the forefront of international business almost since its founding by Thomas Watson in 1924. Until recently, it was deeply entrenched primarily in the developed nations of Europe and Japan. Under its old international strategy, control was centralized and local operations in countries and regions were mini-replicas of the parent company.

This ended in 2007 when then-CEO Samuel J. Palmisano decided to shift the company's center of gravity to outside of the United States. In the years following, IBM has attempted to become a "globally integrated enterprise," which in our terms is a transnational strategy. IBM now sets up value chain activities wherever it can find the right price and right talent. IT is in India. The global supply chain management works out of China and the global financing back office is in Brazil. There are 86 software development centers spread over the globe.

Such change is not easy. Analysts such as Fran Gens of IDC see this change a daunting management challenge requiring major shifts in corporate culture and the resulting turmoil for many employees. The United States, Western Europe, and Japan lost nearly 20,000 jobs while IBM now has over 50,000 employees in India and 10,000 in China. However, commensurate with this shift, IBM now makes two-thirds of its revenues outside of the United States. The focus is not only on highgrowth markets such as China and India, but also on smaller markets such as the Czech Republic, the Philippines, and Vietnam.

One of the reasons a transnational strategy became more appropriate for IBM was its shift from being a hardware company to being a services and software company. In spite of internal resistance, Palmisano sold the PC business to the Chinese company Lenovo. Along with sale of the disk drive and other hardware businesses, IBM generated considerable cash to use for other investments such as its $3.5 billion purchase of PricewaterhouseCoopers Consulting. With its focus now on generating software and helping people use it in an array of industries, IBM is more nimble in that it is easier for the company to move data and information from platforms throughout the world.

*Sources: Based on Ham, Steve. 2007. "IBM's global hold." BusinessWeek, August 13; Lohr, Steve. 2010. "Global strategy stabilized IBM during downturn." The New York Times, April 19; Lohr, Steve. 2011. "Even a giant can learn to run." The New York Times, December 31.*

**EXHIBIT 6.3**   Multinational Strategies, Value Chain Locations of Competitive Advantages, and Pressures for Globalization or Local Responsiveness

| Global/Local Responsiveness Pressures | Primary Source of Competitive Advantage in Value Chain | |
|---|---|---|
| | Upstream | Downstream |
| High pressures for globalization | Transnational strategy or international strategy | Regional strategy compromise |
| High pressures for local responsiveness | Regional strategy compromise | Multidomestic strategy |

© Cengage Learning

and sales in a fourth. Coordination of these activities across national borders and in different parts of the world is costly and difficult.

In contrast to the transnational strategist, the international strategist believes that centralizing key activities such as R&D reduces coordination costs and produces economies of scale. The cost savings from these economies of scale offset the lower costs or higher-quality raw materials or labor that the transnationalist can find by locating worldwide.

Once multinational managers choose their basic internationalization strategic approach—that is, their multinational strategy—they must also select the strategy or strategies necessary to enter different countries. The following section discusses these options in detail.

## Entry-mode Strategies: The Content Options

Regardless of their choice of a general multinational strategy (e.g., multidomestic or transnational), companies must also choose exactly how they will enter each international market. For example, multinational managers must decide whether to export only or to build a manufacturing plant in the target country. The strategies that deal with how to enter foreign markets and countries are called entry-mode strategies. This section reviews several popular entry-mode strategies, including exporting, licensing, strategic alliances, and foreign direct investment.

## Exporting

Exporting is the easiest way to sell a product in the international market. The effort can be as simple as treating and filling overseas orders like domestic orders, often called passive exporting. At the other extreme, a multinational company can put extensive resources into exporting with a dedicated export department or division and an international sales force. The export options beyond passive exporting are discussed next.

Although exporting is often the easiest entry-mode strategy, it is also an important one. In the United States, most export sales, as measured in dollars, go to large companies. The aircraft manufacturer Boeing, for example, receives over half of its revenues from exports. However, most U.S. exporters are small companies. As we will see in the next chapter, exporting is often the only strategy available to small businesses.

Most governments understand the importance of exports to the economy. In the United States, several federal agencies work closely with states to assist small companies interested in exporting.

## Export Strategies

Once a company moves beyond passive exporting, it can adopt two general export strategies: indirect and direct exporting.

Small firms and new exporters usually find indirect exporting the most viable option. In indirect exporting, intermediary or go-between firms provide the knowledge and contacts necessary to sell overseas. Indirect exporting provides a company with an export option without the risks and complexities of going it alone.

The most common intermediary types are the export management company (EMC) and the export trading company (ETC). An export management company (EMC) usually specializes in a particular type of product or in a particular country or region, and it may have both product and country specializations. Usually for a

**Entry-mode strategies**
Options multinational companies have for entering foreign markets and countries.

**Passive exporting**
Treating and filling overseas orders like domestic orders.

**Indirect exporting**
Intermediary or go-between firms provide the knowledge and contacts necessary to sell overseas.

**Export management company (EMC)**
Intermediary specializing in particular types of products or particular countries or regions.

commission, it provides a company with ready-made access to an international market. For example, a U.S. apple producer who wished to export to Japan would seek an EMC specializing in fruit products for the Asian market. Good EMCs have established networks of foreign distributors and know their products and countries very well. An **export trading company (ETC)** is similar to an EMC and provides many of the same services. The ETC, however, usually takes title to the product before exporting; that is, the ETC first buys the goods from the exporter and then resells them overseas. The most important advantage of an EMC or an ETC is that a company can quickly get into a foreign market at a low cost in terms of management and financial resources.

In contrast to indirect exporting, **direct exporting** is a more aggressive strategy in which exporters take on the duties of the intermediaries; that is, the exporters make direct contact with companies located in the foreign market. Direct exporters often use foreign sales representatives, foreign distributors, or foreign retailers to get their products to end users in foreign markets. At the highest level of investment, direct exporters may set up their own branch offices in foreign countries.

Foreign sales representatives use the company's promotional literature and samples to sell the company's products to foreign buyers. Sales representatives do not take title to products, nor do the direct exporters employ them. Rather, sales representatives have contracts with companies that define their commissions, their assigned territories, the length of agreements, and other details. Unlike foreign sales representatives, foreign distributors buy products from domestic sellers at a discount and resell the products in a foreign market at a profit. Typically, the foreign distributor is an intermediary selling to foreign retailers rather than to end-users.

## Licensing

International **licensing** is a contractual agreement between a domestic licenser and a foreign licensee. A licenser usually has a valuable patent, technological know-how, a trademark, or a company name that it provides to the foreign licensee. In return, the foreign licensee provides royalties to the domestic licenser. Licensing provides one of the easiest, lowest-cost, and least risky mechanisms for companies to go international. Licensing, however, is not just for small companies or for companies with limited capital. Even the giant multinationals use licensing when the conditions are right. Unlike its other theme parks around the world, Disneyland Tokyo is a licensing agreement with the owners, Oriental Land Company. Oriental Land Company licenses the rights to use the Disney characters and settings in return for paying Disney a percentage of the gate.

The licensing agreement or contract provides the legal specifications of the relationship between the licensee and the licensor. These contracts can be quite complex. They deal with everything from specific descriptions of the licensed product or technology to how the licensing agreement will end. Usually specialized attorneys from both countries work to prepare a document that is valid in both countries. Exhibit 6.4 shows the content of a typical licensing agreement.

## Some Special Licensing Agreements

Many international firms enter foreign markets using agreements similar to the basic licensing agreement. Like the more general forms of licensing, these agreements allow firms to operate in foreign countries without extensive capital investments.

**International franchising** is a form of comprehensive licensing agreement. The franchisor grants to the franchisee the use of a whole business model, usually

**EXHIBIT 6.4**   Content of a Licensing Agreement

| What Is Licensed | Conditions of Use | Compensation | Other Provisions |
|---|---|---|---|
| *Know-how:* Special knowledge or technology | *Who:* Which companies can use the licensed property (and whether the use is exclusive) | *Currency:* In what currency | *Termination:* How to end the agreement |
| *Patents:* The right to use inventions | *Time:* How long the license lasts | *Schedule:* When payments must be made | *Disputes:* What type of dispute resolution mechanism will be used |
| *Trademarks:* Brand names, such as Levi's | *Where:* In what countries the license can or cannot be used | *Method:* Payments may be lump-sum, installments, royalties as a percentage of profits | *Language:* What the official language of the contract will be |
| *Designs:* The right to copy the design or production of final products | *Confidentiality:* Provisions to protect trade secrets or designs | *Minimum payments:* Agreements regarding minimum royalty | *Law:* What country's contract law will apply |
| *Copyrights:* The use of intellectual property, such as book material or CDs | *Performance:* What exactly the licensee has to do | *Other:* Fees for technical assistance, product improvements, training, etc. | *Penalties:* What penalties are in place for lack of performance by either party |
| | *Improvements:* Rights of the licensee and licenser regarding improvements in licensed property | | *Reports:* What and when the licensee must report |
| | | | *Inspections and audits:* The rights of the licenser |

*Sources: Adapted from Beamish, Paul J., Peter Killing, Donald J. Lecraw, and Allen J. Morrison. 1994. International Management. Burr Ridge, IL: Irwin; Doherty, A. M. 2009. "Market and partner selection process in international retail franchising." Journal of Business Research, 62, 528–534; Root, Franklin R. 1994. Entry Strategies for International Markets. New York: Lexington Books.*

including trademarks, business organization, technologies, and know-how and training. Some worldwide franchisors, such as McDonald's, even provide company-owned stores. To standardize operations, franchisees agree to follow strict rules and procedures. The franchisor, in turn, receives royalties and other compensation, usually based on sales revenue. U.S. companies such as Holiday Inn, McDonald's, 7-Eleven, and Kentucky Fried Chicken dominate the use of franchising as an international entry-mode strategy.[12] The next Case in Point gives some background on worldwide franchising strategy.

An international company sometimes contracts with local foreign firms to produce its products overseas. Similar to the licensing agreement, the foreign companies use the international firm's technology and specifications to make products for their local market or for other markets. However, unlike the typical licensing agreement, the international firm still sells the products and controls marketing. This form of agreement is called **contract manufacturing**. It represents another means of quick, low-cost entry, especially for small markets not warranting direct investment.[13]

In **turnkey operations**, the international company makes a project fully operational before turning it over to the foreign owner. It is called "turnkey" because the multinational firm builds the project and trains local workers and managers on how to operate it. After this, the multinational firm gives the owners an operational project, which they start simply by "turning the key."

Turnkey operations occur usually in public construction projects done by multinational companies for host governments. For example, an international

**Contract manufacturing**
Producing products for foreign companies following the foreign companies' specifications.

**Turnkey operations**
Multinational company makes a project fully operational and trains local managers and workers before the foreign owner takes control.

## Tesco: A Switch to the Franchise Entry-Mode for Its F&F Clothing Stores

Tesco is the largest British retailer and the third largest multiproduct retailer in the world. It operates in 13 markets besides the United Kingdom and has over 2,400 foreign subsidiaries, many of which are franchises. One of Tesco's retail stores is F&F, a clothing and accessory store. Until 2010, Tesco sold its F&F brand clothing in its hypermarkets. In 2010, it opened its first stand-alone store in Prague and the second in the Czech Republic in 2011. Its third store in Central Europe opened in 2012 in Warsaw, Poland. It is now a leading fashion brand in Central Europe.

In January of 2012, Tesco changed the entry-mode strategy for F&F to a franchise model with the objective of turning this fashion label into a major global brand. It plans to work with local partners to locate stores in shopping malls and units in hypermarkets and department stores. Notes F&F CEO Jason Tarry, "The franchise model is a natural extension of the work we have been doing to turn F&F into a truly global fashion brand. We have in a very short time created a

market leading fashion brand in Central Europe, now worth over GBP 400m [~$600 million]. Now we have the opportunity to grow our brand further, in markets where Tesco does not have a presence." The franchise model allows F&F to achieve faster world recognition than would be possible with other entry mode choices.

There first franchisee is Fawaz Abdulaziz Al Hokair & Co, the largest owner of shopping malls in Saudi Arabia, which operates over 80 retail franchises in 11 countries. The first store opened in the Haifa Mall in Jeddah just four months after the agreement was signed. CEO Tarry commented, "Al Hokair is an excellent partner for F&F. It offers local expertise, knowledge, and franchise experience that will really make a difference for local customers."

*Sources: Based on Whiteaker, Jon. 2012. "Tesco unveils F&F franchise model," Retail Gazette. January 17; www.tescoplc. com. 2012. "Tesco opens first F&F store in Saudi Arabia." May 11; www.tescoplc.com. 2012. "Tesco fashions F&F franchise concept." January 17.*

construction company such as Bechtel might build a hydroelectric power plant for a Middle Eastern government. Besides building the plant, the construction company would provide training for workers and management to make certain that the plant is fully operational in the hands of local people.

## International Strategic Alliances

**International strategic alliance**
Agreement between two or more firms from different countries to cooperate in any value chain activity from R&D to sales.

**International strategic alliances** are cooperative agreements between two or more firms from different countries to participate in business activities. These activities may include any value chain activity, from R&D to sales and service.

Gaining increasing popularity during the last decade, international strategic alliances have become one of the dominant entry-mode strategies for multinational firms. Even firms such as IBM and General Motors, which have resources for and traditions of operating independently, have turned increasingly to international strategic alliances as basic entry-mode strategies.[14] Because of the importance of strategic alliances, a separate chapter (9) provides more detail on the methods to design and manage joint venture operations.

## Foreign Direct Investment

**Foreign direct investment (FDI)**
Multinational firm's ownership, in part or in whole, of an operation in another country.

Although international joint ventures (IJVs) are a special form of direct investment (i.e., ownership is involved), usually **foreign direct investment (FDI)** means that a multinational company owns, in part or in whole, an operation in another country.

Unlike the IJV, the parent companies do not create a separate legal entity. FDI reflects the highest stage of internationalization, as it involves not only the largest investment costs and the highest risks, but also the most likelihood of greater returns.

Multinational companies can use FDI to set up, from scratch, any kind of subsidiary (R&D, sales, manufacturing, etc.) in another country. This is called a **greenfield investment**. Alternatively, they can engage in FDI by acquiring existing companies in another country. A greenfield startup allows a company to use its own management and technical systems and hire and train workers to use these systems. In contrast, an acquisition provides a quicker startup, with access to an existing workforce and organization. However, the integration of the acquisition into the parent company can be difficult, especially since both organizational and national cultures differ.

According to the *World Investment Report*,[15] the rapid pace of technological change and the liberalization of foreign investment policies by numerous countries are the major driving factors leading to more acquisition as a form of FDI. Worldwide, greenfield investments are much larger than acquisitions in terms of value. Emerging markets tend to host greenfield investments, with over two-thirds of the total value in recent investments going to those economies. Acquisitions are more common in developed nations. However, recently, companies from emerging market nations such as India are increasingly making acquisitions in the developed world, with the Tata Group leading the way for Indian companies.[16]

Some multinational companies set up foreign operations only to extract raw materials to support their production at home. This type of backward vertical integration is common in the steel, aluminum, and petroleum industries. Other companies set up foreign operations primarily to find low-cost labor, components, parts, or finished goods. These subsidiaries ship finished products or components home or to other markets. Ford, for example, assembles some automobiles in Mexico and Thailand, primarily for export. Market penetration, however, is the major motivation to invest abroad. Companies invest in foreign subsidiaries to have a base for production or sales in their target countries.[17]

The scale of FDI often changes as firms gain greater returns from their investments or perceive less risk in running their foreign operations. For example, a multinational manufacturing firm may begin with only a sales office, later add a warehouse, and still later build a plant or acquire a local company with the capacity just to assemble or package its product. Ultimately, at the highest scale of investment, the firm owns a full-scale production facility, which it can build or acquire.[18]

Despite the importance of FDI, most of the economic downturn period of 2008–2009 saw falling FDI levels. As economies contracted, many companies reduced the amount of their investments overseas. However, early 2011 saw significant increases in both greenfield and acquisition FDI, but neither reached the levels of 2007.[19]

Although multinational companies have many options regarding how to participate internationally, the most difficult questions have to do with choosing the right entry-mode strategy or strategies for a company and its products. The next section addresses these questions in detail.

**Greenfield investments**
Starting foreign operations from scratch.

## Formulating an Entry-mode Strategy

As with any strategy, formulating an entry-mode strategy must take into account several issues, including the basic functions of each entry-mode strategy; general strategic considerations regarding the company and its strategic intent, products, and markets; and how best to support the company's multinational strategy. We will next deal with each of these issues in turn.

## Basic Functions of Entry-mode Strategies

### Deciding on an Export Strategy

Exporting is the easiest and cheapest entry-mode strategy, although it may not always be the most profitable. However, it is a way to begin to internationalize or to test new markets. Most companies continue to export even as they adopt more sophisticated entry-mode strategies. However, an exporting company must answer this question: Which form of exporting should it choose?

Each export strategy has some advantages and some drawbacks. As with most business decisions, the commensurate financial risk and the need to commit resources can offset the greater potential profits of direct exporting.[20] In addition, there are considerations regarding the needs and capabilities of the company. The following diagnostic questions can help multinational managers select the best export strategy for their companies:[21]

- *Does management believe it must control foreign sales, customer credit, and the eventual sale of the product to the customer?* If yes, choose a form of direct exporting.
- *Does the company have the financial and human resources for creating an organizational position or department to manage export operations?* If not, choose a form of indirect exporting.
- *Does the company have the financial and human resources to design and execute international promotional activities (for example, international trade shows and foreign language advertisements)?* If not, rely on the expertise of intermediaries; choose a form of indirect exporting.
- *Does the company have the financial and human resources to support extensive international travel or possibly an expatriate sales force?* If yes, choose a form of direct exporting.
- *Does the company have the time and expertise to develop its own overseas contacts and networks?* If not, rely on the expertise of intermediaries; choose a form of indirect exporting.
- *Will the time and resources required for the export business affect domestic operations?* If not, favor direct exporting.

### When Should a Company License?

The decision to license is based on three factors: the characteristics of the product selected for licensing, the characteristics of the target country in which the product will be licensed, and the nature of the licensing company.

*The Product* The best products to license use a company's older or soon-to-be-replaced technology. Companies that license older technologies avoid giving potential competitors the licensor's innovations while using the license to profit from earlier investments.

Often, licensed products no longer have domestic sales potential, perhaps because the domestic market is saturated or domestic buyers anticipate new technologies. However, old technologies may remain attractive to the international market for several reasons. First, in countries where there are no competitors with recent technology, strong demand may still exist for the licensed product, even if based on older technology. Second, the foreign licensees may not have production facilities capable of producing the latest technology. Third, from the licensee firm's point of view, it may still have an opportunity to learn production methods or other information from a licensor's old technology.[22]

*The Target Country* The situation in the target country may make licensing the only viable entry-mode strategy. Factors that add costs to a product often make licensing more attractive than exporting. Trade barriers, such as tariffs or quotas, add costs to finished goods that can make exporting unprofitable. In this situation, rather than transferring a physical product, a company can transfer the intangible know-how through a license. For example, an international brewing company that exports kegs of beer may face stiff import tariffs in target markets. However, by licensing the brewing process to a local brewer, the international brewer transfers the expertise of its brewing processes to the licensee while avoiding tariffs or import quotas.

Other issues associated with the target country affect the licensing decision. Sometimes it is the only option. For some military and high-technology products, local governments require that the production remain in the country. In other situations, licensing is the low-risk option. Political instability or the threat of a government takeover of companies in the industry can make the lower risks of licensing more attractive. Because a firm neither contributes equity nor transfers products to the host country, it only risks losing the licensing income in an unstable environment. Finally, the market may simply be too small to support any investment larger than licensing.[23]

*The Company* Some companies lack adequate financial, technical, or managerial resources to export or to invest directly in foreign operations. With licensing, however, the company does not have to manage international operations. There is no need for an export department, a foreign sales force, or an overseas manufacturing site. The company's managers do not need to know much about operations in the foreign country or how to adapt their product to local needs. The licensee assumes these chores and responsibilities. Thus, licensing is a low-cost option. It does not demand much from the licensing company, and it often is the most attractive option for small companies.[24]

Having more than one product makes it more advantageous for a company to license. Multiproduct companies can license their more peripheral or sideline products but not their key or most important products. This protects their core technologies from potential competitors but still allows additional profits from licensing.[25]

*Some Disadvantages of Licensing* Although a low-cost and low-risk strategy, licensing presents four major drawbacks.[26]

First and most important, licensing *gives up control*. Once an agreement is signed and the trademark, technology, or know-how is transferred, there is little the licensor can do to control the behavior of the licensee, short of revoking the agreement. For example, a licensee may not market the product adequately or correctly.

Second, a company may create a *new competitor*. The licensee may use the licensor's technology to compete against the licensor not only in the licensee's country but also elsewhere in the world market. Even though a contract may prohibit future use of the technology or its use in other countries, local laws may not support this type of clause in the licensing agreement. In addition, even with the protection of local laws, the cost of foreign litigation may make enforcement too costly to pursue.

Third, *low income* generally results. Royalty rates seldom exceed 5 percent. Often licensees are less motivated to sell a licensed product with its shared profits than to sell its own homegrown products.

Fourth, there are *opportunity costs* to licensing. The licensee removes the opportunity to enter the country through other means, such as exporting or direct investment. Usually the licensing contract grants licensees the exclusive right to use trademarks or technologies in their countries, excluding even the licensor.

## Why Do Companies Seek Strategic Alliances?

Given the importance of strategic alliances to multinational companies, we consider them separately in Chapter 9.

## Some Advantages and Disadvantages of FDI

All but the most experienced international firms usually try other forms of entry-mode strategies before they select foreign direct investment. Exporting, licensing, or alliances can prepare a firm for FDI and can minimize the chances of failure. In any case, however, multinational managers must consider carefully the advantages and disadvantages of FDI. Exhibit 6.5 summarizes the advantages and disadvantages of FDI.

Once a multinational manager has considered the general merits of each possible entry-mode strategy, there are several broader strategic issues for multinational

---

**EXHIBIT 6.5**     **Advantages and Disadvantages of FDI**

| Advantages | Disadvantages |
|---|---|
| Greater control of product marketing and strategy | Increased capital investment |
| Lower costs of supplying host country with the firm's products | Drain on managerial talent to staff FDI or to train local management |
| Avoiding import quotas on raw material supplies or finished products | Increased costs of coordinating units dispersed worldwide over long distances |
| Greater opportunity to adapt products to the local markets | Greater exposure of the investment to local political risks as expropriation |
| Better local image of the product | Greater exposure to financial risks |
| Better after-market service | |
| Greater potential profits | |

*Source: Adapted from Root, Franklin R. 1994.* Entry Strategies for International Markets. *New York: Lexington Books.*

managers to consider: (1) their company's strategic intent regarding profits versus learning, (2) the capabilities of their company, (3) local government regulations, (4) the characteristics of the target product and market, (5) geographic and cultural distance between the home country and target country, and (6) the tradeoff between risk and control.[27]

The strategic intent of a multinational will likely determine its entry-mode strategy. If it is interested in short-term profit, the multinational manager can compare the costs and benefits of the various entry-mode strategies and select the most profitable. However, many companies enter international markets with a low emphasis on short-term profit. Other goals—such as being first in a market with potential or learning a new technology—often motivate their internationalization efforts. For example, many firms have entered China and the former Eastern bloc countries with the knowledge that profits will be possible only in the distant future.

The multinational has to assess its capabilities to determine its extent of internationalization. For many companies, exporting is the only viable option, but companies should also consider human resource issues. Do they have the managers to run a wholly owned subsidiary, transfer to a joint venture, or even supervise an export department? Production capabilities may be important if the company needs to adapt its products to foreign markets.

The product targeted for the international market affects the entry-mode decision in several ways. For example, products that spoil quickly or that are difficult to transport might be poor candidates for exporting, whereas products that need little adaptation to local conditions might be good candidates for licensing, joint ventures, or direct investment. Another key issue relates to how and where the product is sold. This means that a company must address the question of how to get the product to market. Can the firm use local channels of distribution? If not, it might explore exporting or joint ventures. If it can develop its own channels of distribution, direct investment might be the best strategy.

Geographic or cultural distance plays an important role. Physical distance raises several issues. When the producing country is far from the consuming country, excessive transportation costs may limit the export option. Even with direct investment for production, sometimes components or raw materials have to be shipped to the producing country. However, cultural distance can often be just as important—if not more so. Cultural distance is the extent that national cultures differ on fundamental beliefs, attitudes, and values. Usually, when two countries have distinctly different cultures, the foreign company initially avoids direct investment. Instead, joint ventures, for example, are attractive because they allow local partners to deal with the many local cultural issues. Licensing and exporting further remove the foreign company from direct dealings with the local culture. Next, we discuss the control-versus-risk tradeoff.

## The Control-Versus-Risk Tradeoff: The Need for Control

A company going international must determine how important it is to monitor and control overseas operations. Key areas for concern over control are product quality in the manufacturing process, product price, advertising, and other promotional activities, where the product is sold, and after-market service. Companies such as McDonald's that use uniform product quality for competitive advantage often have high needs for control. FDI usually provides the greatest control.

**EXHIBIT** 6.6   Risk-Versus-Control Tradeoff

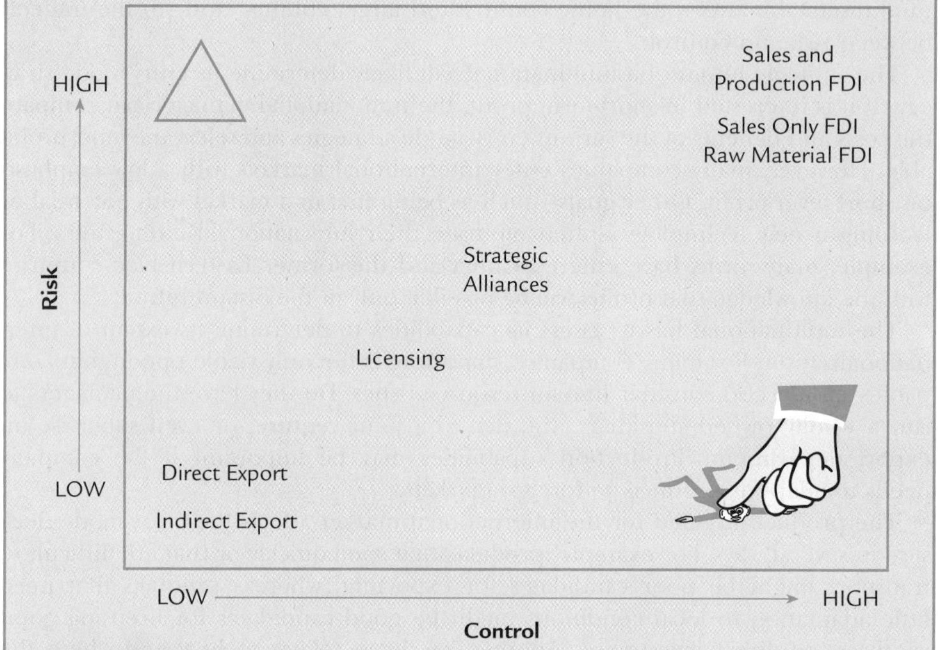

*Source: Adapted from Root, Franklin R. 1994.* Entry Strategies for International Markets. *New York: Lexington Books.*

Usually, entry-mode choices that increase control entail greater risk. For example, exporting and licensing are low-risk ventures, but they surrender control over the product or service to another party. The various forms of FDI allow firms to maximize control, but they also expose the firm to the greatest financial and political risks. Exhibit 6.6 shows the tradeoffs between risk and control for common international entry-mode strategies.

Exhibit 6.7 presents a decision matrix that summarizes the preferred entry-mode strategies for companies facing different conditions. However, it is important to remember that entry-mode strategies can vary by product and by country and a multinational company may mix and change strategies as the situation evolves. Consider the Multinational Management Challenge below, which shows how a small company evolved in entry-mode operations to meet new challenges.

Ultimately, and perhaps most important, entry-mode strategies must align with the multinational strategy, a subject that the next section addresses.

## Entry-mode Strategies and Multinational Strategies

Should a transnational strategist use mostly FDI? Should an international strategist use mostly exporting? There are no simple answers to these questions.

The reason a company is in a host country dictates its choice of a general multinational strategy. Transnational strategists seek location advantages and may be

**EXHIBIT 6.7    Decision Matrix for Formulating Entry-mode Strategies**

| Company Situation | | Entry-mode Strategies | | | | |
|---|---|---|---|---|---|---|
| | | Indirect Export | Direct Export | Licensing and Contracts | IJVs and other Alliances | FDI |
| STRATEGIC INTENT | Learn the market | | | 👍 | 👍👍 | 👍👍👍 |
| | Immediate profit | 👍👍👍 | 👍👍👍 | 👍👍 | 👍 | 👍 |
| COMPANY RESOURCES | Strong financial position | | | | 👍👍 | 👍👍👍 |
| | International expertise | | | | 👍👍👍 | 👍👍👍 |
| LOCAL GOVERNMENT PRODUCT | Favorable regulations | | 👍 | 👍 | 👍👍👍 | 👍👍👍 |
| | Difficult to transport | | | 👍👍 | 👍👍 | 👍👍 |
| | Easy to adapt | 👍👍 | 👍👍 | 👍👍 | 👍 | 👍👍 |
| GEOGRAPHY | Long distance between markets | | | 👍👍 | 👍👍 | 👍👍 |
| CULTURE | Significant differences between cultures | 👍👍 | 👍 | 👍👍 | 👍👍👍 | 👍 |
| NEED FOR CONTROL | High | | | | 👍 | 👍👍👍 |
| RISK | Low | 👍👍👍 | 👍👍👍 | 👍👍 | 👍 | 👍 |

👍 = Favorable conditions for entry-mode strategy

👍👍 = More favorable conditions for entry-mode strategy

👍👍👍 = Most favorable conditions for entry-mode strategy

*Source: Adapted in part from Root, Franklin R. 1994.* Entry Strategies for International Markets. *New York: Lexington Books.*

in any country for any value chain activity. Multidomestic and regional strategists seek local adaptation, and they must determine whether this is best achieved by modifying home country exports or by locating the entire value chain from R&D to service in each country. Therefore, the basic diagnostic question for the multinational manager is which entry-mode strategy best serves the firm's objectives for being in the country or region. In this sense, entry-mode strategies represent the "nuts and bolts" of how a company is actually going to use international markets and country locations to carry out its more general multinational strategies. Exhibit 6.8 describes how companies with various multinational strategies might use the different entry-mode options.

## Multinational Management **Challenge**

### Knowing When to Modify Your Entry-Mode Strategy: The Case of Domes International

For developing countries in need of efficient, inexpensive housing, a Mississippi-based company with its International Sales Office in Memphis, Tennessee, has just the thing: domes. Domes International, Inc., manufactures its bulbous structures out of molded fiberglass. Some look like igloos, others like marshmallows. Among the most attractive benefits of fiberglass domes is their low maintenance. Termite resistant and energy efficient, they also protect against dangerous weather conditions, including severe monsoons that cause horrific damage and loss of life in certain areas of the world.

When Domes International decided to expand internationally, it was already selling houses to the U.S. military for faraway bases on tropical islands. Director of International Business Development and Marketing Steve Pope was assigned the job. He is also president of World Discoveries, Inc., an export-management company based in Memphis that Domes contracted for its global manufacturing operations.

For help, Pope contacted the U.S. government's Export Assistance Centers in Memphis, Tennessee, and Jackson, Mississippi. After talking with trade specialists at the centers, Pope and his company decided to focus on India. After some market research and investigation on how to do business with the Indian government, he connected with officials from the state of Gujarat, who needed to house thousands of homeless families. The state placed an order, and later the Indian military did as well.

Pope and his partners soon realized that they needed a facility in India to assemble components shipped from the United States. Having a local facility is a "win-win," Pope says, because the "jobs created help the local economy, while we benefit stateside by providing the higher-end components." These early experiences led to more sales as Domes International began to adapt the product to fit local needs. Domes uses include offices, schools, military barracks, and warehouses. Even a religious group is interested in replacing their more expensive marble temples with fiberglass domes. "You never know what new opportunities might arise when you're on the ground observing what people need" noted Pope.

In another case, a government client for a school building pointed out that people in one part of the state considered round structures with a hole in them as kind of a temple of doom and gloom. "Local folks wouldn't go near them. So we developed flat fiberglass panels and added ribs and steel struts for strength." It became a more acceptable box, not a dome, Pope explains.

"There's no doubt that Domes International is a better company as a result of our experience in India," Pope says. "We are much more flexible and also innovative. The client wanted a less expensive structure, so we went back to our labs and came up with an insulation solution that met their needs. Now we use these discoveries to improve core products and to offer more variations. We are much more confident going into new situations—listening, adapting, and finding the best solution. That we've been able to transform through our experiences overseas in just a few years is amazing."

*Source: Based on excerpts from http://export.gov/basicguide/eg_main_043073.asp.*

**EXHIBIT 6.8**   **Entry-mode Strategies and Multinational Strategies**

| Strategies | Multinational Strategies | | | |
|---|---|---|---|---|
| | **Multidomestic** | **Regional** | **International** | **FDI** |
| Exporting | Export uniquely tailored products to different countries | Export similar products to each region served | Export home-produced global products worldwide | Export global products made in the most advantageous locations to any other country |
| Licensing | License local companies to produce products with flexibility to adapt to local conditions | License local companies to produce products with flexibility to adapt to regional conditions | License only when export barriers or other local requirements preclude imports from the home country | License only when export barriers or other local requirements preclude imports from optimal production locations or when local risk factors or other barriers preclude FDI |
| Strategic cooperative alliances | Use when partner's knowledge is required for local adaptation of product or service | Use when partner's knowledge is required for regional adaptation of product or service | Use alliances for upstream value chain activities when required by own resources (e.g., investment cost); use downstream alliance under same conditions as licensing | Use alliance for upstream value chain activities when required by own resources (e.g., investment cost or knowledge); use downstream alliance under same conditions as licensing |
| FDI | Own full value chain activities in each country—from raw materials to service | Own full value chain activities in regions—distribute activities within regions for location advantages | Use for downstream sales and after-market services | Invest anywhere in the world for location advantages in sourcing, R&D, production, or sales |

© Cengage Learning

# Political Risk

In the previous section, we looked at some of the ways in which companies can participate in international markets. However, an additional concern that multinationals have to assess and deal with focuses on the political risk associated with a country when making entry decisions. Government policies and instabilities make political risk a more crucial factor than ever in investment decisions today, especially when considering emerging market countries. While emerging markets present significant potential, many of them suffer from high degrees of political risk. In this final section, we look at political risk and what multinational companies can do to offset it.

**Political risk** is the impact of political decisions or events on the business climate in a country, such that a multinational's profitability and feasibility of its

**Political risk**
The impact of political decisions or events on the business climate in a country such that a multinational's profitability and the feasibility of its global operations are negatively affected.

global operations are negatively affected.[28] For example, consider Russia's politically motivated jailing of Mikhail Khodorkovsky, the business tycoon;[29] the Ukraine's disputed recent elections resulting in presidential uncertainties;[30] the Brazilian government's insistence that both government agencies and private citizens use only open source software; and the turmoil in countries like Iran, Lebanon, and Sudan. In such cases, government actions or related incidents raise uncertainties in the business climate, and multinational firms have to consider carefully whether those uncertainties might constrain their investments.

Why should a multinational company be concerned about political risk? Historically, many multinational companies have understood that political risk can have a serious impact on profitability. In fact, for companies like Royal Dutch/Shell, which often enters highly unstable countries because of their oil reserves, political risk is so important that the company dedicates whole departments to assessing it. However, changes in the global situation have accentuated the need for an increased understanding of political risk. For instance, although many multinational companies find that outsourcing production to locations such as India or Kenya can reduce costs, they also are discovering that workers in such locations often work in very harsh conditions that can greatly exacerbate the risk of social unrest.[31] Furthermore, the world is dependent on energy sources in locations with high political risk (e.g., Venezuela, Saudi Arabia, Nigeria), and political instability in these societies can have dramatic effects on multinational firms. Additionally, because the world is so interconnected, political uncertainties in one country can have substantial reverberations around the world. Consider the next Case in Point.

---

### CASE IN POINT

## Political Risk in South America: Nationalizations of Foreign-Owned Companies

Cristina Fernandez succeeded leftist leaning Hugo Chavez as president of Argentina in 2011. Initially she seemed less anti-private and foreign-owned business than her predecessor. However, more recently, she took the bold action of nationalizing 51 percent of YPF, a company owned by Spain's Repsol. This was a popular move with many Argentinians because Repsol was seen as not maximizing YPF's tapping of the Argentina's vast oil reserves. However, it was also a double-edged sword, as Spain is the biggest investor in Argentina and *The Economist* predicts that many Spanish banks, utilities, and telecoms may look to leave Argentina.

Just two weeks after the nationalization of YPF in Argentina, Evo Morales, president of Bolivia, announced that he would "take back what is ours," and nationalized Spain's Red Electrica Espanola (REE). REE supplies over 70 percent of the country's power. Since taking office in 2006, Morales has used May Day celebrations to nationalize different sectors of the economy. In his first year in office he took over natural-gas fields, forcing foreign companies to turn over their production to

the state-owned firm Yacimientos Petrolíferos Fiscales Bolivianos. Next, the Bolivian government seized the British company Ruralec, which owned most of Bolivia's electricity-generating power stations.

Although countries typically promise fair compensation to the parent company when they take over foreign operation, the compensation is often less than the estimated value of the firm. Regarding the recent REE nationalization, company spokesman Antonio Prada noted: "We regret the Bolivian government's decision, which was based on motives that are unknown to us. These actions go against the free market and the rule of law that should govern international investment." Consider the message these nationalization actions send to multinational companies regarding the increased political risk to their investments.

*Sources: Based on Arostegui, Martin and Alex Macdonald. 2012. "Bolivia seizes Spanish power firm." The Wall Street Journal. May 2; Economist. 2012. "Nationalising YPF: Cristina scrapes the barrel." April 21; Economist. 2012. "Expropriations in Bolivia: Just when you thought it was safe." May 5.*

As the Case in Point demonstrates, given the importance of political risk, it is useful to understand some of the factors that influence political risk in any society. Bremmer argues that all the factors that can politically stabilize or destabilize a country play important roles in political risk assessments.[32] Some of the most common factors are changes in the government, a sudden shift in governmental policies or ideology, social volatility, the passage of new laws, leadership changes and the related potential for unrest, and the level of corruption.[33] How can a multinational company assess these various factors? The next Multinational Management Brief lists some important questions that a multinational company must ask before it decides to invest in a country.

Not all companies can afford to dedicate departments to understanding political risk as Royal Dutch/Shell does. In these cases, various agencies can provide risk assessment ratings to multinational companies, which can consult them in making decisions about the appropriateness of investment decisions. One of the most popular companies is Political Risk Services, which offers easily accessible country risk ratings to multinational firms. Exhibit 6.9 shows the PRS risk ratings for selected countries.

Given the impact of political risk on operations and profitability, multinational companies must take the appropriate steps to assess and manage it. Several options are available. Some private organizations offer political risk insurance, and the governmental agency Overseas Private Investment Corporation (OPIC) provides insurance against various risks such as political violence, foreign currency inconvertibility, and expropriation, as well as other types of interference with business operations. However, the insurance can be expensive because it may not always be easy to quantify the risks, and, for some forms of insurance, insurers may not be able to offer protection at all. For example, many insurance underwriters are now hesitant to insure foreign-owned natural-resource-extraction companies

## Multinational Management **Brief**

### Political Risk Assessment

Political risk assessment is a very subjective and difficult task. However, experts suggest that asking a number of key questions can provide preliminary insights into the political risk of a market that a multinational firm is choosing to enter:

- How durable and resilient is the political system?
- How peaceful have governmental transitions been in the past?
- What roles do other nongovernmental organizations, such as trade unions, churches, and the press, play in the country's political stability?
- Could internal factors, such as social, ethnic, or religious tensions, result in social unrest or civil war?
- What is the level of corruption?
- How reliable is the rule of law?
- What is the likelihood that the country can be hit by natural disasters such as tsunamis or earthquakes?

*Sources: Based on Bremmer, Ian. 2005. "Managing risk in an unstable world." Harvard Business Review, June, 51–60; Wade, Jared. 2005. "Political risk in Eastern Europe." Risk Management Magazine, March, 52(3): 24–29; https://www.prsgroup.com/PRS_Methodology.aspx#calculate.*

**EXHIBIT** **6.9**

Political Risk in Selected Countries (1 = no risk, 0 = highest risk)

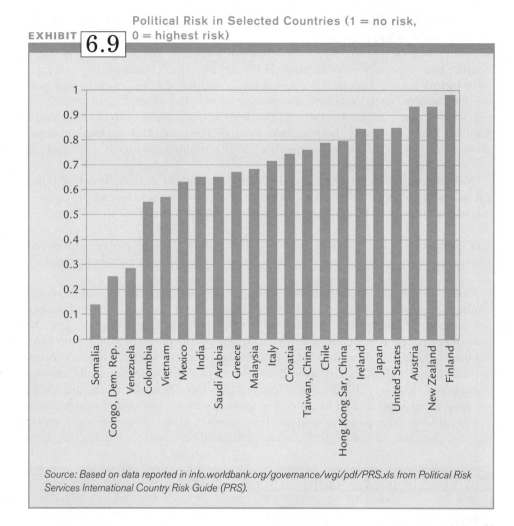

Source: Based on data reported in info.worldbank.org/governance/wgi/pdf/PRS.xls from Political Risk Services International Country Risk Guide (PRS).

operating in Latin American countries such as Bolivia, Ecuador, and Venezuela.[34] In such countries recent government actions have greatly constrained the business operations of multinational firms.

Multinational companies can also rely on local partners to mitigate political risks. For instance, Japan's Sumito Chemical entered into a $4.3 billion joint venture with Saudi Arabia's Aramco to build a major petrochemical plant in Saudi Arabia.[35] Such ventures may help a company deal with local political risk. Furthermore, in a case study of various international firms, Lankova and Katz showed that multinational companies often can take a high-involvement strategy by developing a network of government, business, and public partners to help them face local political risks.[36]

Multinational companies clearly will continue to invest in countries with high levels of political risk. Many of the emerging markets with the highest potential (e.g., Egypt, Colombia, Jordan) have high levels of political risk,[37] but such markets usually present tremendous potential. Furthermore, as Bremmer argues,[38] some of these markets may be so unstable that further instability does not have much influence. Political risk assessment is a very subjective exercise and can vary greatly by region or industry. Consequently, multinational firms must adequately assess political risk and then devise appropriate measures to manage it.

## Summary and Conclusions

The multinational manager faces an array of complex strategic issues. In the previous chapter, you saw how basic strategic management issues apply to the situations faced by multinational firms. In this chapter, you built on that knowledge to see how multinational managers confront strategic issues unique to the multinational situation.

All multinational managers, in both large and small companies, must deal with the dilemma of local responsiveness versus the global solution. The choice of a solution to this dilemma is called a multinational strategy, and each such strategy has its costs and benefits.

There are benefits to favoring local responsiveness, a form of differentiation. Through either the multidomestic or the regional strategy, the multinational company can meet the needs of customers by country or region. Tailoring products or services for each country, the pure multidomestic strategy is the most costly, but it allows the company to deal specifically with differences in culture, language, and political and legal systems. The regional strategy, however, goes only part of the way toward local adaptation. Regional adaptation is balanced against the efficiencies of doing things similarly in a whole region. Some firms will combine these strategies, focusing on larger countries with a multidomestic approach and treating smaller countries in a region similarly.

International and transnational strategists see the world as one market. They try to have global products with global marketing. The goal is to produce high-quality products as efficiently as possible. The transnational strategist differs from the international strategist primarily by using worldwide locations or platforms to maximize efficiency and quality. The transnational will do anything anywhere.

For the multinational company, entry-mode in the international market may occur anywhere in the value chain. At some point, all multinational firms must choose entry-mode strategies that focus on the downstream activities of selling their products or services. All entry-mode strategies, from exporting to FDI, can be used for sales. Exporting focuses on sales, although there may be other strategic benefits, such as learning about the market. However, the other entry-mode strategies, including licensing, strategic alliances, and FDI, serve other value chain activities, including sales. For example, a multinational company might use a strategic alliance for R&D and sales in one country and FDI for production and sales in another country.

In a globalizing world, the complexities of choosing multinational and entry-mode strategies present significant challenges to multinational managers. For example, the nature of the product, the government and political systems where the company locates, the risk of the investment, and the need of the company to control operations (to name only a few issues) come into play in formulating strategic choices for the multinational company. The Cases in Point showed how practicing managers faced and responded to the challenge of formulating multinational and entry-mode strategies.

Finally, political risk is becoming an increasingly important component of investment decisions. The final section discussed some of the components of political risk and the ways in which multinational firms can manage it.

## Discussion Questions

1. Discuss the conditions in which a transnational or international firm is likely to perform better than a multidomestic or regional strategist. Contrast this with the opposite situation, where the multidomestic firm is more likely to be successful.

2. Contrast the transnational and international strategies in their approach to location advantages.

3. Pick a product and analyze its globalization potential, using Yip's diagnostic questions.

4. How might a small manufacturing company become a global marketer?

5. You work for a small company that has an innovative, low-cost production method for laser disks. A Chinese firm approaches your CEO to license the technology. The CEO asks you to write a report detailing the potential risks and benefits of this deal.

6. You work for a small company that has an innovative, low-cost production method for laser disks. A Belgian firm approaches your CEO to form a joint venture with your company. The CEO asks you to write a report detailing the risks and potential benefits of this deal.

7. Discuss some key issues to consider when choosing an entry-mode strategy.

8. What is political risk? How can a multinational company manage political risk?

## Multinational Management **Skill Builder**

**Step 1.** You have been contacted by a local company, which is a major producer of soy, an agricultural component that can be used for many purposes. Research the major products produced using soy.

**Step 2.** The CEO of the company wants to go international. The company is small and has limited resources. Discuss the many options available to the company. Provide a rationale for which method would work the best.

**Step 3.** Research some more to find which countries import the most soy. Prepare a report discussing which countries would be best for the local company to sell to and the way that they should go about entering the market(s).

## Multinational Management **Internet Exercise**

**Step 1.** Search the internet for the terms "transnational strategies" and "multidomestic strategies."

**Step 2.** Identify examples of each that you find.

**Step 3.** Summarize these examples and compare the companies to the general descriptions used in the text.

## *Endnotes*

[1] Humes, Samuel. 1993. *Managing the Multinational: Confronting the Global-Local Dilemma*. New York: Prentice Hall.

[2] Ghoshal, Sumatra. 1987. "Global strategy: An organizing framework." *Strategic Management Journal*, 8, 424–440.

[3] Doz, Yves L. 1980. "Strategic management in multinational companies." *Sloan Management Review*, 21, 2, 27–16; Ghemawat, Pankaj. 2007. Managing differences: The central challenge of global strategy." *Harvard Business Review*, March, 59–68; Porter, Michael E. 1986. "Changing patterns of international competition." *California Management Review*, 28, 2; Porter, Michael E. 1990. *Competitive Advantage of Nations*. New York: Free Press.

[4] Ghoshal.

[5] Ghemawat.

[6] Bartlett, C. A., and S. Ghoshal. 2002. *Managing Across Borders: The Transnational Solution*. Boston: Harvard Business School Press.

[7] Porter.

[8] Weber, Joseph. 2009. "Boeing to rein in Dreamliner outsourcing." www.businessweek.com. January.

[9] Hill, Charles W. L. 2011. *International Business*. McGraw-Hill.

[10] Morrison, Allen J., David A. Ricks, and Kendall Roth. 1991. "Globalization versus regionalization: Which way for the multinational?" *Organizational Dynamics*, Winter, 17–29.

[11] Yip, George S. G. and Tomas M. Hult. 2012. *Total Global Strategy*, 3rd ed. Upper Saddle River, NJ: Prentice Hall.

[12] Root, Franklin R. 1994. *Entry Strategies for International Markets*. New York: Lexington Books.

[13] Ibid.

[14] Beamish, Paul J., Allen J. Morrison, Philip M. Rosenzweig, and Andrew Inkpen. 2011. *International Management*. McGraw-Hill.

[15] United Nations Conference on Trade and Development (UNCTAD). 2000. *World Investment Report: Cross-Border Mergers and Acquisitions and Development*. New York: United Nations.

[16] United Nations Conference on Trade and Development (UNCTAD). 2011. *World Investment Report 2011: Non-Equity Modes of International Production and Development*. New York: United Nations.

[17] Root.

[18] Beamish et al.

[19] UNTC, 2011.

[20] U.S. Department of Commerce. 2008. *A Basic Guide to Exporting*. http://export.gov/basicguide: Wolf, Jack S. 1992. *Export Profits: A Guide for Small Business*. Dover, NH: Upstart Publishing Company.

[21] Wolf.

[22] Beamish et al.

[23] Ibid.

[24] Root.

[25] Beamish et al.

[26] Root.

[27] Ibid.

[28] Clilck, Reid W. 2005. "Financial and political risks in U.S. direct foreign investment." *Journal of International Business Studies*, 36, 559–575.

[29] Ibid. Wade, Jared. 2005. "Political Risk in Eastern Europe." *Risk Management Magazine*, March, 52(3): 24–29.

[30] Bremmer, Ian. 2005. "Managing risk in an unstable world." *Harvard Business Review*, June, 51–60.

[31] Wade.

[32] Bremmer.

[33] Ibid.

[34] Ceniceros, Roberto. 2006. "Political risk insurers leery of Latin America." *Business Insurance*, May 29, 40(22): 21–22.

[35] Baker, Greg. 2006. "Peace Dividends." *Financial Management*, March, 16–18.

[36] Lankova, Elena, and Jan Katz. 2003. "Strategies for political risk mediation by international firms in transition economies: The case of Bulgaria." *Journal of World Business*, August 38(3): 182.

[37] Davis, Chris. 2006. "Emerging markets still a good bet despite recent volatility: Long-term outlook remains strong but be careful, investors told." *South China Morning Post*, May 28, 15.

[38] Bremmer.

# Polaris 2008

Richard Ivey School of Business
The University of Western Ontario | **IVEY** | Institute for Entrepreneurship

**College of Commerce**
National Chengchi University

The 2008 Chinese New Year was still a few days off, but Polaris Financial Group (Polaris) Chairman Wayne Pai had already set off some fireworks. At the security firm's weekly management meeting, Pai had announced the approval of Polaris's investment plans in Singapore, Vietnam, and Abu Dhabi by the Financial Supervisory Commission (the highest administrative commission for Taiwan's banking, securities, and insurance sectors) of the Executive Yuan (Taiwan's highest administration office). This approval launched the further globalization of the Polaris Financial Group, a rapidly growing firm with operations in Taiwan and Hong Kong.

In Taiwan's securities exchange market, Wayne Pai's—and Polaris's—name was synonymous with innovation and entrepreneurship. Pai had led Polaris Securities Co. Ltd. (Polaris Securities) to a stand-out position in Taiwan's securities exchange market by launching online stock trading with a remarkable synergy of complementary assets. Pai had then transferred the business model to Polaris Securities (Hong Kong) Ltd. (Polaris Securities [HK]), including innovative information technology, affluent financial experiences and good customer services. Past successes aside, after the meeting, Pai and the rest of the senior leadership team contemplated whether Polaris's Taiwan and Hong Kong models could be duplicated to Singapore, Vietnam, and Abu Dhabi. These new markets would likely demand new investments in some areas and provide opportunities to further leverage their existing assets.

## Polaris Securities' Background

On July 22, 1988, Pai established Polaris Securities Co. Ltd. as a stock brokerage firm, with capital of NT$200 million.[1] Two years later, in June 1990, Polaris Securities obtained a license from the governing agency to be a full-service securities firm. In 1996, it was listed as an over-the-counter firm, and on September 16, 2002, its stock was approved for listing on the Taiwan Stock Exchange. By early 2008, total paid-in capital of Polaris Securities exceeded NT$19 billion, making it the major source of revenue for the Polaris Financial Group (see Exhibit 1 for Polaris Securities' major business operations; see Exhibit 2 for Polaris Securities' organizational chart). In 2008, total asset value of the Polaris Financial Group totaled more than NT$300 billion.

Pai had not only solidly established the securities firm but under his leadership, the Polaris Financial Group had swiftly reformed and restructured several times within the competitive Taiwan environment. For example, Pai had taken the initiative and merged three other securities firms—Da-Shun, Shi-Dai, and Hua-Yu — with Polaris Securities. Polaris had also purchased the Central Insurance Company in Taiwan, worked with the world's biggest futures company to set up Polaris MF

**EXHIBIT 1    Major Business Operations of Polaris Securities**

1. Consignment trading of securities in a centralized securities exchange market.

2. General trading of securities in a centralized securities exchange market.

3. Underwriting securities.

4. Consignment trading of securities in an over-the-counter market.

5. General trading of securities in an over-the-counter market.

6. Related agent services of securities.

7. Margin purchase and short sale of securities.

8. Futures introducing broker.

9. Consignment trading of foreign securities.

10. Securities firms to do futures dealing.

11. Short-term bill business.

12. Other related securities activities approved by a competent government agency.

*Source: The Polaris Financial Group*

Global Futures Co., Ltd. and purchased the Overseas Bank in Taiwan, which was later sold to Citigroup.

The stated business goal of the Polaris Financial Group was to help investors obtain more wealth management information and conduct their financial transactions. Polaris offered customers various financial and investment products and services, including margin purchases, assistance in issuing initial public offerings (IPOs), firm underwriting public subscriptions, financial consulting, corporate restructuring, securities and futures services, and other related professional investment services.

The major entities that comprised the Polaris Financial Group included Polaris Securities Co. Ltd., Polaris MF Global Futures Co., Ltd., Polaris Securities Investment Trust, Polaris Pu-Tai Investment Consulting, Polaris Futures Co., Ltd., Polaris Holdings (Cayman) Ltd., Polaris Insurance Agent Co., Ltd., Bao-Ju Insurance Agent Co., Ltd., and other companies in which Polaris owned more than 50 percent of the shares (see Exhibit 3).

Although Polaris was a large company with 1,930 employees, its founder and president, Wayne Pai, who strongly believed in resourcefulness and entrepreneurial skills, dominated its management style. Polaris, for example, had revolutionized online trading in Taiwan and had grown its overall market presence through this initiative. Pai also believed that expanding globally would make Polaris an important company on the world's financial services' stage; leveraging Polaris's information technology assets was part of Pai's plan to support this expansion.

## The History of Online Trading in Taiwan

Growth of Taiwan's securities market had been very strong prior to 1998, with many mid- and small-sized Taiwanese firms setting up as many branch offices as possible to compete for market share. After mid-1997, however, Taiwan's security firms found that opening branches did not acquire new customers but increased the operating costs. By 2000, the daily trading volume on the Taiwan Stock Exchange averaged NT$120 billion, and 1,100 security firm branch offices were operating in and around Taiwan.[2]

At the same time, online trading was becoming an important force in the United States and other economies. The Taiwanese company Da-Xin Securities (later Ji-Xiang Securities) realized the increased cost of branch offices could be countered by following the U.S. trend, although Taiwan's government had not yet approved online transactions. Da-Xin Securities introduced online stock trading on June 6, 1997, and on October 17, 1997, the Taiwanese government formally approved online stock trading, revising Taiwan's related regulations on November 6, 1997.

Similar to the situation for many U.S. firms, online stock trading did not immediately become a business success in Taiwan. Initially, some major Taiwanese securities firms, such as Yuan-Ta and Ri-Sheng, did not actively promote the online business because their securities brokers, who were worried about the

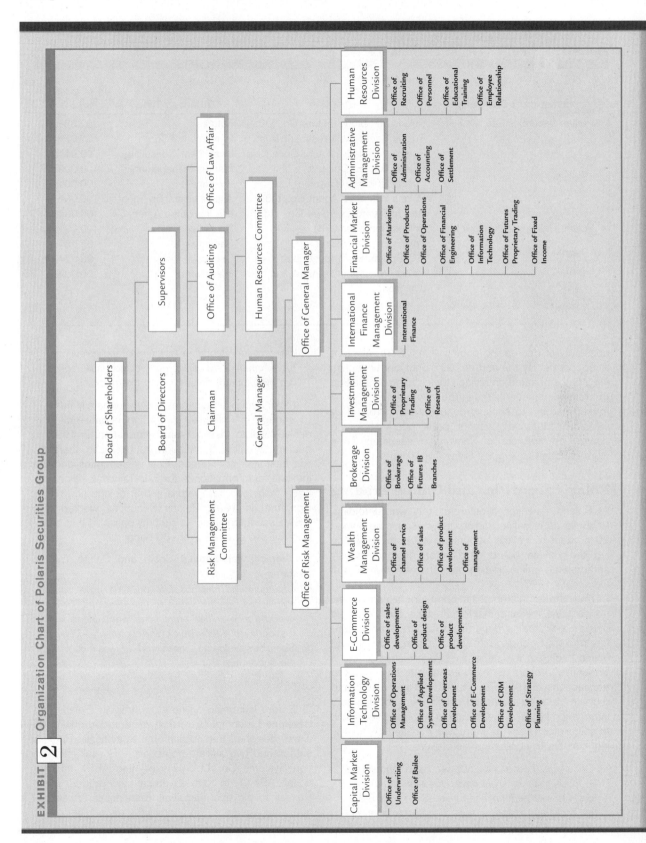

**EXHIBIT 3** Polaris Financial Group

| Investment Company | Subsidiary | Business Type | % of Share Holding |
|---|---|---|---|
| Polaris Securities Co., Ltd. | Polaris MF Global Future Co., Ltd. | Futures | 52.58% |
| | Polaris Securities Investment Trust | Investment & Trust | 52.07% |
| | Polaris Pu-Tai Investment Consulting | Investment Consulting | 99.91% |
| | Polaris Futures Co., Ltd. | Futures Management | 100.00% |
| | Polaris Holdings (Cayman) Ltd. | Investment | 100.00% |
| | Polaris Insurance Agent Co., Ltd. | Assets Insurance Agent | 100.00% |
| | Bao-Ju Insurance Agent Co., Ltd. | Life Insurance Agent | 100.00% |
| Polaris Holdings (Cayman) Ltd. | Polaris Securities (HK) | Securities | 100.00% |
| | Polaris Capital (Asia) Ltd. | Securities | 98.50% |
| | GC Structured Products Ltd. | Securities | 98.62% |
| | Polaris Investment Management (Cayman) Ltd. | Investment | 100.00% |

*Source: The Polaris Financial Group*

possibility of decreasing commissions, were reluctant to cooperate. By the end of 1997, only four securities firms had embarked on online stock trading. In addition to brokers' objections, the introduction of online stock trading had led to security concerns being voiced by investors. Moreover, without profit guarantees, the boards of directors of Taiwanese securities firms were reluctant to support these investments.

## Polaris Securities and Online Trading

At Polaris, however, a different story was unfolding. Pai believed in online trading and, because he owned 20 percent of Polaris Securities' stock, his influence led the Polaris board of directors to unanimously authorize an online trading project to be launched in December 1997.

Pai insisted on a combination of tangible and virtual transactions, meaning that Polaris did not set up a new online stock trading department, but required securities brokers to engage in both traditional trading and online trading at the same time. Pai envisioned Polaris Securities' brokers as the seed team to launch online transactions. In 1997, Pai scrupulously interviewed and recruited a seed team and asked them to distribute information flyers on the streets to introduce the public to online stock trading.[3] Moreover, Pai used the following example to encourage his brokers:

*Once, one of our brokers was seriously ill and stayed in the hospital for eight days. However on the third day, his sale performance ranked 3rd in our Office of Brokerage. How did he do it? Most of his*

*clients trade through the Internet and telephone. Consequently, his sales performance still ranked 3rd even though he was sick in the hospital.*

Major securities customers were generally hesitant to engage in online stock trading because of perceived risks to their personal information. In 1997, to guarantee online transaction security and therefore win customer confidence, Polaris Securities and the Institute for Information Industry in Taiwan jointly developed "a golden key" with a secret design and digital signature. In 1999, Polaris Securities worked with RSA Security to launch a security passport that changed the secret code every 60 seconds.

### Vertical Value-added Chain and Online Trading Systems

*Chairman Pai has absolute decision power and employees do not object to his decisions. However, he also values employees' good ideas and responds to them quickly. Accordingly, Polaris Securities welcomes ideas and suggestions from the bottom up.*

*—Chang-Xueng Li[4]*

Before launching online stock trading, Polaris had developed a complete vertical value-added chain and a well-designed trading platform. Specifically, Pai had established two affiliate companies—Russell Information Systems Co., Ltd. (Russell) and APEX International (APEX)—to form a vertical value-added chain. Russell, in the upstream, was responsible for collection, management, and analysis of original data.

APEX, in the midstream, applied the information to develop financial models. Finally, Polaris utilized the information and models to offer various investment consulting services and financial products to its customers. As chairman, Pai requested that Polaris's trading platform cover operational activities among the front desk, middle office, and back office. Pai's goal was that not only software design in the front desk could offer customers investment consulting services and financial products but information technology systems in the middle office, and back office could properly match, confirm, clear, and settle related business activities Exhibit 4.

Pai also insisted on utilizing information technology to help innovate trading systems and offer other financial services.[5] For example, Polaris continued improving the trading platform to meet customer needs, introducing changes every two or three years. In May 1999, Polaris Securities introduced the "Blue Wizard," which is a freeware of an online stock trading system enabling users to promptly keep an eye on the stock market fluctuation. Thanks to Internet information technology, the Blue Wizard successfully attracted huge numbers of customers. Polaris Securities' trading volume exceeded more than NT$20 billion at the releasing month, outperforming other securities companies.

**EXHIBIT 4**    System Infrastructure of Polaris Financial Group

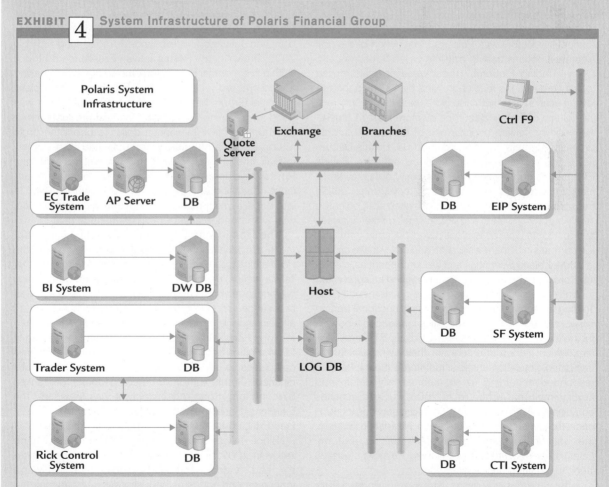

*The abbreviation explanations are as follows: DB: Database; AP Server: Application Server; SF: Sales front Desk; EIP: Enterprise Information Portal; Ctrl F9: Content Provider/Content Collator; BI: Business intelligence; DW: Data warehouse.*

*Source: The Polaris Securities Group.*

In 2001, Polaris Securities launched the first Chinese version of a multinational trading platform called "Polaris Financial Airport," which linked with 11 major stock exchanges in six regions of the world, offering investors 24-hour trading services. This trading platform brought about a large-scale business increase in the Polaris Securities overseas plural commission business,[6] ranking Polaris as one of the top three firms in the Taiwan securities market. Furthermore, Polaris Securities worked with the Central News Agency, offering large amounts of financial news to investors. Because the Central News Agency frequently updated its news content, the financial information offered by Polaris Financial Airport was always up-to-the-minute.

By the end of 2002, Polaris led the market. Key to its competitive victory was Polaris's introduction of the first electrified options trading platform called "Options Lotto Online Trading Platform." This pioneering platform led to Taiwan's options market growing by 13 times the following year. This growth also increased the options trading volume of Polaris Securities by more than 11 times.[7] Accordingly, Taiwan became one of the top 20 futures exchange centers in the world. In 2003, Polaris Securities developed a wealth management software, Polaris EWinner, through which investors could obtain all stock market information free of charge, save considerable transmission fees, access an unlimited self-selected stock-reporting system and obtain stock market analyses and forecasts. This software allowed investors to master the current stock market situation and easily make orders. In 2004, Polaris Securities and Da-Xin Securities, a leading Korean online trading company, signed an agreement to jointly develop a flexible and speedy customized Home Trading System, offering investors multifunctional trading services. In 2005, Polaris Securities introduced a powerful arbitrage profit trading system, Polaris BT Trade System, which helped investors set their own parameters, combined simulation analysis, monitored the market and responded according to an automatically determined arrangement and schedule. In 2006, Polaris Securities combined wealth management banking services to introduce the Smart FP Polaris Wealth Navigation System, the first wealth management online trading platform. Later, other securities firms followed Polaris's steps by launching related businesses.

After introducing online stock trading in 1998, Polaris Securities offered investors various trading channels and promoted its services to more potential clients, leading to online transactions accounting for more than 15 percent of the total securities market.[8] As of 2008, Polaris ranked first in the Taiwan financial market in terms of market shares of online stock trading, online futures and online options trading.

Beyond its innovative trading platform, the Polaris Financial Group had actively introduced new financial products to Taiwan. Following development experiences in other countries and trends in foreign financial markets, Pai believed that one of Polaris's competitive advantages should be the research capabilities and sales abilities for introducing derivative products to investors in Taiwan. Accordingly, Polaris had worked with local well-known universities in the early 1990s, making personnel and academic connections in the fields of finance and information technology. Therefore, when the Taiwanese government lifted restrictions on issuing warrants in 1997, Polaris became the first securities firm in Taiwan to issue Polaris 01 real estate warrants.[9] Moreover, Polaris launched Taiwan's first exchanged-traded fund (ETF) in 2003, known as the Polaris Taiwan Excellence 50 Fund. Within five months, Polaris took the ETF public, breaking a world record for taking an ETF public.[10] The Polaris Financial Group, based on its financial capabilities, was good at designing customized financial products structured on the New Taiwanese dollar to boost the profit return. Polaris's structured products had also outperformed the market. Polaris further worked with the Russell Investment Group, the world's biggest investment consulting and pension management institute, to introduce a multi-manager fund that helped investors with well-rounded asset allocation management.[11]

**The Hong Kong Experience** Based on the advantages of financial innovation and online transaction, the Polaris Financial Group had not only outperformed other Taiwan financial groups[12] but had displayed outstanding performance abroad as well. Polaris had copied its Taiwan experience in innovative information technology and affluent financial experiences and exported it successfully to Hong Kong. When Polaris first entered Hong Kong in 2004, Polaris Securities (HK) ranked 150th in securities companies in the local market. Currently, the Polaris Financial Group, with its excellent performance, ranked 37th in Hong Kong. Accordingly, it was awarded "The Excellent Service Award of Best Securities Firm"[13] (see Exhibit 5 for a list of other honors and awards).

Since Taiwan's entry into the World Trade Organization in 2002, the Taiwanese financial services industry had faced increased globalization. Taiwan's manufacturing industry had already internationalized, with offices and factories established in China and other countries. Taiwan's financial services industry needed to follow in the steps of these manufacturers and establish branch offices offering related financial services in other countries. Opening branch offices in

**EXHIBIT** 5   Honors and Awards of Polaris Financial Group

**Polaris Securities Co., Ltd.**

- Golden Goblet Award for Outstanding Talents in Business Leadership
- 2006 - Outstanding Financial Institution in Risk Management Award, *Asia Risk* magazine
- 2006 - Award for 2006 Annual Outstanding Trading in Taiwan, *The Asset* magazine
- 2005 - Golden Goblet Award for Outstanding Talents in Securities Industry
- 2005 - Golden Goblet Award for Outstanding Talents in Futures Industry
- 2004 - The Benchmark Enterprise in Securities Industry, *CommonWealth Magazine*
- 2003 - Golden Goblet Award for Outstanding Talents in Securities Industry
- 2003 - Outstanding Securities Firm in Taiwan, *AsiaMoney* magazine
- 2003 - Golden Goblet Award for Special Contribution

**Polaris Securities Investment Trust**

- Golden Goblet Award for Outstanding Financial Products Innovation
- Outstanding Assets Management Company in Taiwan, *Asia Investor* magazine
- Golden Goblet Award for Outstanding Talents in Investment Consulting
- 2004 - Outstanding Assets Management Company in Taiwan, *Asia Investor* magazine
- 2003 - Award for Best Product Innovation, *Asia Asset Management* magazine
- 2003 - Golden Goblet Award for Outstanding Talents in Investment Trust and Investment Consulting

**Polaris MF Global Future Co., Ltd.**

- Golden Goblet Award for Outstanding Talents on Futures Industry
- Ranked 1st in Revenues Earned by Securities Firms in Domestic and Foreign Markets
- Ranked 1st in Market Share of Securities Firms in Domestic and Foreign Markets
- 2004 - Ranked 1st in Clearing Awarded by Taiwan Securities Exchange
- 2003 - Ranked 1st in Clearing Awarded by Taiwan Securities Exchange
- 2003 - Golden Goblet Award for Outstanding Talents in Futures Industry

**APEX International Financial Engineering Co., Ltd.**

- 2006 - Ranked 11th among the Top 1000 Service Industries with high growth in net profits after tax, *Business Weekly* magazine
- 2006 - Ranked 19th among Fast 50 hi-tech companies with high profits in Taiwan, Deloitte & Touche
- 2002 - Financial award for innovation and technology R&D plan from Hsin-Chu Science Park
- 2002 - Financial award for New Financial Products and Risk Management Techniques by the Taiwanese Ministry of Economic Affairs
- 2001 - Financial award for Intelligent Assists Management Techniques by the Taiwanese Ministry of Economic Affairs

*Source: The Polaris Financial Group.*

the neighborhood of Taiwanese manufacturers' overseas offices would give Taiwanese financial services firms a better understanding of how businesses operated in China and other countries, which would lead them to offer the appropriate financial services. The Polaris Financial Group was aware of this need and had been actively reaching for foreign markets.[14]

The Polaris Financial Group was looking to expand into the Greater China region.[15] As an initial step, in 1993, Polaris had established an office in Hong Kong, the most prosperous of the cities on the two sides of the Taiwan Strait and the ideal place, it seemed, to boost Polaris's influence among Asia's Chinese population. Polaris Securities (HK) had obtained several authorizations to practice in Hong Kong: an asset management license and other licenses specifically for dealing and advising in securities and for dealing in futures and commodities. Polaris Securities (HK) had also become a participant in the Hong Kong Stock Exchange with four trading seats.

To expand its corporate scope, Polaris Securities (HK) had adapted Taiwan Polaris's innovative information technology, financial experiences, trading platform, and customer services to the Hong Kong market. For example, Polaris Securities (HK) launched in Hong Kong a simplified Chinese version of the Polaris EWinner, trading software that facilitated investors in their online transactions. Because the language interface was a simplified Chinese version, investors in both Hong Kong and China could use it. Polaris Securities (HK) also worked with the Credit Suisse Group to introduce a back office trading system that offered investment products in seven markets around the world, including the United States, Japan, Hong Kong, Singapore, Taiwan, China and South Korea. The trading system offered investors a trading mechanism, trading information, a financial mechanism and trading opportunities. Polaris Securities (HK), through trading systems in Taipei and Hong Kong, set up a trading center across both sides of the Taiwan Strait. Trading center transactions dealt with a range of financial products, including securities, futures, options, structured products, Euro convertible bonds, and Global Depositary Receipts. The trading center offered its customers 24-hour cross-country multifunctional financial services, operated through a back office clearing and settlement system among different companies, markets, products, and foreign currencies.

### Time for Decision-making

*The past does not amount to the future. People cannot live on past successful experiences. The best choice is to proceed forward.*

—*Wayne Pai*

The Polaris Financial Group expected to apply Polaris Securities' experiences to overseas markets. The firm's reasons for exploring individual markets varied. For example, the Hong Kong market gave Polaris the opportunity to collect international capital and acted as a stepping stone for entering China, which was enjoying remarkable growth in its financial market. Many Taiwanese manufacturers had established factories in Vietnam, and because many of these manufacturers trusted compatriot services, Polaris was eager to set up offices there to offer related financial services. Exploring the Singapore market involved obtaining an issuing license for emerging stocks in Singapore while learning about Singapore's financial development. Although Abu Dhabi was an off-shore financial center offering a platform for international capital flow, the city allowed the Polaris Financial Group to easily collect capital for later development.

## The Challenge

Developments in Vietnam, Singapore, Abu Dhabi, and other emerging markets posed a challenge for Polaris. Although the experiences of Polaris Securities and Polaris Securities (HK) provided a valuable background for the strategic initiatives in these countries, each market was characterized by its own laws and regulations, investors' habits, information technology infrastructure, and front, middle, and back office systems. Pai wondered how best to proceed. He knew he had to not only cope with individual market differences but also leverage Polaris's existing assets and experiences.

### CASE DISCUSSION QUESTIONS

1. What critical success factors led to Polaris's launch of online stock trading and online transactions in Taiwan?
2. How did Polaris transfer its Taiwanese success to Hong Kong?
3. What advice would you give Wayne Pai?

### CASE NOTES

[1]The exchange rate in 1988 is approximately US$1= NT$1.27.

[2]Ya-wei Lin. 1999. Gong-Cheng, Polaris, and Da-Xin are the top three electronic securities firms. *Business Weekly*, 599, May 17, pp. 102–103.

[3]Mei-zhen Ren. 1999. Polaris heads all firms in on-line stock trading. *Business Weekly*, 610, August 2, pp. 126–128.

[4]Chang-Xueng, Li. 1999. Polaris securities and the electrification of financial service industry—To engage in continuous innovation in commercial models and to put emphasis on employees' core

competence. *An Industry EB Model Case Study—Research Results in the Scientific and Technological Plan*, Taipei: Institute for information industry, pp. 2.26–2.35.

[5]Ibid.

[6]The overseas plural commission business, through domestic securities firms, helped domestic investors with an overseas commission business license to purchase and sell securities and financial products in overseas markets.

[7]Zi-Qiao Lin 2007. Wayne Pai, a pioneer in Taiwan finance market, leads Polaris' overseas expansion. *Capital CEO Magazine*, Hong Kong: South China Media 44, November, pp. 24–31.

[8]Ya-chin Huang 2002. Securities firms fighting for online trading business. *Win-Win Weekly*, 309, November 25, pp. 82–83.

[9]Xian-Da Si-Tu 2003. *Analysis on Strategic Management Case Studies: Concepts and Cases*. Taipei: Zhi-Sheng Culture, p. 164.

[10]Zi-Qiao Lin.

[11]Jun-hui Lin 2007. Multi-functional manager in fund management sweeps the market. *Timing Financial and Economic Network*, February 1, http://www.yi123.com.tw/forum_1494.html, accessed November 17.

[12]See Exhibit 5.

[13]Zi-Qiao Lin.

[14]Jie-zhi Wu 2001. Polaris securities explore its business in China with low profile. *Win-Win Weekly*, 225, April 8, pp. 110–111.

[15]*Greater China* is a term referring collectively to both the territories administered by the People's Republic of China (including Hong Kong and Macau) and territories administered by the Republic of China (Taiwan and some neighboring islands). This term is most commonly used in the investment and economics community, referring to their growing economic interaction and integration.

# 7

# Small Businesses and International Entrepreneurship: Overcoming Barriers and Finding Opportunities

## Learning Objectives

*After reading this chapter you should be able to:*

- Understand the basic definitions of small business and entrepreneurship.

- Explain how small businesses can begin as global start-ups or follow the stages of internationalization.

- Understand how small businesses can overcome barriers to internationalization.

- Identify when a small business or entrepreneur should consider going international.

- Describe how small businesses or entrepreneurs can find customers, partners, or distributors abroad.

- Understand how new venture wedge strategies can be used in foreign markets.

- Explain the factors driving entrepreneurship at an international level.

*Preview*    C A S E    I N    P O I N T

### Small Businesses in China

China's economic success has been primarily due to small businesses. Whereas most of the economic output was coming from poorly run state-owned enterprises a decade ago, small businesses now contribute almost 60 percent of China's output. According to rough estimates, Chinese small businesses employ almost 75 percent of the urban work force. These small companies have often thrived on the business of a few clients, or through the sale of large quantities of small-margin products.

The ongoing economic crisis has had a serious impact on these dynamic Chinese small businesses. Almost 62,400 companies shut down in the Guangdong province. In all of China, many companies closed, laying off millions of people. For instance, Ye Jianquing, a Chinese entrepreneur, saw a rapid decline in orders from his European and U.S. customers. His small business, which manufactures sunglasses, has seen orders decline by 80 percent from 2007 to 2008. He is now branching out to other products, such as key rings and prescription glasses, hoping to survive.

Experts predicted that the Chinese economy's performance would be heavily dependent on how its small businesses deal with the economic slowdown. The government recently recognized their importance, and government officials have actually requested that banks lend more money to them. In fact, a recent interview with Stephen Yiu, chair of KPMG China, suggests that lack of funds from banks is probably one of the most significant barriers to the growth of small businesses in China. As such, it is not surprising to learn that the Chinese government is actually considering the launch of a new equity exchange. The new exchange will allow investors to trade shares in small technology firms. Such efforts are consistent with the Chinese government's goals of extending credit to smaller firms that have had more difficulty surviving in the current difficult environment.

*Sources: Based on Asia News Monitor. 2012. "China: Finance, small business cited as keys to growth," April 23, online edition; Chao, L., and A. Batson. 2009. "China's small factories struggle." Wall Street Journal, January 31, A6; Wall Street Journal. 2012. "China weighs new equity exchange." March 23, online edition.*

mall businesses contribute significantly to most national economies. As the Preview Case in Point shows, China has become an economic power primarily due to its small businesses, which support the economy by contributing to economic output and providing jobs for millions of workers. In fact, reports suggest that small businesses accounts for 98.9 percent of the total number of businesses and around 65.6 percent of industrial output (Cao, Hartung, Forrest, and Shen, 2011). Even in the developed nations of Europe, North America, and Japan, more than 98 percent of all businesses are small. In these countries, small businesses employ more than 50 percent of the workforce and produce nearly 50 percent of the countries' GNPs.

The U.S. economy is also very dependent on its small businesses. In fact, during the periods of downsizing by large firms in the United States, small companies created more than two-thirds of the new jobs.[1] How important are small businesses to the U.S. economy? Consider the following facts regarding American small businesses:[2]

- Small businesses represent 99.7 percent of all employing firms, employing about half of all private employees.
- Small businesses generate about 60 to 80 percent of all new jobs annually.
- Small businesses employ almost 41 percent of all high-tech workers.
- Small businesses pay almost 45 percent of the private payroll.
- Small businesses represent 97 percent of identified exporters, producing 29 percent of export value in 2007.
- Small businesses have generated 13 to 14 times more patents per employee than large patenting firms.

Given the importance of small businesses to the growth of most national economies and to the increasing globalization of business, it is not surprising that small businesses seek opportunities outside their national boundaries, just as their larger brother and sister firms do. When going international, small businesses can use the same participation strategies and multinational strategies available to larger businesses. They can export, form a joint venture, license, and engage in FDI. Small businesses can also act like multidomestic strategists in product adaptation, or they can develop transnational networks for supply, manufacturing, and distribution. In Korea, for example, small businesses account for approximately 40 percent of exports and 65 percent of Korean manufacturing FDI.[3]

Because they are small and often controlled by their entrepreneurs or founders, small businesses face circumstances different from those of larger multinational corporations. This chapter presents examples and reviews the barriers that small businesses face and must overcome in internationalization. It also shows how basic entrepreneurial strategies can serve small businesses in taking their products or services to the global marketplace.

Have you ever considered starting your own business? Consider the following Case in Point.

# What Is a Small Business?

There are many definitions of a small business. The United Nations and the Organization for Economic Cooperation and Development (OECD) define small- and medium-sized businesses as those having fewer than 500 employees.[4] The popular press usually considers small businesses as those with fewer than 100 employees.

**Small business**
UN definition: fewer than 500 employees. Popular press definition: fewer than 100 employees. The U.S. Small Business Administration's definition varies by industry and takes into account both sales revenue and number of employees.

## Small Business Administration and Questions to Ask Yourself

Small businesses are critical to growth in most countries. As a result, many countries have their own governmental organizations to facilitate the creation and survival of new businesses. In the United States, the Small Business Administration (SBA) fulfills this role. The organization provides assistance to individuals interested in starting their own businesses and helps these individuals navigate the many stages of a new business creation. Are you interested in starting your own business? If so, the SBA advises that you prepare answers to the following questions:

- Are you ready to spend the time, money, and resources to get the business started?

- What kind of business do you want, and what products and/or services will your business provide?

- Why do you want to start a business?

- What is your target market and who is the competition?

- What is unique about your business idea?

- How much money will you need and how long will you have to finance before you make a profit?

- Will you need a loan?

- How will you price and market your product?

- How will you legally structure the business?

- How many employees will you need?

- Where will you house the business?

- What do you need to do to ensure that your taxes are being paid correctly?

*Source: Based on Small Business Administration. Twenty questions before starting a business. http://www.sba.gov.*

The U.S. Small Business Administration (SBA) has a more complex definition. Its definition of small varies by industry and takes into acccount both sales revenue and the number of employees. For example, to be classified as small by the SBA, annual receipts cannot exceed $17 million in the general construction industry but may range up to $22 million in wholesale trade industries. In manufacturing industries, the maximum number of employees for small businesses ranges between 500 and 1,500, depending on the specific industry.[5]

# Internationalization and the Small Business

**Small business stage model**
Incremental process of internationalization followed by many small businesses.

**Global start-up/ born-global firm**
Company that begins as a multinational company.

How do small businesses go international? This section examines two ways. First, some organizations follow the stages of international involvement, with each stage leading to greater involvement. This incremental approach to internationalization is called the **small business stage model**. Second, organizations can begin as global companies. They begin international operations at the same time they start up domestically. A company that goes global from day one of its life is called a **global start-up** or **born-global firm**. The next two sections discuss these processes.

## The Small Business Stage Model of Internationalization

Traditionally, small business internationalization follows the stage model; that is, small companies take an incremental approach. These companies begin as passive exporters, filling international orders but not actively seeking such sales. It is assumed that these companies typically consider exporting only after they have a strong domestic base.[6] However, later they may add an export department or an international division, with a more proactive approach to international sales. Joint ventures and other forms of direct investment follow. The stage model probably applies to the majority of small business efforts at internationalization. Most, but not all, small businesses do not have the managerial and financial resources for immediate globalization.

The typical stages of internationalization for a small entrepreneurial business are:[7]

- *Stage 1—Passive exporting:* The company fills international orders but does not seek export business. At this stage, many small business owners do not realize that they have an international market.

- *Stage 2—Export management:* The CEO or a designated manager specifically seeks export sales. Because of resource limitations, most small businesses at this stage rely on the indirect channel of exporting (see Chapter 6). However, this stage is often a major change in orientation for the entrepreneur or small business manager. Exporting is seen as an opportunity for new business.

- *Stage 3—Export department:* The company uses significant resources to seek increased sales from exporting. Managers no longer see exporting as a prohibitive risk. The key for most small businesses is finding a good local partner for distribution.

- *Stage 4—Sales branches:* High demand for the company's product in a country or region justifies setting up a local sales office. Small businesses must have the resources to transfer home managers to expatriate assignments or to hire and train local managers and workers to run the operations.

- *Stage 5—Production abroad:* Production moves a company beyond downstream value chain activities. It allows companies to gain local advantages, such as easy local product adaptation or production efficiencies. Companies may use licensing, joint ventures, or direct investment. This is often a very difficult stage for a small business because the cost of a failed direct investment can put the survival of the whole company at risk.

- *Stage 6—The transnational:* Small size does not preclude a business from developing a globally integrated network that characterizes the transnational corporation. As we will see, some entrepreneurs begin their small businesses as transnationals.

Many small and some large companies find the incremental process of internationalization adequate for their strategic position. Following the stage model allows companies to minimize their exposure to risk and to develop their international expertise gradually. In contrast, other entrepreneurial companies have products that often require them to go international immediately or to move rapidly through the internationalization stages. In the next section, we discuss the growing phenomenon of global start-ups to show how rapidly some beginning businesses become global operations.

## Small Business Global Start-Ups, or Born-Global Firms

Global start-ups occur when companies begin as multinational companies. In fact, by definition, the born-global company must pursue a global vision from inception and globalize rapidly.[8] Impossible? Not in today's international marketplace. The next Multinational Management Challenge shows how one company was able to go global from its founding.

## Multinational Management **Challenge**

### Can You Go Global from Day One? Surftech Did.

Randy French founded Surftech as a small manufacturer of molded surfboards. With his background as a surfboard shaper and pioneer in windsurfing, he has turned his passion into a transnational business. He has experimented with different materials to make surfboards not only lighter but also much stronger. With boards that cost around $800, Surftech targets the high end of the surfing market. However, its boards are manufactured in molds, unlike the typical high-end product, which is hand-crafted and shaped by skilled artisans. After demonstrating that his boards could perform as well as handmade types, French convinced 25 of the top shapers in the world to make molds for his products. With an innovative manufacturing process and top designers on board, he needed a production platform that could produce the boards in quantity. Like many transnational cousins, he found it—not in his native California, but in Thailand, with a company skilled in producing sailboards.

Designers (shapers) from around the world produce masters. Then a mold is built, and, four months later, boards ship from Thailand to warehouses in the United States (Florida, Hawaii, and California); Australia; Japan; New Zealand; and the United Kingdom.

Surftech sold only 75 boards during its first year of business. However, French consistently pursued the world's top surfers. The company now has the endorsement of most of these individuals and sold between 18,000 and 20,000 boards in 2006. Today, Surftech partners with many of the world's top surfers, vindicating French's belief that he could build a lighter, stronger, and higher-performing board.

*Sources: Based on Pitta, Julie. 2003. "Kowabunga! A surfin' safari supply chain." http://www.worldtrademag.com; Surftech. 2012. http://www.surftech.com.*

Born-globals are critical to the international business environment. In fact, some have even argued that traditional multinationals have a lot to fear from born-globals. Born-globals are often very flexible and fast moving, especially in high-technology areas, because they tend to be very knowledge intensive.[9] Such companies are thus often able to introduce innovations that may change the business environment.

How do companies following the small business model compare with born-global firms? Exhibit 7.1 shows some of the major differences.

Although not always possible for a new venture, the global start-up is an increasingly popular choice for many new companies—when the conditions are right. Although all entrepreneurial ventures are risky, global start-ups are riskier than domestic ventures. Nevertheless, even with the increased risk and complexity of immediately going international, global start-ups may offer the only avenue of success for new ventures in rapidly globalizing industries.

### Small-Business E-Commerce

*To a large extent, technology has helped to level the playing field for small companies. Today, a small business in rural Maine can export machine parts to 38 countries using the Internet. A woman in Mississippi can export food products to Canada. Handcrafted bowls from Colorado can be sold in Japan.*[10]

**EXHIBIT 7.1**    Comparison of Small Business Model Firms and Born-Global Firms

| Attribute | Born-Global Firm | Small-Business Model |
|---|---|---|
| Managerial vision | Global from founding | International market developed after solid domestic market base |
| Previous global experience | Significant among founders | Low degree of previous global experience |
| Networking | Strong use of personal and business networks at both domestic and international level | Looser network with only foreign distributors playing a key role in internationalization efforts |
| International market knowledge | High from founding of firm | Low and slowly accumulating based on domestic market knowledge |
| Degree of innovation | High, though product differentiation based on leading-edge technology and technological innovativeness | Less innovative approach |
| Nature of international strategy | Niche-oriented and proactive international strategy to gain market share in key markets around the world | Broader market approach and more reactive strategic approach |
| Environmental approach | Fast and flexible | Less flexible |
| Nature of relationship with foreign customers | Strong customer orientation and close or direct customer relationships | Indirect relationships through intermediaries at early stages of internationalization |

Sources: Based on Rialp, Alex, Josep Rialp, David Urbano, and Yancy Vaillant. 2005. "The born-global phenomenon: A comparative case study research." Journal of International Entrepreneurship, 3, 133–171; Vapola, T. J., P. Tossavainen, and M. Gabrielsson. 2008. "The battleship strategy: The complementing role of born globals in MNC's new opportunity creation." Journal of International Entrepreneurship, 6, 1–21.

Regardless of whether a small business uses a stage development model or a global start-up model of going international, a website configured for e-commerce is a low-cost and quick way to sell products across national borders. However, besides the use of a website, the Internet provides small companies with the ability to undertake many other activities. Consider the next Case in Point.

Although G.ho.st ended up closing, the Case in Point nevertheless shows that small companies can be easily created using the power of today's Internet technology. Chapter 10 provides a more detailed treatment of the challenges associated with cross-border e-commerce. However, some of the major benefits follow.[11]

## Advantages

- Ability of small firms to compete with other companies both locally, nationally, and internationally.

- Possibility and opportunity for more diverse people to start a business.

- Convenient and easy way of doing business transactions (not restricted to certain hours of operation; open 24 hours a day, 7 days a week).

- An inexpensive way (compared to the cost of paper, printing, and postage prior to the Internet) for small businesses to compete with large companies.

- Availability of domestic products in other countries.

### Global Hosted Operating System

Zvi Schreiber, born and educated in the United Kingdom, came up with the idea of accessing personal documents from multiple computers after watching his daughter laboriously e-mail files to herself. He then decided to form Global Hosted Operating System (G.ho.st). G.ho.st was based in Ramallah, Palestine, and CEO Schreiber lived in Jerusalem. In fact, he had never visited the company headquarters in Ramallah because he is Israeli. How did he form the small business?

Schreiber used the many opportunities offered by the Internet. When he came up with the idea, he decided to hire Palestinians as a way to further his peace ambition and to create jobs for Palestinians. He Googled "Palestinian software executives," and Google led him to Murad Tahboub, who runs an IT-outsourcing company in Ramallah. Tahboub agreed to help start G.ho.st. and about 30 Palestinian software engineers worked in Ramallah. While Schreiber and his three Israeli workers worked in West Jerusalem, the rest of the engineers worked in Ramallah, a town ten miles from Jerusalem, with the two towns separated by a concrete barrier.

Schreiber then organized a meeting where all of the employees met. It was the first time that both the Palestinian and Israeli employees of G.ho.st. had met to talk about their families and a new product launch. Unfortunately, G.ho.st recently closed due to lack of funding and competition from other similar services such as Google Drive and Google docs.

*Sources: Based on Lev-Ram, M. "A fighting chance." Fortune Small Business. 2009. March 19, 2, 62–63; Mossberg, W. S. 2012. "Google Stores, Syncs and Edits in the cloud." Wall Street Journal, April 25, online edition.*

However, in spite of the expanding opportunities for small businesses to internationalize, psychological and resource-related barriers remain in place. The next section reviews some of the obstacles that often prevent small businesses from going international.

## Overcoming Small Business Barriers to Internationalization

Conventional wisdom argues that small businesses face many barriers that prevent them from becoming multinational companies. Small size often means limited financial and personnel resources to dedicate to international activities. Small size can also mean a lack of sufficient scale to produce goods or services as efficiently as larger companies. Small companies often have top managers with limited international experience and possibly negative attitudes toward becoming multinational. Such managers view international ventures as too risky and not potentially profitable. Negative managerial attitudes and past success at home lead to organizational cultures with a strong domestic orientation.

Although many barriers to internationalization seem internal, small businesses also have to face contextual and other environmental issues that magnify the difficulties pertaining to international operations. These difficulties emerge from a variety of factors. For more insights into such factors, consider the next Case in Point.

In spite of the difficulties with internationalization, many small companies aggressively enter international markets and succeed. Next, we consider examples of how small businesses and entrepreneurs have overcome the barriers to establish successful multinational operations.

CASE IN POINT

# The World Bank and the "Doing Business" Project

The World Bank sees new business creation as extremely critical and has devoted significant resources to the "Doing Business" project. The "Doing Business" project assesses the environment worldwide and computes scores of the ease of starting a business in any country. The basic assumption is that economic activity can only happen in environments where there are good rules that are both transparent and accessible to all. If business regulations are fair and easy to comply with, people can more easily start new businesses and reap their efforts. However, in cases where business regulations are cumbersome and getting permits is dependent on whom you know, there are significantly more barriers to starting new businesses.

What factors does the World Bank consider when computing the barriers (or ease) of starting small businesses? Among the 10 factors assessed objectively in the local environment, a number of key factors include:

- *Starting a business:* time and cost needed to formally incorporate and start a business.

- *Getting credit:* the ease with which credit can be accessed through the existence of credit bureaus and the safeguard of both borrowers and lenders.

- *Registering property:* the number of procedures needed for someone to purchase property and to transfer the property title to his/her name.

- *Enforcing contract:* the time, cost, and complexity involved in resolving a contract dispute between two parties.

**Ease of Doing Business Ranking for Selected Countries (out of 183 countries)**

| Country | Ease of Doing Business Ranking |
|---|---|
| Singapore | 1 |
| Hong Kong | 2 |
| New Zealand | 3 |
| United States | 4 |
| Denmark | 5 |
| Saudi Arabia | 12 |
| Australia | 15 |
| South Africa | 35 |
| Spain | 44 |
| Bulgaria | 59 |
| Poland | 62 |
| Italy | 87 |
| China | 91 |
| Vietnam | 98 |
| Russia | 120 |
| Brazil | 126 |
| India | 132 |
| Madagascar | 137 |
| Zimbabwe | 171 |
| Chad | 183 |

*Source: Based on* World Bank. 2012. Doing Business Report. 2012. http://www.doingbusiness.org.

*continued*

> • ***Investor protection:*** the degree to which investors (specifically minority investors) are protected from the misuse of corporate assets.
>
>   As the above shows, the World Bank "Doing Business" project is a very comprehensive project assessed at understanding barriers to small businesses. As small businesses from one country consider going international, they are well advised to consider the World Bank scores to determine which countries are most attractive. The exhibit above shows the rankings of selected countries on the ease of doing business.

## Developing a Small-Business Global Culture

**Global culture**
Managerial and worker values that view strategic opportunities as global and not just domestic.

A **global culture** occurs when an organization has managerial and worker values that view strategic opportunities as global and not just domestic. At all levels of the organization, members share a common language to describe international operations. This common language gives organizational employees a framework to interpret and understand their company's actions in the international arena.[12]

Generally, increased international competition and exposure to international markets have forced large companies, such as those in the automobile industry, to develop more of a global culture. The need for survival has made it necessary for top executives of all nationalities to respond to global competition. Small businesses, however, often ignore international opportunities because key decision makers, given the culture of their organizations, see only their domestic competition. In a truly global culture, entrepreneurial owners develop an international mindset for themselves and for their companies. Thinking globally permeates everything that happens in the company. People believe that national boundaries are not so relevant and that the company can do business and conduct value chain operations (e.g., R&D, manufacturing, raising capital) anywhere in the world.

Several characteristics of the key decision makers in an organization affect the development of a global culture:[13]

- *Perceived psychological distance to foreign markets:* This is the extent to which managers believe that foreign markets are "just too different" for involvement. As the Focus on Emerging Markets feature illustrates, Australian small businesses found the psychic distance from the Central and European markets to be a significant constraint.[14] However, when key managers overcome this belief, a global culture can then develop.

- *International experience:* Managers with little training in foreign languages and little international travel often resist internationalization. However, managers with previous international experiences, even if just from personal travel and sightseeing, have a greater propensity to recognize global opportunities. Often even a chance meeting during a foreign vacation can trigger an international small business venture.

- *Risk aversion:* Managers who are unwilling to take risks have difficulty supporting internationalization. Going international requires an entrepreneurial spirit and thus the willingness to face risks.

- *Overall attitudes toward international strategies:* Some managers simply find the idea of international strategies too threatening to the status quo. Others see international opportunities as beneficial to the company and to their careers. A global culture will develop when the owner/entrepreneur promotes company values that support and reward the search for international opportunities.[15]

CASE IN POINT

### CEOs' Influence in Australian Born-Globals

A criticism of studies of born-global companies has been the ignorance of the history leading to the creation of the born-global enterprise. Most prior studies focused on the characteristics of the firm and ignored the critical aspects of the CEO that may contribute to rapid internationalization. A recent study of 15 small and medium Australian enterprises reveals how critical the CEO is to success in global markets. The study finds that rapid internationalization is not always necessarily caused by the opportunities available to the company's executives. Rather, most of the CEOs in these firms had significant experience in their industry. However, most importantly, many of these executives had significant global experience through assignments in various countries. Furthermore, many of the founders also had significant network ties with individuals in the markets in which they wanted to expand. Additionally, the study also showed that the accumulation of knowledge by the CEO over time led to much faster internationalization as opposed to the more slow pace of internationalization at the beginning. In other words, expansion to one or two new global markets provided significant know-how that allowed more rapid expansion to a larger number of countries.

*Source: Based on Chadra, Y., C. Styles, and I. F. Wilkinson. 2012. "An opportunity-based view of rapid internationalization." Journal of International Marketing, 20, 1, 74–101.*

Furthermore, as Exhibit 7.1 showed, born-global firms likely have global cultures. In such companies, the founders or top managers already have very high levels of international experience,[16] and they use that experience to influence all facets of operations. The next Case in Point shows how the CEO's influence is critical in creating a global culture.

## Changing Attitudes of Key Decision Makers

Both the stage model and the global start-up model depend on the attitudes of the primary decision makers in small and medium-sized businesses. For companies that internationalize their business in stages, each stage demonstrates the key executives' increasing commitment to internationalization. Early in this process, managers perceive foreign markets as risky, with high costs to enter and low potential benefits. Because of these negative attitudes toward internationalization, most international sales for small- and medium-sized businesses come from countries that are close in culture and in geography. For example, most Canadian companies begin exporting first to their geographically and culturally similar neighbor to the south. These cautious early moves help top managers overcome initial skepticism regarding international markets. In the later stages, these attitudes change, with the international market often perceived as more profitable than the domestic market.[17] Exhibit 7.2, for example, shows that exporters and nonexporters in the U.S. industrial equipment industry have quite different attitudes regarding internationalization.

Positive attitudes toward overseas markets are perhaps more necessary for global start-ups than for companies that move slowly into the international marketplace. Experts argue that successful global start-ups require the founders to communicate an appropriate vision to everyone in the organization.[18] Managers use their global vision to help their companies become multinational from birth.

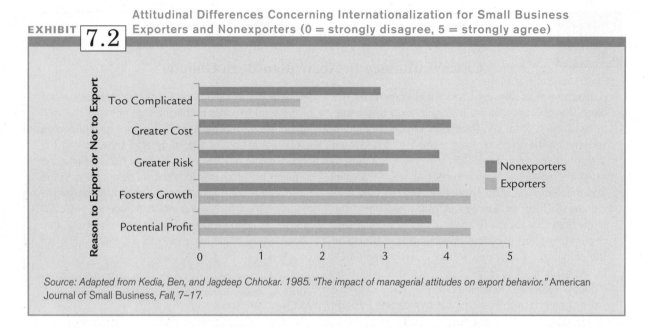

**EXHIBIT 7.2** Attitudinal Differences Concerning Internationalization for Small Business Exporters and Nonexporters (0 = strongly disagree, 5 = strongly agree)

Source: Adapted from Kedia, Ben, and Jagdeep Chhokar. 1985. "The impact of managerial attitudes on export behavior." American Journal of Small Business, Fall, 7–17.

## Gaining Experience: Duties and the Personal Life of the Small-Business CEO

The effects of internationalization on the personal life and duties of the CEO may play a more important role in the international activities of small and medium-size companies than in larger firms. The owner of a small business is often the CEO and the driving entrepreneurial force in the business. Running a small business is always extremely time-consuming and challenging, even when the firm is involved only in the domestic market.[19] However, internationalization demands significantly more commitment, and, when the internationalization effort affects the CEO, it threatens the whole fabric of the organization.[20]

For a small firm, opening new markets is often the CEO's personal responsibility. Although small company CEOs spend only 20 percent of their time managing export and other international functions, they must be willing to incur more than economic costs for the venture.[21] They must be ready to pay social and business costs because their responsibilities for the new international venture often entail increased travel and stress. Many CEOs feel that these activities adversely affect family life, and they dislike being away from the daily management of their businesses.[22] In addition, the job of the small business CEO may change when the company becomes multinational. A study of Canadian manufacturers that had recently begun exporting found that more than 50 percent of the CEOs felt that their duties had changed since their companies had gone international. The impact seemed to affect CEOs more than workers. Only slightly more than 20 percent of the employees in the same companies had their jobs restructured and needed retraining due to the firms' international business.[23]

As new multinational managers, the Canadian CEOs also believed that they needed skill upgrading for international business. Exhibit 7.3 shows key skills that the CEOs felt they needed.

## Is Size a Barrier for Small Business Internationalization?

Large firms tend to enter export markets more than small companies. They have more resources to absorb the risk of exporting and often have a greater incentive

**EXHIBIT 7.3** Training and Knowledge Needs of Small-Firm CEOs Entering Internationalization

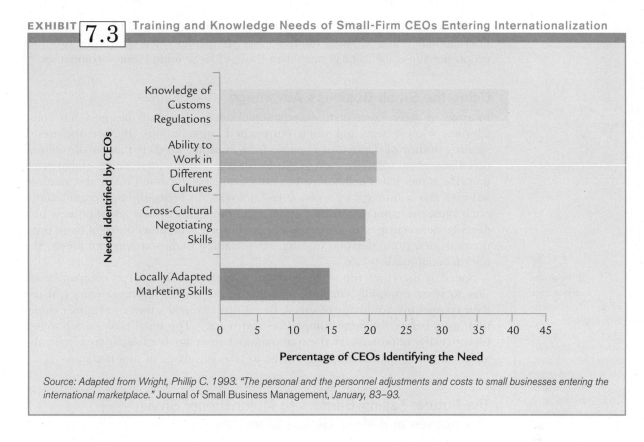

Source: Adapted from Wright, Phillip C. 1993. "The personal and the personnel adjustments and costs to small businesses entering the international marketplace." Journal of Small Business Management, January, 83–93.

to export when domestic markets become saturated.[24] As the Emerging Markets Feature made clear, large firms have other advantages, such as access to more qualified individuals with the ability to negotiate with geographically dispersed partners.[25] In contrast, small businesses often have to rely on a few individuals, who become involved in grueling travel. Large firms have more resources to invest in cross-cultural training to better understand the countries in which they operate, with their local business and national cultures. Such training tends to be less likely for small firms with limited resources.

Many academic researchers and small business managers thus argue that only large companies have the resources to become multinationals.[26] In fact, most studies find that the larger the business, the more likely the firm exports its products.[27] Even among exporting firms, the large companies tend toward committed exporting and the smaller ones tend toward passive exporting. Large firms also serve more national markets. For example, one study of Canadian firms found that companies with total sales of more than $50 million exported on average to 27 markets, while smaller firms averaged only slightly more than 12.[28]

These statistics show that small companies do suffer from the **liabilities of smallness**; in other words, compared to large firms, small businesses find it more challenging to obtain and secure the necessary resources they need to internationalize.[29]

However, the liabilities of smallness may exist only during the initial internationalization stage. Large size makes it easier for a company to begin exporting or making direct investments, but once firms choose to take on an international venture, experts suggest that the international sales intensity of small firms may equal or even exceed that of large firms.[30] **International sales intensity** is the amount of

**Liabilities of smallness**
The challenges facing small businesses in getting access to the resources necessary to internationalize.

**International sales intensity**
Amount of international sales divided by total sales of the company.

international sales divided by the total sales of the company. Once involved in international ventures, small multinational companies often gain sales revenues proportionally equal to or greater than those of large multinational companies.[31]

## Using the Small Business Advantage

In spite of some barriers to internationalization, the small business has some advantages over large and often entrenched organizations. In fact, the trend-spotting author of *The Global Paradox,* John Naisbitt, predicts that small multinational businesses will have even greater advantages in the increasingly global economy. He argues that small companies can change products and internal operations faster to take advantage of evolving technologies. In contrast, large organizations often must overcome extensive bureaucratic procedures when adopting new products or new management operations. The bureaucratic procedures of large organizations slow down decision making, often leading to missed opportunities in the international marketplace.

Speed is therefore the small business advantage. When large companies are slow to react to rapidly changing conditions, fast-moving entrepreneurs can use their competitive advantage of speed. Being first to market, they can capture significant sales before the large competitors can react.[32] The small business advantage is particularly important for the multinational company because, increasingly, the global economy mandates rapid change to take advantage of new markets.

**Small business advantage**
Fast-moving entrepreneurs can use their competitive advantage of speed. Being first to market, they can capture significant sales before large competitors react.

## The Future: Falling Barriers to Multinational Small Businesses and More Global Start-Ups

Many of the barriers to small business internationalization are becoming easier to overcome. Government programs that support small business exporting and sales are expanding. High-impact trade agreements, such as NAFTA and the WTO, make trade less complex and reduce the resource requirements that previously held back many small firms. The rapid growth of international business information produced by governments and other sources, such as the World Wide Web, provides a wealth of readily available information to entrepreneurs regarding international opportunities. The Internet makes the world a click away. In turn, this knowledge of international business opportunities encourages more entrepreneurs to consider global start-ups and makes it easier for established small businesses to become multinationals. Consider the next Case in Point.

As the Case in Point shows, many support programs are available to help small businesses succeed. The resultant increase in the number of small businesses engaged in international activities will make it easier for other businesses to develop a global culture. Potential international entrepreneurs will not only have a better knowledge of business opportunities abroad but will also be able to copy the cultures of other successful small multinational companies. In addition, as managers gain experience in international business, negative attitudes among small business owners and entrepreneurs toward international sales will decrease.

Overall, therefore, going international should become easier for the small firm. In fact, many experts suggest that the only way a small firm can survive and grow is by going international. Consider that exporting, the first phase in internationalization, can bring several important long-term advantages for the small business.[33] Exporting allows the small firm to increase sales volumes and income, thereby providing much needed cash flow. More important, exporting allows the small firm to

CASE IN POINT

## The Start-Up Nation

In a book published in 2009, Senor and Singer called Israel a "start-up nation." Why this label? An examination of statistics shows that Israel has a very high rate of entrepreneurship. This entrepreneurial spirit has been facilitated by many factors. According to the World Bank "Doing Business" project, it is very easy to set up a business in Israel. In fact, Israel ranks 34 out of the 188 countries scored. However, there are a number of support factors that have facilitated this explosion of start-ups. First, advances in information technology have meant that people can buy computing power very cheaply if needed. In fact, Israel has a large number of technology start-ups and the relative ease of buying computing needs has favored such development. For example, smart phone apps designers can now easily rent server space without having to buy computing power. Second, both the government and local industries understand the importance of support for start-ups. Accelerator programs where entrepreneurs can be helped to shape their ideas and seek funding are accelerating. For instance, UpWestLabs has started a program to help new technology start-ups by providing seed money and also provide access to advisers and experts. Furthermore, UpWestLabs plans to bring about 5 to 10 of these Israeli start-ups to Silicon Valley for a 10-week training. Third, most countries see the lack of early stage venture capital as a significant barrier to growth. Therefore several funds were created with public money to provide financial assistance to start-ups. Finally, Israel is now hosting a large number of conferences aimed at aiding start-up. Consider the rapid-pitch events at the DLD conference in Tel Aviv, where 30 entrepreneurs had five minutes each to present their start-up companies to experts and potential investors. More than 300 companies applied for the 30 spots and the chosen companies receive very good advice and funding.

*Source: Based on* Economist. 2012. *"What next for the start-up nation?" January 21, 69–70.*

better understand global markets through contact with new cultures and the development of new contacts. Such activities can help the small firm's future foray into new markets and its competitive advantage.

The next section provides a series of diagnostic questions that can help small business owners and managers make the internationalization decision. The section after that describes how small businesses can make the contacts with customers and potential partners necessary to succeed in foreign sales.

# When Should a Small Business Go International?

The small business must respond to many of the same questions as the large business does when considering multinational options. However, the limited number of products or services—and the limited resources—of most small firms make certain drivers of internationalization more important for them.

Affirmative answers to the following questions suggest that a small business is ready to become a multinational company:

- *Do we have a global product or service?* A global product or service can be sold worldwide with minimal changes for each country. Because small businesses seldom have the resources to adapt a product to local needs, producing a standard worldwide product makes globalization easier. As discussed in Chapter 6, if customers have similar needs or if customers seek a product or service from anywhere in the world, then an opportunity for globalization exists.[34]

- *Do we have the managerial, organizational, and financial resources to internationalize?* Internationalization, even with the more simple participation strategies, requires significant availability of financial and personnel resources. Exhibit 7.4 gives some of the questions concerning resource requirements that a small business needs to address.

- *Even if we do have the resources, are we willing to commit them and face the risks of internationalization?* Small company managers must view internationalization as they would start-up ventures. For the right company, with the right products, the eventual returns from a new international venture may exceed the investment and make the exposure to risk worthwhile. To seek the potential returns, managers must overcome the related psychological and cultural boundaries.

- *Is there a country in which we feel comfortable doing business?* Without the resources to understand the cultural and business practices in many countries, small business managers often first seek international opportunities in national cultures similar to their own.

- *Is there a profitable market for our product or service?* Even with good products or services, a key question focuses on which countries to enter. For example, research by managers at Ekkwill Tropical Fish Farm indicated that collecting fish was a popular hobby in many countries. One-third of its production now goes to markets in Asia, Latin America, Canada, and the West Indies.[35]

**EXHIBIT 7.4** Questions to Consider in the Small Business Decision to Go International

**Management Objectives**
- What is the reason for going international?
- How committed is top management to the internationalization decision?
- How quickly does management expect the internationalization effort to pay off?

**Management Experience and Resources**
- What in-house international expertise does the firm have (international sales experience, language capabilities, etc.)?
- Who will be responsible for the international organizational component of the company (e.g., export department)?
- How much senior management time should be allocated?
- What organizational structure is required?

**Production Capacity**
- How is the present capacity being used?
- Will international sales hurt domestic sales?
- What will be the cost of additional production at home or in a foreign location?
- What modifications of the product or service are required?

**Financial Capacity**
- What amount of capital can be committed to international production and marketing?
- What level of operating costs for international operations can be supported?
- What other financial requirements may compete with the internationalization efforts?

*Source: Adapted from U.S. Department of Commerce. 2012. Basic Guide to Exporting. Washington, D.C.: Government Printing Office.*

- *Which country should we enter?* A thorough strategic analysis is required. Firms need to identify potential threats and opportunities by country. For example, current and future demand for a product may vary by country. Each country also has different competitors and barriers to entry (e.g., tariffs, complex distribution systems). Exhibit 7.5 summarizes the steps that small businesses can follow to find customers abroad.

- *Do we have a unique product or service that is not easily copied by large multinational companies or local entrepreneurs?* Although small firms may have the advantage of speed to market, large multinationals may use their advantage of economies of scale to imitate an innovation, using a lower-priced product. To maintain their competitive advantage over large firms, small multinational companies must have rare (i.e., not easily copied) and valuable resources—factors that allow the company to produce a product or service valued by customers. These rare and valued resources may include technical superiority, innovation, or high quality.[36]

- *Do location advantages exist upstream in the value chain?* Internationalization of a small firm need not be just a downstream activity, such as marketing.

**EXHIBIT 7.5**    Steps in Picking a Foreign Market

1. **Screen potential markets:**
   - Get statistics that show the extent of the relevant products exported to or produced in potential countries.
   - Identify five to ten countries with large and fast-growing markets for the products. Examine the trends in the market in past years and in different economic circumstances.
   - Identify additional countries with small, newly emerging markets, which may provide first mover advantages.
   - Target three to five of the most promising markets. Mix established markets with emerging markets, depending on management's tolerance for risk.

2. **Assess targeted markets:**
   - Examine market trends for the company's products or services and for related products or services that could affect demand.
   - Identify demographic trends (e.g., income, age, education, population, etc.) that identify the users of the company's products or services.
   - Estimate the overall consumption of the product or service and the supply provided by foreign and domestic producers.
   - Identify sources of competition from domestic producers and other foreign competitors, including price, quality, features, and service.
   - Identify local channels of distribution.
   - Assess what modifications of the product or service are required.
   - Identify cultural differences that may influence participation strategies.
   - Identify any foreign barriers to exporting or other participation options (e.g., tariffs, limitations on percentage of ownership, home country export controls, etc.).
   - Identify any foreign or home country incentives to enter the market.

3. **Draw conclusions and make the choice.**

*Source: Adapted from U.S. Department of Commerce. 2012. Basic Guide to Exporting. Washington, D.C.: Government Printing Office.*

When there are advantages of lower cost or higher quality in supply or manufacturing, small multinational companies can seek the same location advantages available to large companies by sourcing raw materials or manufacturing in other countries.

- *Can we afford not to be a multinational?* Even for a small business, several factors may make becoming a multinational company necessary for survival. A shrinking home market may require a firm to internationalize to maintain sales revenue. Finding international sources of lower costs of raw material or production facilities may be necessary to match competitors' prices and to maintain profit margins. Small multinational companies may find the positive image of being a multinational firm necessary for attracting new customers and investors.

The next section reviews the participation strategies available to the small multinational company.

# Getting Connected to the International Market

## Participation Strategies

Small- and medium-sized multinational companies have the same participation options as do large firms, including exporting, licensing, joint ventures, and foreign direct investment. Usually, however, the small business turns to exporting as its major international participation strategy. For the small firm without knowledge of potential foreign customers or sufficient resources to set up an overseas sales office, indirect exporting makes the most sense. These firms use the services of ETCs or EMCs to get their products to the international market.

## Finding Customers and Partners

To go international, small businesses must find ways to reach their foreign customers, either by direct contact or by teaming up with foreign partners (distributors, joint venture partners, or licensees) who deal with the ultimate customers. As with large multinational companies, there is no set formula for finding partners or customers. Much depends on the nature of the product, the countries involved, and the nature and resources of the company. However, some standard techniques are readily available to small multinational companies. In this section, we show some of these common **customer contact techniques**.

**Customer contact techniques**
Trade shows, catalog expositions, international advertising agencies and consulting firms, government-sponsored trade missions, and direct contact.

- *Trade shows:* National and international trade shows give small businesses inexpensive mechanisms to contact potential customers or business partners. Trade shows give businesses the opportunity to set up displays of their products and to provide brochures and other documents that describe their product or service. Businesses may rent space at the shows individually or as part of a large group. The U.S. Commerce Department runs a virtual trade show, and the Web site offers constant access to U.S. suppliers and international buyers. The website shows product descriptions, photos, and videos.[37]

- *Catalog expositions:* Catalog expositions are similar to trade shows except that a business does not have its product or people at the show, but rather product catalogs, sales brochures, and other graphic presentations of a firm's goods or services. Some U.S. embassies and consulates provide catalog expositions for U.S. goods. Because a company need only send printed matter, catalog expositions provide a low-cost way of testing international markets.

- *International advertising agencies and consulting firms:* International advertising agencies and consulting firms have offices throughout the world, often with specialists in different products or services. International advertising agencies can provide advertising and promotional services geared to a particular national environment. Consulting firms often have a good knowledge of local regulations, competitors, and distribution channels, but a business that uses these services can expect to pay significant compensation. However, local market expertise and contacts may make the expenditure worthwhile.

- *Government-sponsored trade missions:* To foster growth in international trade, governments often sponsor trade missions, which represent companies or industries looking to open new markets in the countries visited. Host governments usually provide introductions to potential local sales representatives, distributors, and end users.

- *Direct contact:* Although the option is often more difficult and costly, small business entrepreneurs and managers can seek channel partners, joint venture partners, and end users directly. If the managers/entrepreneurs can find key intermediaries—that is, potential alliance partners or distributors—or can directly access potential customers, then direct contact may work best.

Beyond these methods, the Web also provides access to prospective customers. Consider the next Multinational Management Brief.

## Multinational Management **Brief**

### Using the Web to Find New Customers: Alibaba.com

Alibaba.com is a prominent Chinese website, positioning itself as the virtual intermediary between Chinese exporters and foreign buyers. It was founded in 1999 by Jack Ma, a former English teacher. He saw where the Chinese economy was headed and created Alibaba.com to take advantage of the related opportunities. Alibaba.com has grown rapidly and provides numerous services to its customers. Chinese users, which make up most of Alibaba.com's customer base, pay a service fee to have their products listed on their websites. Alibaba.com provides other assistance, such as photo displays or videos, and anyone in the world can access these products for a fee. As another important service, Alibaba.com supplies product listings and translation services to foreign customers interested in importing from China. For a fee, foreign buyers can view product listings and decide which company they want to do business with. Alibaba.com thus provides a very efficient way to meet new customers. Rather than attending trade shows in China or using an actual intermediary, firms can use the Web service, which provides a very efficient and quick way to find new suppliers and customers. While Alibaba.com has enjoyed tremendous growth, more recent trends suggest that it is facing increased competition from companies such as Google and the Chinese equivalent, known as Baidu.

*Sources: Based on Chao, L. 2009. "How Alibaba.com keeps growing." Wall Street Journal, April 24, 16; Economist. 2012. "So long, for now"; Alibaba.com. February 25, 78.*

*Australian Exporters:* Australianexporters.net is a searchable list of Australian exporters listing each company and its products, contacts, and size. The site also features an exporting guide.

*Busytrade:* A well-organized trade lead website that offers a large collection of trade leads, products, company listings, and trade show announcements.

*BRIC—Capital Goods for BRIC Buyers:* This is an online marketplace connecting Brazilian, Russian, Indian, and Chinese buyers with global suppliers. The intent is to facilitate trade between BRIC countries and international suppliers.

*ChinaBusinessWorld.com:* Listings of Chinese and foreign-based suppliers, buyers, and products, all classified into categories, as well as a listing of the most recent buying trade leads.

*Export.gov:* This site has a worldwide database about potential leads in any country or region and industry. Registration is required.

*Tradeinindia:* Dedicated to India, the site offers news briefs, country export-import opportunity listings, a bulletin board, and importer and exporter company directories.

*BuyKorea:* Offers free trade leads and customized tender notification service.

*MBEndi—African Trading Space:* This site is hosted by the premier African business information site. Posted trade inquiries can be searched by product and offer type.

*Nudeal:* A Canadian-based company that offers both local and international trade leads and company directory listings.

*OpenRussia:* Buy/sell offers from Russian companies, as well as information relating to customs clearance and the documents required for foreign trade activities.

*Taiwantrade:* An online trading hub designed for business-to-business contact for small and medium-size enterprises, with the aim of using the latest Web technology to link buyers and sellers around the world to conduct business online.

*Wbiz.net:* A trading place for exporters and importers featuring business offers, product listings, and company directories.

*Source: Michigan State University. http://globaledge.msu.edu/ibrd/. 2012. Used with permission.*

Exhibit 7.6 shows some of the sources on the World Wide Web that any multinational company can access to find trade leads.

## Ready to Go and Connected: A Synopsis

The preceding sections provided the diagnostic questions that small business owners can ask in order to decide when to take their businesses international. These questions focused first on whether a firm has the right products and adequate resources to go international. They then prompted entrepreneurs to consider the competition and the country environments where they hope to do business.

If the company is ready to go international and the foreign opportunities are attractive, then a variety of mechanisms are popular among small multinational businesses to make international contacts for customer and partners. The previous section reviewed many of the readily available sources. However, an enterprising small businessperson will find that many more sources exist and that detailed research *will* increase the likelihood of the international venture's success. Finding the right overseas partner may be the most crucial decision of all.

Even with the right company, the right product, and a potential customer, a small business needs a wedge to break into a new market. The next section shows how small businesses can use traditional entrepreneurial wedge strategies in starting and building an international venture.

# New Venture Strategies for Small Multinational Companies

New ventures, whether global start-ups or new international operations for an ongoing business, need some type of entry wedge to gain an initial position in a new market. Karl Vesper, the renowned expert on new ventures, defines the **entry wedge** as "a strategic competitive advantage for breaking into the established pattern of commercial activity."[38] This section examines how some of the common entrepreneurship entry wedges work for the small multinational business. The section also includes numerous examples of small businesses using entry wedges for their multinational activities.

## New Product or Service and First Mover Advantage

A basic entrepreneurial wedge strategy that focuses on being the first to introduce a new product or service is the **first mover advantage**,[39] whereby the entrepreneur moves quickly into a new venture and establishes the business before other firms can react. To succeed, the new product or service must be not only innovative but also comprehensive. "Comprehensive" means that the product must meet customer expectations in areas such as warranty, customer service, and expected components. Without a comprehensive introduction, the new product or service is easy for competitors to imitate.

**Technological leadership** provides the most common source of first mover advantage. The first company to use or introduce a new technology often has the best understanding of how to make a product, having done the initial research and development and having the greatest familiarity with the product's characteristics. Such firms can build on this knowledge to keep ahead of competition by using their head start to introduce new product developments and innovations.

Several other situations give first movers an advantage. They may have initial access to natural and social resources, such as mining rights and close relationships with research universities. The first movers can choose the best locations not only for raw materials but also for proximity to customers. Finally, and perhaps more important in international business, first movers can have the best access to social relationships. Social relationships lead to the personal contacts necessary to build effective channels of distribution and to trust and commitment from business partners and customers.

The final advantage of being first comes from **switching costs**, which a customer incurs in turning to a competitor's products. Customers become familiar with products, and they often invest time and effort learning to use them. For example, many people do not switch between Apple- and Windows-based computers because they already know one operating system. In addition, because of brand loyalty, many customers may not want to undergo the discomfort of switching to another brand of a product or service.

## Copycat Businesses

**Copycat businesses** follow the me-too strategy, adopting existing products or services. Competitive advantage comes from varying the nature of product or service characteristics or from how the company provides the product or service.[40] Successful copycats do not copy existing businesses identically. They find a niche or a

**Entry wedge**
Company's competitive advantage for breaking into the established pattern of commercial activity.

**First mover advantage**
That of the entrepreneur who moves quickly into a new venture and establishes the business before other companies can react.

**Technological leadership**
Being first to use or introduce a new technology.

**Switching costs**
Expenses incurred when a customer switches to a competitor's products.

**Copycat businesses**
Those following the me-too strategy, whereby they adopt existing strategies for providing products or services.

slight innovation to attract customers away from existing businesses. Sometimes the innovation can be as simple as a new location that is more convenient for customers. How can companies find their niche and follow a copycat strategy? Here are some suggestions to copycat successfully:[41]

- *Be the first to change to a new standard:* New standards of quality or internationally recognized specification standards offer powerful entry wedges for new competitors.

- *Go after the toughest customers:* Often established firms shy away from some customer groups. Customers who are very price- or quality-sensitive may constitute an opportunity for a niche market.

- *Play to minor differences in customer needs:* Established firms often ignore minor differences in customer needs and leave the door open to a competitor who will cater to such differences.

- *Transfer the location:* A business that works in one part of the country may work equally well in another part of a country, or in another country. The success of U.S. franchises like McDonald's throughout the world shows that this strategy is viable for creating a new business.

- *Become a dedicated supplier or distributor:* A dedicated supplier finds a firm that needs the vendor's goods or services and focuses all its efforts on that major customer. For example, a small firm in Washington State provides cargo containers for Boeing airplanes. This small company serves Boeing directly and sells indirectly to users of Boeing jets throughout the world.

- *Seek abandoned or ignored markets:* The major players in any industry do not always serve every market fully and well.

- *Acquire existing business:* Acquiring an existing business is a common startup strategy for small businesses in domestic markets, but opportunities also exist in foreign countries to acquire businesses. In particular, formerly state-controlled businesses in Eastern Europe provide potentially good acquisition targets for entrepreneurs from around the world.

As you may have realized, entrepreneurship plays a big role in small business creation. In the final section, we consider some key aspects of international entrepreneurship.

# International Entrepreneurship

An **entrepreneur** creates new ventures that seek profit and growth. An entrepreneur deals with the risk and uncertainty of new and untested business. **New ventures** exist when a company enters a new market, offers a new product or service, or introduces a new method, technology, or innovative use of raw materials. Risk results from new ventures because their possible outcomes, such as survival and profitability, are variable. Some companies survive and others die. Some companies make a profit and grow, and others remain small. Uncertainty results because the founder can never fully predict which outcome will befall the new company.[42]

**International entrepreneurship** refers to the "discovery, evaluation and exploitation of international market opportunities."[43] Why should an international management student be concerned about international entrepreneurship? Most experts consider entrepreneurship the driving force of all small businesses. Without the entrepreneurial spirit, few small businesses would exist anywhere in the

**Entrepreneur**
Someone who creates new ventures that seek profit and growth.

**New ventures**
Entering a new market; offering a new product or service; or introducing a new method, technology, or innovative use of raw materials.

**International entrepreneurship**
The discovery, evaluation, and exploitation of market opportunities.

world. If we want to fully understand the small businesses in any nation, we need to examine the level of entrepreneurship there. In any country, at some point the local entrepreneurs have to face the risk and uncertainty of starting up the business. Entrepreneurship is therefore the driver of innovation and economic development anywhere.[44] For instance, countries like the United States and the United Kingdom underwent rapid industrialization because their country context allowed entrepreneurial activities to flourish, not only creating new jobs but also generating new wealth and growth. Today, many individuals around the world are becoming entrepreneurs to solve social problems. Consider the next Case in Point.

Another important reason for understanding international entrepreneurship is the fact that many multinational firms rely on small businesses and their owners to do business when entering a new country. Small businesses can often provide critical products or services, thereby facilitating entry. Consider the challenges facing Handango when it entered the Japanese market.[45] Handango discovered that Japanese consumers do not use credit cards for purchases, and it had to partner with a local small business to provide alternative payment options for its Japanese consumers. Low, Henderson, and Weiler argue that entrepreneurs play a very important role in bringing new ideas and innovations to the marketplace;[46] so small businesses can assist multinational companies in developing or offering new

---

### CASE IN POINT

## Entrepreneurship and Doing Good

Entrepreneurship is drastically changing how philanthropy is viewed today. In fact, many people seek not only to make money by being entrepreneurial but also to solve social problems. Entrepreneurship plays an important role in the voluntary sector.

- Riders for Health was created in Africa when motorbike enthusiasts found that vehicles used by health care providers were not being properly maintained. The organization now helps to provide health care to more than 1 million individuals in inaccessible places, often using a motorbike.

- Shane Immelman was appalled to see that many poor school children in South Africa did not have desks. He invented a lap desk that provides a stable surface on the child's lap. By featuring advertisements on the laps, he has been able to supply the lap desks for free. However, better-off people have been buying them, and exports to other less developed countries have also started.

- Vinod Kapur's dream is to feed India's rural poor. He has therefore dedicated most of his life to breeding a "superchicken," and he has developed one that is resistant to disease, capable of

surviving on farm scrap, and strong enough to fight predators. Most importantly, the chicken provides twice as much meat and five times as many eggs as other breeds. Kapur has also built an important supply chain to make sure that the chickens are accessible to people.

- A group of Swedish students in Kenya have come up with a new method to manufacture sanitary pads. While female students in the developed world have taken such pads for granted, they can often be priced too high for female students in many African nations. As a result, because of the taboo and potential embarrassment associated with menstruation, these students often miss school. The Swedish team of students is using local plants to manufacture sanitary pads that are affordable to all.

*Sources: Based on* Business Week. *2012. "Social entrepreneurship: Why mentors matter." March 9, online edition;* Economist. *2009. "Saving the world." March 14, "Special Report on Entrepreneurship," 19–20; World Challenge. 2011. "Innovators across Africa drive down price of sanitary pads." http://www.theworld challenge.co.uk/down_to_business/news/read/85/Innovators_across_Africa_drive_down_cost_of_sanitary_pads.*

products. For example, Pixalert, a small Dublin-based company, developed innovative image recognition software that can alert a company when employees are viewing inappropriate pictures online.[47] Viewing inappropriate images on the job results in a significant drop in productivity and creates a potential corporate liability in the context of sexual harassment issues. Whereas traditional filters cannot detect images installed from flash drives or other means, such as instant-messaging, Pixalert's system can monitor any image viewing through image analysis.[48]

Understanding entrepreneurship in emerging markets is also critical. Consider the following Focus on Emerging Markets.

---

## **Focus** on Emerging Markets

### Entrepreneurship and Emerging Markets

Most emerging markets are now slowly liberalizing their economies and are becoming increasingly integrated into the global economy. In fact, the largest of the world's emerging economies now make up a third of the world's largest 25 economies. Furthermore, these economies are also growing three times faster than developed economies. However, despite such impressive growth, understanding of entrepreneurship in such emerging economies has remained limited. Most experts nevertheless agree that it is critical to understand entrepreneurship in such societies. Most of these countries will not be able to solely survive on large or governmental organizations. Many will need to rely on the entrepreneurial ingenuity of their citizens to maintain such growth.

A recent review of international entrepreneurship research provides some insights into what is currently known about entrepreneurship in emerging economies. A total of 88 studies were identified, covering emerging economies in Africa (e.g., South Africa, Ghana, Nigeria, etc.), East Asia and the Pacific (e.g., China, South Korea, Taiwan), Central and Eastern Europe (e.g., Poland, Hungary, Slovenia, etc.), Latin America (Costa Rica, Chile, etc.), and South Asia (e.g., India, Bangladesh, and Sri Lanka). The review centered on what was different from entrepreneurship research in developed markets as well as the determinants of entrepreneurship in these emerging markets.

The review revealed several interesting findings about entrepreneurship in emerging economies. First, most of the studies showed the importance of networks (social and organizational) in influencing the entrepreneurial process in emerging economies. Such findings are not surprising given that emerging economies often face institutional voids and other deficiencies where people cannot simply rely on institutions to ensure that things go as planned. A second key finding is that emerging market entrepreneurship research is more focused on individual entrepreneurial characteristics such as self-commitment, dynamism, and experience, rather than having the usual focus on firm or industry level characteristics when starting a new business. This suggests that individual desire to be entrepreneurs and overcome constraints is much more critical than other environmental factors when creating new businesses in emerging markets.

*Source: Based on Kiss, A. N., W. M. Danis, and S. T. Cavusgil. 2012. "International entrepreneurship research in emerging economies: A critical review and research agenda." Journal of Business Venturing, 27, 266–290.*

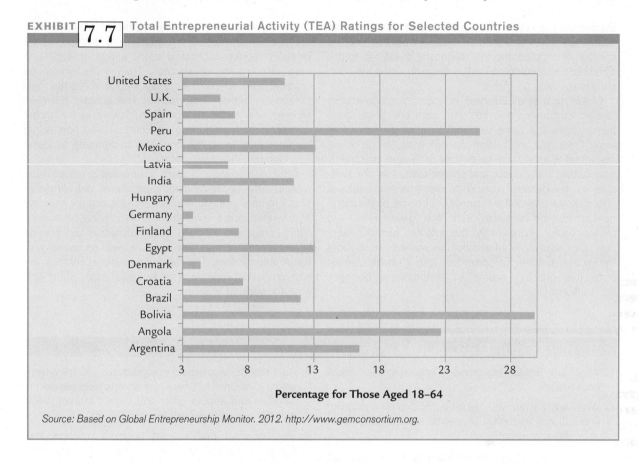

**Percentage for Those Aged 18–64**

*Source: Based on Global Entrepreneurship Monitor. 2012. http://www.gemconsortium.org.*

Finally, multinational companies may make location decisions based on how entrepreneurial a country's inhabitants are. In that context, Global Entrepreneurship Monitor (GEM) is an ongoing study of entrepreneurship activity around the world. The GEM research team has developed several measures of entrepreneurship and studies the cultural and institutional conditions supporting the driving forces of contemporary economies. Exhibit 7.7 shows the total entrepreneurial activity (TEA) ratings for selected countries.[49] The TEA represents the number of entrepreneurs (measured by start-ups) per 100 members of the population in a country.

## Summary and Conclusions

Small businesses are important to the economies of all nations. Often they provide the most jobs, the greatest economic growth, and the best innovation. Increasingly, small businesses must face the challenges of becoming multinational companies and entering the international marketplace. Small businesses do, however, encounter unique problems and prospects when entering global competition. In this chapter, we have extended the study of multinational and participation strategies to focus on situations with particular application to small multinational companies.

After defining the basic characteristics of a small business and of entrepreneurship, we reviewed the processes by which small businesses go international: through stages or through global start-ups. Increasingly, global start-ups are replacing stages of internationalization, especially for high-tech entrepreneurial companies in fast-changing industries.

A small business must overcome the traditional barriers to its internationalization. The chapter discussed how small businesses develop a global culture, change the attitudes of key decision makers, gain crucial international experience, and overcome size-related barriers. The chapter also presented the diagnostic questions that a small businessperson can ask in deciding when the company is ready to go global.

Crucial to a small business is finding ways to access foreign customers and business partners. Small businesses have the same participation strategy options as large firms, but they often do not have the in-house resources to identify or go directly to foreign customers. Fortunately, many public and private resources are available to businesses wishing to become multinational. This chapter provided an overview of some of the pertinent resources available from the government and private sector. Increasingly, the Internet provides easy and quick access to information on markets throughout the world. Exhibit 7.6 provided just a small sample from this growing source of multinational business information.

For the small business, entering the international market is an entrepreneurial venture, and entrepreneurial ventures require successful entry wedge strategies to have any chance of success. Traditionally, books on entrepreneurship consider entry wedge strategies only in terms of the domestic market. This chapter, however, showed how such strategies could work in the global marketplace. Several Cases in Point showed how actual entrepreneurs used the strategies to compete successfully with large international rivals.

A full appreciation of small businesses is not possible without also understanding international entrepreneurship. Entrepreneurship is important to a country because it generates jobs and wealth. It is also critical to multinational companies because small businesses can provide large companies with new ideas, as well as crucial products and services. The degree to which countries are entrepreneurial varies, and we looked at some of the reasons for such differences.

## Discussion Questions

1. Why are small businesses important for most economies?

2. What are the advantages of a small business going international through incremental stages rather than as a global start-up?

3. The Surftech Multinational Management Challenge showcased a successful global start-up. Discuss the conditions that made this strategy the correct choice.

4. Identify two or three small business barriers to internationalization. If you were a recently hired manager of a small business facing great opportunities in a foreign market, how would you go about overcoming these barriers?

5. As a recent business college graduate, you have been asked by a small business manager to help her decide whether she should enter the export market. What questions would you ask her and why?

6. Discuss ways that a small business manager can make the contacts necessary to implement an exporting strategy.

7. Consider three of the suggested strategic moves for copycat businesses. What additional difficulties will a company face in using these strategies in the international market as opposed to the domestic market?

8. What is international entrepreneurship? What benefits do international entrepreneurs bring to multinational companies?

## Multinational Management **Internet Exercise**

### The World Bank "Doing Business" Project

1. Go to the World Bank "Doing Business" project at http://www.doingbusiness.org and find the latest report on the ease of doing business worldwide. Which countries are on the top 10 list of ease of doing business? Which countries are on the bottom 10? What do the countries that rank highest have in common? What do those that rank lowest have in common?

2. What are the findings of the latest report of the "Ease of Doing Business" project? Is the world becoming

generally easier to start businesses? Which regions showed the most progress? Why?

3. Discuss each of the 10 factors used to compute the "Ease of Doing Business." Why are each of these factors included? Do you agree that each factor is equally important?

4. How can multinationals use the findings of the "Ease of Doing Business" project?

## Multinational Management **Skill Builder**

### Take a Product International

**Step 1.** Your instructor will divide the class into groups.

**Step 2.** Select an agricultural or industrial product produced in your region of the country. If possible, interview a small businessperson concerning his or her perspectives on the international opportunities for the company's product. In the United States, one way of finding a potential business owner is through the small business development centers attached to many U.S. universities. Your instructor may assign you a business or product.

**Step 3.** Using the steps shown in Exhibit 7.5 and information from World Wide Web sources (such as those in Exhibit 7.6) and your library, identify a foreign market or markets for the product or products.

**Step 4.** Using Web sources (such as those in Exhibit 7.6), identify potential trade shows, trading partners, or other intermediaries (e.g., ETCs) that would help you get the product to the international marketplace.

**Step 5.** Present your findings to your class, as well as to the small businessperson, if possible.

## *Endnotes*

1 Organization for Economic Cooperation and Development (OECD). 2002. *OECD Small and Medium Enterprise Outlook*. Paris: OECE Publication Services.

2 U.S. Small Business Administration. 2009. "Advocacy: The voice of small business in government." June. http://www.sba.gov/advo.

3 OECD.

4 Ibid.

5 Scarborough, Norman M., and Thomas W. Zimmer. 1996. *Effective Small Business Management*. Upper Saddle River, NJ: Prentice Hall.

6 Rialp, Alex, Josep Rialp, David Urbano, and Yancy Vaillant. 2005. "The born-global phenomenon: A comparative case study research." *Journal of International Entrepreneurship*, 3, 133–171.

7 Dollinger, Marc J. 1995. *Entrepreneurship*. Burr Ridge, IL: Irwin.

8 Vapola, T. J., P. Tossavainen, and M. Gabrielsson. 2008. "The battleship strategy: The complementing roles of born globals in MNC's new opportunity creation." *Journal of International Entrepreneurship*, 6, 1–21.

9 Ibid.

10 U.S. Small Business Administration. 1999. *E-Commerce: Small Businesses Venture Online*. Washington, D.C.: Government Printing Office.

11 Ibid.

12 Caprioni, Paula J., Stefanie Ann Lenway, and Thomas P. Murtha. 1994. "Understanding internationalization: Sense-making process in multinational corporations." In Tamir Agmon and Richard Drobnick, eds. *Small Firms in Global Competition*, New York: Oxford University Press, 27–36.

13 Dichtl, Drwin, Hans-Georg Koeglmayr, and Stefan Mueller. 1990. "International orientation as a precondition for export success." *Journal of International Business Studies*, 1st quarter, 23–40.

14 Freeman, Susan, and Imogen Reid. 2006. "Constraints facing small western firms in transitional markets." *European Business Review*, 18 (3): 187–213.

15 Ibid.

16 Rialp et al.

17 Calof, Jonathan L., and Wilma Viviers. 1995. "Internationalization behavior of small- and medium-sized South African enterprises." *Journal of Small Business Management*, October, 71–79; Miesenbock, Kurt J. 1988. "Small business and internationalization: A literature review." *International Small Business Journal*, 6, 42–61.

18 Oviatt and McDougall.

19 Dalin, Shera. 2005. "Owning a business isn't a 9-to-5 job." *St. Louis Post-Dispatch*, October 30, E6.

20 Wright, Phillip C. 1993. "The personal and the personnel adjustments and costs to small businesses entering the international market place." *Journal of Small Business Management*, January, 83–93.

21 Beamish P. W., and H. J. Munro. 1987. "Exporting for success as a small Canadian manufacturer." *Journal of Small Business and Entrepreneurship*, 4, 38–43.

22 Wright.

23 Ibid.

24 Bonacorsi, Andrea. 1992. "On the relationships between firm size and export intensity." *Journal of International Business Studies*, 4th quarter, 605–633.

25 Freeman and Reid.

26 Bonacorsi.

27 Christensen, C., Angela da Rocha, and Rosane Gertner. 1987. "An empirical investigation of the factors influencing export success of Brazilian firms." *Journal of International Business Studies*, Fall, 61–78.

28 Calof, Jonathan L. 1993. "The impact of size on internationalization." *Journal of Small Business Management*, October, 60–69.

29 Lu, Jane W., and Paul W. Beamish. 2006. "Partnering strategies and performance of SMEs' international joint ventures." *Journal of Business Venturing*, 21, 461–486.

30 Calof.

31 Bonacorsi.

32 Scarborough and Zimmer.

33 Hilton, Gregory. 2005. "Knocking down export barriers to smaller firms." *Business and Economic Review*, July–September, 51(4): 18–20.

34 Yip, George S. 2001. *Total Global Strategy*. Englewood Cliffs, NJ: Prentice Hall.

35 Knowlton, Christopher. 1988. "The new export entrepreneurs." *Fortune*, June, 6, 98.

36 Barney, J. B. 1991. "Firm resources and sustained competitive advantage." *Journal of Management*, 17, 99–120.

37 Barry, Doug. 2000. "From Appalachia to India: U.S. small businesses are going global." *Business Credit*, 102(6): 49–50.

38 Vesper. Karl M. 1980. *New Venture Strategies*. Englewood Cliffs, NJ: Prentice Hall.

39 Dollinger.

40 Vesper.

41 Dollinger.

42 Ibid.

43 Baker, Ted, Eric Gedajlovic, and Michel Lubatkin. 2005. "A framework for comparing entrepreneurship processes across nations." *Journal of International Business Studies*, 36, 492–504.

44 Busenitz, Lowell W., Carolina Gomez, and Jennifer W. Spence. 2000. "Country institutional profiles: Unlocking entrepreneurial phenomena." *Academy of Management Journal*, October, 43(5): 994–1003.

45 Bright, Beckey. 2005. "How do you say 'Web'? Planning to take your online business international? Beware; E-commerce can get lost in translation." *Wall Street Journal*, May 23, R11.

46 Low, Sarah, Jason Henderson, and Stephan Weiler. 2005. "Gauging a region's entrepreneurial potential." *Economic Review–Federal Reserve Bank of Kansas City*, 3rd quarter, 90(3): 61–89.

47 Hosford, Christopher. 2006. "Selling strategies for small business." *Sales and Marketing Management*, April, 158(3): 30–33.

48 Ibid.

49 Minniti, Maria, William D. Bygrave, and Erkko Autio. 2005. "Global Entrepreneurship Monitor 2005 Executive Report." *GEM*, 1–67.

# Aregak Micro-Credit Organization in Armenia

Mariam Yesayan, executive director of Aregak Micro-Credit, crossed Yerevan's Republic Square, walked a few steps down Abovyan Street, and turned in at Arami Street, heading toward her office next to the Georgian Embassy. She reviewed in her mind the events of the last nine years since she had launched Aregak to provide small loans to low-income women in several small villages in Armenia. The loans were designed to assist them in starting up small entrepreneurial ventures. The nongovernmental organization (or NGO, the term often used to describe nonprofit organizations internationally) had met all of her expectations, but it was now 2006 and she knew she must decide whether to remain an NGO or apply to the Armenian government to be a licensed and regulated for-profit organization.

## Background on Mariam Yesayan

Mariam Yesayan was a native Armenian who grew up in Yerevan, the capital of Armenia. Mariam was well-educated, having received her education in the Armenian public school system as well as attending Yerevan State University where she got a degree in education. She also studied at the Gorki Institute of World Literature in Moscow, and received a degree in journalism. As was required during Soviet times, Mariam started working immediately. At the age of 21, she was well on her way—touching lives in Armenia. That year she began teaching at the Yerevan State University.

It was not until the collapse of the Soviet Union that NGOs started arriving in Armenia. The first two that Mariam worked for were ASDI/VOCA (Agency for Promoting Sustainable Development Initiatives) and the Save the Children organization. The main purpose of ASDI was to educate and train individuals so that they could make a living for themselves. Save the Children was worldwide, and Mariam worked for them in many different areas of Armenia. The organization strived to create short-term employment for families with the help of community involvement.

After ten years of working for the same NGO, Mariam felt she needed a radical change in her career. She yearned for more practical work and more benefits for her family, so she began the search for a position that would help her meet those needs. Her quest ultimately led to her changing jobs every two years until she found one to her satisfaction. The jobs she had all dealt with U.S./AID programs and community development. Along the way, Mariam worked with companies like the World Bank and UMCOR (United Methodist Committee on Relief), which was the parent of the organization that she would later initiate.

## Aregak Micro-Credit Organization

In 1996, Mariam Yesayan began working for UMCOR in Armenia. By the fall of 1997, she had established the Aregak Micro-Credit Organization to provide small loans to economically challenged women in three small villages north of Yerevan.

Her rationale in beginning this program was to supplant the aid programs that came into Armenia after the collapse of communism, which had become permanent handouts. Many of these programs, Mariam believed, made the people dependent in the long term, and psychologically vulnerable. She believed that it was important to the self-worth of individual women to be empowered to become self-sustaining.

Armenians at this time were very depressed because of the earthquake of 1988 that killed 28,000 people and left many more homeless; by the embargo by Turkey and Azerbaijan, which stopped the flow of all oil and gas supplies into the country; and by the unemployment rate, which had reached 80 percent shortly after the fall of communism.[1] After the earthquake, there was no electricity throughout the country for a long period of time, leaving the people in darkness and heightening their sense of being cut off from the rest of the world.

In her earlier work with the United Nations, Mariam had done research on sustainable projects to support vulnerable population groups, and this was her first acquaintance with microfinance programs. Bank loans at this time were neither accessible nor affordable.

***The Process for Developing Clients*** Mariam began the organization by applying for loans from UMCOR to fund small loans to prospective women entrepreneurs. She got three people to help her, and they all drove up to three small villages north of Yerevan.

To make the women feel comfortable, they wore some of their oldest clothes and began conversations with the women to try to change their attitude about being dependent on other people or aid agencies. They found that the best way to meet large groups of women in these villages was to show up at someone's business or home who had a television set and had women crowded around it, watching Brazilian or American soap operas such as *Santa Barbara*. In these places, they knew they had a captive audience.

The psychological work with clients at this stage of development was important because the people faced depression about the high unemployment rate in the country, and they believed there was no longer light at the end of the tunnel—unless it was a train barreling toward them. The large Armenian eyes all looked vacant and without hope. Mariam and her coworkers began to talk to the women about developing small, sustainable businesses with the money Aregak would lend them. They were attempting to promote self-confidence and a belief in personal success among the women. Mariam would say to the women, "We can create opportunities together." Soon the women began to believe and filled out the papers to apply for a loan.

When the women began to ask about what they would have to put up as collateral for the loan, Mariam replied that they would not need collateral; their own good name and character would be the only collateral they needed. One client said to Mariam, "If I use my car as collateral for a bank loan and I can't pay the loan back, I may lose my car, but I can do without it for a while and finally get another one. But if I lose my good character by not paying back the Aregak loan, I can never get that back." The loans were negotiated at an interest rate between 20 and 25 percent, which was consistent with bank loan rates at the time.

***Outcome of the Program*** Mariam could hardly wait for a month to pass until the time arrived for her and her coworkers to return to the villages where they had given loans to the women to collect the portion of the principal and interest that was due. She wondered how many would be there to pay on their loans, so she arrived two hours early and waited. To her great joy, all of the women who had received loans came on time to repay that month's portion. Mariam would later discover that the default on the Aregak loans was only 2 percent over the entire nine years of operation. This

was encouraging because the people to whom Aregak had made loans did not have to pledge any collateral for their credit.

Soon Aregak began offering assistance with business planning and credit consulting, which were programs that Armenian banks could not offer at that time. By 2006, the number of employees at Aregak had increased to 180; there were 27 service centers in Armenia and Nagorno Karabakh (a piece of Armenia cut off in Ajerbaijan); Aregak had developed over 21,000 clients (mostly but not exclusively women), they had over $9 million in their outstanding portfolio of loans, over 450 communities were being served, and approximately 35 scholarships of $350 each were being offered to talented children of the entrepreneurs they had funded.

## Alternative Sources of Financing in Armenia

In the early 1990s in Armenia, there was a crisis in the banking sector. This was shortly after the time that the state bank had been abolished and private commercial banks were being established. The newly privatized banking sector was still underdeveloped and fragile. Because many citizens had been financially hurt by the failure of the Soviet banking system and a later currency collapse, they were mistrustful of all lending institutions. In addition, many of the private citizens who established commercial banks did not know how to give loans, and the people did not know how to apply for them.

Only in the late 1990s did banks start to operate independently and give loans, but they were still charging very high interest rates. In the late 1990s, banks were charging 40 percent interest per year. By early 2003, the rate had dropped to 24 percent, and then by October of 2003 it had finally dropped to 20 percent per year.

In addition to high interest rates, individuals and companies who applied for bank loans were required to secure the loans with collateral. They might have to pledge their house or car to secure the financing for their business. This meant that they could lose these valuable assets if they defaulted on their loans. It was very difficult for an Armenian man to get a bank loan at this time, and it was almost impossible for a woman who possessed few assets.

By 2003, more than half of the private capital of Armenian banks belonged to foreign investors, and this percentage continued to increase. This trend indicated that the Union of Armenian Banks was becoming a regional financial center. Armenian financial legislation also assisted in the process by no longer hindering currency circulation inside and outside the country, and there was no limitation on the free sale of currency. The downside was that domestic as well as foreign money was going abroad because it was difficult to make investments in such a risky country as Armenia had become.

## The Microfinance Industry

Microfinance is said to have evolved as an economic development approach intended to benefit low-income women and men. Included in microfinance are both financial and social improvements. Many industries provide education in financial literacy to their clients, training and investing in client confidence development, and teaching on entrepreneurship and management techniques. Thus "microfinance is not simply banking, it is a development tool."[2]

Although the exact number of microfinance institutions remains a mystery, researchers are able to conclude that the number of such institutions in the early years of the twenty-first century was in the thousands, if not millions. In 2005, there were more than 600,000 institutions in Indonesia alone.[3] The Microcredit Summit Campaign (MCS) annually published a collection of data, providing an analysis on the current position of the microfinance fight against poverty. According to the Microcredit Summit Campaign Report of 2005, 3,164 microcredit institutions were reported to be serving over 92 million clients, the majority of which lived in Asia. Of those 92 million, nearly 67 million were among the world's poorest populations when they took their first loan. The poorest population was defined by the MCS as "those who are in the bottom half of those living below their nation's poverty line, or any of the 1.2 billion [people] who live on less than US$1 a day adjusted for purchasing power parity (PPP)."[4] As of 2004, it was estimated that approximately 333 million people were indirectly affected by the microfinance loans made to some of the world's poorest populations, a number equivalent to the combined populations of Norway, the United Kingdom, Switzerland, the Netherlands, Spain, France, Germany, and Italy.[5] Some of the largest and most developed microfinance programs included the Grameen Bank, ACCION, FINCA, Opportunity International, and PreCredit.[6]

The Consultative Group to Assist the Poor (CGAP), a donor consortium connected with the World Bank, said that in 2004 large development aid agencies promised about $1 billion to the microfinance industry. Additionally, many large amounts were provided by private donors. Other costs, such as technical support, were generally sought after at low or even zero cost (*The Economist*, November 2005).[7] Typically, donors focused their support on microfinance institutions with goals to achieve financial sustainability and strong outreach. The industry began in the 1980s and has grown significantly in revenue, market share, and client population.

Remaining steady amid industry changes, however, clients continued to invest newly acquired funds and previously established talents into new trades. Clients could be found in both rural and urban areas, in both developed and developing countries. Generally, clients were self-employed, with work ranging from farming to cutting hair, repairing shoes to sewing handbags, street vending to craft making. Seeking to avoid government regulations and stipulations, many microfinance institutions have remained self-regulated, nonprofit organizations in an effort to remain versatile. Their mission has been to show seemingly hopeless people that someone believed in them. For Mariam Yesayan and Aregak, this mission had been the source of motivation for service to their clients—far beyond profit or recognition. Often it was this simple confidence lenders received that made them successful in doing something for which they had great talent. However, many struggling institutions have been forced to seek funding from the government, despite the fact that this put them at risk of being regulated. This was one of the difficult decisions Aregak faced.

***Industry Service: Women and Men*** More than 66 million people among the world's poorest have been served by a microfinance institution. Of those, nearly 56 million were women—a total of 83.5 percent. Microcredit programs have generally marketed their services to female entrepreneurs. One reason for this has been that men in developing countries, or even developed countries, have been more likely to find employment without third-party assistance. Some organizations, such as Pro Mujer, are solely "dedicated to women's development through provision of credit."[8] However, many institutions have also offered loans and financial assistance to men, even in developed nations such as the United States.

***NGOs and For-Profit Operations*** Many nongovernmental organizations (NGO) specializing in microfinance have been faced with a major decision: to seek government funding and be subject to its regulations or to forego state assistance and remain self-regulating. Some organizations have remained nonprofit, while others have chosen to become for-profit entities. In some cases, a nation's government has required all microfinance institutions in that country to become regulated for-profit entities. In nations where this is not a requirement (such as Armenia), organizations have still chosen to exchange their non-governmental status for any or several reasons. The first such reason was the opportunity to mobilize savings. Most unregulated nongovernmental microfinance institutions around the world and in the United States have been unable to collect savings in order to prevent consumers from fraudulent activity. Second, most regulated microcredit programs have been able to tap into formal capital markets, including commercial banks and global investment funds, which normally would not contribute to unregulated or nongovernmental microcredit institutions. Finally, submitting to the government's operational regulations supported governmental efforts to prevent scamming and poorly practiced programs from developing.

Government restrictions against NGOs typically included, but were not limited to, laws against nonprofits conducting financial transactions or a requirement for all money lending agencies to be state owned. The controlling officials have indirectly chosen to change the mission of the organization from a service-oriented enterprise into a for-profit firm. Whether an organization became government regulated or not determined the path of the organization.

***Microfinance in Developed Countries versus Developing Countries*** Microfinance institutions' market in developed nations has been fairly substantial. The Microcredit Summit Report 2005 stated that 3,044 microcredit programs reported doing work in the developing world, serving a total of more than 92 million clients. The 120 institutions that reported work in the industrialized, developed world claimed to reach almost 233,000 people. Armenia fell into the "Europe and NIS (Newly Independent States)" category, which was said to have 72 programs at work. According to Microcredit Summit Campaign Report 2005 statistics, approximately 3.5 million of the world's poorest families lived within Europe and the Newly Independent States, yet only 60,000 of these families were reached by microcredit projects. In other words, as of 2005, only 1.7 percent of the poorest families living in Europe and the Newly Independent States, including Armenia, had been reached by established microfinance institutions.[9] According to Mariam Yesayan, Aregak controlled about half of Armenia's microfinance market, reaching about 10,000 clients.

## The Decision

Mariam Yesayan walked past the Georgian Embassy next to her office and entered Aregak's headquarters at 42 Arami Street. She waved to the person sitting at the reception desk on the right and then began climbing the stairs on the left to the third floor. After reaching her office, she put the materials she had worked on at home down on her desk and sat in her desk chair. She immediately continued the thoughts she had begun while walking across Republic Square. She knew she must decide soon whether to let Aregak retain the status it had held as a nonprofit organization for the past nine years, or file papers to let it become a for-profit organization regulated by the government. She knew the decision was important because it would shape the strategy of the organization in the future.

### CASE DISCUSSION QUESTIONS

1. Summarize the process Mariam Yesayan used in approaching women about loan opportunities through Aregak.
2. Compare opportunities for funding for women entrepreneurs through the commercial banking system in Armenia with funding opportunities available to them through the Aregak program in the late 1990s.
3. Explain the reason for a default rate on loans of only 2 percent with Aregak in spite of the fact that the loans were not collaterized.
4. Discuss the importance of microfinance programs in the progress of developing nations.
5. In what way might Mariam Yesayan be considered a "social entrepreneur"?
6. Debate the issue of whether Mariam Yesayan should take steps to license Aregak as a nonprofit organization in Armenia, which would bring with it regulation by the government, or remain an NGO (nongovernmental organization) as it had been originally structured.

### CASE NOTES

[1] Benedetto, Joe. 2002. "Where will the jobs be?" *Design Engineering*, April, 48(3): 14.

[2] Ledgerwood, J. 1999. *Microfinance Handbook: An Institutional and Financial Perspective*. Washington, D.C.: World Bank.

[3] Daley-Harris, S. (2005). Microcredit Summit Campaign Report 2005. http://www.microcreditsummit.org.

[4] Ibid.

[5] Ibid.

[6] *Economist*. 2005. "The hidden wealth of the poor: A survey of microfinance," and "From Charity to Business."

[7] Ibid.

[8] Pro Mujer. http://www.promujer.org.

[9] Daley-Harris.

# Tata Motors

Professor Prashant Salwan, Indian Institute of Management - Indore

## Introduction

Economically lower-class Indians felt empowered when they walked into a Tata Motors (TML) showroom in Mumbai, India, on April 21, 2009, and reserved their first family car for Rs 1,00,000 (US $2,000). In that month, India was under the spell of two global influencing acts. The first was the holding of general elections in which the world's largest democracy was going to the polls. The second was the first day on which the world's cheapest car was available for purchase. No one had thought it possible to sell a car with all the required safety features and design for just under US $2,000. Tata Motors, a company that changed the basic automotive business model, had products ranging from the costliest—Jaguar and Land Rover—to the world's cheapest car, the Nano. Tata Motors is the only automobile company in the world offering products ranging all the way from the smallest car to the luxury segment.

The success of Tata Motors lies in its international growth strategy (Appendix I), "to consolidate position in the domestic market and expand international footprint through development of new products by:

* Leveraging in-house capabilities.
* Acquisitions and strategic collaborations to gain complementary capabilities."

In 2009, Tata Motors had operations in 35 countries around the world (Exhibit 1), and it was on the 100 New Global Challengers list released by Boston Consulting

---

### Appendix I  Growth Strategy of TML

1984 : India's first LCV (407 truck)

1996 : India's first SUV (Safari)

1998 : India's first passenger car—Indica

2004 : Acquisition of Tata Daewoo, Korea

2005 : India's first mini-truck (Ace)

2005 : Acquisition of stake in Hispano, Spain

2007 : Formed an industrial JV with Fiat

2007 : JV in India with Marcopolo of Brazil

2007 : JV in Thailand with Thonburi

2008 : People's car—Tata Nano

2008 : Acquisition of Jaguar Land Rover

**EXHIBIT 1** International Markets for Tata Motors

| Passenger Vehicle International Markets | Commercial Vehicle International Markets |
| --- | --- |
| Venezuela | Chile |
| Senegal | Algeria |
| Ghana | Nigeria |
| Congo | Ghana |
| South Africa | Zambia |
| Ethiopia | Angola |
| Tanzania | Mozambique |
| Kenya | Uganda |
| Russia | Mauritius |
| Ukraine | Australia |
| Spain | Turkey |
| Italy | Egypt |
| Poland | Russia |
| Turkey | Ukraine |
| SAARC | Spain |
| Thailand | Italy |
| Malaysia | Poland |
| Middle East | SAARC |
| | Thailand |
| | Malaysia |
| | Middle East |
| | Senegal |
| | Ghana |
| | Congo |
| | South Africa |
| | Ethiopia |
| | Tanzania |
| | Kenya |

Group. TML became the largest player in the 8-ton heavy truck segment in South Africa and the second-largest player in the 2- to 4-ton segment in South Africa. TML is the largest player in light buses and the second-largest in light trucks. The story of global expansion of Tata Motors started in 2004.

# Domestic Economy

The Indian economy in the year 2004 had a growth rate of 8.0 percent. Indian gross domestic product (GDP) grew by 4.4 percent in fiscal year (FY) 2001, by 5.8 percent in FY 2002, and by 4.3 percent in FY 2003, with an expected future growth rate of 7.0 percent in FY 2005, 9 percent in 2006, and 11 percent in 2007. However, according to Goldman Sachs, India will have the highest growth rate in GDP in comparison with other emerging economies until 2045–2050.

## Governmental Initiation

The government of India in the years 2002–2003 invested heavily in infrastructure, implementing the following six-point strategy:

1. Strengthening and four-laning of high-density corridors.

2. Golden Quadrilateral (5,846 kilometers).

3. NSEW Corridor (7,300 kilometers).

4. Road connectivity to major ports.

5. Private sector participation in financing construction and maintenance.

6. Improvement, maintenance, and augmentation of the existing national high-ways network.

This investment was expected to enhance commercial vehicle penetration in India. Furthermore, in 2008, India became the:

• Second-largest two-wheeler market in the world.

• Fourth-largest commercial vehicle market in the world.

• Eleventh-largest passenger car market in the world and is expected to be the seventh-largest market by 2016.

## Demographic Shift in India

It was expected that by 2009, 60 percent of India's population would be 25 years of age and less. The consumption of food and beverage, which was 62.5 percent in the years 1970–1971, came down to 44.5 percent in 2001 and was trending toward further reductions. The consumption of transportation was 2.8 percent in the years 1970–1971 and grew to 13.5 percent in the year 2000–2001. The increasing per-capita disposable income is leading to a subsequent decline in the proportion of spending on basic necessities and an increasing proportion on transportation. Transportation became the second-largest spending category in 2002.

## Domestic Automobile Industry

According to Goldman Sachs' BRIC Team, there will be a significant increase in the middle-class population in India, coupled with an increase in per-capita GDP (in terms of purchasing power parity, PPP), and the team expects India to hit the "sweet spot of car ownership" between 2015 and 2025.

These structural changes have totally altered the commercial vehicle market; there will be a structural shift toward heavy commercial vehicles (HCV). The demand for buses will increase substantially, especially for large, luxury buses.

# International Automobile Market

## Global Automobile Trends

International automobile markets are at crossroads. Factors like consumer prefer-ences, competitive dynamics, the cyclical nature of product design, environmental factors, and regionalism are all factors affecting the global strategy of automobile giants.

Motorization and population increases are the two most influential factors in automakers' strategic product management. In countries where population is increasing but motorization is saturated, auto companies have to consolidate their present position as well as launch new products to attract new, young customers. In areas where both factors are increasing, they have to invest in services, supply chain, and new product launches.

In the United States, Western Europe, Japan, and South Korea, there was an average sales reduction of 20 percent from 2007 to 2009. The sales growth was unaffected in China but grew in India and Eastern Europe.

The global automobile industry is varied not only in strategic orientation but also in customer preferences. For example, for an American automaker, styling means boxiness, a large nose/deck, and an emphasis on size. For a European, it can mean roundness, a short nose/deck, and emphasis on aerodynamics and space efficiency. The engine body, from an American point of view, will be large and powerful engine, a heavy body with slow response. For a Japanese car, the engine can be small, with a light body; the emphasis is on fuel economy and sharp response. In terms of value added, a European wants total balance, while the Japanese want options and many features as standard equipment. The overall image for an American vehicle is that of an all-purpose road cruiser—large, comfortable, powerful; for a European the automobile is a driving machine—responsive, precise, sophisticated.

The automobile companies make more profit in selling luxury cars rather than in selling small cars. The revenue shares for participants in the automobile value chain are as follows: suppliers have a 60 percent share of the recommended retail price, assemblers have 10 percent, marketing logistics another 10 percent, and dealers 20 percent. Vehicle manufacturers in mature markets derive about 20 percent of revenues and 40 percent of operating profits from sales of spare parts.

# Tata Group

Tata Group has been one of the largest and most respected industrial houses of India, with a pioneering track record over 130 years. In FY 2004 Tata Group had over 80 companies with leadership presence in most of the sectors. Its revenues were approximately Rs 615 billion (US $13.4 billion, equivalent to 2.6 percent of India's GDP at current prices), and its net profit was Rs 57 billion (US $1.3 billion).

## Tata Motors

In 2004, Tata Motors was India's largest automotive company in terms of revenue. Tata Motors was the market leader in commercial vehicles and the second-largest player in passenger vehicles. In 1954, it began manufacturing vehicles. The firm has demonstrated very strong R&D skill sets with the capability of developing vehicle platforms indigenously at a relatively low cost. In 2003, Tata Motors had three manufacturing facilities, in Jamshedpur, Pune, and Lucknow. In 2004, it acquired Daewoo Motors and added the Gunsan plant in South Korea, its first outside India. It had the widest range of product offerings in the Indian market, consisting of commercial vehicles, multiutility vehicles, and passenger cars.

## International Business Initiatives by Tata Motors in 2004

In 2004, exports were 15 percent of revenues, and Tata Motors made a target of increasing the exports by 20 percent in 2006.

Ravi Kanth, Managing Director TML, thought that the best strategy for Tata Motors was focused positioning and marketing in selected countries.

- *South Africa:* The market was 360,000 units annually and was comprised of passenger cars and pickup trucks. Tata Motors positioned itself as a seller of a "value for money" product there. The production plan was to make the products in India and ship them to South Africa in 2005. The initial target was 2,000 or more by the third quarter of that year.

- *Sri Lanka:* The commercial vehicle volume was approximately 13,800, primarily medium to heavy commercial vehicles (MHCVs) and light commercial vehicles (LCVs). The competition in Sri Lanka was from secondhand imports of Japanese vehicles. Tata Motors had to cut the Japanese market in Sri Lanka. The plan was to export around 700 vehicles in the third quarter of 2005 and approximately 1,800 units in 2005.

- *Russia and East Europe:* Targeting the LCV truck market in Russia, Tata Motors started operations in 2004 in the Ukraine through bus assembly.

Tata Motors replicated these strategies in other key markets of Southeast and South Asia, Southern Europe, the Middle East, and Africa.

## Organic Growth Strategies of Tata Motors

To develop and sustain a competitive advantage, Tata Motors developed a two-pronged strategy. First, it expanded its capacity. In 2004, the utilization was around 75 percent for commercial vehicles (CVs) and utility vehicles (UVs), and 100 percent for the Indica plant, which made passenger cars (PCs). Indica's PC capacity was expanded by 50 percent by the end of 2005. In the same year, CV capacity was expanded and new products were developed (small pickups and intercity and intra-city buses). By 2006–2007, new platforms had been created for global trucks, a new utility vehicle, and compact cars. For the people's car, there were new engine offerings and commensurate expansion in R&D capability. The goal was for expansion into new markets and product categories, both domestically and internationally.

## Inorganic Growth Planning of Tata Motors in 2004

Tata Motor's philosophy of inorganic growth was as follows:

- Acquiring an international company for (a) access to markets, (b) access to new technology and R&D capability, and (c) growth in international business.
- Marketing tie-ins for (a) distribution and (b) cobranding.
- Asset purchases for (a) new products, (b) new technology, and (c) new capacities.
- Strategic alliances for (a) product swaps and (b) R&D alliances.

There were further challenges for Tata Motors, such as cost pressures on input materials like steel, engineering plastics, aluminum, copper, and so on. As of April 2005, the company also felt the impact of emission compliance measures. Eleven cities in India have migrated to Euro III, while the rest of the country will migrate to Euro II emission norms. The cost of meeting the emission standards may lead to an increase in price, leading to sluggish demand conditions in 2006. Fuel price increases are also a factor.

Furthermore, the automotive business model was changing. Automobile manufacturers were making money not only by selling cars but also by maintaining them and selling accessories.

Tata Motors acquired Daewoo Commercial Vehicle Co. (DWCV) of Korea and made it a 100 percent subsidiary on March 30, 2004. The HCV was a product segment of DWCV and a complementary product for Tata. The acquisition gave Tata access to assembly technology for high-end trucks, the potential for leading the domestic market in high-end trucks, and an entry to the South Korea market for medium and intermediate commercial vehicles. Tata had a market share of 25 percent as well as an additional annual production capacity of 20,000 units. The purchase was a very profitable venture, earning Tata US $5.4 million on a turnover of US $222 million in fiscal year 2003 on a 21 percent of Daewoo's capacity utilization.

## Positioning of Tata Motors in the Global Markets

Ravi Kanth, Tata's Managing Director, had to decide on a positioning strategy for Tata Motors in the global markets. Tata Motors aspired to be among the top global manufacturers in the product group of medium and heavy trucks. In pickup trucks, Tata had to establish a presence in the global segment and couple that with a high domestic demand potential. Tata also targeted the niche global markets in the compact car segment.

## Enhancing Capabilities: Partnering with World-Class Players

Tata Motors is no stranger to global partnering:

1. In a joint venture with Marcopolo (Tata Motors, 51 percent; Marcopolo, 49 percent), the goal was to take advantage of product development and participation in mass transport opportunities in Indian and international markets. The target is to produce 150,000 buses (24- to 54-seaters) in five years using India's low-cost advantage.

2. In an alliance with Fiat, (a) Fiat distributes products in India and (b) the two companies engage in a joint manufacturing venture (Tata Motors, 50 percent; Fiat, 50 percent) in India. Tata gained access to world-class car engine technology. Both companies gained access to a production capacity of 100,000 cars and 250,000 units of engines and transmissions for use globally.

3. To capitalize on the regional trading block ASEAN and local country competencies, Tata formed a joint venture in Thailand with Thonburi Thailand (Tata Motors, 70 percent; Thonburi, 30 percent). In Phase I, the production capacity was 12,500 units per annum. In March 2008, Xenon was launched in Thailand, and an eco car project started.

4. To deal with customs in South Africa, Tata Motors formed a subsidiary (Tata Motors, 60 percent; Tata Africa, 40 percent). The products manufactured will be passenger and commercial vehicles.

Despite this track record, many were surprised when Tata Motors acquired Jaguar Land Rover for US $2.3 billion. Tata had its reasons for the purchase: (a) the opportunity to participate in two fast-growing auto segments (premium and small cars) and to build a comprehensive product portfolio with an immediate global footprint; (b) to increase business diversity across markets and product segments; (c) to get a unique opportunity to move into a premium segment with access to world-class iconic brands; (d) to fit Land Rover naturally above Tata's utility/sport utility/crossover offerings for the 4 × 4 premium category and to broaden the brand portfolio with Jaguar's performance/luxury vehicles; and (e) to enjoy long-term benefits from component sourcing, low-cost engineering, and design services.

For any company to survive, its organizational structure must be excellent and coupled with a suitable business model, effective cost control mechanisms, appropriate products and services, ample resource capabilities, process, and quality, as well as with organic and inorganic growth strategies.

## CASE DISCUSSION QUESTIONS

1. What are some of the features of the Indian market that make it an attractive domestic market to Tata Motors?
2. Prepare a SWOT analysis for Tata.
3. What does a five forces model look like for Tata in the global automotive market?
4. What are the key success factors for a global automobile major?
5. As mentioned in the case, the international success strategies for Tata were "to consolidate position in the domestic market and expand international footprint through development of new products by leveraging in house capabilities, acquisitions, and strategic collaborations to gain complementary capabilities." Did Tata achieve these goals? Please elaborate your answers with examples from the case.
6. Ravi Kanth said that international success will take place through focused positioning and marketing in selected countries. Do you agree with his viewpoint?

# The Fleet Sheet

Marlene M. Reed Professor, School of Business,
Samford University, Birmingham, Alabama
Rochelle R. Brunson Department Chair, Management Development
Alvin Community College, Alvin, Texas

At precisely 8:00 A.M. on Monday, April 3, 2000, faxes began printing out simultaneously in the offices of English-speaking companies all over the Czech Republic. Among the news of the Czech Republic translated into English that day was an interesting political insight gleaned from two newspapers:

> "The Washington Post *wrote that Madeleine Albright is the weakest U.S. Secretary of State since the early 1970s and is now only popular in Prague. Euro quips that that's not so bad: the only place Vaclav Havel is now taken seriously is in Washington."*[1]

It was this kind of honest, straightforward evaluation of the Czech economy and government that had made the *Fleet Sheet* so popular to foreign companies and their managers. For Erik Best, founder of the *Fleet Sheet,* there were many decisions to be made concerning the future of the company as well as his own future.

He had begun the business on February 22, 1992, because of a perceived short-term need by Western companies rushing into Czechoslovakia after the Velvet Revolution for economic and political information that they could understand. He had envisioned that in a few years these companies would train Czech nationals to take over their operations in the country, and the English-speaking Westerners would withdraw. That had not happened, and he now wondered if he had a "going concern" that lacked a sound organizational and legal structure to survive into the future. He also wondered how long an operation such as his would continue to be a viable venture because of rapidly-changing technology and greater access to news through the Internet. Erik was now 37 years old, and he knew he needed to make some decisions for the future.

## Erik's Education and Early Work Experience

Erik was born in North Carolina, and when he was 11 years old, his family moved to Montana. He went to high school there and wrote for the high school newspaper. He also became a part-time staff sports writer for the *Missoulian*—the local newspaper. Near the end of his senior year in high school, Erik was offered a journalism scholarship to Vanderbilt University; however, he turned it down because at that time he was not sure he wanted to be a journalist. In the back of his mind, he had thought for some time that he wanted to be involved in business or politics or perhaps both. He decided to attend Georgetown University, and he received a degree in Foreign Service from Georgetown in 1985. In the summers while working on his undergraduate degree at Georgetown, he also studied the Russian language at Middlebury College in Vermont, a school well known for its concentration on international affairs. He subsequently received a Master's Degree in Russian from Middlebury in the Summer of 1985. Perhaps the educational experience that had the greatest impact upon Erik's life was a required four months' stint in Moscow. When he had completed his degree at Middlebury, he entered the M.B.A. program at the University of North Carolina at Chapel Hill and received his M.B.A. degree in 1987.

## The Move to Prague

Erik Best, a fluent speaker of the Russian language and one conversant in other Slavic languages, became enamored with the historic changes taking place in Eastern Europe. Never in the twentieth century had the opportunity existed to be a part of such a great transformation. Never before in history had countries formerly living under a Socialist government with centrally planned economies tried to make the transition to a free market economy where Adam Smith's "Invisible Hand" would be responsible for moving resources into their most advantageous usage.

Therefore, when the offer was made to Erik by the M.B.A. Enterprise Corps to join them in their work in Czechoslovakia, he quickly accepted. In February of 1991, Erik packed his bags and moved to Prague. He immediately fell in love with the country and found the Czech language very similar to Russian. In explaining his love of Prague to others, Erik would state, "I have always loved music, and there is no city in the world so rich with music as Prague. There are classical concerts daily in concert halls, churches, town squares, on the breathtaking Charles Bridge, private chambers, large public halls and under street arches. There are violinists and accordianists playing on street corners and in Metro stations. I have heard that there are more musicians per capita in the Czech Republic than anywhere else in the world. After all, it was in Prague that Mozart wrote the opera *Don Giovanni* and found greater acclaim than in his own Austria. It was also the home of composers Dvorak and Smetana. This is one of the reasons I feel at home in this city."

## The Situation in Eastern Europe

In the early 1990s, the breakup of centralized Socialist economies was occurring all over Eastern Europe. Simultaneously, there was a rapid growth of the private sector in Russia and the surrounding countries of Poland, Czechoslovakia, and Hungary. One of the challenges in the burgeoning market economies was creating small businesses out of large enterprises and also launching entirely new ventures where none had been before. In fact, the development of the small business sector had been the most successful manifestation of the movement to a market economy. Small businesses had also been the greatest success story in the privatization process. Auctions of small businesses and the restitution of property in these countries had led to the restoration of some family businesses.

However, numerous problems beset these newly-created companies. In some cases, the venture was merely additional work added to one or two other jobs to keep the entrepreneur afloat with increasingly higher inflation rates and increasingly stagnant wage rates. Many small businesses were forced into operating illegitimately to deal with unfair and cumbersome legal procedures in the regulatory environment, or to avoid the attention of the Mafia or corrupt officials. It became very difficult to work out a secure contract for lease of property, and the banking system was not equipped to deal with the needs of small business.[2]

Another serious problem was the lack of experience in running private businesses that existed in Eastern Europe. Most hopeful entrepreneurs had lived all of their lives in a Socialist economy and had no training or knowledge related to the way in which one becomes an entrepreneur. It was into this environment that many organizations from the West sent consultants to assist with the revitalization of the economy as a free market. The M.B.A. Enterprise Corps was one such operation.

## Origination of Idea for the *Fleet Sheet*

After working in Prague for a year, it became clear to Erik that international companies that had established offices and operations in the Czech Republic had difficulty in obtaining accurate and timely information on political and economic trends in the country upon which to make business decisions. From his work as a management consultant, he knew that decision makers in companies are very busy, and those operating in the Czech Republic would need information that was very concise and written in English. At the time, no such product was available in the country. It occurred to him that a 1-page faxed bulletin would be the best format for such a paper. The fax was also an inexpensive medium to use. He knew that in the beginning there would not be much news to report, and a 1-page sheet of paper would probably hold all he needed to print.

By early 1992, he had worked out all of the details to begin the business, and on February 22nd he published the first issue. Erik believed that if he had 4 or 5 subscribers in the first month, the product would be successful. In fact, approximately 15 to 20 subscribers signed up in the first month of operations. By early Spring of 2000, there were somewhere in the neighborhood of 1,000 subscribers receiving the *Fleet Sheet* on a regular basis.

Believing that the life cycle of his product would be relatively short, Erik took little thought to establishing a permanent structure for his business. He set it up as a sole proprietorship, and did not bother with a business plan since the operations of the company were uncomplicated and easy to establish. By 2000, he had 8 staff members in the company. Some of the staff came in the very early morning to review newspapers and begin translating the news from Czech to English. Other members of the staff came in around 7:30 A.M. and were involved in distribution and client support. Erik assumed the major responsibility for picking out the most important news to be translated and distributed in the *Fleet Sheet*. He believed a key competitive advantage of the *Fleet Sheet* was its emphasis on a quality product that reported useful Czech economic and political news. Occasionally, the *Sheet* had made a person unhappy by interpreting something incorrectly. However, if Erik agreed with the person's argument, he would admit it and print a retraction. He had found it important to listen to customer complaints and recognize the needs of the customer. He attempted to treat his readers as equal partners. The name for his paper came from the fact that it was issued in a timely manner, and also in reference to Fleet Street in London where all of the major newspapers once resided before moving to the Docklands.

## The Pricing Strategy

Erik realized immediately that the major publication constraint would be the number of people he could physically fax copies of the *Fleet Sheet* to in a short period of time. This was primarily due to the fact that he knew there would be a limitation on the number of telephone lines that he could get. He also knew that another constraint was the budget of the companies and when they needed to have the news. The larger multinational companies, he speculated, would be willing to pay a higher price to get the information very early in the morning. On the other hand, smaller companies beset with fewer complicated decisions would probably be willing to pay a lower price to have the information later in the day. Some businesses might need the information only once a week.

On the basis of this assessment, Erik constructed a pricing structure that averaged $3 to $4 per day for the customer who wanted the *Fleet Sheet* faxed to him or her early in the morning, and for the smaller companies who needed the *Fleet Sheet* faxed to them only once a week, the price would drop $.50 to $.75 an issue. There would be intermediate pricing between the two end points. Therefore, the large companies and lawyers for whom "time is money," could have access to all of the Czech political and economic news early in the morning so that they could make astute and timely decisions based upon realistic information. The companies that did not need information in a timely manner could enjoy the benefit of a discounted price for the information. The graduated pricing strategy would also make the distribution of the paper manageable. It seemed to be an effective pricing strategy: pricing based upon when the subscriber receives the news. The attractiveness of the pricing strategy was that anyone could afford the *Fleet Sheet*.

In order to insure the timeliness of the paper, Erik initially guaranteed the larger companies that if they did not receive their fax of the *Fleet Sheet* before 9:00 A.M. each day, it would be free. However, the fax was never late, and Erik simply dropped this guarantee since no one worried about getting a fax late.

## Marketing of the *Fleet Sheet*

The marketing of the *Fleet Sheet* was multi-pronged. The first thing that Erik did was to advertise in English-language publications such as the *Prague Post, Business Central Europe* (published by *The Economist*), *The American Chamber of Commerce Newsletter* and in the Czech press in very select publications read by the elite. He was surprised that his subscribers had been not only people from English-speaking countries, but also the Dutch, French, German, and even some Czech companies that realized having the news abbreviated for them saved valuable time.

The company also engaged in direct marketing. They found out about new companies moving to town from the American Chamber of Commerce, people Erik met, personal contacts, and by word of mouth. With all new contacts, the company immediately apprised them of the product they were offering. Erik found that his satisfied subscribers let other people know about the service, and many new customers came from referrals. One reason his subscribers had been well satisfied was because Erik made an effort to dig into the important issues facing businesses in the Czech Republic. He also attempted to give people analysis rather than a simple reporting of the news. He found that clients read the *Fleet Sheet* because of the selection of articles that were covered.

A more recent addition to his marketing activities had been using e-mail to whet the appetite of potential subscribers. (See Exhibit 1, "e-mail Synopsis of *Fleet Sheet*.") Whenever anyone e-mailed him, Erik immediately added their name to a list of people who receive a summary of the day's *Fleet Sheet* articles twice a week. The purpose of this was to acquaint them with the value of subscribing to the

EXHIBIT [1]  E-Mail Synopsis of Fleet Sheet

Sub: **In today's Fleet Sheet**

Date: 11/20/00 12:43:19 AM Central Standard Time

From: info@fleet.cz (Fleet Sheet/E. S. Best)

To: info@fleet.cz

From today's Fleet Sheet:

(MFD/1) The four-party coalition won a big victory in the Senate elections yesterday, gaining seats in 16 of the 19 races in which it had candidates. ODS and CSSD lost their Senate majority and will not be able to elect the chairman of the Senate or push through constitutional changes on their own. The top position in the Senate is now held by Libuse Benesova of ODS, but she lost to Helena Rognerova of the 4C. ODS won just eight of the 27 Senate seats at stake, and CSSD managed only one victory. An independent candidate won the final seat. The communists (KSCM) failed to win any seats. One seat had been decided in the first round in favor of the 4C. Of the 81 total Senate seats, the 4C now has 39, 22 for ODS, 15 for CSSD, three for KSCM and two for independents. Voter turnout was less than 20 percent. Vaclav Klaus responded to this by saying the Senate should be reformed so that its elections become part of the regional elections. (MFD/8) Jiri Leschtina of MFD says it will be interesting to see whether the Senate results lead anyone from within ODS and CSSD to break the loyalty pact and take a firm stance against Klaus and Zeman.

\*

(HN/2) The results of the Senate elections reduce the chance that Vaclav Klaus will succeed Vaclav Havel as President. The results suggest that a candidate close to the 4C and Havel has a better chance. The results also make it unlikely that the constitutional amendment to reduce the powers of the President will win approval. If passed, the President's power to pick Bank Board members would be limited.

\*

(HN/3) CEO Jaroslav Mil of CEZ said that if price were the top priority, the sale of the state's stakes and the regional electricity distributors could bring Kc 200–300bn in privatization. If synergies were sought with the natural-gas distributors, he said, the amount could be higher. However, if things such as maintaining employment and coal output play a role, this amount cannot be expected, he said. In this respect, he said he could imagine a requirement that a certain amount of output be guaranteed by the buyer. He also said he sees no reason why one Czech company should not be able to offer gas, water, and electricity. He also indicated that he expects more use of nuclear power in the future. (HN/P9) CEZ's stock hit a low for the year of Kc 85 and might fall more.

\*

(MFD/2) Klaus got a bit touchy at ODS campaign headquarters yesterday after the first results of the Senate elections were announced. When an MFD photographer made a call during Klaus' live interview on Czech TV, Klaus grabbed the man's cellphone out of his hand and tossed it into the corner."How can he dare (talk on the phone) while I'm being interviewed?" Klaus asked. (MFD/3) Milos Zeman, for his part, refused to face defeat and didn't even show up at CSSD campaign headquarters.

*Fleet Sheet* for daily faxes. Understanding the animosity some people have to receiving "junk e-mails," Erik added a notice at the bottom of the e-mail that explained:

*If you do not wish to receive such messages in the future, please simply let us know and we will remove your name from our list.*

Few people ever asked to have their names removed, and many signed up as regular subscribers. This was probably because the e-mail was only sent to individuals whom Erik believed would have an interest in Czech news.

In the late 1990s, Erik developed a website for his company. The web address was http://www.fleet.cz. (See Exhibit 2, "*Fleet Sheet*" Home Page and Final Word.)

**EXHIBIT 2**  *Fleet Sheet* Home Page and Final Word

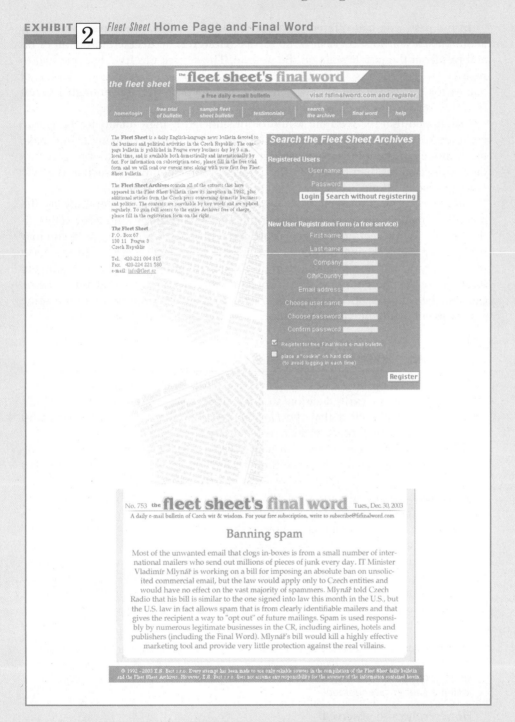

He believed that the website had enormous market potential for his company. It would now be possible for the company to place a page on the website that was a sampling of the *Fleet Sheet* for interested individuals and companies. Erik believed this had the potential to generate an even greater number of subscribers than did the e-mail synopses.

In the past, Erik had offered the entire archives on disk. A company would pay about $500 a year to subscribe to the service. However, he decided to put all of his archives from the past 8 years on the website. The service was free, but one had to register to have access to it. This registry began to generate a good source of names for the e-mail synopses which were intended to develop enough interest from the reader to cause him or her to subscribe to the fax service.

Erik hoped that his Web site would be of sufficiently high quality for people to continue to read it. He was gambling on the belief that a company could make more money in the long run by using its archives as a marketing tool to generate more subscriptions than by selling the archives as some companies such as the *Wall Street Journal* had done.

People occasionally asked Erik why he didn't go to e-mail entirely as the medium for publishing and distributing the *Fleet Sheet*. His response was, "There is the problem of protecting intellectual property. Unless you can encrypt it, you may have a copyright infringement of your material. In fact, Stephen King's most recent story which was published originally on the Internet was encrypted, but someone broke the code. Another problem with encryption is that the message can only be sent to a specific person—not a company. Therefore, there are some real problems with encrypting the information on the Internet."

## Hurdles for the Business

Unlike most start-up businesses, the *Fleet Sheet* was profitable from the very beginning. Erik made an early decision to rent office space and computers initially. Whenever it became clear that the *Fleet Sheet* was a viable business, he did invest in some assets for the company such as necessary equipment.

Concerning the success of the company, Erik mused, "The revenues of the company have grown every year because the Czech Republic was seen early as the darling of the West, and they also received a great deal of media attention. Under more realistic conditions, many of the companies would not have come here." However, in the last couple of years of the 1990s, there had been a decline in subscribers. Erik often contemplated how recent world economic events might be affecting the circulation of the *Fleet Sheet*.

As to the last hurdle, Erik commented, "We have had to fend off 6 or 7 competitors who began to offer the same service that we were offering—a faxed bulletin with important political and economic news. It was a blatant rip-off of our product. The success of the *Fleet Sheet* drew other companies into the market."

Erik speculated:

*The drastic price reduction the competition offered in the beginning served to lower the overall revenue size of the market. I have often wondered if there is a big enough market to support ONE such publication over the long run, much less numerous competitors in a smaller revenue pool.*

However, he also observed:

*The reason we survived was due to the overall quality of the paper. Business people know quality when they see it, and they immediately know that the Fleet Sheet is professionally done.*

Government regulations which had been devastating to many businesses in the Czech Republic had been minimal for the *Fleet Sheet*. The company did not require a large number of licenses or drug approvals as did the large pharmaceutical companies operating in the country. However, it had been faced with government bureaucracy—especially in the distribution of their product. The government informed them that they had to send the *Fleet Sheet* to hundreds of libraries at the company's own expense. This, of course, would have made the company non-profitable and no one would have read the paper anyway. They decided to take a risk and send the paper to only selected libraries where they believed there was a greater chance of someone actually reading the *Fleet Sheet*. Fortunately, the regulation was changed in the early part of 2000 so that the company would no longer be required to distribute the paper in this manner.

In the late 1990s, Erik decided to add an advertisement to the *Fleet Sheet*. The ad was priced at $400 a day and was rotated among 4 or 5 different companies' ads. (See Exhibit 3, "*Fleet Sheet* with Ad.") If he should decide to add another advertisement, Erik would probably have to add another page to the fax. Faxing charges are minimal; the primary cost would be additional staff to prepare another page. However, he wondered if the primary focus of the paper—relevant information in a concise format—would be maintained. People don't mind taking the time to read 1 page of the most concise political and economic news of the day, but would they read 2 pages?

In the Spring of 2000, there were around 800 subscribers to the *Fleet Sheet* paying an average of $2.50 each per day to receive the publication. In addition, each additional subscriber brought in 90% in profits and only 10% in variable costs. Erik speculated about whether a new format with two pages would actually reduce—rather than increase—subscribers.

Erik had always used Adobe Acrobat to format the paper, and the faxed paper was very easy to read. If he went to an e-mail publication of the paper altogether, there could be a text format that would not be limited to one or two pages. But he wondered if that would affect the integrity of the product. They had done so well in the past with the concise format of a 1-page fax. Would people actually sit at their computers and read through a lengthy e-mail the way they read through a newspaper or fax that they can hold in their hands? Erik speculated, "If you could produce the same experience of reading a newspaper on the Internet, it would be good. However, our present computer monitors prevent this from occurring." Erik also wondered how a company could build a brand name and attract a loyal readership over the Internet. On the Internet, one must click through so many pages to get to the desired material that the opportunity cost of one's time becomes very expensive.

When Erik began his venture in 1992, he firmly believed it would be a short-term operation bridging the gap until a new economy was established and other sources of information became available. With that in mind, he had spent little time pondering an appropriate legal structure for the business. He had initially set the business up as a sole proprietorship, but now he wondered if he should have established it as an LLC. He would also have developed a long-term strategy for the company. He wondered if it was too late to develop a business plan for the *Fleet Sheet* and alter its legal structure. He knew he would have to fill out some forms and notify the United States government of his actions, but perhaps he should do that. Erik wondered if a change in the legal structure of the organization would have capital gains tax implications if he decided to sell the business. He never assumed the business would last this long or he might have spent more time in planning rather than starting the business up in two weeks.

EXHIBIT **3**   *Fleet Sheet* with Ad

## the fleet sheet

No. 2999    *Today's news, today*   Prague, Tues., Dec. 30, 2003

| | | |
|---|---|---|
| Euro (fixing) | 32.505 | -0.015 |
| Dollar | 26.009 | -0.235 |
| Pound | 46.168 | -0.125 |
| Slovak crown 100 | 79.011 | -0.036 |
| 3-month Pribor | 2.07 | 0.00 |
| Dow Jones | 10450.0 | +1.2% |
| DAX | 3952.7 | +1.3% |
| Nikkei | 10500.6 | +0.8% |
| České Radiokom. | 345.50 | +0.6% |
| Český Telecom | 287.50 | -0.3% |
| ČEZ | 145.25 | +1.7% |
| Erste Bank | 3210.0 | +1.9% |
| Komerční banka | 2414.00 | +1.2% |
| Philip Morris ČR | 15398.0 | +1.6% |
| Unipetrol | 66.39 | +1.9% |
| PX 50 | 656.9 | +1.15% |

### Business

(MFD/1) A poll by SC&C found that many Czechs associate EU accession next year with higher prices. Some price increases will take effect immediately in Jan., while others will be timed to coincide with EU accession on May 1. Consumers are stocking up on such things as gasoline, alcohol and prepaid phone cards at the old prices. The SC&C poll found that 26.8% of respondents fear price increases next year, compared to 16.7% who fear losing their job and 9.9% who fear accession. Most respondents consider 2003 to be an average year. Most young respondents thought it was a good year, while older respondents and low wage-earners tended to be more pessimistic. (MFD/B4) EU entry will mean higher prices for imports from some non-EU countries of such things as bananas, rice, tuna, bicycles and CDs. (MFD/6) MFD pictures Klaus in a cartoon working on his New Year's address. "Bad things come in threes," he says. "First the floods, then the drought, then EU entry."

(MFD/7) Oskar said it expects a single-digit decrease in calling levels during the first months of next year, due to the sharp VAT increase. T-Mobile said it expects calling traffic to return to its previous level after a few months. Český Telecom expects about 100,000 people to give up their fixed lines because of the higher tax.

(HN/1) Some building & loans have been unable to handle all the customers seeking to sign contracts by the end of the year, before the state subsidy declines next year. ČMSS said that it expects to serve as many as 10,000 customers a day this week. About 2m new contracts are expected this year. Next year, though, this should drop to just six figures, according to ČMSS. Building & loans will use the promise of loans to attract new customers next year. (LN/6) Some clients are using very high target savings levels - such as Kč 1m - as a way to guarantee the higher state subsidies for many years to come.

(HN/13) Pre-Christmas internet sales quadrupled this year. Czech shoppers bought more-expensive items on line, such as DVD players and digital cameras.

(HN/18) Landowners claim that a planned new law for specifying the price and length of their leases of land to farmers is unconstitutional. One version of the bill would allow farmers to continue to pay today's artificially low rates. Farmers welcome the law and favor long lease periods.

(MFD/9) Škoda Auto is offering bonuses of up to Kč 90,000 on Octavias. (EU/62) Škoda does not expect its planned new Octavia to cannibalize its sister brands.

(HN/1) The terms for reserving and paying for tickets to next year's hockey championships were so tight that many people risk losing their reservations. Tickets went on sale shortly before Christmas and had to be paid for within seven days. Due to the

holidays, payment orders needed to be submitted many days in advance. Sazka said it will wait an extra day or two and will then put any tickets that have not been paid for on sale in early Jan. (MFD/D1) Some people are threatening to sue Sazka for not honoring ticket reservations that were made in the summer. Sazka blamed the situation on the Hockey Union.

(HN/13) The CR attracted 40 investments this year into IT and service centers, from companies such as Accenture, DHL, Honeywell and ExxonMobil. Investment into the 15 largest of them will exceed Kč 17bn. (DHL accounts for Kč 16bn of this, and HN gives no figure for Accenture, Honeywell and ExxonMobil.) These 15 investments are expected to lead to 4,386 new jobs. (EU/62) Separately, Škoda Auto Chairman Vratislav Kulhánek said the decade-long tax breaks given to foreign investors are "perverse." Many of the companies would come anyway, he said, and CzechInvest pays no attention to whether the new investments will threaten the existence of thriving businesses. CzechInvest's policies in general need to be examined, he said.

(HN/17) One of the pillars of Český Telecom's strategy is to remain in a business only if it is No. 1 or No. 2 on the market, according to HR Director Imrich Gombar. Layoffs will be closely linked to this. Job cuts are planned preliminarily for the end of each of the first three quarters of 2004. On average, employees will get about eight months' wages as severance pay.

(HN/2) Charges are expected to be filed early next year in what HN calls the biggest corruption affair since 1989. Karel Srba, Pavel Jaroš, Alex Šatánek and other former top-level employees of the foreign ministry are suspected of profiting from state contracts. [HN's article was written by Sabina Slonková. Srba has already been found guilty of conspiring to kill her.]

(HN/17) Czech Railways chose Kapsch again to supply a GSM-R network.... Due to changes in U.S. rules, large PR agencies active here will no longer disclose their annual results.... Ruhrgas will shift its 24% stake in Pražská plynárenská Holding to E.ON. (EU/8) The SEC launched a Kč 100m computer system for detecting trading fraud. (MFD/5) On Jan. 10, Mountfield will launch discounts of "up to 100%" on garden tools and swimming pools.

### Politics

(P/1) Stanislav Gross said KDU-ČSL Chair Miroslav Kalousek should join the cabinet. Kalousek said he is willing to enter into talks with ČSSD and US-DEU about a fourth cabinet seat for KDU. He ruled out any reshuffling of KDU's three seats.

(MFD/2) Czech TV will air a taped three-

minute toast by Václav Havel at midnight on New Year's Eve. Václav Klaus will give his live New Year's address 13 hours later. (MFD/4) Separately, architect Bořek Šípek said he will wait for Klaus' term to expire to carry through with his idea of erecting 25 small buildings in the Castle grounds for representing EU countries. The project is supported by Havel but has been rejected by the current Castle administration.

(HN/4) Jiří Svoboda, who led the Communist Party for three years in the early 1990s, said the shift of voters away from ČSSD to the Communists is due mainly to two things. First, ČSSD makes one decision as a party and another on the cabinet level (such as in the case of the Iraq war), and this confuses voters. Second, voters perceive that the use of "repressive elements," such as wiretaps, is on the rise, and this reminds them of pre-1989 days.

(HN/3) Interior Minister Stanislav Gross said he has the feeling that Viktor Kožený does not meet the conditions set forth in the election law for running for office. Kožený has said that he plans to run for the European Parliament next year.

### Society

(MFD/4) Two youths shot by security guards while allegedly trying to force their way into a nightclub in Most have died, and a third was charged with disorderly conduct. The guards have so far not been charged. A police car was called to the scene, but the officers reportedly remained in the vehicle while the shots were fired.

(MFD/1) Another flu epidemic is expected after New Year's, and it could be worse than the pre-Christmas epidemic. MFD quotes an epidemiology official from Ústí nad Labem as saying that anyone with a fever should seek medical attention.

(HN/13) About 25,000 Czechs are spending the holidays at the beach, up 25% from last year. Accommodations are cheap, income is up, the weather at the beach is warm, and there isn't much snow in the mountains. Favored destinations include Egypt, the Canary Islands and Thailand.

Published by 9 a.m. Mon-Fri except holidays by E.S. Best s.r.o., P.O. Box 67, 130 11 Prague 3. Tel. 420 221 004 315 Fax 420 224 221 580 info@fleet.cz Unauthorized use or copy prohibited. © 2003

MK ČR E 6108 MIČ 46593 ISSN 1210-5279 89KČ www.fleet.cz

## Erik's Dilemma

Erik wondered if this business could survive indefinitely into the future. He also wondered what factors would have an impact on its remaining as a "going concern." Some foreign companies had already begun to close their offices in the Czech Republic because of the difficulties of doing business there, and the German banks were beginning to focus on Germany and not other countries. Even if the multinationals decided to stay in the country and there continued to be a market for the *Fleet Sheet,* he wondered what format it might take in the future. And then there was the question of the Internet. Would people have such quick access to data on the Internet that a service such as his would become obsolete?

Erik also thought about future competition. Would other companies try to offer the service he was offering at a lower price? Would subscribers be enticed by lower prices even though the quality of the product might be inferior?

When Erik had first begun his business, he was not making what he considered an adequate salary; and he often speculated that it would be very easy to close the business and go to work somewhere else. However, by the Spring of 2000, the business was doing so well that he was making a very good salary that might be difficult to duplicate somewhere else. Erik thought it humorous to contemplate all of the problems that one encounters when a business becomes successful.

## CASE DISCUSSION QUESTIONS

1. What are the potential difficulties of starting a business in a transition economy?
2. Prepare a SWOT analysis for the *Fleet Sheet*.
3. What are the key success factors of the *Fleet Sheet*?
4. What is the relationship among education, experience, personal skill, and entrepreneurship for Erik Best?
5. What did you learn about entrepreneurship from this case?
6. Erik Best did not prepare a business plan for starting the *Fleet Sheet*. What type of operation would benefit most from a business plan?

## CASE CREDIT

Used with permission of the authors, Professor Marlene M. Reed, Samford University, and Rochelle R. Brunson, Alvin Community College. Exhibits used courtesy of Erik Best and the *Fleet Sheet*.

## CASE NOTES

[1] Vaclav Havel was the gifted writer who was elected the first President of Czechoslovakia after the dissolution of Communism and was serving his last term in office.

[2] Lyapura, Stanislav, and Allan A. Gibb. 1996. "Creating small businesses out of large enterprises." *Small Business in Transition Economies.* London: Intermediate Technology Publications, Ltd., 34–50.

# Management Processes in Strategy Implementation: Design Choices for Multinational Companies

Cuiphoto/Shutterstock.com

# 8

# Organizational Designs for Multinational Companies

## *Preview*   C A S E   I N   P O I N T

### Takeda's Global Centers of Excellence

Takeda is a global research-based pharmaceuticals company. It is Japan's largest pharmaceuticals company and is considered a global leader in the industry. The firm produces drugs to treat common ailments, such as diabetes and hypertension, but has products for treating other diseases, such as peptic ulcers and cancer. Takeda considers ethical drugs as its core business. It has a sales network that reaches patients in around 70 countries. It currently has 17 production plants located in 14 different countries.

Recently, the company announced important changes in its corporate structure. It streamlined executive reporting relationships by creating new corporate-level functions. Takeda is creating a new R&D center of excellence, to be run by a newly appointed chief scientific officer, along with a new international operations role. The individuals appointed to these new positions all have executive reporting relationships directly to the president. Furthermore, Takeda is moving its development headquarters from Osaka, Japan, to Deerfield, Illinois.

These changes were motivated by Takeda's desire to become a global company with highly integrated operations. The company hopes that these changes will allow it to maximize its international product potential and presence. Additionally, the headquarters move is seen as the means for Takeda to optimize its development functions. Takeda sees these changes as extremely critical if it wants to take advantage of the global market potential. Given that drug dispensing is greatly affected by local conditions, Takeda decided that these changes would allow it to better serve the needs of high-growth markets globally.

*Source: Based on PR Newswire. 2009. "Takeda to create Global Centers of Excellence." March 30; Takeda. 2012. http://www.takeda.com/.*

The best multinational strategies do not ensure success. Implementation of a multinational business strategy requires that managers build the right type of organization; that is, managers must try to design their organizations with what they believe are the best mechanisms to carry out domestic and multinational strategies. As shown in the Preview Case in Point, the global pharmaceutical company Takeda hopes that its organizational changes will provide the right support for its global strategies in the next decade. In this chapter, you will see other design choices and consider the complexities of organizing for international competition.

This chapter discusses the organizational design options available for the implementation of multinational strategies. What is organizational design? **Organizational design** is how organizations structure their subunits and use mechanisms for coordination and control to achieve their strategic goals. This chapter shows how having the right organizational design is crucial to multinational companies achieving their multinational strategic goals.

The choices involved in setting up an organization are complex and varied. Each organizational design has costs and benefits related to the best way to deliver a product or service to the domestic or international customer. Consider the following Case in Point.

As the Preview Case in Point shows, international expansion is a very complex process. Some organizational designs for multinational companies favor flexibility. These designs provide managers with the organizational tools to deliver products adapted to different national or regional markets or to take advantage of resources located in various regions of the world. Other organizational designs favor

**Organizational design**
How organizations structure subunits and use coordination and control mechanisms to achieve their strategic goals.

---

## CASE IN POINT

### Wal-Mart and India

Many experts predict that India is poised to become one of the world's next superpowers. India has enjoyed stability over the past decade as well as impressive economic growth. Per capita income is up, while rural poverty has gone down. However, despite this growth, India still presents uncertainties for investors, as recent governments attacked foreign investors. Facing a severe decline in investments, more recent governmental change has been accompanied by changes to provide a more favorable environment for investors. Outsiders are now being encouraged to set up supermarkets in various Indian states.

One of the companies ready to take advantage of this change is Wal-Mart. Wal-Mart had previously formed a 50-50 joint venture with Bharti Enterprises for cash and carry stores (back-end wholesale stores). However, given the government's decision to allow more foreign investment, Wal-Mart is now considering a stronger partnership with Bharti to open front-end stores. The Swedish multinational IKEA is also pondering stronger investments in India as the more restrictive policies of the past are eliminated. For instance, the government is now waiving its mandatory 30 percent sourcing requirements from local manufacturers when foreign companies open stores. Sourcing from Indian small and mediumsized enterprises is not possible in all industries.

As both Wal-Mart and IKEA decide to invest in India, they will be faced with many organizational design and coordination issues. How should the foreign retail outlets be structured? What form of partnership makes most sense with Indian companies? How much autonomy should the foreign subsidiaries be given? How can operations be coordinated globally to ensure that they are conducted as efficiently as possible?

*Sources: Based on* Economist. *2012. "Special Report: India. Aim Higher." September 29, 3–5; Rishi, R. 2012. "Wal-Mart may be first to buy into retail FDI story." September 17,* Financial Express, *online edition.*

efficiency. These designs provide managers with organizations best suited to delivering low-cost products worldwide.

This chapter first presents a survey of organizational design and a summary of basic background knowledge on organizational structure. Building on this information, the chapter then discusses the organizational structures used by multinational companies. Because organizational structure effectively breaks the business down into logical entities, it is necessary to implement coordination and control mechanisms to integrate the entities, and the chapter summarizes the mechanisms available to do that. Finally, knowledge is crucial in today's increasingly competitive and ambiguous environment. In the final section of the chapter, we look at knowledge management as it relates to design issues.

# The Nature of Organizational Design

The two basic questions involved in designing an organization are: (1) How shall we divide the work among the organization's subunits? and (2) How shall we coordinate and control the efforts of the units we create?[1]

In very small organizations, everyone does the same thing, and does everything. There is little reason to divide the work. However, as organizations grow, managers divide work first into specialized jobs; people perform different tasks. Later, when many people are doing the same tasks and a supervisor is required, managers divide their organizations into specialized subunits. In small organizations, the subunits are usually called departments. In large organizations, divisions or subsidiaries become the major subunits.

Once an organization has specialized subunits, managers must develop mechanisms to coordinate and control their efforts. For example, a manufacturing company must make sure that the production department produces the goods to be available when the marketing department promised the customers. Similarly, a multinational company must ensure that its foreign operations support the parent company's strategic goals. Some companies monitor their subunits very closely; they *centralize* decision making at company headquarters to make certain that the production and delivery of products or services conform to rigid standards. Other companies give subunits greater flexibility by *decentralizing* decision making. Later in the chapter, we will discuss why multinational companies might choose tight or loose control.

Why should multinational companies be concerned about organizational design? In today's world, characterized by hypercompetition and ambiguous industry boundaries, it has never been more crucial to pay attention to organizational design issues. Many companies, including GM, IBM, Sears, and Kodak, suffered major setbacks and saw their profits fall dramatically in the last couple of decades because of their poor organizational designs. While global competition demanded flexibility and speed, these companies had very bloated bureaucratic structures that made it difficult to adapt rapidly to a changing environment.[2] A properly aligned organizational design allows a multinational company to respond quickly to altered conditions.

## A Primer on Organizational Structures

Before you can understand the organizational structures necessary to implement multinational strategy, you need a basic knowledge of organizational structure. To provide this background, the next section gives a brief summary of the fundamental structural options available to managers in designing their organizations. Students who have had course work on organizational design will find this a review.

Organizations usually divide work into departments or divisions based on functions, geography, products, or a combination of these criteria. Each way of organizing has its advantages and disadvantages. A company's choice of subunit forms is based on management's beliefs concerning the best structure or structures to implement the chosen strategies. In this chapter, some of the advantages and disadvantages of each choice will be explained.

## The Basic Functional Structure

In a **functional structure**, departments perform separate business functions, such as marketing or manufacturing. The functional structure is the simplest of organizations and typical of small businesses. However, even large organizations often have functional subunits. Because most organizations use charts to display their organizational structures, the chapter shows each type of organization using exhibits of hypothetical or real organizational charts. Exhibit 8.1 shows an organizational chart for a generic functional structure.

Organizations choose a functional structure primarily for efficiency. The functional structure gets its efficiency from economies of scale in each function because there are cost savings when a large number of people do the same job in the same place. For example, the organization can locate all marketing or all manufacturing people in one subunit, with one staff support group, one telephone system, and one management system. However, because functional subunits are separated from each other and serve functional goals, coordination among them can be difficult, and responses to changes in the environment can be slow. The functional structure works best, therefore, when organizations have few products, few locations, or few types of customers. It also works best when the organization faces a stable environment in which the need for adaptation is minimal.[3]

A variety of situations can undermine the effectiveness of the functional structure. It can lose effectiveness and efficiency when organizations have many products, serve different customer groups, or locate in widely dispersed geographical areas. The most common reaction by managers to these situations is to organize departments or divisions by product or geography.

## The Basic Product and Geographic Structures

The structural arrangements for building a department or subunit around a product or a geographic area are called the **product structure** and the **geographic structure**, respectively. Exhibits 8.2 and 8.3 show simple product and geographic structures.

**Functional structure**
Has departments or subunits based on separate business functions, such as marketing or manufacturing.

**Product structure**
Has departments or subunits based on different product groups.

**Geographic structure**
Has departments or subunits based on geographical regions.

**EXHIBIT 8.1** Basic Functional Structure

Headquarters

RESEARCH AND DEVELOPMENT · PRODUCTION · MARKETING · ACCOUNTING AND FINANCE

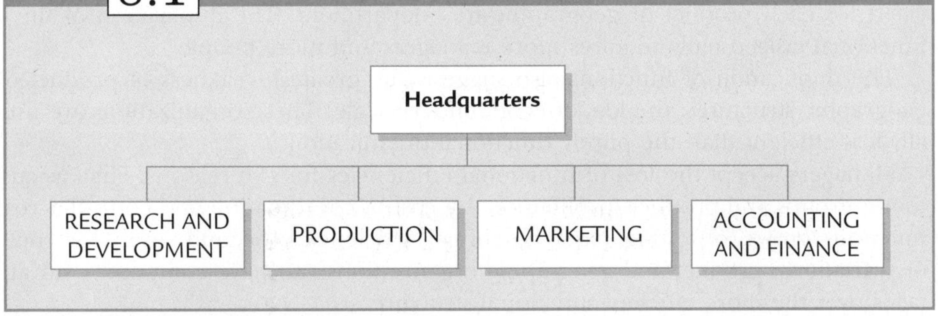

© Cengage Learning

**EXHIBIT** **8.2**    Basic Product Structure

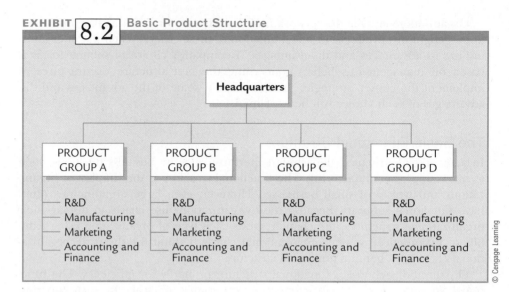

**EXHIBIT** **8.3**    Basic Geographic Structure

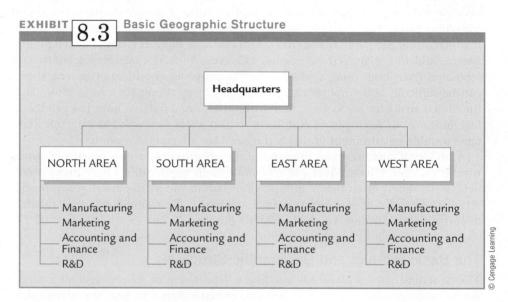

Product or geographic organizations must still perform the functional tasks of a business (e.g., marketing, accounting). In contrast to functionally structured firms, however, organizations structured around products or geographic locations do not concentrate functions in dedicated subunits. Instead, functional tasks are duplicated for each product or geographic-area department. The duplication of these functional tasks usually requires more managers and more people.

The duplication of functions also suggests the greatest weakness of product or geographic structures: the loss of economies of scale. These organizations are usually less efficient than the purely functional organization.

Managers accept the loss of functional efficiencies for two reasons. First, as customer groups and products proliferate, the cost of coordination and control across functions grows, offsetting basic functional efficiencies. Second, even for small organizations, product and geographic organizations can have competitive advantages over the more efficient functional structure.

Organized by region or some other geographic unit, geographic structure allows a company to serve customer needs that vary by region; that is, the business sets up a minifunctional organization in each region. Rather than having one large functional organization serve all customers, the small, regional subunit focuses all its activities on serving the unique needs of the local customer. Because the subunits concentrate on specific customer groups, managers can more easily and quickly identify customer needs and adapt products accordingly.

Managers choose product structures when they believe that a product or a group of products is unique enough to require specialized functional efforts. This structure creates strong coordination across the functional areas to support the product group. Driving the selection of product structures are the products' unique or changing technologies, or the association of distinct customer groups with different products.

Few organizations adopt purely organizational forms. Each organization has its unique trade-offs based on efficiency, product types, and customers' needs. Companies design their organizations with mixtures of structures that they believe will best implement their strategies. These mixed-form organizations, which can include functional, geographic, and product units, are called hybrid structures.

**Hybrid structures**
Mix functional, geographic, and product units.

# Organizational Structures to Implement Multinational Strategies

When a company first goes international, it seldom changes its basic organizational structure. Most companies act first as passive exporters, simply filling orders using the same structures, procedures, and people used in domestic sales.

Even with greater involvement in exporting, companies often avoid fundamental organizational changes. Instead, they use other companies to provide them with international expertise and to run their export operations. As explained in Chapter 6, export management companies and export trading companies manage exporting for companies that do not have the resources or skills to run their own export operations.

Similarly, the choice of licensing as a multinational participation strategy has little impact on domestic organizational structures. The licensor need only negotiate a contract and collect the royalties. The licensor's corporate attorneys may negotiate the licensing contract, and its managers may monitor the licensing contract. However, the licensee's organization must deal with most of the organizational problems of bringing a product or service to the foreign market.

When international sales become more central to a firm's success, then sophisticated multinational and participation strategies usually become a significant part of a company's overall business strategy. As a result, companies must restructure themselves appropriately to manage their multinational operations and implement their multinational strategies. The following sections focus on the options for such companies.

## The Export Department

When exports contribute a significant percentage of sales and the company wishes to increase its control over export operations, managers often create a separate export department. Consider the next Case in Point, which shows that many small companies—in this case, those involved in green exports—are likely to establish an export department.

**Export department**
Coordinates and controls a company's export operations.

## Green Exports

Green technologies are an important component of today's global economy. Many countries are encouraging their consumers to switch to alternative energy sources, such as solar or wind. According to experts, the global environmental market is valued at about $729 billion. Furthermore, a recent study showed that companies that have green supply chain management tend to have better performance compared to companies with lower efforts at being green. Clearly, companies involved in this industry will have many opportunities in the future both in terms of improving their processes and also in terms of increased revenues.

One of the downsides for such businesses, however, is that they are often small and lack capital. Many of them strive to establish export departments as their exports grow because an export department makes the company better able to manage the export process and customers. With an export department, a small company can better understand the local needs of customers and better respond to such needs.

The U.S. governmental organization Ex-Im Bank, an independent federal agency, is now dedicated to helping small businesses export environmentally friendly products. For instance, it provided financial support to Powerlight Corporation to export solar tracking technologies to Germany and South Korea. Powerlight hopes that it can grow and eventually establish an export department.

*Sources: Based on Conlin, L. M. 2008. "Banking on green exports." Journal of Commerce, November 10; Lee, S. M., S. T. Kim, and D. Choi. 2012. "Green supply chain management and organizational performance." Industrial Management and Data Systems, 112(8), 1148–1180.*

By having an export department, top management shows its belief that the investment of human and financial resources in exporting is necessary to sustain and build international sales. The export department deals with all international customers for all products. Managers in the export department often control the pricing and promotion of products for the international market, and the people within it may have particular country or product expertise. Export department managers have the responsibility to deal with export management companies, with foreign distributors, and with foreign customers. When the company uses a direct exporting strategy, sales representatives located in other countries may also report to the export department management. Exhibit 8.4 shows a hypothetical organization with a functional structure and an export department.

As companies evolve beyond the initial participation strategies of exporting and licensing, they need more sophisticated structures to implement the necessary complex multinational strategies. These more complex structures include the international division, the worldwide geographic and products structures, the worldwide matrix structure, and the transnational network structure.

Before discussing these structures in detail, some background is necessary on the types of subunits multinational companies set up in foreign countries.

### Foreign Subsidiaries

**Foreign subsidiaries**
Subunits of the multinational company located in another country.

The more complex multinational organizational structures support participation strategies that include direct investments in a foreign country, which require setting up an overseas subunit of the parent firm. These subunits are called foreign subsidiaries. Foreign subsidiaries are subunits of the multinational company located in countries other than that of the parent company's headquarters. Foreign subsidiaries are a growing component of international business. For example,

**EXHIBIT** 8.4   Functional Structure with an Export Department

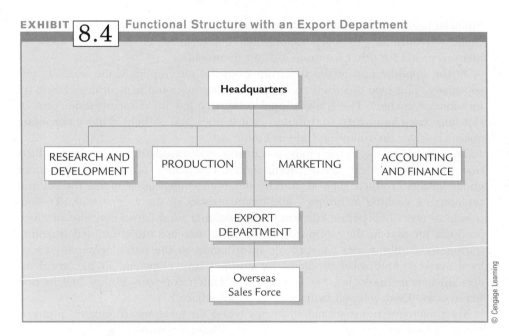

the United Nations estimates that worldwide, there are more than 65,000 multinational corporations with more than 850,000 foreign subsidiaries employing nearly 25 million people.[4] Siemens, the German giant, reported 900 fully owned and 400 majority-owned subsidiaries in its 2005 statements. The multinational organizations Total and Asea Brown Boveri (ABB) report associations with more than 1,000 entities each, and General Electric reports ownership in more than 8,000 subsidiaries.[5]

## Subsidiaries

Multinational firms vary their control over their subsidiaries.[6] Some retain control by maintaining a board that is active in subsidiary management. Such forms of control tend to be typical of joint ventures in emerging markets in India and China, where the multinational firm wants to control the subsidiary's activities. Another form of control is the rubber stamp board, which tends to be required by law. Such boards are more likely to be formal, and they merely approve the subsidiary's activities. However, most multinational companies use a third form of control by which the multinational firm avoids managing the local subsidiary and leaves management decisions up to it. The latter arrangement is seen as necessary to ensure that local subsidiaries stay as efficient as possible.

Multinational companies use several types of foreign subsidiaries. For companies pursuing a multidomestic strategy, the foreign subsidiary often becomes a scaled-down version of the parent company.[7] This type of subsidiary is called the **minireplica subsidiary**. It uses the same technology and produces the same products as the parent company, but it runs on a smaller scale. By producing products or services strictly for the local market, the minireplica can adapt to local conditions and support the multidomestic strategy.

Minireplicas use few expatriate managers. Local managers run the organization, often with little influence from headquarters. Because of its autonomy from headquarters, the minireplica is usually a profit center. In a profit center, corporate headquarters evaluates local managers based on the unit's profitability, using

**Minireplica subsidiary**
Scaled-down version of the parent company, using the same technology and producing the same products as the parent company.

financial performance information such as return on investment. Seldom do mini-replicas contribute to corporation-wide goals such as providing R&D or manufacturing for other locations around the world.

**Transnational subsidiary**

*Has no company-wide form or function; each subsidiary does what it does best or most efficiently anywhere in the world.*

At the opposite end of the spectrum from the minireplica is the transnational subsidiary. This type of subsidiary supports a multinational firm strategy based on location advantages. The transnational subsidiary has no company-wide form or function. Each subsidiary contributes what it does best to help achieve corporate goals. Consider the following Case in Point.

To respond to local conditions, a transnational subsidiary may make products that it adapts to local tastes. Multinational companies often make consumer goods locally. Products such as laundry detergents need adjustments for cultural preferences, washing techniques, and characteristics of the water supply. To contribute to overall corporate efficiency, transnational subsidiaries may also produce products for sale in the worldwide market. To increase organizational learning, transnational subsidiaries can provide information to the parent company about local markets, help solve problems for another unit elsewhere in the world, or develop new technologies. For instance, the Dutch company Philips had its first stereo color TV developed by its Australian subsidiary.[8]

To implement transnational strategies based on location advantages, multinational companies may place subsidiaries in different countries to take advantage of factor costs (e.g., cheap labor or raw materials), to capitalize on other resources (e.g., an educated workforce or unique skills), or to gain access to the country. For example, DuPont gives worldwide control of its Lycra business to its Swiss subsidiary to benefit from its concentration of unique production and management skills.

Some foreign subsidiaries begin as only sales offices and later take on other functions. Before manufacturing a product in another country, companies

## CASE IN POINT

### Universities and International Expansion

While it is usually clear why companies go international, more recent studies have been investigating universities. With globalization, there are more opportunities for universities to expand overseas to take advantage of local and regional markets. For instance, there has been significant expansion into countries such as the United Arab Emirates, China, Singapore, and Qatar. However, such expansion is a very risky, high-growth strategy that can result in significant losses and reputational damage. Consider the case of the University of New South Wales, which decided to close its branch campus in Singapore after just two months. This withdrawal resulted in losses of over US$38 million for the university.

One of the most popular ways for a university to expand overseas is by establishing a transnational subsidiary. A recent report suggests that there were at least 181 branch campuses worldwide. Understanding why universities decide to open foreign branches is therefore important. A foreign branch campus is an educational facility that is owned by a foreign institution and where students receive degrees from the foreign institution.

A recent study found that universities will often set up foreign branches as a way to address loss of revenue resulting from less governmental support at home. Furthermore, some countries actually offer incentives for universities to set up branches. China has encouraged international cooperation to provide quality education locally. High-prestige universities such as Cambridge, the University of Pennsylvania, and Yale have opened foreign branch campuses because they want to control the education being offered and maintain their reputations.

*Source: Based on Wilkins, S. and J. Huisman. 2012. "The international branch campus as transnational strategy in higher education." Higher Education, 64, 627–645.*

frequently test the market by opening a foreign sales office. If the market looks promising, companies invest in the plant and equipment to manufacture locally. In contrast, other subsidiaries begin as and remain suppliers of raw materials for the parent company or other subsidiaries. These units often have no manufacturing or sales capacities. For example, major oil companies such as British Petroleum use many of their subsidiaries only to supply raw materials. Finally, some multinational companies use their subsidiaries as offshore production or assembly plants for export back to the headquarters' country.

Most subsidiaries are neither pure minireplicas nor pure transnationals. Rather, foreign subsidiaries take many forms and have many functions. Multinational companies choose the mix of functions for their foreign subsidiaries based on several issues, including (1) the firm's multinational strategy or strategies, (2) the subsidiaries' capabilities and resources, (3) the economic and political risk of building and managing a subunit in another country, and (4) how the subsidiaries fit into the overall multinational organizational structure.

Foreign subsidiaries are the structural building blocks for running multinational operations; that is, once companies move beyond simple exporting, foreign subsidiaries become key parts of the organizational designs that multinational companies use to implement their multinational strategies. With the background knowledge of the nature of foreign subsidiaries, we will now consider how multinational companies use organizational structures to implement their multinational strategies.

## International Division

As companies increase the size of their international sales force and set up manufacturing operations in other countries, the export department often grows into an international division. The international division differs from the export department in several ways. It is usually larger and has greater responsibilities. Besides managing exporting and an international sales force, this division oversees foreign subsidiaries that perform a variety of functions. Although usually the subsidiaries are sales units, units that procure raw material and produce the company's products are also common. The international division has more extensive staff with international expertise. Top management expects the international people to perform functions such as negotiating licensing and joint venture agreements, translating promotional material, or providing expertise on different national cultures and social institutions.

Exhibit 8.5 gives an example of an international division in a domestic product structure. In this example, the division handles all products, controls foreign subsidiaries in Europe and Japan, and manages a general sales force in the rest of Asia.

The international division structure has declined in popularity among large multinational companies.[9] For multiproduct companies operating in many countries, it is not considered an effective multinational structure.[10] However, for companies of moderate size with a limited number of products or country locations, the international division remains a popular and potentially effective organizational firm.

To deal with the shortcomings of the international division structure, multinational companies have several options: the worldwide product structure, the worldwide geographic structure, the matrix structure, and the transnational network structure. The following section discusses the worldwide geographic and product structures.

## Worldwide Geographic Structure and Worldwide Product Structure

In the worldwide geographic structure, regions or large-market countries become the geographic divisions of the multinational company. Consider the next Multinational Management Brief.

**International division**
Responsible for managing exports, international sales, and foreign subsidiaries.

**Worldwide geographic structure**
Has geographical units representing regions of the world.

**EXHIBIT 8.5**    International Division in a Domestic Product Structure

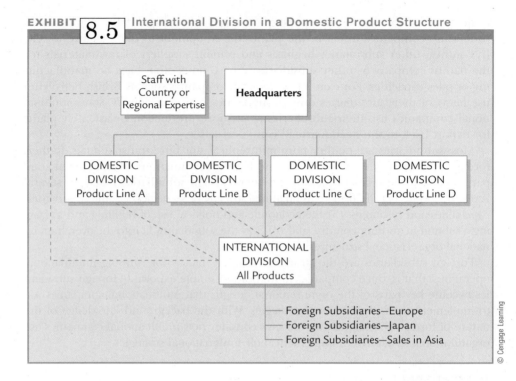

© Cengage Learning

---

## Multinational Management **Brief**

### Cooper-Standard Automotive

Cooper-Standard Automotive is a leading global automotive supplier headquartered in Michigan. It was established in 1960 and now employs about 19,000 people located in approximately 70 locations in 80 countries. The company manufactures products such as body sealing systems and other fluid handling systems. It also provides complete cooling and heating management systems for all types of cars, including hybrids and electric vehicles. It also develops powertrain and other bodymount systems to minimize vibration in cars and thus ensure occupant comfort.

Cooper-Standard was originally organized along its product lines, but in 2009, it began changing to a geographic structure. Rather than have the company divided along product lines, the firm will operate two divisions. One division (North America) will cater to the North American market, and the International Division will be in charge of Europe, South America, and Asia. The company is also discontinuing its body and chassis and fluid system divisions.

Cooper-Standard hopes that these changes will allow it to keep its global products. However, the change to a geographic structure means that it will also be better able to respond to the needs of its customers. Customers in different geographic areas may have different needs and objectives and such a geographic structure will enable Cooper-Standard to respond to these needs and objectives more effectively.

*Sources: Based on Cooper-Standard. 2012. http://www.cooperstandard.com; PR Newswire. 2009. "Cooper-Standard Automotive reorganizes operations into geographic structure." March 26.*

As the Multinational Management Brief shows, the primary reason to choose a worldwide geographic structure is to implement a multidomestic or regional strategy, which requires a company to differentiate its products or services by country or region and therefore to have an organizational design with maximum geographic flexibility. The semiautonomous regional or country-based subunits of the worldwide geographic structure provide the flexibility to tailor or develop products that meet the particular needs of local or regional markets. Often differences in an area's product or service needs or in channels of distribution increase the need for a geographic structure. Exhibit 8.6 shows a geographic structure used by Royal Vopak, a Dutch multinational company that specializes in the distribution of chemicals.

For all practical purposes, even given a multidomestic strategy, country-level divisions usually exist only when a country's market size is sufficiently large or

**EXHIBIT 8.6**    Royal Vopak's Worldwide Geographic Structure

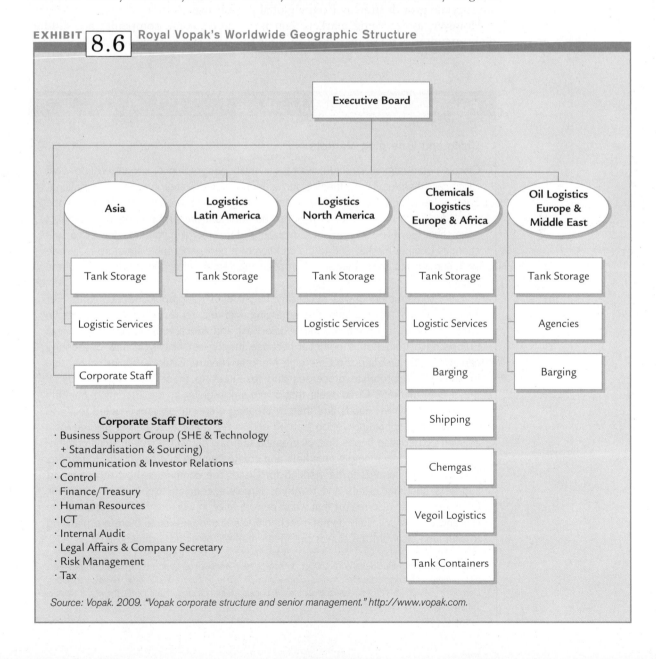

Source: Vopak. 2009. "Vopak corporate structure and senior management." http://www.vopak.com.

important to support its own organization. Separate divisions often make economic sense for large-market countries such as the United States, France, Germany, or Japan. Regional divisions combine small similar countries, such as a Southern European division for Italy, Spain, and Portugal.

For the regional strategist, combinations of countries are as large as possible. The combinations are based on similarities in customer requirements, balanced against the efficiencies of uniform products. However, interestingly, Toyota made some important changes to its geographic structure. Both its sales operations and planning operations groups had been organized by region (domestic and overseas), but then the company decided to integrate both operations by combining its domestic and overseas divisions.[11] As a global company, Toyota wanted more coordination among the various regions, including Japan, to implement the most appropriate growth strategy from a global perspective.

However, as emerging markets gain importance, some companies are shifting their attention to these markets. Consider the next Focus on Emerging Markets.

## **Focus** on Emerging Markets

### Cisco and Emerging Markets

Cisco's organizational structure was traditionally geographic, or organized into what Cisco calls theatres. These theatres included the United States, Americas International, Europe, the Middle East and Africa, Asia Pacific, and Japan. This organization made sense for Cisco because these regions had sufficient demand and need for product adaptation. However, the recent explosion in the emerging markets for Cisco and changes to other markets led to the creation of a new geographic structure to include an Emerging Markets Theatre, a European markets theater, and a U.S. and Canada theater.

Cisco's restructuring was necessary because of geographic developments. For instance, Cisco realized that the emerging markets represented by countries in Latin America, the Caribbean, the Middle East and Africa, and Russia and Eastern Europe have tremendous potential because they invest heavily in new networking capabilities. By creating the Emerging Markets Theatre, Cisco is hoping to be able to apply the appropriate processes and resources to meet the unique needs of these new markets. Cisco feels that the many regions in the Emerging Markets Theatre have similar needs and that, by creating a special division devoted to these regions, it can apply knowledge learned across the markets to deliver tailored local solutions. Cisco also hopes that, by creating the new division, it can show its commitment to these new emerging markets and create demand and growth for the future.

This strategy seems to be working for Cisco. The company's most recent report suggests quarterly profits and revenues largely exceeding expectations. However, Cisco executives also realize that weak performance in western markets such as the U.S and Europe will likely dampen technology spending. Cisco is therefore planning to shift workers from the slower European markets to emerging markets.

*Sources: Based on* Business Wire. *2005. "Cisco System announces three new geographic theatres: New 'emerging markets' theatre created to drive growth." June 6; Cisco. 2012. http://www.cisco.com; Dembosky, A. 2012. "Cisco defies gloom as it boosts dividends and beats profit targets. Financial Times, August 16, online edition.*

**EXHIBIT 8.7**  Worldwide Product Structure

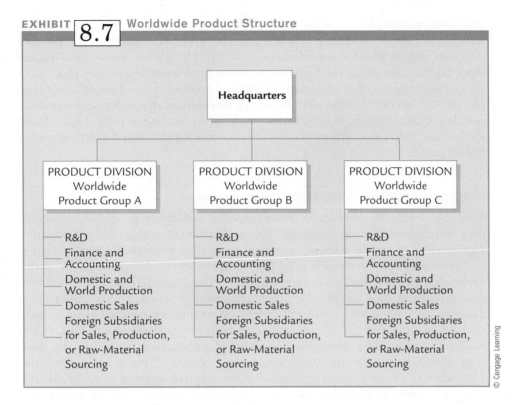

© Cengage Learning

Product divisions form the basic units of **worldwide product structures**, as shown in Exhibit 8.7. Each product division assumes responsibility for producing and selling its products or services throughout the world. The product structure therefore supports strategies that emphasize the production and sales of worldwide products. It is usually considered the ideal structure to implement an international strategy, in which the company attempts to gain economies of scale by selling worldwide products with most of the upstream activities based at home.

The worldwide product structure supports international strategies because it provides an efficient way to organize and centralize the production and sales of similar products for the world market. This type of structure sacrifices regional or local adaptation strengths derived from a geographic structure to gain economies of scale in product development and manufacturing. For example, Ford Motor Company implemented its Ford 2000 strategy by scrapping Ford of Europe and centralizing product engineering and design in Detroit. It created product groups, called Vehicle Centers, that had worldwide responsibility to develop new trucks and cars. This product-oriented design resulted in substantial cost savings by using fewer global suppliers and eliminating duplication in product development.[12] However, the current view is that, with its worldwide product organization, Ford lost touch with local customers in Europe.[13] A danger for Ford—or any other company that emphasizes product over geography—is that the cost savings from efficient production may not offset revenue losses when products fail to please the local market.

Foreign subsidiaries in the worldwide product structure may produce worldwide products/components, supply raw materials, or specialize only in local sales. However, they serve product goals determined by the product division headquarters. Production or supply subsidiaries often have little concern for their local markets.

**Worldwide product structure**
Gives product divisions responsibility to produce and sell their products or services throughout the world.

The sales subsidiaries exercise minimal local adaptation of the headquarters-directed worldwide marketing strategy. Manufacturing subsidiaries in the product structure may produce component products for the global market and export them back to the division's home country for final assembly. In this case, sister sales subsidiaries may then reimport the finished product for local sales.[14] For example, the U.S. aircraft manufacturer Boeing produces many of its aircraft components outside the United States. Its subsidiaries return these components to the United States for final assembly. Later, airlines in many of the producing countries buy the completed Boeing planes.

## Hybrids and Worldwide Matrix Structures

Both the worldwide product structure and the worldwide geographic structure have advantages and disadvantages for multinational strategy implementation. The product structure best supports strategies that emphasize global products and rationalization (worldwide products using worldwide, low-cost sources of raw materials, and worldwide marketing strategies). The geographic structure best supports strategies that emphasize local adaptation (managers are often local nationals and are sensitive to local needs). Most multinational companies, however, adopt strategies that include concerns both for local adaptation and for the economic and product development benefits of globalization. Consequently, most large multinationals have hybrid structures, or mixtures of product and area units. The nature of the product determines whether emphasis is given to the product or geographic side of the company (how global the products are) as well as the nature of the markets (how complex and different the major markets are).

At Sony Corporation headquarters, for example, worldwide product group managers exercise broad oversight over their businesses. However, Sony also focuses on regional needs by dividing global operations into four zones: Japan, North America, Europe, and the rest of the world. The consumer products giant, Unilever PLC, has a regional structure with local managers in three areas: Africa/Middle East, Latin America, and East Asia/Pacific. However, managers in Europe and North America report to worldwide product coordinators.[15] Similarly, Unilever gives the greatest power to the global product units when customers have similar needs worldwide. When customer needs vary by country or region, the company emphasizes geographic unit power with product groups under local management.[16]

To balance the benefits of geographic and product structures and to coordinate a mix of product and geographic subunits, some multinationals create a worldwide matrix structure. Unlike hybrid organizations, the worldwide matrix structure, shown in Exhibit 8.8, is a symmetrical organization, with equal lines of authority for product groups and for geographic divisions. Consider the next Multinational Management Brief.

Ideally, the matrix provides the structure for a firm to pursue both local and global strategies at the same time. Geographic divisions focus on national responsiveness, and product divisions focus on finding global efficiencies. The matrix structure works well only when there are nearly equal demands from the environment for local adaptation and for product standardization, with its associated economies of scale. Without these nearly equal demands, the organization tends to evolve into a product or geographic structure, based on which side is more important for competitive advantage.

In theory, the matrix produces quality decisions because two or more managers reach consensus on how to balance local and worldwide needs. Managers who

**Worldwide matrix structure**
Symmetrical organization, usually with equal emphasis on worldwide product groups and regional geographical divisions.

**EXHIBIT 8.8** Worldwide Matrix Structure

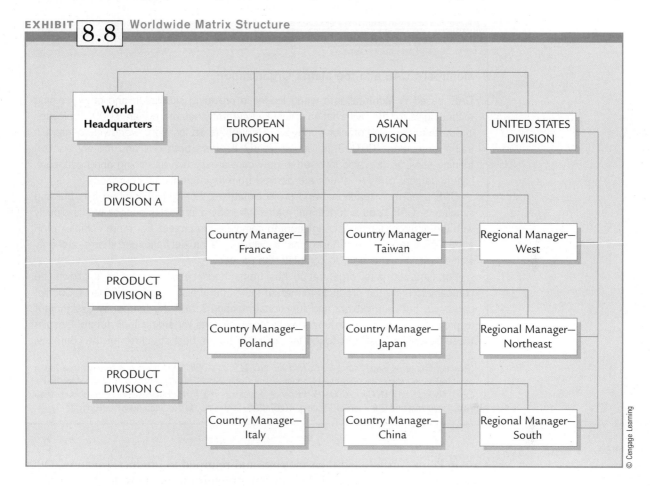

© Cengage Learning

hold positions at the intersection of product and geographic divisions are called two-boss managers because they have a boss from the product side and a boss from the geographic side of the organization. Product bosses tend to emphasize goals such as efficiency and using worldwide products, whereas geographic bosses tend to emphasize local or regional adaptation. The conflict between these interests is intended to balance globalization and localization pressures. As such, for managers at all levels, the matrix requires continual compensation for product and geographic needs.

To succeed at balancing the inherent struggles between global and local concerns, the matrix requires extensive resources for communication among the managers. Middle- and upper-level managers must have good human relations skills to deal with inevitable personal conflicts originating from the competing interests of product and geography. Middle-level managers must also learn to deal with two bosses, who often have competing interests. Upper-level managers, in turn, must be prepared to resolve conflicts between geographic and product managers.

Is the matrix worth the effort? During the 1980s, the matrix structure was a popular organizational solution to the global–local dilemma. More recently, however, the matrix has come under fire because consensus decision making between product and geographic managers has proved to be slow and cumbersome. In many organizations, the matrixes became too bureaucratic, with too many meetings and too much conflict. Some organizations, such as the Royal Dutch/Shell Group (see the next

## Multinational Management **Brief**

### Montreal's CAE and the Matrix Organization

CAE, based in Montreal, is a world leader in providing simulation and other training technologies for the civil aviation industry. It currently has more than 8,000 employees in approximately 100 offices worldwide. Through its 45 locations worldwide centers, it trains more than 100,000 individuals yearly. It offers both civil and military aviation training services. It is also involved in new core areas such as mining and healthcare. Ninety percent of its revenues are derived from its international operations.

CAE uses both functional and project matrixes. For instance, when it is building simulators, CAE uses a functional matrix whereby a project manager works closely with the different functional engineers to complete the project. For more complex projects, CAE uses a project-based matrix, whereby a project manager shares authority with a functional manager to complete the project.

For CAE, a matrix organization has tremendous benefits because it allows the company to bring the products to market faster, but it also creates difficulties. Conflict can occur between project and functional managers, and the temporary assignment to projects can also create uncertainty for employees regarding their future. Despite these difficulties, CAE has found the matrix to be the best structure for the company.

*Sources: Based on Appelbaum, S., D. Nadeau, and M. Cyr. 2008. "Performance evaluation in a matrix organization: A case study (Part One)." Industrial and Commercial Training, 40(5), 236–241; Appelbaum, S., D. Nadeau, and M. Cyr. 2008. "Performance evaluation in a matrix organization: A case study (Part Two)." Industrial and Commercial Training, 40(6), 295–299; CAE. 2012. http://www.cae.com.*

Case in Point), abandoned their matrixes and returned to product structures. Other organizations have redesigned their matrix structures to be more flexible, involving speedier decision making. In the more flexible matrixes, management centralizes key decisions in the product side or the geographic side of the matrix, depending on the need. For example, geographic areas with unique characteristics may require the freedom to tailor strategies. Facing such a situation, AT&T and Owens-Corning Fiberglas Corporation created highly autonomous units in China. They believe that the local Chinese and Asian markets are so dynamic that local managers (both Chinese and expatriates) need a great deal of freedom to seek opportunities.[17]

The evolving intensity and complexity of competition in international business have led to the evolution of strategies beyond geography and product foci. We saw earlier that this resulted in the transnational strategy. To carry out a transnational strategy effectively, a new organizational form has also arisen: the transnational network structure.

## The Transnational Network Structure

The **transnational network structure** is the newest solution to the complex demands of being locally responsive while taking advantage of global economies of scale and seeking location advantages, such as host country sources of knowledge. Like the matrix, the transnational network tries to gain all the advantages of the various structural options, combining functional, product, and geographic subunits. However, unlike the symmetrical matrix structure, the transnational network has no basic form. It has no symmetry or balance between the geographic

**Transnational network structure**
Network of functional, product, and geographic subsidiaries dispersed throughout the world, based on the subsidiaries' location advantages.

C A S E   I N   P O I N T

## Change at Shell and Philips

In 1995, Cornelius A. J. Herkstruter, chair of the Royal Dutch/Shell Group, announced a radical restructuring of his company. In a speech delivered simultaneously to corporate headquarters in London and The Hague, he declared that the matrix was out. Instead, global product divisions, such as exploration, production, and chemical, will report to teams of senior executives. These executives will have centralized decision-making power, no longer sharing it with country or functional managers.

Shell's old matrix was quite complex. For the multinational firm, most matrix structures combine two organizational designs, usually geography and product. Shell's matrix was three dimensional, with some managers having functional, product, and area bosses! For example, a finance executive could have a functional boss (e.g., chief financial officer), a country-level boss, and a product boss (e.g., chemical products).

Herkstruter believed that, over the years, Shell's complex matrix had resulted in too much bureaucracy. The matrix required too many managers. In addition, the meetings and consensus process of the matrix slowed decision making. To remain competitive in the oil industry, Shell had to cut many management positions and be quicker to identify business opportunities.

Philips, the Dutch electrical giant, was one of the earliest multinational companies to use the matrix structure, which combined product and country divisions. For instance, the head of the washing machine division in Italy had to report both to the head of that division and to the top washing machine head in the Netherlands. This created major difficulties for Philips, and there were continuous accountability problems. For instance, it was not easy to determine whether the country head or product head was responsible for profits and losses in a country. As a result, Philips reorganized into a number of units around the company's main businesses, and the national offices are now held accountable for these units.

*Sources: Based on Dwyer, Paula, and Heidi Dawley. 1995. "The passing of the Shell man: An era ends as Royal Dutch Shell vows to centralize power." BusinessWeek Online, international edition, April 17; Economist. 2006. "Survey: The matrix master." January 21; Shell. 2012. http://www.shell.com.*

and product sides of the organization. Instead, the network links different types of transnational subsidiaries throughout the world. Nodes, the units at the center of the network, coordinate product, functional, and geographic information. Product group units and geographic area units have different structures, and often no two subunits are alike. Rather, transnational units evolve to take advantage of resources, talent, and market opportunities wherever they exist in the world. Resources, people, and ideas flow in all directions.

The Dutch multinational Philips Electronics N.V. is only one example of a transnational network.[18] Working in 60 different countries, the company makes products as diverse as defense systems and light bulbs. There are eight product divisions with more than 60 subgroups based on product similarity. The product divisions have subsidiaries throughout the world, and the subsidiaries may focus on only one product or on an array of products. Subsidiaries can specialize in R&D, manufacturing, or marketing for world or regional markets. Some subsidiaries engage only in sales. Some units are highly independent of headquarters, while headquarters tightly controls other units.

In terms of geography, Philips divides the world into three groups. So-called key countries, such as the Netherlands and the United States, produce for local and world markets and control local sales. Large countries such as Mexico and Belgium have some local and worldwide production facilities and local sales. Local business countries are smaller nations that are primarily sales units and that import products from the product divisions' worldwide production centers in other countries.

All these design choices attempt to optimize efficiency, organizational learning, and local responsiveness.[19]

Exhibits 8.9 and 8.10 show two different perspectives on how one can look at Philips' very complex transnational network structure. One exhibit views geographic

**EXHIBIT 8.9**    Geographic Links in the Philips Transnational Structure

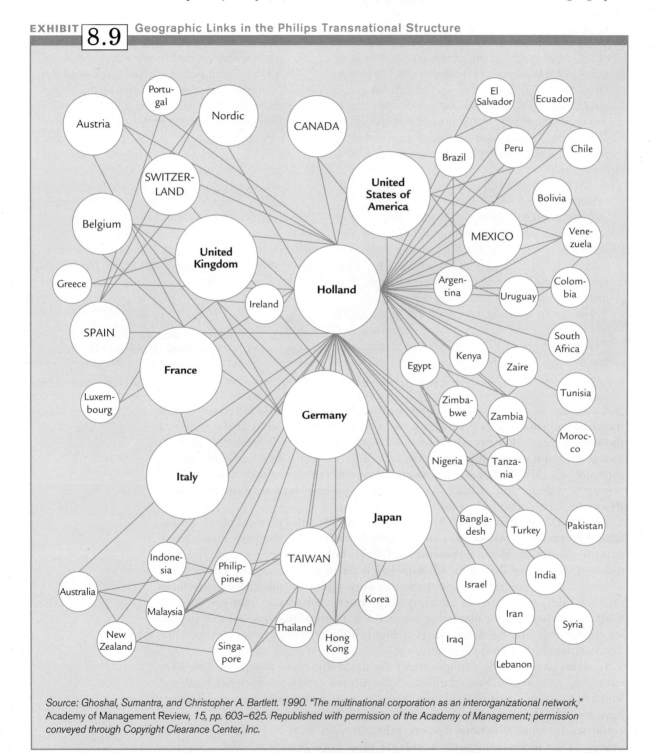

*Source: Ghoshal, Sumantra, and Christopher A. Bartlett. 1990. "The multinational corporation as an interorganizational network,"*
Academy of Management Review, *15, pp. 603–625. Republished with permission of the Academy of Management; permission conveyed through Copyright Clearance Center, Inc.*

EXHIBIT **8.10**    Product Links in the Philips Transnational Structure

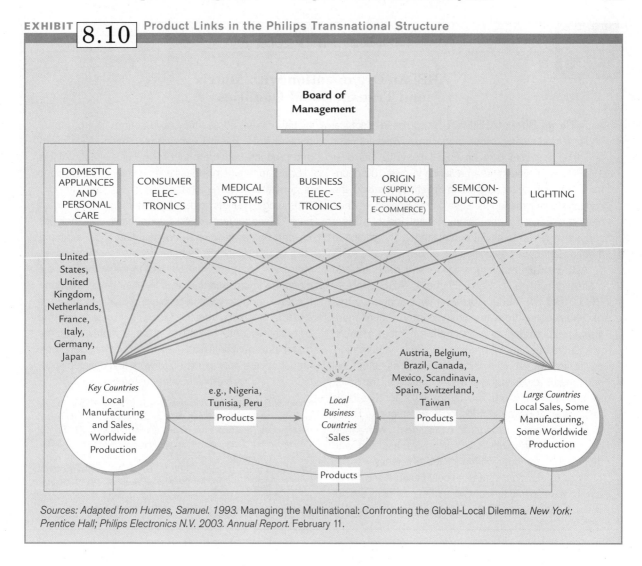

Sources: Adapted from Humes, Samuel. 1993. Managing the Multinational: Confronting the Global-Local Dilemma. *New York: Prentice Hall; Philips Electronics N.V. 2003. Annual Report.* February 11.

links among locations, and the other looks at the functions of different locations. Another company often considered to have the prototypical transnational structure is ABB. The next Case in Point discusses the transnational network structure of ABB, termed a "loose matrix" by its former CEO.

The basic structural framework of the transnational network consists of three components: dispersed subunits, specialized operations, and interdependent relationships.[20] The transnational network structure uses the flexible transnational subsidiary as the basic structural unit. **Dispersed subunits** are subsidiaries located anywhere in the world where they can benefit the company. Some subsidiaries take advantage of low factor costs (e.g., low labor costs); other units provide information on new technologies, new strategies, and consumer trends. All subunits try to tap worldwide managerial and technical talent.

**Specialized operations** are operations that subunits can specialize, whether it is in product lines, research areas, or marketing areas. Specialization builds on the diffusion of subunits by tapping local expertise or other resources anywhere

**Dispersed subunits**
Subsidiaries located anywhere in the world where they can benefit the company.

**Specialized operations**
Subunits specializing in particular product lines, research areas, or marketing areas.

## ABB: An Organization with Matrix and Transnational Qualities

Asea Brown Boveri (ABB) is a Swiss-based electrical equipment company that is bigger than Westinghouse and that hopes to take on GE. It currently has over 135,000 employees and a presence in over 100 countries. Although headquartered in Zurich, Switzerland, the company's top managers speak only English at their meetings. English is the common language, but it is a second language to all but one manager. The choice of meeting language personifies the global culture of ABB.

ABB's organization is a loose and decentralized matrix, according to Percy Barnevik, ABB's former CEO. ABB has about 100 country managers, most of whom come from the host country. Global managers head product divisions from a number of product segments: transportation, process automation, environmental devices, financial services, electrical equipment, and electric power generation, transmission, and distribution. The matrix calls for two-boss managers at some 1,100 local companies. These local company managers must deal with their country-level boss on local responsiveness and with their global manager on worldwide efficiency.

The organization is transnational because the matrix is not balanced and the functions of the subunits are not uniform. Depending on the situation, either country or

global product bosses may have control. The organizational culture of ABB encourages sharing technology and products within product lines. For example, ABB's U.S. steam turbine business uses techniques developed in Switzerland to repair the machines built with U.S. technology. There is no bias against things "not invented here." Management expects even locally run factories to participate in global coordination. For example, 31 power transformer factories, located in 16 countries, share all their performance data monthly through the global segment headquarters in Mannheim, Germany. If even one factory has a problem, global headquarters expects solutions from all factories. Furthermore, the company recently moved to a loose matrix structure that makes sustainability a key aspect of its operations. Managers are now expected to work and develop products that improve efficiency for customers.

*Sources: Based on Karunakaran, N. 2012. "How ABB is tweaking products to make sustainability and integral part of its business model."* The Economic Times (Online), *August 31; Taylor, William. 1991. "The logic of global business: An interview with ABB's Percy Barnevik."* Harvard Business Review, *March–April, 91–105; Rapoport, Garla. 1992. "A tough Swede invades the U.S."* Fortune, *June 29, 76–79; Ferner, Anthony. 2000. "Being local worldwide: ABB and the challenge of global management."* Relations Industrielles, *Summer, 527–529.*

and everywhere in the company's subsidiaries. Philips, for example, has eight research labs located in six countries. Some units have broad mandates, such as Philips' central laboratory in Eindhoven. Other units focus on specific areas, such as the laboratories for solid-state electronics work at Redhill in the United Kingdom.[21]

**Interdependent relationships**

Continuous sharing of information and resources by dispersed and specialized subunits.

**Interdependent relationships** must exist to manage the dispersed and specialized subunits, and units share information and resources continuously. To do this, transnationals usually build communication systems based on the latest technology. For example, GE Appliances' CEO J. Richard Stonesifer begins each Friday at 7:00 a.m. in a videoconference with colleagues in Asia. For the next five hours, he follows the rising sun with more videoconferences with managers from the Americas to Asia.[22] Ford creates virtual teams of design engineers from Europe, Japan, and the United States. These engineers communicate electronically, sharing both written material and design drawings.

The next Multinational Management Brief gives additional real-world examples of such transnational activities.

## Multinational Management **Brief**

### Transnational Activities

Because the transnational model has no fixed organizational components and activities, consider how the following companies include transnational activities in their organizational designs.

- *Flattened hierarchies for quick decision making:* ABB operates in more than 140 countries but still has only one layer of management between the top ranks and the business units.
- *Decentralized R&D for short product life cycles:* Nokia, the Finnish cell phone maker, puts R&D at the plant level at five factories around the world. Concurrent engineering takes place, and the culture supports sharing any valuable engineering information with plants in all country locations.
- *Using a loose matrix structure to make sustainability key to operations:* ABB is now realigning its operations to make sustainability a key aspect of everything the company does. Every business decision is scrutinized in terms of sustainability goals and all aspects of operations are designed to be sustainable.
- *Finding global products:* Texas Instruments created a team with the mandate to search the company worldwide for possible global products.
- *Tapping worldwide talent:* ABB designs locomotives in Switzerland and tilting trains in Sweden. Singapore engineers designed a new pager for Motorola.
- *Integrating the workforce:* To build a collaborative culture between workers in Singapore and workers in its sister plant in the United States, Motorola brought the workers to a Colorado resort for Outward Bound–style team-building games.
- *Using e-mail, information systems, Voice-Over-Internet Protocol, and WIKIs (server software that allows users to create or change website content):* Unilever PLC has 31,000 employees worldwide communicating by e-mail or Lotus Notes. The Mexican company Cementos Mexicanos can tell with one keystroke the energy use in an oven from its Spanish subsidiary.
- *Using web-based collaboration systems, such as WebEx or Lotus Notes:* Dallas-based Fluor, a publicly owned engineering services company, has more than 46,000 employees worldwide with major offices in eight countries and operations in 50 international locations. It uses various web-based collaboration systems such as Lotus Notes and SkillSoft for collaboration and online learning. Aperian GlobeSmart's cultural diversity training tool can be helpful in providing culture training.

*Sources: Based on Bolch, M. 2008. "Going global." Training, 45(4), 28–29; BusinessWeek Online. 1994. "Grabbing markets from the giants," November 18; BusinessWeek Online. 1994. "Tearing up today's organization chart," November 18; Copeland, Michael V. 2006. "The mighty micro-multinational." Business 2.0, July, 107–114; Forteza, Jorge H., and Gary L. Neilson. 1999. "Multinationals in the next decade." Strategy & Business, 16, 3rd quarter, 1–11; Karunakaran, N. 2012. "How ABB is tweaking products to make sustainability an integral part of its business model." The Economic Times (Online), August 31.*

# Beyond the Transnational: Is There a New Structure for the Multinational?

Some evidence suggests that the transnational network is not the end of the evolution of the multinational's structure. Professor Yves Doz and his colleagues argue that a new structure is emerging called the **metanational**.[23] The meta-national

**Metanational structure**
An evolution of the transnational network structure that develops extensive systems to encourage organizational learning and entrepreneurial activities.

company is "a large, entrepreneurial multinational firm that is able to tap into hidden pockets of innovation, technology, and market now scattered around the world, especially in emerging markets."[24]

In many ways, the metanational structure is like the transnational network. The metanational is a networked organization with different types of platforms around the world, and, like the transnational, it is a centerless organization that reduces hierarchy and places critical decision making in the peripheral units or nodes throughout the world. The difference with the metanational is its overriding objective to learn from anywhere in the world and to share this knowledge with the rest of the company. The metanational organization uses the latest in virtual connectivity to link team members worldwide.

The characteristics of the metanational structure are:[25]

- Nonstandard business formulas for any local activity.
- Looking to emerging markets as sources of knowledge and ideas, not just for local labor.
- Creating a culture and an advanced communication system that support global learning.
- The extensive use of strategic alliances to gain knowledge for varied sources.
- High levels of trust between partners to encourage knowledge sharing.
- A centerless structure that moves strategic functions away from headquarters and to major markets.
- A decentralization of decision making away from headquarters and to the managers who serve the key customers and strategic partners.

# Multinational Strategy and Structure: An Overview

Exhibit 8.11 shows the relationship between various multinational strategies and types of organizational structure. The connections between the boxes show typical ways that multinational structures evolve.

Strategies of national or regional responsiveness (i.e., the multidomestic or regional strategies discussed in Chapter 6) suggest the use of geographic structures. Given an international strategy, managers should consider a product organization and have worldwide products.

Most companies support their early internationalization with export departments or international divisions. Later, as Exhibit 8.12 suggests, and depending on the globalization of their strategy, companies evolve into worldwide product or geographic structures. After this, because of the dual demands of local adaptation pressures and globalization, many companies move toward a matrix or transnational network structure. Most companies, however, never quite reach the pure matrix, transnational, or metanational state. Instead, they typically adopt hybrid structures with some matrix and some transnational qualities. With the globalization of ever more products and the competitive efficiencies they bring, large multinational companies are giving product divisions increased power and creating more transnational subsidiaries.

Up to this point, we have discussed how to divide the organization into units that best support the chosen strategies. Next, we will see how these units are brought together to accomplish organizational goals.

**EXHIBIT** 8.11 **Multinational Strategy, Structure, and Evolution**

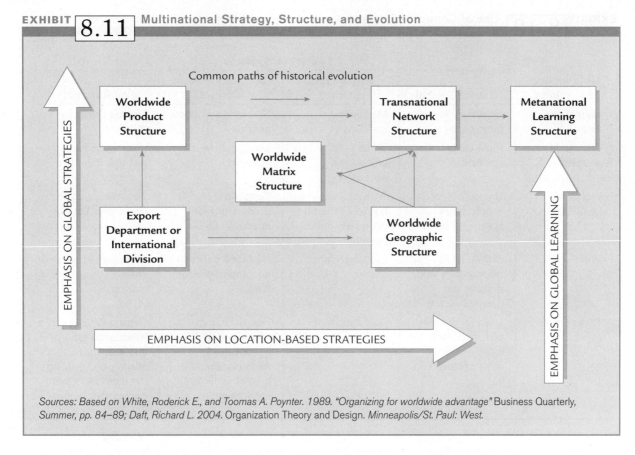

Sources: Based on White, Roderick E., and Toomas A. Poynter. 1989. "Organizing for worldwide advantage" Business Quarterly, Summer, pp. 84–89; Daft, Richard L. 2004. Organization Theory and Design. Minneapolis/St. Paul: West.

## Control and Coordination Systems

In addition to selecting different types of subunits to perform specialized tasks and responsibilities, top managers must design organizational systems to control and coordinate the activities of these subunits. This is a difficult task. Foreign subsidiaries differ widely in terms of geographic location, local markets, cultures, and legal systems, as well as in terms of the talents and resources available to the subsidiary.[26] This section reviews such systems.

For multinational companies, organizational control consists of the procedures used to focus the activities of subsidiaries in directions that support the company's strategies. **Control systems** help link the organization vertically, up and down the organizational hierarchy. Control systems serve this purpose in two basic ways. First, they measure or monitor the performances of subunits regarding their assigned roles in the firm's strategy. Second, they provide feedback to subunit managers regarding the effectiveness of their units. Measurement and feedback help top management communicate strategic goals to subordinates. In addition, measurement and feedback—combined with reward systems (e.g., promotion and pay)—help managers direct subordinates' behavior in appropriate directions.

**Coordination systems** link the organization horizontally. They provide information flows among subsidiaries so that they can coordinate their activities. For example, in implementing its strategy, Ford plans to use advanced information systems so that designers in Europe, the United States, and Japan can coordinate their efforts in designing cars for the world market. Engineers will be able to communicate directly and share complex design information instantaneously.

**Control system**
Vertical organizational links, up and down the organizational hierarchy.

**Coordination system**
Horizontal organizational links.

**EXHIBIT 8.12**  Use of Control Mechanisms in Multinational Organizational Structures

| Multinational Structures | Control Systems | | | |
| --- | --- | --- | --- | --- |
| | **Output Control** | **Bureaucratic Control** | **Decision-Making Control** | **Cultural Control** |
| International division | Most likely to be profit center | Must follow company policies | Some centralization possible | Treated like other divisions |
| Worldwide geographic | Profit center most common | Some policies and procedures necessary | Local units have autonomy | Local subsidiary culture often more important |
| Worldwide product | Unit output for supply; sales volume for sales | Tight process controls for product quality and consistency | Centralized at product division headquarters | Possible for some companies but not always necessary |
| Matrix | Shared profit responsibility with product and geographic units | Less important | Balanced between geographic product units | Culture must support shared decision making |
| Transnational network | Used for supplier units and some independent profit centers | Less important | Few decisions centralized at headquarters; more decisions centralized in key network nodes | Organizational culture transcends national cultures; supports sharing and learning; the most important control mechanism |

© Cengage Learning

## Design Options for Control Systems

There are four broad types of control systems: output control, bureaucratic control, decision-making control, and cultural control.

**Output control systems** assess the performance of a unit based on results, not on the processes used to achieve the results. In multinational companies, top management and local management usually negotiate output goals for foreign subsidiaries, and the goals must support the overall corporate strategy. Control occurs because headquarters evaluates subsidiaries and rewards local managers depending on how well the subsidiaries achieve the output goals.

Responsibility for profit is the most common output control. As already noted, a **profit center** is the name given to a unit controlled on the basis of profit or loss. Companies compare such units by looking at each profit center's profit or loss. The minireplica subsidiary is often a profit center. Profit center subsidiaries usually set their own strategies, hire local workers, and act independently from the multinational company's headquarters. Top managers judge the success of the unit and its managers on the basis of the profits generated for the parent company.

Besides profit, other outcomes—such as market share, developing new technologies, and supplying high-quality raw materials—provide performance targets used to control multinational subsidiaries. For example, companies with transnational strategies and structures may evaluate each of their subsidiaries differently. One subsidiary may be evaluated based on its development of worldwide products, and another may be evaluated on its market penetration by capturing market share.

**Output control system**
Assesses the performance of a unit based on results, not on the processes used to achieve the results.

**Profit center**
Unit controlled by its profit or loss performance.

**Bureaucratic control systems** focus on managing behaviors, not outcome, within an organization. Typical bureaucratic control mechanisms include budgets, statistical reports, standard operating procedures, and centralization of decision making.[27] These systems work as follows:

- *Budgets set financial targets for expenditures during specific time periods.* Budgets control subsidiary behavior by providing rules that limit how much the subsidiary can spend on an activity. They focus on controlling costs and usually emphasize efficiency goals; that is, efficient subunits produce more output (service or products) on a fixed budget than inefficient subunits.

- *Statistical reports provide information to top management on non-financial outcomes.* For example, a service organization might report on the number of customer complaints each week. A manufacturing organization might report on the number of units produced or the number of units rejected by quality control.

- *Standard operating procedures (SOPs) provide the rules and regulations that identify the approved ways of behaving.* For example, SOPs might prescribe that all subsidiaries should follow a standard practice for personnel evaluations.

**Decision-making control** represents the level in the organizational hierarchy where managers have the authority to make decisions. Upper management seldom makes all the decisions in an organization. In decentralized organizations, lower-level managers make a large number of important decisions. In centralized organizations, higher-level managers make most of the important decisions. In most worldwide product structures, control over the functional and strategic activities (i.e., production, finance, marketing, and product strategies) is centralized in the product division headquarters. Local country-level subsidiary managers deal only with local administrative, legal, and financial affairs.[28] In contrast, decentralized decision making is more common in worldwide area structures; local country or regional subsidiaries have considerable autonomy from headquarters. Transnational network structures do not exhibit a tendency for decision-making control in one direction or the other. The transnational company has several headquarters, each controlling different types of decisions depending on local expertise and the strategic situation. Depending on the strengths of a subsidiary, decision making may be centralized in the headquarters' nodes or passed down to lower levels.

**Cultural control systems** use organizational culture (Chapter 2) to control employees' behaviors and attitudes. Strong organizational cultures develop shared norms, values, beliefs, and traditions among workers. Such cultures encourage high levels of commitment and support for the organization. Workers and managers understand management goals and direct their efforts in support of them. Many experts now argue that a strong organizational culture may be the only way to link a dispersed multinational company with managers from many different national cultures.

Cultural control is the favored control mechanism for transnational network structures. Although transnational organizations use bureaucratic and output-control mechanisms, the uncertainties and complexities of the international environment make these relatively formal mechanisms less effective than culture. For example, budgets or output goals set at the Paris headquarters may not be timely for changing situations in Budapest or Singapore. Instead, headquarters relies on local managers' commitment to corporate goals and trusts that they will adjust appropriately to local conditions.

**Bureaucratic control system**
Focuses on managing organizational processes through budgets, statistical reports, standard operations procedures, and centralization of decision making.

**Decision-making control**
Level in the organizational hierarchy where managers have the authority to make decisions.

**Cultural control system**
Uses organizational culture to control the behaviors and attitudes of employees.

Multinational companies use all these control mechanisms to varying degrees, depending on their structure. Exhibit 8.12 shows the relationships between the control mechanisms and the basic multinational organizational structures.

## Design Options for Coordination Systems

There are six basic horizontal coordination systems: textual communication (memos or reports in electronic or paper form), direct contact, liaison roles, task forces, full-time integrators, and teams.[29] We discuss first the mechanisms that provide the least amount of coordination and then continue to the mechanisms that offer the greatest amount of coordination.

All organizations use textual communication, such as e-mail, memos, and reports, to coordinate the activities of subunits. Units report on their activities, keeping other units aware of problems, output levels, innovations, or any other important information. With the increased availability of low-cost computer equipment, most memos and reports no longer appear on paper. Companies use e-mail or postings to local websites. Such electronic communication is particularly popular for multinational companies because they need rapid interaction over long distances and across many time zones.

**Direct contact** means that managers or workers interact face to face. For multinational companies, direct contact often requires sophisticated videoconferencing and knowledge of a common language. For example, GE Medical Systems uses nearly 1,000 hours of teleconferencing in a year. Ford has computer-aided design and manufacturing links between two continents to allow its engineers in Europe and the United States to communicate design and engineering ideas.[30]

**Liaison roles** are the specific job responsibilities of a person in one department to communicate with people in another department. A liaison role is only part of a manager's job responsibilities. For example, in a multinational company, one manager in each country subsidiary might be given the responsibility of coordinating marketing efforts within a region.

**Full-time integrators** have roles similar to liaison roles, but coordination is their sole job responsibility. Often product managers are full-time integrators. Product managers coordinate the development of their products with design teams, their production with the manufacturing departments, and their sales and promotion with marketing. In the multinational company, product managers often serve as links between the production units and local country operations.

**Task forces** are temporary teams, usually linking two or more departments, created to solve a particular organizational problem, such as entering a new market. For example, to take advantage of new market opportunities in China, Unilever assembled a group of Chinese-speaking troubleshooters selected from its 100 country operations and sent them to China. The troubleshooters built plants and planned strategy and organization, and then returned to their home countries when they had completed their task.[31]

**Teams** are the strongest coordination mechanisms. Unlike task forces, which have a short life, teams are permanent units of the organization. Teams come from several organizational subunits to specialize in particular problems. For example, a team doing new product development might include a scientist from R&D and managers from production and marketing. In a multinational example, Texas Instruments uses permanent special-project teams, called Nomads, to set up chip fabrication plants anywhere in the world, from Italy to Singapore.[32]

**Direct contact**
Face-to-face interaction of employees.

**Liaison roles**
Part of a person's job in one department to communicate with people in another department.

**Full-time integrator**
Cross-unit coordination is the main job responsibility.

**Task force**
Temporary team created to solve a particular organizational problem.

**Team**
Permanent unit of the organization designed to focus the efforts of different subunits on particular problems.

As with the control options, most multinational companies use several, if not all, of the coordination mechanisms at one time or another. However, matrix and transnational network structures have a very high need for coordination. In these types of organizations, one sees a great use of the more elaborate control mechanisms of task forces, full-time integrators, and teams. For transnational networks, with their extensive geographic dispersion of subunits, teams are increasingly virtual units, with members seldom meeting face to face. Given the importance of team coordination mechanisms, we consider them in more depth.

## Teams

As multinational companies strive to meet both local and global customer needs by integrating the design and development expertise from around the world, they are making increased use of teams.[33] Consider the following Multinational Management Brief.

As the Multinational Management Brief below shows teams give global companies the ability to better coordinate the work and expertise of widely dispersed individuals, to develop and launch new products, and to become more flexible. For example, International Truck and Engine Corporation created cross-functional project teams of employees located in Canada, the United States, and Mexico to develop its new products.[34] By bringing together the top employees in engineering, manufacturing,

---

## Multinational Management **Brief**

### Teams and Multinationals

Teams are becoming increasingly popular in multinational companies. Many see teams as the means to deal with the challenges stemming from globalization. As multinationals face increasingly competitive and diverse environments, teams are seen as the way to allow individuals located across countries and regions to coordinate their activities and achieve common goals. Furthermore, as you will see later, many multinationals are also making increased use of virtual teams to coordinate work in the absence of face-to-face communication.

Consider the case of Boeing and its most recent product, the Dreamliner. Boeing relied on a large number of external suppliers to help design the Dreamliner. Many of these suppliers were located outside of the United States and the company had to make extensive use of teams to ensure that the plane's development was progressing as needed. Consider, for instance, the challenges the company faced with respect to the use of materials in the plane. New materials often require extensive testing as engineers find ways to control properties of the materials being tested. However, Boeing developed an innovative materials design team that enabled employees worldwide to collaborate. For example, any design changes made in Japan could immediately be seen by engineers in the United States. National Steel of Singapore also used to teams to find ways for the company to become more sustainable. Employees organized in teams came up with ways to save energy and many of their ideas were then implemented.

*Sources: Based on* Business Times. *2012. "Keeping the business on the boil." September 19, online edition; Wadia, C. 2012. "Competing faster."* Technology Review, *11; Zander, L., A. I. Mockatis, and C. L. Butler. 2012. "Leading global teams."* Journal of World Business, *47, 592–603.*

**Global virtual team**

Groups of people from different parts of the world who work together by using information and communication technologies such as intranets, Web meetings, WIKIs, e-mail, and instant messaging.

finance, and project management in these cross-functional teams, International Truck and Engine Corporation hopes to find ways to bring products to market more rapidly while increasing productivity. Furthermore, the new global workplace is seeing an increased use of **global virtual teams**, which are groups of people from different parts of the world who work together using information and communication technologies such as intranets, Web meetings, WIKIs, e-mail, and instant messaging.[35]

Although global teams are popular, they face significant challenges, many of which are associated with having team members with diverse cultural backgrounds located in different parts of the world. Previous surveys and empirical research have identified challenges such as the diversity of languages and cultural differences among team members.[36] Such challenges often make it difficult for the teams to collaborate.

Despite these challenges, multinational companies can take steps to ensure that their global teams collaborate to function effectively, as follows.[37]

- *Build relationships and trust:* Important steps have to be taken to encourage global team members to get to know each other and build trust. For instance, initial face-to-face meetings should be organized not only to let team members learn about each other but also to set project goals and roles. Some even suggest that the first meeting should last at least three days. However, if traveling is too expensive, conference calls or other means can be used regularly. It is advisable to use the time at the start of such meetings to encourage global team members to get to know each other personally. This can be done by assigning a full-time communication specialist who can plan and manage both information flow and communication across teams. For example, a communication specialist may request team members to provide more extensive feedback when necessary or educate them about the pros and cons of the various forms of communication, such as e-mail and videoconferencing.

- *Pay attention to project planning and hold project progress meetings regularly:* Ensuring that projects are completed on schedule and on budget is difficult enough with domestic teams. However, the added complexity of having team members located around the world suggests that multinational companies need to devote significant resources to planning the project. All team members should be made aware of the goals and time line of the project, and the project leader should send clear messages about the key issues and how they relate to the strategic objective. Furthermore, regular team meetings should be held to inform team members of progress. Corrective actions can also be implemented as necessary.

- *Cultural, language, and active-listening training:* Global teams can function only if team members are all on the same wavelength. Multinational companies need to devote resources to training global team members appropriately and to assessing their level of cultural competency. Language training may also be appropriate for a level of language commonality among all team members. For instance, the prescriptions discussed in Chapter 13 on international negotiation regarding communication with non-native speakers may be helpful. Also, global teams may fail because they consider lengthy discussions a waste of time. Group members must be trained to be sensitive to different communication styles, to practice active listening, and to avoid overlooking important issues.

This section completes our consideration of organizational design by showing how managers can control and coordinate subunits. In the final section, we look at knowledge management, a design issue that is becoming crucial for most multinational companies.

# Knowledge Management

In Chapter 7, we saw that most multinational companies face a very chaotic and unfocused environment. Industry boundaries are ambiguous, and companies are facing intense competition. Product life cycles are being increasingly compressed, and most multinational companies are experiencing severe information overload.[38] To face such challenges, companies must make optimal use of the available knowledge—that is, the filtered information of value to a company—to build an innovative culture. Knowledge is the most important source of sustainable competitive advantage as multinational companies face shifting markets, rapid product cycles, and hypercompetition.[39] Companies must therefore implement systems to manage knowledge.

In this final section, we examine some of the critical design issues related to knowledge management.

**Knowledge management** consists of the systems, mechanisms, and other design elements of an organization that ensure that the right form of knowledge is available to the right individual at the right time.[40] Consider the next Case in Point.

Why is it so critical for companies to manage their knowledge closely? For domestic companies, adequately managing existing knowledge can be instrumental in generating new knowledge, which can then lead to innovation and value creation.[41] However, as the Case in Point demonstrates, for multinational companies, knowledge management is even more critical because they face unique challenges. Many multinationals now have to face forces for both international integration and local differentiation while achieving global innovation. Multinational companies

**Knowledge management**
Systems, mechanisms, and other design elements of an organization that ensure that the right form of knowledge is available to the right individual at the right time.

## CASE IN POINT

### Knowledge Management in Various Multinationals

Knowledge management systems are keys to the success of multinationals. Telenor Mobile of Norway was one of the world's pioneers in mobile phones, introducing the world's first automatic cellular service as far back as the 1980s. Its entry strategy was to develop joint ventures with local telecommunication companies. In many cases, Telenor was buying into companies at the start-up stage, proving its technical expertise as the basis for the joint ventures. However, as mobile phone technology became more standardized, the company was losing its competitive advantage based on technical expertise.

Telecommunication companies like Telenor realized that the only way to succeed was to develop systems that could identify the best practices in the markets they were operating in and spread those practices across their operations. Telenor therefore devised a knowledge management system whereby local best practices were identified and collected in a central system. Local affiliates identified best practices, and Telenor then attempted to implement the practices in other locations. Without such a

knowledge management system, Telenor would not have been able to benefit from the knowledge of its many foreign partners.

The insurance industry also benefits tremendously from knowledge management systems. DKVA is a German insurance company responsible for health care claims by German citizens living in other parts of the European Union. It processes about 1.2 million claims per year and must handle a 10 to 15 percent dispute rate. DKVA designed a knowledge management system to help with its claims. It selected a Process360 optimization solution whereby users can find out where all their claims and payments are. The system also allows DKVA to find out the stage of a dispute, as well as print invoices and retrieve other critical documents. Most importantly, the system is flexible enough to accommodate the frequent changes in health coverage and payment rules that characterize the European Union.

*Sources: Based on Britt, P. 2008. "KM reaps benefits worldwide for insurers." KMWorld, October, 20, 26; Goodermam, P. N., and S. Ulset. 2007. "Telenor's third way." European Business Forum, Winter, 31, 46–48.*

therefore need to be able to implement systems that are capable of combining worldwide local knowledge in order to innovate and then to transfer the innovation to new products for international markets.

Appropriately managing knowledge can give multinational companies the means to create the global flexibility they will need to survive and prosper.[42]

To develop an effective knowledge management system, the first step is to identify potential barriers to knowledge sharing within the organization. Barriers can exist at various levels, including individual and organizational levels.[43] Sharing knowledge across companies located in different parts of the world introduces a number of cross-cultural and geographic distance-related challenges. Exhibit 8.13 summarizes some of the most important individual, organizational, and cross-cultural problems.

The next step is for multinational companies to assess the degree to which these barriers exist and implement appropriate actions to reduce their effects. For instance, the multinational firm can take the appropriate steps to communicate with employees about the need to share knowledge. Individual employees should be motivated and encouraged to capture and disseminate the appropriate knowledge to others in the organization as needed, and they should be rewarded when they do so.[44] Furthermore, the organizational structure should be aligned with the need for knowledge management. Tall, hierarchical structures are obvious barriers to information flow, and important steps need to be taken toward a flatter and more fluid structure. Finally, an important aspect of knowledge management is the use of computer-based technology.[45] Computer and web-based technologies allow multinational companies to create simple data repositories of explicit knowledge (i.e., knowledge that can be stored and shared), and they enable firms to use their

**EXHIBIT** 8.13   Knowledge Management Barriers

**Individual barriers:**

- Lack of time or interest to share knowledge.
- Lack of understanding of importance of sharing knowledge.
- Lack of trust in others.
- Use of hierarchical position or power to encourage sharing of explicit, rather than tacit, knowledge.
- Poor communication skills.

**Organizational barriers:**

- Lack of communication of importance of knowledge management.
- No strategic alignment between organization's mission and objectives and knowledge-sharing strategy and initiatives.
- Lack of sufficient mechanisms (both online and face to face) to share knowledge.
- Lack of reward systems to foster and encourage knowledge sharing.
- Communication flows restricted to one direction as reflected in the organizational hierarchy.
- Internal strife and conflict among business units.

**Cross-cultural barriers:**

- Language barriers.
- Cultural differences.
- Time zone and other geographic distance-related challenges.

*Sources: Based on Riege, Andreas. 2005. "Three-dozen knowledge-sharing barriers managers must consider." Journal of Knowledge Management, 9(3), pp. 18–35; Voelpel, Sven C., and Zheng Han. 2005. "Managing knowledge sharing in China: The case of Siemens ShareNet." Journal of Knowledge Management, 9(3), pp. 51–63.*

tacit knowledge through such tools as networking, collaborative commerce, and other decision support systems. DuPont uses Lotus Notes to allow its R&D personnel to collaborate and consult with other in-house and outside experts.[46] So it is important for multinational companies to invest in building the integrative platform for individuals located around the world.

## Summary and Conclusions

Good strategies alone will never guarantee successful multinational operations. Good implementation is equally important. Perhaps the most important part of strategy implementation is having the right organizational design to carry out strategic intents, goals, and objectives. This chapter provided a review of how multinational companies use organizational designs to implement multinational strategies. Organizational design entails the choice of subunits (how to divide work) and the choice of coordination and control mechanisms (how to focus the efforts of the subunits).

The chapter reviewed the basics of organizational structure. Functional, product-oriented, and geographic structures were described and pictured. They also were compared and contrasted for their strengths and weaknesses. A knowledge of these basic structures is necessary because function, product, and area structures are the building blocks for the organizational structures used by multinational companies.

As companies internationalize their strategies, they usually progress from using an export department or international division to more complex organizational structures. More complex structures call for foreign subsidiaries to conduct value chain activities (e.g., manufacturing) in other countries. Some of these subsidiaries are minireplicas—small reproductions of the home country organization. Other subsidiaries are transnational; they can do anything or be anywhere depending on the local strengths and the parent company's needs. Companies use different types of subsidiaries depending on the structures they choose.

If companies adopt a multidomestic or regional multinational strategy, they usually favor a worldwide geographic structure, which emphasizes responding to local markets. In contrast, the worldwide product structure supports an international strategy; it facilitates building and selling global products. Hybrid and matrix structures support companies with mixtures of strategies for different products and businesses. These structures combine some of the benefits of both the geographic and the product structures. The transnational network structure goes beyond the matrix and hybrid. It has no set form, and its subsidiaries respond uniquely to global efficiency pressures, company learning needs, or local needs, as the strategic situation dictates. The step beyond the transnational network structure is the metanational structure, whose organizational learning and virtual information sharing become the drivers of the organization.

Organizational designs are not complete without integration mechanisms. These mechanisms link subunits and coordinate their activities. Control systems, such as bureaucratic and cultural controls, link the organization vertically. Coordination mechanisms, such as task forces and teams, link the organization horizontally. Multinational organizations use all these integration mechanisms, but for the multinational company, cultural control is often considered most important. A strong organizational culture helps the multinational company bridge the national cultures of its employees.

Finally, an important component of today's multinational companies consists of knowledge management systems. Knowledge management systems allow the multinational company to encourage the sharing of valuable expertise of individuals located around the world. To implement such systems successfully, the multinational organization must assess barriers to knowledge sharing and implement knowledge networks.

## Discussion Questions

1. You work for a company with three major products, and your CEO has decided to sell these products in the international marketplace. She asks your advice in setting up an organizational structure. What issues would you discuss with her regarding the company's international strategy before making any recommendations?

2. What are the advantages of a worldwide product structure over a worldwide area structure? What type of company would most likely choose each type?

3. What are the costs and benefits of having a matrix structure?

4. What transnational activities might be possible for a small company with only an export department or an international division?

5. Identify some areas in multinational companies where cultural control might work better than bureaucratic control.

6. What cultural values must a metanational company encourage so that alliance partners and dispersed subsidiaries share knowledge?

7. What are virtual teams? What benefits can virtual teams bring to multinational companies?

8. What are some of the typical problems multinationals face when using teams as integration mechanisms? What can multinational companies do to address these problems?

9. What are knowledge management systems? How can they be appropriately designed?

## Multinational Management **Internet Exercise**

1. Go to any major multinational's website (e.g., Siemens, Shell, McDonalds).

2. Find the company's organizational structure. What type of organizational structure exists at the company?

3. Do you think that the structure is appropriate for the multinational? Why or why not?

4. What sort of challenges do you see from the particular form of organizational structure used?

## Multinational Management **Skill Builder**

### Build an Organization Structure for P&G

**Step 1.** Procter & Gamble (P&G) is a major multinational corporation headquartered in the United States. Review the popular business press (e.g., *Wall Street Journal, Fortune, Economist, Business-Week*) over the last year for articles on P&G's operations around the globe.

**Step 2.** Given this background information, design a multinational structure that you think can best implement P&G's strategies for different products. Exhibits 8.14 and 8.15 show an overview of P&G's geographic locations and major global products.

**Step 3.** Prepare a written or oral report showing your design and providing a rationale for your structural choices.

**EXHIBIT 8.14**    P&G's Worldwide Locations and Starting Dates of Operations

| | | | | |
|---|---|---|---|---|
| Algeria, 2001 | Denmark, 1992 | Indonesia, 1970 | Panama, 2000 | Tanzania, 1997 |
| Argentina, 1991 | Egypt, 1986 | Ireland, 1980 | Peru, 1956 | Thailand, 1985 |
| Australia, 1985 | El Salvador, 1988 | Israel, 2001 | Philippines, 1935 | Turkey, 1987 |
| Austria, 1966 | Estonia, 1995 | Italy, 1956 | Poland, 1991 | Uganda, 1995 |
| Azerbaijan, 1998 | Federal Republic of | Japan, 1973 | Portugal, 1989 | Ukraine, 1993 |
| Bangladesh, 1995 | Yugoslavia, 1996 | Kazakhstan, 1996 | Puerto Rico, 1947 | United Arab |
| Belarus, 1995 | Federation of Bosnia- | Kenya, 1985 | Romania, 1994 | Emirates, 2001 |
| Belgium, 1955 | Herzegovina, 1998 | Korea, 1988 | Russia, 1991 | United Kingdom, |
| Brazil, 1988 | Finland, 1971 | Latvia, 1995 | Saudi Arabia, 1957 | 1930 |
| Bulgaria, 1994 | Former Yugoslav | Lebanon, 1959 | Singapore, 1969 | United States, |
| Canada, 1915 | Republic of Macedonia, | Lithuania, 1997 | Slovak Republic, | 1837 |
| Caribbean Islands, | 1998 | Malaysia, 1969 | 1993 | Uzbekistan, 1996 |
| 1986 | France, 1954 | Mexico, 1948 | Slovenia, 1996 | Venezuela, 1950 |
| Chile, 1983 | Germany, 1960 | Morocco, 1958 | South Africa, 1994 | Vietnam, 1994 |
| China, 1988 | Ghana, 1998 | Netherlands, 1964 | Spain, 1968 | Yemen, 1995 |
| Colombia, 1982 | Greece, 1960 | New Zealand, 1985 | Sri Lanka, 1996 | |
| Costa Rica, 1995 | Guatemala, 1985 | Nicaragua, 1985 | Sweden, 1969 | |
| Croatia, 1991 | Honduras, 1985 | Nigeria, 1992 | Switzerland, 1953 | |
| Czech Republic, | Hong Kong, 1969 | Norway, 1993 | Syria, 1998 | |
| 1991 | Hungary, 1991 | Pakistan, 1989 | Taiwan, 1984 | |

*Source: Adapted from Procter & Gamble. 2003.* Facts About P&G 2002–2003 Worldwide. *Cincinnati: Procter & Gamble.*

EXHIBIT **8.15**   **P&G's Global Product Groups and Product Types**

| Product Groups | Product Types | Net Sales ($ millions) |
|---|---|---|
| Baby, feminine, and family care | Baby diapers, baby wipes, baby bibs, baby change and bed mats<br>Toilet tissue, paper towels, and facial tissue<br>Feminine protection pads, pantiliners, and tampons | 11.9 |
| Beauty care | Cosmetics<br>Deodorants<br>Fragrances<br>Hair coloring<br>Skin care | 11.6 |
| Fabric and home care | Bleach<br>Care for special fabrics<br>Dish care<br>Fabric conditioners<br>Household cleaners<br>Laundry detergent<br>P&G chemicals<br>Cosmetics | 8.1 |
| Food and beverage | Beverages<br>Snacks | 3.8 |
| Health care | Oral and personal care<br>Pet health and nutrition<br>Prescription drugs<br>Water filtration | 5.0 |

*Source: Adapted from Procter & Gamble. 2003. Facts About P&G 2002–2003 Worldwide. Cincinnati: Procter & Gamble.*

## *Endnotes*

[1] Jones, Gareth R. 2009. *Organizational Theory, Design and Change.* Upper Saddle River, NJ: Pearson-Prentice Hall.

[2] Ibid.

[3] Duncan, Robert. 1979. "What is the right organization structure? Decision tree analysis provides the answer." *Organizational Dynamics,* Winter.

[4] United Nations Conference on Trade and Development (UNCTAD). 2003. *World Investment Report.* New York and Geneva: United Nations.

[5] Brellochs, Jochen, and Ulrich Steger. 2006. "Most multinationals now derive most of their value from subsidiaries. So, why do so few have robust systems in place to ensure that principles of governance are applied consistently across their organizational networks?" *Financial Times,* June, 2, 4.

[6] Ibid.

[7] Beamish, Paul W., J. Peter Killing, Donald J. Lecraw, and Allen J. Morrison. 1994. *International Management.* Burr Ridge, IL: Irwin.

[8] Bartlett, Christopher A., and Sumantra Ghoshal. 1989. *Managing Across Borders: The Transnational Solution.* Boston: Harvard University Press.

[9] Humes, Samuel. 1993. *Managing the Multinational: Confronting the Global-Local Dilemma.* New York: Prentice Hall.

[10] Stopford, J. M., and L. T. Wells, Jr. 1972. *Managing the Multinational Enterprise.* New York: Basic Books.

[11] Toyota. 2006. "Toyota announces board of directors and organizational changes." June 23. http://www.toyota.co.jp.

[12] *BusinessWeek Online.* 1994. "Borderless management: Companies strive to become truly stateless." May 23; Treece, James B., Kathleen Kerwin, and Heidi Dawley. 1995. "Ford: Alex Trotman's daring global strategy." *BusinessWeek Online,* April 3.

[13] *Economist.* 2000. "Ford in Europe: in the slow lane." October 7; *Economist.* 2002. "From baron to hotelier." May 9; Lublin, Joann. 2001. "Division problem—place vs. product: It's tough to choose a management model—Exide tore up system based on countries for one on centered battery lines—rolling over European fiefs." *Wall Street Journal* (Eastern edition). June 27, A1.

[14] Beamish et al.

[15] *BusinessWeek Online.* 1994. "Borderless management: Companies strive to become truly stateless." May 23.

[16] *Economist.* "From baron to hotelier."

[17] *BusinessWeek Online.* 1994. "High-tech jobs all over the world." November 18.

[18] *Economist.* 2006. "Survey: The matrix master." January 21.

[19] Ghoshal, Sumantra, and Christopher A. Bartlett. 1990. "The multinational corporation as an interorganizational network." *Academy of Management Review,* 15, 603–625; Humes, S. *Managing the Multinational: Confronting the Global-Local Dilemma;* Philips Electronics N.V. 2003. *Annual Report.* February 11.

[20] Ghoshal and Bartlett.

[21] Ibid.

[22] *BusinessWeek Online.* "High-tech jobs all over the world."

[23] Doz, Yves, J., Jose Santos, and Peter Williamson. 2001. *From Global to Metanational: How Companies Win in the Knowledge Economy.* Boston: Harvard Business School Press.

[24] Fisher, Lawrence M. 2002. "ST Microelectronics: The metaphysics of a metanational pioneer." *Strategy & Business,* 19, 3rd quarter, 2–10.

[25] Ibid.

[26] Cray, David. 1984. "Control and coordination in multinational corporations." *Journal of International Business Studies,* Fall, 85–98.

[27] Daft, Richard L. 2004. *Organization Theory and Design.* Minneapolis/St. Paul: West; Jones.

[28] Beamish et al.

[29] Daft.

[30] *BusinessWeek Online.* "Borderless management: Companies strive to become truly stateless."

[31] *BusinessWeek Online.* "Tearing up today's organization chart." November 18.

[32] *BusinessWeek Online.* "High-tech jobs all over the world."

[33] Barczak, Gloria, Edward F. McDonough III, and Nicholas Athanassiou. 2006. "So you want to be a global project leader?" *Research Technology Management,* May–June, 49(3), 28–35.

[34] Rosswurm, Gretchen, and Patricia Bayerlein. 2004–2005. "Overcoming barriers to global success at International." *Strategic Communication Management,* December–January, 9(1), 14–17.

[35] Brake, Terence. 2006. "Leading global virtual teams." *Industrial and Commercial Training,* 38(3), 116–121.

[36] Barczak, Gloria, and Edward F. McDonough III. 2003. "Leading global product development teams." *Research Technology Management,* November–December, 46(6), 14–18; Barczak, McDonough III, and Athanassiou, "So you want to be a global project leader?"; Rosswurm and Bayerlein.

[37] Barczak, McDonough III, and Athanassiou, "So you want to be a global project leader?"; Kumar, Janaki Mythily. 2006. "Working as a designer in a global team." *Interactions,* March–April, 25–27; Rosswurm and Bayerlein.

[38] Davis, Joseph G., Eswaran Subrahmanian, and Arthur W. Westerberg. 2005. "The 'global' and the 'local' in knowledge management." *Journal of Knowledge Management,* 9(1), 101–112.

[39] Ibid.

[40] Wang, Junxia, Hans Peter Peters, and Jiancheng Guan. 2006. "Factors influencing knowledge productivity in German research groups: Lessons for developing countries." *Journal of Knowledge Management,* 10(4), 113–126.

[41] Voelpel, Sven C., and Zheng Han. 2005. "Managing knowledge sharing in China: The case of Siemens ShareNet." *Journal of Knowledge Management,* 9(3), 51–63.

[42] Davis, Subrahmanian, and Westerberg.

[43] Riege, Andreas. 2005. "Three-dozen knowledge-sharing barriers managers must consider." *Journal of Knowledge Management,* 9(3), 18–35.

[44] Ibid.

[45] Holsapple, Clyde W. 2005. "The inseparability of modern knowledge management and computer-based technology." *Journal of Knowledge Management,* 9(1), 42–52.

[46] Davis, Subrahmanian, and Westerberg.

# Managing Strategic Growth At Sjöland & Thyselius AB

It seemed extraordinary that, in 21 years, Rune Thyselius, chair and cofounder of Sjöland & Thyselius AB (S&T), and his partner, CEO Magnus Sjöland, had grown their business from a two-person programming firm to an important Swedish defense enterprise with 160 employees. Based in Stockholm, S&T offered a range of services, from management consulting, military training systems, construction engineering, and communication technologies to owning and running Scandinavia's only wind tunnel. Some reaching that level of success might have been ready to slow down and mull over an exit strategy, but Sjöland and Thyselius were looking to grow.

Their first large-scale international project was well under way in the United Arab Emirates (UAE), and other opportunities in the international defense arena were possible. But was the firm ready for an international expansion? What internal actions would be necessary to create an organizational structure capable of supporting successful globalization? Should it continue to seek business in the UAE or target other markets? What organizational structure and which capabilities would be required to expand globally?[1]

## The Early Years

Born in 1962, Rune Thyselius was the son of an engineer and a stay-at-home mother who later went to work for the municipality. He grew up in the southern part of Stockholm. His father worked at Ericsson, the telecom firm, for his entire career, which for Thyselius had two consequences—he adopted his father's natural interest in science and engineering, and, unlike his sister, who also worked at Ericsson, Thyselius wanted to avoid working for a large firm:

> *I strived for the opposite of what I saw happening to my dad: He got promoted to department manager and building operations, then the firm restructures, and everything is gone. So you do the same thing again in another department. I mean, it is like writing in the sand. So I thought to myself: Why not try the opposite?*

Until it began to be phased out in the 1990s, all adult Swedish males, including Thyselius, were conscripted for service in the military for an average of 11 months. He did not enjoy his time as a soldier. Although he was originally designated conscript platoon leader, his allergy to grass prevented this, and Thyselius quickly realized that taking orders was not his cup of tea: "In terms of personality, I don't fit in as a soldier in the mass of other soldiers. I have always gone my own way. And I paid the price for that in some situations. I go my own way and if no one comes along, I go alone."

From 1981 to 1985, Thyselius studied electrical engineering and computer sciences at the well-reputed Royal Institute of Technology in Stockholm, known not least for its relation to the Nobel Prize Award. While at school, he became friends with Magnus Sjöland, a math major, and the two soon became interested in starting their own business. They launched a venture in 1985 and earned their first revenues the following year with a project for the Swedish

Defense Materiel Authority (FMV), the Swedish armed forces procurement organization.

Upon graduation, each went his separate way, Thyselius to Ericsson and Sjöland to FOA, the former name for the Swedish Defense Research Institute (later FOI). After 15 months at Ericsson, Thyselius returned to the Royal Institute to pursue a PhD and to research the interaction between humans and computers. Although he soon realized he was too impatient for research, his position left him time to develop skills in other areas. For example, he started offering training in computer programming. At the time, programming skills were a scarce resource. He trained employees at Ericsson and FMV, within their aerospace divisions in particular. Thyselius's prime motivators were doing what interested him and what he perceived as "developing himself," so at 25 years of age, he abandoned his PhD studies. He and Sjöland reunited and founded S&T in 1989, to offer computer programming courses in Stockholm.[2]

Given Sjöland's connections at FOA, it was natural for the new entrepreneurs to turn to the defense industry for customers. Despite its population of some 9 million, Sweden, neutral and non-member of NATO, had been a country with a large military defense of its own. Its proximity to the Soviet Union and long coastline made it virtually the northern half of a potential European battle theatre. When the Second World War caught Sweden and other countries with a small and declining military defense, armed forces expansion began and continued for years after.

S&T was an early adopter of the Internet and the first in Sweden to offer training in Java, the programming language, and eventually to develop technical systems. It soon became apparent that its market could be expanded to include large companies outside the defense industry such as Ericsson. As they gained clients, Thyselius and Sjöland concentrated on Ericsson and hired doctoral students from the Royal Institute to keep up with work for other customers. Although their focus on developing a programming code especially for the Swedish armed forces naturally limited their market, the two founders experienced no limits in demand for their services. Thyselius described the early years: "Oh, when we started in 1989—it was fantastic. We earned something like (Swedish krona) SKE400 [in U.S. dollars, approximately USD50] per hour; all hours we could work, I mean, it was fantastic."

## Technology Industry

As the Internet began to evolve, the programming and IT industry grew dramatically. One of the fastest-rising segments of the software industry was enterprise resource planning (ERP), the automated business processes that helped the back office manage a corporation's day-to-day operations. The front office became the next priority, with emphasis on supply chain management. As technology became more advanced and vendors proliferated, end users tended to need third-party help to design, install, integrate, and maintain their equipment for e-commerce, and because the best computer professionals tended to work for computer firms, non-computer businesses found it more cost-efficient to outsource such tasks to computer service companies.

Sometimes called the Silicon Valley of Europe, Sweden was at the forefront of the Internet boom during the 1990s and saw a dramatic increase in the value of programming and Internet firms, leading many start-ups to attempt fast growth. S&T, however, did not take part in that trend, partly because it prioritized work toward existing customers in the defense industry and partly because it strived for quality and long-term growth rather than the quick benefit of being branded an "Internet firm."

Industry developments, however, influenced the firm. The tech boom made competition for employees intense. IT companies with seemingly endless pots of money had invested in in-house restaurants and on-site gyms with tae kwon do and yoga classes. Swimming pools, table tennis, massage therapists, dry-cleaning drop-off services, and dog walkers were only some of the perks companies showcased to attract techies. Thyselius recalled the difficulties in attracting talent in this competition, and the founders' solution to hire family:

> In 1991 we spoke to the first potential employees, but it didn't work because nobody wanted to work in such a small firm. In 1992, we needed to recruit and eventually hired Magnus's wife. Then her younger brother joined us for 10 years—and met his wife at S&T, too, by the way.

## From Home Office to Building

Eventually Sjöland and Thyselius were able to hire outside the family, and in 1993, the firm got its own office. A secretary was hired, and business started taking off, with an annual growth of 50% for four years. At the same time, S&T attempted to cater more to civilian industries, but during the Swedish economic downturn in the early 1990s, demand was low for civilian projects. But demand from the Swedish armed forces continued unabated.

Outgrowing the office a couple years later, S&T moved to larger premises. Then, in 1995, S&T opened its first subsidiary in Gothenburg, Sweden's second largest city, located on the west coast. The first non-founder CEO was hired at the end of the 1990s, and several employees from his former firm were hired too.

During the dot-com bubble, forces within the firm pushed for growth in civilian industries. Demand for civilian projects increased, but so did competition for highly skilled employees; there was a significant gap between the number of technology users and the number of expert programmers at the time. "A lot of people still thought that a computer engineer should earn more than an engineer in chemistry or electronics, without any rational reasons," Thyselius said. "And that still is a bit of a problem in the IT business—too high salaries in relation to the earnings, even if it has improved." This made it even more difficult for the firm to find competent employees, especially without risking compromise in terms of quality.

As the dot-com bubble burst in 2000, and many Internet companies shut off their computers and closed their doors, S&T remained profitable and was well positioned to grow. Giving priority to existing customers over new ones, S&T continued to use its resources to deliver to the Swedish Defense Forces, thus further establishing the firm within the defense sector.

## Growth Through Acquisition

Another trend that followed the tech bubble affected S&T's business: The Swedish Defense Forces experienced successive cutbacks in number of troops, resulting in diminished demand for the company's services. To balance that, S&T searched for opportunities in other areas through acquisitions. The strategy behind the growth was a combination of actively searching for suitable firms and opportunistically responding to reasonable prices. "So when we started looking at acquisitions," Thyselius said, "All our acquisitions have come at a low price, really." At the same time, this meant diversifying the firm.[3]

In 2005, Erik Andersson, CEO of a software company called InterIT Konsult (InterIT), approached Thyselius and Sjöland about a possible sale. The purchase would allow S&T to reach new customers outside the military area. InterIT had barely survived the IT crisis and still struggled to make profits—a poor performance that kept the acquisition price modest. Although some InterIT employees left following S&T's takeover, many stayed including the CEO, and the acquisition was considered successful.

In 2006, S&T's acquisition of Grandezza, a management and IT consulting firm in Stockholm, allowed S&T to broaden its offering; Grandezza developed into one of its cash cows. That same year, a telecom project manager based in Lund (in southern Sweden) was acquired as a one-man firm, and around him, the firm Site of Knowledge was formed; it managed to grow to eight employees during the first year following acquisition.

Two years later, in one of its largest acquisition deals, S&T bought the Swedish government's wind tunnel and renamed it the Sjöland & Thyselius Aerodynamic Research Center Sweden AB (STARCS). Because that acquisition also included a certain financial support from the Swedish Defense Research Agency (FOI), it provided S&T some time to acquire new customers.

The wind tunnel played a pivotal role in the firm. Being inherited from FOI, it carried credibility from the history of the Swedish jet fighter development program. Sweden was one of the few European countries developing and producing its own fighter aircraft. Some countries—Germany, France, the UK, and Italy—had wind tunnels of their own, but few other European did (even fewer countries in other parts of the world, and no other firms in the Nordic countries boasted wind tunnels). The lack of wind tunnels made this a high-profile resource, in turn providing S&T with contacts to potential customers and offering add-on projects from other firms in the S&T corporation.

In itself, the wind tunnel represented a resource that would cost approximately USD100 million to build from scratch, not to mention the employees' wealth of experience. In that sense, the wind tunnel could work as an entry into many firms and countries that otherwise would deal only with much larger, international firms. As Thyselius explained:

> The wind tunnel plays a central role in putting us on the map. It gives us contact to Saab in a completely different way. That is the most important difference. So now we are administering a part of the Swedish industrial heritage, which carries weight both with the Defense Department, FMV, and Saab. It has a certain weight. You are for real. No one else has such a thing.

At the end of 2008, S&T acquired Projektgaranti, a construction and real estate consulting firm, broadening the types of project management in which S&T was involved. That same year, the firm Sellegi Technologies was purchased; the intention was to integrate Sellegi into Site of Knowledge and make the CEO of Sellegi responsible for business development in the combined unit. In spring 2009, S&T acquired 51% of Stockholm firm Perakustik, which built ceilings for offices and schools. It was acquired on personal recommendations and was a completely new line of business.

The wide array of acquisitions had the corporation competing in a variety of industries; the strategy of growing through opportunity had the consequence of spreading firm resources over a wide range of activities. Both owners were aware that there was little conscious positioning in markets and no grand plan or common strategy behind the firm's success. Overall, the growth was more of trial and error, or, as Thyselius put it, *carpe diem*, than a clear strategy. There had been many discussions between Thyselius and Sjöland about which way to go. There were successes, but also mistakes: In hindsight, decisions not to expand into the Internet business and not to invest in the Swedish real estate market during the 1990s meant losing out on highly profitable markets. Nevertheless, the continuous success boiled down to managing as Thyselius described:

> *It is because of the ability to keep things together. Not having any loose ends. Managing challenges during a crisis. That is what has saved us. We have made mistakes: We did not grasp that interest rates would sink and real estate prices would skyrocket. We could have positioned ourselves as a dot-com firm, for instance. But we didn't think of adopting the st.com or st.co.uk domains because we did not grasp that it could have been very, very profitable. We have had our .se domain since 1992 and the domain business did not take off until around 1995. We probably could have earned a million dollars on one of those addresses. So keeping things together is what explains our success.*

## S&T Organizational Structure

By 2011, S&T was a holding company owning 12 firms of different sizes and industries, mainly in the defense industries and around project management and IT. The long period of growth had created a successful company which, as Thyselius proudly stated, "never produced any losses." But there could be room for improvement. For instance, even in those areas where there might be synergies between firms, cooperation within the corporation was low.

At the top of the corporation was the holding company, Sjöland & Thyselius Holding, consisting of the founders, a financial controller, two accountants, and a receptionist (see **Figure 1** for company structure). The holding company owned stakes in a total of 12 firms of different sizes. Six of those firms were somewhat larger, three of which were geared toward the

defense industry and three toward civilian industries. The defense industry part represented an estimated 60% of turnover. S&T Datakonsulter offered consulting services mainly to the defense industry; S&T Systemteknik developed IT systems mainly to the defense industry but also to civilian customers; and STARCS ran the only wind tunnel in the Nordic countries. S&T Systemteknik and Datakonsulter were highly profitable. The wind tunnel itself delivered little cash flow but provided both contacts and international recognition.

Additionally, three firms worked in project management and consulting primarily in the civilian sector: Projektgaranti, Grandezza, and Site of Knowledge, as well as six firms with between one and ten employees.

## Management Style and Culture

In some ways, the company's culture reflected Thyselius's personality. It was the foundation of the firm, and Thyselius believed the culture should be both supportive and demanding. First and foremost, the culture emphasized a work ethos: Deliver results. As the firm had no set strategy, expressed overall goals, or common budget, the idea was to give managers freedom to develop their own businesses, although in the direction that matched the interests of the overall firm. Thyselius stressed the importance of managers feeling that they were the bosses of their own firms. But there was one set rule: "It is forbidden to allow losses," Thyselius said. "If you make losses it means that operations are not working and that you allow negligence and stupidities."

Also important to the culture was a belief in welcoming and personally rewarding HR policies for all employees. That approach seemed to work as illustrated by the fact that the first secretary, Agneta, hired in 1993, still worked in the company in 2011. The founders insisted on personally meeting every candidate for hire in all the firms. It was company policy that they meet students writing their degree project and that each should feel welcome and be given the status of hired on a project basis. One manager ignored the policy, and Thyselius described the situation:

> *Then you realize that they are challenging the rules. All of a sudden, it turns out that one of our managers had hired a degree project student—without talking to us. Hello?! We regard degree project students as regular employees who get to join us at conferences and things like that. So we are as picky with project works as other employees. So that was not good.*

**FIGURE 1**   S&T Holding and Its Daughter Firms

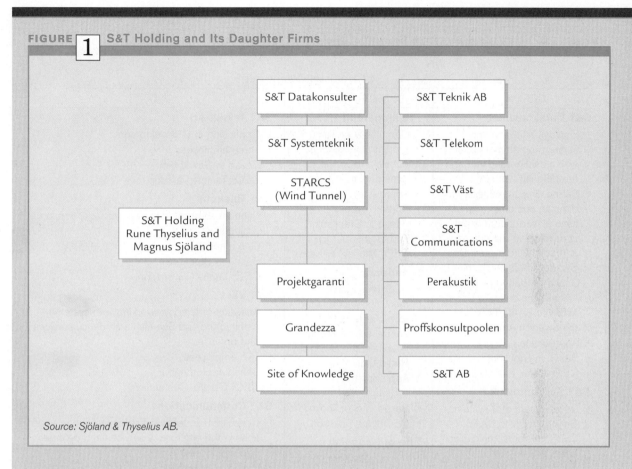

Source: Sjöland & Thyselius AB.

Thyselius explained that the practice was connected to their focus on quality—"to produce quality you have to hire qualified persons"—so hiring was controlled by top management. It was also reflected in a set of credos (Exhibit 2) that included stressing personal development and a good work environment. On their first day of work, every new hire was greeted with flowers on his or her desk to signal they were welcome.

There was emphasis on the importance of having a mix of people. The firm had around 25% female employees in 2011, a figure Sjöland and Thyselius were working hard to increase (the industry average was between 6% and 7%). A leading Swedish weekly business journal noted S&T among other firms for its flexibility in allowing people to work from home or bring their children to work.[4] Thyselius described the policies:

*We are very open; we do not have a lot of opinions that things should be a certain way. It makes it easier for women if they can bring children. [The Swedish weekly] Veckans Affärer wanted an interview about that. "So you can bring children also when they are ill [and are not allowed in kindergarten]?" Yes; that is the most common reason. "But are you not afraid that employees get ill?" Yes, well, you can be afraid of everything.*

In that way, the culture mirrored Thyselius's personal ambition and hard work, mixed with a desire to set his own agenda and an expectation that people pull toward a common goal rather than wait to be pushed. At the same time, several other important reasons contributed to the success of the firm. Initially, it was innovative in terms of offering new programming languages, but it grew into an adaptive and flexible organization with expertise in the defense industry. Describing that development, Thyselius said S&T had moved from an IT firm working with defense into a defense corporation working with IT. He explained: "We know this environment. We have some specialties, such as building fighting vehicle simulations or if Saab would consider outsourcing any of their command and control systems to [the jet fighter] JAS Gripen, we could take care of that."

**EXHIBIT 1**   Managing Strategic Growth at Sjöland & Thyselius AB

### S&T Holding: Companies

| DEFENSE | CIVILIAN | IT |
|---|---|---|

**DEFENSE**

**S&T Datakonsulter**
- Employs analytics and senior programmers often with a background in IT and the defense industry.
- Selling almost exclusively to defense customer, e.g. have played a central part in developing the control and command system for Swedish jet fighter airplane Gripen produced by SAAB.
- A consulting business selling mainly to SAAB, FMV, and the Swedish Armed Forces.
- Approximately 25 employees.
- Based in Stockholm.
- CEO: Peter Johansson.

**S&T Systemteknik.**
- Development of IT systems. Selling mainly to SAAB, FMV, but also some civilian sales, among them Ericsson.
- Contains the original activities from when S&T started, and still does in-house development work (as opposed to consulting at the client).
- Approximately 25 employees.
- Based in Stockholm.
- Manager Erik Andersson.

**STARCS**
- Considered a strategic asset and core company operating in the defense industry.
- Approximately 26 employees.
- Based in Stockholm.
- CEO: Mikael Karlsson.

**CIVILIAN**

**Projektgaranti**
- Completely civilian project management consultants in the construction industry.
- Approximately 35 employees.
- Based in Stockholm and Gothenburg.
- CEO: Michael Nilsson.

**Grandezza**
- Traditional management consulting firm with clients in the energy sector clients, hospitals, the Swedish Radio Ltd.
- Approximately 25 employees.
- Based in Stockholm.
- CEO: Lars Eriksson.

**Site of Knowledge**
- Primarily senior consultants with business, process development, and quality management consulting, mainly towards clients in telecom.
- Approximately 15 persons.
- Based in Lund.
- CEO: Magnus Olsson.

**IT**

**S&T Teknik AB**
- Consulting in IT-development.
- Three employees.
- Based in Stockholm.
- CEO: Tommy Persson.

**S&T Telekom**
- Telecom sector and project manager in export projects.
- One employee.
- Based in Stockholm.
- CEO: Lennart Svensson.

**S&T Väst**
- Analytics of telecom working with systems architecture and Swedish emergency services and defense.
- Two employees.
- Based in Gothenburg.
- CEO: Gunilla Gustafsson.

**S&T Communications**
- Consultants in technical communications solutions in the emergency services and defense.
- Five employees.
- Based in Stockholm.
- CEO: Johan Pettersson.

**Perakustik**
- Construction services
- Receives sales and marketing support from other parts of S&T
- Approximately ten employees.
- Based in Stockholm.
- CEOs: Gunnar Jonsson and Peter Bengtsson.

**Proffskonsultpoolen**
- Consulting in the computer space. S&T owns 25% and no operational engagement in the firm.
- One employee.
- Based in Stockholm.

**S&T AB**
- A firm set up to channel all exports in defense part of the firm.
- One employee.
- Based in Stockholm.
- CEO: Rune Thyselius.

---

**EXHIBIT** 2   Managing Strategic Growth At Sjöland & Thyselius AB

### Company Credos[1]

The firm has developed a set of credos; a number of guidelines for how the firm is to be run, and what the firm stands for. These are

- We are a knowledge firm. The innovative engineer is our hero.
- We work long-term for our customers, employees, and cooperation partners [other firms]. That, in turn, means that:
  - We are results-focused and deliver on time.
  - We have high business ethics and we keep our promises.
  - We work closely with and listen to our customers.
- We give our staff the great responsibility and authority to work to satisfy the customer.
- Sjöland & Thyselius shall be a firm where it is fun to work, with a culture open to different views, with respect for the individual and with challenging tasks [to employees].

[1]Translated from company website, http://www.st.se/ (accessed March 18, 2011).

---

Rather than attempting to be first with new technologies, S&T instead applied existing knowledge or technology to the defense environment. That in turn dictated the kind of individuals who worked in the organization, they were talent seeking a mix of freedom and growth opportunity within a smaller firm. Some were managers, others engineers, all with a unique understanding of sales and operations in the defense industry. Thyselius said:

*A lot of it is good people. If you want to work in a small firm in the defense sector you do not have much choice. We are, I would argue, the leading small firm in the Swedish defense sector. That is one thing. Another is people who are so good at what they do that they can hire people by means of their own personal trademark. Mattias Larsson is, I mean, he is "Mr. Fighting Vehicle Simulator" in Sweden. If he goes to a competitor, then they would have "Mr. Fighting Vehicle Simulator," not us, and that would be bad.*

### S&T Governance

Cooperation between the two founders simply worked out. By 2008, after each had had several roles in the firm, it was decided that Sjöland would work with external issues, such as growth, sales, and government contacts, and Thyselius would act as CFO, controlling the different firms in the holding company, and sales, but primarily supporting the companies.

Thyselius described Sjöland as the more social partner, building relationships within industry organizations and developing and managing contacts with

Swedish authorities and employees. Sjöland was also more interested in STARC and had invested a great deal of time managing Site of Knowledge. He was less interested in traveling, but he was responsible for external contacts in Sweden.

Thyselius described himself, on the other hand, as more interested in working with exports and development of the simulator, sales, and traveling. The pair's interests and competencies therefore complemented each other over the years, and they had a good relationship. Thyselius summarized:

*What happens is that you work as hard as you can, but you do not see what your partner does. So we have two things in common, so to speak: "The other one talks too much, and I do all the work!" [laughs] And when you realize that there is very much truth in that you do not see what the other one does, you have reached a certain level in your cooperation: He actually does work I do not see.*

The entrepreneurs' governance practices were influenced by the corporate culture. The cultural emphasis on room for personal development also extended to managers in the companies, and the management and governance structure emphasized local responsibility in each firm. Thyselius and Sjöland respected individual decision making, but rather than merely expecting profits, they took an operative interest in the firms when they felt it was warranted. If they thought a firm was being poorly run or was allowing gender balance to slide, they might direct managers to invest more in employee competence development.

# Defense Industry

Although active in several industries, S&T's main emphasis was on the *defense* industry, as opposed to the *arms* industry, which deals in weaponry, ammunition, and related technologies. The defense industry is much broader, encompassing all supplies to government military organizations, everything from computers and analysis systems to clothes.

As with many industries, defense industry capability was of strategic national importance, so the process of buying and selling was highly regulated, and the ability to meet regulatory demand was a barrier to market entry. Because such competencies did not necessarily extend to other industries, however, expansion might incur additional compliance costs.

The international defense industry was dominated by multinational firms much larger than S&T: Sales figures for BAE Systems in the UK and Lockheed Martin and Boeing in the United States exceeded USD30 billion each in 2008.[5] Previously, S&T had sold mainly to the Swedish Defense Forces, but as with much of Europe after the collapse of the Soviet Union, Sweden was cutting down its substantial air force and reducing its number of soldiers. Thyselius described the situation:

*It is an inherent problem that a defense firm cannot grow with its customer. On the contrary, customers are shrinking. On the other hand, a larger part of it is based on IT, and that makes us hang in there. And then, if you can take some market share, you grow.*

To grow in a shrinking national market, the firm had to either expand internationally or take market shares from national competitors, and as a whole, the market for arms had increased in previous years.[6] Thyselius identified the source of global demand for defense products as developed countries, which were already well equipped and countries in which the economy more recently had allowed for defense investments.

Demand was influenced by a few interrelated trends. As demand decreased after the cold war, costs rose, resulting in fewer but larger development projects but also an increase in off-the-shelf public procurement—large orders from a small number of suppliers. As a result, long-lasting and potentially profitable development projects were rare, and an increasing portion of military budgets was spent in global competition. Thyselius summed it up:

*It is a European trend that defense forces want fewer suppliers, such as in the UK, where they are buying from 75 instead from 5,000 companies. That is a threat to smaller suppliers—especially if*

*procuring goes international. Therefore, you suddenly compete with the large players from abroad, instead of only the players from your own country, with whom you have learned to coexist. And that is a clear risk for a small company.*

The trend toward larger contracts with fewer firms and the resultant subcontracting threatened close relationships with the end customer. Without those close relationships, the flow of information decreased severely, which hampered business in several ways. For one, if the main contractor controlled the information a development firm received, it could keep the most attractive deals to itself and withhold from subcontractors critical information about a customer's long-term strategic plan.

In addition, demand itself sometimes was fuzzy. In some cases, the customer could perceive and articulate its needs, but as systems grew complex and customer expertise grew thin, specification development increasingly required supplier consultation, which in turn necessitated a long-term customer relationship, as Thyselius described:

*In many instances, defense customers do not know what they want or need, which makes it hard to make a worldwide public tender offer. So, whereas they are aware of a basic need, it is difficult to know unless you go and speak to them.*

Over time, a system producer could develop a concept customized for a particular defense force, so close contact with end customers was crucial to future projects. "To have any power in product development, you need contact with the end customer," Thyselius said. "But, of course, the large firms are not stupid; contact with the end customer is the first thing the larger firms monopolize."

As global military procurement moved toward increasing formalization, clearer views were expressed by politicians in many countries regarding which countries they deemed acceptable to sell military equipment. The reasons behind what countries were considered good and others suspect were not always clear-cut. Thyselius's view was that these preconceptions were historical, political, or cultural, which created a degree of ambiguity regarding potential future sales volumes.

In industrialized countries, the market was saturated; growth potential was in countries with an emerging industry and the economic resources to equip their defense forces. From outside an emerging country, it was not always clear who made what decisions and on what grounds. In some countries, the business culture added another dimension to the challenge, such as those based less on official public tenders, as in the United States or Sweden, than on business contacts and personal relations. "Contacts— who is related to whom," Thyselius said. "In many regards, societies can be built upon what family you belong to, and relations come with that—good as well as bad, even if generations have passed."

## Competition

Within Sweden, S&T faced two kinds of competition: firms offering consulting, engineering, and programming services to both the civilian and defense markets, including several of Sweden's leading IT consulting firms, and firms that were more clearly military in origin.

Despite its size, Sweden had produced several notable arms and defense system suppliers: Kockums, producer of world-class conventional submarines; Saab, airplanes; Bofors, arms and artillery; and Hägglunds, armored fighting vehicles exported to Norway and Switzerland.[7] Some had been acquired or partly acquired, such as Kockums by ThyssenKrupp of Germany and Saab partly by British Aerospace (BAE). Other competitors were somewhat smaller than Saab but larger than S&T, such as Generic, HiQ, ÅF, and Combitech, and several were smaller, including Frontend and Syntell.

But competition in this market was rarely straightforward. Typically, a supplier could not offer a complete solution, because the size and complexity of a deal might be beyond its capacity or specialty, so competition often gave way to partnership. Similarly, a larger firm might buy special parts to deliver larger systems, transforming competitors into supply chain partners. For instance, Saab made command and control systems for military use and was a competitor to S&T in some procurement procedures, a partner in some, and a customer in others. Actors on the defense market could be customers, competitors, or potential suppliers to each other, depending on the project.

This was also true in the international arena. Raytheon, the American firm, sold missiles to a customer to whom S&T was selling a surveillance system; thus, both firms served the same customer. Raytheon, however, also made similar surveillance systems for missile firing ranges, making them a competitor.

There was one market, however, where S&T was one of only a few players—wind tunnel services. Aerodynamic analysis, therefore, was a market in which S&T could compete. Two conditions were important. One regarded the competence to produce results. Several

countries shared the ambition to develop wind tunnel capabilities, but, according to Thyselius, it would take up to 20 years to develop the skills to make full use of a wind tunnel because most knowledge was proprietary and therefore developed from scratch. So even if there were competitors, not all would have the capacity to produce valid results from analyses.

The second factor was political influence. Given the geopolitical importance of, say, the development of new military aircraft, many nations were conscious and cautious of where tests were conducted. Test secrecy was often of primary concern, and some deals were structured specifically to avoid dependence on one party. Brazil, for instance, used both a Russian and an American wind tunnel to split the risk of leaking secrets entirely to either party, as Thyselius explained:

> Brazil has a large air industry, Embraer, but no wind tunnel, so they work both with Russia and the U.S., approximately 50% each, to balance it. And you know that if you send something to the U.S., your American competitors are likely to know what you are doing. And the same thing in Russia. So there are no real secrets on that level.

In that sense, STARC, with politically neutral Sweden's long history of successfully developing military aircraft, possessed a rather unique position in the eyes of non-NATO countries (or any other countries not part of an alliance), and firms such as American aircraft developer McDonnell-Douglas were not considered potential customers of S&T wind tunnels for secrecy reasons.

## Industry Regulation and Official Contacts

The defense industry was highly regulated. Even if not under the same strict rules and regulations as actual arms sales, several systems in the defense industry at least required approval by Swedish government authorities for export from Sweden.

Not providing weapons meant that S&T's products did not fall under the weapons exports regulations, but some related products and services did. The Swedish weapons export act allowed export of weapons if there were security or defense policy reasons and if did not conflict with either Swedish foreign policy or guidelines accepted by the EU and the UN. In particular, the act stated that export should not be allowed to countries at war and gave special attention to human rights of the customer country.[8] So regulations depended on whether the country was actively involved in a war and whether Sweden supported its government. Added to this, Thyselius described the role of perception among countries:

*There exists a common view in the global defense industry that some countries are good to do business with and others bad, not always clearly connected to what the country does or not; it might just be a perception, but nevertheless it is very important.*

A committee within the Swedish parliament had authority over whether a country's arms or defense systems could be sold; product decisions were made on a case-by-case basis, and political changes could alter conditions for both sales and exports over time. So contacts within government bodies were important.[9] Because of Sjöland's skills as a social networker, S&T had well-developed connections with decision makers at different levels of the Swedish political hierarchy. Sjöland took a leading role in industry organizations and was chairman of the industry association for small- and medium-size Swedish firms.

At the same time, taking too large a role in a defense industry organization could cause problems due to conflicts of interest. The organization was informed, for instance, when the government was doing an export trip; to both represent the organization and gain access to several contacts for S&T would be unethical. The fact that Sjöland had always taken care not to mix official tasks with business was important. Thyselius explained:

*Sweden is a country of organizations; If you are chairman of the board of such an industry organization, you get a completely different set of new contacts. It becomes legitimate for the other part, often authorities. They do not generally like to meet firms—that is not quite perceived as all right. But representatives of organizations, that is totally okay! But [Sjöland] is very strict in what he represents, and that might be one of the reasons he has done so well in that role.*

## International Opportunity

By 2008, it grew increasingly clear that the firm had an opportunity to enter the international market. In itself, the project had come out of contacts and coincidence. A Swede with roots in the Arab world had been hired by FOI to develop contacts in the UAE. He managed to skillfully develop relations with an organization closely connected to the UAE government called Emirates Advanced Investments. After the 2006 Swedish general election, attitudes in the government toward selling weapons changed, and FOI had to abandon the project, so the employee moved to S&T instead, taking the contacts with him. He was instrumental in making and closing the deal to sell surveillance systems for a test range.

In addition to the product purchase, the firm provided education to analyze the system's results. S&T's first major international order of USD9 million was secured in August that year. In comparison to the total Swedish weapon exports of the same year of approximately SEK13.5 billion,[10] this was very small, but for S&T that deal boosted international sales to new heights.

Additionally, future opportunities were obvious: Such large sales would increase the brand name abroad, the financial strength provided would open new opportunities, and, not least, it would be something challenging for Thyselius. Selling abroad would require substantial efforts in meetings and marketing, all demanding a local presence and language skills; in other words, substantial resources. Travel time alone would make running a business relationship between Sweden and the UAE difficult.

As stated before, customers in the defense industry were not always fully informed about products. Many products were secret and at the cutting edge of technology, hence not summarized in a catalogue. Instead, marketing efforts from the seller and development of requirements of the buyer were often developed in parallel. In addition, differences in business and political culture made customer decision making unclear. In all, a local presence, an understanding of the language and cultural skills were required to develop long-term and trustful relations and increase the likelihood of future sales. In this instance, the UAE customer was eager to buy, making it an even more interesting situation, and requiring someone to manage the differences.

That project was not the only effort to sell in the UAE. Independent of the surveillance system, Grandezza had secured an order to audit a joint venture between the UAE and a French life science corporation that was running unsatisfactorily. In addition, discussions about wind tunnel tests were being held with China, South Korea, Thailand, Singapore, and Brazil (see **Table 1** for 2010 country profiles). Not every country has the capacity to do wind tunnel tests, even if it has an airplane industry; business might comprise testing or developing an entire wind tunnel. Although tempting, it had yet to occur:

*In a wind tunnel you can make tests. But you can also sell a wind tunnel to anyone with around USD100 million to spare. It takes around 10 years if you want some university education and so on. It is quite a*

TABLE 1    Economic data by country (in 2010 U.S. dollars except as noted).

| Country | GDP (in billions of U.S. dollars) | Export of G&S (% of GDP) | Import of G&S (% of GDP) | Merchandise Trade (% of GDP) | Ease of Doing Business Rank[11] |
|---|---|---|---|---|---|
| *Brazil* | $1,573.41 | 11 | 11 | 18.2 | 124 |
| *China* | $4,985.46 | 27 | 22 | 44.3 | 78 |
| *Korea* | $832.51 | 50 | 46 | 82.5 | 15 |
| *Singapore* | $182.23 | 221* | 203* | 282.9 | 1 |
| *Thailand* | $263.77 | 68 | 58 | 108.5 | 16 |
| *UAE* | $230.25 | 93** | 71** | 136.8 | 37 |

*=2008 U.S. dollars **=2005 U.S. dollars

Sources: "The World Bank Group Country Data Profiles," http://www.enterprisesurveys.org/ and The World Bank and the International Finance Corporation, Doing Business 2011: Making a Difference for Entrepreneurs (report), http://www.doingbusiness.org/~/media/FPDKM/Doing%20Business/Documents/Annual-Reports/English /DB11-FullReport.pdf (accessed April 21, 2011).

*difficult thing to run. So that is what we talk to Brazil about; not tests, but selling a wind tunnel.*

## What to Do Next?

As their two-man operation grew into several organizations employing approximately 160 people, Sjöland and Thyselius had much to decide about the company's future.

Having grown in different directions, S&T firms had little internal coordination among businesses and very limited managerial resources at the corporate level. There was also the issue of unprofitable companies. Site of Knowledge had recorded losses in mid-2009, which was no surprise, given the problems in the market: When mobile phone producer Sony Ericsson drastically reduced its number of consultants, prices had to be lowered. Sjöland invested a lot of time supporting Site of Knowledge, which kept him from work he could do in other areas.

Perakustik also struggled to be profitable. Management blamed the 2009 economic crisis, but Thyselius saw signs that management was unaccustomed to marketing its services and was not "hungry" enough. Corporate tried to throw some resources at the issue, deploying a manager from one of the consulting firms to help with selling, but it proved unsatisfactory.

A similar issue was growing at Sellegi. That manager blamed the crisis on Sony Ericsson and pointed to a lack of sales support from corporate. Thyselius offered resources, but the manager failed to use the extra selling help, and Thyselius drew the conclusion that something else was lacking. By the end of 2009,

the firm was sold back to its previous owner, and S&T broke even, a relief to Thyselius. Divesting Perakustik could be equally prudent. A third-party firm had expressed interest in acquiring it, something Thyselius considered an option:

*If what we have done does not bear fruit and we have not had resources in terms of time to do more, and the fundamental operations do not develop well, then, it is best to get rid of it. It is a little too small to spend so much time and energy on.*

The lack of cooperation among firms in the corporation manifested itself in a troubling way. Thyselius expected managers of firms within S&T to show personal drive. The manager of one S&T company both delivered good results and was ambitious for more, having expressed the desire to take on responsibilities for another S&T company. That company's manager, however, was not interested in having his firm taken over. Thyselius had to deal with the conflict. In addition, the same ambitious manager had broken a few of the firm's rules, having hired someone without letting Thyselius and Sjöland meet the candidate and installed an incompatible lock on his office door, which was also against office policy.

The manager's behavior was not a simple problem to solve. Neither Sjöland nor Thyselius was interested in coordinating the firms' managers. Both saw the need for the role but considered it a step back rather than a challenge. And even if part of the problem could be explained by difficulties in finding good managers, finding another manager for the defense sector would be even more problematic. Thyselius knew well that even small firms required managers with a broad skill set that included management, accounting, sales, HR, and competence development.

Increasing coordination among firms would mean a break from both the spontaneous growth concept and how managers were used to being treated. An increase in centralization would risk reducing the freedom of managers. Thyselius explained:

*That's it: Driving the strategic development of the Swedish operations and operationally becoming the manager of the CEOs in a much clearer way. And that restricts their freedom of action much more clearly. This also meant a risk. For instance, losing the manager of Datakonsulter would risk also losing customers and consultants.*

Several decisions lay ahead. If Thyselius and Sjöland concluded that the time was right for diving headlong into the international defense industry, they would need S&T Holding running smoothly and at full tilt—which would require more coordination among firms. And what should they do with the unprofitable subsidiaries? How should they deal with the ambitious, unorthodox, yet highly successful manager? Should they continue to seek more business in the UAE? What about their possible wind tunnel connections? Should they broaden their global expansion efforts to other regions of the world? There was much to work out.

## CASE NOTES

[1] The case data is based on a strategy workshop held February 18–19, 2010, and interviews held with Rune Thyselius on April 6, 2010, and February 14, 2011, unless stated otherwise.

[2] Thyselius did return to school to earn his MBA from the Stockholm School of Economics in 2003 and an SERA training certificate for senior managers in the European defense industry from the Higher National Defense Study at the French Military Academy in 2010.

[3] Acquisition data has been augmented by data from the company website, http://www.st.se/ (accessed January 18, 2011).

[4] *Veckans Affärer* (in Swedish), April 24, 2010, http://www.va.se/nyheter/2010/04/27/barntillatet-pa-jobbet-linda-ahlstroms-fe/ (accessed January 17, 2011).

[5] Stockholm International Peace Research Institute website, "The SIPRI Top 100 Arms-Producing Companies, 2009," http://www.sipri.org/research/armaments/production/Top100 (accessed January 18, 2011).

[6] Stockholm International Peace Research Institute website, "14 March 2011: India World's Largest Arms Importer According to New SIPRI Data on International Arms Transfers," http://www.sipri.org/media/pressreleases/armstransfers (accessed March 14, 2011).

[7] Sweden was ranked in the top 10 on the SIPRI list of arms transfers in 2010. Stockholm International Peace Research Institute website, http://www.sipri.org/databases/armstransfers/armstransfers?searchterm=list+of+arms+tr (accessed March 14, 2011).

[8] Regeringskansliet, "Exportkontroll av krigsmateriel" (translated from Swedish), http://www.sweden.gov.se/sb/d/10675/a/21898 (accessed January 17, 2011).

[9] It should be noted that corruption was considered extremely low in Sweden. On an international ranking of corruption, Sweden was 4th after New Zealand, Denmark, and Singapore. Canada ranked 9th, Germany 14th, the United States 19th, and France 24th. Figures for 2009. Transparency International website, Corruptions Perceptions Index 2009, http://www.transparency.org/policy_research/surveys_indices/cpi/2009/cpi_2009_table (accessed January 18, 2011).

[10] According to Swedish government figures, http://www.sweden.gov.se/sb/d/10675/a/21898 (accessed January 18, 2011).

[11] The ranking of 183 countries was based on nine factors: construction permits, property registration, obtaining credit, protecting investors, work force, taxes, border trade, contract enforcement, and closing a business.

# International Strategic Alliances: Design and Management

9

## Preview CASE IN POINT

### Strategic Alliances in Emerging Markets

Emerging markets such as India, China, Russia, Brazil, and South Africa continue to enjoy good health largely due to maturing economic policies. Many of the emerging markets have taken steps to control potentially damaging economic factors such as inflation while maintaining strict monetary and fiscal policies. These emerging markets present tremendous potential for multinational companies because multinational companies take advantage of the significant cost benefits and the rising middle classes in these countries. Consider that, in the next decade, more than 800 million people in China, India, Russia, and Brazil will qualify as members of the middle class, with more than $1 trillion to spend on products.

Many multinational companies also find that, if they want to take advantage of such markets, they need to form strategic alliances with local companies. For example, McDonald's signed a significant deal with the Chinese company Sinopec, which runs almost 30,000 gas stations and is growing by about 500 stations annually. McDonald's is hoping to create thousands of drive-through restaurants at many of Sinopec's locations. It anticipates that the alliance will give it a powerful means to attract the young and affluent Chinese, who are more likely to drive.

In 2012, Starbucks opened its first store in Mumbai through an US$80 million Indian joint venture with Tata Global Beverages. Starbucks already has over 500 stores in China and this is just one part of a wider Asian expansion by the company, which has been planning for the Indian market since 2006. Even though recent changes in Indian law allow India's Foreign Investment Promotion Board (FIPB) to approve 100 percent ownership by foreign investors, this shows that many multinational companies seek local partners to overcome the difficulties faced when entering such a complex market. Other recent joint venture entries into India include a 51/49 joint venture between the U.S. clothing retailer Brooks Brothers and Mukesh Ambani's Reliance Brands, and a similar relationship between the Italian jeweler Damiani's and its Indian partner Eurostar.

## Learning Objectives
*After reading this chapter you should be able to:*

- Know the steps for implementing successful international strategic alliances.

- Describe how multinational companies link value chains in international strategic alliances.

- Understand the importance of choosing the right partners for alliances.

- Know the important characteristics to look for in potential alliance partners.

- Distinguish between equity-based international joint ventures and other types of international cooperative alliances.

- Know the basic components of an international strategic alliance contract.

- Understand the control systems and management structures used in alliance organizations.

- Appreciate the unique problems in human resource management faced by managers in alliance organizations.

- Realize the importance of interfirm commitment and trust for building successful international strategic alliances.

- Understand how multinational companies assess the performance of their international strategic alliances.

- Know when companies should dissolve or continue their alliances.

*Sources: Based on Bajaj, Vikas. 2012. "Starbucks opens in India with pomp and tempered ambition."* New York Times, *October 19; Crabtree, James, James Fontanella-Khan, and Barney Jopson. 2012. "Starbucks plans $80m Indian joint venture."* Financial Times, *January 30; Jain, Dipti. 2012. "Damiani, Brooks Bros ventures get FIPB nod."* Times of India, *October 20; Litterick, David. 2006. "Fast food McDonald's takes meals on wheels to China."* Daily Telegraph, *June 21, 1.*

As the Preview Case in Point shows, emerging markets will likely continue to enjoy good economic health and provide tremendous potential for multinational companies. Because strategic alliances are fast and flexible ways to gain complementary resources, they are increasingly among the most popular strategies that companies use to develop new products and to expand into these new geographic areas or markets. In fact, recent studies by Accenture (formerly Andersen Consulting) found that major multinational companies expect alliances to account for up to 40 percent of company value in the next five years. In addition, they observed greater increases in joint ventures in developing economies.[1] However, the same study found that top management considered only 30 percent of the alliances as outright successes.

Why do alliances fail to meet expectations? The most common reason is a poorly designed or managed alliance organization—not a poor strategic choice in entering the alliance. Increasingly, strategic alliances involve companies from two or more nations. Foreign partners often have the most attractive resources or skills that make them the partners of choice. However, partnering with a company from a different nation only compounds the management difficulties. As a result, the student of multinational management needs an understanding of international strategic alliance operations and management.

Although strategic alliances are attractive for a variety of reasons, they are inherently unstable and entail significant management challenges. Estimates of failure rates range from 30 to 60 percent. Partners may fail to deliver or may disagree on how to run the business, and even profitable alliances can be torn by conflict. Successful alliances must make strategic sense, but they also require good implementation. In this chapter, you will see the steps necessary to implement a successful strategic alliance. In our discussion, we will follow the model of these steps presented in Exhibit 9.1.

## Where to Link in the Value Chain

The many benefits of strategic alliances include gaining access to a local partner's knowledge of the market, meeting government requirements, sharing risks, sharing technology, gaining economies of scale, and accessing lower-cost raw materials or labor. The objectives a firm hopes to achieve determine where multinational companies link in the value chain.

Exhibit 9.2 shows two value chains and the areas in which companies commonly link to gain strategic benefits.

Alliances that combine the same value chain activities often do so to gain efficient scales of operations, to merge compatible talents, or to share risks. These alliances are attractive when no one company is big enough, has the necessary talent, or is willing to take on an enormously risky venture. In R&D alliances, for example, high-tech multinational companies often use joint research and development to merge different technical skills or to share the risks of developing new or costly

**EXHIBIT** **9.1** Implementing a Strategic-Alliance Strategy

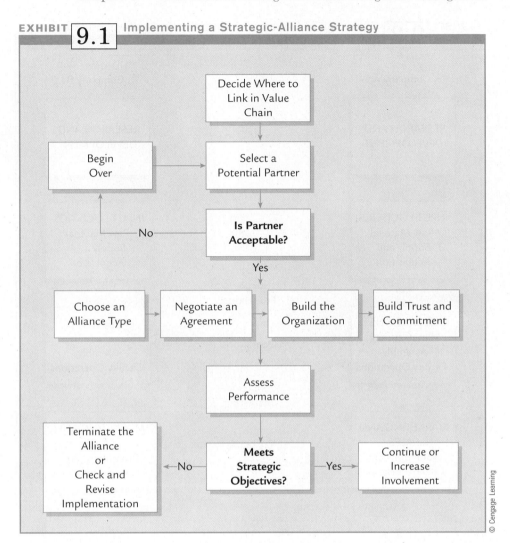

© Cengage Learning

technologies. For companies like Toshiba, cross-national alliances are central to their strategy. Toshiba uses alliances with companies like Apple and IBM to complement and enhance its technological strengths. Why not do it alone? R&D in high technology is a highly risky and expensive venture, which no one company wants to attempt by itself. Just the costs of chip design and fabrication alone run in the billions.

In operations alliances, multinational companies often combine manufacturing or assembly activities to achieve a profitable volume of activity. For example, General Motors of the United States and Renault SA of France have an alliance to develop and market pickup trucks and vans targeted at the light commercial market.[2] As shown in the next Case in Point, these companies have worked together for over a decade to produce light commercial trucks for the European market. Leadership skills and a focus on results and values have made this alliance between GM and Renault a success.[3]

Marketing and sales alliances allow multinational companies to increase the scope and number of products sold and to share distribution systems. Sometimes partners even share logos. In the KLM/Delta alliance, the companies share

**EXHIBIT 9.2** Examples of Linking Value Chains in Strategic Alliances

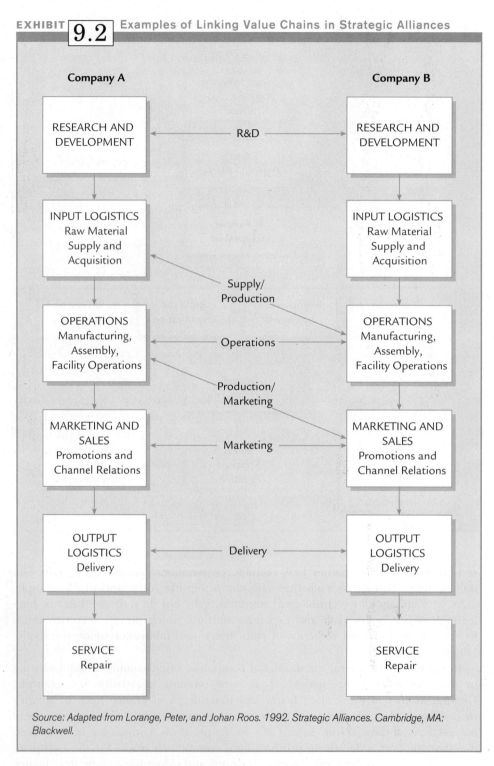

Source: Adapted from Lorange, Peter, and Johan Roos. 1992. *Strategic Alliances*. Cambridge, MA: Blackwell.

advertising that notes their joint reservation-and-route systems. In the automobile industry, alliance partners often share each other's dealer systems.

Output alliances deliver a service and are perhaps the most popular in the airline industry. International alliances—such as the 18-airline member SkyTeam

## CASE IN POINT

### Evolution of the GM/Renault Strategic Alliance

GM from the United States and Renault from France reached an agreement for a cooperative alliance for the co-development and shared production of a utility van aimed at the commercial market. The first van came off the line in 2001, and by 2012, the companies working together had produced nearly 2 million vehicles. Renault handles the design, development, and engine supply, while GM Europe manufactures at its plant in Luton, United Kingdom. Because the relationship was so successful, the joint venture partners decided to produce additional vehicles at a plant owned by Renault's joint venture with Nissan. GM sells the van as the Vivaro model, and Renault sells it as its Trafic model. Nissan now sells the same van as the Interstar.

*Sources: Based on GM Authority. 2010. "Open/Vauxhall continues van collaboration with Renault," September 27, http://gmauthority.com; GM Europe/Renault Press Release. 2006. "General Motors Europe and Renault pursue cooperation on LCVs," http://www.renault.com/SiteCollectionDocuments/Communiqu%C3%A9%20de%20presse/en-EN/Pieces%20jointes/11497_CP-VU_GB.pdf; Just-auto.com. 2011. "UK: Luton immediate future secure as Vauxhall confirms Vivaro build," March 2; Wardsauto. 2006. "GM, Renault maintain joint van production," March 9, http://wardsauto.com.*

Alliance—deliver their services jointly through a process called code sharing (the sharing of reservation codes). In this way, passengers can buy an international ticket in one airline's country, fly to the partner's country, and get continuing flights with the same ticket on the partner's airline.

Alliances linking upstream and downstream components of the value chain can serve the objectives of low-cost supply or manufacturing. In some supply/operations alliances, one partner provides low-cost sources of supply or components, and the other partner does the manufacturing. Operations/marketing links can work similarly. One company trades a source of low-cost manufacturing for another company's eventual sales. For example, because of increasing wages in their own countries, many Japanese and Korean companies formed production/marketing alliances with low-wage Southeast Asian companies. Production and assembly occur at the low-cost site, and the Japanese and Korean companies do the downstream marketing and sales.

For U.S. companies, the majority of international strategic alliances occur in operations. Exhibit 9.3 shows the mixture of value chain links for the nearly 800 publicly announced international strategic alliances created by U.S. multinational companies during a four-year period.[4]

The links discussed so far and illustrated in Exhibits 9.2 and 9.3 are only some of those possible for international strategic alliances. In building alliances, each company must determine which of its value chain activities can be enhanced by the relationships, thereby helping the firm achieve its strategic objectives. Having made that decision, management faces what is generally considered the most important step in implementing a strategic alliance: choosing the right partner.

# Choosing a Partner: The Most Important Choice?

Most experts attribute the success or failure of strategic alliances to how well the partners get along. Especially early in the relationship, each party must believe that it has a good partner who can deliver on promises and be trusted. The next

**EXHIBIT** **9.3**   Value Chain Links in U.S. International Strategic Alliances

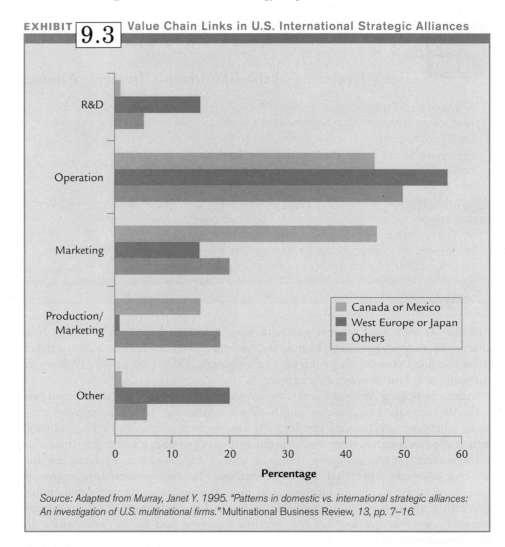

*Source: Adapted from Murray, Janet Y. 1995. "Patterns in domestic vs. international strategic alliances: An investigation of U.S. multinational firms."* Multinational Business Review, *13, pp. 7–16.*

Case in Point shows some of the difficulties that can occur when a company makes mistakes in partner selection.

Experts identify several key criteria for picking an appropriate alliance partner:[5]

**Strategic complementarity**
The alliance partners' strategies are complementary.

- *Seek strategic complementarity:* Before forming the strategic alliance, prospective partners must have a good understanding of each other's strategic objectives for the venture. Each should know what the other hopes to achieve, both in the short term and in the long term. It is not necessary, however, that partners have the same objectives. Although similar strategic objectives, such as rapid growth, are beneficial, objectives can be complementary. For example, a U.S. or Japanese firm may have an advanced technology for manufacturing computer components that is attractive to a Chinese firm. The Chinese firm may dominate the Chinese market and could provide a potential powerful sales and distribution outlet for a partner. These companies have complementary strategic objectives. The U.S. or the Japanese company desires growth in its Chinese market share, and the Chinese company seeks access to the other side's technology.

**Complementary skills**
Skills that enhance but do not necessarily duplicate an alliance partner's skills.

- *Pick a partner with complementary skills:* Partners must contribute more than money to the venture. Each partner must contribute some skills or resources that complement those of the other partner. J. Michael Geringer asserts that technical complementarity is the most important criterion.[6] A typical

## CASE IN POINT

### Picking the Wrong Partner

TNK-BP is a Russian oil company and one of the leading producers of crude oil in the world. TNK-BP was originally a 50/50 joint venture owned by British Petroleum and the Alfa, Access, Renova group, which is owned by a consortium of Russian billionaires. AAR claimed that the joint venture agreement precluded BP from doing any of its Russian oil business outside TNK-BP. However, since most of TNK sites were older, this resulted in excluding BP from exploring some of the newer and potentially more lucrative Arctic sea sites. Twice BP approached other Russian companies to collaborate on Arctic explorations.

In January of 2011, BP approached Rosneft, the state-controlled oil company, with a proposal to explore for oil in the Arctic. With that move, an already bad relationship collapsed. Board members quit, decision making for the organization became crippled, and the Russians sued BP for breaching their agreement.

The Russian consortium concluded, "It has become apparent that the parity ownership structure has become inoperable given fundamental differences over strategy and governance between A.A.R. and BP." By June 2012, Russian billionaire Mikhail Fridman, the CEO of TNK-BP, resigned. Three months later, state-controlled Rosneft agreed to buy out both partners and the joint venture divorce was finalized.

Picking the wrong partner had major consequences for both AAR and BP. BP retained a 20 percent share in the new company, now under Rosneft control, but it remains to be seen how BP's minority holding will benefit BP.

*Sources: Based on Julia Werdigier and Andrew E. Kramer. 2012. "PB to exit its venture in Russia." New York Times, June 1, www .nytimes.com; http://tnk-bp.ru/en/company/; Economist. 2012. "PB and Rosneft, Unhappy families." October 20, www.economist .com.*

complementary alliance, for example, occurs when one company (usually the foreign country) contributes technical skills and another company (usually a host country company) contributes marketing skills. Another recommendation is to find partners with similar but not identical products or markets, thus avoiding the difficulties of working with direct competitors.[7]

- *Seek out companies with compatible management styles:* Lord Weinstock, the managing director for 27 years of Britain's General Electric Company (GEC, not related to the U.S. company GE), is a strategic alliance expert. He has seen many alliances succeed and fail. One recent example, an alliance of GEC with Germany's Siemens, flopped. Consultants noted that Siemens is an engineers' company, consistent with many values in German business culture, and GEC is a financiers' company. The managers simply did not get along. Weinstock noted that for alliances to succeed "You have to suppress the ego—it's absolute poison in a joint venture."[8]

- *Seek a partner that will provide the right level of mutual dependency:* As in any marriage, mutual dependency means that companies must rely on each other to contribute to the relationship. With a good match, partners feel a mutual need to supply their unique resources or capabilities to the alliance. Both partners see their contribution as critical to the success of the relationship and ultimately to the success of the alliance. The best level of mutual dependency is balanced, wherein both companies feel equally dependent on the outcome of the venture. Geringer suggests maintaining this mutual dependency by building safeguards into the agreement, such as types of "alimony" payments and restrictions on entering the same business over a specified period.[9] The alimony payments would require payments to the partner if the relationship breaks up before a specified period.

- *Avoid the so-called anchor partner:* **Anchor partners** hold back the development of a successful strategic alliance because they cannot or will not provide their share of the

**Anchor partner**
A partner that holds back the development of a successful strategic alliance because it cannot or will not provide its share of the funding.

funding. Prospective partners should carefully study each other's financial position and investment plans. A potential partner with a weak division or expansion in other areas may drain financial support from the alliance. If a potential partner is financially weak but still attractive for other reasons, precautions are advised. For example, a contract might specify that the division of the alliance's profits (or other alliance outputs) among the partners will vary in proportion to their financial contributions.

**Elephant-and-ant complex**
Occurs in strategic alliances when two companies are greatly unequal in size.

- *Be cautious of the elephant-and-ant complex:* The **elephant-and-ant complex** occurs when two companies are greatly unequal in size. In such cases, serious potential problems can result. First, the larger firm may dominate the smaller one, controlling the strategies and management of the alliance. Second, the corporate cultures probably differ significantly. For example, bureaucracy and slower decision making usually characterize large, old companies. Small companies are often more entrepreneurial and informal. Thus, because of cultural differences, a small firm's executives may see the large firm's managers as ignoring immediate problems. The large partner's executives may see the small firm's managers as less professional. For instance, an analysis of the strategic alliance between Telia and Telenor, Sweden's and Norway's largest telecommunication companies, respectively, shows that the elephant-and-ant complex may have played a role in its failure.[10] A close look at the alliance shows that Norwegian nationalistic feelings emerged when the country's largest telecom company, Telenor, was being treated poorly by Sweden's Telia. The elephant-and-ant complex was reflected in the perception that a big country company (Sweden, the elephant) was bullying a small country company (Norway, the ant). In spite of these potential problems, however, elephant-and-ant alliances can succeed. When other factors exist, such as complementary skills, managers find ways to overcome size differences. Exhibit 9.4 contrasts some of the incentives and concerns for small businesses in elephant-and-ant international strategic alliances.

- *Assess operating policy differences with potential partners:* Marriage partners need to work out how to squeeze the toothpaste, when to have dinner, who makes the beds, who cleans the house, and all the other operational details of running a household. Similarly, would-be partners in a strategic alliance are likely to have

**EXHIBIT 9.4** International Strategic Alliances for Small Multinational Companies: Incentives and Concerns

| Incentives | Concerns |
|---|---|
| • Gain legitimacy<br>Act as a seal of approval | • Relative level of contribution<br>Must commit relatively more assets than large firm |
| • Develop links in distribution channel<br>Use large firm's existing channels | • Entering a large scale of operations<br>Lack of experience with large-scale operations |
| • Access to resources<br>Sped-up access to market | • Risk of unequal proprietary information disclosure<br>Easier access to small firm's information |
| • Diversification of risk<br>Sharing risk with richer partner | • Mismatch of interacting managers<br>Small-firm entrepreneur with large-firm functional or product specialists |
| | • Loss of control<br>Concerns of large firm's dominating relationship |

*Sources: Adapted from Ghisi, F. A., J. A. G. da Silveria, T. Kristensen, M. Hingley, and A. Lindgreen. 2008. "Horizontal alliances amongst small retailers in Brazil." British Food Journal, 110(4/5): 514–538; Peridis, Theodoros. 1992. "Strategic alliances for smaller firms." Research in Global Strategic Management, 3, 129–142.*

operational differences in how their companies are run on a day-to-day basis. Accounting policies, human resource management policies, financial policies, reporting policies, and the like may all differ because of organizational or cultural differences. For example, potential European partners may want to shut down operations during certain holiday periods, or Japanese partners may want the strategic alliance to respect the age hierarchy of management. For the strategic alliance to function smoothly, before the strategic alliance comes into operation, partners should agree on mutually satisfactory operational policies.

• *Assess the difficulty of cross-cultural communication with a likely partner:* Even if partners speak each other's languages, cross-cultural communication is never as easy as it is within one's own culture or organization. Managers must expect slower communication and more errors in understanding. For example, in a joint venture between a Japanese company and the U.S. aircraft manufacturer Boeing, the agreement required that fuselage panels have a "mirror finish." The Japanese workers interpreted this specification literally. They polished the metal to a mirror finish. The result was excessively high labor costs and the need for further discussion to resolve the meaning of "mirror finish."[11]

The next Multinational Management Brief discusses some of the key questions to ask when picking a partner.

## Multinational Management **Brief**

### Picking an Alliance Partner

Picking an alliance partner is a very important task, and it can be a difficult one. Some experts see choosing a partner as one of the key factors that can determine the success or failure of an alliance. Based on extensive research with joint venture managers from both successful and failed joint ventures, experts suggest that multinational companies need to ask a number of questions about the potential partner. The answers to these questions are regarded as "make-or-break." The interview participants advised companies to avoid the cross-border alliance if managers must answer no to any of the following questions regarding the potential partner:

• Does the partner have the necessary resources?
• Will the partner provide access to these necessary resources?
• Can both partners agree on clear goals and objectives for the strategic alliance?
• Have there been attempts to minimize potential for competition and friction with the partner?
• Does the potential partner have any alliances with your competitors?
• Does the potential partner share with you a vision about how the cross-border strategic alliance might evolve?
• Is the partner willing and able to contribute the necessary skills and resources to ensure that the alliance is successful?
• Does the partner have a history of success with previous strategic alliances?
• Have you compared the potential partner with other partners in terms of value creation?
• Does the cross-border alliance fit with your vision of your future alliance network?

*Sources: Based on Beamish, P.W. and Nathaniel C. Lupton. 2009. "Managing joint ventures." Academy of Management Perspectives, 23, 75–94; Holmberg, S. R., and J. L. Cummings. 2009. "Building successful alliances." Long Range Planning, 42, 164–193; Jagersma, Peter Klaas. 2005. "Cross-border alliances: Advice from the executive suite." Journal of Business Strategy, 26(1): 41–50.*

After finding potentially satisfactory partners, multinational managers from all companies involved must decide on the form of the alliance. Next, we consider the popular choices in types of international strategic alliances.

# Choosing an Alliance Type

There are three main types of strategic alliances:[12] informal international cooperative alliances, formal international cooperative alliances (ICAs), and international joint ventures (IJVs). Exhibit 9.5 outlines the major differences among the types. We consider each of these next.

## Informal and Formal International Cooperative Alliances

**Informal international cooperative alliance**

An agreement between companies to cooperate on any value chain activity that is not legally binding.

**Informal international cooperative alliances** are agreements between companies from two or more countries that are not legally binding. They can be agreements of any kind and can provide links between companies anywhere on their value chains. For example, a local company might agree informally to market and sell a foreign firm's products in exchange for exclusive distribution rights. Although neither firm is legally bound to continue the relationship, the companies might use the informal agreement as a test of their ability to work together in future, more formal agreements. If the informal alliance does not work, it can be ended at any time.

Because there is often no contract that offers legal protection, managers usually limit the scope of their involvement with the other company. They are usually reluctant to dedicate sizable resources to the relationship, such as product changes for the partner's benefit. In addition, multinational companies in informal alliances resist revealing a company's proprietary information—that is, information

**EXHIBIT 9.5**    Types and Characteristics of International Strategic Alliances

| Alliance Type | Degree of Involvement | Ease of Dissolution | Visibility to Competitors | Contract Required | Legal Entity |
|---|---|---|---|---|---|
| Informal international cooperative alliance | Usually limited in scope and time; a marriage of convenience | Easy, at the convenience of either side | Often unknown to competitors | No | None |
| Formal international cooperative alliance | Deeper involvement requiring exchange of proprietary company knowledge and resources | More difficult to dissolve before end of contract because of legal obligations and commitment of resources by companies | Often visible to competitors through announcements in business press but details can be secure | Yes | None |
| International joint venture | Deep involvement requiring exchange of financial, proprietary company knowledge and managerial resources | Most difficult to dissolve because companies invest significant resources and have ownership in a separate legal entity | High visibility because joint venture company is a separate legal entity | Yes | Yes, separate company |

© Cengage Learning

that a firm considers its own and wants to keep secret from competitors. An example might be special manufacturing processes.

The **formal international cooperative alliance (ICA)** calls for a high degree of involvement among partners. This type of alliance usually requires a formal contract specifying exactly what each company must contribute, which could be managers, technical specialists, factories, information or knowledge, or money. To achieve a strategic gain that a single company cannot attain by itself, companies must usually share some knowledge, skill, or specialized resources through a formal ICA. This sharing of proprietary information or knowledge raises the level of involvement of the partners. Both companies must give away something valuable to the partner to get something in return. In addition, in combination with the obligations specified in the contract, the sharing of proprietary knowledge makes backing out of a formal alliance more difficult than it is for alliances with informal agreements. Sometimes, firms structure formal cooperative alliances by one firm taking an equity or ownership share in the other with an agreement to cooperate on several activities.

Formal ICAs with equity sharing are very popular in the automobile industry. The Nissan/Renault alliance is considered the model.[13] For example, Nissan owns 15 percent of Renault, which in turn owns 44 percent of Nissan. The companies purchase most of their parts together. They share engineering expertise, such as Nissan's strength in gasoline engines and Renault's strength in diesel engines.

> **Formal international cooperative alliance (ICA)**
> A nonequity alliance with formal contracts specifying what each company must contribute to the relationship.

## International Joint Ventures

An **international joint venture (IJV)** is a self-standing legal entity owned by parent companies from different countries; the participating companies have an equity or ownership position in an independent company. The simplest IJV occurs when two parent companies have 50/50 ownership of the venture. International joint ventures are becoming increasingly popular as a means for global companies to join forces by sharing resources.[14]

Not all joint ventures have only two partners, even though two-partner joint ventures are probably the most common. When a large number of companies form a joint venture, the resulting legal entity is often called a consortium. Airbus Industries, for example, is a consortium that includes Aerospatiale from France, Messerschmitt Boklow Blohm from Germany, British Aerospace, and Construcciones Aeronáuticas from Spain.

Companies need not have equal ownership to form a joint venture. Often one partner has a majority ownership. In some countries, the law requires the local partner to be the dominant owner. In such cases, for example, in a two-company venture, the foreign company cannot own more than 49 percent of the IJV's stock. Companies may also increase or decrease their ownership shares; agreements may require a foreign company to surrender its ownership after a specified time. The first McDonald's in Russia, for example, was a joint venture designed to revert eventually to sole Russian ownership. Some parent companies also increase or decrease ownership depending on the IJV's performance or the parent company's strategic goals. One company may buy out its partner and take over the joint venture as a wholly owned subsidiary.

One difficulty in determining the initial ownership of a joint venture arises from equity contributions other than cash. Companies may contribute equal monetary shares to a venture to have equal equity positions, but they may also bring nonfinancial resources. If the partners accept that the contributed resources have an economic value, then the resources become part of a firm's

> **International joint venture (IJV)**
> A separate legal entity in which two or more companies from different nations have ownership positions.

equity contribution. For example, one parent company in a 50/50 joint venture may contribute only its advanced technology, whereas the other partner may furnish all of the financing.

Formal ICAs and IJVs require formal agreements. Next, you will see some of the issues considered by multinational managers in negotiating alliance agreements.

# Negotiating the Agreement

For an IJV or a formal ICA, contractual agreements have to be negotiated and signed. Similar to licensing agreements, alliance contracts are the legal documents that bind partners together. The formal agreements, however, are never as important as the ability of managers to get along. Exhibit 9.6 shows some of the questions that must be addressed as **IJV negotiation issues**.

**IJV negotiation issues**
Points such as equity contributions, management structure, and "prenuptial" agreements regarding the dissolution of the relationship.

In general, experts recommend that negotiation teams with technical and negotiation experience handle an alliance agreement. This cross-cultural negotiation follows the steps explained in Chapter 13.

Once a firm has a partner and an agreement, it must build the organization to run the alliance, a process that includes organizational design and human resource management issues. First, we consider structure and design.

---

**EXHIBIT** $\boxed{9.6}$     Selected Questions for a Strategic Alliance Agreement

**For Both ICAs and IJVs:**

- What products or services does the alliance produce?
- Where is the new alliance located?
- Under which country's law does the agreement operate?
- What are the basic responsibilities of each partner? The responsibilities in question might include which company provides the production technology, the plant location, the training of the workforce, and the marketing expertise.
- What are the partners' contributions of senior managers?
- What are the partners' contributions of other employees?
- How will royalties or profits be divided?
- How should the company be controlled?
- How is the company organized?
- Who owns new products or technology developed by the new company?
- To whom and where will the strategic alliance sell its products?
- Is a prenuptial agreement needed?
- How can the alliance be dissolved?

**Primarily for IJVs:**

- What is the name of the new IJV company?
- What are the equity contributions of each partner?
- What is the makeup of the IJV's board of directors?

# Building the Organization: Organizational Design in Strategic Alliances

Design depends on the type of alliance chosen. Informal ICAs often require no formal design, and managers from the participating companies cooperate without formal control. Formal ICAs may require a separate organizational unit housed in one of the companies, with employees from all the parents. However, some formal ICAs may share information or products with minimal organizational requirements. For example, two airlines may book each other's routes but need no common organizational entity. IJVs, however, are separate legal entities, and they require a separate organization to carry out the alliance's objectives.

In this section, we consider two key issues in managing an alliance organization: decision-making control and management structure. These design issues are applicable mostly to IJVs, but also apply to formal ICAs that require organizational settings.

## Decision-Making Control

Parent companies must consider two major areas of decision making when designing their alliance organizations: operational decision making and strategic decision making. Operational decisions include management decisions associated with the day-to-day running of the organizations, such as the size of production runs and the hiring of assembly line workers. Strategic decisions focus on issues that are important to the long-term survival of the alliance organization, such as opening a new plant and introducing a new product.

Majority ownership of an IJV does not necessarily mean that the parent company controls its operational and strategic decision making. Similarly, providing the location for a formal ICA does not entitle a partner to such control. Depending on each partner's skills, parent companies may agree to distribute the managerial decision-making duties among partners.

In the IJV, strategic decision making usually takes place at the level of the IJV's board of directors or the top management team. So, to gain more control over strategic decision making, some IJV parent companies place more of their managers on the board of directors or top management team. IJV parent companies that wish to control the IJV's operational decision making usually have most of their people serving as mid- to lower-level managers.

In nonequity ICAs, strategic decision making usually remains with the parent companies. Alliance managers focus on operational decision making related to delivering the product or to knowledge from the parent companies.

## Management Structures

The mix of strategic and operational decision-making control among alliance partners is often complex and unique. However, to formalize the decision-making control, partners must choose a management structure that formally specifies the division of control responsibilities among partners. Multinational companies typically use five management control structures for their ICAs or IJVs:[15]

- *Dominant parent:* The **dominant parent** is usually the majority owner of an IJV or, in some cases (especially when majority ownership is not possible), the major contributor of critical resources to an ICA. In this structure, one parent controls or dominates strategic and operational decision making. Its managers

**Dominant parent**
Majority owner or contributor who controls or dominates the strategic and operational decision making of the alliance.

hold most of the important positions in the IJV or ICA organization. For IJVs, the dominant parent treats the IJV as if it were just another one of its subsidiaries.

- *Shared management:* In the **shared management structure,** both parents contribute approximately the same number of managers to positions such as the board of directors, the top management team, and the functional areas of management (e.g., production or marketing).

- *Split control:* The **split-control management structure** is similar to the shared management structure in that partners usually share strategic decision making. However, at the functional level (e.g., marketing, production, and R&D), partners make decisions independently. Often one partner has a unique skill or technology that it does not want to share completely, and so it insists on independent decision making in these protected areas.

- *Independent management:* In the **independent management structure,** the alliance managers act more like managers from separate companies. This structure is characteristic of mature IJVs—which must be legally separate organizations—and seldom occurs in ICAs. Especially for operational decisions, IJV managers have nearly complete decision-making autonomy. Because of their independence, IJVs with this structure often recruit managers and other employees from outside the parent companies' organizations.

- *Rotating management:* Managers from the various partners rotate through the key positions in the management hierarchy. For example, the alliance's top manager or management team may change each year, with each partner appointing its own managers. The rotating management structure is popular with alliance partners from developing countries. It serves to train local management and technical talent and to transfer the expertise to the developing country.[16]

## Choosing a Strategic Alliance Management Structure

Many characteristics of the alliance relationship influence the choice of a management structure. Usually, a parent that has a dominant equity position or contributes the most important resources to the alliance favors a dominant management structure, at least for strategic decision making. Alliance partners with equal ownership shares (for IJVs) or equal resource contributions (for ICAs) tend to avoid the dominant management structure. Instead, they adopt one of the more balanced managerial control systems, such as the shared, split, or rotating structures.

Management structures can change as companies' needs or contributions to the alliance change. For automobile manufacturers, the Chinese government requires joint ventures. Historically, the foreign companies provided the expertise and technology and the Chinese companies provided the labor and production site. However, as Chinese automobile companies have evolved, their needs for influence on the organizational design have changed.[17] The next Multinational Management Challenge shows how four joint ventures deal with such changes. How would you react?

Additional considerations in the choice of a management structure relate to the strategic and organizational characteristics of the parent companies and the nature of their industry; that is, parent company and industry characteristics make certain management structures more effective or more attractive to the companies involved.[18] A summary of alliance research summarized several of the factors that multinational managers take into account when designing a management structure for their international strategic alliances:[19]

*Shared management structure*
Occurs when both parent companies contribute approximately the same number of managers to the alliance organization.

*Split-control management structure*
Partners usually share strategic decision making but split functional-level decision making.

*Independent management structure*
Alliance managers act like managers from a separate company.

## Multinational Management **Challenge**

### Finding the Right Management Structure

Recently, China passed the United States as the world's largest car market. Not surprisingly, most major manufacturers want a piece of the action. However, government regulations require a joint venture for entry into the Chinese market. Experts argue that having the right management structure is crucial to success.

One recent study shows that a mixture of split and shared management style seems to work successfully, as it can be adjusted as the venture evolves. The study looked at 50/50 automotive IJVs involving state-owned Chinese companies with companies from Europe, Japan, and Korea. Although technically all control was shared due to the 50/50 control, overseas partners exercised tight control over new product development, procurement, cost management, quality control, and HRM. Shared control existed with manufacturing planning, pricing, and budgeting. As the Chinese strategic objectives have switched from learning from partners to profits, they have sought increased control in new product development, manufacturing planning, pricing, procurement, quality control, and budgeting.

All the IJVs studied were considered successful by both Chinese and foreign managers. The researchers concluded that acceptance of changing organizational designs is required to maintain stability and performance of the relationship. The challenge for these ventures will be how to manage the evolution of local partners' bargaining power, especially if China changes the law and allows 100 percent foreign ownership in the automobile industry.

*Sources: Based on Li, P., G. Tang, H. Okano, and C. Gao. 2011. "Management controls in automotive international joint ventures involving Chinese parent companies." Chartered Institute of Management Accountants Research Executive Summary Series, 7, 1–5; Reuters. 2012. "China ex-minister says foreign auto JV policy 'like opium': Report." September 3.*

- If partners have *similar* technologies or know-how and they contribute this knowledge *equally* to the alliance, they prefer a shared management structure.
- If partners have *different* technologies or know-how and they contribute this knowledge *equally* to the alliance, they prefer split management structures.
- If the alliance has more strategic importance to one partner, a dominant management structure is likely.

For joint ventures in particular:

- Mature joint ventures move to independent structures as the IJV's management team gains expertise.
- Joint ventures in countries with a high degree of government intervention produce IJVs with local partner dominance.
- Independent management structures are likely when the market is expanding, the venture does not require much capital, or the venture does not require much R&D input from its parents.

A strategic alliance is like a marriage. Without mutual trust and commitment, the relationship will fail. We now examine how these issues are handled in strategic alliances.

# Commitment and Trust: The Soft Side of Alliance Management

A common theme among managers from both failed and successful strategic alliances is the importance of building mutual trust and commitment among partners. No matter how beneficial and logical the venture may seem at its start, without trust and commitment, the alliance will either fail entirely or fail to reach its strategic potential.[20]

## The Importance of Commitment and Trust

**Commitment** in a strategic alliance means taking care of each other and putting forth extra effort to make the venture work. **Attitudinal commitment** means that partners are committed and willing to dedicate resources and effort and to face risks to make the venture work. Formally, attitudinal commitment is the psychological identification with the relationship and a pride of association with the partner and with the alliance. Attitudinal commitment in international strategic alliances is demonstrated in many ways: a fair financial commitment; a commitment to support the partner's strategic goals; a commitment to the partner's employees; and a commitment to understand the culture, politics, and economics of the partner's country. If all partners involved in the alliance demonstrate this kind of commitment, the venture develops based on the principle of **fair exchange**;[21] that is, all partners believe that they receive benefits from the relationship that equal their contributions.

Why is commitment important? The marriage of two or more distinct companies from different cultures creates a strong potential for conflict and mistrust. Without a sense of mutual obligation to each other and to the alliance, partners often fail to work out problems. Instead, they retreat to their own companies or cultures, leaving issues unresolved and often feeling that the venture is not worth the effort. As Henry Lane and Paul Beamish point out,[22] "A successful relationship requires constant attention and nurturing. As one executive explained, 'Good local partners have to be cherished and taken care of.'"

Commitment also has a practical side. **Calculative commitment** comes from the evaluations, expectations, and concerns about the future potential for gaining rewards in a relationship. Businesses require tangible outcomes for a relationship to continue. A study of commitment in IJVs suggests that commitment increases when both partners achieve their strategic goals, which may be financial or related to market entry or learning a new technology. However, it is not necessary that partners have the same strategic goals for the relationship to endure or grow in commitment.[23] Perhaps, like any marriage, if partners select each other carefully, it is easier to develop complementary strategic goals and the eventual commitment to the relationship.

Trust and commitment usually go hand in hand. As with commitment, there are two forms of trust. **Credibility trust** is the confidence that the partner has the intent and ability to meet its obligations and make its promised contributions. **Benevolent trust** is the confidence that the partner will behave with goodwill and with fair exchange.[24]

The development of trust between alliance partners may take time. Partners often begin a relationship suspicious of each other's motives. Fears and questions are typical: Do they want to steal my technology? Are they trying to take me over? Am I building a new competitor? Am I giving away too much? Will they or can they provide what we agreed on? Such initial suspicions make trust difficult.

---

**Commitment**
In a strategic alliance, when partners take care of each other and put forth extra effort to make the venture work.

**Attitudinal commitment**
The willingness to dedicate resources and efforts and to face risks to make the alliance work.

**Fair exchange**
In a strategic alliance, when partners believe that they receive benefits from the relationship equal to their contributions.

**Calculative commitment**
Alliance partner's evaluations, expectations, and concerns regarding the potential rewards from the relationship.

**Credibility trust**
The confidence that the partner has the intent and ability to meet promised obligations and commitments.

**Benevolent trust**
The confidence that the partner will behave with goodwill and with fair exchange.

**EXHIBIT** 9.7    Trust/Commitment Cycle

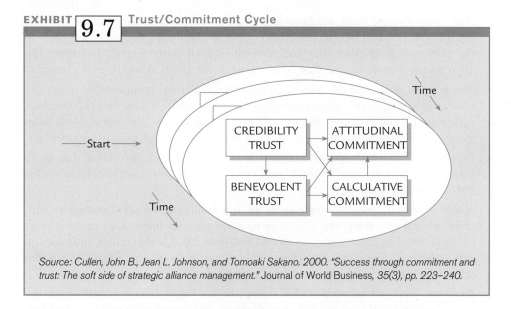

Source: Cullen, John B., Jean L. Johnson, and Tomoaki Sakano. 2000. "Success through commitment and trust: The soft side of strategic alliance management." *Journal of World Business, 35(3), pp. 223–240.*

Most experts on trust believe that it develops in what are called trust cycles. Just like people in relationships, partners in IJVs and ICAs often feel vulnerable. This early vulnerability makes partners tentative in their involvement in the relationship and reluctant to reveal true motives, business know-how, or technology. Gradually, as each side deals repeatedly with the other, suspicion declines and reciprocal trust grows.[25] Exhibit 9.7 illustrates the trust and commitment cycle in strategic alliances.

Why is trust important? Successful cooperation requires alliance participants to contribute quality inputs into the alliance organization. When partners do not trust each other, they hold back information or take unfair advantage of each other, given the opportunity. In such cases, the alliance seldom produces all the expected mutual benefits. Consider the alliance between Telia and Telenor, Norway's and Sweden's largest telecommunication companies, respectively. The lack of trust was so critical that it led to the breakdown of the alliance. Although the CEOs had trust in each other during the pre-alliance phase, it did not carry over to the individuals involved in the implementation.[26]

Trust is also necessary because formal contracts can never identify all the issues that arise in strategic alliances. It is impossible to write a contract with sufficient detail to cover every foreseeable situation. Much of what happens between alliance partners develops informally as the alliance matures. In addition, the technology and know-how of organizations entail tacit knowledge, which includes rules, procedures, and ways of doing things that are parts of the organization's culture. Tacit knowledge is not written down, and often people are not aware that it exists. As a result, for two organizations to share sensitive knowledge and go beyond the details of a formal contract, trust must exist. What happens if trust is lost and evolves into a distrust cycle?

## Building and Sustaining Trust and Commitment

Multinational managers need to consider several key factors to build and sustain commitment and trust in international strategic alliances:[27,28]

- *Pick your partner carefully:* Picking a partner must include consideration of more than potential strategic complementarity and resource contributions. Alliance partners must believe that they can trust each other, and they must believe that mutual commitment is possible.

- *Know your strategic goals and those of your partner:* Mutual revelations of strategic goals build a crucial step in the trust cycle and allow partners to realize early in the relationship whether they can commit to each other's goals. However, alliance partners must realize that strategic goals for the ICA or IJV may change.

- *Seek win-win situations:* To achieve and maintain mutual commitment in an alliance, each side must gain something of importance from the relationship. Although the outcomes from the alliance need not be the same, both sides must perceive them as a fair exchange if commitment and trust are to evolve.

- *Go slowly:* Participants in international strategic alliances must realize that problems arise and take time to work out. Trust and commitment develop in cycles, not necessarily all at once.

- *Invest in cross-cultural training:* As in all international ventures, managers with cross-cultural sensitivity and language competence will likely have more success in understanding their partners' needs and interests. Quality cross-cultural interactions between partners' employees enable them to avoid conflict and misunderstandings, leading to greater trust and commitment.

- *Invest in direct communication:* To overcome national, business, and organizational cultural differences, alliance partners are more successful at building trust and commitment when they deal with issues face to face.

- *Find the right level of trust and commitment:* Exhibit 9.8 shows the tradeoff between the vulnerability that comes with trust and commitment and their benefits.

Companies form IJVs or ICAs for benefits in the short term, in the long term, or both. Consequently, companies must assess whether the alliance is living up to

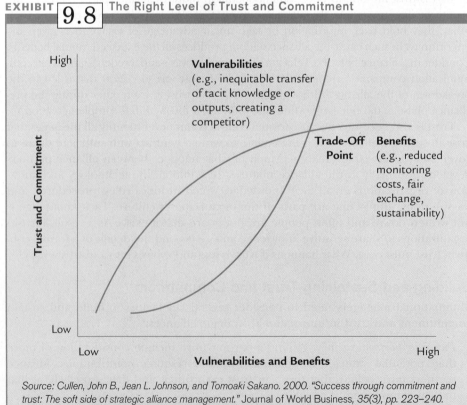

**EXHIBIT** **9.8**    The Right Level of Trust and Commitment

*Source: Cullen, John B., Jean L. Johnson, and Tomoaki Sakano. 2000. "Success through commitment and trust: The soft side of strategic alliance management." Journal of World Business, 35(3), pp. 223–240.*

expectations. In the next section, we consider the complex problems of assessing the performance of international strategic alliances.

# Assessing the Performance of an International Strategic Alliance

Like all business ventures, strategic alliances should contribute eventually to their parents' profitability. When the strategic intent of the alliance is to produce immediate results, assessment of the alliance's performance is not difficult. Standard financial and efficiency measures of performance, such as profit, sales revenue, or number of units produced, are common. Often such alliances, particularly IJVs, become stand-alone profit centers that provide direct financial benefits to the parents. Profit center alliances produce and sell their own products on the open market. Parents evaluate such alliances as they would their other corporate divisions, based on traditional financial profitability ratios, such as return on investment.

Other types of strategic alliances provide mostly indirect strategic contributions to parents, and the alliance organizations may never generate profits. Instead, they produce other valued outputs, such as new technologies with potential benefits for their parents. Indirect benefits from strategic alliances may come from penetrating risky markets, learning new markets or technologies, developing new technologies, overcoming local political barriers, developing a presence in a market, or supporting other competitive tactics. Consider the next Multinational Management Brief, which shows alliance performance measurement in the risky world of new drug therapy development.

Eventually, all companies hope to make money from their ICA or IJV investments. The alliance itself may not produce the profit, but the knowledge gained may allow the parents to succeed in the future. In the meantime, however, how can upper management assess the performance of a strategic alliance and of the managers responsible for it? What is distinctive about **IJV and ICA performance criteria**?

**IJV and ICA performance criteria**
Often must include criteria other than financial criteria, such as organizational learning.

## Multinational Management **Brief**

### Non-Financial Performance Criteria in a Strategic Alliance

Oxford Bio Therapeutics (OBT) and pharmaceuticals giant GlaxoSmithKline (GSK) entered into a strategic alliance. OBT focuses on the development of innovative cancer-fighting drugs through antibody-based approaches. Because of its expertise in the development of such drugs, GSK has entered into the alliance to benefit from OBT's expertise in drug development. In exchange for up-front payments and other financial support that may add up to about $370 million, OBT will develop drugs up to the clinical proof of concept. GSK will then use its own expertise to take the drug through the clinical testing phase and eventual commercialization. In return, OBT will receive royalties on sales of the product.

The success of this alliance depends on the development of new and financially rewarding drugs, but it cannot be measured directly, such as in terms of profit. To ensure that the alliance progresses smoothly, GSK has devised milestones and will compensate OBT as it reaches the milestones: a specified discovery, followed by development, regulatory compliance, and commercialization. Success for both GSK and OBT will be measured in terms of these milestones, with the hope that the new drug will be a commercial success.

*Source: Based on PR Newswire. 2009. "Oxford Bio Therapeutics and GlaxoSmithKline form strategic alliance to develop novel cancer therapeutic antibodies." May 18.*

Financial measures alone are seldom good indicators of performance for strategic alliances created for indirect strategic benefits. Depending on the unique objectives of the alliances, parent companies must develop more subjective performance criteria, such as creating harmony among the partners, identifying product adaptations for a new market, or capturing market share to gain first-mover advantages over their competitors.[29]

Research emphasis on the relational aspects of alliances has spurred interest in other forms of alliance performance measures.[30] For instance, some have proposed "alliance satisfaction" as a measure of performance, and others emphasize measures like goal accomplishment. Still others have argued for alternatives to more direct measures of performance, such as duration of the alliance, with early termination suggesting failure.[31] However, most measures are problematic, and the best measure depends on the nature of the alliance. For instance, duration may not be an appropriate measure because most alliances are formed with the intent that they will be dissolved once the partners' goals have been achieved. Early termination may imply that the goals have been achieved sooner than expected.

Assessing the performance of an alliance demands that parents match the alliance's strategic objectives with the measures used for assessment. If immediate profit is the strategic goal, then profit must be part of the assessment. If the goals are long term, such as learning a new market or technology, then immediate profit must be deemphasized in favor of other performance measures.

Exhibit 9.9 shows a list of potential performance measures that parent companies use to evaluate their strategic alliances.

Not all alliances achieve their strategic intent. The next section addresses how managers must plan for handling a nonperforming alliance.

**EXHIBIT 9.9** Selected Performance Criteria for Strategic Alliances

| Management Processes | Competitive |
|---|---|
| Good partner relationships; no conflict, or conflict handled well<br>High worker morale<br>Meeting goals of social responsibility<br>Development of human resources<br>Dealing with the local government | Gaining market share<br>Minimizing knowledge leakage to partners (of knowledge not intended for partners)<br>Affecting competitors (e.g., preventing them from gaining a foothold in the country) |
| **Organizational Learning** | **Marketing** |
| Understanding a new market<br>Learning a new technology<br>Improving R&D cycle times<br>Developing new management techniques<br>Developing innovative technologies<br>Generating other potential opportunities | Total sales<br>Customer satisfaction<br>Insights into customer needs<br>Facilitating the sale of other products |
| | **Financial** |
| | Return on investment (return on assets)<br>Return on assets |

*Sources: Adapted from Anderson, Erin. 1990. "Two firms, one frontier: On assessing joint venture performance." Sloan Management Review, Winter, 19–30; Gomes-Casseres, Ben. 1998. "Strategy before structure." Alliance Analyst, August.*

# If the Alliance Does Not Work

If the alliance fails to meet strategic goals, managers have two basic choices (see Exhibit 9.1). Providing that they keep their same strategic intent, they can negotiate an end to the agreement or improve their implementation.

The art of managing strategic alliances is in knowing when to quit and when to invest more time and resources in building the relationship. There are really no hard and fast rules, and each case is unique. Consider the examples in the next Focus on Emerging Markets, which shows some of the difficulties Pepsi and other companies faced with ending joint ventures in China.

## **Focus** on Emerging Markets

### Pepsi has a Contentious Divorce from Its Chinese Partner; Some Firms Fair Better

> *Divorce is not a pleasant thing; you only go through it where there is no alternative. We have found them impossible to work with. They have totally destroyed any basis for cooperation.*
>
> —*Wah-Hui Chu, president of Pepsi China, regarding a local IJV partner*

The attraction of gaining access to a city of 10 million led Pepsi to create a joint venture with Sichuan Radio and Television Industrial Development Co., a subsidiary of the province's Bureau of Radio, Film, and Television. Although the Chinese company had no knowledge of the beverage industry, most foreign investments in China require local partners, so Pepsi saw this as a way to gain local government favor. Pepsi's Chu noted, "They came to us and said they could secure government approval to set up the business, and off we went. It wasn't a pure commercial decision. You could call it an arranged marriage." Pepsi invested $20 million in the factory, which resulted in only 27 percent ownership. However, it retained the right to 50 percent of the board.

Unfortunately, after some initial success, the international joint venture between Pepsi and the Sichuan provincial government in China, Sichuan Pepsi-Cola Beverages Co., deteriorated. Once a symbol of China's economic reforms, the IJV became an embarrassment for both partners. How could such a promising venture go into the distrust cycle?

Pepsi's side:

- The partner looted the company, using funds for fancy vacations and cars. Managers submitted multiple copies of receipts to pad reimbursements.
- The general manager of the IJV, appointed by the local partner, did not follow company policies regarding sales areas.
- The partner changed the ownership structure.
- The partner blocked Pepsi's auditors from looking at factory books.

The local side:

- Managers dismissed talks of the improper use of company monies.
- "We must sell outside the markets assigned by Pepsi to make a profit—managers' bonuses depend on it."
- Pepsi's accusations are exaggerations of long unresolved conflicts designed to lead to the replacement of the factory's management.
- Pepsi is practicing "commercial hegemonism."

*continued*

Eventually, Pepsi filed papers to dissolve the partnership.

Many joint ventures in China fail due to misunderstandings regarding the evolution of the intents of the Chinese partners. Initially, many Chinese firms were interested in acquiring technology and management know-how. However, as the ventures evolve, Chinese partners seek more independence to pursue profits. If unanticipated, this move has often led to conflicts.

The list of failed IJVs includes companies from almost every industry, for example, steel (Fletcher Challenge), media (News Corporation), automobiles (Peugeot), spirits (Remy Martin), and beer (Foster's). However, some firms were clever enough to plan for divorce; as McKinsey consultant Jonathan Woetzel noted, "For a joint venture to be successful, you have to plan for it to die." Unlike Pepsi, Coca-Cola and Starbucks recently bought out their Chinese partners in amicable divorces.

*Sources: Based on Ambler, T., M. Witzel, and C. Xi. 2009. Doing business in China. New York: Routledge. Goodman, Peter S. 2002. "Pepsi seeks 'divorce' in China: Subsidiary seeks to dissolve partnership that runs bottling plant in Sichuan Province." Washington Post, September 28, E0; Economist. 2007. "Wahaha-haha! The lessons learned from Danone and HSBC's troubled partnerships in China." April 19, www.economist.com.*

**Escalation of commitment**

Companies continue in an alliance relationship longer than necessary because of past financial and emotional investments.

A particular danger in all questionable alliance relationships is the escalation of commitment,[32] which means that companies continue in relationships longer than necessary because of past financial and emotional investments. Consider the next Multinational Management Brief, and the possibility of the escalation of commitment for Toyota as it risks the success of a product line on the ability of a small firm to deliver solely battery power engines.

Improving the implementation means going over each step in the implementation process to determine what, if any, changes can be made. Perhaps, for example, partners failed to develop an appropriate design for the alliance organization or chose a weak alliance manager. Of course, if one side decides that it simply has the wrong partner, it must dissolve the relationship and, if necessary, seek another.

A recommended strategy of alliance formation is to plan for the end of the alliance from its beginning. Alliance contracts can contain a kind of prenuptial agreement that specifies how the alliance can be dissolved. This agreement describes the procedures to end the alliance and states the periods during which both sides must agree to keep the alliance alive. It may also specify penalties for early termination by either side. The advantage of including such an agreement up front, before the alliance begins, is that negotiations occur in a positive and friendly stage of the relationship, not later, when there is often conflict between the partners and a high level of distrust.

The death of a strategic alliance should not be confused with a failed relationship. Many alliances are intended to be short term. Once partners achieve their strategic goals, they both go their own ways. For example, an alliance may end after a new technology is developed, a new market is penetrated, or a temporary product gap is remedied. In addition, IJVs are often acquired by one of the partners and move to the next level of direct investment.

Next, we consider the role of the parent company in managing a portfolio of IJVs.

## Multinational Management **Brief**

### Escalation of Commitment: Will Toyota Know When or If to Pull Out?

Toyota is shaking up its "go-it-alone" corporate culture. For decades, Toyota had limited alliances with other automobile manufacturers, in an industry known for alliances. Toyota used its vast treasury and worked within its *keretsu* (a group of Japanese companies linked by cross-ownership) to develop new products. This has changed, however, as Toyota is embarking on a more risky strategy by forming an array of alliances to fill gaps in its product line. Mitsushige Akino, of Ichyoshi Investment Management Company in Tokyo, notes, "If Toyota doesn't reach out to other companies for help in technology, they won't be able to sustain market share."

Product recalls and unprecedented natural disasters are partial drivers of this strategic change. So, too, is the arrival of new CEO Akio Toyoda, the grandson of the company founder. Those who know the CEO say that he has a higher risk approach to the company than previous CEOs.

One alliance that is particularly risky and could possibly force Toyota to continue to pump money into the partner if something goes wrong is its partnership with Tesla Motors, a small California start-up specializing in batteries and electric cars. Toyota is ceding Tesla the production of its totally electric RAV4-EV. The car uses a Tesla engine and a Toyota body. Toyota has already invested more than $50 million, and hints of millions more for future electric vehicles. Telsa is still untested as a car producer, and Toyota will need to exercise caution should problems arise. The pressure to escalate commitment to "fix" things is strong after a $50 million initial investment.

*Sources: Based on* Automotive News. *2011. "Toyota's alliances with BMW, Tesla signal end of go-it-alone strategy." December 16, www.autonews.com; Eisenstein, Paul A. 2012. "New RAV4-EV shows Toyota no longer willing to go it alone." Detroit Bureau, May 7, www.thedetroitbureau.com; Ohnsman, Alan, Anna Mukai, and Yuki Hagiwara. 2011. Bloomberg, December 15, www.bloomberg.com.*

## Learning to Partner: Building a Dedicated Strategic Alliance Unit and Key Lessons from Cross-Border Alliances

Alliances are so common in today's global business environment—the Global 500 companies average 60 each—that companies are developing specialized units to manage their design. These specialized units provide processes and procedures that, for example, help managers identify the need for an alliance, evaluate partners, negotiate agreements, structure the alliance organizations, and develop specific performance indicators.

Experienced multinational companies that have had many alliances are taking the experience of what has worked and what has failed and developing templates of successful practices. For example, a recent study showed that multinational companies with alliance-management units, such as HP and Lucent Technologies, outperform companies without them.[33] However, alliance management units do not work for all companies. Typically, only very large multinational companies have enough alliances to dedicate the resources necessary to create such a specialized unit.

As we saw in this chapter, strategic alliances are likely to become more crucial in the future as multinational companies take advantage of emerging markets as well as try to lower costs. To conclude this chapter, we look at some key lessons learned from successful cross-border alliances based on Peter Jagersma's interview and survey of key individuals involved in successful cross-border alliances:[34]

- *Understand and appreciate business and cultural differences:* Successful cross-border alliances can be possible only if the partners recognize cultural and business differences and adapt to them.
- *Keep strong executive support:* Successful cross-border alliances consistently retain strong executive support. Involvement of the executive shows commitment and support of the alliance.
- *Communicate:* Communication is crucial to the cross-border alliance's success. Nothing is worse than two partners having different visions for the alliance.
- *Commitment, trust, and dedication:* In successful cross-border alliances, the partners are committed to the alliance and willing to commit the resources and personnel (including senior management time) to make it work.
- *Have checkpoint as the alliance is being implemented:* Build in go/no-go checkpoints to ensure that the partners are informed and satisfied with progress and development.
- *Review the alliance's viability:* Multinational companies need to review any alliance frequently to determine whether the alliance is viable and beneficial.

## Summary and Conclusions

The use of international strategic alliances as a major participation strategy continues to grow in the global business environment. Implementing this strategy demands a sound knowledge of the problems and prospects associated with alliance management. This chapter provided a basic understating of the related issues, including where to link in the value chain, how to select a partner, how to design an alliance organization, HRM practices in an alliance, how to build trust and commitment, how to assess performance, and what to do if the alliance fails.

Perhaps the most important decision in managing successful strategic alliances is picking the right partner. Choosing a compatible partner with the appropriate skills determines the eventual fate of most alliances.

Strategic alliances have no set structure for ownership, decision-making control, or management control. Partners must negotiate structures that support their mutual strategic goals. Most experts also consider trust and commitment as making up the foundation for IJV or ICA success, second only to picking the right partner. Commitment and trust take on such importance because not everything can be stated in a contract. For long-term success, partner companies must trust each other to deliver the agreed-upon outputs and to not take advantage of partners in the relationship.

Because alliances' strategic goals are varied and subtle, the performance of an IJV or ICA is often difficult to determine. Usually, companies expect a strategic alliance to generate more than short-term financial returns. Other objectives, such as organizational learning and market penetration, often figure strongly in performance assessment.

Strategic alliances are inherently unstable and many will fail. Consequently, when an international strategic alliance fails to meet strategic goals, multinational managers must be prepared to improve their implementation efforts or to abandon the alliance. However, many strategic alliances die natural deaths when they meet their strategic objectives or are bought out by one of the parent companies.

International strategic alliances are now so common among the major multinational companies that many have formalized the process of implementing them and their organizations. Eli Lilly, for example, calls its unit the Office of Alliance Management.

## *Discussion Questions*

1. What are the characteristics of a good partner in a strategic alliance? How do these partner traits help make an alliance successful?

2. Which of the alliance contract issues explained in the text do you think are most important? Why?

3. Discuss some costs and benefits of the different management structures. Under what conditions should a firm choose a particular structure?

4. What types of personnel are usually assigned to strategic alliances? For each type of personnel, what kind of impact does the IJV assignment have on future careers?

5. What are some of the difficulties of assessing IJV or ICA performance? How do these differ for companies with different strategic goals?

6. Why are trust and commitment so important to strategic alliances? How can a partner demonstrate trust and commitment to a joint venture?

## Multinational Management **Internet Exercise**

Most multinational companies have many joint ventures or strategic alliances. Your task is to identify the alliances of a company you select.

**Step 1.** Pick two Global Fortune 500 companies.

**Step 2.** Go to the corporate websites and look at their annual reports.

**Step 3.** From the reports, see how many alliances the companies have and identify several for additional study.

**Step 4.** Use a search engine to search for information on these alliances.

**Step 5.** Draw conclusions on how important these alliances are to the company's strategy.

## Multinational Management **Skill Builder**

**Compare and Contrast International Joint Venture Contracts**

This exercise prompts you to examine the complexities of joint venture contracts. Focus on contracts for international joint ventures.

**Step 1.** Go to http://contracts.corporate.findlaw.com/ and search for joint venture or alliance contracts. Many are available and include well-known companies.

**Step 2.** Select two contracts for alliances in the same industry, and make a summary list of the major points covered.

**Step 3.** Compare and contrast these contracts regarding inclusiveness and detail of points covered versus the flexibility of the relationship.

**Step 4.** Summarize your findings.

## *Endnotes*

[1] Accenture. 2009. http://www.accenture.com; Brunier, Frédéric. 2011. *Joint Ventures in Banking: A Source of Growth and High Performance.*

[2] Kimberley, William. 2001. "Renault and GM target the light truck market." GM Automotive Design and Production. December. http://www.autofieldguide.com, accessed 2001; GM Europe/Renault press release. 2006. "General Motors Europe and Renault pursue cooperation on LCVs," http://www.renault.com/SiteCollectionDocuments /Communiqu%C3%A9%20de%20presse/en-EN/Pieces%20jointes /11497_CP-VU_GB.pdf.

[3] *Strategic Direction.* 2006. "Create successful international mergers and alliances," 22(1): 25–28; GM Europe/Renault press release. 2006. "General Motors Europe and Renault pursue cooperation on LCVs," http://www.renault.com/SiteCollectionDocuments/Communiqu%C3%A9%20de%20presse/en-EN/Pieces%20jointes/11497_CP-VU_GB.pdf.

[4] Murray, Janet Y. 1995. "Patterns in domestic vs. international strategic alliances: An investigation of U.S. multinational firms." *Multinational Business Review,* 13: 7–16.

[5] Geringer, J. Michael. 1988. *Joint Venture Partner Selection.* Westport, CT: Quorum Books.

[6] Ibid.

[7] Main, Jeremy. 1990. "Making global alliances work." *Fortune,* December 17, 121–126.

[8] Ibid.

[9] Geringer.

[10] *Strategic Direction.*

[11] Geringer.

[12] Lorange, Peter, and Johan Roos. 1992. *Strategic Alliances.* Cambridge, MA: Blackwell.

[13] *The Economist.* 2010. "All together now: The Renault-Nissan alliance has become a template for the car industry," June 10, www.economist.com.

[14] Kealey, Daniel L., David R. Protheroe, Doug MacDonald, and Thomas Vulpe. 2006. "International projects: Some lessons on avoiding failure and maximizing success." *Performance Improvement,* March, 45(3): 38.

[15] Gray, Barbara, and Aimin Yan. 1992. "A negotiations model of joint venture formation, structure, and performance: Implications for global management." *Advances in International Comparative Management,* 7: 41–75; Killing, J. P. 1988. "Understanding alliances: The role of task and organizational complexity." In F. J. Contractor and P. Lorange, eds. *Cooperative Strategies in International Business,* 241–245. Lexington, MA: Lexington Books.

[16] Vernon, R. 1977. *Storm over Multinationals.* Cambridge, MA: Harvard University Press.

[17] Bosshart, Stephan, Thomas Luedi, and Emma Wang. 2010. "Past lessons for China's new joint ventures," *McKinsey Quarterly,* December, 1–6.

[18] Ibid.

[19] Ibid.

[20] Taylor, Andrew. 2005. "An operations perspective on strategic alliance success factors: An exploratory study of alliance managers in the software industry." *International Journal of Operations & Production Management,* 25(5/6): 469–490.

[21] Lane, Henry W., and Paul W. Beamish. 1990. "Cross-cultural cooperative behavior in joint ventures in LDCs." *Management International Review,* 30, Special Issue, 87–102.

[22] Ibid.

[23] Cullen, John B., Jean L. Johnson, and Tomoaki Sakano, "Success through commitment and trust: The soft side of strategic alliance management." Cullen, John B., Jean L. Johnson, and Tomoaki Sakano. 1995. "Japanese and local partner commitment to IJVs: Psychological consequences of outcomes and investments in the IJV relationship." *Journal of International Business Studies,* 26(1): 91–116.

[24] Johnson, Jean L., John B. Cullen, Tomoaki Sakano, and Hideyuki Takenouchi. 1996. "Setting the stage for trust and strategic integration in Japanese–U.S. cooperative alliances." *Journal of International Business Studies,* 27: 981–1004.

[25] Ibid.; Ring, Peter Smith, and Andrew, H. Van De Ven. 1992. "Structuring cooperative relationships between organizations." *Strategic Management Journal,* 13: 483–498.

[26] *Strategic Direction.*

[27] Cullen, Johnson, and Sakano, "Success through commitment and trust."

[28] Barmford, Jim and David Ernst. 2002. "Measuring alliance performance." *McKinsey on Finance,* 5: 6-10; Lei, David. 1993. "Offensive and defensive uses of alliances." *Long Range Planning,* 26: 32–44.

[29] Anderson, Erin. 1990. "Two firms, one frontier: On assessing joint venture performance." *Sloan Management Review,* Winter, 19–30.

[30] Rahman, Noushi. 2006. "Duality of alliance performance." *Journal of American Academy of Business,* September, 10(1): 305–311.

[31] Ibid.

[32] Cullen, Johnson, and Sakano, "Japanese and local partner commitment to IJVs."

[33] Dyer, Jeffrey H., Prashant Kale, and Harbir Singh. 2001. "How to make strategic alliances work." *Sloan Management Review,* 42: 37–44.

[34] Jagersma, Peter Klaas. 2005. "Cross-border alliances: Advice from the executive suite." *Journal of Business Strategy,* 26(1): 41–50.

# Tata Motors and Fiat Auto: Joining Forces

*"This is the beginning of what promises to be a far-reaching, long-term relationship between Fiat and Tata."*[1]

— *Ratan Tata, Chairman, Tata Motors, in 2006.*

*"While Tata Motors will get technology to develop economically priced small cars and entry-level sedans and an entry into untapped markets, Fiat India can continue to have a presence in the Indian market without much investment."*[2]

— *Kalpesh Parekh, Auto analyst, ASK Raymond James,[3] in 2006.*

## Introduction

In July 2006, major Italian automaker Fiat Auto S.p.A. (Fiat Auto), and the Indian automaker Tata Motors (TM), signed a Memorandum of Understanding (MoU) to form a joint venture to produce passenger cars, engines, and transmissions in India. These products were intended both for the Indian and the international market. Earlier, in January 2006, the two companies had signed a marketing and distribution agreement under which TM marketed select models of Fiat cars through a few of its dealers. The joint venture was seen as a major development in the Indian automobile industry.

Both TM and Fiat Auto had a long history in automobile manufacturing. Until the 1990s, TM was mostly a manufacturer of commercial vehicles. It entered the passenger car market in the 1990s with the *Indica*, a 1400 cc small car with a diesel engine,[4] which went on to become a success and placed TM among the top three passenger vehicle manufacturers in India. However, in 2002, because of a fall in the demand for commercial vehicles, TM reported a loss. As a part of its turnaround strategy, it improved its internal efficiencies and also decided to focus on overseas markets to reduce the impact of demand fluctuations in the domestic market. In 2003, TM returned to profitability. By 2005, it had a market presence in Thailand, Senegal, South Africa, Turkey, Europe, and West Asia. However, in spite of its impressive growth, TM was still a small player at the global level.

Fiat Auto, which built its first car in 1899, also had an illustrious history in the automobile world. After World War II, it became a major manufacturer of small cars in Italy, and later on in Europe. Until the 1990s, Fiat Auto dominated the small car market in Europe and other parts of the world.[5] In India, Fiat cars were imported even as far back as 1905. In the 1950s, the Fiat Group entered into a license agreement with India-based Premier Automobiles Ltd. (PAL) to manufacture its cars.[6] Fiat Auto formally entered the Indian market in 1997 through a joint venture with PAL.

In the early 2000s, Fiat Auto ran into losses as it was slow in adapting to the changed economic environment in Italy in particular and Europe in general.[7] Its market share in the Italian and European car markets declined. Around the same period, Fiat Auto's share in the Indian automobile market also fell drastically. In 2002, the company adopted a turnaround strategy which included several measures like cutting costs, restructuring debts, launching new models, increasing advertising spend, and focusing on markets where the demand for small cars was high. India being a major market for small cars, Fiat Auto decided to revive its operations in the Indian market. And the joint venture with TM was a step in that direction.

Most analysts were of the opinion that the joint venture would benefit both parties; TM would gain in terms of better accessibility to technology, design, and global markets, while for Fiat Auto, it would mean a larger presence in India, one of the world's fastest growing auto markets, without heavy investments. However, there were others who felt that the joint venture would end in brand dilution and product cannibalization for both parties. Also, with Honda, Toyota, GM, Mitsubishi, M&M/Renault, Nissan, Skoda, etc., chalking out plans to enter the small car segment, especially the premium small car segment, it seemed likely that the TM-Fiat Auto joint venture would face intense competition in the coming years.

## Tata Motors

TM had its origins in Tatanagar Shops,[8] which was acquired by Tata Sons Ltd.[9] on June 1, 1945, from the Government of India (GoI). Tata Sons renamed the company Tata Locomotive and Engineering Company Ltd. Initially, the company produced steam locomotive boilers and later graduated to producing complete loco-motives and other engineering products. From 1960 onward, it was referred to as Telco (Tata Engineering and Locomotive Company Ltd.).

Telco began production of medium commercial vehicles in 1954. The company gradually grew under the leadership of J.R.D. Tata (Chairman between 1945 and 1973) and Sumant Moolgaokar (Moolgaokar) (Chairman between 1973 and 1988). Telco set up a second factory in Pune in the 1970s. The company started manufacturing heavy commercial vehicles in 1983 and light commercial vehicles in 1986. Telco also increased its exports over the years. In 1988, Ratan Tata replaced Moolgaokar as Telco's Chairman. Under Ratan Tata, the company stepped into the passenger car segment. Telco began to test several indigenously developed car models in the late 1980s and the early 1990s.

Until 1990, India had a licensing and regulatory regime that stifled competition in the automobile industry. Due to this, the automobile market was a seller's market, with customers having to endure long waiting periods while purchasing new vehicles.

However, all this changed with the liberalization of the Indian economy in 1991. The seller's market was transformed into a buyer's market. The 1990s saw the entry of several major global automobile manufacturing companies into India. In 1991, Ratan Tata took over as Chairman of the Tata Group.

In 1991, the first utility vehicle (described as a cross between a truck and a car) under the Tata marquee called the *Sierra* was launched. This was followed by the *Estate* in 1992. In the same year, Telco opened a new factory at Lucknow. In 1994, the company entered into a joint venture agreement with Daimler-Benz AG for the manufacture of Mercedes Benz passenger cars in India,[10] an agreement which continued until 2001. The same year, it also launched a multi-utility vehicle (MUV) called the *Sumo*.

In 1998, Telco launched the *Safari*, India's first sports utility vehicle (SUV). The same year, the company also introduced the *Indica*,[11] a small hatchback with an indigenously developed diesel engine.[12] The launch of the *Indica* was a defining moment for Telco as it was not only the company's first small car, but also India's first indigenously developed small car.[13]

At the time of launch of the *Indica*, the small car market in India was dominated by the *Maruti 800*, a small hatchback manufactured by Maruti Udyog Ltd. (MUL).[14] The *Indica* was priced aggressively to attract *Maruti 800* customers. This forced MUL to lower the retail price of the *Maruti 800*, which made small cars more affordable to the Indian middle class and consequently expanded the

market for small cars. Telco changed the rules of the game in the Indian automobile market by providing customers of the *Indica* with options like air conditioning, power steering, alloy wheels, and electric windows features which until then had been available only in premium cars.

By 1999, with 115,000 bookings, it was clear that the *Indica* was a success. Even as the car was a commercial success, Telco received several complaints from customers on aspects such as excessive tire wear, engine vibration, and problems with gears. Telco then re-engineered the car totally and launched it as the *Indica V2* (or version 2). This version fixed most of the technical problems that had plagued the *Indica* and it went on to become very popular with customers.

Even though Telco was making impressive inroads into the passenger car market, the year 2001 saw the company recording a net loss of about Rs. 5 billion—its first loss in 57 years. This was attributed to the Indian commercial vehicles market contracting by about 40 percent during the year. As Telco was the market leader in the commercial vehicles (light and heavy) segment with a market share of 74 percent (in 2001), the impact of this on the company was particularly severe.

As part of a turnaround strategy, Telco focused on improving internal efficiencies and restructuring its debts. It also took measures to increase productivity. These efforts helped it to cut costs by Rs. 9.60 billion within two years (Telco was able to reduce the cost of raw materials by 65 percent and of interest costs by 25 percent). "Our turnaround initiatives during the past two years were focused on aggressive cost reduction, right-sizing the organization, financial restructuring, gains in volume and market share, re-engineering processes, organizational transformation, and launching new products,"[15] said Praveen Kadle (Kadle), executive director (Finance), Telco.

The company improved its overall efficiency, which allowed it to break even at a much lower level of capacity utilization than before (31 percent for commercial vehicles and 48 percent for cars). It adopted the platform-sharing system, where different vehicle models shared the same manufacturing system and some key components, which cut down costs as well as the time-to-market. In 2002, it launched the *Indigo*, a mid-size three-box car, which shared a platform with the *Indica*.

In 2002–2003, Telco registered a net profit of Rs. 3 billion. In this period, the company worked out a two-pronged strategy for growth and to protect itself from future downturns in markets. The first component of the strategy was to enter and establish itself in overseas markets. This, in addition to aiding growth, was expected to help the company ride out demand fluctuations in the domestic market. "The international markets mitigate risk and provide a growth opportunity,"[16] said Kadle. The second part of the strategy was to produce new products in new segments and to increase the focus on small passenger vehicles.

## The Growth Strategy

**Going Global** In December 2002, Telco signed a manufacturing and supply agreement with the UK-based MG Rover Group.[17] Under the agreement, Telco was to supply the *Indica*, suitably modified to meet the applicable regulatory standards, to MG Rover, which would then sell it in the UK and in Continental Europe as the *City Rover*. Telco also planned to simultaneously market the *Indica* in Europe through its own distribution network. Ratan Tata said, "This agreement will enhance the volume throughput of the Indica plant [at Pune] significantly. More importantly, we look at it as an endorsement by a major international company of Tata Engineering's [Telco] capabilities in general, and the world-class acceptability of the Indica in particular."[18]

In keeping with its global aspirations, Telco was renamed as Tata Motors (TM) in September 2003. "It's all about growth and a bit of international aspiration. We are driving a change in mindset through this new name, embarking on a journey that will be increasingly global,"[19] said a Tata spokesperson.

In October 2003, TM won a US$ 19 million tender for the supply of 500 buses to Senegal. It then set up a bus assembly unit in Thies, Senegal.

In 2004, TM set up a regional office and a special sales team in the UAE to boost its commercial vehicles business in West Asia. In March 2004, TM acquired Korea-based Daewoo's commercial vehicles business. One of the reasons for this acquisition was to gain an entry into the high-volume Chinese market. "About 60 percent of Daewoo's total exports goes to China, and it is already working with a company there to make trucks in China for the local market. So we would use Daewoo as leverage to strengthen our position in the Chinese market,"[20] said Kadle.

TM had been selling its medium commercial vehicles and buses in the South African market through Tata Automobile Corporation South Africa (TACSA) since 1997. In 2004, the company invested Rs. 40 million in a bus assembly unit in Johannesburg. TM also launched its passenger cars–the *Indica* and the *Indigo*–in the South African market that year. The cars were sold through a network of 20 dealers. According to reports, TM aimed to capture 7 percent of the South African passenger vehicle market by 2007–08.

TM was listed on the New York Stock Exchange (NYSE) in September 2004.[21] "We are confident that the company will benefit from the capital market access that this listing provides,"[22] said Ratan Tata.

By the end of 2004, TM's agreement with MG Rover came under a cloud with Rover selling far fewer *City Rovers* than expected. Eventually, the agreement came to an end in April 2005, when Rover was shut down because of financial problems.

However, TM continued to scout for new opportunities overseas. In March 2005, it acquired a 21 percent stake in Hispano Carrocera SA,[23] a Spanish bus manufacturing company, giving it controlling rights in the company and an option to buy the remaining stake at a later date. "This strategic alliance with Hispano Carrocera will give us access to its design and technological capabilities to fully tap the growing potential of this segment in India and other export markets. Besides, it provides us with a foothold in developed European markets,"[24] said Ravi Kant (Kant), executive director (commercial vehicle business unit), TM.

In February 2005, TM launched the *Indica* in Turkey through a network of 16 dealers.

In September 2005, TM entered into an agreement with Thai Rung Union Car Plc., Thailand's largest pick-up truck modifier,[25] to set up a manufacturing unit for pick-ups in Thailand. Thailand was the largest manufacturing base for utility vehicles after the United States and a major market for utility vehicles.[26] With this venture, TM also hoped to gain access to the ASEAN region.[27] TM also made known its plans to set up a production base for hybrid and low-cost small cars in this region in the future.

**New Product Initiatives** Alongside its global forays, TM launched several new products, some of which created new categories in the Indian market. In 2004, it unveiled plans to launch the *Indiva*, a seven-seater multipurpose vehicle (MPV). In September 2004, TM launched the *Indigo Marina*, a station wagon, positioned as a premium car that combined the luxury of a sedan with the convenience of an MPV. "We believe that the Indigo Marina will create a new segment in the market. Tata Motors has always endeavored to grow the market by prying open new segments,"[28] said Dr V. Sumantran, executive director, engineering research centre and passenger car business unit, TM. The same year, it also launched an improved version of the *Indica V2* and the *Sumo Victa*, an improved version of the *Sumo*.

At the Geneva Motor Show in March 2005, TM unveiled the *Xover*, a concept car which was a fusion of a car and a SUV. After gauging customer reactions,

TM planned to take a decision regarding the commercial launch of the car in Europe, India, and some other markets.

In May 2005, TM launched the *Ace*, a sub-one ton mini-truck that was uniquely positioned between three-wheeled cargo carriers and light commercial vehicles. The vehicle generated intense interest as it offered more load carrying capacity than the three-wheeled vehicles, and at a reasonable price. Moreover, the *Ace* catered to a segment of the auto industry that was believed to be less cyclical than the light, medium, and heavy commercial vehicles segments. In this period, TM also launched the *Safari Dicor*, the *Indigo SX series* (a luxury variant of the *Indigo*), the *Indica V2 Turbo Diesel*, the *TL 4X4* (India's first Sports Utility Truck), and the *Novus* (a range of commercial vehicles).

In September 2005, TM announced plans to launch a Rs. 100,000 car within three years.[29] "The vehicle would seat four to five people and have a rear engine. It will not be a scooter, three-wheeler or an auto-rickshaw made into a car,"[30] said Ratan Tata. The product was to be positioned between two-wheelers and the existing entry-level cars.

At the end of 2005, TM continued to be the market leader in the US$ 5 billion Indian commercial vehicle market (truck and bus) with about 58 percent market share (*See Exhibit I for the market share of TM in commercial vehicles market in India*). The company was the world's sixth largest commercial vehicle manufacturer,[31] and the third biggest car maker in India after MUL and Hyundai (*See Exhibit II for the market share of TM in the Indian passenger vehicles market*). International business, including exports, accounted for 18 percent of its revenues (in 2005–06).

## Fiat Auto

Fiat came into existence on July 11, 1899.[32] The company was established by Giovanni Agnelli (Giovanni) together with a group of investors. The first Fiat car manufacturing facility was opened in 1900 in Corso Dante, Italy. Giovanni became the managing director of the company in 1902. In 1908, the company started exporting cars to the United States, France, Australia, and the U.K.

By 1911, the Fiat Group had diversified into the production and marketing of commercial vehicles, marine engines, trucks, and trams and by 1925, it had entered the steel, railways, power, and public transportation businesses.

The Fiat Group's auto division used mass production to keep production costs low. By the late 1950s, the Group had set up several new manufacturing plants abroad for automobiles as well as for farm machinery. In 1966, Gianni Agnelli (Agnelli), the grandson of Giovanni, became the Chairman of the Fiat Group. In later years, the Group expanded its operations into areas such as aerospace and telecommunications with varying degrees of success. In 1967, in its first acquisition, the Fiat Group purchased Autobianchi.[33] In 1969,[34] it purchased controlling interests in Ferrari and Lancia.[35]

In 1976, the Fiat Group's auto division entered the automobile market in Brazil. It also established production facilities in the country. Later, it entered the Argentinean automobile market. Over the years, the Group invested heavily in these two markets.

In the 1970s, the Fiat Group's numerous operations were spun off as independent companies. In 1979, the automobile division of the Group (consisting of Fiat, Lancia, Autobianchi, Abarth,[36] and Ferrari) was incorporated as an independent company called Fiat Auto S.p.A. By the late 1970s, Fiat Auto had plants in Italy, Poland, Brazil, and Argentina. In 1986, Fiat Auto took over Alfa Romeo,[37] a sports car manufacturer. In 1993, it acquired Maserati,[38] another sports car manufacturing company.

By the late 1980s, Fiat Auto was facing severe competition from Japanese auto manufacturers in several markets. During this period, Fiat Auto withdrew from the American and Australian markets.

In the early 1990s, Agnelli was made a senator for life in recognition of his role in developing Italy's economy. At that time, the Fiat Group accounted for almost 5 percent of Italy's Gross Domestic Product (GDP) and was also Italy's biggest employer and something of a national icon.

## Fiat India

The Fiat Group's association with the Indian automobile market goes back to 1905, when it appointed Bombay Motor Cars Agency as the sales agent for its cars in India. In the 1950s, the Fiat Group entered into a license and service agreement with PAL, which allowed PAL to manufacture the *Fiat 500* in 1951, the *Millicento* in 1954, and the Fiat 1100 in 1964. The Fiat 1100 model was later marketed in India as the *Premier Padmini*. The *Premier Padmini*, launched in 1968, went on to become very popular in India. PAL manufactured and marketed the *Premier Padmini* until 2000. PAL also launched the 118 NE which combined the body shell of the Fiat 124 with a Nissan engine. This model was not very successful.

In 1995, Fiat Auto established a wholly-owned subsidiary in India–Fiat India Auto Ltd (FIAL). FIAL entered into a 51:49 joint venture with PAL to form Ind Auto Ltd. The joint venture company manufactured the *Uno*, a

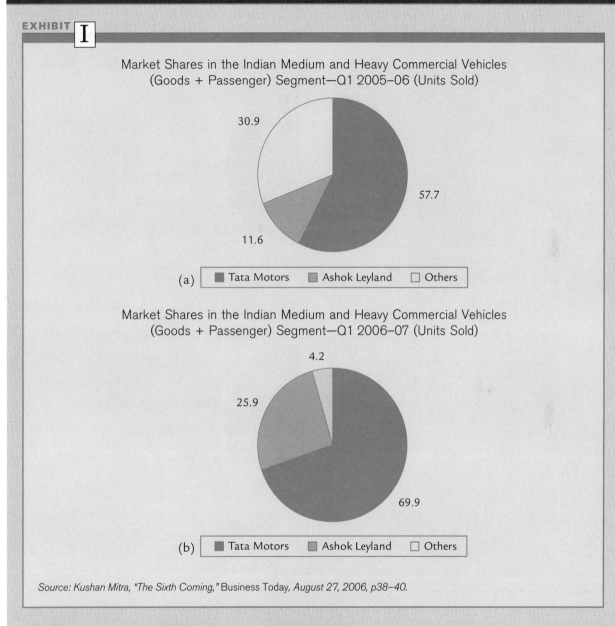

EXHIBIT I

Market Shares in the Indian Medium and Heavy Commercial Vehicles (Goods + Passenger) Segment—Q1 2005–06 (Units Sold)

(a)    ■ Tata Motors    ■ Ashok Leyland    □ Others

Market Shares in the Indian Medium and Heavy Commercial Vehicles (Goods + Passenger) Segment—Q1 2006–07 (Units Sold)

(b)    ■ Tata Motors    ■ Ashok Leyland    □ Others

*Source: Kushan Mitra, "The Sixth Coming," Business Today, August 27, 2006, p38–40.*

small hatchback, at a plant in Kurla, Mumbai. The production of the *Uno* started in 1996. In 1997, FIAL increased its stake in the joint venture to 97 percent, took over the Kurla plant, and created a new dealer network. Ind Auto Ltd. was renamed as Fiat India Pvt. Ltd. (Fiat India). In 1998, Fidis S.p.A., Fiat Auto's subsidiary in the auto finance business, entered into a joint venture with Sundaram Finance Ltd.,[39] to form Fiat Sundaram Auto Finance Ltd. (FISAF) to finance Fiat cars.

Though the *Uno* received favorable reviews for its design and was considered to be a car that offered good value for money, it was not a commercial success. Reportedly customer interest in the product declined over a period of time due to poor customer service and promotion. Fiat India launched the *Siena* in 1999 and the *Palio* in 2001.

## Financial Problems at Fiat Auto

By the late 1990s, Fiat Auto was in deep trouble. Its problems had been building up for years. One of the main reasons for its problems was that, over the years,

EXHIBIT  II

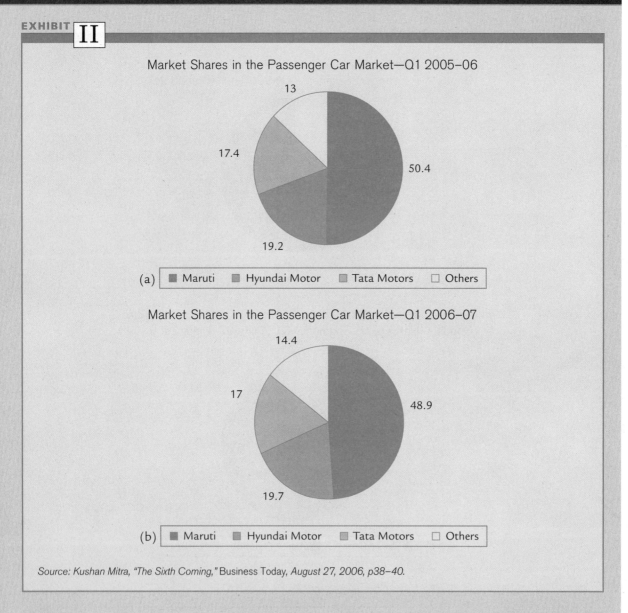

Market Shares in the Passenger Car Market—Q1 2005–06

13

17.4

50.4

19.2

(a)    ■ Maruti    ■ Hyundai Motor    ■ Tata Motors    □ Others

Market Shares in the Passenger Car Market—Q1 2006–07

14.4

17

48.9

19.7

(b)    ■ Maruti    ■ Hyundai Motor    ■ Tata Motors    □ Others

*Source: Kushan Mitra, "The Sixth Coming,"* Business Today, *August 27, 2006, p38–40.*

it had failed to move beyond the small car segment to the segments for bigger cars, where margins were higher. Italy's adoption of the Euro, the common currency of the European Union, also had an adverse effect on Fiat Auto. The Italian government's decisions to withdraw the concessions and subsidies given to the company, and at the same time, give foreign auto companies free access to the Italian market, severely affected the company's revenues and profitability. "The terrible story of Fiat [Fiat Auto] reflects the protectionism, ineffectiveness, corruption, and compromise typical of the way Italy has done business for the past 30 years,"[40] said an Italian entrepreneur. However, as much as to the macro-economic factors, auto analysts attributed the decline of Fiat Auto to the poor quality and performance of its cars.

Apart from increasing foreign competition, the late 1990s also saw the demand for cars falling in Italy and some other European countries. The European car industry was burdened with excess capacity, and Fiat Auto started incurring losses in its European operations because of falling sales and increasing costs. Other auto companies too were affected and some of them even shut down their plants in Europe. Fiat Auto, which had invested heavily in expanding the markets in Latin America, suffered another blow when the region faced a financial crisis in 1998–99. Due to all these developments, the company found itself in deep financial trouble.

Paolo Fresco (Fresco) became chairman of Fiat Auto in 1998, by which time its market share in Italy had fallen to 41 percent from around 62 percent in 1984. In 2000, the Fiat Group entered into a joint venture agreement with General Motors (GM).[41] While GM took a 20 percent share in Fiat Auto, the Italian company took a 6 percent share in GM. The deal included a put option, valid between January 2004 and July 2009, which required GM to acquire the Group's auto business, failing which GM would have to pay a penalty of US$ 2 billion to the Fiat Group.

By 2002, Fiat Auto had accumulated losses of US$ 2.5 billion, including a loss of $1.3 billion in 2001. The Fiat Group as a whole had debts of almost € 33.4 billion (in 2002).

In 2002, Fiat Auto's market share was down to 28 percent in Italy, and a mere 7 percent in Europe.[42] Its share price had also fallen by almost 50 percent over a ten-year period. In the same year, the company embarked on a restructuring program to deal with the crisis caused by declining sales, increasing losses, and rising levels of debt.

The crisis at Fiat Auto prompted the Italian government to consider buying a stake in the company. However, private banks, which were the major creditors of the Fiat Group, preferred a market-guided restructuring for the company. The Fiat Group received about € 3 billion in credit from the private banks with a requirement to either sell or turn around its auto business. The Group also transferred a major share in Fidis Retail Italia (FRI),[43] a subsidiary in the auto finance business, to the banks.[44]

In an effort to cut costs, Fiat Auto announced its intention to trim its workforce. The proposal met with stiff resistance not only from the labor unions but also from the Italian government. However, the company went ahead and in 2002, cut more than 8,100 jobs at its factories in Italy. It also increased investment in R&D and new product development.[45]

The Fiat Group also sold some of its industrial assets to pay off loans. In 2003, the Group sold its insurance and aviation businesses and in February 2004, its engineering and power businesses (*See Exhibit III for the corporate structure of the Fiat Group*).

Through the early 2000s, Fiat Auto saw the entry and exit of four chief executives. These frequent changes in leadership had their impact on the restructuring process. In June 2004, Sergio Marchionne (Marchionne) became the CEO of Fiat Auto. He initiated further cost-cutting measures, and fired managers whose performance was unsatisfactory. He also drew up a schedule for new model launches, refurbished Fiat Auto's European showrooms, and increased advertising expenditure. In this period, Fiat Auto also adopted a strategy to develop new feature-rich models, which could be sold at higher prices.

These measures were taken to revive the fortunes of Fiat Auto so that the Group would not have to sell the company to GM. However, with losses mounting, the Fiat Group was forced to consider the put option. GM, whose European operations (which primarily consisted of the *Opel* and *Vauxhall* brands) were themselves making losses, was not keen to acquire yet another loss-making car manufacturer. Therefore, it started negotiations with the Fiat Group to extricate itself from the deal. On May 13, 2005, the agreement between GM and the Fiat Group was dissolved and GM paid the Group US$ 2 billion (€ 1.55 billion) as penalty. GM also returned its stake (10 percent) in Fiat Auto to the Fiat Group.

Amidst the growing consolidation in the global auto industry, Fiat Auto's market share continued to shrink rapidly. Fierce competition and high levels of overcapacity in the developed countries made Fiat Auto look to markets in developing countries, especially India and China. Fiat Auto's expertise in small cars gave it an advantage in these markets, where small, cheap cars were in great demand. Also, generally, the cars sold in developing countries were much simpler (in that they offered fewer features as options, and used less complex technology) than those sold in mature markets, resulting in lower product development costs.

However, in the mid-2000s, Fiat Auto's Indian operations were faring badly, even though the company had, over the years, invested more than Rs. 20 billion. The *Palio* was initially very successful, and Fiat India even started work on a second manufacturing facility at Ranjangaon, Maharashtra. However, the car's popularity waned very quickly. Fiat India's other products–the *Siena* (later relaunched as the *Petra*), and the *Palio Adventure* also fared badly. The company faced a situation where its sales declined and its plant was underutilized. To add to its problems, the Kurla plant (which had an annual capacity of 60,000 cars) was severely damaged by floods in the middle of 2005, bringing production at the plant to a halt.[46]

In March 2005, Paulo Castagna (Castagna) was appointed as the managing director of Fiat India. Around this time, several Indians were appointed to top management positions. In June 2005, Fiat India

**EXHIBIT III**    Corporate Structure of the Fiat Group

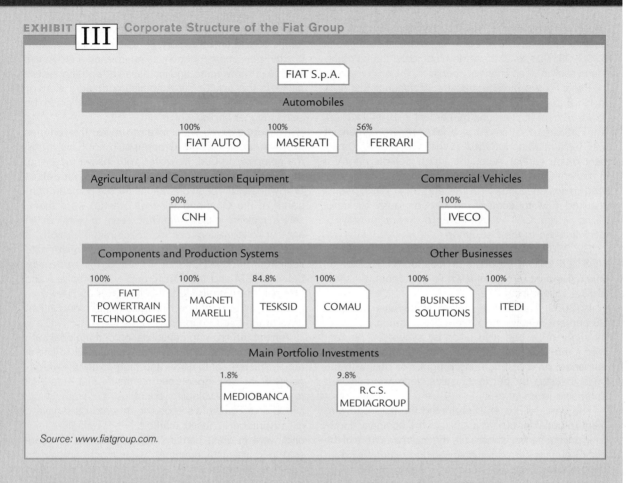

Source: www.fiatgroup.com.

initiated a 12-month revival plan. "India is a strategic market for Fiat [Auto] and we will take all measures to make it profitable for us. We are taking a long-term view of the market and hope to turn around the current position,"[47] said Castagna.

In 2005, Fiat Auto made a fresh infusion of about Rs. 2 billion into its Indian operations. The company also made efforts to rationalize the dealer and service network, removing non-performers. "We are concentrating from the commercial side…. restructuring and deepening relations with the dealer,"[48] said Castagna. The company also announced plans to introduce new models in India in the near future.

As a part of its initiative to cut costs and reduce risks, Fiat Auto was also working with other major auto makers on product development, market development, etc. The company had entered into partnerships with global auto manufacturers like Ford Motor Co., PSA Peugeot Citroen, etc. In the second half of 2005, there were reports that Fiat Auto was considering teaming up with TM.

## Tata Motors and Fiat Auto: Joining Forces

On September 22, 2005, TM announced that it was signing a Memorandum of Understanding (MoU) with Fiat Auto to explore the possibility of cooperation across different areas in the passenger car market. The two auto makers were examining the possibility of joint product development, manufacturing, sourcing, and distribution of products, aggregates, and components.

A 15-member joint team consisting of senior officials from both organizations was set up to study the viability and the specifics of the nature of cooperation, both in the short and the long term. "If found feasible, the two companies will enter into definitive agreements in the course of the coming months,"[49] said an official statement.

Both companies appeared optimistic about the possibilities from the alliance. "We are delighted to be in dialogue with the Fiat Group on the range of possibilities between the two corporations,"[50] said Ratan Tata. For Fiat Auto, this alliance was in keeping with its global strategy. "The possible strategic cooperation agreement with Tata Group represents another step in our clearly defined strategy that calls for targeted alliances across the automobile value chain. It is consistent with successful ventures established with premier partners,"[51] said Marchionne.

In October 2005, Giovanni De Filippis was appointed as managing director of Fiat India in place of Castagna.

In January 2006, the TM-Fiat Auto alliance moved another step forward, with the announcement of a shared dealer network in 11 Indian cities, representing 70 percent of Fiat India's market. Under the deal, TM dealers would sell Fiat cars from March 2006. Moreover, the two companies also examined synergies in overseas distribution so that Fiat Auto could give marketing support to TM through its retail network in Europe. "The two big companies have come together looking at opportunities not confined to India but spreading to other places of the world,"[52] said Ratan Tata.

The new TM-Fiat Auto India dealer network consisted of 25 TM dealers and three Fiat India dealers. The 28 dealers were to sell Fiat's *Palio* and *Palio Adventure* in addition to all TM passenger cars–the *Indica, Indigo, Indigo Marina, Sumo*, and *Safari*–through 44 outlets. These dealers were to offer service and spare parts for both Fiat and TM cars. Moreover, the co-operation extended to vehicle finance as well. According to the deal, Fiat cars were to be financed through Tata Motor Finance, the finance division of TM.

The two companies also announced that discussions were on to identify new areas for co-operation. Officials said that new agreements would be reached as and when their feasibility was established. It was also announced that Fiat Auto would give TM access to its technology and there was also a possibility of the two companies sharing platforms in the future. "This is not a joint venture, but this is the start of a relationship which could go beyond even a joint venture. It is a relationship which is beginning to form. We want to give it time,"[53] Ratan Tata said.

Fiat Auto's alliance with TM took place against the backdrop of a revival in sales in Europe. The company earned a quarterly trading profit for the first time in nearly four years in the last quarter of 2005. This came about mostly because of the high sales of its new model–the *Grande Punto*. In the first half of 2006, Fiat Auto earned an operating profit of US$ 184 million from revenues of US$ 14.8 billion (*See Exhibit IV for financials of Fiat Group and revenues by sector*).

Meanwhile, TM continued with its forays into international markets. In May 2006, the company entered into a 51:49 joint venture with Brazil-based Marcopolo to build buses and coaches for the Indian as well as the overseas markets,[54] at a production facility to be set up in India at an investment of Rs. 1.5–2 billion.

In mid-2006, Fiat India began using the paint booth facility at its Kurla complex for painting the *Tatamobile 207*, TM's pickup. This was done to increase the utilization of Fiat India's facilities. "We are painting 3,000–4,000 bodies of the Tatamobile on a monthly basis, thus optimizing the paint booth facility. The idea is to be self-sufficient through internal means and the paint booth plays an instrumental role in sourcing revenue for the company,"[55] said Filippis. Around this time, the alliance between the two companies was further strengthened by Ratan Tata joining the board of Fiat S.p.A.[56]

In July 2006, TM signed another MoU with Fiat Auto for setting up a joint venture in India to manufacture passenger vehicles, engines and transmissions. The joint venture was to manufacture both TM and Fiat vehicles for the Indian and overseas markets. Fiat India transferred its facility at Ranjangaon, where 100,000 cars and 250,000 engines and transmissions were to be produced, to the joint venture. The two companies were expected to jointly build Fiat cars in the B and C segments (The *Fiat Grande Punto* and a new Fiat sedan) and its successful small diesel engine for Indian as well as export markets. "Fiat [Auto] has technology … and the opportunities are endless,"[57] said Ratan Tata. The joint venture was expected to commence production in late 2007 or early 2008.

Fiat Auto and TM also commissioned a 60-day study aimed at exploring industrial and commercial cooperation in Latin America. The study was to examine the prospect of using Fiat Auto's production units in Cordoba, Argentina, to manufacture Tata vehicles, especially utility vehicles and pick-ups, and market them in South America and other markets.

The July MoU was an indication of the growing commitment and co-operation between the two companies to work together and use their combined strengths to capture key markets. "Both companies have complementary strengths, convergent objectives, and shared values. Together, we can meaningfully address markets in India and other select geographies, combining technologies, products, and human skills of both organizations,"[58] said Ratan Tata.

The companies also had plans to expand the dealership network in India. Though the two companies did not reveal their investments in the venture, analysts estimated that it would be around of Rs. 2.2 billion.

Moreover, the Fiat Group intended to take TM's assistance in establishing a market for its truck unit

EXHIBIT **IV**

### Fiat Group Financials 2004–05 *(in millions of euros)*

| Particulars | 2005 | 2004 | 2003 | 2002 |
|---|---|---|---|---|
| Net Revenues | 46,544 | 45,637 | 47,271 | 55,649 |
| Trading Profit | 1,000 | 50 | – | – |
| Operating Result | 2,215 | (585) | (510) | (762) |
| Income/(loss) before taxes | 2,264 | (1,629) | (1,298) | (4,817) |
| Net Income/(loss) before interest | 1,420 | (1,579) | (1,948) | (4,263) |
| Group interest in net income/(loss) | **1,331** | **(1,634)** | – | – |

*Source: www.fiatgroup.com.*

### Fiat Group's Revenues by Sector *(in millions of euros)*

| Particulars | 2005 | 2004 |
|---|---|---|
| Fiat Auto | 19,533 | 19,695 |
| Maserati | 533 | 409 |
| Ferrari | 1,289 | 1,175 |
| Fiat Powertrain Technologies | 1,966 | – |
| Agricultural and Construction Equipment (CNH Global) | 10,212 | 9,983 |
| Trucks and Commercial Vehicles (Iveco) | 9,489 | 9,047 |
| Components (Magneti Marelli) | 4,033 | 3,795 |
| Metallurgical Products (Teksid) | 1,036 | 910 |
| Production Systems (Comau) | 1,573 | 1,711 |
| Services (Business Solutions) | 752 | 976 |
| Publishing and Communications (Itedi) | 397 | 407 |
| Holding Companies, Other Companies and Eliminations | (4,269) | (2,741) |
| **Total for the Group** | **46,544** | **45,637** |

*Source: www.fiatgroup.com.*

Iveco in India.[59] Iveco earlier had a stake in Ashok Leyland (the second largest commercial vehicle manufacturer in India), through which it had sold its cargo range of trucks in India. However, with sales being less than satisfactory, the range was phased out within a few years of its launch. TM and Fiat were also looking for other areas where they could partner. "There will be additional alliances that we will disclose as they are concluded,"[60] said Marchionne.

## Advantages of the Alliance

Even though Fiat India had been present in India for close to a decade, it had the lowest market share among the 11 players—including later entrants like Skoda India—in the growing car market.[61] Though the company's cars like the *Palio* were initially quite successful, Fiat's image suffered due to its dealers. Fiat customers were reported to have faced problems

because of the non-availability of spare parts and lackadaisical customer service. Such problems had an adverse impact on the company's image, and it struggled to compete effectively in the Indian automobile market. The alliance with TM was expected to improve its dealership network and customer service without the company having to make significant investments. The goodwill enjoyed by TM, and the company's reach were expected to improve Fiat's image in India. "This alliance enables us to increase our customer base in India and also provide superior service and facilities to our existing customers,"[62] said Marchionne.

Through the alliance, Fiat India also planned to source spare parts for its vehicles from TM. The Tata Group was a cost effective supplier of auto components and had several manufacturing companies under the TACO Group.[63] Fiat Auto also had plans to increase the level of component sourcing for its overseas operations from India to US$ 10 million in 2006. Component sourcing was expected to be a major area of cooperation between the two companies.

According to auto analysts, while the alliance was expected to cut manufacturing costs for Fiat India (since the manufacturing at the Ranjangaon facility would use the cost efficient production processes of TM), TM was also expected to improve efficiency. "The tie-up between Tata Motors and Fiat will provide better synergy for both the companies in terms of operational efficiency and better utilization of resources,"[64] said HC Raveendra of KR Choksey, a Mumbai-based broking firm.

Though TM was a force to reckon with in the diesel passenger car segment of the Indian auto market, it did not possess the latest in diesel engine technology. In contrast, Fiat Auto's expertise in diesel engine technology, specifically in the common rail technology,[65] was world-renowned. The joint venture was expected to strengthen TM's position in the diesel passenger car segment. Among the engines to be made under the joint venture was the 1.3 liter next-generation JTDi diesel engine.[66] Fiat Auto also announced that it would introduce a small diesel engine in India. Auto analysts expected this to be used in the Rs. 100,000 small car that TM was planning to launch in 2008.

Though TM was the leader in the diesel segment of the Indian auto market, its presence in the petrol segment was limited. TM's *Indica* petrol version contributed only 5 percent to its total car sales. The company was therefore keen on upgrading its petrol engine technology. "We are looking at getting a larger piece of the petrol market than we have and that is something we must also do. We cannot only be dependent on the diesel when the proliferation of diesel products is greater than ours alone,"[67] said Ratan Tata. Through the alliance with Fiat Auto, TM expected to gain access to next generation petrol powertrains.[68] According to auto industry sources, the TM-Fiat Auto joint venture was set to produce two petrol engines called the 'Fire' range.[69] Both engines were expected to be used in future models from TM and Fiat.

The joint venture also planned to co-develop new car models. This was expected to help TM to learn and benefit from Fiat Auto's expertise, gained through years of producing small cars and sedans. "The alliance with Fiat [Auto] could help Tata get technologies and designs for new models in future. It's a win-win deal for both,"[70] said Kalpesh Parekh, an analyst with ASK Raymond James.

The Ranjangaon plant was expected to add to TM's production capacity. The new capacity was being added at a critical time for the company as its manufacturing facility at Pune had been working at full capacity.

India was one of the fastest growing car markets in the world, with most of the growth taking place in the small car segment. In the 2000s, car sales in India had grown by almost 20 percent annually. In addition, in 2005–06, the GoI had announced a cut in excise duty on small cars which was expected to make India the world's manufacturing hub for small or compact cars. The joint venture was expected to help TM and Fiat Auto compete effectively against MUL and Hyundai Motor Company (Hyundai)–who were aggressively increasing their production capacities–and to capture a larger share of the small car market in India.

The joint venture was expected to improve TM's competitiveness in global automobile markets, as the company would be able to sell its cars in several regions of Europe, through Fiat Auto's distribution network. After the termination of the agreement with the Rover group, TM had been selling the *Indica* in Europe on its own. Fiat Auto was expected to take up the distribution of the car in Europe through its outlets, reciprocating the distribution of Fiat cars by TM in India. Since Europe was a major market for small cars, TM expected to gain substantial benefits from the arrangement. "We live in a boundary-less world. We hope to grow beyond the shores of India,"[71] Ratan Tata said.

Fiat Auto also had a very strong market presence in Brazil and Argentina, whereas TM had almost no presence in Latin America. "Fiat [Auto] has plants in various parts of the world like eastern Europe and Latin America. Both are areas that we would like to be in and where they have ideal capacity presence, that is another opportunity of working together,"[72] said Ratan Tata. If the talks were successful, models like the *Sumo* and the *Tatamobile 207* would be marketed in South America and in other overseas markets.

## Threats

Even though both firms gained several advantages by co-operating, they also faced significant threats. The TM-Fiat Auto alliance was expected to face intense competition from other automobile manufacturers in India, some of who were in the midst of forming their own alliances.

In February 2005, Renault SA formed a 49:51 joint venture with Mahindra & Mahindra Ltd. The alliance was to launch the *Logan*, a sedan, which would compete against TM's *Indigo*. Toyota Motor Corp. and its subsidiary Daihatsu Motor Co. Ltd., had plans to launch a new small car for the Indian market.

More significantly, MUL was all set to challenge TM's diesel supremacy, by entering the diesel car market in a big way. It was planning to invest Rs. 32 billion to set up a new car plant and diesel engine production facility. In 2006, MUL announced that it would launch three new small car models in the next five years. Also, Nissan and Suzuki (which owned 54.2 percent of MUL) had entered into an alliance in June 2006. Under this alliance, MUL was to produce a small car (the Nissan *Moco*). There were also reports that Nissan had plans to enter the Indian small car market on its own.

Another potential threat came from GM India. In 2005 and 2006, GM India was able to improve its market share in India, with successful launches of the *Chevrolet Optra* and the *Chevrolet Aveo*. It planned to launch the *Chevrolet Spark*, a small car, in India, in mid-2007.

There were reports that Hyundai planned to launch diesel variants of its popular models–the *Getz* and the *Santro*. It also had plans to launch a new small car by the end of 2007. Honda Motor Co. planned to launch a small hatchback car, for which it was to build a new production facility. Hindustan Motors had plans to launch the Mitsubishi *iCar* in India in 2007.[73] Similarly, while Volkswagen was expected to announce its India plans in late 2006, the Indian arm of its Czech subsidiary, Skoda India, which had already made a mark in the premium sedan market in India, was toying with the idea of launching the *Roomster*, a compact five-seater.

TM's ambitions in the highly competitive European automobile market were also fraught with difficulties. Even though the company had demonstrated its ability to compete effectively against global players in the Indian domestic market, this did not imply that its major export product, the *Indica*, was of high quality. The *Indica* was believed to have succeeded in India primarily because of the price advantage it offered over other models. However, in the European markets, quality was a far more significant issue than in the Indian market.

Another worrisome consequence of the plans for joint production and distribution was the prospect of brand dilution for both companies.[74] TM felt that the joint venture would strengthen its global expansion initiatives without adversely affecting its market share in India. "Fiat [India] operations are small when compared to ours…We will have access to their technology, new aggregates and we will market some of their products,"[75] said Ratan Tata.

TM did recognize the threat from Fiat Auto's Petra to its *Indigo* model and planned not to offer the *Petra* through its dealers. The Petra, though priced higher than the *Indigo*, reportedly offered better ride quality and other benefits.[76] A TM spokesman gave the reason for the exclusion of the *Petra* as, "The combined portfolio had been picked keeping in mind the need for

**EXHIBIT** **V** Tata Motors: Financials

| (In millions of Rupees) As on (Months) | 31-Mar-06(12) | 31-Mar-05(12) | 31-Mar-04(12) |
|---|---|---|---|
| **Profit/Loss Statement** | | | |
| Net Sales | 200,374.90 | 171,539.80 | 128,955.50 |
| Operating Income (OI) | 204,880.70 | 172,658.20 | 131,273.00 |
| OPBDIT | 20,793.20 | 19,470.30 | 17,894.50 |
| OPBDT | 18,529.70 | 17,928.80 | 16,279.20 |
| OPBT | 13,320.30 | 13,427.20 | 11,936.80 |
| Non-Operating Income | 7,217.80 | 3,097.30 | 1,067.90 |
| Extraordinary/Prior Period | −1,421.50 | −511.30 | −3,935.80 |
| Tax | 3,827.80 | 3,643.70 | 965.50 |
| Profit after tax(PAT) | 15,288.80 | 12,369.50 | 8,103.40 |
| Cash Profit | 20,498.20 | 16,871.10 | 12,445.80 |
| Dividend-Equity | 4,979.40 | 4,521.90 | 2,821.10 |

Source: www.myiris.com.

EXHIBIT **VI** Tata Motors: Sales

| Unit Sales | 2005–06 | 2004–05 | % Change |
|---|---|---|---|
| Medium & HCV | 136,964 | 135,337 | 1.2 |
| LCV | 108,084 | 74,253 | 45.6 |
| Utility Vehicles | 39,783 | 37,032 | 7.4 |
| Passenger Cars | 169,512 | 152,943 | 10.8 |
| Total | 454,343 | 399,565 | 13.7 |

Source: Kushan Mitra, "The Sixth Coming," Business Today, August 27, 2006, p38–40.

complementary products and models that contributed best to strengthening the Fiat brand in the local market."[77]

## Outlook

India was one of the fastest growing automobile markets in the world, with passenger car sales forecast to reach two million units per annum by 2010. As of 2006, small cars made up more than two-thirds of India's passenger car market. Even in the future, at least in the short to medium term, the small car segment was expected to remain the largest segment of the market. Therefore, in spite of the intense competition, the TM-Fiat Auto joint venture was aiming to make an impact in this high-volume segment. "Obviously Tata-Fiat [Auto] JV is entering an over-crowded and a price sensitive segment. But this [small car] segment which contributes to more than 60 percent of the total car sales will remain a key segment in the Indian car market for many years,"[78] said an auto analyst. Also, the fact that only eight in a thousand Indians owned a car meant that there was a huge potential for growth.

As of 2006, both TM and Fiat Auto were financially sound (See Exhibit V for the financials of TM). Fiat Auto reported a 56 percent rise in second-quarter (April–June 2006) profits partly due to the encouraging sales of its new model–the Grande Punto. The Grande Punto had increased Fiat Auto's market share in Western Europe to 7.9 percent from 6.6 percent a year earlier. The company also intended to launch several new models in 2007, like the next generation Stilo and Ducato. Fiat Auto had also formed partnerships with some of the other global car majors. For example, it announced new industrial ventures in Russia with Severstal Auto and in China with SAIC Motor Corporation Ltd. TM also saw a rise in sales and exports during this period (see Exhibit VI for the sales of TM).[79]

Fiat Auto aimed to increase its market share in India to 5 percent by 2010. In August 2006, Fiat India shut down its Kurla plant. It planned to completely relocate its manufacturing operations to Ranjangaon.

In September 2006, there were newspaper reports that Fiat Auto was evaluating whether it could share the Indica platform for a new low-cost car it intended to sell in Europe and in other markets–a proposal that went even beyond the scope of the July 2006 MoU. "It will be in the short term as they [TM] have already done most of the work. We will add our know-how, and maybe the money,"[80] said Marchionne. There were also reports that Fiat Auto might invest in TM's Rs. 100,000 car project, and that TM might build cars for some of Fiat Auto's luxury marquees like Alfa Romeo. (See Exhibit VII for the all models of Fiat Auto.) Kant said, "Nothing is ruled out and that includes Fiat [Auto]'s top-end models like the Alfa Romeo."[81] The new developments indicated the potential in the joint venture, and the possibilities that remained to be explored.

EXHIBIT **VII** Fiat Group: Automobile Models

| | Marquee | Models |
|---|---|---|
| 1 | Fiat | Panda, Idea, Stilo, Grande Punto, Mutipla, Croma, and Sedici. |
| 2 | Lancia | Ypsilon, Musa, Thesis, Lybra, and Phedra. |
| 3 | Alfa Romeo | Alfa 147 GTA, Alfa 156, Alfa 159, Alfa 166, Alfa GT, Alfa Sportwagon, Alfa Spider, and Brera. |
| 4 | Maserati | Quattroporte, Gransport, Gransport Spyder, GT, Cambiocorsa, and MC12. |
| 5 | Ferrari | F430, F430 Spider, 599 GTB Fiorano, and 612 Scaglietti. |

Source: Compiled from various sources.

CASE DISCUSSION QUESTIONS

1. What is Fiat's current situation in India?
2. What is the business opportunity in India? Do you think that Fiat needs a partner?
3. Do you think Fiat and Tata make for good partners? Compare the Fiat-GM relationship with the Fiat-Tata relationship.
4. Is the business case convincing for the joint venture? Back your answer up with a financial analysis.
5. How would you assess the negotiation process between Fiat and Tata?
6. What would you recommend for the alliance to be successful?

REFERENCES AND SUGGESTED READING

1. Lou Ann Hammond, "Who owns whom," www.car list.com, *September 07, 2006.*
2. Lijee Philip & Nandini Sen Gupta, "La dolce deal?" www.economictimes.indiatimes.com, *August 04, 2006.*
3. "Tata Motors, Fiat chart a winning formula," www.economictimes.indiatimes.com, *July 27, 2006.*
4. Gail Edmondson, "Fiat's comeback - Is it for real?", www.businessweek.com, July 26, 2006.
5. "Tata Motors, Fiat in 50:50 JV for cars, engines," www.finanacialexpress.com, July 26, 2006.
6. Razib Ahmed, "Tata Motors made good profit but not enough!" www.southasiabiz.com, *May 19, 2006.*
7. "Car makers beware, the Tata-Fiat tag team is here," www.rediff.com, January 14, 2006.
8. Sudhakar Shah, "Tata partnership with Fiat would play to strengths," www.wardsauto.com, September 28, 2005.
9. "Rs 1 lakh car in 3 yrs: Tata," www.indiacar.net, September 01, 2005.
10. Raghuvir Srinivasan, "Tata Motors: India's own wheels," www.thehindubusinessline.com, January 28, 2004.
11. "The new and improved Tata twins," www.tata.com, November 09, 2003.
12. S. Muralidhar, "More wheels in each segment," www.thehindubusinessline.com, July 27, 2003.
13. "What now for Fiat?" www.bbc.co.uk, January 24, 2003.
14. Biswajit Chowdhury, "An auto giant in distress," www.flonnet.com, December 21, 2002.
15. "Comeback kid," www.tata.com, June 24, 2002.
16. "Ciao, Paolo," www.economist.com, June 13, 2002.
17. Sudipta Basu, "Riding the global wave," www.tata.com.
18. "Crisis at Fiat Auto worsens," www.eiro.eirofound.eu.int.
19. www.tata.com.
20. www.thehindubusinessline.com.
21. www.fiat.com.
22. www.indiacar.net.
23. www.siam.com.
24. www.autocarindia.com.

CASE CREDIT

This case was written by **Namratha V. Prasad** and **Sachin Govind**, under the direction of **S.S. George**, ICMR Center for Management Research (ICMR). It was compiled from published sources, and is intended to be used as a basis for class discussion rather than to illustrate either effective or ineffective handling of a management situation.

©2007, ICMR. All rights reserved.

To order copies, call 0091-40-2343-0462/63 or write to ICMR, Plot # 49, Nagarjuna Hills, Hyderabad 500 082, India or e-mail info@icmrindia.org.

**www.icmrindia.org**

CASE NOTES

[1] "Fiat and Tata announce joint venture in India," www.detnews.com, July 26, 2006.

[2] "La dolce deal?" www.economictimes.indiatimes.com, August 04, 2006.

[3] ASK Raymond James Securities India Pvt. Ltd. (ASK RJ) is a joint venture between ASK Investment and Financial Consultants Ltd. (India), Raymond James Financial Inc. of the US, and Bharat Shah, an investor. It offers portfolio management services and investment advisory services.

[4] A small car, in the Indian context, is a car of length not exceeding 4,000 mm and with an engine capacity not exceeding 1,500 cc for diesel cars and not exceeding 1,200 cc for petrol cars. They are the most fuel-efficient cars available in both diesel and petrol variants, and also the cheapest.

[5] In 1968, Fiat surpassed Volkswagen as the largest carmaker outside the United States, with 157,000 employees producing 1.75 million cars a year. Fiat continued to expand through much of the 1970s and 1980s. (Source: www.time.com)

[6] Premier Automobiles Ltd. (PAL) was established by Walchand Hirachand in 1942. In 1946, in association with U.S.-based Chrysler, the company assembled De Soto and Plymouth cars. As of 2006, the company was making auto components.

[7] In the early 2000s, the European Union's new requirements for open competition came into force. This and the dismantling of protectionist measures changed the economic environment for businesses in the EU region.

[8] Tatanagar is a part of the city of Jamshedpur. The East Indian Railway had a locomotive manufacturing facility at that place called the Singhbhum Shops or the Tatanagar Shops.

[9] Tata Sons Ltd., a holding company, is a successor to the first trading company founded by Jamsetji Tata (the founding father of the Tata business empire). The Tata Sons Ltd. board is made up of the

chairmen or CEOs of major operating Tata Group companies, and the elected chairman of the board of Tata Sons Ltd. is recognized as the Group Chairman. The company is based in Mumbai.

[10] Daimler-Benz AG, founded in 1926 in Germany, was a leading manufacturer of automobiles, motor vehicles, and engines. In 1998, it merged with U.S.-based Chrysler Corp. to form Daimler-Chrysler AG. It sells passenger cars/SUVs under Mercedes-Benz, Maybach, Smart, Chrysler, Dodge, and Jeep brands and commercial vehicles under Fuso, Sterling, Orion, Setra, Freightliner, Mercedes-Benz, Thomas, and Western Star brands.

[11] A type of automobile design wherein the passenger cabin included additional cargo space accessed through a hatch tail gate or a flip up window.

[12] The engine design was based on the TUD5 Peugeot engine. Telco claimed to have further refined and optimized the engine to deliver higher standards of efficiency and emission.

[13] Telco paid for services to develop technology in accordance with its specifications. Styling was sourced from Italy, engine design from France, and instrumentation from Japan. But the design process and implementation of the manufacturing and supply lines was done by Telco. The *Indica* was launched within three years of conception, at a development cost of about $400 million as against the international norm of $1.2 billion required to develop a new car.

[14] Maruti Udyog Ltd. was established through an Act of the Indian parliament in February 1981. In 1982, it entered into a license and joint venture agreement with Suzuki Motor Company (later renamed as Suzuki Motor Corp.). In 1992, SMC raised its stake to 50% and in 2002, to 54.2%. With this, MUL became a subsidiary of SMC.

[15] "The new and improved Tata twins," www.tata.com, November 09, 2003.

[16] Ibid.

[17] Rover Company Ltd. (Rover), an automobile manufacturer, was set up in 1904. Over its 100-year history it changed hands several times. It was taken over by BMW, a German automobile company, in 1994. In 2000, BMW sold it to the Phoenix Corporation. MG (a sports car manufacturing company) was then merged with Rover to form the MG Rover Group. It was taken over by China-based Nanjing Automobile Group, a Chinese automobile company, in July 2005.

[18] "Tatas to ship Rover-branded Indicas," www.blonnet.com, December 21, 2002.

[19] "Rechristened thus," www.tata.com, September 28, 2003.

[20] "Fencing with the West," www.cfoasia.com, April 2004.

[21] The company listed its depository shares on NYSE through the conversion of its existing international Global Depository Shares (GDSs) into American Depository Shares (ADSs). The company's symbol on the NYSE is 'TTM'. Citibank NA was the depository. With the listing, the company was required to publish its financial results annually under both the US GAAP and the Indian GAAP.

[22] "Tata Motors drives into Wall Street," www.tata.com, September 28, 2004.

[23] The Spanish company had a market share of 25% in the bus market in Spain, and sold its buses in Europe and several other countries outside Europe. It had its own in-house product development facility for buses and coaches.

[24] "Tata Motors to acquire 21 per cent stake in Hispano Carrocera," www.tata.com, February 25, 2005.

[25] A modifier alters the specifications of a vehicle to suit his client's special needs. Most governments prescribe the standards for modification so that the 'modified' vehicle adheres to safety and other norms.

[26] "Can India become a global sourcing hub for small cars?" www.thehindubusinessline.com, May 09, 2004.

[27] The Association of Southeast Asian Nations (ASEAN) is a political and economic organization of countries located in Southeast Asia. The members of ASEAN include Brunei, Cambodia, Indonesia, Laos, Malaysia, Myanmar, Philippines, Singapore, Thailand, and Vietnam.

[28] "Tata Indigo Marina set for launch on September 15, 2004," www.tata.com, September 14, 2004.

[29] Tata Motors had first mentioned that it was working on a Rs. 100,000 car project at the 2003 Geneva Motor Show. However, in September 2005, the company made an official announcement regarding the project and indicated a time frame for its implementation.

[30] "Tatas' Rs 1-lakh car to be gearless," www.rediff.com, August 31, 2005.

[31] According to www.tatamotors.com.

[32] Fabbrica Italiana Automobili Torino or Italian car factory of Turin.

[33] Bianchi (later renamed Autobianchi) was established by Edoardo Bianchi in 1899. The cars were built for the luxury segment with great attention to detail. It produced a very small number of successful small cars. Autobianchi later came under the control of Lancia.

[34] Ferrari was founded by Enzo Ferrari in 1929 to manufacture race cars. Ferrari S.p.A. was established in 1946 to produce street legal cars. The Fiat Group acquired a 50% stake in Ferrari in 1969, which went up to 90% in 1988. In 2002, the Group sold 34% of its stake to Mediobanca, a bank. As of 2006, the Fiat Group had expressed its intention to acquire the bank's stake.

[35] Lancia was an Italian automobile manufacturer founded in 1906 by Vincenzo Lancia. Lancia was famous for many innovations in the automobile industry, including the first full-production V6 engine (in the 1950 Aurelia), V8 and V12 engine configurations, etc.

[36] Karl Abarth was a car enthusiast who remodeled cars. Fiat entered into an agreement with Abarth in the mid-1950s, where Fiat supplied partly constructed cars and Abarth would finish them at his workshop. The remodeled cars were sold as Fiat Abarths. The first car under the Fiat-Abarth brand was the 750 Berlina, based on the Fiat 600.

[37] Alfa Romeo was established in 1907 as Darracq Italiana. It was renamed as ALFA (Anonima Lombarda Fabbrica Automobili) around 1909 and then as Alfa Romeo in 1920. It came under Fiat Auto in 1986.

[38] Maserati was an Italian manufacturer of racing cars and sports cars established by six Maserati brothers in 1914. It was acquired by the Fiat Group in 1993. In 1997, as part of a restructuring effort, Maserati was brought under Ferrari. In 2005, Maserati was brought back as a direct subsidiary of Fiat S.p.A., the flagship company of the Fiat Group.

[39] Sundaram Finance Ltd., part of the TVS Group, was established in 1954. It is involved in car and commercial vehicle finance, home loans, software solutions, tire finance, deposits and mutual funds, etc.

[40] "Fiat: Running on empty," www.businessweek.com, May 13, 2002.

[41] General Motors was the world's largest automaker. It was established in 1908 in United States.

[42] Fiat had a 14 percent share in the European car market and a 60 percent market share in the Italian car market in the early 1990s. (www.time.com)

[43] The Fiat Group sold 51 percent of its stake in FRI to four banks–Capitalia, Banca Intesa, San-Paolo-ISI, and UniCredito–for € 370 million.

[44] "Fiat agrees sale of Fidis to banks," www.italiaspeed.com, March 14, 2003.

[45] In 2004, Fiat Auto announced that it would invest US$ 4.92 billion on R&D over four years (2008).

[46] Production resumed only in the first half of 2006.

[47] "Fiat works on 12 month revival plan," www.indiacar.com, September 01, 2005.

[48] Ibid.

[49] "Tata Motors, Fiat tie up to explore cooperation in passenger car segment," www.thehindubusinessline.com, September 23, 2005.

[50] Ibid.

[51] Ibid.

[52] "Pact with Fiat our window to the world: Tata," www.tata.com, January 14, 2006.

[53] "Tata Motors, Fiat in joint drive—Marketing tie-up is first step towards deeper relationship," www.thehindubusinessline.com, January 14, 2006.

[54] Marcopolo, founded in 1949 in Brazil, manufactured bodies for a whole range of coaches, e.g. microbuses, and inter-city and touring coaches. It had manufacturing plants in Brazil, Argentina, Colombia, Mexico, Portugal, and South Africa. It also exported its coaches to more than 60 countries of the world.

[55] "Fiat paints Tatamobile bodies at its plant," www.blonnet.com, June 28, 2006.

[56] Fiat S.p.A. is the holding company in the Fiat Group.

[57] "Fiat and Tata plan India venture," www.news.moneycentral.msn.com, July 24, 2006.

[58] "Tata-Fiat JV to make passenger cars," www.indianexpress.com, July 26, 2006.

[59] Iveco, a subsidiary company in the Fiat Group, was a leading manufacturer of trucks and buses in Europe.

[60] "Fiat and Tata plan India venture," www.news.moneycentral.msn.com, July 24, 2006.

[61] Apart from TM and Fiat India, MUL, Hyundai, Ford, GM, Mahindra & Mahindra, Skoda, Mercedes Benz, Honda, and Toyota were the other players in India. BMW was also setting up a factory in India and was to begin sales in 2007.

[62] "Tatas, Fiat tie up to sell vehicles," www.tribuneindia.com, January 13, 2006.

[63] TACO was established in 1995 by the Tata Group. The group includes Tata Autocomp Systems Ltd., joint ventures with several global auto manufacturing players and two subsidiaries (plastics and stampings).

[64] "Tata Motors, Fiat in 50:50 JV for cars, engines," www.finanacialexpress.com, July 26, 2006.

[65] Common rail is a modern variant of direct fuel injection system for diesel engines.

[66] This engine won the Engine of the Year Award in 2005.

[67] "Tata's grand vision," www.tata.com, January 15, 2006.

[68] The powertrain for a vehicle consists of all the components, including the engine, transmission, driveshafts, differentials, and the final drive (drive wheels, caterpillar track, propeller, etc), that produce power and help the vehicle travel over road, water, or in air.

[69] The first was a 1.2 liter, 8 valve, 75 horsepower engine and the other was a 1.4 liter, 16 valve, 95 horsepower petrol engine.

[70] "Tata Motors in pact with Fiat," www.newstodaynet.com, January 17, 2006.

[71] "Tata, Fiat to share car dealer networks," www.expressindia.com, January 13, 2006.

[72] "Tata's grand vision," www.tata.com, January 15, 2006.

[73] Hindustan Motors was making Mitsubishi brand cars including the popular *Lancer* since 1998 under a tie-up with Mitsubishi Motor Corporation, Japan.

[74] Brand dilution happens when products that are not a natural fit are offered in the market place under a particular company's corporate identity. This also affects the company's brand positioning when the new product gives out messages which differ from the company's own communications.

[75] "Tata Motors-Fiat alliance gets ready for a long drive," www.telegraphindia.com, December 07, 2006.

[76] "Turnaround artist," www.bsmotoring.com, August 07, 2004.

[77] "Tata Motors, Fiat India to share dealer network," www.thehindubusinessline.com, March 07, 2006.

[78] "La dolce deal?" www.economictimes.indiatimes.com, August 04, 2006.

[79] Tata Motors exported 4,257 vehicles in February compared with 3,290 vehicles in the same month in the previous year, representing an increase of 29.4 percent. The cumulative sales from exports in the current period amounted to 44,031 vehicles, a growth of 66 percent over the corresponding period in the previous year.

[80] Parvathy Ullatil, "Fiat, Tata mull platform sharing," *The Economic Times*, September 06, 2006.

[81] "Tata Motors plans big push," www.economictimes.com, September 09, 2006.

# Multinational E-Commerce: Strategies and Structures

# 10

## *Preview* CASE IN POINT

### The Global Internet Economy

The Internet and electronic commerce (e-commerce) are drastically changing how international business is done. The Internet allows any company to create a virtual and global presence to conduct operations around the world, and it allows a multinational company to dramatically alter the way it presents and communicates with global customers. Web presence can give any company the ability to advertise and present useful information that is critical in influencing purchasing decisions. In fact, product-based websites are becoming increasingly important as an advertising medium. Furthermore, the Internet enables companies to analyze their value chain to become more efficient and competitive by implementing e-commerce initiatives all along it. Additionally, the world is seeing an explosion in the use of smart phones, which is revolutionizing the way consumers are buying products. Moreover, the growth of social computing such as Facebook and Twitter also means that multinationals have to contend with both challenges and opportunities emanating from these new media.

This trend is predicted to accelerate in the future. Consider the following facts regarding the Internet economy and e-commerce:

- Because of the economic slowdown, the IT industry will likely grow slower in 2013 than in 2011. However, despite the slowdown, it is estimated that technology spending will still grow by 6 percent, with a 9 percent increase in hardware spending and a 3 percent increase in software.

- Emerging economies will likely dominate much of the IT sector. It is estimated that 1 out of 5 personal computers will be sold in China. Other emerging economies, such as India and Thailand, will see significantly higher shipments.

- Latin America will continue to see strong growth. Given the generally low PC penetration in this region, PC sales are estimated to grow at 10 percent.

- The Internet will see the biggest growth for advertising for companies. As such, while advertising spending on TV will grow by 6.1 percent, Internet advertising spending will grow by 15 percent in 2012.

## *Learning Objectives*

*After reading this chapter you should be able to:*

- Define the forms of e-commerce.
- Understand the structure of the Internet economy.
- Identify the basic component of a successful e-commerce strategy.
- Know the basic multinational e-commerce business models.
- Identify the practicalities of running a multinational e-commerce business.
- Understand the function of enablers in multinational e-commerce operations.

- By 2016, almost half of the world's population (3 billion) will be Internet users globally.

- The economic impact of the Internet economy continues to grow. The Internet economy is expected to rank in the top six industry sectors in countries such as China and South Korea.

- Online advertising is expected to grow 12 percent a year to around $125 billion in 2016 in the world's G20 countries.

- Consumer-to-consumer Internet commerce continues to grow at an astonishingly fast pace. For example, more products were purchased on China's leading e-commerce website, Taobao, than from China's top traditional retailers.

*Sources: Based on Dean, D., S. DiGrande, D. Field, A. Lundmark, J. O'Day, J. Pineda, and P. Zwilenberg. 2012. "The Internet economy in the G-20." BCG Perspectives, http://www.bcgperspectives.com; Economist Intelligence Unit. 2012. "The World in 2012." Information Technology and Media, 121.*

Although still small in comparison to the traditional economy, the Internet economy is booming, growing faster than any other business trend in history. As shown in the Preview Case in Point, the Internet economy is growing exponentially and has become a worldwide phenomenon. Consequently, multinational managers must be knowledgeable in all aspects of e-commerce and prepared to use the Internet as a global platform for multinational business transactions.

Earlier chapters discussed many of the intricacies involved in developing multinational strategies and building the organizations to implement them. This chapter will show that new opportunities exist for companies to expand their multinational operations via the Internet.

Many of the issues involved in doing multinational business over the Web are similar to those faced by traditional multinational companies. However, the next generation of multinational managers must address unique challenges in formulating and implementing multinational strategies for the Internet economy.

This chapter will provide essential background on the nature of e-commerce and the Internet economy. First, it considers basic e-commerce strategies, structures, and operations. Second, it discusses issues unique to the multinational company, including the costs and benefits of globalizing via the Internet, basic multinational e-commerce models, and practical issues associated with multinational e-commerce, such as website design. After reading this chapter and considering the array of multinational management issues considered earlier, you should gain a sound understanding of and appreciation for the e-commerce challenges multinational companies must face now and in the near future.

# The Internet Economy

## What Is E-Commerce?

**E-commerce**
The selling of goods or services over the Internet.

**E-commerce** is the selling of goods or services over the Internet. These goods or services include those delivered offline, such as when UPS ships a book purchased through Amazon.com to a customer anywhere in the world, and those delivered online, such as when a consumer downloads computer software. When most people talk about e-commerce, they focus on two types of transactions. The first type is

CASE IN POINT

## IT and Manufacturing

The developments in IT and IT-related technologies have enhanced the ability of companies to collaborate on all aspects of the value chain. Furthermore, IT-related developments have enabled companies to start relying more on automation and robots. Rather than see robots as substitutes for people, new robots are being designed to work with humans. For instance, robots are now being designed to fetch and carry parts, sort items, and even clean up.

Furthermore, recent developments in other IT technologies such as social media will present companies with even more opportunities in the future. In fact, some experts see the current explosion in IT as the third industrial revolution. Consider the case of Quirky, a company based in New York City. With the help of its online community, the company strives to develop two new products every week. Typically, a user in its online community submits an idea for a product. If enough

people like the product idea, Quirky product development teams will design a prototype. Users can review the prototype and help decide on the design and pricing. Quirky then works with manufacturers in Asia that produce the product. The product is sold via Quirky's website. If it becomes a success, the product is then also sold in retail shops. Quirky thus provides a means for the online community to help develop new products. The company also helps with the patenting process while charging 30 percent for generated revenues. Its most successful product to date is the Pivot Power, a $29.99 electrical extension with adjustable sockets. This product allows users to plug in several large chargers at once, something that would be difficult or impossible with traditional electrical extensions.

*Sources: Based on* Economist. *2012. "All together now." April 21, 18–19;* Economist. *2012. "Making the future." April 21, 19–20.*

business-to-consumer transactions, such as buying toys from eToys. The acronym **B2C** is commonly used to refer to these transactions. The second type consists of the buying and selling done among businesses, or business-to-business transactions. This is the **B2B** component of e-commerce. B2B transactions make up 70 to 85 percent of current e-commerce business. The high proportion of B2B relative to B2C is expected to continue in the future.[1]

One of the most important reasons for the significance of B2B e-commerce comes from the revolution in supply chain management made possible by electronic links between businesses and suppliers. Information sharing between business customers and suppliers allows vendors to know what their customers want and enables businesses to know price, availability, and product characteristics immediately. Consider the above Case in Point.

As the above Case in Point shows, the use of IT is enabling new opportunities for innovation. For example, Ericsson, the Swedish mobile phone giant, has gone to paperless procurement. It uses the company's local network, or intranet, to find approved suppliers. The intranet provides links to these suppliers' websites, and a purchase is made within predefined levels. Prior to this system, Ericsson spent an average of $100 on every order processed. The reduction in paperwork has reduced the average transaction cost to $15.[2] Similarly, Microsoft uses an intranet procurement process called Microsoft Market that reduced its business purchase transaction costs from $60 to $5.[3] Exhibit 10.1 shows how e-commerce activities work along the value chain.

Longitudinal research in the United States confirms the pervasiveness of Internet usage. A large number of firms were studied, and the most interesting finding showed that all companies experienced increased Internet use all along the value chain. The companies surveyed were making increased use of the Internet

**B2C**
Business-to-consumer transactions.

**B2B**
Business-to-business transactions.

**EXHIBIT 10.1**    E-Commerce Value Chain

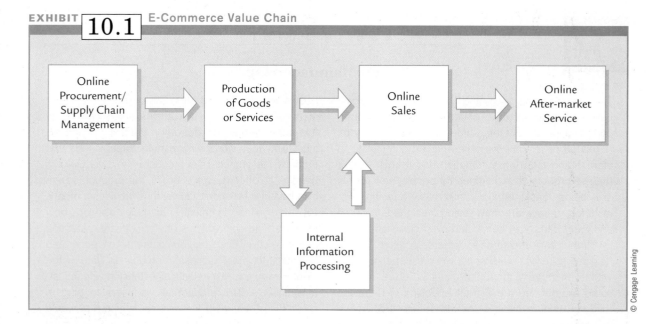

© Cengage Learning

to facilitate such value chain activities as human resources, sales, advertising, and other operations.[4] This study showed that we will likely see more e-commerce in all these activities.

In addition to these e-commerce models, the Internet has spawned other forms of business transactions; for example, eBay is a global player in the **C2C** (consumer-to-consumer) business of auctions. Anyone can sell something online and/or place bids for items. Other forms of business transactions to consider are **C2B** (consumer-to-business), such as price comparison websites like AddALL, which searches online bookstores throughout the world to provide price comparisons and shipping and delivery information.

What is the current global presence of e-commerce? A recent Organisation for Economic Co-operation and Development (OECD) report suggests that measuring the presence of e-commerce is becoming increasingly difficult.[5] A significant reason for such difficulty is that some of the latest Internet activities cannot be measured by traditional Internet metrics. Consider that most of the important trends pertain to the use of smart phones, cloud computing, and social networking. Many of these new activities cannot necessarily be measured by metrics such as miles of fiber optics or Internet Protocol (IP) addresses. Measuring the presence of e-commerce will likely grow in difficulty in the future.

However, reports from the OECD use two indicators. One is the number of secure servers. A secure server is an Internet host that allows users to send encrypted data so that those outside the connection cannot see the information. Such servers are necessary for e-commerce to thrive because they encourage users to send credit card information over the Internet. A second indicator of the presence of e-commerce is the number of Internet hosts. Any computer connected to the Internet with its own IP address is considered a server in OECD statistics. An IP address is a unique address that a computer has on the Web so that other Internet users can access the public information available there.

Despite the difficulty of measuring the Internet economy, one of the convenient ways of measuring the economic impact of the Internet is by estimating its contribution to a country's Gross Domestic Product (or GDP). This measure

**C2C**
Consumer-to-consumer transactions.

**C2B**
Consumer-to-business transactions.

**Secure server**
Internet host that allows users to send and receive encrypted data.

**Internet host**
Computer connected to the Internet with its own IP address.

gives an estimate of the importance of the Internet economy relative to the overall economy. A recent report suggests that the importance of the Internet will continue to grow.[6] For instance, while the Internet economy accounted for 8.3 percent of GDP in the United Kingdom in 2010, it is estimated that it will account for around 12.4 percent of that nation's GDP in 2016. To give you more insights into these changes, Exhibit 10.2 shows the importance of the Internet economy in 2010 and projections for 2016 for selected countries. As mentioned earlier, the growth in the use of the Internet e-commerce is so dramatic that its impact is difficult to estimate. Some say that the Internet will have more impact on the world than the Industrial Revolution. In fact, as we saw earlier, the Internet is already revolutionizing the way companies manufacture products. Companies such as Quirky are relying on social networking and online communities to develop and sell new products. To give you more insight into the importance of the Internet, Exhibit 10.3 shows the trend in the number of households with Internet access in different parts of the world, according to recent estimates.[7] Such consistent growth suggests tremendous opportunities for multinational companies to use the Internet as a tool for conducting business worldwide at any point in the value chain, from the procurement of raw materials to eventual sales. China also presents companies with significant opportunities. Consider the next Focus on Emerging Markets.

**EXHIBIT 10.2**   Internet Economy as a Percentage of GDP for Selected Countries

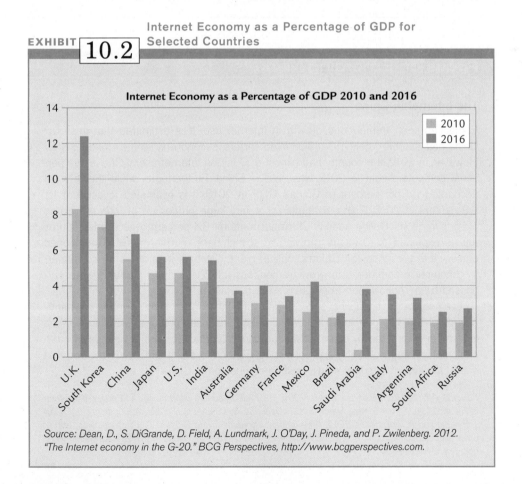

Source: Dean, D., S. DiGrande, D. Field, A. Lundmark, J. O'Day, J. Pineda, and P. Zwilenberg. 2012. "The Internet economy in the G-20." BCG Perspectives, http://www.bcgperspectives.com.

**EXHIBIT** **10.3**     **Percentage of Households with Internet Access**

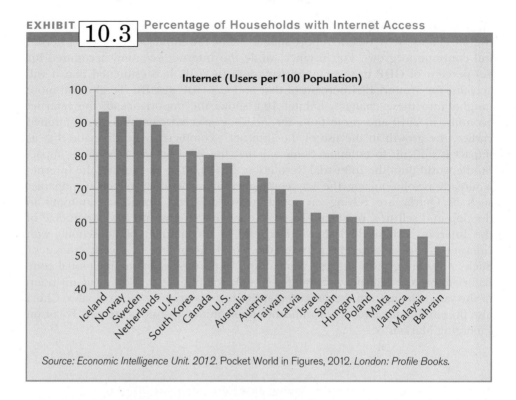

*Source: Economic Intelligence Unit. 2012. Pocket World in Figures, 2012. London: Profile Books.*

## Focus on Emerging Markets

### The Internet in China

China has seen tremendous growth in Internet use. It is estimated that in 2006, China had approximately 110 million Web surfers, second only to the United States. However, in 2012, the country had almost 500 million Internet users. One in five personal computers sold in 2012 was sold in China. Furthermore, while the Internet accounted for 5.5 percent of China's GDP in 2010, it is estimated to account for 6.9 percent in 2016. China accounts for a very large proportion of Internet-related exports in goods. Online retail in China accounts for 3.4 percent of total retail figures and is expected to continue growing at a fast pace. Furthermore, as mentioned earlier, the presence of China's online giant, Taobao, has allowed consumer-to-consumer e-commerce to grow tremendously. In 2012, more products were purchased from Taobao than from China's top 5 retailers.

Even so, multinationals have to contend with challenges. China's Web is constantly being monitored by people who filter and delete prohibited phrases. The Chinese Web is also being targeted by scam artists and criminals ready to take advantage of naive customers through phishing and spamming. Furthermore, a recent study showed that nearly 13 percent of social media posts are censored in China.

*Sources: Adapted from Barboza, David. 2006. "110 million surfers can buy sex and drugs, but reform is still illicit." New York Times, March 8, C1; Dean, D., S. DiGrande, D. Field, A. Lundmark, J. O'Day, J. Pineda, and P. Zwilenberg. 2012. "The Internet economy in the G-20." BCG Perspectives, http:// www.bcgperspectives.com; Economist Intelligence Unit. 2012. "The World in 2012." Information technology and Media. 121.*

### Broadband and the Broadband Surplus

It is undeniable that information and other communication technologies result in productivity growth for most countries. A recent review of the literature suggests that investment in Information and Communication Technologies (ICT) has a positive and significant effect on productivity. ICT is pervasive, as it is applicable in a wide array of uses. However, ICT also allows wide experimentation and exploration that can result in lower costs and higher innovation for companies. ICT therefore has many advantages both at the company and country levels.

A recent report suggests that countries that invest in broadband enjoy an even greater "productivity surplus" than access to the Internet through other means. Most countries provide access to the Internet initially through dial-up. However, as more users embrace broadband, the price of broadband falls and more users become adopters of broadband. As more people use broadband,

they get access to faster Internet service. This also provides better access to online applications that enhances the economic impact of broadband. Broadband also provides significant advantages to companies, as they have access to easier means by which to sell products, while at the same time, faster Internet allows for higher levels of collaboration as well as greater efficiency. A recent study of 30 OECD countries provides evidence of the bonus effects of broadband. The study found that having access to broadband contributes an additional 1 percent of GDP per capita.

*Sources: Based on Greenstein, S., and R. McDevitt. 2012. "Measuring the Broadband Bonus in Thirty OECD Countries." OECD Digital Economy Papers, No. 197, OECD Publishing. http://dx.doi.org/10.1787/5k9bcwkg3hwf-en; Kretschmer, T. 2012. "Information and Communication Technologies and Productivity Growth: A Survey of the Literature." OECD Digital Economy Papers, No. 195, OECD Publishing. http://dx.doi.org /10.1787/5k9bh3jllgs7-en.*

The OECD sees broadband development as a critical aspect of the Internet and e-commerce.[8] Broadband is a combination of digital technologies that enables data and other digital services to be transmitted rapidly, often simultaneously. It is seen as a major reason why people access information and technology products and services. The OECD believes that, in turn, such use can result in economic growth, facilitating social and cultural development and even innovation. Consider the above Case in Point.

As you can see from the above Case in Point, broadband provides many advantages at both the level of an individual company, and at the level of a nation as a whole. Broadband also allows small- and medium-sized firms to benefit from heightened efficiency through sped-up information exchanges. The OECD also argues that broadband use can benefit governments through the efficient and increased availability of services such as health, education, and other social services.[9]

Before considering the strategy and structure of using e-commerce in multinational business, the chapter next provides background material on the nature of the Internet economy.

# Fundamentals of E-Commerce Strategy and Structure

Although e-commerce is evolving quickly, the failures of many e-commerce start-ups demonstrate that the Internet economy is not without risks. Each layer of the Internet economy has its threats and opportunities. Exhibit 10.4 provides a summary of them. In this section, you will learn the current strategies used by successful e-commerce companies to overcome some of these challenges.

EXHIBIT **10.4**     E-Commerce Business Models: Openings and Barriers for Going Global

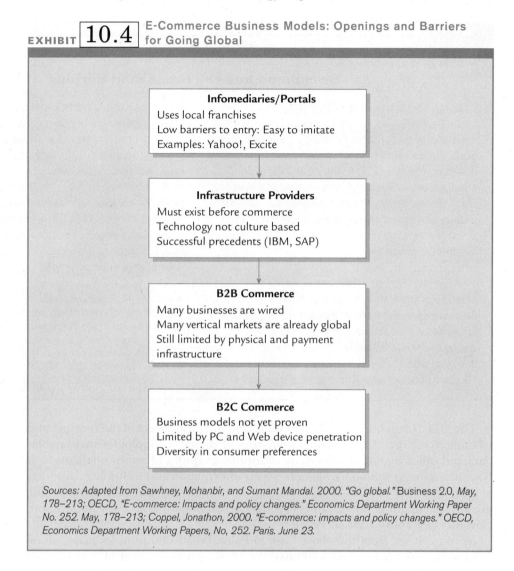

**Infomediaries/Portals**

Uses local franchises
Low barriers to entry: Easy to imitate
Examples: Yahoo!, Excite

**Infrastructure Providers**

Must exist before commerce
Technology not culture based
Successful precedents (IBM, SAP)

**B2B Commerce**

Many businesses are wired
Many vertical markets are already global
Still limited by physical and payment infrastructure

**B2C Commerce**

Business models not yet proven
Limited by PC and Web device penetration
Diversity in consumer preferences

*Sources: Adapted from Sawhney, Mohanbir, and Sumant Mandal. 2000. "Go global." Business 2.0, May, 178–213; OECD, "E-commerce: Impacts and policy changes." Economics Department Working Paper No. 252. May, 178–213; Coppel, Jonathon, 2000. "E-commerce: impacts and policy changes." OECD, Economics Department Working Papers, No, 252. Paris. June 23.*

## Steps for a Successful E-Commerce Strategy

E-commerce strategizing is a new and evolving management challenge, and the multinational manager must build on sound, basic strategizing as a prelude to multinational operations. Experts suggest seven fundamental requirements:[10]

1.  **Leadership:** Successful e-commerce is possible only through dynamic and strong leadership. At a minimum, CEO and senior executives should strongly believe in the benefits of an e-commerce approach. They should also have expertise to objectively assess the company's position on e-commerce in order to craft the most appropriate e-commerce strategy.

2.  **Build on current business models and experiment with new e-commerce models:** Search for ways to use the e-commerce business to reduce costs or to enhance traditional services. E-commerce transactions can be cheap but can add value to customers. Customers can get timely updates like the American Airlines Alert, an e-mail service to notify customers of changes in schedules.

However, some companies are taking their e-commerce to new and innovative levels. Consider the following Multinational Management Brief.

3. **Meet the challenge of developing an e-commerce organization:** The basic choice involves the distinction between a separate autonomous entity for e-commerce business and a seamless integration into the current model. The integrated model works best when the customer finds it difficult to separate e-commerce from the existing form of business. The integrated model also requires senior management's commitment to using the Internet aggressively as part of the company's strategy, and the entire firm must be prepared to embrace the e-commerce model, as did Egghead Software when it moved entirely to a web-based business.

4. **Allocate resources:** A successful e-commerce strategy must commit financial, human, and technological resources to developing e-commerce capabilities. If these capabilities do not exist within the organization, then selected e-commerce operations are outsourced to third parties or to strategic alliance partners.

5. **Have an e-commerce strategy:** Companies should not implement e-commerce haphazardly. A company can use some of the strategic management techniques discussed in Chapter 5 to implement a strong strategic e-commerce plan. Some of the most recent data suggest that a well-positioned brand name is very

---

## Multinational Management **Brief**

### Nike and E-Commerce

Nike is currently one of the most innovative companies when it comes to using the Internet and e-commerce to boost its performance. For example, while many companies still rely on traditional advertising, Nike has slowly shifted its focus away from advertising on TV to a more direct dialogue with its customers. It spent nearly $800 million on nontraditional advertising in 2010, a much greater percentage of its advertising budget than any other top 100 U.S. advertiser. Instead of mega TV advertising, it now focuses on smaller online advertising campaigns that enable the company to make stronger connections with its customers.

Nike has also taken advantage of the opportunities offered by e-commerce to boost sales. For instance, it developed Nike +, whereby jogging data was synchronized with an iPod. By using a sensor powered inside Nike running shoes, runners can have access to running data that let them know how much longer they need to run or suggest the type of music they might listen to. However, the workout details can then be input on Nikeplus.com, where users can get more training tips while comparing their performance with others'. Furthermore, the Nike + website allows Nike to study its customers, and this helps drive sales for the running division.

Nike is also working on the idea of Digital Sport, which takes Nike + into other sports. The company is building a large network of customers across different sports. These customers can then be provided with more targeted and accurate advertising campaigns that can result in enhanced sales. Many industry insiders admire Nike's new digital approach, arguing that the company has in-depth knowledge of what consumers want because of its online communities.

*Source: Based on Cendrowski, S. 2012. "Nike's new marketing mojo." Fortune, February 27, 80–88.*

important for repeat purchases. However, companies need to ensure that they offer reliable customer service because that is often seen as more critical than a strong brand. It is also not always necessary to offer the same products online as in physical locations. Companies such as Office Depot typically offer more products online, whereas others, such as Costco, have smaller and more specialized product offerings.

6. **Develop appropriate e-commerce systems:** To fully benefit from e-commerce, there has to be a cultural transformation in how information flows through the organization. The company has to work hard to remove traditional barriers and to ensure increased coordination and information flows among the various functional areas, such as manufacturing, sales, service, and shipping. Any company that is serious about e-commerce must also align human resource policies and compensation with e-commerce goals.

7. **Measure success:** Companies need to have metrics in place to measure e-commerce success. Obvious output success measures include website hits, the number of new e-commerce customers, e-commerce revenue, and the number of customers learning about new products to purchase through other channels. Companies also can assess process success measures, such as the degree of top management commitment to e-commerce and e-commerce integration across internal and external operations.

The Internet economy has spawned numerous new companies. At the same time, it has provided opportunities for traditional companies to use this evolving business tool. Next, you will see one of the major issues faced by traditional companies when they engage in e-commerce.

## E-Commerce Structure: Integrated or Autonomous

Each company needs to decide how e-commerce fits into its existing organizational design and management systems. Writing in the *Harvard Business Review,* Ranjay Gulati of Northwestern University and Jason Garino of the Boston Consulting Group call this the "right mixture of bricks and clicks."[11] They mean that companies must decide how much to integrate their evolving Internet operations into their traditional business operations. In the evolving e-commerce jargon, traditional business operations are often called the **brick-and-mortar** part of the company.

The degree of integration between brick-and-mortar operations and the Internet business can occur anywhere in the value chain, from the procurement of raw materials to after-sales service. Additionally, the degree of integration can range from the nearly seamless operation of an Office Depot to the mostly independent operations of Barnes & Noble and Barnesandnoble.com.

Each choice has its benefits. The independent operation can move faster and be more entrepreneurial when freed from corporate bureaucracy. It can seek funding from the deep pockets of venture capitalists willing to invest in e-commerce companies. The integrated operation, on the other hand, can benefit from the cross-promotion of shared products, shared customer information, increased large-quantity purchasing leverage, and economies of scale by using the same distribution channels.[12]

The choice between seamless integration and a fully autonomous unit is not simple and is seldom clear-cut. The best option for most companies is something in between. Consider the next Case in Point.

**Brick-and-mortar**
Traditional or nonvirtual business operation.

C A S E   I N   P O I N T

## Research Online and Purchase Offline (ROPO)

A recent report of G20 countries provides evidence of the necessity of having the right combination of brick-and-mortar vs. online outlets. The report shows that a significant proportion of consumers researched online and then purchased offline (ROPO). According to the report, ROPO represented almost 8 percent of consumer spending in 2010. For example, groceries tend to be typical ROPO purchases in China. In the United States, consumers engage in ROPO purchases for cars. In India, consumers prefer ROPO purchases for technology items, while in Brazil, consumers make ROPO purchases for products such as electronics, appliances, and travel.

Why should multinationals be concerned about ROPO? The report mentioned above suggests that consumers are increasingly using the Web for informational purposes prior to purchase. As such, multinationals will need to appreciate the informational role of a website while also emphasizing that such products are offered in their brick-and-mortar stores. Furthermore, as we will see later, e-commerce is not necessarily as widespread in all countries. Barriers such as poor delivery infrastructure and low Internet penetration, for example, may necessitate a brick-and-mortar presence. However, a website to support such operations may be necessary to entice such consumers to make purchases.

*Source: Based on Dean, D., S. DiGrande, D. Field, A. Lundmark, J. O'Day, J. Pineda, and P. Zwilenberg. 2012. "The Internet economy in the G-20." BCG Perspectives, http://www.bcgperspectives.com.*

As with most strategy implementation issues, managers must evaluate their company's situation to make an informed decision. Exhibit 10.5 shows a decision model with the questions that managers must consider when choosing the best level of integration for an e-commerce unit.

Although Exhibit 10.5 provides useful guidance regarding the appropriate level of integration, experience suggests that more companies in the United States are taking steps to integrate their online and offline channels.[13] Customers are getting more sophisticated about their purchases and often use channels that offer the best prices. These customers get frustrated if they are not informed of appropriate pricing or inventory differences between a retailer's online and offline offerings. Below are some of the ways companies can integrate their online and offline operations.[14]

- *Keep customers informed:* Most retailers find it impossible to maintain the same pricing and inventories on their websites and in their stores. However, this discrepancy does not have to be a source of frustration for consumers. Companies often find that their customers appreciate being informed of such differences.

- *Share customer data across channels:* Companies are realizing the benefits of sharing customer data across channels. For instance, retailers can send tailored product e-mails based on store purchases. Segmentation campaigns can be compared across channels (online versus in the store) to get better insights into customer purchasing behaviors.

Although the level of e-commerce integration is a crucial decision, numerous other operational challenges must be considered.

## Additional Operational Challenges for an E-Commerce Business

What challenges can a company anticipate when developing an e-commerce business? Towers Perrin, the New York consulting firm, surveyed more than 300 major companies from the United States and Europe. The survey, the Towers Perrin Internetworked Organization Survey, found that although many companies see

**EXHIBIT**   **10.5**   **Key Decisions in Web Business Integration**

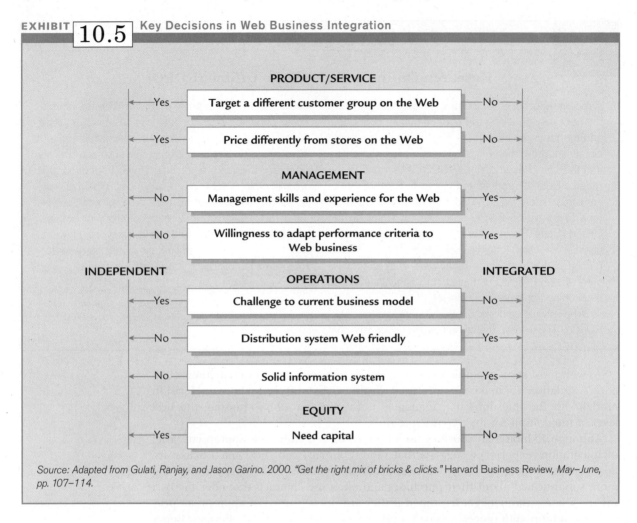

Source: Adapted from Gulati, Ranjay, and Jason Garino. 2000. "Get the right mix of bricks & clicks." Harvard Business Review, May–June, pp. 107–114.

the advantages of e-commerce, they also foresee many problems and challenges. This section summarizes the important findings of the Towers Perrin survey.

- Many companies have difficulty finding partnerships and alliances with customers or third parties.
- Because of the shortage of people with e-commerce skills, it is difficult to attract, retain, and develop employees in an e-commerce unit.
- Training and development in e-commerce are not yet adequate.
- Finding ways to provide individuals with growth opportunities and job satisfaction drives employee retention in e-commerce.
- Deciding which e-commerce functions to outsource is difficult. Most survey companies outsource many functions, but they are reluctant to do so for functions involving direct customer contact.

Depending on the degree of Internet penetration, different countries may face different challenges. Consider the next Multinational Management Brief.

As the next Multinational Management Brief shows, there are sometimes significant barriers to e-commerce implementation. Eliminating some of these barriers will necessitate new policies at the governmental level to educate companies

## Multinational Management **Brief**

### E-Commerce Barriers in Saudi Arabia

As mentioned earlier, having an Internet economy has significant advantages for countries. The Internet allows significant development that results in lower costs for companies and enhanced innovation. It is therefore not surprising to see that most economies want to implement e-commerce strategies. However, the success of such implementation is dependent on the barriers that the nation faces. Overcoming such barriers is therefore important.

A recent study examined the barriers facing e-commerce implementation in Saudi Arabia. While Saudi Arabia remains a competitive nation and has been a significant recipient of investments worldwide, it still remains at an early stage of e-commerce implementation. To identify key barriers, the authors surveyed 237 key IT executives in 237 companies. The study identified the following barriers:

- Lack of awareness of e-commerce technology and benefits of e-commerce
- Shortage of skilled IT human resources
- Small size of market
- Insufficient e-commerce infrastructure
- Lack of trust between customers and companies and concern for data security
- Difficulty in integration of current system with e-commerce

*Source: Based on Ahmad, I., and A. M. Agrawal. 2012. "An empirical study of problems in implementation of electronic commerce in Kingdom of Saudi Arabia."* International Journal of Business and Management, 7, 15: 70–80.

---

about the potential of e-commerce as well as education in IT. However, others will involve company training.

How can companies meet these and other challenges? Towers Perrin also suggests different strategies depending on whether the company is a pure e-business or a unit of a traditional business. Pure e-business companies must:

- Develop information and management systems to respond to rapid growth.
- Maintain rapid decision making, creativity, innovation, and flexibility.
- Build external relationships with e-commerce support companies and customers.
- Attract and retain e-commerce-capable talent.
- Develop an effective management team.

Traditional companies with e-commerce units must:

- Build a common vision and commitment to the e-commerce operation throughout the organization.
- Change the organizational structure to emphasize quick reconfiguration of assets and capabilities.
- Change the organizational culture to create a supporting environment for e-commerce.
- Attract and retain e-commerce-skilled employees.
- Alter HR programs to suit the different skill requirements of e-commerce employees.

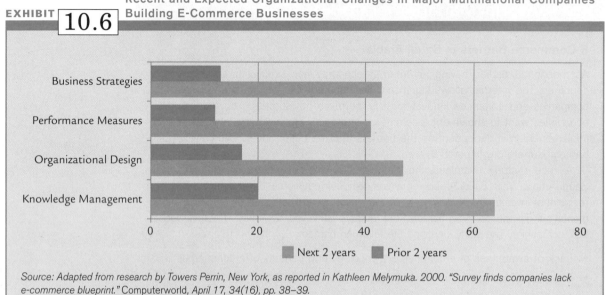

*Source: Adapted from research by Towers Perrin, New York, as reported in Kathleen Melymuka. 2000. "Survey finds companies lack e-commerce blueprint." Computerworld, April 17, 34(16), pp. 38–39.*

Exhibit 10.6 shows the organizational changes multinational companies are making to implement their e-commerce strategies.

As companies and institutions take advantage of e-commerce and its applications, they face a new and important challenge: **e-commerce security**,[15] which is the degree to which customers feel that their private, personal information is safe in the hands of the online companies collecting it. Hundreds of millions of people around the world provide personal information on the Internet as they browse or purchase products and services online.[16] How such information is collected and stored and what is done with it are sources of concern for most Internet users. Furthermore, attacks on popular websites are increasing rapidly, resulting in the theft of credit card numbers of thousands of customers. Specific industries, such as online banking, are suffering significant Internet attacks through phishing and Trojan horses.[17] Banking regulators suggest that online bank fraud may drain from 2 to 5 percent of a bank's overall revenue. Furthermore, recent observations suggest that cyber-criminals are becoming increasingly sophisticated.[18] Instead of attacking operating systems and Internet services on the Web, cyber-criminals now focus on applications and network operating systems. Cyber-criminals are also emphasizing specific vulnerabilities within certain companies. In this respect, e-commerce security is at risk for a not-so-obvious reason: software piracy. Consider the next Case in Point.

As the Internet becomes a crucial medium of international trade and commerce, countries are being urged to improve Internet security. The European Union and ASEAN (Association of Southeast Asian Nations, including Singapore, Thailand, Malaysia, and Indonesia) are being encouraged not only to improve Internet security, but also to minimize abuse because many online scams and instances of phishing tend to originate in some of these member countries.

Multinationals are also being encouraged to beef up their Internet security. Specifically, most companies need to be concerned about a number of information security issues:[19] (1) confidentiality (making sure that private information is protected), (2) availability (ensuring that information is accessible to authorized users), (3) integrity (ensuring that the information collected is accurate and

**E-commerce security**
Degree to which customers feel that their private and personal information is safeguarded by companies collecting it.

## Software Piracy and E-Commerce Security

Software piracy—the illegal copying of software—has many important disadvantages for the e-commerce industry. Software companies incur revenue losses, for one thing. Research shows that for every $1 of software sold in a country, local IT service companies lose $3 to $4 in revenue due to spillover. Pirated software also costs jobs for local employees. One of the worst problems is the increased potential of cyber crime and security issues. Legally acquired software is regularly updated. However, the users of pirated copies do not get the latest updates, allowing hackers to take advantage of new vulnerabilities.

A recent report suggests that software piracy is also occurring as more companies migrate to the cloud. Cloud computing services such as webmail and word-processing over a browser are increasing in importance. However, the report also suggests that around 30 percent of users in rich countries and 45 percent in poorer countries have the potential of sharing log-in details for paid services. Although the report further details that such estimates may be high, it is important to acknowledge that such piracy can also occur in this new medium.

Where is software piracy most problematic? Research suggests that the lowest-piracy countries are the United States, Japan, New Zealand, and Luxembourg, with about a 20 percent piracy rate. However, countries such as Bangladesh and Armenia have among the highest piracy rates, at 90 percent. Countries in Central and East Europe and in Latin America have piracy rates up to 66 percent. The European Union and North American regions have the lowest rates at 35 percent and 21 percent, respectively. A more recent study suggests that software piracy is less likely in countries that have higher well-being and are more individualistic.

*Sources: Based on* Economist. *2012. "Heads in the cloud: Online software piracy." July 25, online edition;* U.S. Newswire. *2009. "A fifth of PC software in the U.S. is pirated." May 12, http://www.bsa.org; Yang, D., M. Sonmez, D. Bosworth, and G. Fryxell. 2009. "Global software piracy: Searching for further explanations."* Journal of Business Ethics, *87, 269–283.*

reliable), and (4) authentication (having systems in place to ensure that persons using the systems are legitimate). Companies are also under increased pressure to protect the privacy of individuals as more and more personal information is being collected, stored, and shared by companies in industries such as health care, banking and finance, travel, and the government.[20]

Experts thus suggest the use of (1) firewalls,[21] antivirus protection software,[22] (2) data encryption and several levels of authentication for users,[23] and (3) abiding by privacy rules to address Internet security issues.[24]

The preceding sections reviewed the basic strategies, structures, and challenges managers face when developing an e-commerce business. The following sections will discuss some of the additional challenges faced when companies choose to go multinational with their e-commerce operations.

## Globalizing Through the Internet

The increase in information exchanges and efficiency due to the Internet and e-commerce has made it possible for companies to reach customers worldwide. However, the Internet also makes possible the emergence of a new form of multinational company, the born-global firms.[25] From the day they are created, born-global firms are able to obtain a significant portion of their revenues from sales in international markets (see Chapter 7).

Although a website immediately gives the entire world access to a company's products or services, many of the challenges of globalization faced by traditional brick-and-mortar companies remain. A company still must solve the global-local dilemma (Chapter 6). Managers must decide whether the company's products or services are global in content and delivery or require localization at the national or regional level. E-commerce companies also must address the traditional multinational business problems relating to national and business cultures and national institutional contexts (e.g., currencies/payments, local laws, and infrastructure for delivery or procurement). Other chapters will consider these issues in more detail. This section adds to the understanding of multinational strategy formulation and implementation by considering some issues unique to the e-commerce operation.

## Multinational E-Commerce Strategy Formulation: The Nature of the Business

What kind of e-business is easiest to take global? To a large degree, the kind of company depends on the types of products or services offered through e-commerce. According to e-commerce experts Mohanbir Sawhney and Sumant Mandal,[26] e-commerce companies work in three areas: (1) some move bits of computerized information; (2) others move money in payment flows; and (3) still others move physical products. Each type of operation requires an infrastructure to support the transaction. Telecommunications infrastructures support moving parts. A payment infrastructure allows the movement of money. Moving physical goods requires physical infrastructure. The ease of taking e-commerce international depends mostly on the mix of infrastructures required.

Sawhney and Mandal argue that there is a hierarchy of difficulty in e-commerce depending on infrastructure requirements. Portals and info-mediaries provide gateways to the Internet. Portals are primarily search engines to locate websites, and infomediaries go a step further by providing not only links but also information, such as current news. They were also the first e-business forms to have a global presence.

At the next level are businesses such as travel services, digital music, and software vendors. Although they do not move physical objects, they still must rely on local infrastructure to receive payment for their products. The technical and managerial challenge comes from dealing with issues such as credit card payments (fraud and the lack of use in some areas), currency conversion, and a bewildering array of tax jurisdictions. Most difficult to globalize are e-commerce businesses that rely on a physical infrastructure. Like their brick-and-mortar counterparts, these businesses must ship goods to fulfill customer orders and manage their supply chains located throughout the world. In addition, they must deal with the challenges of receiving payments through a variety of payment infrastructures.

For e-businesses that require a physical infrastructure in host countries, large multinational firms with an existing global presence often have an advantage as they enter into e-commerce. They have in place either brick-and-mortar units or the resources to establish physical bases and localized websites. Small firms and firms new to the complexities of multinational commerce face more challenges in establishing an international presence.

## Basic Opportunities and Threats of Multinational E-Commerce

In deciding whether to globalize their e-commerce operations—either as an existing brick-and-mortar company or as a pure e-commerce company—managers need to weigh the attractions and deterrents of international e-commerce.[27] Again, this is a traditional strategy formulation problem and managers must consider the opportunities and threats before deciding on a strategy. However, the e-commerce environment has some unique characteristics. Consider the following.[28]

The major attractions of e-commerce globalization are:

- *Cost reduction:* Reaching international customers via the Web can be relatively inexpensive.
- *Technology:* The technology to reach anyone with an Internet-linked computer is readily available.
- *Efficiencies:* Electronic communication and processes can be very efficient.
- *Convenience:* The Web is in operation seven days a week and 24 hours a day, regardless of location.
- *Speed of access:* Once a website is running, a company's products or services can be accessed immediately from anywhere in the world.

Some deterrents include:

- *The return/receipt burden and cost of delivery:* If the pattern follows catalog sales, businesses should expect a 30 to 40 percent return rate for online purchases.[29]
- *Costs of site construction, maintenance, upgrades:* Website construction and maintenance in multiple languages, currencies, and tax locations can cost companies millions of dollars per year.
- *Channel conflicts:* Distributors and retailers that sell a company's products may be undermined by competition from a company's website that sells directly to end users—a major fear of many automobile dealers if the manufacturers were to sell directly. Consider what is happening to travel agents as more people buy tickets online directly from the airline companies.
- *Easily copied models:* Local competitors can easily see and copy a multinational's product, service, or business model if it is displayed on the Web.
- *Cultural differences:* Understanding global customers and overcoming cultural barriers and language differences can be difficult on the Web. Websites not only must be multilingual, but they must also present a format that is culturally appropriate.
- *Traditional cross-border transaction complexities:* These issues include pricing for exchange rates, varying taxes, and government regulations.
- *Standard or local websites:* Companies must decide whether to standardize websites or tailor them to local contexts.
- *Customer trust and satisfaction:* Companies must determine whether customers abroad will trust and be satisfied with e-commerce in general and with their websites in particular.

The next Case in Point gives an example of how one company overcame cultural differences to succeed in Japan.

## Picking a Market

Clay Shirky suggests that Web entrepreneurs should target countries based on two factors.[30] First, attractive markets for e-commerce are those with market inefficiencies. Shirky claims that many formerly state-controlled markets have suboptimal economic performance. In these markets, e-commerce shopping allows buyers to obtain better quality and lower prices because they are free from state control.

### CASE IN POINT

## Adapting E-Commerce to Cultural Differences

Most experts agree that using the Internet to go international can be a good way to gain access to new markets. Selling online allows a company to weather slowdowns in local markets while diversifying into new territories. However, going global through the Internet means more than just offering websites in local languages. Multinationals need to take into consideration other factors, such as culture, customs, and technical sophistication, while adapting their products to meet local needs. Research shows that 52 percent of online buyers will buy only from websites using their own language. Thus, although experts agree that Internet access is spreading and more consumers are becoming comfortable with e-commerce, significant cultural differences pose serious challenges to e-commerce. In fact, a recent report suggests that the Internet is going even more local, reflecting national characteristics and other social and political influences unique to different countries.

Consider the case of Handango, which decided to expand into Japan after it noticed that Japanese customers were purchasing from its U.S. websites. Although the company was encouraged to find that there were no shipping restrictions for its products, it quickly faced significant barriers. For instance, Japanese consumers prefer to make online payments using a method called *konbini*, which requires consumers to go to a local convenience store to make a cash payment. The clerk then transfers the money to the vendor's online account. Handango decided to form a partnership with a local consumer electronics company to handle marketing and sales.

*Sources: Adapted from Bright, Becky. 2006. "E-commerce: How do you say 'Web'? Planning to take your online business international." Wall Street Journal, May 23, R11; Dean, D., S. DiGrande, D. Field, and P. Zwillenbegr. 2012. "The connected world." Boston Consulting Group Perspectives, http://www .bcgperspectives.com; Murphy, S. 2008. "A touch of local flavor." Chain Store Age, May, 144.*

Second, target markets with attractive demographic characteristics. These include locations with an Internet population of at least 5 percent, a high literacy rate (to predict the future growth of the Internet population), a country that participates in at least one free trade agreement, and a government with a viable legal system.

In Shirky's opinion, e-commerce potential is great in South America because of the Mercosur trade group, as well as in Southeast Asian countries with membership in the ASEAN trade group. He also suggests that the European Union is the next boom area for e-commerce because countries such as France, Italy, and Germany retain market inefficiencies from pre-Union days. The open borders and common currency in the EU should make for fertile ground for e-commerce growth.

Not all countries are equally e-commerce ready. The population must have access to computers and infrastructure links to the Internet. Governments and financial institutions must be ready to protect and process e-commerce transactions. Exhibit 10.7 shows a ranking of the Web Index of selected countries. The Web Index was developed by the World Wide Web Foundation to rank countries according to their progress and use of the Web. The Web Index is a composite measure that gives an indication of the impact and value of the Web in these countries. It also provides an indication of the opportunities presented to multinationals in such countries.[31]

The enormous growth in global e-commerce shows that its benefits clearly outweigh its risks, as firms increasingly use the Internet to globalize their operations. In the rapidly growing Internet environment, however, competition is heating up. Achieving a sustainable competitive advantage is difficult when competitors can easily copy business models.

**EXHIBIT 10.7    Web Index for Selected Countries**

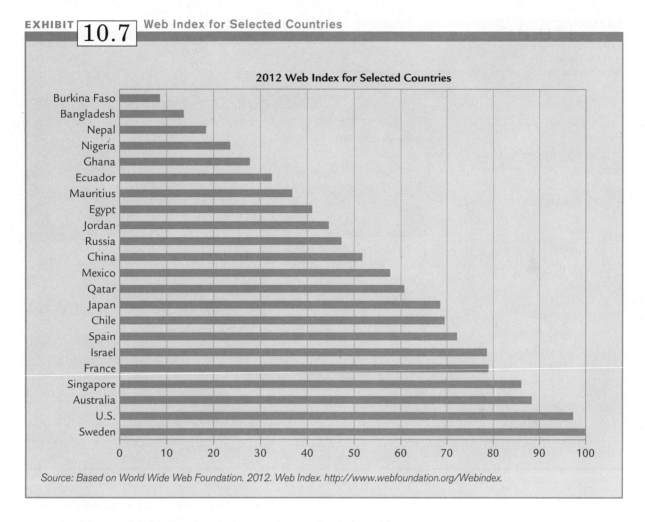

2012 Web Index for Selected Countries

*Source: Based on World Wide Web Foundation. 2012. Web Index. http://www.webfoundation.org/Webindex.*

## Multinational E-Commerce Strategy Implementation

Successful implementation of a multinational e-commerce strategy requires building an appropriate organization and developing the necessary technical capabilities to conduct electronic transactions. The following sections provide an overview of the options available to multinational managers.

## The Multinational E-Commerce Organization

How is a multinational e-business organized? Amazon.com and Yahoo! provide the most likely models.[32] These organizations are three-tiered, mixing global and local functions.

1. Corporate headquarters represents the global core that supplies the vision, strategy, and leadership driving the electronic marketing of worldwide products or services.

2. Headquarters also provides shared services, such as the network infrastructure. Managers at headquarters and in the shared functional areas have worldwide responsibility for their operations.

3. Local subsidiaries, which actually deliver the goods, take charge of functions that are better done locally, such as managing the supply chain and dealing

**EXHIBIT** **10.8**    **Organizational Structures of the Multinational E-Corporation**

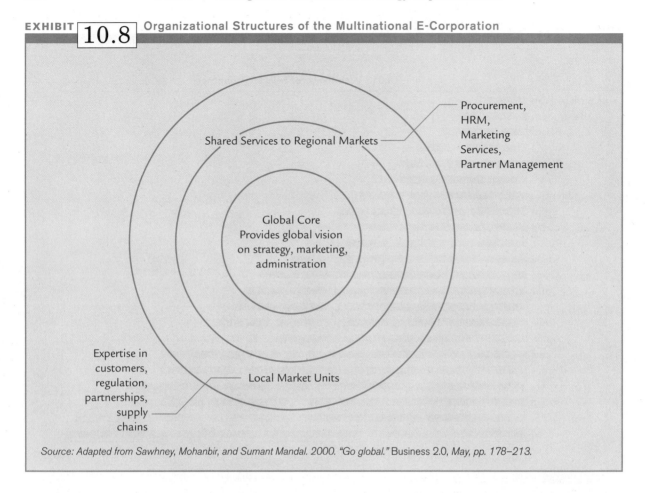

Procurement,
HRM,
Marketing
Services,
Partner Management

Shared Services to Regional Markets

Global Core
Provides global vision
on strategy, marketing,
administration

Expertise in
customers,
regulation,
partnerships,
supply
chains

Local Market Units

*Source: Adapted from Sawhney, Mohanbir, and Sumant Mandal. 2000. "Go global." Business 2.0, May, pp. 178–213.*

with regulations. These organizations try to solve the global-local dilemma with the integration of similar technical functions, such as Web server design, while making necessary adaptations such as website translations.[33] Exhibit 10.8 illustrates the levels and functions of this type of organization.

## Technical Capabilities and Implementation Options for Multinational E-Commerce

Components of a successful multinational online presence require electronic capabilities and support throughout the value chain.[34] Such capabilities are:

- Software to process pricing in multiple currencies. (The most sophisticated software not only supports payment processing systems that show prices in multiple currencies but also accepts payment in the customer's preferred currency.)

- Systems that calculate and show purchase information on international shipping, duties, and local taxes such as the VAT (value-added tax common in Europe).

- Systems that check regulatory compliance with local and international laws.

- The ability to give support in multilingual service centers.

- Fraud protection.

- Electronic payment models in addition to credit cards (not used as commonly as in the United States).

In addition, local realities influence how a multinational approaches its international markets. Many areas of the world do not process data the same way. In some countries, for instance, last names may actually come first. Similarly, not all countries use credit and debit cards—a significant problem for e-commerce. The following Case in Point shows how 7-Eleven and other companies manage their electronic payment models without the use of credit cards.

## Websites: Localize or Standardize?

As more and more multinationals use product-based websites and corporate websites to present, sell, and communicate with the public and their consumers, the issue of website adaptation is becoming critical.[35] As in the local-global dilemma, multinationals have to decide whether they want a **standardized website** (the company's websites are fairly similar in layout and design around the world) or a **localized website** (the values, appeals, symbols, and even themes in the communication content are adapted to a local culture).[36]

For some companies, the localization of websites is minimal. Dell Computer has websites in 50 countries using 21 different languages, but it uses the same layout for the sites in all countries. In contrast, Chipshot.com, which sells golf equipment online, tailors its sites to local cultural needs. In Japan, to take advantage of the Japanese golfer's sensitivity to brand names, the Chipshot site shows brand names conspicuously and emphasizes the availability of custom-made clubs. By comparison,

**Standardized Website** Website that is similar in design and layout around the world.

**Localized Website** Website that is adapted to local cultures.

---

### CASE IN POINT

### Last Names and Making Payments

Despite the globalizing nature of the Internet and e-commerce, the Internet remains a very "local" phenomenon. For instance, countries do not all process data in the same way. Consider the case of a large conference held at an international hotel in Asia. The hotel had all 200 guests registered but could not find the names in its system. When the hotel examined how it processed the data, it found that the names were entered as first name and last name. However, many of the conference attendees went by family name and given name. Such a simple problem was a major hassle for the hotel, and the data processing was subsequently revised.

Another issue is that e-commerce in many parts of the world is restricted because the use of credit or debit cards is not common. How do you pay electronically without a card? Even in an advanced industrial nation such as Japan, credit card use is much less common than in the United States. For example, in Japan, fewer than 10 percent of the transactions involve credit card payments. In Japan, people often pay utility bills at convenience stores. Thinking creatively, 7-Eleven Japan

took advantage of the existing payment structure for Web purchase payments. Japanese users of 7dream.com can select "Payment at 7-Eleven Store" as an option, allowing them to pick up their purchases and pay for them at any of the 8,000 7-Elevens in Japan.

Similarly, Handango found that many of its German consumers would leave in the middle of their order. The company soon learned that Germans have a strong cultural bias against debt and using credit cards. Handango eventually partnered with a local company to allow German customers to wire money directly from their bank accounts.

*Sources: Adapted from Bright, Becky. 2006. "E-commerce: How do you say 'Web'? Planning to take your online business international." Wall Street Journal, May 23, R11; Dean, D., S. DiGrande, D. Field, and P. Zwillenbegr. 2012. "The connected world." Boston Consulting Group Perspectives, http://www.bcgperspectives.com; Litchy, T. R., and R. A. Barra. 2008. "International issues of the design and usage of websites for e-commerce: Hotel and airline examples." Journal of Engineering and Technology Management, 25, 93–111; Sawhney, Mohanbir, and Sumant Mandal. 2000. "Go global." Business 2.0, May, 178–213.*

the U.S. site appeals to the more cost-conscious U.S. customers by emphasizing the 50 percent discount.[37]

Should companies standardize or localize? The practitioners and academic literature are fairly silent on the subject, but studies are starting to provide some guidance on the question. Consider the following Case in Point, which examines cultural differences and how they impact websites worldwide. The Case in Point also shows how McDonald's websites differ around the world. The study in that case provides evidence of the influence of cultural factors on website design and layout.

Developing a global website entails challenges to organizations beyond cultural sensitivity and language differences. Many firms discover that they need to adapt their organizations to the information flow and customer demands created by Web locations accessed from anywhere in the world. The resultant changes in organizational structure and in internal information systems make the company more globally integrated.

The results of the Forrester Research survey, reported in Exhibit 10.9, suggest that organizational challenges are among the most important issues affecting website globalization.

## CASE IN POINT

## McDonald's Websites around the World

It is undeniable that a country's national culture and institutions have an impact on how websites are designed. In fact, a recent report showed how multinationals' websites differ in different countries. For example, the study found that the website language in different countries is often more than merely a translation from the multinational's home country. Even with languages, some form of localization is necessary.

Another study examined websites of McDonald's worldwide. McDonald's multinational corporation currently operates more than 33,500 restaurants, with around 1.7 million employees in 119 countries. Given McDonald's effort to customize its products to meet local needs, the company not surprisingly tailors its websites to satisfy local preferences. In an interesting study, Wurtz compared McDonald's websites in high-context cultures (i.e., where communication is not direct but includes implicit messages contained in body language and silence) and in low-context cultures (i.e., where communication occurs primarily through explicit statements, such as text and speech). Comparing high-context countries such as Japan, India, and South Korea with low-context countries such as Denmark, Germany, Finland, Norway, and the United States, Wurtz found strong evidence of McDonald's website adaptation to local cultures. For instance, the author found more animation centered on people in the websites of high-context cultures, showing a preference for complexity in communication, while low-context websites are more static and use less animation. Navigation on low-context websites tends to be more linear, while on high-context websites more new browser windows open with less transparent guidance. The author also examined some aspects of Hofstede's cultural dimensions and how they influence Web design. For instance, the highly individualistic Swiss and German websites display images of individuals listening to music and relaxing (a very individual activity). In contrast, the Indian website shows a man running with a child in a shopping cart, emphasizing the family ties and group approach typical of collectivistic societies.

*Sources: McDonald's. 2012. http://www.mcdonalds.com; Nacat, R. and S. Burnaz. 2012. "A cultural content analysis of multinational companies' web sites." Qualitative Market Research: An International Journal, 14, 3, 274–288; Wurtz, Elizabeth. 2005. "A cross-cultural analysis of Websites from high-context cultures and low-context cultures." Journal of Computer Mediated Communications, 11, 25–43.*

**EXHIBIT 10.9    Major Problems Identified in Web Site Globalization**

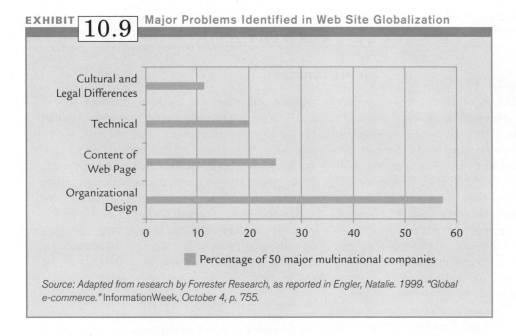

Percentage of 50 major multinational companies

*Source: Adapted from research by Forrester Research, as reported in Engler, Natalie. 1999. "Global e-commerce." InformationWeek, October 4, p. 755.*

## To Build or Outsource Technical Capabilities?

Similar to companies' choosing an export strategy (directly or indirectly, with the aid of export management companies), e-commerce companies seeking to globalize their operations have two basic options. They can run all the e-commerce functions themselves, or they can outsource them to e-fulfillment specialists, called **e-commerce enablers.** Enablers provide services and software that translate websites and calculate shipping, value-added taxes, duties, and other charges unique to each country. They take on functions such as receiving the customers' purchased goods, storing, packing, and eventual shipping to the customer. As with good export management firms, successful order fulfillment enablers understand local business culture and know how to comply with taxation and regulatory requirements.[38]

Enablers exist because many companies—from small to quite large—do not have the internal resources or capabilities to conduct all the required e-commerce functions. In addition, in such a rapidly changing, competitive environment, few companies have the time to develop such strategic capabilities. For example, Forrester Research estimates that 85 percent of U.S. e-retailers cannot fill international orders because they do not have the capability to deal with the complexities of shipping across borders. Even some very large companies, such as Nike and Blockbuster, outsource to enablers.

Many enablers specialize in helping companies globalize their e-commerce. Companies such as Global Site and Idion help create multilingual versions of websites for their customers. These companies have automated the translation process so that updates to websites can occur rapidly. This type of service has become so popular that Forrester Research expects a 50 percent per year increase in it.

In addition to e-commerce enablers that provide transaction services, numerous companies offer Web translations, some of which have automated the translation process. A challenge of translation is to keep up with the frequent, often costly changes in global websites. Culturally sensitive enablers go beyond simple translations. Like any advertisement or promotion in different countries, the website

**E-commerce enablers**
Fulfillment specialists that provide other companies with services such as website translation.

## CASE IN POINT

### Smart Phones

The increasing popularity of smart phones suggests that more people are likely to use such phones to access the internet. In fact, consumers in emerging markets are much more likely to be familiar with mobile phones than landlines. Data from the G20 nations show that only 21 percent of connections to broadband were made from fixed connections such as a laptop or computer. Meanwhile, 2,134 million connections were made from mobile connections.

This explosion in the use of smart phones has important implications for multinationals. Consumers in emerging markets, for instance, rely on smart phones for informational and purchase purposes. Multinationals will increasingly need to optimize their websites for smart phones. Furthermore, there are strong efforts now to replace cards as a means of payment with smart phones. Many countries in Asia and Europe are already seeing the use of smart phones as means of payment instead of cash or card payments. Multinationals will also need to invest in the technology to ensure that such transactions can occur. Finally, smart phones are increasingly being used to research and compare products and to buy the products. Most multinationals will need to offer products in such multi-channels if they want to take advantage of such opportunities. This will become increasingly critical in developing and emerging markets that are seeing drastic decreases in prices of smart phones.

*Sources: Based on Dean, D., S. DiGrande, D. Field, and P. Zwillenbegr. 2012. "The connected world." Boston Consulting Group Perspectives, http://www.bcgperspectives.com; Helft, M. 2012. "The death of cash." Fortune, July 23, 118–128.*

must be sensitive to cultural and religious differences. Colors, symbols, pictures, and variance in the local use of the same language may cause undesirable reactions depending on locale.

How will e-commerce and the Internet evolve for multinationals? Many experts agree that the explosion of discussion forums, blogs, and social networking sites is creating tremendous new opportunities for companies.[39] Consumers are using user-generated content (UGC) such as product reviews to make purchasing decisions. Multinationals will be well advised to understand and accommodate this new medium. Many multinationals are already using UGC to their advantage, and this trend is bound to continue. Furthermore, the explosion of the use of smart phones will also revolutionize e-commerce. Consider the above Case in Point.

## Summary and Conclusions

This chapter introduced the concepts of e-commerce in general and of multinational e-commerce in particular. It discussed the basic forms of e-commerce, including B2C, B2B, C2C, and C2B. Currently, B2B dominates the Internet economy, but B2C is expected to gain a major share of e-commerce transactions. Overall, e-commerce is expanding astronomically. Although the United States currently dominates e-commerce, statistics show that other areas of the world are quickly catching up.

The fundamentals of e-commerce strategy emphasize building on traditional business models and experimenting with cost reductions and areas of differentiation that Internet use might provide. There is no easy formula for building a successful e-commerce business. Innovative and creative managers will find ways to use e-commerce tools to improve their firms' cost leadership or differentiation strategies. Because the World Wide Web makes e-commerce models transparent and easy to copy, only the most innovative and rapidly moving companies are likely to survive.

Companies conducting multinational operations via the Internet face most of the same challenges as brick-and-mortar multinational companies. The problems remain of the global-local dilemma and of conducting business in different cultural and institutional environments. The Web, however, provides instant access to the world for all companies willing to navigate the e-commerce world. It will probably become one of the most important drivers of globalization in the future.

## *Discussion Questions*

1. Define e-commerce and discuss the types of e-commerce transactions.

2. Identify and discuss the levels of the Internet economy. How has the Internet created new types of businesses?

3. Compare and contrast the costs and benefits of a fully integrated brick-and-mortar and e-commerce company.

4. What are the advantages of e-commerce businesses over traditional brick-and-mortar businesses when taking their operations global? What are the disadvantages?

5. Discuss the advantages and disadvantages of outsourcing global e-commerce activities to enablers.

6. Discuss the characteristics of a successful multinational web page.

## Multinational Management **Skill Builder**

**The Boston Consulting Group Perspectives on the Digital Economy**

1. Go to the Boston Consulting Group Perspectives website, http://www.bcgperspectives.com, and locate the "The Digital Manifesto: How Companies and Countries Can Win in the Digital Economy," located at https://www.bcgperspectives.com/content/articles/growth_innovation_connected_world_digital_manifesto/.

2. Read the article. Discuss how the "new" Internet is different from the "old" Internet.

3. What are some of the major opportunities and challenges facing both companies and countries as they contemplate this new digital world?

4. What can multinationals do to better adapt in the new Internet environment?

## Multinational Management **Skill Builder**

**Build a Web Store**

**Step 1.** Your instructor will divide the class into groups.

**Step 2.** Select an agricultural or industrial product produced in your region of the country. If possible, interview a small businessperson concerning his or her perspectives on the international opportunities for the product. In the United States, one way of finding a potential business owner is through the small business development centers attached to many U.S. universities. Your instructor may assign you a business or product.

**Step 3.** Using the steps shown in Exhibit 7.5 (Chapter 7), information from Web sources, and your library, identify a foreign market or markets for the product or products.

**Step 4.** Build a simulated or actual website in your own language that shows the company's products or services. If you have the technical capabilities and are working with a real business, you can build a Web store. Simple no-cost or low-cost versions of Web storefronts can be downloaded from sources such as http://www.authstores.com/. Periodically search the Web for additional free e-commerce sources because new sites frequently become available.

**Step 5.** Translate your website into the language(s) of your target country or countries. Use the free translation software available on the Web via Google or another search engine.

**Step 6.** Test your translation and site layout with native speakers. If it is a real site, wait for orders.

**Step 7.** Present your site and its performance to your class and to the small businessperson, if possible.

## *Endnotes*

1. Andersen, Poul Houman. 2005. "Export intermediation and the Internet: An activity-unbundling approach." *International Marketing Review*, 22(2), 147–164.

2. ebusinessforum.com. 2000. "Ericsson: The promise of purchasing cards." December 18. http://www.ebusinessforum.com.

3. Neff, Dale. 2001. *e-Procurement*. Upper Saddle River, NJ: Prentice-Hall.

4. Koh, Chang E., and Kyungdoo "Ted" Nam. 2005. "Business use of the Internet: A longitudinal study from a value chain perspective." *Industrial Management + Data Systems*, 105(1/2), 82–95.

5. Lehr, W. 2012. Measuring the Internet: The Data Challenge. OECD Digital Economy Papers, No. 194, OECD Publishing. http://dx.doi.org/10.1787/5k9bhk5fzvzx-en

6. Dean, D., S. DiGrande, D. Field, A. Lundmark, J. O'Day, J. Pineda, and P. Zwilenberg. 2012. "The Internet economy in the G-20." BCG Perspectives, http://www.bcgperspectives.com.

7. Economic Intelligence Unit. 2012. *Pocket World in Figures, 2012*. London: Profile Books.

8. Organization for Economic Cooperation and Development (OECD). 2009. *Measuring the Internet Economy 2008*. Paris: Organization for Economic Cooperation and Development.

9. Ibid.

10. Epstein, Marc J. 2005. "Implementing successful e-commerce initiatives." *Strategic Finance*, March, 86(9), 22–29; Venkatraman, N. 2000. "Five steps to a dot-com strategy: How to find your footing on the Web." *Sloan Management Review*, Spring, 15–28.

11. Gulati, Ranjay, and Jason Garino. 2000. "Get the right mix of bricks & clicks." *Harvard Business Review*, May–June, 107–114.

12. Ibid.

13. Beasty, Colin. 2006. "Retail's 2 worlds: Tips on integrating online and offline channels." *Customer Relationship Management*, March, 10(3), 30–35.

14. Ibid.

15. Kim, Hyunwoo, Younggoo Han, Sehun Kim, and Myeonggil Choi. 2005. *Journal of Information Systems Education*, Spring, 16(1), 55–64.

16. Peslak, Alan R. 2006. "Internet privacy policies of the largest international companies." *Journal of Electronic Commerce in Organizations*, 4(3), 46–62.

17. Grimes, Roger. 2006. "E-commerce in crisis: When SSL isn't safe." *InfoWorld*, May 1, 28(18), 26.

18. Claburn, Thomas. 2005. "New path of attack." *InformationWeek*, No. 1066. November 28.

19. Gordon, Lawrence, and Martin P. Loeb. 2006. "Budgeting process for information security expenditures." *Communications of the ACM*, January, 49(1), 121–125.

20. Karat, Clare-Marie, Carolyn Brodie, and John Karat. 2006. "Usable privacy and security for personal information management." *Communication of the ACM*, January, 49(1), 56–57.

21. Fahmy, Dalia. 2005. "Making financial data more secure." *Institutional Investor*, December, 1; Grimes.

22. Chandra, Akhilesh, and Thomas Calderon. 2005. "Challenges and constraints to the diffusion of biometrics in information systems." *Communications of ACM*, December, 48(12), 101–106.

23. Mientka, Matt. 2006. "Behavioral biometric to improve e-commerce security." *AFP Exchange*, January–February, 32–33.

24. Peslak.

25. Knight, Gary A., and Tamer Cavusgil. 2005. "A taxonomy of born-global firms." *Management International Review*, 45, 15–35.

26. Sawhney, Mohanbir, and Sumant Mandal. 2000. "Go global." *Business 2.0*, May, 178–213.

27. Rosen, Kenneth T., and Amanda L. Howard. 2000. "E-retail: Gold rush or fool's gold?" *California Management Review*, Spring, 42(3), 72–100.

28. Cyr, Dianne, Carole Bonanni, John Bowes, and Joe Ilsever. 2005. "Beyond trust: Web site design preferences across cultures." *Journal of Global Information Management*, October–December, 13(4), 25–54; Singh, Nitish, George Fassot, Hongxin Zhao, and Paul D. Boughton. 2006. "A cross-cultural analysis of German, Chinese and Indian consumers' perception of Web site adaptation." *Journal of Consumer Behavior*, 5, 56–68; Singh, Nitish, Olivier Furrer, and Massimiliano Ostinelli. 2004. "To localize or standardize on the web: Empirical evidence from Italy, India, Netherlands, Spain and Switzerland." *Multinational Business Review*, 12(1), 69–87.

29. Rosen and Howard.

30. Shirky, Clay. 2000. "Go global or bust." *Business 2.0*, March 1, 145–146.

31. World Wide Web Foundation. 2012. Web Index. Http://www.webfoundation.org/Webindex.

32. Sawhney and Mandal.

33. Ibid.

34. Hudgins, Christy. 1999. "International e-commerce." *Network Computing*, November 15, 10(23), 75–50.

35. Singh, Furrer, and Ostinelli.

36. Singh, Furrer, and Ostinelli.

37. Engler, Natalie. 1999. "Global e-commerce," *InformationWeek*, October 4, 755.

38. Wilkerson, Phil. 2000. "Enabling global e-commerce." *Discount Store News*, April 17, 39(8), 15–16.

39. *Retailing Today*. 2008. "UGC, CGC: The hot new buzz words both online and off," December, 5.

# Yumcha.Com.AU

Richard Ivey School of Business
The University of Western Ontario

**IVEY** | Institute for Entrepreneurship

*Rohan Belliappa wrote this case under the supervision of Prof. Nicole Haggerty solely to provide material for class discussion. The authors do not intend to illustrate either effective or ineffective handling of a managerial situation. The authors may have disguised certain names and other identifying information to protect confidentiality.*

*Richard Ivey School of Business Foundation prohibits any form of reproduction, storage or transmission without its written permission. Reproduction of this material is not covered under authorization by any reproduction rights organization. To order copies or request permission to reproduce materials, contact Ivey Publishing, Richard Ivey School of Business Foundation, The University of Western Ontario, London, Ontario, Canada, N6A 3K7; phone (519) 661-3208; fax (519) 661-3882; e-mail cases@ivey.uwo.ca.*

*Copyright © 2010, Richard Ivey School of Business Foundation*

*Version: (A) 2010-05-27*

On November 1, 2007, Mardi Tan, founder and executive director of Yumcha.com.au (Yumcha), was anxiously looking at the timeline she had set for her new social networking venture. There were many decisions to be made and actions still to be implemented for the launch of the new website. While it had been nearly seven years since she had won an entrepreneurship award for the idea, Tan was determined to launch the site by June 2008 as she was running out of time and money. She knew that she would need to use creativity and innovation to differentiate her enterprise in an increasingly competitive environment. There were also key questions concerning the firm's information systems and organization strategy and how it would fit with Yumcha's overall business strategy.

## Australia

Australia is a developed country with a prosperous multicultural society, having excellent results in many international comparisons of national performance such as human development, quality of life, health care, life expectancy, public education, economic freedom and the protection of civil liberties and political rights.[1] As a continent, Australia is considered part of the Asia-Pacific region. Its multicultural society and open immigration policies have resulted in a large percentage of its urban residents being born outside the country. The 2006 Australian Census indicated a national population of just under 20 million people, of which 1.7 million declared Asian ancestry.

## The Target Demographic

In 2000, when the first Yumcha business plan was written, the Australian Bureau of Statistics (ABS) indicated approximately 6.4 million Australian adults were Internet users; furthermore, a 1998 ABS survey indicated that the Chinese community in Australia was the second largest Internet-using group by ethnic community. Noticing that a number of other communities—all with smaller populations than that of Asian-Australians—had dedicated community websites, Tan felt that there may be a business opportunity in developing Australia's first website serving its Asian community.

In December 2000, this first version of the Yumcha website (Yumcha 1.0) resulted in Tan earning the New South Wales Young Entrepreneur of the Year award in the Shell-Livewire entrepreneurship competition. A prestigious award in the Australian business community, it provided credibility to Tan's efforts as she set about launching and growing the venture. In 2000, Tan conducted a survey of 200 individuals identifying themselves as Asian-Australian; the responses indicated strong demand for an online community portal. There was no structured way for Asian professionals to congregate as a group outside community-based organizations and religious gatherings. The survey, which was distributed amongst members of Asian social clubs and church groups, indicated that there was strong interest in meeting other Asian professionals in Australia beyond just their immediate group. Yumcha was seen as a way for these individuals to gain access to the Asian community beyond traditional social structures.

A survey of potential advertisers indicated demand for advertising space targeting Asian-Australians; these potential advertisers included educational institutions looking to recruit Asian students from overseas markets, large financial institutions looking to target well-established Asian professionals in Australia with investment, credit card and life insurance products, English language course providers, Asian-themed event promoters and government agencies with events or services targeting the Asian community (annual cultural events, immigration services). Tan had to ensure that the website reached its potential to be an attractive advertising platform for these companies; she wondered what metrics would be most suitable to measure and present to potential advertisers.

Yumcha 1.0 had a simple user interface, whereby after logging in to their account, a user would see an Asian-themed screen with a text-based list of other members stating their professional title and company, as well as links enabling two types of communications: a private messaging system to connect with other members and a 'virtual business card' system, where one member could publicly send a message with their professional contact information to another member. This version of the site had no administrative back end, meaning that it was updated as a conventional website with no means to administer memberships, advertising or advanced features such as blogs or online stores. Major website updates were virtually impossible without the assistance of programmers, whose services were outside Tan's budget at the time. Tan was disappointed that the available technology was too expensive, difficult to use and unreliable for what she felt was possible from the site. She had been contacted by major Australian companies looking to advertise on the site, but was unable to provide banner advertising and track its results due to the constraints of technology at the time.

By early 2002, Tan decided to set the Yumcha idea aside to pursue other professional opportunities, as the website did not have the functionality that she was seeking and the cost of maintaining it was beyond her means. In 2007, however, after encouragement by friends and business contacts, she decided to revive the idea. With the evolution of Web 2.0[2] and the availability of numerous online tools to administer social networking websites, Tan felt she could better capitalize on the business opportunities provided by the Yumcha concept. While Yumcha 1.0 offered a very simple screen interface to members, Yumcha 2.0 offered more Web 2.0 features, such as forums concerning topics of interest to

members, individual blogs, the ability to share and discuss media articles, an online bookstore, job postings and the ability to share media such as photographs and videos. With the advent of social networking templates used on websites such as Facebook, LinkedIn and MySpace, Yumcha 2.0 provided each member with their own page, which enabled them to include biographical information. It also used a simple administrative back end system, which enabled Tan to administer the site herself without reliance on an outside developer; this meant that she could upload and track advertising results, moderate website activity and make major updates herself, maximizing her flexibility whilst reducing development costs from programmers.

## Yumcha

*Yum cha* is a Cantonese word. Its literal translation means to "drink tea." However, figuratively Yum cha refers more to an experience: the social experience of dining on dim sum and drinking Chinese tea. For the Yumcha website, the goal was to create an online social experience similar to the physical social experience that occurs when eating dim sum and drinking tea with a group of friends.

The Yumcha website was developed with a vision to be the pre-eminent Asian-Australian community portal. Its mission statement was the following: "To provide a premium quality website to fulfill the informational and networking needs of the Asian-Australian community and maximize exposure for advertisers seeking to target this demographic group on the Internet."

### Building the Social Networking Website

As of November 2007, after Tan made the decision to revive Yumcha, she had a few decisions to make: How would this website make money? What value proposition would enable her to meet her mission statement and reach out to her key target market?

Tan also had to decide on a cost-effective means to build the site and maintain it on an ongoing basis. While she worked a full time job as a teacher, her budget was limited. She had to decide whether to choose a developer within her hometown of Sydney, or use one of the developers she had located on a global sourcing site which enabled developers worldwide to bid on project work for sites such as Yumcha. Examples of such websites included Scriptlance and GetAFreelancer: these sites allowed independent web developers, programmers, consultants and site builders around the world to promote their capabilities. Based on price quotation and peer reviews on the website, clients such as Tan could get an idea of the cost and quality of the work offered. Such platforms were not widely available when Yumcha was first launched in 2000. Many options were far less expensive than the quotes being offered in Australia for web development services. If Tan chose one of the international developers, however, she knew she would be taking on the extra risk of not being able to visit the contractor in person to enforce project deliverables; additionally, it would be difficult to legally enforce any work contracts if the developer was in a country with a legal system different to that of Australia.

### The Developer Decision

Tan decided to look overseas after her first developer, based in Sydney, created a back end administration system far too complicated for her to use and at a very high price. She was outraged when, in July 2007, he suggested that the Yumcha site architecture was too complex for her to manage alone, and that he should take ownership of the entire site for himself and give Tan a share of revenues. After terminating the individual's contract, Tan knew she would have to be careful with the contractors she chose for the website.

Tan had made a decision not to pursue venture capital funding so as not to lose ownership control of the organization, and also to avoid being beholden to the agendas of her investors; therefore, funded by her own income, budget was a significant consideration in choosing a developer. In her research on Scriptlance and GetAFreelancer, she narrowed her decision down to three developers. She outsourced minor project work to all three, with the intent of evaluating their performance before selecting a final lead developer for the site.

The first developer, Ravi, was based in Bangalore, India. Hired in July 2007 through Scriptlance, he offered the lowest price for the development projects Tan had put on tender on the website; however, in a few minor projects, which involved setting up the basic visual layout of the new Yumcha website, Ravi was frequently late in his deliverables. As Tan said, the constant Google Chat quote from Ravi was, "It will be done," followed by no response for one to two weeks after the promise. While the price was right, Tan knew she had to race against the clock to get the website successfully launched with Ravi. She could not perpetually keep the website in development and Ravi, rather than being an asset to her work, risked being a significant source of delay.

The second developer, Arjad, was based in Tehran, Iran. Initially, Tan was delighted with his work as he was timely, cost-effective and provided stunning visual effects for the website. Hired in October 2007 after Tan's frustrations with Ravi, he received strong peer reviews on Scriptlance and seemed to be a good fit; however, after about a month it became apparent that Arjad was more concerned with creative independence than serving Tan's requirements as the customer. When Tan would email requests for visual changes or alterations to features on the website, Arjad would reply with opinions on the changes, rather than carrying out the work as requested. He also questioned Tan's choices of visual layout and suggested his own visuals which were far outside the scope of their agreement, resulting in delays to implementing Tan's launch action plan. While Tan was firm in her requests, the delays were mounting due to Arjad's assumed creative liberties. The difficulties in communication were compounded by the fact that mediums such as Google Chat and email were used; since English was not Arjad's first language, Tan often found it difficult to understand what he was trying to communicate concerning the site's requirements.

The final option was Chris, based in Los Angeles. Chris was prompt in his delivery of projects, and being an expert in the software powering the back end of Yumcha, was also a source of helpful advice to Tan in working through the subtle technicalities. While not as creative a programmer as Arjad, and significantly more expensive than both Arjad and Ravi, Tan felt that she had "one less fire to fight" knowing that Chris was on a project.

## Developments in Social Networking

In 2007, seven years after drawing up the business plan for Yumcha, the online social networking landscape had evolved significantly. New websites such as Facebook, MySpace, LinkedIn, Oriented and others had established an online presence and growing member base (see Exhibit 1). When Tan decided to re-launch Yumcha in 2007, she acknowledged that these were competitive threats that did not exist when Yumcha was first launched in 2000. Yumcha would have to ensure that it had a relevant differentiation strategy from these incumbents. Tan also acknowledged that many end-users had by now become used to a certain 'look and feel' experience when using a social networking website.

**Facebook** was a social networking website operated and privately owned by Facebook, Inc. Founded February 1, 2004, it had US$716 million[3] in funding and was expected to be the largest social networking website by mid-2009 with 175 million members[4], surpassing its nearest rival MySpace. Users could add friends, send messages and update their personal profiles to notify friends about themselves.

**EXHIBIT 1**    Performance Metrics for Select Social Networking Sites

### Top 20 Social Network Sites, January 2009[5]

| Site | Jan-09 Unique Audience (000) | Jan-09 Time per Person (hh:mm:ss) | Jan-08 Unique Audience (000) | Jan-08 Time per Person (hh:mm:ss) | Yearly Growth Unique Audience | Yearly Growth Time per Person |
|---|---|---|---|---|---|---|
| Facebook | 62,444 | 2:50:04 | 23,346 | 1:01:31 | 167% | 176% |
| Myspace.com | 60,603 | 1:35:47 | 59,613 | 2:20:03 | 2% | -32% |
| Classmates Online | 19,452 | 0:09:07 | 13,992 | 0:08:53 | 39% | 3% |
| LinkedIn | 14,705 | 0:14:05 | 6,456 | 0:10:56 | 128% | 29% |
| Reunion.com | 12,458 | 0:05:10 | 3,968 | 0:04:13 | 214% | 23% |
| Windows Live Home | 10,250 | 0:02:12 | 8,285 | 0:06:21 | 24% | -65% |
| Club Penguin | 5,721 | 0:36:43 | 4,706 | 0:07:38 | 22% | 381% |
| AOL Community | 4,574 | 0:12:43 | 4,323 | 0:33:13 | 6% | -62% |
| Twitter.com | 4,556 | 0:09:03 | N/A | N/A | N/A | N/A |
| Ning | 3,777 | 0:15:02 | 1,172 | 0:06:08 | 222% | 145% |
| Tagged.com | 3,770 | 1:03:59 | 2,130 | 0:05:33 | 77% | 1053% |
| Imeem | 3,541 | 0:06:12 | 2,549 | 0:05:14 | 39% | 18% |
| Bebo | 3,028 | 0:13:37 | 2,203 | 0:16:41 | 37% | -18% |
| Last.fm | 2,873 | 0:03:17 | 1,233 | 0:08:48 | 133% | -63% |
| MyYearbook | 2,464 | 2:00:15 | 1,809 | 1:02:43 | 36% | 92% |
| Flixster | 2,399 | 0:05:35 | 2,871 | 0:05:01 | -16% | 11% |
| Meetup.com | 2,226 | 0:08:18 | 2,271 | 0:16:08 | -2% | -49% |
| CarDomain Network | 1,828 | 0:04:06 | 1,166 | 0:05:07 | 57% | -20% |
| Care2.com | 1,820 | 0:02:53 | 1,327 | 0:05:20 | 37% | -46% |
| Gaia Online | 1,731 | 1:59:35 | 1,121 | 2:44:45 | 54% | -27% |

*Source: Nielsen Online.*

According to the Nielsen standard of usability, this success was attributed to various factors, including the following:[6]

1. **Learnability**—Facebook is easy to use and has been designed to be intuitive for its anticipated user base.

2. **Efficiency**—Because of technology choices—specifically the use of AJAX tools, Facebook users can perform actions quickly, including friend and application searches.

3. **Memorability**—graphic design choices and consistency in use of their chosen layout, ensure that Facebook users can navigate the site easily.

4. **Error-handling**—The AJAX tools largely hide systems errors from users and provide instant feedback to the design team to resolve.

5. **Satisfaction**—Facebook users are largely satisfied with the design and accessibility of the site.

Major criticisms of Facebook included uncertainties concerning its protection of user privacy, anger by advertisers over having corporate logos displayed on the member pages of controversial individuals, child safety and the difficulty of terminating accounts once created. Enabling third-party advertisers to access and utilize user photos uploaded to Facebook was also a significant area of controversy. Facebook had been sued by companies claiming that it unlawfully used their intellectual property.[7]

**MySpace** was the original social networking site before Facebook. Located in Beverly Hills, California, it was owned by Fox Interactive Media, which itself was owned by News Corporation. While MySpace was a very popular site for social networking, Facebook posed a considerable threat to their dominance. MySpace was expected to be overtaken internationally by its main competitor, Facebook, in mid-2008 based on monthly unique visitors, and by mid-2009 on the basis of total membership. Users and commentators indicated that MySpace's shortcomings included a cluttered look and frequent error messages due to incorrect coding on user-generated profile pages[8].

**LinkedIn** was a business-oriented social networking site. It began "in the living room of co-founder Reid Hoffman in the fall of 2002."[9] As of September 2007, LinkedIn had 15 million members worldwide. Its venture capital partners included a host of blue chip investors and notable Internet pioneers. Its management committee included top-ranking graduates of leading technical and business education institutions worldwide.[10] In 2007, the site added individual profile pages, ostensibly as a means to keep up with and emulate Facebook. Criticisms of the site suggested that LinkedIn lacked the rich social experience provided by Facebook, and that it had always been about collecting professional networks data and not about building up professional network through extensive socializing. Building the relationships that LinkedIn displayed happened elsewhere, such as in-person interactions or in work settings or even on Facebook.[11]

**Oriented.com** was a global network of international professionals interested in Asian business and partnerships, with more than 30,000 members worldwide. Its signature service was "Happy Hours," simultaneously held in real time on the last Thursday of every month in more than ten cities around the world, providing offline networking opportunities for its members. These offline networking events were acknowledged as a major reason for the site's popularity, as the general look and feel of the Oriented.com website was considered cluttered and not overly user-friendly.

The emergence of these organizations raised two problems for Yumcha; firstly, how would Yumcha differentiate itself with a unique value proposition. If Yumcha was to offer networking and information relevant to Asian-Australian professionals, there was nothing stopping Facebook or another like-minded entrepreneur from creating sub-groups related to the same topic area. There was nothing preventing any of these competitors from establishing links amongst individuals that might otherwise do so on Yumcha.

Secondly, Tan was concerned that as each competitor website evolved, and in all likelihood improved its services, Yumcha would be expected to do the same; if so, how would she maintain the flexibility in her information technology (IT) infrastructure to be able to quickly evolve the site at minimal expense, disruption and effort?

## Developing Yumcha Version 2.0

Tan decided to leverage the emerging social networking trend, as well as developments in social networking technology, as an advantage; there was still no dedicated Asian-Australian community portal in Australia. She remembered that the Jewish community numbered 102,000 in Australia and had over 120 dedicated websites; the Asian community, which numbered over 1.5 million, had none. Having worked for a large Japanese company for a number of years, Tan wanted to return to Australia and live the entrepreneurial life of working from home, no longer having to answer to a boss. While in Japan, she was a member of mixi.co.jp, a Japanese-language website which enabled networking amongst Japanese professionals.

Australia was increasingly connected to the Asian region, with Sydney having hosted the Asia Pacific Economic Conference (APEC) in 2007, the largest-ever gathering of political leaders in the nation. The country's commercial interests were increasingly tied to Asia, displacing its traditional partners the United States and United Kingdom. Japan, China, the Republic of Korea and India were Australia's top four export markets in 2008-2009[12].

In developing Yumcha 2.0, Tan wanted to keep her initial commitments and overhead expenses low — her office would be at her Sydney home, and the only immediate hardware requirements would be her desktop and laptop. She did not approach any external funders for capital, as she did not want to give up ownership or be constrained by any debt-related covenants in running her business. She felt that all the key tasks for Yumcha could be performed at a minimal cost and funded by her existing income from being a teacher and jazz singer.

Another important consideration was her choice of platform—or software—which would be used to run the entire website. Two options were available to Tan: phpFox and SocialEngine. Both phpFox and SocialEngine were social networking scripts designed for anyone to create their own social networks. They were written in PHP programming language and could be customized to suit the individual needs of the site. The caveat, however, was that while they appeared simple to configure, one needed programming experience or a budget to hire a programmer familiar with customizing the script language to a particular site.

While both options offered the same business functionality in terms of features they could provide, phpFox was considered the standard social networking software for new start-ups in 2007. In looking for developers, Tan found that the significant majority of programmers were phpFox specialists, and that SocialEngine, while considered to be a more stable program resulting in fewer site crashes on average, was too new to the market and therefore not widely adopted. PhpFox was more affordable, and Tan's three potential developers had expressed a preference for phpFox; however, Tan knew that site stability would be an important consideration when finalizing her information system strategy.

## The Product

The new Yumcha website would provide relevant information, networking opportunities and ancillary services of interest to Asian-Australian professionals. Revenue would be sourced from user membership fees and from advertisers targeting Asian-Australian Internet users. The growth strategy would involve leveraging avenues such as Google AdWords, Facebook groups, LinkedIn and Twitter updates to recruit members. Tan was insistent that no high upfront promotion costs be incurred to minimize the personal financial burden; she felt that there had been enough developments in Internet technology over the last few years to build a technically-sound website and see it shepherd its growth organically through resourceful use of existing online advertising mediums.

The revenue for Yumcha would come from advertisers (see Exhibit 2). The aim was to keep advertising rates low, while ensuring strong value in exchange for the fee. While revenue was the bottom line, Tan was aware that the higher the number of members, the more advertising revenue she could generate; thus, Yumcha would operate with free membership in its early days.

## The Experience

Users would sign up for an account, granting them access to the site. After signing in, they had a dedicated profile page, as well as access to different

---

**EXHIBIT 2**    Yumcha.com.au Advertising Rates (as submitted to prospective advertisers)

Yumcha.com.au is Australia's premier networking site for Australian-Asian professionals. Launched in August 2009, the site has attracted much attention and has reached its maxim of attracting astute and discerning professionals within the Asian community both in Australia and abroad. We have achieved this success by delivering a new unique service that taps into the global Zeitgeist of the social networking phenomenon and the ongoing trend of 25–40 year old professionals using the internet to expand their business and social networks.

**Site Statistics:**
As Yumcha.com.au has only recently launched in August 2009, we will be providing detailed statistics as they are collected.

**Banner Formats & Rate Card for one month tenancy:**
468 X 60 (<15Kb), 1 Month (or 31 days) = AU$400.00
250 X 250 (<25Kb), 1 Month (or 31 days) = AU$400.00
150 X 150 (<10Kb), 1 Month (or 31 days) = AU$350.00
Monthly tenancy display advertisements will allow your advertisement to be seen on the screen at all times. During peak advertising periods, e.g. Christmas, Valentine's Day, etc. we guarantee a minimum display rotation of 1 in 5.

**Newsletter Monthly Sponsorship: $350 per issue.**
Your banner and logo will be featured prominently acknowledging your company's sponsorship of the monthly newsletter.

**Newsletter Advertorial: $250.**
A written piece on your company/services will be posted as an unmarked advertorial. Advertorials are subject to approval in accordance with Yumcha.com.au guidelines and appropriateness for our target audience.

**Banner Ad Creation**
For companies that do not have their own banners, Yumcha.com.au can provide a fully customized, unique web banner solution for $200.00 including GST. This banner ad is not restricted to use on Yumcha and can be used anywhere you want to advertise on the internet.

sections of the site, including other member profiles, blogs, articles, job postings and discussion groups.

Tan found that there was strong initial interest in joining the site; however, new user activity decreased over time, and most members returned infrequently. She needed to develop strategies to ensure that users remained active on the site after joining.

## Strategic Objectives

Yumcha would remain in a beta phase following its target launch date in June 2008. The beta phase of new software was its testing phase before an official release. An 'open beta' phase of a new software offering made it available to the general community, with the aim to identify prospective weaknesses or bugs in the program during its normal course of use. This gave Yumcha an opportunity to run as a business and iron out any unforeseen issues while improving existing business processes.

After completing the beta phase, the objective was to have 15,000 paid members, with 5,000 by August 2010 and a further 10,000 joining by August 2011. Membership would be free initially, with the aim to attract more advertisers due to a larger membership base. All members would gain access to Yumcha's offerings, which included the following:

- Connecting with other members,
- Browsing and posting job vacancies,
- Accessing events advertised on Yumcha within Australia,
- The ability to share links, blog, upload photos and video.

Exhibit 3 provides sample screenshots of the Yumcha website.

## Revenue Generation and Growth

Tan's most pressing concern was how to grow revenues from membership and advertising sales. To do so, she used a number of marketing avenues, both online and offline. Online, she used a suite of advertising tools including promotion through search engine optimization technology (ensuring that Internet searches for keywords relevant to Yumcha resulted in higher listings), Facebook user groups and a Twitter site dedicated to Yumcha. These required no marketing budget, and aligned with

**EXHIBIT 3**   Sample Screenshots from Yumcha.com.au

**EXHIBIT** 3 **Continued**

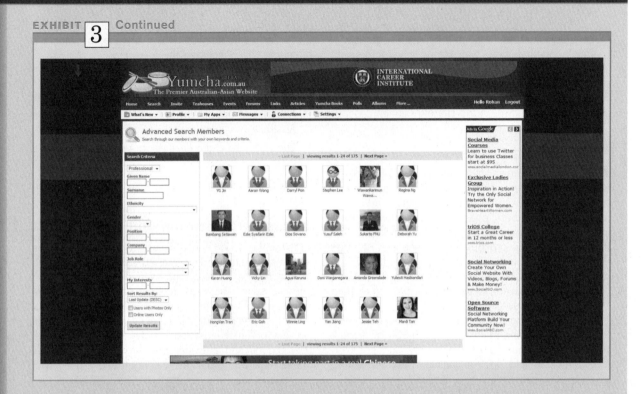

Tan's objectives of running a start-up site with minimal upfront costs.

Offline, Tan tapped into her extensive business network, built up over years working with major Asian firms and government agencies, and her own extensive social network in Sydney, Australia. Given Australia's proximity to nations such as Singapore, China and Japan, Tan was able to get support from government missions in Sydney for the initiative. The government of Singapore, for example, was known for proactively looking to engage with its neighbors, ideally through professional and academic networks to recruit top talent to its shores. Their Contact Singapore office in Sydney was well resourced, with the mission to encourage businesses and qualified professionals to consider moving to Singapore.

## Yumcha Events

Tan wondered if offsite events in real time could be organized to increase Yumcha revenues and exposure for its advertisers. Initial surveys showed many people in Sydney had signed up to be invited to these events, and perhaps there was value to be had in developing an online and offline presence for Yumcha.

## Conclusion

As Tan thought through the issues facing this new venture, she knew she had to ensure that her business strategy was clearly defined, and that it drove her information and organizational strategy decisions. Many questions still ran through her mind: Who was the best developer to support Yumcha's launch? Should she risk going with the international developers, or go with Australian options? What exactly was Yumcha's optimal value proposition? Were there offline networks that she had not tapped? How could she differentiate Yumcha to ensure a unique value proposition, and then communicate this to her target market? What types of organizations should she approach to sponsor the entity? She was excited about the available opportunities and options, but knew she would have to use her limited resources wisely to successfully develop the project to its full potential.

### CASE DISCUSSION QUESTIONS

1. What were some of the rationale of Ms. Tan's decision to launch Yumcha? Do you think it was a wise decision given the existence of many other social networking websites such as Facebook etc?

2. What were some of the challenges Ms. Tan faced in finding developers from around the world? Do the behaviors of the developers reflect their national culture?
3. What can Ms. Tan do to ensure that the developers deliver as needed? How can she balance the cost versus benefits associated with the developers?
4. What other challenges do you anticipate Ms. Tan will face as she launches the site?

### CASE NOTES

1. As of November 1, 2007, Cdn$1 = AU$1.05.
2. The term "Web 2.0" is commonly associated with web applications that facilitate interactive information sharing, interoperability and collaboration on the World Wide Web.
3. http://www.askdavetaylor.com/angel_investors_venture_capital_startups_funding.html, accessed May 27, 2010.
4. http://news.cnet.com/8301-1023_3-10164458-93.html, accessed May 27, 2010.
5. As of the time that this case was written, Yumcha had not yet implemented a structure to collect this information.
6. Regnard Raquedan, "Why is Facebook So Successful? Usability holds the key," Standard Web Standards, available at http://webstandards.raquedan.com/?p=251, accessed April 30, 2010.
7. Susan Decker and David Glovin, "Google, Facebook Sued Over Phone Social-Networking," *BusinessWeek*, March 9, 2010, www.businessweek.com/news/2010-03-09/google-facebook-sued-over-phone-social-networking-patent.html, accessed April 30, 2010.
8. Facebook Overtakes MySpace (Again) http://mashable.com/2009/02/19/facebook-bigger-than-myspace-in-us/ accessed April 30, 2010.
9. LinkedIn Company History, available at http://press.linkedin.com/history, accessed on April 30, 2010.
10. http://press.linkedin.com/management, accessed April 30, 2010.
11. Anne Zelenka, "LinkedIn Needs to Reach Out," GigaOm, December 10, 2007, http://gigaom.com/2007/12/10/linkedin-needs-to-reachout/, accessed April 30, 2010.
12. Australian Department of Foreign Affairs and Trade: http://www.dfat.gov.au/trade/focus/-081201_top10_twoway_exports.html, accessed April 30, 2010.

# Transition at Whirlpool Tatramat: From Joint Venture to Acquisition

T his case gives a description of the evolution of Whirlpool's participation strategy in Slovakia. Beginning first with a joint venture, Whirlpool eventually takes control of the whole operation.

## The Joint Venture Partners

### Whirlpool Corporation

Whirlpool Corporation is one of the world's leading manufacturers and marketers of home appliances, such as washing machines, refrigerators, and kitchen ranges. Its growth, from a domestic manufacturer in the United States to a firm with worldwide presence, is the result of a strategic decision taken in the mid-1980s.

Unable to find adequate growth potential in the United States appliance market, the company began its global expansion. By 1998, the company manufactured products in 13 countries and marketed them in approximately 170 countries. It employed over 59,000 people worldwide, and its net sales reached $10.5 billion.[1] Over ten years, the company had doubled the number of its brands, its employees, and its revenues, and had tripled the number of countries in which it had manufacturing sites (Table 1).

Whirlpool's Western European operations started in 1989, when Whirlpool and N.V. Philips of the Netherlands formed a joint venture, Whirlpool Europe B.V. (WEBV). Its mission was to manufacture and market appliances in Europe. Originally, Whirlpool held a 53 percent stake in the joint venture; in 1991, it became the sole owner through the acquisition of the remaining shares.

Whirlpool Europe B.V. soon became the third largest household appliance producer in Europe, behind the Swedish company AB Electrolux and the German joint venture Bosch-Siemens Hausgerate GmbH. After its acquisition of Philips's shares, Whirlpool began production in several European countries (France, Italy, Germany, and Sweden). These sites achieved economies of scale by producing a minimum of 600,000 pieces per year per factory. However, the Western European market soon experienced a recession, which was reflected in disappointing sales and profits, unlike at that time those in the United States.

**TABLE 1  A Decade of Whirlpool's Internationalization, 1988 and 1998**

| Item | 1988 | 1998 |
|------|------|------|
| Countries with manufacturing sites | 4 | 13 |
| Brands | 14 | 25 |
| Employees | 29,100 | 59,000 |
| Revenues (billions of dollars) | 4.4 | 10.5 |

*Source: Whirlpool Corporation. 1998. Vision, 1, 2 (March–April) and information provided by Whirlpool Slovakia.*

After the fall of the Berlin wall and the revolutionary wave in Central and Eastern European (CEE) countries, WEBV started looking for opportunities in the transition economies of Eastern Europe. Given the competitive pressure in Western Europe, as well as pressures on manufacturing costs, WEBV capitalized on the idea of opening new markets as well as using the low-cost competitive advantage of CEE by investing in Poprad, Slovakia.

Whirlpool Europe not only ranked as the third largest producer and marketer in Western Europe, but it also was the leader in CEE, where it had one manufacturing center (in Poprad, Slovakia) and ten sales offices. Whirlpool's strategy for Europe has evolved over time. During the 1990s, Whirlpool focused on closing the "value gap" between the costs of appliances relative to consumers' disposable income in Western Europe as compared to other major world markets, such as North America. That strategy was by and large successful, although at that time the whole industry was under cost pressures, as economic growth in Europe stagnated and consumers turned to lower-cost, less-featured products.

Through new products, the company undertook a dramatic restructuring of its entire line during the second half of the 1990s. Using extensive consumer and trade customer research, new products were introduced in every appliance category. In 1997, an estimated 60 percent of revenues came from these new products. In February 1998, Whirlpool CEO David Whitman commented on the situation in Europe: "Europe proved to be a bright spot for us in 1997, following two years of turbulent times. Our performance in Europe has consistently improved, quarter after quarter, following cost-reduction and productivity improvement efforts begun in 1996. Additionally, we continued to expand our business in Central Europe and other emerging markets by drawing from our expertise throughout our other European operations. As a result, Whirlpool remains the leading brand across the whole region."[2]

## Tatramat

Karol Scholz founded Tatramat in 1845 as a producer of nails and currycombs for grooming horses. After World War I, the company switched to producing domestic kitchen goods; after World War II, the company was nationalized. Under the 45 years of socialism, the company expanded to produce zinc-coated and painted barrels, water heaters, electric ovens, and automatic washing machines. It began production of automatic top-loading washing machines (under license with VIVA of France) in 1969, and front-loading washing machines in cooperation with Elektronska Industrija of Yugoslavia in 1972. In Czechoslovakia, it was the number one manufacturer of automatic washing machines (202,500 units in 1990) and domestic water heaters (146,900 units). At the beginning of the 1990s, Tatramat employed approximately 2,300 people. It controlled 88 percent of the automatic washing machine market in Czechoslovakia, a near monopoly. The company derived about 12 percent of its revenues from exports. In 1990, its sales reached $48 million. The operating profit was about $3.2 million, resulting in an operating margin of 6.8 percent. Tatramat's washing machines were designed to meet the requirements of the Czechoslovak market.

In the late 1980s, Western brands were often too expensive, too complicated, or simply too large to appeal to the average Czechoslovak buyer. Tatramat also had an established distribution and servicing network in Czechoslovakia. This, along with a wide spread of the brand, meant cheaper distribution costs, cheaper servicing costs, and lower advertising costs relative to imported brands. In addition, there was an untapped market for washing machines in Czechoslovakia. At the beginning of the 1990s, the penetration level for washing machines was only 58 percent. It was expected to rise to the levels of Western Europe (approximately 90 percent) within a decade. The demand for major consumer appliances was expected to increase gradually in Czechoslovakia and in neighboring countries as the region reoriented itself toward a market economy.

After the Velvet Revolution in 1989 in Czechoslovakia, Tatramat, as well as other Czech and Slovak companies, went through major changes. The communist government was overthrown and Czechoslovakia began to build a democratic society and a market economy. Although restructuring was difficult, and the year of 1990 was particularly hard, Czechoslovakia was considered to be among the leading and most successful countries in transition. Martin Ciran, the director of Tatramat and, subsequently, Whirlpool Slovakia, described the situation of Tatramat at that time as follows:

*After 1988, State export subsidies that covered the difference between high domestic costs and low prices on foreign markets were gradually abolished in our country. It hit the sales of our main export article, frontloaded washing machines very strongly. At that time we realized that our products were not competitive on the open European market. We concentrated on top loaded washing machines because our main customers were all interested in top-loaders and we were able to increase the production of only one product at a time. Obviously, top-loaders and front-loaders were produced using different technology. In 1989–1990, we introduced abroad our new product, the MINI, fully designed by Tatramat. It was a failure because of its low quality and high price. It was simply an old concept; a new machine, but an old concept. Afterwards, we started to think about how to increase the competitiveness of our products. We considered the purchase of technology or licensed production. In 1989, prior to the revolution, I began looking for partners to supply technology for top-loading washing machines. We received bids from Philips, Thompson, and Zanussi. We intended to improve the technical standards of our production as well as to increase production capacity. We realized that it was not enough to produce only 200,000 units per year, because studies showed us that we had to produce more than 300,000 per year to achieve scale economies.*

Martin Ciran and other managers of the company visited the leading manufacturers of white goods in Western Europe and saw that even 300,000 washing machines per year were probably not enough. The best companies produced 600,000 to 1 million units per year. They decided hence to change their products, to increase production, to share costs, and to cut unit costs for the company to survive. Martin Ciran went on:

*In the meantime, the COMECON market collapsed. We totally lost our foreign markets for washing machines and boilers; domestic demand also went down as a result of the difficulties of the first years of transition. There were fewer apartments built, fewer weddings.... People had other troubles and preferences than the purchase of a washing machine. We lost markets, we lost customers. In 1990, we fired about 100 people; in 1991, we fired 900, from an original of 2,300. We were lucky, because such a major lay-off did not lead to any special discontent. Employees got good compensation according to the law and some of them started to run their own small private businesses, which had not been allowed under socialism. It was also a time of so-called small privatization—the privatization of small shops, services, etc. formerly owned by the State, which attracted some of our employees, too.*

One of the primary challenges in the Czechoslovak transition and in the shift toward a market economy was privatization. On October 1, 1990, the Slovak Ministry of Economy transformed Tatramat from a state enterprise into a state joint stock company. At that time, ownership of assets, in the form of shares, was transferred to the National Assets Fund, under the administration of the Slovak Ministry of Privatization. As a joint stock company, the intention was to privatize Tatramat through vouchers. Companies owned by the National Assets Funds could establish joint ventures with foreign investors only after approval by the Slovak Ministry of Privatization.

Martin Ciran recalled:

*We were transformed from a State-owned company into a State-owned joint stock company, one of the first companies in Czechoslovakia. In the meantime, the separate Czech and Slovak Governments became much stronger and federal Czechoslovak Government lost most of its power. It meant that our superior authorities were no longer the federal authorities in Prague but the Slovak authorities in Bratislava. The change of the form of the company also resulted in more power in the hands of management. We started to have a real feeling for new responsibilities, and we could do a lot of things without the approval from the State or State authorities. Although short of ownership, we had more competence and power. We could, for example, negotiate with foreign companies. After we recognized that the price for a license or a new technology was very high, we started thinking about capital investment or about a partner for a joint venture. It took us half to three-quarters of a year to understand that it would not be enough to produce new machines without access to markets. Under the new conditions brought by the revolution, it was possible to think about other forms of cooperation or alliance with foreign companies, not only about licensing. At that time, Volkswagen was preparing a deal with Skoda in the Czech Republic and with BAZ in the Slovak Republic, with the assistance of Credit Suisse First Boston. We also prepared a memorandum about us, followed by an offer for cooperation. This memorandum was sent in January 1991 to all prospective investors known worldwide, all leading companies in white goods. I cannot say that all the people in the company were eager for such cooperation with Western companies as I and my closest team were, but everybody felt it was necessary to do something.*

After receiving the memorandum, Whirlpool, Electrolux, Bosch-Siemens, and Thompson all declared their interest in possible cooperation. It is to be recalled that, at the end of the 1980s and at the beginning of the 1990s, Tatramat produced about 200,000 washing machines per year: 100,000 top-loading washing machines (the so-called MINI, 95 percent sold in the Czechoslovak market) and 100,000 front-loading machines (25 percent for the Czechoslovak market, 75 percent for exports, primarily to the socialist countries of Poland, Bulgaria, Yugoslavia, and the German Democratic Republic; only 5,000 were sold in Western markets). At that time, various problems surfaced in the factory and its environment: high fixed costs, low productivity and quality, backward technology, products unsuitable for foreign markets, the abolition of state export subsidies, the collapse of the COMECON market, and a drop in demand on the domestic market. Tatramat sales dropped from around 350,000 units in 1988 to around 220,000 units in 1991 (Table 2). Finally, the devaluation of the Czechoslovak crown in 1990 tripled production costs.

At that time, Tatramat's management realized that a single purchase of technology would not solve all its problems. Market access was needed, as well as a partner who

**TABLE 2**    Tatramat Sales, 1988–1991 ( thousand units)

| Item | 1988 | 1989 | 1990 | 1991 |
|---|---|---|---|---|
| Washing machines | 200.0 | 199.1 | 210.6 | 144.1 |
| Water heaters | 151.8 | 143.7 | 133.3 | 76.2 |

*Source: Information provided by Tatramat.*

would be able to guarantee it. Tatramat's idea shifted from a purchase of technology or licensed production to capital investment or a joint venture. During the search for the right partner, it was realized that Whirlpool was the firm most interested in improving Tatramat's management and including Tatramat in its global network.

# Motivations for an Alliance Between Whirlpool Europe B.V. and Tatramat

In 1990, the managers of WEBV realized that the changes in CEE brought about new opportunities and challenges for their company. They were attracted by the possibility of gaining new markets, as well as obtaining production facilities and a skilled labor force. Their facilities were not efficient, but they were low cost in comparison to Western Europe. The privatization of state-owned factories opened the way for potential ownership and control. However, WEBV was not driven only by external reasons. It was also forced to look at new opportunities because of its internal problems: more limited success in Western Europe than expected, disappointing operating margins, and the need to decrease costs.

## Strategic Options for Whirlpool

To solve some of these problems, WEBV could use various strategic options: exporting, joint venture, acquisition, or greenfield investment in CEE. Every option had some advantages and disadvantages:

### Exporting

- *Advantages:* Sales would increase, without assuming high risks.
- *Disadvantages:* Production costs would not be reduced; tariff barriers would remain.

### Joint venture

- *Advantages:* Access would be had to an existing facility, an existing brand, an existing labor force, an established market share, existing distribution facilities, an established local supplier base; low production costs; contact with authorities through the local partner; the potential to increase ownership control at a later stage.
- *Disadvantages:* Control would be shared, relationships and trust need to be built, labor force training would need to change local attitudes, need to overcome negative attitude toward the local brand name.

### Acquisition

- *Advantages:* Full control plus all advantages of a joint venture.
- *Disadvantages:* More resistance from the target firm and local government. In Czechoslovakia, takeovers had no precedence, resulting in more prejudice and in less motivation or cooperation by the local partner; the facility and the labor force would be more difficult to change.

### Greenfield

- *Advantages:* New facility, full control, own trained labor force, low costs.
- *Disadvantages:* No labor force at hand, more training needed, local competition, more obstacles from the government and local authorities, more expatriate staff would be needed, no inherited market share, no previous brand name recognition.

A takeover would have been the best choice for Whirlpool. However, the legal system of Czechoslovakia and the resistance of the local managers as well as the Government did not allow going for this form immediately. Therefore, the most realistic choice for Whirlpool from a strategic point of view was a joint venture, with the possibility of a gradual increase in investment until a final takeover.

## Strategic Options for Tatramat

Tatramat's reasons for entering into the joint venture could be summarized as follows: drop in domestic demand, collapse of export markets in CEE, high and growing costs, obsolete technology, risk of massive layoffs, and a need to increase production to reach scale economies. To solve its problems, Tatramat had to choose between two strategic options: licensing or joint venture. Both options had some advantages and disadvantages:

### Licensing

- *Advantages:* New technology, no partner to be accommodated, full control, access to training in technology, continued production of both washing machines and water boilers under Tatramat's control.
- *Disadvantages:* No market access, possibly high technology and license fees, no other know-how or skills inflow, no capital inflow.

### Joint venture

- *Advantages:* Technology, capital, training capacity, know-how, and market access.
- *Disadvantages:* Profits and control to be shared, eventually leading to a loss of control over the enterprise.

A joint venture seemed to be a better choice in comparison to a licensing agreement. Because the potential partners wanted only the washing machine unit, Tatramat's contribution could be only this part of production. The main question that remained was what to do with the water boiler segment. Other problems could be solved through gradually selling Tatramat's ownership to Whirlpool or by becoming a supplier to the joint venture.

### Form of the Deal

As seen from this analysis, the most suitable form for both partners was a joint venture. Tatramat was nevertheless concerned by the three conditions set by Whirlpool: the possibility of a gradual increase of Whirlpool's share in the joint venture, Whirlpool's unwillingness to include water boiler operations in the joint venture, and the call for an increase in the tariff protection of the local washing machine market. Tatramat was in a weak position vis-à-vis Whirlpool, and it decided to accept fully the first two conditions. It even managed to lobby for import tariffs.

# Anatomy of the Deal: Main Problems and Outcomes

After complex negotiations, the contractual basis for the joint venture was created at the end of 1991, and it began operations in May 1992. Whirlpool contributed know-how in technology, production, and marketing to the joint venture, and

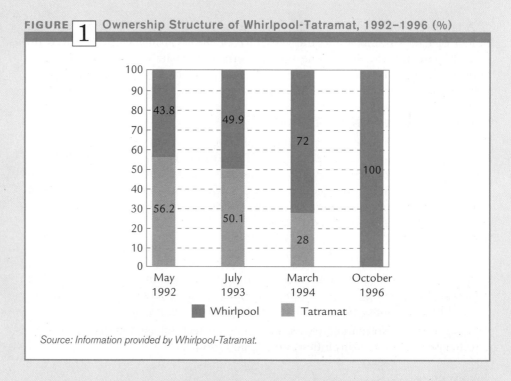

**FIGURE 1**    Ownership Structure of Whirlpool-Tatramat, 1992–1996 (%)

*Source: Information provided by Whirlpool-Tatramat.*

also bought 43.8 percent of the shares for $6 million (Figure 1). Tatramat's non-financial contribution consisted of intellectual property rights in the area of washing machine production, goodwill, buildings, machinery, land, and contracts. It kept 56.2 percent of the shares of the joint venture. The original agreement was signed for ten years.

With Whirlpool's investment, the original Tatramat company split into three separate entities: (1) the joint venture Whirlpool-Tatramat became the number one washing machine producer in both the Slovak and Czech Republics; (2) Tatramat itself continued to produce water heaters; and (3) Tatramat-Quasar, a small joint venture with an Italian partner, continued to produce vending machines.

Whirlpool-Tatramat became a separate organization with its own sales staff and after-sales service. Whirlpool-Tatramat produced two types of top-loading washing machines: the old Tatramat MINI (under Tatramat's brand name), and the Whirlpool T-12 (under the Whirlpool-Philips brand name). The first T-12 rolled off the line in October 1992. Even though results improved over time, the number of units produced in 1993 (59,000 MINIs and 39,000 T-12s) was below expectations.

Not only quantity but also quality became a critical problem in Poprad. As WEBV envisaged broadening Poprad's role to an international production platform for Western markets, the quality of Poprad's products had to meet the strict demands of Whirlpool and its customers. Quality had improved at Poprad during the years 1992 and 1993 but not enough, forcing them to sell to mostly Czech and Slovak customers.

Employment levels significantly dropped after the establishment of the joint venture. Initially, 550 employees were transferred from Tatramat to the joint venture, and the remaining 750 employees stayed on the payroll of the Slovak parent company. In the case of management staff, Tatramat did not want to lose its best employees to Whirlpool-Tatramat, and therefore any transfer of white-collar workers was subject to its approval.

By 1993, employment at the joint venture was down to 219.[3] However, productivity increased from 153 units per employee in 1992 to 199 units in 1993.

In July 1993 Whirlpool transferred $1.5 million to the joint venture, increasing its share in the joint venture to 49.9 percent (Figure 1). This amount was invested into a partial transfer of "hard" technology.

The external conditions of the joint venture also experienced a drastic change. In 1993, as a consequence of the division of Czechoslovakia, the local market for Whirlpool-Tatramat, with its location in Slovakia, diminished by two-thirds with the loss of the Czech Republic. However, Tatramat's brand name still enjoyed high name recognition in the Czech Republic, and the company maintained distribution facilities there. To catch up with the political changes, including new borders, and to avoid losses resulting from worsened operational conditions, Whirlpool-Tatramat established its own affiliate in the Czech Republic in May 1993.

Despite the loss of about $1.5 million in the first full year of operations, Whirlpool increased its share in the joint venture to 72 percent in February 1994 (Figure 1). Before Whirlpool's stake reached two-thirds of the joint venture, Tatramat had the right to nominate the chairperson of the board of directors and two other board members, compared to two seats for Whirlpool. After having obtained the two-thirds majority, Whirlpool got the chairpersonship plus two additional seats. Moreover, as soon as Whirlpool reached two-thirds in the joint venture, the joint venture agreement allowed it to decide, without the approval of Tatramat, on most important issues, such as plans, major contracts, and financing. As Martin Ciran, managing director of Whirlpool-Tatramat since the beginning of its operations, recalled: "We were aware of the necessity of performance improvement, but we did not want to have our hands tied up by Tatramat, which faced big economic troubles at that time."

In 1994, production experienced moderate growth, with the production of T-12 more than doubling to 95,000 units (Table 3). The joint venture also produced the 11,000 MINIs that year, but it was the last year that the model was manufactured. The MINI was abandoned due to poor design, quality, declining sales, and thin margins. Initially, in 1992 and 1993, the Whirlpool-Tatramat assembled washing machines from kits imported from Amiens, France, where the T-12 was also made. The joint venture produced only the T-12 in 1995 and 1996.

In October 1996, Whirlpool bought out the remaining shares and became the sole owner of the company (Figure 1). The name was changed to Whirlpool Slovakia, and its headquarters and national sales office were moved from Poprad to the capital city, Bratislava. The following year the company exceeded, for the first time, the production targets outlined in the original joint venture agreement. A new front-loading model, the Tatry, was introduced in 1997 and production reached over half a million washing machines in 1998 and nearly one million by the year

**TABLE 3**   Whirlpool-Tatramat's and Whirlpool Slovakia's Production, 1992–2000 ( thousand units)

| Type | Brand | 1992 | 1993 | 1994 | 1995 | 1996 | 1997 | 1998 | 1999 | 2000 |
|------|-------|------|------|------|------|------|------|------|------|------|
| MINI | Tatramat | 74 | 59 | 16 | – | – | – | – | – | – |
| TL* | Whirlpool Ignis | 5 | 39 | 93 | 8,149 | 267 | 349 | 381 | 495 | 585 |
| FL | Whirlpool Ignis | – | – | – | – | – | 1 | 140 | 275 | 360 |
| Total |  | 79 | 98 | 111 | 219 | 267 | 350 | 521 | 770 | 945 |

*Note: TL: top-loaders, FL: front-loaders. The model T-12 has been produced since the beginning. In 1998, other top-loaders (Kireco and Alliance) were introduced.

Source: Information provided by Whirlpool Slovakia.

2000. Although the capacity at Poprad made it the smallest of Whirlpool's European manufacturing centers, it remains the lowest-cost production facility.

# Operational Issues

Since 1994, Poprad has begun to integrate vertically, producing more of its components in-house in an effort to reduce its reliance on the expensive Amiens components. Components account for 80 percent of a machine's costs. This, together with transport distance, customs regulations, and problems with timely delivery from the Amiens site, led to a decision to source as much as possible locally. While local content was only 3 percent in the first year, it reached 12 percent in 1994, 37 percent by the end of 1995, and 60 percent by the middle of 1997. This share has been maintained since then. In the mid-1990s, the plant had only 14 local suppliers; by 2000, it had 35.

With the creation of a local supplier network, the company succeeded in increasing production flexibility, reducing costs, and avoiding import restrictions such as duty and import surcharges.

The total equity investment of Whirlpool, including the initial investment and the equity increases, reached about $11 million (including technology capitalized at $3 million) by 1996. The joint venture invested $14 million into production in 1992 to 1995. In the years 1996 through 1998, the company planned significant investments into new front-loading machines (the so-called Delta). This project was supposed to introduce a completely new front-loading machine for the European market. Later, Project Delta was changed to Project Tatry, with less investment and different technology, producing low-end front-loading washing machines. Investment into this model reached about $10 million by 1997. To prepare for the launching of this product, changes had to be made to production areas and technology, and a semirobotic line for assembling was installed.

The total amount of Whirlpool investment into the Poprad plant reached $36 million by the year 2000. In comparison to hard technology, soft technology transfer has been more pronounced. Whirlpool introduced its management and incentive structures in Poprad. The company stressed the importance of communication with workers. Face-to-face meetings with management took place, explaining human resources practices previously unknown to the employees. After the first shock from Western management style in 1992 and 1993, employment gradually grew.

The human resources department adopted new policies, such as performance evaluation, pay for performance, a "recognition policy" to reward hard work and innovation, and gain-sharing schemes in which additional wages were linked to company profits. It also emphasized the need for improving inter- and intradepartmental communication and for training on specialized topics, such as teamwork, decision making, and individual thinking.

White-collar workers were trained in basic business skills, market economics, quality management, supplier quality, ISO 9000, English, computer skills, and Whirlpool philosophy and corporate culture. These training programs were intended to increase managers' commitment to the firm and to spread the new corporate philosophy among workers. People were taught how to communicate, organize their workplace, and increase productivity and the quality of work.

Additionally, the human resources department provided introductory courses on the Whirlpool Excellence System (WES). These courses were popular among Whirlpool Slovakia employees. According to the managers, it became a valuable tool for improving the work of the company. The region of Poprad had an unemployment rate of about 17 percent, and for Whirlpool this meant the possibility to ensure flexible work practices.

The human resources department received 400–500 job applications annually. Seventy percent of the candidates completed high school education. Currently, workers' wages consist of a fixed part (73 percent on average) and a collective bonus (27 percent), depending on productivity, flexibility, quality, and the level of absenteeism. A collective bonus was chosen as a way of encouraging cooperation among employees to work more efficiently at a lower level of absenteeism.

Since work there is considered to be intense, most employees at the Poprad plant are young, with an average age of 28 years. The average manager is 38 years old, which is also considered to be young. This may reflect the fact that only young people were willing to join a terra incognita—a joint venture—when the joint venture was established in 1992. They were trained by Whirlpool and were able to take their new positions quickly. In comparison to the Slovak average, they are well paid. During the first six years of Whirlpool's operations in Slovakia, only one employee had left the company. Currently, there is only one expatriate in Slovakia, an Italian national who serves as plant director in Poprad.

The joint venture was established with the aim to reach the productivity levels that were typical of other Whirlpool plants in Europe. The productivity in Poprad's plant increased significantly from 153 pieces per employee in 1992 to 199 in 1993 and to 323 in 1994. It reached 927 pieces per employee in 1997, which is far above the expectation and levels in similar plants (Table 3). Product quality has been a critical aspect of production at Poprad. As WEBV intended to expand Poprad's role as an international production center to serve Western markets, Poprad's products had to meet Whirlpool's global quality requirements. Quality improvements in Poprad have been attributed to the training of employees in quality concepts, in-process checks, and vertical integration, including greater internal control over the quality of components. During production, every machine is tested electronically, and 10 percent are taken off the assembly line and tested for 50 cycles. Additionally, 3 percent out of the 10 percent taken from the line are taken to the factory reliability lab where they are run through 250 cycles (corresponding to one year's usage) or 2,500 cycles (ten year's usage).

During the two first years (1992–1993), the company operated only in the Czech and Slovak markets because product quality at that time was too low to guarantee exports. In 1994, the company started to sell in Poland, Hungary, and Argentina. In 1995, it entered into the Western European market. In 2000, about 90 percent of the output of Poprad was exported through the corporate distribution network. On balance, Whirlpool-Tatramat proved to be successful. Its performance has gradually improved. Its WES score rose from 238 in 1993 to 702 in 1997. Even the best Whirlpool plant in Europe managed to score only slightly better in 1997 (850). According to Whirlpool managers, the performance of Poprad has remained at the same high level since then.

# Reasons for the Takeover of the Joint Venture by Whirlpool

The following reasons for the full takeover of the joint venture by Whirlpool could be identified:

*   *The global strategy of Whirlpool.* Whirlpool and Tatramat were two unequal partners with two different goals. Since the beginning, the goal of Whirlpool was a

gradual increase of its share in the joint venture with the aim of taking it over. It is consistent with its worldwide strategy of acquisitions and global control.

- *The economic problems of Tatramat.* Tatramat was not able to keep its share in the joint venture. In 1993, when it was time for the first significant investment to increase productivity, Tatramat was unable to contribute. This situation propelled a gradual increase in the share of Whirlpool in the joint venture. Under the worsened conditions, the goals of Tatramat to continue washing machine production and to survive the transition could be reached only at the expense of losing control over the joint venture. The hopes of Tatramat's management to obtain the dividends from a profitable joint venture and to improve its own difficult economic situation were not realized.

At the beginning of its operations, the joint venture was in the red, and the only way for Tatramat to get some cash was to sell its shares to the other partner. With this deal, each party nevertheless satisfied at least some of their needs: Whirlpool established production in a low-cost country, benefited from the local skilled labor force, reached a new market, and created a new export base for other countries. Tatramat avoided going into bankruptcy and received cash and knowledge in various areas, including marketing, management, and production.

# Factors of Success at Whirlpool Slovakia

## A Manager's Point of View

According to Martin Ciran:

> The very comprehensive and detailed joint venture agreement consisting of 30 pages and four appendices worked out by English lawyers from the Scadden Arps Company was one of the reasons for the success of the company. In each case of a misunderstanding, we referred to this agreement, and it really showed us the way out. On the other hand, you have several cases in Slovakia where a joint venture broke up because of a non-qualified agreement. After the collapse of the centrally run economy, the establishment of joint ventures was marked by a lack of hands-on experience on the Slovak side. Due to a shortage of reputable and experienced law firms, we chose a foreign company to draft the agreement and it was really worthwhile.

There is still more to that story. Martin Ciran described other success factors:

> Based on the joint venture agreement and the follow-up development of the ownership structure, the parent company Whirlpool practically had full managing and decision-making power in the company. Its approach has been very transparent and we got all the necessary knowledge and skills through training and technology transfer. On the other hand, Whirlpool's headquarters in Italy had agreed to the use and application of this knowledge. I would say mutual trust has been one of the basic points of our success. Furthermore, our people have been eager to learn and to apply new procedures. It was also essential that top management of the joint venture was young and not "afflicted by socialist working practices." It identified very quickly with the Whirlpool philosophy and corporate culture. The managers have transferred these values to other employees. We have implemented a new management system known as the Whirlpool Excellence System, quickly and successfully. In my opinion, the greatest change since the Tatramat days has not been in technological innovation or investment but in employee attitudes. The new thinking of our employees and their accomplishments in improving the working conditions at the facility and in making the production

*lines more flexible set the company apart from most of the other firms in Slovakia today. On top of that, the next very important success factor has been "not over investing." In other words, our company has a big cost advantage in comparison to Western European producers because of low debts. With high investment we would lose this advantage.*

## A Broader Approach to Success Factors

Even though Martin Ciran mentioned many success factors, it is necessary to add that the story started with the investment of Whirlpool into a local monopoly producer. Hence, an immediate market share was guaranteed for the joint venture. This was important especially at the beginning of the operations when it was not possible to export products abroad due to their low quality. The monopoly position was also guaranteed in the joint venture agreement stipulating a noncompetition clause. It did not allow the Slovak parent company to produce washing machines and excluded competition between affiliates and parent companies. Whirlpool could also realize classical first mover advantages. The combination of a monopoly position, low-cost production, and first mover advantages has contributed to the success of Whirlpool Slovakia. It is interesting to note that Whirlpool insisted on market protection, but this was automatically abolished in the Czech Republic after the split of Czechoslovakia and did not play any special role in Slovakia. The firm maintained its market share simply because imported goods were too expensive for the average Slovak costumer at the beginning of the 1990s. There were no other classical incentives (such as tax holidays) provided to Whirlpool.

# The Performance of the Slovak Parent Company

The managers of Whirlpool were satisfied with the evolution of Whirlpool-Tatramat and later Whirlpool Slovakia. However, the situation in the Slovak parent company, Tatramat, has proved to be more complex. With the creation of the joint venture Whirlpool-Tatramat and the splitting of the old Tatramat into washing machines and boilers production, the parent company Tatramat entered into a period of difficulties. The parent company Tatramat tried to adjust to its joint ventures with foreign partners. At the beginning of the 1990s, in addition to Whirlpool-Tatramat, it established Tatramat-Quasar, which produced vending machines with an Italian partner. At a later stage, it also established Scame-Tatramat with an Italian partner to produce plastic parts. As activities moved out from the parent firm into the joint ventures, Tatramat experienced a large decline in its labor force, especially in the first half of the 1990s, and at one point even faced bankruptcy. As initially expected, the sense of rivalry, jealousy, and competition between Whirlpool-Tatramat and its Slovak parent company evolved during the first year of operations: Tatramat, located in the neighborhood of Whirlpool, has become its main local supplier. According to the Slovak managers of Whirlpool, Whirlpool's orders placed in Tatramat and its ventures created employment for about 200 persons there. Besides that, they argued that Whirlpool contributed to the creation of 400 more jobs in other Slovak companies. This means that one workplace established in Whirlpool created another job in supplier, service, or distribution companies doing business with or for Whirlpool. In the end, Tatramat survived its period of transition. In 2000, it reported a turnover of about $11 million, of which 75 percent came from export sales. It recorded a pretax profit of $0.15 million (compared with a loss of $0.6 million in 1997) with 520 employees.

# Conclusions

The acquisition of Tatramat by Whirlpool is only one example out of many: Since the middle of the 1990s, the strategy of investors in Slovakia has changed, especially among large multinational corporations (MNCs). The new trend is characterized by incremental takeovers. In several instances in the late 1990s, MNCs (including the biggest investor in manufacturing, Volkswagen) steadily increased their equity shares in joint ventures in Slovakia. There are a number of reasons for this new trend:

- The global strategies of MNCs.
- The weak, unequal position of the local partners in comparison to their foreign partners.
- The conflicts between the Slovak and foreign partners over the joint venture strategy.
- Conflicts over the control of key or common services such as energy, telecommunications, and security (joint ventures are usually situated in the former plants of Slovak parent companies).
- Conflicts over pricing and transferring profits abroad.
- A lack of experience by local companies in how to deal with these issues (under socialism, cooperation with Western companies was not permitted).
- The inability or unwillingness of the Slovak partners to maintain their shares in the joint ventures.
- Financial difficulties of the Slovak partners, forcing them to sell their shares in the joint ventures to their foreign partners.
- The success of MNCs in establishing their own communication channels with the authorities, in building positive public relations and in finding local managers for top positions, resulting in less reliance on local partners in these areas.
- The recognition by MNCs that the transition process is irreversible and thus risk sharing with local partners was no longer necessary.

Most multinational companies that first established a joint venture with local partners in Slovakia have, in the meantime, moved into the acquisition of shares (Whirlpool-Tatramat, Volkswagen-BAZ, Alcatel SELTesla, Henkel-Palma, Hoechst-Biotika, etc.). There are only a few exceptions, usually based on legal constraints, such as state participation in the telecommunication industry. Moreover, this situation is typical not only for Slovakia, but also for many other transition economies in CEE.

Like the best-known examples in Slovakia (Whirlpool and Volkswagen), similar developments occurred, for example, in Hungary with General Electric-Tungsram, in Poland with Gerber, and in the Czech Republic with Philip Morris. As soon as multinational companies became sole owners, they tended to invest more into technology (however, they usually tried not to "over invest," i.e., not to lose the cost advantage and not to replace cheap labor by machinery). Most governments seem to have no policy to prevent an "incremental takeover." Moreover, entry into the European Union and the acceptance of its legal framework may further limit the possibilities to block such acquisitions.

# Epilogue: Whirlpool Slovakia in the New Century

At the turn of the century (years 1999, 2000, 2001), Whirlpool Slovakia produced around 1 million units yearly. In 2002 the production reached 1.2 million units, half of that top-loaders and another half front-loaders. In 2003 production reached 1.5 million pieces and the company employed more than 800 employees. Since 2004 Whirlpool Europe decided to shift all the production of washing machines in the group to Slovakia (e.g., 300,000 units from Amiens, 150,000 from Polar), and the capacity was removed from Neukirchen to Poprad.

From 2004 until 2008, Whirlpool Slovakia produced almost 2 million units each year (slightly more top-loaders than front-loaders every year); for example, in 2008 the total production was 1.97 million washing machines. In 1998 the company produced the millionth piece in its history, and in 2008 the 15 millionth washing machine produced in Poprad ran off the production line.

In 2004–2008, the company employed about 1,200 people directly, and about 1,800 employees worked in the Poprad area for the suppliers of Whirlpool Slovakia (such as Tatramat, Pascal, Sagit, Cima, AZD). Three to four percent of the yearly production is sold on the domestic market; about 96–97 percent of the production is shipped to Africa, Asia, Latin America—to almost 30 countries.

Planned yearly capacity for Whirlpool Slovakia is 2.2 million units; some managers even talked about 4 million units in the future.

*Plainly, the operation of Whirlpool has changed from a market-seeking to a fully low-cost-seeking operation.*

The year 2008 meant a new landmark in the history of Whirlpool Slovakia. The company has opened a new central warehouse of 24,000 square meters in Lozorno in Western Slovakia, to which the Whirlpool products from nine European factories and China are shipped and from where about 1.5 million of Whirlpool white appliances for Czech, Slovak, Hungarian, and Austrian markets are distributed.

There is an interesting story related to the acquisition of Polar in Poland: Polar was on the radar screen of Whirlpool Europe early in the nineties, but at that time the top management decided not to engage the company because of the strong trade unions and low willingness of the then Polish management to work with a foreign investor. Later, Thomson Electric, a French company, acquired Polar, but the deal ended up in economic problems: When Whirlpool Europe was buying Polar, it had the value $28 million and was $14 million in debt; so the company put itself for sale for $42 million. At that time Whirlpool Europe was trying to find a company in Central and Eastern Europe where it could localize refrigerators production for all of Europe (based on a very good experience from Slovakia, where a major production site for washing machines was created).

There was a cheap refrigerator company for sale in Slovakia, the former Calex company whose value decreased after an unsuccessful joint venture with Samsung. The local Slovak management, led by Martin Ciran, was trying to persuade Whirlpool Europe to buy it. Even though the success of Whirlpool in Slovakia was undeniable and the country at that time had a very progressive government introducing many market-oriented reforms and one of the best business environments in Europe, Whirlpool Europe decided to buy a much more expensive

Polish facility instead. The reasons may be seen in risk diversification and the relatively big size of the Polish market.

*Plainly, Central and Eastern Europe has become more and more attractive for big MNCs as a location of production for the whole European market. The advantages of the CEE countries, such as relatively cheap and skilled labor, even increased since 2004 when Poland and Slovakia (together with other CEE countries) entered the European Union.*

Since that time many producers, especially from outside of the EU (the United States, Asia), established their major European production and distribution centers in CEE (e.g., Sony, Samsung, Hundayi, Kia, Panasonic).

## CASE DISCUSSION QUESTIONS

1. Would you have recommended a greenfield investment strategy for Whirlpool Slovakia rather than a joint venture? Explain your answer.
2. Would you have recommended a direct acquisition of Tatramat for Whirlpool rather than a joint venture? Explain your answer.
3. How would you assess the control versus risk tradeoff by Whirlpool?

## CASE CREDIT

Sonia Ferencikova. 2002. "Transition at Whirlpool-Tatramat: From joint venture to acquisition." *Transnational Corporations,* 1, 1, pp. 69–98. Used with permission of the author.

## CASE NOTES

[1]Whirlpool Corporation. 1996. *Annual Report 1996.* Benton Harbor, MI: Whirlpool Corporation.

[2]Whirlpool Corporation. 1998. *Annual Report* 1997. Benton Harbor, MI: Whirlpool Corporation, p. 4.

[3]William Davidson Institute. 1994. *Whirlpool Tatramat, a.s.* Mimeo. Ann Arbor, MI: William Davidson Institute, University of Michigan School of Business Administration.

[4]Maruca, Regina Fazio. 1994. "The right way to go global: Interview with the Whirlpool CEO David Whitman." *Harvard Business Review,* 72, March–April, pp. 135–145.

[5]Steinmetz, Greg and Carl Quintanilla. 1998. "Tough target." *Wall Street Journal Europe,* 16, 50, p. 1.

[6]Whirlpool Corporation. 1998. Vision, 1, 2 (March–April).

[7]Whirlpool Corporation. 1999. *Annual Report 1998.* Benton Harbor, MI: Whirlpool Corporation.

# Strategy Implementation for Multinational Companies: Human Resource Management

*part four*

Cuiphoto/Shutterstock.com

# 11 International Human Resource Management

## Learning Objectives

*After reading this chapter you should be able to:*

- Know the basic functions of human resource management.

- Define international human resource management.

- Understand how international human resource management differs from domestic human resource management.

- Know the types of workers that multinational companies use.

- Explain how and when multinational companies decide to use expatriate managers.

- Know the skills necessary for a successful expatriate assignment.

- Understand how expatriate managers are compensated and evaluated.

- Appreciate the issues regarding expatriate assignments for female managers.

- Know what companies can do to make expatriate assignments easier for their female expatriates.

- Understand the relationship between choice of a multinational strategy and international human resource management.

*Preview*  CASE IN POINT

### Fast-Track Global Multinationals

U.S. companies and other multinationals around the world are increasingly relying on expatriates to run their overseas operations. As these companies search for new customers and markets abroad, they have a growing need for managers with the necessary skills for global assignments. In fact, recent studies by a large number of consulting firms, among them Mercer Consulting, suggest that an increasing number of multinationals are relying on expatriate assignments to achieve their goals. Clearly, properly managing expatriates presents both significant opportunities and challenges.

Companies with serious ambitions to become key global competitors are devoting significant resources to managing international assignments. Consider the expatriate management program of DuPont, which routinely sends its employees on international assignments. For example, engineers from Mexico and the United States may be sent to work in a chemical plant in China. Such international assignments pose challenges because DuPont must deal with multiple nationalities within the same assignment. Instead of allowing each country or division to set its own policies, DuPont is finding that having a standardized international assignment policy works well for its 300 to 400 international assignments each year. DuPont's Global Transfer Center of Expertise manages all aspects of the program, from preparing the candidates for the international assignment to finding educational opportunities for the candidates' children.

Many companies are also seeing a key trend in expatriate assignments. Consider the case of the U.K.-based multinational KPMG. The company has around 300 expatriates filling posts abroad. However, it also has around 350 inbound expatriates working in the United Kingdom. The most telling trend for KPMG has been the dramatic increase in postings in countries such as China (25 percent increase), South Africa (52 percent increase) and Brazil. In contrast, expatriate postings to countries such as the United States and the rest of Europe have dropped.

*Sources: Based on Hamm, S. 2008. "International is't just IBM's first name." Business-Week, January 28, 36–40; Minton-Eversole, T. 2009. "Overseas assignments keep pace." HR Magazine, 72–74; Mercer Consulting http://www.mercer.com; Syedain, H. 2012. "From expats to global citizens." People Management, January, online edition.*

The Preview Case in Point shows that more and more multinationals are seeking internationally experienced managerial talent to run their operations in the global market. Furthermore, as the BRIC countries continue their sustained growth, multinationals are also fielding an increasing number of employees in these countries. This emphasis on building such talent comes from the increasing popularity of multinational strategies in response to a globalizing world economy. However, there are many challenges inherent in this approach. A key ingredient of implementing any successful multinational strategy includes using compatible human resource management (HRM) policies. Multinationals will have to get creative to manage the workforce adequately.

This chapter first presents a basic definition of international human resource management and shows how it differs from its strictly domestic counterpart. The chapter then discusses how multinational companies must choose a mixture of employees and managers of different nationalities to set up operations overseas. Particular attention is given to the role, selection, training, and evaluation of multinational managers in international assignments. Also explained are issues regarding women with international postings and the uniquely difficult conditions that female expatriates face. The chapter concludes with a discussion of the four basic orientations of international human resource management and how each supports multinational strategies.

# International Human Resource Management Defined

Business organizations necessarily combine physical assets (e.g., buildings and machines) and financial assets, as well as technological and managerial processes, to perform work. However, without people, the organizations would not exist. Managing and developing human assets are the major goals of **human resource management (HRM)**, which deals with the overall relationship of the employee with the organization. The basic HRM functions are recruitment (identification of qualified individuals for a vacant position), selection (choosing an individual for the position), training (providing opportunities to help the individual perform), performance appraisal (assessing the individual's performance), compensation (providing the adequate reward package), and labor relations (the relationship between the individual and the company).[1]

## International Human Resource Management and International Employees

When applied to the international setting, the HRM functions make up **international human resource management (IHRM).** When a company enters the international arena, all the basic HRM activities remain, but they take on added complexity for two reasons. First, the employees of multinational organizations include a mixture of workers of different nationalities. Second, multinational managers must decide how necessary it is to adapt the company's HRM policies to the national cultures, business cultures, and social institutions where the company is doing business.

## Types of Employees in Multinational Organizations

IHRM must take into account several types of employees in the multinational organization. Expatriate employees come from a country that is different from the one

**Human resource management (HRM)**
Recruitment, selection, training and development, performance appraisal, compensation, and labor relations.

**International human resource management (IHRM)**
All the HRM functions, adapted to the international setting.

**Expatriate**
Employee who comes from a country that is different from the one in which he or she is currently working.

**Home country national**
Expatriate employee who comes from the parent firm's home country.

**Third country nationals**
Expatriate workers who come from neither the host nor home country.

**Host country nationals**
Local workers who come from the host country where the unit (plant, sales unit, etc.) is located.

**Inpatriate**
Employees from foreign countries who work in the country where the parent company is located.

**Flexpatriates**
Employees who are sent on frequent but short-term international assignments.

**International cadre**
Managers who specialize in international assignments.

**Commuter assignments employees**
Are employees who live in one country but spend at least part of the working week in another country.

in which they are working. Expatriate employees who come from the parent firm's home country are called **home country nationals.**

Expatriate workers who come from neither the host nor the home country are called **third country nationals.** Local workers who come from the host country where the unit (plant, sales unit, etc.) is located are **host country nationals.** Usually, home country and third country expatriates belong to the managerial and professional staff rather than to the lower-level workforce. The globalization of the workforce also is breeding a special type of expatriate called the **inpatriate.** Inpatriates are employees from foreign countries who work in the country where the parent company is located. Recent trends also suggest a new breed of workers known as **flexpatriates.**[2] Flexpatriates are employees who are sent on frequent short-term international assignments. Finally, multinational companies have created a separate group of managers who specialize in international assignments, called the **international cadre,** or *globals.* Members of the international cadre have permanent international assignments. They are recruited from any country and are sent to worldwide locations to develop cross-cultural skills and to give the company a worldwide perspective.[3] Finally, a new breed of employees is now emerging. **Commuter assignments employees** are employees who live in one country but spend at least part of the working week in another country; they represent a trend that is growing in popularity. Syedain (2012) reports that 45 percent of European companies and 35 percent of American companies are now making use of such commuter assignment employees (Syedain, 2012).

# Multinational Managers: Expatriate or the Host Country

U.S. companies employ more than seven million people outside the United States. Although most of these employees are lower-level workers, they require a significant number of managers. When are the management positions filled by expatriates? When are they filled by host country nationals? Deciding how many expatriates or local managers to use depends mostly on a company's multinational strategy. Transnational strategists see their managerial recruits as employable anywhere in the world. Multidomestic strategists tend to favor local managers or use expatriates only for short-term assignments. Regardless of multinational strategy, management teams usually contain a mixture of expatriate and host country nationals. For a particular position, a firm might approach its staffing decisions by answering questions like the following:[4]

- *Given our strategy, what is our preference for this position (host country, home country, or third country national)?* For example, a company with a regional strategy may favor the use of third country nationals as country-level managers.

For expatriate managers (parent country or third country nationals):

- *Is there an available pool of managers with the appropriate skills for the position?* To use expatriate managers, a company must have qualified and available managers within its own ranks, or it must be able to recruit qualified parent company or third country managers to fill open positions.

- *Are these managers willing to take expatriate assignments?* Not all managers will take assignments abroad. Some managers believe that international assignments can hurt their advancement at home. Increasing numbers of managers have employed spouses, making it impossible to take international assignments. However, such mindsets will likely change in the future. Consider the following Case in Point.

C A S E   I N   P O I N T

### Generational Differences and International Assignments

A frequent assumption of traditional expatriate research is that employees are reluctant to go on foreign assignments. Such reluctance comes from the perception that such assignments may hurt one's career. However, recent surveys suggest that there are potential generational differences regarding how different generations view such international assignments. Baby boomers (born between 1946 and 1964), the generation now nearing retirement, were likely to take international assignments. However, they preferred to be "looked after" with significant packages and most were encouraged to take international assignments with generous relocation packages. In contrast, Generation X (born between 1965 and 1980) were also happy to go international, given the right package. However, they expected to look after themselves.

Most multinationals are now concerned about the millennials (born after 1981), individuals who will make up the majority of international assignments within the next 10–15 years. These individuals have a very different mindset than previous generations. Rather than viewing international assignments as an unnecessary evil, they are more likely to see such assignments as necessary and a taken-for-granted aspect of employment. Furthermore, they are also more likely to see companies as being without boundaries. As such, compared to previous generations, they are much more likely to be open to international assignments and also see such assignments as critical to their personal development. Additionally, in contrast to previous generations that would be motivated mostly by financial incentives to go abroad, millennials are more likely to seek interesting assignments that present opportunities. Thus, as the need for talent intensifies, multinationals will have to become increasingly creative in offering the right packages as they compete for rare talent.

To give you insights on how willing millennials are to take international assignments, Exhibit 11.1 shows the percentage of such individuals willing to work outside of their home countries as surveyed in different countries.

*Sources: Based on PriceWaterHouseCoopers. 2012. "Talent mobility 2020." Accessed online http://www.pwc.com; and Syedain, H. 2012. "From expats to global citizens." People Management, January, online edition.*

---

- *Do any laws affect our assignments of expatriate managers?* Some countries have strict restrictions on foreigners taking employment. Temporary work visas may be difficult or impossible for employees to obtain.

For host country managers:

- *Do our host country managers have the expertise for the position?* To use host country managers, the local labor pool must have available managers with the training and expertise to fill open positions. Host country managers often lack the expertise of managers from multinational companies.

- *Can we recruit managers with the desired skills from outside our firm?* Even if qualified managerial talent exists in a country, a foreign multinational might not have the reputation or the local connections to attract host country managerial talent. For example, in Japan, many college graduates are reluctant to work for foreign multinationals because they do not provide the security of Japanese companies.

## Is the Expatriate Worth It?

IHRM decisions regarding the use of expatriate managers must take into account the costs of the assignments. The total compensation of expatriate managers often is three to four times higher than home-based salaries and benefits. Extremely costly locations such as China can be even higher. In China, for example, a

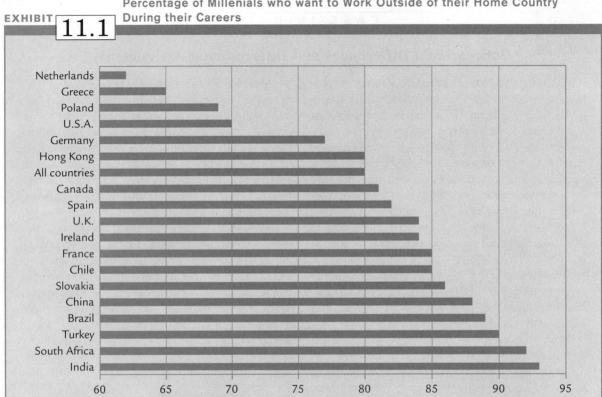

**EXHIBIT 11.1**

Percentage of Millenials who want to Work Outside of their Home Country During their Careers

*Source: Based on PriceWaterHouseCoopers. 2010. "Talent mobility 2020." Accessed online http://www.pwc.com.*

bilingual senior U.S. executive can expect a base salary approaching $400,000; hardship allowances as high as 35 percent of salary; two free houses (one in Hong Kong for the weekends and one in China); and chauffeur-driven cars.[5] An expatriate manager with a base salary of $100,000 and a family of four can cost as much as $360,000 in Tokyo, $275,000 in Hong Kong, $210,000 in Singapore, and $250,000 in London. Consider that a Pacific Northwest manufacturing company was spending about $500,000 for its expatriate's salary.[6]

The compensation packages of expatriates depend on the cost of living in the host country. The Economist Intelligence Unit also develops a cost-of-living index based on the most expensive cities in the world. They use New York as the base to determine how much more expensive other cities are. Exhibit 11.2 shows the 10 most and least expensive cities as ranked by the Economist Intelligence Unit. As the exhibit shows, of the many cities surveyed by the Economist, Zurich is the most expensive city for multinational companies to send expatriates. Furthermore, many of the world's most expensive cities are located in more mature markets. In contrast, many of the world's least expensive cities are located in emerging markets such as India and other middle Eastern nations.

In addition to the high costs of relocating expatriates, more multinationals are now concerned about expatriate safety worldwide. Consider the following Focus on Emerging Markets.

Even with such high costs, the success of an expatriate assignment is not guaranteed. U.S. companies in particular have poor records of expatriate success when

**EXHIBIT 11.2**    **Expatriate Success Factors and Selection Methods**

| Ten Most Expensive Cities | Ten least expensive Cities |
|---|---|
| Zurich, Switzerland | Muscat, Amman |
| Tokyo, Japan | Dhaka, Bangladesh |
| Geneva, Switzerland | Algiers, Algeria |
| Osak Kobe, Japan | Kathmandu, Nepal |
| Oslo, Norway | Panama City, Panama |
| Paris, France | Jeddah, Saudi Arabia |
| Sydney, Australia | New Delhi, India |
| Melbourne, Australia | Tehran, Iran |
| Singapore, Singapore | Mumbai, India |
| Frankfurt, Germany | Karachi, Pakistan |

*Source: Based on Economist Intelligence Unit. 2012. "Worldwide cost of living 2012." http://www. eiu.com.*

## Focus on Emerging Markets

### Expatriates and Safety

More multinationals now have to contend with the costs associated with keeping their expatriate workers safe. Consider the case of Chinese multinationals. As the scope of Chinese investments has grown abroad, Chinese citizens have increasingly become targets in troubled countries. For instance, assailants in Egypt recently kidnapped around 25 Chinese workers. In Sudan, around 29 Chinese workers were kidnapped by Sudanese rebels. As the Chinese continue to toil to break into markets traditionally ignored by Western companies, they are thus becoming easy targets for those seeking financial benefits.

Western and U.S. multinationals also have to fear for their expatriates. Consider the potential for violence and unrest in countries where expatriates are being posted. For instance, the recent bombing in Mumbai, India, has shed light on the potential for terrorism. Mexico has seen over 5400 people murdered because of the drug wars. The potential for kidnappings has increased; executives for companies such as Adobe and Satyam have been kidnapped in high-risk areas. In Moscow, a suicide bomber killed 42 people and paralyzed the airport.

Multinationals are clearly responsible for ensuring the safety of their employees. To prevent kidnapping in Brazil, executive-level expatriates are offered chauffeured, bullet-proof cars followed by vehicles with bodyguards. Other companies are purchasing annual memberships in companies that can provide quick emergency services in foreign locales. Consider that in the United Kingdom, employers are responsible for the health and safety of their employees anywhere in the world. In 2008, the Corporate Man-slaughter Act was passed, placing the responsibility for safety and health on employers. Companies are therefore well advised to properly train their employees to deal with emergencies and other unexpected events such as earthquakes, demonstrations etc.

*Sources: Based on Martin, H. 2011. "Training for safety abroad." May, http://www.trainingjournal.com; Mueller, S. 2006. "Shoring up protection for overseas employees." Risk Management, 53(3): 38–41; Spegele, B., P. Wonacott, and N. Bariyo. 2012. "China's workers are targeted as its overseas reach grows." Wall Street Journal, February 1, online edition.*

compared with European and Japanese multinational companies. Surveys show that U.S. multinationals often have failure rates for managers in overseas assignments ranging from 10 to 40 percent,[7] while other international surveys reveal that 83 percent of companies surveyed experienced expatriate failure.[8] A more recent study showed that 21 percent of companies surveyed had expatriates leave in the middle of their international assignments.[9] Clearly, ensuring expatriate success is a major challenge for companies.

Although it has been traditionally assumed that expatriates fail because they are not adequately prepared for their foreign assignments, other factors come into play. Often, failures occur because companies do not have human resource management policies compatible with expatriate policies.[10] Many organizations tend to neglect appropriate human resource practices when they send their employees overseas. Failure can take many other forms.[11] Some expatriates may be reassigned to the home country for poor performance. Others may choose to return because of their own or their family's difficulties adjusting to the local culture. Expatriates may willingly choose to return because they find themselves ineffective in their jobs. Some companies also see their expatriates end their assignments prematurely to take jobs with other companies. Therefore, typical reasons for U.S. expatriate failure include individual, family, cultural, and organizational factors:[12]

### Individual

- Personality of the manager.
- Lack of technical proficiency.
- No motivation for international assignment.

### Family

- Spouse or family members fail to adapt to local culture or environment.
- Spouse or family members do not want to be there.

### Cultural

- Manager fails to adapt to local culture or environment.
- Manager fails to develop relationships with key people in the new country because of the complexity of cultivating networks with diverse people.

### Organizational

- Excess of difficult responsibilities as part of the international assignment.
- Failure to provide cultural training and other important preassignment training, such as language and cultural-acquisition training.
- Failure of company to pick the right people for the job.
- Company's failure to provide the level of technical support that domestic managers are used to.
- Failure of company to consider gender equity when considering candidates.

Because of the problems associated with using expatriates, some U.S. multinational companies have questioned the practice. The high costs of locating expatriates in overseas assignments, the high costs of failed assignments, and the difficulties of finding U.S. managers with skills like language fluency combine to discourage companies.

In contrast, many multinational companies, especially those with transnational or regional strategies, view international assignments in a broader, longer-term perspective. To compete successfully in the twenty-first century, such companies see international assignments as having a key strategic role. Consider the following benefits:

- *International assignments help managers acquire the skills necessary to develop successful strategies in a global context:* Strategic management in the coming decades will require managers who understand global competition, customers, suppliers, and markets. Seldom can managers make effective strategic decisions without considering worldwide implications. Without international management experience, the future top managers may not develop talents, such as understanding foreign customers or foreign governments. Recognizing such challenges, companies like Colgate-Palmolive provide a variety of international assignments, both for high-potential managers and for managers who recently have graduated from college.[13] Consider the following Multinational Management Brief.

- *Expatriate assignments help a company coordinate and control operations that are dispersed geographically and culturally:* Expatriates with a shared vision and objectives for the corporation serve as links to communicate corporate needs and values to culturally and geographically diverse local subsidiaries. Expatriates also have firsthand knowledge of local situations and communicate local needs

---

## Multinational Management **Brief**

### Importance of International Assignments

IBM is now a global multinational with over 375,000 employees worldwide. Although it still has about 127,000 employees in the United States, it also has a sizable number of employees in countries such as Japan (25,000), India (75,000), Brazil (13,000), Britain (20,000), and France (11,000), among many others. Since 2004, IBM has been transforming itself into a truly globally integrated enterprise. Prior to this transformation, IBM was operating its subsidiaries in 160 countries like mini-IBMs. However, this system was very costly because IBM was not taking advantage of its global workforce. Its philosophy now is that it will get the job done where the job can best be done. IBM also understands the importance of emerging markets. It has invested in more than 100 of these countries while also opening 100 new branch offices beyond the BRIC.

To achieve this global integration, IBM has realized that it is crucial to send its employees on international assignments to transmit the corporate values. Consider the case of IBM Brazil. When resources were tight in Brazil, the Brazilians favored projects from local customers, while IBMers from other countries pushed for their own clients in those other countries. American Robert Payne was sent to address this conflict. IBM sent the 22-year IBM executive to facilitate the global integration process. By encouraging the employees to think of the company's interests in the long term, he was able to reduce some of the conflict. IBM has sent other expatriates to other key subsidiaries to help integrate the company's operations.

*Source: Based on Hamm, S. 2008. "International isn't just IBM's first name." BusinessWeek, January 28, 36–40; IBM. 2012. Annual report. http://www.ibm.com.*

and strategic information to headquarters. In contrast, an overuse of host country managers may create employees who identify primarily with the host country subunit rather than with the global organization.[14]

- *Global assignments provide important strategic information:* Because of the length of typical expatriate assignments (two to five years), compared with short visits from headquarters, expatriate managers have sufficient time to gather complex information.[15] For example, in politically risky countries, an experienced expatriate manager can provide the top management of the parent company with critical and timely information, which might include key trends in the host country's political, economic, and financial environments.[16]

- *Global assignments provide crucial detailed information about local markets:* Expatriates have incredible in-depth knowledge of local markets.[17] This information needs to be part of the strategic planning of companies because it can be extremely critical for companies with a wide geographic presence. For instance, Colgate-Palmolive's expatriates' detailed knowledge of local markets enabled them to determine that small sachets of detergent sell better in Africa than the typical 64-ounce bottle sold in the United States. Similarly, interviews of 16 Austrian expatriates in Polish banks revealed that the bankers acquired significant knowledge of local market conditions such as the legal system.[18]

- *Global assignments provide opportunities for management development:* As we saw earlier, expatriates from the millennial generation will expect some form of international assignment during their work lifetime. As such, global assignments can also provide opportunities for the company to develop their managers while also providing managers with challenges that may be intrinsically motivating (Pinto, Cabral-Cardoso, and Werther, Jr., 2012).

- *Global assignments provide important network knowledge:* Because expatriates meet many people, such as clients, suppliers, and people within the subsidiary, they create an important network in the host country. Because they are the main contacts between the host and the parent companies, they also may develop a new network at the home company. Such networks can be very useful because they can create new business opportunities and help the subsidiary function smoothly.[19]

Next, the chapter considers how to use the expatriate manager to maximize strategic advantage.

# The Expatriate Manager

Once a company makes the decision to use expatriate managers or to develop a full-time international cadre, successful multinational organizations develop IHRM policies that maximize their effectiveness. This section discusses the effective selection, training and development, performance appraisal, compensation, and repatriation of the expatriate multinational manager.

## Selecting Expatriate Managers

Selecting the wrong person for any job can lead to failure and can be a major expense for the company.[20] This problem is even more pronounced for expatriates because a failed expatriate assignment can cost the company from two to five times the assignee's annual salary.[21] In fact, it is estimated that each expatriate failure through early departure can cost a company more than $1 million.[22] Furthermore, it has even been argued that improperly selected employees who cannot perform adequately but who remain on assignment can be more damaging to the company than those who leave prematurely.[23] Companies are therefore becoming more aware of the strategic need to select the right person for the job the first time. Consider the following Focus on Emerging Markets.

Traditionally, multinational companies have assumed that domestic performance predicts expatriate performance. This assumption leads companies to search for job candidates with the best technical skills and professional competence. When these factors become the major, if not the only, selection criteria for international assignments, companies often overlook other important criteria.[24] However, as the

---

## Focus on Emerging Markets

### Expatriate Assignments in China

China continues to attract foreign investment and remains a destination of choice for multinationals worldwide, but it is also one of the most challenging destinations for expatriates. In fact, various studies rank expatriate failure in China as twice as high as in other countries, while others have found failure rates as high as 70 percent. Given the potential for such high rates of failure, it is clear that multinationals need to pay special attention to expatriates being sent to China to ensure that they have every chance of succeeding.

Why is expatriate success in China so much harder to achieve than in other countries? Many surveys suggest that expatriates sent to China are not necessarily prepared for such assignments. Consider that many expatriates are usually from countries with limited government involvement, and their focus is on driving sales. As such, they do not have much experience dealing with the government and often get frustrated when facing bureaucratic interference. Furthermore, expatriates often assume that the key to gain government support for their projects is periodic "wining" and "dining" of government officials. However, expatriates in companies such as the U.K.-based Hong Kong Shanghai Bank take a much more holistic view. They will often take great pains to show how China can benefit from their projects, but will also seek feedback from the various city officials about their local bank branch and what types of future directives they should expect. Such efforts build a much stronger connection with government officials.

Another inaccurate assumption made by expatriates sent to China is that because China has frequent reports of corruption, bribery, and unsafe products, that following business ethics standards is not necessary. However, more experienced expatriates are now realizing that foreign companies are held to a much higher standard than local companies. As such, expectations of foreign companies are much more rigorous than local ones. Well-advised executives are now ensuring that employees are trained to properly respect global ethics standards. As such, more expatriates are instituting clear nonnegotiable standards and clearly communicating these standards to employees. Companies are also appointing compliance officers to make sure that they are complying with local rules, but also to investigate and address corporate misconduct issues.

Given the above difficulties, it is therefore not surprising to see that some companies are now hiring locals to fill critical jobs. Such companies want executives who can deal with the government without help from translators. Chinese natives are more likely to be integrated in the culture and thus more likely to succeed.

*Sources: Based on Kwoh, L. 2012. "Asia's endangered species: The expat." Wall Street Journal, March 28, B6; Lund, D., and Degen, R. J. 2010. "Selecting candidates and managing expatriate assignments in China." Global Business and Organizational Excellence, November/December, 60–72; Paine, L. S. 2010. "The China rules." Harvard Business Review, June, 103–108.*

above Focus on Emerging Markets shows, succeeding in China may not necessarily hinge on technical skills. What other criteria are important for selecting the best people for expatriate assignments?

Several experts on international HRM have identified **key success factors for expatriate assignments.**[25] In addition to professional and technical competence, these factors are relational abilities, family situation, motivation, and language skills.

- *Technical and managerial skills:* Often an expatriate assignment gives managers more tasks and greater responsibilities than similar-level assignments at home. Additionally, the geographical distance from headquarters can result in the manager's having more decision-making autonomy. Only managers with excellent technical, administrative, and leadership skills have a strong likelihood of success in such positions.

- *Personality traits:* A foreign assignment inevitably comes with a host of unexpected problems and new situations. To be able to deal with such uncertainties and novelty, the expatriate has to be flexible, be willing and eager to learn new things, be able to deal with ambiguity, have an interest in other people and cultures, and have a good sense of humor. Extroversion also is critical to success.[26] Extroverts are more likely to be sociable and talkative, and thus motivated to communicate and develop relationships with locals. Relationships with locals can not only help expatriates adjust better in the new country, they can also provide access to important information regarding appropriate behavior.

- *Relational abilities:* Relational abilities help employees avoid a major pitfall of international assignments: the failure to adapt to different cultures. People with good relational skills have the ability to adapt to strange or ambiguous situations. They are culturally flexible and sensitive to cultural norms, values, and beliefs. They also have the ability to modify their own behaviors and attitudes to fit in with a new culture. They favor collaborative negotiation styles and avoid direct confrontation.

- *Family situation:* Selection for an international assignment also must weigh the potential expatriate's family situation. An overseas assignment affects the spouse and children as much as the employee, so a family situation favorable to the assignment is crucial for expatriate success. Key factors to consider are the spouse's willingness to live abroad, the impact of the potential posting on the spouse's career and the children's education, and the spouse's relational skills. Because of the increasing number of dual-career couples, multinational companies may need to offer two positions or compensation for the spouse's lost income to ensure a successful assignment.

- *Stress tolerance:* Adapting to a new culture and work environment can be extremely stressful. The ability to tolerate stress is a crucial quality that can help an expatriate succeed on an international assignment.[27] Expatriates who can maintain their composure in the face of extreme stressors are more likely to succeed in their new assignments.

- *Language ability:* The ability to speak, read, and write the host country language enhances many of the other key success factors. Managers with good language skills are well prepared to apply their technical and managerial skills. They have heightened success in dealing with local colleagues, subordinates, and customers. Knowledge of the local language also increases the understanding of the local culture and reduces the stress of adapting to a new cultural environment.

- *Emotional intelligence:* Research suggests that emotional intelligence is a crucial success factor.[28] Emotional intelligence is the ability to be aware of oneself, to understand and relate to others, and to be empathetic and manage one's emotions. Expatriates inevitably need to relate to others and manage their own presence. Those with high emotional intelligence are likely to be able to relate to locals and show the appropriate emotions when adjusting locally.

Selecting an expatriate manager with the appropriate array of skills demands more effort than selecting domestic managers. There are more key success factors to consider than in domestic assignments. Most successful multinationals use a combination of selection techniques to identify people with the appropriate talent for an expatriate posting. Some popular techniques are interviews, standardized tests of intelligence or technical knowledge, assessment centers (testing centers where candidates solve simulated managerial problems), biographical data, work samples, and references. Exhibit 11.3 shows some of the key success factors and selection techniques used in the expatriate selection process.

**EXHIBIT 11.3** Expatriate Success Factors and Selection Methods

| Key Success Factors | Selection Methods | | | | | |
|---|---|---|---|---|---|---|
| | Interviews | Standardized tests | Assessment centers | Biographical data | Work samples | References |
| **Professional/technical skills** | | | | | | |
| ➤ Technical skills | ✓ | ✓ | | ✓ | ✓ | ✓ |
| ➤ Administrative skills | ✓ | | ✓ | ✓ | ✓ | ✓ |
| ➤ Leadership skills | | | | | | |
| **Relational abilities** | | | | | | |
| ➤ Ability to communicate | ✓ | | ✓ | | | ✓ |
| ➤ Cultural tolerance and empathy | ✓ | ✓ | ✓ | | | |
| ➤ Tolerance for ambiguity | ✓ | | ✓ | | | |
| ➤ Flexibility to adapt to new behaviors and attitudes | ✓ | | ✓ | | | ✓ |
| ➤ Stress adaptation skills | ✓ | | ✓ | | | |
| **International motivation** | | | | | | |
| ➤ Willingness to accept expatriate position | ✓ | | | ✓ | | |
| ➤ Interest in culture of assignment location | ✓ | | | | | |
| ➤ Commitment to international mission | ✓ | | | | | |
| ➤ Fit with career development stage | ✓ | | | ✓ | | ✓ |
| **Family situation** | | | | | | |
| ➤ Spouse's willingness to live abroad | ✓ | | | | | |
| ➤ Spouse's relational abilities | ✓ | ✓ | ✓ | | | |
| ➤ Spouse's career goals | ✓ | | | | | |
| ➤ Children's educational requirements | ✓ | | | | | |
| **Language skills** | | | | | | |
| ➤ Ability to communicate in local language | ✓ | ✓ | ✓ | ✓ | | ✓ |

*Sources: Adapted from Black, J. Stewart, Hal B. Gregersen, and Mark E. Mendenhall. 1992. Global Assignments. San Francisco: Jossey-Bass; Ronen, Simcha. 1986. Comparative and Multinational Management. Hoboken, NJ: Wiley.*

The importance of the expatriate success factors is not the same for all expatriate job assignments. Each factor has a different priority depending on four assignment conditions:[29] assignment length, cultural similarity, required communication with host country nationals, and job complexity and responsibility. Each of these conditions affects the selection criteria:

- *Assignment length:* The amount of time an expatriate expects to remain in the host country may range from short postings of a month or less to several years. Selection for short-term assignments usually focuses primarily on technical and professional qualifications. What are the trends for assignment length? Consider the following Multinational Management Brief.

- *Cultural similarity:* Cultures vary widely, but certain cultures are similar to each other. The cultural similarity of Japan and Korea, for example, is higher than that of the United States and Taiwan or France and Saudi Arabia. Thus, finding the right French or U.S. expatriate for an assignment in the Middle East or Asia requires more emphasis on family factors, relational skills, and language skills. Managers from similar cultures usually find adaptation much easier.

- *Required interaction and communication:* Some jobs require a lot of interaction and communication with host country nationals, such as subordinates, suppliers, customers, and joint venture partners. Increased relational skills and knowledge of the host country language and culture become important in such situations.

- *Job complexity and responsibility:* In jobs with complex tasks and great responsibilities, the personal abilities of the manager often have significant effects on the success of projects. For this reason, even though professional and technical skills are important, the more important the job is to the organization, the more the candidate's skills and previous success in related work will count in the selection decision.

## Multinational Management **Brief**

### Expatriate Assignment Length

ecent surveys indicate that the nature of assignment length is changing. Traditionally, companies viewed assignments in a linear fashion, ranging from short term to long term. However, many new forms of assignments are now emerging, ranging from frequent travelers, commuters, and the increased use of technology to enhance virtual presence. As more companies rely on global collaboration technologies, the future will be less likely to see the traditional high-remuneration, long-term assignments in favor of more short-term and flexible assignments that make heavy use of collaboration technologies. In a recent survey, more than 25 percent of companies are now relying on more short-term assignments, compared to only 17 percent of companies relying on long-term trends. To give you more insights on these trends, Exhibit 11.4 shows the growth of short-term assignment regions. It is clear that all regions are seeing more companies adopting more short-term forms of assignments.

*Source: Based on O'Neil, J., and D. Mikes. 2012. "Latest trends in international assignment policies and practices." Mercer Consulting, http://www.mercer.com.*

EXHIBIT **11.4**

**What Percentage of Companies are Using more Short Term Assignments?**

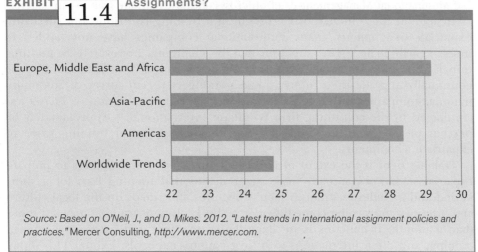

*Source: Based on O'Neil, J., and D. Mikes. 2012. "Latest trends in international assignment policies and practices."* Mercer Consulting, *http://www.mercer.com.*

EXHIBIT **11.5**

**Selecting Expatriates: Priorities for Success Factors by Assignment Characteristics**

| Expatriate Success Factors | Assignment Characteristics | | | |
|---|---|---|---|---|
| | Longer duration | More cultural dissimilarity | Greater interaction and communication requirements with locals | More complex or responsible job |
| Professional/technical skills | High | Neutral | Moderate | High |
| Relational abilities | Moderate | High | High | Moderate |
| International motivation | High | High | High | High |
| Family situation | High | High | Neutral | Moderate |
| Language skills | Moderate | High | High | Neutral |

*Sources: Adapted from Black, J. Stewart, Hal B. Gregersen, and Mark E. Mendenhall. 1992. Global Assignments. San Francisco: Jossey-Bass; Tung, Rosalie L. 1981. "Selection and training of personnel for overseas assignments." Columbia Journal of World Business, 16(1): 68–78.*

Exhibit 11.5 summarizes issues to consider in setting priorities in the expatriate selection process. Each factor is more or less important, depending on the expatriate's job assignment conditions.

The efforts to ensure the best chance of the expatriate manager's success do not end with his or her selection. Expatriates need training and development, which we consider next.

## Training and Development

Strong evidence shows that predeparture **cross-cultural training** reduces expatriate failure rates and increases job performance.[30] The main objective of cross-cultural training is to increase the relational abilities of the future expatriate and, when possible, of the spouse and family. The techniques used and the rigor of the

**Cross-cultural training**
Increases the relational abilities of future expatriates and, in some cases, of their spouses and families.

training depend on the anticipated situations in the assignment. Consider the following Multinational Management Brief on cross-cultural expatriate training in Nigeria.

In spite of the evidence that cross-cultural training contributes to successful expatriate assignments, many multinational companies have not tended to invest heavily in it.[31] This situation may be changing, however. U.S. multinational firms like American Express, Colgate-Palmolive, and General Electric continually upgrade their international training. A recent survey of 264 multinational companies with a total worldwide expatriate population of 74,709 was conducted by the consulting firm Windham International.[32] Approximately 63 percent of the firms surveyed had provided cross-cultural training prior to expatriate assignments.

**Training rigor**
Extent of effort by both trainees and trainers to prepare the expatriate.

**Training rigor** is the extent of effort by both trainees and trainers to prepare expatriates for work abroad.[33] Low rigor means that training lasts for a short period and includes techniques such as lectures and videos on the local culture and briefings concerning company operations. High-rigor training may last more than a month. It contains more experiential learning and extensive language training, and often interactions with host country nationals. Exhibit 11.6 shows various training techniques and their objectives as the rigor of the cross-cultural training grows.

Training vigor depends on the same conditions as the prioritizing of expatriate success factors. Increases in the length of the assignment, the cultural dissimilarity between home and host country, the amount of required interaction and communication with local people, and job complexity/responsibility all suggest a need for increased training rigor.[34] (See Exhibit 11.7.) Because a major reason for expatriate failure relates to family situations, training for a long assignment in a dissimilar culture may include all family members, not just the expatriate.

As the Multinational Management Brief shows on next page, training cannot fully prepare expatriates to face life in the new country. Many companies are now relying on mentor and buddy programs to facilitate integration in the host country.

Once expatriates are on assignment, IHRM does not stop. Multinational managers must have appropriate performance appraisal techniques.

## Performance Appraisal for the Expatriate

Conducting a reliable and valid performance appraisal of expatriate managers poses one of the greatest IHRM challenges for the international company. Seldom can a company transfer the same performance criteria and measures to a host country operation. Here are some of the issues that make expatriate performance appraisals difficult:[35]

- *Fit of international operation in multinational strategy:* As discussed in Chapter 6, companies often enter international markets for strategic reasons other than immediate profit. Learning about a new market and challenging an international competitor may be strategic goals that put a subsidiary in the red but still serve a useful purpose for the organization. In these cases, local managers might look quite ineffective to a company that uses economic performance measures such as return on investment (ROI).

- *Unreliable data:* Data used to measure local subunit performance may not be comparable with the home unit's data or with data from other international operations. For example, local accounting rules can alter the meaning of

## Multinational Management **Brief**

### Cross-Cultural Training in Nigeria

Recent trends and surveys suggest that Africa will play a critical role in trade in the next few years. As more African countries are becoming politically stable while also improving the standard of living of their populations, more multinational companies are seeing Africa as a new market. It is therefore likely that more Western-based multinationals will be sending expatriates to these countries. Such trends underscore the importance of cross-cultural training.

A study of 226 Western-based multinational expatriates based in cities such as Abuja, Lagos, and Warri, Nigeria, investigated the relationship between types of cross-cultural training and expatriate adjustment. Four types of cross-cultural training were considered: 1) general conventional training (information transmitted through unidirectional communication such as that offered in universities and management development centers); 2) specific conventional training (information transmitted through unidirectional communication about a specific culture); 3) general experimental training (participants learn about cultures in general through simulation of real-life and other hands-on situations); and 4) specific experimental training (participants learn about a specific culture through simulation of real-life and hands-on situations).

To examine the impact of such training, the researchers considered three forms of expatriate adjustment: general adjustment (ability of the individual to adapt to life in the foreign country); work adjustment (ability to adapt to work conditions); and interaction adjustment (ability to interact with members of the host country). The survey showed that all four forms of cross-cultural training had a positive impact on all three forms of adjustment. The results of this study provide evidence that all forms of cross-cultural training impact expatriates' adjustment. Such results are important in that multinationals tend to neglect training, often seeing it as an unnecessary expense. Furthermore, the results also showed that the specific experimental form of training was the most effective. It is not surprising to see that the more rigorous experimental programs had the most impact.

*Source: Based on Okpara, J. O., and J. D. Kabongo. 2011. "Cross-cultural training and expatriate adjustment: A study of western expatriates in Nigeria." Journal of World Business, 46, 22–30.*

financial data, or production efficiency can look bad because local laws require full employment rather than the occasional use of overtime.

- *Complex and volatile environments:* The international environment is complex and unstable. Economic and other environmental conditions can change rapidly and often in ways unanticipated by managers back in the home country headquarters. Consequently, reasonable and achievable performance objectives that are developed early can quickly become impossible.

- *Time differences and distance separation:* Although decreasing in importance with more rapid communication and travel options, the separation of local organizations from the home office by geography and time differences remains a problem for evaluating local managers. Often out of sight and out of mind, expatriate and local managers lack the frequency and intensity of communication to keep home office staff adequately informed.

**EXHIBIT 11.6** Building Cross-Cultural Training Rigor: Techniques and Objectives

**Training Rigor**

**High**

**Techniques:** Field trips to host country, meetings with managers experienced in host country, meetings with host country nationals, intensive language training.
**Objectives:** Develop comfort with host country national culture, business culture, and social institutions.

**Techniques:** Intercultural experiential learning exercises, role-playing, simulations, case studies, survival language training.
**Objectives:** Build general and specific knowledge of host country culture, reduce ethnocentrism.

**Techniques:** Lectures, videotapes, reading background material.
**Objectives:** Provide background information on host country business and national cultures, basic information on company operations.

**Low**

*Sources: Adapted from Black, J. Stewart, Hal B. Gregersen, and Mark E. Mendenhall. 1992.* Global Assignments. *San Francisco: Jossey-Bass; Ronen, Simcha. 1986.* Comparative and Multinational Management. *Hoboken, NJ: Wiley.*

**EXHIBIT 11.7** Training Needs and Expatriate Assignment Characteristics

ASSIGNMENT CHARACTERISTICS:
➤ Long assignments
➤ Dissimilar culture
➤ High job responsibility
➤ High need to communicate with locals

**High Training Rigor**

60 hours +

**Moderate Training Rigor**

20–60 hours

**Low Training Rigor**

4–20 hours

ASSIGNMENT CHARACTERISTICS:
➤ Short assignments
➤ Similar culture
➤ Low to moderate job responsibilities
➤ Low need to communicate with locals

*Source: Adapted from Mendenhall, Mark E., E. Dunbar, and Gary R. Oddou. 1987. "Expatriate selection, training and career-pathing: A review and critique."* Human Resource Management, *26(3): 331–345.*

## Multinational Management **Brief**

### Mentorship and Expatriate Buddy Programs

According to surveys, some of the major challenges faced by expatriates when they start their assignments are such things as choosing schools for their children, finding housing, opening bank accounts, finding grocery stores, getting a driver's license, and learning about the community. Unfortunately, many of these challenges cannot be easily addressed in predeparture training. Expatriates usually must deal with such challenges as they start their foreign assignments. Experts thus suggest mentorship and even buddy programs.

In a recent study of 299 expatriates, researchers examined the effectiveness of mentorship programs on key aspects of assignments. The researchers examined the effects of both home country mentors and host country mentors. They found that having a host country mentor positively impacted the expatriates' organizational knowledge, job performance, promotability, and teamwork. They also found that home country mentors were beneficial but had a positive impact only on the expatriates' organizational knowledge, job performance, and promotability.

Given the importance of host country mentors, many global companies, such as KPMG International and Balfour Beatty, have implemented buddy programs to help expatriates adjust to their new surroundings and deal with the challenges. In these programs, expatriates are assigned buddies in their host location. At Balfour Beatty, buddies receive cultural awareness training prior to the expatriates' arrival. Once they arrive, they go through more cultural training with their buddies. Buddies also get time off work to help the newly arrived expatriates shop for houses and select schools. At KPMG, the buddies play an important networking role. They typically invite the expatriates to dinners and help them get adjusted socially. Small companies motivate their expatriates through cash incentives to join local trade and social clubs. In general, global companies are finding that such buddy programs are useful to ensure that the expatriates adjust smoothly in their host locations.

*Sources: Carraher, S. M., S. E. Sullivan, and M. M. Crocitto. 2008. "Mentoring across global boundaries: An empirical examination of home- and host-country mentors on expatriate career outcomes." Journal of International Business Studies, 39, 1310–1326; Krell, Eric. 2006, "Budding relationships." HR Magazine, 50(6): 114–118.*

Without intensive and direct contact, performance appraisals can fail to demonstrate a comprehensive understanding of an expatriate manager's situation.

To overcome the difficulty of conducting performance appraisals of international managers and other employees, experts suggest several steps:[36]

- *Fit the evaluation criteria to strategy:* For example, if the objective is to enter a market for long-term position, it does not make sense to use short-term financial performance measures.

- *Fine-tune the evaluation criteria:* Senior managers need to consider carefully all their objectives for the international operation. They need to visit local sites to understand the problems and situations faced by expatriate and local managers. Recently repatriated managers also can furnish excellent knowledge about local circumstances.

- *Use multiple sources of evaluation with varying periods of evaluation:* The complexity of the international situation demands more information than at-home

**EXHIBIT 11.8**   Evaluation Sources, Criteria, and Time Periods for Expatriate Evaluation

| Evaluation Sources | Criteria | Periods |
|---|---|---|
| Self-evaluation | Meeting objectives • Management skills • Project successes | Six months and at the completion of a major project |
| Subordinates | Leadership skills • Communication skills • Subordinates' development | After completion of major project |
| Peer expatriate and host country managers | Team building • Interpersonal skills • Cross-cultural interaction skills | Six months |
| On-site supervisor | Management skills • Leadership skills • Meeting objectives | At the completion of significant projects |
| Customers and clients | Service quality and timeliness • Negotiation skills • Cross-cultural interaction skills | Yearly |

*Source: Adapted from Black, J. Stewart, Hal B. Gregersen, and Mark E. Mendenhall. 1992.* Global Assignments. *San Francisco: Jossey-Bass.*

appraisals, and high-level management should rely on several sources of information. Exhibit 11.8 shows several common components of expatriate performance appraisals, which include sources of evaluation information, evaluation criteria, and evaluation periods.

The next question is: How do multinational companies determine the fair and adequate compensation of expatriate managers?

## Expatriate Compensation

Expatriate compensation presents significant challenges to companies. On the one hand, companies are being pressured to control the ever-growing costs associated with expatriate assignments with the knowledge that failure can reach exorbitantly high levels.[37] On the other hand, companies need to provide an appropriate compensation package not only to entice expatriates to relocate, but also to retain and motivate expatriate employees.

Compensation packages tend to have many common factors:[38]

- *Local market cost of living:* One of the most important factors in determining expatriate compensation is the cost of living in the host country. Often, companies try to adjust compensation levels so that the expatriate suffers no loss from relocation. As an example, expatriates sent to Japan may have close to 50 percent added to their home pay as services and goods allowances.

- *Housing:* Many multinationals tend to provide some form of housing allowance, with many companies providing free housing. Providing comparable housing is much more difficult than offering cost-of-living allowances because there are major differences in the acceptable sizes of houses. For instance, an American expatriate may move from a 3,000-square-foot house in the United States to a smaller 1,200-square-foot apartment in London.

- *Taxes:* Expatriates may face double taxation because they are taxed in the host country as well as in the home country. Although there are some exceptions, U.S. citizens and residents are taxed on their worldwide income.[39]

Some multinationals therefore have to cover the payment of taxes to ensure that their employees do not experience double taxation.

- *Benefits:* Benefits such as pension and health care remain an important aspect of compensation packages.[40] Many expatriates tend to be frustrated with their benefit packages when they are in the host country. Often, the benefits are not similar to the home situation or they are inadequate in the host country. As a result, companies need to find better ways to provide benefits to their expatriates. Current events around the world also suggest the need for emergency benefits.

Calculating the appropriate compensation package can be a daunting task. Some of the methods used to determine the level of benefits are discussed next.

## The Balance Sheet Approach

More than 85 percent of U.S. multinational companies commonly apply the **balance sheet method** for determining expatriate compensation.[41] This method provides a compensation package that attempts to equate or balance an expatriate's purchasing power in the host country with his or her purchasing power in the home country.[42] The basic aim is that the expatriate should not be in a better or worse position financially as a result of the assignment. To balance the compensation received for the international assignment with compensation received in the home country, multinational companies usually provide additional salary, which includes adjustments for differences in taxes, housing costs, and the costs of basic goods and services. Goods and services are items such as food, recreation, personal care, clothing, education, home furnishings, transportation, and medical care.[43] Exhibit 11.9 provides a simple view of how the balance sheet approach works.

Besides matching the expatriate's purchasing power, companies often provide other allowances and extra benefits, called perquisites. These benefits cover the initial logistics of the international move (such as hotel costs while getting settled), compensation for lifestyle differences between the home and host country, and incentives to take the assignment. Here are some of these additional allowances and perquisites:[44]

- *Foreign-service premiums:* Multinational companies often provide 10 to 20 percent of base pay for accepting the individual and family difficulties associated with an overseas assignment. Approximately 78 percent of major U.S. multinational companies pay this premium.
- *Hardship allowance:* This allowance provides extra money for a particularly difficult posting due to issues such as high risk or poor living conditions.
- *Relocation allowances:* Along with the basic costs of moving a family to an international assignment, many companies pay a flat amount equal to one month's salary at the beginning and end of the assignment to cover miscellaneous costs of relocating.
- *Home leave allowances:* These allowances provide transportation costs for expatriates and their families to return to their home country once or twice a year.

## Other Approaches

The high cost of expatriate compensation and the trend for multinational companies to have workers anywhere in the world have resulted in modifications of the traditional balance sheet approach. Some companies simply pay home

**Balance sheet method**
Attempts to equate purchasing power in the host country with purchasing power in the expatriate's home country.

EXHIBIT **11.9**   A Balance Sheet Approach to Expatriate Compensation

| Domestic Assignment:<br>Expenses and<br>Spendable Income: | | Expatriate Assignment:<br>Expenses and<br>Balanced Spendable<br>Income + Allowances: |
|---|---|---|
| Base Salary | + | Base Salary |
| | = | |
| Taxes | = | Taxes |
| | + | |
| Goods and Services | = | Goods and Services |
| | + | |
| Housing | = | Housing |
| | + | |
| Spendable Income | = | Spendable Income |

Allowances as an incentive to take position, foreign service premium, hardship pay, R&R

Allowances to balance extra tax payments

Allowances to cover cost-of-living differences, housing, children's education, medical costs, automobile, recreation, home leave travel

Allowances for moving expenses, settling-in expenses, initial housing costs, and furnishing allowances

© Cengage Learning

**Headquarters-based compensation system**
Paying home country wages regardless of location.

country wages regardless of location. This approach, called the **headquarters-based compensation system,** works well when home country wages are high compared with the local assignment's cost of living.[45] However, it can be a problem in high-cost locations such as Paris or Tokyo.

Many experts recommend that companies wean expatriates gradually from dependence on perks and allowances that allow them to maintain their home country lifestyles or sometimes to live better overseas.[46] These companies assume that there is nothing special about being an expatriate, especially for longer assignments.[47] After an initial period on assignment, firms reduce allowances, using local or regional markets to determine compensation. Such companies expect the expatriate to become an efficient consumer by adjusting to local lifestyles and costs of living. This approach is called the **host-based compensation system.**

**Host-based compensation system**
Adjusting wages to local lifestyles and costs of living.

The international cadre presents different compensation problems. To address the question of compensation for multiple and continual global assignments, companies develop global pay systems, which are worldwide job evaluation and performance appraisal methods designed to assess the worth of jobs to the company and then equitably reward employees. To some extent, global pay systems resemble the balance sheet system. Allowances still exist for differences in expenses such as cost of living, taxes, settling in, and housing. However, the system does not balance compensation to produce parity with lifestyles in the home country. Rather, companies use a worldwide standard of compensation and make only necessary adjustments to that standard. The objectives are to reduce waste from expatriate perquisites, to eliminate the steep differences in compensation, and to maintain compensation equity for all long-term international cadre managers.[48]

Although international cadre managers are not expected to come home, most other types of expatriate managers return to their parent company in their home country. Returning home is not always as easy as many managers expect, and multinational companies often face the so-called repatriation problem.

**Global pay system**
Worldwide job evaluations, performance appraisal methods, and salary scales are used.

## The Repatriation Problem

Bringing expatriate employees home and back into full participation in the company is a difficult problem for many organizations. For example, studies of North American companies found that 25 percent of managers completing foreign assignments wanted to leave the firm.[49] Turnover may range from 33 percent to as high as 50 percent within two years after return.[50] A recent Cendant Mobility study showed that approximately half of the companies surveyed had no repatriation program. This finding is especially troubling because U.S. employers often spend as much as $1 million to send an expatriate on an overseas assignment. It is therefore imperative for companies to retain returned expatriates.

The difficulties that managers face in coming back to their home countries and reconnecting with their old job constitute the repatriation problem. However, these difficulties can be solved with proper preparation and planning by the expatriate and the company.

Expatriates face at least three basic cultural problems when coming home.[51] Many of these problems relate to the phenomenon called reverse culture shock, whereby people must relearn the subtleties of their own cultural norms, values, and beliefs. First, the expatriate must adapt to what is often a new work environment, as well as to the organizational culture of the home office, leading to low work performance or turnover after the assignment. Second, expatriates and their families must relearn to communicate with friends and coworkers in the home and organizational cultures. Often, as a result of having adapted to their former host cultures, expatriates are unaware that they now use different communication patterns. Third, although surprising for people who have lived most of their lives in their home country, many expatriates need time to adapt to the basic living environment, including its school, food, and weather.

Even when repatriation is not a concern, there are other organizational problems for the expatriate and the company. One survey reported that 61 percent of expatriates felt they were not given the chance to use their international experience. After years in challenging international postings, three-quarters of expatriates reported that their present jobs were demotions. Often, there were no planned career paths for expatriates after returning home.[52] Three months after their return home, one-third of the former expatriates were still in temporary jobs.[53] Finally, expatriates also get used to the autonomy abroad and may no longer feel challenged when they return.

**Repatriation problem**
Difficulties that managers face in coming back to their home countries and reconnecting with their home organizations.

A variety of strategies allow companies to successfully repatriate their managers:[54]

- *Provide a strategic purpose for the repatriation:* Use the expatriate's experiences to further organizational goals. Expatriates often provide excellent sources of information and experiences that companies should plan to use.

- *Establish a team to aid the expatriate:* The HRM department and the expatriate's supervisor can help plan for the expatriate's return. The returning expatriates can be provided with counseling so that they are aware of the challenges of repatriation as well as how business has changed at the local office. The team also can look for obvious reverse culture shock symptoms (boredom, fatigue, withdrawal, frustration, and isolation from coworkers) and provide help as needed.

- *Provide parent company information sources:* Many companies assign mentors or sponsors who keep the expatriate informed of current changes in the company, including job opportunities.

- *Provide training and preparation for the return:* This preparation can begin as early as six months before the return. Visits home and specific training for the next assignment help ease transition difficulties.

Traditionally, in most multinational companies, international assignments have been male dominated. The previous section discusses the reasons for this tendency, whether the practice is ongoing, and several issues that arise when women take on international assignments.

# International Assignments for Women

The most striking fact about women in international assignments is their rarity. Estimates are that only 12 percent of expatriate managers are women.[55] In North America, it is estimated that 14 percent of global assignees are women, whereas women represent 45 percent of management in general.[56] In the United Kingdom it is estimated that only 9 percent of the expatriate population are women.[57] These data show that, although multinational companies are willing to promote women domestically, they are reluctant to post them overseas.[58] Personnel managers believe foreigners would be prejudiced against women managers.[59] In addition, of the women who do get international assignments, very few have top management positions.[60] These findings are even more striking when one considers that North American companies use more women in international positions than do Asian or European companies.[61] All this has led some researchers to suggest that women managers face not only a glass ceiling at home but also an **expatriate glass ceiling.**[62] In other words, multinationals are reluctant to give international assignments to female managers. Furthermore, even if multinationals decide to give women an expatriate position, they run into problems. Consider the following Case in Point.

Why are the barriers so strong against women gaining international positions, even in countries such as the United States, where nearly half of the business school graduates are women? As we see from the Case in Point, some societies have very traditional views of the role of women. Understanding women expatriates in such countries can be problematic. Furthermore, such culturally based gender role expectations for women and men enter into many selection decisions. Some managers question whether family problems, a known predictor of expatriate failure, will be greater for women. They doubt whether women will be willing to take the time away from their families that is necessary to handle an

**Expatriate glass ceiling**
The organizational and structural barriers preventing female managers from receiving international assignments.

## Expatriate Glass Ceiling

Recent events suggest that the work environment for women may be changing in countries that have viewed women as only fulfilling very traditional roles. For instance, Saudi Arabia is finally allowing women to work. On January 4, 2012, more than 7000 lingerie shops were forced to lay off the mostly male workers. These retailers were then forced to hire Saudi women. Furthermore, even in India, more married women are now leaving their children and husbands behind to take global assignments, seeing these assignments as critical to their career development. However, despite such changes, significant barriers remain for women. Consider the following.

Linda Myers decided to take a human resources position with the South Korean conglomerate SK Telecom. However, as soon as she started work at the company in Seoul, South Korea, she started running into barriers. First, she found herself unable to communicate effectively, although she considered herself a skilled communicator. She needed a translator in many meetings and gradually found that she could not be as effective through a third party. Second, she realized that although she was brought in as a change agent, she was having great difficulty in implementing change. She found that the leadership was very nervous about such change. Third, the most important challenge for Linda was the fact that she was a woman in a very male-dominated company. She was constantly aware that she was the only woman at meetings, as most other women in the room were secretaries. Furthermore, SK Telecom had a very strict hierarchy and she quickly learned that she could only talk with others at her level. Eventually, the challenges took their toll, and Ms. Myers's contract was not renewed.

*Sources: Based on Green, S. 2011. "The would-be pioneer." Harvard Business Review, April, 124–126; Knickmeyer, E. 2012. "Saudis push young people, including women into jobs." Wall Street Journal, January 31, online edition; Sharma, S., and Tejaswi, M. J. 2012. "Married women executives opting for foreign stints to boost careers." Economic Times, March 9, online edition.*

expatriate position. They ask: How will the spouse fit in? What will happen if there are dual careers? Some even voice the concern that women are not tough enough to face the physical hazards, isolation, and loneliness of some international postings.[63]

However, the data tend to prove these prejudices wrong. Nancy Adler, a leading expert on women in international management, notes two important myths that lead HR executives and top-line managers to overlook qualified and motivated women for international postings:[64]

- *Myth 1: Women do not wish to take international assignments.* In a survey of women graduating with MBAs, more than three-quarters said that they would choose an international position at some time during their career.

- *Myth 2: Women will fail in international assignments because of the foreign culture's prejudices against local women.* To address this myth, Adler surveyed more than 100 women managers with international postings for North American companies. More than 95 percent of them reported successful expatriate assignments, well above the average success rate for men.

### Successful Women Expatriates: Foreign, Not Female

In a classic article titled "A *Gaijin*, Not a Woman," Nancy Adler debunked one of the key myths regarding women as expatriates.[65] *Gaijin* is the Japanese word for foreigner. From her research, Adler concluded that it is a mistake to assume that people from foreign cultures, even traditionally patriarchal Asian cultures, apply the same gender role expectations to foreign women that they apply to local women.

It seems that people from even very traditional cultures can view foreign business-women so differently from how they view local women that gender becomes irrelevant for business purposes. For example, one businesswoman working in the Sudan was surprised by the behavior of her Sudanese host. She asked him how it was possible that he could serve her food, give her a cushion to sit on, and wash her arms after the meal. Men never do these things for women according to traditional Sudanese gender role expectations. The Sudanese host reasoned, "Oh, it's no problem. Women do not do business; therefore, you are not a woman."[66] After establishing a business relationship, according to Adler, the real issues that arise in cross-cultural interactions depend more on how host country people react to people of another nationality than on how they react to an expatriate's gender.

The next Case in Point describes a situation where a woman's business status determined how Japanese men responded to her.

### The Woman's Advantage and Disadvantage

Some studies suggest that women may have some advantages in expatriate positions, especially in Asia.[67] Being unique has its benefits. Because so few women have expatriate assignments, women who take them report being more visible. Local business-people were more likely to remember them and often sought them out more than the women's male colleagues. North American expatriate women also report that local businessmen from traditional cultures assume that the woman is the best person for the job, reasoning, "Why else would the organization send a woman?"

Women may be more likely to excel in relational skills, a major factor in expatriate success. Women report that local male managers can be more open in communication with a woman than with a man. Local men, even from traditional cultures, can talk at ease with a woman about an array of subjects that include issues outside the domain of traditional male-only conversations. Consequently, being both a businessperson and female gives expatriate women a wider range of interaction options than those available to expatriate men or to local women.[68]

Despite the many obvious advantages women expatriates enjoy, the situation is nevertheless bleak for many of them. In-depth interviews with 50 European female

**CASE IN POINT**

### The Gender-Free *Meishi*

The Japanese and many other Asian cultures exchange business cards (*meishi* in Japanese) during introductions. *Meishi* serve to define status with one's company and determine how one should interact with business associates, including the use of polite forms of language.

Two U.S. professors, a husband-and-wife team working on a research project in Japan, observed how the *meishi* determined the pattern of interaction with the woman. If the man was introduced first or the two were introduced as a married couple, Japanese businessmen and professors would focus attention on the man and treat the wife, politely but obviously, as *oksuma* (wife). However, if the woman also produced her *meishi* at the same time as the husband did, the role of wife was ignored, and the Japanese responded to the woman in terms of her professional rank. She was *sensei* (a polite form of address for professors), and gender or marital status became irrelevant. It seemed particularly important, however, to establish professional rank initially. The Japanese seemed to have more difficulty moving a woman to professional status after they perceived her initially as a wife.

expatriates revealed that they faced much worse situations than their male counterparts.[69] Female expatriates are more likely to:

- *Face the glass ceiling:* Women expatriates have more difficulty being taken seriously in the early stages of their career. They are more likely to face isolation and loneliness.[70] They must work harder than their male counterparts, and they constantly need to prove themselves. Studies have shown that, in some cases, women have to be at much higher positions than their male counterparts before they are assigned international positions.

- *Need to balance work and family responsibilities:* Because of socialization and childhood experiences, research suggests that women expatriates may have a higher burden than their male counterparts to balance family and home responsibilities. There is evidence that female expatriates may be more likely to have to choose between having an international career and having a family, often because of very little support from the partner. Not surprisingly, women managers are less likely to be married and more likely to remain childless than their male counterparts.[71]

- *Need to worry about accompanying spouse:* Many female expatriates felt that they could be successful only if the career of their spouse became secondary. However, because of societal norms, it is still difficult for male partners to accept that their spouses have the primary career. It has been found that female expatriates are more likely to have partners with professional careers and that it is more difficult for the company to accommodate the needs of the male partner because of visa regulations and other host country work policies.[72]

Furthermore, even in societies where women may have advantages because they are viewed differently (e.g., *gaijin* in Japan), they still face significant barriers. For instance, although research found that Western women had some advantages because they were seen as foreigners rather than as women, it also found that these women faced significant barriers, influencing their ability to adjust to the Japanese environment and to perform well in their jobs.[73] However, a more recent study argued that Western women should have an easier time in Japan.[74] It reasoned that Japan has experienced many institutional changes, such as a more flexible market, growth of foreign multinational presence, growth of women in the workforce, and Japan's 1986 Equal Opportunity Act. These changes should result in some convergence between Western and Japanese attitudes toward women and make for a better environment for women. However, results show that many of the barriers found in a similar study a decade ago are still formidable. Foreign women managers still face cultural barriers, making it harder for them to adjust to their new jobs, perform well, and become accepted in Japan.

The next section explains that women are an ever-growing segment of the expatriate population and companies can implement programs to ensure that they have an opportunity to flourish.

# What Can Companies Do to Ensure Female Expatriate Success?

Despite the disadvantages women face, the opportunities for them as expatriate managers are expected to grow, particularly with global companies. Scholars see several factors leading to more women in international assignments.

## Multinational Management **Brief**

### Women Expatriates and Networking

How important is networking to women's success as expatriates? A recent study of 18 expatriate women in the oil, gas, and minerals industry provides some insights into the importance of networking. The study involved interviewing the 18 out of 66 available women expatriate in a British company involved in oil and gas extractions. In 2009, the company had created a women's network initiative aimed at providing assistance to women in their career development. The network was run by five very senior women, three of whom had significant expatriate experience at senior managerial levels worldwide. These women reported directly to the diversity and inclusion committee of the company.

Findings show that the network was seen as extremely critical. Such networks were helpful in 1) providing an understanding of the culture and lifestyle in the expatriate location, 2) providing important social support, 3) providing important advice on dual career and family issues, 4) providing important information about vacancies in new locations thus aiding as a career development tool, 5) providing the necessary contacts to learn about appropriate actions to face challenges at work, and 6) providing the necessary support in easing repatriation and reintegration in the home company.

*Source: Based on Shortland, S. 2011. "Networking: a valuable career intervention for women expatriates."* Career Development International, 16(3): 271–292.

Many global and multinational companies face an acute shortage of high-quality multinational managers.[75] At the same time, perhaps because of the rise in dual-career couples, fewer men are willing to take the assignments.[76] One solution is to tap the available population of women managers. Freed from local cultural barriers that restrict the use of women managers, multinational companies can select the best people for the job regardless of gender. Because of potentially stronger relational skills, women managers often may be better qualified for international positions than their male colleagues.

Because women expatriates are likely to increase in number and are as motivated and willing to take international assignments as men, companies must take the necessary steps to ensure that their female expatriates are successful. Companies should provide other mentors[77] and also offer opportunities for networking with other working women.[78] Finally, multinationals also need to ensure that they can identify and remove barriers.[79] How important is networking to women? Consider the above Multinational Management Brief.

## Multinational Strategy and IHRM

Multinational companies have several options in developing the appropriate IHRM policies for the implementation of multinational strategies. One way to ascertain a company's approach to IHRM is to examine its IHRM orientation or philosophy. Experts identify four IHRM orientations, which we will discuss next. We will then consider how these orientations support the implementation of multinational strategies.

## IHRM Orientations

The four **IHRM orientations** reflect a company's basic tactics and philosophy for coordinating its IHRM activities for managerial and technical workers. The four basic types are ethnocentric, polycentric, regiocentric, and global. Exhibit 11.10 shows how the IHRM orientations relate to some of the basic HRM functions.

## Ethnocentric IHRM Orientation

Given an **ethnocentric IHRM** orientation, all aspects of HRM for managers and technical workers tend to follow the parent organization's home country HRM practices. In recruitment, key managerial and technical personnel come from the home country. Local employees fill only lower-level and supporting jobs. Past performance at home and technical expertise govern the selection criteria for overseas assignments in the ethnocentric IHRM company.[80]

Consistent with the use of home country nationals for management and technical positions, evaluations and promotions use parent country standards. The company assesses managers' performances using the same criteria and measures used for home country units. Because of national context variations, companies may be forced to use different approaches for the evaluation and promotion of host country managers. Such local adaptations, however, often have little effect on the ethnocentric company's procedures for promotions beyond the lowest levels of management. When an ethnocentric IHRM company uses expatriates, training for the international assignment is often limited or nonexistent. Except for top country-level or region-level positions, most international assignments last only a short time, often only for marketing and sales contacts. The use of home company evaluation and promotion standards, the lack of training, and the often short periods of expatriate assignments limit and discourage cultural adjustments for expatriates. Seldom, for example, do expatriate managers from the parent country know the host country's language.

Here are some of the benefits and costs of ethnocentric IHRM policies:

### Benefits[81]

- *Little need to recruit qualified host country nationals for higher management:* Local employees will hold only lower-level jobs or midlevel management jobs. Often a glass ceiling limits the advancement of host country nationals.
- *Greater control and loyalty of home country nationals:* These employees know that the home culture drives their careers. They seldom identify with the local country subsidiaries.
- *Little need to train home country nationals:* Managers look to headquarters for staffing and evaluation and follow headquarters' policies and procedures.
- *Key decisions centralized:* Personnel decisions are made at headquarters.

### Costs

- *Possibly limited career development for host country nationals:* High-potential host country nationals may never get beyond the glass ceiling, and talent is wasted.
- *Host country nationals may never identify with the home company:* Host country nationals are governed by local HRM practices, and they often realize that the glass ceiling exists. Therefore, they typically have more allegiance to the local company than to the home company.

**IHRM orientation**
Company's basic tactics and philosophy for coordinating IHRM activities for managerial and technical workers.

**Ethnocentric IHRM**
All aspects of HRM for managers and technical workers tend to follow the parent organization's home country HRM practices.

**EXHIBIT 11.10** IHRM Orientation and IHRM Practices for Managers and Technical Workers

| IHRM Practice | IHRM Orientation | | | |
|---|---|---|---|---|
| | Ethnocentric | Polycentric | Regiocentric | Global |
| Recruitment and selection | Home country nationals for key positions selected by technical expertise or past home country performance; host country nationals for lowest levels of management only | Home country nationals for top management and technical positions; host country nationals for midlevel management positions; selection of home country nationals similar to ethnocentric; selection of host country nationals based on fit with home country culture, e.g., home country language ability | Home country nationals for top management and technical positions; regional country nationals for midlevel management and below | Worldwide throughout the company; based on best qualified for position |
| Training for cross-cultural adaptation | Very limited or none; no language requirements | Limited for home country nationals; some language training. | Limited to moderate training levels for home country nationals; home and host country nationals use language of business, often English | Continuous for cultural adaptation and multilingualism |
| Management development effects of international assignments | May hurt career | May hurt career of home country nationals; host country nationals' advancement often limited to own country | Neutral to slightly positive career implications; international assignments of longer duration | International assignments required for career advancement |
| Evaluation | Home standards based on contribution to corporate bottom line | Host standards based on contribution to unit bottom line | Regional standards based on contribution to corporate bottom line | Global standards based on contribution to corporate bottom line |
| Compensation | Additional pay and benefits for expatriate assignments | Additional pay and benefits for expatriate assignments; host country compensation rates for host country nationals | Due to longer assignments, less additional compensation for expatriate assignments | Similar pay and benefit packages globally with some local adjustments |

*Sources: Adapted from Adler, Nancy J., and Fariborz Ghadar. 1990. "International strategy from the perspective of people and culture: The North American context." Research in Global Business Management, 1, 179–205; Heenan, D. A., and H. V. Perlmutter. 1979. Multinational Organization Development. Reading, MA: Addison Wesley.*

- *Expatriate managers are often poorly trained for international assignments and make mistakes:* Training is not valued and assignments are usually short.

## Regiocentric and Polycentric IHRM Orientations

Firms with **regiocentric** or **polycentric IHRM** orientations are more responsive to the host country differences in HRM practices. These orientations are similar in that they emphasize adaptation to cultural and institutional differences among countries. They differ only in that the polycentric company adapts IHRM practices to countries, while the regiocentric company adapts to regions. Given their similarity in IHRM philosophy, they are discussed together in this section.

Companies with polycentric IHRM orientations treat each country-level organization separately for HRM purposes. The home company headquarters ordinarily lets each country-level subsidiary follow local HRM practices. The regiocentric organization tends to adopt region-wide HRM policies. Consistent with these orientations, companies recruit and select their managers mostly from host countries or regions. Regiocentric companies may also look within the home company for key people who have mastered the cultures and languages of the countries in their regional locations. Qualifications for managers from the host country follow local or regional practices. However, to communicate with the multinational's headquarters, host country managers usually must be able to speak and write in the home company's national language.

Polycentric and regiocentric multinationals usually place home country nationals in top-level management or technical positions. These home country managers are used to control overseas operations or to transfer technology to host country production sites.[82] As with the ethnocentric IHRM companies, HRM home country policies are applied to expatriates. In addition, unless headquarters values country- or region-specific international experiences, there remains a tendency for international assignments to have negative effects on the managerial careers of home country nationals.[83]

Some benefits and costs of polycentric and regiocentric IHRM policies are as follows:[84]

### Benefits

- *Reduced training expenses:* Using mostly host country nationals or third country nationals from the region reduces the costs of training expatriate managers from headquarters; successful expatriate assignments, especially in a widely different culture, require heavy investments in training.

- *Fewer language and adjustment issues:* The use of host country and third country nationals limits the number of home country expatriate employees who face language barriers and adjustment problems, as local managers speak their area's language. Third country nationals from the region usually come from a similar culture and are more likely to have local language skills. Consequently, no investment in language training is necessary. The multinational company also faces fewer problems in managing expatriate adjustments to local cultures and in bringing home company expatriates back into the headquarters organization.

- *Lessened hiring and relocation costs:* Host country employees and third country nationals from the region are often less expensive than home country expatriates; the costs of expatriates are usually quite high.

**Regiocentric IHRM**
Regionwide HRM policies are adopted.

**Polycentric IHRM**
Firm treats each country-level organization separately for HRM purposes.

Costs

- *Coordination problems with headquarters based on cultural, language, and loyalty differences:* Even when host country or regional managers speak the language of the multinational's headquarters, communication can be difficult and misunderstandings can result. Host country managers may have more loyalty to their local organization than to the multinational parent.
- *Limited career path opportunities for host country and regional managers:* As with ethnocentric HRM practices, host country and regional managers may face a glass ceiling on promotions, that is, limited to advancement within a country or region.
- *Limited international experience for home country managers:* Because international experience often is not valued or rewarded, it does not always attract the best managers. Companies with limited managerial talent in international operations often face difficulties if their industry becomes global, requiring a step-up in international operations.

## Global IHRM Orientations

**Global IHRM**
Recruiting and selecting worldwide, and assigning the best managers to international assignments regardless of nationality.

Organizations with truly **global IHRM** orientations assign their best managers to international assignments.[85] Recruitment and selection take place worldwide, in any country where the best-quality employees can be found. The fit of the manager to the requirements of the job far outweighs any consideration of the individual's country of origin or of job assignment. Capable managers adapt easily to different cultures and are usually bilingual or multilingual. In addition, the international assignment becomes a prerequisite for a successful managerial career in companies with global orientations.

In companies with global orientations, managers are selected and trained to manage cultural diversity inside and outside the company. Employees inside their organization have culturally diverse backgrounds, and the company's multiple country locations provide culturally diverse customers and suppliers.[86] Besides confronting issues of cultural diversity, global managers must meet the coordination and control needs of corporate headquarters.[87] To meet these challenges successfully, managers need continual training in cultural adaptation and in the skills needed to balance local needs with overall company goals.[88]

As with other IHRM orientations, a global IHRM has its costs and benefits:[89]

Benefits

- *Bigger talent pool:* The available talent pool of managers and technical specialists is not limited by nationality or geography.
- *High international expertise:* Multinational companies develop a large group of experienced international managers.
- *Development of transnational organizational cultures:* Managers identify with the organizational culture more than with any national culture.

Costs

- *Difficulty in importing managerial and technical employees:* Host countries often have immigration laws that limit the use of foreign nationals or that make their use very costly.
- *Added expense:* Training and relocation costs are expensive. Expatriate compensation is higher than for host country employees.

## Focus on Emerging Markets

### Expatriate Success in China

Most research on HRM orientation has focused mostly on multinationals based in developed countries expanding into either developed or developing economies. However, the current environment is seeing the emergence of multinationals from emerging markets. Consider the case of India, with companies such as Infosys and Tata. Both companies are becoming formidable competitors in their own right. As such, it is important to see how these smaller emerging market multinationals, which are often at early stages of internationalization, are adopting IHRM strategy.

A recent study suggests that emerging markets multinationals face two forms of liabilities that developed multinationals do not necessarily face. First, in entering a new country, emerging market multinationals face the liability of foreignness whereby they have to work harder in a host country to succeed because they are seen as being foreign. Second, emerging markets multinationals also suffer from the liability of country of origin. Specifically, emerging market multinationals also suffer from the poor image perception of their country of origin.

In the face of such barriers, emerging market multinationals have to approach adoption of IHRM strategy differently. For instance, if they operate in developed markets, they can seldom use the "forward diffusion" strategy typical of developed market multinationals. While developed market multinationals often have superior home country practices that they can transfer to other countries, emerging market multinationals are often more likely to want to learn from practices in developed markets and to transfer those practices to other countries. As such, they are more likely to adopt more polycentric or regiocentric approaches where they hire host country managers with local knowledge. Lessons learned from the various locations are then transferred back to home subsidiaries as an improvement mechanism.

However, if an emerging market multinational is entering other emerging markets, it may not have access to the necessary individuals with the needed technical and management skills at the local level. In such cases, emerging market multinationals are more likely to adopt an ethnocentric approach, whereby they transfer home HRM practices in other subsidiaries worldwide.

*Sources: Based on Thite, M., A. Wilkinson, and D. Shah. 2012. "Internationalization and HRM strategies across subsidiaries in multinational corporations from emerging economies: A conceptual framework." Journal of World Business, 47, 251–258.*

As multinational companies from emerging markets are globalizing, they are also adopting the appropriate IHRM strategy based on the context they are located. However, for such companies, the type of market they are located in provides strong impetus for the type of orientation that is chosen. Consider the above Focus on Emerging Markets.

## *Summary and Conclusions*

This chapter introduced the basic HRM practices of recruitment, selection, training and development, performance appraisal, compensation, and labor relations. When these practices are applied to a company's international operations, they become IHRM, or international human resource management. Besides basic HRM functions, two key issues in IHRM are the mixture of expatriate and host country managers and knowing how to adapt home company HRM practices to the host country's situation. This chapter focused on HRM practices for expatriate employees. The next chapter reviews the differences in national HRM practices. Knowledge of these national differences helps multinational managers adapt IHRM to local conditions.

Expatriate managers present challenges and opportunities to multinational companies. They are costly, often costing two to three times as much as host country managers. They need special training to succeed even though they are not always successful. However, expatriate managers are loyal to the home organization, and they often have skills that are impossible to find in host country managers. It is important for multinational companies to find ways to properly manage their expatriates to fully benefit from the expatriates' experience. As companies face a global shortage of managers, they will increasingly rely on their women managers to take on expatriate responsibilities. Multinationals therefore must heighten their awareness of the significant barriers their women managers face in taking international assignments, and they must do what is necessary to facilitate the female expatriates' experience.

Successful IHRM presents one of the most important challenges to multinational companies in the twenty-first century. Many globalization trends—the development of large-scale trading blocs, the opening of national boundaries for trade, and the increasing prevalence of international strategic alliances—offer multinational companies the opportunity to use human resources unrestrained by political, linguistic, and cultural boundaries. Companies, large and small, that exploit international human resources the most effectively will have strong competitive advantages in an increasingly global economy.

## *Discussion Questions*

1. Identify the components of HRM and describe how they differ for IHRM.

2. Describe the types of nationals employed by multinational firms. Note likely situations when each type would be used.

3. Using the basic components of HRM as a guide, describe the likely practices used by a transnational firm.

4. Contrast the positive and negative issues for using short-term international cadre. Consider both the organization's perspective and the career implications for the individual manager.

5. Discuss the options available for expatriate compensation. Consider how these options might be used for a transnational and a multidomestic company.

6. Discuss how multinational companies can deal with the repatriation issue.

7. How can companies benefit from using women expatriates? Discuss some of the advantages women expatriates have over their male counterparts.

8. Discuss some of the major problems facing women expatriates. What can companies do to make their expatriate experience successful?

## Multinational Management **Internet Exercise**

Mercer Human Resources Consulting has developed a cost-of-living index that companies routinely use to determine how much to pay their expatriates. The index uses New York as a base and compares prices in the host country by weighting price ratios in the expenditure patterns of the expatriate. The index is a measure of the cost of living of American employees assigned to a foreign country. Go to http://www.mercer.com and find the most recent cost-of-living index.

1. How does Mercer Consulting develop the cost-of-living index? What factors does it take into consideration?

2. Which cities are the most expensive? Least expensive? What factors contribute to a city being ranked as most expensive?

3. How does the Mercer cost-of-living index compare with the Economist Intelligence Unit index? Do you see similarities? What are some differences?

4. How can a multinational use any of the above two cost-of-living indices to determine expatriate compensation?

## Multinational Management **Skill Builder**

### A Presentation

You are the vice president of the human resource management department of a large multinational company. Your company has decided to expand overseas. It is possible that you may send expatriates around the world, including to countries such as Australia, Japan, Mexico, Malaysia, India, South Africa, and Chile. You just came back from an important meeting with other VPs and the CEO. The major emphasis during the meeting was deciding which countries to expand into and how to ensure the expatriates' satisfaction with their overseas assignments and overall cost reductions because of efficiency pressures. You have been instructed to report some solutions to these pressing problems. As you prepare your presentation, you know that you need to address the following issues:

**Step 1.** Using as many sources of information as possible, prepare a list of types of information/issues that you can use to show the costs and benefits of sending the expatriates to the preceding countries.

**Step 2.** Demonstrate the types of information and sources you can use for them.

**Step 3.** Demonstrate how capturing the various types of information can be beneficial to the company; and how such information can be used.

**Step 4.** Recommend one or a few countries.

**Step 5.** Present your findings to the class.

---

## *Endnotes*

1. Milkovich, George T., and Jerry Newman. 1993. *Compensation,* 4th ed. Homewood, IL: Irwin; Bohlander, George W., Scott Snell, and Arthur W. Sherman, Jr. 2001. *Managing Human Resources,* 12th ed. Cincinnati: South-Western.

2. Mayerhofer, Helene, Linley C. Hartmann, and Anne Herbert. 2004. "Career management issues for flexpatriate international staff." *Thunderbird International Business Review,* November–December, 46(6): 647–666.

3. Quelch, John A., and Helen Bloom. "Ten steps to a global human resources strategy." *Strategy & Business,* 1st quarter, 2–13. Syedain, H. 2012. "From expats to global citizens." *People Management, January, online edition.*

4. Black, J. Stewart, Hal B. Gregersen, and Mark E. Mendenhall. 1992. *Global Assignments.* San Francisco: Jossey-Bass; Quelch and Bloom; Tung, Rosalie L. 1981. "Selection and training of personnel for overseas assignments." *Columbia Journal of World Business,* 16(1): 68–78.

5. Melvin, Sheila. 1997. "Shipping out." *The China Business Review,* 24, 30–35.

6. Rafer, M. V. 2009. "Return trip for expats." *Workforce Management,* March 16, 1, 3.

7. Ashamalla, Maali H. 1998. "International human resource management practices: The challenge of expatriation." *Competitiveness Review,* 8(2): 54–65.

8. McFarland, Jean. 2006. "Culture shock." *Benefits Canada,* January 30, 1, 31.

9. *Business Wire.* 2006. "International job assignment: Boon or bust for an employee's career?" March 13, 1.

10. Harzing, Anne-Wil, and Claus Christensen. 2004. "Think piece: Expatriate failure: Time to abandon the concept?" *Career Development International,* 9(6/7): 616–626.

11. McCaughey, Deirdre, and Nealia S. Bruning. 2005. "Enhancing opportunities for expatriate job satisfaction: HR strategies for foreign assignment success." *HR Human Resources Planning,* 28(4): 21–29.

12. Ashamalla, Maali H. 1998. "International human resource management practices: The challenge of expatriation." *Competitiveness Review,* 8(2): 54–65; Harzing and Christensen; McCall, Morgan W., and George P. Hollenbeck. 2002. "Global fatalities: When international executives derail." *Ivey Business Journal,* May–June, 74–78; McCaughey and Bruning; Poe, Andrea C. 2002. "Welcome back." *HR Magazine,* 45(3): 94–101;Tung, Rosalie L. 1987. "Expatriate assignments: Enhancing success and minimizing failure." *Academy of Management Executive,* 1(2): 117–126.

13. Fink, Gerhard, Sylvia Meierewert, and Ulrike Rohr. 2005. "The use of repatriate knowledge in organizations." *HR Human Resources Planning,* 28(4): 30–36; Gregersen, Hal B. 1999. "The right way to manage expats." *Harvard Business Review,* March–April, 52–61; Lublin, Joann S. 1992. "Younger managers learn global skills." *Wall Street Journal,* March 3, B1; O'Connor, Robert. 2002. "Plug the expat knowledge drain." *HR Magazine,* October, 101–107.

14. Korbin, Stephen J. 1988. "Expatriate reduction and strategic control in American multinational corporations." *Human Resource Management,* 27(1): 63–75.

15. Gregersen.

16. Boyacigiller, Nakiye A. 1991. "The international assignment reconsidered." In Mark Mendenhall and Gary Oddou, eds. *Readings and Cases in International Human Resource Management.* Boston: PWS-Kent, 148–155.

17. O'Connor.

18. Fink, Meierewert, and Rohr.

19. Ibid. Pinto, L.H., C. Cabral-Cardoso, and W. B. Werther. 2012. Compelled to go abroad? Motives and outcomes of international assignments. *International Journal of Human Resource Management,* 23(11) 2295–2314.

20. Micciche, T. 2009. "Preparation and data management are key for a successful expatriate program." *Employment Relations Today,* Spring, 35–39.

21. Poe.

22 Sims, Robert H., and Mike Schraeder. 2005. "Expatriate compensation: An exploratory review of salient contextual factors and common practices." *Career Development International*, 10(2): 98–108.

23 Selmer, J. 2002. "Practice makes perfect? International experience and expatriate adjustment." *Management International Review*, January, 42(1): 71–87.

24 Tung, "Selection and training of personnel for overseas assignments."

25 Gregersen; Halcrow. Allan. 1999. "Expats: The squandered resource." *Workforce*, July, 3, 28–30; Mendenhall, Mark, and Gary Oddou. 1985. "The dimensions of expatriate acculturation: A review." *Academy of Management Review* 10, 39–47; Poe; Tung, "Selection and training of personnel for overseas assignments."

26 Tye, Mary G., and Peter Y. Chen. 2005. "Selection of expatriates: Decision-making models used by HR professionals." *HR Human Resource Planning*, 28(4): 15.

27 Ibid.

28 Gabel, Racheli Shmueli, Shimon L. Dolan, and Jean Luc Cerdin. 2005. "Emotional intelligence as predictor of cultural adjustment for success in global assignments." *Career Development International*, 10(5): 375–395.

29 Tung, "Selection and training of personnel: Decision-making models used by HR professionals."

30 Black, J. Stewart, and Mark E. Mendenhall. 1990. "Cross-culture training effectiveness: A review and theoretical framework for future research." *Academy of Management Review*, 15, 113–36; Forster, Nick. 2000. "Expatriates and the impact of cross-cultural training." *Human Resource Management Journal*, 10, 63–78.

31 Forster.

32 Winham International. 2000. "Survey highlights." http://www.windhamint.com.

33 Black, Gregersen, and Mendenhall.

34 Mendenhall, Mark, and Gary Oddou. 1988. "Acculturation profiles of expatriate managers: Implications for cross-cultural training programs." *Columbia Journal of World Business*, 21, 73–79; Tung, "Selection and training of personnel for overseas assignments."

35 Dowling, Peter J., Denice E. Welch, and Randall S. Schuler. 1999. *International Human Resource Management*. Cincinnati: Southwestern.

36 Black, Gregersen, and Mendenhall.

37 Sims and Schraeder.

38 Ibid.; *Employee Benefits*. 2006. "Sending perks overseas." February 10, S10.

39 Davis, Debra A. 2005. "Paying the piper: Taxation of global employees." *Journal of Pension Benefits*, Autumn, 13(1): 85.

40 Frazee, Valerie. 1998. "Is the balance sheet right for your expats?" *Workforce*, 3, 19–23.

41 Overman, Stephenie. 2000. "In sync." *HR Magazine*, 45(3): 86–92.

42 Sims and Schraeder.

43 Dowling, Welch, and Schuler.

44 Black, Gregersen, and Mendenhall.

45 Ibid.

46 Frazee; Overman.

47 Sims and Schraeder.

48 Overman.

49 Gregersen.

50 Klaff, Leslie G. 2002. "The right way to bring expats home." *Workforce*, July, 40–44; Poe.

51 Black, Gregersen, and Mendenhall.

52 Klaff.

53 Gregersen.

54 Klaff; Gregersen; Black, Gregersen, and Mendenhall; Tyler, Kathryn. 2006. "Retaining repatriates." *HR Magazine*, March, 51(5): 97–102.

55 Lancaster, Hal. 1999. "To get shipped abroad, women must overcome prejudice at home." *Wall Street Journal*, June 29, B1.

56 Caligiuri, P. M. and R. Tung. 1999. "Comparing the success of male and female expatriates from a U.S.-based company." *International Journal of Human Resource Management*, 10(5): 163–179.

57 Harris, Hillary. 2002. "Think international manager, think male: Why are women not selected in international management assignments?" *Thunderbird International Business Review*, 44(2):175–203.

58 Linehan, Margaret. 2000. *Senior female international managers: "Why so few"*. Ashgate, U.K.: Aldershot.

59 Jelinek, Mariann, and Nancy J. Adler. 1988. "Women: World-class managers for global competition." *Academy of Management Executive*, 11(1): 11–19; Stroh, Linda K., Arup Varma, and Stacy J. Valy-Durbin. 2000. "Why are women left at home: Are they unwilling to go on international assignments?" *Journal of World Business*, 35, 241–255.

60 Izraeli, Dafna, and Yoram Zeira. 1993. "Women managers in international business: A research review and appraisal." *Business and the Contemporary World*, Summer, 35–46.

61 Linehan.

62 Inshc, G. S., N. McIntyre, and N. Napier. 2008. "The expatriate glass ceiling: The second layer of glass." *Journal of Business Ethics*, 83, 19–28.

63 Adler, Nancy J. 1993. "Women managers in a global economy." *HR Magazine*, September, 52–55.

64 Ibid.

65 Adler, Nancy J. "Pacific basin managers: A *gaijin*, not a woman." *Human Resource Management*, 26(2): 169–191.

66 Solomon, Julie. 1989. "Women, minorities and foreign postings." *Wall Street Journal*, June 2, B1.

67 Adler, "Pacific basin managers: A *gaijin*, not a woman."

68 Adler, "Women managers in a global economy."

69 Linehan, Margaret, and Hugh Scullion. 2001. "European female expatriate careers: critical success factors." *Journal of European Industrial Training*, 25(8): 392–418.

70 O'Leary, V. E., and J. L. Johnson. 1991. "Steep ladder, lonely climb." *Women in Management Review and Abstracts*, 6(5): 10–16.

71 Parasuraman, S. J., and J. H. Greenhaus. 1993. "Personal portraits: The lifestyle of the woman manager." In E. A. Fagenson, ed. *Women in Management: Trends, Issues and Challenges in Management Diversity*. London: Sage, 186–211.

72 Davidson, M. J., and C. L. Cooper. 1983. *Stress and the Woman Manager*. London: Martin Robertson.

73 Adler, "Pacific basin managers: A *gaijin*, not a woman."

74 Volkmar, John, and Kate L. Westbrook. 2005. "Does a decade make a difference? A second look at western women working in Japan." *Women in Management Review*, 20(7): 464–477.

75 Thaler-Carter, Ruth E. 1999. "Vowing to go abroad." *HR Magazine*, 44(12): 90–96.

76 Izraeli and Zeira.

77 Linehan and Scullion.

[78] Davidson and Cooper.

[79] Inshc, McIntyre, and Napier.

[80] Mendenhall, Mark E., E. Dunbar, and Gary R. Oddou. 1987. "Expatriate selection, training and career-pathing: A review and critique." *Human Resource Management*, 26(3): 331–345.

[81] Dowling, Peter J., and Denice E. Welch. 1988. "International human resource management: An Australian perspective." *Asia Pacific Journal of Management*, 6(1): 39–65; Reynolds, Calvin. 1997. "Strategic employment of third country nationals." *Human Resource Planning*, 20(1): 33–39.

[82] Adler, Nancy J., and Fariborz Ghadar. 1990. "International strategy from the perspective of people and culture: The North American context." *Research in Global Business Management*, 1, 179–205; Bohlander, Snell, and Sherman.

[83] Adler and Ghadar.

[84] Dowling and Welch; Reynolds.

[85] Quelch and Bloom.

[86] Ibid.

[87] Bartlett, Christopher A., and Sumantra Ghoshal. 1998. *Managing Across Borders*, 2nd ed. Boston: Harvard Business School Press.

[88] Quelch and Bloom.

[89] Dowling and Welch.

# People Management Fiasco in Honda Motorcycles and Scooters India Ltd.

*Dr. Debi S. Saini, professor and chairperson of HRM at Management Development Institute (MDI), Gurgaon, India, prepared this case for class discussion. This case is not intended to show effective or ineffective handling of decision or business processes.*

*The author thanks the many people who helped in construction of this case. The three union office bearers of the HMSI union who visited MDI at his request twice to give interviews; Mr. M. R. Patlan, the Deputy Labour Commissioner of Gurgaon, and his staff, who shared information and provided other help to reconstruct some of the nuances of the case; some anonymous persons who also shared useful information that facilitated cross-checking of the claims of the HMSI union and in building several new formulations. The author also thanks Rakhi Sehgal, a doctoral scholar in sociology, American University, Washington, D.C., for helping him establish contacts with many respondents.*

At the onset of 2006, the president of Honda Motorcycles and Scooters India Ltd. (HMSI), who was also its chief executive officer, had to make some radical decisions on a number of issues confronting the company following the July 2005 altercations with its workers. Not only did he have to repair the damage to the company's image, but he also had to develop a strategy for long-term cooperation with its employees. As he reflected upon the bitter memories of the last 12 months, he wondered

if the company could achieve targets laid out in the aggressive expansion plan developed before the unrest. This included tripling the Gurgaon plant's production capacity to 0.6 million motorcycles and 1.2 million two-wheelers by the end of fiscal 2007–2008.

Neither he, nor perhaps any of the members in his managerial team, could have imagined that workers' seemingly minor grievances would turn into a warlike situation, as they did in July 2005. The company, despite all its efforts, had not been able to prevent the union formation, that too with an affiliation to All India Trade Union Congress (AITUC), which was the trade union wing of the Communist Party of India. With the events taking a nasty violent overtone, the adverse publicity might have done perhaps irreparable harm to the public image of the company. In addition, the drop in the company's sales was also worrying. The company had suffered a production decline resulting in a loss of Rs 1.3 billion[1] as a consequence of the strike and go-slow tactics by the workers, especially during the months of May and June 2005. But there was much more at stake than just the monetary loss. While choosing the company's logo of the wings, the company had aimed to fly high by taking a dominant role in the Indian two-wheeler industry, simultaneously taking advantage of the rapidly growing Indian economy. Given the unexpected turn of events, would the CEO be able to successfully implement strategies that would not only wash away past wounds but would also lay the foundations of a soaring future?

## HMSI: Products and Workforce

HMSI was a wholly-owned subsidiary of Honda Motor Company Limited (HMCL), Japan. The Tokyo-headquartered HMCL was one of the world's leading manufacturers of automobiles and power products. With more than 120 manufacturing facilities in 30 countries, it was also the largest manufacturer of two-wheelers in the world. HMCL was known to have excelled in the adoption of the post-Fordist production system (also called the Toyota Production System).

HMSI was established on October 20, 1999, with an aim to produce world-class scooters and motorcycles in India. The state of the art HMSI factory, located in Gurgaon, was spread over 52 acres. The initial installed capacity was 100,000 scooters per year, which was scheduled to reach 600,000 scooters by the end of 2005. HMSI operated on the principles that were followed by all Honda companies worldwide. Maintaining a global viewpoint, HMSI was dedicated to supplying products of the highest quality, yet at a reasonable price to ensure complete customer satisfaction. These two-wheelers, manufactured with Honda-tested technology, were backed with after-sales service in line with Honda's global standards. Instead of being just vehicles for transportation, HMSI's products were intended to be vehicles for change: change in the way people worked, the way they travelled, and the way they lived.

HMSI had about 3,000 employees in all; of these 2,000 were in the worker category,[2] 1,300 were confirmed workers, while 700 were contract workers. The other 1,000 employees belonged to the supervisory and managerial staff. In addition, 700 persons were working as trainees and 300 were apprentices under the Apprentices Act 1960. Almost every worker or trainee held a certificate from an Industrial Training Institute (ITI) in India. All trainees, after completion of their training, normally got absorbed into the regular workforce, whereas only about 15% of the apprentices were able to get a job with the company after their apprenticeship. Considering the region-cum-industry averages, HMSI had the reputation of being a comparatively good paymaster. In October 2005, monthly wages for workers ranged from Rs 8,150 for unskilled workers to Rs 11,200 for skilled workers, which included a Rs 2,000 allowance for home rental.[3]

## Human Resource Policies at HMSI

The human resource (HR) policies of HMSI were in alignment with the philosophy of its parent company, HMCL. The latter considered itself a unique organization, having adopted some distinctive employment and production practices. It also had certain fundamental beliefs, which, among others, included the value of each individual. HMSI's philosophy advocated two fundamental beliefs: respect for individual differences, and the "Three Joys" that it wanted to promote for all organizational members.

Respect for the individual stemmed from initiative, equality, and trust. The company believed that it was the contribution of each employee that was responsible for a company's success, and which would take the company into the future. Based on its philosophy, respect for the individual translated into independence of spirit and freedom, equality and mutual trust of

human beings who worked for or came in contact with the company. The company claimed that its policies focused on developing each individual's capacity to think, to reason, and, most importantly, to dream.

In line with its parent Honda's philosophy, HMSI conducted all its daily activities in pursuit of the Three Joys: the joy of buying (i.e., the joy of using world-class products), the joy of selling (i.e., the joy of selling world-class products), and the joy of manufacturing (i.e., the joy of producing high-quality products). In addition, as an extension of its key mission, the company had imbibed the "joy of creating" as an important value for itself. The management believed that the joy of creating, which helped staff derive happiness from their daily work, thrilled its employees the most.

The company also promoted association among different categories of employees through provision of similar uniforms and common canteen facilities for all. In fact, all employees were called associates. The induction program of HMSI involved, among others, acclimatizing the employees to the Honda philosophy, which was a clear written statement. The company also talked of a "Honda way," which was not a written statement but was expected to run through the company. It was commonly understood that the Honda way meant "human behavior or way of thinking based on Honda philosophy." For example, one of the prominent Honda ways was perseverance to ensure safety and quality in all aspects. The HR department was expected to organize training programs and facilitate internalization of culture-building so as to promote the Honda way among the employees. Apart from training in Honda philosophy, the company organized other types of training, such as TQM (total quality management) training, training for building team leaders, ISO 9000 training, and 5S training.[4]

The company also published a six-page quarterly newsletter, "Dream Team." Its focus, among others, was on covering the company's achievement in terms of awards, contracts, recognitions, quality certification, new dealers, and kaizen activity. Employee-related matters were restricted to sports competition results and announcements of marriages and childbirths.[5]

### Performance Appraisal System

HMSI had a performance appraisal system for all its employees, including those in the worker category. Appraisal was performed by the section head and the shift in charge, who graded the employee on a rating scale. From this grade, workers were divided into five categories with increments ranging from

Rs 400 to 1,400 per month. The company announced all appraisal results and salary-hikes immediately on the end of the fiscal year. Thus on April 1 of each year, all employees would receive their pay-hike or promotion letters. The promotion opportunities for workers ranged from worker to sub-leader to assistant executive to executive. Since almost no employee was covered by the Payment of Bonus Act, 1961, the company had institutionalized a policy of giving an *ex gratia* of one month's gross pay to every employee as incentive pay around the Diwali festival.[6]

### Works Committee

Since April 1, 2004, the company had constituted a works committee under the Industrial Disputes Act, 1947 (IDA), consisting of 15 workers and 5 management representatives.[7] The management had also constituted some other committees consisting of workers and management representatives. Some of these were the canteen committee, the transport committee, the health committee, and the sports committee. Nominations to these committees were done by the management based on the perceived interest of different persons.

### Employee Welfare

In line with its HR policies, all employees at HMSI, including the managers, wore similar uniforms. The company provided two sets of uniforms, one company cap, and one pair of shoes to each employee every year. HMSI had also taken several initiatives in the area of employee welfare, which ranged from subsidized canteen facilities to attractive hospitalization reimbursement for all employees. Besides the canteen, another key initiative in this regard was transport facilities to and from workers' residences, provided at subsidized rates. The company also had a sports club for employees' use at Sukhrali village in Gurgaon, which had facilities for both outdoor and indoor games. Workers used these facilities to organize matches with employees of other companies in a variety of sports including football, volleyball, table tennis, chess, carom board, badminton, tug of war, high jump, and long jump. In the initial years, the company used to invite workers' families to celebrate the foundation day, but as the size of the workforce increased, the practice was discontinued.[8]

Most of the HMSI workers did not qualify for the Employees State Insurance scheme under the ESI Act, 1948, as their salaries had crossed the maximum salary limit for coverage. The company covered such employees under the Paramount Health Care facility. In addition to out-patient department facilities, this scheme provided re-imbursement for hospitalization expenses. Until September 2005, a worker and his or her spouse and up to two children were covered for Rs 75,000 each for hospitalization insurance, while the worker's mother and father were covered for Rs 150,000 each per annum.[9] In addition, to provide support to an associate at times of financial need, the company had a policy of paying, in cash, Rs 2,100 for the birth of a child (limited to a maximum number of two children) and Rs 3,100 on an employee's marriage. Rs 5,000 was given to the family of an employee on his or her death and Rs 3,000 on the death of an associate's spouse, child, or parent. The company also met its liabilities under various labor laws.

## Seeds of Unionization and After

For a couple of years after commencement of production, things ran smoothly. However, despite all the HR initiatives, it seemed all was not as it had appeared. The first signs of acrimony were voiced in November 2004, when workers expressed resentment at receiving Diwali gifts valued at Rs 600 apiece. Union leaders were quoted to have said, "in the past years also, the value of the Diwali gift was of about Rs 400 to Rs 500. Looking at the stature that our company enjoys in the global market, we all felt belittled at this small gift." A manager added that the perception of unfairness among workers was exacerbated by additional rumors that Hero-Honda,[10] a competitor of HMSI, was giving a refrigerator each to its workers as a Diwali gift. In the end, 99 percent of the HMSI workers refused to accept the Diwali gift, and the company took it back. As an alternative, it offered a coupon of Rs 600, with which workers could buy any gift item of their choice from certain specified dealers, but that too was turned down by the workers. Ten days after Diwali, this money was transferred to their bank accounts.

Other resentments were also festering among the workers. They were made to sign a "movement sheet" whenever they took a break to go to the toilet or drink water. In a much-cited incident, a worker was once denied permission to go to the toilet. When he could no longer bear it, he pulled the line chain to stop the conveyor belt and rushed to relieve himself. When he returned some minutes later, he was dismissed. Also, as in the post-Fordist production system, workers were often required to attend to more than one machine simultaneously; this increased stress levels on the shop floor. The company was also very strict in granting leave. Even when a worker's close relative was seriously ill or circumstances were otherwise serious, leave would not be granted. Apparently, while denying the leave, managers would lecture the employees. Sometimes they would be told to leave the company permanently if they could not perform up to expectations. If a worker wanted to change a shift temporarily for some obligatory reason, it was almost never granted. Almost every day, some worker or another would get a threat of termination. Because there was considerable fear of management's authority, nobody dared to speak up or seek a grievance redress.

Workers also perceived that many managers showed partiality in matters related to job postings. Their favorites were posted in jobs outside the production line. Production-line jobs were far more exerting than any other postings. The enormity of the problem took on serious proportions, and led to considerable bickering among workers. It seemed that while this practice was in place since the beginning, the Japanese top management knew little about it. The Indian managers would not let the workers meet the top management to share their grievances, but rather encouraged the scenario, as it prevented workers from uniting. Union leaders reinforced this view and claimed that managers did so to create friction amongst the common workers. They wanted these postings to be done on the basis of seniority.

At the same time, workers were also unhappy with the idiosyncratic attitude of the vice-president of manufacturing (a Japanese national), who was a strict Honda disciplinarian. Known for his unpredictability, he had a reputation for saying anything to anybody at any time. He was often seen patrolling the shop floor with a 14-foot-long stick that was used for measuring the heights of trolleys. Most workers took a dim view of him and cracked jokes about him behind his back. Once, a worker returned two minutes late from the teatime break. To show his disapproval, the VP kicked this worker in the leg, albeit in a friendly manner. At the time, neither the concerned worker nor the other workers around him reacted at all. However, by evening, the news had spread amongst the others and slogans were raised against the VP. The next day, the VP apologized in front of the workers' gathering. Subsequently, the Indian managers asked some 15 workers to have a meeting with them on the issue. The incident resulted in production stopping for a day and a half. A similar incident occurred when a Sikh officer of the company was wearing a different-colored cap and not the usual company cap.[11] The VP gave a push to his cap, knocking it off him. Although the official concerned felt insulted, he kept quiet.

Although the errant VP was later sent back to Japan, no other action was taken against him. Not satisfied with a mere apology from the VP, in the last week of March 2005 the workers came out with a charter consisting of more than 50 demands. These included an increase of Rs 2,500 per month in wages; a 20 percent annual increment in wages; house rent allowance to be pegged at 70 percent of wage; conveyance allowance of Rs 1,500 per month; a 20 percent bonus on wage plus a dearness allowance; provision for free distribution of one kilogram of milk and 0.5 kilogram of *gur* (jaggery) per worker every day; provision for a union office on the company premises along with all incidental facilities including a telephone; a loan of Rs 200,000 for marriage of a sibling or child; provision of a library on the company premises, and the abolition of the policy of overstay (if the production target for the day was not achieved, workers were required to compulsorily stay back until the target was achieved). Reluctantly, on April 1, 2005, the management offered the workers a compensation package comprising an increment of Rs 3,000 per month, on the condition that the workers not form a union. They refused to accept the management's offer.

When the management did not yield, the workers started collecting money for funding union activities. HMSI management suggested that the workers form an internal committee instead. When workers declined this suggestion, many were individually called into a manager's room and exhorted not to join the union. Letters were sent to certain workers' homes, claiming that they were indulging in undesirable activities. The management allegedly hired some outsider toughs to frighten the workers if they formed a union. But their resolve was too strong. With the help of local union leaders (affiliated with political parties), HMSI workers began making efforts to form a union, and subsequently moved an application for registration of the union to the registrar of trade unions in Chandigarh.[12] The management, not wanting the formation of a union in the organization, tried its best to stop the union registration. It resorted to various means like lobbying with the government of Haryana to help prevent the formation and subsequent registration of the union. As a result, the registrar allegedly denied registration of the union on the ground that the proposed workers' action was initiated in bad taste. The registrar also claimed that it would result in disharmony of relations between the industry and workers in the region at large and would prove detrimental to the growth and development of the industrial belt in and around Manesar.[13]

Consequent to this, the workers resorted to a slow-down of work (go-slow) and refused to put in overtime to complete production targets. The management viewed the new stand of the workers as a serious breach of discipline and suspended four workers on charges of insubordination, tampering with the quality of output, adopting a go-slow policy, indiscipline, and unrest. During the same period, the management also refused to absorb some trainees who had completed their two years of internship. These actions of the management led to widespread discontent among the workers. Most workers, whether permanent or trainees, collected together under the leadership of the suspended workers and started raising slogans. They also *gheraoed* the management within the offices located at the factory premises.[14] During this *gherao,* one person from senior management was manhandled and beaten up. The entire incident of the *gherao* and resulting violence resulted in production being shut down for 30 minutes. The management saw this as a grave and acute case of breach of discipline. It retorted by suspending 50 workers and dismissing the previously suspended four workers without any inquiry. This made the situation in the company still more explosive. Interestingly, in regard to the importance of local laws, the global philosophy of Honda stated as follows:

> *Honda is committed to providing a work environment that is free from unlawful discrimination, including harassment that is based on any legally protected status. Honda will not tolerate any form of harassment that violates this policy. This policy forbids any unwelcome conduct that is based on an individual's age, race, colour, religion, sex, national origin, ancestry, marital status, sexual orientation... or any other basis protected by state, federal or local law.*

In view of the resistance from the management, the registration of the proposed HMSI union was further delayed by more than a month. It was only when the cause of the workers and their application for registration was supported by a letter from AITUC chief Gurudas Dasgupta, a member of Indian Parliament, that the HMSI labor union registration finally took place. This letter, dated May 20, 2005, was addressed to the chief minister of Haryana and requested that he look into the matter to secure early registration of the proposed union. The newly formed union, while adopting the demands raised earlier, also added additional demands to their charter.

## Conciliation Failure and the Intensity of Workers' Action

Eventually, the dispute landed itself for conciliation. Conciliation proceedings were initiated on May 26, 2005, by the deputy labor commissioner of Gurgaon, who served as the conciliation officer in the Gurgaon region for all general-demands disputes. For conciliating matters related to individual disputes, the Gurgaon area was divided into four regions, each headed by a labor-cum-conciliation officer. Six conciliation meetings were held, on June 3, 17, 28, and July 8, 14, and 19, 2005. The HMSI management was represented by two managers belonging to the company's HR department. They remained quiet almost throughout the proceedings. The only contention the management raised was that the company was not required on any ground, whether legal or equitable, to raise the wages of the workers since it was already paying more than the region-cum-industry standards. The representatives of the union, however, chose to stick to their demands. The commissioner thought that the conciliation proceedings failed due to "the uncompromising stand adopted by both the union as well as the management representatives." He submitted a confidential failure report to the Haryana government under section 12(4) of the Industrial Disputes Act, 1947 (IDA) on July 19, 2005.

Concurrently, pending the outcome of the conciliation proceedings, the management asked the workers to sign a statement of good conduct. This statement stipulated that the workers return to work unconditionally and remain disciplined while on the factory premises. The statement also contained a clause stipulating non-pursuance of union activities by the workers while at work. It was this clause that became contentious and which compelled workers not to sign the statement. The management, in retaliation, refused to let the workers enter the factory premises without their signatures on the good-conduct bond.

In order to maintain production schedules, the management hired some temporary workers from its vendor companies. These temporary workers were asked to stay in the factory premises and requisite facilities were provided to them within the factory. Eventually, in June 2005, the management and the union reached an agreement whereby the management agreed to allow the workers to enter the premises of the company and work only under the condition that the terminated staff would not be taken back or reinstated. Furthermore, it was decided that the workers would be allowed entry into the factory premises in batches of 400 and that too only if they signed good conduct bonds. However, further apprehensions continued to plague the management. A few years prior at Hero-Honda Motorcycles Ltd, Dharuhera,[15] a similar situation had arisen and temporary workers from vendor companies were called in to continue the production. The management of Hero-Honda Motorcycles Ltd, under circumstances similar to those faced by HMSI, had entered into an agreement with their employees and allowed batches of 400 workers to enter the premises and resume work. However, after entering the premises, these workers disrupted the work done by the temporary workers from the vendor companies and brought production to a halt. The management at HMSI feared similar consequences at their factory.

While the workers agreed to the management proposition, on the following day, they put up the union flag at the factory gate. HMSI management became cautious and decided to allow only batches of 100 workers to enter the factory premises. Later, the management further retracted and announced that it would take back workers in batches of no more than 50. Anguished workers agreed yet again, but the management eventually decided not to allow any worker to enter the factory. The management also requested and received a good degree of police protection. The potentially explosive situation in the factory resulted in a fear in the minds of the temporary workers who had come from the vendor companies. Many of these workers fled from the factory premises. On June 18, 2005, only 38 temporary workers reported to work. At 1:30 p.m., the management was forced to shut down production for the day.

All these disruptions, in addition to the go-slow tactics adopted by the workers after the union registration, severely affected daily production at the plant. During the months of May, June, and July 2005, production dropped to a mere 10 percent of normal levels, from 2,000 scooters per day to around 200. This was a grave cause for concern to the management, causing HMSI to place a newspaper advertisement for the recruitment of new workers.

## The Dance of Violence and its Aftermath

On July 25, 2005, workers from HMSI and some from neighboring industries staged a rally at offices of the district authorities to press their demands for reinstatement of their dismissed and suspended colleagues. The police prohibited the workers from entering the Civil Lines area, which housed the offices of all major government functionaries of the district, including the district collector. At this point, several masked men began throwing stones. The protesters attacked the deputy superintendent of police, who was beaten mercilessly. They also set fire to the vehicle belonging to the sub-divisional magistrate. Eventually, the police succeeded in controlling the mob. The incident was covered by the television media and generated a great deal of public sympathy for the police. The identity of the masked men was not confirmed, and HMSI workers denied that anyone from their ranks was among them.

After this much-publicized clash, a message was sent to the workers that the administration would meet them and accept their memorandum. They were asked to assemble at the lawns of the secretariat. Once inside the enclosure, on some slight provocation, the police resorted to the use of brute force against the unarmed workers, reportedly in retaliation for the earlier attack on the police. The constabulary forced workers indiscriminately to kneel holding their ears while they were thrashed. The number of workers injured was initially claimed to be 700. While most workers were discharged after first aid, 70 of them suffered severe injuries. Later on, the police arrested a number of workers and booked them under different sections of the Indian Penal Code. The Haryana police also booked the legal counsel of the HMSI union on charges of attempt to murder. The media reported that this use of the worst possible police brutality on the workers, though inexcusable, was not exactly unprovoked (see Exhibit 1 for media pictures of the event). The television images of the savagery exhibited by the police in their attack on the workers brought to many minds the savagery of General Dyer's army at Jalianwala Bagh, perpetrated in the interest of their British masters. P. Sainath, a journalist for the *Hindu*, an English language daily, wrote:

> The scenes from Gurgaon gave us more than just a picture of labor protest, police brutality or corporate tyranny.... The streets of Gurgaon gave us a glimpse of something larger than a single protest. Bigger than a portrait of the Haryana police. Greater than Honda. Far more complex than the "image of India" as an investment destination. It presented us a microcosm of the new and old Indias. Of private cities and gated communities. Of different realities for different classes of society. Of ever-growing inequality.
>
> *P. Sainath, journalist for the Hindu*

While it was admitted that some police officers were beaten by the mob before the police responded

**EXHIBIT 1** Press Images of the July 2005 Union Incident

Picture 1: Police beating HMSI workers on July 25, 2005

Picture 2: An angry relative of an injured worker attempting to hit a policeman for his role in beating HMSI workers

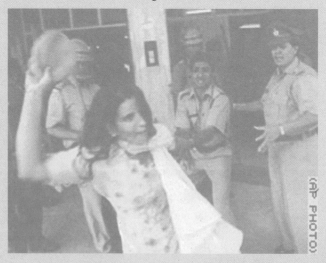

(AP PHOTO)

*continued*

with its brutality, the HMSI union maintained that it was done by outsiders. Violence continued on the next day, reportedly sparked off by enraged members of the public who turned up at the civil hospital and could not find their relatives. Some of these were whisked away by the police and were charged with the previous day's violence. This inflamed matters even further. The police action on workers was severely protested by the print and television media and by politicians in and outside the Parliament. As a result, the inspector-general of police conceded that the incident was an act of gross negligence on the part of the police. The deputy superintendent of police and the sub-divisional magistrate concerned claimed

**EXHIBIT** **1** Continued

Picture 3: HMSI union leaders meet Mrs. Sonia Gandhi,
president of the ruling Congress Party, to seek help
against the police action

that out of the 375-odd persons arrested after the incident, 79 had nothing to do with the strike at HMSI. This was later verified by the records of HMSI.

On July 26, 2005, the day after the unprecedented violence, HMSI closed operations for half a day, but it did not declare a lockout. Consequent to severe protests in different circles, on July 27, the Haryana chief minister ordered a court of enquiry to investigate the violent incident, to be conducted by a retired judge of the Punjab and Haryana High Court.[16] The terms of reference provided for, among others: completing the inquiry within a period of three months; examining the role of outsiders in the incident; examining whether the force used by the police was justified or excessive; and whether the means available to the police were adequate to control the crowd. The Haryana chief minister was also directed by Congress president Sonia Gandhi to hold discussions with the HMSI management and its workers. For more than two weeks,

61 workers remained in jail. They were subsequently released on August 11, 2005.

## The Truce and the Role of the State

On July 30, 2005, an agreement arbitrated by the Haryana chief minister was arrived at between the workers and the management of HMSI. Of course, technically this was a conciliated settlement and not a case of arbitration under the IDA. The agreement stated that the striking workers would resume duty from Monday, August 1, 2005, and that they would not raise any new demands during the next one year. The trade union, which was the bone of contention between the workers and management would, however, continue to operate. The agreement also stated that the 50 suspended workers would be reinstated, as well as the four union leaders whose services had been previously terminated. However, the employees would be reinstated only after they had submitted an unconditional letter of apology.

The four terminated workers were also required to submit a separate assurance letter to the top management. The settlement contained a clause stipulating that the workers promised not to engage in any act of indiscipline and assure normal production. However, the management retained the right to conduct an inquiry into the reasons for termination of the aforementioned four employees and, if the employees were found guilty, the management had the right to transfer them to any other department other than the manufacturing department. The agreement also provided for termination of any employee of HMSI who was convicted in any of the court cases that had been initiated against them by the city administration in connection with the July 25, 2005 incident. The workers were awarded full salary for the months of May and June, 2005. However, from June 27 onwards, the principal of "no work, no pay" would be implemented.[17] It was also provided that the injured workers who were not able to work immediately would be given paid leave.

About the workers' demand to absorb the trainees as permanent employees after the completion of their internship, it was decided that a proper test and a detailed appraisal form would be administered for evaluating their performance before inducting them as permanent staff. Finally, it was decided that the agreement be considered as final conciliation in respect to all demands raised by the workers and that, in the future, both the parties would maintain cordial relations.

## Union–Management Dynamics in the Post-Violence Scenario

The union office-bearers felt that a good degree of change could be seen in the attitude of the managers in the post-July 25 scenario. The management allowed concessions on several fronts. On the day of the tripartite agreement, the management wanted to terminate the services of some 200 contract workers even though the tripartite agreement provided for reinstatement of all workers. But the union was able to convince the management that the company should stick to the agreement. No domestic inquiry proceedings were started against the four dismissed workers who had been taken back, nor were they transferred to other departments as envisaged in the tripartite agreement.

The management had also informally allotted a temporary room to the union leaders, though it was not sufficiently big, and promised them a proper union office after some time. There was also an informal understanding that the union leaders would have the freedom not to work on the shop floor as long as several industrial relations issues were still pending. For example, police had registered cases against 63 workers, including all the seven union office-bearers, for the July 25 violence. This necessitated running around contacting different people to build a sound defense. Meanwhile, the injured workers had their own problems, requiring the intervention of the union. Of the 50 workers who had suffered major injuries, 15 cases were very serious and involved head injuries, multiple fractures, damage to knee caps, etc. The company showed all these injured as absent, and was hesitant to pay them their salaries. According to union leaders, they "had to struggle to ensure that their salaries are paid regularly."

They also had to monitor the worker–supervisor relations closely to see that workers were treated better. Another area of the union leaders' involvement was the issue of absorption of trainees into regular positions. Even as the absorption of all persons who had completed their training into regular service formed part of the tripartite settlement, the management was initially refusing to take most of them on different pretexts. As these trainees had supported the workers' struggle, the union got all of them absorbed into regular jobs. Speaking of the change, S. K. Shafi, the secretary of the union, observed:

> Now, when a worker asks for leave, managers speak with much restraint; their response being far more positive. Workers are able to adjust a half-day shift within the next day with negligible hassles. The number of memos that workers get is negligible. The workers wanted four days' leave on Diwali in November 2005, and consequently closure of the factory for four days. This meant three days' compensatory working on Sunday and/or holidays; the management has hesitantly agreed to this proposal. Further, most factories in Gurgaon were working on 29th September, 2005, when some of the major Indian trade union federations gave a call for industrial strike all over the country in protest against the Central Government's economic policies. Our union, however, observed the day as strike. Though the management felt bad to know its decision, the union compensated the loss by working on a Sunday.

> *S.K. Shafi, secretary of the HMSI workers' union*

Another major achievement by the union was the hike in the coverage of the workers and their family members under the medical insurance scheme. This was a result of negotiations following an incident in September 2005, when the hospitalization expense of a worker's wife cost him Rs 135,000. Although the worker was in extreme distress over the death of his wife, the management refused to pay the excess of the coverage limit. Earlier, nobody would have dared to talk about such an incident with the management. In the changed circumstances, the union negotiated the issue and made the management agree to a family floater coverage scheme of Rs 175,000. This overall limit could be utilized by one or more or all the family members. If the expenses still exceeded this amount, the company agreed to pay up to Rs 100,000. This agreement was reached not through any written settlement with the union, but by way of a change in management policy at the insistence of the union, and came into effect on October 1, 2005.

Another new development was that, whenever there was a workers-related problem or issue, the management invited all seven of the union office-bearers for discussion. This had never been done earlier. For example, the management faced a problem of increasingly stressed workers who had to work overtime to meet the production targets. Overtime was being paid at the rate of double the basic wage rate. Workers found it somewhat attractive to work overtime and make extra money. But this had led to, among others, medical problems. Workers never felt fresh while at work, thus hampering overall productivity. The union's help was sought and a decision was taken to scrap overtime completely, except under exceptional circumstances.

In a landmark incident on September 9, 2005, the "A-shift" in assembly achieved its target of 1,000 scooters for the first time after the union formation. Prior to the unrest, the target was achieved in almost every shift. Union leaders said that the targets could not be achieved due to various interruptions. However, they could not satisfactorily explain why these interruptions had not affected the target achievement earlier. On hearing the target achievement that day, the vice-president of manufacturing, along with the general manager of production, came to the shop floor during the lunch time and commended the achievement of the workers. The next day, sweets were distributed to all workers.

The scheme of inviting workers' families on the founders' day had been stopped as the number of employees had increased, and the practice was becoming unmanageable in view of the fact that Honda workers were from more than 20 different states of India. This practice was revived in late September 2005. Thereafter, family members were invited to the factory at the company's expense in batches and were shown the conditions under which their loved ones worked.

The Diwali gift for the year 2005 was also settled through negotiations. Each employee was given a gift of Rs 2,000 and an incentive bonus in the form of a bank account credit of Rs 4,000. This included all managerial staff. Ironically, unlike the one month's gross pay disbursed for the year 2004, the bonus money for the year 2005 was smaller. The management was able to convince the union that the factory had suffered huge losses and thus the *ex gratia* bonus had to be cut down. The biggest sufferers from this agreement were the managerial employees, who received substantially less than their one month of gross salary in previous years.

Despite these developments, there were still some odd incidents reminiscent of the previous unrest. One took place on September 2, 2005, when two supervisors in the aluminum machine shop treated workers authoritatively and in a provocative manner, just as they had done before. The workers of this department reacted. Some 150 of them came to the union leaders seeking their intervention. When the union leaders went to settle the issue with the senior manager concerned, he spoke angrily with the union leaders too. Workers of the whole shift halted work for around 15 minutes. A union leader later said, "we went to all the departments to exhort the workers to start the work; we did not want work to be interrupted. That day most senior managers had gone to Chandigarh for some work. After they came back, the next day they all felt sorry for the incident and appreciated our intervention in the matter."

Expatiating on the dynamics involved, C. D. Tikar, the general secretary of the union, observed:

*We are committed to the company. We consider it as ours, and always want to do our best for it. The respect for the individual and the joys that the company claims to be practicing are merely in the book. Some of the senior managers want to see a big distance between the top management and the workers. The HR manager never wants that we meet the Japanese top management, as he feels that if he is asked to become transparent in his working, this will prevent him from realizing his hidden objectives including favouring his chosen few. Only some 20 per cent of the managers treat us with the dignity that we expect as members of the company; most others have big egos. The managers as well as the workers need to change. You know, the problems always emanate at the shop floor, but nobody bothers about analyzing their causes and possible solutions in a more practical and acceptable manner. The worker always wants fair and just working of the company. When this does not happen, he reacts.*

*C. D. Tikar, general secretary of the HMSI workers' union*

## Looking Back and Planning for the Future

The company had been performing extremely well since the beginning, and had shown promising results on several fronts (see Exhibit 2). The TNS Automotive Dealers Satisfaction Study, 2004 ranked HMSI as the leader in the two-wheeler category in India with 108 points, followed by Hero-Honda with 96 points. The company also received several recognitions in other spheres. But in the post-July 25 scenario, the company took quite some time to absorb the shock of what had happened. The management wanted to know what had gone wrong and where, and how things could be improved. Some of the issues at hand that needed attention were summarized by an anonymous manager of HMSI as follows:

*The company had a total lack of direction on the people front, which to a great extent is still persisting. Management does not know what to do to overcome the shock of July 25 and its aftermath. Japanese were conversant dealing with the Japanese unions, which were known to be much more tolerant. The company also has a lot of problems of hierarchy consciousness. The present GM–Operations came from Maruti (a Suzuki-controlled automobile company), where he could successfully tackle somewhat similar discontent among workers. The Japanese do not understand the workers' language also. The Director—General Affairs, who also is responsible for overall HR management, came with a lot of ideas, but he could not understand the organizational working from the employees' point of view. When workers had resorted to go-slow, Japanese managers did not know what to do. On the other hand, Indian managers were specialists in production; they did not understand how to handle industrial relations (IR) issues. If D. P. Singh [who was HR chief till some time ago, and had left HMSI, commanded respect among most workers] had not left, perhaps the problems may never have arisen. He had a good rapport with the workers. Another problem was that the Japanese had not given Indian managers much power to take major initiatives in different dimensions. Things have, however, somewhat improved in this regards now after July 25.*

**EXHIBIT 2**   2004 Dealer Satisfaction Study Ranking of Two-Wheelers

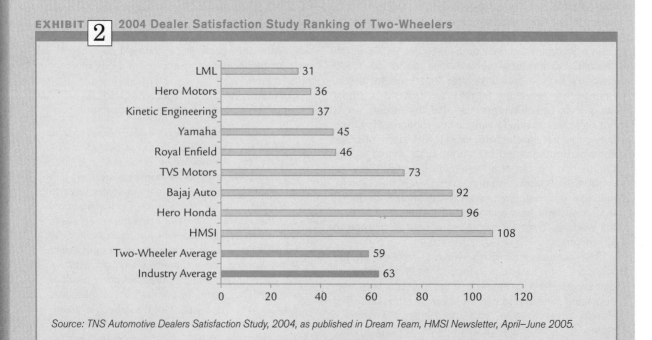

*Source: TNS Automotive Dealers Satisfaction Study, 2004, as published in Dream Team, HMSI Newsletter, April–June 2005.*

As one of the direct consequences of the unrest, the company revamped and intensified its training function. Managers were sent out to attend management development programs (organized by, among others, the Confederation of Indian Industry and the All India Management Association). Training areas included inter-personal skills, negotiation skills, team-building and conflict management, and leadership building. Interestingly, however, the position of assistant manager of training remained vacant.

In view of the damage done to the company's reputation, HSMI was also busy in an image-building exercise. Earlier, the managers were under the impression that Honda products would sell because of the company's image as a global brand. Now it had come to realize that, following the July 25 violence, its advertisements were no longer effective. The company was forced to consider new ways of enhancing their market image. In an innovative attempt, a week-long drive was organized during which henna tattoos of the HMSI logo were applied on women's hands.[18] In its endeavour to reach the far-flung masses across the country, HMSI also ran road shows of two of its popular two-wheeler models, Eterno and Unicorn.

A strategic meeting of the top management and the department heads took place at a country resort to decide the future course of action. They were well aware that, in addition to the assistant manager of training position, the posts of senior manager of industrial relations and senior manager of administration were also lying vacant. An outcome of the meeting was the decision to appoint a new person as the senior manager for both these functions. In September 2005, all union office-bearers were trained by the HR department on building cooperative industrial relations. External trainers were also invited to participate in this program. The company also nominated a committee consisting of seven worker representatives who would bring the workers' grievances to the notice of the management and the union leaders.

The short but bitter history of industrial relations of HMSI had shaken the company's top management. Its CEO was wondering what impact this would have on the ambitious expansion plans that he had drawn out just a few months before the July 25 violence. In preparation for the move forward, he was looking for ways to undo the bitter feelings among the workers, while at the same time deliberating what steps he should implement, not only to repair the damage to the company's image, but also to maintain and enhance productivity.

## CASE DISCUSSION QUESTIONS

1. Identify and discuss the key factors that led to the breakdown of industrial relations at HMSI.
2. Discuss the failures on the part of the Japanese and Indian managers that contributed to the present situation.
3. What HRM strategy was being pursued by the management, and what factors led to its failure?
4. Discuss the provisions of Indian industrial relations law that may have been violated by the HMSI management.
5. How should HMSI go about attending to the issues in people management systems and processes? What HR strategy should it adopt and implement for making lasting improvement in industrial relations?

## CASE NOTES

[1] US$1 = 45 INR on May 1, 2005.

[2] Under the Factories Act 1948, a worker is "a person employed directly or by or through any agency (including a contractor)…in any manufacturing process or in cleaning any part of the machinery or premises used for a manufacturing process or in any other kind of work incidental to, or connected with, the manufacturing process…."

[3] In the state of Haryana, India, the minimum wage rates for unskilled, semi-skilled, skilled, and highly skilled workers in the month of May 2005 were Rs 2,360, Rs 2,470, Rs 2,615, and Rs 2,920 respectively.

[4] The training department, which was a part of its human resource department, was supposed to be headed by an assistant manager; but this position lay vacant for a long time.

[5] A perusal of the past issues of the newsletter revealed that its focus was on targets, safety, exhortations related to, and announcement of, achievements concerning quality, safety, and training programs on defensive and safe driving of two-wheelers. Very few employee-related matters were covered. Nor was there any scope for workers' expression through any letter to the editor related to issues that concerned them.

[6] Diwali is the most important and most widely observed festival of Hindus, who constitute more than 80 percent of the Indian population. Festivities include gift exchanges and purchases of new clothes and household items. The exact date of the festival is decided according to the Hindu calendar, normally falling in the month of November, and, on occasion, in the last week of October.

[7] After the union came into being, the works committee had become merely symbolic.

[8] The practice was reinstated in late September 2005 after union negotiations.

[9] Subsequently, after the union intervention these rates were enhanced.

[10] Hero-Honda is an Indian company, which is a joint venture between the Hero group of companies and HMCL. It is a separate entity and has no connection with HMSI. Hero-Honda also produces motorcycles and scooters. It has two plants, one at Gurgaon (Haryana) and the other at Dharuhera (Haryana). While there is no union in the Gurgaon plant, the Dharuhera plant is unionized.

[11] Sikhs, as a part of their religion wear turbans as a part of their normal daily attire.

[12]Gurgaon falls in the Indian state of Haryana. Chandigarh is the capital city of Haryana, which houses all state offices.

[13]Manesar is an industrial belt of Haryana which includes sections of Gurgaon.

[14]*Gherao* is a Hindi word. It means to encircle. It is often used by employees against managers or officers as a pressure tactic. Persons indulging in a *gherao* surround the person concerned (usually one or more managers) and do not let him/them move at all. Technically, it is illegal as it violates the provisions of the Indian law of crime. It leads to illegal confinement of the person *gheraoed*. But in case any other violence is not practiced, normally no action is taken against those indulging in a *gherao* in the interest of industrial peace.

[15]See footnote 9.

[16]Punjab and Haryana are two Indian states which share the Union Territory of Chandigarh as their capital.

[17]In accordance with an earlier ruling of the supreme court of India in the case of "Bank of India v. T. S. Kelawala" (1990), *Labour Law Reporter*, 313.

[18]The application of henna tattoos is a popular Indian ritual undertaken by women on happy occasions such as weddings or festivals.

# HRM in the Local Context: Knowing When and How to Adapt

# 12

*Preview*　　C A S E　 I N　 P O I N T

## Following Local Traditions

The United States is the only industrialized country without government-mandated vacation time. Employees in U.S. firms average just two weeks of vacation per year. In contrast, their European counterparts receive an average of five to six weeks of vacation annually. Countries such as Italy, France, Germany, Spain, Sweden, and others have regulations that guarantee workers at least a month of paid annual vacation. It is therefore not surprising that U.S. workers are likely to work about 250 more hours a year than workers in Western Europe. Although many U.S. managers see the European vacation as excessive, European managers counter that U.S. organizations have misplaced goals.

Vacation time is not the only labor issue that differs worldwide. Consider the case of maternity leave. A recent study of 177 countries found that 170 of the 177 countries surveyed offer paid maternity leave. Australia, Lesotho, Norway, Papua New Guinea, Portugal, Sweden, and the United States are the only countries that do not provide paid maternity leave. However, Australia, Norway, Portugal, and Sweden do offer shared parental leave as well as paid paternity leave. Only 59 of the 177 economies studied offered paid leave for both parents.

Given the wide differences regarding human resources worldwide, it is important to carefully consider the customs and laws of the countries where employees are located. For example, when Nokia decided to open a new plant, it chose Cluj, a city of 400,000 in Romania. Why Cluj? Nokia found that it is difficult to recruit and retain skilled workers in many emerging cities in India and China. In fact, experts argue that although both India and China have an increasing number of qualified graduates, recruiting quality staff is becoming increasingly difficult. In contrast, Cluj has a plentiful supply of workers who are very eager for these jobs. However, because one of the major success factors in the mobile phone business is maximum productivity, Nokia realized that it had to respect local customs and give workers the appropriate incentives to make the plant succeed. Nokia planned to give workers free food, a gym, and even playing fields. Furthermore, as a show of respect for the local culture, foreign staffers must study Romanian.

## Learning Objectives
*After reading this chapter you should be able to:*

- Have a basic understanding of how the national context affects HRM practices.

- Describe how recruitment and selection practices differ among national contexts.

- Identify possible host adaptations in recruitment and selection practices for a multinational company.

- Explain how training and development techniques are used in different countries.

- Name sources of high-quality workers in different nations.

- Understand how training must be adapted to host country workers.

- Identify how performance evaluation and compensation practices differ in various national contexts.

- Discuss possible host country adaptations in performance evaluations and compensation practices for a multinational company.

- Understand how labor costs vary among nations.

- Appreciate how national context and historical conditions affect the relationship of management and labor in different countries.

*Sources: Based on Beacham, W. 2009. "Competition for talent is still fierce." ICIS Chemical Business, February 2, 8, 5; World Bank. 2012. Doing Business Project: Employing Workers. htpp://www.doingbusiness.org; Ewing, J. 2008. "Nokia's new home in Romania." BusinessWeek, January 28, 41–42; Poe, Andrea C. 1999. "When in Rome ... European law and tradition back generous vacation policies." HR Magazine, 44; HR Magazine Online Archive, http://www.my.SHRM.org; Simmers, Tim. 2005. "Workers in U.S. labor longer with less vacation than others." Business Writer, December 10, 1.*

The Preview Case in Point shows several issues that can affect how multinational companies conduct business in a host country. Similar critical questions might be: How do you hire a worker in Mexico? What educational background can you expect from German workers? Can you lay off workers in Denmark? What would happen in Japan if you promoted a 30-year-old to supervise 40-year-old employees? How many days of vacation should you give to employees in Brazil? Should employees in Chile get paid maternity leave? What kind of relationships should you expect with unions in South Africa?

To avoid costly mistakes in human resource management, multinational companies need to consider several key questions regarding local employees, such as:[1]

- How can we identify talented local employees?
- How can we attract prospective employees to apply for jobs?
- Can we use our home country's training methods with local employees?
- What types of appraisal methods are customary?
- What types of rewards do local people value (e.g., security, pay, benefits)?
- Do any local laws affect staffing, compensation, and training decisions?

To show the impact of the national context (national and business cultures and social institutions) on human resource management, this chapter illustrates varied practices from the United States and other countries. The chapter builds on your understanding of international human resource management (IHRM), discussed in Chapter 11. Reading both chapters will help you, the multinational manager, select and implement appropriate human resource management policies and, when necessary, adapt the policies to the local environment.

How important are HRM systems? Consider the following Case in Point.

The next Case in Point clearly demonstrates the importance of HRM worldwide. Next we consider the major factors that explain why nations differ in the ways that they approach HRM.

## Why Do Nations Differ in HRM?

**National context**
*National culture and social institutions that influence how managers make decisions regarding the strategies of their organizations.*

Cross-national differences in HRM and the pressures to adapt to local conditions arise from the array of factors that make each nation unique. As we saw in Chapter 3, these factors are called the **national context**, and they include such things as the national culture, the country's available labor and other natural resources, the characteristics of political and legal institutions, the types of managers available to firms, social institutions, and national and business culture factor conditions and their combined effects on the business environment. Thus, the national context provides the unique setting for each nation in which managers make HRM decisions. Exhibit 12.1 shows a model of how the national context leads to national differences in HRM policies and practices.

C A S E   I N   P O I N T

## Human Resource Management Practices in Jordan

As we will discuss later in the chapter, human resource management (HRM) is the process of recruiting, training, and compensating while also ensuring that the labor relations of the workers are respected. Some experts suggest that the HRM of any company is likely its most important asset. Well-managed HRM systems ensure that multinationals have access to the human resources they need while, at the same time, ensuring that employees develop their full potential. There is now some consensus that properly designed HRM systems result in stronger-performing organizations and employees. But how is HRM related to job aspects?

A fascinating recent study of employees in Jordan examined how key HRM aspects influence job involvement. Job involvement reflects the degree to which a person identifies with his or her job. People with high job involvement tend to consider their jobs as very important and central to their lives. Job involvement is a critical factor that is related to many other positive work outcomes, such as how satisfied a person is with his or her job. Furthermore, those with high job involvement have fewer absences and are less likely to leave their organizations.

The study of 284 Jordanian employees from a variety of industries such as banking, health services, accounting, and insurance provide some insights into the importance of HRM. It measured different aspects of HRM such as job analysis (duties of a job and the type of employees needed for the job), selection, training, performance appraisal, compensation, and performance management. All aspects of the HRM systems in the companies studied had positive influences on job involvement.

*Source: Based on Abutayeh, B., and M. Al-Qatawneh. 2012. "The effects of Human Resource Management practices on job involvement in selected private companies in Jordan." Canadian Social Science, 8(2): 50–57.*

Chapters 2 and 3 showed that the values and norms associated with national and business cultures result in preferred ways of doing business. These preferences influence all aspects of the organization: strategies, organizational design, and human resource practices. Basic norms and values regarding gender, age, and family and friends influence HRM practices from recruitment to performance appraisal.

Because countries' social institutions differ widely, multinational managers must select and implement HRM practices that meet the demands of a society's social institutions. Just as social institutions relate to how relationships are structured among people, they help define the correct ways of doing business in a country. In the United States, for example, antidiscrimination laws, part of the legal social institution, prohibit many recruitment practices common in Japanese and Korean companies. In Japan, the family system relies on women raising children so that men can work long hours at night or be away from home for extended periods. There are unwritten biases against women holding managerial positions after they have children.

The national context also includes the pool of resources available for firms. The **resource pool** represents all the human and physical resources available in a country. Examples are the quality of labor, the availability of scientific laboratories, and sources of fuel. If all countries had access to the same resources, there would be fewer differences across nations in management practices. Regardless of nationality, if firms could access the same resources, they would copy the strategies and organizations of the most successful competitors in the world. However, the national endowments of physical resources (e.g., supply of raw materials) and other resources (e.g., culturally based motivations to work, educational systems) are unique to each country.

**Resource pool**
All the human and physical resources available in a country.

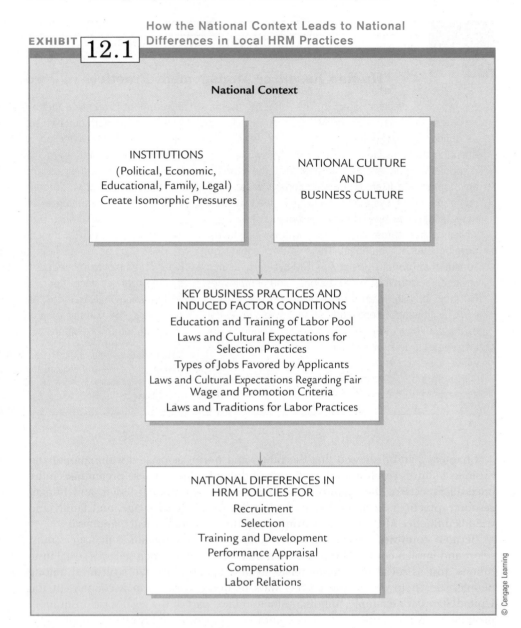

**EXHIBIT 12.1** How the National Context Leads to National Differences in Local HRM Practices

The resource pool represents the factor conditions associated with a country. Five key factors influence the resource pool and, in turn, the management practices favored by firms in a given nation:[2]

1. *The quality, quantity, and accessibility of raw material:* For example, the extensive tracts of fertile land in the United States enable U.S. agricultural firms to compete with low prices and high quality on the world market.

2. *The quantity, quality, and cost of personnel available:* Germany, for example, has large pools of technically trained workers who support the development of industries and firms where high-quality differentiation strategies abound. In contrast, however, German workers are among the most highly paid in the world, thus making low-cost strategies difficult.

3. *The scientific, technical, and market-related knowledge available to firms:* Both Japan and the United States, for example, have abundant stores of scientific and technical knowledge from universities and industry-based R&D. Additionally, in countries like China and Taiwan, the government is taking an active role in reshaping the educational system in order to encourage people to get trained in more knowledge-oriented sectors.[3]

4. *The cost and amount of capital available to firms for operations and expansion:* This factor addresses the question of how firms get financing to run their operations. For example, during the double-digit expansion of the Korean economy, Korean *chaebol* (conglomerates) relied mostly on heavy debt financing from government-controlled banks. In the post-1998 Korean economy, reeling from the shock of failing *chaebol* and a weakened currency, Korean banks were less likely to loan money to debt-ridden companies.

5. *The type, quality, and costs of supporting institutions such as systems of communication, education, and transportation:* Nations differ widely in the supporting resources necessary to run a business. Trained workers are a critical resource, but factors such as reliable phones and the ability to transport goods cheaply and predictably are also important.

Some resources, called natural factor conditions, occur naturally. For example, countries with extensive coal and gas reserves favor the development of industries and firms that require high energy consumption. For example, Canada has abundant sources of the water necessary for the efficient production of aluminum.

Other resources, called induced factor conditions, arise from cultural and institutional pressures. For example, the high cultural value placed on education in many Asian societies helps create a well-trained workforce for countries like Singapore and Korea. Social institutions such as the government can also affect induced factor conditions. For example, the knowledge base available to the Japanese robotics industry is facilitated by the more than 180 Japanese universities that created robotics laboratories and the $20 million a year contributed to program development by the Japanese Ministry of International Trade and Industry.[4]

As the model shows, a country's national and business cultures combine with its social institutions to affect the business environment and certain factor conditions. In turn, this national context determines a company's management practices and policies and eventually its types of HRM adaptations. This chapter outlines the major national context characteristics that affect HRM, which are as follows:

**Natural factor conditions**
National resources that occur naturally, such as an abundant water supply.

**Induced factor conditions**
National resources created by a nation, such as a superior educational system.

• *Education and training of the labor pool:* The type and quality of labor available to companies is a key issue in HRM. A country's educational system provides the raw human resource material for companies. Later you will see how the German system of specialized training dominates key aspects of German HRM.

• *Laws and cultural expectations of selection practices:* The laws of a country and people's expectations tell managers the "right" way to find new employees. In some nations, for example, you are expected to hire your relatives. In other nations, it might be against a company's policies to do so. Sometimes it is considered common and necessary to ask women job applicants if they plan to get married soon, but asking a job applicant such a question in the United States would be illegal and discriminatory. Consider, for instance, the Preview Case in Point that discusses the various legal expectations regarding paid maternity and paternity leave.

• *Types of jobs favored by applicants:* Japanese college graduates prefer to be hired by big companies. They are attracted by the security of working for a large company. Most Chinese businesses are family dominated, and family members expect to work for and with other family members. These examples illustrate cultural values and norms regarding the "best" and "right" places to work.

- *Laws and cultural expectations regarding fair wages and promotion criteria:* Should older workers make more money than younger workers? Should men be promoted faster than women? Should people who enter the company together make the same salary and be promoted together? Should a worker's family situation influence his or her salary? Due to cultural expectations and institutional pressures, the answers to such questions vary according to national context. Values, norms, and institutional expectations influence compensation decisions and the relationship between performance appraisals and compensation. For example, U.S. multinational managers often find that the link between compensation and performance, considered legal and fair in U.S. companies, is considered less important in other nations.

- *Laws and traditions regarding labor practices:* The legal position and power of unions and the historical relationships between management and labor have profound influences on HRM practices in labor relations. For example, in some nations labor-management conflict has long-term historical precedents. However, labor conflict and the popularity of unions among workers differ by national context. Consider the following Multinational Management Brief.

## Multinational Management **Brief**

### Kidnappings in France

France has always had contentious labor relations. Its laws and traditions empower employees to have strong unions and to fight for their rights. In fact, with the 2012 elections, the new government is fighting to implement even more employee-friendly policies. For instance, new regulations will make it close to impossible for companies to fire workers. Companies that fire workers and pay dividends later will likely be fined. Additionally, companies will be encouraged to sell their plants to competitors rather than close such plants. Furthermore, the French population has very little sympathy for businesses, seeing them as the root of many problems. Experts are therefore not surprised to see top-level executives being held hostage by workers who are trying to get better working conditions or better severance packages as they get laid off. In fact, several major companies, Sony and the French tire manufacturer Michelin among them, have had top-level executives held hostage after announcing impending layoffs. Serge Foucher, the head of Sony in France, was released the next day after agreeing to pay better severance packages. Michelin saw two of its top-level executives locked up after it announced plans to close a plant.

Although executive kidnapping is fairly popular in France, workers in other countries typically use less drastic measures to fight for their rights. For instance, sit-ins are very popular in the United States. However, some experts believe that executive kidnappings could easily happen in other countries as workers deal with rashes of layoffs in an economic downturn.

*Sources: Based on* Economist. *2009. "Kidnapped," March 21, 68;* Economist. *2012. "Adieu, la France." June 23, online edition.*

The remainder of this chapter illustrates the impact of national context on HRM practices in several nations. These examples only hint at the extent of differences among national HRM practices. To understand a particular host country's HRM practices, multinational managers must pay careful attention to the relevant values, norms, and laws.

For comparison purposes, each basic task of HRM is treated by contrasting the dominant practices in the United States with those of other nations. The tasks considered are recruitment, selection, training and development, performance appraisal, compensation, and labor relations.

# Recruitment

Exhibit 12.2 summarizes the major steps in recruitment. First, managers determine that there are vacancies, which may occur in anticipation of expansion or as the result of workers leaving the organization. Second, employers determine the types of people and skills necessary for the job. Third, employers generate a pool of applicants.

Recruitment strategies to generate the applicant pool include:

- Walk-ins or unsolicited applications.
- Advertisements placed in newspapers or on the Internet.
- Company website job postings; that is, listings of vacant positions on the firm's website.
- Internal job postings; that is, company listings of vacant jobs targeted at current employees.
- Public and private personnel agencies.
- Placement services of educational institutions.
- Current employee recommendations.

Managers hope that one or more of these recruitment strategies will generate a pool of applicants who are qualified for the vacant job.

**EXHIBIT 12.2**    **Steps in the Recruiting Process**

- Jobs open
- Applicant characteristics identified
- Recruitment strategies applied
  - Walk-ins
  - Newspaper and other advertising (e.g., Internet)
  - Job positions posted in organization
  - State and private employment services
  - Educational institutions
  - Employee referrals
- Applications received

*Sources: Adapted from Bohlander, George W., and Scott, Snell. 2009.* Managing Human Resources; *Cincinnati, OH: South-Western; Werther, William B., and Keith, Davis. 1993.* Human Resources and Personnel Management. *New York: McGraw-Hill.*

Most national differences in recruitment occur in the preferences for types of strategies. National and business cultures determine the "right way" to find employees, but the norms of organizational and occupational cultures also affect recruitment. For example, firms such as Procter & Gamble in the United States have strong norms favoring recruitment from within the firm. Social institutions such as educational systems also affect recruitment. In Japan, for example, personal contacts between university professors and managers are often a prerequisite for university students getting good jobs in big companies.

### Recruitment in the United States

U.S. companies use all types of recruiting strategies, but U.S. managers do not judge all recruitment strategies to be equally effective. Exhibit 12.3 shows the relative effectiveness of recruitment strategies in the United States for four job categories.

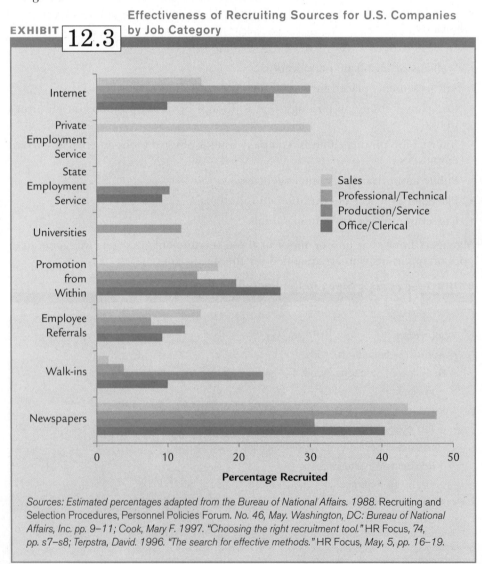

**EXHIBIT 12.3**

**Effectiveness of Recruiting Sources for U.S. Companies by Job Category**

Legend:
- Sales
- Professional/Technical
- Production/Service
- Office/Clerical

X-axis: Percentage Recruited

Sources: Estimated percentages adapted from the Bureau of National Affairs. 1988. Recruiting and Selection Procedures, Personnel Policies Forum. No. 46, May. Washington, DC: Bureau of National Affairs, Inc. pp. 9–11; Cook, Mary F. 1997. "Choosing the right recruitment tool." HR Focus, 74, pp. s7–s8; Terpstra, David. 1996. "The search for effective methods." HR Focus, May, 5, pp. 16–19.

As you can see from Exhibit 12.3, for all types of positions, U.S. managers see advertising—whether it be online or in print—as one of the most effective recruitment channels. College or university recruitment was judged among the most effective only for professional and technical jobs.

Managers believe that employee referrals produce only marginal success. There is some concern in the United States that employee referrals result in the recruitment of only employees with similar backgrounds to current workers. There is also a fear that recruitment by personal contacts (common in many other nations) may result in potential biases against certain groups, such as women and minorities.[5]

The belief in the United States that open and public advertisements are the most effective recruiting strategy reflects U.S. individualistic cultural values. Managers in the United States and in other individualistic societies view prospective workers as unique combinations of skills, and these skills are purchased by the company on the labor market. Public advertisements of jobs maximize the pool of available talent and, from the workers' point of view, support egalitarian norms that all can compete for open jobs. However, this approach is not necessarily preferred worldwide. Consider the next Multinational Management Brief regarding recruitment in Mexico and Barbados.

## Multinational Management **Brief**

### Recruitment in Mexico and Barbados

An important recruitment practice in the United States is to avoid any form of discriminatory language in job advertisements. For instance, it is illegal to advertise jobs expressing preferences in terms of age, gender, physical appearance, and/or marital status. Furthermore, most companies tend to recruit through formal methods, such as advertising in newspapers or using employment agencies. However, not all societies share this emphasis on equality or formality. In fact, inequality is very prevalent in Mexico and in many Latin American countries. In such societies, it is acceptable to advertise jobs reflecting preferences for gender, age, physical appearance, and marital status.

To compare recruitment practices between the United States and Mexico, a study looked at job advertisements of U.S. multinationals operating in Mexico versus those of Mexican companies. The study found that U.S. multinationals operating in Mexico are less likely than Mexican companies to use discriminatory language. Such results show the influence of the U.S. recruitment practices on U.S.-based multinationals.

Another study of recruitment practices in Barbados revealed further differences with U.S. practices. In a study of 49 companies from Barbados from the manufacturing, tourism, and retailing industries, findings showed that both large and small companies located in the Caribbean preferred informal methods of recruitment. Such methods included "word of mouth" or other existing employee referrals. Smaller firms in the sample were even more likely to use such methods in contrast to the U.S. preference for more formal means, such as through newspaper advertising or use of recruitment agencies.

*Sources: Based on Daspro, E. 2009. "An analysis of U.S. multinationals' recruitment practices in Mexico."* Journal of Business Ethics, *87, 221–232; Greenidge, D., P. Allevyne, B. Parris, and S. Grant. 2012. "A comparative study of recruitment and training practices between small and large businesses in an emerging market economy. The case of Barbados."* Journal of Small Business and Enterprise Development, *19(1): 164–182.*

# Recruitment

Whereas the United States favors open forms of recruitment, recruitment in collectivist societies tends to focus on the in-group, such as the family and friends of those already in the organization. Consider, for instance, the earlier Multinational Management Brief and the preference of Barbados companies for informal recruitment methods. Another example, South Korea, ranks moderately low on Hofstede's individualism scale (21st percentile) and has HRM practices that are representative of collectivist cultures. Recruitment in South Korea originated from a mixture of Confucian values and Western pragmatism. Most Korean companies recruit blue-collar workers through **backdoor recruitment**, a form of employee referral; that is, prospective employees are friends or relatives of those already employed. From the company's perspective, friends and relatives represent a good pool of candidates. If prospective employees are relatives or friends, then someone can vouch for their trustworthiness and industriousness. Small companies and those in rural areas tend to rely more on backdoor recruitment rather than on open recruitment.

Like the Japanese system, the South Korean recruitment of managers emphasizes looking for candidates at prestigious universities. Also like the Japanese, Korean companies prefer recent graduates to managers with experience. Companies assume that young people will adapt more easily to fit the company's culture. However, a form of backdoor recruitment occurs at this level, primarily through old school ties. A company tends to favor graduates of a particular university, from which a disproportionate number of the firm's managers might come.

In addition to companies' preference for recruitment strategies, individuals located around the world have preferences in terms of how they look for jobs. These preferences likely evolve from the norms associated with national culture and social institutions. For instance, Korean jobseekers know that many Korean firms prefer forms of backdoor recruitment, and so they are likely to turn to friends and family to find jobs.

To provide additional information on cross-cultural differences in preference for appropriate ways to find jobs, we analyzed data collected through the International Social Survey Program (ISSP), provided by the Inter-University Consortium for Political and Social Research.[6] The ISSP is a cross-national collaboration dedicated to the collection of important data related to work and work orientations.

The ISSP asked respondents who were looking for jobs to indicate what means they were using: registering with public and private agencies, advertising in the newspaper, responding to advertisements, applying directly to employers, and asking relatives or friends. Comparisons of the forms of recruitment confirm that both national culture and social institutions influence recruitment practices by encouraging people in a given society to prefer particular ways to look for jobs.

Exhibit 12.4 illustrates, for selected countries, whether individuals were registered with a public or a private agency in their job-seeking efforts. As the exhibit shows, individuals from, for example, Sweden, Norway, Hungary, and France, were more likely to register with a public agency as one way to find a job. Such findings are not surprising considering that the governments of these countries are actively involved in the day-to-day operation of the country. Both former communist societies (e.g., Hungary, Slovenia) and socialist societies (e.g., Sweden, Spain) are heavily influenced by governmental regulations and policies. It is therefore natural for individuals from these societies to rely on their governments as a way to find new jobs. In contrast, individuals in countries where governments play a lesser role

**Backdoor recruitment**
Prospective employees are friends or relatives of those already employed.

**EXHIBIT 12.4**    Preferred Ways to Look for a New Job: Public versus Private Agency

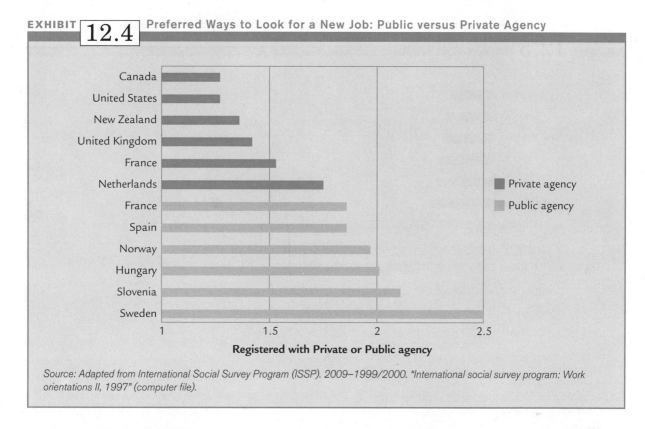

*Source: Adapted from International Social Survey Program (ISSP). 2009–1999/2000. "International social survey program: Work orientations II, 1997" (computer file).*

(e.g., United States, United Kingdom, and New Zealand) are more likely to rely on private agencies. Such results clearly demonstrate the influence of social institutions on preferences for ways to find jobs.

Exhibit 12.5 shows which countries have the highest preference for advertising in newspapers or responding to newspaper advertisements. Both advertising in newspapers and responding to them reflect very open recruitment forms. In both cases, potential employees depend on open competition in the labor market and on how their skills and qualifications compare to those of other people. Not surprisingly, many individualistic countries (e.g., United Kingdom, United States, New Zealand) are found on that list. Individuals in such societies prefer open means because these are the preferred recruitment methods—societies high on individualism favor hiring the person with the right skills for the job regardless of family or other connections. They consider that one of the most likely ways to ensure that the best person is hired is through open advertisements where all pools of skills and qualifications can be considered.

When individuals rely on posting advertisements or on responding to them, they are assuming that universalistic qualifications apply to all. This assumption explains the ratings of such low masculinity countries as Denmark, Norway, and the Netherlands, where cultural norms favor egalitarianism. Such results are also consistent with Trompenaar's view of countries high on universalism (e.g., Canada, the United States, Denmark) where the cultural expectation is based on equality.[7]

Exhibit 12.6 shows, by country, whether individuals prefer direct applications to companies or asking friends or relatives. The exhibit indicates that individuals in countries that are high on individualism or low masculinity (e.g., Canada and

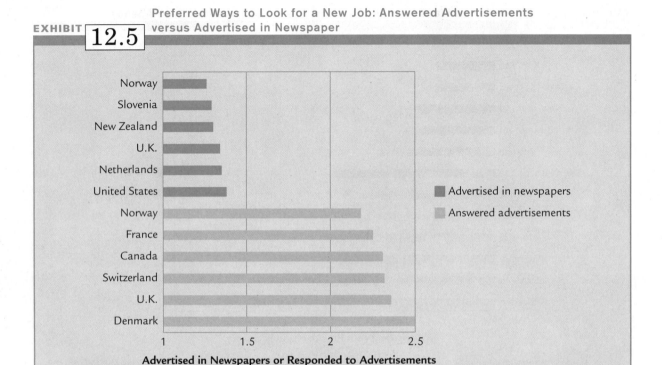

EXHIBIT **12.5** Preferred Ways to Look for a New Job: Answered Advertisements versus Advertised in Newspaper

*Source: Adapted from International Social Survey Program (ISSP). 2009–1999/2000. "International social survey program: Work orientations II, 1997" (computer file).*

Sweden) are more likely to apply directly for jobs. Direct applications are also reflective of open forms of recruitment and cultural norms of individual achievement and equality. In contrast, individuals in socialist societies (e.g., Italy, Poland, and Hungary) prefer to talk to friends or relatives as a means to get a job. Individuals in such societies rely more on friends, relatives, and other connections (i.e., relationships) for work advancement and for other work opportunities. That is, they rely chiefly on their personal connections as a means to find a job.

After attracting a pool of applicants, the next stage in the HRM process is selection.

# Selection

### Selection in the United States

U.S. experts on human resource management identify a series of steps in the selection process.[8] Exhibit 12.7 shows these steps, from the initial application to the final hiring.

The aim of typical U.S. selection practices is to gather quality information on a candidate's job qualifications. The ideal selection then results in a match between the applicant's skills and the job requirements. As in the recruitment process, an individual is seen as a bundle of skills that the organization can purchase. The individualistic culture in the United States promotes a focus on a person's achievements (e.g., education, natural ability, experience), rather than on group affiliations such

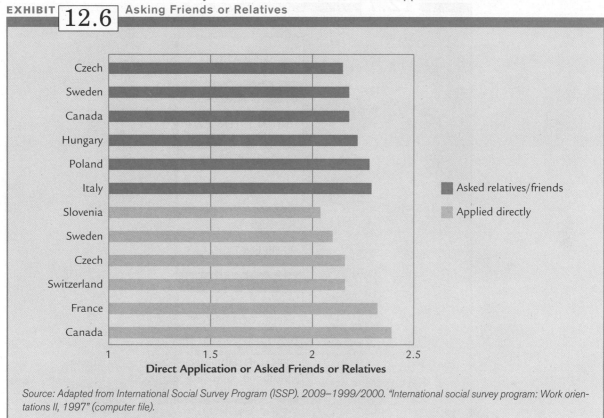

**EXHIBIT 12.6**

**Preferred Ways to Look for a New Job: Direct Application versus Asking Friends or Relatives**

*Source: Adapted from International Social Survey Program (ISSP). 2009–1999/2000. "International social survey program: Work orientations II, 1997" (computer file).*

as the family. As a result, many U.S. companies have prohibitions against nepotism—the hiring of relatives—as well as policies forbidding managers to supervise family members. This focus on personal achievements has obvious effects on how candidates present themselves. Consider the following Case in Point.

Clearly, the next Case in Point shows that there are differences in terms of how applicants present themselves. Furthermore, previous work experience, performance on tests, and perceptions of qualifications in interviews help inform HRM personnel or hiring managers about the applicant's qualifications. To avoid discrimination or favoritism, laws and cultural norms in the United States prescribe that the information gathered during the selection process must be valid; that is, the information gathered from prospective employees must relate to performance on the job. Job qualification tests must predict job performance. For example, lifting 100 pounds would not be a valid selection test for most clerical jobs. Personal information gathered during the selection process, such as height and weight, must also be relevant to the job.

Next, we consider contrasting selection practices in collectivist national cultures.

## Selection in Collectivist Cultures

Hofstede captures the essence of hiring in collectivist cultures:[9] "The hiring process in a collectivist society always takes the in-group into account. Usually preference is given to hiring relatives, first of the employer, but also of other persons

**EXHIBIT 12.7** Typical Steps in U.S. Personnel Selection

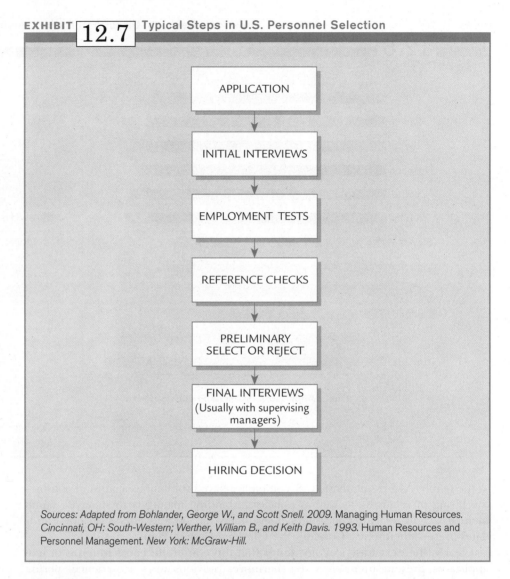

Sources: Adapted from Bohlander, George W., and Scott Snell. 2009. Managing Human Resources. Cincinnati, OH: South-Western; Werther, William B., and Keith Davis. 1993. Human Resources and Personnel Management. New York: McGraw-Hill.

already employed by the company. Hiring persons from a family one already knows reduces risks. Also relatives will be concerned about the reputation of the family and help correct misbehavior of a family member."

In selecting employees, collectivist cultural norms value potential trustworthiness, reliability, and loyalty over performance-related background characteristics. Personal traits such as loyalty to the company, loyalty to the boss, and trustworthiness are the traits that family members can provide. However, large and technically oriented companies may need professional managers and technicians with skills not available inside the family. In these cases, the selection process still prioritizes personal characteristics over technical characteristics. If one cannot have a family member, then the priority is to find employees who have the personality characteristics and background necessary to fit into the corporate culture. Young male recruits are preferred because they have not been corrupted by another company's values, and cultural role expectations are for them to be more dedicated to work than women with children.

### Applicants' Self Presentation in Iceland, Switzerland, and the United States

Because the U.S. selection process is heavily based on personal achievements, applicants for jobs typically have to present themselves in such a way as to impress the recruiters. However, this focus on impression management may also result in self-presentation behaviors. Self-presentation simply refers to the applicant's efforts to present him- or herself in a more positive light by focusing on positive attributes or minimizing negative attributes. In other cases, applicants can also present themselves to appear more interested in the job than they really are. While there are individual differences, most studies show that a large proportion of U.S. applicants tend to engage in self-presentation.

Despite the findings of high levels of self-presentation behaviors in the U.S., few studies have been done in other countries. Experts nevertheless expect that applicants in other countries may not have such high levels of self-presentation. One explanation for such findings is that different countries may value modesty differently. Countries that place a higher value on modesty are likely to have lower levels of self-presentation.

In a recent study, self-presentation was measured for subjects from Switzerland, Iceland, and the United States. Findings showed that the U.S. subjects had generally high levels of self-presentation as compared to those from Switzerland and Iceland. Such findings suggest that multinational HR managers will need to be very careful as they assess applicants through interviews in different settings. The U.S. focus on how candidates present themselves during interviews may not necessarily function in other cultures. If a U.S. multinational adopts uniform selection processes, it may incorrectly gauge the potential of candidates from societies in which applicants rely less on self-presentation. HR managers will therefore need to find ways to incorporate self-presentation into their selection criteria.

*Source: Based on Konig, C. J., L. G. Hafsteinsson, A. Jansen, and E. H. Stadelmann. 2012. "Applicants' self-presentational behavior across cultures: Less self-presentation in Switzerland and Iceland than in the United States." International Journal of Selection and Assessment, 19(4): 331–339.*

For example, in managerial selection in the collectivist Korean culture and in the moderately collectivist Japanese culture, high school and university ties substitute for family membership. At Daewoo Corporation in Korea, the chairman and six of the eight top executives attended Kyunggi High School. Seoul National University graduates make up 62 percent of the highest executives in seven of Korea's most important *chaebol.*[10] Graduates from two public universities (Tokyo and Kyoto) and two private universities (Keio and Waseda) dominate both business and public leadership in Japan. Executives who graduated from elite universities use their personal contacts with university professors to provide information on a recruit's worth to the company. Often, the recruit's area of study at the university is of much less concern than the more subjective assessment of fit with the company.

# Implications for the Multinational: Recruitment and Selection

The recruitment and selection of host country workers and managers require that the managers of a multinational company understand and adapt to local practices. Thus, for example, foreign multinationals in the United States probably have the most success using the typical U.S. recruitment practices: advertising in newspapers and going to college campuses. In other countries, the multinational manager will also need to discover and use local recruitment and selection practices.

Adaptation to local recruitment and selection practices may not always be easy. In societies where backdoor or personal contacts are acceptable recruitment strategies, foreign multinational managers may not have access to the appropriate recruitment channels. In Japan, for example, most foreign multinational companies do not have the personal contacts with Japanese professors that they need to attract the best managerial talent. For U.S. companies, such recruitment methods may violate ethical codes that require competitive access to all open jobs.

What happens when a company does not follow local norms in recruitment and selection? First, it may not get the best employees. Second, it may offend local cultural norms or break host country laws. Therefore, multinational managers must always assess the trade-off between following home practices that get what they believe are the "right" people for the job and the costs and benefits of following local traditions.

Many companies are now making use of electronic human resources (e.HR) to manage their human resources. The use of e.HR has also proved to be very useful for the recruitment function. Consider the next Case in Point, which discusses e.HR for recruitment.

After identifying a pool of applicants and selecting those to be hired, the next step in the HRM process is the training and development of employees.

# Training and Development

Within a country, training and development needs vary widely, affected by different industries, technologies, strategies, organizational structures, and local labor market conditions. However, broad national differences in training and development do exist.

The cross-national differences in training and development are most closely associated with institutional differences in national educational systems, which create large differences in recruits' qualifications in basic skills and in attitudes toward work. For example, more than 90 percent of the 25- to 34-year-olds in Norway, Japan, and Korea finish secondary school. By contrast, Turkey and Portugal have only 24 percent.[11] For another example, consider Germany, which has a strong technical education program and an apprenticeship system that originated with the guild system of the Middle Ages.

Cross-cultural training and development differences are also associated with the type of emphasis placed by national governments.[12] For instance, the Australian government requires companies above a certain size to spend 1.5 percent of their payroll expenses on training. The Chinese government is also heavily involved in training; companies are encouraged to train their workers before they are offered full-time jobs. The Taiwanese have gone even further by establishing 13 public vocational training institutes for those who do not have access to higher education. Cultural values regarding types of educational credentials and other personnel practices, such as lifetime employment, also affect training and development needs. For example, the Japanese retain the ideal of long-term employment, though it is threatened by economic practicalities and often maligned as inefficient. For companies like Ricoh, which continues to avoid layoffs at all costs, long-term employment allows management training and development to take place slowly, through extensive job rotations. Managers learn by doing, with many different job assignments early in their careers.

Exhibit 12.8 gives an overview of work-related training systems in use throughout the world, and Exhibit 12.9 presents some specific details about training in a number of countries.

CASE IN POINT

## Using e.HR for Recruitment

Many companies are now relying on electronic human resources (e.HR) because they see important benefits to using such systems. For instance, electronic human resources can provide employees with ways to access their payroll and other critical employment information. In fact, global companies like Nike, KPN, and Siemens are all using e.HR systems to manage their human resource functions around the world. Consider that Nike's European, Middle Eastern, and Asian headquarters get almost 800 job applications a month for approximately 100 to 120 positions. Nike's policy is that each applicant is a potential employee and customer and that each must be treated as such. However, before e.HR was implemented, there was tremendous stress on the HR department to quickly process the résumés to make hiring decisions. Unfortunately, reviews of the system showed that mistakes were made and that the cost of hires needed to be reduced while the level of talent needed to increase.

The new e.HR system at Nike has been helpful in addressing many of the problems. All applicants can now apply for specific jobs or for future job opportunities through the Nike website, which is linked to other external recruiting sites that enable more potential applicants to be aware of job opportunities. Furthermore, for each new job position, the online system makes the first cut and matches the candidates with the job requirements. As such, Nike managers have access to a candidate short list rather than the large number of hard-copy résumés of the previous system. The e.HR system has enabled Nike to improve the quality of the candidates it considers. Furthermore, applicants are encouraged to update their résumés every six months to show their continued interest in the company. Nike has a constantly growing list of applicants for future positions. The database now contains about 8,500 résumés.

Nike has seen tremendous benefits with the implementation of the e.HR system. The company has saved close to 50 percent of recruitment costs. Furthermore, with the regular résumé updates, the company has relied less on external recruiters because it always has qualified applicants on hand. The system's ability to provide short lists based on job requirements also has improved the quality of hires, and the time to fill vacancies has dropped from 62 to 42 days.

However, despite the heavy use of information technology by multinationals, a recent report suggests that technology still offers untapped potential. Specifically, many technological tools, such as the "Hiring Smart Tool" or "Aviva's Talking Talent," are available. Furthermore, few multinationals are taking advantage of the possibilities offered by social media.

*Sources: Based on Gorsline, K. 2012. "Room for improvement in HR's use of technology." Canadian HR Reporter, 25(12): 9; MacLellan, J. 2009. "Electronic solutions a greener option." Canadian HR Reporter, 22(8): 8; Pollitt, David. 2005. "Recruiting the right project managers at Siemens Business Services." Human Resources Management International Digest, 13(7): 28–30; 2005. "E-recruitment gets the Nike tick of approval." Human Resources Management International Digest, 13(2): 33–35; 2006. "E-HR brings everything together at KPN." Human Resources Management International Digest, 14(1): 34–35.*

Next, as a detailed example, we will discuss training and development differences between the voluntary system of the United States and the cooperative system of Germany.

## Training and Development in the United States

U.S. companies with more than 100 employees invest more than $60 billion in training.[13] Exhibit 12.10 shows the types of skills taught to employees. The most popular training topics are management development and computer skills. However, other types of training, such as those needed for new methods and procedures, reach more people on all levels of the organization. In spite of the billions of dollars invested, training in the United States does not reach all workers. Estimates are that U.S. employers provide training to only 1 out of every 14 workers.[14] Because of perceived weaknesses

**EXHIBIT** **12.8**   Training Systems around the World

| Type | Example Countries | Features and Sources of Institutional Pressures |
|---|---|---|
| Cooperative | Austria, Germany, Switzerland, and some Latin American countries | Legal and historical precedents for cooperation among companies, unions, and the government. |
| Company-based voluntarism/high labor mobility | United States and U.K. | Lack of institutional pressures to provide training. Companies provide training based on own cost benefits. |
| Voluntarism/low labor mobility | Japan | Low labor turnover encourages investment in training without institutional pressure. |
| State-driven incentive provider | Hong Kong, Korea, Singapore, Taiwan, China, Australia | Government identifies needs for skills and uses incentives to encourage companies to train in chosen areas. |
| Supplier | Developing countries in Asia and Africa, transition economies | No institutional pressures for companies to train. Government provides formal training organizations. |

*Source: Adapted from International Labor Organization (ILO). 1999. World Employment Report 1998–99. Geneva: International Labor Office.*

in U.S. secondary education, the pressure on U.S. businesses to supplement basic educational training will increase. Thirty percent of U.S. students do not finish high school, and many graduates do not have sufficient reading and mathematical skills for current and future jobs.[15] For example, 40 percent of the companies in Exhibit 12.11 already see the need to provide remedial and basic education.

The shift in emphasis of the U.S. economy from manufacturing to service is predicted to be an important issue in the future. The service sector tends to be very capital and skill intensive and requires employees to have not only the appropriate technical skills but also critical thinking skills, team-building skills, and learning abilities.[16] This prediction suggests that there may be a widening gap between what companies emphasize in their training programs and the skills required for the future. Compounding the problem are pressures to cut costs, which have resulted in more U.S. companies outsourcing their training needs. Unfortunately, as training is moved out of the organizations, its relevance and applicability to the companies' needs is lessened.

Predictions of high needs for training have resulted in some calls from business and government for German-style apprentice programs. In such programs, the government requires industry to provide vocational training to workers in exchange for tax benefits. However, in the United States, training that is not specifically tailored to a company is often viewed as something that the employee may eventually take to a competitor. This fear makes some companies reluctant to invest in training without a more immediate and positive cost-benefit analysis regarding their own bottom line.[17]

Next, we describe perhaps the most acclaimed model of vocational training.

**Dual system**
A form of vocational education in Germany that combines in-house apprenticeship training with part-time vocational school training, and leads to a skilled worker certificate.

## Training and Vocational Education in Germany

German companies are renowned worldwide for their high-quality technical products. A sophisticated and standardized national system of vocational education and training provides a major human resource for German industry.

**EXHIBIT** | **12.9** | **Key Specific Training and Development Characteristics of Selected Countries**

**Australia**
- Government-introduced 1990 Training Guarantee Act, requires companies to spend 1.5% of annual payroll expenses on training.
- More training provided at managerial level than bluecollar level.
- Not enough initiatives are yet available to assess effectiveness of training programs.

**Canada**
- Because of NAFTA, companies are facing increasing pressures to cut costs, and HR departments are being disproportionately affected.
- Use of outside consultants for training purposes is becoming increasingly prevalent.
- Only half of corporate HRM departments are involved in training.

**China**
- High degree of governmental intervention to encourage companies to train.
- Heavy emphasis is on training and development of managers.
- Training programs are more likely to emphasize corporate values and interpersonal skills.
- Manymultinationals (ABB, Ericcson, Procter &Gamble, Motorola) have established state-of-the-art campus training centers.

**Japan**
- Training and development is planned and executed in disciplined manner at all levels of the organization.
- Training for white-collar and blue-collar workers is fairly similar.
- Skills in coordination and communication are considered as important as technical skills in training programs.

**Korea**
- Emphasis is on molding current and future managers and workers to fit the corporate culture.
- Loyalty, dedication, and team spirit are emphasized rather than job skills.
- The Asian crisis has forced companies to cut down on training costs.
- Governmental policies require companies with more than 150 employees to establish training centers.

**Mexico**
- Increased levels of training are driven by standards established by international investors and other trade agreements (North American Free Trade Agreement, MERCOSUR).
- Major emphasis on on-the-job training and skill development of lower-level employees. Training is seen as becoming increasingly important because often business and cultural practices collide on a variety of manufacturing and other techniques (i.e., JIT).
- Training methods such as on-the-job training are used to familiarize workers with job requirements.

**Taiwan**
- Government has built a vast educational system and established 13 vocational training schools. New curricula stressing creativity and free thought are replacing traditional educational approaches based on memorization and job-specific skills.
- Taiwanese companies are seeing the importance of training as the country shifts to more knowledge intensive sectors.
- Among different training practices, job rotation is perceived as most effective, followed by in-house and outside training.
- Emphasis is on managerial rather than technical training.

*Sources: Adapted from Cantu de la Torre, I., and L. Cantu Licon. 2009. "Focus on Mexico."* Training, *February, 46(2), p. 20; Drost, Ellen A., Colette A. Frayne, Kevin B. Lowe, and J. Michael Geringer. 2002. "Benchmarking training and development practices: A multicountry analysis."* Human Resource Management, *41(1), pp. 67–86.*

There are two forms of vocational education in Germany. One consists of general and specialized vocational schools and professional and technical colleges. The other form, called the **dual system**, combines in-house apprenticeship training with part-time vocational school training, leading to a skilled worker certificate. This training can be followed by the *Fachschule*, whereby a college provides advanced vocational training. Ultimately, one can achieve the status of a **Meister**, or master technician.

**Meister**
In Germany, a master technician.

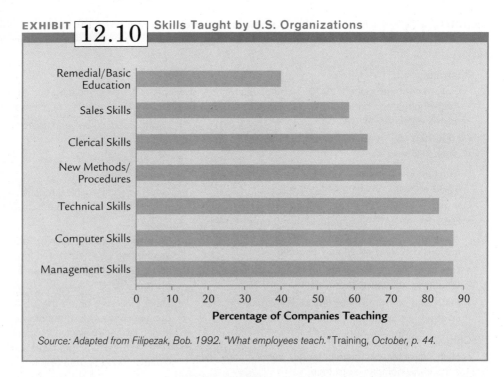

EXHIBIT **12.10** Skills Taught by U.S. Organizations

*Source: Adapted from Filipezak, Bob. 1992. "What employees teach." Training, October, p. 44.*

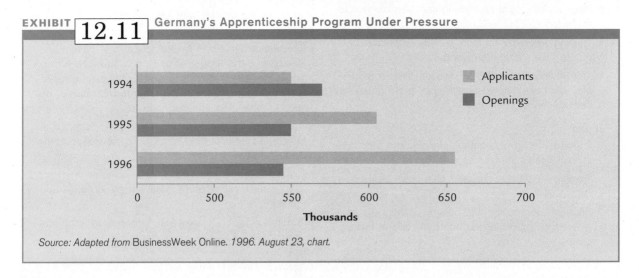

EXHIBIT **12.11** Germany's Apprenticeship Program Under Pressure

*Source: Adapted from BusinessWeek Online. 1996. August 23, chart.*

The dual system is probably the most important component of German vocational training. The training and certificate qualifications are standardized throughout the country. This produces a well-trained national labor force with skills that are not company specific. Apprenticeships exist not only for manual occupations but also for many technical, commercial, and managerial occupations. Apprenticeships are not limited to the young. Older workers often seek apprenticeships and the resulting certificates to enhance their development. There are nearly 400 nationally recognized vocational certificates.[18] Unions, organizations, and the government are now identifying new groups of certificates to represent qualifications for high-tech jobs in the new economy.

The dual system results from a collaboration of employers, unions, and the state. The costs are shared between companies and the state, with the companies paying approximately two-thirds of the costs. Employers have a legal obligation to release young people for vocational training. However, in the downturn of 2008–2009, cutbacks by German companies and high unemployment have resulted in fewer apprenticeships being offered than there are workers applying. Many firms have cut the number of apprentices to cut costs or have called for more company-specific skills (see Exhibit 12.11). Emerging information technology industries are also challenging the system because their job requirements are not served by the traditional German educational structure.[19]

Besides their national system of vocational education, German companies invest heavily in training, with four out of five workers receiving some in-house training. For example, at Mercedes Benz, the company's internal training center offers 180 vocational courses. Besides the 600 young people in vocational training and a modular management-development program, 4,000 employees per year take formal training at the company's training center.[20] However, Germany is not the only country that provides vocational training. Consider the following Multinational Management Brief.

## Multinational Management **Brief**

### Vocational Training Worldwide

While Germany has one of the best-known vocational educational systems in the world, it is not the only country that mandates such training. In fact, the type of vocational training provided in a country is dependent on the type of support provided by the government. There are three different types of vocational training. First, in some countries, the government does not play, or plays only a very minimal, role in vocational training. This market-oriented system exists in countries such as the United Kingdom, the United States, and Japan. In these countries, there is no formal system of education that provides vocational training to students. Most of the vocational training is left to the individual initiatives or company initiatives and the government does not impose rules or regulations. Larger companies tend to dominate vocational training under such systems. In contrast to the market system, the institutional system is one in which the government is solely in charge of vocational training. This system can be found in countries such as France and Italy. There, vocational training is connected to the formal educational system, and entrance into the vocational education is guided by uniform standards set in the general educational system. Finally, the dual system, in which the government works with industries to shape the vocational training system, exists in countries such as Australia, Germany, and Switzerland. There, vocational training takes place under conditions set by the government. Furthermore, training can take place in institutes that are different than those that provide general education. However, participants in vocational training can get degrees and qualifications that are equivalent to those awarded by general education institutions such as universities.

*Source: Based on Shah, I. H., M. Ajmal, F. Rahman, and M. N. Akhter. 2012. "A comparative study on vocational training structure of Pakistan with British and German model." International Journal of Business and Social Science, 2(1): 162–169.*

Having seen examples of training and development in different national contexts, we can now consider how these differences affect the operations of multinational companies.

# Implications for the Multinational: Training and Development

Before setting up operations in a host foreign country, multinational managers must consider the quality of the workers and sometimes of the managers in the host country. They must also examine the feasibility of exporting their company's training techniques to the host country. For example, a transnational company might need workers with basic skills in mathematics and science to staff future plants. Rather than invest in basic education to train a low-cost workforce, the company can locate in countries with the best educational systems. Thus, for example, a multinational company with a requirement for technical workers might examine which educational systems produce the best students in mathematics and science.

The adaptation of management-development practices to different national contexts depends significantly on the intended use of host country managers. If host country nationals are limited to lower management levels, then multinational companies may follow local management-development practices. This would be a likely approach for a multilocal company with a polycentric IHRM orientation. Such companies develop local managerial talent for careers in one country. Host country managers often never expect to work at the multinational organization's headquarters or in another country.

When multinational companies allow and expect host country nationals to rise to higher levels of management, however, the parent company's corporate culture dominates management-development policies, and such multinational companies expect managers of all nationalities to be, for example, Motorola or Ford managers—not British or Mexican or Malaysian.

Next, the chapter examines differences between performance appraisal in the United States and in collectivist cultures.

# Performance Appraisal

Regardless of the national setting, all companies at some point must deal with the human resource problems of identifying people to reward, promote, demote, develop and improve, retain, or terminate. Not everyone can move up the ladder of the organizational pyramid. Not everyone can be a leader. Not everyone will perform at acceptable levels. Even in countries like Japan, with its high value for lifetime employment, the survival of the company often requires layoffs.

The fundamental assumption in the West, and in particular, in individualistic cultures, is that performance appraisal systems provide rational and fair solutions to these human resource problems. In other words, ideally, appraisal systems provide management with objective, honest, and fair data on employee performance. Consequently, human resource decisions such as pay or promotion can be based on these data. Although issues regarding seniority, experience, and security are not ignored, the cultural ideal is a meritocracy in which good performers get more rewards.

## Performance Appraisal in the United States

The U.S. performance appraisal system represents cultural values that espouse links among individual rights, duties, and rewards, as well as a legal system that promotes equal opportunity. Thus, the ideal U.S. system is highly rational, logical, and legal. The textbook view of it contains four elements: performance standards; performance measures; performance feedback; and human resource decisions related to remuneration, promotion, or termination.[21]

- *Performance standards* reflect management's goals regarding the acceptable quality and quantity of work output: work-related knowledge, quality, volume, and initiative. For example, a secretary may be expected to type a certain number of words per minute.

- *Performance measures* are techniques intended for the objective and often comparative assessment of employees on the performance standards. The most popular measures use some form of rating scale.[22] The employee is rated on a variety of traits (e.g., work quality), usually by managers, but occasionally by peers or subordinates. Teacher evaluations by class members and peer evaluations of contributions to a student group project are examples of performance ratings.

- *Performance feedback* usually occurs in a formal interview between superior and subordinate. Three methods are common in the United States.[23] First, in the tell-and-sell method, the supervisor gives feedback and explains the evaluation. Second, in the tell-and-listen method, the supervisor gives feedback and listens to the subordinate's reactions. Third, in the problem-solving method, the supervisor and subordinate work to identify problems and propose solutions for improvement.

- *Human resource decisions* related to the performance appraisal system, in most U.S. organizations, are compensation decisions. Other major but less common uses include performance improvement, feedback, documentation, and promotion.[24]

Because of the concern in the United States that human resource decisions be fair and equitable for all individuals, performance appraisal systems must follow **U.S. legal requirements for appraisals** that ensure fairness by regulating performance evaluation practices.

The U.S. performance appraisal system is rooted in an individualistic culture and an institutional system that aspire to protect equal rights and equal opportunities. Cultural stories like the American dream of rags to riches support the idea that all can achieve wealth and success through their own efforts.

Next, we will see how the institutional systems and cultural values of other nations result in the valuing and evaluation of quite different aspects of work performance.

**U.S. legal requirements for appraisals**
Regulating performance evaluation practices to ensure their fairness.

## Performance Appraisals around the World

Although performance appraisal practices vary widely among countries, they are undertaken with the common purpose of devising ways to control employees so that they give maximum performance.[25] However, while appraisals are based on similar notions in many countries, they are used for many different purposes. The Best International Human Resource Management Practices Project[26] provides extensive evidence on cross-national differences in performance appraisal purposes in Australia, Canada, Indonesia, Japan, South Korea, Latin America, Mexico, China, Taiwan, and the United States.

**EXHIBIT 12.12**

Cross-National Differences in Purposes of Performance Appraisals: Top Five Countries and Regions for Each Category

| Performance Apprai- sal Purpose | Countries | | | | |
|---|---|---|---|---|---|
| Determine pay | Taiwan | Canada | United States | China | Japan |
| Document performance | Australia | United States | Taiwan | Latin America | Canada |
| Plan development activities | Australia | Latin America | Canada | Taiwan | Mexico |
| Salary administration | Latin America | Taiwan | United States | Canada | Indonesia |
| Recognize subordinate | Australia | Taiwan | United States | Canada | China |
| Discuss improvement | Australia | Latin America | Canada | United States | Taiwan |
| Discuss subordinate views | Australia | Canada | Taiwan | United States | Mexico |
| Evaluate goal achievement | Australia | Latin America | Taiwan | Canada | Japan |
| Identify strengths and weaknesses | Latin America | Australia | United States | Canada | Taiwan |
| Let subordinate express feelings | Australia | Taiwan | Canada | China | United States |
| Determine promotion potential | Korea | Latin America | Taiwan | Australia | Japan |

*Source: Adapted from Geringer, J. Michael, Colette A. Frayne, and John F. Milliman. 2002. "In search of 'best practices' in international human resource management: Research design and methodology." Human Resource Management, 41(1), pp. 5–30.*

Exhibit 12.12 shows the top five countries for each performance appraisal purpose. The project asked respondents to rate the importance of 12 purposes of performance appraisals, and the results revealed significant differences among countries. However, the most striking finding is that Australia, Canada, and the United States are among the top five countries for all performance appraisal purposes; these countries are very high on individualism, meaning that they place heavy emphasis on the development of the individual. As such, performance appraisals are seen as the most effective method to gauge how well an employee is doing and how that person's performance can be improved. However, it is also interesting to see that countries and regions such as Taiwan and Latin America figure prominently on the list. Their presence suggests the possible effects of social institutions such as government and trade agreements. Because these countries are emulating Western-based systems to satisfy trade agreements and other competitiveness requirements, they are perhaps seeing performance appraisal systems as critical.

It also is interesting to note that the collectivist societies surveyed (e.g., China, Japan, Korea, Indonesia) were very unlikely to be among the top five countries for each performance appraisal purpose. This suggests that performance appraisals may not be seen as important in all societies. Consider the next Focus on Emerging Markets.

In collectivist cultures, age and in-group memberships (usually family or social status) make up a large component of the psychological contract with the organization; that is, the employer and employee accept as correct and fair the idea that human resource decisions should take into account personal background characteristics

**Focus** on Emerging Markets

### Performance Appraisal in China and India

As more multinationals strive to take advantage of the Chinese market, they will face challenges related to performance appraisals as they assess their Chinese workers. Consider the case of ITT China president William E. Taylor, who was puzzled by the fact that turnover in the Shanghai office was very high. He decided to investigate this issue. When he talked to the local manager, he was given a simple answer: whenever a boss gives an employee a 3 on the 1–5 rating scale on their performance appraisal, the employee either stops talking or quits. Taylor then realized that the performance appraisal system in use was seriously flawed. A rating of 3 in China would make the employee lose face. Further investigation revealed that the individual rating system was also not compatible with preferences in the more collective Southern Europe. Scandinavian countries had problems with the ratings, too. Who gave the manager the right to give someone a 3 where bosses and employees are considered equal?

ITT then made the radical decision to drop the ratings system. It displayed cultural sensitivity by dropping a system that almost 90 percent of companies are using. The results have so far shown that ITT made the right decision. For instance, turnover in the Shenyang plant dropped by half. However, the U.S. plant is still having trouble because metrics-loving engineers in the defense industry still prefer the traditional system.

Performance appraisals were typically viewed as a mere formality in many Indian companies. Although employees may have felt they were doing a good job, they would get rated only yearly and feedback would sometimes be negative. Furthermore, many employees were dependent on their relationships with their supervisors. If relationships were not good, supervisors would often give negative performance appraisals to the employees. Therefore performance appraisals were never viewed as meaningful exercises that would give companies the potential to help their employees improve their performance.

However, things seem to be changing in many Indian companies. For instance, HDFC Life, an insurance company, is training its managers on how to conduct effective appraisals to give meaningful (and, if necessary, negative) feedback. A number of companies, such as Marriott International, have gone to more frequent reviews rather than the yearly review to avoid surprises. Additionally, to make the process fairer, Accenture has now implemented a performance appraisal system that invites feedback from three other stakeholders rather than merely relying on the supervisor. Such changes all aim at making performance appraisals a much fairer and more meaningful exercise in Indian companies.

*Sources: Based on* Economist. *2012. Pedalling prosperity. May 26, 3-5; McGregor, J. 2008. "Case study: To adapt, ITT lets go of unpopular ratings."* BusinessWeek, *January 28, 46; Sangani, P. 2012. "How India Inc. is attempting to revive the lost art of meaningful performance appraisals."* The Economic Times, *February 24, online edition.*

more than achievement. Since who you are and how old you are may count more than how you perform, the usefulness of a Western-style performance appraisal system is less clear. For example, if only family members are eligible for promotion, it makes little sense to evaluate all employees for management potential.

None of this implies, however, that information regarding performance is not communicated to people in collectivist cultures. Members of work groups often know the best and the worst performers. Because it is important to work for the benefit of the group, members may subtly praise or punish other workers based on their performance. Managers also may work indirectly to discourage poor performance. Behaviors such as withdrawing normal favors or working through intermediaries (who are often relatives) are common. For the Japanese, the supervisor can communicate negative feedback for poor work performance simply by ignoring his subordinate. Thus, even without formal appraisal systems, feedback occurs indirectly.

According to Hofstede,[27] managers in collectivist societies often avoid direct performance appraisal feedback. An open discussion of performance may clash with the society's norm of harmony, which takes precedence. For example, during the first eight to ten years of their careers, Japanese managers may never encounter the appraisal system. Even if one exists, it is often secret and does not give direct feedback to the employee. Instead, all beginning managers get the same salary and promotions, based on age and seniority. Reducing competition among managers and maintaining harmony among the group are higher-priority values than identifying or developing high performers.

Steers, Shin, and Ungson point out that the preference for seniority-based promotions is even stronger among Koreans.[28] They note that while job performance is important and most companies have appraisal systems, seniority is the most important factor for advancement. This follows "from the Confucian tradition that strives to preserve harmony (since it is unseemly for younger employees to supervise older ones). It is also easier to use seniority to make promotion decisions than to rely on imprecise personnel evaluation methods to discriminate between a group of high achievers."[29]

Perhaps because of the long-term orientation of Korean culture, Korean performance appraisal systems focus on evaluating and developing the so-called "whole man" for the long-term benefit of the company. They evaluate sincerity, loyalty, and attitude on an equal footing with job performance. Only for senior management, where the logic of an organizational pyramid dictates a small number of top positions, does the performance evaluation focus on actual performance and contribution to the company.[30]

Regardless, at least from an individualistic society's perspective, performance appraisals provide the information necessary for promotion and compensation decisions.

Next, we will see how compensation practices in other national contexts differ from the U.S. model.

## Compensation

Compensation includes wages and salaries, incentives such as bonuses, and benefits such as retirement contributions. There are wide variations both among countries and among organizations concerning how to compensate workers. A country's economic development, cultural traditions, and legal institutions, as well as the role of labor unions, all affect compensation. Consider these examples:

- Japanese workers earn more than three times the wages of workers in other East Asian countries such as Taiwan, Singapore, and Korea.[31]

- Although not required by law, South Korean and Japanese workers expect bonuses at least twice a year.

- In Denmark, more than 80 percent of employees belong to unions, and agreements between unions and employers' associations determine minimal and normal pay.[32]

- In the European Union, there is a statutory minimum of four weeks of vacation. As an example, France has a law that guarantees workers five weeks of paid vacation on an annual basis.[33]

## Compensation Practices in the United States

Conditions external and internal to the company affect the wages and salaries of workers and managers.[34] External factors include local and national wage rates, government legislation, and collective bargaining. Internal factors include the importance of the job to the organization, the affluence of the organization or its ability to pay, and the employee's relative worth to the business (merit).

Taking into account these external and internal factors, most U.S. companies develop formal and systematic policies to determine wages and salaries. The Personnel Policies Forum, a group of personnel managers representing companies of all sizes and from all industries, found that 75 percent of their member companies had formal written policies for wage and salary administration.[35] What are these policies? Consider the following additional results from the Personnel Policies Forum study.

The Personnel Policies Forum study showed that 94 percent of U.S. companies used data from comparative wage and salary surveys to determine compensation in order to ensure that their wages and salaries were competitive in the labor market. Comparative wage and salary surveys tell companies how their compensation packages match up with those of competitors. Two-thirds of the companies check on comparative wage and salary data at least once a year. Nearly 40 percent assess their competitive wage and salary position more than seven times a year.

Perhaps more than any other society, the highly mobile U.S. labor market requires this hefty concern with external equity (i.e., do we pay at or above market level?). The individualistic U.S. culture views careers as private and personal, and mobility, advancement, and higher wages often require leaving a company. Thus, unlike in countries such as Japan and Korea, where company loyalty often prevails over opportunities for higher remuneration, U.S. companies must rely on competitive wages to maintain a quality workforce.

Most U.S. companies also develop procedures to establish that people receive equitable pay for the types of jobs they perform. Seventy-five percent of the companies surveyed by the Personnel Policies Forum have formal systems to evaluate how much particular jobs (independent of the people doing them) contribute to the company.[36] A variety of methods help to establish a hierarchy of jobs based on their worth to the company. Issues such as responsibility, skill requirements, and the importance of the job's tasks to the organization contribute to the worth of a job. Those who occupy the higher-ranked jobs are paid more.

Although the worth of a job to the company largely determines the base pay assigned to a certain position, raises in pay are determined mostly by merit.[37] As discussed in more detail in the following section, this is particularly unlike the seniority-based systems of Korea and Japan.

As part of the total compensation package, benefits have grown substantially in the United States during the last few decades. Major employee benefits in the United States include pension plans, health care benefits, insurance coverage, vacation pay, sick leave, and paid holidays. Social Security insurance, unemployment

## Multinational Management **Brief**

### A Comparison of Some Benefits around the World

| Country | Average Salary (Head of Sales and Marketing) (US $) | Expected Days Off | Local Perks |
|---|---|---|---|
| Brazil | $208,691 | 40 | Chauffeured bulletproof cars followed by bodyguards for top-level employees |
| China | $ 92,402 | 23 | Contribution to housing fund to help employees buy houses |
| France | $188,771 | 40 | Use of company-owned ski chalets and beach houses |
| Hong Kong | $149,905 | 26 | Traditional Chinese medicine health coverage in addition to regular health insurance |
| India | $ 56,171 | 31 | Compensation for health care of aging parents of employees |
| Japan | $148,899 | 35 | Family allowances on top of salary |
| Mexico | $163,591 | 23 | Before Mother's Day weekend, getting the day or half day off to take mothers out to lunch |
| Philippines | $ 95,286 | 19 | "Rice" allowances that employees can convert to perks such as free cell phones |
| United States | $229,300 | 25 | Access to financial planners for top-level employees |
| Russia | $117,135 | 39 | Company-sponsored mortgages |

*Sources: Based on McGregor, J. 2008. "The right perks." BusinessWeek, January 28, 42–43; Mercer. 2012. http://www.mercer.com.*

insurance, family leave, and workers' compensation insurance for work-related accidents are required by law. However, as the next Multinational Management Brief shows, U.S. benefits still lag behind those that a multinational company should expect to pay in Europe.

Next we will look at one of the most comprehensive studies on compensation practices and the perceived trend toward convergence.

## Compensation around the World

Compensation packages vary widely among countries. The Best International Human Resource Management Practices Project represents one of the most extensive cross-national studies of compensation practices to date.[38] The researchers investigated cross-national variations in nine compensation practices in ten countries or regions (Australia, Canada, China, Indonesia, Japan, Korea, Latin America, Mexico, Taiwan, and the United States). Respondents were asked a number of questions pertaining to these compensation practices, both in terms of their assessment of the current state of practice and also the extent to which they felt that these practices should be used in the future.

Results of the study revealed some convergence of compensation practices. For instance, managers of all countries and regions felt that it was necessary that all but one of the nine compensation practices (that pay incentives should be important, pay should be contingent on group/organizational performance, incentives should be a significant amount of pay, job performances should be the basis of pay raises, benefits should be important, benefits should be more generous, and pay should be based on long-term results) be used more in the future.[39] These managers also felt that less emphasis should be placed on using seniority as a determinant of pay decisions. Additionally, all managers felt that a properly designed compensation plan was key to harnessing employee performance and therefore to organizational effectiveness.

These results are particularly striking given that the countries studied have wide variations in terms of both national culture and social institutions, but they provide some practical guidelines for practicing managers. In general, it is suggested that managers make more effective use of the preceding nine compensation practices. For instance, given that the respondents felt that job performance should become more prevalent as the basis for pay raises, it is essential for HRM managers to implement systems that provide a stronger link between job performance and pay raises.

Despite the evidence of convergence in many areas, the study also revealed surprising results. For instance, the researchers expected that the collectivist countries would have higher ratings for the compensation practice "pay is contingent on group or organizational performance." However, findings showed that there were no major differences between collectivistic and individualistic countries on that point. Yet another perplexing result is that there were no significant variations among countries in terms of the compensation practice of using seniority as the basis for pay decisions.

This study suggests that there may be some convergence pressures on compensation practices. As further evidence of convergence, we will see an example of the changing compensation system in Japan. In response to competition, 10 years of recession, and the globalization of Japanese organizations, Japanese firms are moving toward a Western style of compensation management. However, despite such convergence, there are still wide differences between compensation practices. Consider the following Multinational Management Brief.

## Compensation in Japan

As with U.S. firms, Japanese companies determine base salaries to a large degree by the classification of positions. Positions have skill and educational requirements. Those who occupy the more demanding positions receive higher wages and bonuses.

Seniority has two effects on the Japanese compensation system. First, besides educational qualifications, each position has minimum age requirements. As the Japanese worker gains in seniority he, and less often she, becomes eligible to move up to more valued and more highly paid positions. Second, seniority factors

## Multinational Management **Brief**

### Compensation Practices in Russian Companies

As argued earlier, U.S. compensations practices rely heavily on equity and market conditions to determine compensation packages. Most companies have internal systems to equitably determine what wages and salaries should be paid to workers. However, the situation is not the same in Russia. To understand current compensation practices in Russia, it is necessary to understand compensation practices during the Soviet era. During that time, employees were guaranteed jobs and compensation levels were determined by the government. While the compensation scales were developed to ensure that there was low wage differentiation (the ratio between lowest level workers and ministers could not exceed 1:7), the government also gave a large number of nonmonetary benefits such as use of vacation hostels, industry-sponsored hospitals, and other psychological benefits such as awards. Furthermore, governmental officials had a significant say in terms of who had access to these wages and benefits.

Current compensation practices in Russian organizations suggest that there are still some similarities, but also some differences, with the Soviet model. First, wages and other benefits are still determined by influential individuals rather than objectively determined by the HR department. In fact, the recent study of HR practices in companies found that most strategic HR matters are actually undertaken by line managers rather than the HR department. Second, in contrast to the base wages set by the government, current practices suggest that companies have flexibility in setting wages. The current study suggests that most companies have set very low baselines for wages. Third, line managers still control a large number of bonuses that are arbitrarily awarded by line managers. Preference for specific employees still prevails. Finally, the current study also suggests that most Russian companies have implemented systems to ensure maximum flexibility with regards to labor. For instance, there are no performance appraisal systems and employees can easily be laid off or denied wage increases.

*Source: Based on Gurkov, I., and O. Zelenova. 2012. "Human resource management in Russian companies." International Studies of Management and Organizations, 41(4): 65–78.*

into pay decisions, but at a declining rate; that is, seniority counts more for pay raises earlier in one's career and diminishes after age 45. The logic of this system is that more money is required early, when family responsibilities, such as buying a home or paying for children's education, are highest. These responsibilities decrease after middle age. In fact, early in a career it is not uncommon for marital status and family size to affect wages or salary.

In more recent times, merit (as the Japanese interpret it) affects pay raises to a greater degree than under the traditional position/seniority system. Even though the Japanese view of merit does not match exactly the Western view, stressing attitudes as much as job performance, experts on Japanese personnel policies predict that merit and achievement—at least Japanese style—will continue to have a greater impact on Japanese compensation and promotions.[40] Exhibit 12.13 shows the traditional compensation formula as it is being modified for pay raises in many Japanese companies today. The major shift is the weight given to merit over seniority.

**EXHIBIT 12.13**    The Japanese Pay Raise Formula: Changing the Balance

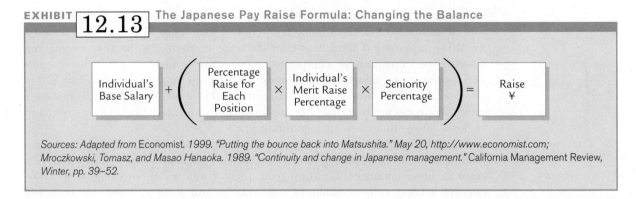

Sources: Adapted from Economist. 1999. "Putting the bounce back into Matsushita." May 20, http://www.economist.com; Mroczkowski, Tomasz, and Masao Hanaoka. 1989. "Continuity and change in Japanese management." California Management Review, Winter, pp. 39–52.

Economic pressures on the Japanese compensation system are growing,[41] partly due to the increasing costs of compensating a large management staff recruited from the Baby Boomer Generation. As a result, some Japanese companies are taking the radical approach of basing management compensation only on merit. Honda was among the first to introduce this type of system, called the **nenpo system**, in 1992. At Honda, there are no cost-of-living raises, housing allowances, family allowances, or automatic pay raises. Instead, superiors determine a manager's pay using yearly performance evaluations that emphasize goals.[42] Although seniority remains important for holding certain positions, trends in Japanese human resource practices show a convergence with practices used in the United States and other Western nations. A recent survey shows that 90 percent of Japanese companies have or plan to introduce performance into their pay and promotion systems.[43]

Along with raises based on age, promotions, and merit, a significant component of Japanese compensation is the **bonus system**. Many Korean companies use similar systems. Bonuses come twice a year, usually during traditional gift-giving seasons. During the high of the Japanese boom economy, employees often received up to 30 percent of their base salary in the form of bonuses. Successful large companies paid up to 100 percent of base salaries in bonuses in particularly good years. However, with the current economic situation in Japan, such levels are now infrequent.

**Nenpo system**
New Japanese compensation system based on yearly performance evaluations that emphasize goals, although the goals are not always the same as in Western companies.

**Bonus system**
In Japan, employees often receive as much as 30 percent of their base salary, usually given twice a year during traditional gift-giving seasons.

# Implications for the Multinational: Performance Evaluation and Compensation

As with recruitment and selection, multinational companies must match their performance evaluation system to their multinational strategies. For example, top U.S. managers for Japanese companies in the United States often report that they must adjust to the HRM practices of their Japanese parents; they are uncomfortable with ill-identified career paths and the lack of specialization. Moreover, many U.S. managers working in Japan believe that headquarters management posts are blocked by the glass ceiling. As Bill Bsand, executive vice president for Hitachi America, notes: "There are very few Americans who work for Hitachi in Japan and usually at a very low level."[44]

A multinational company with locations in several nations may therefore need several compensation systems for host country nationals. For each host country, worker compensation levels must match wage levels in the local labor market. Country-level comparative compensation data are available from many government, private, and international sources. Information on compensation laws is usually available from host country governments. However, multinational managers must also consider regional differences within countries. Both labor costs and regional government laws may be different.

The relatively low cost of labor, managers, and engineers in Eastern European countries and in India lead many multinational companies to seek location advantages in these countries. Children from these countries also score well in cross-national comparisons of ability in mathematics and science. These locations will probably provide excellent future workers in technical occupations. However, multinational companies are also finding that it is harder to retain talented workers in India. Consider the next Focus on Emerging Markets.

Some experts argue that competitive advantages based on wage rates are only short term. They cite the many Japanese, South Korean, and Taiwanese companies that based their early competitive advantages on their own high-quality, low-cost labor. Most of them have moved plants to cheaper locations in China or Southeast Asia. The implication for multinational companies is that, when local wage rates rise, the company will be forced either to keep pace or to seek another low-cost location.

In the next section, the chapter looks at labor relations.

# A Comparative View of Labor Relations

The variations of labor relations arise not only from cultural differences but also from the unique national histories of unionization.[45] Historical factors, such as the state of technological development during early unionization and the point at which governments recognized the legality of unions, influence current union structure and activities. Some unions were developed for ideological reasons, such as overthrowing the capitalist system or representing religious values. Others developed simply to improve wages and working conditions. Management views of unions also differ from country to country. Astute multinational managers should be well versed in the history, structure, and ideology of unions in the countries in which their companies operate. Consider some of the difficulties of labor relations in India, as shown in the next Case in Point.

A major HRM issue is the popularity of unions, as indicated by what is called union membership density.

## Union Membership Density

**Union membership density**
Proportion of workers in a country who belong to unions.

A strong indicator that multinational managers can use to tell how much unions influence companies is the **union membership density**. Union membership density refers to the proportion of workers who belong to unions in a country. Estimates of union membership density are always approximate because some reports do not consider white-collar workers or professional unions.

Union membership in the United States has declined considerably over the last 30 years. Some decline worldwide is due to the end of compulsory union membership in the transition economies of Eastern Europe. However, European and other

**Focus** on Emerging Markets

### Compensation Plans in Indian Multinational Companies

Although India boasts a plentiful supply of skilled labor, cultivating loyalty to retain valuable workers has proved to be a difficult challenge. As local and multinational companies expand their presence in India, demand for talented employees is becoming fierce. Employees are showing themselves very willing to leave their companies to start new positions. Because it is predicted that many sectors will face future shortages, many companies are starting to work harder to design compensation plans to retain their workers.

A survey by the Grow Talent Company shows that companies that are successful at retaining their employees show respect for them through compensation and benefits. For instance, these companies use HR strategies such as bring-your-spouse-to-the-office days, or they have big budgets to celebrate birthdays or weddings. Other companies are finding that engaging their workers' families also strikes a good work-family balance. Yet other multinational companies are finding that offering the possibility of attaining a master's degree in business administration or some form of global experience cultivates loyalty. Finally, many companies are also experimenting with variable pay (as opposed to fixed pay) to retain talented individuals. By tying the performance of employees to their pay, many companies are still able to manage costs while at the same time rewarding their employees if the company does well.

Infosys, India's famous technology services firm, has been able to retain employees through the Employee Relations Program, which typifies Infosys's commitment to work-life balance. The program includes counseling services, athletic competitive events, the celebration of important cultural events, and even health fairs open to the employees' families. The company also supports the strong family ties inherent in Indian culture by inviting family members to visit its campus. This program has allowed Infosys not only to enjoy a very low attrition rate (10 percent), but also to prevent competitors such as IBM and Oracle from taking its trained employees.

Both domestic and multinational organizations are finding that good HR practices have important benefits. Often, the buzz about employers with good HR practices spreads rapidly through the labor market grapevine. As a result, these companies are able not only to retain their workforce but also to attract more applicants for future positions.

*Sources: Based on Chaturvedi, A. 2012. "Companies across sectors hiking variable pay to retain talent." Economic Times, June 9, online edition; Hamm, S. 2008. "Young and impatient in India." BusinessWeek, January, 45–46; Merchant, Khozem. 2006. "Companies in India offer a taste of the sweet life: Keeping skilled workers is a challenge in the buoyant Indian jobs market and businesses are offering an ever-growing range of perks to keep them happy." Financial Times, February 2; Workforce Management. 2006. "The 10 most forward-thinking leaders in workforce management," March 13.*

industrialized countries still have high proportions of workers who are union members. In major industrialized countries, union membership is declining but still averages greater than 50 percent. In countries such as South Africa, with the opening of unions to the formerly barred black population, unions have more than doubled in size.[46] Exhibit 12.14 summarizes unionization density in various parts of the world.

**CASE IN POINT**

## Dealing with Unions in India

India's free market reforms have attracted multinational firms General Electric, Otis Elevator Co., and Unilever, to name only a few. However, these firms are encountering a national context in which strong institutional pressures give power to unions and encourage union militancy.

India has a rich trade union history. The first trade union was created by a social worker when he discovered the exploitative working conditions of workers. Today, India has more than 45 overlapping, sometimes conflicting, and often confusing major labor laws. These laws allow unions to be formed by as few as seven people, and some companies must deal with as many as 50 different labor groups. The laws also make it difficult to fire employees or to close money-losing operations. A company with more than 10 workers needs government permission to fire employees—something almost never given. In fact, Indian labor laws tend to be highly protective of labor, and they have encouraged a very inflexible labor market.

How are multinational companies adapting? Siemens AG, Whirlpool Corp., and Philips Electronics NV are using golden handshakes to buy out workers. Rather than confronting unions directly, these companies offer workers voluntary retirement and payoffs. For example, with little fanfare, Siemens shed 1,300 of 7,500 employees from its bloated Indian operation for a maximum payout of $16,160 per person—low by European standards but high for India. Many multinational managers sense that unions are ignoring such practices because of a growing realization that Indian businesses must be more efficient to compete internationally.

India also sees a very high level of strikes and lockouts. Consider that India's state-run airline, Air India, recently saw pilot strikes that severely disrupted operations. The pilots decided to strike after Air India decided to train some crews that were only flying domestically to fly the Boeing Dreamliner. The 787 Dreamliner planes are destined for the international market and pilots are unhappy because flying international routes carries much higher perks.

Given the high prevalence of strikes and lockouts, some are arguing that Indian labor laws need to be revised to improve productivity and to make industries more profitable. They point to the experience of China, which has transitioned from extreme job security to major reform in the labor laws. Currently, China has a relatively mobile labor market, and surveys show that Chinese workers have benefited from such changes. These experiences may be useful to India as it considers reforms.

*Sources: Based on Bhowmik, S. K. 2009. "India—Labor searching for a direction." Work and Occupation, 36(2): 126–144; Chowdhury, A. 2012. "Air India local flights take a hit." Wall Street Journal, June 19, online edition; Chowdhury, A. and Gulati, N. 2012. "Air India pilots likely to call off 58-day strike." Wall Street Journal, July 3, online edition; Economist. 2003. "Two systems, one grand rivalry." June 21, 21–23; Rai, Saritha. 2006. "Airport workers across India strike to protest plan for privatizations." New York Times, February 2, C5; Karp, Jonathan, and Michael Williams. 1997. "Firms in India use buyouts to skirt layoff rules." Wall Street Journal, October 13, A16.*

## Some Historical and Institutional Differences

Historical conditions during the early days of unionization and the unions' relationships with social institutions like the government tend to influence the activities of contemporary unions. Consider the differences among British, German, French, U.S., Asian, and Indian unions observed by Professor Christel Lane.[47]

British unions began early in the nineteenth century, corresponding to the rise of major factory-based industries. Ignored early on by government, British unions developed without government interference. Not until the 1980s was there much legal control of management–labor conflict. If the union went on strike, neither the company nor the workers had any legal obligation to solve the conflict, such as honoring the workers' right to return to work. According to Lane,[48] the lack of government intervention led management and workers to develop strong

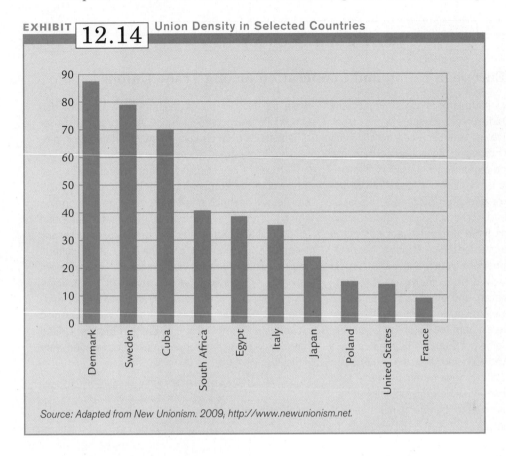

Source: Adapted from New Unionism. 2009, http://www.newunionism.net.

adversarial relationships that remain in existence today in Britain. Lane characterizes the British situation as fragmented and highly conflictual.

Perhaps because German culture ranks high on uncertainty avoidance, labor relationships have a more orderly tradition. The government recognized the union movement in the mid-1880s. The strong role of the state served to develop more harmonious relationships between labor and management. The result in today's Germany is a formalized, legalistic, low-conflict situation with centralized bargaining between large unions and large corporations. Lane argues that the government serves as an intermediary between unions and management.

French unions began much later and developed more slowly than did British or German unions. According to Lane,[49] there were many small companies, and this fragmentation of businesses retarded union growth. In some industries, legal recognition of the right to bargain collectively occurred as late as 1969. The lack of legal protection of French workers and the difficulties of unionization led to highly militant unions. French unions often have strong ideological orientations, and they adopt anti-capitalistic stances based on a belief in the unavoidability of class conflicts between owners and workers. The French ideological unions tend to compete for union members within the same organizations, the consequence of which sometimes has favored management. In many cases, management simply ignores the unions.

British, French, and German unions developed differently. With the creation of the European Union, there has been strong desire among these unions to cooperate, but barriers to such cooperation still exist. Consider the following Case in Point.

## The European Union and Cooperation among Trade Unions

Cooperation among trade unions worldwide occurs fairly frequently. Trade unions cooperate on issues such as exchanging information, collaborating on training programs, producing collective agreements, signing petitions, and organizing strikes. With the creation of the European Union and the "Europeanization" of both labor and products, there has been sustained interest in cooperation among trade unions in Europe. However, there are significant barriers in Europe that have prevented much stronger cooperation. Such barriers originate from the ideological roots of trade unions as well as from differences in production structure, legislation, and other cultural aspects.

The specific barriers relate to historical differences as well as lack of interest from the European Union. For instance, unions in different European countries have ideological differences. Consider that the organization of unions in the United Kingdom and Germany tend to be much looser than in the Nordic countries. Furthermore, Southern unions tend be much more radical, while the Nordic unions tend to view the European Union with much more suspicion. Additionally, employer organizations have also played an important role in preventing unions from cooperating.

A recent study also shows that differences exist at the level of the European Union. The European Union has not put as much effort into promoting cooperation among its unions. Furthermore, there is no European Union institution that has the ability to enforce any legislation. Differences also emanate from cultural sources. There are wide differences in terms of levels of bargaining as well as the extent of trade union coverage. Some countries cover the entire labor markets (e.g., Germany) while others cover only specific industries or companies (e.g., Eastern Europe, United Kingdom). Such differences make cooperation very difficult.

*Source: Based on Larsson, B. 2012. "Obstacles to transnational trade union cooperation in Europe-results from a European survey." Industrial Relations Journal, 43(2): 152–170.*

In the United States before 1926, there was little legal support for union activity. The Wagner Act, passed in 1935, provided the most important legal protection for unions and granted federal protection of the right to organize and bargain collectively. U.S. unions tended early on to focus on the bread-and-butter issues of wages, benefits, and working conditions. They never developed the ideological orientations of the French unions or the formal union–management cooperation of the Germans. Union membership peaked soon after the Wagner Act, during the 1940s. However, with the decline of many traditionally unionized industries and the movement offshore of U.S. manufacturing, union strength in the United States has continually weakened.

In Asia, unionization has taken several different paths. As will be described in more detail later, formerly militant Japanese unions were absorbed into the corporate structure and now largely support management. However, Korean unions have developed a more conflictive relationship with industry and government. For example, recent Korean labor legislation introduced more freedom for companies to fire workers. This led to student unrest and strikes, costing more than $2 billion in lost output in just one month.[50] In tightly controlled economies such as Singapore's, where unionization has gained little ground, there were no days lost to industrial disputes between 1992 and 1994.[51]

In India, the first union was formed in 1918. B. P. Wadia, a social worker, created the union as a response to ongoing worker exploitation. However, that union was short lived because the courts agreed with the companies that the actions of the union were illegal. Mahatma Gandhi was also closely associated with the creation of a textile union. After independence from Britain in 1947, India adopted a socialist model, leading to the strengthening of the unions and a strong public sector. Only recently has the government started liberalizing the economy.[52]

Reflecting their particular ideologies and orientations, unions from different countries tend to adopt different structures. Next, you will see a summary of such structures in use today.

## Union Structures

The type and structure of unions reflect the institutional pressures and historical traditions surrounding unionization. Several major types exist:

* **Enterprise unions** represent all the people in an organization, regardless of occupation or location.
* **Craft unions** represent people from one occupational group, such as plumbers.
* **Industrial unions** represent all the people in an industry regardless of occupational type.
* **Local unions** usually represent one occupational group in one company, but they are often affiliated with larger craft or industrial unions.
* **Ideological unions** represent all workers based on an ideology (e.g., communism) or religious orientation.
* **White-collar or professional unions** represent occupational groups.

Exhibit 12.15 shows selected countries and the popular unions in them.

The nature of union structures in turn influences the collective bargaining process and the general relationship between management and workers.

Enterprise unions are most often associated with Japanese labor relations, although they are not the only unions that exist now or that have existed in Japan. However, most radical Japanese ideological and industrial unions were effectively crushed during the first half of the twentieth century and were replaced

**Enterprise union**
Represents all the people in one organization, regardless of occupation or location.

**Craft union**
Represents people from one occupational group, such as plumbers.

**Industrial union**
Represents all people in an industry regardless of occupational type.

**Local union**
Represents one occupational group in one company.

**Ideological union**
Represents all types of workers based on an ideology (e.g., communism) or religious orientation.

**White-collar or professional union**
Represents an occupational group, similar to craft union.

**EXHIBIT 12.15**   Popular Form of Unions in Selected Countries

| Country | Craft | General | Industrial | White-Collar | Professional | Enterprise |
|---------|-------|---------|------------|--------------|--------------|------------|
| Australia | ✓ | ✓ | ✓ | ✓ | ✓ | |
| Belgium | | | ✓ | | ✓ | |
| Canada | ✓ | | | | | |
| Denmark | ✓ | | | ✓ | | |
| England | ✓ | | | ✓ | | ✓ |
| Finland | | | | ✓ | ✓ | |
| Germany | | | | ✓ | ✓ | |
| Japan | | | | | | ✓ |
| Netherlands | | ✓ | | ✓ | | |
| Norway | ✓ | | ✓ | | | |
| Sweden | ✓ | | ✓ | ✓ | | |
| Switzerland | ✓ | | ✓ | ✓ | | |
| United States | | | ✓ | ✓ | | |

*Source: Adapted from Poole, M. 1986.* Industrial Relations: Heritage and Adjustment. *Oxford: Oxford University Press.*

by enterprise unions. Sometimes critically called company unions, these unions have close associations with management. In fact, one-sixth of the executives in major Japanese companies were previously union executives.[53] Not surprisingly, there is often close cooperation between unions and management, with unions viewing management goals as their own.

German unions favor the industrial form of organization. There are 17 major industrial unions, and collective bargaining generally takes place between the unions and employer associations (groups of employers). At the plant level, an elected **works council** negotiates working conditions directly with the employer, and industry unions negotiate wages at the national or regional level. The next Multinational Management Brief shows how the works council is integrated into management decision making in Germany and is globalizing its influence in tandem with the globalization of German companies.

**Works council**
In Germany, employee group that shares plant-level responsibility with managers regarding issues such as working conditions.

**Codetermination**
Surrender by management to workers of a share of control of the organization traditionally reserved for management and owners.

---

## Multinational Management **Brief**

### Globalization of the Works Council

Codetermination (*Mitbestimmung* in German) means that management surrenders to workers a share of the control of the organization traditionally reserved for management and owners. In Germany, codetermination exists at two levels. At the plant level, workers elect the works council, which has certain prerogatives supported by law, and which shares some decisions with management, such as selection criteria. Some management decisions can be vetoed, such as reassignment. Finally, management must consult and inform the works council on other decisions, such as accident protection. These rights are detailed in the exhibit below.

At the enterprise level, industrial democracy in Germany gives many workers equal representation on the board of directors with those elected by the shareholders. In practice, however, most of these arrangements include policies that favor owners and managers in tight votes. For example, one of the worker-selected representatives must be a manager.

For the Volkswagen Group, the works council has followed its globalization with the formation of the World Works Council in 1999. Although the World Works Council does not have the participatory rights granted German groups by Germany's Industrial Constitution Law, it is funded out of corporate operations and has some power to influence the group's worldwide strategic decisions. Furthermore, the Volkswagen Group is now implementing a Global Labor Charter in all of its international sites. This Global Labor Charter was drafted by the World Works Council and reflects cooperation between management and labor.

The Hoppmann Company, a car dealer and repair shop in Sigen, Germany, has taken codetermination beyond the legal requirement. The company has given workers more power and participation. For example, Hoppmann shares profits 50/50 with its employees. Furthermore, the Hoppmann owner has also transferred all property rights of his company to a foundation that makes decisions regarding the company, and to which profits are routinely transferred. Workers also have full say in major decisions affecting the company.

*continued*

---

**Examples of Decisions and Levels of Participation
by German Works Councils**

| Codetermined with Management | Veto Power over Management | Consulted or Provided Information by Management |
|---|---|---|
| Compensation system | Selection criteria | Major business plans |
| Piecework rates | Training | Introducing new technology |
| Job design | Recruitment | Introducing new equipment |
| Holiday planning | Dismissal | Financial information |
| Accident prevention | Reassignment | |

*Sources: Based on Jochmann-Doll, A., and H. Wachter. 2008. "Democracy at work—revisited."* Management Review, 19, 274–290; Just-Auto Global News. 2012. *"Volkswagen Group puts global charter into practice at international sites." May 15, online edition; Lane, Christel. 1989.* Management and Labour in Europe. *Aldershot, UK: Edward Elgar;* International Labor Organization (ILO). 2000. *"Globalization of works council activities."* World of Work, 36, *http://www.ilo.org/public/english/bureau/inf/magazine/36/.*

---

Given that the most common objective of French unions is to organize along ideological lines, union structure does not necessarily follow industry, occupational, or enterprise categorization. Instead, one union will represent a variety of workers who adhere to the same ideological beliefs. Any one company may have several of these groups organizing workers.

In the United States, the local union remains the major structural feature. Most locals associate with some craft, industry, or mixed national union. There are approximately 170 national unions in the United States. Local craft unions tend to represent workers in a local region, while local industrial unions tend to represent workers at plant level. Although most collective bargaining takes place at the local level, in some instances, such as in the automobile industry, unions attempt to make company-wide or industry-wide agreements.

## Implications for the Multinational: The Search for Harmony

When they use local workers, multinational companies have no choice but to deal with local labor practices, traditions, and laws that must be considered in any strategic decision regarding locating in another country. Consider these examples. In the United States, Japanese companies have avoided locations in the more union-friendly Northern states, favoring instead Southern locations with less union activism. The militant unions in Western Europe have led some multinational companies to look for locations in countries like the Czech Republic, where not only wages but also labor conflict are lower. A country's labor relations situation is therefore an important factor in designing a multinational's IHRM policies.

## Summary and Conclusions

This chapter highlighted fundamental national differences in the HRM processes of recruitment, selection, training and development, performance appraisal, compensation, and labor relations. It also showed how multinational operations are affected by the HRM practices prevalent in host countries.

To understand why HRM practices differ, the chapter presented a model of how the national context affects HRM practices—national culture, business culture, and key social institutions such as education and the legal system.

To show how the model works in different national contexts, the chapter provided numerous illustrations that contrasted U.S. HRM practices with those of other nations. Countries with collectivist cultures were often chosen for comparisons because of their cultural distance from the highly individualistic United States. The contrasts purposefully showed large differences in HRM practices, giving some sense of the variety of HRM practices around the world. However, no one chapter or book could adequately explain all the worldwide differences in human resource management. Thus, the examples given serve only to sensitize multinational managers to the complexity of their task in the HRM area.

The chapter compared U.S. recruitment and selection practices with those in collectivist societies. In contrast to managers used to working with the more public and legalistic U.S. practices, managers from collectivist societies believe that personal contact is the best method to recruit and identify the best employees.

The chapter noted that the training of entry-level workers depends largely on the institutional structure of the educational system. U.S. managers are increasingly concerned that workers do not have the basic educational skills necessary to succeed in complex jobs. In contrast, Germany has perhaps the best system of technical training, based on a collaboration of companies, unions, and the government. Many other countries, including some of the transitioning economies and developing countries, have educational systems that produce workers with good mathematical and science skills.

We also saw that management-development practices are embedded in cultural expectations regarding the relationship of managers with their organizations. U.S.

companies face the dilemma of investing to develop top management talent and then risking that they will go to another company. In collectivist national cultures such as Japan and Korea, managers have a commitment to remain with the organization (they often have little choice). Companies can therefore take a long-term view of investing in extensive management development and training.

To avoid the legal ramifications of race, gender, and age biases, U.S. performance evaluation systems tend to be formal and public. In collectivist societies, in contrast, performance appraisal tends to be informal and relatively secret. In the United States, rewards—in particular, compensation—are linked to the results of performance appraisals. In collectivist societies, factors such as age, family situation, loyalty to the company, and the relationship to the owners often influence rewards more than performance does.

Most multinational companies are attracted to production sites in countries where the wages are low but the talent pool is strong, and so they tend to adopt the host country's wage and salary levels. Numerous sources of information can provide guidance on appropriate compensation strategies. In general, multinational companies need to adapt their practices to be consistent with local norms and customs.

Confronting and dealing with differences in traditions and the volatility of labor relationships are unavoidable activities in running overseas operations. Multinational companies can seldom change a country's traditions of labor relations. Consequently, the volatility of host country labor often becomes a key factor in choosing locations.

Whether a company establishes a joint venture or sets up wholly owned operations in another country, a detailed study of the HRM practices of the local environment is required. Each nation's history, tradition, culture, and social institutions (education and legal and government systems) create unique HRM practices. Moreover, even countries that are culturally similar often have different historical and traditional patterns of labor relations. Thus, a successful multinational manager comes prepared not only with knowledge of the local culture but also with an understanding of how HRM practices evolved to become part of a host country's business environment.

## Discussion Questions

1. Describe and discuss the major factors in the national context that affect a nation's HRM practices.

2. Compare and contrast recruitment and selection strategies in the United States with those in nations with collectivist cultures. Discuss legal and cultural

problems that multinational managers might face using a collectivist approach to recruitment and selection in the United States and using a U.S. approach in collectivist cultures.

3. Some U.S. politicians have called for the development of a German-type apprenticeship training system in the United States. If you were a manager of a U.S. Fortune 500 multinational company, how would you respond to this proposal and why?

4. Discuss the advantages and disadvantages of a permanent employment system for managers. Discuss how this system might work for non-Asian countries other than the United States.

5. You have been given the assignment of setting up a training program for first-level managers in a formerly government-owned Eastern European company. How would you go about developing a curriculum? Why?

6. Compare and contrast the appraisal and compensation systems in the United States with those in collectivist culture nations. Discuss legal and cultural problems that multinational managers might face using a collectivist approach to these systems in the United States and using a U.S. approach in collectivist cultures.

7. Contrast the different types of unions and discuss the challenges each type might pose to a multinational manager.

## Multinational Management **Internet Exercise**

1. Go to the International Labor Organization website (http://www.ilo.org). Read about the mission and goals of the International Labor Organization. Present your findings to the class.

2. Your CEO is very interested in promoting gender equality in the company's various subsidiaries in emerging markets. Review the report produced by the ILO titled "Gender Equality and Decent Work: Selected ILO Conventions and Recommendations that Promote Gender Equality as of 2012," posted on the ILO website. What are some of the major findings of the report?

3. What can your multinational do to promote gender equality in your subsidiaries? Be specific.

4. What are some other key areas that the ILO promotes?

## Multinational Management **Skill Builder**

### The HRM Component in a Multinational Company's Location Decision

**Step 1.** Read the following multinational problem:

You are now a vice president for human resources for the XYZ Company located in the United States. Your company manufactures components for industrial robots. Employees need U.S. high-school-level ability in reading and mathematics to maintain job skills.

You have just come from a meeting where the CEO has asked all functional area vice presidents to prepare a report concerning the location advantages or disadvantages of a country. Marketing and production VPs will look at issues such as potential market size, the availability of raw materials, and supply and sales distribution channels. Your job is to consider the nature of the labor force should your company decide to set up operations in the overseas location. You will need to plan for a host country national workforce of 200 production workers, 10 first-line managers, and 2 midlevel managers.

**Step 2.** Picking teams and countries.

Your instructor will divide you into teams of three to five people. Each team will choose a different country for a prospective location. Your team will act in the role of the vice president for human resources and will prepare the report called for in Step 1. Your instructor may also require that you work within a specific industry.

This is a library research project. Your instructor may provide you with general data sources. You may also use information from the text.

**Step 3.** Prepare reports.

Reports may be written, oral, or both. A typical report analyzes the implications of economic, cultural, and institutional factors as they might affect all of the HRM functions discussed in this chapter. Following are some key topics that must be addressed. Your instructor may assign additional topics.

- *Economic considerations:*

  Comparative wage and salary levels of this country with other countries

  Employment levels, including workforce participation of women and youth

Employer-provided benefits

Characteristics of labor relations (e.g., likelihood of work stoppages)

- *Institutional conditions:*

  Availability of educated workers

  Extent of government intervention in employment—wage levels, benefit requirements, policies for layoffs, mandated holidays, other labor legislation

  Legal power of unions

- *National and business cultures:*

  Effects of dominant religion and language on labor relations

  Cultural effects of the relationship of the employee with the organization—long term, family dominated, preference for large or small organizations, etc.

  Traditions regarding union types and labor

- *Analysis:*

  Costs and benefits of locating in this country

  Solutions for potential problems

  Recommendation to the president

**Step 4.** Present your findings.

Oral reports for this exercise will take between 1 and 2 hours, depending on your instructor's requirements.

*Source: Adapted from Balfour, Alan. 1988–1989. "A beginning focus for teaching international human resources administration." Organizational Behavior Teaching Review, 13(2): 79–89.*

## *Endnotes*

[1] Black, J. Stewart, Hal B. Gregersen, and Mark E. Mendenhall. 1992. *Global Assignments*. San Francisco: Jossey-Bass; Reynolds, Calvin. 1997. "Strategic employment of third country nationals." *Human Resource Planning*, 20(1): 33–39.

[2] Porter, Michael E. 1990. *The Competitive Advantage on Nations*. New York: Free Press.

[3] *Economist*. 2003. "Roll over, Confucius." January 25, 40.

[4] Porter.

[5] Bohlander, George W., Scott Snell, and Arthur W. Sherman Jr. 2001. *Managing Human Resources*. Cincinnati: South-Western.

[6] International Social Survey Program (ISSP). 1999–2000. "International social survey program: Work orientations II, 1997" (computer file).

[7] Trompenaars, Fons. 1994. *Riding the Waves of Culture: Understanding Diversity in Global Business*. Chicago: Irwin.

[8] Bohlander, Snell, William B. Werther, and Keith Davis. 1993. *Human Resources and Personnel Management*. New York: McGraw-Hill.

[9] Hofstede, Geert. 1991. *Cultures and Organizations: Software of the Mind*. London: McGraw-Hill.

[10] Steers, Richard M., Yoo Keun Shin, and Gerardo R. Ungson. 1989. *The Chaebol: Korea's New Industrial Might*. New York: HarperBusiness.

[11] Organisation for Economic Co-operation and Development (OECD). 2000. *Education at a Glance: OECD Indicators*. Paris, France: OECD.

[12] Drost, Ellen A., Colette A. Frayne, Kevin B. Lowe, and J. Michael Geringer. 2002. "Benchmarking training and development practices: A multicountry analysis." *Human Resource Management*, 41(1): 67–86.

[13] Van Buren, Mark E., and Stephen B. King. 2000. "ASTD's annual accounting of worldwide patterns in employer-provided training." *Training & Development*, Supplement, the 2000 ASTD International Comparisons Report, 1–24.

[14] Cook, Mary F. 1993. *The Human Resources Yearbook 1993/1994 Edition*. Englewood Cliffs, NJ: Prentice Hall.

[15] Ibid.

[16] Drost et al.

[17] Bondreau, John W. 1991. "Utility analysis in human resource management decision." In M. D. Dunnette and Latta M. Hough, eds. *Handbook of Industrial and Organizational Psychology*, 2nd ed. Palo Alto, CA: Consulting Psychology Press, 1111–1143.

[18] Arkin, Anat. 1992. "Personnel management in Denmark: The land of social welfare." *Personnel Management*, March, 32–35; International Labor Organization (ILO). 1999. *World Employment Report 1998–99*. Geneva: International Labor Office.

[19] *BusinessWeek Online*. 1996. August 23, chart; International Labor Organization (ILO).

[20] Arkin.

[21] Werther and Davis.

[22] Locher, Alan H., and Kenneth S. Teel. 1988. "Appraisal trends." *Personnel Journal*, 67(9): 139–145.

[23] Bohlander, Snell, and Sherman.

[24] Ibid.

[25] Milliman, John, Stephen Nason, Cherrie Zhu, and Helen De Cieri. 2002. "An exploratory assessment of the purposes of performance in North and Central America and the Pacific Rim." *Human Resource Management*, 41(1): 87–102.

[26] Geringer, Frayne, and Milliman.

[27] Hofstede.

[28] Steers, Shin, and Ungson.

[29] Ibid, 101.

[30] Ibid.

[31] U.S. Department of Labor. 1995. *Hourly Compensation Costs for Production Workers, June 1995*. Washington, D.C.: U.S. Government Printing Office.

[32] International Labor Organization (ILO). 1997. *World Employment Report 1996–97*. Geneva: International Labor Office.

[33] Simmers, Tim. 2005. "Workers in U.S. labor longer with less vacation than others." *Business Writer*, December 10, 1.

[34] Bohlander, Snell, and Sherman.

[35] Bureau of National Affairs. 1988. *Recruiting and Selection Procedures, Personnel Policies Forum*. No. 46, May. Washington, D.C.: Bureau of National Affairs, Inc., 9–11.

[36] Ibid.

[37] Hansen, Fay. 1998. "Incentive plans are now commonplace in large firms." *Compensation and Benefits Review*, 30, 8.

[38] Geringer, Frayne, and Milliman.

[39] Lowe, Kevin B., John Milliman, Helen De Cieri, and Peter J. Dowling. 2002. "International compensation practices: A ten-country comparative analysis." *Human Resource Management*, 41(1): 45–66.

[40] Macharzina, Klaus. 2000. "Editorial: The Japanese model—out of date?" *Management International Review*, 40, 103–106.

[41] *Economist*, 2006. "Greying Japan—The downturn," January 9. http://www.economist.com.

[42] Takahashi, Shunsuke. 1993. "New trends on human resource management in Japan." In Mary F. Cook, ed. *The Human Resource Yearbook 1993/1994*. Upper Saddle River, NJ: Prentice Hall, 137–138; Schmidt, Richard. 1997. "Japanese management, recession style." *Business Horizons*, 39, 70–75.

[43] *Economist*. 1999. "Putting the bounce back into Matsushita." May 20, http://www.economist.com.

[44] Lancaster, Hal. 1996. "How you can learn to feel at home in a foreign-based firm." *Wall Street Journal*, June 4, B1.

[45] International Labor Organization (ILO). *World Employment Report 1998–99*. Geneva: ILO; Poole, M. 1986. *Industrial Relations: Heritage and Adjustment*. Oxford: Oxford University Press.

[46] International Labor Organization (ILO). *World Employment Report 1996–97;* International Labor Organization (ILO). 1997. *World Labour Report 1997–98*. Geneva: International Labor Office.

[47] Lane, Christel. 1989. *Management and Labour in Europe*. Aldershot, UK: Edward Elgar.

[48] Ibid.

[49] Ibid.

[50] *Economist*. 1997. "The trouble with South Korea." January 18, 59–60.

[51] IMD. 1996. *The World Competitiveness Yearbook 1996*. Lausanne, Switzerland: IMD.

[52] Bhowmik, S. K. 2009. "India—Labor searching for a direction." *Work and Occupations*, 36(3): 126–144.

[53] Abegglen, James C. and Stalk, Jr., George. *Kaisha: The Japanese Corporation*. New York: Basic Books.

# People Management, The Mantra for Success: The Case of Singhania and Partners

It was 9:15 a.m. on 25 April 2006. An article published in that day's *Economic Times,* a leading Indian financial daily, had attracted the attention of both Mr. Ravi Singhania and Ms. Manju Mohotra. Singhania was the founder and managing partner of Singhania and Partners,[1] one of the largest full-service national law firms in India; Mohotra was its chief executive. The Indian legal services industry had been booming since the country's economic liberalization, which had started in the 1990s. The exponential growth of this industry was accompanied by an acute talent crunch. The ability to hire and retain talent was becoming a source of competitive advantage, a mantra for success. The news article Singhania and Mohotra read was about the movement of partners between legal services firms. It was yet another testimony to the high attrition rate in the Indian legal services industry. Sitting in Mohotra's office, the article provoked both Singhania and Mohotra to reflect on the adequacy of their firm's people practices.

## Indian Legal Services Industry

"The legal services market includes practitioners of law operating in every sector of the legal spectrum. These include commercial, criminal, legal aid, insolvency, labor/industrial, family and taxation law."[2] Before 1992, a vast majority of Indian lawyers worked in small practices, as Indian law mandated that law firms could neither have more than 20 partners nor could they advertise their services.[3] Additionally, Indian corporations preferred in-house legal advisors as they were more economical compared to external counsels,[4] further rendering the creation of large legal firms less likely. The legal services industry had competitive pricing and legal firms were mostly fragmented and competed in niche domains.

With the liberalization of the Indian economy beginning in the early 1990s came the foreign investors and multinational corporations. Indian law firms soon realized the importance of providing legal services to these new arrivals. But only a few Indian legal firms had the expertise to handle commercial work for multinational corporations.[5] Combined with this paucity of expertise was the high demand for it, created by the fact that the legal system in India was very slow and companies preferred arbitration over going to court in settling disputes. These two factors combined to create an explosive demand for legal services in India.

In spite of the country's accession to the World Trade Organization in 1995, the Indian legal services market remained closed to foreign players. Various political parties were opposed to the idea of opening up this sector to outsiders. Hence the Indian legal services industry was protected—the practice of law was restricted to Indian nationals only.[6] Under the Indian Advocates Act of 1961, foreign law firms were not allowed to open offices in India[7] and were "prohibited from giving any legal advice that could constitute practising Indian law."[8] This prevented foreign lawyers and law firms from establishing offices in India. International law firms were "allowed to function only as liaison offices, or foreign legal consultants."[9]

Law firms were people-intensive organizations and their key capability was the skill, knowledge, and capacity of their employees. The high demand for lawyers that came with the liberalization of the Indian economy, together with the continued shortage of good quality lawyers in many areas of law, meant that the industry faced an acute shortage of legal professionals. With ample employment opportunities in the industry, attrition became a real concern. Effective human resource management became essential for law firms. The increasingly competitive labor market required firms to develop creative approaches to the recruitment and reward of employees. It also brought significant retention challenges. Firms had to find ways of holding on to their employees and of ensuring that they continued to be motivated. It was a challenge for firms to create a legal practice that met both the needs of clients for a high-quality service and the needs of lawyers for a sustainable work–life balance. Typically, firms increased profits by reducing the number of employees and increasing the workload of the remaining employees.

Global spending on legal services in 2005 was over U.S. $390 billion, and was forecast to grow to over U.S. $480 billion by 2010, with the United States accounting for around 49 percent of the global value.[10] Thanks to the highly qualified, low-cost legal workforce, fast-growing economies such as India were likely to become outsourcing destinations, occupying a significant portion of this market.[11] This area of work opened up new avenues for Indian legal professionals, creating even more opportunities for an already scarce high-quality legal workforce. The main focus of legal process outsourcing ("LPO") was in the areas of "legal transcription," "document review," "litigation support," "legal research," "intellectual property," "contract related services," and "secretarial and legal publishing services."[12] The Indian LPO space was divided into captive centers, third party niche service providers and third party multiservice providers, with third party service providers dominating the space. The growth strategy for most service providers was to begin with low-value services and gradually move up the value chain by acquiring and exhibiting domain expertise.[13] The largely untapped LPO sector was in its nascent stages, providing vast business opportunities in high-volume services like document review and legal publishing, and in high-end services such as intellectual property and contract services.[14]

Regional competitors like China, Korea, etc., were increasingly liberalizing their legal services sectors.[15] The Indian government, though concerned by this decision of its regional competitors, had yet to make any formal decisions about the liberalization of Indian legal services. If the proposed liberalization of the legal services sector were to go through and the restrictions on nationality in order to practice in India were removed, it was expected that India would witness the entry of many foreign law firms and legal consultants. Meanwhile, even more foreign investors and multinational corporations were expected to enter India in 2006. This would further increase competition and legal expertise requirements in areas such as foreign direct investment, intellectual property rights, infrastructure financing, human rights, environmental law, etc.[16]

## Singhania and Partners

Singhania grew up surrounded by his father's corporate law and litigation practice in New Delhi, India. From his formative years, Singhania knew that he was going to be a lawyer and have his own practice one day. In 1987, while going to law school, he started his legal career with his father's firm, Singhania & Company.[17] He worked on various cases and helped manage the practice with offices all over India. During these years, Singhania became well versed with the nuts and bolts of the legal services business. His most important lessons were that customer is king and that Singhania's employees were his biggest asset.

Singhania was able to capitalize on the demand for legal services created by the liberalization of the Indian economy. A lot of work came to the firm from overseas clients, particularly from the east coast of the United States. During 1996–1997, Singhania & Company felt that in order to effectively serve clients and gain a competitive advantage, it would be valuable to establish an overseas office; New York City was the chosen location. In October 1997, Singhania moved to New York to set up Singhania & Company's office. Through his interactions with other law firms, he became conversant with the Western style of legal services management, which had a significant impact on his own management style. In November 1999, Singhania moved back to New Delhi to set up his own corporate law and litigation practice under the name of Singhania and Partners—a name very similar to his father's firm. Singhania's father encouraged his decision and advised him to take on Mohotra, who had worked with Singhania & Company, to meet the new challenge of setting up a law firm.

In the beginning it was Singhania, an associate lawyer and Mohotra in a small office in New Delhi. While Singhania managed the core legal services aspects of the business, Mohotra took responsibility for managing the overall business (see Figure 1) and the assignment of personnel to various projects based on their competencies and availability, in consultation with senior management. The marketing activities were handled jointly by both Singhania and Mohotra. Singhania's father sought approval from clients already working with Singhania & Company to move them over to Singhania and Partners. The first few clients that moved to the firm were America Online, Fedders Corporation, Standard & Poor's, and McGraw Hill.

Although the firm did not have any litigation work in hand, Singhania, realizing the potential of a litigation

**FIGURE 1     Singhania and Partners' Organization Chart**

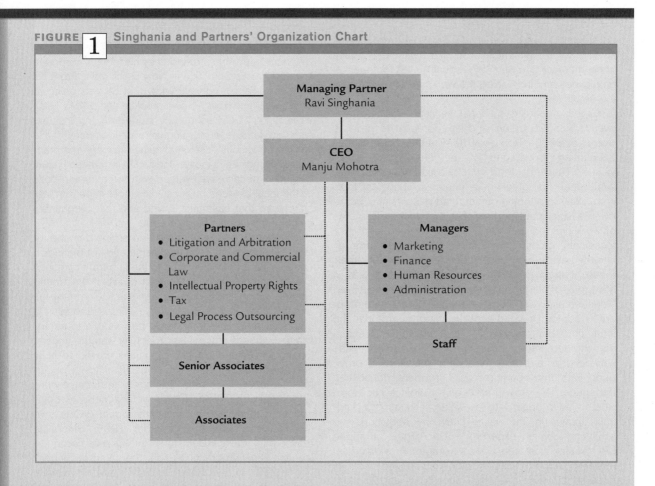

practice, hired Arvind, a litigation lawyer, in early 2000. Sure enough, soon after Arvind came on board, Daewoo approached the firm with a litigation case, giving the firm's litigation practice a boost. In an effort to better serve its clients, between 1999 and 2002 the firm moved to a bigger office in the same building in New Delhi and set up offices in Bangalore, Mumbai, and Hyderabad. At the same time, it also formed affiliations with counsels across several Indian states in order to meet its clients' need to interact with one face for legal services across the country. The firm grew from two lawyers in 1999 to 50 lawyers in 2006, eight of whom were partners. The firm's practice areas included tax, corporate and commercial law, and intellectual property, as well as arbitration and litigation. After the onset of the outsourcing wave, the firm had been approached by potential clients for legal process outsourcing. While Singhania and Mohotra agreed that this was a booming industry, they knew that this was not their core competence and were not sure if they

should try to make it one. So although Singhania and Partners did enter this domain, it did so with great caution and was extremely selective about the quality of work it picked up.

The firm gained considerable experience in cross-border transactions in the areas of mergers and acquisitions, joint ventures, due diligence, and technology transfer, as well as in assisting its clients in establishing wholly owned subsidiaries in India. The practice was built in ways so as to ensure that the clients could realize value from the firm's services. Turnaround time, accessibility to senior members in the firm, meeting deadlines, and providing services in a cost-effective manner were all important to clients and formed the core values of the firm. The firm's systems, in turn, revolved around these core values.

Since Indian law prohibited legal services firms to directly market their services through any means other than the yellow pages, Singhania and Partners increased business by getting work through referrals.

Singhania knew that this could only happen by providing exceptional services to clients. He put systems and processes in place and used technology to provide state-of-the-art infrastructure to serve clients effectively. In order to institutionalize the systems put in place, the firm sought an ISO 9002[18] certification in 1999, which it received in 2000. Foreseeing tremendous growth in the infrastructure and information technology sectors in India, in 2001 Singhania and Partners began focusing on these two sectors. In that same year, India witnessed mega infrastructure deals, with the golden quadrangle project[19] being announced by the government of India. The National Highways Authority of India[20] was at the forefront of these projects, and Singhania and Partners, emerging from intense competition, was appointed its legal counsel.

## Are We at Risk?

When Singhania walked into Mohotra's room, she was engrossed in reading an article in that day's *Economic Times*. She asked if he had read the article. "The one about J. Sagar?" he asked.

"Yes, attrition seems to be becoming a monster in the industry," said Mohotra, and started reading the news out aloud. "'Corporate lawyers Dina Wadia, a former partner of Little & Co.; Nitin Potdar, former partner of Amarchand Mangaldas; and Akshay Chudasama, former partner of AZB and Partners and Lex Inde have signed up with national law firm J. Sagar Associates.' Do you think we need to worry about our people?"

Singhania exclaimed, "I'd rather look at this now than wait for it to become a problem and then address it!"

Mohotra, answering her own question, said, "I don't think we need to be concerned about our people. I don't think anybody in the industry can provide a better environment to work in than we can. We have always thought of our people as our core asset and have treated them accordingly. After all, it's our people who make us a market leader by providing quality service to clients. And accordingly we do everything to retain talent."

"You are right. When we were looking at outsourcing, the important criteria in accepting processes was our people—we absolutely refused to do processes that required form-filling sort of work because it would not stimulate our lawyers," said Singhania. "You do think they remain intellectually stimulated, don't you?"

"We try our best. Apart from the regular work, in the bi-weekly open house we have small presentations on different topics from different legal areas. Even our junior-most lawyers are encouraged to present. It's a great opportunity to learn, build confidence, and grow with the organization! And if there were any dissatisfaction, I would hope for it to come out in the weekly senior management meeting or the bi-weekly open house. We encourage these forums to be utilised for voicing opinions, suggestions, ideas.... Moreover, given our open door policy, anybody can walk in to any senior management's cabin for discussions," continued Mohotra.

Singhania said, "And the career growth is all merit based. A good example is our first litigation lawyer, who started as an associate and is now a partner. Moreover, we don't just rely on annual performance reviews for increments; it is done on an as-and-when-needed basis. And, again, it is all merit based! In fact I remember that recently we increased a new employee's salary by 50 percent even before he got his first paycheck, purely because we felt he provided that kind of value to the firm. He seemed happy."

Mohotra pondered further, "Talking of happiness, I can't forget the staff's excitement when we go for the annual firm retreats. The first year when we went to Naukuchiyatal,[21] it was three days full of fun. We played games, had picnics; it was total unwinding time. It was a great time to bond! And at our most recent camping retreat to Dhanaulti,[22] everybody had a great time. I am already being asked where we will be going this year!"

Singhania contemplated, "Do you think we're paying them enough?" Without waiting for a reply, he continued, "I do believe that we are among the best paymasters in the industry and the year-end bonuses are substantial. And like you said, it is all merit based. All the same, Seth did leave us for more money without even talking to us about it. And he was a good performer."

"You are right, but again, we try our best. We try not to overwork our lawyers. For projects that require five lawyers, we assign seven, whereas others in the industry would like to assign only three. This is because we feel family life is most important. We have also been able to provide a stress-free environment to work in."

Both of them felt much better than they had felt at the beginning of their conversation. Just then Mohotra's phone rang It was Seth. Putting the call on speaker, Mohotra replied, "Good morning Seth. How are you?"

"Fine thanks. Do you have a few minutes?"
"Sure."

"Well, it's a little awkward, but I'll be straightforward. Would you be open to bringing me back on board?"

Singhania and Mohotra silently agreed. "We could talk about it, but I would like to understand the reasons for your decision."

"Well, the foremost reason is that I miss the environment of Singhania and Partners. And … could we meet to discuss?"

"Ummm…. I am traveling this week, so, would you like to come to the office sometime next week and we can chat about it? Say sometime next Tuesday?" replied Manju.

"Sure, ma'am. Is 10:00 a.m. convenient?"

Referring to her diary, Manju replied, "Yes it is. All right, I'll see you Tuesday, 1st May at 10:00 am then."

"Thank you, ma'am. See you then," said Seth, concluding the conversation.

Mohotra and Singhania looked at each other and smiled. Preparing to leave, Singhania thought out aloud, "We seem to be fine for today, but what about tomorrow … especially with all the talk about the entry of foreign law firms into India?"

## CASE DISCUSSION QUESTIONS

1. Discuss Singhania and Partners' HR practices.
2. Evaluate the adequacy of the firm's HR practices. Use the PCMM for this evaluation. What level does it appear to be at?
3. If the organization wants to improve its PCMM level, what steps should it take?

## CASE CREDIT

(©) 2008 by the Asia Case Research Centre, The University of Hong Kong. Preeti Goyal prepared this case for class discussion.

## CASE NOTES

[1] Singhania and Partners' website, http://www.singhania.net, accessed June 20, 2006.

[2] *Business Wire*. 2007. "New report helps you to spot future trends and developments in the global legal services players." March 29.

[3] RocSearch Ltd. 2006. *Indian Legal Services Market: An Analysis*. February.

[4] Ibid.

[5] Ibid.

[6] Ibid.

[7] Ibid.

[8] Sengupta, Reena. 2005. "India's legal market on the cusp of inevitable change LAW SERVICES IN ASIA PART I: Outsourcing," *The Financial Times*.

[9] RocSearch Ltd.

[10] *Datamonitor. 2005. "Global Legal Services—Industry Profile."* December.

[11] RocSearch Ltd.

[12] ValueNotes. 2006. *Offshoring Legal Services to India*. December.

[13] *Business Wire*. 2007. "An In-Depth Analysis of the Indian Vendor Space along with Profiles of All Major Industry Players." July 10.

[14] Ibid.

[15] RocSearch Ltd.

[16] Ibid.

[17] Singhania and Company's Web site, http://www.singhania.com, accessed June 24, 2006.

[18] ISO 9002 is a model for quality assurance for production, installation, and servicing developed and maintained by the International Organization for Standardization, or ISO.

[19] The golden quadrangle project would link the four metropolitan areas of India—Delhi, Mumbai, Chennai, and Calcutta—via a national highway.

[20] The National Highways Authority of India was constituted by the Indian Parliament and is responsible for the development, maintenance, and management of national highways in India.

[21] Naukuchiyatal is a lake resort in the northern Indian state of Uttranchal.

[22] Dhanaulti is a camp resort in the northern Indian state of Uttranchal.

# Cisco Switches in China: The Year of The Manager

*As an expat, your job from the beginning is to leave. The day you arrive is the day you must start to think "What am I going to do to facilitate my leaving? Who is going to work out and who should move up?"*

UVA-OB-0978
January 21, 2010

Ivo Raznjevic, engineering director of the Cisco China Research and Development Center (CRDC), was enjoying an end-of-day round of Ping-Pong he was playing with the office's most competitive player. Between challenging volleys, he couldn't help but make the connection between the game and his job; that for every challenge addressed, another came right back at him. Working themselves out of a job was not that easy.

With buy-in from the top of the Cisco Systems (Cisco) San Jose-based executive team, the CRDC leadership team of which Raznjevic and Gronski were members had started the building of the fledgling organization in Shanghai. The initial development plan was to focus on technologies and products targeting service providers and consumer networking sectors. Cisco had committed to invest $32 million USD in the center. Not intending it to be an overseas R&D center for internal outsourcing Cisco projects, the CRDC leadership team had pushed for innovation and independence from corporate headquarters.

Within a year, the organization had top-notch local engineers who built relationships with U.S. engineers and provided early delivery on CRDC's first few projects. By the fall of 2007, $100 million had been received, and the CRDC team was proud of its success.

But certain personnel issues still weighed on his mind. Should one of Cisco's local female employees be transferred laterally from a test manager position to a development manager position? How should he help his newest manager through his first encounter with Cisco's ranking system? What action—if any—should he take regarding a UK-based senior engineer who sent out a controversial e-mail? He readied his paddle as his opponent paused to serve.

# China Opens Its Doors, and the United States Becomes a Guest

Cisco made its global footprint in China during 1994, when the firm established Cisco China in Beijing. Mainly a sales office, the company's name recognition grew rapidly through contracts to help the state-owned phone companies build nationwide networks.[1] A few years later, the "Huawei affair," a messy lawsuit with a Chinese technology company over intellectual property, that Cisco eventually dropped, left a bitter aftertaste.

In the fall of 2004, Cisco announced a plan to invest $32 million in a new R&D center in Shanghai. The company already had several R&D centers geographically dispersed in North Carolina; Massachusetts; Bangalore, India; and Tokyo, Japan. CEO John Chambers believed that the firm's long-time commitment to "ongoing research and development is the basis for Cisco's innovation."[2] The move was also intended to be symbolic of Cisco's commitment to China— despite the Huawei affair.[3] Soon after the People's Republic of China (PRC) granted the necessary licensing and approval for the center to operate as a *wholly owned foreign enterprise* (WOFE).

Cisco tapped Jan Gronski to establish the Cisco China Research and Development Center. Gronski, a Chinese-speaking PhD, who grew up in Warsaw, Poland and had worked for Cisco since 1996, ran the systems and solutions quality business unit in San Jose and knew most of the senior vice presidents of Cisco's other business units. In the fall of 2004, Gronski relocated to Shanghai, eager to start as managing director of CRDC. With start-up cash[4] and a few engineering jobs in his pocket, Gronski's first job was to assemble his leadership team.

# Don't Apply Unless You Fly

To build the leadership team he wanted, Gronski put a lot of effort into recruiting. He called Daniel Puche, a French Canadian he had worked with in Montreal for awhile. Puche had a PhD in physics and spent several years doing research and working around the world. He then joined Cisco holding various jobs mainly as a development manager and software process expert. Puche recalled:

*Jan called and asked if I'd like to help him open an engineering facility in Shanghai. I said, "No." I turned it down because Jan had an engineering team in Canada, and I was in a position that made things difficult to go. And I didn't want to be away from my family that much. China was an unknown to me.*

*Jan has always been a believer in the way I teach engineering, which is quite different from any others in Cisco, and he told me I would have private run of engineers who would have no resistance to learning things differently. That was an interesting challenge and an opportunity for me to show we could do things just as well or even better than how engineering was done in San Jose. He convinced me and I went with him.*

Gronski also recruited one of his employees, Jerry Chen, to go to Shanghai with them. Chen was a software developer who had been at Cisco since graduating with a master's degree in computer science. Chen said:

*Jan was my boss and liked me. Then he gets an assignment to open a center in China. I grew up in China and left when I was 12 years old. He was chatting with me and said, "Do you want to go back to China and do something?" "Why not?" I answered. I'd never really experienced Chinese culture, so the reason I went back was to experience the cultural differences between the U.S. and China. To me, actually, it was very exciting to get a job working in China.*

On January 2, 2005, Gronski, Puche, and Chen arrived together in Shanghai and started to set up shop. "We landed and there was no center," Chen said. "We didn't even have a place to sit, so we borrowed space at the sales facility." A few weeks later, Ted Curran, an Irishman with degrees in engineering and computer science, joined the group as a technology expert. Curran recalled:

> I didn't know anybody. The team was from all parts of Cisco and different nationalities. I arrived at the airport and had to figure out how to get a taxi to the office. And then try to understand the complexity of building a new team. I'd been involved in team building but never to create a new one.

Ivo Raznjevic, who arrived in February 2005, was the next recruit to complete the initial CRDC team. He grew up in Zagreb, Croatia, when it was one of the Yugoslav republics. Raznjevic earned an undergraduate degree in mathematics in 1989 and a master's degree in computer science. In 1994, he started working for Cisco in San Jose. Raznjevic smiled when he talked about his background: "Who would have thought that being from a communist country would be a job qualification?"

The group was diverse enough to conduct business in at least 11 different languages. "Jan was the only one fluent in Chinese," Curran said. "That made it a great adventure because most of us didn't know the language, the culture, and we didn't pretend to know the culture." Among them they had a broad array of degrees from highly respected institutions that included Oxford University, University of California Santa Barbara, University of Illinois, Université de Montréal, University of New Hampshire, the University of Warsaw, and the University of Zagreb. "We complemented each other," said Curran. "Jan was dogmatic, Daniel was passionate, and Ivo was very strategic." Curran was described as "patient and able to provide a lot of laughter." Little did they realize how much they would need all of those perspectives. Using borrowed furniture and office space, the team settled down to sort out many issues. What was their vision for this center? How would CRDC govern itself? What should it ask Cisco's India facility about best practices? What kind of projects should it take on? What was its strategy for talent management?

## CRDC Governance

In May of 2005, Gronski and Raznjevic returned to Cisco headquarters in San Jose to meet with an oversight group that eventually became the CRDC Strategy Board. Gronski's significant network contacts at the company's vice president level were instrumental to the board's formation. In the end, Charles Giancarlo, Cisco chief development officer and senior vice president, agreed to head the board. His participation was key because he agreed that, to keep talent at the firm, CRDC had to be a place to engage in important work and become a center of expertise, not a place to outsource undesirable work. "Giancarlo supported growing CRDC and made sure it was part of the corporate global strategy," a CRDC business operations manager said.

The board met quarterly to formulate CRDC's strategic direction and facilitate its alignment with corporate's business initiatives. Members of the board included several other high-ranking executives from San Jose and China besides Gronski and Raznjevic.

A CRDC Core Team was also established and included VP-appointed stakeholders from various Cisco support functions (CDO, finance, HR, WPR, legal, and CRDC). The idea was that the Core Team would provide tactical guidance and assistance to execute board-approved CRDC strategy.

In Shanghai, Gronski and senior CRDC managers were the CRDC Management Team (see Exhibit 1 for CRDC governance model). Its goal was to create an R&D center to architect, design, develop, test, and support products and solutions for delivery to Cisco customers worldwide.

# Looking West for Guidance

Cisco's first foray into an R&D center outside the United States was India, so when the CRDC team needed to figure out what the structure of an R&D facility might look like, India provided clues. Attracted by the English-speaking engineering talent India offered, Cisco had opened the Global Development Centre (GDC) 10 years earlier in Bangalore. The GDC grew to employ approximately 300 people by 2005,[5] becoming a low-cost engineering resource for San Jose. Different business units in San Jose allocated work to GDC whose engineers complemented or extended engineering efforts on the product. GDC was not originating work but supporting projects controlled from other parts of Cisco. As a result, the GDC had many groups of various sizes reporting to individual business units in San

**EXHIBIT 1**    CRDC Governance Model

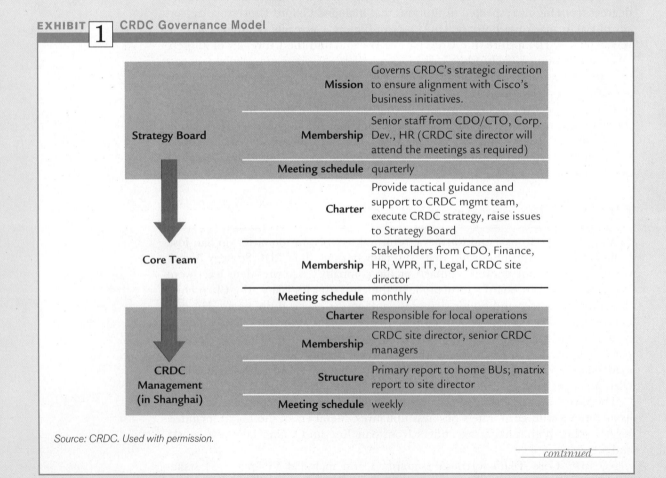

| Strategy Board | Mission | Governs CRDC's strategic direction to ensure alignment with Cisco's business initiatives. |
| | Membership | Senior staff from CDO/CTO, Corp. Dev., HR (CRDC site director will attend the meetings as required) |
| | Meeting schedule | quarterly |
| Core Team | Charter | Provide tactical guidance and support to CRDC mgmt team, execute CRDC strategy, raise issues to Strategy Board |
| | Membership | Stakeholders from CDO, Finance, HR, WPR, IT, Legal, CRDC site director |
| | Meeting schedule | monthly |
| CRDC Management (in Shanghai) | Charter | Responsible for local operations |
| | Membership | CRDC site director, senior CRDC managers |
| | Structure | Primary report to home BUs; matrix report to site director |
| | Meeting schedule | weekly |

*Source: CRDC. Used with permission.*

*continued*

**EXHIBIT 1** Continued

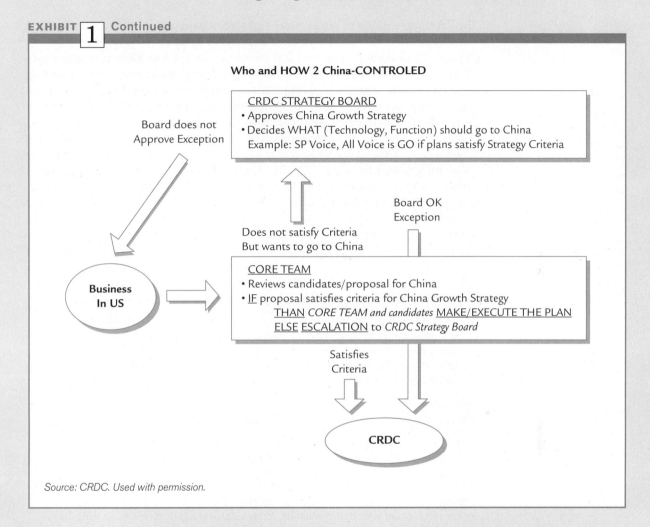

*Source: CRDC. Used with permission.*

Jose. Attrition rates in India were high and the CRDC team suspected that the high turnover was because of how the work was structured.

Believing that engineers would be proud to own something—even if it was small—and work harder (and not leave), the team decided that the China facility needed to be different. "Right away at CRDC we negotiated with upper management in San Jose that we would bring ownership of the projects to China as we built up the capability," Puche recalled. "Our goal was to have ownership with project management, leadership, and so on."

# Finding that First Project

Cisco maintained a defined process within its R&D centers. The first step at developing a project at a Cisco R&D site was to have an idea that excited the decision makers and conceptually won approval—called Concept Commit (CC). The next phase was to have resources approved and available—referred to as Execution Commit (EC). After that, engineers and scientists generally conducted original investigations on a systematic basis to gain new knowledge (research) and/or the application of research findings to create or significantly improve products or processes. This work was done on the development side of the product and service. So at Cisco R&D centers, several software developers thought about how to create a product or process and how to implement it—take ideas from zero and create new things. Once the product or process was developed, it moved over to the test side. Testers spent a lot of time ensuring that things worked. The tester thought about whether the new design met all the necessary requirements and whether or not they could destroy the product or process—did the product deliver good quality to the customer?

The CRDC group knew that the first project would be critical. Raznjevic believed they needed a core project that would bring some money to the company but was not strategic to Cisco. "The ideal scenario would be to find something to own that was losing money in San Jose, move it to China, and make it profitable," Raznjevic said. "We couldn't start with the crown jewels (IOS). Finding a project that was in the red and then moved to China and moved back in the black, not much money nor intellectual property to risk."

Early on the CRDC team had identified a list of possible projects. Because each business unit at Cisco had its own marketing, engineering, testing, and finance people, the CRDC team had to convince business unit managers who owned that project of the value in moving it to China. Puche remembered the issue:

> If you go to establish an R&D center in a country like the UK or Germany, they would get responsibility to do stuff. Why not the same for China? We created a model against the grain of Cisco where engineers working for a particular BU were not directly reporting to that BU but to Gronski and a dotted line to the BU with little intervention on our part except to coach them to do it.

Not surprisingly, relinquishing ownership of the project (see Exhibit 2 for structure) was not easy for business unit managers. Raznjevic recalled:

> How you present information, and to whom, became important. Each project had a list of people involved like the vice president, general manager (GM), senior/junior staff. So we decided which staff meeting to hit—initially this was the three BUs where we knew the GM. We talked to a lot of people to make sure we knew in advance what problem they were having with the project. And there were certain topics we learned just not to mention to general managers in the U.S. because all they wanted was to get it done the cheapest way—not necessarily concerned with our longevity.

## Space Shot

The CRDC management team wanted to provide a pleasant and secure environment for their employees, who would spend 10 or 12 hours a day at the office. Raznjevic preferred that the CRDC lab and offices be housed at a single site. Scouting for good locations and negotiating leases would be a frustrating task in any country, and China was no exception. Several questions guided the search: What was a prime location? Could employees tolerate a long commute to and from the office, or should it be close to where they lived? Should their space be near potential key customers? Perhaps somewhere with a prestigious address? Then there was the issue of how much space was enough. The average footage per employee in the United States was 175–275 square feet.[6] What was the norm in Shanghai, where people were used to living and working closer together than in the United States?

**EXHIBIT 2**   **Cisco Business Organization**

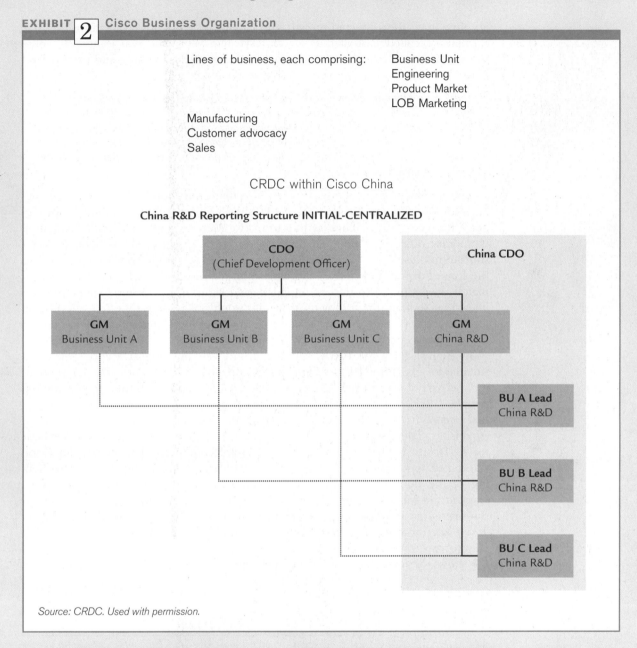

Lines of business, each comprising:   Business Unit
                                       Engineering
                                       Product Market
                                       LOB Marketing

Manufacturing
Customer advocacy
Sales

CRDC within Cisco China

**China R&D Reporting Structure INITIAL-CENTRALIZED**

*Source: CRDC. Used with permission.*

The group planned to double or triple in size over the next five years. Outgrowing a chosen facility would require renting additional space, which would mean having offices all over the place with different lease-end times. On top of that, the Shanghai real-estate market was hot and demand for buildings high. How could the CRDC sign long-term leases and still accommodate growth? How much of its resources should it spend on buildings?

Despite finding a great building in a good location in Pudong Park (on the east bank of the Huangpu River) for the right price and lease arrangements that would accommodate the expected growth, the CRDC was not allowed to move forward. Raznjevic recalled part of that search: "We had WPR, the real estate VP, come to look. They saw a fancy chandelier in the lobby of the building and then walked out—'too opulent'—they said." As Gronski recalled:

*There were other buildings that we went through. Unfortunately there was not a single one that satisfied my requirements—convenient for employees to get to work. The "opulent" one satisfied that criterion, but had some other characteristics which made it less desirable from the corporate view point. In hindsight the "opulence" issue was a red herring. The core problem was the issue of growth. That place had very limited expansion opportunity.*

That interaction was the team's first hint that even though they were in Shanghai, San Jose was not that far away. "WPR didn't believe that we would get any bigger," Raznjevic said. "They didn't think we were serious. We ended up in a temporary office in a poor facility with our people squeezed in there. It was a short-term lease, and we wanted a long-term." A temporary office was found in the Luwan district with a lease available until January 2006 and room for approximately 46 people. "We wanted to get started right away," Gronski said. "And we knew that looking for a long-term facility would take some time." It offered the team a place to train the first group of hired engineers and time to search for a more suitable space.

By August 2005, the CRDC found a brand new building at a good price and suitable for expansion in the Shanghai's Caohejing Hi-Tech Park. The large building was part of an industrial complex outside of Shanghai with the capacity for 160 people. CRDC was able to leverage its position as an anchor tenant (indeed the first occupants) to obtain agreement from the landlord for upgrades and future expansion. They initially rented two and one-half floors. Because it was not built for R&D offices, the site required considerable attention. The floors had to be reinforced to keep the heavy computer equipment from falling through the ceiling of the floor below. There was no air conditioning—a computer necessity. Gaps in the window frames left plenty of room for an outside breeze to enter. In the restrooms, the sink was nowhere near the toilets. The elevators had no ring to signal when it arrived at a floor, no light, and no bell, and there were not enough elevators to transport passengers at peak times. All the retrofitting took time, but the site's expandability justified the extra effort.

# New to This Market Economy

According to Ted Curran, doing business in China required "understanding our many limitations," some of which were apparent from the start. Cisco would have to win the support of several people to help it navigate government structure. For example, each family in Shanghai had a government-issued *hukou*, a residency permit in the form of a booklet containing information about family members and their employers. Each city had its own policies regarding hukou. Without a hukou, a person living in Shanghai was denied access to government-paid entitlements such as medical insurance and would have to pay for health care out of pocket. Another key benefit attached to the hukou was the right to send your children to public schools. The hukou requirement thus influenced the location of the CRDC office: any employee wanting to live closer to their job needed permission from Shanghai authorities to move, so Cisco made sure it could provide hukous for all its employees. Raznjevic said:

> *Dealing with the Shanghai government means understanding certain policies. You can't just decide to move; [you] need [a] permit for that. They don't enforce it, but if you move without hukou you don't get city benefits. That's a big factor because without hukou your child will not go to the good schools unless you pay. Beijing is very good with hukou, whoever we employ can get one. Shanghai decided not everyone could get hukou, just a few selected people we hire. It took some time to deal with that.*

To bring equipment and supplies into Shanghai from San Jose or other parts of the United States meant building relationships with government officials in the Shanghai customs office. Understanding the regulations required patience. Raznjevic explained:

> *There is a problem shipping things in China. To import equipment there is a Chinese company, which is an expert in Chinese importation. It requires a certificate that the equipment is good for importation to Shanghai. [There is] only one company [that the] government considers certified to do this work. Not the most responsive...it takes forever to get these guys. So relations with customs are crucial. You really want to know these people personally.*

And then there were cultural practices the Cisco team had to learn about. For example, buying and giving coupons for moon cakes right before the midautumn festival was an annual Chinese tradition. Companies often issued coupons to their employees and also used this as a way to build business relationships with customers or government officials. People who received the coupons could use them any way they wanted, whether that be selling them, purchasing the moon cakes, or giving the coupons to their family, friends, or colleagues as presents. Gift-giving demonstrated respect and was seen as an important symbol of relationship-building.

In many ways, being an American company put the CRDC team at a disadvantage. American law prohibited the buying of presents that could be perceived as courting favor with Chinese officials. Yet, this was a culture that was particularly inclined to gift-giving. Furthermore, "European companies have no problem with this as an unfair advantage," Raznjevic said. "They have deeper pockets and no law against gift-giving so they have all these deals going on."

Most expats at the CRDC agreed with the notion that China was simply going through what many of the market economy-based countries had experienced in previous years. "I'm sure if you went to Croatia or the U.S. when they are at the beginning of the 19th- or 20th-century stage of capitalism everything worked differently," Raznjevic said. "That's my take—it is the wild west of capitalism." So when foreigners commented on the thick pollution in the air over Shanghai, the expats reminded them of the pollution that filled the air over the northeastern harbors of New York and Boston at the beginning of the industrial age in the United States. A fairer comparison might be China now and the United States back then or even London during the 1950s or 1960s.[7]

# Pay and Promotion

Establishing a salary structure for Cisco was tricky because employees responsible for different functions were paid different wages. The HR department in China insisted that the CRDC pay all employees the same; Raznjevic had to convince

HR that manufacturing paid less than sales. Then there was the difference between when Cisco typically awarded salary increases and when Chinese employees expected their raises, which was during the Chinese New Year (from the first new moon of the year to the full moon, 15 days later).

The freedom to change jobs within the company was another Cisco work procedure that presented a challenge for new employees. The company allowed people to move across business units based on the belief that if an employee was in one place too long, they became "stale," and rotation helped refresh an employee's metric and ability to understand the entire business. Therefore, anyone was able to leave a business unit and apply for jobs in other parts of the organization as a free agent after one year.

Cisco also had a relative ranking system regarding the criteria required for success in the organization. Every six months, managers evaluated employee performance against other employees to differentiate talent. Once employees were ranked, bonuses were granted to all except employees at the bottom level.

Another touchy issue was work titles. In the United States, technical workers in the IT industry were considered very valuable, reached high positions in organizations, and were generally paid extremely well. In China, this was a problem because technology experts were not viewed as a success unless they became a manager. Chinese employees working for the CRDC were frequently asked the question: "Are you a manager yet?"

## Looking for Local Talent

The resource pool for engineering talent in China was immense (see Exhibit 3 for universities and research institutes) and so was the competition for them. Recruiting, interviewing, and evaluating candidates was a huge task that the CRDC team took seriously. They advertised for engineers domestically—targeting groups of people within the industry and those at universities.

The Web was used to reach larger numbers of potential candidates and pinpoint recruiting efforts. ChinaHR.com (partially owned by Monster.com) helped create a recruiting campaign using e-mail and short text messages to mobile phones. That channel allowed CRDC to target those who weren't actively looking for a job but were potential employees of interest with skills the team wanted.

The initial search generated over 4,000 resumes. As a first step in identifying the best candidates, applicants were invited to take a multiple-choice test. The CRDC team was careful to change the test questions frequently. The hiring process produced some surprises, according to Raznjevic:

> Cheating on interviews is pretty amazing. Some people tend to send their friends to take tests so you really have to check if they have identification. A background check takes months and is pretty useless since we get government-controlled information. Lying on resumes is standard; I'd guess many can't be relied on at all. No lying about graduation or degrees, but work history—what did they do and who is referring them. So for example I got a referral and called, "So how long have you known this person?" "We worked together at Cisco." "Really, when did you work at Cisco together?" Her friend had called her to tell her she was applying at Cisco, and she got confused and thought she was supposed to say they had worked together at Cisco.

The written exam vetted the group of 4,000 to identify the 200 top-performing candidates, who were then invited to face-to-face interviews to check their English

**EXHIBIT 3    Universities and Research Centers in Beijing and Shanghai**

| Universities—Beijing Region | |
| --- | --- |
| **Universities** | **Research Institutions** |
| Tsinghua University | Telecommunication Academy |
| | Data Communication National Emphasis Lab |
| Beijing University | Micro-Electronics Research Academy |
| | Word Processing National Emphasis Lab |
| Bupt | Telecommunication Research |
| | Telecommunication and Electronics Academy |
| | JV With Nortel—Technical Research Center |
| | Telecommunication Academy |
| Beijing Aeronautics University | Micro-Electronics Academy |
| Beijing University of Science and Technology | Optical and Electronic Academy |
| | Wireless and Electronics Academy |
| | Integrated Circuit Academy |
| | Data Communication National Emphasis Lab |
| | Machinery Engineering & Control Lab |
| | Signal Gathering & Processing Lab |
| Tianjin University | Electronic Information |
| | Telecommunication |
| | Optical and Electronic Lab |
| Nankai University (Tianjin) | Telecommunication Academy |

| Universities—Shanghai Region | |
| --- | --- |
| **Universities** | **Research Institutions** |
| Shanghai Jiaotong University | Audio and Communication Processing Academy |
| | Communications Storage Research Center |
| | Telecommunication Lab |
| | Micro-Electronics and System Lab |
| Fudan University (Sh) | Micro-Electronics Academy |
| | Data Processing Intelligence Communication Open Lab |
| | Electronic Communication and System Academy |
| | JV With Alcatel |
| | Integrate Circuit and System Academy |
| Tongji University (Sh) | |
| Nanjing University | Telecommunication Engineering Research Center |
| Nanjing Telecom. Univ. | Telecommunication Academy |
| Zhejiang University | Telecommunication Academy |
| | Computer Science and Technology Academy |
| | Optical and Electronic Academy |
| China University of Science and Technology (Hefei) | CAS Quanta Communication Emphasis Lab |
| | Huawei Communication Technology Academy |
| | Telecommunication Academy |
| | Signal Stat. Disposal Center |
| | Communication Disposal Center |
| | Communication and Decision-Making Academy |
| | Intelligence Communication Academy |
| Tianjin University | Electronic |
| | Telecommunication |
| | Optical and Electronic Lab |
| Nankai University (Tianjin) | Communication Technology Academy |

*Source: CRDC. Used with permission.*

language skills, among other things. "We wanted candidates to be able to explain engineering notions in English," said Jan Gronski.

Many of the top American companies with a presence in China targeted the same well-educated engineers as Cisco (see Exhibit 4 for university graduation data), so the CRDC had to develop a strategy to attract talented new graduates. Senior leadership went to campuses and gave career talks. Cisco academic clubs were established at four universities to engage students early during their first or second year of classes.

Besides its name being good for resumes, there were several other reasons why working for Cisco was attractive to many Chinese engineers. In its role as an American multinational company, Cisco provided and paid for good training, offered an opportunity to travel abroad, supplied atypical health insurance and benefits, and used a distinctively different management style. As one Cisco manager explained:

*The Cisco brand name is very successful in attracting experienced industry people. People come from top management companies: Lucent, Alcatel, domestic brands like*

**EXHIBIT 4**    University Graduation Data and Competitors

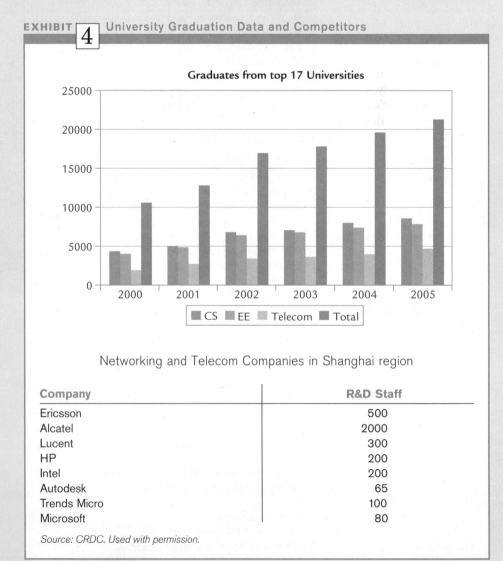

**Graduates from top 17 Universities**

Networking and Telecom Companies in Shanghai region

| Company | R&D Staff |
| --- | --- |
| Ericsson | 500 |
| Alcatel | 2000 |
| Lucent | 300 |
| HP | 200 |
| Intel | 200 |
| Autodesk | 65 |
| Trends Micro | 100 |
| Microsoft | 80 |

*Source: CRDC. Used with permission.*

*GE China and Huawei. Recruiting for the IP communications BU, we were able to attract two managers from Lucent and one from Alcatel who had been there 10 years.*

Still, not all Chinese engineers agreed that working at an American multinational was a good thing. Some thought that the work often was not challenging and that opportunities to move up the corporate ladder were less likely than at a Chinese corporation. Jerry Lu, a software development manager, explained:

*A lot of my friends work for a China company. I have a classmate who has 1,000 direct reports, and he believes we can only get a higher position when we work in a local China company. For example, Cisco has a very high-end router, and even though the application based on that platform needs to be examined, that technology can't be done here in China. This means we are here, we are good, yet it is difficult for us to get that project. If we don't get good projects, we can't grow and move up. At a China company if you are competent you can always get a more difficult project. Not here.*

# Looking for Local Managers

Finding qualified engineers was one thing but finding managerial talent was even more difficult, especially because the team was adamant about using local rather than expatriate managerial talent. Chris Dong, CRDC business operations manager, was the first local managerial hire. He grew up in Beijing and went to college at Tsinghua University. Following graduation, Dong moved to the United States and earned two master's degrees in computer science and applied statistics. Microsoft recruited him as a developer for their Redman, Washington facility, and he climbed the corporate ladder to become a senior manager. In 2001, China's booming economy persuaded many of his friends to move back. Dong returned to Beijing, this time as an entrepreneur, and two years later he rejoined Microsoft China. "Cisco was behind Microsoft in the game, but I knew their R&D was aggressive and would be the next thing to happen when they approached me," Dong said. "It took me a few months to think about it before I moved my family and myself to Shanghai."

Hiring local senior engineers with managerial potential for the CRDC, however, was more difficult than hiring engineers with technical expertise. Although there were highly skilled and capable managers who were Chinese, their managerial approach was authoritative, whereas Cisco was a collaborative environment. "We interviewed some of them, but we knew right away that they wouldn't pass on the culture that we wanted," Raznjevic said.

# Building Local Management

During the buildup period, Jerry Lu, software development manager, was the first local technical hire promoted to the management team at CRDC. Lu earned his PhD in electrical engineering at Nanjing University and worked for Lucent for six years. After a year and a half as a software engineer doing bench research, Lu was promoted to manager. Lu's technical skills earned him deep respect from other engineers at the site, and his promotion was well regarded.

"We have extensive training and coaching for managers," Lu said, "And during that training there is a lot of questions about your style." As an engineer, he did his work and then went home. When first promoted, Lu would check the product schedule and follow up with his reports about whether they were doing what they needed to do for the product. The rest of his time was spent in meetings with other managers, his team, and his boss. Lu disliked attending so many meetings.

In time, he discovered the importance of having collaborative relationships with others to ensure the success of his team's projects. As his management skills developed, Lu learned to let his 17 direct reports think through problems themselves. The importance of meaningful work was something Lu clearly understood would be key to CRDC success.

# Working for the Man

Problems started at 7:00 a.m. and ended at 9:00 p.m. every day, seven days a week. China's greatest challenge was not its productivity or its engineers' skill sets but its situation as a society in transition. Daniel Puche elaborated:

> I don't want to the use the term cultural difference because there is no culture difference. It is just that China is like the rest of the world of the 1950s or '60s, where everything is great. You are the first generation to have a great job, but you don't really know how to behave in a large corporate environment yet. You don't know that you have to be outspoken and take the initiative. Instead you are used to family rules and not making decisions. That's probably the biggest challenge we had. Our engineers had very good ideas and were very smart. They hesitated to be outspoken.

The Chinese tendency to think hierarchically affected the manner in which employees worked and interacted with their boss. In China, specific work hours were defined and when the clock struck quitting time, most engineers felt compelled to promptly leave. "In China, my boss is waiting for me to leave," Jerry Chen said explaining the difference. "In San Jose, you work to get things done, so I need to stay until I finish regardless of the boss." And unlike the United States where people would jump at an opportunity to spend some time with a boss three or four positions above them, CRDC employees felt uncomfortable being around Ivo Raznjevic and the rest of the senior management team. When Raznjevic first tried to sit with employees in the cafeteria, they disappeared! On another occasion, Raznjevic got an e-mail from an engineer who was unhappy. Raznjevic sent one back: "Why don't you come to my office?" The dissatisfied employee was surprised and answered, "Well, you have more important things to do."

Attempting to bridge those differences, CRDC executives came up with various ways of interacting with employees in a non-work-related manner. Jan Gronski began organizing breakfasts with several employees each day. As the workforce size increased, he moved to lunches and then birthday lunches. Raznjevic felt less comfortable with the dining experience and chose sports as a way to engage employees. On each floor of the CHJ building was a common recreational area where Raznjevic started playing Ping-Pong:

> At first they would be playing and see me coming along and stop. "You go ahead and play, we can play later." "No, I can wait," I'd say. And of course I would lose all the time! But Ping-Pong is extremely popular, and they still don't really trust you, but it only took about nine months to reach a comfort level.

The CRDC group started weekly meetings with its engineers that involved design review discussions. Those sessions were eventually nicknamed the Kindergarten Class. Part of its purpose was to cultivate leaders by increasing their decision-making responsibilities. That approach took some time. For example, one of the senior engineers would say little in the meeting and then approach his manager afterwards to say, "This is wrong, it will not work, and this is what we should be doing." And although the engineer was right, he would not say it in the meeting. Raznjevic believed that behavior could be changed if Chinese employees were put in a position to make decisions about engineering and the employees reporting to them. This way they would develop as managers and learn to express stronger opinions. Puche believed that a lot of businesses in China failed because of the American presence there checking on what employees were doing instead of coaching them on how to lead.

# Patience and Persistence

Back at the Ping-Pong table, Raznjevic was unable to return the smash his opponent had just launched. Hopefully, he would be better at responding to the issues he was confronting.

## Should Jasmine Zhou run the SW development team?

Once timid and deferential, Zhou had developed into a strong test manager with advancement potential, and they were proud of her development; however, she was being considered for a lateral move to a managerial position on the development side—a potential move that was arousing controversy. First, there was a natural rivalry between the test and development side of research and development. Although both developers and testers generally had similar educational backgrounds and were highly skilled and trained, there was tension between them. There was a perception in China that testers were not as qualified as developers. Developers often thought testers were failed developers, while testers, who spent a lot of time ensuring that the product worked, frequently felt their quality assurance was crucial but unappreciated.

Zhou who held a master's degree in computer science and had started her career as a developer for Nortel Canada in southern China, quickly had transferred to another department as a tester. She worked on wireless technology at Nortel for a year and a half before joining Cisco as a test engineer in January 2005. Moving her from testing to development management would likely pose a potential problem. The situation was further complicated by a development engineer who wanted—and felt he deserved—the position. If Raznjevic and his team selected Zhou, they would have to exercise great tact when informing the other engineer.

## How should he advise Ehud Oentung?

Oentung, an American of Chinese origin raised in Indonesia, earned his electrical engineering degree at the University of Maryland and worked for Verizon, Bell Atlantic, and Cisco in Herndon, Virginia. From there, he transferred to the CRDC and became a software manager on the development side. Cisco's ranking system for measuring success in the organization used a set of criteria that made Oentung uncomfortable: Every six months, managers evaluated employee performance against other employees to differentiate talent. "Even if you are the bottom it doesn't mean you haven't been doing good work," Oentung said. "Every six months we have to pick someone to do better." During the most recent performance review cycle, Oentung had one engineer who ranked the lowest, which meant that this individual would not get a bonus. Razjnevic recalled Oentung saying, "I didn't want to do it." How should he coach Oentung to deliver his employee a difficult message?

## How should he handle a recent e-mail situation?

The Chinese concept of losing face in the eyes of others was something the non-Chinese managers thought they knew about, but a particular e-mail incident suggested to Raznjevic that intellectual understanding only went so far. One of the senior CRDC engineers sent out an e-mail with an idea, a practice that Raznjevic encouraged, and immediately one of the United Kingdom-based managers replied, copying everyone, and said, "You are completely incorrect and false in this area." Within minutes of the e-mail coming out there was an audible silence that Raznjevic could detect from his office. He watched as people looked around the cubicles trying to understand why this happened. All the junior engineers that worked with the CRDC engineer felt he had lost face.

Knowing he needed a few moments to collect himself and think, Raznjevic had headed for the Ping-Pong table. Now, he continued to volley.

### CASE DISCUSSION QUESTIONS

1. Discuss some of the challenges Raznjevic faced as an expatriate when he decided to move to Shanghai. How did he convince others to join him on this foreign assignment?
2. What are some implications of the move for the office in San Jose? Would this move be viewed positively by the home office given that some R&D work was being transferred to Shanghai?
3. What are some of the major HRM challenges facing CISCO as they open offices in Shanghai? Be specific about the various HRM functions such as recruitment, compensation and management etc.
4. What can CISCO do to manage the challenges discussed in question 2? What lessons do you learn about HRM practices in China?

### CASE NOTES

[1] Peter Burrows, Manjeet Kripalani, and Bruce Einhorn, "Cisco: Sold on India," *Businessweek*, November 28, 2005, http://www.businessweek. com/magazine/content/05_48/b3961055.htm (accessed September 17, 2008).

[2] 2006 Cisco annual report.

[3] Bruce Einhorn, "Selling Cisco to China's Tech Talent Pool," *Businessweek*, September 17, 2007, http://www.businessweek.com/globalbiz/content/sep2007/gb20070913_971883.htm (accessed September 17, 2008).

[4] Gronski said it was hard to tell how much money he had. He knew that Cisco had committed $32 million over a three-year period and that he could go ahead and hire.

[5] "Cisco invests US$50 million for new campus in Bangalore," EMS-Now, October 25, 2005, http://www.emsnow.com/newsarchives/archivedetails.cfm?ID=10684.

[6] Lee Anne Obringer, "How Finding Office Space Works," HowStuffWorks, http://money.howstuffworks.com/office-space3.htm.

[7] King's College London, "Air Pollution in London," http://www.londonair.org.uk/london/asp/information.asp?view=howbad, (accessed August 10, 2009).

# Strategy Implementation for Multinational Companies: Interaction Processes

Cuiphoto/Shutterstock.com

# 13 International Negotiation and Cross-Cultural Communication

*Preview* CASE IN POINT

### Deals That Failed

Mergers and acquisitions remain at an all-time high. In fact, reports suggest that in 2007, the volume of mergers and acquisitions reached more than $4.74 trillion. However, success in mergers and acquisitions is highly dependent on companies approaching the process with the requisite skills. Without the appropriate skills, negotiations could end and any hopes of merger or acquisition abandoned. Consider the following negotiation mishaps.

When Kiel AG, a Swiss multinational conglomerate, discovered that Georgia-based Edwards Engineering, Inc. (EEI), was for sale, Kiel's management felt that they had found the right company to acquire in the United States. There was a construction boom in the southeastern United States that Kiel viewed as a strategic opportunity. Moreover, EEI was a successful company, whose founder, Tom Edwards, was close to retirement and willing to sell. Kiel made an initial offer close to the asking price, and the outlook for the purchase looked positive. Kiel president Herbert Kiel even came to the United States to conduct the negotiations personally. However, after four difficult days of negotiations, the Kiel team went home and talks ended.

What happened? In a typical U.S. American way, Edwards was open and friendly in the negotiations. He was eager to sell the business. He was direct and forthright about the strengths and weaknesses of his business. He made every effort to provide information requested and to adjust his proposals to Kiel's positions. But the U.S. style didn't work.

Edwards confused the Swiss. They approached the negotiations in a formal and measured way. They perceived Edwards' openness as dangerous and untrustworthy. They responded by asking to review documents and by hiring a major U.S. accounting firm to audit the EEI books. Edwards, on the other hand, found the audit insulting and time-consuming. He was annoyed by Kiel's continuously polite but unresponsive answers to his proposals. Ultimately, neither side played the negotiation game the way the other expected. Distrust grew, and an otherwise good deal ended in failure.

*Sources: Based on Bryan, Robert M., and Peter C. Buck. 1989. "When customs collide: The pitfalls of international acquisitions." Financial Executive, 5, 43–46; Goman,*

*Carol Kinsey. 2002. "Cross-cultural business practices."* Communication World, *February–March, 22–25; Copeland, L., and L. Griggs. 1985.* Going International. *New York: Random House; Muehlfeld, K., Sahib, P. R. and Witteloostuijn, A. V. 2012. "A contextual theory of organizational learning from failures and successes: A study of acquisition completion in the global newspaper industry, 1981–2008."* Strategic Management Journal, *33, 938–964; Whately, Arthur. 1994. "International negotiation case." In Dorothy Marcic and Sheila Puffer, eds.,* Management International, *St. Paul, MN: West, 73–74.*

I nternational negotiation is the process of making business deals across national and cultural boundaries, and it precedes any multinational business project. However, as shown in the Preview Case in Point, without successful negotiation and the accompanying cross-cultural communication, there are seldom successful business transactions.[1]

Consider some of the following examples, in which the successful outcome of the business opportunity depends on successful international negotiations. Companies that sell overseas must negotiate with foreign distributors and sales organizations. Companies that participate in an international joint venture must negotiate a contract to establish the alliance. Companies that receive raw materials from overseas sources must negotiate with local suppliers to provide raw materials at an acceptable cost. Companies that set up manufacturing operations in other countries often must negotiate with foreign governments to get necessary permissions. Finally, as in the Preview Case in Point, companies that wish to acquire businesses in other countries must negotiate successfully with the current owners.

As the world's market becomes increasingly global, companies will need to become adept at conducting international negotiations. As we discussed in Chapter 1, the predictions that the economic "center of gravity" of the world markets would shift to the emerging markets of China, Brazil, Turkey, India, and Mexico has now become reality.[2] These countries also are expected to show strong technology-driven growth and provide major opportunities for U.S. organizations. However, understanding how the significant cultural differences between the United States and these countries affect international negotiations will be increasingly crucial if U.S. multinational companies want to capitalize on such opportunities.

This chapter provides a survey of the basic processes that guide international negotiation: successful preparation, building relationships with foreign partners, using persuasion tactics, gaining concessions, and reaching a final agreement. We will also consider how to identify and avoid the common "dirty tricks" of negotiators and what personal characteristics make a good international negotiator.

# The Basics of Cross-Cultural Communication

Successful international negotiation requires successful cross-cultural communication. Negotiators must understand (or have interpreted) not only the written and oral language of their counterparts but also other components of culturally different communication styles. Mistakes in this area often go unnoticed by the communicator, but they can do damage to international relationships and negotiations. Mistakes or misinterpretations of the subtle gestures of hand and face, the use of silence, what is said or not said, and the intricacies of dealing with age and status often prove to be pitfalls for the multinational businessperson.

To help you negotiate and communicate more successfully in your role as a multinational manager, we will review some of the major issues in cross-cultural communication: the relationship between language and culture, differences between high- and low-context cultures, cultural differences in communication styles, nonverbal communication through body movements and the use of personal space, when and how to use interpreters, how to speak to nonnative speakers of your language, and how to avoid cross-cultural communication errors based on faulty attributions.

## Language and Culture

There are approximately 3,000 basic languages in the world, with many dialects.[3] Language is so essential to culture that many consider linguistic groups synonymous with cultural groups. Multinational managers should also note that many countries—Canada and Belgium, for example—have more than one national language. Even within political boundaries, these national languages often represent diverse communication and negotiation styles of many cultural groups. In addition, the choice of the wrong language may touch on areas of extreme cultural sensitivity.

The interrelationship between language and culture is so strong that some experts suggest that a society's language determines the nature of its culture. This is known as the **Whorf hypothesis**, developed by the anthropologist and linguist Benjamin Lee Whorf.[4] Whorf argued that words provide the concepts for understanding the world. According to Whorf, all languages have limited sets of words. These restricted word sets, in turn, constrain the ability of the users to understand or conceptualize the world. Because language structures the way we think about what we see, it determines cultural patterns.

In his famous and at the time futuristic novel *1984,* George Orwell used Whorf's premise that those who controlled the available vocabulary would control the world. Not all experts agree with Whorf, and some argue the opposite: culture comes first and requires the development of certain concepts and thus certain words. However, no one debates that there is a close interrelationship between language and culture. Most experts agree that the twenty-first-century global leader must necessarily have language skills to bridge cultural differences.[5]

How critical is language? Consider the following Case in Point.

## High- and Low-Context Languages

The anthropologist Edward T. Hall identified an important distinction among the world's languages based on whether communication is explicit or implicit.[6] Hall focused on how different cultures use the context or the situation in which communication takes place to understand what people are saying. Languages in which people state things directly and explicitly are called **low context**. The words provide most of the meaning, and you do not have to understand the situation. Languages in which people state things indirectly and implicitly are called **high context**. Communications have multiple meanings that one can interpret only by reading the situation. So important are the ideas of high and low context that many people refer to the entire culture as being high or low context.

Most Northern European languages, including German, English, and the Scandinavian languages, are low context. People use explicit words to communicate direct meaning. Thus, for example, if a German manager says "Yes," she is stating a clear affirmative. In addition, most Western cultures attach a positive value to

**Whorf hypothesis**
Theory that language determines the nature of culture.

**Low-context language**
Language in which people state things directly and explicitly.

**High-context language**
Language in which people state things indirectly and implicitly.

### CASE IN POINT

## Languages and Global Trade

While there is no doubt that culture and language are difficult to separate in international trade, ultimately people from different countries use language to negotiate. Parties do not have transactions in the culture; rather it is the language that different parties use to transact. As such, languages are critical tools that are used to engage in international trade. When two parties from different countries meet, they need to choose a common language to negotiate, to express the needs for specific goods and to make a counteroffer to negotiate an acceptable transaction agreement. Flows of foreign direct investment and international trade would have not flourished without the use of common languages worldwide. Furthermore, languages are powerful in that they have the capacity of lowering transaction costs for people from different countries by facilitating understanding between people. Languages provide the means to specify contracts that reduce uncertainties and build trust in transactions.

A recent study examined the degree of language distance between countries and the extent of trade and foreign direct investment. For instance, Chinese and English are seen as being in the top 15 percent of language dissimilarity, meaning that these languages are very different from each other. The study found that there is a strong relationship between language distance and trade and foreign direct investment. In other words, the larger the distance between two countries, the less likely they are to engage in trade and foreign direct investment.

*Source: Based on Selmier, W.T., II and Oh, C. H. 2012. "International business complexity and the internationalization of languages." Business Horizons, 55, 189–200.*

clear and direct communication. This inclination is particularly apparent in negotiations, where low-context languages allow clear statements concerning what a negotiator wants out of the relationship.

In contrast, Asian languages and Arabic are among the highest-context languages in the world. In Asian languages, often what is left unsaid is just as important as what is said. Silent periods and the use of incomplete sentences require a person to read the situation in order to interpret what the communicator does not say. Arabic introduces interpretation into the language with an opposite tack. Extensive imprecise verbal and nonverbal communication produce an interaction where reading the situation is necessary for understanding. Exhibit 13.1 shows a ranking of languages by their degrees of high and low context.

Communication between high- and low-context people is a challenge. Translated words that have explicit meanings to a low-context speaker may have a multitude of meanings to a high-context speaker. For example, Japanese speech is full of words that encourage a speaker to continue and to repeat the message, often in a slightly different way. One of these words, *hai*—literally "yes" in English—means yes in the English sense only if other components of the situation also mean yes. *Hai* can also mean: "Yes, I hear you," "Yes, say it again," "Yes, give me more information," "Yes, please continue with the conversation," or "Yes, I don't really want to say no, but it should be obvious to you that the answer is no." Consider the next Focus on Emerging Markets.

The types of nonverbal communication we consider here are body movements (kinesics), the use of personal space (proxemics), and forms of communication that rely on senses, such as touching (haptics), eye contact (oculesics), and smell (olfactics).

Such difficulties in translation suggest that, when negotiations take place between high- and low-context cultures, both sides must realize that communication may have errors. Moreover, even good translations may require contextual interpretations for effective communication.

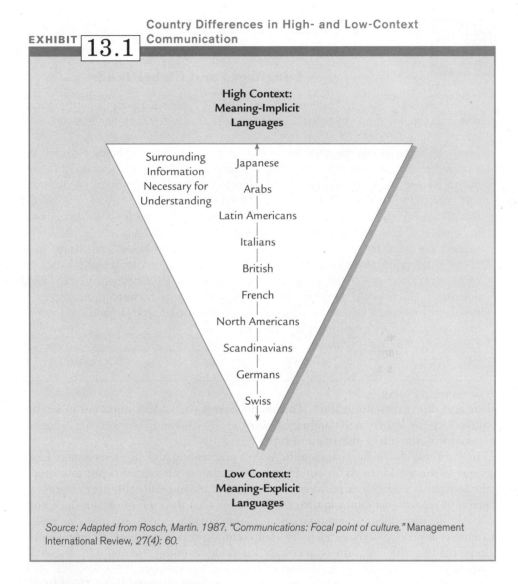

**EXHIBIT 13.1** Country Differences in High- and Low-Context Communication

Source: Adapted from Rosch, Martin. 1987. "Communications: Focal point of culture." Management International Review, 27(4): 60.

Differences in languages can have other effects on international negotiations. Consider the next Case in Point.

## Basic Communication Styles

In addition to high- and low-context language use, other cultural differences in communication can influence cross-cultural interactions and negotiations. In some cultures, people speak very directly; they tend to state opinions and ask questions that come right to the point and lack ambiguity. This is called **direct communication**. In other societies, people consider it impolite to ask a direct question or state an opinion. In indirect communication, people attempt to state their opinions or ask questions by implied meaning. Successful and polite communication allows the receiver to understand a statement without the communicator stating directly his or her intentions. Consider the direct communicator who asks, "Will we reach a deal tonight?" Consider the response of the indirect communicator who says, "Tonight we will go to a superb restaurant, which best represents our

**Direct communication**
Communication that comes to the point and lacks ambiguity.

## **Focus** on Emerging Markets

### The Chinese and Yes

Despite the slowdown, most experts agree that the Chinese economy will keep growing and will continue to present Western multinationals with significant opportunities. An important component of success with grasping opportunities in China is through understanding of Chinese culture in negotiations. Consider that the Chinese negotiator will often answer yes to negotiators asking a question. However, while *yes* implies agreement in Western culture, it can carry many more complex meanings in China. *Yes* can sometimes be used to make sure that the conversation goes on. In fact, when there is confusion, many believe that if people keep talking, the meaning will eventually be understood. *Yes* is thus used as a means to keep the conversation flowing. However, it can also be a way for the Chinese to save face. Sometimes, because of language barriers, the Chinese pretend to understand the meaning by saying yes. This is done to avoid feeling embarrassed. However, the Chinese can also say yes in these situations to prevent the negotiator from losing face as a result of asking an unclear question. Furthermore, it is considered an honor to be asked something, and it is therefore rude or bad manners to reject someone.

In sum, *yes* for the Chinese can be very ambiguous and have many meanings. It can mean "maybe," "back up," "I'm thinking," "give me time to think," "let me get back to you with an answer," or "yes." The astute negotiator is the one who can read between the lines and understand the appropriate understanding of *yes.*

*Source: Based on Doucet, M. 2008. "What part of yes don't you understand?" Mechanical Engineering, November, 46–47; Economist. 2012. Pedalling prosperity. May 26, 3–5.*

---

### CASE IN POINT

## **Differences Between the Chinese and English Languages**

As companies try to take advantage of the tremendous opportunities presented by China, they will have to deal with the challenges of language comprehension. Almost a quarter of the world's population, including Chinese, Japanese, and Korean speakers, read logographic characters that represent meanings rather than sound. In contrast, in many other languages, such as those using Latin alphabets (e.g., English, Spanish), Arabic, and Hindi, the words represent sounds rather than meaning. This difference in reading process has been shown to have important implications for how people remember things and even how they process thoughts.

The difference also has important implications for how U.S. negotiators approach presentations to their Chinese counterparts. For instance, research shows that Chinese individuals are likely to respond more positively to visual cues, such as font selection, whereas people from the United States are more likely to respond to

the speaker's voice. As such, it is important for U.S. negotiators to use as many visual stimuli as they can to make their presentations more effective. Other research shows that Chinese subjects were more likely to remember brands and to associate brand names with logos when information was presented visually. U.S. negotiators are thus encouraged to rely on visual information if they want their Chinese counterparts to remember aspects of their presentations. Instead of focusing on the presentation style of the negotiator, it may be more beneficial to improve the content.

*Sources: Based on Economist. 2012. Pedalling propserity. May 26, 3–5; Kambil, Amit, Victor Wei-the Long, and Clarence Kwan. 2006. "The seven disciplines for venturing in China." MIT Sloan Management Review, Winter, 47(2): 85–89; Lieberthal, Kenneth, and Geoffrey Lieberthal. 2003. "The great transition." Harvard Business Review, October, 13–27; Tavassoli, Nader T., and Jin K. Han. 2002. "Auditory and visual brand identifiers in Chinese and English." Journal of International Marketing, 10, 13–28.*

**EXHIBIT** **13.2** **Cultural Differences in Communication Styles**

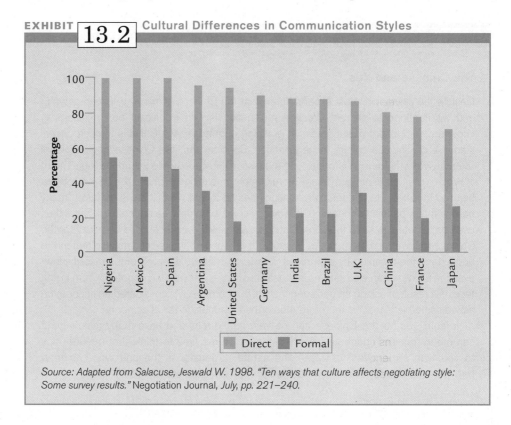

Source: Adapted from Salacuse, Jeswald W. 1998. "Ten ways that culture affects negotiating style: Some survey results." Negotiation Journal, July, pp. 221–240.

national cuisine." This answer usually means, "I am not ready to do business with you until I get to know you better." Exhibit 13.2 shows a ranking of direct communication styles for several countries.

Another cultural trait of communication style that often affects or surprises those communicating with people from the United States is the lack of **formal communication** expected. As you can see in Exhibit 13.2, people from the United States are among the least formal in communication. The casual use of first names and informal dress, and the dispensing with of titles, characterize U.S. communication styles. Most other cultures communicate, especially in business settings, with more formality. They take care to acknowledge rank and titles when addressing each other. There is also more formality of dress for men and women, as well as sensitivity to ceremony and procedures in social interactions. In many countries, for example, adult men never wear short pants unless engaged in an exercise or sport activity.

At several points, we have noted that communication consists of more than verbal interaction. Multinational managers and negotiators must be aware of cultural differences in both verbal and nonverbal communications. The next section provides background on nonverbal communication.

## Nonverbal Communication

**Nonverbal communication** means communicating without words. Often it is not necessary to speak to communicate with someone. People gesture, they smile, they gaze into another's eyes, they hug, they kiss—they engage in a whole array of behaviors that supplement or enhance spoken communication. How important are nonverbal signs? Consider the next Multinational Management Brief.

**Formal communication**
Communication that acknowledges rank, titles, and ceremony in prescribed social interactions.

**Nonverbal communication**
Face-to-face communication that is not oral.

## Multinational Management **Brief**

### Nonverbal Communication

As more employees increasingly interact with their counterparts from foreign locales, understanding nonverbal communication is becoming even more critical. A classic study revealed that only 7 percent of the total impact of a message is based on the words used. The rest is based on the tone of voice (38 percent) and various other types of nonverbal communication aspects (facial expressions, body language, etc., make up 57 percent). A more recent study also shows the importance of nonverbals. In that study, Cypriots were exposed to different facial expressions. Specific facial expressions, such as showing positive emotions, were often associated with the perception of being a leader. Furthermore, the study showed that there is the possibility that the same facial expressions may also be perceived differently worldwide.

Clearly, it is critical for multinationals to appreciate the complexities involved in nonverbal communication. Consider the case of a CEO who showed up at an oil refinery in an expensive suit to address rank-and-file employees dressed in their blue overalls. Before starting his speech, he took his watch off and placed it in front of the lectern. Although he started the speech with, "I am happy to be with you today," the nonverbal signs communicated, "I don't like coming to dirty places, and I have only 20 minutes to spend with you." Multinational negotiators should thus be very cognizant of nonverbal communication and use appropriate body language and other nonverbal signs.

*Source: Based on Gorman, C. K. 2008. "Lost in translation."* Communication World, *July/August, 25, 31–33; Trichas, S. and Schyns, B. 2012. "The face of leadership: Perceived leaders from facial expression."* The Leadership Quarterly, *23, 545–566.*

## Kinesics

**Kinesics** means communicating through body movements. Every culture uses body posture, facial expressions, hand gestures, and movement to communicate nonverbally. Most Asian cultures, for example, use bowing to indicate respect for older people or people of higher status. The person of lesser status must bow at a lower angle than the person of higher status.

It is easy to misinterpret the meanings of body movements in another culture. Like oral communication, there is no universal code for what body movements mean in all societies. For example, U.S. Americans communicate a relaxed atmosphere by putting their feet up. The manager with feet on the desk is saying, "I am relaxing, and you can too." However, people from many other cultures consider such behavior rude or even insulting. Most German managers would consider putting one's feet up on the desk uncivilized. Showing the soles of the feet is among the most outrageous insults to most Arabs.[7]

Facial expressions occur in every human interaction. People smile, frown, squint, sneer, and engage in a range of facial movements. Some scholars argue that certain facial expressions are biological and do not vary across cultures. For example, the quick raising and lowering of eyebrows when people greet each other seems to occur in many different cultural settings.[8] In addition, people born deaf or blind have most of the common facial expressions, suggesting that at least some are inborn.[9]

**Kinesics**
Communication through body movements.

Body posture relates to the way people stand, walk, and sit. Each culture encourages and discourages different body postures depending on the situation. A trip on a Japanese subway, for example, quickly reveals the proper way of sitting—straight forward, legs together, head slightly down, and (for women) handbag placed squarely on the lap. Cultural norms determine whether people slouch, stand, or sit erect, as well as the speed and cadence of the walking gait.

All cultures use hand gestures to embellish and add emphasis to oral communication. Some cultures use expressive gestures, and others use subtle gestures. The same gestures often mean different things from one society to another, a common source of embarrassment for international communicators. For example, the gesture with the thumb and forefinger joined in a circle means "okay" in North America and money in Japan, but it is obscene in Brazil. The thumbs-up gesture means everything is going well for North Americans and many Europeans, but it is a rude gesture in West Africa. Even the "V" for victory sign made with two fingers held upward, popularized by the British prime minister Winston Churchill during World War II, has a rude meaning for the British and the French if the palm is facing inward. Nodding the head means yes in most of the world, but it means no in Bulgaria.[10]

The important point to remember for international negotiators and multinational managers is that it is easy to misinterpret gestures. A safe communication strategy is to minimize their use. You should use only the gestures that you understand well. Eventually, as you get to know a culture better, acceptable and appropriate gestures will become second nature.

## Proxemics

**Proxemics**
The use of space to communicate.

**Proxemics** focuses on how people use space to communicate. According to some experts, the basic senses of sight, smell, hearing, and touch allow people to perceive and sense differences in space.[11] Naturally, there are large cultural differences in how people react to sounds, sights, smells, and personal contact. Each culture has appropriate distances for various levels of communication, and most people are uncomfortable if those distances are ignored. Violations of space may even be considered offensive.

The personal bubble of space around each individual may range from 9 inches to more than 20 inches. North Americans are most comfortable with 20 inches, whereas groups from Latin and Arab cultures generally prefer a closer spacing. It is not uncommon to see a North American continuously backing up to maintain a comfortable 20 inches when interacting with someone from the Middle East or Latin America.

**Haptics or touching**
Basic form of human interaction, including shaking hands, embracing, or kissing when greeting one another.

Personal space may also affect the design of offices. In the next Multinational Management Brief, the exhibit shows a typical Japanese office, where the desks are in contact and managers work closely together. In contrast, Germans are even more protective of their personal office space than North Americans. They prefer heavy office furniture that people cannot move to get too close. A German newspaper editor stationed in the United States was highly intolerant of the U.S. habit of moving chairs closer in certain social situations. He finally reacted by having his visitor's chair bolted to the floor, keeping people at a comfortable and "proper" distance.[12]

**Oculesics**
Communication through eye contact or gaze.

**Olfactics**
Use of smells as a means of nonverbal communication.

## Haptics or Touching, Oculesics, and Olfactics

Nonverbal communication also can occur through touching, smelling, and seeing. **Haptics** or touching is communication through body contact. **Oculesics** refers to communication through eye contact or gazing. **Olfactics** is the use of smells as a means of nonverbal communication.

Haptics is related to proxemics and is a basic form of human interaction. In greeting one another, people may shake hands, embrace, or kiss. In routine interaction, people may touch or pat each other in a variety of ways. The type of touching deemed appropriate is deeply rooted in cultural values. For example, Russian men often kiss other men outside their family as a form of greeting. Brazilian men hug in greeting. Japanese schoolgirls routinely walk holding hands with other girls, although touching among strangers is less accepted. In some cultures, people expect a firm handshake, whereas in other cultures, the handshake is limp. Generally, Latin European and Latin American cultures accept more touching than do Germanic, Anglo, or Scandinavian cultures. Axtell has classified the degree of touching among countries into categories,[13] such as no touching (e.g., Japan, United States, England, and many Northern European countries), moderate touching (e.g., Australia, China, Ireland, and India), and touching (e.g., Latin American countries, Italy, and Greece).

The degree of comfort with gaze and eye contact (oculesics) also varies significantly around the world. In some countries, like the United States and Canada, people are very comfortable and expect eye contact to be maintained for a short moment during conversations. In contrast, in countries like China and Japan, eye contact is considered very rude and disrespectful; in fact, the way to show respect in such societies is by avoiding eye contact. Yet in other societies like France and the Middle East, maintaining eye contact for long periods of time is socially acceptable.

To avoid blunders, negotiators must be aware of a society's degree of comfort with eye contact. For instance, U.S. negotiators should know that a prolonged stare from the French is not rude or hostile but rather shows interest. Similarly, when negotiating with the Chinese, it is important to avoid direct gazing or eye contact so as not to place the Chinese negotiators in an uncomfortable position.

Finally, different countries have different views of smell (olfactics). Societies like the United States and United Kingdom tend to be very uncomfortable with body odors. In fact, people from the United States tend to consider body odor offensive and will avoid talking to someone who has body odor. However, in contrast, Arabs are much more accepting of body odors and consider them natural.[14] Negotiators need to be aware of such diverse perspectives on smell and accept and adapt to them.

This section concludes our discussion of the basic forms of nonverbal communication. The following section deals with three practical issues in cross-cultural business communications: when to use interpreters, how to speak with someone whose language is not your own, and how to recognize and avoid incorrectly applying your own cultural assumptions to people's motivations.

## Practical Issues in Cross-Cultural Business Communication

Cross-cultural negotiations and communications nearly always face a language barrier because one or both parties must communicate in a foreign language. International managers are always at an advantage if they speak more than one language fluently. People from the United States are among the worst when it comes to learning a second language, whereas Europeans are much more likely to be bilingual or multilingual. U.S. businesspeople are fortunate that English is the most common language of business. However, even if English is the local business language and you negotiate in English, communication and understanding of the local culture always improves if you speak the local language. An important preparation for any international assignment, therefore, is gaining at least rudimentary skills in the language of the country.

## Using Interpreters

To make sure that all parties understand agreements, international negotiation often requires the use of interpreters. The **interpreter's role** is to provide a simultaneous translation of a foreign language while a person speaks. This role requires greater linguistic skills than speaking a language or translating written documents. Good interpreters not only are bilingual, but also have the specialized knowledge and vocabulary to deal with technical details of business transactions.

Even if some of the negotiators understand or speak both languages, it is often a good idea to use interpreters. It detracts from a negotiation team member's negotiation task if he or she must also serve as the team's interpreter. In addition, even if all members of the negotiating team are competent speakers of both languages, professional interpreters can be present to ensure the accuracy and common understanding of written and oral agreements.

However, even with interpreters, the intended message is not always conveyed efficiently. Consider the following Multinational Management Brief.

---

## Multinational Management **Brief**

### Interpreters and HRM

As more multinationals venture into South American countries and more U.S. multinationals rely on employees who are not necessarily native speakers, the potential for language misunderstanding is high. Consider the case of a human resource officer discussing the details of the company's benefit plan with new employees. Because many of the new employees do not speak English, a Spanish translator is translating the details of the health and insurance plan and the retirement system. However, the human resources officer is confronted only with blank stares and she realizes that many of her points are not getting across. Where did the human resource officer go wrong?

A closer examination of the case shows that there is a significant gap between translation and communication. While a retirement plan seems attractive to someone from the English-speaking world, many individuals from Latin America abhor such programs. Many of them do not trust banks and find putting money in banks to be culturally uncomfortable. Furthermore, the idea of trusting their company to invest for them is also very unusual for individuals from Latin America. Additionally, Latin Americans are used to relying on children and other relatives for retirement purposes. Any plan whereby employees are required to entrust the company with their own salaries is usually viewed with suspicion.

The case illustrates the cultural context of communication. While the Spanish translator was able to translate the message, communication was not effective. The cultural nature of retirement and the suspicion around entrusting wages to the company were not properly addressed. Interpreters must take into consideration these complexities. The Human Resource Officer found that if she took the time to be patient and educate the employees about the importance and benefits of a retirement plan, they become more receptive.

*Source: Based on Rimalower, G. 2012. "Owls are not always wise: How to improve communication with non-English speaking employees." Employee Benefit Plan Review, April, 5–6.*

As the above Multinational Management Brief shows, it is important for any negotiator to meet and work with the interpreter to ensure that talks proceed smoothly. For instance, U.S negotiators are well advised to have interpreters review their notes and other information they intend to share with the other party. Such proactive efforts may greatly help the U.S. negotiators anticipate problems. Axtell,[15] Chaney, and Martin suggest the following tips:[16]

- Spend time with the interpreter so that he or she gets to know your accent and general approach to conversations.
- Go over technical and other issues with the interpreter to make sure that they are properly understood.
- Insist on frequent interruptions for translations rather than translations at the end of statements.
- Learn about appropriate communication styles and etiquette from the interpreter.
- Look for feedback and comprehension by watching the listener's eyes.
- Discuss the message beforehand with the interpreter if it is complex.
- Request that your interpreter apologize for your inability to speak in the local language.
- Confirm through a concluding session with the interpreter that all key components of the message have been properly comprehended.

To simplify the increasing diversity of languages in business organizations, some multinational companies use one language as the corporate tongue. Increasingly, this language is English because it is the most common second language. Examples of companies using English are Philips Electronics and DHL Worldwide Express. Using English allows these companies to have a more consistent corporate culture, while dealing with the linguistic diversity of their employees and customers. Yet even these major multinational companies have permanent translators on staff to manage such issues as interaction with the international press, the translation of local product information, and negotiations with other companies.

Although the use of company-wide languages simplifies some of the multinational's communication problems, it creates other linguistic challenges. One of the greatest challenges is communicating with nonnative speakers. The next section gives practical suggestions on how to do that.

## Communication with Nonnative Speakers

In the multinational organization, it is very likely that you will be speaking with and writing to employees, customers, and business associates in their second or even third language. In this situation, communications scholars recommend several techniques that make communication easier and more accurate:[17]

- *Use the most common words with their most common meanings:* A good source of these words is a book for a beginning language course.
- *Select words with few alternative meanings:* If this is impossible, use the word with its most common meaning.
- *Strictly follow the basic rules of grammar:* Follow the rules more than you would with native speakers.
- *Speak with clear breaks between words:* It is often difficult for a nonnative speaker to hear distinct words, especially amid background noise.

- *Avoid "sports" words or words borrowed from literature:* In U.S. English, for example, phrases such as "he struck out" should be avoided.
- *Avoid words or expressions that are pictures:* Some words or expressions, such as "knee deep in the big muddy" in U.S. English, require listeners to have a mental image of the picture.
- *Avoid slang:* Slang is often based on age and region, and the nonnative speaker may have learned the language from people from other regions. For example, British English slang is quite different from U.S. English slang.
- *Mimic the cultural flavor of the nonnative speaker's language:* For example, use more flowery communication with Spanish-speaking listeners than with Germans.
- *Summarize:* Paraphrase and repeat basic ideas.
- *Test your communication success:* Do not ask, "Did you understand?" Instead, ask your listener what he or she heard. Ask the listener to paraphrase what you said.
- *When your counterpart does not understand:* Repeat the basic ideas using different words. Use more common nouns and verbs.
- *Confirm important aspects in writing:* Make sure that all important information is written to avoid any misunderstanding or confusion.

Sensitivity to cross-cultural communication provides a solid foundation for a multinational negotiator. Next, the chapter provides you with the essential background to develop your knowledge of international negotiations and to prepare you for negotiating in the global business environment.

# International Negotiation

International negotiation is more complex than domestic negotiation. Differences in national cultures and in political, legal, and economic systems often separate potential business partners. Consequently, most international businesspeople find it necessary to modify the negotiation styles of their home country. If they wish to succeed in the multinational arena, they must develop a style of negotiation based on the flexible application of sound principles. This section develops your understanding of those principles by describing the steps in a successful international negotiation.

## Steps in International Negotiations

Most experts recognize that international negotiation requires a number of steps.[18] Although each negotiation is unique and may combine two or more steps or repeat some, the process involves five steps leading to the final step, which is an agreement. (See Exhibit 13.3, which shows a seventh step, postagreement, which will be discussed later in the chapter.) The **negotiation steps** are preparation, building the relationship, exchanging information and the first offer, persuasion, concessions, and the agreement. The most important step in international negotiation is preparation, and the culturally naive negotiator almost always fails to bring home an adequate agreement.

**Negotiation steps**
Preparation, building the relationship, exchanging information, first offer, persuasion, concessions, agreement, and postagreement.

## Step 1: Preparation

A winning international negotiating strategy requires significant preparation. Prior to the negotiations, the well-prepared international negotiator gathers extensive information on the negotiation issues, on the setting in which the negotiation will

**EXHIBIT 13.3**    Steps in International Negotiations

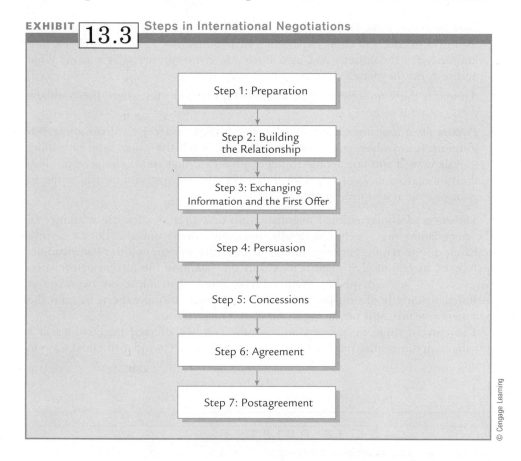

© Cengage Learning

take place, and on the firm and people involved. In this stage, you must answer questions such as, "Where do I stand?" in order to understand your company's position in the negotiation process. However, after you understand your own position, you also want to understand your counterpart's position by answering questions such as, "What do they want?" or "What is important to them?"

Experts on international negotiation identify numerous essential questions and issues to consider before the negotiation:[19]

- *Determine if the negotiation is possible:* To begin the negotiation process, you must believe that you have at least some areas of agreement with your negotiating counterparts.

- *Know exactly what your company wants from the negotiation:* What does the company hope to achieve in the negotiation? What are the minimally acceptable conditions of an agreement? Make a list of your specific needs or demands. Which specific demands have more negotiating power?

- *Be aware of what can be compromised:* It is very unlikely that you will get everything you want from the negotiation. Think in advance about the compromise and concessions that you can make. By thinking ahead, you reduce the likelihood of giving up too much or making concessions on the wrong issues.

- *Know the other side:* What does the other side bring to the situation? Can the other organization deliver what your company wants? What are the goals of the other side? Are they dealing with competitors, and do the competitors have any advantages? What are they willing to negotiate? How badly do they want the deal?

- *Send the proper team:* Do the negotiators have the appropriate knowledge of the technical details, sufficient experience in negotiations, language abilities, and knowledge of the country and its culture? Have they prepared as a team? What authority do they have?

- *Agenda:* Is there an agreed-upon agenda? Can it lead somewhere the company does not want to go?

- *Prepare for a long negotiation:* Avoid being rushed to accept a disadvantageous solution. Know when you must leave, but don't tell the other side. Be willing to walk away if you are unable to negotiate a deal that you both agree on. Furthermore, avoid making a deal for the deal's sake. Desperation usually results in poor judgment and unfavorable decisions.

The successful international negotiator not only prepares for the substance of the negotiation (e.g., technical details, company needs) but also does extensive research on the nature and negotiation styles of the foreign culture. For example, a study of successful U.S. negotiations with the Japanese found that careful preparations led to high-quality results. Preparations that improved negotiations included reading books on Japanese business culture, hiring experts to train the negotiation teams, and practicing in simulated negotiations.[20]

The current surge in mergers and acquisitions has affected negotiations in a way that emphasizes the need for adequate preparation. Consider the next Case in Point.

## CASE IN POINT

## Negotiations and Risk

The current economic situation has given many multinationals the opportunity to acquire companies that were previously out of reach. In fact, it is predicted that the pace of mergers and acquisitions will remain steady. Furthermore, multinationals in countries such as China are also relying increasingly on mergers and acquisitions to gain access to new markets. Because of such trends, negotiation teams are feeling increased pressure to complete the deal of a lifetime. However, without adequate preparation, such acquisitions can be very risky. Experts agree that the implementation of a merger is as critical as getting the deal signed. For instance, what should a multinational do as customers reduce purchases or suppliers go bankrupt? Unfortunately, negotiators often downplay or ignore such risks to get the deal signed as soon as possible. Multinational negotiators are therefore encouraged to take the time to prepare and to get as much information as possible so they can ask the important questions regarding risk:

- Treat risk as an integral part of the discussion rather than avoiding it.

- Break the risk into components to show how solutions can be devised to address these issues.

- Understand that risks and problems can be addressed jointly.

- Allow the counterparties to express their concerns.

Rather than hurry the negotiating along, multinationals are well advised to prepare adequately to fully address problematic issues that may arise.

*Sources: Based on Ertel, D. 2009. "Negotiating the risk or risky negotiations?" Financial Executive, April, 40–42; Muehlfeld, K., P. R. Sahib, and A. V. Witteloostuijn. 2012. "A contextual theory of organizational learning from failures and successes: A study of acquisition completion in the global newspaper industry, 1981- 2008." Strategic Management Journal, 33, 938–964; Sun, J. 2012. "Analysis of mergers and acquisition strategy of multinationals in China and Chinese enterprises countermeasures." Cross-cultural Communication, 8(2): 56–60.*

Although it is impossible to understand the negotiating styles of all the world's cultures, managers can anticipate certain key differences among cultures. This section identifies some of those common differences: in the goals of the negotiation, in the personal styles of the negotiators, in the communication styles of the negotiators, in the negotiators' sensitivity to timing and pacing of the negotiation, in the forms of agreement typical in the society, and in the common types of negotiating team organization. The examples from different countries discussed next show the extreme differences in these areas,[21] but keep in mind that many countries fall between these cases.[22]

- *Negotiation goal—signing the contract or forming a relationship:* Most Chinese and Japanese businesspeople consider the prime objective of negotiation to be the formation of relationships. A negotiation may produce signed agreements, but the signed paper represents only the formal expression of the relationship between the companies, and sometimes of the personal relationships between the individual negotiators. The contract exists only as an initial step in the relationship, one that may lead to longer-term mutual benefits. In legalistic societies, such as the United States, the detailed, signed contract is the most important goal of the negotiation. Commitment is less personally binding but relies instead on the force of law. The sanctity of the contract is a valued legal principle in U.S. courts.

- *Formal or informal personal communication style:* Business cultures differ widely on the acceptability of informal styles. Australians, like people from the United States, easily adapt to using first names and having informal conversations. As shown in Exhibit 13.2, however, Nigerian, Spanish, and Chinese negotiators react negatively to the informality of using first names among short-term business acquaintances.

- *Direct or indirect communication style:* We saw in the section on communication that the extent to which communication is direct and verbal, rather than indirect and nonverbal, varies widely by culture. The rules of politeness and styles of interaction in different cultures encourage or restrict the ability of negotiators to come directly to the point. For example, the Japanese will seldom say "No" directly. Instead, if something is "very difficult," it is probably impossible. Conversely, a speaker of a more explicit language might interpret such aversion to direct speech as an effort to hide something.

- *Sensitivity to time—low or high:* The pace of negotiation and the time given to each phase of it intertwine with the objective of the negotiation. Cultures place different values on how much time is devoted to the pursuit of goals. For people from the United States, closing the deal means signing a contract, and time is money. As a result, Americans tend to get down to business as soon as they can. In contrast, Asian cultures place value on creating a relationship rather than simply signing a contract. These cultures tend to want to take time to get to know the other parties better to determine whether a long-term relationship is worthwhile. Attempts to speed up negotiations tend to be viewed with suspicion that the other party may be trying to hide something.

- *Forms of agreement—specific or general:* A negotiated agreement may consist of general principles or of very detailed documents that attempt to anticipate all possible outcomes of the relationship. In many countries, such as Japan, the preferred contract states only general principles, not detailed rules and obligations. The Japanese argue that, because it is impossible to foresee all possible contingencies, a detailed agreement is dangerous and unnerving. The contract may obligate someone to do something that eventually becomes impossible due to unforeseen circumstances. In contrast, broad agreements, preferably based on strong personal relationships, allow for fair adjustments if circumstances change. Pressing for legalistic, detailed coverage of all contingencies, as people from the United States typically do, leads many people from other cultures to believe that their U.S. partners have little trust in the relationship. Exhibit 13.4 shows the differences among nations in cultural preferences for a broad agreement.

- *Team organization—a team or one leader:* The senior U.S. negotiator often has, within specified boundaries, the final authority to make commitments for his or her company and to close the deal. This style of organization fits the U.S. mode of rapid negotiations and the goal of reaching a signed contract. In international negotiations, a small U.S. negotiation team with one leader faces a much larger team, where the true decision maker might not be present or, if present, might say very little. Russians, Japanese, and Chinese prefer large teams and rely chiefly on consensus decision making.

- *Attitude toward negotiation—win-lose or win-win:* Because of the role of culture, different nationalities tend to approach the negotiation with their own mindsets. Some cultures view the process as one in which both parties can benefit (win-win), and others see it as a necessity that one side wins while the other loses (win-lose). For instance, Salacuse reports that 100 percent of Japanese approached negotiations with a win-win mindset,[23] whereas only 33 percent of the Spanish executives surveyed had the same view. By understanding the approach, you can be aware of your situation.

- *High or low emotions:* As we saw in Chapter 2, societies differ in terms of the acceptability and appropriateness of emotional displays. For instance, Latin Americans and the Spanish are said to usually show their emotions through

**EXHIBIT 13.4** Cultural Differences in Preference for Broad Agreements

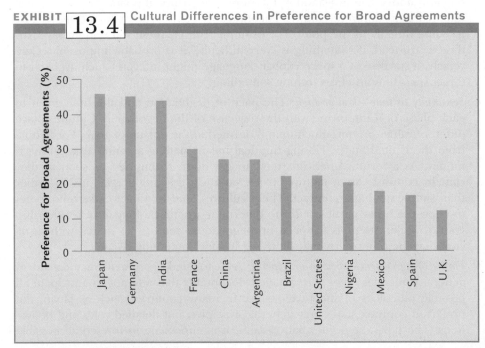

negotiations, whereas the Japanese and Germans tend to be reserved. Knowing the appropriateness of emotional display is also necessary to ensure that the negotiation progresses smoothly.

Lack of preparation for cultural differences in international negotiations can lead to many problems. For example, the negotiating style typical of the highly individualistic U.S. culture seldom works well in collectivist cultures. Both U.S. managers and managers from other cultures who are negotiating with a U.S. firm should prepare to avoid some of the pitfalls of the U.S. negotiating style. Exhibit 13.5 contrasts some common U.S. negotiating characteristics with those from other national cultures. U.S. negotiators have what John Graham and Roy Herberger call the "John Wayne" style of negotiation.[24] As Exhibit 13.5 shows, U.S. negotiators are independent, aggressive, and direct. Although this style makes sense in the individualistic U.S. culture, it contrasts sharply with the negotiating styles from nations with other

**EXHIBIT 13.5    Preparation: Understanding Negotiators from Other Countries**

| U.S. Negotiation Style | Rationale | Contrasting Negotiation Style | Rationale |
|---|---|---|---|
| "I can go it alone." | Why spend the money for more people than necessary? | Bring a team. | More people provide social pressure. |
| "Just call me John." | Formalities are unnecessary. | Be extremely formal. | Rank and status count in language. |
| "Pardon my French." | Why bother? English is the international language. | Understand English but use interpreters anyway. | Gives extra time to listen and formulate responses. |
| "Get to the point." | Why beat around the bush? | Build the personal relationship and exchange information first. | Personal relationships and trust are more important than contracts. |
| "Lay your cards on the table." | Give and expect honest information up front. | Don't reveal the real position at first. | A bit of trickery or avoiding saying "No" is okay. |
| "Don't just sit there, speak up." | Long periods of silence are unacceptable. | Long periods of silence are acceptable, especially in response to an impasse. | Time is necessary to react. |
| "One thing at a time." | A final agreement is a sum of agreements on each issue. | A holistic approach leaves all points open for discussion until the end. | Issues are always interconnected. |
| "A deal is a deal." | A commitment is final down to the last detail. | Today's commitment can be voided if tomorrow's circumstances are different. | Negotiation partners must understand that absolutes are impossible and things change. |
| "I don't need to check with the home office." | Negotiators should have the authority to make the deal. | I must check with the home office first. | To complete the negotiation, you have to convince not only me but also my boss on another continent. |

*Source: Adapted from Graham, John L., and Roy A. Herberger, Jr. 1983. "Negotiators abroad—Don't shoot from the hip." Harvard Business Review, 61, 160–168.*

---

## Multinational Management **Brief**

### What to Expect When Negotiating with Arabs

While most of the world reeled from the recession, many of the Middle Eastern Arab states weathered it fairly well. For instance, many of the governments of the Gulf Cooperation Council, an alliance of six Arab states in the Gulf region, created large financial reserves. These countries took advantage of the high oil prices to add to wealth funds. Furthermore, despite pessimism in countries like Saudi Arabia, experts predict changes that will significantly liberalize trade. Experts thus predict that more Western multinationals will be negotiating with Arab states to take advantage of opportunities that they offer.

There are five key characteristics of negotiations with people from Arab nations:

1. *A subjective view:* Arabs look at the world as subjective. Reality is based on perception, not on facts. A common frustration for Westerners is that logical flaws in arguments have less impact than expected. If the facts do not fit someone's beliefs, then that person may reject the facts and consider only his or her own view of the situation. In particular, personal honor is more important than fact.

2. *The type of relationship expected:* A good personal relationship is the most important foundation for doing business with Arabs.

3. *Information on family and connections:* Social connections and networks are crucial in the highly personalized Arab societies. This should not be interpreted as useless information, but rather it may represent the key to finalizing a business deal.

4. *Persuasion:* For Arab negotiators, personalized arguments are more effective than logical arguments. Emphasis on friendship and personal appeals for consideration are common. Showing emotion by raising the voice, repeating points with enthusiasm, or even pounding the table is acceptable. An emotional argument shows the sincerity of the concern.

5. *The time required to complete the process:* From the perspective of Western businesspeople, negotiations with Arabs take considerable time. Time is not fixed for Arabs. There are no fixed beginnings and endings of events. Everyone expects delays.

*Sources: Based on* Economist. *2012. "The long day closes." June 23, 27–30;* Canadian Business. *2009. "The United Arab Emirates: Gateway to the Gulf," Summer, 82, 143–144; Nydell, Margaret K. 1997.* Understanding Arabs: A Guide for Westerners. *Yarmouth, ME: Intercultural Press.*

---

cultural values and norms. The above Multinational Management Brief shows what to expect in negotiations with Arabs.

After thorough preparation, a negotiator is ready to begin direct communication with the counterparties. In the next section, we will see how these interactions evolve in the negotiation process.

## Step 2: Building the Relationship

**Building a relationship**
The first stage of the actual negotiation process, when negotiators concentrate on social and interpersonal matters.

After initial planning, the next step consists of **building a relationship** between the negotiating parties. At this stage, negotiators do not focus on the business issues but rather concentrate on social and interpersonal matters. Negotiation partners get to know each other personally. They develop opinions regarding the personalities of the negotiators: what they are really like, what their real goals are, and whether they can really be trusted.

This phase often takes place at a location different from the formal negotiation site. The first step in a Japanese negotiation, for example, is often drinking tea in a room outside the formal office. Only the exchange of business cards and small talk take place during this encounter. In most countries, including Japan, restaurants, bars, and cultural tours often provide the context for relationship-building activities. The simple act of drinking tea underscores the importance of appropriately approaching the relationship building stage. Consider the following Case in Point.

The duration and importance of the relationship-building stage vary widely by national culture. U.S. negotiators are notorious in their attempts to get down to business after brief and perfunctory socializing.[25] German negotiators also get to the point quickly. When foreign negotiators bring up issues not related directly to the negotiation objective, U.S. negotiators often view this as a waste of time and an inefficient use of company resources. The pressure on U.S. managers is to get to the point, make the deal, and come home—particularly when they are overseas. International travel and hotels are costly, and many U.S. companies believe that a manager's time is better spent at home, getting on with implementing the negotiated deal.

The goal of U.S. negotiators is to get the details of the agreement in a written contract, with specific requirements and due dates. From this perspective, there is little need to develop personal relationships. In the U.S. legalistic view, "The partner must agree to a legally binding document." Other legal systems, however, do not see the contract as binding in its detail. For example, for many Chinese managers, a contract provides only the foundation on which to build the relationship, with details to be worked out later. As with most Asian societies, the Chinese

## CASE IN POINT

### Role of Tea in Various Societies

While tea may seem like an ordinary beverage, the act of drinking tea plays a special role in many cultures. As more multinationals get involved in other societies, properly appreciating the importance of tea to some cultures is very important. Tea is one of the world's three most popular beverages worldwide, but there is wide variation in the customs related to tea drinking. Consider the very spiritual role that tea drinking plays in Japan. The process of and etiquette surrounding tea preparation and rituals have been passed down from generation to generation. The tea ceremony is heavily focused on building relationships and geared towards the notions of peace, respect, quiet, and restraint. Both the host and the guest have to view the tea drinking ceremony with utmost respect. While experts recognize that tea drinking may be becoming less formal, negotiators must still treat the tea drinking ceremony with great respect and follow the appropriate rules.

Tea also plays a very important role in Chinese culture. While there are variations in rituals among the various regions, tea is still used to develop relationships with friends. The tea is usually savored slowly and there is great emphasis on the mood of the meeting. As such, properly appreciating tea drinking in China can also show respect for the culture and the host and promote relationship building.

Tea drinking is not limited to Asian cultures. England also enjoys a strong tea-drinking culture. While tea drinking is very frequent, more formal tea drinking rituals such as high tea indicate the importance of tea to the British. Tea drinking in England is also a way to develop relationships, and negotiators need to give the activity the desired importance.

*Source: Based on Jinxia, L. V., and S. Zhaodan. 2012. "A comparative study of tea customs." Cross-Cultural Communication, 8(2): 128–133.*

---

## Multinational Management **Brief**

### Negotiating with the Chinese: The Need for Cooperation

Understanding Chinese negotiators is critical, given the importance of the region to global trade. Chinese negotiators are known to prefer to take time to develop a relationship rather than merely focusing on the negotiation. The Chinese are more apt to work with the other party to explore contradictions and ambiguities. Additionally, the negotiation may be just the beginning of a long-term relationship. In contrast, for the U.S. negotiators, the emphasis is on completing the negotiations, a task-oriented focus that minimizes the importance of relationships.

The Chinese regard relationships differently. Researchers had four foreign managers communicate with 120 Chinese participants. The foreign managers communicated either with warm-heartedness or indifference, and they proposed either mutual or independent rewards for the negotiation. Results showed that participants who interacted with the managers displaying warm-heartedness were more likely to feel that they had cooperative goals and were more confident in future collaboration. The employees who dealt with the managers with mutual rewards were more likely to find that the managers' ideas were reasonable.

These results suggest that foreign managers negotiating in China should display warm-heartedness, which can take the form of listening carefully, understanding nonverbals, and showing interest by asking caring questions. It is also recommended that negotiators communicate their interest through sincere conversations, smiles, and using soft voices. Outcomes of the negotiations should also be structured so that they are win-win.

*Source: Based on* Economist. *2012. Pedalling propserity. May 26, 3–5; Yinfeng, N. C., D. Tjosvold, and W. Peiguan. 2008. "Effects of warm-heartedness and reward distribution on negotiation."* Group Decision Negotiation, *17, 79–96.*

---

believe that investing the time to build personal relationships must come first. Consider the above Multinational Management Brief.

Building a good relationship among the negotiating parties provides a foundation for working out an eventual deal. As illustrated in the Multinational Management Brief, in many Asian societies, it is extremely important to build trust and relationships. Even in individualistic societies such as the United States, personal trust among negotiators is important. However, a business negotiation must eventually specify who is going to do what, when, and for what price. The next section shows how negotiators begin to address these issues.

**Task-related information**
Actual details of the proposed agreement.

**First offer**
First proposal by parties of what they expect from the agreement.

## Step 3: Exchanging Information and the First Offer

At this stage, both parties exchange information on their needs for the agreement. This so-called **task-related information** pertains to the actual details of the proposed agreement. Typically, both sides make a formal presentation of what they desire out of the relationship, such as the quantity, characteristics, and price of a product. Both sides usually present their **first offer**, which is their first proposal of what they expect from the agreement.

At this stage, national and business cultures influence what information is given and requested, how the information is presented, and how close the initial offer is

**EXHIBIT** `13.6`    Information Exchange and First Offer Strategies

|  | Arab Countries | Japan | Mexico | Russia | United States |
|---|---|---|---|---|---|
| Information exchange | Focus is on information about the relationship and less on technological details. | Extensive requests are made for technical information. | Focus is on information about the relationships and less on technical details. | Great attention is paid to detail. | Information is given directly and briefly, often with a multimedia presentation. |
| First offer or counteroffer | 20% to 50% of goal | 10% to 20% of goal | Fair for both parties and close to goal | Extreme and purposefully unfair | 5% to 10% of goal |

*Sources: Adapted from Chaney, Lillian H., and Jeanette S. Martin. 1995.* Intercultural Business Communication. *Upper Saddle River, NJ: Prentice Hall; Yale; Richmond, B. 1992.* From Nyet to Da: Understanding the Russians. *Yarmouth, ME: Intercultural Press.*

to the actually expected or hoped-for specifications in the agreement. Exhibit 13.6 shows a comparison among nations regarding information exchange and first offer strategies. Note, for example, the difference between the typical U.S. initial negotiation point (off the real goal by 5 to 10 percent) and the more extreme starting points used by Arab negotiators.

In the information-presentation stage, the negotiator must properly understand the audience and adapt the presentation to the audience's needs. There is some evidence that cultures have different preferences for the type of information being presented and that some countries in both Asia and Europe value depth.[26] Negotiators must know the negotiation aspects in-depth. If they display ignorance, the other party may be offended. In contrast, some cultures, such as Arab and Mexican cultures, may focus more on relationships. In such cases, presenters may need to focus more on the relational aspects of the presentation. If the information presented is too technical or difficult to understand, the other party may feel intimidated and more reluctant to make a deal,[27] so presenters must make sure that appropriate information is presented.

Negotiators need also to be attentive to the emotional aspect of the offer. Consider the next Multinational Management Brief.

After the first offer, the core of the negotiation begins. Negotiators move beyond first offer strategies and attempt to reach accord on the actual nature of the agreement. The next section outlines some of the tactics used in the next step.

## Step 4: Persuasion

In the **persuasion stage**, each side in the negotiation attempts to get the other side to agree to its position. This is at the heart of the negotiation process. Numerous tactics are available to international negotiators. Although all negotiators use somewhat similar tactics to argue for their side, their emphasis and mix of tactics vary according to their cultural background.

We will review two general types of tactics: (1) standard verbal and nonverbal negotiation tactics and (2) some dirty tricks.

**Persuasion stage**
Stage when each side in the negotiation attempts to get the other side to agree to its position.

## Multinational Management **Brief**

### Emotions and Negotiation Offers

Understanding negotiators in the Arab world is becoming increasingly critical. Many of these societies present significant opportunities to multinationals. Consider that Dubai has some of the world's most spectacular shopping malls. Despite social unrest, Saudi Arabia is currently experiencing drastic changes that may open the doors to more opportunities in the near future. More multinational employees will therefore have to negotiate with individuals from these societies.

Displays of emotions play a big role in terms of creating first impressions and the eventual acceptance of an offer. For instance, for Asians, saving face is a key aspect of negotiations. Negotiators who display emotions consistent with saving face are more likely to be viewed in a positive light. One of the key requirements for saving face is respect. For East Asians, respect can be shown through humility, deference to authority, and minimal disagreement. In contrast, emotions that show lack of respect, such as arrogance, direct confrontation, and open disagreements, are not likely to show respect for face.

In an interesting study, Hong Kong and Israeli negotiators were presented with positive emotions (humility and minimal disagreement) and negative emotions (arrogance and direct confrontation). Consistent with cultural expectations, the East Asian negotiators were more likely to accept offers from the individuals displaying positive emotions, who were viewed in a better light because they were acting consistently with normative expectations. In contrast, Israeli culture values directness and in-your-face argumentation. Unlike the Hong Kong negotiators, the Israeli negotiators were indifferent to the displayed emotions and were as likely to accept offers from negotiators displaying both positive and negative emotions.

Clearly, culture affects how emotions are interpreted in negotiations. Multinationals need to ensure that people sent to negotiate display the appropriate emotion whenever possible.

*Sources: Based on* Canadian Business. *2009. "The United Arab Emirates: Gateway to the Gulf."* Summer, 82, 143–144; Economist. *2012a. "Mall of the masses." April 14, online edition;* Economist. *2012b. "The long day closes." June 23, 27–30; Kopelman, S., and A. S. Rosette. 2008. "Cultural variation in response to strategic emotions in negotiations."* Group Decision Negotiation, 17, 65–77.

## Verbal and Nonverbal Negotiation Tactics

**Verbal negotiation tactics**
Promises, threats, recommendations, warnings, rewards, punishments, normative appeals, commitments, self-disclosures, questions, commands, saying no (refusals), interruptions.

John L. Graham, an expert on international negotiations, identifies several **verbal negotiation tactics** common in international negotiations:[28]

- *Promise:* If you do something for me, I will do something for you.
- *Threat:* If you do something I don't like, I will do something you don't like.
- *Recommendation:* If you do something I desire, good things will happen to you (e.g., people will buy your product).
- *Warning:* If you do something I don't like, bad things will happen to you (e.g., other companies will know you cannot do business here).
- *Reward:* I am going to do something beneficial for you (without conditions).
- *Punishment:* I am going to do something you will dislike—without conditions (e.g., end the negotiations immediately).

- *Normative appeal:* This is the way we do or do not do business here (e.g., "You must learn the Japanese way").

- *Commitment:* I agree to do something specific (e.g., meet a delivery date).

- *Self-disclosure:* I will tell you something about myself or my company to show you why we need to close the deal.

- *Question:* I ask you something about your company or yourself.

- *Command:* This is an order that you must follow.

- *Refusal:* Just saying no.

- *Interruption:* I talk when you talk.

Exhibit 13.7 shows examples of cultural differences in these tactics among Japanese, U.S., and Brazilian negotiators.

Cultural differences in nonverbal communication styles also influence negotiations. Nonverbal communication, through such things as body posture, facial expression, hand gestures, and the use of personal space, is a natural part of any international negotiation. For example, a hand gesture or a facial expression might be a subtle way to indicate agreement or disagreement. In addition, foreign nonverbal communication might also create (purposely or not) situations that make a negotiator uncomfortable. For example, people from cultures with a comfortable speaking distance of 1 meter (about 3 feet) might have difficulty concentrating on negotiations when someone stands inside their comfort range.

As explained earlier in this chapter, the interpretation of nonverbal communication is tricky for people of different cultural backgrounds. For example, in dealings with the Japanese, a proposal might be met with downcast eyes and no response, a reaction that U.S. negotiators often interpret as a rejection. The Japanese, however, take whatever time they need to think and formulate a proper

**EXHIBIT 13.7**    Frequencies of Verbal Negotiating Behaviors: A Comparison of Brazilian, U.S., and Japanese Negotiators

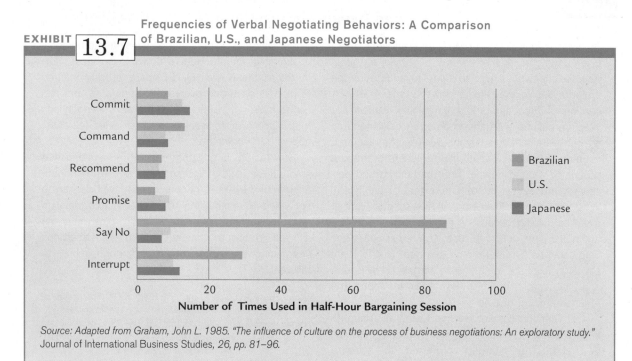

Source: Adapted from Graham, John L. 1985. "The influence of culture on the process of business negotiations: An exploratory study." Journal of International Business Studies, 26, pp. 81–96.

response. Unlike most U.S. negotiators, they feel no pressure to fill the gaps in conversation. Stressed by the silence, U.S. negotiators may continue to talk, causing the Japanese to hesitate even more. Feeling that their position is rejected, U.S. negotiators often offer unnecessary concessions.[29]

Although many Asian societies use silence to communicate that they are still deliberating, other cultures allow hardly any time for introspection. One study found that, in 30 minutes of negotiation, the Japanese had more than five periods of complete silence of ten seconds or longer, nearly twice as many as U.S. negotiators. Brazilians, on the other hand, were never silent for more than ten seconds.[30] Yet another aspect of the persuasion stage is time. Consider the next Case in Point about possible bargaining tactics with Arabs.

The more direct tactics of negotiation are often supplemented by tactics that not all people consider fair. The next section shows you some of them and possible responses.

## Dirty Tricks in International Negotiations

In both international and domestic negotiations, people can use many tactics to gain an upper hand. All negotiators want to get the best deal for their company, and they use a range of ploys or tactics to get what they want. However, people from different cultures consider some negotiating tactics **dirty tricks**, which are negotiation tactics that pressure opponents to accept unfair or undesirable agreements or concessions.[31]

The nature of cross-cultural negotiation makes the perception of dirty tricks almost unavoidable. Cultures differ on the norms and values that determine

**Dirty tricks**
Negotiation tactics that pressure opponents to accept unfair or undesirable agreements or concessions.

---

### CASE IN POINT

## Time and Impact on Negotiations

As mentioned in an earlier Multinational Management Brief, many multinationals are expected to begin negotiations with Arabs to take advantage of the opportunities in the region. However, the Arab perception of time can affect bargaining. Specifically, Western culture is organized around clock time; that is, events are scheduled by the clock. In contrast, Arab countries have event-time cultures, where events are scheduled around people. Their bargaining and persuasion process is different from that of the typical Westerner. In fact, Western societies tend to want to avoid bargaining because it requires significant time and human interaction. In contrast, Arab societies see bargaining as a trust-building exercise. They will not shy away from spending time to bargain on all issues, and negotiators need to be ready to spend the required amount of time.

Consider the case of Bechtel Corporation negotiating with the Kuwait Oil Company to rebuild Kuwaiti oil fields. The Kuwaitis preferred to socialize extensively, drinking tea and developing interpersonal relationships before getting down to business. Furthermore, the Kuwait Oil Company officials wanted to discuss each and every issue separately and feel comfortable before moving to the next. Negotiations took place over 15 weeks, and both sides felt satisfied with the outcome.

So Western negotiators need to understand that time can be used as a bargaining tool. When negotiating with the Arabs, negotiators are well advised to be willing to commit the time to build and maintain relationships. Furthermore, wide margins must be allowed to ensure that sticking to rigid deadlines negotiating does not doom the negotiations to failure.

*Source: Based on Alon, I., and J. M. Brett. 2007. "Perceptions of time and their impact on negotiations in the Arabic-speaking Islamic world." Negotiation Journal, 23, 55–73; Economist. 2012a. "Mall of the masses." April 14, online edition; Economist. 2012b. "The long day closes." June 23, 27–30.*

acceptable strategies for negotiation. As compared to people from the United States, Brazilians, for example, expect more deception and truth-stretching during the initial stages of negotiation.[32] It is therefore also critical to pay special attention to the presenters to detect whether information is being presented truthfully.

In many countries, unlike the typical situation for U.S. negotiators, the negotiating team lacks the authority to complete a contract. Just when one party believes the deal is final, the other party responds by saying that a higher authority must approve the contract before the deal is complete. The agreement often comes back with modifications, psychologically pressuring the other side to accept numerous minor modifications.

Here are some examples of common ploys in international negotiations (that some may consider dirty tricks), with possible response tactics:[33]

- *Deliberate deception or bluffing:* Negotiators present flagrant untruths either in their facts or in their intentions for the negotiation. For example, one foreign negotiating team spent a week in a hotel pursuing a deal, only to find out later that they were part of a dirty trick being played by the local company. The local company was already negotiating in earnest with another foreign company and had brought in the second foreign company only to scare the negotiators.
  *Possible response:* Point out directly what you believe is happening.

- *Stalling:* Negotiators wait until the last minute before the international negotiating team plans to go home. They then push for quick concessions to close the deal.
  *Possible responses:* Do not reveal when you plan to leave. When asked, say that you plan to stay as long as it takes. Alternatively, state when you will leave, with or without the deal.

- *Escalating authority:* Negotiators make an agreement but then reveal that it must be approved by senior managers or the government. The objective is to put the other team under psychological pressure to make more concessions.
  *Possible response:* Clarify decision-making authority early in the negotiating process.

- *Good-guy, bad-guy routine:* One negotiator acts agreeable and friendly while a partner makes outrageous or unreasonable demands. The good guy suggests that only a small concession will appease the unreasonable bad guy.
  *Possible response:* Do not make any concessions. Ignore the ploy and focus on the mutual benefits of the potential agreement.

- *You are wealthy, and we are poor:* Often used by negotiators from developing countries, this tactic attempts to make concessions seem trivial. Small companies may also use this tactic when dealing with larger companies.
  *Possible response:* Ignore the ploy and focus on the mutual benefits of potential agreement.

- *Old friends:* Negotiators act as if the companies and their negotiators have long-enduring friendships. They feign hurt feelings if their counterparts disagree or do not agree to their requests.
  *Possible response:* Keep a psychological distance that reflects the true nature of the relationship.

Successful international negotiators recognize and deal with dirty tricks and other ploys. Besides the suggested strategies, experts recommend other general responses to dirty tricks.[34] First, stick to your standards and avoid using the tricks yourself. This encourages negotiating counterparts to be more forthright. Second, point out the dirty tricks or ploys when they are used. This discourages their use later in the negotiation. Third, try to avoid fighting back directly. Fourth, be ready to walk out of the negotiation if the other side fails to play fairly. This may involve some cost, but it is probably better than a bad deal for your company. Finally, realize that ethical systems differ by culture, and understand that your opponents may not feel that they are really doing something wrong or immoral.

Although negotiators use a variety of tactics to argue their points, the goal remains to make a business deal. In the next section, we will examine the final steps in negotiation that bring the process to a successful conclusion.

## Steps 5 and 6: Concessions and Agreement

**Final agreement**
Signed contract, agreeable to all sides.

Successful negotiations result in the **final agreement**, which is the signed contract, agreeable to all sides. The agreement must be consistent with the chosen legal system or systems. The safest contracts are legally binding in the legal systems of all the signers. Most important, people from different national and business cultures must understand the contract in principle. Partners must have a true commitment to it that goes beyond the legal stipulations.

**Concession making**
Process requiring each side to relax some of its demands to meet the other party's needs.

For most negotiations to reach a final agreement, each side must make some concessions. **Concession making** requires that each side relax certain demands to meet the other party's needs. It usually means giving in on the points of less importance to you to achieve your major objectives.

**Sequential approach**
Each side reciprocates concessions made by the other side.

Styles of concession making differ among cultures, and none are necessarily the most successful. Experts point out that North American negotiators take a **sequential approach**.[35] Each side reciprocates the concessions made by the other side. North Americans have a norm of reciprocity, which means that one party should meet a concession made by the counterparty by making a concession. In many cultures, however, people consider a concession as a sign of giving in, of weakness, and an encouragement to extract more concessions. In addition, in the typical U.S. negotiating strategy, partners consider each issue as a *separate* point. Negotiators expect each side to give and take on the individual issues in sequence, and they complete the agreement when the sequential concession making resolves all issues.

**Holistic approach**
Each side makes very few, if any, concessions until the end of the negotiation.

In contrast, a **holistic approach** is common in Asia. The parties make very few, if any, concessions during discussions of each point. Only after all the participants discuss all the issues can concession making begin. When dealing with holistic negotiators, North Americans are often perplexed to learn that a point that they believed was negotiated arises again in the discussion of the overall package.

To illustrate cross-national differences in concession-making styles, Hendon, Roy, and Ahmed surveyed 10,424 executives from more than 21 countries over a 15-year period (1985–1999).[36] They presented the executives with seven different patterns in a hypothetical situation: They are negotiating and have to distribute $100 within one hour, and their counterparts are unaware that they will give away the $100. The executives also have to make distribution decisions at the end of each of the four 15-minute periods in an hour, at the end of which they have to have given away exactly $100. The seven patterns presented to the executives are as follows:

- *Pattern 1:* Give away $25 at the end of each of the four 15-minute periods.
- *Pattern 2:* Give away $50 at the end of each of the first two 15-minute periods, leaving no concession for the last two 15-minute periods in the hour.

- *Pattern 3:* Give away $100 at the end of the negotiation, with no concessions during the first three 15-minute periods.

- *Pattern 4:* Give away $100 at the end of the first 15-minute period, with no concessions for the remaining three 15-minutes periods.

- *Pattern 5:* Give away increasing amounts in the order of $10, $20, $30, and $40 at the end of each of the 15-minute periods, in that order.

- *Pattern 6:* Give away decreasing amounts in the order of $40, $30, $20, and $10 for the end of each of the 15-minute periods, in that order.

- *Pattern 7:* Give away $50 at the end of the first 15-minute period, $30 at the end of the second 15-minute period, $25 at the end of the third 15-minute period, and take back $5 at the end of the negotiation.

Results of the study showed that the various regions studied agreed on Patterns 4 and 7 as being their least favorite concession patterns. Executives from the 21 regions represented by the five regions of North America, British Commonwealth (e.g., the United Kingdom, Australia, South Africa); more-developed Southeast Asian countries (i.e., Taiwan, Singapore, and Malaysia); less-developed nations of South East Asia (i.e., Philippines, Papua, New Guinea); and Latin America overwhelmingly agreed that they disliked these patterns. Pattern 4 is known as the naive negotiating style, where the bottom line is revealed at the beginning of the negotiation; practitioners do not recommend it because it makes the negotiator vulnerable—the bottom line is revealed too fast. Pattern 7, known as the renegotiation style, is also discouraged because it signals that the negotiator gave away too much.

However, the results were more interesting in that the preferred concession patterns among these regions varied widely. For instance, the North Americans seemed to prefer Pattern 3 the most, whereas none of the other regions liked this pattern. Pattern 3 is known as the tough hard-nosed concession style and is consistent with the macho culture of the individualist societies of North America. Concessions are made only at the end when everything else has failed. This strategy is, however, discouraged because concessions need to be made occasionally to break deadlocks and to keep the negotiation progressing.

The less developed Southeast Asian region preferred Pattern 5, known as the escalating pattern, in which increasing levels of concession are made as the negotiation progresses. Although this seems to be a popular style, practitioners nevertheless discourage its use. The major problem with this style is that the negotiating counterparty may get greedy and expect more and more concessions or even prolong negotiations in order to get more.

The British Commonwealth, advanced Asian, and Latin American nations all preferred Pattern 6. This is known as the de-escalation pattern; the negotiator is sending the message that fewer and fewer concessions can be made. However, the experienced negotiating counterparty may try to get as much as possible early in the negotiations.

These preference patterns suggest that negotiators can be better prepared by understanding the styles of their counterparty. Such knowledge can be invaluable because the appropriate strategies can be adopted to get the maximum advantage from the concession-making style.

Approaches to the negotiating steps vary not only by culture but also by a general philosophy regarding negotiating strategy. The next section discusses two approaches to negotiation, along with their implications for international negotiations.

## Basic Negotiating Strategies

There are two basic negotiating strategies: competitive negotiating and problem-solving negotiating.[37] The competitive negotiator views the negotiation as a win-lose game. One side's gain must result in the other side's loss. Problem-solving negotiators, in contrast, search for possible win-win situations wherein the outcome of the negotiation is mutually satisfactory to both sides.

**Competitive negotiation**
Each side tries to give as little as possible and tries to win the maximum for its side.

In **competitive negotiation**, each side tries to give as little as possible. They begin with high and often unreasonable demands. They make concessions only grudgingly. Competitive negotiators use dirty tricks and any plot that leads to their advantage. They spend more energy defending their positions while attempting to get the other side to make all the concessions.

Competitive negotiation seldom leads to long-term relationships built on mutual trust and commitment. Additionally, starting from inflexible positions often leads to outcomes that satisfy neither side. Thus, both sides develop negative attitudes toward each other, and often the losers seek revenge, reneging on the agreement when the opportunity arises.

**Problem-solving negotiation**
Negotiators seek mutually satisfactory ground that is beneficial to both companies.

The foremost tenet of **problem-solving negotiation** is separating positions from interests.[38] Negotiators do not think of defending their company's position as the major goal of the negotiation. Rather, they seek mutually satisfactory ground that is beneficial to both companies. Problem-solving negotiators avoid dirty tricks and use objective information whenever possible. They often find that actively seeking to please both sides results in the discovery of new ways to achieve mutual gains. Why is understanding negotiation style critical? Consider the following Case in Point.

Exhibit 13.8 summarizes and contrasts how the competitive negotiator and the problem-solving negotiator differ in their approaches.

In international negotiations, there are three important points regarding the use of competitive or problem-solving strategies.

First, in cross-cultural bargaining, the ease of misreading the other side's negotiation strategy increases dramatically. For example, the formal politeness used by many Asian negotiators may look like problem solving to U.S. negotiators. The tendency of Brazilian negotiators to talk or to exaggerate may look like competitive bargaining to people from cultures with ritual politeness. However, in either of the examples, culturally based rules of social interaction can mask either a highly inflexible position or a true openness to problem solving.

Second, cultural norms and values may predispose some negotiators to one of the approaches. Exhibit 13.9 shows some recent evidence from a cross-national study on cultural differences in the preference for a problem-solving negotiation style.

Third, most experts on international bargaining recommend a problem-solving negotiating strategy. They believe that problem solving leads to better long-term contracts and relationships. Problem solving is more likely to achieve the multinational's goals of mutual benefits from international trade. In contrast, competitive negotiations exacerbate the inevitable conflicts and misunderstandings that occur in cross-cultural interaction.

**Postagreement**
An evaluation of the success of a completed negotiation.

## Step 7: Postagreement

A commonly ignored step by U.S. negotiators is the **postagreement** phase, which consists of an evaluation of the success of a completed negotiation. Because of their inherent task orientation, negotiators tend to ignore the benefits of

## CASE IN POINT

## Understanding the Nigerian Negotiating Style

Among African nations, despite violence and instability, Nigeria is poised to benefit from globalization and provide increased opportunities to multinationals. For instance, consider that Africa's richest man on the Forbes list of billionaires comes from Nigeria. Aliko Dangote is currently dealing in a variety of products from cement to pasta and prayer mats. He built his fortune on products other than oil. Other reports suggest that Nigeria also has some of the continent's most successful entrepreneurs. Understanding the Nigerian approach to negotiations is therefore important.

A recent report provides some insights into how to approach the Nigerians. Nigerians place strong emphasis on the family and achieving meaning of life through social relationships. As such, multinationals are well advised to start negotiations through a third party that already has a relationship with the Nigerian party. Furthermore, Nigerians are very slow at developing trust. Negotiators thus have to take the time to develop relationships and trust and not rush into negotiations. Furthermore, the Nigerians tend to be very oriented toward hierarchy. It is therefore recommended that multinationals send individuals who have higher positions. Additionally, Nigerians tend to be more formal at the outset of negotiations. Multinationals are thus more likely to succeed if they first assume more formal positions and later becoming more informal as the relationship develops.

The report also provided some recommendations on the preferred Nigerian negotiating style. Negotiators often adopt a distributive style whereby the negotiators often believe that for them to win, others have to lose. Such negotiators often see the other party as in conflict and focus on maximizing their own goals and interests. In contrast, the integrative style negotiator sees mutually beneficial ways to negotiate and often want to find ways to seek win-win solutions. Current research on Nigeria suggests that Nigerians have high mastery, whereby they tend to want to control their environment and outcomes to further group or individual interests. As such, Nigerian negotiators tend to be more distributive, focusing on winning the negotiations to achieve self-interested outcomes. As multinationals send individuals to negotiate with Nigerians, it is also critical to appreciate the Nigerian negotiating style.

*Sources: Based on* Economist. *2012a. "Africa's richest man." June 23, online edition;* Economist. *2012b. "Africa's entrepreneurs: Parallel players." June 23, online edition; Spralls III, S. A., Okonkwo, P., and Akan, O. H. 2011. "A traveler to distant places should make no enemies: Toward understanding Nigerian negotiating style."* Journal of Applied Business and Economics, *12(3): 11–25.*

postagreement as they get ready to move on to the next deal. Additionally, the short-term and impatient nature of U.S. negotiators also encourages them to ignore engaging in a postagreement session.[39]

The postagreement stage can be very beneficial because it allows the garnering of valuable insights into the strengths and weaknesses of the approach used during the negotiation. Such knowledge can be very important for organizational learning and for success in future negotiations. By analyzing each step, the negotiators can determine where things went well and where improvements are needed. However, beyond information critical to learning, postagreement analysis can enable members of a negotiating team to develop a closer relationship with their counterparts. As more U.S. companies increasingly negotiate with Asian countries, taking a long-term relationship approach is necessary. For instance, for the Chinese, agreement on a deal is not the end of the negotiation but rather the beginning of an opportunity to develop trust and strengthen the relationship. U.S. negotiators will need to become more adept at post-agreement work in order to further enhance their relationship-building skill.

Superior products or services, combined with good negotiating, lead to sound multinational business relationships. However, people must do the negotiating.

**EXHIBIT 13.8** Competitive and Problem-Solving Negotiation

| Stages in Negotiation | Competitive Negotiating Strategy | Problem-Solving Negotiating Strategy |
|---|---|---|
| Preparation | Identify the economic or other benefits that the company needs from the deal. Know the position to defend. | Define the interests of the company. Prepare to overcome cross-cultural barriers to defining interests. |
| Relationship building | Look for weaknesses in the other side. Find out as much as possible about your competition. Reveal as little as possible. | Separate the people in the negotiation from the problem. Change negotiators if necessary. Adapt to the other side's culture. |
| Information exchange and first offer | Give as little as possible. Give only task-related information. Make your position explicit. | Give and demand objective information that clarifies interests. Accept cultural differences in speed and type of information needs. |
| Persuasion | Use dirty tricks and any ploys that you think will work. Use pressure tactics. | Search for and invent new options that benefit the interests of both sides. |
| Concession | Begin with high initial demands. Make concessions slowly and grudgingly. | Search for mutually acceptable criteria. Accept cultural differences in the starting positions and in how and when concessions are made. |
| Agreement | Sign only if you win and get an iron-clad contract. | Sign when the interests of your company are met. Adapt to cultural differences in contracts. |

*Sources: Adapted from Adler, Nancy J. 1991. International Dimensions of Organizational Behavior, 2nd ed. Boston: PWS-Kent; Kublin, Michael. 1995. International Negotiating. New York: International Business Press.*

**EXHIBIT 13.9** Cultural Differences in Preference for a Problem-Solving Negotiation Strategy

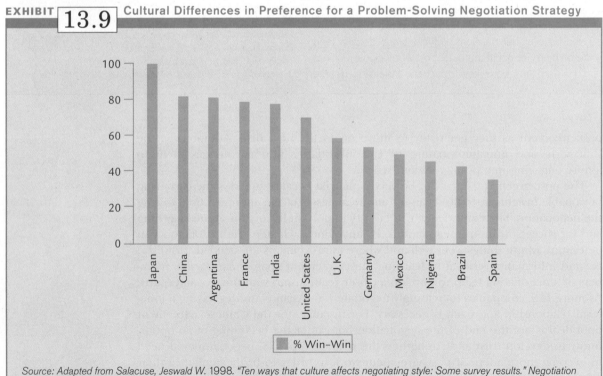

% Win–Win

*Source: Adapted from Salacuse, Jeswald W. 1998. "Ten ways that culture affects negotiating style: Some survey results." Negotiation Journal, July, pp. 221–240.*

In the next section, we will consider the characteristics of the successful international negotiator.

# The Successful International Negotiator: Personal Characteristics

Successful international negotiators are comfortable in a multicultural environment and skilled in interpersonal relationships. They have a variety of **personal success characteristics** that enhance their abilities to adjust to the stress of cross-cultural negotiations:[40]

- *Tolerance of ambiguity:* Even if they are familiar with the culture of their counterparty, an international negotiator is still a cultural bridge between people from different national and organizational cultures. Consequently, both the process of negotiation and the ultimate outcome are never entirely predictable. Individuals who take comfort in the certainty of outcomes should probably avoid international negotiations. During the negotiation process, success requires that negotiators remain patient and nonjudgmental and go with the flow.

- *Flexibility and creativity:* The international negotiator must expect the unexpected. Explicit goals for the outcome may not work. Unanticipated proposals may be offered. Counterproposals may not come. Even the site of the negotiation may be entirely different from the planned location.

- *Humor:* Situations arise in intercultural exchanges that are sometimes embarrassing or humorous. Humor often breaks tension and allows both sides to deal with cultural ambiguities. For example, a U.S. businesswoman in Japan was shocked to see a lobster, which she was eating at the time, demonstrate its freshness by attempting to walk off the plate. Her Japanese hosts were much amused at her shock. She joined in their laughter as they teased her about eating "active" food.

- *Stamina:* Long travel times, jet lag, different foods, different climates, hotel living, and culture shock stress the physical stamina of even experienced international negotiators. Negotiators must overcome these physical challenges and still listen, analyze, observe, and socialize during the negotiation exchange. Only negotiators with a strong constitution succeed.

- *Empathy:* Empathy means putting yourself in the place of your foreign colleagues—understanding the world from their perspective. This does not mean that a negotiator must agree with all counterparties on all issues, but rather that he or she must have a sincere concern for their feelings and perspectives. Empathy facilitates the negotiation because it softens the impact of interpersonal errors and cultural misunderstandings.

- *Curiosity:* Curiosity opens the door to new information. Managers with a genuine curiosity and respect concerning other cultures often discover subtleties that a task-oriented negotiator misses.

- *Bilingualism:* Knowing the counterparty's language is an asset. However, sometimes linguistic ability alone is not enough. Even people who speak a language fluently may not understand significant aspects of a country's business culture. In particular, a good negotiator needs to understand how the business culture affects styles of negotiation.

**Personal success characteristics** Flexibility, creativity, humor, stamina, empathy, curiosity, tolerance of ambiguous situations, and knowledge of a foreign language.

A final personal characteristic is discussed in the following Multinational Management Brief.

---

## Multinational Management **Brief**

### Negotiations and Phone Conferences

A growing number of multinationals now rely on telephone conferences (rather than face-to-face conferences) to conduct meetings. As globalization continues apace, some negotiations may also take place through telephone conferences. Future negotiators will therefore need to become more skilled at conducting some negotiations over the telephone. To understand the skills needed to become more adept at conducting telephone conferences, it is important to first understand the differences between face-to-face and telephone conferences.

A recent study of data from European countries such as the Czech Republic, Finland, Germany, Italy, Netherlands, Spain, and South Africa provides some insights on such differences. The study found that the lack of nonverbals is a key issue that reduces the effectiveness of communication. This results in fewer interruptions, less overlaps and pauses in telephone conference calls compared to face-to-face conferences. Furthermore, the study also showed that small talk tends to be very limited as people cannot have side conversations as they typically do in regular face-to-face communication. The use of the telephone means that people cannot have several individualized conversations.

The implication of telephone conversations is that negotiators have to be more skilled at building relationships and trust. The lack of small talk may prevent participants from discussing peripheral issues or "breaking the ice." Furthermore, because of the lack of nonverbals, telephone conference negotiators will need to work harder to ensure that the intended meanings are what the participants understand. However, it is likely that negotiators are more likely to participate in face-to-face meetings if they want to be involved in successful negotiations.

*Source: Based on Halbe, D. 2012. "'Who's there'? Differences in the features of telephone and face-to-face conferences."* Journal of Business Communication, *49(1): 48–73.*

---

## Summary and Conclusions

In this chapter, we examined the negotiating process and elements of cross-cultural communication in international business. The negotiating process involves preparation, building relationships with counterparts, persuading others to accept your reasonable goals through verbal and nonverbal negotiating tactics, making concessions, and finally reaching an agreement. Successful negotiators prepare well and understand the steps in negotiation. They also avoid the use of dirty tricks and competitive negotiating strategies.

The people who become successful negotiators are bilingual and have good cross-cultural communication skills. In addition, they are tolerant, flexible, empathic, and curious. They react to the stress of international negotiations with humor and stamina.

Oral cross-cultural communication demands that one learn the language or use interpreters, especially in complex negotiations. High-context languages also require that people learn to interpret situations that may not be apparent from analysis of the spoken component.

Nonverbal communications through body movements, proxemics, and touching vary widely among cultural groups. International negotiators and managers must learn to interpret these behaviors in sensitive and empathic ways. This often requires looking at the world through the prism of the other culture.

Avoiding attribution errors is a key to cross-cultural communication. International managers need sensitivity to their own behaviors and to the behaviors of their foreign counterparts to avoid misinterpreting the meanings surrounding their forms of communication. For example, a dirty trick in one culture may be a perfectly acceptable tactic in another.

---

## *Discussion Questions*

1. Identify the steps in the negotiating process.

2. How does the U.S. "John Wayne" style of negotiation influence the steps in the negotiating process?

3. Pick two countries and discuss the cultural differences in how people might use verbal negotiating tactics.

4. What is an attribution? How do attributions influence cross-cultural communication?

5. How can attributions influence the perception of dirty tricks?

6. Identify some cultural differences in body movements. How might these influence a negotiating session?

7. How might a manager successfully influence his or her subordinates in a high-context culture?

8. Discuss each of the seven stages of negotiation. Which stage do you feel is the most important? Why?

---

## Multinational Management **Internet Exercise**

### Entertaining an Indian Negotiating Team

Your CEO recently informed you that an Indian multinational is interested in buying your products. However, you will need to meet with a team of Indian negotiators to work on the details of the deal. You are in charge of developing a relationship and entertaining the Indian team.

1. Search the web for useful information on acceptable and unacceptable business practices and etiquette in India. You can use a website such as Executive Planet (http://www.executiveplanet.com).

2. What are the key dimensions/aspects that you need to inform your CEO about?

3. What would you tell your colleagues about how to entertain Indians?

4. What are some styles of business and social interaction that you will make sure to ask your colleagues to avoid?

---

## Multinational Management **Skill Builder**

### Negotiating an International Contract: A Simulation

**Step 1.** (1 minute) Read the following scenario.
This exercise simulates an international negotiation between Sportique Shoes, a North American manufacturer of athletic shoes, and Tong Ltd., a shoe manufacturer from the fictitious Southeast Asian country of Poreadon. Both countries are members of the World Trade Organization. Because of increasing price competition in the shoe industry, Sportique Shoes is seeking a low-cost manufacturing facility overseas. In preliminary correspondence, Tong Ltd. has offered the lowest price. It is also common knowledge that Poreadon has a high-quality and motivated workforce.

A negotiating team from Sportique Shoes, charged with the task of beginning negotiations, arrives today to negotiate with the Tong Ltd. management team for a contract to manufacture Sportique's shoes for the next year.

**Step 2.** (10 minutes) Your instructor will divide the class into two teams. One team will represent the management of Sportique Shoes. The other team will represent the management team of Tong Ltd. Go to separate rooms or separate parts of one classroom.

Independently of the two teams, four people will be assigned the roles of World Bankers (two) and Administrators (two). These four people do not participate in the negotiation; rather, they observe, keep time, manage the finances, and take notes on the progress of the negotiation.

The objective of both the Sportique Shoes team and the Tong Ltd. team is to achieve the best contract for their company.

**Step 3.** (15 minutes) Each team will receive a packet of materials from the instructor. Read the Timeline, Negotiation Tasks, Cultural Background, and Negotiation Roles at this time. Decide who will play which roles.

**Step 4.** (10 minutes) Read the general rules for the following simulation:

    **A.** The contract must cover four points:
1. Delivery dates for product shipments.
2. Quantity to be delivered at each shipment.
3. Price per 100 shoes manufactured.
4. Penalties for lateness.

    **B.** Finances
1. Each team member must contribute $ 1.00 to each company's Capital Account. Your instructor may change or eliminate this requirement, depending on the circumstances of your course. The Capital Account is managed by each team's CFO.
2. The CFO delivers 40 percent of each company's Capital Account to the World Bank, which will finance future operations and requires this payment as an indication of good faith negotiations. The World Bank calls this money your Good Faith Account.
3. Forty percent of your Good Faith Account will be returned to each team after a successful contract is signed

and delivered to your instructor. Should you fail to reach an accord in the time allocated, you will forfeit your entire Good Faith Account to the World Bank. (It will be donated to a local charity.) You may recover the additional 60 percent of your Good Faith Account by meeting certain objectives as stated in the Contract Negotiation Objectives.

    **C.** General Contract Objectives and Financial Implications
1. Each team should try to negotiate a contract that is consistent with its cultural values and economically favorable for its company.
2. Long-term financial gains and losses can result from what you negotiate. As in real life, these are not completely certain during the negotiation. However, the closer you are to reaching your objectives, the more likely it is that you will gain in the negotiations. For each point of negotiation, there are ranges of possible outcomes; some are neutral and both teams win, and some result in financial gain for one or the other side. After you negotiate your contract, your instructor will inform you of the economic results of your negotiations. For each point on which a team gains a favorable outcome, the other team will contribute 10 percent of its remaining Capital Account to the other team's Capital Account. For each point on which the contract results in balanced outcomes (you both win), the World Bank will contribute a flat fee of $1.00 to each company's Capital Account.

**Step 5.** (10 minutes) Read the Contract Negotiation Objectives provided by your instructor.

**Step 6.** (20 minutes) Plan a negotiation strategy with your team members.

**Step 7.** (10 minutes) Make a first offer.

**Step 8.** (60 minutes) Negotiate!

**Step 9.** (30 minutes) World Bankers and Administrators balance accounts between teams. Entire group debriefs.

## *Endnotes*

1  Hise, Richard T., Roberto Solano-Mendez, and Larry G. Gresham. 2003. "Doing business in Mexico." *Thunderbird International Business Review*, 45, 211–224.

2  De Mattos, Claudio, Stuart Sanderson, and Pervez Ghauri. 2002. "Negotiating alliances in emerging markets—Do partners' contributions matter?" *Thunderbird International Business Review*, 44, 710–728.

3  Terpstra, Vern, and Kenneth David. 1991. *The Cultural Environment of International Business*. Cincinnati: South-Western.

4  Whorf, Benjamin Lee. 1965. *Language, Thought, and Reality*. Hoboken, NJ: Wiley.

5  Babanoury, Claire. 2006. "Collaborative company research projects: A blueprint for language. *The Journal of Language for International Business*, 17(1): 15–28.

6  Hall, Edward T. 1976. *Beyond Culture*. Garden City, NY: Anchor Press.

7  Ferraro, Gary P. 1994. *The Cultural Dimension of International Business*. Upper Saddle River, NJ: Prentice Hall.

8  Eibel-Eibesfeldt, I. 1971. "Similarities and differences between cultures in expressive movement." In Robert E. Hinde, ed. *Behavior and Environment: The Use of Space by Animals and Men*. London: Cambridge University Press, 297–312.

9  Ferraro.

10  Axtell, R. E. 1998. *Gestures*. Hoboken, NJ: Wiley; Chaney, Lillian H., and Jeanette S. Martin. 2005. *Intercultural Business Communication*, 4th ed. Upper Saddle River, NJ: Prentice Hall.

11  Hall, Edward T., and Mildred Reed Hall. 1990. *Understanding Cultural Differences*. Yarmouth, ME: Intercultural Press.

12  Ferraro.

13  Axtell.

14  Chaney and Martin.

15  Axtell.

16  Chaney and Martin.

17  Harris, Philip R., and Robert T. Moran. 1991. *Managing Cultural Differences*. Houston: Gulf.

18  Adler, Nancy J., and Allison Gundersen. 2007. *International Dimensions of Organizational Behavior*, 4th ed. Boston: PWS-Kent; Graham, John L., and Roy A. Herberger Jr. 1983. "Negotiators abroad—Don't shoot from the hip." *Harvard Business Review*, 61, 160–168.

19  Copeland, L., and L. Griggs. 1985. *Going International*. New York: Random House; Dolan, John Patrick. 2005. "Strategies to negotiate any sale." *Agency Sales*, January, 35(1): 24; Dolan, John Patrick. 2005. "How to prepare for any negotiation session." *Business Credit*, March, 107(3): 18; Salacuse, Jeswald W. 1991. *Making Global Deals*. Boston: Houghton Mifflin.

20  Tung, Rosalie L. 1984. "How to negotiate with the Japanese." *California Management Review*, 26, 62–77.

21  Salacuse.

22  Ibid; Salacuse, Jeswald W. 2005. "Negotiating: The top ten ways that culture can affect your negotiation." *Ivey Business Journal Online*, March–April, 1–6.

23  Salacuse, "Negotiating: The top ten ways that culture can affect your negotiation."

24  Graham and Herberger, Jr.

25  Salacuse, "Negotiating: The top ten ways that culture can affect your negotiation."

26  Chaney and Martin.

27  Inman, William. 2006. "What are you talking about?" *Industrial Engineer*, January, 38(1): 36–39.

28  Graham, John L. 1985. "The influence of culture on the process of business negotiations: An exploratory study." *Journal of International Business Studies*, 26, 81–96.

29  Adler and Gundersen.

30  Graham.

31  Adler and Gundersen.

32  Graham, "The influence of culture on the process of business negotiations: An exploratory study."

33  Adler and Gundersen; Elahee, Mohammad N., Susan L. Kirby, and Ercan Nasif. 2002. "National culture, trust, and perceptions about ethical behavior in intra- and cross-cultural negotiations: An analysis of NAFTA countries." *Thunderbird International Business Review*, 44, 799–818; Fisher, Roger, and William Ury. 1981. *Getting to Yes*. New York: Penguin; Kublin, Michael. 1995. *International Negotiating*. New York: International Business Press.

34  Adler and Gundersen; Dolan, "How to prepare for any negotiation session."

35  Adler and Gundersen; Kublin.

36  Hendon, Donald W., Matthew H. Roy, and Zafar U. Ahmed. 2003. "Negotiation concession patterns: A multi-country multiperiod study." *American Business Review*, January, 75–83.

37  Kublin.

38  Bazerman, Max H., and Margaret A. Neale. 1991. *Negotiating Rationally*. New York: Free Press.

39  Palich, Leslie E., Gary R. Carinini, and Linda P. Livingstone. 2002. "Comparing American and Chinese negotiating styles: The influence of logic paradigms." *Thunderbird International Review*, 44, 777–798.

40  Kublin.

# Cross-Cultural Negotiation: Americans Negotiating a Contract in China

MARKUS PUDELKO, TÜBINGEN UNIVERSITY

This comprehensive fictitious case covers the essential aspects and facets of a cross-cultural negotiation, in this case between an American and a Chinese company. The difficulties, problems, and misunderstandings both sides are facing are particularly stressed. In addition, the case's unique contribution is in presenting cross-cultural negotiation from both perspectives, the American and the Chinese. The presentation of both perspectives is structured in the same way, facilitating a direct comparison. This multi-perspective approach is rather distinctive in so far as cross-cultural negotiation tends to be regarded in most texts of Western origin exclusively from the angle of the Western side. However, it is only through a better understanding of the respective "other" party that performance in cross-cultural negotiation can be significantly improved.

In order to facilitate group work, the various aspects covered in this case are clearly divided into various sections. This allows the class to be split up into different groups, which can each discuss specific sections in more detail and subsequently present their results to the entire class.

The case should be useful in all courses that cover cross-cultural negotiation, that is mainly in Management Across Cultures and International Business courses. The case has been written primarily for business students at the MBA level and for participants in executive education programs. However, students in advanced undergraduate classes should also benefit substantially from this case.

## Introduction

**Mr. Jones:** I had just come back to our headquarters in Alabama from two months of negotiations in Shanghai. We hoped to set up a Joint Venture (JV) with a Chinese state-owned vehicle component company. It was our intention to outsource some of our production to China to reduce our costs. When I was assigned to

lead our negotiation team, I realized this could substantially boost my career and I was determined to bring these negotiations to a successful end.

Of course I was aware of the fact that the Chinese are known for being tough negotiators, but so what I thought, we Americans are certainly tough as well when it comes to business. And I was probably chosen because I have a reputation for my no-nonsense, straightforward, and sometimes even aggressive way of negotiating. What I had subsequently to discover however was that the Chinese are not tough, which would have been fine with me, they just don't know how business is done these days and they just try to cheat and play unfair games wherever possible. They still have a lot to learn if they want to be successful on the world markets. Anyway, we decided to pull out of the negotiations. You just can't trust them.

**Mr. Wang:** We were negotiating over the last two months with a major vehicle component company from Alabama, USA. We hoped to set up a JV which would have allowed us to improve substantially our technological knowledge base. Of course we knew about Americans always being direct to the point of rudeness and indeed we had to put up with a lot of just uncivilized behavior. Anyway, we did our best to build up a long-term relationship. And after many difficulties we were almost there, but then the Americans lost their nerve and pulled out. You just can't trust them.

## Preparing for the Negotiations

**Mr. Jones:** Before flying over to Shanghai we did our homework very thoroughly. We made inquiries about the Chinese company and had a pretty good picture about their production facilities, product quality, and their amazingly low production costs. We thought about each little detail and knew exactly what specific information we needed. So, all that we wanted from our Chinese counterparts at the start of the negotiations were specific answers to specific questions and once we had all the missing numbers we could have simply put them into our equations and come up with a proposal which would be fair for both sides.

I stress fairness because successful negotiations are essentially a positive sum game. You learn that in every MBA program. We should all know each other's interests and viewpoints and as adults we should be able after some tough negotiations to come to a mutually satisfactory solution. All that it takes is a little bit of trust, openness, frankness, and transparency. But, as it turns out, these are terms which apparently don't exist in Chinese.

**Mr. Wang:** Before the Americans came over we had done our homework very thoroughly. We made inquiries about the American company and had a pretty good picture about their overall business philosophy, their corporate culture, the people running the company, and their sophisticated production technology from which we could learn much. We were keen to get to know them and hoped to enter a long-term partnership built on mutual trust. We prepared their arrival carefully, arranging meetings with everyone whom they should meet. Business is in the end about people and for people to get to know each other it takes time and we were willing to invest this time. But as it turns out, Americans don't care for people and trust, all they care about is the bottom line.

## Upon Arrival

**Mr. Jones:** Upon arrival we were very impressed and positively surprised by the reception we received. A delegation was waiting for us already at Pudong Airport and once we arrived at the company's headquarters a huge banner across the gate was put up to welcome us. In the consecutive days, we had many meetings, not just with people from the Chinese company but even with local government officials. So, we felt greatly honored. And in the evenings we had one banquet after the other.

While appreciating the hospitality of our hosts, we were kept completely ignorant about the schedule and agenda: we had no idea what we would be doing the next day, whom we were going to meet and talk to, or even when the official negotiation would start. And we became increasingly impatient, also because my boss back home called me every day to find out where we were with the negotiations and every time I had to tell him that we hadn't even started yet.

Then we noticed that during all this friendly chitchat with our hosts, they dropped from time to time and in seemingly casual ways questions about our business plan. In order to maintain the good atmosphere we were quite willing to answer openly. But whenever we asked questions the topic quickly changed again to the quality of Chinese food or the "long-established" friendship between China and America.

**Mr. Wang:** In order to show our guests how much we valued their visit, we invested a lot of time and effort to make them feel welcome. We took them out to lavish dinners, organized meetings with government and party officials, so that they could report home that they were treated with great honor. Being introduced to people with high rank and influence increases your own status and opens doors and what matters more than status and access to important people?

In their ignorance and short-sightedness, all they could think of was their business presentation and kept asking when we would start the negotiations, and even got quite annoyed by some changes of agenda, without any understanding that sometimes we ourselves didn't have the detailed schedule either. This was decided by our bosses. By openly showing their annoyance and asking us questions about the agenda we didn't know the answers to, they made us lose face. How rude!

And what was this talk about when to start negotiations? As far as we were concerned the negotiations started with the first handshake. By the time we formally sat down for formal discussions we had already learned a lot about them and their actual intentions. But for the Americans only facts and figures presented in formal presentations or written down in documents seem to count. And if they felt increasingly under time pressure, which they naively even openly admitted, well that's part of the game.

## General Principles

**Mr. Jones:** Fortunately, after more than a week the first real business meeting was scheduled. It was with the CEO, Mr. Chen, of the company. He is of a much higher rank and may be twenty years older than I am so I rehearsed my entire presentation carefully, in order not to make any mistakes. But then again, the whole meeting didn't touch upon any material content of our contract, instead we wasted time discussing the history of Chinese civilization and the promising business environment in China.

Finally the CEO stressed the important purpose of this meeting was to reach an agreement upon the general principles between both partners. And when I tried to raise some detailed issues, Mr. Chen just laughed and referred to Chairman Mao's meeting with U.S. Secretary of State, Henry Kissinger. At Kissinger's mere mention of political issues, Chairman Mao stopped him in courtesy, saying "You can talk about any detail with Prime Minister Zhou later on, but with me only about general principles."

I didn't quite understand what this talk of "general principles" was all about, but I just went along. So, Mr. Chen highlighted the importance of mutual understanding, good-will, trust, a long-term relationship, the importance for the Chinese side to learn from us technological know-how, and so on and so forth. I said yes to everything, but also mentioned our interests. Later on a communiqué was even drafted. I noticed that our interests were hardly mentioned, but in the interest of keeping a good atmosphere I was happy to sign the document, after all it was just a legally non-binding statement of some intentions.

As I found out later, that was a huge mistake. Much later on in our negotiation of concrete details, whenever we refused to make any more concessions, the Chinese would refer to these general principles, pointing out our failure to understand the spirit of those general principles which were clearly spelled out and warned us not to jeopardize our mutual understanding. How they managed to build up the connection between every detail of the contract and these non-binding wishy-washy general principles was just far beyond any of us.

**Mr. Wang:** After one week we invited Mr. Jones and his delegation to see our CEO, Mr. Chen. We were not overly impressed that the American CEO did not fly over for this meeting. After all this was the meeting where the "general principles" for the JV were to be agreed upon: the most important part of the negotiations. This was for us a sign of disrespect and insincerity, but in order not to spoil the atmosphere we didn't mention it at all.

Apparently, Mr. Jones yet again failed to understand the importance of this meeting and foolishly agreed to everything we suggested. And when he refused to make concessions later on in the negotiations and we referred back to what he himself agreed upon when discussing the "general principles," he made it clear to us that he didn't care much about them. But these mutually approved principles constituted the foundation of our entire cooperation. How can you trust someone who ignores general principles which are based on trust? All that mattered for the Americans were the details of the actual contract. Only those with bad intentions hide behind paragraphs of some contract.

## Patience

**Mr. Jones:** When it finally came down to negotiating the details of our contract, it appeared that our Chinese counterparts always controlled the pace of the negotiations, using delays very purposefully to put us under pressure. The Chinese never missed any chance to ask for concessions, and it seems the only thing they're willing to sacrifice is time. Whenever we thought we had made some progress, the Chinese had to double-check with their superiors and even government and party officials and that could take forever. And when we asked to resume the talks, they replied that consistent with the general principles of "mutual understanding," we should make more efforts to understand the slowness of Chinese bureaucracy.

However, whenever we had to get advice from our headquarters back in the States and the response took a bit longer than foreseen, then this was unacceptable to the Chinese. They thought that, as we were from such an efficient and advanced capitalist country, there could be no other reason for delays than some malice intentions. So much for the principle of mutual understanding!

**Mr. Wang:** We actually felt quite annoyed and almost insulted by the insistence of the Americans on discussing specific details, coming to an agreement, and moving on. What is the point of hurrying and discussing some details of a contract if you haven't even got to know the people well with whom you will actually have to implement the contract. That matters much more than some details which would need to be adapted over time anyway, because things just develop and change. And how can you adapt if there is no mutual understanding?

Also we can't just take decisions at the negotiating table, as we often need approval, not only from our superiors but also from certain government agencies and this takes time. Of course we can't always admit to this openly, it makes us lose face, but they should have understood that negotiating teams in China don't have the autonomy Americans have. Decisions in Chinese companies are often taken by people in the background.

## Friendship, Trust, Harmony, and Contracts

**Mr. Jones:** One thing we felt really strange about was the constant insistence on friendship and long-term trust relationships between the two sides throughout the negotiation process. Whenever the Chinese "offered" something we considered as a matter of course anyway, they made a big story out of it, implying that it was only because of our friendship that they "offered" us this "favor." And whenever they wanted something we considered as out of question they tried to pressure us with the hint that refusing would endanger our friendship. As far as I am concerned, I never considered these Chinese (or for that matter any other persons I ever negotiated with) as friends. We have common interests to start negotiations, during the negotiations themselves we certainly have more opposite interests and to sort this out is a question of professionalism, not of friendship.

Another of their constantly repeated buzzwords is harmony. In the beginning we were always very polite, soft spoken, and even tolerated some attempts from the Chinese side to take advantage of us. But the more we gave them, the more they wanted and so we became increasingly direct in communicating where our limits were. And at times that included some outburst and door slamming. But the next day it was all forgotten and we moved on.

With all their talk about trust, one thing the Chinese never seemed to fully trust was what has been written in a contract. They constantly asked to whom they should turn if something went wrong. But if "something went wrong," that can only mean that one of the two parties broke the contract, and that should be solved by required legal procedure. But the Chinese insisted on adding some clauses about arbitration through a third party into the contract, again with the emphasis on mutual understanding and trust. But how can you trust someone who apparently already thinks about breaking the contract before it is actually signed?

**Mr. Wang:** We Chinese do business on the basis of personal relationships, friendship, and trust and not on the basis of some written document. We give ourselves a long time before doing business with someone, but once we believe we can enter a business relationship, then we stick to it and we would never give it up, only because, say, someone would offer us for some deal a better price.

Although it didn't seem at all a problem for the Americans, they behaved at times quite rudely. Even if you don't agree with the other side, you should always control your anger and maintain harmony. How can the Americans still get along when they just had a furious argument the day before? To keep harmony is our way to express intention to build up long-term relationship. We wouldn't mind taking more time and patience when problem arises, so long as both sides remain calm and discuss in a peaceful way. However, the Americans only cared for speed in the negotiation.

Then the Americans who were always so interested in the specifics of the contract, were very reluctant to introduce arbitration clauses in case some changes occur which need to be taken into consideration. They said: "If something goes wrong, we have to go to court." How can you trust someone who wants to sue you if a problem comes up? If you really are interested in a long-term business relationship, no contract in the world can foresee all eventualities. It's like a marriage. Its success is based on trust, not on a contract.

## Guanxi

**Mr. Jones:** If one thing is known to Westerners about Chinese business culture it is the concept of *guanxi*. Of course all over the world connections and networks do matter in business, but the Chinese take it to an extreme and apply it to virtually every aspect in society. In order to get planning permission for the plant we intended to build, our Chinese partner encouraged us to take the senior officials of the local planning approval commission out for a luxurious dinner. Building up good connections might shorten the application process from several months to just a couple of weeks. However, what our Chinese business partners labeled as building up connections sounded to us very much like corruption. It is our company's strict policy not to engage in any kind of such activities, no matter where in the world.

Apparently, also the recruitment and promotion policy of our Chinese business partner was mainly determined by *guanxi*. Sons and daughters of business partners and influential bureaucrats clearly received preferential treatment. Once engaged in the JV we would have had to make an end to all that to make sure that only the best candidates got recruited or promoted. What a mess, to clean all this up!

**Mr. Wang:** As always the Americans only thought about business in terms of abstract concepts. We don't dispute the validity of these concepts, but we take a more holistic approach and don't forget that business is done in the end by people, and people have to get along with each other. Everything comes down to give and take and what matters is that in the end there is a balance between the favors you receive and do. We like to do someone a favor, as we know the person will feel morally obliged to return the favor at one point. Therefore we also like to repay a favor as soon as possible, so that we don't feel indebted anymore.

Moral obligations are much smoother, flexible, and adaptable than contractual obligations. We don't like to sue each other, which seems to be a national sport in the United States. If you go to court, all parties involved lose face. And a system which is built on moral obligations can only work if a high degree of ethical standards are observed. That is why we get so upset, if the Americans equal *guanxi* with corruption. I freely admit that we have the problem of corruption in China, but this is because of the abuse of power by bureaucrats, not because of the importance we attach to mutual obligations, which goes back to Confucius. Why do you think overseas Chinese are so successful in so many countries? It is because of trust and sense for obligation, in short because of *guanxi*.

America might be at the moment the most powerful country in the world, but their values are not as universal as they might think. And our American business partners, with their usual combination of arrogance and ignorance, did not follow our advice to build up *guanxi* with the planning commission and I am sure they would still be waiting today for approval.

## Overseas Chinese

**Mr. Jones:** Considering the difficulty we anticipated to have in communicating with our Chinese counterparts, we had a fellow in our negotiation team who was of Chinese origin. We thought that his fluency in Chinese and his deeper understanding of the Chinese way of doing things would be useful. And indeed, we benefited greatly from his accurate interpretation and prediction of responses from the Chinese. Even though both sides had professional interpreters, his role was appreciated also by the Chinese, as he was able to better interpret conflicting standpoints and mediate between both sides.

However, it didn't take long before we ran into problems. Whenever there was some dispute over the contract details, our Chinese counterparts began to pressure him to sort out things in their favor. Never mind that he was born in the United States, was an American citizen and was working for an American company, they just saw him as one of theirs and couldn't grasp that he represented the other side. This was not China against America, this was a negotiation between two companies and he was an employee of our company, so what did they expect? It's completely ridiculous that the Chinese felt entitled to ask so much from him just because he was of Chinese origin.

**Mr. Wang:** There was this U.S.-born Chinese guy on the American negotiation team, and we interpreted his presence as a sign of sincerity and goodwill on the part of the Americans and their wish to establish a good relationship with us. Finally someone who would appreciate how business is done here. So we focused on trying to make him understand our position. But instead of acting like a bridge between the two sides, he showed no sympathy whatsoever for us. He was coming from rich America and should have had more consideration for our situation. And when he overheard us discussing in Chinese, he must have passed on what he heard to his bosses. So, the man we thought of as a friend was nothing but a spy. Not exactly the right way to establish trust.

## Honesty

**Mr. Jones:** Our Chinese partners constantly stressed the values of trust and harmony in business. But how can you expect to be trusted if you are not completely honest. And the Chinese were the masters of deception and game play. Of course no one puts his cards on the table, but there is a difference between holding back some crucial information and telling stories which are not true. Overall we were quite frank with what we wished to see to come out of the negotiation, because we were convinced we were in a win-win situation and we wanted to build up trust. But we didn't get anything back for our honesty. In the end I think they considered our honesty as a weakness.

**Mr. Wang:** Life in society would not be possible without honesty. You should never lie to your parents, relatives, or close friends. But in a business negotiation you have to act strategically. To our great surprise, the Americans turned out unbelievably naïve with being overly honest. With all their money and technological know-how they might think they can afford to be completely honest, but if you start out at the weaker end, one needs to compensate for this by being cleverer. At one point the American negotiation leader even called us dishonest. What an insult! Only because we were cleverer by not revealing everything, we are not dishonest. And what the Americans mistook for honesty and frankness was often nothing but impolite and rude behavior.

## Face/Shame

**Mr. Jones:** The Chinese concept of "saving face" soon began driving us mad. In a business negotiation you have to think logically, you need to be objective and look at the facts. In the interest of the project you have to be able to criticize and accept criticism. Once we were discussing the optimal way of setting up machines in the factory. It was a purely technical detail. The head of the Chinese negotiation team, Mr. Wang, made a proposal which simply didn't make sense. We had it all figured out and based on our calculations. I calmly but firmly explained to him that what he suggested was simply nonsense. He became angry and left the meeting. What is this? First not getting the math right and then getting upset? If we hadn't picked up on this, we could have incurred lots of costs which would have been of no interest to anyone. I might have been more diplomatic, but I wasn't putting him down, I only made my point.

Still, I apologized later on and he replied I shouldn't worry, there was no problem. But the following day when I just confused two figures, he corrected me like a teacher would a schoolboy, looking triumphantly to his team. Apparently, he tried to regain face by shaming me. What childish behavior! What we never could quite comprehend when communicating with the Chinese is how much they care about the formal way of communication, instead of its actual content. No problem to tell a blunt lie, if you only do it with a polite smile!

**Mr. Wang:** Being completely fixated on profits and efficiency, our American counterparts showed no respect to people. Once I made a point which was probably not well thought through. It was just a detail, no reason fighting over. But instead of just leaving it for the moment and telling me later on, Mr. Jones lectured me for 10 minutes about why I was wrong, thus causing me embarrassment in front of my entire team. I think he was not even aware of the fact that I lost face, but that is even worse: the Americans always seem to think that their way of behavior represents the universal standard and everything else are just folkloristic oddities which should be abandoned for the sake of the only right (American) way. And in addition, Mr. Jones is 10 years younger than I am. How dare he treat me with so little respect!

## Haggling

**Mr. Jones:** What amazed us quite a lot was the fact that the Chinese adopt exactly the same strategy in business negotiation as in shopping on the street market. The seller demands an unreasonably high price, followed by some intense haggling which usually ends at around half of the initial asking price. In the end, both parties feel happy, even though they could

have settled for half the price right away without wasting all the time on fierce negotiation. It took us quite a while to realize what satisfaction the Chinese take from asking and receiving concessions. The bargaining ability is something the Chinese take pride in, and they enjoy practicing it no matter if it is for obtaining better conditions in a multi-million contract or for getting cheaper vegetables for dinner. At each item on the agenda, our Chinese counterparts started out with some totally unacceptable conditions, waited for our counter-offer, which was much closer to a realistic solution, and then continued asking us for concessions with an unbearable patience.

Before coming to China an expert on Chinese business suggested to me to read *The Art of War,* written by Sun Tzu more than 2000 years ago. At that point I laughed at this advice, but it turned out I should have taken it more seriously, as the Chinese themselves interpret negotiation as psychological warfare and use the war metaphor quite frequently when talking about negotiations. Chinese just don't understand the concept of a positive sum game. They only think in terms of losing or winning. How can you enter a JV if you are always perceived as the rival and not as the partner?

**Mr. Wang:** We are surprised how little negotiation skills the Americans had. They always were so upfront with their real intentions that we could easily get concessions when we pushed the right buttons. And we could read from the expressions on their faces like an open book. I thought the Americans were so good at poker, but apparently not. In negotiation you should never reveal what you think.

Also, the Americans reacted always so nervously if there was a delay in the negotiation. Whenever we agreed on something important we told them we needed approval from our superiors which was also often the case. We just don't have the decision-making authority the Americans are used to. Anyway, as they often reacted so impatiently, we delayed sometimes the process on purpose. And in particular when they became irrationally agitated and furious we always got the concession we wanted.

Skillful negotiation is about ascertaining the genuine intention of the other side, and preparing responding strategies so as to reap the most benefits from the final result. This is what real negotiation encompasses, which is far more than "haggling" as the Americans refer to our tactics. Of course, for a long-term partnership both sides need to be satisfied, but it is always good to be a little more satisfied than the other side.

## Strategic Behavior

**Mr. Jones:** Negotiating with the Chinese feels almost like walking in complete darkness—you never know what their next move will be, you can't even figure out whether they are content with your proposal or not. Always seemingly modest and courteous, we never knew what they were thinking. Whenever we suggested something and explained in detail why this should be good for both sides, they never contradicted, always nodded, frequently said "yes," but in the end, they often just ignored what we just laid out or said they needed to refer this to their superiors and come back to us, which they never did.

And every time they pushed us for another concession, they started by emphasizing the importance of looking at the long-term benefits, as if we were just myopic and unwise not to agree with the conditions more favorable to them. And when asked what these long-term benefits would be, they usually vaguely described them as the possibility of much more lucrative contracts in the "near future." Whatever that means.

**Mr. Wang:** One of the most crucial criteria in our society to judge a person's social status and social skills is the ability to control one's own emotions. The more someone plainly shows satisfaction or irritation, the more people will regard this person as shallow, undignified, and inexperienced. Americans with their noisy directness and openness will never understand this. This has put us into an advantageous position, as we always knew where we were with them, but they had no clue about our position. As a result, they also felt less and less confident and more willing to compromise.

Americans like to feel dominant. They like to talk a lot and explain this and that. So we let them talk, we listen and nod encouragingly. The more you listen the more you learn, but the more you talk the more you reveal your position. At the end of a negotiation day, our American friends were happy, because they felt they were in charge and we were happy because we understood their intentions better.

## What Means "Yes" and "No"

**Mr. Jones:** What frustrated us most was the fact the Chinese negotiators were never prepared to give a definitive answer, everything remained "subject to approval" of their superiors. And even if we got what we thought was a definite agreement, the Chinese were not the slightest embarrassed to reopen a subject we thought to have settled. So, a "yes" could mean anything, including "no."

While we often got a "yes" without knowing what it meant, we never got a clear "no." Only after a while we understood that phrases such as "it's possible, so long as ..." or "this would be very difficult" were equivalent to "forget it." In short, you never knew what was going on. When we said "yes" we meant it and they could count on it. And also when we said "no," we meant it as well, but the Chinese never took "no" for an answer. Sometimes I felt like I was in a kindergarten!

**Mr. Wang:** Reality is just too complex for simple "yes" or "no" answers. Everything depends on everything else and everything is in flow, so what matters is the overall picture. The Americans are always so proud of their analytical approach. But to "analyze," means to "take apart" and you simply can't just tear things apart and treat them as independent from each other. This is for us a sign of an immature view of the complexities of reality. We don't analyze reality, we take a holistic view, in order to comprehend the totality of the problem. Therefore, we could never comprehend how upset the Americans became when we asked to revise a certain point. Negotiations are a circular and iterative process, not a linear and sequential one!

## Chinese Lack of Technological Know-How

**Mr. Jones:** Another point we were never able to comprehend was the following: Often we detected a certain feeling of cultural superiority with the Chinese who appeared to look down on us. But then, at times, they fully surprised us by putting themselves down to the verge of self-humiliation. This was specifically the case when the negotiation touched upon technology and R&D. Here the Chinese openly admitted how backwards their technological standards were, which was all due to foolish Chinese politics in the past. Now they had to catch up and so our Chinese partners expressed straightforwardly their admiration for our advanced technology and their willingness to "learn from the Americans," pleading for our help. Deeply impressed by the Chinese ambitions, we felt it, to certain extent, as our moral duty to contribute with our technology to the development of this amazing country.

However, things soon went completely wrong when, after exploring the possibilities of our cooperation on the technology level, we moved on to the estimated costs of R&D, licensing fees, and others. What shocked us was that the Chinese refused to even consider paying for anything, and said they were truly disappointed at our intention to charge them for our technological know-how which was in clear opposition to the spirit of trust and good relations. They argued that it wouldn't cost us anything to just provide them with the know-how, as we already had the technology. Besides we are from a rich company and a rich country, while they were from a poor state-owned company in a still-developing country. The fact that we had spent hundreds of millions of dollars on R&D and that our company is fiercely competing with other big corporations on the world market and that we have to act in the best interest of our shareholders and can therefore not just give away technology for free was incomprehensible to our Chinese partners.

I think they somehow still had this notion in the back of their mind that for centuries foreigners traveled from all parts of the world to China, bringing with them their knowledge and goods which they freely offered as tribute and sign of respect to the Chinese who perceived themselves as the only real civilization on earth and the center of the world. Well, not with us!

**Mr. Wang:** We were deeply disappointed with the Americans' attitude about passing on technological know-how. We very much admire the American ingenuity to develop new products and we were eager to learn from them. But they apparently only wanted to engage in the JV to use cheap Chinese labor. And when we discussed technology transfer and expressed our interest in learning from them, they asked for outrageously high fees which we would never have been able to pay. We are from a still poor country and the Americans shouldn't try to take advantage of this and exploit us. I think they were acting very selfishly and immorally.

## Criticism

**Mr. Jones:** The Chinese never accepted any constructive criticism, however well intended. I admit, we Americans might be more direct than the Chinese and this might cause some friction, but why is it that we always have to adapt to them?

**Mr. Wang:** We were just tired of the Americans lecturing us all the time. They kept making critical comments about everything, about our interpreter who had a strong accent which made it difficult to understand him, about people in the streets who seldom obey traffic rules, about air pollution in the cities, and so on. At one point they even touched upon sensitive issues such as democracy, human rights, and Taiwan. How

dare they mingle into our internal affairs? That's none of their business.

## Conclusion

**Mr. Jones:** Despite all the obstacles and everything we had to put up with, we were almost there! We had gone through all points and agreed with much difficulty on each item. The day for the formal signature of the contract was set and our CEO planned to fly in for this event. We were all enthusiastic to finally go back home. At this point the Chinese negotiation leader came to us, apologized to us and said that some "little points" still had to be revisited on the request of his superiors. And it turned out that these "little points" were absolutely fundamental and purely unacceptable to us. I was absolutely furious and called him a dishonest game player. He realized that he might have gone too far, but it was too late. I told him that the deal was off. The next day we flew home. With people who behave in this way one can't do any business.

**Mr. Wang:** For us Chinese a negotiation starts with the first handshake and hasn't finished until the contract is signed. But the Americans seemed to be all content to have gone through their checklist with all their little items and only thought about going home. For us, however, it makes sense to leave everything open to further possible adjustment up to the very final stage, so that we can always re-consider earlier agreements. We can't just say "yes" or "no" to a little issue and then move on until you reached the end of the agenda. This is just a sign of naivety and immaturity.

And of course it is standard tactical negotiation behavior to try to score some final points at the very end, taking advantage of the tiredness of your negotiation partners. One of the advantages to negotiate on your home turf is that at the end the others are eager to return home and often willing to make some last minute concessions. Of course I didn't expect the Americans to fully agree to my proposals, but just a little concession would have been sufficient. They are rich enough to make one more compromise and I would have been regarded by my superiors as a clever negotiator to obtain some last minute concessions. Mr. Jones should have known that. But instead, he became all angry, shouted at me, and thus completely lost face. It is very unfortunate, but even in the future we cannot take up the negotiations again. With people who behave in this way one can't do any business.

1. What are the different approaches both parties take toward business negotiations?
2. What are the mistakes both parties have committed in this cross-cultural negotiation process, and what should they have done better?
3. What are the key characteristics of a successful cross-cultural negotiator?
4. How could both sides have prepared better to anticipate the problems faced in the negotiation?

CASE CREDIT

This case was written by Markus Pudelko, now Professor of International Business at Tübingen University, with assistance from Brian Stewart, former diplomat in China and from 1981 to 1998 adviser to American and British companies entering the Chinese market; from Sally Stewart, former Head of Department of Management at the University of Hong Kong; and from Xunyi Xu, student of Economics at Fudan University. Copyright 2005 Markus Pudelko. All rights reserved.

# Motivation in Multinational Companies

14

## Motivating Workers in China and India

As more multinationals move into China and India to take advantage of the opportunities in these countries, they are creating an intense competition for good workers. These multinational companies are finding it no easy task to attract the upwardly mobile Chinese and Indian professional with strong technical and international management skills. As domestic companies reform their operations, they are pursuing these same individuals. In China, where the average wage is $250 a month, money talks, especially in recruitment and retention. Skilled secretaries get monthly salaries that match or even double the yearly national average. When companies do not match the local market wages, job performance drops and turnover increases. In India, companies are giving significant pay raises to retain talented workers. Furthermore, many of the IT companies such as WIPRO and Infosys are finding it very difficult to retain expatriates. Many expatriates become frustrated as they find the pace of work and Indian companies' way of doing things intimidating and challenging.

In the case of China, however, recent trends show that pay is no longer the best motivator for workers. As many of the safety nets of the centrally controlled government (e.g., low-cost housing, health care, guaranteed jobs) have disappeared, budgeting for such items is slowly eating away at people's incomes. Additionally, corruption has become rampant. Chinese workers are becoming disenchanted with the uncertainties inherent in a capitalist society, and many job seekers are applying for civil servant or other government jobs to benefit from job security.

Other surveys suggest that multinational companies will have to become more creative to motivate their talented Chinese workers. As salary levels between cities and increases start to level off, multinational companies need to go beyond pay to motivate their workers. Some companies are finding that they need to provide adequate training programs, while others are refining their performance management systems to incorporate stronger pay-for-performance philosophies. A recent survey by Watson Wyatt showed that Chinese workers are increasingly looking for safer and healthier work

## Learning Objectives

*After reading this chapter you should be able to:*

- Recognize how people from different nations perceive the basic functions of working.

- Explain how people from different nations view the importance of working.

- Understand how the national context affects the basic processes of work motivation.

- Apply common theories of work motivation in different national contexts.

- Design jobs for high motivational potential in different national cultures.

environments where the organization shows genuine concern for their professional development.

Multinationals in India are experiencing similar circumstances. Unlike their parents, young Indian professionals do not necessarily value security and stability in a job. They grew up in an age of economic optimism and thus demand more of their employers. Multinationals need to develop plans to ensure that these new workers' energies are harnessed. However, these new employees come with high expectations. If they feel that their employers are not treating them well in terms of salary or advancement, they do not hesitate to find work in other companies or change careers. Multinationals thus have to devise appropriate plans to retain and motivate these new Indian employees.

*Sources: Based on Dominic, B. 2009. "Asia's future and the financial crisis." McKinsey Quarterly, 1, 102–105; Chaturvedi, A. 2012. "Companies across sectors hiking variable pay to retain talent." Economic Times, June 9, online edition; Chen, Kathy. 2006. "Free market rattles Chinese; Economists' ties questioned; Job seekers eye state positions." Wall Street Journal, January 26, A9; Hamm, S. 2008. "Young and impatient in India." Business Week, January 28, 45–48; Leininger, Jim. 2004. "The key to retention: Committed employees." China Business Review, January–February, 31, 16–17, 38–39; Phadnis, S. 2012. "Indian IT companies like Wipro, HCL, Infosys and Mindtree find it tough to hold on to expats." Economic Times, June 27, online edition.*

All managers must motivate their subordinates to accomplish organizational goals. However, as the Preview Case in Point showed, motivational techniques present significant challenges for companies. The motivational methods based on pay used previously by multinational companies in China or India are no longer working. New trends suggest that multinational companies need to constantly be aware of what workers seek in their work environment and adjust rapidly to satisfy those needs. As more multinational companies and domestic companies compete for the same talented workers, they are encountering increased pressure to find new ways to motivate and retain workers.

To provide the background necessary to understand how to motivate workers in multinational organizations, this chapter reviews differences in work values and in the meaning of work, discusses major theories of motivation and their multinational applications, and reviews U.S. and European views of designing jobs to produce high levels of motivation.

## Work Values and the Meaning of Work

Before we can understand how to motivate or lead people from different national cultures, we must have some knowledge about what work means to people from different societies. Two basic questions need to be answered: How important is work in people's lives? What do people value in work?

### How Important Is Work in People's Lives?

To answer this question, a number of major international research projects studied thousands of workers from several countries. These studies included workers in all types of occupations: professional, managerial, clerical, service, and production.[1] The most recent study, the World Values Surveys and European Values Surveys (WVS/EVS),[2] contains information on people's attitudes toward work and life from the 50 countries that include the majority of the world's population.

One question addressed in the Meaning of Work study is the degree to which people are attached to work. Work centrality is "the degree of general importance that working has in the life of an individual at any given point in time."[3] Work centrality represents the importance of work in a person's life when compared with other activities, including leisure, family, community, and religion.

Few studies have examined the country-level factors that lead to cross-national differences in work centrality. However, Parboteeah and Cullen used a combination of national culture (Chapter 2) and social institutions (Chapter 3) to examine work centrality differences in 26 nations.[4] They examined five social institutions, namely, the extent of socialism, the degree of industrialization, the degree of union strength, the accessibility of education, and the extent of social inequality, and they found that all five social institutions had negative effects on work centrality. In addition, the study looked at three of Hofstede's national culture dimensions.[5] Results showed that uncertainty avoidance and masculinity had negative effects on work centrality. In contrast, the cultural dimension of individualism had positive effects on work centrality.

The study showed that the traditional attachment to work typical of most industrialized societies may be changing. Such changes are consistent with Inglehart, Basanez, and Moreno's observation of a postmodern shift in many industrialized societies.[6] They argue that industrialized societies have long thrived on values that encouraged work centrality, economic achievement, individualism, and innovation but that these values have now reached their limits. In the postindustrialized societies, people are now more concerned with quality-of-life issues and individual self-expression.

Higher levels of work centrality are closely correlated with the average number of hours worked per week in the country (Chapter 12). That is, people from countries with great work centrality usually work long hours. The average Japanese worker, for example, puts in more hours than his or her counterpart in most other industrialized nations. Hence, managers may be able to apply management techniques that favor job-related incentives in order to motivate workers in societies with high work centrality. Consider the following Multinational Management Brief.

In general, high levels of work centrality may lead to dedicated workers and effective organizations. However, as the next Multinational Management Brief shows, high levels of work centrality can also have adverse effects on workers. Evidence suggests that the number of hours worked by the Japanese is declining and that many workers are complaining of burnout, perhaps indicating a change in work centrality for that country.[7]

In addition to work centrality, the levels of work obligation norms are important. In general, societies with high work obligation norms expect their citizens to view work as an obligation or a duty. These societies are more likely to have individuals who work longer hours. Exhibit 14.1 shows the levels of work obligations in various societies surveyed by the World Values Survey.[8] As the exhibit shows, many of the emerging economies, such as India, Turkey, Poland, and Bulgaria, show very high levels of work obligation norms. Such findings are encouraging for multinational companies with substantial investments in these countries. Many of these emerging economies now have much stricter monetary and fiscal policies and more stable financial systems.[9] The high work obligation norms, coupled with a more structurally sound financial environment, suggest that multinational companies will face a workforce with a very favorable view of work.

**Work centrality**
Overall value of work in a person's life.

**Work obligation norms**
Degree to which work is seen as an obligation or duty to society.

## Multinational Management **Brief**

### *Karoushi* and *Karojisatus*: Sudden Death or Suicide from Overwork

In Japanese, *karoushi* translates in English as "sudden death from overwork." *Karojisatus* is suicide from overwork. As we saw in Chapter 12, the Japanese work more hours than people from most other countries do. They also have the highest work-centrality score.

This psychological and time commitment to working probably accounts for some of the Japanese economic growth. However, there is some indication that the benefits may have physical and psychological costs. As most of the managers who led Japan through its period of growth reach later middle age, the costs to them of long working hours and other Japanese business practices (long hours of drinking and smoking with colleagues after work) may be taking its toll. Early evidence suggests that death from work-related stress is on the rise. Police estimate the number of work-related suicides at 1,300 annually, but they have no official classification for this type of death. Some lawyers representing surviving family members put the estimate higher.

However, besides death from overwork, Japan is also facing worker suicides caused by overwork. According to Japanese officials, 81 cases of worker suicides were attributed to stress over the 2007–2008 fiscal year. Over 40 percent of these deaths involved workers in their twenties and thirties. Furthermore, although Japanese officials only reported 66 suicides in 2011, experts suggest that the number is vastly underestimated. Japanese officials are alarmed because suicides will probably increase as the work environment incorporates more temporary workers who are more likely to commit suicide. Furthermore, recent reports suggest that the working population in Japan continues to shrink. This also implies greater pressure on the future workforce as fewer employees are available to maintain the productivity level. Finally, downsizing coupled with increased workload will also likely put more pressure on workers.

*Sources: Based on Economist. 2006. "Greying Japan—The downturn." January 7; Economist. 2012. "The vanishing workforce." February 24, online edition; Caryl, Christian. 2006. "Turning un–Japanese." Newsweek, February 20; Japan Times. 2012. "Worker's comp for mental illness," July 1, online edition; Jiji Press English News Service. 2008. "Worker suicides keep increasing in Japan." August 4; Tubbs, W. 1993. "Karoushi: Stress-death and the meaning of work." Journal of Business Ethics, 12, 869–877.*

Exhibit 14.1 also shows that more developed economies, such as the Netherlands, the United States, and Germany, have much lower work obligation norms. Such results are consistent with Inglehart, Basanez, and Moreno's post-industrialization shift.[10] Decades of prosperity have reduced the importance of a strong work ethic, and individuals in these societies no longer view work as a duty. However, other factors may also explain low work obligations. Consider the following Multinational Management Brief.

**Extrinsic work values**

Preference for the security aspects of jobs, such as income and job security.

## What Do People Value in Work?

The WVS/EVS study also looked at work values: what people expect from work. Two important work values are extrinsic work values and intrinsic work values. Individuals with **extrinsic work values** express a preference for security from their jobs, in terms of income, job security, and less demanding work, among other factors. In contrast,

**EXHIBIT 14.1** **Work Obligations Norms for Selected Countries**

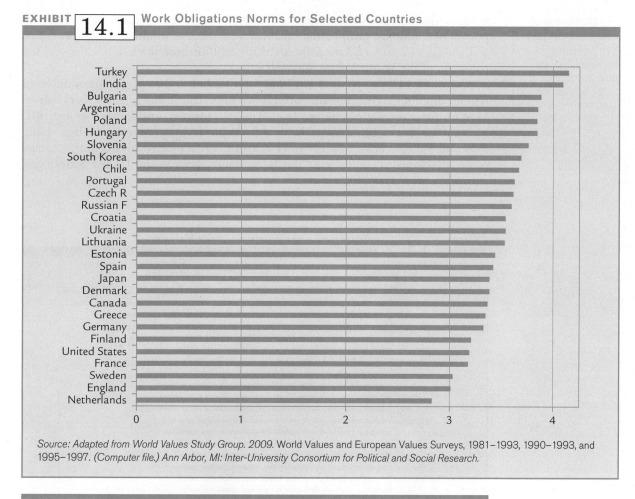

*Source: Adapted from World Values Study Group. 2009.* World Values and European Values Surveys, 1981–1993, 1990–1993, and 1995–1997. *(Computer file.) Ann Arbor, MI: Inter-University Consortium for Political and Social Research.*

## Multinational Management **Brief**

### Cubans and Work Obligations

Cuba has long operated under communism. Fidel Castro centralized power, expropriated private property, and closed both family businesses and foreign ventures. During the 1970s, Cuba relied on Soviet subsidies to survive. However, although the Soviet Union collapsed and caused harm to the island, the Venezuelan government came again to the rescue. Fidel Castro was able to exchange Cuban doctors for oil and this brought new life to the communist regime.

With the recent arrival of Fidel's brother, Raul Castro, Cuba is turning towards capitalism. However, work obligations for Cuban remain low. A major reason for such attitudes is that Fidel Castro mostly took away incentives for people to work while at the same time not sanctioning those who do not work. It is therefore not surprising to see a recent report that claims that Cubans often do not work too hard at their jobs and seem content to be chatting or talking on the phone. Decades of social programs such as free education, generous pensions, and free world-class health care have also meant that Cubans did not have to worry too much about how to make ends meet. However, the recent changes suggest that Cubans will soon have to face the reality where work becomes more important in their lives.

*Source: Based on* Economist. *2012. Cuba: Revolution in retreat. March 24, 3–12.*

**Intrinsic work values**

Preference for openness-to-change job aspects, such as autonomy and opportunities to take initiative and be creative.

workers with **intrinsic work values** express preferences for openness to change, the pursuit of autonomy, growth, and creativity, and the use of initiative at work.

Exhibits 14.2 and 14.3 show the extrinsic and intrinsic work values for selected countries of the World Values Survey.[11]

As Exhibit 14.2 shows, the most important finding is that people from different nations did not express the same preference for extrinsic and intrinsic work values. Most of the emerging economies (e.g., Turkey, Hungary, and India) rate extrinsic work values very highly. This probably reflects the situation in many of these countries where the security aspect of work is instrumental to survival. In contrast, many of the developed societies (e.g., the Netherlands, France, the United States) rate extrinsic work values much lower.

**EXHIBIT 14.2**   **Preference for Extrinsic Work Values**

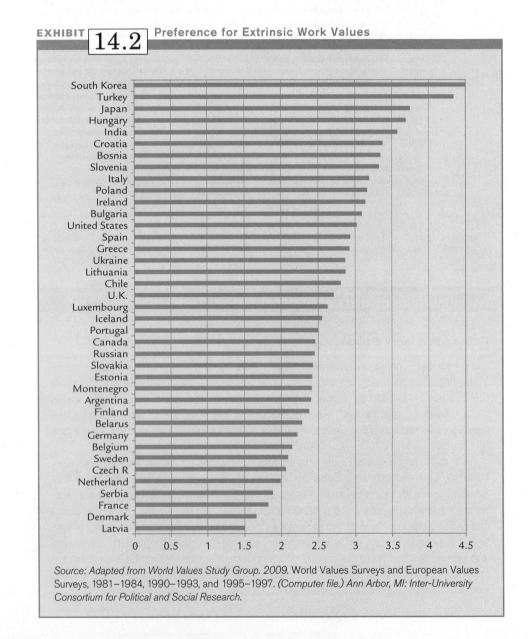

*Source: Adapted from World Values Study Group. 2009.* World Values Surveys and European Values Surveys, 1981–1984, 1990–1993, and 1995–1997. *(Computer file.) Ann Arbor, MI: Inter-University Consortium for Political and Social Research.*

**EXHIBIT 14.3**   Preference for Intrinsic Work Values

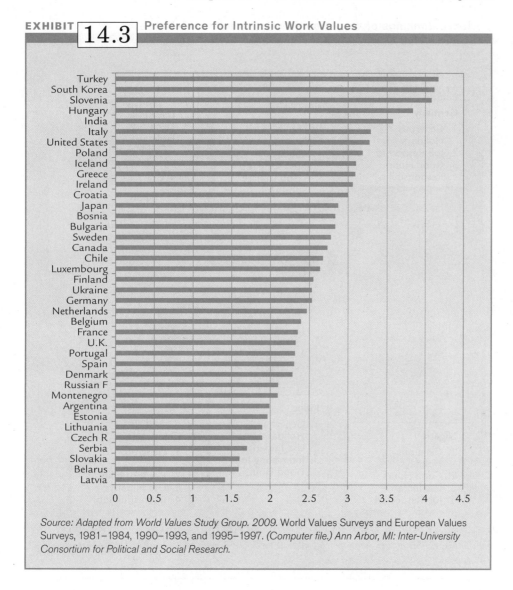

Source: Adapted from World Values Study Group. 2009. World Values Surveys and European Values Surveys, 1981–1984, 1990–1993, and 1995–1997. (Computer file.) Ann Arbor, MI: Inter-University Consortium for Political and Social Research.

Similar to extrinsic work values, findings for intrinsic work values show that people from different societies have varying preferences (see Exhibit 14.3). A surprising finding, however, is that many of the countries that rated extrinsic work values highly also rated intrinsic work values highly. This suggests that many of the emerging economies may view all work aspects positively, while people from developed nations do not see work in a positive light. Consequently, when crafting their motivational strategies for a local workforce, multinational managers must not assume that people from different nations express the same preferences for work values.

The WVS/EVS research team asked workers to note what characteristics of a job they believe are important. As shown in Exhibit 14.4, the priorities given to different job characteristics vary by country. Note, for example, that Japan and Russia differ from the world trend of giving a high priority to holidays. In spite of pay being a dominant function of work for many of the transitional and developing nations, no country rated pay as the most important work characteristic.

**EXHIBIT 14.4**  Importance Rankings of Work Characteristics in Nine Countries

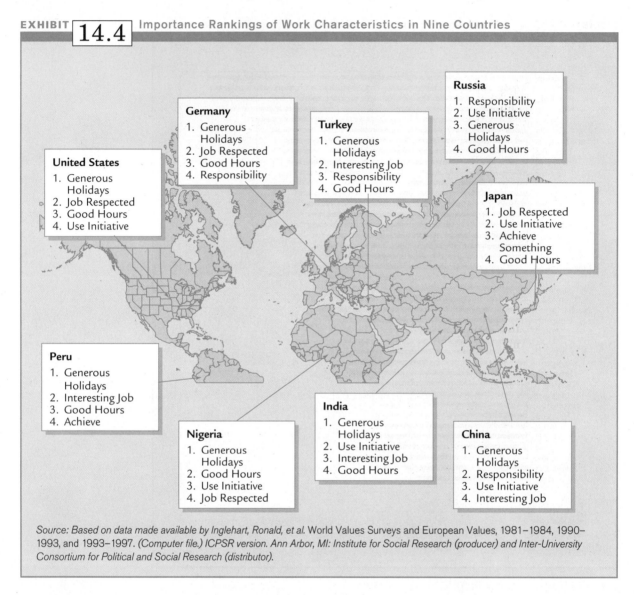

**United States**
1. Generous Holidays
2. Job Respected
3. Good Hours
4. Use Initiative

**Germany**
1. Generous Holidays
2. Job Respected
3. Good Hours
4. Responsibility

**Turkey**
1. Generous Holidays
2. Interesting Job
3. Responsibility
4. Good Hours

**Russia**
1. Responsibility
2. Use Initiative
3. Generous Holidays
4. Good Hours

**Japan**
1. Job Respected
2. Use Initiative
3. Achieve Something
4. Good Hours

**Peru**
1. Generous Holidays
2. Interesting Job
3. Good Hours
4. Achieve

**Nigeria**
1. Generous Holidays
2. Good Hours
3. Use Initiative
4. Job Respected

**India**
1. Generous Holidays
2. Use Initiative
3. Interesting Job
4. Good Hours

**China**
1. Generous Holidays
2. Responsibility
3. Use Initiative
4. Interesting Job

*Source: Based on data made available by Inglehart, Ronald, et al. World Values Surveys and European Values, 1981–1984, 1990–1993, and 1993–1997. (Computer file.) ICPSR version. Ann Arbor, MI: Institute for Social Research (producer) and Inter-University Consortium for Political and Social Research (distributor).*

The Meaning of Work study and the more current WVS/EVS study give us a good initial picture of how work values differ in national contexts. They suggest the following conclusions:

- In some societies, work is central and absorbs much of a person's life. People in such societies willingly work long hours and have a strong commitment to succeeding at work. However, in many industrialized countries that have traditionally been seen as valuing high work centrality (e.g., the United States and Japan), people may be changing their views of work. In contrast, less developed societies may have a workforce that places significant importance on the role of work in their lives.

- All people hope to receive certain benefits from work. Regardless of national context, money is a necessity, but it is not enough. Other emotional and practical benefits derived from work may have higher priorities. The benefits people hope to get from their jobs vary by national context.

- Societies differ in the degree to which they regard work as an obligation to society. Societies that have high work-obligation norms are more likely to have individuals working longer to conform to such duties.

- Many of the emerging economies that value extrinsic work values such as income and job security also place a high value on intrinsic work values. Multinational companies need to provide jobs that not only offer adequate compensation but also offer job satisfaction.

- The first key to successful motivational strategies in multinational companies is understanding the differences among countries in the functions of work, work centrality, and the priorities given to different job characteristics.

Multinational managers must understand that people from different countries often have their own reasons for working and certain priorities regarding the important attributes of their jobs. Although this knowledge is important to have, is it all a manager needs to motivate and manage a multinational workforce successfully? Probably not. To use the knowledge of national differences in work attitudes for motivational purposes, the manager needs to understand how basic motivational principles work in the multinational environment. To give you this background, the next sections provide reviews of the basic work motivation process, of popular theories of work motivation, and of applications of work motivation theories to multinational settings.

# Work Motivation and National Context

## The Basic Work Motivation Process

Why do some people set goals that are more difficult and put forth more effort to achieve them than others? Why do some students seek A's while other students feel satisfied with C's? Why do some workers seek jobs that are more difficult and work harder at them, even if the pay is not higher? These questions address the issue of motivation.

Motivation concerns all managers. Managers want their subordinates motivated to achieve organizational goals. Toward this end, managers choose incentives (e.g., pay, promotion, recognition) and punishments (e.g., salary reduction), and they design work (e.g., with simple or complex tasks) based on their assumptions and knowledge concerning what motivates people.

If a manager believes that her subordinates work only to meet their basic needs, such as feeding and clothing themselves and their families, she may use wages and bonuses as her major motivational tool. Alternatively, if a manager believes that people work to find fulfillment in doing a challenging job well, she might assign subordinates complex, varied, and interesting tasks. Managers usually respond positively to people (e.g., with raises) who help the organization achieve its goals and negatively (e.g., with bad evaluations) to employees who fail to help the organization achieve its goals.

The left side of Exhibit 14.5 presents a picture summarizing the psychological processes that most experts use to explain work motivation. A brief explanation of these underlying psychological processes follows.

Psychologists see motivation as a psychological process that results in goal-directed behaviors that satisfy human needs. A need is a feeling of a deficit or lack that all people experience at some time. Although needs differ for individuals and for cultural groups, all people seek to satisfy them. A need might be very basic,

**Motivation**
A psychological process resulting in goal-directed behavior that satisfies human needs.

**Need**
Feeling of deficit or lack that all people experience at some time.

**EXHIBIT** 14.5     The Basic Work Motivation Process and the National Context

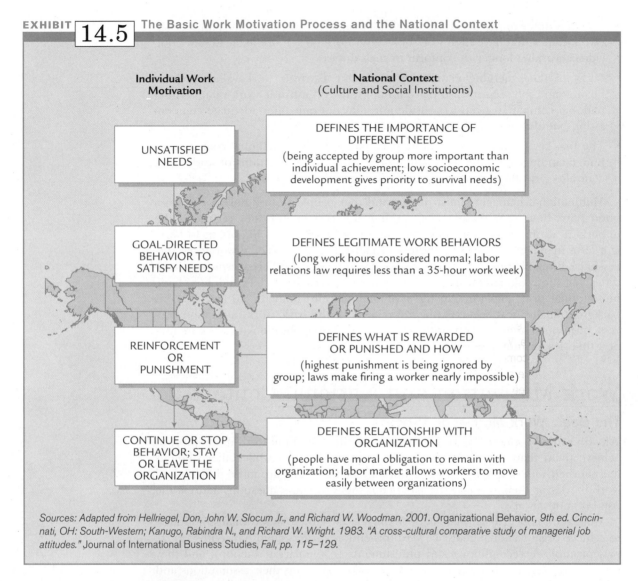

Sources: Adapted from Hellriegel, Don, John W. Slocum Jr., and Richard W. Woodman. 2001. Organizational Behavior, 9th ed. Cincinnati, OH: South-Western; Kanugo, Rabindra N., and Richard W. Wright. 1983. "A cross-cultural comparative study of managerial job attitudes." Journal of International Business Studies, Fall, pp. 115–129.

such as being hungry for the next meal. A need might be more complex, such as the need to be the best at something. To satisfy the hunger need, you may go to work to earn money to buy food. To satisfy an achievement need, you might practice ice skating daily with the ultimate goal of becoming an Olympic champion. In each case, a person uses **goal-directed behaviors** (i.e., work or practice) to satisfy unfulfilled or unsatisfied needs (i.e., hunger or the need for achievement). Goal-directed behaviors are behaviors that people use with the intention of satisfying a need.

Although satisfying needs is a general condition for human motivation, people use the work setting to satisfy many needs. For example, for most people, work is necessary to provide food and shelter. In addition, as you saw from the WVS/EVS study, working provides people with an opportunity to satisfy needs such as affording leisure, having interesting things to do, having responsibility, having a chance to use initiative, and developing relationships with other people. Many theories of work motivation have a basic assumption that people will work harder if they can satisfy more of their needs on the job.

**Goal-directed behavior**

Behavior that people use with the intention of satisfying a need.

## Focus on Emerging Markets

### Motivating Workers at Tata Group

As India continues attracting investment and world talent, attention is being paid to some of India's most well-known corporations, such as Infosys, Reliance, and Tata. These companies have shown that they can produce goods and services to compete in the world market. This increased attention to Indian conglomerates has brought some interest in the Tata Group and its unique approach to motivating workers.

The Tata Group has been around for more than 130 years and is still pursuing its nineteenth-century mission of making India an industrial power. Today, the Tata Group is a family conglomerate that is involved in such business sectors as cars and steel, software and consulting, and even luxury hotels. Tata has recently started producing one of the cheapest cars in the world, the Tata Nano. Furthermore, Tata has also continued expansion into foreign markets. For instance, its expansion into Britain has now made Tata the largest manufacturer there. However, despite thriving in a brutal global economy, the Tata Group has stayed true to its liberal roots of first taking care of its workers.

Consider, for example, the town of Jamshedpur, which was created by one of the founders of Tata. When the town was created in Calcutta, it was based on socialist principles. The company built schools, churches, parks, and a hospital, and provided housing to workers. In addition to satisfying many of the workers' obvious needs, the company provided generous employee benefits. It cut the workday to eight hours and undertook efforts to make the work environment better. To this day, the steel mill and the surrounding town are thriving as Tata tries to modernize them. Furthermore, although India is generally prone to having regular strikes, Tata's steel arm has gone decades without one.

This concern for workers is replicated across all of Tata's businesses. Although many of the company's executives have MBAs from Western universities, they are very aware of Tata's mission and view layoffs and downsizing as very "un-Tata." Tata works hard to ensure that workers have access not only to basic needs but also to a good work environment. Such principles are still based today on the founder's philosophical beliefs.

*Sources: Based on Birmingham Post. 2009. "Indian firms in driving seat to give best staff new Tata Nano car," April 27, 27; Economist. 2012. "Tata for now." September 10, online edition. Patel, Vibhuti. 2005. "India, Inc.: No longer just an outsourcing hub for low-level jobs, India is luring American talent and unprecedented new investments by tech giants Microsoft and Intel." Newsweek, December 19, http://www.msnbc.msn.com/id/10455090/site/newsweek; Wehrfritz, George, and Ron Moreau. 2006. "A new kind of company: Tata coddles workers, not managers, keeps its distance from Wall Street—yet thrives in brutal global industries as a uniquely Indian kind of multinational." Newsweek, http://www.msnbc.msn.com/id/8359069/site/newsweek.*

The above Focus on Emerging Markets shows how the world-class Indian conglomerate Tata Motors uses both satisfaction of needs and work setting to motivate its workers.

Because most goal-directed behaviors take place in a social context, motivation includes more than satisfying needs; that is, when we do things that affect others, people react positively or negatively. In reinforcement theory, we call these reactions reinforcement and punishment. **Reinforcement** means that the consequences that follow a person's behavior encourage the person to continue the behavior.

**Reinforcement**
Reactions to a person's behavior that encourage the person to continue the behavior.

**Punishment** means that the consequences that follow a person's behavior encourage the person to stop the behavior. In the work setting, for example, managers use reinforcement, such as bonus pay, to encourage certain behaviors, such as increased daily output. Managers also use punishment, such as docking pay, to discourage behaviors, such as missing days of work. Based on whether they meet their needs at work and how managers react to their behaviors at work, employees may put more or less effort into work, feel satisfied or dissatisfied, or stay with or leave the organization.

# National Context and Work Motivation: A Brief Introduction

Although certain basic needs are common to all humans (e.g., the need for food and shelter), national context (culture and social institutions) influences all steps of the motivational process. The right side of Exhibit 14.5 shows the effects of the national context on the work-motivation process. Each box contains two examples. One example shows an effect of national culture on the motivation process. The other example shows an effect of social institutions on the motivational process. More explanation and examples follow.

Cultural values, norms, and supporting social institutions—important aspects of any society's business context—influence the priority that people attach to work in general and the types of needs that people hope to satisfy at work. For example, early education and childhood games encourage people in collectivist societies to develop a need to belong to groups. National context also helps to define behaviors that provide legitimate ways to satisfy needs. For example, in countries such as Japan, where work is central to a person's status and self-image, seeking a job in the largest and most prestigious company satisfies a need for achievement.

The national context influences reactions to goal-directed behaviors at work. For example, if a Japanese worker brags about her performance, she is likely to be sanctioned by her work group. The Japanese have a saying: "The nail that stands out gets hammered down." Finally, national culture and social institutions influence the levels of satisfaction workers expect to receive in an organization and how committed they are to their organization and its goals. For example, in countries where labor is well-organized and militant, resistance to increases in work productivity is considered legitimate. Consider the next Case in Point, in which national cultural context clearly influences the techniques that can be used to motivate workers in Thailand.

This brief overview of work motivation and the effects of national context provide only an introduction to the complexities of motivating international workers. Next, the chapter expands on the basic model of work motivation. In the following sections, we will review several motivation theories and discuss how national context influences the application of each motivation theory and how the multinational manager can use it.

# Theories of Work Motivation in the Multinational Context

Work-motivation theories attempt to show how basic motivational processes apply to a work setting. Managers can use the theories to develop systematic approaches to motivating employees on the job. There are two basic types of motivational

### CASE IN POINT

## Motivating Thais: Cultural Influences

As multinational companies increase their investments in Thailand, being able to understand and motivate Thai workers is becoming crucial. In fact, recent trends suggest that Thailand continues to be a destination of choice for many countries, including the United States. For example, the Ford–Mazda AutoAlliance Thailand assembly plant manufactures cars and pickup trucks for sale in more than 130 markets. Toyota is also seriously pursuing efforts to open a gearbox plant in Thailand. Between 2004 and 2007, imports from Thailand grew by more than 15 percent, as U.S. companies extended their supply chains into Thailand to take advantage of high productivity and low cost.

A Hofstede study revealed that Thailand has a high score on collectivism, moderately high scores on uncertainty avoidance, and a low score on masculinity. Motivational do's and don'ts garnered from practical experience in Thailand suggest that cultural influences may be very helpful in determining what works and what does not.

The high score on collectivism suggests that Thais are very attentive to the needs of in-groups. They generally function better in groups, and harmonious relationships are preferred. Not surprisingly, care must be taken not to criticize individual employees openly. Furthermore, senior Thais deserve *hai-kiat* (respect), and arguing with them in front of junior staff can be devastating. *Sia ñah* (losing face) is the ultimate humiliation and must be avoided.

The moderately high score on uncertainty avoidance implies that Thais prefer structure in their jobs and organizations to make things more certain and predictable. Unclear instructions or an organizational structure without clear lines of communication can be very demotivating. Managers are thus advised to provide clear structure.

Finally, the low score on masculinity, or the more feminine nature of the culture, suggests a preference for family and quality of life as opposed to work. It is imperative to understand Thais' appreciation of work and to avoid training on weekends or expecting Thais to invest their personal time in the company. Motivational practices should focus on integration of the family.

*Sources: Based on Field, A. M. 2009. "Fall from grace." Journal of Commerce, February 9, 56–60; Hofstede, Geert. 2001. Culture's Consequences: International Differences in Work-Related Values, 2nd ed. London: Sage; M2 Presswire, 2006. "Research and markets: An analysis of the latest happenings in the automotive manufacturing industry from around the world," January 11; Niratpattanasai, Kriengsak. 2002. "How to make work miserable." Bangkok Post, November 22, 1; Sawyer, Christopher A. 2006. "Ford making Tracs for Thailand." Automotive Design & Production, February, 28; Thapanachai, Somporn. 2006. "Oldest Californian firm picks Saraburi." Bangkok Post, February 21, 1.*

theories: need theories and process theories. The following section summarizes the major need theories of motivation, which have the most international applications. A later section considers process theories.

## The Need Theory of Motivation

The **need theory** of motivation rests on the assumption that people can satisfy basic human needs in the work setting; that is, people are motivated to work because their jobs satisfy both basic needs, such as money for food and shelter, and higher-level needs, such as personal growth.

There are four popular need theories of motivation:

1. Maslow's hierarchy of needs
2. ERG theory
3. Motivator-hygiene theory
4. Achievement motivation theory

**Need theory**
Theory of motivation that assumes people can satisfy basic human needs in the work setting.

**EXHIBIT** 14.6    Need Theories of Motivation

| Source of Need Satisfaction on the Job | Maslow's Needs Hierarchy | ERG Theory | Motivator-Hygiene Theory | Achievement Motivation |
|---|---|---|---|---|
| • Advancement<br>• Use of ability<br>• Meaningful work<br>• Achievement<br>• Interesting job | Self-actualization | Growth | Motivators<br>• Advancement<br>• Growth<br>• Achievement | Need for achievement |
| • Recognition<br>• Influence<br>• Esteem | Esteem | | | Need for power |
| • Coworker support<br>• Supervisor support<br>• Social interaction | Affiliation | Relatedness | Hygiene factors<br>• Working conditions<br>• Job security<br>• Salary | Need for affiliation |
| • Work conditions<br>• Benefits<br>• Security | Security | Existence | | |
| • Base pay | Physiological | | | |

*Sources: Adapted from Daft, Richard L. 1991.* Management, *2nd ed. Chicago: Dryden; Gordon, Judith R. 1987.* A Diagnostic Approach to Organizational Behavior. *Boston: Allyn &; Bacon; Hellriegel, Don, John W. Slocum Jr., and Richard W. Woodman. 2001.* Organizational Behavior, *9th ed. Cincinnati, OH: South-Western.*

This section briefly reviews each theory. You can find more detailed reviews of these and other theories of motivation in courses and texts in organizational behavior. Exhibit 14.6 gives a summary and comparison of these four theories and also shows the characteristics of jobs that can satisfy the types of needs identified by them.

## Maslow's Hierarchy of Needs

The psychologist Abraham Maslow offered perhaps the most famous need theory of motivation.[12] The **hierarchy of needs theory** states that people have five basic types of needs: physiological, security, affiliation, esteem, and self-actualization. Physiological needs include basic survival such as food, water, air, and shelter. Security needs include safety and the avoidance of pain and life-threatening situations. Affiliation needs include being loved, having friendship, and belonging to a human group. Esteem needs focus on respect, recognition by others, and feelings of self-worth. Self-actualization needs, the highest level in Maslow's theory, are those associated with maximizing personal achievement.

Maslow believed that the five basic needs follow a hierarchy from the lower to the higher levels. First, people seek to satisfy lower-level needs, such as the physiological need for food and shelter. After they fulfill these lower-level needs, people seek to satisfy higher-level needs, such as the need for esteem. According to Maslow, once a need is satisfied, it no longer motivates. Thus, for example, if your base pay is adequate for survival, it has no motivational value. Then other characteristics of the work situation, such as working in teams to meet affiliation needs, become motivational. Consider the following Multinational Management Brief.

**Hierarchy of needs theory**
States that people have five basic types of needs: physiological, security, affiliation, esteem, and self-actualization.

---

## Multinational Management **Brief**

### Employee Motivation in Greece and Zambia

Understanding what employees expect from their work is very useful for multinationals. Motivation can take place through extrinsic motivators (salary, working conditions, job security) and intrinsic motivators (opportunities for creativity, opportunities to use initiative, and how others perceive the job).

By satisfying work expectations, companies can ensure that their employees are motivated to do their best. In a study of the Greek public sector, researchers were able to determine the key motivators. When surveyed employees were asked what they perceived to be the most important motivators, the answer was extrinsic work motivators. This finding suggests that Greek employees see that satisfaction of their basic needs is very critical. As long as basic needs are not being fully satisfied, Maslow's hierarchy of needs suggests that satisfaction of such basic needs will motivate workers.

Consider another study that examined the situation of public health workers in Zambia. These workers have been receiving very low salaries, as the government has been continuously slashing their pay. As a result, existing Zambian health workers are not very motivated to stay on the job and the attrition rate has been very high. To address the challenges of a severe shortage of health workers, the Zambian government has now implemented measures to start encouraging employees to come back to the health sector. Many of the new policies pertain to the satisfaction of basic needs. For example, the government has started providing housing allowances, rural hardship allowances (to make sure workers stay in hard to reach locations), and other allowances. This also suggests that employers need to first satisfy basic needs before other needs become motivating.

*Sources: Based on Gow, J., G. George, S. Mwamba, L. Ingombe, and G. Mutinta. 2012. "Health workers satisfaction and motivation: An empirical study of incomes, allowances and working conditions in Zambia." International Journal of Business and Management, May, 7, 10, 37–48; Human Resource Management International Digest. 2008. "Does the board know whether it is the money, or the love?" 16(3): 14–16.*

---

The current opinion on Maslow's approach suggests that, while there are two groups of needs representing higher- and lower-level needs, the need hierarchy does not work in sequence. Moreover, not all available jobs in a country provide the activities required to meet all levels of needs.[13]

### Alderfer's ERG Theory

Clay Alderfer developed **ERG theory** as a simplified hierarchy of needs having only three levels (see Exhibit 14.6 for a comparison with Maslow's theory):[14] growth needs, relatedness needs, and existence needs. Growth needs are similar to Maslow's self-actualization and esteem needs. Work is motivating when it provides the opportunity for personal growth, such as by using one's creativity. Relational needs are similar to Maslow's affiliation needs. Getting support from one's work group satisfies relational needs. Existence needs are lower-level needs and represent basic survival needs.

In ERG theory, the frustration of a need motivates behavior to satisfy the need. In addition, a person who cannot satisfy a higher-level need will seek to satisfy

**ERG theory**
Simplified hierarchy of needs: growth needs, relatedness needs, and existence needs.

lower-level needs. For example, if the satisfaction of growth needs is impossible on the job, satisfaction of relational needs becomes the prime motivator.

### Motivator-Hygiene Theory

Proposed by Frederick Herzberg, the **motivator-hygiene theory** assumes that a job has two basic characteristics, motivators and hygiene factors.[15] Motivating factors are the characteristics of jobs that allow people to fulfill higher-level needs. For example, a challenging job might allow someone to meet his or her need for heightened levels of achievement. Hygiene factors are characteristics of jobs that allow people to fulfill lower-level needs, such as when good benefits and working conditions satisfy security needs.

Motivating factors arise from the content or the actual tasks that people perform on the job. Hygiene factors focus on the context or the setting in which the job takes place. Therefore, for example, tasks that allow you to use your abilities are motivators. However, the size of your desk and the color of your office are context or hygiene factors. Unlike other need theories, which assume that the desire to satisfy any type of need can motivate, Herzberg argued that satisfying lower-level needs at work (i.e., the hygiene factors) brings people only to a neutral state of motivation. To move employees beyond just a neutral reaction to the job, managers must build motivators into the context of a job (e.g., provide interesting tasks). Thus, only the opportunity to satisfy higher-level needs increases motivation.

### Achievement-Motivation Theory

The psychologist David McClelland identified three key needs as the basis of motivation:[16] achievement, affiliation, and power (see Exhibit 14.6). However, most of McClelland's influential work focused on achievement motivation. **Achievement-motivation theory** suggests that some people (approximately 10 percent in the United States) have the need to win in competitive situations or to exceed a standard of excellence. High achievement-motivated people like to set their own goals. They seek challenging situations but avoid goals that they feel are too difficult. Because they like to achieve success in their goals, high achievers desire immediate feedback. They like to know how they are performing at every step leading to a goal.

McClelland believed that achievement motivation is fixed in early childhood and that different cultures have different levels of achievement motivation. Some evidence supports McClelland's contention of different levels of achievement motivation in different cultures. However, there is no clear evidence regarding whether nations with more achievement-motivated people have better economic performance.[17]

### Needs and National Context

There are both similarities and divergence in the needs that people from different nations seek to satisfy by working. Similarities of needs across cultures occur because people tend to group needs into similar clusters or categories;[18] that is, regardless of national background, people see their work-related needs *grouped* in ways that match the broad groups proposed by need theories of motivation.

However, national groups vary in two ways on how people see needs being satisfied at work. First, people from different nations do not give the same priorities to the needs that might be satisfied at work. For example, as shown in Exhibit 14.7, Hungarians give a high priority to satisfying physiological needs through higher base pay. This is not true for people from some other countries, such as China or Holland. Second, even if workers from different countries have similar needs, they may not give the same level of importance to satisfying these needs. For example, one cross-national comparison found that interesting work (something that satisfies growth needs) ranked as the most important work goal for Japanese, British, and Belgian workers. However, interesting work was still relatively more important for Belgian workers than it was for Japanese and British workers.[19]

Can multinational managers use need satisfaction as a motivational tool? Yes, it can serve as a motivational tool, if multinational managers take into account the particular needs that people in a nation seek to satisfy in the work setting. Consider the following Case in Point, which gives examples of companies that increased motivation by linking organizational goals to the local employees' needs.

What differences in need satisfaction might multinational managers expect to find in different countries? Exhibit 14.7 illustrates some of the differences in the priorities given to job-related sources of need satisfaction by people from a group of nations.[20] The exhibit divides the rankings of job-related sources of need satisfaction into three groups: high (H) for the top third, middle (M) for the middle third, and low (L) for the bottom third. Exhibit 14.7 also shows the job-related sources of need satisfaction in terms of Maslow's need hierarchy. For cross-referencing to other need theories, see Exhibit 14.6, which shows how Maslow's need hierarchy relates to other need theories.

**EXHIBIT 14.7**

Rankings of the Importance of Job-Related Sources of Need Satisfaction for Seven Countries (H = upper third, M = middle third, L = bottom third, 1 = highest rank)

| Job-Related Sources of Satisfaction for: | China | Germany | Holland | Hungary | Israel | Korea | United States |
|---|---|---|---|---|---|---|---|
| **Self-actualization needs** | | | | | | | |
| • Advancement | M | M | H | L | H | H | H |
| • Use of ability | H | H | H | H | M | H | H |
| • Meaningful work | M | H | M | M | M | M | M |
| • Achievement | 1 | M | H | H | 1 | 1 | H |
| • Interesting job | H | 1 | 1 | H | H | H | 1 |
| **Esteem needs** | | | | | | | |
| • Recognition | M | L | M | H | M | M | M |
| • Influence | M | L | M | L | L | L | L |
| • Esteem | H | M | M | M | H | L | H |
| **Affiliation needs** | | | | | | | |
| • Coworker support | M | H | H | M | M | H | L |
| • Supervisor support | M | H | M | M | H | H | M |
| • Interaction | L | L | M | M | L | L | L |
| **Security needs** | | | | | | | |
| • Work conditions | L | L | L | M | L | M | L |
| • Benefits | L | H | L | M | M | M | M |
| • Security | L | H | M | M | L | H | M |
| **Physiological needs** | | | | | | | |
| • Base pay | L | M | L | H | M | M | L |

*Source: Adapted from Elizur, Dov, Ingwer Borg, Raymond Hunt, and Istvan Magyari Beck. 1991. "The structure of work values: A cross cultural comparison." Journal of Organizational Behavior, 12, pp. 21–38.*

## Finding the Right Needs in Central and Eastern Europe

Central and Eastern European countries remain attractive destinations for foreign investment. Most major foreign investors coming from neighboring Germany and Austria, as well as U.S. investors, see these growing markets as very lucrative. However, despite being in the region for a decade, foreign investors still face challenges.

For instance, taking over a formerly state-owned firm in Poland turned out to be a motivational challenge for the Finnish paper and power equipment firm Ahlstrom Fakop. Morale and sales were low, and the new management searched for ways to improve the situation. The first try, offering incentive pay, produced no results. As workers who had recently entered a market economy, the East European employees of Ahlstrom Fakop had needs other than money. Decades of communism had ingrained an expectation of a guaranteed job. When told that their jobs were secure if sales and productivity targets were met, workers responded positively with increases in both. It seems that the anxiety produced by the transition to a market economy made keeping a job more important than bonuses for productivity.

When Dow Chemical took over a crumbling chemical plant in the former East Germany, it inherited a bloated workforce and the knowledge that it would need to lay off 400 workers. To ease the culture shock of the transition to a market-based company and to increase productivity, Dow built a motivational system based on trust and individual initiative. Many workers adapted well to the system, using the newfound independence to achieve heightened levels of performance and promotions. However, some floundered, confused by managers who did not watch their every move and a distrust of those with power.

A recent study of Polish information technology workers also provides some understanding of worker motivation. The study suggests that the hygiene factors (context surrounding the job) are extremely critical for these workers; they are not necessarily motivated by salary. Rather, Polish IT workers tend to respond better when the social context within which the work is organized—where, for example, the team working on a project—is well organized.

Trends suggest that many multinational companies are now facing a challenge of a new kind. After being in the former East Germany for a decade, many companies are finding that the pool of inexpensive talent is slowly drying up. Local companies have made substantial progress and are competing with foreign companies for the same local talent. As a consequence, attracting and retaining talented employees are becoming the most important challenges. Such trends suggest that properly understanding Eastern European workers will become even more critical in the future.

*Sources: Based on Dougherty, Carter. 2006. "Eastern Europe at crossroads."* International Herald Tribune, *January 19; Dougherty, Carter. 2006. "Europe's young economies grow up but retain appeal: Even as costs rise, investors keep going east."* International Herald Tribune, *January 18; Fargher, S., S. Kesting, T. Lange, and G. Pacheco. 2009. "Cultural heritage and job satisfaction in Eastern and Western Europe."* International Journal of Manpower, *29(7): 630–650; Lubienska, K., and J. Wazniak. 2012. "Managing IT workers."* Business, Management and Education, *10(1): 77–90; Warren, Susan. 2000. "Five-year mission: For Dow, a dirty job in Germany presented a chance to clean up—to court eastern Europe, it wrestled a dinosaur from the Communist era—Razing 'the glittering hall.'"* Wall Street Journal, *May 19, A1.*

As Exhibit 14.7 shows, people from different nations do not necessarily prioritize their sources of need satisfaction at work as suggested by need theories. For example, although most need theories suggest that higher-level needs (e.g., self-actualization) should be most important regardless of national background, many sources of satisfying self-actualization needs had only moderate importance. Only the need for interesting work fell into the top third classification for all seven countries. High levels of potential need satisfiers on the job were found at all levels of the need hierarchy. In Germany, for example, perhaps because of the social institutional support for labor, job characteristics that could satisfy security and affiliation needs were as important as those related to self-actualization needs.

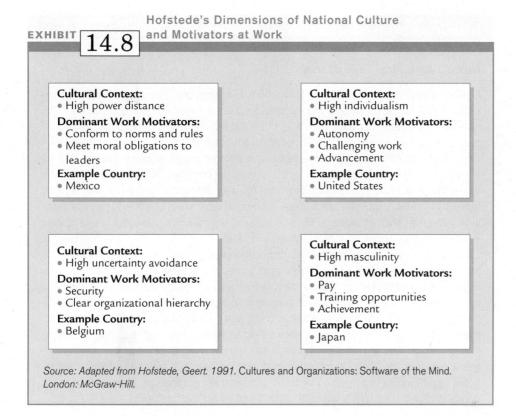

**EXHIBIT 14.8**   Hofstede's Dimensions of National Culture and Motivators at Work

**Cultural Context:**
- High power distance

**Dominant Work Motivators:**
- Conform to norms and rules
- Meet moral obligations to leaders

**Example Country:**
- Mexico

**Cultural Context:**
- High individualism

**Dominant Work Motivators:**
- Autonomy
- Challenging work
- Advancement

**Example Country:**
- United States

**Cultural Context:**
- High uncertainty avoidance

**Dominant Work Motivators:**
- Security
- Clear organizational hierarchy

**Example Country:**
- Belgium

**Cultural Context:**
- High masculinity

**Dominant Work Motivators:**
- Pay
- Training opportunities
- Achievement

**Example Country:**
- Japan

*Source: Adapted from Hofstede, Geert. 1991.* Cultures and Organizations: Software of the Mind. *London: McGraw-Hill.*

Many multinational managers work in emerging or formerly state-controlled economies, where there is little available information on the often-evolving employee attitudes toward work. How can the manager anticipate need differences in such countries? In these cases, skillful managers must anticipate worker needs based on cultural norms and values and institutional conditions. Hofstede's work gives some additional hints on how a multinational manager might do this.[21] Exhibit 14.8 shows some of the motivators at work, as identified by Hofstede, for different types of national cultures (see Chapter 2). Hofstede's work suggests that satisfying high-level needs at work may apply better to highly individualistic cultures. In addition, he cautions that need satisfaction may not be a motivator at all in some high-power-distance countries dominated by norms of service to the elite.

## Applying Need Theories in Multinational Settings

Here are some points to consider in adapting need theories of motivation to the international context:

- *Identify the basic functions of work in the national or local culture:* Where work is not central, people may satisfy their needs outside the work setting, limiting the manager's use of need satisfaction as a motivational tool.

- *Identify the needs considered most important by workers in the national or local culture:* The evidence presented in this chapter shows that need priorities differ by national context. Managers should identify cultural differences in potential need satisfiers at work and focus on providing jobs that satisfy them. Consider the next Multinational Management Brief.

## Multinational Management **Brief**

### Nokia's New Plant in Romania

Nokia decided to close its factory in Bochum, Germany, because it was becoming too expensive. When looking for a replacement location, it considered several places in the usual emerging markets, such as China and India, but it chose Cluj, Romania. Why Cluj? Nokia found that wages are quickly rising in countries such as China and India. However, Nokia found that Cluj had a plentiful supply of eager workers looking to take advantage of opportunities offered by a multinational company. Nokia could not expand its facility in Komarom, Hungary, because most of the local workforce was already tapped. In contrast, Cluj still had a largely untapped workforce, and it is home to a technical university that provides a ready supply of engineering graduates. In fact, over 8,000 individuals showed up at a job fair, and Nokia had plans to hire only 500 people.

Nokia expects to keep most of its new employees in Cluj by satisfying local needs. Most of the residents of Cluj are emerging from poverty resulting from the dictatorial regime. Nokia expects that it can satisfy workers by providing competitive wages, but the firm wants to look beyond cost and work to retain these employees. As multinationals have dealt with similar issues in India and China, they found that wages can rise quickly and workers are then quickly willing to work for the highest offer. To ensure that the employees are retained, Nokia is offering many other perks at the plant: a cafeteria with free food, a gym, and other features. Furthermore, Nokia is offering international opportunities not usually available in Romanian companies. By satisfying such needs in its workers, Nokia hopes to attract and retain the best employees.

*Source: Based on Chaturvedi, A. 2012. "Companies across sectors hiking variable pay to retain talent."* Economic Times, *June 9, online edition; Ewing, J. 2008. "Nokia's new home in Romania."* Business-Week, *January 28, 40–42.*

- *Sources of need fulfillment may differ for the same needs:* Even if people from different cultures have the same needs, they may find different sources of fulfillment on the job. For example, people from different cultures may consider interesting work the most important need, but they may have quite different ideas about what is interesting work. Hofstede's work suggests that individualism and power distance represent important dimensions of national culture that affect how people find need satisfaction at work.

- *Understand the limitations of available jobs to satisfy needs:* Although satisfying higher-level needs is possible in most industrialized countries, the same may not be true in many developing nations. Existing jobs may provide only the satisfaction of basic needs for survival.

To increase the motivation of host-country workers or to solve other motivational problems, multinational managers can consider approaches to motivation other than need theories. Next, the chapter will provide reviews of additional theories of motivation and their applications to multinational settings.

## Process and Reinforcement Theories of Motivation

In this section, we briefly review the process theories of motivation known as expectancy theory, equity theory, and goal-setting theory. More complex than need theories, **process theories** assume that motivation arises from needs and values *combined* with an individual's beliefs regarding the work environment. Besides the popular versions of these theories, this section reviews reinforcement theory and its application to multinational settings. These approaches to motivation receive fewer applications in the international setting than do need theories. However, we can draw some tentative conclusions regarding how they work in national settings. For a complete review of these theories, students should consult any current organizational behavior textbook.

## Expectancy Theory

Victor Vroom proposed a view of motivation that is more complex than simple need satisfaction.[22] This theory and its later variants are known as **expectancy theory**. Vroom proposed that work motivation is a function not only of an individual's needs or values, but also of an individual's beliefs regarding what happens if you work hard. Expectancy theory assumes that part of motivation is an individual's desire to satisfy his or her needs. However, the level of motivation also depends on people's beliefs regarding how much, or if, their efforts at work will eventually satisfy their needs.

The three factors that make up expectancy theory are expectancy, valence, and instrumentality. The theory often is presented in the form of the following equation:

$$\text{Motivation} = \text{Expectancy} \times \text{Valence} \times \text{Instrumentality}$$

*Expectancy* is an individual's belief that his or her effort will lead to some result. For example, if you believe that intensive study over a weekend will lead to a high grade, you have a high expectancy in that situation. *Valence* is the value you attach to the outcome of your efforts. For example, a student may value a high grade in a class compared to the pleasure of going skiing over a weekend. *Instrumentality* refers to the links between early and later results of the work effort. For example, there is a link between one outcome of studying, a grade on a test, and a later outcome, a final grade for a course. If the test was worth only 1 percent of the final grade, instrumentality would be low; that is, how one performs on a minor test has little effect on a final grade.

Thus, in expectancy theory, motivation is much more than the value people attach to work outcomes. Beliefs regarding whether an effort will lead to success and whether the results of effort will lead eventually to valued outcomes also come into play.

Some suggest that expectancy theory serves best as a diagnostic tool to determine why workers are motivated or not motivated.[23] The manager must ask three questions: First, do workers believe that their efforts will lead to the successful performance of a task? Second, do workers believe that present success at some task (e.g., no defects for a week) will lead to success at some future valued outcome (e.g., getting a raise)? Third, do employees value the outcomes that follow from their efforts at work? Consider the following Multinational Management Brief.

*Applying Expectancy Theory in Multinational Settings*   There are two key issues in applying expectancy theory in the multinational company. The first is to identify which outcomes people value in a particular national or local cultural setting; that is, the multinational manager must find and use rewards with positive valence for employees. The second is to find culturally appropriate ways of convincing employees that their efforts will lead to desirable ends.

**Process theories**
Theories of motivation arising from needs and values combined with an individual's beliefs regarding the work environment.

**Expectancy theory**
Assumption that motivation includes people's desire to satisfy their needs and their beliefs regarding how much their efforts at work will eventually satisfy their needs.

## Multinational Management **Brief**

### Performance Appraisal in India

The basic logic behind performance appraisals is to provide work feedback to employees. Employers assume that employees can use such feedback to improve in the future. A key aspect of this assumption is related to the application of expectancy theory. Specifically, if employees feel that they have achieved the desired effort (they have high expectancy), they will be more motivated in the future to continue engaging in such productive behavior. Alternatively, performance appraisal can be accompanied by other remedial measures for those employees with low expectancy.

In India, most performance appraisals are typically a once-a-year phenomenon. However, annual performance appraisals are problematic because feedback is only provided infrequently. Employees may think they are doing well and then receive negative feedback. Furthermore, annual performance appraisals may also disproportionately focus on recent achievements and disappointments while altogether ignoring earlier achievements and problems.

In response to these challenges, many multinationals are now engaging in more frequent performance appraisals. For example, companies such as Deutsche Bank India and Nivea India have both adopted mid-year appraisals. These new appraisals aim at making employees more accountable for their actions. At Azko Nobel India, a manufacturer of paints and coatings, the feedback is continuous. The Human Resources team reviews the performance of employees and provides guidance to increase employee expectancy.

*Source: Based on Singh, N. 2012. "Mid-year appraisals good for staff motivation." The* Economic Times, *June 7, online edition.*

In the Case in Point on page 620, we saw that the workers from a former Eastern Bloc country had a higher valence for secure jobs than they did for bonus pay. When managers from the Finnish parent company recognized this, they promised job security (the workers' ultimate goal) in return for the workers' putting more effort into productivity. As expectancy theory would predict, when the workers became convinced that their efforts would lead to their valued goal of security, their motivation increased.

### Equity Theory

**Equity theory**
Proposal that people perceive the fairness of their rewards vis-à-vis their inputs based on how they compare themselves to others.

**Equity theory** focuses on the fairness that people perceive in the rewards that they receive for their efforts at work, which can include pay, benefits, recognition, job perquisites, and prestige. Under this theory, the "efforts" people put into the job are not only the quality and quantity of their work, but also such factors as their age, educational qualifications, seniority, and social status.[24]

Equity theory proposes that people have no absolute standards for fairness in the input/output (effort/reward) equation. Rather, people perceive the fairness of their rewards relative to their inputs, based on how they compare themselves to others. For example, if two people have the same experience and do the same job, but do not have the same pay, then one is in overpayment inequity and the other is in underpayment inequity. Equity theory predicts that workers who believe that they are under-rewarded reduce their contribution to the company (e.g., take longer breaks). Workers in an inequitable situation produced by over-rewards increase their work input, at least in the short run.

How does equity theory apply to the international setting? Consider the next Case in Point.

*Applying Equity Theory in Multinational Settings*  The first issue to consider in the multinational applications of equity theory is the importance of equity norms in a society. Developing reward systems based on equity norms may not be motivating when other norms for rewarding people have more importance than equity.

Psychologists identify three principles of allocating rewards whose use varies in different cultural settings: the principle of equity (based on contributions), the principle of equality (based on equal division of rewards), and the principle of need (based on individual needs).[25] A review of cross-national reports on the three principles of reward allocation suggests the following:

- *Equity norms prevail in individualistic cultures:* In particular, managerial practices in the United States such as bonus pay, management by objectives, and most U.S. performance appraisal systems use the equity norm. Rewards are based on

---

### CASE IN POINT

## Equity and Expatriates

As more multinationals enter the Chinese market to take advantage of opportunities in China, they will inevitably send more expatriates to manage local operations. Nowhere is inequity more apparent than when local workers compare their salaries to those of expatriates. The significant gap is due to the practice of paying expatriates home market rates while local employees are paid according to local labor market. Research has provided ample evidence of the perceived inequity and injustices associated with this large gap. Multinationals are thus very wary of this gap and its effects on local employee productivity, and they are looking for ways to minimize the perception.

A study by Chen, Choi, and Chi of international joint ventures and compensation disparities provides some insight into the applications and subtleties of equity theory in an international context. The study examined Chinese employees' perception of fairness compared with that of their expatriate counterparts in international joint ventures. As expected, it was found that local Chinese employees perceived less fairness when comparing their incomes with expatriates than when comparing them with other locals. However, the study also showed that other factors can neutralize part of the felt inequity. For instance, it was found that the local employees' perception of fairness

increased if they were paid more than local employees in other international joint ventures. Additionally, if the employees endorsed ideological explanations that expatriates are necessary and important to the Chinese economy and position in the global environment, their perception of fairness toward expatriates was higher. Finally, the study also showed that employees who perceived that expatriates were interpersonally sensitive and nice to them perceived higher fairness with regard to these expatriates' compensation packages.

A more recent study shows that the perceived inequity can be reduced if expatriates are seen as more trustworthy. While adjusting the salary of locals to reduce the gap may not always be realistic, multinationals can find other ways to reduce the effect of the perceived wage inequity. For instance, if foreign plants can implement practices to enhance expatriate trustworthiness, local employees feel less inequity.

*Sources: Based on Chen, C. C., J. Choi, and S. C. Chi. 2002. "Making justice sense of local expatriate compensation disparity: Mitigation by local referents, ideological explanations, and interpersonal sensitivity in China-foreign joint ventures." Academy of Management Journal, 45, 807–817; Economist. 2012. Pedalling prosperity. May 26, 3–5; Leung, K., X. Zhu, and G. Ge. 2009. "Compensation disparity between locals and expatriates: Moderating the effects of perceived injustice in foreign multinationals in China." Journal of World Business, 44, 85–93.*

performance. Good work deserves good pay.[26] In contrast, in societies where status comes from group membership rather than achievement, rewards based on performance may not make sense. High-status groups are expected to get higher rewards regardless of their performance levels.

- *Equality norms prevail over equity norms in collectivist cultures:* In societies with strong equality norms, at least for the members of one's group or team, group members prefer equal rewards for all. For example, one study of an Israeli company found that 40 percent of the workers perceived a bonus system as unfair even though it increased their income. They suggested that fair rewards should go to the team instead of to individuals.[27]

  However, as the Chen et al. study shows, in some collectivistic societies like China, equity may be potentially becoming more important.[28] As China has adopted a more open-door, market-oriented economic approach, it is possible that employees are beginning to prefer equitable situations based on their performance. Managers must carefully assess local conditions to determine if equity is preferred.

- *The principle of need may prevail over equity in certain conditions:* One study found, for example, that Indian managers preferred rewards based on need over rewards based on either equality or equity.[29] Collectivist cultures in particular may place more value on other people's needs than on an individual's contributions.

Exhibit 14.9 shows an example of how the fairness of equity or equality rewards can affect even students' responses to grades relative to contributions. The information comes from a study in which Korean, Japanese, and U.S. students assigned peer evaluation grades for contributions to group projects. Although some equity norms seemingly worked for all students, U.S. students clearly linked rewards to

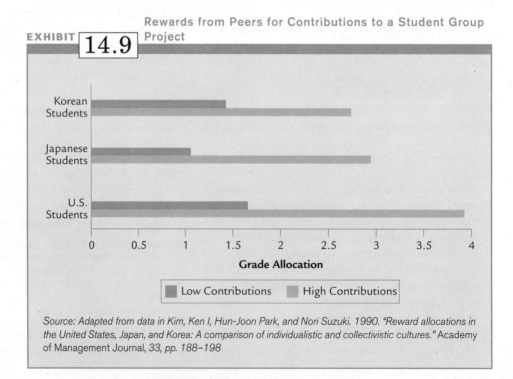

**EXHIBIT 14.9**

Rewards from Peers for Contributions to a Student Group Project

Low Contributions     High Contributions

*Source: Adapted from data in Kim, Ken I, Hun-Joon Park, and Nori Suzuki. 1990. "Reward allocations in the United States, Japan, and Korea: A comparison of individualistic and collectivistic cultures." Academy of Management Journal, 33, pp. 188–198*

performance much more than did the students from the two Asian societies.[30] Clearly, U.S. students were more likely to get rewards for high performance from their peers.

The final issue to consider in applying equity theory is the cultural differences in beliefs regarding the sources of a person's contributions to work. In some cultures, age, social status, and family membership may be more important inputs to work than the actual effort and performance on the job. In many Asian countries, for example, most people would consider it very unfair if a young worker received more pay than an older worker—particularly if the two did the same job. Research suggests that, in addition to performance criteria, collectivist cultures judge pay fairness based on factors such as seniority, education, and family size.[31]

## Goal-Setting Theory

**Goal-setting theory** assumes that people want to achieve goals. When they meet or exceed a goal, people feel competent and satisfied. When they fail to meet a goal, they feel dissatisfied. Thus, the mere existence of a goal is motivating.[32]

Goal-setting theory has several principles,[33] and the theory's proponents argue that managers who follow these principles can motivate employees to meet organizational objectives:

- *Set clear and specific goals:* Employees need to know and understand what management expects them to accomplish.

- *Assign difficult but achievable goals:* If goals are too difficult, there is little incentive to try to achieve them. If goals are too easy, employees may not take them seriously.

- *Increase employee acceptance of goals:* At least in the United States, studies tell us that employees who participate in goal setting have a greater acceptance of managerial goals.[34]

- *Provide incentives to achieve goals:* Tying rewards (e.g., salary, bonuses) to goal achievement increases the acceptance of the goals.[35]

- *Give feedback on goal attainment:* To be motivated and to achieve their goals, people must understand how well they are doing.

*Applying Goal-Setting Theory in Multinational Settings*  Some experts believe that goal setting works to some degree regardless of location.[36] Setting goals does affect behavior in a positive direction. However, cultural expectations vary regarding whether subordinates should participate with managers in setting the goals and whether it is better to set goals for groups or for individuals.

In individualistic cultures, such as in the United States, setting individual goals may prove more effective than setting goals for a work group. People from individualistic cultures do not easily share responsibility for group outcomes. Thus, they do not find goals assigned to groups as motivating as goals that are assigned to them personally. In contrast, workers in collectivist cultures may respond better to high levels of participation in goal setting than people from individualistic cultures. In societies with cultural values supporting the necessity of belonging to a group, participation may have a greater chance of enhancing the worker's ownership and commitment to goals.

Finally, in cultures with high power distance, worker participation in setting goals may not produce any positive effects. Workers expect the leader to set the goals and tell them what to do.[37]

**Goal-setting theory**
Assumption that the mere existence of a goal is motivating.

**EXHIBIT** **14.10**    Cultural Effects on Performance by the Degree of Participation in Goal Setting

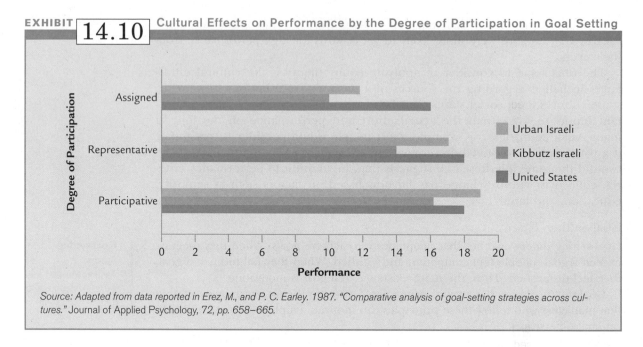

Source: Adapted from data reported in Erez, M., and P. C. Earley. 1987. "Comparative analysis of goal-setting strategies across cultures." Journal of Applied Psychology, 72, pp. 658–665.

Exhibit 14.10 demonstrates some of the outcomes that can occur when people from different cultures have varying degrees of participation in the goal-setting process. This exhibit is based on a study of U.S. and Israeli university students.[38] Three groups of students performed simulated job tasks. For the first group, goals were assigned. For the second group, a representative from the group expressed the students' opinions on goals to the leader. For the third group, all members participated in setting goals. Because Israeli culture is more collectivist and lower in terms of power distance than U.S. culture, the experimenters expected that goal assignment would not work very well for the Israeli students.

Participation in goal setting improved the performance of all groups. However, perhaps because U.S. students come from a highly individualistic and moderate-power-distance national culture, they performed almost as well with assigned goals as they did when given the opportunity to participate in goal setting. This was not true for the Israeli students, who come from a more collectivist and lower power distance culture. The Israeli students did much better with participation. The implication is that subordinate participation in goal setting is an effective motivational tool in collectivist nations, but it is less important in individualistic or high-power-distance national cultures.

### Reinforcement Theory

**Operant conditioning**

Model that proposes that if a pleasurable consequence follows a behavior, the behavior will continue, whereas if an unpleasant consequence follows a behavior, the behavior will stop.

Most managerial applications of reinforcement theory focus on **operant conditioning**, which represents a basic way people learn. The famous psychologist B. F. Skinner identified most of the principles underlying operant conditioning.[39] The operant conditioning model proposes that behavior is a function of its consequences. If a pleasurable consequence follows a behavior, the behavior will continue. If an unpleasant consequence follows a behavior, the behavior will stop.[40] Unlike most other theories of motivation, operant conditioning focuses on observable behavior and not on the psychological processes (e.g., meeting needs) that affect people's motivation. Consider the next Case in Point.

## CASE IN POINT

### The Japanese Salaryman and Reinforcement Theory

It is widely believed that the Japanese salary is a major reason why Japan has been able to experience such sustained growth. The salaryman is the white-collar employee who is fully dedicated to the company. In fact, the salaryman was part of the managerial class who chose to work for a company rather than for a career. As a fresh university graduate, the company would inculcate the employee with its values and provide training, perks, and other benefits that would historically provide for a comfortable life. In return, the employee would dedicate his life to the company.

The salaryman's ongoing commitment to the company was ensured through many types of reinforcement. If employees conformed to norms, they were rewarded. However, if norms were broken, employees faced severe negative consequences. Consider the practice of drinking late into the night a few times a week. Most employees feel obliged to go along with such activities to avoid retribution for not participating. Drinking with the boss is seen as a way to show loyalty and to build camaraderie, and those who conform are given a positive reward. Another practice involves the use of holidays. Most

salarymen take only a fraction of their paid holidays to show their devotion to the company. Those who take longer holidays are punished by being denied pay raises and promotions. Finally, a salaryman works for only one company. Switching jobs is close to impossible because many factors, including seniority-based wages and the loss of pensions, make changing jobs difficult.

Experts nevertheless agree that Japan is seeing new economic conditions that may lead to the traditional salaryman becoming a dying breed. In fact, some experts are questioning whether Sony's new Chief Executive Officer has what it takes to turn around the Japanese electronics firm. The Sony board appointed a known insider as CEO. However, many see Kazuo Hirai, the new CEO, as a Sony salaryman who seems cautious and overly interested in protecting the firm's tradition. In this extremely competitive environment, some experts suggest that a visionary outsider would have worked better for Sony.

*Sources: Based on* Economist. *2012. "Same old or new different." February 1, online edition;* Economist. *2008. "Sayonara, salaryman." January 5, 68–70.*

The operant-conditioning model has three steps, as are shown in Exhibit 14.11 with a managerial example. The antecedent comes first and stimulates behavior. The behavior follows the antecedent, and the pleasant or unpleasant consequences follow the behavior. The exhibit shows a simple example based on work attendance. In the antecedent, management sets an attendance goal. The employee behaves by either coming to work or missing work. Management then provides pleasant or unpleasant consequences for the behavior.

Positive reinforcement occurs when management responds with a rewarding consequence, but the consequence is deemed rewarding only if it increases the desired behavior. Not all people respond to the same positively intended consequences in the same way. Although often confused with punishment, negative reinforcement increases desired behavior by eliminating some negative consequence; that is, people behave in a certain way to avoid something unpleasant. For example, you may put on a heavy coat to avoid the pain of extreme cold. Punishment occurs when something unpleasant occurs after a behavior. The exhibit shows that docking pay is an unpleasant consequence that follows the behavior of not coming to work. Extinction occurs when a manager ignores a behavior, but managers must be careful to avoid extinction when other rewards (e.g., a paid day off) may be operating.

In most management applications of reinforcement theory, positive reinforcement is used to encourage the desired behaviors, and managers have an array of organizational rewards. These include material rewards (e.g., pay), benefit rewards (e.g., company car), status rewards (e.g., prestigious office), and social rewards (e.g., praise).[41]

**EXHIBIT 14.11**

**Management Example of Operant Conditioning Process and Types of Consequences**

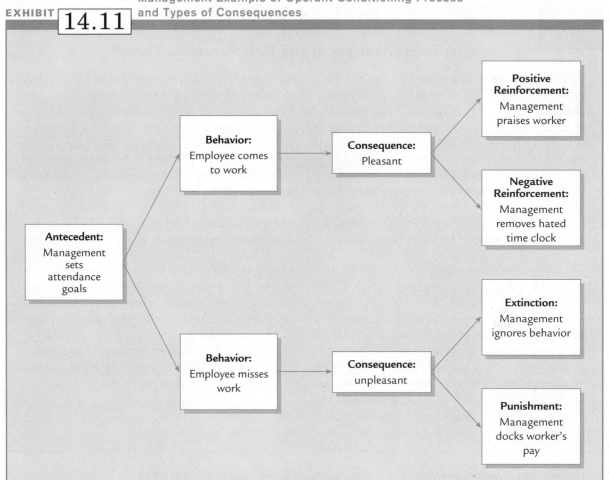

© Cengage Learning

*Applying Reinforcement Theory in Multinational Settings* For behaviors that are easily observable and measurable, such as attendance, the evidence from most U.S. studies suggests that positive reinforcement works.[42] However, finding appropriate organizational reinforcers remains a major difficulty in applying reinforcement theory to diverse national groups. Given that people from various nations expect different rewards from work, groups may respond to different reinforcers. Furthermore, managers must be able to determine whether it is always necessary to use certain forms of punishment for observable behaviors such as absences.

The challenge for the multinational manager is not only to understand how work values influence potential rewards but also to identify the organizational rewards available in a national setting. National cultures and social institutions define acceptable and legitimate rewards. Consider these two examples. In highly unionized countries such as Germany, pay and benefits are fixed nationally and are not available as organizational rewards targeted to specific behaviors. In Japan, employees often consider public praise embarrassing; it implies that one is somehow better than his or her colleagues. This embarrassment and the potential ostracism by the work group would result not in a reward but in punishment, unintended by the culturally ignorant manager.

Evidence exists, however, that when multinational managers can find culturally and institutionally appropriate reinforcers, reinforcement theory works. For example, companies in Mexico City often use punishment to control tardiness—a one-day suspension without pay for every three days tardy during a 30-day period. When one company replaced the punishment system for tardiness with a positive reinforcement program, giving bonuses for punctuality, tardiness fell from 9.8 percent to 1.2 percent.[43]

## Key Points in the Multinational Application of Process and Reinforcement Theories

The multinational manager should consider several key points when using process and reinforcement theories of motivation in different cultural settings:

- *Expectancy theory:* The key is identifying the appropriate work rewards that have positive valence for employees in a national setting.
- *Equity theory:* The multinational manager must assess the importance and meaning of the principle of equity in a national context. Equality norms or norms that base rewards on need may be as or more important than equity.
- *Goal-setting theory:* Depending on cultural norms, goal setting may be more effective when assigned to groups rather than to individuals. Participation in goal setting may have a more positive effect in collectivist cultures than in individualistic or high-power-distance cultures.
- *Reinforcement theory:* The rewards people value at work, in a given cultural context, may influence the types of reinforcers that are useful to managers. In addition, the institutional environment, such as the degree of economic development and the labor relations system, affects the types of available rewards in a society.

# Motivation and Job Design: U.S. and European Perspectives

Job design attempts to make jobs more motivating by changing the nature of their functions and tasks. Early theories of job design focused primarily on making jobs more efficient through procedures such as time and motion studies. The objective was to make a job as fast and as efficient as possible, with little concern for the psychological state of the worker. Contemporary views of job design take into account the psychological effects on the worker produced by the types of tasks associated with a job. Theories on ways to design jobs for high motivation focus on how job characteristics allow a worker to meet or satisfy motivating needs.

## A U.S. Approach: The Job Characteristics Model

Although there are several approaches to redesigning work for increased motivation, one of the most popular in the United States is the **job characteristics model**.[44] This model suggests that work is more motivating when managers enrich core job characteristics, such as requiring more than one skill. In turn, these core job characteristics affect the psychological states of a worker that are critical to motivation. For example, one such psychological state is whether the worker believes the job is meaningful. Proponents of the job characteristics model argue that, if the core job characteristics lead to appropriate psychological reactions, then jobs have a high potential to motivate workers.

The job characteristics model sees three critical psychological states as motivating. First, a person must believe that the job is meaningful. A meaningful job is perceived as important or valuable. Second, a person must believe that he or she is responsible or accountable for the outcome of the work. Third, a person must understand how well he or she has performed.

**Job characteristics model**
Suggests that work is more motivating when managers enrich core job characteristics, such as by increasing the number of skills a job requires.

Core job characteristics that lead to motivating psychological states are:

* *Skill variety:* A job with skill variety requires the use of different abilities and activities.
* *Task identity:* Task identity increases when a person can complete a whole piece of work from beginning to end.
* *Task significance:* Task significance increases when a job has important effects on other people.
* *Autonomy:* People control their own schedules and job procedures.
* *Feedback:* Feedback occurs when the job allows timely information on a person's performance.

Not all people respond positively to jobs with enriched job characteristics. The model suggests that jobs with high motivational potential work best for people who have a strong need for personal growth and who have the appropriate knowledge and skills to perform the job well. Exhibit 14.12 gives a picture of how the model works when a job has a high potential for motivating workers.

**EXHIBIT 14.12**   A Motivating Job in the Job Characteristics Model

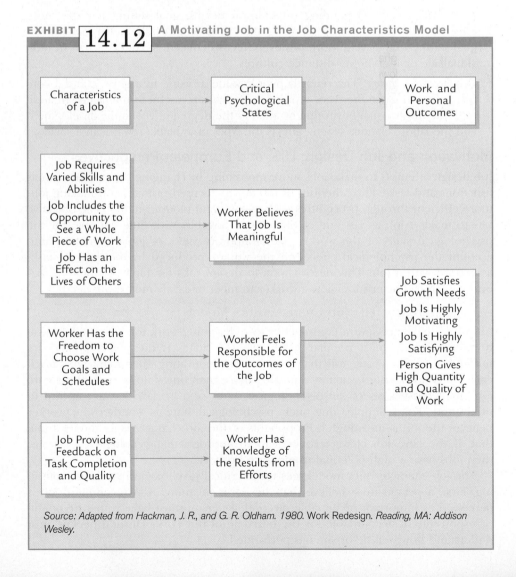

*Source: Adapted from Hackman, J. R., and G. R. Oldham. 1980. Work Redesign. Reading, MA: Addison Wesley.*

CASE IN POINT

## The Job Characteristics Model: A Comparison of Mauritian and Australian Hotel Workers

Mauritius, a small island off the east coast of Madagascar, remains one of the African countries experiencing significant economic development. It is often seen as one of the only full democracies in Africa. An important contributor to its economic development is a vibrant tourism sector. Many of the world's leading hotel groups, such as One & Only Resorts, Club Med, and Hilton Hotels, have world-class resorts on the island. The tourism sector employs a significant number of Mauritians, and hotels work hard to motivate their employees.

In an innovative study, Lee-Ross provides some insights into application of the job characteristics model when comparing Mauritian and Australian hotel workers. The author argues that because Mauritian workers have higher power distance, higher uncertainty avoidance, and lower individualism than their Australian counterparts, they are less likely to be given jobs that display high levels of core job characteristics. For instance, the author argues, Mauritian workers are not likely to be given work that requires taking initiative or becoming involved in decision making because high power distance means that they are less likely to disagree with their supervisors. High uncertainty avoidance also implies that they are not very comfortable with situations involving high levels of autonomy. Because of their cultural attributes, therefore, Mauritian workers are less likely to be given jobs with high core

job characteristics. The study supports this argument, showing that Australian workers perceive higher levels of core job characteristics than their Mauritian counterparts.

However, although the job characteristics model suggests that people with high levels of core job characteristics are likely to be motivated (e.g., the Australians), the study showed that both Mauritian and Australian workers had similar levels of motivation. The authors suggest that the high power distance of Mauritians encourages them to agree with authority and even to be deferential to customers. This allows Mauritian workers to satisfy their predisposed cultural obligations of deference to those in positions of authority. By behaving consistently with their cultural predispositions, Mauritian hotel employees experience levels of motivation similar to their Australian counterparts.

Such results show that the job characteristics model is clearly culture dependent and needs to be adapted to fit cultural predispositions.

*Sources: Based on* Economist. *2012. "A glass half-full." March 31, online edition; Lee-Ross, Darren. 2005. "Perceived job characteristics and internal work motivation. An exploratory cross-cultural analysis of the motivational antecedents of hotel workers in Mauritius and Australia."* Journal of Management Development, *24, 253–266; Stott, Bridget. 2006. "Mauritius ready to open doors to paradise."* Observer, *February 19, 21.*

---

One of the major criticisms of the job characteristics model is that it is U.S. based and thus works only for societies that display similar cultural attributes. The Case in Point seems to support that criticism.

### A European Approach: Sociotechnical Systems

The **sociotechnical systems (STS) approach** to building a job's motivational potential was originally developed in England and some Scandinavian countries.[45] The STS approach attempts to mesh both modern technology and the social needs of workers, but it does not consider workers just as individuals. Rather, individual workers are part of a social system (i.e., organizational structure, culture) that must be blended with technologies.[46] The STS approach focuses on the **autonomous work group,** which is a team or unit that has nearly complete responsibility for a task. The most famous example is Volvo's Kalmar plant, where autonomous work groups have responsibility for particular components of the automobile (e.g., doors). In autonomous work groups, worker teams control many aspects of their jobs traditionally governed by management, such as the tasks assigned to individuals and the pace of work.[47]

**Sociotechnical systems (STS) approach**
Focuses on designing motivating jobs by blending the social system (i.e., organizational structure, culture) with technologies.

**Autonomous work group**
Team or unit that has nearly complete responsibility for a task.

The STS approach builds into a job many of the same motivational job characteristics proposed by the U.S. job characteristic model. However, in a crucial difference with the U.S. approach, the team's tasks become the focus of job enrichment, not the individual worker's tasks.[48] The team decides individual task assignments and thus increases skill variety. The team makes autonomous decisions on a variety of job-related matters, such as which task to complete first. The team has task identity because it is producing a whole product. And the team gets feedback from its work, often by conducting its own quality inspections.

## Choosing Job Enrichment Techniques in Multinational Settings

How can a multinational manager choose the best techniques to design motivating work? Some experts suggest that the choice should depend on whether the culture is individualistic or collectivist.[49] Approaches created in the United States tend to focus on how the *individual* reacts to core job characteristics. They have a cultural bias in favor of individualistic cultures. Approaches designed in collectivist cultures, including the sociotechnical systems approach and the quality circles popular in Japan, focus on the job characteristics of the *team*. They have a cultural bias in favor of collectivist cultures. Although proponents of both forms of enrichment can point to success stories in several nations, experts recommend a team focus for job enrichment in collectivist cultures and an individual focus in individualistic cultures.

One explanation of why team-based job enrichment may not work well in individualistic cultures is that people from individualistic cultures just do not work as well in

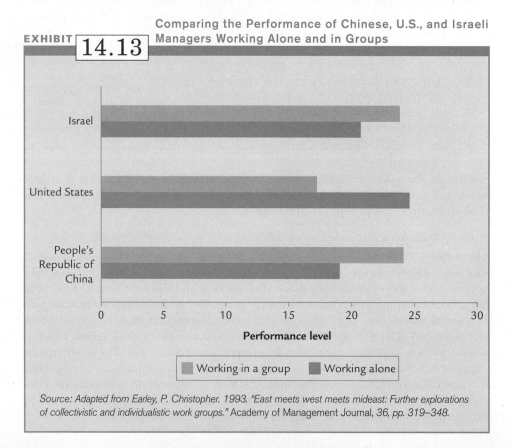

**EXHIBIT 14.13** Comparing the Performance of Chinese, U.S., and Israeli Managers Working Alone and in Groups

*Source: Adapted from Earley, P. Christopher. 1993. "East meets west meets mideast: Further explorations of collectivistic and individualistic work groups." Academy of Management Journal, 36, pp. 319–348.*

groups. Exhibit 14.13 gives an example of this phenomenon. It shows a comparison of three culturally diverse groups of managers working in groups or alone. As you can see, unlike the managers from the collectivist cultures, U.S. managers performed much worse in groups than they did alone.

Why does performance drop off with the use of teamwork in individualistic cultures? Some experts explain this by noting that people from individualistic cultures often engage in social loafing; that is, people put out less effort when they work in groups. They do this for three reasons. First, working in groups, people do not feel responsible for group outcomes and feel less pressure to perform. Second, workers in groups often believe that the group will make up for any slack in their personal efforts. Third, especially in highly individualistic cultures such as the United States, people give their own work and interests priority over those of the group. However, in individualistic cultures, social loafing has less of a detrimental effect on a group's performance when individuals rather than the groups are held accountable for performance.[50]

**Social loafing**
People put out less effort when they work in groups.

In sum, this chapter shows how challenging it is to motivate individuals in different cultural settings. We conclude with a recent development that is making motivation even more challenging. Consider the following Case in Point.

---

## C A S E   I N   P O I N T

### Teleworking in Egypt

The recent advances in information technology and computing power are making teleworking more of a reality in multinationals today. Teleworking refers to employees working from a remote location that is equipped with telecommunications technology to allow employees to transfer their work to the employing firm. Many multinationals have embraced teleworking as a means to reduce costs while also giving employees better flexibility. Such flexibility can also result in employees being better able to manage work-family conflict while also boosting employee morale. Teleworking can also address absenteeism and other turnover problems.

Despite the advantages, teleworking presents significant challenges to companies. Teleworkers usually work outside of the office and may not be as attuned to the company culture. Furthermore, companies have found that assessing productivity of teleworkers may not be as easy. Additionally, motivating teleworkers can be very challenging, as workers do not get access to the same organizational resources. They may also feel that they have fewer career opportunities for promotion and career advancement because of their isolation.

Given these challenges, more multinationals will find it problematic to motivate such workers. However, a recent study of 199 Egyptian teleworkers provides some insights as to what factors may be effective. The study revealed that job security is a critical factor that enhances productivity. Because workers feel disconnected from the firm, they need the certainty of the job to ensure that they give as much of themselves as possible. Furthermore, the level of management support for teleworking also enhances motivation. In other words, if managers feel that teleworking is beneficial and they provide the necessary resource to allow teleworkers to succeed, these workers are more likely to feel that they are productive. Interestingly, when companies allow their teleworkers to set their own working time and to find a balance between work and family, teleworkers were more likely to perceive higher productivity. Such work flexibility also shows that the company cares about their teleworkers.

*Source: Based on Aboelmaged, M. G., and M. E. Subbaugh. 2012. "Factors influencing perceived productivity of Egyptian teleworkers: an empirical study."* Measuring Business Excellence, *16(2): 3–22.*

## Summary and Conclusions

Motivating workers in diverse cultural settings is a constant challenge for multinational managers. As companies both large and small become more global and transnational in their strategic and human resource orientations, the challenge of increasing worker motivation in multinational settings will become even greater. For multinational companies to remain competitive in the global environment, each company and its managers must find ways to motivate an increasingly diverse workforce.

As a guide to developing motivational techniques in multinational settings, this chapter addressed several key issues. First, the chapter showed some of the available information on international differences in work centrality, work obligation norms, and extrinsic and intrinsic work values in several different nations. Second, the chapter reviewed the basic processes of work motivation and how these processes are influenced by the national context. Third, it reviewed classic theories of motivation (including need, process, and reinforcement theories) and the multinational applications of each approach. In these sections were specific and practical suggestions on how to apply these theories in different national contexts. Fourth, and finally, the chapter considered both U.S. and European approaches to designing jobs with high motivational potential.

Most of the views of motivation discussed in this chapter were "made in the U.S.A." U.S. academics created the theories and performed much of the supporting research. The approaches to motivation discussed here are also standard fare in U.S. university courses on organizational behavior. However, the dominance of the United States as the country of origin for many motivational theories does not invalidate their multinational applications—*if* a manager makes appropriate adjustments for national contexts and various subcultures. Many of the psychological theories that underlie common U.S. approaches to motivation have culture-free assumptions and research support; that is, they attempt to explain human behavior independently of cultural setting.

However, even if psychological processes that underlie motivational theories are culture independent, the applications of motivation theories are not. Even when people respond to work using the same underlying psychological processes, the national context continues to influence other factors, such as what people find rewarding at work and what people feel is fair and moral. For example, a person from the United States and a Brazilian may respond similarly to the psychological process of positive reinforcement; their behaviors increase when consequences are pleasant. But they do not necessarily view the same reinforcers offered by management as rewarding. Nations vary widely in their predominant views regarding the functions and meaning of work and in the rewards that people hope to get from work.

A brief discussion of motivation can only sensitize the multinational manager to the subtleties of applying any motivational technique in a given national setting. Although managers may begin their approach to motivating workers with an awareness of the broad stereotypes concerning national cultures, each job situation requires an understanding of unique organizational, regional, and occupational cultures as well as the individual differences of each employee.

## Discussion Questions

1. Compare the job characteristics approach to job design and the sociotechnical systems approach. Pick a national culture with which you are familiar (besides your own), and discuss which approach would be most likely succeed and why.

2. How might a country's educational and political system affect the effectiveness of redesigning work as a motivational tool?

3. Discuss differences in the attributes of work considered the most important in different nations. How might these differences influence the application of expectancy theory and reinforcement theory to the work setting?

4. Discuss the differences between the need and process theories of motivation. Which type do you think is more applicable to multinational management and why?

5. Discuss the three principles of fairness of rewards. Do you think that equity theory could work in societies where other principles besides equity operate? If so, how would you apply equity theory as a manager in these countries?

6. Under what conditions would you recommend involving groups in setting goals? Discuss the cultural influences on goal setting using Hofstede's original four dimensions of national culture.

## Multinational Management **Internet Exercise**

1. Go the Hofstede cultural dimension website at http://geert-hofstede.com/geert-hofstede.html.

2. Click on the "Organizational Culture" link. Discuss the eight types of Organizational Culture as described by Hofstede.

3. Are some countries more likely to have some of the specific organizational cultures than others? Why?

4. Discuss how you would motivate employees in each of the different types of cultures.

## Multinational Management **Skill Builder**

### Planning Motivational Strategies for Different Countries

**Step 1.** Read the following multinational problem.

You have just completed your first year as a management trainee for the XYZ company. Your company manufactures components for industrial robots. You have just come from a meeting with the vice president for personnel. She has told you that XYZ has decided to open a manufacturing plant in the country of_____. Because of your background in international business, top management has chosen you to be the new plant manager. The VP tells you that this is a significant opportunity and challenge since you would have to wait at least five more years to get this level of responsibility at home. Personnel experts are already in, working on recruitment, selection, and training. Your major job will be to motivate the local workers to reach the plant's full capacity as soon as possible. Given your knowledge of the local culture and social institutions, the VP asks you to prepare a report specifying the motivational strategies that you might use on your new assignment.

**Step 2.** Pick teams and countries.

Your instructor will divide you into teams of three to five people. Each team will choose or be assigned a different country for a plant location. Your team will act in the role of the new expatriate plant manager. If your instructor chooses, this may also be an individual assignment. This project may be a library research project or an in-class assignment based on information from the text.

**Step 3.** Prepare reports.

Reports may be written, oral, or both. They are to analyze the likely effectiveness of motivational approaches given different economic, cultural, and institutional factors in the country in question.

Each report must discuss the strengths and weaknesses of applying the following motivational theories in the selected country:

- Need theory
- Expectancy theory
- Goal-setting theory
- Equity theory
- Reinforcement theory
- Job design

**Step 4.** Present your findings to the class.

**Step 5.** Class discussion.

Alternative approach: The whole class works with one country, and each team deals with one approach to motivation.

### *Endnotes*

1 Meaning of Work International Research Team. 1987. *The Meaning of Working: An International Perspective.* New York: Academic Press.

2 World Values Study Group. 1994. *World Values Surveys and European Values Surveys, 1981–1984, 1990–1993, and 1995–1997.* (Computer file.) Ann Arbor: Inter-University Consortium for Political and Social Research.

3 Meaning of Work International Research Team.

4 Parboteeah, K. Praveen, and John B. Cullen. 2003. "Social institutions and work centrality: Explorations beyond national culture." *Organization Science,* 14, 137–148.

5 Hofstede, Geert. 2001. *Culture's Consequences: International Differences in Work-Related Values,* 2nd ed. London: Sage.

6 Inglehart, Ronald, Miguel Basanez, and Alejandro Moreno. 1998. *Human Values and Beliefs: A Cross-Cultural Sourcebook.* Ann Arbor: University of Michigan Press.

7 Grant, Linda. 1997. "Unhappy in Japan." *Fortune,* January 13, 142.

8 World Values Study Group.

9 *Economist.* 2006. "Emerging economies—Climbing back." January 21.

10 Inglehart, Basanez, and Moreno.

[11] World Values Study Group.

[12] Maslow, A. 1970. *Motivation and Personality.* New York: Harper & Row.

[13] Pinder, C. C. 1984. *Work Motivation.* Glenview, IL: Scott, Foresman.

[14] Alderfer, C. P. 1972. *Existence, Relatedness and Growth: Human Needs in Organizational Settings.* New York: Free Press.

[15] Herzberg, F., B. Mausner, and B. B. Snyderman. 1959. *The Motivation to Work.* Hoboken, NJ: Wiley.

[16] McClelland, David C. 1961. *The Achieving Society.* Princeton, NJ: Van Nostrand Reinhold.

[17] Ronen, Simcha. 1986. *Comparative and Multinational Management.* Hoboken, NJ: Wiley.

[18] Ronen, Simcha. 1994. "An underlying structure of motivation need taxonomies: A cross-cultural confirmation." *Handbook of Industrial and Organizational Psychology,* 4, 241–269.

[19] Harpaz, Itzhak. 1990. "The importance of work goals: An international perspective." *Journal of International Business Studies,* 1st quarter, 75–93.

[20] Elizur, Dov, Ingwer Borg, Raymond Hunt, and Istvan Magyari Beck. 1991. "The structure of work values: A cross cultural comparison." *Journal of Organizational Behavior,* 12, 21–38.

[21] Hofstede, Geert. 1991. *Cultures and Organizations: Software of the Mind.* London: McGraw-Hill.

[22] Vroom, Victor H. 1964. *Work and Motivation.* Hoboken, NJ: Wiley.

[23] Gordon, Judith R. 1996. *Organizational Behavior.* Upper Saddle River, NJ: Prentice Hall.

[24] Adams, J. S. 1963. "Toward an understanding of inequity." *Journal of Abnormal and Social Psychology,* 67, 422–436.

[25] Erez, Miriam. 1994. "Toward a model of cross-cultural industrial and organizational psychology." *Handbook of Industrial and Organizational Psychology,* 4, 559–607.

[26] Gluskinos, U. M. 1988. "Cultural and political consideration in the introduction of western technologies: The Mekorot Project." *Journal of Management Development,* 6, 34–36.

[27] Ibid.

[28] Chen, C. C., J. Choi, and S. C. Chi. 2002. "Making justice sense of local expatriate compensation disparity: Mitigation by local referents, ideological explanations, and interpersonal sensitivity in China–foreign joint ventures." *Academy of Management Journal,* 45, 807–817.

[29] Berman, J. J., and P. Singh. 1985. "Cross-cultural similarities and differences in perceptions of fairness." *Journal of Cross-Cultural Psychology,* 16, 55–67.

[30] Kim, Ken I., Hun-Joon Park, and Nori Suzuki. 1990. "Reward allocations in the United States, Japan, and Korea: A comparison of individualistic and collectivistic cultures." *Academy of Management Journal,* 33, 188–198.

[31] Hundley, Greg, and Jooyup Kim. 1997. "National culture and the factors affecting perceptions of pay fairness in Korea and the United States." *International Journal of Organizational Analysis,* 5(4): 325–341.

[32] Locke, E. A., and G. P. Latham. 1990. *A Theory of Goal Setting and Task Performance.* Upper Saddle River, NJ: Prentice Hall.

[33] Hellriegel, Don, and John W. Slocum, Jr. 2007. *Organizational Behavior,* 11th ed. Cincinnati: South-Western.

[34] Erez, M., P. C. Earley, and C. L. Hulin. 1987. "The impact of participation on goal acceptance and performance: A two-step model." *Academy of Management Journal,* 12, 265–277.

[35] Locke, E. A., G. P. Latham, and M. Erez. 1988. "The determinants of goal commitment." *Academy of Management Review,* 13, 23–39.

[36] Erez, M., and P. C. Earley. 1987. "Comparative analysis of goal-setting strategies across cultures." *Journal of Applied Psychology,* 72, 658–665.

[37] Erez.

[38] Erez and Earley.

[39] Skinner, B. F. 1938. *The Behavior of Organisms: An Experimental Analysis.* New York: D. Appleton-Century.

[40] Luthans, Fred, and Robert Kreitner. 1985. *Organizational Behavior Modification.* Glenview, IL: Scott, Foresman.

[41] Hellriegel and Slocum.

[42] Luthans and Kreitner.

[43] Herman, J. 1973. "Effects of bonuses for punctuality on the tardiness of industrial workers." *Journal of Applied Behavioral Analysis,* 6, 563–570.

[44] Hackman, J. R., and G. R. Oldham. 1980. *Work Redesign.* Reading, MA: Addison-Wesley.

[45] Trist, E., and H. Murry. 1993. *The Social Engagement of Social Science: An Anthology, Vol. II: The Socio-Technical Perspective.* Philadelphia: University of Pennsylvania Press; Thorsrud, E. 1984. "The Scandinavian model: Strategies of organizational democracy." In B. Wilpert and A. Sorge, eds. *International Perspectives on Organizational Democracy.* Hoboken, NJ: Wiley, 337–370.

[46] Cummings, T. G. 1978. "Self-regulating work groups: A socio-technical synthesis." *Academy of Management Review,* 3, 625–634.

[47] Gordon.

[48] Erez, M., and P. C. Earley. 1993. *Culture, Self-Identity and Work.* New York: Oxford University Press.

[49] Ibid.

[50] Earley, P. Christopher. 1989. "Social loafing and collectivism: A comparison of the United States and the People's Republic of China." *Administrative Science Quarterly,* 34, 565–581.

# Wipro Technologies Europe (B)

> *The first challenge for me in Europe has been to convince people that whatever has been our modus operandi for success in the US cannot be translated into Europe; it has got to be a different strategy.*

—*Sudip Nandy, July, 2001*

Sudip Nandy got busy—there was work to do to grow Wipro Technologies Europe into 42 percent of the parent company's total IT business. He knew from experience that designing and implementing change had the potential to be a laborious 'on your hands and knees' kind of trip. Paul had given Nandy a whole lot of rope to make strategies that were quite contra to what the firm had successfully used before. A year after he began in the European operations, Nandy had a clearer picture of the actions, activities, and successes they had already accomplished.

## Patterns, Principal Ideas, and Potholes

First Nandy decided to look for people "who have sufficient grasp of the abstract, tolerance for ambiguity, and the patience to be able to grow with us for one year." He searched for critical core personal characteristics, including some typical of people from India, "For instance, your resilience, your ability to remain calm, your ability to deal with uncertainty, such as juggling changes in schedules." Nandy added, "I think those are good things. I remember an article that was written abroad saying that Indians do very well elsewhere because they deal better with uncertainty, because people from India are used to uncertainty." Nandy also worked with his Indian team to be open to the new relationships with their European counterparts. He commented, "I know that locals will force us to think differently, do things differently, get more blatant at times, get more subtle at other times."

An early and critical step was structuring how the work would be done. In Wipro's operational model almost all sales and customer interactions involved team interactions. The sales person led Wipro into the account. A combination of one to three others, some from within Europe and some from India, would be "the core team." The sales lead followed when the contract negotiations got underway. Then the ongoing project management phase continued. "Our motto is always 30/70 percent on an average—30 percent on site with the customer and 70 percent away. Of that 30 percent I want a local to be the leader," Nandy said. In this model, however, Wipro had assumed that a single person made the initial sales calls and explored the client's needs. According to Nandy, "Our sales people are far more technical than what you normally would anticipate, so they are able to take first, second, and third level calls on their own. Only when it gets deeply technical do they call a consultant to come in with them."

Creating a proper induction program for his new European hires was critical. Nandy decided to send each new employee to India at the outset of their employment and on a regular basis—every three to four months "to recharge, not the batteries, but the contacts." Nandy continued:

> *And again to understand what we are. You don't get a feeling for what we are unless you go there.*

*We are like a factory, which is our main strength, and the factory is in India. So many things have got to be put in place for local hires to make them really become as much Wiprocentric and Wipro as possible, because I think they are excellent salesmen in their own country. They understand what the customer's need is far better. I think the only thing to do is to understand exactly what our value proposition is and how to tweak it for the local customer.*

Nandy implemented numerous changes as he continued to lead. He decided to provide an early review at the three-month mark for each new hire. In these reviews Nandy solicited feedback from the European employee on what kind of company Wipro was to work for. He explicitly encouraged employees to express critical content to support improvement of Wipro's processes as they applied to European employees and business.

Nandy tightened the definition of the kinds of contracts wanted. This change assured that the new sales person avoided chasing a client and hearing the Wipro manager of that vertical say, "No, we don't want that kind of work." In addition, he had the sales people report contacts to him weekly, and he included the head of the business unit involved. Nandy also worked with Wipro's systems people to expedite the further automation of all sales information so that it could be more easily shared and to avoid any sense of there being an "old boys' network" for access to information. In all these initiatives a "culture of close monitoring and review" was being built. Nandy summarized:

*I am also pushing everyone to get a quick success because everything is, you know, in a honeymoon*

*period until you have got the first order. Once you have the first order and you start delivering, you realize there are three hurdles you have got to cross which you did not know of and you have to fall flat. So if they get a quick order then they go through that cycle and they know how to deliver and get the revenues. I think then they have made the first break. You know, you have made your first swing so it's much easier.*

Nandy also decided to experiment with using Six Sigma processes for his sales, marketing, and relationship management teams. Wipro was already a leader in using Six Sigma for its technology operations (see Exhibit 1). The process was developed to reduce errors in software programs, but Nandy thought Six Sigma could help deepen relationships for colleagues working together in Europe, and assure continuous improvement in the sales, contracting, and account management processes they used. As Nandy described:

*I think it is a really important thing because software people are very strong individuals. Each of them thinks that their way of writing the code is the best way of writing, each of them thinks that their analysis is the best analysis and as a company, we can't be successful unless we work in teams. So I think one of the biggest tools is our Six Sigma process. Six Sigma forces people to work as a team because they have to put the criteria down for measuring the benefit in a monetary term or cycle time production term at the end of the whole process, so it has to benefit everyone as part of the team. We are using Six Sigma more and more. After the first one was pushed*

**EXHIBIT 1**    **Premji's Leadership Laws**[1]

1. Vision: is like a lighthouse, showing the way and pointing out hazards. It must be slightly beyond reach, but must not be an impossible dream.

2. Values: if vision gives direction, values set boundaries. Values need leaders to be absolutely transparent in whatever they do.

3. Energy: the leader must work both hard and smart, long and intensely. It's the only way to keep on top of the demands.

4. Confidence: self-confident leaders assume reasonability for their mistakes and share credit with their team members.

5. Innovation: ideas have limited shelf-life. The leader must create a culture of continuous innovation.

6. Teambuilding: the leader must attract best minds and create a sense of ownership in them. Not just by stock options but through emotional engagement.

[1] *Rohit Saran and Stephen David. "Azim H. Premji; The World's Richest Indian". India Today, 03 June 2000.*

*down people's throats—you have to come for the training—I am finding people happily coming on Saturdays for Six Sigma training. When we take on a new project, we have a Six Sigma team get together and then we go through exercises for a half day module. So it has been a great tool.*

## Building Cultural Competence for Indian Staff

In India, Wipro Technologies tried to build cultural understanding among the India-based staffers who worked on projects with European clients. Before anybody traveled anywhere their first time, Wipro Technologies made corporate training a prerequisite. The program consisted of one- to two-day, country-specific cross-cultural awareness courses that described business cultures by nationality. Wipro also built content based on feedback from those employees who had gone abroad without training. Returning ex-patriots shared their experiences and generally agreed they could have been much more effective had they gone through a cross-cultural program before leaving India. As senior executive trainer and designer of these courses, Bharathi Srinivason, explained:

*We switched over to training before traveling because we learned that people should have this sensitivity. Our people are interacting with clients over the phone, over the mail, and other communications, so we thought it was important for any individual who joins the company. Unless our people attend the training sessions they cannot travel—they don't get their tickets if they don't enter this program, to that level it has become mandatory.*

Indian employees also were enrolled in language programs. The idea was to understand what a German or French client was saying and to be able to speak a few sentences, ask a few questions. Differences between British English and U.S. English were also highlighted.

## Teaching the Client How to Partner with Wipro and Work with Indians

Another plan that Nandy hoped would create success in Europe involved clients. Nandy asked his sales people to encourage clients who lacked experience working with South Asian partners to learn more about Indian culture. One strategy was to request as a term of the contract that the client pay for their own learning through use of a consultant Wipro designated. The person involved was an American cultural trainer familiar with Indian business culture. So when Wipro won the contract to provide

information systems design and management for the Scottish Parliament, the consultant's services were written into the contract. She worked with the designated internal partners at the Parliament who did most of the interacting with Wipro Technologies' India-based people during the life of the contract.

The idea that customers needed to learn about Wipro and Indian business culture was not Nandy's invention, although his way of addressing the issue was new. Ranjan Acharya, Wipro Technology's Bangalore-based vice president of corporate and human resource development, described how the company first expanded its learning circle to include the customer:

*I remember there was one company in the United States that invited our people to come and talk to their people every Friday on what India was all about. In their own way they were trying to learn how to deal with us and understand us as much as we were trying to understand them and interact with them.*

*We decided we had to give a wider exposure to people. Get our people to stay there, get customers to come here, send some people from there to here and here to there.*

Nandy found that using the consultant really helped. While (following Premji's lead) Wipro Ltd. and Wipro Technologies adopted mostly "American-style" management, human resources, and quality processes, there were some critical cultural norms typical of Indian culture that customers needed to understand. Nandy described differences and said, "One is that the boss doesn't call all the shots, and another thing is that I think we speak of confrontation, but many, most of us, can't handle confrontation." Also, the concept of work and its relation to social time or fun was very different. In France, Wipro's Indian employees learned that it was okay to go with the client for a three-hour lunch, whereas in Germany, people tended to get down to business much more quickly. European customers and employees of all cultures faced a shock, however, when they went to Bangalore, Wipro's Learning Center and corporate headquarters, for seminars or training. Nandy described:

*I had two European employees who just came back from training in India. They said, "You know there is this saying about death by a thousand cuts—Chinese torture. By the end of the first three days of training in Bangalore, it was death through a thousand PowerPoints because we had gone through training from 8:00 in the morning to late in the evening with each guy coming and giving 50 PowerPoints." If the same training was in some other country, probably they would*

*Source: Wipro Human Resources-Bangalore*

*combine it with an equal amount of leisure time or chit chat or speaking to people face-to-face in order to get to know each other.*

Nandy realized his employees were astonished when they experienced India and so were the customers. He said, "They stay for one day and we give them at least ten presentations. Each one lasts an hour, with a short lunch, and a coffee, with no time to take a stroll or anything." So the company learned from the interactions between customers and India and employees and India. Nandy continued, "It's a two way process—therefore we are learning from that."

## The First Year Results

That dreary March day in his office, Nandy felt good about what his team of Indian employees had accomplished in the first year of his leadership. He had hired locals so his group had gone from 100 percent Indian to 20 percent European employees and 80 percent Indian. This put Nandy half way to his goal on personnel balance. The business had grown 120-130 percent. But Nandy knew the next growth was going to be even harder and the next hires even more challenging. So far his team included 19 people: two French, one Dutch German to be based in Germany, one Swiss German based in Switzerland, two English, one Irish, and eleven Indians plus himself. Wipro

Technologies needed account-relationship people and employees who could follow after the sales people, particularly for accounts in Sweden, Finland, and Italy. Nandy felt very strongly that such people needed to be fully fluent, if not native speakers, in the clients' language—not simply people familiar with that business context and able to speak the language as a second language. He needed people capable of understanding a greater level of subtlety to distinguish the differences between "what the client wants and what the client needs." Nandy was unsure what additional strategies (see Exhibit 2) he was going to develop for this next phase but he had some ideas.

## CASE DISCUSSION QUESTIONS

1. Review India's scores on Hofstede's cultural dimensions. Do you think that the critical personal characteristics that WIPRO is looking for will be difficult to find in the Indian context? Why or why not?
2. What are some of the key steps WIPRO has taken to enhance its effectiveness? Are these consistent with Indian culture?
3. How can you motivate workers in an emerging market characterized by low employee loyalty to companies and high competition for talent among companies?
4. Will the measures implemented at WIPRO be effective? Why or why not?

# Leadership and Management Behavior in Multinational Companies

15

## *Preview*    C A S E   I N   P O I N T

### Same Problem, Different Styles

Consider the fictional example of the leadership styles of two CEOs of pharmaceutical companies, one in the United States and the other in Japan. They must lead their subordinates in dealing with a crisis regarding a potentially deadly batch of headache medicine produced by one of their overseas subsidiaries. Although the characters and companies are fictional, the styles are based on real leaders.

| Ms. Moore, a U.S. CEO | Sakano-san, a Japanese CEO |
|---|---|
| **7:00** Ms. Moore, CEO of Thorndike Pharmaceuticals, leaves for work with her daughter. | Sakano-san, CEO of Kobe Pharmaceuticals, eats a breakfast of a raw egg and rice. Sakano-san's wife wakes their two children in enough time for their 45-minute subway ride to school. |
| **7:30** Ms. Moore leaves her daughter at a private junior high school for girls. | |
| **7:45** Ms. Moore receives a cell phone call from the Thorndike Pharmaceuticals European area manager to tell her of a death and the nonfatal poisoning of several people in France as a result of their taking tainted headache medication produced by their company. The European area manager asks what he should do. Moore says she will get back to him. | |
| **8:00** Ms. Moore calls her executive secretary and tells him to plan for an 8:30 videoconference with relevant U.S. and European managers and legal staff. | Sakano-san exchanges a polite bow with his driver and begins his limousine ride to Kobe Pharmaceuticals. |

## Learning Objectives
*After reading this chapter you should be able to:*

- Know the characteristics of global business leadership.

- Describe traditional North American models of leadership, including trait theory, behavioral approaches, and contingency theory.

- Explain the Japanese performance maintenance model.

- Apply the cultural contingency model of leadership.

- Develop sensitivity to national cultural differences in preferred leadership traits and effective leadership behaviors.

- Discuss how national culture affects the choice of leader influence tactics.

- Discuss how national culture influences subordinates' expectations regarding appropriate behaviors and the traits of leaders.

- Explain the role of transformational leadership in multinational settings.

- Understand how national culture affects a leader's attributions regarding subordinates' behaviors.

- Diagnose cultural situations and suggest appropriate leadership styles to fit them.

| Ms. Moore, a U.S. CEO | Sakano-san, a Japanese CEO |
| --- | --- |

**8:30** Ms. Moore has a videoconference with the management team and briefs its members on the crisis.

**8:45** Corporate attorneys brief Ms. Moore and the top management team on legal options and liabilities.

**9:00** The director of public relations calls Moore, asking how she can deal with the press.

**9:05** The plant manager of the French facility that produced the tainted drug calls and asks what he should do about the protesters outside the gate.

**9:45** Fearing further deaths and injury, the VP of European operations temporarily shuts down all production of the tainted drug and recalls all drugs produced after a certain date.

Sakano-san meets with executives from Bayer to discuss an international joint venture.

**10:00** Ms. Moore asks the finance and accounting department to figure out how much this is going to cost.

Around this time, a trusted midlevel manager, a student of Sakano-san's old Tokyo University professor, informs Sakano-san discreetly that a problem exists and that staff members are developing a solution. Sakano-san nods his understanding. Staff members engage in consensus building (*nemawashi*) to develop a plan of action to deal with the crisis.

**10:05** Top management and legal staff meet with Ms. Moore to give her an update.

**10:30** Ms. Moore gives an interview to the press.

**11:30** Ms. Moore has a hurried lunch at her desk. She takes calls from the legal department and from the VP for European operations while eating.

Subordinates formally brief Sakano-san on the problem and their plan to deal with it. He acknowledges the information and thanks them for their quick work.

**For the remainder of the day and to well after 8:00 p.m.** Ms. Moore continues at this hectic pace of meetings and phone calls. She calls her husband at 4:00, reminding him to pick up their daughter at school.

With the knowledge that his staff is working on dealing with the crisis, Sakano-san continues his regular business day: a two-hour luncheon meeting with government officials to discuss long-term R&D goals for the industry. He ends his day talking with a chemical supply company CEO at 1:00 a.m. in a private bar in Tokyo's entertainment district, Roppongi.

*Source: Based on the format in a fictional story in Doktor, Robert H. 1990. "Asian and American CEOs: A comparative study."* Organizational Dynamics, *Winter, 46–56.*

**W**hat is leadership? The Western-based view defines leadership as the influencing of group members to achieve organizational goals. However, it is important to understand whether this definition is acceptable in most cultures. In that respect, the Global Leadership and Organizational Behavior Effectiveness project (GLOBE, described in more detail later) sheds some light on the issue. The project gathered about 200 researchers from 60 countries, and after hours of discussion, the GLOBE's universal definition of leadership emerged. The researchers agreed that leadership is "the ability of an individual to influence, motivate, and enable others to contribute toward the effectiveness and success of the organizations of which they are members."[1]

The European Foundation for Quality Management (EFQM),[2] an important association dedicated to fostering quality in European companies, has also attempted to define leadership within the European context. It sees leadership as the process by which individuals "develop and facilitate the achievement of the mission and vision, develop values required for long-term success and implement these via appropriate actions and behaviors, and are personally involved in ensuring that the organization's management system is developed and implemented."[3]

As we see from the GLOBE and EFQM definitions, leadership is more than simply holding a management position. Improving one's leadership skills in a domestic company is a difficult enough challenge, but becoming an excellent leader in a multinational company is an even greater one. In fact, as you will see in this chapter, being an excellent leader is a key aspect of success in any organization. Consider the following Case in Point.

**Leadership**
Ability of an individual to influence, motivate, and enable others to contribute toward the effectiveness and success of the organizations of which they are members.

---

## CASE IN POINT

### Leadership and Supply Chain Implementation in Korean Firms

As you read the chapter, you will see that leadership is an extremely critical aspect of any organization's success. By acting appropriately, a leader can retain and motivate employees to do their best. However, leadership does not only affect employees. The implementation of key projects in any company is also affected by company leaders.

In a recent study of 142 Korean firms, the authors examined the characteristics of leadership and effective supply chain implementation. As noted in Chapter 5, a supply chain is simply the list of activities that company undertakes to manufacture products from the design aspect to after sales support. Companies devote significant resources to ensuring that supply chain activities are designed appropriately, as well as to ensuring desirable supply chain outcomes such as low cost, flexible market responsiveness, and trust with customers.

In the study, the authors argue that integrative leadership on the part of the CEO, chief information officer, and supply chain officer is critical for successful supply chain implementation. Integrative leadership refers to the extent to which these key executives have high levels of collaboration and interact in a dynamic manner. The results of the study in Korea showed that integrative leadership is indeed related to many key supply chain outcomes. Integrative leaders share critical operational and strategic information that allows the company to better implement its supply chain to achieve better value for customers while also enhancing the flow of information within the company.

*Source: Based on Youn, S., Yang, M. G. and Hong, P. 2012. "Integrative leadership for effective supply chain implementation: An empirical study of Korean firms." International Journal of Production Economics, 139, 237–246.*

As the next Case in Point shows, leadership is a critical function in any company. This chapter will therefore show that successful multinational leaders choose effective leadership styles based on an understanding of how national culture and a country's social institutions affect leadership. The chapter covers two important areas. First, it provides a summary of theories of leadership offered by experts from different countries. Second, it offers key examples of how leaders of different national backgrounds behave in their home cultures. As the Preview Case in Point shows and as this chapter will describe, managers working in different cultures may achieve similar goals using widely different leadership styles.

# Global Leadership: The New Breed

The rise of transnational companies and the dependence of even the smallest companies on international trade have created a need for a new type of leader. This **global leader** must have the skills and abilities to interact with and manage people from the diverse cultural backgrounds that populate his or her multinational company.

Let us consider some of the characteristics of this new breed of leader. According to experts on managing cultural differences, the successful global leader is:[4]

> **Global leader**
> One who has the skills and abilities to interact with and manage people from diverse cultural backgrounds.

- *Cosmopolitan:* Sufficiently flexible to operate comfortably in pluralistic cultural environments.

- *Skilled at intercultural communication:* Conversant in at least one foreign language and understands the complexities of interaction with people from other cultures.

- *Culturally sensitive:* Experienced in different national, regional, and organizational cultures needed to build relationships with culturally different people while understanding his or her own culture and cultural biases.

- *Capable of rapid acculturation:* Able to rapidly acculturate or adjust to different cultural settings.

- *A facilitator of subordinates' intercultural performance:* Aware of cultural differences in work and living and able to prepare subordinates for successful overseas experiences.

- *A user of cultural synergy:* Takes advantage of cultural differences by finding a synergy that combines the strengths of each cultural group and by using performance standards understandable across cultural groups, resulting in increased levels of organizational performance than those produced by culturally homogeneous companies. Consider the following Case in Point.

- *A promoter and user of the growing world culture:* Understands, uses, and takes advantage of the international advances in media, transportation, and travel that support the globalization of business.

- *Emotionally intelligent:*[5] Able to accurately perceive his or her emotions and to use them to solve problems and to relate to others.

How can multinationals train global leaders? Consider the next Multinational Management Brief.

The remainder of this chapter provides a background on leadership. Few managers will reach the levels and experience of truly global managers, but all managers can benefit by gaining a better understanding of leadership, thereby developing the strengths of a global leader.

### Role of Leaders in Successful Mergers and Acquisitions

A recent article provides some insights into the role of leaders in ensuring the success of mergers and acquisitions. In that article, the authors compare Rolf Eckrodt (CEO of the DaimlerChrysler-Mitsubishi merger) with Carlos Goshn (CEO of the Renault-Nissan merger) and find that Goshn made much better use of cultural synergy than Eckrodt. Goshn's use of cultural synergy was offered as a potential explanation of why the Nissan-Renault merger succeeded while the DaimlerChrysler-Mitsubishi merger failed. Specifically, Goshn had better awareness of his role as a leader and this allowed him to be more sensitive to the cultural differences. When Renault acquired Nissan, Goshn expected that there would be a clash between his French management style and Nissan's predominant organizational culture. Rather than imposing his own style, he created cross-functional teams from both companies. These teams were given the power and authority to implement changes to facilitate the acquisition. Goshn met with the teams on a monthly basis and employees were fully involved in the change process. Because Goshn wanted to implement many changes at Nissan, this team approach allowed him to get the buy-in of Nissan and changes proceeded very smoothly.

In contrast, Eckrodt was not as sensitive to cultural differences. He did not make much use of teams and left much of the power and authority in the hands of expatriate managers. Furthermore, being from a high power distance society, managers at Mitsubishi were less likely to question and disagree with decisions. The Mitsubishi managers were actually more likely to passively resist change and did not show their displeasure with the changes. Eckrodt mistook such passivity for acceptance and the merger eventually failed.

*Source: Based on Gill, C. 2012. "The role of leadership in successful international mergers and acquisitions: Why Renault-Nissan succeeded and DaimlerChrysler-Mitsubishi failed."* Human Resource Management, *May–June, 51(3): 433–456.*

# Three Classic Models: A Vocabulary of Leadership

The three basic models of leadership entail leadership traits, leader behavior, and contingency leadership. Knowledge of these views of leadership will help you understand the terms used to describe leadership options in a multinational setting.

Like the motivation theories discussed in Chapter 14, most, but not all, of these leadership models originate in North America. However, this chapter focuses on the multinational applicability of leadership models, not just on their North American applications.

## Leadership Traits

Trait models of leadership evolved from the debate regarding whether leaders are born or made. Early leadership theorists looked at successful leaders in business, politics, religion, and the military, such as Alexander the Great and Muhammad. They concluded that such leaders were born with unique characteristics that made them quite different from other people. This view of leadership is known as the **great person theory**.

Although leadership theorists never identified an exact list of leadership traits, decades of research have uncovered some differences between leaders and their subordinates.[6] At least in the United States, successful leaders exhibit the following traits: high intelligence and self-confidence, great initiative, assertiveness and

**Great person theory**
Leaders are born with unique characteristics that make them quite different from other people.

## Multinational Management **Brief**

### Intel's and Dow Corning's Leadership Training Program

Intel, the Silicon Valley–based semiconductor giant, obtains 70 percent of its revenues from outside the United States. It currently has employees located in more than 48 nations. Given the global nature of its operations, Intel places crucial importance on the ability of its managers to deal with cross-cultural differences. In that context, it has a very innovative leadership program that requires all of its midlevel leaders to be exposed to other cultures.

The design of the leadership training program is the result of substantial cooperation among employees from places such as China, Russia, the United States, and Israel. The program incorporates seminars emphasizing the development of leadership skills, such as setting pace and implementing business plans. Although the seminars do not necessarily include cultural training, the program requires teams of six to nine midlevel leaders from various regions to create new product proposals at the end of the training. In doing so, Intel forces the participants to consider cultural differences by working with individuals from many different societies. Such experiences ensure that attendees have a chance to deal with cultural variations as they work on the project.

For Dow Corning, the U.S.-based multinational corporation that specializes in silicone-based technology products, it identifies high performers in each country it operates and provides training to these high-potential individuals. For example, although it has only been in India for 12 years, it has refined its leadership strategy to identify high-potentials early on. These high-potential individuals are then put through a rigorous experiential training program that encourages them to get involved in specific projects or businesses. These future leaders are also asked to argue and present to the top management teams why they should be considered as high potential and what they expect to achieve during their careers at Dow Corning. Such programs have paid off for the company. While many companies in India struggle to keep talent, Dow Corning is able to keep most of its high-potential performers.

*Sources: Based on Ghosh, L. 2012. "We select people who are resilient, says HR Director of Dow Corning." Economic Times, online edition, August 15; Hamm, S. 2008. "Young and impatient in India." BusinessWeek, January 28, 45–48; Thomke, Stefan H. 2006. "Capturing the real value of innovation tools." MIT Sloan Management Reviews, Winter, 47, 24–32; Times of India. 2009. "RMSI, Intel among best work places in India," June 10.*

persistence, a great desire for responsibility and the opportunity to influence others, and a high awareness of the needs of others. However, unlike the great person theory of leadership, contemporary views of leadership traits do not assume that leaders are born. Although leaders are different, aspiring leaders can achieve this difference through training and experience.

## Leadership Behaviors

### U.S. Perspectives on Leadership Behaviors

Although leaders have different traits than their subordinates, North American studies of leadership traits have concluded that traits alone do not make a leader. The *behaviors* leaders use to manage their employees may be more important.

Classic studies of leadership behaviors in the United States came from two U.S. universities: Ohio State University and the University of Michigan. Based on hundreds of studies of North American managers, these teams of researchers identified two major types of leadership behaviors.[7] One study included behaviors that focus on completing tasks by initiating structure. Leaders who have a principal concern for initiating structure are called task-centered leaders. A **task-centered leader** gives specific directions to subordinates so that they can complete tasks. This type of leader establishes standards, schedules work, and assigns employees tasks. A second type of leader, a **person-centered leader,** focuses on meeting the social and emotional needs of employees. Such consideration behaviors include showing a concern for subordinates' feelings and taking subordinates' ideas into account.

The distinction between person-centered and task-centered leader behaviors also applies to how leaders make decisions. Leaders who adopt an **autocratic leadership** style make all major decisions themselves. Those who employ a **democratic leadership** style include subordinates in the decision making. Most experts accept that a range of leadership behaviors exists between the authoritarian leader, who makes all decisions, and the purely democratic leader, who delegates all decision making to the group.[8] For example, the **consultative or participative leadership** style often falls midway between the autocratic and democratic leadership styles. Do some cultures prefer specific leadership decision making styles? Consider the next Case in Point.

Taking a somewhat broader perspective than just leadership behavior, Rensis Likert, a famous management and leadership theorist, identified four styles of management that reflect a similar distinction between the task and the person.[9]

**Task-centered leader**
One who gives subordinates specific standards, schedules, and tasks.

**Person-centered leader**
One who focuses on meeting employees' social and emotional needs.

**Autocratic leadership**
Leaders make all major decisions themselves.

**Democratic leadership**
Leader includes subordinates in decision making.

---

### CASE IN POINT

## Leadership Decision-Making Style in India and South Korea

Many South Korean companies have traditionally been run autocratically. This is not surprising given the paternalistic rule that corporations play in South Korea. Consider the case of Hyundai, one of South Korea's powerhouses. Chung Mong Koo, Hyundai's chairman, and his team of executives have managed the firm using a very autocratic style. It has been claimed that the executive team micromanages details and seldom listens to advice. Furthermore, the executives do not display much tolerance for disagreement. This style is running into major problems in U.S. operations. Both Hyundai and its sister company, Kia, have fired many American executives. Critics argue that the very autocratic style has frustrated American executives, who are used to a participative leadership style. For instance, Hyundai and Kia both have South Korean coordinators whose role is to monitor decision making. American managers resent this system because they have to get the approval of

the South Korean coordinators for even small decisions. This has resulted in many top executives getting fired.

India also has high power distance and subordinates therefore tend to be more submissive and to expect orders. However, a recent article suggests that this may be changing. Many Generation Y employees (the twenty-somethings) at India's large companies tend to be fearless and full of "spunk." Many are very self-confident and will publicly criticize. Furthermore, they tend to be more entrepreneurial and want balance in life. These behaviors and attitudes are in stark contrast to those of previous generations, who were more submissive and rarely likely to voice their opinions.

*Source: Based on Bhattacharya, S. 2012. "How young executives are redefining parameters of work and challenging bosses' notions."* The Economic Times, *online edition, August 12; Welch, D., D. Kiley, and M. Ihlwan. 2008. "My way or the highway at Hyundai."* BusinessWeek, *March 17, 48–51.*

**EXHIBIT 15.1**    Likert's Four Styles of Management

| Management Behaviors | Exploitative Authoritative (System 1) | Benevolent Authoritative (System 2) | Consultative (System 3) | Participative (System 4) |
|---|---|---|---|---|
| General leadership style | Autocratic, top-down | Paternalistic but still autocratic | Less autocratic, more attention to employees | Employee centered |
| Motivation techniques | Punishments, some rewards | More rewards, but still punishment dominated | Reward dominated | Employees set own goals and appraise results |
| Communication style | Downward, little use of teamwork | Downward, with some limited teamwork | Employees give opinions | Extensive multiway communication both laterally and vertically |
| Decision-making style | Decisions made at top of organization | Management sets boundaries | Management consults but makes final decision | Group or team makes most decisions |
| Control mechanisms | Process and output managed from the top | Management sets boundaries | More output control than process | Team appraises results |

*Source: Adapted from Likert, R., and Jane Likert. 1976.* New Ways of Managing Conflict. *New York: McGraw-Hill.*

**Consultative or participative leadership**
Leader's style falls midway between autocratic and democratic styles.

These patterns are exploitative/authoritative, benevolent/authoritative, consultative, and participative. Exhibit 15.1 shows how each management style relates to a general leadership orientation, preferred motivational techniques, communication style, decision-making style, and controlling style.

Based on early studies of U.S. workers, we can conclude that leaders choose behaviors that focus on initiating structure for task completion or on meeting the social and emotional needs of workers. Which style of leader behavior is best? Perhaps it all depends on the situation. In later sections, you will see that contemporary U.S. leadership theories challenge the assumption that one style of leadership behavior fits all situations. Before considering that issue, however, we will look at leadership as perceived in Japan.

## Japanese Perspectives on Leader Behaviors

**Performance-maintenance (PM) theory**
Japanese perspective on balancing task- and person-centered leader behaviors.

The **performance maintenance (PM) theory** of leadership represents a Japanese perspective on leader behavior. Created in Japan but similar to many U.S. leadership theories, PM theory has two dimensions.[10] The performance function (P) is similar to task-centered leadership; the manager guides and pressures subordinates to achieve increasing levels of group performance. The performance (P) side of PM leadership has two components. First, the leader works for or with subordinates to develop work procedures, called the planning component. Second, the leader pressures employees to put forth the effort and to do good work; this is the pressure component. The maintenance function (M) is similar to person-centered leadership. It represents behaviors that promote group stability and social interaction.

One key difference exists between the Japanese PM approach and the U.S. perspective on task- and person-centered leadership. The Japanese PM leader focuses on influencing groups. The U.S. task- or person-centered leader focuses on influencing individuals.

PM theory suggests that groups perform best when both P and M are present. That is, a leader can pressure a group to increase levels of performance as long as the leader also supports the social interaction needs of the group, the M function. The theory suggests that the positive effects of combining the P and M leadership components should work in all cultural settings. However, in adapting to national differences, many Japanese companies use modified versions of PM theory to manage their overseas operations.[11]

The next section presents an overview of a more complex view of leadership, called contingency theory. It shows the historical progression of leadership theory beyond the simple trait and behavior models.

## Contingency Theories

The early models of leadership tended to look for leadership universals: managers and researchers wanted to know which leadership traits or behaviors defined excellent leadership in all situations. After years of study, experts concluded that "it all depends"; in other words, no one leadership style works best for all situations. This conclusion led to an approach to leadership known as **contingency theory**, which assumes that the appropriate type of styles and leaders depends on the situation. To lead successfully, managers must choose different leadership styles in different situations.

How does contingency theory work? Consider the next Multinational Management Brief.

**Contingency theory**
Assumption that different styles and leaders are appropriate for various situations.

## Multinational Management **Brief**

### Management at LG

The preference of South Korean multinationals for autocratic styles of leadership is consistent with the Confucian-influenced Korean culture: "Father knows best." However, other multinationals, such as LG, are making changes to this approach. LG, a major electronics multinational, used to be one of the most Korean of South Korea's conglomerates, or *chaebols*. The company's chief executive, Nam Yong, believes that changing the decision-making style is critical in enabling LG to succeed in its global markets. Unlike other South Korean multinationals, LG has been steadily hiring foreigners to diversify its managers. Foreign executives and top managers now represent over 25 percent of the company's leadership, and the new executives are gradually changing the leadership styles at LG. However, Nam Yong's recent comments reflect his contingency style approach to leadership. He recently wrapped up a stormy strategy meeting where tempers flared—a very rare occurrence in a culture that values agreement and consensus. Nam Yong told his chief marketing officer, Dermot Boden, an Irishman working in Seoul, "You know, we argue a lot. Why don't we argue more often?" This strategy seems to be paying off. LG is now the world's second-largest liquid crystal display manufacturer and is achieving prominence in many other electronics sectors. The company has developed a new type of display technology that is expected to be used in the next iPhone.

*Sources: Based on Ihlwan, M. 2008. "The foreigners at the top of LG." BusinessWeek, December 22, 56–58; Lee, J. 2012. "LG Display starts producing new panels." Wall Street Journal (online), August 23; Welch, D., D. Kiley, and M. Ihlwan. 2008. "My way or the highway at Hyundai." BusinessWeek, March 17, 48–51.*

The next section reviews two important North American contingency theories of leadership: Fiedler's theory of leadership and path-goal theory. These theories identify several factors that influence the effectiveness of certain leadership styles in different situations. They also provide the basic framework that multinational managers can use to adapt their leadership styles to work in different national contexts. For additional reviews of other contingency theories of leadership, consult standard organizational behavior textbooks.

## Fiedler on Leadership Effectiveness

**Fiedler's theory of leadership**
Proposal that success of task- or person-centered leader depends on relationships between the leader and subordinates, the degree that subordinates' tasks are easily and clearly defined, and the officially granted organizational power of the leader.

Fred Fiedler, an expert on leadership, developed one of the most popular early contingency views of leadership.[12] **Fiedler's theory of leadership** proposes that managers tend to be either task- or person-centered leaders. The success of these leadership styles depends on three contingencies, or characteristics, of the work situation: the relationships between the leader and subordinates (e.g., the degree to which the subordinates trust the leader); the degree to which subordinates' tasks are easily and clearly defined (e.g., tasks for assembly line work usually are clearly defined); and the officially granted organizational power of the leader (e.g., the formal power of a position, such as a ship's captain).

As with all contingency theories, effective leadership occurs when the style matches the situation. What situations suggest a task- or person-centered leadership style? Exhibit 15.2 shows the predicted effectiveness of task- and person-centered leadership in different conditions. Task-centered leadership works best when the work situation includes a positive relationship between the leader and subordinates, highly structured tasks, and high levels of organizational power. It also works best in just the opposite conditions, such as when the job requirements are unclear. Person-centered leadership is required in mixed conditions, such as when a leader has low formal power but good relationships with subordinates.

The theory's logic suggests that task-centered leadership works best in situations that are favorable or unfavorable for a leader. In favorable situations, the leader does not need to worry about the psychological needs of subordinates. They already feel positive about their work, the tasks are clear, and the leader is powerful. The leader tells people what to do, and they do it willingly. In unfavorable situations, such as when job requirements are unclear or subordinates are uncooperative, the leader must focus on getting subordinates to complete the job. In mixed situations, however, employee commitment and satisfaction become more important, and a successful leader must focus time on people rather than on just getting tasks done.

**EXHIBIT 15.2** Predictions of Leader Effectiveness under Different Conditions

| Leadership Style | Leader Effectiveness | | |
|---|---|---|---|
| Person-centered | Ineffective | Effective | Ineffective |
| Task-centered | Effective | Ineffective | Effective |
| Contingency conditions | Good relations between leader and group<br>Structured tasks<br>Low power in leader's position<br>(generally favorable for the leader) | Mixed | Poor relations between leader and group<br>Unclear job requirements<br>Low power in leader's position<br>(generally unfavorable for the leader) |

*Source: Adapted from Fiedler, F. 1978. "Contingency model and the leadership process." In L. Berkowitz, ed. Advances in Experimental Social Psychology, 11th ed. New York: Academic Press, 60–112.*

## Path-Goal Theory

Another popular contingency theory, **path-goal theory,** identifies four types of leadership styles that a manager might choose depending on the situation:

**Path-goal theory**
Four types of leadership styles that a manager might choose depending on the situation.

- *Directive style:* Give subordinates specific goals, schedules, and procedures.
- *Supportive style:* Show a concern for satisfying subordinates' needs and establishing good relationships.
- *Participative style:* Consult with subordinates, ask for suggestions, and encourage participation in decision making.
- *Achievement-oriented style:* Set goals and reward goal accomplishment.

In path-goal theory, the key contingency or situational factors that determine the choice of the best leadership styles are the nature of the subordinates and the characteristics of the subordinates' tasks. Exhibit 15.3 presents a simplified overview of path-goal theory.

The path-goal theory projects many outcomes from the complex interactions between leadership and the contingencies. A complete review of path-goal theory is beyond the scope of this chapter; however, here are some key leadership suggestions based on path-goal theory:[13]

- When subordinates have high achievement needs, successful leaders adopt the achievement-oriented style.

**EXHIBIT 15.3**   A Simplified Model of Path-Goal Theory

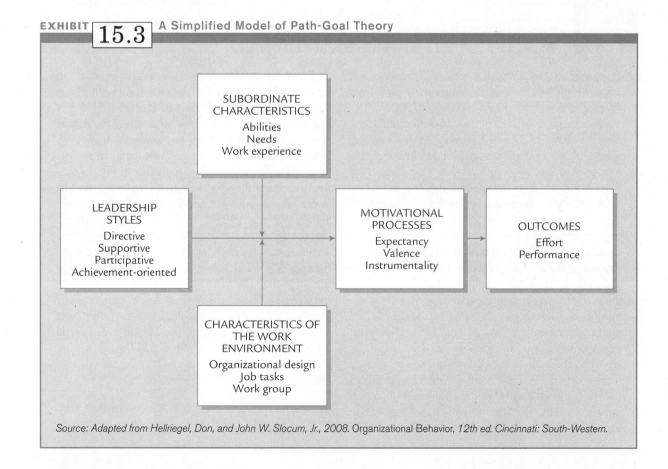

*Source: Adapted from Hellriegel, Don, and John W. Slocum, Jr., 2008.* Organizational Behavior, *12th ed. Cincinnati: South-Western.*

- Subordinates with high social needs respond best to the supportive leadership style.
- When the subordinates' job is unstructured, the theory suggests using a directive style (the leader details very specific job tasks and requirements) or an achievement-oriented style (the leader gives subordinates responsibility to discover solutions).

## Traits, Behaviors, and Contingencies

Given our review of North American and Japanese views of leadership traits, behaviors, and contingency theory, we know that leaders have different characteristics than their subordinates. However, it seems that leaders can develop the required characteristics if they do not come naturally. Leaders have a variety of behaviors that they can use to get the job done. These range from task- to person-centered styles and include decision-making styles from autocratic to democratic.

Most experts now believe that no one leadership trait or behavior works in all situations. The contingency theory of leadership suggests that a successful leader must diagnose the situation and pick the behaviors or develop the leadership traits that fit best. The recent turnaround at Toyota shows how the company's current founder, Akio Toyoda, assessed the situation to determine what leadership style would work best. Consider the following Case in Point.

The next sections will explain how national culture and social institutions, such as a country's educational system, affect the choice of an appropriate leadership style.

### CASE IN POINT

### Leadership Style at Toyota

Toyota recently experienced a number of disasters that many thought would irreversibly damage the company's standing and reputation as a carmaker. In 2009–2010, it ordered a giant recall as a result of unintended acceleration in some of its cars. It also had to deal with the effects of the tsunami that had hit Japan. All of this happened under the watch of the new CEO, Akio Toyoda, the grandson of the company's founder.

To deal with these crises, Toyoda took a contingent approach to his own leadership approach. He understood that Toyota had become very complacent as a result of its size, and as a result of Japanese national culture. The company was very inflexible and any decision could only be made after going through the usual bureaucratic channels. Furthermore, being a Japanese company, Toyota did not delegate too much power to its U.S. sales and operations. As a consequence, its U.S. operations were dogged by slow decision making and an inability to deal with crises. For instance, American managers had to follow a long bureaucratic process to report defects in cars. Such complaints about defects in cars were often met with skepticism in Japan.

Toyoda understood that his leadership style had to be changed if he expected to lead Toyota out of the crisis. Toyota had to become faster, more nimble, and less bureaucratic. For instance, when the massive tidal wave disrupted production, he organized a meeting with the general managers and gave them the authority to make decisions without reporting upward. In contrast to cultural expectations, he removed several layers of management. Additionally, he now meets weekly with his advisers and decisions are made on the spot. Top executives are now no longer rotated across functions such as purchasing, product engineering, or manufacturing. Rather, top executives now remain in their specialties to benefit from their experience. Finally, Toyoda is very different from previous Toyota CEOs. He is a certified test car driver and tests almost 200 Toyotas on an annual basis. He is also a strong supporter of the $375,000 Lexus LFA. He hopes that the car will show that Toyota can also be a serious sports car manufacturer.

*Source: Based on Taylor III, A. 2012. "Toyota's comeback kid." Fortune, February 27, 72–79.*

# National Context as a Contingency for Leadership Behaviors

Most experts on leadership in multinational companies argue that a contingency perspective is required;[14] that is, successful leadership in multinational companies requires that managers adjust their leadership style to fit the situation. This adjustment must occur in response not only to traditional contingency factors, such as subordinates' characteristics, but also to the cultural and institutional contexts of the country locations.

The next Focus on Emerging Markets illustrates the effects of culturally contingent management behavior by showing some of the preferred leadership behaviors in selected Latin American countries. It also describes how one U.S. company ran equally successful plants in Mexico and the United States using two different management styles.

The first step in understanding how to adjust your leadership to a multinational situation is understanding what local managers do to lead successfully in their own countries. The second step is using that knowledge to modify your leadership style appropriately; that is, although it is unlikely that an expatriate manager can ever lead in exactly the same way as local managers, knowledge of how successful local leaders behave can suggest the necessary modifications in a multinational leader's behavior.

## The National-Context Contingency Model of Leadership: An Overview

As a guide both for understanding leadership behaviors in different national contexts and for modifying your leadership behaviors in different cultural contexts, this section presents the **national-context contingency model of leadership** (summarized in Exhibit 15.4). This model explains how culture and related social institutions affect leadership practices. Similar to the classic contingency theories of leadership, the model shown in Exhibit 15.4 begins with the basic contingency assumption that to be successful, leaders must modify their behaviors or develop particular leadership traits, depending on two key contingencies: the characteristics of their subordinates and the nature of their work setting.

**National-context contingency model of leadership**
Shows how culture and related social institutions affect leadership practices.

In the multinational setting, however, the components of the contingency leadership model (leader behavior and traits, subordinates' characteristics, and the work setting) are affected by the national context (the national culture, business culture, and social institutions). Here is how the national context affects leadership behaviors, traits, and contingencies:

- *Leader behaviors and traits:* National culture, business culture, and social institutions define the array of preferred and acceptable leader behaviors and traits for managers. Consider the following examples. In high-power-distance countries, leaders and subordinates expect the manager to act with authority. Educational systems like the French *grandes écoles* train managers to believe that they should act as an elite social class. If the host country's legal system gives power to unions to participate in management decisions, then managers must adjust their leadership behaviors to this situation (Chapter 12).

- *Subordinates' characteristics:* National and business cultures influence workers' needs and levels of achievement motivation (Chapter 14). Additionally, a country's socio-economic development and institutional support for education affect the quality and availability of training and education for workers (Chapter 12). Consequently, leaders must modify their styles to fit the types of workers in a given nation.

## Focus on Emerging Markets

### Leadership Styles in Latin America and Mexico

Despite the worldwide recession, trends suggest that Latin American economies will continue to grow and present many opportunities. Although many of these economies are facing significant challenges, they also have the opportunity to continue experiencing impressive growth. Such opportunities are likely to continue encouraging more investments. As multinational companies begin operations in Latin America, they need to adapt their leadership styles to the cultural demands of employees.

Many Latin American countries share a cultural heritage because of their common Spanish colonial history. As a result, many Spanish institutional traditions, such as authoritarianism and paternalism, are strong today. Hofstede also found that many Latin American countries share high power distance, high uncertainty avoidance, and high masculinity. These historical and cultural facts have implications for leaders.

The traditional Latin American leader, *el patron,* is expected to be autocratic and directive, seldom delegating work or using teams. Such leaders use the formal top-down organizational hierarchy to communicate, are relationship oriented, and are expected to be aggressive and assertive. An exploratory study in Argentina, Chile, the Dominican Republic, Mexico, Peru, Puerto Rico, and Venezuela confirmed that the leaders in these countries were more likely to adhere to *el patron* behaviors.

Other studies suggest that appropriate leadership behaviors and styles are dependent on culture. In a study using two plants of a U.S. manufacturer, one in the United States and the other in Mexico, two researchers from the University of San Diego found that different leadership styles produced the same level of success. The exhibit below shows their results based on the classification of management styles developed by Likert. Neither plant used a participative management style. The U.S. plant achieved success with a consultative management style. The Mexican plant succeeded with a management style falling into the authoritative range on all of Likert's management behaviors. The equally effective performances of the plants suggest that national culture may be an important contingency factor in choosing a leadership or management style. Furthermore, the results confirm the suitability of authoritative leadership styles and behaviors in Latin American countries.

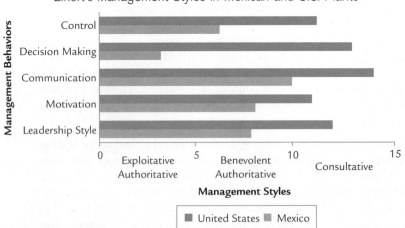

Likert's Management Styles in Mexican and U.S. Plants

*Sources:* Based on Economist. *2012. "Latin America's big tests." The World in 2012, 53; Morris, Tom, and Cynthia M. Pavett. 1992. "Management style and productivity in two cultures." Journal of International Business Studies, 1st quarter, 169–179; Romero, Eric J. 2004. "Latin American leadership: El patron & el lider moderno." Cross Cultural Management, 11(3): 25.*

- *Work setting:* Culture and social institutions affect the choices managers make in designing organizations and subunits. The organizational characteristics in turn affect the leader's options in the work setting; that is, task characteristics, such as routine work, and organizational characteristics, such as formalized jobs, constrain

**EXHIBIT 15.4**   A National-Context Contingency Model of Leadership

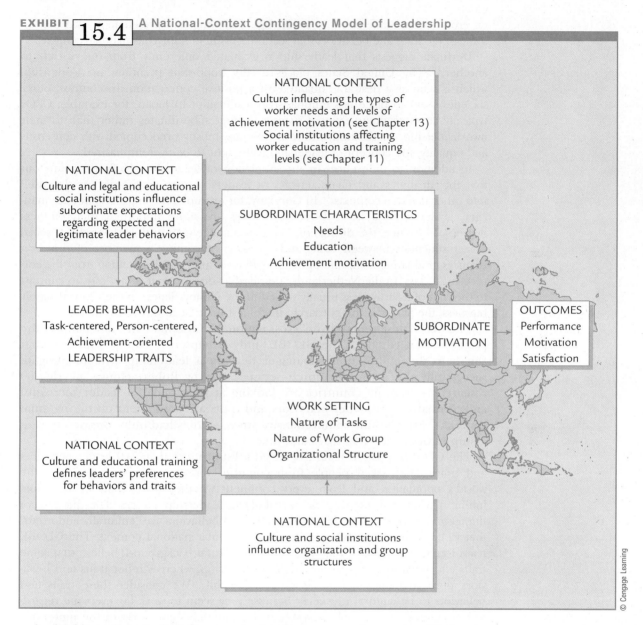

leadership options. In fact, the organizational context can be so powerful that, in some situations, certain leader behaviors may not even be necessary.[15] For example, a highly formalized organization may not require much direct leader supervision.

The next sections expand on the cultural contingency model of leadership. They provide more examples and detail on how national culture, business culture, and social institutions affect the choice of leader behaviors or traits.

## Leadership Traits and Behaviors in National Context

There is considerable evidence that people prefer certain traits and behaviors in their leaders depending on their cultural backgrounds. The many cultures in the world have different images of what distinguishes successful leaders. However, there is also evidence that some leader behaviors and traits are cultural universals; that is, they are endorsed or accepted by almost all people. The following section provides more detail on cross-national differences in leadership. Following that presentation, you will see some of the traits and behaviors that seem successful in numerous national contexts.

Dorfman suggests that leadership is evaluated differently from one society to another.[16] The United States places a very important premium on leadership, which is seen as a desirable quality with a positive connotation. In contrast, other societies seem to place less emphasis on leadership. In Japan, for example, CEOs typically attribute organizational success to their subordinates rather than to their own leadership. In Holland, where people are mostly preoccupied with consensus and equality, the concept of leadership is thought to be overemphasized.

In addition to differences in the evaluation of leadership, Hofstede points out that the attributes and characteristics of leaders do not necessarily translate well into other national contexts.[17] In Germany, for example, the engineer, not the manager, is the cultural hero. Doctoral degrees are more important than business degrees. In France, the distinction between management and worker reflects social class distinctions between *cadres* and *noncadres*. Becoming a member of the *cadre* requires graduating from one of the *grandes écoles* and, usually, coming from the correct social class. In the Netherlands, a desired leadership trait is modesty, in contrast to the trait of assertiveness usually valued in the United States. In the Chinese family business, the leader is the patriarch, the oldest male head of the family.

The very latest research on cross-national differences in leadership is the project called GLOBE. The GLOBE study (Chapter 2) contains insights that can help the multinational manager develop a leadership style to navigate successfully the maze of cultural settings. Led by Robert House, nearly 200 researchers from 60 countries are looking at what makes a leader successful and to what extent leader behaviors and traits are contingent on the national context.[18] Prior to this comprehensive study, studies had only considered leadership in only a few countries at a time.

The GLOBE research team assembled a list of more than 100 leader behaviors and traits. They asked people from countries representing the majority of the world's population and from every continent whether these traits or behaviors inhibit a person's leadership or contribute to leadership success. The first task of the team was to see which leadership traits and behaviors are "culturally endorsed," that is, considered best for a leader in a particular national context. The GLOBE team found that most people, regardless of cultural background, believe that some traits and behaviors lead to outstanding leadership, whereas other traits and behaviors prevent managers from leading successfully. We consider these traits and behaviors to be cultural universals because they seem to work for everyone regardless of cultural or national background. Exhibit 15.5 shows a list of the universally acceptable or disliked behaviors and traits identified by the GLOBE study. The implication for the multinational manager is that one can adopt these traits or behaviors and behave within cultural expectations almost anywhere in the world.

Another way of looking at the leadership traits and behaviors is to consider groups of them that represent different leadership styles. Earlier in the chapter, we examined the classic distinctions among leadership styles, focusing on the person versus the task leader and on the degree of participation. The GLOBE research team identified leadership styles that are particularly relevant to leadership in other cultural settings. Some are similar to the classic leadership style distinctions. We consider five here: team-oriented, self-protective, participative, humane, and autonomous.

The team-oriented style characterizes a leader who is an integrator, who is diplomatic and benevolent, and who works collaboratively with the team. The self-protective leader is self-centered, status conscious, procedural, and a face-saver. The participative leader is a delegator and encourages subordinate participation

EXHIBIT **15.5**    Culture-Free Positively and Negatively Regarded Leadership Traits and Behaviors from 60 Countries

| Positively Regarded Traits and Behaviors | | Negatively Regarded Traits and Behaviors |
|---|---|---|
| Trustworthy | Dependable | Loner |
| Just | Intelligent | Asocial |
| Honest | Decisive | Not cooperative |
| Plans ahead | Effective bargainer | Nonexplicit |
| Encouraging | Win–win problem solver | Egocentric |
| Positive | Skilled administrator | Ruthless |
| Dynamic | Communicator | Dictatorial |
| Motivator | Informed | |
| Confidence builder | Team builder | |

*Source: Adapted from Den Hartog, Deanne N., Robert J. House, Paul J. Hanges, Peter W. Dorfman, S. Antonio Ruiz-Quintanna, and 170 associates. 1999. "Culture specific and cross-culturally generalizable implicit leadership theories: Are attributes of charismatic/transformational leadership universally endorsed?" Leadership Quarterly, 10, 219–256.*

in decisions. The humane style characterizes leaders who have modesty and a compassionate orientation. Finally, the autonomous leader—individualistic, independent, and unique—is expected to act in a self-interested fashion.

To compare leadership behaviors, we use the GLOBE's study grouping of countries by clusters,[19] which offers a convenient way to summarize information regarding how countries are similar as well as how they differ.[20] We consider 10 clusters: the Anglo cluster, the Confucian Asia cluster, the East Europe cluster, the Germanic Europe cluster, the Latin America cluster, the Latin Europe cluster, the Middle East cluster, the Nordic Europe cluster, the Southern Asia cluster, and the Sub-Saharan cluster.

Exhibit 15.6 shows the countries included in each cluster, and Exhibit 15.7 shows how each style varies across clusters representing a large sample of nations

EXHIBIT **15.6**    GLOBE's Study Clusters and Countries Included in Each

| Anglo | Latin Europe | Eastern Europe | Latin America | Confucian Asia |
|---|---|---|---|---|
| Australia | Israel | Albania | Argentina | China |
| Canada | Italy | Georgia | Bolivia | Hong Kong |
| Ireland | Portugal | Greece | Brazil | Japan |
| New Zealand | Spain | Hungary | Colombia | Singapore |
| South Africa (White) | France | Kazakhstan | Costa Rica | South Korea |
| United Kingdom | Switzerland (French | Poland | El Salvador | Taiwan |
| United States | Speaking) | Russia | Guatemala | |
| | | Slovenia | Mexico | |
| | | | Venezuela | |

| Nordic Europe | Germanic Europe | Sub-Saharan Africa | Middle East | Southern Asia |
|---|---|---|---|---|
| Denmark | Austria | Namibia | Qatar | India |
| Finland | Switzerland | Nigeria | Morocco | Indonesia |
| Sweden | Netherlands | South Africa (Black) | Turkey | Philippines |
| | Germany (former East) | Zambia | Egypt | Malaysia |
| | Germany (former West) | Zimbabwe | Kuwait | Thailand |
| | | | | Iran |

*Source: Adapted from Gupta, Vipin, Paul J. Hanges, and Peter Dorfman. 2002. "Cultural clusters: Methodology and findings." Journal of World Business, 37, 11–15.*

representing Asia, Africa, Europe, the Middle East, and North America. As shown in the exhibits, there are differences in the various leadership styles based on cultural differences. For instance, it is not surprising to find that team-oriented leaders are preferred in Latin European, East European, and Southern Asian

**EXHIBIT 15.7**     Culturally Contingent Beliefs Regarding Effective Leadership Styles

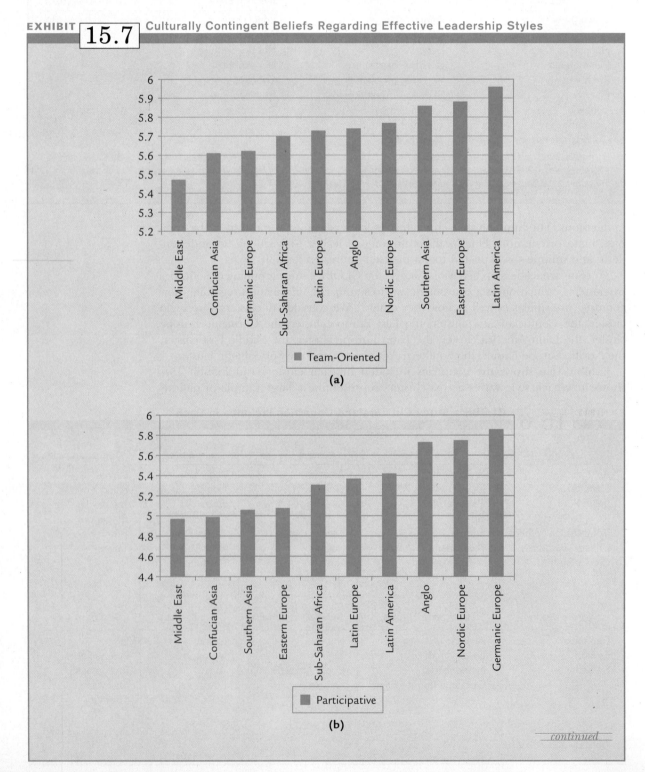

(a)

(b)

*continued*

**EXHIBIT 15.7** Continued

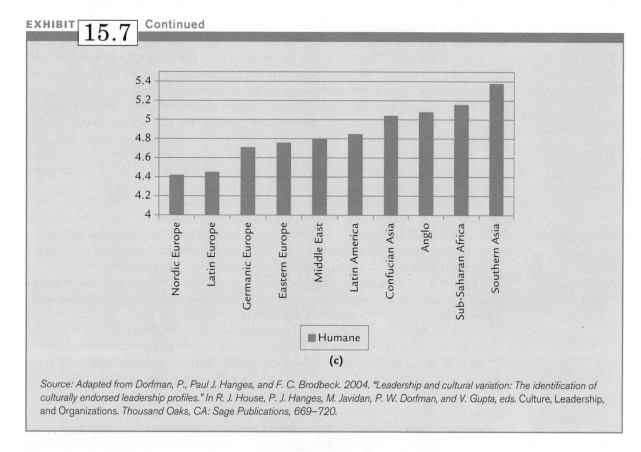

**(c)**

*Source: Adapted from Dorfman, P., Paul J. Hanges, and F. C. Brodbeck. 2004. "Leadership and cultural variation: The identification of culturally endorsed leadership profiles." In R. J. House, P. J. Hanges, M. Javidan, P. W. Dorfman, and V. Gupta, eds.* Culture, Leadership, and Organizations. *Thousand Oaks, CA: Sage Publications, 669–720.*

societies. Latin European societies have had a history of socialist governments, corresponding with collectivism rather than individualism.[21] Similarly, Southern Asian societies are high on collectivism, and leaders who are willing to be collaborative and diplomatic and who respect the group and the collective are likely to succeed.[22] Surprisingly, East European societies prefer high team-oriented leaders. However, these societies have had long periods of communism when people have had to rely on each other to satisfy basic needs. It is also possible that the presence of many multinational companies in these countries and the use of teams are gradually encouraging East Europeans to view team-oriented leaders in a better light.

The participative leader delegates and encourages subordinates to participate in decisions. Exhibit 15.7 shows that the Anglo, Nordic European, and Germanic European clusters have the highest score on this dimension. Germanic and Nordic European countries all have systems that emphasize economic development through cooperation between workers and employers rather than confrontational means.[23] This desire for cooperation and harmony between labor and capital means that effective leaders are seen as those who are willing to listen to their subordinates and accept their input. Anglo cultures tend to be very individualistic, and individualism is synonymous with people valuing their freedom and having a say in decisions that affect them. Leaders who allow subordinates to have their say through participative leadership are more likely to be viewed as effective.[24] Furthermore, all these cultures have low power distance; that is, subordinates are encouraged to have a say in decision making.

The humane-oriented leader is fair, altruistic, friendly, generous, and caring.[25] All country clusters rate the humane leader highly, suggesting that this leadership orientation is almost universally seen as a very desirable trait in successful leaders. Exhibit 15.7 shows that the Southern Asian cluster scored the highest on this leadership dimension. The score can be attributed to the generally benevolent and humane orientation of most Southern Asian societies, such as India, Thailand, and Malaysia. Consider the following Focus on Emerging Markets.

As for the autonomous leader, most country clusters see autonomy as an impediment to effective leadership. Results were similar for the self-protective leader. The clusters with the highest score on autonomy are the Germanic and East European clusters. Their scores, however, were slightly higher than 4, indicating that these clusters were generally indifferent as to the propensity of autonomous leadership to either contribute to or impede effective leadership. The scores for the self-protective leadership were all fairly similar and were all lower than 4, indicating that all country clusters felt that self-protective leadership hindered effective leadership. Taken together, results for autonomous and self-protective leadership are consistent with Den Hartog et al.'s findings that certain leadership characteristics, such as being a loner or egocentric, are negatively regarded universally.[26]

Leadership characteristics and behaviors vary across countries because different national contexts produce differences in the repertoire of behaviors and traits available to managers. Both superiors and subordinates see the leader's task or person orientation based on culturally and institutionally defined sets of leader behaviors; that is, each national context has its own acceptable ways to communicate a leader's concerns for tasks or people. To lead successfully in multinational companies, managers must be particularly sensitive in using locally appropriate leadership behaviors

---

## **Focus** on Emerging Markets

### Leadership Style at Tata

Large Indian multinationals are well known for their human approach to leadership. They often have very benevolent leaders who take good care of their workers. This is not surprising given the results of the GLOBE study. Consider the case of Tata and its leader, Ratan Tata. While other companies were engaging in mass layoffs, the 137-year-old company has stayed true to its roots and treat employees very humanely. While India tends to have frequent strikes, Tata Steel has gone around 80 years without a strike. Furthermore, Tata still maintains Jamshedpur, the steel town it started from the jungle a century ago. The company still pays for full health and education expenses for its employees. In that town, it still maintains schools and a 1000-bed hospital.

How is Tata faring with this humane approach to leadership? The evidence suggests that Tata is doing fine. It continues to expand worldwide. For instance, it is now one of the biggest manufacturers in the United Kingdom, with around 40,000 employees. It now owns the Jaguar/Land Rover brands and has been successful in that industry. Many experts note that Tata does not stray too far from its humane roots even if it expands in other countries.

*Sources: Based on* Economist. *2011. "Tata for now." September 10, online;* Hindustan Times. *2012. "Mahindra: Tata a source of inspiration." August 13, online edition; Wehfritz, G. and R. Moreau. 2005. "A kinder, gentler conglomerate: Tata coddles workers, not managers, yet thrives in global industries as a uniquely Indian-style company."* Newsweek, *October 31, online edition.*

to communicate their intended leadership styles. The next section shows that even the basic tactics leaders use to manage subordinates vary by national context.

## National Context and Preferred Leader Influence Tactics

Beyond broad approaches to leadership behaviors, one can look at the specific tactical behaviors leaders use to influence subordinates. U.S. managers favor seven major **influence tactics.**[27] Here they are, with examples for each:

1. *Assertiveness:* Being forceful, directive, and demanding.
2. *Friendliness:* Being friendly, humble, and receptive.
3. *Reasoning:* Using logical arguments, providing reasons, and using plans.
4. *Bargaining:* Offering favors and exchanges.
5. *Sanctioning:* Using threats, rewards, and punishments.
6. *Appeals to a higher authority:* Appeals for help to higher authorities and sending problems to higher authorities.
7. *Coalitions:* Building support for ideas by networking and using friendships.

> **Influence tactics**
> Tactical behaviors leaders use to influence subordinates.

What influence tactics are used in other national contexts? One research study found that most managers, regardless of cultural background, use the same general types of influence tactics. However, different nationalities favor some over others.[28] For example, the British prefer bargaining, while the Japanese favor reasoning. Exhibit 15.8 shows the favored tactics of Taiwanese, Japanese, Australian, and British managers.

## National Context and Subordinates' Expectations

Leaders cannot lead without the cooperation of subordinates. The national context also affects **subordinates' expectations** regarding who can be a leader, what a leader should do, and what a leader may or may not do. All levels of culture—national, business, occupational, and organizational—influence the types of leader behaviors that subordinates consider appropriate or fair. For example, at the level of organizational culture, even university students differ in the range of leader behaviors they perceive as acceptable for professors. At some universities, two 25-page papers for a semester class are a fair expectation. At other universities, students would resent this assignment and perceive it as unfair. Just as a leader's behaviors communicate his or her person or task orientation, subordinates accept or reject certain behaviors as legitimate prerogatives of leadership. For example, North American workers consider leadership behaviors associated with applying pressure to work, considered normal in Japan, as harsh or punitive.[29]

> **Subordinates' expectations**
> Expectations regarding what leaders should do and what they may or may not do.

What makes a behavior acceptable in one country but not in another? The cultural and institutional settings provide a framework for people to interpret leader behaviors. For example, labor relations laws in some European countries mandate that managers consult with workers regarding key strategic issues, such as plant closures (Chapter 12). At the level of national culture, Hofstede suggests that the cultural value of power distance has profound effects on subordinates' expectations regarding leaders.[30]

Exhibit 15.9 shows Hofstede's ideas on how subordinates from countries with three different levels of power distance respond to leadership issues. In countries with high power-distance values, including many of the Latin and Asian countries, subordinates expect autocratic leadership. The leader often assumes the status of a

**EXHIBIT** 15.8   Preferred Leader Influence Tactics in Four Countries

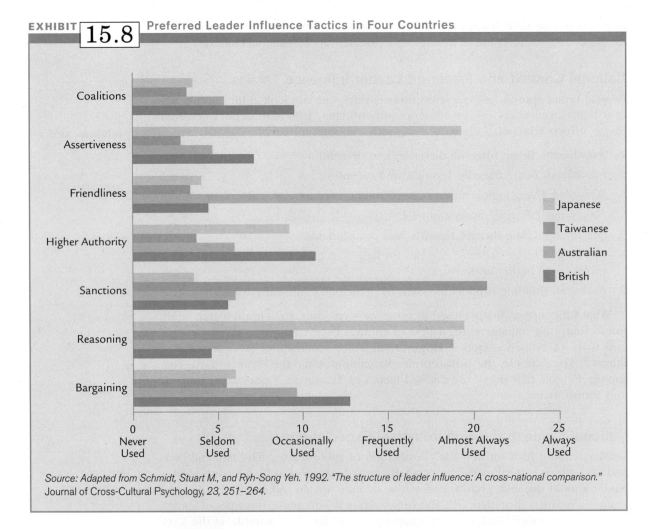

Source: Adapted from Schmidt, Stuart M., and Ryh-Song Yeh. 1992. "The structure of leader influence: A cross-national comparison." Journal of Cross-Cultural Psychology, 23, 251–264.

**EXHIBIT** 15.9   Subordinates' Expectations under Three Levels of Power Distance

| Leadership Issue | Low Power Distance (United Kingdom) | Medium Power Distance (United States) | High Power Distance (Mexico) |
|---|---|---|---|
| Subordinates' dependence needs | Weak dependence on superiors | Moderate dependence on superiors | Heavy dependence on superiors |
| Consultation | Strongly expected as part of superior's role | Expect consultation but will accept autocratic leadership | Expect autocratic leadership |
| Ideal superior | Democrat | Moderate democrat | Benevolent autocratic or paternalistic father figure |
| Laws and rules | Apply to superiors and subordinates | Apply to all, but superiors have some privileges | Superiors above the law and take advantage of privileges |
| Status symbols | Viewed as not appropriate | Accepted as symbolic of authority | Very important contributions to the authority of superiors |

Sources: Adapted from Hofstede, Geert. 1980. "Motivation, leadership, and organization: Do American theories apply abroad?" Organizational Dynamics, Summer, 42–63; Hofstede, Geert. 1984. Culture's Consequences: International Differences in Work-Related Values. Newbury Park, CA: Sage Publications.

father figure and acts as a caring but authoritarian master. A leader is different and is expected to show visible signs of status (e.g., a chauffeur-driven car). In low-power-distance countries, such as Sweden and Norway, subordinates expect the leader to be more like them. Good leaders should involve subordinates in decision making and should forgo excessive symbols of status.

Besides power distance, other cultural values likely affect subordinates' expectations. Hofstede's work suggests that strong masculinity norms often lead to the acceptance of authoritarian leadership, although perhaps this is a paternalistic authoritarianism in the case of the Japanese. Strong uncertainty-avoidance norms may cause subordinates to expect the leader to provide more detail when giving directions. For example, workers may expect leaders to say exactly what they want, how, and when.[31]

The next Multinational Management Brief gives more examples of international differences in subordinates' preferences for leadership behaviors.

The classic contingency view of leadership and the national-context contingency model of leadership can guide multinational managers as to when and how to adapt leadership styles given the particularities of national context.

## Multinational Management **Brief**

### Subordinate Expectations and Trust in China

Despite some challenges, many expect that China will continue experiencing growth. Understanding leadership and subordinate expectation in China is therefore critical. China's culture is characterized by a preference for familial orientation and harmony. People generally want to maintain harmonious relationships with others as a way to save face. So it is logical to expect that subordinates will prefer leadership behaviors that promote harmony.

In a study of full-time Chinese employees, researchers examined task- and person-centered leaders and their subordinates' reactions. A person-centered leader (called consideration leadership style in the study) is a leader who leads through mutual trust and respect for subordinates' ideas and feelings. In contrast, a task-centered leader (or initiating structure) is focused on getting the task done. The results of the study showed that leaders were more likely to display a person-centered leadership style than task-centered style. The results are not surprising, given the Chinese preference for human interactions and harmony. The study also showed that the person-centered leader was more likely to encourage Chinese employees to display organizational citizenship behaviors whereby they perform beyond what is expected. However, the results showed that not only is the task-centered leadership style important, but that it is very important if employees are expected to share knowledge. Such results are attributed to the fact that Chinese culture favors a paternalistic and authoritarian approach. Task-centered leaders can expect their subordinates to comply given their propensity to display obedience to leaders' orders. Such results show that the best Chinese leaders tend to display high levels of both person-centered and task-centered leadership.

*Source: Based on* Economist. *2012. "Pedalling prosperity: Special Report on China's Economy." May 26, 3–18; Huang, Q., R. Davison, H. Liu, and J. Gu. 2008. "The impact of leadership style on knowledge-sharing intentions in China."* Journal of Global Information Management, *16(4): 67–91.*

We now extend our discussion to consider additional contemporary views of leadership and their applications to multinational settings.

# Contemporary Leadership Perspectives: Multinational Implications

This section of the chapter reviews two contemporary approaches to leadership: transformational leadership and the attribution approach. It considers how these views apply in multinational settings.

## Transformational Leadership

Most experts argue that, to achieve a great organization, managers must adopt a higher form of leadership known as transformational leadership. Of importance to the multinational manager is the finding by the GLOBE researchers that transformational leadership is considered superior in almost all societies. What makes a transformational leader? What do transformational leaders do that separates them from ordinary leaders?

Studies have identified several behaviors and characteristics of transformational leaders.[32] The transformational leader:

- *Articulates a vision:* Presents in vivid and emotional terms an idealized vision of the future for the organization—what it can and should become—and makes this vision clear to followers.
- *Breaks from the status quo:* Has a strong desire to break from tradition and to do things differently, is an expert in finding ways to do things differently, and challenges subordinates to find new solutions to old problems.
- *Provides goals and a plan:* Has a vision that is future oriented and provides clear steps for followers to transform the company.
- *Gives meaning or a purpose to goals:* Places the goals in emotionally laden stories or a cultural context so that subordinates see the need to follow the leader's ideals and to share a commitment to radical change, and helps subordinates envision a future state of a better organization.
- *Takes risks:* Is willing to take more risks with the organization than the average leader.
- *Is motivated to lead:* Seeks leadership positions and displays strong enthusiasm for the leadership role; acts as a role model.
- *Builds a power base:* Uses personal power based on expertise, respect, and the admiration of followers.
- *Demonstrates high ethical and moral standards:* Behaves consistently and fairly with a known ethical standard.

Transformational leaders succeed because subordinates respond to them with high levels of performance, personal devotion, reverence, excitement regarding the leader's ideas, and a willingness to sacrifice for the good of the company.[33] However, true transformational leaders are rare. They seem to arise when organizations need change or face a crisis. In the next Multinational Management Brief, you can see how transformational leadership works in Malaysia.

Although transformational leaders exist in all countries, the same leadership traits and behaviors may not lead to successful transformational leadership

## Multinational Management **Brief**

### Transformational Leadership in Malaysia

Malaysia has experienced impressive growth as an emerging economy. Consider the 88-floor tower recently built by its state-owned oil company, Petronas. Malaysia presents tremendous opportunities, and it is therefore important to understand leadership in that society.

Although transformational leadership is viewed differently across societies, it is clearly valued worldwide. In a large-scale study of Malaysian CEOs, researchers provided evidence of the value of transformational leadership. The researchers examined how a transformational leader affects organizational performance as well as the ability of a company to adopt best practices of the industry. The study showed not only that transformational leaders indeed influenced their firms' performance positively, but also that it positively influenced Malaysian companies' ability to adopt best practices in the industry. A transformational leader is better able to reflect and examine what competitors are doing in order to adopt their best practices. Such results show that the transformational leader is more open to new ideas and to comparing the company's own performance with that of other companies.

*Source: Based on* Economist. *2012. "New masters of the universe." January 21, online edition; Idris, F., and K. A. M. Ali. 2008. "The impacts of leadership style and best practices on company performances: Empirical evidence from business firms in Malaysia."* Total Quality Management, *19(1/2): 163–171.*

everywhere. Charisma requires tapping into basic cultural values and evoking national cultural myths and heroic deeds.[34] For example, Hitler built part of his perceived charisma by tapping into the heroic myths and symbols of German culture; Gandhi capitalized on Indian culture in his struggles with the British.[35] In addition, traits associated with charisma—such as risk taking—and behaviors necessary to communicate a transformational vision may have different consequences depending on national setting.

Den Hartog et al. provide perhaps the most definitive test of the proposition that transformational or charismatic leadership is universally endorsed as the key to effective leadership.[36] As part of the GLOBE project, they examined data from 62 different cultures and found that charismatic leadership attributes, such as encouraging, trustworthy, positive, confidence builder, and motivational, were all perceived as universal attributes. Although no attempts were made to link these differences to cultural factors, the study showed that some aspects of transformational leadership may be viewed similarly in many cultures.

GLOBE project researchers also looked at whether possessing traits of a charismatic leader contributed to effective leadership.[37] The charismatic leader is decisive, performance oriented, visionary, inspiring for subordinates, and willing to sacrifice for the organization.

Next, we will examine a final perspective on leadership and its application to multinational operations.

## Attributions and Leadership

The **attributional approach to leadership** emphasizes the leader's attributions regarding the causes of subordinates' behaviors. We all make attributions when

**Attributional approach to leadership**
Emphasis on what leaders believe causes subordinates' behaviors.

we observe someone's behavior and attach a reason or motivation to it. For example, when a student walks quickly across campus, we may assume (correctly or incorrectly) that she is late for class, or we might believe that the student is hungry and going to lunch.

The most important attribution for leaders is that of responsibility for work performance. In determining how to respond to subordinates' behaviors, leaders make two key distinctions: the external attribution and the internal attribution. The *external attribution* explains a person's behavior based on factors outside the person and beyond the person's control (e.g., natural disasters, illness, faulty equipment). For example, a leader uses an external attribution when assuming an employee is late because of a severe storm. The *internal attribution* explains a person's behavior based on the characteristics of the person (e.g., personality, motivation, low ability). For example, a leader makes an internal attribution when assuming an employee was late because he is lazy.

In making such an attributional decision, the leader responds to the subordinate based on that assumption. If the subordinate's behavior is based on an internal attribution, the manager tends to correct or reward the worker. If, on the other hand, the attribution is external, the leader modifies the work environment. Consequently, according to this view, successful leadership requires making the correct attributions regarding subordinates' behavior.[38]

In most Western nations, people tend to make internal attribution. As a result, managers more often believe that people behave in certain ways because of internal motivations, such as laziness or ambition, not because of outside factors, such as poor working conditions. This assumption is so strong in Western culture that it is called the **fundamental attribution error.**[39]

**Fundamental attribution error**
Assumption by managers that people behave in certain ways because of internal motivations rather than outside factors.

As in international negotiation, where mistakes in attribution can be a major source of misunderstanding, the challenge for the multinational leader is to understand the cultures of subordinates enough to avoid such errors. The next Multinational Management Challenge shows how a U.S. manager working in Mexico and his Mexican subordinate imposed their own culturally biased attributions regarding the use of time, authority, and interpersonal relations. The Challenge shows what can happen when superiors and subordinates attach the wrong motivations to each other's behaviors. How would you advise these managers?

## Getting Results: Should You Do What Works at Home?

The contingency view of leadership—that leadership works differently depending on national context—suggests that managers cannot assume that the leadership styles or traits that worked successfully in their home countries will result in equally successful leadership in a foreign country.

What happens if leaders do not adapt to local conditions? The results of at least one study suggest that home-based leadership styles do not work very well in other cultural settings.[40] Based on this study, Exhibit 15.10 shows the correlation between managerial performance and leadership behaviors for two groups of U.S. managers, one working in the United States and one working as expatriates in Hong Kong. A +1.0 indicates a perfect correspondence between the leadership behavior and the performance of the leader's unit; a 0 indicates no relationship; and a negative number indicates that leader's behavior reduced performance levels. As you can see from the example, typical U.S. leadership behaviors did not

## Multinational Management **Challenge**

### Getting Attributions Right

Paul Jones makes some observations regarding his leadership challenges during his first year as a manager in Mexico. Jones's observations are countered by the perceptions and attributions of Sr. Gonzalez, a subordinate manager at Jones's plant.

| Paul Jones: | Sr. Gonzalez: |
|---|---|
| First day: "It is well past 9:00 a.m. and the office staff just arrived. I must emphasize punctuality at the next staff meeting." | "Mr. Jones wants us to behave as if we were robots. He seems crazy about the clock. Doesn't he realize that there are legitimate reasons to be late?" |
| "I just toured the plant, and Gonzalez pointed out various problems. He really pressed me to meet all the supervisory staff, but there are many more pressing problems." | "Mr. Jones did not take the time or make the effort to meet the supervisors. Doesn't he realize that this neglect really hurt their feelings?" |
| Second month: "My managers keep asking me for advice, or, worse, asking me to solve their problems. Don't they realize that this lack of taking responsibility reflects poorly on their performance?" | "Mr. Jones does not seem to realize that many managers feel he is the boss and he must make the decisions." |
| "I had to correct a first-line supervisor today when he was incorrect in teaching a worker how to operate a machine. The whole plant seemed to stop and listen. These people need to get over their fear of criticism." | "Mr. Jones's actions today created an extreme embarrassment for one of my supervisors. Jones criticized him in public! Now all the supervisors are afraid to do anything for fear of a public reprimand." |
| "I thought things were looking up. My managers recently produced a beautiful document on how to improve procedures. Three weeks later, much to my astonishment, only one manager had made any attempt at implementation." | "Doesn't Mr. Jones realize that the managers were waiting for him to tell them when to begin?" |
| "I figured maybe I should try a 'U.S.-style' meeting—shirt sleeves, feet up on the desk, and open communication. But the managers just stood around looking embarrassed. I don't understand." | "Mr. Jones did not act like a plant manager at all. Can you imagine a plant manager putting his feet up on the desk? How uncivilized!" |

*Source: Kras, Eva S. 1995.* Management in Two Cultures. *Yarmouth, ME: Intercultural Press.*

work as well in Hong Kong as in the United States. In particular, the highly involved hands-on leadership style that worked very well in the United States had little impact on the performance of Hong Kong workers.

A possible reason that many managers (especially from the United States) fail in international assignments may be their inability to modify their behavior and adopt

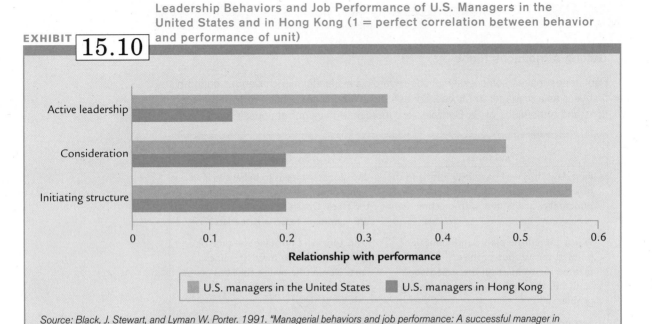

Leadership Behaviors and Job Performance of U.S. Managers in the United States and in Hong Kong (1 = perfect correlation between behavior and performance of unit)

**EXHIBIT 15.10**

Source: Black, J. Stewart, and Lyman W. Porter. 1991. "Managerial behaviors and job performance: A successful manager in Los Angeles may not succeed in Hong Kong." Journal of International Business Studies, 1st quarter, 99–113.

leadership styles to be congruent with the cultural setting. This difficulty in adaptation is not surprising. As noted in Chapter 12, selection for an expatriate assignment usually requires prior success as a manager in the home country. Thus, before getting international assignments, most expatriate managers likely demonstrated successful leadership at home. As a result, without adequate cross-cultural training and awareness, many previously successful managers will continue to apply their native countries' leadership behaviors in their international assignments.

### The Cultural Context and Suggested Leadership Styles

Probably because of the extreme variability among cultures and nations, there are few prescriptive theories of multicultural leadership; there is no simple formula identifying how to lead in every national context. However, some writings by Hofstede and Rodrigues suggest some general recommendations.[41] Using the dimensions of national culture considered most important by Hofstede for organizations—power distance and uncertainty avoidance—Exhibit 15.11 shows these experts' recommended leadership styles for different cultural settings.

Power distance is important for leadership because it affects both subordinates' and superiors' expectations regarding the leader's degree of directiveness or task orientation. In high power-distance countries, leaders generally behave autocratically. Subordinates also feel, "You are the boss, so tell us what to do." Hofstede suggests that managers from low power-distance countries can usually adjust to a high power-distance country without much difficulty;[42] they just develop a more authoritarian leadership style. However, he suggests that it is more difficult for managers from high power-distance countries to become less authoritarian and more participative or person-centered.

The uncertainty-avoidance norm also affects the range of acceptable leadership styles.[43] In high-uncertainty-avoidance national cultures, both leaders and

**EXHIBIT** **15.11**    National Culture and Recommended Leadership Styles

**Cultural Context:** Low power distance and low uncertainty avoidance
**Leader Type:** The democrat
**Recommended Leadership Styles:** Supportive, participative, and achievement
**Example Country:** Great Britain

**Cultural Context:** High power distance and low uncertainty avoidance
**Leader Type:** The master
**Recommended Leadership Styles:** Directive and supportive
**Example Country:** China

**Cultural Context:** Low power distance and high uncertainty avoidance
**Leader Type:** The professional
**Recommended Leadership Styles:** Directive, supportive, and participative
**Example Country:** Germany

**Cultural Context:** High power distance and high uncertainty avoidance
**Leader Type:** The boss
**Recommended Leadership Style:** Directive
**Example Country:** France

*Source: Adapted from Hofstede, Geert. 1991.* Cultures and Organizations: Software of the Mind. *London: McGraw-Hill; Rodrigues, Carl A. 1990. "The situation and national culture as contingencies for leadership behavior: Two conceptual models."* Advances in International Comparative Management, *5, 51–68.*

subordinates often feel more comfortable when the leader removes ambiguity from the work setting. In countries such as France, this may take the form of *le directeur* telling subordinates exactly what to do. In countries such as Germany, substitutes for leadership such as professional training may make the work setting predictable and allow leaders more discretion for participation.

Ultimately, multinational managers must diagnose the institutional, organizational, and cultural situations that may affect the success of their leadership style. Too many contingencies exist to predict what may work in all situations, but successful global leaders remain flexible and highly sensitive to national context.

## *Summary and Conclusions*

All managers who work for multinational companies should strive to become global leaders, unconstrained by national or cultural limitations and able to adjust to any national context. Toward this goal, this chapter provided background information on the nature of leadership, information crucial to understanding leadership options in a multinational setting.

First, the chapter defined leadership and introduced the global leader. Then it reviewed three classic North American views of leadership based on leadership traits, leadership behaviors, and contingency theory. Trait theories identify the personal qualities of leaders. Leadership behavior theories identify the behaviors that signify certain leadership styles; these styles are usually considered person or task centered. Contingency theories identify characteristics of the supervisor, organization, and subordinates that determine the appropriate leadership style in a given situation. The chapter also showed that the Japanese and Indians have similar views of leadership.

The national-context contingency model of leadership extended traditional contingency theories to show how culture and social institutions affect the leadership process. Culture affects the preferences that leaders have for certain styles. Culture and the nation's social institutions affect subordinates' expectations regarding the leadership behaviors considered fair or appropriate.

Using the most recent findings from the GLOBE study, you saw numerous examples of national differences in preferred leadership traits and behaviors.

The national context also affects leadership contingencies indirectly. Culture and social institutions, such as a nation's educational system or economic system, influence the characteristics of the workforce available in a country and the nature of typical companies there. In turn, the types of available workers and the typical designs of organizations and jobs limit the successful leadership options for the multinational manager. In addition to developing a national-context contingency view of leadership, the chapter reviewed the international implications of contemporary views of leadership, focusing on the transformational leader and leadership attributions.

Finally, the chapter applied elements of the national-context contingency model of leadership to suggest leadership styles for expatriate managers in selected countries. Specifically, we showed that the power-distance norm and the uncertainty-avoidance norm suggest different choices in leadership styles. Although it is impossible to identify all cultural and situational factors that affect the choice of leadership style, a careful reading of this chapter should sensitize the multinational manager to the array of complex culture issues facing today's global leader.

## Discussion Questions

1. Define leadership. How might people from different national cultures define leadership? What are the implications of these definitions for multinational leaders working in the affected countries?

2. Discuss how the cultural norms of power distance and uncertainty avoidance affect the preferred leadership styles in different nations.

3. Pick a national culture with which you are familiar and identify leadership traits and behaviors that would be detrimental to organizational effectiveness.

4. From the perspective of the subordinates, discuss why culturally inappropriate leadership behaviors might be demotivating.

5. Discuss whether transformational leadership qualities are culture free. In other words, are transformational leaders similar regardless of cultural background, or is there a different type of transformational leader for each cultural group?

6. Compare and contrast the U.S. leadership-style model with the Japanese performance-maintenance model. Use national culture dimensions to explain your findings.

## Multinational Management Internet Exercise

1. Go to http://www.grovewell.com/GLOBE/ and click on the Quiz.

2. What are each of the leadership attributes? Which ones do you believe are universally viewed?

3. Take the quiz. Which attributes did you correctly see as universally viewed? Which ones did you get wrong? Why?

4. Are the general findings of the GLOBE study consistent with what you saw in your country?

## Multinational Management Skill Builder

### Leadership Challenges in Mexico

Step 1.　Read the following scenario:

You have been approached by a U.S. multinational company that is considering opening a manufacturing facility in Mexico. The company will most likely employ Mexican employees, although management will come from the United States. Your consulting services are required to ensure that U.S. management and leadership are effective in the Mexican environment. You have been asked the following questions:

• What sources of cultural and social institutional differences between the United States and Mexico are likely to pose significant challenges to U.S. managers as they lead Mexican workers?

- What specific forms may these challenges take?

- What do you propose to help your client and its managers face these problems?

- What specific forms of training or immersion programs would you recommend?

**Step 2.** After gathering the necessary information, prepare a presentation to answer the questions.

## Endnotes

1 Dorfman, P. 2003. "International and cross-cultural leadership research." In J. Punnett and O. Shenkar, eds. *Handbook for International Management research,* 2nd ed. Ann Arbor: University of Michigan.

2 European Foundation for Quality Management. 2009. http://www.efqm.org.

3 McCarthy, Grace. 2005. "Leadership practices in German and UK organizations." *Journal of European Industrial Training,* 29(2/3): 217–261.

4 Harris, Philip R., and Robert T. Moran. 2000. *Managing Cultural Differences.* Woburn, MA: Gulf Professional Publishing; Rosen, Robert, Patricia Digh, Marshall Singer, and Carl Phillips. 2000. *Global Literacies: Lessons on Business Leadership and National Cultures.* New York: Simon & Schuster.

5 Alon, Ilan, and James M. Higgins. 2005. "Global leadership success through emotional and cultural intelligences." *Business Horizons,* 48, 501–512.

6 Yukl, Gary. 1998. *Leadership in Organizations.* Upper Saddle River, NJ: Prentice Hall.

7 Likert, R. 1961. *New Patterns of Management.* New York: McGraw-Hill; Stogdill, Ralf M., and Alvin E. Coons. 1957. *Leader Behavior: Its Description and Measurement.* Columbus: Bureau of Business Research, Ohio State University.

8 Tannenbaum, R., and W. H. Schmidt. 1958. "How to choose a leadership pattern." *Harvard Business Review,* March–April, 95–102.

9 Likert, R. 1967. *Human Organization: Its Management and Value.* New York: McGraw-Hill.

10 Peterson, M., Mary Yoko Brannen, and Peter B. Smith. 1994. "Japanese and U.S. leadership: Issues in current research." *Advances in International and Comparative Management,* 9, 57–82.

11 Misumi, J., and M. F. Peterson. 1985. "The performance-maintenance theory of leadership: Review of a Japanese research program." *Administrative Science Quarterly,* 30, 198–223.

12 Fiedler, F. E., and J. E. Garcia. 1987. *New Approaches to Effective Leadership.* Hoboken, NJ: Wiley.

13 House, R. J., and M. L. Baetz. 1979. "Leadership: Some empirical generalizations and new research directions." *Research in Organizational Behavior,* 1, 341–424.

14 House, R. J., N. S. Wright, and R. N. Aditya. 1997. "Cross-cultural research on organizational leadership: A critical analysis and a proposed theory." In P. C. Earley and M. Erez, eds. *New Perspectives in International Industrial Organizational Psychology.* San Francisco: New Lexington, 536–625; Rodrigues, Carl A. 1990. "The situation and national culture as contingencies for leadership behavior: Two conceptual models." *Advances in International Comparative Management,* 5, 51–68.

15 Kerr, S., and J. M. Jermier. 1978. "Substitutes for leadership: Their meaning and measurement." *Organizational Behavior and Human Performance,* 22, 375–404.

16 Dorfman.

17 Hofstede, Geert. 1993. "Cultural constraints in management theories." *Academy of Management Executive,* 7, 81–93.

18 House, R. J., Paul J. Hanges, Mansour Javidan, Peter W. Dorfman, and Vipin Gupta. 2004. *Culture, Leadership, and Organizations.* Thousand Oaks, CA: Sage Publications; Brodbeck, Felix, and Associates. 2000. "Cultural variation of leadership prototypes across European countries." *Journal of Occupational and Organizational Psychology,* 23, 1–29; Dorfman.

19 Dorfman, P., Paul J. Hanges, and F. C. Brodbeck. 2004. "Leadership and cultural variation: The identification of culturally endorsed leadership profiles. In R. J. House, P. J. Hanges, M. Javidan, P. W. Dorfman, and V. Gupta, eds. *Culture, Leadership, and Organizations.* Thousand Oaks, CA: Sage Publications, 669–720.

20 Gupta, Vipin, Paul J. Hanges, and Peter Dorfman. 2002. "Cultural clusters: Methodology and findings." *Journal of World Business,* 37, 11–15.

21 Jesuino, Jorge Correia. 2002. "Latin Europe cluster: From south to north." *Journal of World Business,* 37, 81–89.

22 Gupta, Vipin, Gita Surie, Mansour Javidan, and Jagpdeep Chhokar. 2002. "Southern Asia cluster: Where the old meets the new?" *Journal of World Business,* 37, 16–27.

23 Szabo, Erna, Felix C. Brodbeck, Deanne N. Den Hartog, Gerard Reber, Jurgen Weibler, and Rolf Wunderer. 2002. "The Germanic Europe cluster: Where employees have a voice." *Journal of World Business, 37,* 55–68.

24 Ashkanasy, Neal M., Edwin Trevor-Roberts, and Louise Earnshaw. 2002. "The Anglo cluster: Legacy of the British empire." *Journal of World Business,* 37, 28–39.

25 House, Hanges, Javidan, Dorfman, and Gupta.

26 Den Hartog, Deanne N., Robert J. House, Paul J. Hanges, Peter W. Dorfman, S. Antonio Ruiz-Quintanna, and 170 associates. 1999. "Culture specific and cross-culturally generalizable implicit leadership theories: Are attributes of charismatic/transformational leadership universally endorsed?" *Leadership Quarterly,* 10, 219–256.

27 Kipnis, D. S., M. Schmidt, and I. Wilkinson. 1980. "Intraorganizational influence tactics: Explorations in getting one's way." *Journal of Applied Psychology,* 65, 440–452.

28 Schmidt, Stuart M., and Ryh-Song Yeh. 1992. "The structure of leader influence: A cross-national comparison." *Journal of Cross-Cultural Psychology,* 23, 251–264.

29 Peterson, Brannen, and Smith.

30 Hofstede, Geert. 1984. *Culture's Consequences: International Differences in Work-Related Values.* Thousand Oaks, CA: Sage.

31 Ibid.

32 Ibid; Conger, J. A., and James G. Hunt. 1999. "Overview—Charismatic and transformational leadership: Taking stock of the present and future (Part I)." *Leadership Quarterly,* 10, 112–117; Conger, J. A. 1991. "Inspiring others: The language of leadership." *Academy of Management Executive,* 5, 31–45.

33 Greenberg, Jerald, and Robert A. Baron. 1995. *Behavior in Organizations.* Upper Saddle River, NJ: Prentice-Hall.

34 Kets de Vries, M. F. R. 1988. "Origins of charisma: Ties that bind the leader to the led." In J. A. Conger and R. N. Kanungo, eds. *Charismatic Leadership.* San Francisco: Jossey-Bass, 237–252.

35 Erez, Miriam P., and Christopher Earley. 1993. *Culture, Self Identity and Work.* Oxford: Oxford University Press.

[36] Hartog et al.

[37] House, Hanges, Javidan, Dorfman, and Gupta.

[38] Heneman, R. L., D. B. Greenberger, and C. Anonyuo. 1989. "Attributions and exchanges: The effects of interpersonal factors on the diagnosis of employee performance." *Academy of Management Journal,* 32, 466–476.

[39] Mullen, B., and C. A. Riordan. 1988. "Self-serving attributions for performance in naturalistic settings: A meta-analytic review." *Journal of Applied Social Psychology,* 18, 3–22.

[40] Black, J. Stewart, and Lyman W. Porter. 1991. "Managerial behaviors and job performance: A successful manager in Los Angeles may not succeed in Hong Kong." *Journal of International Business Studies,* 1st quarter, 99–113.

[41] Hofstede, Geert. 1991. *Cultures and Organizations: Software of the Mind.* London: McGraw-Hill; Rodrigues.

[42] Ibid.

[43] Ibid.

# Cheung Yan: China's Paper Queen

It was August 2008, and Cheung Yan (张茵), the 51-year-old chairperson and co-founder of the Nine Dragons Paper Holdings Company ("Nine Dragons"), could look back upon a successful year. Nine Dragons had, three months earlier, acquired a controlling interest in a Vietnamese paper mill, thereby expediting the company's entry into the Southeast Asian markets.[1] For Cheung, this was just another milestone in an illustrious career. In November 2006, *Forbes* magazine had ranked Cheung the richest woman (and the fifth-richest person) in China, with a fortune of US$ 1.35 billion.[2] By any measure, Cheung was a truly successful business leader. The firm she had founded just over a decade ago, in 1995, was by June 2007 a pulp and paper powerhouse—it had 13 giant papermaking machines, about 8,600 full-time employees, US$1.4 billion in annual revenue and US$300 million in profits.[3]

Cheung started off modestly by setting up a small scrap paper brokerage in Hong Kong in 1985. When the market did not appear large enough for someone of her ambition, she left for the United States in 1990. In the United States, with her new husband, she started a paper recycling unit called America Chung Nam. This unit collected waste paper from the United States and shipped it to China. Cheung soon realized that there was a huge opportunity for her in China—there was an ever-rising demand for export packaging there. Thus, in 1995, with a bank loan and the support of her husband and brother, Cheung established Nine Dragons in Dongguan, China. The unit started off modestly with two paper machines and made 600,000 tons of kraft linerboard per year.[4] By 2006, the company had an annual production capacity of 3.3 million tons of containerboard, with ten paper machines running and five more under construction.[5] With a huge expansion program in place, it was expected that by 2009, Nine Dragons, in which Cheung and her family had a 72% stake, would be Asia's top producer of packaging paper, and the first in the world in terms of production capacity.

In a male-dominated industry in Asia, how had Cheung succeeded in being celebrated globally as a business leader? What were the qualities and abilities that made her such an effective strategic leader?

## Cheung Yan and the Making of Nine Dragons

Cheung Yan (also called "Zhang Yin") was one of eight children born in Lioaning province, northeast China. Her father was an army official who was imprisoned during China's Cultural Revolution. Cheung lacked formal education and experienced early hardship when she started work in a textile company, supporting her mother and seven siblings on a mere US$6 a month.[6] She left the textile plant in the early 1980s for a job with a small paper trading company in southern China.

In 1985, the 28-year-old Cheung relocated to Hong Kong as an accountant at a Chinese trading company, which, however, closed within a year.[7] Instead of looking for another job, Cheung, with just about US$4,000, set up a waste-paper trading business. She saw an opportunity in China's chronic paper shortages. At that time, straw was the main raw material for the manufacture of paper in China because recycled paper was unpopular due to its high moisture content. Hence, Cheung's first success was realized when she managed to procure high-quality waste paper to send to China. Cheung's partner in Hong Kong, Ng Weiting, said that Cheung was successful because she was "driven and tough, and had figured out how to get the best performance out of those who worked for her."[8]

By 1990, Cheung found the Hong Kong market too small for her ambitions, and despite the fact that she spoke very little English, she left for the United States. In her view, "vision and methods matter more than language."[9] It was in the United States that Cheung really saw the huge potential of the Chinese paper-making market. Along with her new husband, Liu Ming Chung,[10] she started a paper trading unit called America Chung Nam in 1990. America Chung Nam collected paper for recycling from all over the United States and shipped it to China, where it was used for manufacturing boxes for packaging. By 2004, the company, which had shipped 2.6 million tonnes of recovered paper to China, was named the top U.S. exporter to China by the *Journal of Commerce*.[11]

Cheung enjoyed her stint in the United States and said that she benefited a lot from her experience there. She found that the Americans shared her long-term views about businesses and had high credibility, keeping to their promises.

As Cheung kept shipping these numerous containers of paper from the United States back to China, she realized the immense potential for manufacturing paper in China's fast-growing economy. An early effort was made to enter this business through a passive investment in a Chinese paper-making company which, however, failed. Cheung returned to China in 1995.

With the help of her husband and younger brother, Zhang Cheng Fei, Cheung availed of financing from a bank and set up Nine Dragons in Dongguan, an industrial hub located in the Pearl River Delta area near Hong Kong.

> *Fortunately, I had the wholehearted support from the bankers because of Nine Dragon's vision of the business and the valuable assets of the company, so I was able to get the funding. I believed that one day China would be like Europe or the USA. So that's why I started to invest in the first paper machine in Dongguan with an international approach—meaning that I imported the machines from overseas, components from the USA and Europe, and also the scale of the machines was much bigger than my peers at that time.*

— Cheung Yan, chairperson of Nine Dragons[12]

Cheung's business model was classically simple: it followed a cycle where her companies would procure tons of waste paper from the United States and Europe (essentially developed countries where the quality of waste paper was high), and ship it to China. Freight costs of shipping to China were cheap, as container vessels transporting goods to the United States often returned empty. In China, this waste paper was recycled and used for making boxes in which Chinese-made products would be packed, and then shipped out, invariably to the same Western market from which the raw material had been sourced. When these boxes were thrown away, the cycle would begin again. As Cheung said, her inspiration came from a statement made by someone in the business, "Waste paper is like a forest: paper recycles itself, generation after generation."[13]

On 3 March 2006, Nine Dragons went public and was listed on the main board of the Hong Kong Stock Exchange. The three founders continued to be actively involved: Cheung as the chairperson; Liu, her husband, as the deputy chairperson and chief executive officer; and Zhang, her younger brother, as the deputy chief executive officer.

## Nine Dragons

In China, the paper industry was strewn with manufacturers who were typically small, inefficient and environmentally unfriendly. Cheung's vision was the opposite of the market trend—she wanted Nine Dragons to be the biggest, most efficient and environmentally friendly paper company.

As of August 2008, Nine Dragons was the largest producer of containerboard products in China in terms of production capacity. It offered a large range of products in three major categories of packaging paper products—linerboard (kraft linerboard, test linerboard, and white top linerboard), high performance corrugating medium and coated duplex board [see Exhibit 1]. The company and its subsidiaries thus served "as a one-stop shop for a wide range of packaging paperboard products."[14] Its paper machines were located in two locations in China: Guangdong and Jiangsu. There were two more units planned at Chongqing and Tianjin. The group also had operations in Sichuan to produce high value specialty paper and pulp.[15] It further produced unbleached kraft pulp through a joint venture in Inner Mongolia. In May 2008, the company acquired a 60% controlling interest in an existing paper mill in Vietnam, thereby getting a foothold into the South-East Asian markets [see Exhibit 2 for significant milestones].

The Nine Dragons group showed consistent growth in turnover and profits. For the financial year ending on 30 June 2007, revenues increased by approximately 24% over the previous year to US$1,436 million. The annual gross profit too increased by about 35% to US$369 million, while the net profit registered an increase of 47% to US$300 million [see Exhibit 3 for further financial details].

For the six months ending on 31 December 2007, the group continued to perform exceedingly well. The total revenue amounted to US$976.7 million, an increase of 44.2% over the corresponding period of the previous year. Similarly, the gross profit increased by 30.9% to approximately US$230 million over the corresponding period of the previous year, and the profit attributable to the shareholders grew 11.4% more than the same period of the previous year to US$154 million. This success was attributed to Nine Dragon's competitive advantage, that is, economies of large-scale production and the lower costs associated with it.

**EXHIBIT 1**   Nine Dragon's Products

Nine Dragons' main products included linerboard (kraft linerboard, test linerboard, and white top linerboard), high performance corrugating medium, and coated duplex board.

**Linerboard**

Kraft linerboard was the unbleached linerboard manufactured from unbleached kraft pulp and recovered paper.

Test linerboard was a more environmentally friendly, lower-cost linerboard made completely from recovered paper.

White top linerboard was a three-ply sheet, with one layer bleached, and allowed for superior printing.

**High performance corrugating medium**

This product had superior strength as compared to standard corrugating medium, thereby reducing the amount of weight and material used, and the customers' shipping costs.

**Coated duplex board**

This product had a glossy coated surface, and was basically used for small boxes that required high quality printing.

*Source: Nine Dragons Paper (Holdings) Ltd. 2008. "Our business." http:/www.ndpaper.com/eng/business/products.htm, accessed October 6, 2008.*

In terms of operational efficiency, Nine Dragons continually looked at technological improvements to achieve higher product quality. To improve operations and management, the company had adopted advanced management techniques and systems, such as enterprise resource planning (ERP).[16]

**Vision for the Future**

The plan was for Nine Dragons to be the "world's leading fully integrated paper manufacturer, from forestry to paper."[17] The company hoped to expand its annual capacity of the overall packaging paperboard from

**EXHIBIT** **2**    Milestones in Nine Dragons' History

| | |
|---|---|
| July 1998 | The first paper machine (PM-1) achieves a successful test run, marking the entry of Nine Dragons in the Chinese paper industry. |
| June 2000 | PM-2 commenced operations. |
| May 2002 | PM-3 commenced operations, raising the total annual production capacity of the company to over 1 million tonnes per year. By this time, further land had been purchased in the Taicang and Dongguan areas of China, so that the production could cover a wider geographical network of the Pearl River Delta and the Yangtze River Delta. |
| October 2003 | PM-4 commenced production, breaking the productivity records of stand-alone units round the world at that time. |
| November 2003 | PM-5 commenced operation. |
| February 2004 | Established Nine Dragons Xing An Pulp and Paper (Inner Mongolia) Co. Ltd. ("ND Xing An") as an equity joint venture with China Inner Mongolia Forestry Industry Co., Ltd., which owns abundant forestry resources. |
| October 2004 | PM-6 and PM-7 commenced production of high performance corrugating medium, which expanded the variety and market reach of the company. |
| April 2005 | PM-8 has a successful test run. |
| May 2005 | 210MW thermal power generating units successfully commence on-grid power generation, thereby becoming the largest in the industry in terms of power generation capacity. As a result, the total thermal power generating capacity of the Dongguan production base of the company increased to 350MW, comparable to a medium scale power plant. This assured Nine Dragons a stable and sufficient electricity supply, and also eased the pressure on the local electricity supply, thereby winning government and public recognition. |
| December 2005 | PM-9 and PM-10 begin production of corrugating medium. |
| March 2006 | Nine Dragons is successfully listed on the main board of the Hong Kong Stock Exchange and included in the MSCI Standard Index, the MSCI Global Value and Growth Index, and the Hang Seng Index. |
| November 2006 | Plans are announced for the third production site in Chongqing, to meet the rising containerboard demand in the region. |
| January 2007 | PM-11 commences production, bringing the company's total annual production capacity in coated duplex board to 950,000 tonnes, the largest in China. Also, another two machines, PM-12 and PM-13, commence production of high performance corrugating medium. |
| August 2007 | PM-14 and PM-15 commence operations, and the total annual designed capacity of the containerboard products reaches 5.35 million tpa. |
| September 2007 | Nine Dragons finalizes the location of its fourth production base in Tianjin, improving the geographical coverage in China. It is expected to commence operations in 2009. |
| May 2008 | The company starts the development of highvalue specialty paper production and bamboo and wood pulp manufacturing. It also enters Vietnam by acquiring a 60% controlling interest of Cheng Yang Paper Mill Co. Ltd. in Vietnam. |

*Source: Nine Dragons Paper (Holdings) Ltd. 2008. "About ND paper," http://www.ndpaper.com/eng/aboutnd/major_achievements.htm, accessed October 6, 2008.*

**EXHIBIT 3**   Nine Dragons' Income Statement from 2006 to 2008 (US$ Millions)

|                                | 30 June 2007 | 30 June 2006 | 30 June 2005 | 30 June 2004 |
|--------------------------------|-------------:|-------------:|-------------:|-------------:|
| Sales                          | 1436.30      | 1153.72      | 704.51       | 387.41       |
| Cost of Goods Sold             | (1067.08)    | (882.03)     | (593.48)     | (307.43)     |
| Gross Profit                   | 369.22       | 271.69       | 111.03       | 79.98        |
| Other Gains                    | 45.44        | 52.12        | 3.52         | 0.77         |
| Selling and Marketing Expenses | (28.53)      | (25.23)      | (13.36)      | (8.79)       |
| Administrative Expenses        | (51.29)      | (34.15)      | (19.71)      | (9.83)       |
| OPERATING PROFIT               | 334.84       | 264.44       | 81.48        | 62.14        |
| Finance Costs                  | (9.18)       | (43.04)      | (26.25)      | (12.42)      |
| Profit before Tax              | 315.65       | 221.39       | 55.23        | 49.71        |
| Income Tax Expense             | (14.85)      | (16.98)      | (8.82)       | (7.69)       |
| NET INCOME                     | 300.80       | 204.41       | 46.41        | 42.02        |

*Source: Nine Dragons Paper (Holdings) Ltd. 2007 "Annual report." http://www.ndpaper.com, accessed September 12, 2008.*

5.35 million tons per annum (tpa) as of June 2007 to 10.15 million tpa by 2009.

To pursue this vision, the following initiatives were planned:[18]

- To expand the containerboard production capacity, such that the company could continue to capitalise on the large scale economies of the paper making industry to become the largest packaging paperboard manufacturer in the world.

- To widen the product range to include high performance products through which the company could get a stronghold in the high value categories market.

- To stabilize recovered paper costs (the main raw material expense of the company) by sourcing from a wider set of geographical locations across the globe, and participating in pulp production and forestry projects.

- To work towards a comprehensive and balanced geographical coverage in China, from where most of the company's business was sourced.

- To expedite the entry into the ASEAN markets, in particular, Vietnam, Laos, and Cambodia, through investment in a paper mill in Vietnam.

In April 2007, the company successfully raised about US$25 million for future core business expansion.

## Cheung Yan: The Leader

### Strategic Direction

Cheung clearly and simply articulated her vision as: "My desire has always been to be the leader in an industry."[19] However, for someone to have this ambitious vision and actually succeed at it would require considerable effort and determination.

> My success didn't come so easily and simply. It's a lot of hard work over the past twenty years. The industry is good. That is a prerequisite definitely. And I have a passion for the business. I like the paper recycling business.
>
> — Cheung Yan, chairperson of Nine Dragons[20]

Cheung's vision and strategy were clear—economies of scale mattered, and the bigger the better. Unlike many family-owned businesses in Asia, her company had not over-diversified. Nine Dragons continued to specialize in paper products and the paper market alone. She looked at Nine Dragons as a legacy, "a long-term business with a 100 years' foundation."[21]

***As a Woman*** In the male-dominated paper manufacturing industry in China, Cheung maintained that gender inequality had never been a concern for her, and claimed that men had always respected her.

> I didn't feel I was affected by any sex[ual] discrimination in the business community. Actually I felt that whether it was in China or whether it was in the USA, males and female[s] are actually now equal. And in my career development, I didn't feel that as a woman I experienced any difficulty because of that. And my belief is in any business transaction, it's not [gender] that makes the difference. It's actually [ … ] your intelligence [ … ].
>
> — Cheung Yan, chairperson of Nine Dragons[22]

In her opinion, a problem only arose when a woman lost confidence and put herself down, thinking that being a woman meant that she was inferior.

### Managing the Resource Portfolio

*Human Capital* Cheung believed that Nine Dragon's people were one of its critical success factors. She had defined the spirit of the company as "Spirit and Dedication, Cooperation and Aspiration, Excellent Product Quality, Enviable Market Reputation."[23]

Some of the measures followed by the company to ensure staff satisfaction and loyalty included:[24]

- A fair performance management system to realize staff potential.

- Opportunities for transfers and promotions to improve overall staff development.

- Provision of comfortable staff residences.

- A staff communication system where new recruits could meet management three times during the probation period so that assistance in settling in could be offered.

- Adoption of an opinion feedback system to strengthen communication and handle staff advice and complaints promptly.

- Strict adherence to a fair appraisal system based on performance.

- Ensuring competitive remuneration and incentive schemes adjusted annually to market levels.

Cheung claimed to be critical of "heavy-handed family-style management" and had tried to run her company professionally, with three non-family members appointed as general managers responsible for all aspects of the business.[25] However, as of June 2007, she, her husband, and her brother (the three original founders of the company) continued to have a major say in the company's affairs. Cheung was the chairperson responsible for the overall corporate development and long-term strategy, supervising the functions and performance of the Board. Her husband, Liu, was the deputy chairperson and chief executive officer responsible for the overall corporate management and planning of the company's businesses, the development of new technologies, and human resources management. He also assisted Cheung in managing government relations. Cheung's brother, Zhang, was the deputy chief executive officer and executive director, responsible for the management of the company's operations and the business of marketing, finance, procurement, and information

technology (IT). In February 2006, Cheung appointed her 25-year-old son, Lau Chun Shun, as a non-executive member of the Board of Directors. This move was criticized by analysts for nepotism, but vehemently defended by Cheung, who said that her son was qualified and exposed to the paper recycling business, and Nine Dragons was, in any case, a family company.[26] She did, however, say that while he would "take priority in being considered as a successor," it would only happen when he could prove that he was capable of doing so.[27]

*Government Relations* Cheung had always worked at maintaining good relations with the government and claimed that "there had never been any conflict with the government."[28] In the 1990s, the Chinese government was actively promoting foreign investment, and Nine Dragons, founded as a subsidiary of America Chung Nam to be able to benefit from preferential government policies such as tax cuts,[29] fell into that category. Moreover, as the container box manufacturing industry was still nascent then, the company had been further encouraged by the government.

In 2007, the government stipulated the Paper Industry Development Policy to ensure that there was no monopolistic behavior and to promulgate open market competition. Cheung publicly supported this stance through the company's annual statement.

As of June 2007, Cheung had been recognized as a member of the National Committee of the Chinese People's Political Consultative Conference, vice-chairperson of the Women's Federation of Commerce of the All-China Federation of Industry and Commerce, executive vice-president of the Guangdong Overseas Chinese Enterprises Association, and an honorary citizen of the City of Dongguan.[30]

### Effective Organizational Culture

Cheung had demonstrated an entrepreneurial mindset. Nine Dragons was dramatic evidence of her having pursued opportunities to become a first-mover in the industry. She had also supported innovativeness by being open to new ideas and creative processes, whether in improving technology or in going public with her family-held business. She had displayed her risk-taking abilities on several occasions, and said, "I can withstand a lot of pressure."[31] Whether in the United States, or later in China, Cheung was truly proactive, anticipating market needs. Because of her competitive aggressiveness, she had often outperformed her rivals.

Nine Dragons had been awarded the ISO Quality and Environmental Standard Certifications and the OHSAS 18001 certification[32] in recognition of its superior occupational health and safety standards. In August 2008, Cheung admitted that her company imposed fines on its workers to ensure work safety, and that these fines had amounted to approximately US$152,000 in the previous year. She was responding to a report filed by the Hong Kong-based group called Students and Scholars Against Corporate Misbehaviour ("SACOM") and two Hong Kong University Student Unions, which had described her factory as "shameful among Hong Kong funded companies" for its unsafe working conditions, poor welfare, and violation of labor laws.[33] Cheung vehemently denied the criticism and also went on to mention that the company had so far paid out about US$3,068,000 in bonuses for outstanding performances and to those who had contributed to work safety. She said that her company was capital- and technology-intensive, rather than labor-intensive.

*The feed-in plant is what the SACOM has condemned most; however, I can assure [you] that the working conditions in the plant are at least equal to or even better than those in developed countries.*

— Cheung Yan, chairperson of Nine Dragons[34]

The Guangdong provincial trade unions agreed with Cheung, and said that there were no major violations like those mentioned in the SACOM report, but "minor mistakes" like fines did exist, which the company had begun to amend.

## Ethical Practices

In an environment where Cheung would be faced with numerous ethical conflicts, she simply claimed, "I'm an honest businesswoman."[35] In her view, anyone could see the company's results and books—after all, she said, "I run a listed company and I'm transparent. I have nothing to hide."[36]

Following Nine Dragons' listing on the Hong Kong Stock Exchange in 2006, the company's annual statement certified its adherence to the Code on Corporate Governance Practices as set out by the Hong Kong Stock Exchange.

In terms of a corporate governance structure, the company's Board of Directors served as the core, with a separate stratum of management employees looking after the day-to-day operations.[37] As of June 2007, the Board had nine directors, of which four were executive directors—Cheung; her husband, Liu; her brother,

Zhang; and her husband's cousin. Cheung's son, Lau, was a non-executive Board director, and the other four non-executive Board directors were independent.

***Corporate Social Responsibility*** It was Cheung's belief that corporate development had to be accompanied by social responsibility. During the financial year 2007, the company made donations totaling about US$ 1.02 million to local charities and included subsidies to students from poor regions in China to pursue further studies in the mainland's education institutions.[38]

In terms of environmental responsibility, the company had from the very start invested substantially into facilities aimed at protecting the environment. The paper manufacturing industry was known to be a polluting one as it used substantial quantities of chemicals. Nine Dragons aimed at not just meeting the stringent industry standards set by the Chinese government, but rather becoming a role model for the industry. "No environment, no paper" was Nine Dragons' widely publicized philosophy. In December 2006, the company was awarded the "Green/Environmental Creditable Enterprise" by the Guangdong Environmental Protection Bureau in recognition of these efforts.[39]

Cheung believed that in the long run, Nine Dragons had benefited from being environmentally friendly from the very start as government policies were such that those paper makers who could not comply with these standards were being forced to leave the industry, thereby helping Nine Dragons consolidate their market position.[40] Cheung claimed that she had started appreciating the importance of environmental protection early in her life, particularly during her stints in Hong Kong and the United States.

## Organizational Controls

Cheung has played a critical part in managing the balance between the strategic controls and the financial controls of the company. While ensuring that the consistently profitable Nine Dragons remains financially stable, she also made appropriate investments for future viability. For instance, recognizing that the company's reliance on good quality waste paper from the United States could be a real risk in the future, she invested in a joint venture in Inner Mongolia to ensure a steady supply of kraft pulp required to manufacture containerboard.

Nine Dragons did not restrict itself to investing in just the paper machines—rather, looking towards the future, it invested in two power plants that provided it with power and steam, it acquired land use rights in case of further development and expansion, and it went ahead and constructed a shipping pier to reduce port charges and avoid potential transportation bottlenecks.

**Financial Perspective** Seen from a shareholder's point of view, Nine Dragons had a strong cash flow and healthy return on equity and return on assets. Cheung and family (with about 72% shareholding in the company), were perhaps the most tangible evidence of the company's strong financial balance sheet, with a net worth of approximately US$3.4 billion in August 2007.[41]

**Customer Perspective** Cheung had correctly predicted the huge demand for the paper that Nine Dragons produced. Prices remained firm, and net profit margins increased steadily from 6% in 2005 to 20% for the quarter ending in March 2007.[42] The company also used its extensive customer network to assemble a library of data which would help forecast future customer needs and demand.

**Internal Business Processes** By 30 June 2007, Nine Dragons had successfully installed 13 paper-making machines, and the average utilization rate of these machines was an impressive 94.6%.[43]

To boost morale, remuneration packages were competitive and performance-linked incentives were offered. As Cheung said, her company's lowest-paid worker earned between about US$220 and US$350 a month last year (2007), in addition to pension and other benefits, compared to the average monthly income of about US$140 for workers in the city (Dongguan).[44]

**Learning and Growth** Cheung would have kept a close watch on new requirements in the market. For instance, to meet the "3R" principles of "Reduce, Reuse, Recycle," the company planned to launch lightweight, high performance corrugating medium- and light-weight linerboard products in China, in a move that would make the company a pioneer in introducing this product category into China, and help broaden the product range.[45]

To improve employee skills, Nine Dragons' staff were encouraged to pursue further studies. Staff were sent to university for advanced studies. The company also collaborated with Zhongshan University in Guangzhou to launch EMBA and MBA courses as part of their staff incentive schemes. Further, students who had dropped out of school in the poor regions of China were provided assistance to study in the South China University of Technology, and then hired after graduation.

## Cheung Yan: The Successful Leader

*My achievement was a natural consequence of the building of values in my enterprise. The Nine Dragons development was a step-by-step process. Today the achievements are all derived from excellent management in the company and my own*

*long-term vision about the market. It is from the raw material market that I had a good vision of the potential of the Chinese paper market and started to build a business and become successful. In my management, I emphasized a humanized approach and also an approach that you may say is an amalgamation of the Chinese and Western management.*

— *Cheung Yan, chairperson of Nine Dragons*[46]

Cheung was proud of her capacity to meet challenges. She often attributed her success to the long-term vision she had about the industry and company. Woo, an analyst at BNP Paribas, agreed, calling her a "visionary."[47] It was also believed that Cheung's "ebullient personality made her a great saleswoman and a savvy deal maker."[48]

How did Cheung, a woman from modest beginnings, succeed in being globally recognized as one of the foremost strategic business leaders of Asia? What are the special qualities and abilities she possesses that has allowed her to successfully transform her vision and dreams into reality? What must she now do to ensure that Nine Dragons continues to grow from strength to strength?

### CASE DISCUSSION QUESTIONS

1. What is strategic leadership?
2. What would constitute key strategic leadership actions? What are the key elements of a "Balanced Scorecard"?
3. How has Cheung Yan seen such success as a strategic leader? What are the qualities she possesses?

### CASE CREDIT

Havovi Joshi prepared this case under the supervision of Prof. Stephen Ko for class discussion. This case is not intended to show effective or ineffective handling of decision or business processes.

### CASE NOTES

1. Data sourced from Nine Dragons Paper (Holdings) Ltd. 2007. "Annual report."
2. Flannery, R. 2006. "China's richest dragon lady." November 13. http://www.forbes.com/global/2006/1113/060.html, accessed August 23, 2008.

3  Data sourced from Nine Dragons Paper.

4  Linerboard refers to the outside and inside surfaces of the corrugated panels that constituted a box. These are generally made from a mixture of kraft and recycled pulp. Kraft linerboards contain at least 80 percent virgin kraft pulp fibres.

5  Taylor, B. 2006. "Roaring dragon: China's Nine Dragon's paper emerges as a high volume recovered fiber destination." *Recycling Today,* November 1. http://www.forbes.com/global/2006/1113/060.html, accessed August 24, 2008.

6  *The Economist.* 2007. "Face value, paper queen." June 7. http://www.economist.com/people/displaystory.cfm?story_id=9298884, accessed October 6, 2008.

7  Cheng, A. 2007. "The packaging of Zhang Yin: Other people's trash has made her fortune." *Business Report,* January 21, http://www.busrep.co.za/index.php?fArticleId=3636278, accessed September18, 2008.

8  Barboza, D. 2007. "China's queen of trash finds riches in wastepaper." *International Herald Tribune,* January 15. http://www.iht.com/articles/2007/01/15/business/trash.php, accessed September16, 2008.

9  *The Economist.*

10  Liu Ming Chung, Cheung's second husband, was a dentist by profession. He was born in Taiwan and grew up in Brazil.

11  Beck, M. 2005. "America Chung Nam: Committed to the paper loop." *Recycling International,* June. http://www.environmental-expert.com/Files%5C6496%5Carticles%5C4543%5Carticle3.pdf, accessed September 17, 2008.

12  Rao, A. 2007. "Cheung Yan interview on Talk Asia." June 3 edition. http://cnn.com/2007/WORLD/asiapcf/06/03/talkasia.cheungyan/index.html, accessed September 12, 2008.

13  Barboza, D. "China's queen of trash."

14  Nine Dragons Paper (Holdings) Ltd. 2008. "About ND paper." http:/www.ndpaper.com/eng/aboutnd, accessed September 12, 2008.

15  "Pulp" is the material from which paper is made when ground and suspended in water.

16  ERP is a method used to integrate an organization's data and processes.

17  Nine Dragons Paper (Holdings) Ltd. 2008. "Chairlady's statement in the 2007/08 interim report." http://www.ndpaper.com/eng/aboutnd/profile.htm, accessed September 12, 2008.

18  Nine Dragons Paper (Holdings) Ltd. 2008. "Annual report." http://www.ndpaper.com, accessed September 12, 2008.

19  Barboza, D. 2007. "Blazing a paper trail in China: A self-made billionaire wrote her ticket on recycled cardboard." January 16. http://query.nytimes.com/gst/fullpage.html, accessed August 23, 2008.

20  Rao.

21  Ibid.

22  Ibid.

23  Nine Dragons Paper (Holdings) Ltd. "Chairlady's statement."

24  Nine Dragons Paper (Holdings) Ltd. "About ND paper."

25  Flannery, R.

26  Barboza, D. "Blazing a paper trail in China."

27  Rao.

28  Ibid.

29  Siegerist, M. 2007. "China's no. 1 business woman." August 1. http://www.erim.eur.nl/portal/page/portal/2B188840788F43B32E0401BAC4D012257?p_ite, accessed September 29, 2008.

30  Nine Dragons Paper (Holdings) Ltd. 2008. "Annual report."

31  Cheng, A. 2007. "The packaging of Zhang Yin."

32  OHSAS 18001 certification was created by an association of specialist consultancies and certification bodies, and certified that the management system for the health and safety of the workforce complied with prescribed global best practices.

33  Lisheng, Z. 2008. "Nine Dragons paper admits firing workers." *China Daily,* August 5. http://www.chinadaily.com.cn/china/2008-05/08/content_6669958.htm, accessed 29 September 29, 2008.

34  Ibid.

35  Barboza, D. "Blazing a paper trail in China."

36  Cheng, A. 2006. "Pulp making beckons China's richest woman." *International Herald Tribune,* November. http://www.iht.com/articles/2006/11/07/bloomberg/sxpulp.php, accessed September 16, 2008.

37  Nine Dragons Paper (Holdings) Ltd. 2008. "Annual report."

38  Ibid.

39  Ibid.

40  Government policies in China had become stricter as the new middle class was becoming more concerned about the state of the environment.

41  Flannery, R. 2007. "China's 40 richest." August 10. http://www.forbes.com/business/2007/10/08/china-40-richest-ent-cx_rf_1008chinasrich.html, accessed October 8, 2008.

42  *The Economist.*

43  Nine Dragons Paper (Holdings) Ltd. 2008. "Annual report."

44  Lisheng, Z.

45  Nine Dragons Paper (Holdings) Ltd. "Chairlady's statement."

46  Rao.

47  Barboza, D. "Blazing a paper trail in China."

48  Barboza, D. "China's queen of trash."

# The Bamínica Power Plant Project: What Went Wrong and What Can Be Learned

*This project was like the Hotel California. "You can check out anytime you want but you can never leave."*

*There were several times along the way where we could have stopped the project but we did not have the willpower, discipline, or maturity to do it…. There was no single fatal flaw in the project. There were a bunch of things that made it ugly at the end of the day…. My view is that when you do things at the speed of light you don't have time to read the warning signs.*

*We allowed a transaction to go through that had a lot of pieces that should have been more heavily scrutinized and fixed because we were very hungry for a deal. The people in charge weren't able to identify all the risks. The people who could have done that were pushed away from the transaction.*

Various Comments from a Bamínica Project Developer

Tom Stephens, Executive Vice President, Global Development for Power-Gen Inc. (PowerGen), was evaluating the company's eight-year involvement in the Bamínica power plant project, which was now operated by a joint venture controlled by PowerGen. Stephens considered the Bamínica power plant one of PowerGen's most diffcult and challenging projects. There had been problems in many different areas, including site selection, joint venture management, fnancing, plant construction, equipment suppliers, community relationships, and customer payments. Although the power plant was proftable, the various problems had consumed a disproportionate amount of PowerGen management time given the size of the project. As Stephens reviewed the project's history and many challenges in mid-2011, he hoped he could identify some key learning areas to apply to future projects.

## PowerGen

PowerGen, Inc., a global power company with generation and distribution businesses, operated across fve continents. Founded in 1987 in Houston, Texas, Power-Gen built its first power plant in 1989 in Louisiana. Over the next six years, PowerGen built four more plants in the United States. The company then began looking for international opportunities.

In the early 1990s, global markets for power plant projects began to open up. PowerGen built its first plant outside the United States in Argentina and then expanded to the United Kingdom, Indonesia, China, Hungary, Brazil, Ghana, Cameroon, and several Caribbean nations, including Bamínica. Although most of the power plants used thermal fuel sources, in 2011 the company was actively involved in a range of projects using renewable fuel such as biomass, hydropower, solar, and wind.

# Electricity Supply in Bamínica

Bamínica, a Caribbean nation with a population of about 4.5 million, had experienced robust economic growth from 2002 to 2007. During the 2008 to 2009 period, growth slowed to about 3.0% and then picked up to about 7% in 2010. Economic growth was led by exports from free-trade zones and strong performance from the construction and economic sectors. However, there was an estimated 150 MW defcit in electricity generation capacity and power outages were frequent. It was common for businesses in Bamínica to maintain backup power systems and it was acknowledged that problems with power were hampering economic growth. The head of the power company, the Corporación Bamínica de Electricidad (CBE), admitted that because of old equipment, problems with billing, and widespread power theft, only about 60% of the power actually produced was paid for. The CBE was operating on a deteriorating asset base and could not keep up with growth in demand. CBE's cost was about 12-15 cents/kWh. Electricity demand was expected to grow 9% over the next decade. Private power projects were necessary if electricity demand was to be met.

# Overview of the Bamínica Project

The project was a barge-mounted 185 MW combined cycle baseload plant located at Puerto Salinas on the north coast of Bamínica. The project would be one of the largest privately owned, project-fnanced power plants in Latin America and, when completed, provided more than 20% of the country's average electric generation capacity. The project was owned by PowerGen/Jones Cogeneration Limited Partnership (PJCLP), a joint venture between PowerGen and Jones International (JI). Originally, each partner had a 50% ownership interest. In 2011, JI's ownership was 15% and PowerGen's share was 85%.

The plant was mounted on two seaworthy barges. One barge contained a 138k kV substation and a Western Electric 75 MW turbine generator designed to burn No. 2 diesel fuel. The second barge contained a Waste Heat Recovery Steam Generator, two auxiliary boilers, and a 110 MW Western Electric steam turbine generator. The boilers burned No. 6 fuel oil. Seawater was used for cooling and then discharged into the sea outside the port area. The shore facilities included 2 × 60,000 barrel No. 6 fuel oil tanks, 2 × 60,000 barrel No. 2 fuel oil tanks, a fuel pumping facility, a utility-pipe corridor, a fuel unloading facility, a parking area, space for a cooling water discharge line, and office space. The project met all local and World Bank environmental standards.

The sole power purchaser was CBE, a general utility with generation, transmission, and distribution in Bamínica. The power purchase agreement (PPA) had a 19-year term and was structured in U.S.-style, with energy payments that allowed for pass-through to CBE of all fuel costs at market prices and operations and maintenance and capacity payments intended to cover all other project costs and provide a return on investment. The Bamínica government guaranteed the peso (the local currency) convertibility and all CBE obligations under the PPA agreement and further supported the guarantee by providing a $24 million letter of credit. CBE payments were dollar denominated.

The project cost was $204 million. Long-term debt for the project consisted of loan agreements with International Finance Corporation (IFC) and several other lenders, including government development banks of Germany, Holland, and the U.K. The plant became operational in simple cycle mode in 2004 and in combined cycle mode in 2006.

# Project Initiation

PowerGen first became interested in Bamínica in early 2003. Several PowerGen people, including Don Williams and Jack Kirk, went to Bamínica on an exploratory visit. Williams and Kirk worked in PowerGen's development group, which was responsible for initiating and constructing projects. Williams, an engineer, was in his late 50s and had worked for various energy companies over his career. Kirk was a former U.S. military offcer and was in his late 30s. Prior to joining PowerGen two years earlier, he had not had any private sector experience.

In April 2003, Williams returned to Bamínica and spent a week driving around the country. His objective was to learn as much as he could about Bamínica culture, the government, the land, other power plants, and business prospects. Based on that trip, the development team decided that PowerGen could potentially develop a diesel-powered plant of about 150 MW on the north coast.

The CBE encouraged PowerGen to make a proposal. With Jack Kirk in charge, PowerGen began preparing a proposal for the CBE. Kirk was responsible for development in Central America and the Caribbean. Prior to joining PowerGen, Kirk was a colonel in the U.S. Army. He had no project development experience or business background. Kirk joined PowerGen in 2001 and had not yet closed any deals.

In July 2003, just a few days before the proposal was to be submitted, the team discovered that Jones International (JI) and the CBE had signed an agreement in March 2003 to develop a power plant on the north coast. At this point PowerGen knew nothing about JI, a company run by Richard Jones as a one-man business. JI's only previous development was a 200 MW cogeneration facility running on natural gas in Texas. The proposed Bamínica facility would be a copy of the Texas plant but built on barges.

The PowerGen team concluded that there was room for only one plant on the north coast, so ceased work on their proposal and left Bamínica. In August 2003, Don Williams called Richard Jones. PowerGen knew that JI had signed a PPA with the CBE and had an obligation to secure a construction contract within a certain period of time. Suspecting that JI did not have the capital to develop the project, Williams thought that perhaps JI and PowerGen could work together. The conversation went as follows:

PowerGen (Williams): We want to congratulate you on your win with the CBE.

Jones: Thank you very much. I had heard about you guys and knew you were in competition against us.

PowerGen: Perhaps there is something we can do to cooperate.

Jones: I already have the PPA. Why do I need you people?

PowerGen: Well, the PPA has a pretty short window for fnancing—maybe we can fnd some way to help?

Jones: Thanks, but I already have the PPA and I don't anticipate any problems getting fnancing.

PowerGen subsequently learned that Jones had been to about 15 banks and none were interested in financing the project. In late August, two-and-a-half weeks after the initial PowerGen-Jones conversation, Jones called PowerGen and suggested a partnership. According to Williams:

*Richard Jones sent us a confidentiality agreement to sign and it was the most screwed up agreement you have ever seen. We should never have signed it. Although the agreement never caused us any problems, it was defnitely a red flag in the way it was drafted.*

*There were lots of problems with the PPA. Richard Jones went to Bamínica and got most of them fixed. In the end the PPA was not bad. But, combined with a customer who interpreted it differently than us and the problems with the plant, it was a disaster.*

*We were probably Jones's last resort. We had the ability to finance the whole project out of cash. That was one of the attractions. We told Richard that if we liked the project, we would use PowerGen's cash and put it together on a fast track basis. When we went to the board we were confdent that we could finance this thing out.*

In October, PowerGen received board approval to proceed with a joint venture with JI. In November, without notice to PowerGen, Jones executed a turnkey construction contract with Western Electric for $117.25 million.

*It was a bad construction contract that we immediately tried to change for the benefit of the owners. It was so one-sided it was leaning over. The only right the sponsor had was to pay. Jones said that he had to sign with Western Electric because he had a time limit to perform in the PPA. We tried to get Western Electric to make changes but they basically folded their arms and said no. For example, I wanted the operations and maintenance manuals in Spanish. Western Electric said no. Western Electric would not let us review contract details and our management refused to dig their heels in. At the end of the day, Jones and Western Electric colluded to get what Western Electric wanted.*

*Throughout this period there were various opportunities for PowerGen to kill the deal but nobody did because the expected returns were off the charts.*

Jack Kirk had a very free hand in developing the project and was under pressure to complete a deal. That was usual in PowerGen. Developers were expected to find and close deals and were incentivized to do so. Bonuses tied to projected project performance were a signifcant share of developer compensation for energy infrastructure projects. Developers who did not close deals and finish projects rarely lasted long at PowerGen. Bonuses were typically paid at two stages: at the completion of project fnancing, and at the start-up of the project. Lead project developers determined how the bonus was shared across the development team.

*Kirk was running around unsupervised because we had various other bigger deals under way. As well, Kirk was trusted. He was a guy with ice water in his veins. He was not afraid to stand up to the Bamínica government. You did not have to be around him long to have confidence in him. He seemed to have the capabilities of a PowerGen developer.*

Prior to the Bamínica deal, Kirk worked on a project in Colombia that did not get PowerGen approval. Because he was a senior developer and had not yet closed any deals, "Kirk's future was largely dependent on the Bamínica project."

*During the negotiation process, Jack Kirk made all the decisions and put the package together. He listened to everybody but at the end of the day he was the driver. Jack called the shots and had a pretty free hand. Once it was put together and the outside counsel and the finance people were brought in, then it went to the board.*

This view of Kirk's autonomy is refected in comments from another PowerGen manager who had some involvement early in the deal:

> I took a strong position on several points. I thought we were going in the wrong direction in that (a) we were creating a situation that was unstable, and (b) we were overpaying and giving Jones too much for what he was bringing to the table. I said we needed to be more aggressive in designing the joint venture and particularly who controlled the venture, and insisting on changes to the PPA and the construction contract. In terms of experience, slickness, business sophistication, street smarts, and a willingness not to be constrained by normal ethical standards, Jones had us at a disadvantage. I thought we needed some more experience on our team. Kirk had been pretty successful in the military and was used to running his own show. He did not like interference from other people. He went to Rebecca [the head of PowerGen Latin America] and said, "I want this guy off my back." So, I was overruled.

# The Partnership Agreement

Within PowerGen, Richard Jones quickly developed a reputation for being diffcult to deal with and a somewhat unusual personality:

> Richard Jones is an unbelievably crazy guy. You match up a wild man who believes his own b.s. with a developer who is desperate for a deal, and what do you get? We did a bit of research on Jones and learned through various law frms that he was very litigious. It turned out to be true. Richard would say in letters to us that "You will recall in our last meeting that we agreed a, b, c." when in fact we agreed x, y, z. We had to respond to everything he did, almost on a daily basis.
>
> It was a very diffcult negotiation with Jones. Because of that we didn't have as strong a partnership agreement as we should have. When the deal was cut, we did not have a lawyer sitting there full time. Part of the problem was the inexperience of Jack Kirk. There were no other deals in Latin America at that time and there was a lot of pressure to get this one going.

In late November, PowerGen and JI signed the agreement for the PowerGen/ Jones Cogeneration Limited Partnership (PJCLP). According to the agreement, PowerGen Construction would oversee construction.

> We knew there were problems with the construction contract. Jones thought he understood the risks because he had developed a plant in Texas. We knew that if we were interested in this transaction, we needed to get control very quickly over the unilateral decisions being made. We entered into a partnership agreement under which PowerGen was able to get vast control so that the project could get financed. As long as PowerGen had to front the money for Jones, the concept was that after the banks converted their construction finance to non-recourse project finance, we would try to control the project.
>
> Even though the construction contract was signed between Jones and Western Electric, our outside lawyer told us not to sign. We stayed up all night with Western Electric and Sylvanto [Western Electric's construction partner] making changes to get the contract to the bare minimum. But, with the returns, we thought we could live with it. We also kept telling ourselves that Western Electric was a marquee company and they'd do the right thing. Wrong, big mistake. Western Electric was trying to make money selling turbines and they would shove them down your throat.
>
> In the final negotiations with Jones, we tried to get him to make two representations: one, that the PPA was legal, valid, and enforceable under Bamínica law; and two, that there were no FCPA violations. We told Jones that he had to bear the risk if any of his people bribed someone. Jones did not like that. We also told him that if the PPA was not enforceable, it was also his problem. In the end we got weaker representation on these issues than we should have.

*It also became apparent to us that Jones was going to ride our coattails and that this was a mouse on the coattails of an elephant. We tried not to act like an elephant but he continually used that against us. He's a crafty guy and he played us like a piano for a while.*

## Partnership Details

The agreement was set up with PowerGen and JI each holding a 1% general partner interest (see Exhibit 1 for ownership structure as of 2011). Both partners initially had a limited partner interest of 49% each. Richard Jones's stake was subject to reduction unless he came up with a certain amount of money at financial close to

**EXHIBIT 1**   Jones/PowerGen Cogeneration Limited Partnership after Jones 35% Equity Share Transferred to PowerGen

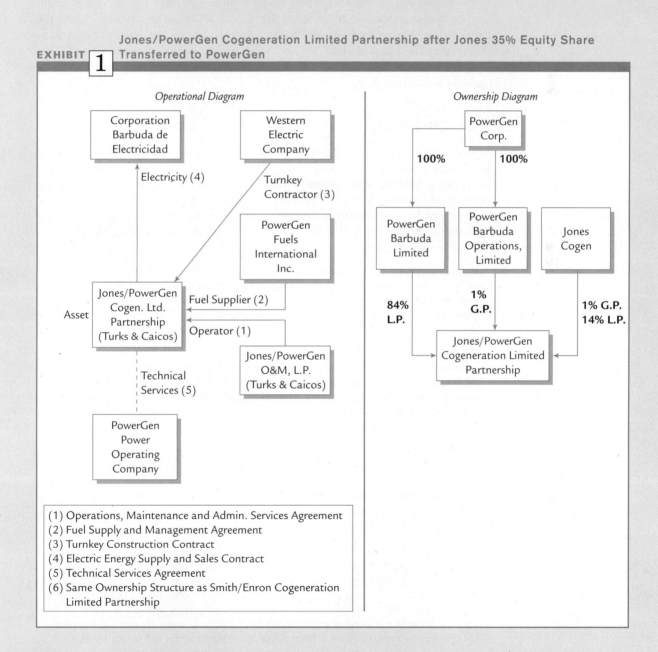

(1) Operations, Maintenance and Admin. Services Agreement
(2) Fuel Supply and Management Agreement
(3) Turnkey Construction Contract
(4) Electric Energy Supply and Sales Contract
(5) Technical Services Agreement
(6) Same Ownership Structure as Smith/Enron Cogeneration Limited Partnership

repay PowerGen for carrying his out-of-pocket equity from inception to financial close (the stake was subsequently reduced). The agreement provided the following:

1.  Each partner will always agree and discuss major issues, except for financing, which was exclusively in PowerGen's control.

2.  Unanimous approval of the partners required for: liquidation, sale of the business, changing the name of the company, entering into agreements with partner affliates, modifying the construction budget upwards, and modifying the distribution of development fees.

3.  For all other decisions, Jones and PowerGen will collaborate.

Notwithstanding the PowerGen supervote for financing, Jones's *de facto* involvement from the beginning was that he acted like a 50% shareholder. As well, "Until the financial close, PowerGen bent over backwards to accommodate Jones's concerns, to a fault. After the fnancial close, we no longer had to be so accommodating." Also, the agreement did not include clear exit terms, something that would become contentious at a later date.

## Site Selection

According to the PPA, the government was to provide a site for the project and provide the necessary regulatory authorizations. The government provided a site near Puerto Salinas. The site was inadequate because it would require tearing down an old bodega on the waterfront. The local government objected to the development because they had their own plans for the area. So, another site had to be found quickly because there were time deadlines in the PPA. Simple cycle power had to be available by May 2004.

> *Some people said that since the site was not suitable, the clock should roll over until we found a site. Some of us were not comfortable with this view. We had already given the order to Western Electric. The turbine and the barge were being built. God forbid that the barge arrives and we don't have a site. There were not a lot of choices for sites. We looked farther away from Puerto Salinas but that would have meant building a transmission line, which would have been very diffcult.*

Another site was located but it also had problems. Finally, a third site that CBE recommended was found. It was zoned for industrial use with the approval of the Bamínica government and the CBE against the protests of a nearby hotel. The site was at the western edge of a bay on the leeward side of a port. The hotel was on a ridge, north of the plant in a straight line. The design of the plant included exhaust stacks which were about the same height as the hotel restaurant. When the plant was under construction and during the testing phase, there was a lot of noise throughout the day and night because silencers were not included in the design of the steam relief system. In addition, although the emissions normally blew to the south, away from the hotel, there were times when the wind shifted and the emissions blew north over the hotel. Just beyond the hotel was an upscale residential neighborhood occupied primarily by foreigners.

> *We did a lot of emissions modeling to assure ourselves that we would not cause any problems. Our greatest concern was noise from the steam blows and the aesthetics of the property. We spent a great deal of money on landscaping and painting the tanks. We tried to make the place attractive. The folks at the hotel liked what we did but they did not like the noise. And, I believe the operators ignored directions and did a steam blow when the wind was blowing directly over the hotel. We never knew for sure if the particulate fallout came from our plant or other plants about a mile and a half across the bay.*

# Construction

The PowerGen development team was responsible for completing the construction and then turning the plant over to PowerGen's asset management group. There were construction problems from the beginning, leading to a series of disputes and arguments between PowerGen and the contractors. For example, one dispute began like this:

*In your own [Western Electric] literature you say that it is preferred that the client put in fuel treatment, which means centrifuges. I said to Western Electric, "Where is the centrifuge." Western Electric said we don't need one and it was not included in the price. If you want one, you pay for it. So we did, for more than a half million dollars. The proposal that Western Electric signed had dual fuel filters. When we got the actual unit it had one filter. Western Electric said that they changed their standard. I had to buy them myself. Before they were installed I can't count the number of days that we had to shut the plant down because the fuel filter was plugged. They just dug their heels in and said we are Western Electric and we do it this way.*

*We initially thought we would not have to do a lot of oversight. We were reasonably confident that the contractors would deliver. We had never worked with Western Electric before this project. We had good feelings about them—they were supposed to be a first-rate company.*

To satisfy the lenders, PowerGen's construction company oversaw the construction. Unfortunately, Power-Gen overlooked some serious construction issues and Jack Kirk was not interested in hearing about construction problems. Then, Kirk left the company to join a competitor.

*Our own PowerGen construction guys were not leading the parade; they were standing on the curb watching the parade go by with full confidence that we've got the best in the world and they are going to do it right. Unfortunately, Western Electric did not have their A team on the ground. They were under pressure to get things done quickly so they cut corners. I didn't figure this out until late in the game. They did a sloppy job.*

*We were also under pressure to get the project finished. For one thing, we had contractual deadlines that we had to meet. The project was to be transferred to PowerGen Global Power and we were told to stop screwing with the project and get it transferred over.*

*Throughout the construction phase, Richard Jones and his company did little or nothing. Richard was always the missing man. He was off sailing his sailboat or hunting or fishing. He might return our call or he might not. He wanted to be part of the decision-making team but he was never around to make a decision.*

# The Project Start-up

The project was designed in two phases. The frst phase was a simple cycle power plant on a barge that generated about 75 MW. This phase was completed six months after the contract was signed. The second phase was a combined cycle power plant that included two boilers. This phase was supposed to be completed by June 2005.

The second barge was brought in, and when the performance test was run, there was major failure in the gas turbine and boilers. The result was a lengthy period of repair and disputes with the contractors. It was several months before the cause of the problem was identifed and the repairs were completed. PowerGen concluded that contaminated water and other anomalies were present in the preparation for the start-up. Water quality, something Western Electric should have controlled, was not carefully monitored during commissioning and the boiler suffered extensive corrosion damage.

There were major disputes with Western Electric and Sylvanto about who was responsible for the installation problems, why they occurred, and if claims were under warranty or not. There was a major insurance issue because of a lapse in coverage. It was unclear if a major claim was a Western Electric/Sylvanto responsibility or a PJCLP responsibility.

Construction problems delayed the second phase start-up until January 2006.

# Financing

PowerGen committed to a very aggressive deadline to have the power plant operating. PowerGen financed the initial development, with the understanding that long-term non-recourse financing would replace PowerGen's debt. From the beginning, Bamínica was acknowledged as a diffcult place to get projects financed because (1) the government had a history of not paying its debts; (2) there was a thin foreign exchange market; and (3) there were weak banking laws.

The project was designed to be 25% equity and 75% debt. The original cost was $204 million and the goal was to raise $153 million. The plan was to have a single financial closing with two lenders: the World Bank's International Finance Corporation (IFC), with about $25 million and a bond underwriter for the remainder.

A bond underwriter was selected and began due diligence. When problems with the CBE and payments for the electricity arose (see the next section), the bond underwriter withdrew from the project, leaving a huge hole in the financing. By this time PowerGen had spent about $100 million on the project.

The IFC agreed to increase its financing to $75 million. The remaining financing came from six different lenders, with the result that seven different financial closings were required. Each closing required an entire set of documents (legal opinions, permits, mortgage registrations, and so forth). As well, it took almost nine months longer than planned to replace PowerGen's financial exposure.

> Because of all the problems, there was a low level of confidence as to when the project would perform. Everyone knew the customer was bankrupt. We were worried that if we waited one week, the lenders might run away from the project. So, as soon as a lender said yes, we went to closing. That increased the legal budget exponentially. The reason the lenders remained in the project was because there was a lot of confidence in PowerGen and the contractors and there were expectations that the Bamínica government would stand behind the project.
>
> Richard Jones made our life diffcult because he did not want to trust us, perhaps because he felt we were not getting the best deal for the joint venture. After we negotiated with the lenders, we often had to negotiate with our own partner about the financing terms. We had to convince him that it was the best deal for the partnership. The problem was that our incentives were not aligned properly. From Jones's point of view the project was fully financed by PowerGen. He did not have the same incentives as PowerGen in raising third party debt. If we did not find financing and the project tanked, PowerGen would have been out of a lot of money. Jones did not have money in the project to lose. The third party debt was cheaper than PowerGen was charging the project and, in Jones's view, PowerGen was benefiting because of this. Every time something changed he viewed this as an opportunity to improve his position.

The final closing was in April 2006 when lenders assumed the project risk, with the exception of a PowerGen debt service guarantee of $9.6 million and approximately $32 million of liability for certain contingent litigation and construction risk. At this time, total capital in the project was $205 million and the third party debt portion was $150 million.

# The CBE Does Not Pay

Prior to the start-up of the second phase, there had been some minor disputes with the CBE about how PJCLP would be paid for the power, about the heat rate, the cost of fuel, and the measurement of power output. The delayed second phase start-up increased the contractual diffculties with the CBE. After the second phase startup in January 2006, the plant performed well for the first month and the invoice to the CBE became due. By contract, the monthly invoice from simple cycle to combined cycle went from about $1 million per month to $7 million. Under the contract, PJCLP had agreed that during the simple cycle phase the invoice would mainly cover operating costs. Once the second phase was completed, the capital return and profit billings would begin.

CBE did not have the funds to pay the first invoice. The contract allowed PJCLP to shut down the plant if payment was not received. PJCLP gave the government 10 days' notice and then shut down the plant in March 2006. It took 20 days to get the plant restarted and an agreement reached about payment. In June 2006, a new government was formed in Bamínica. The outgoing government decided they had been ill-treated by PJCLP, and again PJCLP was not paid. At this time there were disputed payments of about $5 million dollars. PJCLP responded by filing an arbitration claim. By August 2006, the new Bamínica government was in place and had not yet responded to the claim. In September the government filed a counterclaim. By the end of 2006, the disputed amount from the PJCLP side was about $19 million.

The problem, according to a PowerGen executive, was as follows:

*Under their interpretation of PPAs, the CBE thinks they are entitled to pay based on what is delivered, notwithstanding a contractual obligation to make capacity payments and incentives or disincentives regarding the generator's performance. Even if the shutdown of the generator was caused by grid failure in Bamínica, they would take the position that "You are failing to deliver the capacity that we expected and consequently we are not paying you."*

*We concluded that the government and the CBE do not honor their word or the written contract. They try to find ways to weasel out of it. Part of it is their nature, and part of it is the fact that they don't have any money.*

In contrast, another PowerGen manager commented:

*The contract may have been too overreaching in some areas. For example, was it reasonable to expect them to pay when the plant could not perform? The CBE was an unsophisticated buyer and did not understand how the PPA really worked.*

Throughout this period, management turnover in the CBE did not help:

*JI originally signed an agreement with the general administrator of the CBE, who was authorized by the president to sign a PPA . After we got involved there was a steady turnover in administrators. Some of them stayed for only a few months. The rumor was that each administrator signed a project and got a retirement deal. On one occasion we had a Monday meeting with the administrator about an issue that had to be resolved quickly. As I was having breakfast I read in the local newspaper that Sunday night the administrator was fired. Now I have a guy who doesn't know anything about the deal. I went to his office and he did not want to meet me. He said, "I have been here for less than 24 hours—I can't take this to my president." Did they understand the contract? Most of them probably never even read it.*

According to public statements from the head of the CBE, payments were not made because the facility had not run up to speed and CBE did not owe nearly as much as PJCLP claimed. PJCLP was not the only company with which CBE was in dispute. Another firm that entered Bamínica about a year after PowerGen threatened to shut down its 220 MW plant because of unpaid bills.

By the end of 2006, an ICC arbitration panel was established, with the arbitration to take place in Mexico. Meetings with the arbitration panel began in early 2007. All parties agreed on a settlement but in early 2008 the Bamínica government changed the CBE management. The new management created a new committee in charge of negotiating with PJCLP and the new committee refused to acknowledge any of the earlier negotiations. By the end of 2009, an agreement was finally reached on the disputed payments.

## Settlement with the Contractors and New Problems

The plant had a series of operating problems from the start-up. Of the five major pieces of equipment, problems were experienced with each one. In addition to the start-up problems, a steam turbine blade broke in 2006. In the interim period of six months between failure and repair, the turbine was run with one less blade, reducing capacity by 10-15%. By the end of 2006, a settlement was reached with Western Electric and Sylvanto. These firms agreed to pay for the direct restart cost and to replace the steam turbine (equipment and installation costs). They also agreed to an extended warranty on the turbine and boilers. PJCLP and the contractors also agreed to jointly seek insurance claims and to jointly share any settlement. This agreement was contingent on getting approval from the lenders because part of the settlement would be release from other claims. PowerGen thought this was a good deal and asked the lenders for their approval. The new turbine was scheduled to be installed by April 2007.

The lenders would not approve the settlement. Their view was that there had been so many problems that they did not want to release anyone. PJCLP decided that the settlement would go forward without lender approval because it would not have a material adverse effect on the lenders or the project. The lenders were not pleased because they hoped PowerGen would come up with additional guarantees, which PowerGen refused to do. Nevertheless, up to this point, PJCLP had met its financial obligations to the lenders.

Not long after the settlement with the contractors, the plant began experiencing a series of tube leaks in both boilers. Each tube leak required the boiler to be shut down for at least 24 hours of repair. During the repairs it was noticed that there was buildup of slag on the tubes. The slag blocked the tubes as heat exchangers, which meant the boilers became less effcient. Various procedures were unsuccessfully tried to remove the slag, including hydro blasting and chipping the slag off the boilers. As it turned out, the boilers were not suited to the heavy fuel used by the project because they were designed for natural gas. Although the slag was common for the fuel used by PJCLP, the spacing of the boiler tubes must be wide enough to prevent a buildup on the tubes and cleaning the slag must be possible. The boilers installed had neither of these features. Unfortunately, PowerGen had no experience with boilers and did not identify the design problems created by Western Electric and its subcontractors.

The result was that PowerGen began a series of meetings with Sylvanto to determine how to fix the boilers, which had cost about $6 million. The cost to replace the boilers was estimated to be about $20 million. Earlier, Sylvanto had informed PowerGen in writing that the proposed boilers would run on the fuel selected for the project. When the problems first emerged, Sylvanto's response was that PJCLP was not running the plant properly. Technical consultants were hired to show that the problem was the boilers, not PJCLP. Finally, the contractors agreed that the boilers were the wrong type for the fuel. It was not possible to change the fuel because it would destroy the economic viability of the project. In 2009, another settlement agreement was being negotiated to get new boilers. PJCLP would pay the incremental cost of the newly designed boilers (about $4 million) and the contractors and their insurance carrier would pay an additional $16 million for installation along with refurbishing the existing boilers in the interim period of two years.

## Richard Jones's Ownership Is Reduced

The original deal with Richard Jones was that in order to become a 50% shareholder, he would have to pay cash for 40%. The other 10% would come from his origination of the deal. At the financial close in April 2006, Jones paid for 5%. An agreement was reached that gave Jones 18 months to raise $17 million required for the remaining 35% share. In November 2007, the deadline came and Jones did not have the money. Jones asked for an indefinite deferral and PowerGen said no. PowerGen also initiated arbitration with Jones to establish its claim. Jones countersued and claimed that PowerGen had conspired to prevent him from buying his share. A six-month arbitration process was resolved in June 2008 when Jones withdrew his lawsuit and his 35% stake was transferred to PowerGen. Jones raised another lawsuit in Bamínica alleging that PowerGen fraudulently induced him to give up his share of the project. Jones claimed damages of $169 million. In January 2000, the suit was dismissed. In 2011, Jones remained a 15% shareholder in the joint venture.

## Management

Three people reported to the PJCLP executive director: the plant manager, the financial manager, and the commercial manager. The financial and commercial managers were Bamínica nationals and had been with PJCLP from the beginning. The first executive director, hired in September 2006, was an Ecuadorian and former World Bank employee. He had been the general manager of a utility in Quito. He was a strong source of technical expertise and understood the IFC. However, he was not a good politician and was ineffective in building community and government relations. A new executive director was appointed in January 2008. PJCLP was the new director's first assignment in a power company. Prior to PJCLP, the director had been general manager for several mining companies in Latin America and had worked in Bamínica. He was strong in building community relations.

Turnover in plant managers was a problem and meant that a long-term operational strategy was slow to evolve. The first permanent plant manager also began in September 2006 and was an American of Hispanic origin. He had previously worked in power plants in Michigan. He was characterized as a "difficult case" and eventually ended up with little support inside or outside the company. He was also viewed as a bit scary in that he carried a gun and was suspected of having a drinking problem. He left voluntarily in January 2008. He was followed by a temporary plant manager who stayed for about three months. In June 2008, another permanent plant manager was hired. This manager was born in Panama and had been a plant manager in Argentina and Africa.

# Community Relations

As the payment dispute with CBE increased, CBE used the media aggressively. PJCLP was blamed for causing major power shortages in Bamínica because of its operational problems. CBE was able to successfully blunt PJCLP's efforts to publicize CBE's poor payment practices by arguing that PJCLP did not deserve to get paid. To overcome the media campaign, PJCLP began an aggressive community relations program. According to a PowerGen executive:

> *Public opinion in Bamínica was not particularly important because the public was powerless. The administration runs the country the way they want to run it. Bad press in the country does not have much effect on the relationships with the Bamínica government. Bad press is more important outside the country.*
>
> *Community relations is another story. We built a relationship with the First Lady, a woman in her 70s. We were close to the mayor and some of the council members in Puerto Salinas. We held seminars using people from the university to explain the technical issues, we invited school children to tour the plant, and we sponsored local sports*

**EXHIBIT 2** PowerGen/Jones Cogeneration Limited Partnership Balance Sheets December 31, 2009 and 2010

| Assets | 2010 | 2009 |
|---|---|---|
| Current assets: | | |
| Cash | US$ 9,964,741 | US$ 2,296,976 |
| Accounts receivable net of allowance of US$136,198 | 59,897,787 | 38,317,364 |
| Inventories, mainly fuel and parts | 4,577,327 | 3,447,421 |
| Prepaid insurance | 894,293 | 1,347,472 |
| Total current assets | 75,334,148 | 45,409,233 |
| | | |
| Pre-operating expenses | 17,542,651 | 18,661,923 |
| Property, plant and equipment | 175,483,806 | 180,717,632 |
| | 193,026,457 | 199,379,555 |
| | US$268,360,605 | US$244,788,784 |
| **Liabilities and Partnership Equity** | | |
| Current liabilities: | | |
| Current portion of long-term debt | US$ 15,077,649 | US$ 13,336,312 |
| Accounts payable | 16,858,589 | |
| Accounts payable to related companies | 19,158,511 | 21,633,360 |
| Accrued interest payable | 4,809,250 | 1,512,285 |
| Other accrued liabilities | 4,702,396 | 3,093,830 |
| Total current liabilities | 60,606,395 | 39,575,787 |
| | | |
| Deferred income from capacity fees | 5,780,049 | 2,709,201 |
| Long-term debt | 135,066,438 | 143,915,521 |
| | 140,846,487 | 146,624,722 |
| | | |
| Partnership equity: | | |
| Partner contributed capital | 51,077,600 | 51,077,600 |
| Undistributed partnership earnings | 15,830,123 | 7,510,679 |
| Total equity | 66,907,723 | 58,588,279 |
| | US$268,360,605 | US$244,788,788 |

teams. *We did some training with the fire department. We bought some used fire equipment and clothing from a fire company in Fort Worth and gave it to the fire department. We bought tires for the ambulance. When we bought emergency equipment for the plant, I bought two of everything and gave half to the ambulance service. This was all done very quietly.*

*Unfortunately, after the project was transferred to the PowerGen operators, community relations efforts did not improve. No natural allies were created to carry us through good and bad times. The thought was, "We have an operating project. We have to go run it just as we would in the States."*

## Hotel Claims

During the construction period, the adjacent hotel initiated a lawsuit against the noise. The lawsuit was settled with a payment of $1 million by PJCLP in 2005. During the construction of the second phase, the hotel began losing customers. In 2007, the hotel was permanently closed. The hotel owners, a wealthy and well-connected Bamínica family, filed an arbitration claim against PJCLP claiming that the plant had been built illegally and that the plant site should never have been developed as an industrial site. The claim maintained that the permits from the government had been given improperly.

The acknowledged cost and value of the hotel, even according to the hotel accountants, was not more than $5 million. In 2008, a Bamínica arbitration panel awarded the hotel $13.6 million against the project. The panel had three members

**EXHIBIT 3** PowerGen/Jones Cogeneration Limited Partnership Statements of Income and Undistributed Partnership Earnings Year Ended December 31, 2009 and 2010

|  | 2010 | 2009 |
|---|---|---|
| Income: |  |  |
| Energy income | US$ 51,552,207 | US$ 46,655,458 |
| Capacity, operation and maintenance fees | 38,566,090 | 37,049,085 |
| Total revenues | 90,115,297 | 83,704,543 |
|  |  |  |
| Cost and expenses: |  |  |
| Operating costs | 46,865,643 | 42,682,139 |
| Depreciation of machinery and equipment | 5,667,430 | 5,367,238 |
| Amortization of prepaid insurance | 2,217,571 | 2,066,118 |
| Amortization of pre-operating expenses | 1,134,984 | 970,878 |
| Administrative expenses | 12,322,451 | 9,817,533 |
|  | 68,208,079 | 60,903,906 |
| Net operating income | 21,910,218 | 22,800,637 |
|  |  |  |
| Interest income | 4,819,080 | 1,786,228 |
| Interest expense | (18,398,256) | (17,032,683) |
| Exchange loss | (11,598) | (31,783) |
| Other |  | (11,720) |
| Other income (expenses) | (13,590,774) | (15,289,958) |
|  |  |  |
| Net income | 8,319,444 | 7,510,679 |
| Undistributed partnership earnings at the beginning of year | 7,510,679 |  |
|  |  |  |
| Undistributed partnership earnings at the end of year | US$ 15,830,123 | US$ 7,510,679 |

but before the decision was complete, the chairman of the panel was appointed to the Bamínica Supreme Court. By law, the chairman was unable to participate in the arbitration. The remaining two panelists completed the arbitration. PJCLP appealed the arbitration ruling in the Bamínica courts, claiming that without a third panelist, the arbitration was invalid according to Bamínica rules of arbitration. In 2011, the arbitration was not settled.

# The Project in 2011

Looking forward, Tom Stephens hoped to take advantage of the learning from the Bamínica project. One of the interesting outcomes was that despite all the problems and challenges, the project was profitable (see Exhibits 2 and 3 for project financial statements). Perhaps a key lesson was to take a long-term view and not let any one issue derail the entire project.

## CASE DISCUSSION QUESTIONS

1. Discuss some of the major challenges that PowerGen faced as they developed the Baminica Power Plant project.
2. What factors can explain these challenges? Were these challenges due solely to institutional or cultural factors?
3. What went wrong when PowerGen was negotiating with Richard Jones? Did Richard Jones use any of the dirty negotiation tactics discussed in the negotiation chapter?
4. What steps should PowerGen have taken to ensure that the negotiations went smoothly? Why did they agree to the partnership despite the problems?
5. What would you do now? Would you end the project?

# Old Corporate Ways Fade as New Korean Generation Asserts Itself

Until a few years ago, there was an unwritten rule about working hours at South Korea's leading food and beverage company. "Everyone sat at their desks, fidgeting and waiting for their superiors to leave. Assistant managers waited for managers to leave. The managers waited for the bosses upstairs to leave," said Kim Jang-ok, 40, a customer service manager at Cheil Jedang Corp. So for Kim, Lee Wook-jae presents a cultural shock. Lee, a 27-year-old assistant marketing manager, doesn't wait for the bosses. He leaves when he pleases.

He also comes to work in khaki pants and an open-necked shirt, a cell telephone dangling from a cord around his neck. His black hair is dyed chestnut brown with yellow strains. "I want to be judged by what I do for the company, not by my hairstyle," Lee said. Thanks to young office workers such as Lee, a growing number of companies are abandoning South Korea's rigid corporate culture for a global one.

But staid old Korea, Inc. isn't dead. Most companies still prefer top-down management. Sons inherit businesses from fathers. Most employees address each other by their titles. Suits with ties are standard attire in most offices. The rise of Internet start-ups with their casual and egalitarian ways, the new generation of assertive youths entering the job market, and the disintegration of some of the country's top conglomerates have undermined old hierarchies. Lee, who majored in business management at Ohio State University, is among thousands of Koreans returning home every year armed with U.S. college diplomas and Western ways. "When I first dyed my hair some months ago, everyone in the office looked at me as if I did something wrong," said Lee. "After a while, they accepted it. Now they even comment on how well my latest color came out."

Women are making halting progress too in male-oriented corporate Korea. They still earn less and are promoted less, but "We no longer deliver coffee for male workers. That ended three or four years ago. We get more chances to demonstrate our abilities" said Kim Yoon-hee, 28, a colleague of Lee's at Cheil Jedang. "Still, many men look uncomfortable to talk business with women," she said. "When I sit down for contract negotiations, for example, some of the men across the table first give me a look that says, 'What is this woman doing here?'"

The old system was shaken to its roots during the Asian economic crisis of the late 1990s. People began questioning whether staffers trained to think alike were flexible enough to react to sharp global market changes. "It was not uncommon for the one-man boss to shout at a lower-ranking official briefing him, 'Who's this fool? Get out!'" said Choi Hae-pyong, describing his management experience at an electronic components arm of South Korea's largest conglomerate, Samsung. At 39, Choi is beyond dying his hair but is still adventurous enough to have quit Samsung last year with two colleagues to start their own business, making components for flat-panel computer screens. At Samsung, he said, "They put brutal pressure on employees to force good results. But under such a system, you try to keep the status quo and not make any mistakes. You don't try to be creative. Now I no longer have the safety of working in big business. But at least now I work for myself. I feel good," Choi said.

These days, more companies are urging their employees to get lean and creative. Big corporations such as Cheil Jedang, LG Electronics, and SK encourage workers to shed sober suits and stiff ties. They have also abolished many executive posts to speed up decision making. At Cheil Jedang, gone are big desks and long titles for managers. Individual merit determines wage increases and promotion. Workers who used to say "Mr. Manager Kim" now say "Mr. Kim." Employees in casual attire sit with legs crossed and talk business—in stark contrast to other big business offices where employees still work in suits and ties, and young staffers bow to the boss or stand at attention. "In the past, everybody dressed and looked more or less the same. Everybody got promoted at the same time and had the same salary increases," said Kim, the customer service manager. "In the old days, you got to the senior managers only when you were summoned," he said. "Now, we see young employees going directly to senior managers with opinions. For example, they come to me to ask for more responsible jobs, rather than the dull work of typing data into the computer."

Until recently, working for the nation's top conglomerates conferred status. Now, more college graduates prefer Internet start-ups and foreign businesses. "Loyalty to the company used to be a big motto, and your life centered on what you did at the company," said Ha Il-won, a midlevel manager at a construction arm of the SK conglomerate. "But the Asian financial crisis shattered our illusion about lifetime employment at one company. We became more individualistic." Previously, companies hired students with good school grades and required them to pass a written test. Today, many recruiters are just as likely to choose independent people who have traveled or worked abroad. "Interviewers were more interested in listening to what I had to say than asking standard questions. They asked me what I thought of antiglobalization activists," said Park Ji-sook, 24, a French major who was hired by LG Electronics while protests were going on against the World Trade Organization meeting in Seattle in late 1999. Park said she spoke well of the activists' success in attracting media attention to their demands through the well-publicized protests.

The company made her an editor of its Internet Web site.

CASE DISCUSSION QUESTIONS

1. What institutional factors are driving changes in Korean business culture?
2. How can organizations in a culture that values respect for age differences manage the changes that occur when organizational necessities require younger managers to supervise older managers?
3. How will Korean companies manage more individualistic employees without losing the competitive advantage of a loyal workforce?

REFERENCE

1. Choe, Sang-Hun. 2001. Associated Press. http://www.asianweek.com/2001_02_02/biz4_koreanbizculture.html.

# A

**Achievement versus ascription** How a society accords or gives status.

**Achievement motivation theory** Suggestion that only some people have the need to win in competitive situations or to exceed a standard of excellence.

**Anchor partner** A partner that holds back the development of a successful strategic alliance because it cannot or will not provide its share of the funding.

**Asia-Pacific Economic Cooperation (APEC)** A confederation of 19 nations with less-specific agreements on trade facilitation in the Pacific region.

**Attitudinal commitment** The willingness to dedicate resources and efforts and to face risks to make the alliance work.

**Attributional approach to leadership** Emphasis on what leaders believe causes subordinates' behaviors.

**Autocratic leadership** Leaders make all major decisions themselves.

**Autonomous work group** Team or unit that has nearly complete responsibility for a task.

# B

**B2B** Business-to-business transactions.

**B2C** Business-to-consumer transactions.

**Backdoor recruitment** Prospective employees are friends or relatives of those already employed.

**Balance sheet method** Attempts to equate purchasing power in the host country with purchasing power in the expatriate's home country.

**Benevolent trust** The confidence that the partner will behave with goodwill and with fair exchange.

**Bonus system** In Japan, employees often receive as much as 30 percent of their base salary, usually given twice a year during traditional gift-giving seasons.

**Brick-and-mortar** Traditional or non-virtual business operation.

**Buddhism** Religious tradition that focuses primarily on the reality of world suffering and the ways in which all beings can be freed from suffering.

**Building a relationship** The first stage of the actual negotiation process, when negotiators concentrate on social and interpersonal matters.

**Bureaucratic control system** Focuses on managing organizational processes through budgets, statistical reports, standard operations procedures, and centralization of decision making.

**Business culture** The norms, values, and beliefs that pertain to all aspects of doing business in a culture.

**Business-level strategies** Strategies for a single-business operation.

# C

**C2B** Consumer-to-business transactions.

**C2C** Consumer-to-consumer transactions.

**Calculative commitment** Alliance partner's evaluations, expectations, and concerns regarding the potential rewards from the relationship.

**Capabilities** The ability to assemble and coordinate resources effectively.

**Capitalist or market economy** System where production is decentralized to private owners who carry out these activities to make profits.

**Christianity** Religion based on the life and teachings of Jesus.

**Codetermination** Surrender by management to workers of a share of control of the organization traditionally reserved for management and owners.

**Collectivism** A set of cultural values that views people largely on the basis of the groups to which they belong.

**Commitment** In a strategic alliance, when partners take care of each other and put forth extra effort to make the venture work.

**Commuter assignments employees** Are employees who live in one country but spend at least part of the working week in another country.

**Comparative advantage** The advantage arising from cost, quality, or resource advantages associated with a particular nation.

**Competitive advantage** When a company can outmatch its rivals in attracting and maintaining its targeted customers.

**Competitive negotiation** Each side tries to give as little as possible and tries to win the maximum for its side.

**Competitive scope** How broadly a firm targets its products or services.

**Competitive strategies** Moves multinational firms use to defeat competitors.

**Competitor analysis** Profile of a competitor's strategies and objectives.

**Complementary skills** Skills that enhance but do not necessarily duplicate an alliance partner's skills.

**Concession making** Process requiring each side to relax some of its demands to meet the other party's needs.

**Consultative or participative leadership** Leader's style falls midway between autocratic and democratic styles.

**Contingency theory** Assumption that different styles and leaders are appropriate for various situations.

**Contract manufacturing** Producing products for foreign companies following the foreign companies' specifications.

**Control system** Vertical organizational links, up and down the organizational hierarchy.

**Convenient relativism** What occurs when companies use the logic of ethical relativism to behave any way they please, using the excuse of differences in cultures.

**Coordination system** Horizontal organizational links.

**Copycat businesses** Those following the me-too strategy, whereby they adopt existing strategies for providing products or services.

**Corporate social responsibility** The idea that businesses have a responsibility to society beyond making profits.

**Corporate-level strategies** How companies choose their mixture of different businesses.

**Counter-parry** Fending off a competitor's attack in one country by attacking in another country, usually the competitor's home country.

**Country clusters** Groups of countries with similar cultural patterns.

**Craft union** Represents people from one occupational group, such as plumbers.

**Credibility trust** The confidence that the partner has the intent and ability to meet promised obligations and commitments.

**Cross-cultural training** Increases the relational abilities of future expatriates and, in some cases, of their spouses and families.

**Cultural beliefs** Our understandings about what is true.

**Cultural control system** Uses organizational culture to control the behaviors and attitudes of employees.

**Cultural intelligence** Ability to interact effectively in multiple cultures.

**Cultural norms** Prescribed and proscribed behaviors, telling us what we can do and what we cannot do.

**Cultural paradoxes** When individual situations seem to contradict cultural prescriptions.

**Cultural relativism** A philosophical position arguing that all cultures, no matter how different, are correct and moral for the people of those cultures.

**Cultural rituals** Ceremonies such as baptism, graduation, the tricks played on a new worker, or the pledge to a sorority or fraternity.

**Cultural stories** These include such things as nursery rhymes and traditional legends.

**Cultural symbols** These may be physical, such as national flags or holy artifacts. In the workplace, office size and location can serve as cultural symbols.

**Cultural values** Values that tell us such things as what is good, what is beautiful, what is holy, and what are legitimate goals in life.

**Culture** The pervasive and shared beliefs, norms, and values that guide the everyday life of a group.

**Customer contact techniques** Trade shows, catalog expositions, international advertising agencies and consulting firms, government sponsored trade missions, and direct contact.

# D

**Decision-making control** Level in the organizational hierarchy where managers have the authority to make decisions.

**Defensive competitive strategies** Attempts to reduce the risks of being attacked, to convince an attacking firm to seek other targets, or to blunt the impact of any attack.

**Democratic leadership** Leader includes subordinates in decision making.

**Deontological ethical theory** A focus on actions that, by themselves, have a good or bad morality regardless of their outcomes.

**Developed countries** Countries with mature economies, high GDPs, and high levels of trade and investment.

**Developing countries** Countries with economies that have grown extensively in the past two decades.

**Differentiation strategy** Strategy based on finding ways to provide superior value to customers.

**Direct communication** Communication that comes to the point and lacks ambiguity.

**Direct contact** Face-to-face interaction of employees.

**Direct exporting** Exporters take on the duties of intermediaries and make direct contact with customers in the foreign market.

**Dirty tricks** Negotiation tactics that pressure opponents to accept unfair or undesirable agreements or concessions.

**Dispersed subunits** Subsidiaries located anywhere in the world where they can benefit the company.

**Distinctive competencies** Strengths that allow companies to outperform rivals.

**Dominant parent** Majority owner or contributor who controls or dominates the strategic and operational decision making of the alliance.

**Dual system** A form of vocational education in Germany that combines in-house apprenticeship training with part-time vocational school training, and leads to a skilled worker certificate.

# E

**E-commerce** The selling of goods or services over the Internet.

**E-commerce enablers** Fulfillment specialists that provide other companies with services such as website translation.

**E-commerce security** Degree to which customers feel that their private and personal information is safeguarded by companies collecting it.

**Economic analysis** In relation to an ethical problem, this analysis focuses on what is the best decision in terms of a company's profits.

**Economic system** System of beliefs (concerning work, property, and wealth); activities (extraction, production, and distribution); organizations (business firms, labor unions); and relationships (ownership, management) that provide the goods and services consumed by the members of a society.

**Education** Organized networks of socialization experiences that prepare individuals to act in society.

**Elephant-and-ant complex** Occurs in strategic alliances when two companies are greatly unequal in size.

**Emerging markets** Countries that are currently between developed and developing countries and are rapidly growing.

**Enterprise union**  Represents all the people in one organization, regardless of occupation or location.

**Entrepreneur**  Someone who creates new ventures that seek profit and growth.

**Entry wedge**  Company's competitive advantage for breaking into the established pattern of commercial activity.

**Entry-mode strategies**  Options multinational companies have for entering foreign markets and countries.

**Equity theory**  Proposal that people perceive the fairness of their rewards vis-à-vis their inputs based on how they compare themselves to others.

**ERG theory**  Simplified hierarchy of needs: growth needs, relatedness needs, and existence needs.

**Escalation of commitment**  Companies continue in an alliance relationship longer than necessary because of past financial and emotional investments.

**Ethical analysis**  An analysis that goes beyond focusing on profit goals and legal regulations.

**Ethical convergence**  The growing pressures for multinational companies to follow the same rules in managing ethical behavior and social responsibility.

**Ethical relativism**  The theory that each society's view of ethics must be considered legitimate.

**Ethical universalism**  The theory that basic moral principles transcend cultural and national boundaries.

**Ethnocentric IHRM**  All aspects of HRM for managers and technical workers tend to follow the parent organization's home country HRM practices.

**Ethnocentrism**  When people from one culture believe that theirs are the only correct norms, values, and beliefs.

**European Union (EU)**  Austria, Belgium, Bulgaria, Britain, Denmark, Finland, France, Germany, Greece, Ireland, Italy, Luxembourg, the Netherlands, Portugal, Romania, Spain, and Sweden, plus Norway and Switzerland in the related European Free Trade Area.

**Expatriate**  Employee who comes from a country that is different from the one in which he or she is currently working.

**Expatriate glass ceiling**  The organizational and structural barriers preventing female managers from receiving international assignments.

**Expectancy theory**  Assumption that motivation includes people's desire to satisfy their needs and their beliefs regarding how much their efforts at work will eventually satisfy their needs.

**Export department**  Coordinates and controls a company's export operations.

**Export management company (EMC)**  Intermediary specializing in particular types of products or particular countries or regions.

**Export trading company (ETC)**  Intermediary similar to EMC, but it usually takes title to the product before exporting.

**Extrinsic work values**  Preference for the security aspects of jobs, such as income and job security.

# F

**Fair exchange**  In a strategic alliance, when partners believe that they receive benefits from the relationship equal to their contributions.

**Fiedler's theory of leadership** Proposal that success of task- or person-centered leader depends on relationships between the leader and subordinates, the degree that subordinates' tasks are easily and clearly defined, and the officially granted organizational power of the leader.

**Final agreement**  Signed contract, agreeable to all sides.

**First mover advantage**  That of the entrepreneur who moves quickly into a new venture and establishes the business before other companies can react.

**First offer**  First proposal by parties of what they expect from the agreement.

**Flexpatriates**  Employees who are sent on frequent but short-term international assignments.

**Focus strategy**  Applying a differentiation or low-cost strategy to a narrow market.

**Foreign Corrupt Practices Act (FCPA)** Forbids U.S. companies to make or offer illegal payments or gifts to officials of foreign governments for the sake of obtaining or retaining business.

**Foreign direct investment (FDI)** Multinational firm's ownership, in part or in whole, of an operation in another country.

**Foreign subsidiaries**  Subunits of the multinational company located in another country.

**Formal communication**  Communication that acknowledges rank, titles, and ceremony in prescribed social interactions.

**Formal international cooperative alliance (ICA)**  A nonequity alliance with formal contracts specifying what each company must contribute to the relationship.

**Full-time integrator**  Cross-unit coordination is the main job responsibility.

**Functional structure**  Has departments or subunits based on separate business functions, such as marketing or manufacturing.

**Fundamental attribution error** Assumption by managers that people behave in certain ways because of internal motivations rather than outside factors.

# G

**General Agreement on Tariffs and Trade (GATT)**  Tariff negotiations among several nations that reduced the average worldwide tariff on manufactured goods.

**Generic strategies**  Basic ways that both domestic and multinational companies keep and achieve competitive advantage.

**Geographic structure**  Has departments or subunits based on geographical regions.

**Global culture**  Managerial and worker values that view strategic opportunities as global and not just domestic.

**Global IHRM**   Recruiting and selecting worldwide, and assigning the best managers to international assignments regardless of nationality.

**Global integration solution**   Conducting business similarly throughout the world and locating company units wherever there is high quality and low cost.

**Global leader**   One who has the skills and abilities to interact with and manage people from diverse cultural backgrounds.

**Global Leadership and Organizational Behavior Effectiveness (GLOBE) project**   A recent large-scale project based on Hofstede's model and aimed at determining 9 cultural dimensions of 62 countries.

**Global mindset**   Mindset that requires managers to think globally but act locally.

**Global pay system**   Worldwide job evaluations, performance appraisal methods, and salary scales are used.

**Global platform**   Country location where a firm can best perform some, but not necessarily all, of its value chain activities.

**Global start-up/born-global firm** Company that begins as a multinational company.

**Global virtual team**   Groups of people from different parts of the world who work together by using information and communication technologies such as intranets, Web meetings, WIKIs, e-mail, and instant messaging.

**Globalization**   The worldwide trend of cross-border economic integration that allows businesses to expand beyond their domestic boundaries.

**Globalization drivers**   Conditions in an industry that favor transnational or international strategies over multidomestic or regional strategies.

**Global-local dilemma**   Choice between a local-responsiveness or global approach to a multinational's strategies.

**Goal-directed behavior**   Behavior that people use with the intention of satisfying a need.

**Goal-setting theory**   Assumption that the mere existence of a goal is motivating.

**Great person theory**   Leaders are born with unique characteristics that make them quite different from other people.

**Greenfield investments**   Starting foreign operations from scratch.

# H

**Haptics or touching**   Basic form of human interaction, including shaking hands, embracing, or kissing when greeting one another.

**Headquarters-based compensation system**   Paying home country wages regardless of location.

**Hierarchy of needs theory**   States that people have five basic types of needs: physiological, security, affiliation, esteem, and self-actualization

**High-context language**   Language in which people state things indirectly and implicitly.

**Hinduism**   Acceptance of the ancient traditions of India that are based on the Vedic scriptures.

**Hofstede model of national culture** A model mainly based on differences in values and beliefs regarding work goals.

**Holistic approach**   Each side makes very few, if any, concessions until the end of the negotiation.

**Home country national**   Expatriate employee who comes from the parent firm's home country.

**Host country nationals**   Local workers who come from the host country where the unit (plant, sales unit, etc.) is located.

**Host-based compensation system** Adjusting wages to local lifestyles and costs of living.

**Human resource management (HRM)** Recruitment, selection, training and development, performance appraisal, compensation, and labor relations.

**Humane orientation**   An indication of the extent to which individuals are expected to be fair, altruistic, caring, and generous.

**Hybrid structures**   Mix functional, geographic, and product units.

# I

**Ideological union**   Represents all types of workers based on an ideology (e.g., communism) or religious orientation.

**IHRM orientation**   Company's basic tactics and philosophy for coordinating IHRM activities for managerial and technical workers.

**IJV and ICA performance criteria** Often must include criteria other than financial criteria, such as organizational learning.

**IJV negotiation issues**   Points such as equity contributions, management structure, and "prenuptial" agreements regarding the dissolution of the relationship.

**Independent management structure** Alliance managers act like managers from a separate company.

**Index of economic freedom**   Determines the extent of governmental intervention in a country.

**Indirect exporting**   Intermediary or go-between firms provide the knowledge and contacts necessary to sell overseas.

**Individualism**   A relationship between the individual and the group in society that privileges individual traits and achievements.

**Induced factor conditions**   National resources created by a nation, such as a superior educational system.

**Industrial society**   Characterized by the dominance of the secondary or manufacturing sectors.

**Industrial union**   Represents all people in an industry regardless of occupational type.

**Industrialization**   Cultural and economic changes that occur because of how production is organized and distributed in society.

**Influence tactics**   Tactical behaviors leaders use to influence subordinates.

**Informal international cooperative alliance**   An agreement between companies to cooperate on any value chain activity that is not legally binding.

**Inpatriate** Employees from foreign countries who work in the country where the parent company is located.

**Interdependent relationships** Continuous sharing of information and resources by dispersed and specialized subunits.

**Internal versus external control** Beliefs regarding whether one controls one's own fate.

**International business ethics** Unique ethical problems faced by managers conducting business operations across national boundaries.

**International cadre** Managers who specialize in international assignments.

**International division** Responsible for managing exports, international sales, and foreign subsidiaries.

**International entrepreneurship** The discovery, evaluation, and exploitation of market opportunities.

**International franchising** Comprehensive licensing agreement where the franchisor grants to the franchisee the use of a whole business operation.

**International human resource management (IHRM)** All the HRM functions, adapted to the international setting.

**International joint venture (IJV)** A separate legal entity in which two or more companies from different nations have ownership positions.

**International sales intensity** Amount of international sales divided by total sales of the company.

**International strategic alliance** Agreement between two or more firms from different countries to cooperate in any value chain activity from R&D to sales.

**International strategies** Selling global products and using similar marketing techniques worldwide.

**Internet host** Computer connected to the Internet with its own IP address.

**Interpreter's role** To ensure the accuracy and common understanding of written and oral agreements.

**Intrinsic work values** Preference for openness-to-change job aspects, such

as autonomy and opportunities to take initiative and be creative.

**Islam** Religion based on the submission of the will to Allah (God).

**ISO 14000** The current name for the environmental protection standards of the International Organization for Standardization.

**ISO 9001:2000** The current name for the technical and quality standards of the International Organization for Standardization.

# J

**Job characteristics model** Suggests that work is more motivating when managers enrich core job characteristics, such as by increasing the number of skills a job requires.

# K

**Key success factors (KSFs)** Important characteristics of a company or its product that lead to success in an industry.

**Key success factors for expatriate assignments** Relational abilities, family situation, motivation, and language skills.

**Kinesics** Communication through body movements.

**Knowledge management** Systems, mechanisms, and other design elements of an organization that ensure that the right form of knowledge is available to the right individual at the right time.

# L

**Leadership** Ability of an individual to influence, motivate, and enable others to contribute toward the effectiveness and success of the organizations of which they are members.

**Legal analysis** In relation to an ethical problem, this type of analysis focuses only on meeting legal requirements of host and parent countries.

**Less developed countries (LDCs)** The poorest nations, often plagued

with unstable political regimes, high unemployment, and low worker skills.

**Levels of culture** The levels of cultural influence, including national, business, and occupational and organizational culture.

**Liabilities of smallness** The challenges facing small businesses in getting access to the resources necessary to internationalize.

**Liaison roles** Part of a person's job in one department to communicate with people in another department.

**Licensing** Contractual agreement between a domestic licenser and a foreign licensee. (Licenser usually has a valuable patent, technological know-how, a trademark, or a company name that it provides to the foreign licensee.)

**Local union** Represents one occupational group in one company.

**Local responsiveness solution** Responding to differences in the markets in all the countries in which a company operates.

**Localized Website** Website that is adapted to local cultures.

**Location advantages** Dispersing value chain activities anywhere in the world where the company can do them best or cheapest.

**Long-term (Confucian) orientation** An orientation toward time that values patience.

**Low-context language** Language in which people state things directly and explicitly.

**Low-cost strategy** Producing products or services equal to those of competitors at a lower cost.

# M

**Market transitions** Changes that societies go through as they move from socialism toward a market-based economy.

**Masculinity** Tendency of a society to emphasize traditional gender roles.

**Meister** In Germany, a master technician.

**Metanational structure** An evolution of the transnational network structure that develops extensive systems to encourage organizational learning and entrepreneurial activities.

**Minireplica subsidiary** Scaled-down version of the parent company, using the same technology and producing the same products as the parent company.

**Mixed economy** Combines aspects of capitalist and socialist economies.

**Moral languages** Descriptions of the basic ways that people use to think about ethical decisions and to explain their ethical choices.

**Motivation** A psychological process resulting in goal-directed behavior that satisfies human needs.

**Motivator-hygiene theory** Assumption that a job has two basic characteristics: motivators and hygiene factors.

**Multidomestic strategy** A strategy that emphasizes local responsiveness issues.

**Multinational company (MNC)** Any company that engages in business functions beyond its domestic borders.

**Multinational management** The formulation of strategies and the design of management systems that successfully take advantage of international opportunities and that respond to international threats.

# N

**National context** National culture and social institutions that influence how managers make decisions regarding the strategies of their organizations.

**National culture** The dominant culture within the political boundaries of the nation-state.

**National-context contingency model of leadership** Shows how culture and related social institutions affect leadership practices.

**Natural factor conditions** National resources that occur naturally, such as an abundant water supply.

**Need** Feeling of deficit or lack that all people experience at some time.

**Need theory** Theory of motivation that assumes people can satisfy basic human needs in the work setting.

**Negotiation steps** Preparation, building the relationship, exchanging information, first offer, persuasion, concessions, agreement, and post-agreement.

**Nenpo system** New Japanese compensation system based on yearly performance evaluations that emphasize goals, although the goals are not always the same as in Western companies.

**Neutral versus affective** The acceptability of expressing emotions.

**New ventures** Entering a new market; offering a new product or service; or introducing a new method, technology, or innovative use of raw materials.

**Nonverbal communication** Face-to-face communication that is not oral.

**North American Free Trade Agreement (NAFTA)** A multilateral treaty that links the United States, Canada, and Mexico in an economic bloc that allows freer exchange of goods and services.

**Occupational cultures** Distinct cultures of occupational groups such as physicians, lawyers, accountants, and craftspeople.

**Oculesics** Communication through eye contact or gaze.

**Offensive competitive strategies** Direct attacks, end-run offensives, preemptive strategies, and acquisitions.

**Olfactics** Use of smells as a means of nonverbal communication.

**Operant conditioning** Model that proposes that if a pleasurable consequence follows a behavior, the behavior will continue, whereas if an unpleasant consequence follows a behavior, the behavior will stop.

**Organizational culture** The norms, values, and beliefs concerning an organization that are shared by members of the organization.

**Organizational design** How organizations structure subunits and use coordination and control mechanisms to achieve their strategic goals.

**Output control system** Assesses the performance of a unit based on results, not on the processes used to achieve the results.

**Outsourcing** The deliberate decision to have outsiders or strategic allies perform certain activities in the value chain.

# P

**Particularism** Dealing with other people based on personal relationships.

**Passive exporting** Treating and filling overseas orders like domestic orders.

**Path-goal theory** Four types of leadership styles that a manager might choose depending on the situation.

**Performance maintenance (PM) theory** Japanese perspective on balancing task- and person-centered leader behaviors.

**Performance orientation** The degree to which the society encourages its members to innovate, improve their performance, and strive for excellence.

**Personal success characteristics** Flexibility, creativity, humor, stamina, empathy, curiosity, tolerance of ambiguous situations, and knowledge of a foreign language.

**Person-centered leader** One who focuses on meeting employees' social and emotional needs.

**Persuasion stage** Stage when each side in the negotiation attempts to get the other side to agree to its position.

**Pervasive** The idea that culture affects almost everything we do, everything we see, and everything we feel and believe.

**Political risk** The impact of political decisions or events on the business climate in a country such that a multinational's profitability and the feasibility of its global operations are negatively affected.

**Polycentric IHRM** Firm treats each country-level organization separately for HRM purposes.

**Porter's five forces model** A popular technique that can help a multinational firm understand the major forces at work in the industry and the industry's degree of attractiveness.

**Postagreement** An evaluation of the success of a completed negotiation.

**Postindustrial society** Characterized by emphasis on the service sectors.

**Power distance** Expectations regarding equality among people.

**Preindustrial society** Characterized by agricultural dominance and shaping of the economic environment.

**Prescriptive ethics for multinationals** Suggested guidelines for the ethical behavior of multinational companies.

**Primary stakeholders** Groups or entities directly linked to a company's survival, including customers, suppliers, employees, and shareholders.

**Problem-solving negotiation** Negotiators seek mutually satisfactory ground that is beneficial to both companies.

**Process theories** Theories of motivation arising from needs and values combined with an individual's beliefs regarding the work environment.

**Product structure** Has departments or subunits based on different product groups.

**Profit center** Unit controlled by its profit or loss performance.

**Proxemics** The use of space to communicate.

**Punishment** Consequences of a person's behavior that discourage the behavior.

# R

**Regiocentric IHRM** Regionwide HRM policies are adopted.

**Regional strategy** An approach that manages raw material sourcing, production, marketing, and support activities within a particular region.

**Regional trade agreements** Agreements among nations in a particular region to reduce tariffs and develop similar technical and economic standards.

**Reinforcement** Reactions to a person's behavior that encourage the person to continue the behavior.

**Related diversification** A mix of businesses with similar products and markets.

**Religion** Shared set of beliefs, activities, and institutions based on faith in supernatural forces.

**Repatriation problem** Difficulties that managers face in coming back to their home countries and reconnecting with their home organizations.

**Resource pool** All the human and physical resources available in a country.

**Resources** Inputs into the production or service processes.

# S

**Secondary stakeholders** Groups or entities less directly linked to a company's survival, including the media, trade associations, and special interest groups.

**Secure server** Internet host that allows users to send and receive encrypted data.

**Sequential approach** Each side reciprocates concessions made by the other side.

**7d culture model** A seven-dimension model based on beliefs regarding how people relate to each other, how people manage time, and how people deal with nature.

**Shared cultural values, norms, and beliefs** The idea that people in different cultural groups have similar views of the world.

**Shared management structure** Occurs when both parent companies contribute approximately the same number of managers to the alliance organization.

**Small business** UN definition: fewer than 500 employees. Popular press definition: fewer than 100 employees.

The U.S. Small Business Administration's definition varies by industry and takes into account both sales revenue and number of employees.

**Small business advantage** Fast-moving entrepreneurs can use their competitive advantage of speed. Being first to market, they can capture significant sales before large competitors react.

**Small business stage model** Incremental process of internationalization followed by many small businesses.

**Social inequality** Degree to which people have privileged access to resources and positions within societies.

**Social institution** A complex of positions, roles, norms, and values organizing relatively stable patterns of human resources that sustain viable societal structures within a given environment.

**Social loafing** People put out less effort when they work in groups.

**Socialist or command economy** Production resources are owned by the state and production decisions are centrally coordinated.

**Sociotechnical systems (STS) approach** Focuses on designing motivating jobs by blending the social system (i.e., organizational structure, culture) with technologies.

**Specialized operations** Subunits specializing in particular product lines, research areas, or marketing areas.

**Specific versus diffuse** The extent to which all aspects of an individual's life are involved in his or her work relationships.

**Split-control management structure** Partners usually share strategic decision making but split functional-level decision making.

**Standardized Website** Website that is similar in design and layout around the world.

**Stereotyping** When one assumes that all people within a culture behave, believe, feel, and act the same.

**Strategic complementarity** The alliance partners' strategies are complementary.

**Strategy** The central, comprehensive, integrated, and externally oriented set of choices determining how a company will achieve its objectives.

**Strategy formulation** Process by which managers select the strategies to be used by their company.

**Strategy implementation** All the activities that managers and an organization must perform to achieve strategic objectives.

**Subordinates' expectations** Expectations regarding what leaders should do and what they may or may not do.

**Sustainable** Characteristic of strategies that are not easily defeated by competitors.

**Switching costs** Expenses incurred when a customer switches to a competitor's products.

**SWOT** The analysis of an organization's internal strengths and weaknesses and the opportunities or threats from the environment.

# T

**Task force** Temporary team created to solve a particular organizational problem.

**Task-centered leader** One who gives subordinates specific standards, schedules, and tasks.

**Task-related information** Actual details of the proposed agreement.

**Team** Permanent unit of the organization designed to focus the efforts of different subunits on particular problems.

**Technological leadership** Being first to use or introduce a new technology.

**Teleological ethical theory** A theory that suggests that the morality of an act or practice comes from its consequences.

**Third country nationals** Expatriate workers who come from neither the host nor home country.

**Time horizon** The way cultures deal with the past, present, and future.

**Training rigor** Extent of effort by both trainees and trainers to prepare the expatriate.

**Transformational leadership** Managers go beyond transactional leadership by articulating a vision, breaking from the status quo, providing goals and a plan, giving meaning or a purpose to goals, taking risks, being motivated to lead, building a power base, and demonstrating high ethical and moral standards.

**Transition economies** Countries in the process of changing from government controlled economic systems to free market or capitalistic systems.

**Transnational network structure** Network of functional, product, and geographic subsidiaries dispersed throughout the world, based on the subsidiaries' location advantages.

**Transnational strategy** An approach that seeks location advantages and economic efficiency through operating worldwide.

**Transnational subsidiary** Has no companywide form or function; each subsidiary does what it does best or most efficiently anywhere in the world.

**TRIAD** The world's dominant trading partners: the European Union, the United States, and Japan.

**Turnkey operations** Multinational company makes a project fully operational and trains local managers and workers before the foreign owner takes control.

# U

**U.S. legal requirements for appraisals** Regulating performance evaluation practices to ensure their fairness.

**Uncertainty avoidance** How people react to what they perceive as different and dangerous.

**Union membership density** Proportion of workers in a country who belong to unions.

**Universalism** Dealing with other people based on rules.

**Unrelated diversification** A mix of businesses in any industry.

**Utilitarianism** The argument that what is good and moral proceeds from acts that produce the greatest good for the greatest number of people.

# V

**Value chain** All the activities that a firm uses to design, produce, market, deliver, and support its product.

**Verbal negotiation tactics** Promises, threats, recommendations, warnings, rewards, punishments, normative appeals, commitments, self-disclosures, questions, commands, saying no (refusals), interruptions.

# W

**White-collar or professional union** Represents an occupational group, similar to craft union.

**Whorf hypothesis** Theory that language determines the nature of culture.

**Work centrality** Overall value of work in a person's life.

**Work obligation norms** Degree to which work is seen as an obligation or duty to society.

**Works council** In Germany, employee group that shares plant-level responsibility with managers regarding issues such as working conditions.

**World Trade Organization (WTO)** A formal structure for continued negotiations to reduce trade barriers and a mechanism for settling trade disputes.

**Worldwide geographic structure** Has geographical units representing regions of the world.

**Worldwide matrix structure** Symmetrical organization, usually with equal emphasis on worldwide product groups and regional geographical divisions.

**Worldwide product structure** Gives product divisions responsibility to produce and sell their products or services throughout the world.

# NAME INDEX